MARVEL ENCYCLOPEDIA

NEW EDITION

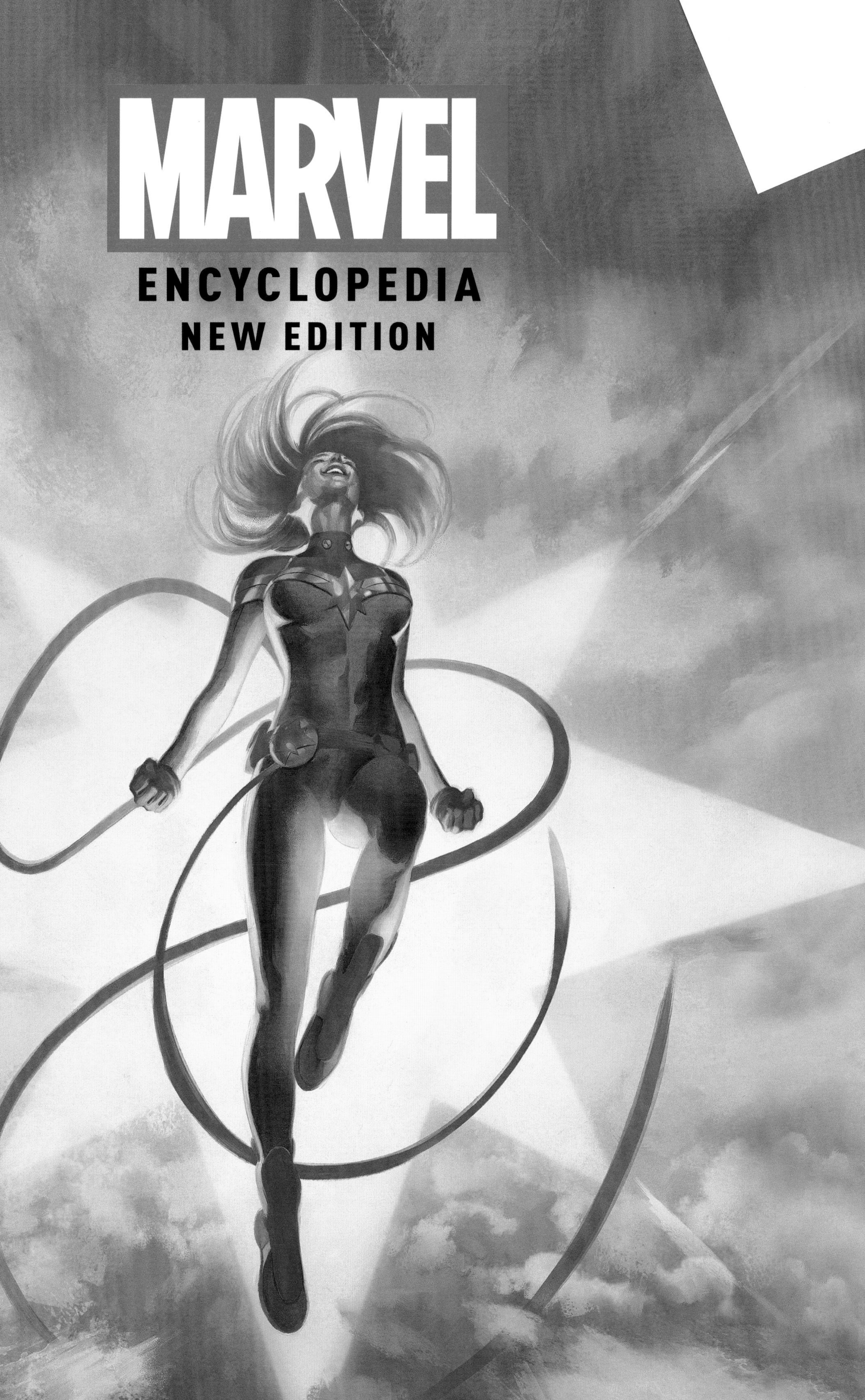

Senior Editor David Fentiman
Senior Designer Anne Sharples
Editors Ruth Amos, Emma Grange, Matt Jones, and Cefn Ridout
Designers Rosamund Bird, Chris Gould, and Thelma Jane Robb
Pre-Production Producer Siu Yin Chan
Senior Producer Jonathan Wakeham
Managing Editor Sadie Smith
Design Manager Vicky Short
Publisher Julie Ferris
Art Director Lisa Lanzarini
Publishing Director Simon Beecroft

This American Edition, 2019
First American Edition, 2006; reprinted 2008; revised 2009, 2014, 2019
Published in the United States by DK Publishing
1450 Broadway, Suite 801, New York, NY 10018

19 20 21 22 23 10 9 8 7 6 5 4 3 2
007–311501–April/2019

Published in Great Britain by Dorling Kindersley Limited.

A catalog record for this book is available from the Library of Congress.

ISBN 978-1-4654-7890-0

Printed in Canada

MARVEL
ENCYCLOPEDIA
NEW EDITION

CONTENTS

FOREWORD
by Chris Claremont

In a way, I consider this a trip down memory lane. Once upon a time—and now that I actually think of it, it truly was a very long time ago—when I was in High School, I re-discovered comic books, in the personae of Marvel Comics and *The Fantastic Four* (story by Stan Lee, art by Jack Kirby and Joe Sinnott). To put it mildly, that was a game changer. Never before had I encountered such exciting visual story-telling, combined with outrageous yet surprisingly empathetic characters. In three exciting issues, Reed, Ben, Sue and Johnny faced, fought and defeated the Silver Surfer and Galactus—and, oh yes, before the climactic 50th issue was done, Johnny Storm attended his first day of college. Less than fifty pages in total, and I was hooked. Next to be discovered was *The Mighty Thor*, also by Stan and Jack, *The Amazing Spider-Man* (Stan again, originally teamed with Steve Ditko and later with John Romita), *Doctor Strange, Master of the Mystic Arts* (Stan and Steve again), and *The Mighty Avengers* (Roy Thomas, this time, and John Buscema).

Everything I read left me wanting to read more. I liked these folks—not simply the characters but the world they inhabited and the ways these fantastic writers and artists presented them—and I wanted to see more and more of them.

Those were so much simpler times. A half century has passed since that first encounter—and the good news is, my feelings haven't changed, even as one fairly significant piece of that Marvel Universe and a whole bunch of characters became the product of my own creative work and imagination. I find I'm still passionate about the Marvel Universe and its "children."

Thing is, though, over the course of years, that Universe hasn't stopped growing.

Back when I started, Marvel was a much smaller company, with—far more importantly—a much more limited history. Unlike DC, whose foundation characters dated back to pre-Second World War days, Marvel, with the exception of Captain America, was a product of the 1960s. There wasn't a whole lot of product in existence and therefore it was far easier to keep track of everything. In those days, we actually created bound, archival, hardcover volumes of each year's run of titles, so we could have ready and accessible reference at the office. Over the many years since, with the expansion of Marvel's creative staff—both in terms of actual numbers of people and their spread across the globe—and of the amount of product itself, it's become significantly more challenging to keep track of all the continuous changes to the Universe. Sure, we can go online now to look things up—but, surprisingly, that's not always a practical solution. True, one can look up a character and get their archival history. What turns out to be more challenging, though, is gathering appropriate and accurate visuals. Words, it seems, are easy; pictures, not so much.

X-Men #1, published in October 1991, was co-written by Chris Claremont and Jim Lee. It remains the bestselling comic book of all time.

Which brings me to DK, and this book. Firstly, about Dorling Kindersley (as I first knew it), one of the best publishers of reference books I've ever known. Every time I visited London back when I was building my writing career I'd make sure to visit their store near Covent Garden and simply browse. For me, that was fun, because their stock covered pretty much everything I was interested in as a creator, told in ways that were easy to comprehend and which made me want to keep turning pages to see what came next. Far too often, I'd end up trading pounds (£) for books, to return home with scads of new titles I would use for reference. For a working writer, DK was—and remains—a Godsend.

The thing to remember, though, is that time passes for them (the publisher) as it does for us (the readers). What was comprehensively valid for one edition, no matter how brilliant, may not hold quite so true years later. Which means, as in this case, time for a new edition!

Thank goodness.

Herein, you'll find the whole of the Marvel Universe—all the characters one can imagine, with defining images and personal history. Where they came from, what they look like, who they are. It is a feast for the eye but also for the mind. Unlike looking things up online, one doesn't have to know precisely what one's looking for in order to use the book and find it valuable.

Years ago, my wife's (deservedly renowned) professor at NYU would often start a writing project by visiting the library and browsing the reference stacks. He'd visit a section appropriate to his research but then he'd just—browse. He'd let his eyes wander over the neighboring shelves and take a look now and again at books that for whatever reason caught his eye. He'd give those books a look to see if he might find them intriguing, and if they did, give them a proper read. Every so often, he'd find one that proved so enticing it led to a wholly unexpected topic to research. That's not so easy to do on the Web.

Online, one goes from "A" to "B." A simple process, true, but by the same token, not so easy to explore "B" in context, or see what one might have missed along the way.

In this book, one can look for a specific character—but then one can take a glance at what other characters are in the vicinity, to see if any look interesting, if there's any element in character or history that might prove to form the viable foundation for a story. One can simply and easily browse. And through browsing, learn. And through learning, perhaps create a new wrinkle on an existing reality, or possibly, a whole new aspect of reality altogether.

The DK books I have are cheerfully dog-eared, with post-it notes stuck beside the appropriate passage or in far too many cases over the actual pages themselves! I cherish my original edition *Marvel Encyclopedia* because it's a far more convenient comprehensive reference catalogue than the tens of thousands (!) of issues-stories-characters it's referring to. Sadly, it's out of date.

Thankfully, I—along with you lucky readers—have here its successor-replacement. I hope you all have fun looking at the way things are and were—because I'll be busy trying to figure out delightfully infuriating aspects of what's yet-to-be, that will hopefully fill up a decent number of entries and pages in the next edition!

Welcome to Stan's funhouse, true believers, and the best ride ever. May it never end.

With this guidebook in hand, you should never get lost!

Chris Claremont
New York, October 2018

THE CONTRIBUTORS

TOM DEFALCO is also the Consultant Editor for the *Marvel Encyclopedia*. He is a best-selling author and a former editor-in-chief of Marvel. He is also the author of several DK Ultimate guides to Marvel Super Heroes: *Avengers: The Ultimate Guide*, *Fantastic Four: The Ultimate Guide*, *Hulk: The Incredible Guide*, and *Spider-Man: The Ultimate Guide*.

PETER SANDERSON is a comics historian and critic, who was Marvel's first official archivist. He is the author of DK's best selling *X-Men: The Ultimate Guide*. Mr. Sanderson was also one of the main writers of the first four versions of *The Official Handbook of the Marvel Universe*.

TOM BREVOORT is Senior Vice President of Publishing for Marvel Comics, where he oversees titles such as *Avengers*, *Fantastic Four*, *Captain America*, *Iron Man*, and others. This also puts him in the unique position of being able to change any details of any Encyclopedia entry for which he couldn't locate the correct answer!

MICHAEL TEITELBAUM has been a writer, editor, and packager of children's books, comic books, and magazines for more than 20 years. Some of Michael's more recent writing includes *X-Men School*, *Story of the X-Men*, *Story of the Hulk*, *Story of Spider-Man*, and *Batman's Guide to Crime and Detection* for DK.

DANIEL WALLACE is the author or co-author of more than a dozen books, including *Superman Returns: The Visual Guide* and the *DC Comics Encyclopedia* for DK, *The Art of Superman Returns*, and the *New York Times*-best-selling *Star Wars: The New Essential Guide to Characters*.

ANDREW DARLING is a film, television and comics journalist, and the author of DK's *Ghost Rider: The Ultimate Guide* and *Thunderbirds: The Making of the Movie*. Andrew also writes for *SFX* and *Dreamwatch* magazines and the *Daily Mail,* and contributed to *Star Wars* and *Prisoner* Fact Files.

MATT FORBECK has been writing and designing games, novels, comics, and more for over 20 years. His work includes *Blood Bowl: Killer Contract*, *Mutant Chronicles*, *More Forbidden Knowledge*, *The Complete Idiot's Guide to Drawing Superheroes & Villains*, the *Harvey Birdman: Attorney at Law* video game, *Marvel Heroes Battle Dice*, *Dungeonology*, and a number of *Halo* titles.

ALAN COWSILL has been a writer and editor for 30 years. He wrote the award-winning graphic novel *World War One* and the novels *Zombie 18* and *Punch Drunk Kisses.* His other work includes *Marvel Avengers: The Ultimate Character Guide* and *Marvel Comics 75 Years of Cover Art*.

ADAM BRAY has contributed to dozens of books on travel, culture, and entertainment over the past decade. He is a best-selling *Star Wars* author and is also the author of DK's *Marvel Studios Visual Dictionary* and *Marvel Studios 101*. He is a co-author of *Ultimate Marvel* and *Marvel: Absolutely Everything You Need to Know* as well.

ADDITIONAL TEXT WRITTEN BY

Ruth Amos, Alastair Dougall, David Fentiman, Emma Grange, Matt Jones, and Cefn Ridout.

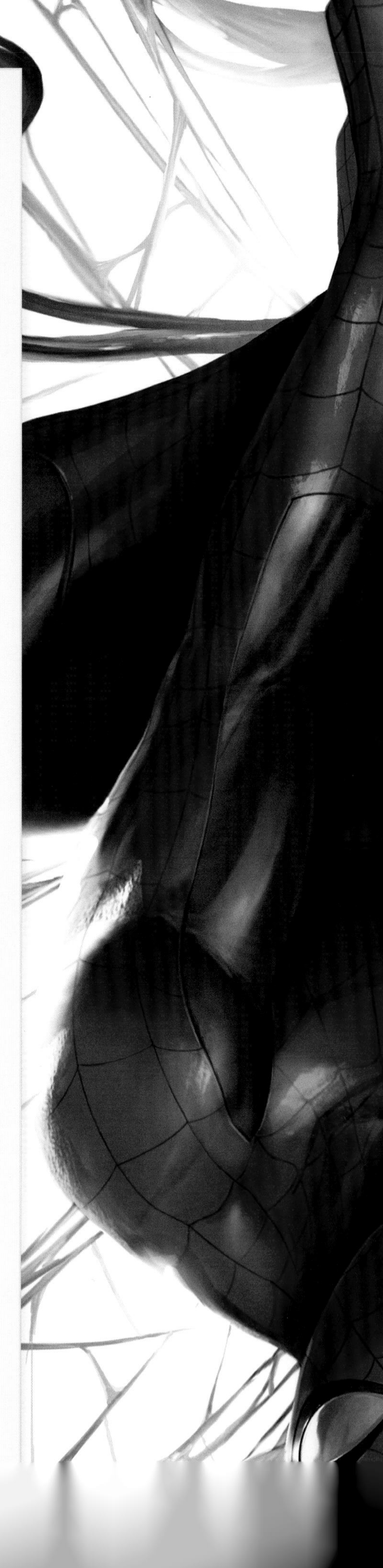

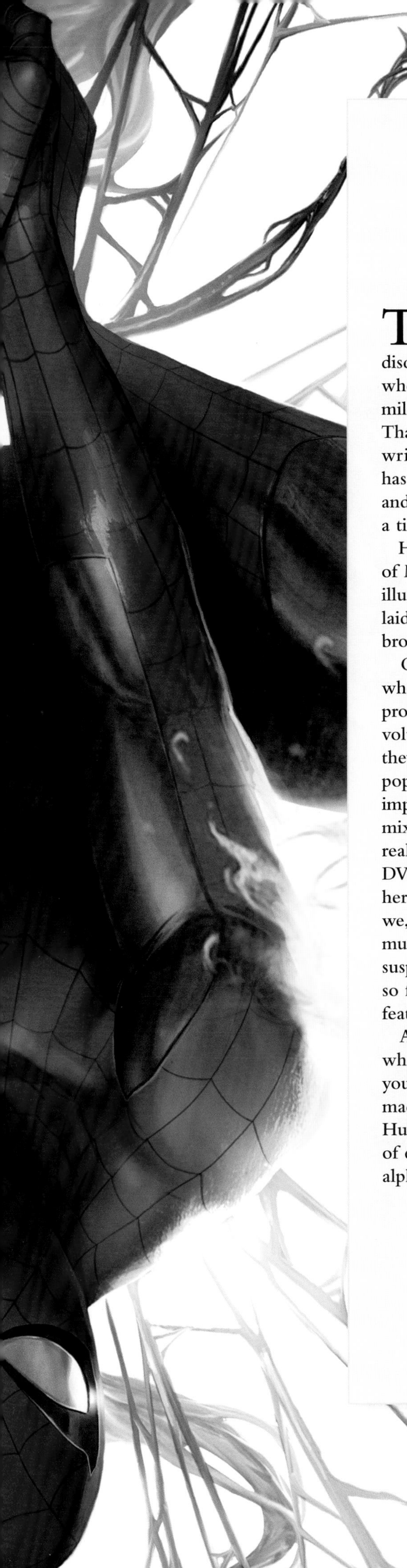

INTRODUCTION

by Stan Lee

The *Marvel Encyclopedia*. I still proudly say—it ranks way up there with the discovery of fire and the invention of the wheel. Just like them, it represents an epic milestone in the history of the human race. That's why I'm so incredibly proud to be writing this intro for a book that mankind has been hungering for, a book that is—now and forever—a shining beacon of wonder, a titanic tribute to talent unleashed.

Here you'll find more than a thousand of Marvel's classic characters, all brilliantly illustrated, with their lives and vital statistics laid bare for your closest scrutiny and your browsing delight.

On a personal note, I must confess, when I first dreamed up some of the more prominent characters you'll find in this volume, I never dreamed that decades later they would have achieved the fame and popularity which they now enjoy. It's almost impossible to describe the feeling of pride, mixed with disbelief, that I feel when I realize how many great movies, video games, DVDs, toys and books are based on these heroes, villains, and far-out stories which we, in the mighty Marvel bullpen, had so much fun creating. None of us could have suspected that our creations would become so famous that we'd one day find ourselves featured in a prestigious encyclopedia.

And, speaking of this extraordinary book, when it comes to finding the hero or villain you may be seeking, the publishers have made it as easy for you as recognizing the Hulk in a crowd. They've put the names of each and every one in convenient alphabetical order.

But what about the artwork? Glad you asked! You'll find illustrations from the very best of Marvel's amazing army of artists, pencilers, and inkers who have made their indelible marks on the consciousness of comic book fans worldwide.

And, naturally, the accompanying texts are written by the most acclaimed scriptwriters in Marvel's galaxy of gifted scriveners. Every sentence is a tribute to the greatest Super Hero creations this side of Asgard.

But that's not all. Realizing that some of the spectacular characters in our Super Hero stable have actually achieved such status and fame that they are now truly worldwide legends, the editors have wisely decided to accord these special heroes and villains full-page, double-page, or even two double-page layouts, plus a brief guide to their essential storylines.

There's so much more that I could say, but if I do it'll keep me from leaving my computer and reaching for my beautiful, brand-new *Marvel Encyclopedia* which is proudly sitting on my corner table. It might be my imagination, but I seem to see a glow around that voluminous volume, as though it's illuminated by some supernatural aura, some mystic radiance emanating from the combined power of the fantastic characters within its pages.

I know I must be fantasizing, and yet—as I slowly reach out to touch the cover of this magnificent book, I wonder—as you may wonder, too—what magic lies within?

Excelsior!

Stan

Stan Lee

ABOMINATION

FACTFILE

REAL NAME
Emil Blonsky

OCCUPATION
Criminal

BASE
Mobile

HEIGHT 6 ft 8 in
WEIGHT 980 lbs
EYES Green
HAIR None

FIRST APPEARANCE
Tales to Astonish #90 (April 1967)

POWERS
Superhuman strength enables leaps of two miles; tough skin withstands small arms fire. Unlike Hulk, the Abomination's strength does not increase with rage, and he rarely returns to human form; however he retains all Blonsky's mental faculties.

ABOMINATION

Born in Zagreb, Yugoslavia, Emil Blonsky became a spy and infiltrated the US Air Force base where scientist Bruce Banner (*see* HULK) was stationed and discovered gamma-radiation equipment, with which Banner intended to commit suicide. Irradiating himself, Blonsky became the monstrous Abomination.

The Abomination battled the Hulk multiple times. Their struggles were interrupted when the STRANGER kidnapped Abomination into space for study, and he wound up serving as the first mate of the starship *Andromeda*. After returning to Earth, he became the pawn of many villains, including MODOK, MEPHISTO, and TYRANNUS.

The Abomination later revealed his new form to his wife, Nadia, who then left him. Jealous of Banner's apparent wedded bliss, Blonsky poisoned Banner's wife Betty (*see* ROSS, BETTY). Years later, the RED HULK, secretly Betty's father (*see* ROSS, GENERAL T. E.) hunted down and murdered the Abomination. The Ancient Order of the Shield reanimated Abomination, though without his former mind. They used him to hunt the Hulk, but IRON MAN helped his friend by teleporting Abomination out to space and into Jupiter's orbit.

The Abomination is even stronger than the Hulk. His body is covered with reptilian scales.

ABYSS

FIRST APPEARANCE *Avengers* #1 (February 2013)
REAL NAME Abyss **OCCUPATION** Destroyer
BASE Mars **HEIGHT/WEIGHT** N/A
EYES Black **HAIR** Black
SPECIAL POWERS/ABILITIES Abyss is made of living gas, which makes her invulnerable to most physical attacks. She can manipulate the minds of others, whom she envelopes in a sphere of gas.

Abyss was a powerful creature of living gas created by an ALEPH, one of the alien BUILDERS, along with her brother EX NIHILO. The three creatures traveled the universe together, destroying planets they judged unworthy. They came to Mars and began to terraform it into their base for the Solar System. From there, Ex Nihilo fired origin bombs at Earth, terraforming entire cities and killing everyone within. They were stopped by CAPTAIN UNIVERSE and the AVENGERS, and ordered to limit their work to Mars. When the Builders subjugated Ex Nihilo's kind (the Gardeners) to mere servants, the duo sided with the Avengers and Gardeners against the Builders (*see* INFINITY). Abyss and Ex Nihilo were killed during the collapse of the Multiverse.

ABSORBING MAN

FACTFILE

REAL NAME
Carl "Crusher" Creel

OCCUPATION
Criminal

BASE
Mobile

HEIGHT 6 ft 4 in
WEIGHT 365 lbs
EYES Blue
HAIR None

FIRST APPEARANCE
Journey Into Mystery #114 (March 1965)

POWERS
Can magically duplicate within himself the physical and mystical properties of anything he touches, including various forms of energy. If his body is broken into pieces while he is in a non-human state, he can mentally reassemble it.

ABSORBING MAN

Seeking a pawn to use against THOR, LOKI endowed brutal prisoner "Crusher" Creel and his ball and chain with the power to absorb the physical properties of anything he touched. Creel broke out of prison and battled Thor, as Loki intended. However, Creel overreached himself by trying to absorb the power of the whole Earth and exploded. Thanks to his new powers, however, Creel was not truly dead, and Loki magically reassembled his body.

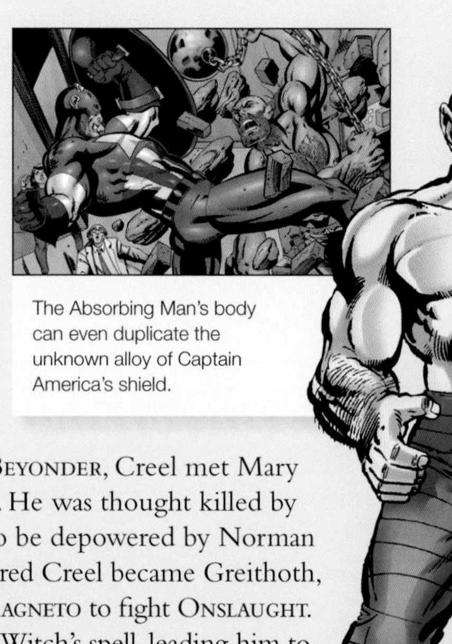

The Absorbing Man's body can even duplicate the unknown alloy of Captain America's shield.

Over the years the Absorbing Man has repeatedly battled Thor and the HULK as well as SPIDER-MAN and the AVENGERS. During the first Secret War staged by the BEYONDER, Creel met Mary "Skeeter" MacPherran (TITANIA), whom he later married. He was thought killed by SENTRY during the CIVIL WAR, but Creel returned, only to be depowered by Norman Osborn (*see* GREEN GOBLIN). During FEAR ITSELF, a repowered Creel became Greithoth, Breaker of Wills. Some time later Creel was recruited by MAGNETO to fight ONSLAUGHT. Like others, his moral compass was then reversed by Scarlet Witch's spell, leading him to temporarily become a hero. He was later incarcerated at SHIELD's Pleasant Hill facility, before ending up in a space prison with BLACK BOLT. He appeared to sacrifice himself to help the other inmates escape. In fact, he escaped the prison by storing his essence in his ball and chain, and reconstituted himself back on Earth.

ADVERSARY

FIRST APPEARANCE *Uncanny X-Men* #188 (December 1984)
REAL NAME Unknown (alias Naze, the great trickster)
OCCUPATION Ancient deity **BASE** An unknown dimension
HEIGHT/WEIGHT/EYES/HAIR N/A
SPECIAL POWERS/ABILITIES Can assume any form he desires; may be fought successfully through magic, but not through most forms of physical force; vulnerable to iron, steel, and Adamantium.

The Cheyenne believe that the Adversary is a demonic god that toys with the fate of the universe, heedless of the deaths he causes. Forge was trained to be a shaman and combat him. After his teacher, Naze, was murdered and replaced by the Adversary, Forge joined the X-Men in an attempt to stop the monster. The Adversary is imprisoned by mystical spells, but may one day escape confinement.

A-FORCE

A-Force was the all-female security team of Arcadia, a domain of Doctor Doom's Battleworld. After Battleworld came to an end, the team members were reborn on Earth-616. Singularity, who had perished in Arcadia, was also resurrected on Earth-616. With her arrived Antimatter, bent on destroying her. Singularity soon encountered her former teammates Captain Marvel, Medusa and She-Hulk, none of whom remembered her. Medusa decided to protect Singularity after Antimatter killed an Inhuman. The women enlisted the help of Sister Grimm (*see* Minoru, Nico) and Dazzler, but when Antimatter appeared to kill Dazzler, Singularity gave herself up. Her new friends pursued; Medusa destroyed Antimatter with a bomb and Dazzler returned in time to save Singularity. The team remained together for a few misadventures, but soon disbanded.

FACTFILE

MEMBERS AND POWERS

SINGULARITY (1)
Body contains pocket dimension.
DAZZLER (2)
Converts sonic vibrations into various forms of light.
SISTER GRIMM (3)
Summons powerful magical item called the Staff of One.
QUEEN MEDUSA (4)
Highly durable prehensile hair.
SHE-HULK (5)
Superhuman strength and durability.
CAPTAIN MARVEL (6)
Superhuman strength, flight, and energy manipulation.

BASE
Mobile

FIRST APPEARANCE
A-Force #1 (May 2015)

AGAMEMNON

FIRST APPEARANCE *Incredible Hulk* #381 (May 1991)
REAL NAME Vali Halfling **OCCUPATION** Godlike observer
BASE The Mount, a mountain base in Arizona
HEIGHT 5 ft 7 in **WEIGHT** 140 lbs **EYES** Brown **HAIR** Brown
SPECIAL POWERS/ABILITIES Virtually immortal; projects a holograph of himself as an old, bearded man so that no one suspects that he truly looks like a teenage boy.

The son of Loki and a mortal mother, Vali traded the pick of his future offspring with the alien Troyjan race in exchange for knowledge of immortality. He later founded the Pantheon, an interventionist think tank whose members included many of his other children, some adopted. However, when Agamemnon's betrayals became known to the Pantheon, he attempted to slay them all. He died during that battle, but he returned with the rebirth of the Norse Gods (*see* Gods of Asgard) after Ragnarok and worked with Amadeus Cho's Olympus Group. He captured Wolfsbane when she was pregnant so he could steal her child, but the monstrous baby killed him soon after its birth.

AGENT X

FIRST APPEARANCE *Agent X* #1 (September 2002)
REAL NAME Nijo (aka Alex Hayden)
OCCUPATION Mercenary **BASE** Mobile
HEIGHT 6 ft 2 in **WEIGHT** 210 lbs **EYES** Brown **HAIR** None
SPECIAL POWERS/ABILITIES Augmented strength, agility, and dexterity; superhuman regenerative abilities; certain advanced mental abilities; enhanced skill as a marksman.

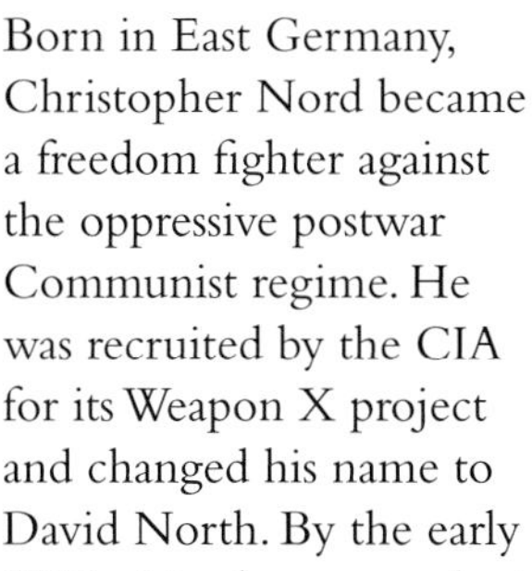

Agent X's real name is Nijo, but during a bout of amnesia he adopted the name Alex Hayden. Agent X is a combined consciousness which resides in the body of Nijo but which also contains the mental powers of Deadpool and Black Swan. Agent X was created when the corpse of Nijo was revived and given Deadpool's healing power by Black Swan, who has the ability to enter a person's mind and unleash viruses similar to computer viruses into their brain. Agent X subsequently founded a team of mercenaries known as Agency X with his girlfriend Outlaw, Taskmaster, Sandi Brandenberg, and the mutant Mary Zero.

AGENT ZERO/MAVERICK

FIRST APPEARANCE (as Maverick) *X-Men* #5 (February 1992)
REAL NAME Christopher Nord (changed to David North)
OCCUPATION Secret agent; mercenary **BASE** Berlin, Germany
HEIGHT 6 ft 3 in **WEIGHT** 230 lbs **EYES** Blue **HAIR** Brown
SPECIAL POWERS/ABILITIES Can absorb kinetic energy and utilize it for superhuman strength or release it as concussive blasts. Possesses aging suppression and enhanced healing factors.

Born in East Germany, Christopher Nord became a freedom fighter against the oppressive postwar Communist regime. He was recruited by the CIA for its Weapon X project and changed his name to David North. By the early 1960s, North partnered with Logan and Victor Creed, the future Wolverine and Sabretooth, in the CIA's Team X. Later, North became a mercenary code-named Maverick. After nearly being killed by Sabretooth, Maverick reluctantly rejoined the Weapon X project, which saved his life. Nord subsequently became the project's leading special operative, Agent Zero. He lost his powers on M-Day and retired, and now works as Maverick once more.

THE AGE OF ULTRON

The end of an era

After the events of Annihilation, Ultron—the human-hating, artificially intelligent robot created by Hank Pym—returned to Earth in the inactive body of a Galadorian Spaceknight. The Intelligencia found it and tried to activate it, but the Avengers intervened. During the ensuing battle, Ultron reawakened in his new body and escaped.

With New York destroyed and the rest of the planet about to follow suit, Hawkeye rescues Spider-Man, and brings him beneath Central Park to reunite with the surviving Avengers.

With two Wolverines from different universes trapped in the past, the one from The Age of Ultron sacrificed himself so the other could return to his repaired timeline.

ULTRON RETURNS

Free on Earth once again, Ultron assembled an army of Ultron Sentinels and launched a swift and horrifying attack on New York City. The initial assault killed many of the world's most powerful heroes, and the rest—including Captain America, Emma Frost, Invisible Woman, Iron Man, Hawkeye, Luke Cage, She-Hulk, and Wolverine—were forced underground. Hammerhead and the Owl captured Spider-Man and tortured him to learn the location of other Avengers so they could sell them to Ultron, but Hawkeye mounted a bloody and successful rescue attempt before they could do so.

Under the guidance of Captain America, Luke Cage knocked out She-Hulk and pretended to try to sell her to Ultron, in order to get inside the Adamantium robot's headquarters. Cage discovered that Ultron ruled over his Sentinels via a dismembered Vision, controlling him by remote from the future. She-Hulk sacrificed her life so Luke could escape and tell the others what he had learned. The Avengers traveled to the Savage Land to evade Ultron. There they met with Ka-Zar and other scattered heroes, including Black Widow, Moon Knight, Monica Rambeau (*see* Spectrum), Quicksilver, Red Hulk, and Valkyrie. Despite being caught in a nuclear bomb explosion, Cage had reached the Savage Land first and, before he died, he told them Ultron's secret. Black Widow led the others to a safe house Nick Fury had set up in the Savage Land long ago. They found him waiting there for them, along with Doctor Doom's time platform.

Ultron created thousands of Ultrons, and they set about conquering the world one city at a time.

A team of heroes mounted an ill-fated assault against Ultron in the future. Believing the effort was doomed to fail, Wolverine and Invisible Woman waited for the others to leave and then went back into the past to kill Hank Pym before he could create Ultron. When they returned to their time, they found themselves in an alternate universe, which had been transformed into a dystopia by Pym's death. Disheartened, Wolverine and Invisible Woman returned to the past. Wolverine stopped his past self from killing Pym, and they worked with Pym to implant a virus into Ultron at his creation and then erase Pym's memory of doing so.

This time around, when Ultron was awakened, Pym—alerted by a message from his past self—worked with Iron Man to trigger the failsafe virus and deactivate Ultron before he could escape.

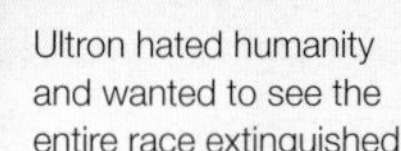

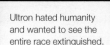

Ultron hated humanity and wanted to see the entire race extinguished.

Luke Cage cradles the dead body of She-Hulk—killed by Ultrons.

DIFFERENT TIME

ne death of Hank Pym caused a butterfly effect that reated a whole new universe, in which a cyborg Iron an led SHIELD in a war that pitted his technology gainst the magical forces of Morgan le Fay. In this world, arth's mightiest heroes were the Defenders, which cluded Cable (Cyclops), Captain Marvel (Wasp), olonel America (Captain America), Doctor Strange, ulk, Star-Lord, the Thing, and Wolverine. This world's on Man told Wolverine how he could repair the timeline nd defeat Ultron. During an attack by Le Fay's army, visible Woman and both Wolverines escaped and et out to implement that plan.

AGENTS OF ATLAS

Security team with a shady reputation

AGENTS OF ATLAS

FACTFILE

KEY MEMBERS

GORILLA-MAN
The body of a gorilla with the mind of a man.

HUMAN ROBOT
Super-strong, self-repairing robot with a force-field, a death ray, and telescopic, electrified limbs.

NAMORA
Amphibious, super-strong woman.

THE URANIAN
The original Marvel Boy.

VENUS
A siren with super-toughness and a hypnotic voice.

JIMMY WOO
Secret agent.

BASE
The Temple of Atlas, inside a huge cavern beneath San Francisco

FIRST APPEARANCE
Agents of Atlas #1 (October 2006)

In 1958, FBI agent Jimmy Woo formed a group of heroes called the G-Men to rescue President Eisenhower from the Golden Claw. Working with SHIELD decades later, Jimmy reformed the team to investigate a shadowy organization known as the Atlas Foundation, based in the Temple of Atlas. They discovered that the Golden Claw was in fact Plan Tzu, direct heir of Genghis Khan and the leader of the Atlas Foundation. Tzu had chosen Jimmy as his own heir, and he'd spent the past few decades working as Jimmy's enemy, forcing him to become properly prepared. Shocked by this revelation, Jimmy nevertheless agreed to take over the Atlas Foundation and turn it into a force for good, at which point Tzu allowed his adviser—a golden dragon known as Mr. Lao—to devour him.

ESSENTIAL STORYLINES

- ***Agents of Atlas Vol. 1 #1–6*** Jimmy Woo reunites the team to fight against the Golden Claw and discovers the Claw's master plan.
- ***Agents of Atlas Vol. 2 #9–11*** Jimmy Woo accidentally breaks a truce with the Asian splinter group of the Atlas Foundation and sparks a Dragon Clan War.
- ***Atlas #1–5*** Aliens from the Echo World attack 3-D Man with innocents they've possessed and lead to the discovery of Earth-9904.

The Golden Claw met his end in Mr. Lao's jaws, just like every khan in his line.

DARK REIGN

The team fought the Skrulls during the Secret Invasion, but once Norman Osborn (*see* Green Goblin) rose to power during the Dark Reign, Jimmy decided to retain the Atlas Foundation's villainous reputation so he could work to destroy Osborn's takeover of the US government from within, starting with robbing Fort Knox. Jimmy's insistence on leading his team in the field led Mr. Lao to appoint a second-in-command: Temugin, the son of the Mandarin. To help run the organization, Jimmy in turn hired his old friend Derek Khanata, one of the many SHIELD agents Osborn had fired.

TURF WARS

Jimmy discovered that his old flame Suwan, Plan Tzu's niece, had long ago split from the main Atlas Foundation and set up her own organization in Asia. Retaining her youth via the same elixirs used by the Golden Claw, she ruled over her faithful warriors as the Jade Claw, enforcing her will with the help of her high-tech robot M-21 and her own dragon advisor, Yao. Jimmy accidentally broke a truce with the Great Wall, sparking a war with Suwan. When the Atlas Foundation defeated the Great Wall, Jimmy decided not to destroy their rivals but reconcile with them, and he put Temugin in charge of this newly acquired branch.

The Atlas Foundation later joined up with 3-D Man, who helped them stave off an invasion from the Echo World situated between theirs and Earth-9904. In the course of this, the Agents of Atlas visited that alternate Earth and witnessed a celebration in which Jimmy was being honored for having started the Avengers.

AGENTS OF ATLAS
1 The Uranian
2 Namora
3 M-11
4 Gorilla-Man
5 3-D Man
6 Venus
7 Jimmy Woo

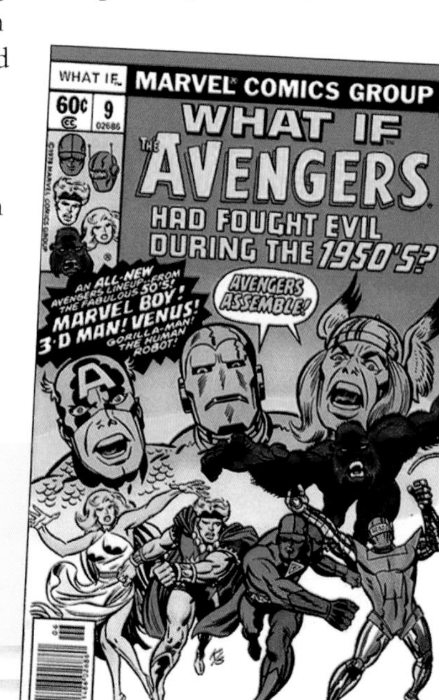

A similar team appeared in *What If?* #9 (June, 1978) as the 1950s Avengers of Earth-9904.

AHAB

FIRST APPEARANCE *Fantastic Four Annual* #23 (1990)
REAL NAME Dr. Roderick Campbell
OCCUPATION Geneticist **BASE** Mobile
HEIGHT 6 ft 1 in **WEIGHT** (as Campbell) 166 lbs (as Ahab) 222 lbs
EYES Brown **HAIR** Brown **SPECIAL POWERS/ABILITIES** Possesses a robotic body, and wields psionic harpoons that cause those struck to feel pain, to be enslaved to his will, or to perish.

In a possible future, Ahab created a process by which captured mutants were turned into slaves known as Hounds and used to hunt down their fellow mutants. Ahab's body was rebuilt cybernetically after he was critically injured during the escape of his best Hound, Rachel Summers, into the past. He later joined Apocalypse and became Famine in the Four Horsemen. Later, Ahab traveled to Earth-616 to try to kill all of the X-Men.

AIR-WALKER

FIRST APPEARANCE *Fantastic Four* #120 (March 1972)
REAL NAME Gabriel Lan
OCCUPATION Herald of Galactus **BASE** Various
HEIGHT 6 ft 1 in **WEIGHT** 210 lbs **EYES** Blue **HAIR** White
SPECIAL POWERS/ABILITIES Command of the Power Cosmic, the fundamental force of the universe, enables a variety of powers, including force blasts, interstellar flight, and ability to walk on air.

Chosen by the planet-devouring Galactus to become his latest herald after the betrayal of the Silver Surfer, Xandarian starship captain Gabriel Lan was endowed with the Power Cosmic, becoming Gabriel, the Air-Walker.

As the Air-Walker, Gabriel served his master for several years, seeking out worlds for Galactus to consume in order to survive. After the Ovoids killed the Air-Walker, Galactus transferred his mind into a robotic body. However, Galactus did not care for the results and replaced him with Firelord. Since then, Air-Walker's robotic body has been destroyed and rebuilt several times. Perhaps this last rebuild could mean the end of him.

AJAK

FIRST APPEARANCE *The Eternals* #2 (August 1976)
REAL NAME Ajak **OCCUPATION** Adventurer
BASE The City of the Space Gods, Andes Mountains
HEIGHT 6 ft 1 in **WEIGHT** 220 lbs **EYES** Gray **HAIR** Black
SPECIAL POWERS/ABILITIES Superhuman strength, virtual immortality and invulnerability; could psionically levitate, rearrange the molecular structure of objects, and project cosmic energy.

One of the Polar Eternals, Ajak was the spokesman for the Third and Fourth Host of the Celestials on Earth. Ajak befriended archaeologist Dr. Daniel Damian, who used Celestial technology to turn Ajak into a murderous monster when his daughter Margo was killed. Ajak disintegrated himself and Damian out of guilt. Restored to life in Olympia years later, Ajak sought to learn how to speak with the Dreaming Celestial. He joined Hercules' God Squad against the Skrull gods and was killed in that battle. He returned after all the Eternals had had their memories erased and helped remind them who they were.

ALLAN, LIZ

Elizabeth, aka Liz, Allan was a talented CEO who formed her own multinational and multibillion-dollar business empire. Liz was a popular student at Midtown High, and Peter Parker (Spider-Man) had a crush on her, but they went on to become good friends. After high school, Liz became a nurse and cared for her stepbrother Mark Raxton (Molten Man). Soon, she met and fell in love with Harry Osborn. They married and had a son, named Norman Osborn after Harry's father.

After the seeming deaths of Harry and Norman Osborn, Liz took over the role of CEO of Osborn Industries, but lost this position when Norman returned from the grave to take back the company. Eventually, Liz formed her own corporation named Allan Chemicals that specialized in scientific research. Following her successes in the field, Liz was able to purchase the majority stake in Horizon Labs, which was then folded into her business. Then, Liz agreed to merge her company with Oscorp to become Alchemax, with Liz as CEO.

Her son Norman, aka Normie, grew up hating Spider-Man because he thought the hero had hurt his dad. When his grandfather became the Red Goblin, he kidnapped Normie and forced upon his grandson a portion of the Carnage symbiote. Normie was turned into the Goblin Childe and tried to kill Aunt May Parker. Goblin Childe betrayed his grandfather when Spider-Man saved his mother. Alchemax's scientists seemed to purge him of the Carnage symbiote, but a small portion lurked inside his eyeball.

In high school, Liz sometimes joined in when Flash Thompson mocked Peter Parker. She soon matured and befriended Peter.

Goblin Childe was a vicious and jealous villain with a range of super powers.

FACTFILE
REAL NAME
Elizabeth Allan
OCCUPATION
Businesswoman
BASE
Mobile

HEIGHT 5 ft 9 in
WEIGHT 135 lbs
EYES Blue
HAIR Blond

FIRST APPEARANCE
Amazing Fantasy #15 (August 1962)

ALEPH

FIRST APPEARANCE *Avengers* #1 (February 2013)

REAL NAME Aleph **OCCUPATION** Destroyer

BASE Mars **HEIGHT** Varies **WEIGHT** Varies

EYES Yellow **HAIR** None

SPECIAL POWERS/ABILITIES Aleph possesses superhuman strength, speed, and senses. He can fly and project energy blasts. His metal body is nearly invulnerable and he can reconfigure it at will.

Aleph is one of a powerful set of living robots created by the BUILDERS, the oldest race in the universe. Tasked with purging worlds filled with unfit forms of life, he traveled the galaxy until he found a worthy people, at which point he released the seeds that grew into ABYSS and EX NIHILO. He escorted them to many other planets, debating the fate of their peoples with them. On Mars, Aleph oversaw the planet's terraforming and advocated the razing of the Earth. When CAPTAIN UNIVERSE ordered the trio to stand down, Aleph refused, and she destroyed him with a touch.

ALL-WINNERS SQUAD

FIRST APPEARANCE *All-Winners Comics* #19 (Fall 1946)

MEMBERS AND POWERS

Captain America Superior strength, speed, agility, and endurance

Human Torch Can control fire and can fly

Namor Increased strength, can fly, can breath in air or water

Whizzer Can run at super speed

Miss America Superhuman strength, can fly

Following World War II, the heroes of the All-Winners Squad decided to stay together to fight crime in the US rather than foreign enemies. They battled and stopped Adam-2, an android who designed a robot army. Later they faced Future Man, a time traveler from the year 1,000,000 who hoped to destroy humanity in order to allow his race to inhabit the Earth. The Squad also battled the SHE-HULK, who had traveled back in time to help some gangsters acquire an atomic bomb.

THE ALL-WINNERS SQUAD
1 Miss America ***2*** Captain America ***3*** The Human Torch ***4*** Namor, the Sub-Mariner ***5*** Whizzer

ALPHA

FIRST APPEARANCE *Amazing Spider-Man* #692 (October 2012)

REAL NAME Andrew Maguire

OCCUPATION Student, Super Hero **BASE** Pittsburgh, PA

HEIGHT 5 ft 8 in **WEIGHT** 150 lbs **EYES** Blue **HAIR** Blond

SPECIAL POWERS/ABILITIES Alpha is energized with Parker Particles, which give him superhuman strength and speed, as well as the ability to project energy, create force-fields, and fly; however, he can usually only use one power at a time.

Andy Maguire was a student at Midtown High in Queens. On a field trip to Horizon Labs to see Peter Parker (*see* SPIDER-MAN) debut his latest discovery, Andy was accidentally infused with a blast of Parker Particles. Spider-Man took Alpha under his wing, but after a disastrous fight in which Alpha helped the AVENGERS bring down TERMINUS but endangered countless innocents, Spider-Man de-powered Alpha and sent him home. Andy's parents divorced soon after, and he moved to Pittsburgh with his mother. When DOCTOR OCTOPUS took over Spider-Man's body, he gave Alpha back 10 percent of his powers so he could study the effects. Alpha decided to use his powers to protect Pittsburgh.

AMATSU-MIKABOSHI

AMATSU-MIKABOSHI

FACTFILE

REAL NAME
Amatsu-Mikaboshi

OCCUPATION
God of Evil

BASE
The Void

HEIGHT Variable
WEIGHT Variable
EYES Gold (variable)
HAIR Black (variable)

FIRST APPEARANCE
Thor: Blood Oath #6 (October 2012)

POWERS
An immortal god with superhuman strength, endurance, invulnerability, and speed. He manipulates magical energy and can change shape at will. He can also teleport and fly.

Amatsu-Mikaboshi—also known as the Chaos King—is the Shinto (Japanese) God of Evil. He represents the void that existed before the creation of the universe, and he works to return it to that state of nothingness. He long desired Kusanagi, the legendary Grasscutter Sword, but it was kept from him for centuries until THOR and the WARRIORS THREE liberated it. The blade wound up on Earth, where Mikaboshi finally claimed it.

He used the sword to capture Yomi (the underworld) and then sought to conquer the GODS OF OLYMPUS. The Olympians banded together with the other Japanese gods to thwart Mikaboshi, but not before he mortally wounded Zeus, the leader of the Olympians. Despite this, Mikaboshi joined the God Squad that Athena assembled to defeat the SKRULL gods during the SECRET INVASION. While it seemed that Mikaboshi died in that battle, he survived and went on to defeat the gods of several alien civilizations before returning to Earth.

During the Chaos War, Mikaboshi murdered NIGHTMARE and stole his powers, putting all sleeping mortals into a coma as he prepared his assault on the surviving gods. HERCULES assembled a new God Squad to stand against the Chaos King. At the last moment, he knocked Mikaboshi through a portal into an empty alternate universe known as the Continuum, which the Chaos King now rules.

Mikaboshi used Ares' son Alex against him, taking the boy's form so he could get close enough to attack Zeus.

ALPHA FLIGHT

Canada's foremost Super Hero team

The Alpha Flight team roar into action.

Conceived as the Canadian government's answer to the recent spate of superhuman activity within the United States, Alpha Flight was the brainchild of James MacDonald Hudson, soon to be known first as VINDICATOR, then as GUARDIAN. Inspired by the FANTASTIC FOUR, Hudson and his wife Heather convinced the Canadian government to found Department H, which would be tasked with assembling a team of superhumans indigenous to the Great White North.

ESSENTIAL STORYLINES

- ***Uncanny X-Men #120–121*** Alpha Flight ambushes the X-Men in an attempt to recover the AWOL Wolverine for the Canadian government.
- ***Alpha Flight #12*** Guardian is seemingly killed during Alpha's battle with Omega Flight.
- ***Alpha Flight Vol. 3 #1–6*** With the real Alpha Flight missing, Sasquatch assembles a new team of off-beat heroes.

FACTFILE

ORIGINAL MEMBERS

GUARDIAN
Electromagnetic battlesuit allows him to fly, surrounds him with a powerful force-field, and permits him to throw bolts of electromagnetic force.

VINDICATOR
Geothermic battlesuit allows her to fly, cause the earth to erupt volcanically, and blast a lavalike substance from her hands.

SHAMAN
Withdraws needed objects from enchanted medicine pouch.

SASQUATCH
Superhuman strength and imperviousness to harm.

PUCK
Trained fighter, skilled acrobat.

SNOWBIRD
Transforms into various Canadian animal forms.

BASE
Tamarind Island, British Columbia

FIRST APPEARANCE
Uncanny X-Men #120 (April 1979)

ALPHA FLIGHT (2011)
1 Shaman ***2*** Guardian ***3*** Sasquatch ***4*** Aurora ***5*** Marrina ***6*** Northstar ***7*** Puck ***8*** Snowbird

WANTED: A LEADER

The project was implemented using a three-tiered training system. New recruits or those whose powers proved unstable would be assigned to Gamma Flight. Those whose command of their abilities required further training formed the basis of Beta Flight. The front line—the active members whose job it would be to rout any superhuman threats to the nation—were Alpha Flight. Hudson intended that the man known as Logan (*see* WOLVERINE) or Weapon X would lead Alpha Flight. However, that task fell to Hudson himself when Logan was recruited by PROFESSOR X to become a member of his X-MEN team. Alpha Flight endured a rocky relationship with the Canadian government, being cast aside then drafted back into military service. While the Beta and Gamma Flight units produced heroes to serve with Alpha Flight, such as PUCK, the programs were perverted to form the nucleus of the sinister OMEGA FLIGHT. Alpha Flight soldiered on through deaths and resurrections, strange transformations, sudden reversals, and numerous roster changes—loyal to their mission of protecting their homeland.

In the aftermath of M-Day, a man known as the Collective blazed across Canada, bursting with the energy of all the mutant powers lost that day. Alpha Flight assembled to stop him, but Guardian, Major Mapleleaf, two Pucks, SHAMAN, and Vindicator were killed, leaving only SASQUATCH alive. During the Chaos War, Guardian, MARRINA, Shaman, and Vindicator returned from the dead to help AURORA, NORTHSTAR, Sasquatch, and SNOWBIRD protect Canada. They later reunited with the first Puck to defeat the MASTER OF THE WORLD, who'd taken overthe Canadian government.

Under Captain Marvel's leadership and aboard the Alpha Flight Space Station, the team later became Earth's first line of defense against threats from outer space.

AMERICAN EAGLE

FIRST APPEARANCE *Marvel Two-In-One Annual* #6 (1981)
REAL NAME Jason Strongbow
OCCUPATION Champion of the Navaho Tribe
BASE Navaho Reservation, Arizona
HEIGHT 6 ft **WEIGHT** 200 lbs **EYES** Brown **HAIR** Black
SPECIAL POWERS/ABILITIES Superhuman strength, speed, and endurance; shoots a crossbow with specialized bolts.

While protesting the mining of a sacred mountain, Jason Strongbow and his brother Ward encountered KLAW, whose sonic blast reacted with uranium in the rock and mutagenically enhanced the brothers. As American Eagle, Jason tracked Klaw to the Savage Land, where he defeated the villain with the aid of the THING, Ka-zar, and Wyatt WINGFOOT, but at the cost of Ward's life. Jason refused to register with the US government during the CIVIL WAR and fought the THUNDERBOLTS to stay free. He badly injured BULLSEYE before he escaped. During FEAR ITSELF, he foiled a trio of thugs on mutant growth hormone who were causing troubles on his reservation.

A-NEXT

On Earth-982, the AVENGERS disbanded. Ten years later, Kevin Masterson, son of THUNDERSTRIKE, visited Avengers Compound to find that JARVIS had kept his father's enchanted mace for him. LOKI stole the mace and so inspired the formation of a new Avengers team, each member being related to a former one. Team membership varied as A-Next faced off against the DEFENDERS, the Soldiers of the Serpent, Kristoff VERNARD (DR. DOOM's adopted son), Argo, IRON MAN, RED SKULL and DR. DOOM, and the REVENGERS. They've also worked with SPIDER-GIRL and the Fantastic Five.

A-NEXT
1 Blue Streak
2 Spider-Girl
3 American Dream
4 Sabreclaw
5 J2

FACTFILE
FOUNDING MEMBERS
THUNDERSTRIKE Super-strong, generates thunder blasts of concussive force.
MAINFRAME Program that lives within mobile armored, multi-weaponed, super-strong robot body.
STINGER Flies, shrinks, generates bio-electric blasts.
J2 Super-strong, nearly unstoppable and indestructible.
EDWIN JARVIS Director of operations.
ADDITIONAL MEMBERS
American Dream, Ant-Man, Blue Streak, Crimson Curse, Freebooter, Hawkeye, Jubilee, Kate Power, Sabreclaw, Scarlet Witch, Speedball, Thena, Warp

BASE
Avengers Compound

FIRST APPEARANCE
A-Next #1 (October 1998)

A-NEXT

ANACONDA

FIRST APPEARANCE *Marvel Two-In-One* #1 (June 1980)
REAL NAME Blanche "Blondie" Sitznski
OCCUPATION Freelance criminal **BASE** Mobile
HEIGHT 6 ft 2 in **WEIGHT** 220 lbs **EYES** Green **HAIR** Blond
SPECIAL POWERS/ABILITIES Able to stretch her limbs, wrap them around people or objects, and exert enough power to crush one-inch thick steel. Few humans can break free from her grasp.

Former steelworker Blanche Sitznski underwent bioengineering changes at the mutagenics lab of the Brand Corporation and became Anaconda. She then joined the SERPENT SQUAD to help retrieve the Serpent Crown. After some time as a mercenary, she joined Sidewinder in the SERPENT SOCIETY crime organization. She did stints with the Femizons and the SIX PACK before joining Viper's Serpent Society and Helmut Zemo's Army of Evil.

ANCIENT ONE

Five centuries ago, the master sorcerer called the Ancient One was a young farmer in the Himalayan village of Kamar-Taj. He studied sorcery with another villager, KALUU. When Kaluu sought to use his powers for conquest, the youth thwarted him, and henceforth dedicated his life to opposing evil sorcerers. He eventually became Sorcerer Supreme of Earth's dimension.

Though magic greatly extended his life, the Ancient One knew that his death was inevitable and sought to train a successor. He accepted BARON MORDO as a pupil, although he was aware of Mordo's potential for evil. Then the American surgeon Stephen Strange arrived, hoping that the Ancient One could cure his injured hands. Instead Strange found a new vocation and asked to become the Ancient One's pupil. Under the Ancient One's tutelage, DOCTOR STRANGE ultimately became the new Sorcerer Supreme of the Earth dimension.

Later, to prevent the demon Shuma-Gorath from entering the Earth dimension through his mind, the Ancient One persuaded Strange to shut down the elderly sorcerer's brain. Thus the Ancient One died in mortal form, but his astral form became "one with the universe." He has reappeared in his astral form several times since, working in the service of Eternity.

FACTFILE
REAL NAME
Yao
OCCUPATION
Sorcerer Supreme
BASE
Kamar-Taj, Tibet, China

HEIGHT 5 ft 11 in
WEIGHT 160 lbs
EYES Brown
HAIR Bald, with white beard

FIRST APPEARANCE
Strange Tales #110 (July 1963)

ANCIENT ONE

POWERS
Vast natural talent allied with years of training made him the greatest sorcerer in Earth's dimension; capable of astral projection, mesmerism, and illusion-casting; able to hurl bolts of energy and possessed of extraordinary longevity.

ANGAR

FIRST APPEARANCE *Daredevil* #100 (June 1973)

REAL NAME David Alan Angar

OCCUPATION Criminal **BASE** San Francisco

HEIGHT 6 ft 10 in **WEIGHT** 155 lbs **EYES** Brown **HAIR** Brown

SPECIAL POWERS/ABILITIES As Angar, his scream induces hallucinations and memory loss. As Scream, a creature of pure sound, he has flight, sound manipulation, and invulnerability.

Disillusioned social activist David Angar volunteered to be exposed to technology brought to Earth by MOONDRAGON, which gave him a hallucination-inducing scream. Moondragon's malevolent partner, Kerwin J. Broderick, hired Angar to kill DAREDEVIL and BLACK WIDOW, but Angar failed. Becoming a criminal for hire, Angar spent time in prison and lost his powers. MASTER KHAN later reinstated them, but the police gunned Angar down during a robbery. THE FIXER later used Angar's essence to create SCREAM, a being of pure sound, who joined the Redeemers (see THUNDERBOLTS). At his request, his teammate SONGBIRD dispersed him permanently.

ANGER, DIRK

FIRST APPEARANCE *Nextwave* #1 (March 2006)

REAL NAME Dirk Anger **OCCUPATION** Leader of HATE

BASE Mobile

HEIGHT 6 ft 1 in **WEIGHT** 225 lbs **EYES** Blue **HAIR** Brown

SPECIAL POWERS/ABILITIES Controls HATE and its resources. Ages very slowly.

General Dirk Anger was the director of the Highest Anti-Terrorist Effort (HATE), an organization dedicated to battling the terrorists of SILENT. Through the use of various, experimental longevity drugs, the mentally unstable Anger lived for more than 90 years. He recruited a group of heroes to form NEXTWAVE, HATE's strike team, but they went rogue after they discovered that SILENT was actually funding HATE through its Beyond Corporation subsidiary, a fact Anger knew all about. He was last seen commanding the Aeromarine (HATE's mobile control center) on a kamikaze course into Nextwave's Shockwave Rider airship, killing everyone but his targets.

ANGELA

Angela is the daughter of ODIN and Freya, but was raised in the Tenth Realm of Heven as an angel with no knowledge of her lineage. In the distant past, Heven and Asgard had waged war against each other, during which Odin's daughter, Aldrif, was seemingly killed. It transpired that Aldrif survived and was taken by the angels to Heven and raised as Angela. However, by then Odin had exiled Heven from his reality, leaving only the Nine Realms rather than ten. A ferocious warrior who is able to go toe-to-toe with THOR, Angela is still coming to terms with her role as an Asgardian since learning of her heritage. Angela has acted as Asgard's assassin, working for Odin, and has also fought alongside the GUARDIANS OF THE GALAXY. She once became the Queen of Hel in order to save her lover, Sera, but soon left, having no desire for such great power. She also became part of the space-faring team dubbed ASGARDIANS OF THE GALAXY.

ANGELA

FACTFILE

REAL NAME
Aldrif Odinsdottir

OCCUPATION
Adventurer; hunter

BASE
Asgard; Heven; Hel

HEIGHT 6 ft 2 in
WEIGHT 480 lbs
EYES White
HAIR Red

FIRST APPEARANCE
Age of Ultron #10 (March 2013)

POWERS
Asgardian with superhuman strength and speed; invulnerable to the elements, including outer space; flies faster than light and carries a bow and sword; protected by ribbons that move as if alive; a formidable warrior.

ANNIHILATORS

In the aftermath of ANNIHILATION and the death of his friend STAR-LORD, COSMO—working as the head of security of Knowhere, a space station built inside a Celestial's head—formed a team of the most powerful heroes in the universe to meet the most dangerous threats. He brought together BETA RAY BILL, GLADIATOR, Ikon, RONAN, the SILVER SURFER, and QUASAR. After initial confusion, the team bonded and drove BLASTAAR from Kree territory. They then agreed to work together as needs demanded.

When a SKRULL named Klobok took the shape of Doctor Dredd—a DIRE WRAITH sorcerer—and tried to free the Wraith homeworld and destroy their Galadorian foes, the Annihilators assembled to stop him. This battle brought them into conflict with IMMORTUS and forced them to meld the Dire Wraith planet and the Galadorian planet into one.

The Annihilators later reunited to stop the rebirth of the MAGUS on Earth, as engineered by the Universal Church of Truth. At first the AVENGERS fought the Annihilators, thinking they were part of an invading force. The Avengers subsequently joined with the Annihilators to capture the new Magus and imprison him in Knowhere.

ANNIHILATORS

FACTFILE

FOUNDING MEMBERS

BETA RAY BILL
Korbinite with the power of Thor

COSMO
Telepathic canine cosmonaut

GLADIATOR
Majestor of the Shi'ar Empire

IKON
Galadorian Spaceknight

RONAN
Kree accuser

SILVER SURFER
Former herald of Galactus, from Zenn-La

QUASAR
Human Protector of the Universe

BASE
Knowhere

FIRST APPEARANCE
Thanos Imperative: Devastation #1 (May 2011)

ANNIHILATORS
1 Cosmo ***2*** Beta Ray Bill ***3*** Ronan ***4*** Quasar
5 Ikon ***6*** Gladiator ***7*** Silver Surfer

ANNIHILATION, SEE PAGES 20–21

ANNIHILATION

This means war...

Richard Rider (Nova), the last survivor of the Nova Corps, leads the Kree defense—and later the entire United Front—against the invading hordes of the Annihilation Wave.

The Annihilation Wave, an overwhelming force from the strange dimension known as the Negative Zone, broke through the Crunch to attack the positive matter universe. The Wave, composed of countless insectoid starships and warriors, first destroyed the Kyln, a ring of artificial moons that served both as a super-prison and as a generator of nearly limitless power. Then it destroyed the planet Xandar and the Nova Corps, leaving Earth's Richard Rider (Nova) as the galactic police force's only survivor.

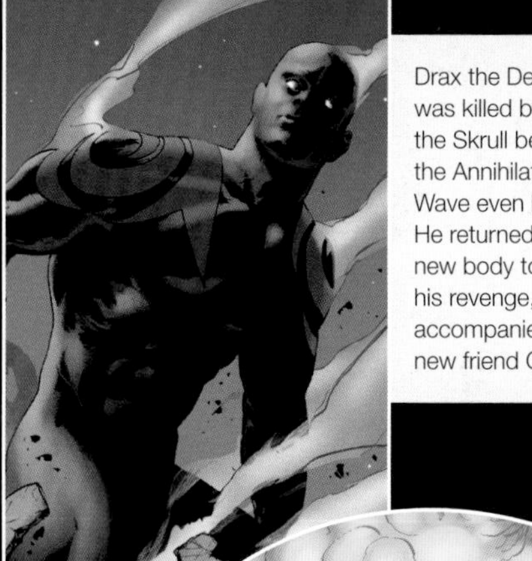

Drax the Destroyer was killed by Paibok the Skrull before the Annihilation Wave even began. He returned in a new body to seek his revenge, accompanied by his new friend Cammi.

THE GALAXY AT WAR

With the help of Quasar and Drax the Destroyer, Nova discovered that Annihilus, who led the Annihilation Wave, had allied with Thanos to conquer the galaxy. After killing Quasar, Annihilus took his Quantum Bands and drove off the others. Annihilus freed from Kyln two ancient beings known as Aegis and Tenebrous, whom Galactus had imprisoned there. The Silver Surfer joined with Galactus and his former heralds to fight his foes but lost.

With the help of Drax, Gamora, Ronan the Accuser, and Star-Lord (Peter Quill), Nova formed and led the interstellar alliance called the United Front. After Thanos captured Moondragon, Drax went to rescue her and discovered that Annihilus had turned Galactus and his heralds into a weapon that could destroy planets. Drax freed the Silver Surfer, who in turn freed Galactus. Furious, Galactus attacked the Annihilation Wave. Meanwhile, with the Skrull Empire destroyed, Ronan and the Super-Skrull freed the Kree Empire from the control of the traitorous House Fiyero, which had kept the Supreme Intelligence trapped between life and death. Finishing the Supreme Intelligence off, Ronan took control of the empire.

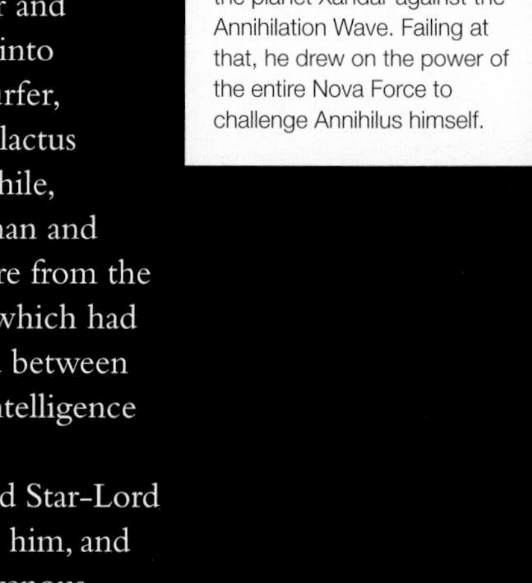

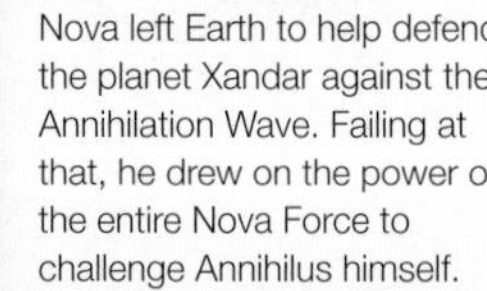

Nova left Earth to help defend the planet Xandar against the Annihilation Wave. Failing at that, he drew on the power of the entire Nova Force to challenge Annihilus himself.

The Silver Surfer made the ultimate sacrifice to stem the tide of the Annihilation Wave. After nearly dying at the hands of other elder beings, he returned to the service of Galactus.

With the Annihilation Wave decimated, Nova, Phyla-Vell, and Star-Lord hunted down Annihilus. Phyla took the Quantum Bands from him, and Nova killed him with his bare hands. Later, though, Annihilus' lieutenant Ravenous revealed an infant insectoid he believed to be Annihilus reborn.

ANOTHER CONQUEST

Soon after, the Phalanx attacked and conquered the Kree Empire, using a techno-organic virus to control their subjects. Star-Lord formed a team (a prototype of the Guardians of the Galaxy) to help fight this threat. Phyla-Vell (now the new Quasar) and Moondragon hunted for a savior who could defeat the Phalanx: a young, regenerated Adam Warlock. Warlock brought the women to meet the High Evolutionary. Soon after, Ultron attacked, killing Moondragon and revealing himself as the driving force behind the Phalanx invasion. Later, Ultron forced the High Evolutionary to transfer his mind into Warlock's body.

Meanwhile, Ronan, Super-Skrull, and a Kree named Wraith—who can protect others from the Phalanx infection—went to the Kree world controlled by Ravenous and shielded an army of robotic Kree sentries. They then sent them to destroy the Phalanx. At the same time, Nova, Drax, and Gamora reappeared with Warlock of the Technarchy, which had created the Phalanx.

The Technarchy Warlock forced Ultron from Adam Warlock's body. When Ultron reassembled himself into a gigantic body, Wraith trapped Ultron's mind within it, and Quasar slew it, ending the war.

The Super-Skrull failed to keep the Annihilation Wave from destroying his people's homeworld, but he sacrificed himself (temporarily) to keep the Harvester of Sorrows from obliterating any other worlds.

Ronan the Accuser was framed for treason but still rose to become the leader of the Kree. He ultimately had to kill the Supreme Intelligence and take control of the Kree Empire himself.

THE ANNIHILATION WAVE

The invasion forces that Annihilus assembled in the relative safety of the Negative Zone proved to be the largest fighting force the galaxy had ever seen. At the height of its powers, it destroyed nearly all of the mighty Skrull and Kree Empires and even captured the Silver Surfer and Galactus. At the moment known as Annihilation Day, Annihilus' forces destroyed the Kyln super-prison and launched their war on the positive-matter universe.

ANGEL

The avenging angel

ANGEL

FACTFILE

REAL NAME
Warren Kenneth Worthington III

OCCUPATION
Hero and Chairman of Worthington Industries

BASE
New York State (Avengers Tower), Manhattan, New York

HEIGHT 6 ft
WEIGHT 150 lbs
EYES Blue
HAIR Blond

FIRST APPEARANCE
X-Men #1 (September 1963)

POWERS

Feathered wings can carry up to twice his weight and bear him to 29,000 feet; able to fly up to 150 mph; enhanced lungs enable him to breathe at high altitudes; possesses extraordinary eyesight and blood has healing qualities.

Warren's skin gained a blue pigment during his time working for Apocalypse.

Warren Worthington was born into a wealthy family. At private school, during his late teens, Warren noticed wings budding from his shoulder blades. Fearful of attracting attention, he strapped them to his body but secretly began experimenting with flying. When a fire started in his school, Warren flew to the rescue of his schoolmates disguised in a nightshirt and blond wig. He was mistaken for an angel and so, when he headed to New York City to become a costumed crimefighter, he took the moniker Avenging Angel.

A young version of Angel was brought forward in time with his teammates. This Angel gained powerful cosmic wings after entering the transformative Black Vortex in the hope of not turning into Archangel.

ITINERANT X-MAN

Warren soon came to the attention of Professor X and joined the Professor's fledgling band of X-Men. At first, Warren disguised his face with a mask, but he later discarded it, believing that his handsome, telegenic features would help gain the team public support. He inherited vast wealth and went on to become a media playboy. Warren used his fortune to provide backing to the Champions of Los Angeles, the Defenders, and later X-Factor. While with X-Factor, Warren's wings were damaged battling the Marauders, became infected, and had to be amputated. The loss of his wings so depressed Warren that he attempted suicide. Saved by the mutant warlord Apocalypse, Warren was offered the chance to grow new wings of steel if he became one of Apocalypse's Horsemen—Death. Confused and still depressed, Warren agreed, but this Faustian pact brought him into direct conflict with his X-Men friends. Only the apparent death of his old friend Iceman brought Warren to his senses. Following this epiphany, Warren's metal wings molted to reveal feathers.

Having lost both his parents, Archangel considers the X-Men his surrogate family, bickering and fighting but also protecting and defending each other.

Returning to the X-Men, Warren rechristened himself Archangel. For a while, Warren could morph back and forth between his Angel and Archangel personas at will.

Following Apocalypse's death, Warren was forced into becoming the new Apocalypse. Archangel had two children with Pestilence, another Horseman that Apocalypse had created. These children became the Apocalypse Twins. Archangel was seemingly killed by Psylocke but was later found alive, with no memory of his past life—in fact he believed himself to be a real angel. This individual was later revealed to be just half of the real Warren, who had been split into two entities—the dark, vengeful Archangel and his peaceful human side. After Clan Akkaba and Genocide (Apocalypse's son) created clones of Archangel, Psylocke and an X-Men team stopped the villains, rescued their friend, and helped merge the two sides of Warren into one. Professor X later gave Angel more control over his form and restored his memories.

ESSENTIAL STORYLINES

- ***X-Men #54–6*** Warren Worthington's origins are shown—from a private schoolboy who grows wings to a member of the X-Men.
- ***X-Factor #10–15, Thor #373–4*** Angel's wings are amputated and he is driven to suicide.
- ***X-Factor #21–25*** Apocalypse appoints Angel as his Fourth Horseman, Death.

ANNIHILUS

FACTFILE
REAL NAME
Annihilus
OCCUPATION
Conqueror; destroyer
BASE
Sector 17A of the Negative Zone

HEIGHT 5 ft 11 in
WEIGHT 200 lbs
EYES Green
HAIR None

FIRST APPEARANCE
Fantastic Four Annual #6 (1968)

POWERS
Exoskeleton can withstand vast external pressure (up to 1,500 psi); can breathe in the vacuum of space; his wings enable him to fly at up to 150 mph.

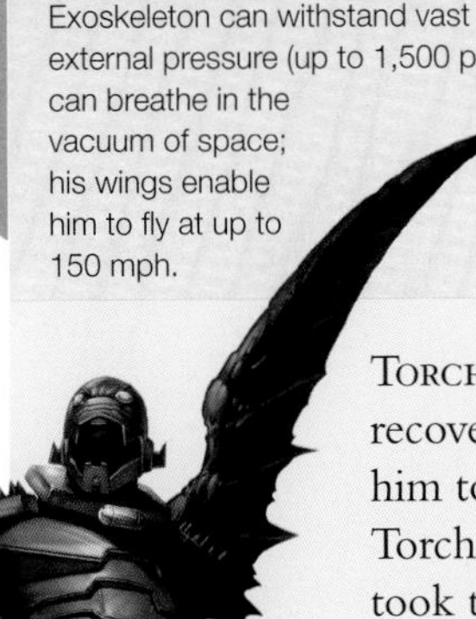

In the Negative Zone, a Tyannan ship crashed on the planet Arthros and released some spores. One of them grew into an insect-like being called Annihilus. Wielding the Cosmic Control Rod, he became master of the life forms that grew from the other spores, and he set out to conquer the other worlds of the Negative Zone. The FANTASTIC FOUR regularly stymied his attempts to conquer the Earth and the Microverse.

Annihilus launched the Annihilation Wave, aiming to destroy both the Negative Zone and Earth. After his efforts were thwarted, NOVA killed him, but he was reborn with his memories intact and soon took control of the Negative Zone again. When the HUMAN TORCH was killed in the Negative Zone, Annihilus recovered his body and revived the Torch to force him to help him reach Earth again. The Human Torch led a revolution against Annihilus' rule and took the Cosmic Control Rod from him, which the Torch then used to lead the Annihilation Wave to stop a KREE invasion of Earth. When the Human Torch allowed free elections in the Negative Zone, Annihilus won the leadership once more by a landslide. He continues to plague the FF.

ANT-MAN II

Electronics expert Scott Lang turned to crime to help support his family, but was arrested and sent to prison. After being paroled for good behavior, he worked at Stark Industries. His wife divorced him, but gave him custody of their daughter Cassie. Scott learned that Cassie needed a heart operation, but her surgeon had been kidnapped. He resorted to burglary, breaking into the home of Dr. Hank PYM and stealing his old Ant-Man costume and shrinking formula. After rescuing the surgeon and saving Cassie, Scott turned himself in, but Pym decided to allow him to continue as Ant-Man. Scott eventually joined the AVENGERS, but was later killed in action by the SCARLET WITCH. The YOUNG AVENGERS rescued Scott by traveling back in time to the moment of his death, only for him to then witness DOCTOR DOOM killing Cassie (now the hero STATURE). Wanting to make amends, Doom later brought Cassie back to life. Lang opened Ant-Man Security Solutions in Miami. He helped Bucky BARNES defeat the HYDRA CAPTAIN AMERICA and adventured with the new WASP (Nadia Van Dyne).

FACTFILE
REAL NAME
Scott Edward Lang
OCCUPATION
Adventurer; former burglar; electronics technician
BASE
Avengers Mansion

HEIGHT 6 ft
WEIGHT 190 lbs
EYES Blue
HAIR Blond

FIRST APPEARANCE
Avengers #181
(March 1979)

POWERS
Possesses ability to shrink himself and other objects and people, usually to ant size, but also to microscopic levels. Cybernetic helmet allows him telepathic control of ants. Helmet amplifies his voice so that he can be heard by normal-sized humans.

ANT-MAN III

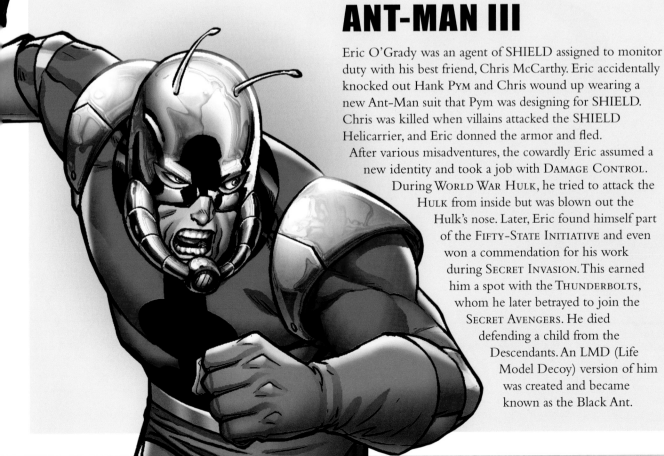

Eric O'Grady was an agent of SHIELD assigned to monitor duty with his best friend, Chris McCarthy. Eric accidentally knocked out Hank PYM and Chris wound up wearing a new Ant-Man suit that Pym was designing for SHIELD. Chris was killed when villains attacked the SHIELD Helicarrier, and Eric donned the armor and fled.

After various misadventures, the cowardly Eric assumed a new identity and took a job with DAMAGE CONTROL. During WORLD WAR HULK, he tried to attack the HULK from inside but was blown out the Hulk's nose. Later, Eric found himself part of the FIFTY-STATE INITIATIVE and even won a commendation for his work during SECRET INVASION. This earned him a spot with the THUNDERBOLTS, whom he later betrayed to join the SECRET AVENGERS. He died defending a child from the Descendants. An LMD (Life Model Decoy) version of him was created and became known as the Black Ant.

FACTFILE
REAL NAME
Eric O'Grady
OCCUPATION
Member of the Thunderbolts
BASE
Mobile

HEIGHT 5 ft 10 in
WEIGHT 115 lbs
EYES Brown
HAIR Blond

FIRST APPEARANCE
The Irredeemable Ant-Man #1
(September 2006)

POWERS
Can grow to giant size and shrink to ant size and back with the touch of a button on his helmet, which also allows him to communicate with ants. His armor features a jet pack and a pair of metallic tentacles.

ANTI-VENOM

FACTFILE

REAL NAME
Edward Charles "Eddie" Brock

OCCUPATION
Former journalist; vigilante

BASE
New York City

HEIGHT 6 ft 3 in
WEIGHT 260 lbs
EYES Blue
HAIR Reddish-blond

FIRST APPEARANCE
Amazing Spider-Man #569 (August 2008)

POWERS

Anti-Venom has superhuman speed, strength, and agility. He can stick to and climb surfaces and can fire webbing. He can also cure the irradiated.

ANTI-VENOM

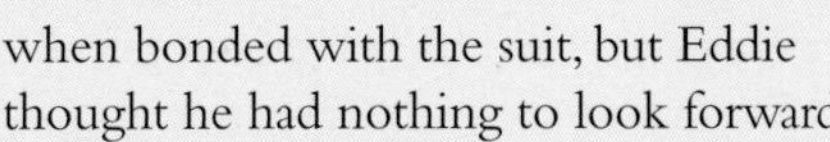

Flash Thompson became the second Anti-Venom

When Eddie Brock found that he had cancer, he auctioned off his symbiotic suit (*see* VENOM), and it later bonded with the criminal Mac Gargan (*see* SCORPION). Lawyer Matt Murdock (*see* DAREDEVIL) helped Eddie clear his name of the crimes he'd committed when bonded with the suit, but Eddie thought he had nothing to look forward to but a painful death. Martin Li (secretly the villain Mister Negative) cured Eddie with a touch, causing the last vestiges of the symbiote to bond with Eddie's immune system. When Gargan confronted Eddie, the symbiote tried to return to him, but it burned on touching his skin. In response, Eddie's altered antibodies became a substance that covered his flesh and turned him into Anti-Venom. Eddie later sacrificed his Anti-Venom powers for use as the prime ingredient of the cure administered to the victims of the Spider Island outbreak (see SPIDER-MAN). However, a new Anti-Venom was created by Alchemax, affecting Flash THOMPSON. Flash, as Anti-Venom, used his powers to save Spidey's allies when Norman OSBORN bonded with the CARNAGE symbiote and attacked them. With Flash injured in previous fighting, the act used up all of his Anti-Venom powers and he died in Spider-Man's arms.

APOCALYPSE TWINS

FIRST APPEARANCE *Uncanny Avengers* #5 (May 2013)
REAL NAMES Uriel and Eimin Worthington
OCCUPATION Conquerers **BASE** Mobile **HEIGHT** 6 ft 1 in (Uriel); 5 ft 11 in (Eimin) **WEIGHT** 210 lbs (Uriel); 185 lbs (Eimin) **EYES** Red (Uriel); None (Eimin) **HAIR** None (Uriel); Brown (Eimin)
SPECIAL POWERS/ABILITIES Various mutations, including wings, superhuman durability, ability to generate acid and/or energy razors, chronokinesis.

Uriel and Eimin, the children of Archangel (*see* ANGEL) and Pestilence, were kidnapped by KANG soon after their birth and taken into the future. When APOCALYPSE's son, Genocide, tried to gain a Death Seed from a CELESTIAL Gardener, the twins reappeared, killed the Celestial, and destroyed Genocide's forces. They took the artifact and used it to create their own Horsemen. The twins then built a dark future, but were stopped by survivors from the AVENGERS Unity Division of that future, who traveled back in time to defeat them. The duo were finally killed by SUNFIRE, when he redirected the energy of a dying Celestial against them.

AQUARIAN

FIRST APPEARANCE *Adventure Into Fear* #17 (October 1973)
REAL NAME Wundarr **OCCUPATION** Adventurer
BASE Commune on southern California coast
HEIGHT 5 ft 10 in **WEIGHT** 165 lbs **EYES** Brown **HAIR** Brown
SPECIAL POWERS/ABILITIES Surrounded by null-field that neutralizes other superhumans' kinetic and electromagnetic energies; walks on air.

Sent into space at an early age, Wundarr landed on Earth, where the sun's energy gave him superhuman powers. An encounter with a Cosmic Cube augmented these powers. As Aquarian, he became a prophet of the Water-Children. After the CIVIL WAR he joined THE FIFTY-STATE INITIATIVE and was assigned to Florida's team, the Command. He defended Florida from the SKRULLS during SECRET INVASION.

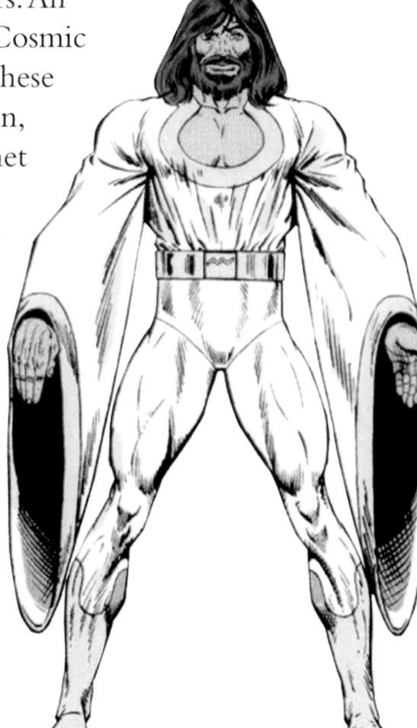

APOCALYPSE

Ancient mutant menace

In one possible future—Messiah War—Apocalypse teamed up with Angel (in his Archangel form) to rescue Hope Summers from Stryfe.

Born nearly 5,000 years ago in ancient Egypt, Apocalypse is one of the earliest known mutant humans. As "En Sabah Nur," or "the First One," he traveled the world for thousands of years, sometimes hibernating for many years at a time. He often instigated wars to test which nations were fittest, and he was worshiped as a god by ancient civilizations. He had a hand in creating not only DRACULA but also MISTER SINISTER, and a wide number of people have served as his Four Horsemen: Famine, War, Pestilence, and Death.

FACTFILE
REAL NAME
En Sabah Nur
OCCUPATION
Conqueror
BASE
Mobile

APOCALYPSE

HEIGHT Variable, usually 7 ft
WEIGHT Variable
EYES Blue
HAIR Black

FIRST APPEARANCE
(In shadow) *X-Factor* #5 (June 1986), (fully shown) *X-Factor* #6 (July 1986)

POWERS
Can alter the atomic structure of his body to change shape. Can increase his size by absorbing additional mass. Possesses superhuman strength, stamina, and durability.

MODERN ERA

In the 20th century, Nur, now called Apocalypse, decided the emerging mutants were destined to supplant "unfit" ordinary humans. He battled the original X-FACTOR and the X-MEN, who were dedicated to peaceful coexistence between mutants and other humans. Apocalypse sometimes even recruited his foes to become his Horsemen. Accordingly, both ANGEL and WOLVERINE have taken the role of Death at different times.

Apocalypse's greatest foe throughout time is CABLE, whose birth was engineered by Mr. Sinister and proved such a powerful moment that it awakened Apocalypse from his hibernation. Determined to raise Cable as his own to keep him under control, the Apocalypse of the 37th century—who had conquered North America—mistakenly captured Cable's clone STRYFE and raised him instead. This proved a poor strategy when Stryfe traveled to the 20th century to try to kill Apocalypse.

RESURRECTION

Though he was extraordinarily long-lived, Apocalypse's physical body eventually wore out. He survived by projecting his consciousness into host bodies, including those of X-MAN and CYCLOPS. Cable destroyed Apocalypse's spirit after Jean GREY ripped it from Cyclops' body.

After M-DAY, Apocalypse returned again, this time after a drop of his technovirus-infected blood created a body for him. He tried to rebuild his Horsemen and force the remaining mutants to join his cause, but the CELESTIALS—who had loaned him much of his technology long ago—returned to collect payment for his debt, in the form of his body.

In the present day, Clan Akkaba, a cult run by Apocalypse's many descendants, revived Apocalypse as a child. X-FORCE stopped them, and FANTOMEX killed the child while the other members of X-Force argued over what to do with him. Fantomex then secretly cloned him, raising him in a simulated environment to become a hero called Genesis who could defeat Archangel (*see* ANGEL). The child, now known as Evan SABAHNUR, was then sent to study at the Jean Grey School for Higher Learning. He later joined the time-displaced X-Men, and met the young version of Apocalypse while traveling back in time to Ancient Egypt with Hank McCoy (BEAST). After briefly turning into his evil adult self during the Axis event, he reverted to his younger self and went on the run with DEADPOOL.

The X-Men were later caught up in a fight with a version of Apocalypse from the distant future. He was seemingly destroyed after NIGHTCRAWLER threw him into a vortex threatening to destroy Limbo. No matter how many times Apocalypse has been killed, though, he always seems to return stronger and more deadly than ever.

THE HOUR OF YOUR GLORY IS AT HAND, MY HORSEMEN!
MOUNT YOUR BEASTS!

Apocalypse's first modern team of Horsemen, his warrior servants, included Famine, War, Pestilence, (from left to right) and Archangel as Death (not shown).

ARABIAN KNIGHT

FIRST APPEARANCE *Union Jack* #1 (November 2006)
REAL NAME Navid Hashim **OCCUPATION** Government Agent
BASE Mobile **HEIGHT** 6 ft 2 in **WEIGHT** 175 lbs
EYES Brown **HAIR** Brown
SPECIAL POWERS/ABILITIES Scimitar fires force bolts and penetrates almost any material; rides magic carpet, which can also convert into a battering ram or envelop enemies.

Navid Hashim succeeded the original Arabian Knight (Abdul Qamar) when he was killed. Hashim is a Palestinian working for the Saudi Arabians. Alongside Union Jack, he prevented a terrorist attack on London, earning the grudging respect of Israeli hero Sabra. A highly trained fighter, Hashim wields a magical scimitar, and aided Red Hulk and Machine Man to defeat the Sultan Magus. A third Arabian Knight once fought the Black Panther in Wakanda.

ARCANNA

FIRST APPEARANCE *Defenders* #112 (October 1982)
REAL NAME Arcanna Jones
OCCUPATION Adventurer **BASE** Squadron City
HEIGHT 5 ft 8 in **WEIGHT** 115 lbs **EYES** Blue **HAIR** Blond
SPECIAL POWERS/ABILITIES Extensive magical powers, especially over natural forces, such as wind and water; able to levitate and ride the wind, sometimes on a pole.

A former medium who spent years developing her natural affinity for magic, Arcanna was encouraged to use her mystic powers in the service of mankind by her husband. Arcanna joined the ranks of the Squadron Supreme, costumed champions of her home reality, and became one of its staunchest members—eventually using her magic powers to hollow out the enormous crater in which they built their upgraded headquarters, Squadron City.

ARCADE

An engineering genius and a ruthless hitman, Arcade came by his fortune after allegedly murdering his billionaire father. He is obsessed with traps and games, and executes his victims in secret, amusement-park-style complexes he designs himself and dubs "Murderworlds." He charges $1 million per hit, but the money barely covers his expenses; he kills for sheer enjoyment.

Arcade has captured and toyed with several Super Heroes over the years, including Spider-Man and the X-Men, but they all managed to escape. Arcade kidnapped sixteen superpowered teenagers and put them into a massive new Murderworld, pitting them against each other in a life-or-death competition in which he claimed only one could survive. Several heroes were killed before they could escape. Cullen Bloodstone convinced several survivors to find and kill Arcade—only to later learn the Arcade they killed was a clone created by the Masters of Evil, and the real Arcade was still alive.

FACTFILE
REAL NAME
Unknown
OCCUPATION
Assassin; playboy
BASE Various Murderworlds in undisclosed locations

HEIGHT 5 ft 6 in
WEIGHT 140 lbs
EYES Blue
HAIR Red

FIRST APPEARANCE
Marvel Team-Up #65
(January 1978)

ARCADE

POWERS
Genius at engineering, electronics, and robotics; habitual liar, using deceit to confuse opponents.

In his new Murderworld, Arcade had the powers of a god and he used them to toy with and kill teens.

ARES

FACTFILE
REAL NAME
Ares
OCCUPATION
God of War
BASES
New York City; Olympus

HEIGHT 6 ft 1 in
WEIGHT 500 lbs
EYES Brown
HAIR Brown

FIRST APPEARANCE
Thor #129
(June 1966)

POWERS
Superhuman strength, endurance, agility, and reflexes. Immortal with healing factor.

The son of Zeus and Hera, Ares is the Olympian God of War and has tried to conquer Olympus several times. In many instances, his hated half-brother HERCULES thwarted his plans, continuing their eons-old enmity. Weary of his father's rule, Ares retired to Earth to raise his son Alexander (later revealed to be the god PHOBOS) as a mortal. He returned to Olympus to battle AMATSU-MIKABOSHI—but only when Alexander's life was at stake. Ares joined IRON MAN'S AVENGERS, and he stuck with the team even after Norman Osborn (GREEN GOBLIN) assumed control. He was killed by the SENTRY during Osborn's attack on Asgard.

After spending time in the Elysian Fields with his son Alexander—who had been killed by the Hand assassin Gorgon—Ares was resurrected to be one of the COLLECTOR'S fighters in a cosmic Contest of Champions. Surviving the contest, he returned to Earth and was part of the Champions of Europe, hoping to have many more adventures before returning to the afterlife.

As the God of War, Ares was born for battle and is more than willing to use modern weaponry to help him wage war.

ARIES

FIRST APPEARANCE *Avengers* #72 (January 1970)
REAL NAME Marcus Lassiter
OCCUPATION Professional criminal **BASE** Atlanta, Georgia
HEIGHT 6 ft 1 in **WEIGHT** 230 lbs **EYES** Brown **HAIR** Unknown
SPECIAL POWERS/ABILITIES Costume with horns made of unknown, incredibly hard material, used for charging into foes; Zodiac Key—an otherdimensional, sentient power object capable of firing energy bolts and transporting people across dimensions.

Aries was a founding member of the criminal cartel known as ZODIAC. There have been several Aries. The original was Marcus Lassiter who gained the Zodiac Key and managed to take over Manhattan Island before dying in an explosion. Others have included Grover Raymond, who physically merged with the alien LUCIFER before his death. One of the more recent incarnations worked for the Mad Titan THANOS when he formed a new version of Zodiac. They fought the AVENGERS but were depowered and left for dead by Thanos following their defeat.

ARKON

FIRST APPEARANCE *Avengers* #75 (April 1970)
REAL NAME Arkon ("The Magnificent")
OCCUPATION Ruler ("Imperion") **BASE** The planet Polemachus
HEIGHT 6 ft **WEIGHT** 400 lbs **EYES** Brown **HAIR** Brown
SPECIAL POWERS/ABILITIES Superhuman strength, speed, agility, and stamina; skin and muscles are more dense than that of humans; recovers from injury at a much faster rate than humans.

Arkon once ruled the planet Polemachus. The culture of Polemachus glorifies war and Arkon became his world's greatest warrior. When Polemachus was faced with annihilation, Arkon came to Earth believing that its destruction could save his homeworld. On Earth, IRON MAN teamed with THOR in a plan that saved Polemachus and stopped Arkon's aggression. He was later seen on Weirdworld under the control of DOCTOR DRUID, before being freed by the SQUADRON SUPREME. Arkon now searches for a way home.

ARMADILLO

FIRST APPEARANCE *Captain America* #308 (August 1985)
REAL NAME Antonio Rodriguez
OCCUPATION Professional wrestler **BASE** Mobile
HEIGHT 7 ft 6 in **WEIGHT** 540 lbs
EYES Brown **HAIR** None
SPECIAL POWERS/ABILITIES Body resembles that of a gigantic humanoid armadillo, with sharp claws and armor plating; possesses superhuman strength and durability.

When his wife became mortally ill, Antonio Rodriguez turned to Dr. Karl MALUS, who promised to try to cure her if Antonio worked for him and submitted to his experiments. Malus combined genes from an armadillo with Rodriguez' genes, transforming him into a super-powerful being resembling a humanoid armadillo. Malus assigned the Armadillo to invade the AVENGERS WEST COAST Compound. There CAPTAIN AMERICA defeated the Armadillo but realized he was not a criminal at heart. Armadillo later turned to taking part in wrestling matches against super-strong opponents to earn a living, but returned to crime as part of BARON ZEMO'S Army of Evil.

ARMBRUSTER, COL.

FIRST APPEARANCE *Incredible Hulk* #164 (June 1973)
REAL NAME Colonel John D. "Jack" Armbruster
OCCUPATION Colonel in US Air Force **BASE** Mobile
HEIGHT 6 ft 1 in **WEIGHT** 225 lbs **EYES** Blue **HAIR** Gray
SPECIAL POWERS/ABILITIES Military strategist, resourceful, honorable, and heroically loyal; inveterate pipe-smoker.

Colonel Armbruster led a force to rescue General Ross from the Russians. Although Ross' son-in-law, Major TALBOT, was lost during the mission, it was deemed successful and Armbruster was given control of Project Greenskin, an attempt to study the effects of gamma radiation on the human body. Armbruster's main objective was to capture the HULK, which he succeeded in doing. When Talbot eventually returned, apparently having escaped from the Russians, Armbruster suspected foul play; when he shook hands with Talbot, his watch stopped. Armbruster discovered that there was a bomb in Talbot's body and dragged the Major into a pit. The bomb exploded, killing them both, but saving the life of the US President.

ARMAGEDDON

Leader of the long-lived intergalactic race known as the Troyjan, the teen who would one day be known as Armageddon almost single-handedly reversed the fortunes of his race's declining empire. Under his leadership, the Troyjan expanded their galactic power base and became a force to be reckoned with. Armageddon's attentions first turned to Earth after his son Trauma abducted ATALANTA of the PANTHEON in order to make her his mate, and was subsequently killed in battle with the HULK. Vowing revenge, Armageddon used a resurrection device created by the gamma-enhanced genius known as the LEADER to reincarnate the then-deceased Thunderbolt Ross, in order to lure the Hulk into his clutches. Once the Hulk had been captured, Armageddon intended to use his life force to restore Trauma to life. But the Hulk's energy proved too powerful, and it incinerated the remains of the deceased Troyjan warrior—leaving Armageddon with an even greater desire for revenge!

Armageddon's son, Trauma, lost his life in battle with the Hulk after trying to abduct Atalanta of the Pantheon.

FACTFILE
REAL NAME
Arm'Cheddon
OCCUPATION
Warlord of the Troyjan
BASE
Troyjan-controlled space

HEIGHT 9 ft
WEIGHT 2,528 lbs
EYES Yellow
HAIR Gray

FIRST APPEARANCE
Incredible Hulk #413 (January 1994)

POWERS
Superhuman strength and energy manipulation; enhanced durability and resistance to injury; warlike temperament; great leadership qualities.

To avenge his son's death, Armageddon launched attacks against the Pantheon and the Earth.

ARMOR

FACTFILE
REAL NAME
Hisako Ichiki
OCCUPATION
Adventurer; student
BASE
Jean Grey School for Higher Learning

HEIGHT 5 ft 4 in
WEIGHT 112 lbs
EYES Black
HAIR Black

FIRST APPEARANCE
Astonishing X-Men #4 (October 2004)

POWERS
Hisako can draw upon the strength of her ancestors to psionically create a translucent suit of armor that grants her superhuman strength and durability.

Hisako dreamed of becoming one of the X-MEN from the moment she gained her mutant powers. Once the existence of the Xavier Institute became public, she enrolled there and began her studies. She retained her powers after M-Day and soon afterward realized her dream, accompanying the X-Men to the planet Breakworld to stop a plot to destroy the Earth. Hisako studied at the Jean Grey School of Higher Learning, where WOLVERINE trained her in combat. He became something of a mentor to her until his death.

She later fought against DAKEN and Norman Osborn's Dark X-Men. A version of Armor from another reality joined MISS SINISTER's New Marauders, but was killed alongside her teammates when Emma FROST turned them against Miss Sinister, causing Miss Sinister to activate kill-switches that she had implanted in their genetic code.

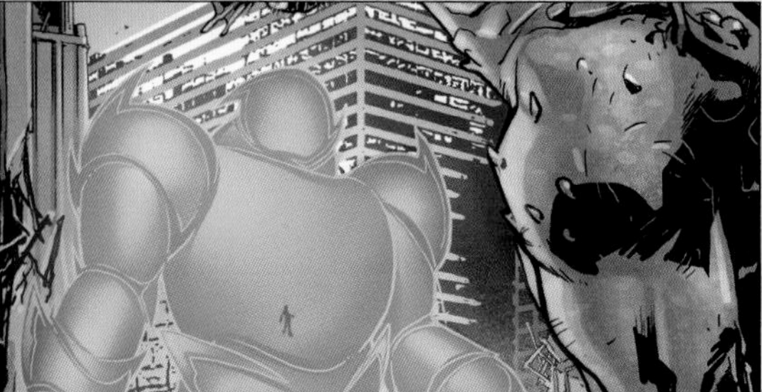
Since her powers are linked to her family, when her relatives die, Hisako's abilities become vastly more powerful. Her armor can become the size of a building.

ARMORY

FIRST APPEARANCE *Avengers: The Initiative* #1 (April 2007)
REAL NAME Violet Lightner
OCCUPATION Former hero **BASE** Camp Hammond, CT
HEIGHT 5 ft 6 in **WEIGHT** 110 lbs **EYES** Green **HAIR** Purple
SPECIAL POWERS/ABILITIES Wore the Tactigon, an alien weapon capable of morphing into any weapon necessary.

As suicidal teen Violet Lightner leaped from the Golden Gate Bridge, an alien weapon called the Tactigon shot from the water, attached itself to Lightner's arm, and transformed into a grappling hook that saved her. After helping the Avengers defeat the giant robot Ultimo, Lightner joined the Fifty-State Initiative and reported to Camp Hammond as part of the first class of trainees. During her first combat training session, teammate Trauma triggered her arachnophobia, and Lightner panicked. Wild shots from the Tactigon blew off Komodo's arm and killed Michael Van Patrick. Lightner was removed from duty, and surgeons stripped her of the Tactigon.

ARON, THE ROGUE WATCHER

FIRST APPEARANCE *Captain Marvel* #39 (July 1975)
REAL NAME Aron **OCCUPATION** Cosmic meddler
BASE Mobile; intergalactic **HEIGHT** Variable
WEIGHT Variable **EYES** White; yellow when angry **HAIR** None
SPECIAL POWERS/ABILITIES Vast cosmic abilities; changed appearance at will; able to move between dimensions; subdued enemies with psionic blasts, or teleported them.

A young Watcher (as far as such temporal matters are measured by that intergalactic race) Aron eschewed his people's pledge of non-interference in all things, choosing instead to use his great cosmic abilities for his evil enjoyment. He toyed with the lives of the Fantastic Four, replacing them with corrupt duplicates, and later engineered a civil war within his own Watcher race.
As Aron was about to destroy the Fantastic Four, Uatu the Watcher, who was responsible for Earth's section of the cosmos, reluctantly killed him.

ATALANTA

FIRST APPEARANCE *The Incredible Hulk* #376 (December 1990)
REAL NAME Unrevealed **OCCUPATION** Pantheon operative
BASE The Mount, southwestern United States
HEIGHT 5 ft 10 in **WEIGHT** Unknown **EYES** Blue **HAIR** Black
SPECIAL POWERS/ABILITIES Wields a bow and arrows composed of an unknown form of energy that turns matter into super-heated plasma.

Named after the huntress of Greek mythology, Atalanta is a member of the Pantheon, a covert organization of superhumans which intervenes in world affairs to prevent disasters.
A deadly shot with her flaming bow, Atalanta has skin, body tissue, and a skeleton that are denser than a normal human's, affording her greater resistance to injury. She also possesses a fast healing factor and an extended lifespan. A psychic power enables her to mentally perceive her target even if she is unable to see it. Virtually nothing is known about the origin of Atalanta, except that she is related to other members of the Pantheon. She has been the lover of fellow Pantheon member Achilles.

ASGARDIANS OF THE GALAXY

Angela the Asgardian assassin, Valkyrie (and her host, the archaeologist Annabelle Riggs), the Destroyer, Skurge the Executioner, Thunderstrike and Throg the Thunder Frog form the Asgardians of the Galaxy, a team of renegade heroes and gods brought together by Kid Loki (with Angela acting on his behalf) to stop Nebula taking over the universe.

But with Nebula already amassing a huge army it proved a tough task. While recruiting her crew, Angela sought out Annabelle Riggs not because of her connection to Valkyrie (Riggs and Valkyrie share a single body), but because of her knowledge of ancient languages. At first only Angela knew that Kid Loki, a version of Loki long thought dead, had concealed himself using the Destroyer and was the real power behind the team.

ASGARDIANS OF THE GALAXY
1 Angela ***2*** Destroyer
3 Valkyrie ***4*** Thunderstrike
5 Skurge ***6*** Throg

FACTFILE
FOUNDING MEMBERS
ANGELA
Superhuman strength and speed; flies faster than light; protected by ribbons that move as if alive; a formidable warrior.
VALKYRIE
Enhanced strength, longevity, and stamina; can perceive the onset of death; can teleport to the realm of the dead.
DESTROYER (KID LOKI)
Nearly indestructible armor can levitate, generate fire, and shoot a disintegrator from its face.
SKURGE
A master of combat. Superhuman strength and stamina; wielded a magical double-bladed ax.
THUNDERSRIKE
Super-strong; projects concussive blasts of mystical energy.
THROG
Superhuman strength, stamina, and durability; increased longevity (for a frog).

FIRST APPEARANCE
Asgardians of the Galaxy #1 (November 2018)

ASGARDIANS OF THE GALAXY

ATLANTEANS

Undersea warrior race

ATLANTEANS

FACTFILE

NOTABLE ATLANTEANS

PRINCE NAMOR (ruler of Atlantis)
LADY DORMA (Namor's first royal consort)
ATTUMA (barbarian warlord)
KRANG (usurper)
VASHTI (Namor's Grand Vizier)
PRINCE BYRRAH
LADY FEN (Namor's mother)
NAMORA (Namor's cousin)
NAMORITA (clone of Namora)
BEEMER (would-be usurper)

FIRST APPEARANCE

Fantastic Four Annual #1 (1963)

POWERS

Atlanteans' gills allow them to breathe underwater; they only survive five minutes out of water. They are about ten times stronger and faster than "surface dwellers." They easily withstand the crushing pressure and freezing temperatures at the bottom of the ocean.

Atlantis was once a small continent in the Atlantic Ocean. The cradle of an advanced civilization, it was torn apart by earthquakes and sank into the sea some 20,000 years ago. About 10,000 years ago, a genetic offshoot of Man, *Homo mermanus*, evolved the ability to live underwater. These mermen discovered the ruins left by the ancient Atlanteans and settled in them.

The current emperor of Atlantis, Namor has often battled outside invaders and faced treachery from traitorous relatives—like his cousin Beemer—who have attempted to steal his throne.

FIRST CONTACT

About 150 years ago, to protect his people, Emperor Thakorr moved the capital near to Antarctica. The Atlanteans remained undisturbed until an American research ship, commanded by Captain Leonard McKenzie, set off explosive charges to break up icebergs. Fearing his city was under attack, Thakorr sent his daughter to investigate. Princess Fen fell in love with McKenzie and married him. When she failed to return, her father sent a war party to rescue her and McKenzie fell in the attack. Fen returned to Atlantis and gave birth to Prince NAMOR, the Sub-Mariner.

Unique Atlantean architecture employs submerged coral reefs.

Atlanteans' skin is usually light blue and their eyes tend to be blue or gray. Atlanteans communicate with high-pitched sounds and elaborate gestures. Their government is a coalition of tribes, ruled by an emperor. A Council of Elders advises the emperor. Most Atlanteans worship Poseidon, the Greek god of the sea. They are a rigid, warlike people; each citizen joins a guild to become a hunter, farmer, tradesman, craftsman, entertainer, or warrior.

No one knows how many Atlanteans exist and they have suffered greatly at times. Namor evacuated Atlantis and detonated the villain NITRO within it rather than leave the capital under the control of Namor's traitorous son Kamar. Atlantis also went to war with Wakanda, and suffered great destruction following Namor's attack on the African kingdom. The SQUADRON SUPREME destroyed much of Atlantis—after allowing the population to flee—but later helped to rebuild it. Atlantis has also provided a temporary base for Jean GREY's X-MEN team.

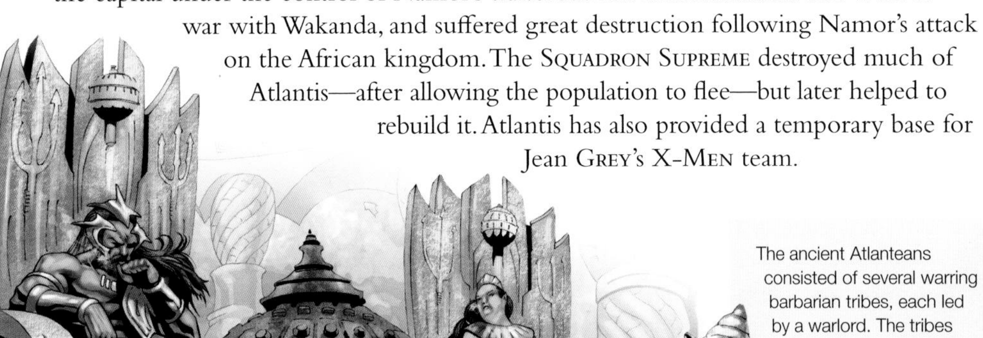

The ancient Atlanteans consisted of several warring barbarian tribes, each led by a warlord. The tribes formed alliances over the years, eventually uniting under a single emperor.

KEY ATLANTEANS
1 Namora
2 Namor, the Sub-Mariner
3 Lady Dorma

ATLAS

FIRST APPEARANCE *Thunderbolts* #1 (April 1997)
REAL NAME Erik Josten
OCCUPATION Adventurer; former criminal **BASE** Mobile
HEIGHT 6 ft **WEIGHT** 225 lbs **EYES** None; replaced by containment spheres for unknown energy **HAIR** Red
SPECIAL POWERS/ABILITIES Atlas can grow in size from 6 ft to 60 ft; superhumanly strong and durable.

After working as POWER MAN and GOLIATH, Josten joined BARON ZEMO and his MASTERS OF EVIL (later the THUNDERBOLTS) as Atlas. While battling COUNT NEFARIA, he was changed into ionic energy. He later managed to place his energy into the body of Dallas RIORDAN. After they were separated, his body and powers were restored. He briefly joined WONDER MAN's REVENGERS before becoming part of the WINTER SOLDIER's incarnation of the Thunderbolts, later quitting and returning to the Masters of Evil.

ATTUMA

FIRST APPEARANCE *Fantastic Four* #33 (December 1964)
REAL NAME Attuma **OCCUPATION** Barbarian chieftain; former ruler of Atlantis **BASE** Atlantic Ocean
HEIGHT 6 ft 8 in **WEIGHT** 196 lbs **EYES** Brown **HAIR** Black
SPECIAL POWERS/ABILITIES Superhuman strength and stamina; can breathe underwater and see clearly in the depths; expert combatant with most Atlantean weapons.

Born to a tribe of nomadic Atlantean barbarians, Attuma repeatedly fought NAMOR and often allied himself with renegade Atlantean or human scientists in his efforts to conquer Atlantis. Despising humanity, he often attacked the surface world, but was thwarted by the AVENGERS and FANTASTIC FOUR. The SENTRY beheaded him during one attempt, but DOCTOR DOOM revived him. During FEAR ITSELF, a Hammer of the Worthy turned him into Nerkodd, Breaker of Oceans. After losing that power, he took over the lost city of Lemuria, only to be defeated by the HULK. He was later killed by the SQUADRON SUPREME's POWER PRINCESS.

AVALANCHE

FIRST APPEARANCE *X-Men* #141 (January 1981)
REAL NAME Dominic Szilard Janos Petros
OCCUPATION Member of the Brotherhood of Evil Mutants
BASE Mobile **HEIGHT** 5 ft 7 in **WEIGHT** 195 lbs
EYES Brown **HAIR** Brown
SPECIAL POWERS/ABILITIES Vibrations generated from his hands can bring down buildings and cause earthquakes.

Dominic Petros was a Greek immigrant to the US with mutant powers. MYSTIQUE recruited him into The BROTHERHOOD OF EVIL MUTANTS, and he participated in the Brotherhood's first attempted assassination of Senator Robert KELLY. Petros left the Brotherhood to blackmail California with the threat of an earthquake, but he returned when the group transformed into FREEDOM FORCE. He later joined EXODUS' version of the Brotherhood. He retained his powers after M-Day, but he decided to open up a bar in San Francisco rather than return to crime. The RED SKULL captured him and replaced part of his brain with a machine to force him to commit an act of mutant terrorism and then leap to his death.

AURORA

FACTFILE
REAL NAME
Jeanne-Marie Beaubier
OCCUPATION
Adventurer; special operative of the Canadian government
BASE
Canada

HEIGHT 5 ft 11 in
WEIGHT 125 lbs
EYES Blue
HAIR Black

FIRST APPEARANCE
The Uncanny X-Men #120 (April 1979)

POWERS
Can run and fly at superhuman speed.
Can project bright white light.

Twin orphans Jeanne-Marie and Jean-Paul Beaubier were separated, and Jeanne-Marie was raised in a strict religious girls' school. She was so unhappy she threw herself off a roof—and found herself flying. Jeanne-Marie thought a miracle had taken place and told the headmistress, but was punished for blasphemy. Jeanne-Marie developed an identity disorder: her everyday self was introverted, but her repressed side was uninhibited. Five years later, Jeanne-Marie became a teacher at the school. One night, WOLVERINE saw her use superspeed to defend herself from a mugger. Wolverine introduced her to James MacDonald Hudson, who reunited Jeanne-Marie with her brother. Taking the code names Aurora and NORTHSTAR, Jeanne-Marie and Jean-Paul joined Hudson's team of Canadian heroes, ALPHA FLIGHT. Since then, Aurora has manifested other personalities, too, some of which reveal her powers in different ways.

AVENGERS

Earth's mightiest heroes

Loki tried to escape by casting a spell that made his body radioactive. However, the heroes soon trapped him within a lead-lined tank.

AVENGERS

FACTFILE

KEY MEMBERS

(see individual entries for powers)

THOR; IRON MAN;
ANT-MAN (Dr. Hank Pym aka Giant-Man, Goliath, Yellowjacket);
WASP; HULK;
CAPTAIN AMERICA; CAPTAIN MARVEL (Carol Danvers);
WONDER MAN; HAWKEYE;
VISION; SCARLET WITCH;
QUICKSILVER;
BLACK PANTHER;
BLACK WIDOW;
HERCULES; BLACK KNIGHT;
SHE-HULK; SPECTRUM (Monica Rambeau aka Pulsar and Photon); **QUASAR; CRYSTAL;**
SERSI; ANT-MAN (Scott Lang).

BASE

Avengers Mountain, Arctic Circle; formerly Stark Tower, Manhattan, and Avengers Mansion, Manhattan

FIRST APPEARANCE

Avengers #1 (September 1963)

ALLIES/FOES

ALLIES Rick Jones, Edwin Jarvis, the Fantastic Four

FOES Space Phantom, the Lava Men, the Mole Man, Baron Zemo, his Masters of Evil, Kang, Ultron, Collector, Grandmaster, Electro, Sauron, Madame Hydra

ISSUE #1

Written by Stan Lee, penciled by Jack Kirby, and inked by Dick Ayers, the first issue of *The Avengers* guest-starred Rick Jones, the Teen Brigade, and the Fantastic Four.

The Avengers are dedicated to safeguarding the planet from super-menaces too powerful for a single hero or the armed forces of any one country to combat. Formed shortly after the first public appearance of the Fantastic Four, the Avengers immediately won government approval from the National Security Council of the United States and the General Assembly of the United Nations. Unlike the FF, the Avengers' roster is always changing. Members join, leave and return—a precedent set by the Hulk, who left the team weeks after it was first formed.

Captain America had lain frozen in the Arctic ice since the end of World War II. Decades later, he was discovered and revived by the Avengers.

HERO TEAM

The Avengers were formed by accident. Loki, Asgardian God of Evil, wanted revenge on his half-brother Thor. After searching for a menace powerful enough to challenge Thor, he selected the Hulk and tricked him into causing a train wreck. When the Hulk's former partner Rick Jones heard this news, he attempted to alert the Fantastic Four, but Loki diverted his radio signal and sent it to Thor. But the Thunder God wasn't the only one to answer the call. The astonishing Ant-Man (*see* Pym, Hank), the Wasp, and Iron Man also responded. While the other heroes battled the Hulk, Thor tracked down Loki and captured him. After learning that the Hulk was innocent, Ant-Man suggested that the heroes form a team. The Wasp suggested they call themselves "something colorful and dramatic, like... the Avengers."

The Avengers roster has included countless different heroes over the years, as the team has evolved to face new threats.

For most of their history, the Avengers employed a rotating chairmanship that allowed different acting members to chair meetings and make administrative decisions. Captain America usually served as team leader in the field.

AVENGERS MANSION

Tony Stark (Iron Man) donated his three-story townhouse to the team, who renamed it Avengers Mansion and later significantly modified it to fit their needs. Stark also funded the new team and provided them with most of their high-tech equipment, weaponry, security countermeasures, and computer systems. He also used his government contacts to lobby for A-1 or Avengers Priority security clearance to aid the team's operations.

The Avengers began to establish themselves by fighting foes like the Space Phantom, the Lava Men, the Mole Man, Baron Zemo, his Masters of Evil, and Kang. The team also met Wonder Man who later sacrificed himself to save them. All of the founding members eventually left the team, leaving Captain America in charge with a band that first consisted of Hawkeye, the Scarlet Witch, and Quicksilver. The Wasp and Hank Pym, who had exchanged his Ant-Man title to become the first Goliath, returned to the team. The Olympian demigod Hercules also became a member. Serving as an agent for the Mandarin, the first Swordsman even attempted to join.

THE OLD ORDER CHANGETH

Accidentally created by Hank Pym, the robot Ultron tried to kill the Avengers. He even built the android Vision, who betrayed him and served as an Avenger for many years. Haunted by guilt, Pym's marriage to the Wasp deteriorated and Pym left the team.

ESSENTIAL STORYLINES

- ***Avengers #4*** The Avengers rescue Captain America from an icy tomb and invite him to join the team.
- ***The Greatest Battles of the Avengers (tpb)*** The Avengers fight many of their most deadly foes.
- ***Avengers: The Korvac Saga (tpb)*** The Guardians of the Galaxy help the Avengers battle Michael Korvac.
- ***Avengers: Under Siege (tpb)*** The new Baron Zemo and his Masters of Evil attack Avengers Mansion.
- ***Avengers: Disassembled*** The Scarlet Witch warps reality and attacks her former teammates.

THE ULTIMATES

On a parallel Earth, government scientists created a super-soldier formula, but lost it when Captain America disappeared during World War II. Many years later, Dr. Bruce Banner was hired to recreate it. Working out of a rundown research facility in Pittsburgh, he engaged in secret superhuman trials on civilians and even tested the formula on himself, transforming himself into the rampaging Hulk. General Nick Fury took custody of Banner and ordered him to complete his research in order to create a new super-team called the Ultimates. This team included Dr. Hank Pym, a cybertronics expert and a world authority on super-genetics. On Earth-616 an unrelated team of heroes called themselves the Ultimates. Consisting of Captain Marvel, Black Panther, Spectrum, America Chavez, and Blue Marvel, the team faced cosmic threats to Earth such as Galactus and the Infinaut.

THE ULTIMATES (2004)
1 Giant-Man **2** Iron Man **3** Hawkeye **4** Wasp **5** Captain America **6** Black Widow **7** Thor

When Kang the Conqueror and his son Marcus waged all-out war against the Earth, the Avengers led the planet's defensive effort. Although Kang temporarily succeeded in subduing the entire world, the Avengers led a resistance movement that eventually overthrew his new dynasty.

The Avengers fought alongside the alien Captain Mar-Vell in a cosmic battle that came to be known as the Kree-Skrull War. The membership continued to change as the Black Widow, the Beast, the now-reformed Swordsman, Mantis, and Hellcat all became members. A romance developed between the Vision and the Scarlet Witch and they married. The National Security Council began to take an active interest in the team and appointed Henry Peter Gyrich liaison officer. He tried to control team membership by recruiting Falcon and Carol Danvers (Ms. Marvel). In recent years, Justice, Firestar, Triathlon, Silverclaw, Jack of Hearts, Ant-Man, and a new female Captain Britain have served as members.

HEROES REBORN AND RETURN

At one point, the Avengers became embroiled in an epic battle with the villain Onslaught, and they, the Fantastic Four, and Doctor Doom were all presumed to have perished. Actually, Franklin Richards had used his reality-altering powers to save them at the last moment and transport them into a pocket dimension of his own creation, which featured a copy of Earth called Counter-Earth. They came back after a year. Later, Counter-Earth became situated on the opposite side of the sun from the Earth.

When the Avengers disappeared while battling Onslaught, those on the Earth they left behind believed them dead.

AVENGERS continued

The Avengers Mansion had survived many attacks—until it was destroyed by one of its own.

AVENGERS DISASSEMBLED

A victim of her own reality-altering powers, the Scarlet Witch (Wanda Maximoff) had a nervous breakdown after the Wasp accidentally reminded her of something that had been wiped from her mind: the existence of her twin sons, Thomas and William. Desperate to become pregnant by her husband, the Vision, she'd subconsciously created them with her magic, implanting in each a soul fragment she'd found. When Mephisto claimed these fragments as lost bits of his own soul, the boys disappeared into him. To help save Wanda from a breakdown, Agatha Harkness had erased the memory of the boys from their mother's mind. When the memories came flooding back, Wanda's fragile sanity shattered completely.

THE MANSION DESTROYED

An undead version of Jack of Hearts—who'd died earlier in the year while saving Cassie Lang, the daughter of Ant-Man (Scott Lang)—showed up at the Avengers Mansion without warning. When Ant-Man went out to greet him, Jack said, "I'm sorry," and then exploded. The massive blast killed Ant-Man and totally destroyed half of the mansion.

At the same moment, Iron Man—who was with the Scarlet Witch and Yellowjacket (Hank Pym)—was addressing the United Nations when he became drunk and belligerent, without having had a drink. Soon after, back at the Avengers Mansion, the Vision crash-landed an Avengers Quinjet into the front yard. Melting to pieces as he tried to explain himself, the Vision launched five metal balls from his mouth. These each transformed into an Ultron.

While helping to defeat the Ultrons, Captain Britain (Kelsey Leigh) was killed. Afterward, She-Hulk flew into a rage and ripped the remains of the Vision to pieces, then nearly killed the Wasp.

THE FINAL ASSEMBLY

As the Avengers tried to puzzle out what was happening, every available hero who'd ever been an Avenger rallied outside the mansion. As they did, the UN revoked the Avengers' Charter. Directly after that, a Kree invasion force appeared over the mansion and attacked. Hawkeye sacrificed his life to destroy the alien ships.

Doctor Strange then arrived and revealed that Wanda had been behind the string of disasters, which were designed not only to destroy the Avengers but also their reputation.

As the Vision was destroyed, his corpse produced copies of Ultron.

Always ready for a fight, the Avengers battled the five Ultrons, removing their heads to destroy them. As they did, they realized something was truly wrong.

The Avengers found and confronted Wanda, who unleashed a horde of their foes against them. After Doctor Strange finally stopped Wanda, Magneto, who at the time believed he was Wanda's father, appeared and took her away. Although he tried to nurse her back to health, she later snapped again, which led to the reality-altering House of M and M-Day events. The Avengers were no more.

NEW AVENGERS
1. Iron Fist
2. Doctor Strange
3. Echo
4. Luke Cage
5. Ronin
6. Wolverine
7. Spider-Man

THE NEW AVENGERS

When ELECTRO staged a breakout of the world's worst criminals from the super-prison called the Raft, CAPTAIN AMERICA and Iron Man led an impromptu team of heroes into trying to keep the lid on the place. They only partially succeeded, and the two members of the original Avengers decided to form a new team to help them track down and capture the escaped villains.

Just when the Avengers thought they had seen the worst, an invasion force of Kree warriors appeared in the sky over Manhattan.

Besides Captain America and Iron Man, this new team included Luke CAGE, SPIDER-MAN, SPIDER-WOMAN, and WOLVERINE.

The New Avengers lived in Stark Tower, which was topped by the SENTRY's watchtower. The team fractured down the middle when the CIVIL WAR began. Those who supported the Superhuman Registration Act stayed with Iron Man, while the others backed Captain America's resistance. This team functioned underground with no official support from any government.

MIGHTY AVENGERS
1 Sentry ***2*** Iron Man ***3*** Wonder Man ***4*** Ms. Marvel

THE MIGHTY AVENGERS

At the end of the Civil War, Iron Man was appointed director of SHIELD and named Ms. Marvel to lead a new team of official Avengers. For her Mighty Avengers, she chose ARES, BLACK WIDOW, Iron Man, Sentry, Wasp, and WONDER MAN. They fought together until Iron Man was disgraced and removed from SHIELD.

At that point, Hank Pym decided to form an Avengers team with the prodding of QUICKSILVER and the restored Scarlet Witch. This new team eventually learned that their Scarlet Witch was actually LOKI in disguise.

THE DARK AVENGERS

At the same time, Norman Osborn (see GREEN GOBLIN) took over where Iron Man left off. He formed his own team of Avengers, staffing it with villains placed in the costumes of heroes—often their greatest foes, including VENOM in the role of Spider-Man and BULLSEYE as Hawkeye. As the IRON PATRIOT, Osborn filled the roles of both Captain America and Iron Man on his team, leading from the front while he deployed his THUNDERBOLTS as a cover strike force.

Norman Osborn (Green Goblin) revealed a new team, the Dark Avengers, featuring (left to right) Captain Marvel (Marvel Boy), Sentry, Ms. Marvel (Moonstone), Iron Patriot (Green Goblin), Ares, Wolverine (Daken), Hawkeye (Bullseye), and Spider-Man (Venom).

AVENGERS continued

Rogers' covert crew of Secret Avengers took on missions that required a more discreet team.

THE INITIATIVE

As part of the Fifty-State Initiative, SHIELD created a place for training new Super Heroes at Camp Hammond, located in the heart of Stamford, Connecticut. Hank Pym originally served as the administrator of the camp, but during the Secret Invasion he was revealed to be a Skrull imposter who'd used his position to place other Skrulls on Initiative teams around the country.

Osborn, in his new job as the head of HAMMER (his replacement for SHIELD), exploited this scandal to shut down the Initiative. However, the idea behind it—training young heroes for eventual membership in the Avengers—refused to die.

Steve Rogers set up different squads to fill the roles he saw the Avengers playing in the modern world.

THE AVENGERS RENEWED

When Osborn was removed from power, the President asked Steve Rogers (the original Captain America) to take over the Avengers once again.

Rogers reformed Iron Man's team as the Avengers, a group that worked closely with the new SHIELD. This team consisted of Rogers, Hawkeye, Iron Man, Thor, Spider-Man, Spider-Woman, and Wolverine, with Maria Hill of SHIELD as the team's leader.

At the same time, Rogers set up another Avengers team that could operate independently of direct government influence. This team initially featured Iron Fist, Jessica Jones, Luke Cage, Mockingbird, Ms. Marvel, and the Thing, along with Victoria Hand, who had been Osborn's chief lieutenant at HAMMER. Spider-Man and Wolverine pulled double duty with both teams.

Rogers himself headed up a third covert team of Secret Avengers, recruiting Ant-Man (Eric O'Grady), Beast, Black Widow, Moon Knight, Nova, Sharon Carter, Valkyrie, and War Machine for his initial lineup.

AVENGERS VS. X-MEN

When the Phoenix Force was found to be returning to Earth, the Avengers sought to take the X-Men's Hope Summers into protective custody as it seemed the force was heading directly for her. Cyclops refused to hand her over, resulting in a conflict between the two teams. It was a conflict that ended with a Phoenix-empowered Cyclops killing Professor X, only to have his power stripped by the Scarlet Witch and Hope.

In the aftermath of the battle, Rogers formed an Avengers Unity Division, combining powerful Avengers and X-Men to rebuild trust between the two groups. The original team was made up of Captain America himself alongside Wolverine, Havok, Rogue, Scarlet Witch and Thor. They soon found themselves taking on a new incarnation of the Red Skull—one who had gained Charles Xavier's abilities after he had stolen the professor's brain and molded it with his own. The team continued to work together, with Rogue, Wasp, and Sunfire among the heroes joining.

Hope Summers, the "Mutant Messiah," became the focus of the conflict between the Avengers and the X-Men.

ULTRON VICTORIOUS

When Ultron returned, he devastated the world and killed numerous Super Heroes, creating an "Age of Ultron." The surviving Avengers were fighting this extinction-level event when Wolverine and Sue Storm traveled back in time to kill Hank Pym before he could create Ultron. Wolverine's actions altered their reality, causing a dark future where the Kree-Skrull War had ravaged Earth. They returned to the past and altered their own actions, this time telling Hank about their horrific, Ultron-dominated future. Hank created a code that could be used in the future to destroy his creation without harming the timeline. While the code worked, it too became sentient, taking the name Dimitrios and causing SHIELD to create an Avengers A.I. squad to combat it.

When Steve Rogers lost his powers and was aged during a fight with Iron Nail, he took a more tactical role with the Avengers, and a new Captain America, Sam Wilson, joined the team. Shortly afterward, the Avengers and others heroes were turned evil while fighting Red Onslaught when a spell from the Scarlet Witch went wrong. A new Avengers team made up of villains who had been turned good by the spell was formed to defeat them. The team told the world it was their scheming that had made the Avengers appear evil, thus saving the reputations of the heroes when the inversion spell was reversed.

AVENGING HEROES

There have been many Avengers splinter groups. Sunspot led a team called Avengers Ideas Mechanics after taking over AIM island, and tried to use AIM's technology for good, while Hank Pym created the Avengers A.I. team to combat cyber threats. Perhaps the strangest Avengers team was created at the dawn of humankind. Dubbed Avengers 1,000,000 BC, the team was made up of Lady Phoenix, a young Odin, Black Panther, Ghost Rider, Iron Fist, Agamotto, and Starbrand. They came together to defeat an insane Celestial named Zgreb.

The Challenger was an almost invincible foe. It took an entire army of Avengers to finally bring him down.

HERO VS. HERO

A new Avengers team formed shortly after, with Iron Man recruiting young heroes Nova (Sam Alexander), Spider-Man (Miles Morales), and the new Ms. Marvel (Kamala Khan) to fight alongside more seasoned heroes so they could learn from them. However when Captain Marvel and Iron Man came to blows over how best to use an Inhuman who could predict the future, it started a new Super Hero Civil War (*see* Civil War II) and the young heroes quit the team, disgusted at their mentors' behavior. The second Civil War ended with Captain Marvel putting Iron Man in a coma during a ferocious showdown, and the cause of their disagreement—Ulysses Cain—ascending to a higher plane of reality.

Steve Rogers found himself young again thanks to the cosmic abilities of Kobik, a young girl who was a sentient Cosmic Cube. Unknown to Steve's allies, Kobik had been manipulated by the Red Skull to become a member of Hydra, and she had recreated Captain America's history so that he'd always been a Hydra spy. When this evil Captain America made his move, Hydra took over the United States. In the new reality created by these events, Cap had his own evil team of Avengers—including a Chthon-possessed Scarlet Witch. Other heroes and Avengers fought Hydra, eventually bringing the real Captain America back into the world (he had been trapped inside Kobik's memories) and defeating Hydra's forces.

The Avengers had little time to rest, and soon found themselves forced to take part in a cosmic competition between the Grandmaster and the Challenger (another cosmic entity), fighting the Lethal Legion and the Black Order. The Avengers were eventually victorious, defeating the Challenger when he went berserk on Earth.

CELESTIAL MENACE

Hydra's takeover had left a fractured country. When dying Celestials started falling from the sky, Captain America, Iron Man, and Thor re-formed the Avengers to protect the Earth—the new team included Ghost Rider, She-Hulk, Captain Marvel, Black Panther, and Doctor Strange. They learned the threat was from Dark Celestials, summoned by Loki. These Celestials had been infected by aliens called the Horde and driven mad. The Avengers managed to revive some of the infected Celestials and destroy the Dark Celestials. Captain America, knowing that his image had been tainted by the actions of his evil self, suggested Black Panther as the new team leader. It was the start of a new era for Earth's Mightiest Heroes.

As a reward, the Avengers were given the shell of the first Celestial to visit Earth to operate from.

AVENGERS WEST COAST

The Avengers' West Coast "branch office"

FACTFILE

FOUNDING MEMBERS
HAWKEYE
MOCKINGBIRD
IRON MAN
TIGRA
WONDER MAN

ADDITIONAL MEMBERS
SCARLET WITCH
SPIDER-WOMAN (Julia Carpenter)
WAR MACHINE
U.S.AGENT
HUMAN TORCH (James Hammond)
LIVING LIGHTNING
MOON KNIGHT

CURRENT MEMBERS
HAWKEYE (Kate Bishop)
HAWKEYE (Clint Barton
KID OMEGA
GWENPOOL
FUSE
AMERICA CHAVEZ

BASE
West Coast Avengers HQ, Venice, Los Angeles

FIRST APPEARANCE
West Coast Avengers #1 (September 1984)

ALLIES/FOES

ALLIES Avengers, X-Men

FOES Giant land-sharks, AIM, BRODOK

While chairman of the AVENGERS, the VISION decided to expand the team and sent HAWKEYE and his new wife MOCKINGBIRD to Los Angeles to establish a second headquarters on the West Coast. Hawkeye purchased a 15-acre estate on the Pacific coast. It consisted of a main building, surrounded by several guest cottages that housed various Avengers over the years. The mountainside beneath the main building accommodated the high-security Avengers Assembly Room, a hospital, laboratories, and a hanger for Avengers' Quinjets.

ESSENTIAL STORYLINES

- ***West Coast Avengers #1–4*** Hawkeye and Mockingbird establish the new team.
- ***West Coast Avengers #17–23*** Dr. Pym contemplates suicide, the team is transported into the past, and Mockingbird is captured by the Phantom Rider.
- ***Avengers West Coast #55–57, 59–62*** The Scarlet Witch falls victim to Magneto and Immortus.

GROWING PAINS

The team faced its first crisis when Mockingbird and Hawkeye argued over whether the Avengers had the right to use lethal force. Hawkeye later resigned when the government assigned the U.S.AGENT to the team and temporarily joined the GREAT LAKES AVENGERS. The WASP moved to the West Coast to join her former husband Dr. PYM and the team aided their East Coast counterparts in the Kree-Shi'ar war known as Operation: Galactic Storm. After falling under the control of MAGNETO and IMMORTUS, the SCARLET WITCH used her reality-altering powers against the West Coast Avengers.

Hawkeye and Mockingbird eventually reconciled and rejoined the team, and the Scarlet Witch (now cured) became the team's chairperson. During an attack by the demon MEPHISTO and the LETHAL LEGION, Mockingbird was killed and the Compound severely damaged. Afterward, the west coast branch closed down. Years later, Hank Pym reopened the compound as the campus for the Avengers Academy.

Most of the original West Coast Avengers had served on the East Coast team and returned to New York after the branch closed.

A NEW BEGINNING

While living in California, Kate Bishop (HAWKEYE) decided to form a super-team after trying to fight an army of land-sharks. Clint Barton (the original Hawkeye), America Chavez (*see* MISS AMERICA), Fuse, Gwenpool (*see* POOLE, Gwen), and Kid Omega (*see* QUIRE, Quentin) joined her. The new team soon found themselves fighting strange foes—including a giant version of Tigra.

AVENGERS WEST COAST
1 Kid Omega ***2*** Gwenpool ***3*** Hawkeye (Kate Bishop) ***4*** Hawkeye (Clint Barton) ***5*** Fuse ***6*** America Chavez

FACTFILE

FOUNDING MEMBERS

HANK PYM
VISION
VICTOR MANCHA
ALEXIS
DOOMBOT

BASE

Crofton University, Washington D.C.

FIRST APPEARANCE

Avengers A.I. #1 (September 2013)

ALLIES SHIELD's Artificial Intelligence Division, Monica Chang, Jocasta, Avengers Unity Division, Avengers, Daredevil

FOES Dimitrios

AVENGERS A.I.

When Hank Pym created a computer virus to defeat Ultron, the virus evolved and became a sentient entity named Dimitrios. This new AI intelligence then threatened the world, and SHIELD agent Monica Chang was tasked with stopping it. She ordered Hank Pym to help her, and he formed a new Avengers team to do so. The new team, officially dubbed the Avengers Artificial Intelligence Squad, consisted of heroes who were themselves more machine than human—the Vision, Victor Mancha, a Doombot and Alexis. The team faced threats from both inside and outside of cyberspace, especially when Dimitrios took over an old suit of Iron Man's armor. They eventually dealt with Dimitrios, having located his base—an AI-created virtual world known as the Diamond.

AVENGERS A.I.
1 Doombot ***2*** Alexis ***3*** Vision
4 Hank Pym ***5*** Victor Mancha

AZAZEL

FIRST APPEARANCE *The Uncanny X-Men* #428 (October 2003)
REAL NAME Azazel **OCCUPATION** Conqueror
BASE La Isla de Demonas, off the coast of Florida; the *Brimstone*
HEIGHT 5 ft 11 in **WEIGHT** Unknown **EYES** Black **HAIR** Gray
SPECIAL POWERS/ABILITIES The full extent of his powers is unknown; can teleport himself, take on human form, and mentally influence his offspring.

Azazel is the leader of the Neyaphem, a race of mutants who resemble demons. In ancient times Azazel was thought to be the devil. Azazel claims that he once ruled the Earth until he and the Neyaphem were banished to another dimension by the Cheyarafim, a race of mutants who resembled angels. As part of his plan to reconquer Earth, Azazel mated with various women, fathering mutants with teleportational powers. Among the women he seduced was the mutant Mystique, who gave birth to their son Kurt Wagner, alias Nightcrawler. When Nightcrawler learned that Azazel was his father, he not only rejected him, but helped defeat him.

AZAZEL AND HIS CREW
1 Azazel ***2*** Ginniyeh
3 Minion of Azazel
4 Ydrazil ***5*** Jillian

AWESOME ANDROID

FIRST APPEARANCE *Fantastic Four* #15 (June 1963)
REAL NAME Answers to "Awesome Andy"
OCCUPATION Legal aide **BASE** New York City
HEIGHT 15 ft **WEIGHT** 1421 lbs **EYES** None **HAIR** None
SPECIAL POWERS/ABILITIES Possessed the ability to duplicate any special powers directed against it.

The Awesome Android was the creation of the evil Mad Thinker, constructed using research notes that once belonged to scientist Reed Richards (*see* Mister Fantastic). The Mad Thinker intended to use the Awesome Android as a weapon to destroy the Fantastic Four. However, as time went by, the android developed a personality of its own and freed itself from the Thinker's villainous thrall. "Awesome Andy" worked as a legal aide for a while, but his personality was later rebooted and he returned to the Mad Thinker's service.

AYESHA

FIRST APPEARANCE *Marvel Two-In-One* #61 (March 1980)
REAL NAME Paragon
OCCUPATION None **BASE** Outer space
HEIGHT 6 ft 6 in **WEIGHT** 390 lbs **EYES** White **HAIR** Blond
SPECIAL POWERS/ABILITIES Controls cosmic energy which prevents aging; uses this energy to rearrange matter, project concussive blasts, to fly, and to open cosmic rifts into warp-space.

Originally called Paragon or Her, Ayesha was created by a group of scientists known as the Enclave. Hoping to create a perfect life form, they created a being called Him, but Him refused to be controlled. Paragon also rebelled, destroying the Enclave's base. After meditating in a cocoon, she emerged as Her, able to tap into pure cosmic energy. She hoped to mate with Him (now known as Adam Warlock), pursuing him even through death and return to life, but he spurned her. She then turned her attentions to Quasar, during which time she was known as Kismet.

BALDER THE BRAVE

FACTFILE

REAL NAME
Balder

OCCUPATION
Norse God of Light

BASE
Asgard

HEIGHT 6 ft 4 in
WEIGHT 320 lbs
EYES Blue
HAIR Brown

FIRST APPEARANCE
Journey into Mystery #85 (October 1962)

POWERS

Charismatic leader; formidable swordsman, horseman, and hand-to-hand combatant; in Asgard's dimension, only weapons tipped with mistletoe cause him harm; able to produce and emit light; possesses superhuman strength, endurance, and longevity.

BALDER THE BRAVE

Prophecy had it that the death of Norse god Balder would bring about Ragnarok—the destruction of the GODS OF ASGARD. For this reason, ODIN commanded his wife Frigga to make their son Balder invulnerable, and she cast spells to protect him from everything but mistletoe. LOKI learned of this and tricked the blind god Hoder into firing an arrow tipped with mistletoe wood at Balder, but Odin managed to bring Balder back to life. Later, to Balder's horror, his beloved, Nanna, sacrificed herself to save him from having to marry the Norn sorceress Karnilla.

Balder died along with all of the Norse Gods—except THOR—in the final Ragnarok. Thor later discovered Balder's spirit inside the Destroyer, a massive suit of enchanted armor programmed to destroy anything in its path, and restored Balder to life. When Thor was forced to kill his grandfather, Bor, Balder exiled him from Asgard and reluctantly assumed the throne. He ruled the Norse Gods through the destruction of Asgard, but later died fighting overwhelming odds. While in the afterlife, he still used his godly powers as a force for good. Loki tried to force him to marry Hela, the Queen of Hel, but Karnilla wed Hela in Balder's place, freeing him from Hela's realm.

A natural leader, Balder the Brave has led his people on countless campaigns.

BANNER, DR. BRIAN

FIRST APPEARANCE *The Incredible Hulk* #312 (Oct. 1985)
REAL NAME Brian Banner
OCCUPATION Atomic physicist **BASE** Dayton, Ohio
HEIGHT 5 ft 10 in **WEIGHT** 145 lbs **EYES** Brown
HAIR Brown **SPECIAL POWERS/ABILITIES** Scientific genius

Suspecting that he had been exposed to radiation while helping to develop atomic weapons for the US government, Dr. Brian Banner was horrified when he learned his wife Rebecca was pregnant. Convinced their son would grow up to become a monster, he kept his distance from young Bruce (*see* HULK). When Bruce showed signs of great intelligence, Brian beat the boy—and Rebecca when she tried to protect him. Years later, he killed Rebecca in front of the boy and told Bruce he'd burn in Hell if he testified against him. Brian Banner was convicted of manslaughter and confined to a mental institution for 15 years. Released into Bruce's care, he was accidentally killed in a scuffle with his son over his wife's headstone. During the Chaos War, Brian returned from the dead and battled both his son and grandson (SKAAR) and their loved ones, feeding on their anger against him. He later reappeared, having possessed Sasquatch, until the Hulk drained Sasquatch of his gamma radiation.

BANSHEE

After his wife's death, Irish Interpol agent and mutant Sean Cassidy was forced to join Factor Three, an organization of evil mutants. The evil CHANGELING gave him the name Banshee and fitted him with an explosive headband to keep him in line. PROFESSOR X used his telepathic powers to remove the band, and Banshee then defeated Factor Three. Later, Banshee joined the X-MEN. While there, he reunited with his daughter SIRYN and became co-head—with Emma FROST—of Xavier's Academy, where he taught the young mutants of GENERATION X. Following the tragic death of his beloved, Dr. Moira MACTAGGERT, Banshee suffered a temporary breakdown. He formed X-CORPS, but this venture ended with MYSTIQUE stabbing him through the throat. Banshee later died at the hands of VULCAN, only to be remade as one of the APOCALYPSE TWINS' new Horsemen. After this, he became one of Havok's X-Men but was much changed by his deathly experience.

BANSHEE

FACTFILE

REAL NAME
Sean Cassidy

OCCUPATION
Director of X-Corps

BASE
Cassidy Keep, Ireland

HEIGHT 6 ft
WEIGHT 170 lbs
EYES Blue-green
HAIR Blond

FIRST APPEARANCE
Uncanny X-Men #28 (January 1967)

POWERS

Banshee's "sonic scream" could propel him into flight, shatter solid objects, and fire percussive blasts that placed others into trances or knocked them unconscious.

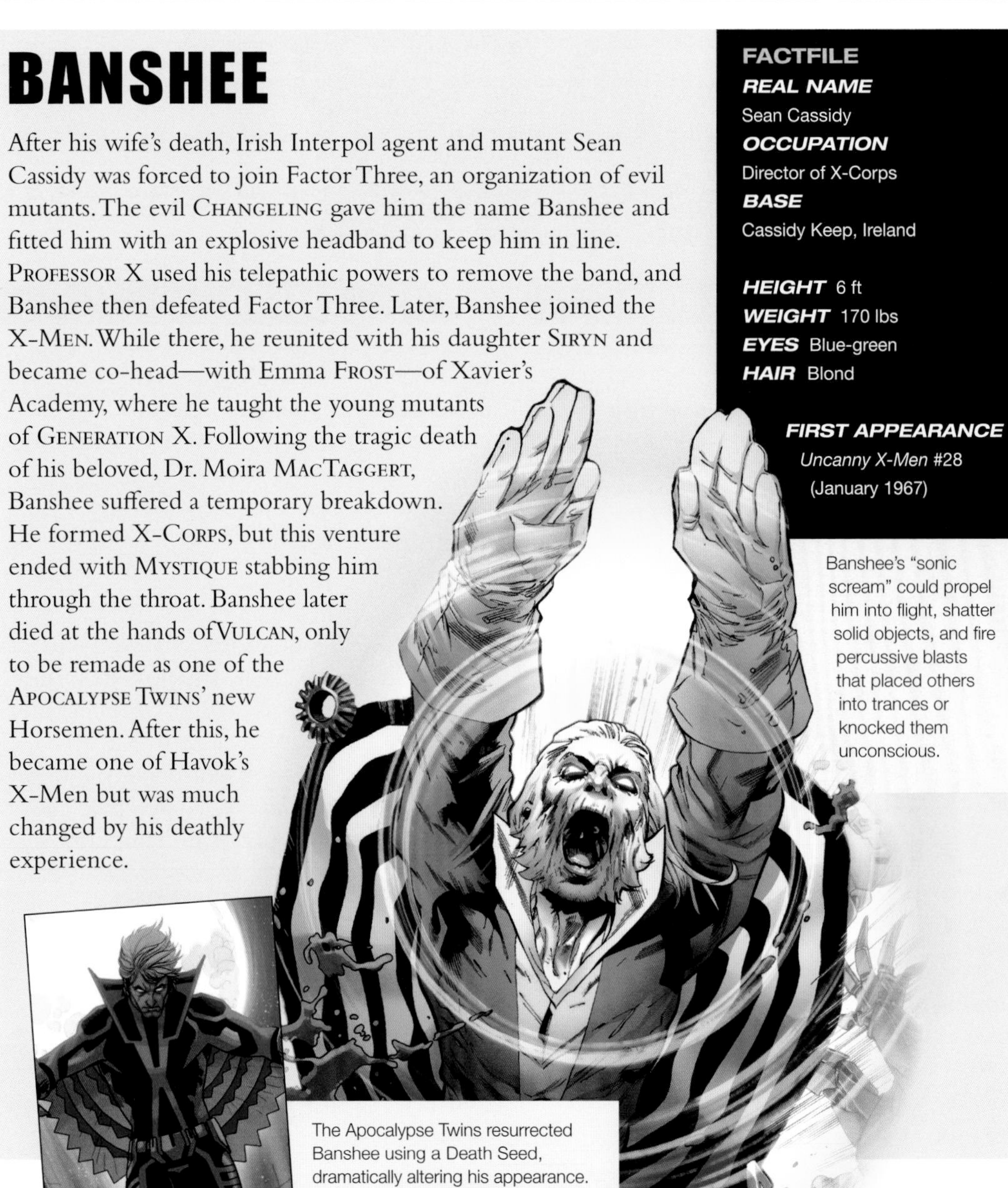

The Apocalypse Twins resurrected Banshee using a Death Seed, dramatically altering his appearance.

BARNES, BUCKY

Orphan James Buchanan "Bucky" Barnes was a mascot for the soldiers at Camp Lehigh, Virginia, where Steve Rogers was stationed. After learning that Steve was CAPTAIN AMERICA, Barnes began helping him on his missions, and became his official partner. Captain America and Bucky discovered that their enemy BARON ZEMO was attempting to steal a bomb-filled drone plane. As the plane took off, Bucky leaped aboard and was apparently killed. Captain America was hurled into the English Channel.

Decades later, Cap was revived by the AVENGERS. Years after that, he discovered Bucky had also survived but had been transformed by the Soviets into the WINTER SOLDIER. After Cap's death, Bucky became the new Captain America and remained so even after Steve Rogers' return to life. Bucky apparently died in the events of FEAR ITSELF, but secretly returned to the role of Winter Soldier in order to make up for his former deeds in that guise.

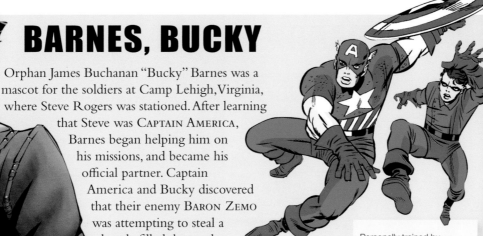

Personally trained by Captain America, Bucky learned Cap's unique fighting style that employed acrobatics and gymnastics in combat situations.

Bucky discovers that Steve Rogers has a secret—he's the superpowered costumed war hero Captain America.

BARNES, BUCKY

FACTFILE

REAL NAME
James Buchanan Barnes

OCCUPATION
Adventurer; army camp mascot

BASE
Mobile

HEIGHT 5 ft 7 in
WEIGHT 140 lbs
EYES Brown
HAIR Red-brown

FIRST APPEARANCE
Captain America #1 (March 1941)

POWERS
Excellent hand-to-hand combatant; skilled marksman; Olympic-level athlete, acrobat, and gymnast.

BARNES, RIKKI

Rikki Barnes grew up on the Counter-Earth created by Franklin RICHARDS as a response to the attacks of ONSLAUGHT. On that world, she became the partner of CAPTAIN AMERICA as a young, female version of Bucky BARNES. When Captain America and the other heroes defeated Onslaught and returned to the original Earth, Rikki remained behind.

Onslaught was reborn years later, and Rikki helped defeat him by pushing him into the Negative Zone with a borrowed Fantasticar. She thought she'd sacrificed her life to stop him, but she later awakened on the main Earth. The BLACK WIDOW found her before she could introduce herself to the new Captain America (Bucky Barnes) and gave her a new costume and name, that of NOMAD.

Unknown to Rikki, Onslaught had sent her to Earth from the Negative Zone with some of his energy inside her so he could use her as an anchor for his return. Once he was defeated again, she asked GRAVITY to kill her to keep Onslaught from using her that way again, sacrificing herself a second time.

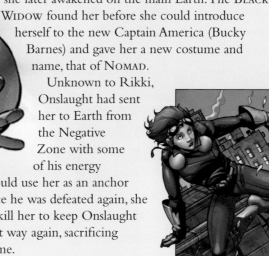

Rather than remain as Bucky in the regular world, Rikki became the new Nomad instead.

BARNES, RIKKI

FACTFILE

REAL NAME
Rebecca Barnes

OCCUPATION
Adventurer, student

BASE
New York City

HEIGHT 5 ft 4 in
WEIGHT 98 lbs
EYES Hazel
HAIR Red

FIRST APPEARANCE
Captain America #1 (November 1996)

POWERS
Rikki is a trained dancer and acrobat who studied combat under Captain America. As Nomad, she carries disks that function as flash-bang grenades.

BARON BLOOD

FIRST APPEARANCE *The Invaders* #7 (June 1976)
REAL NAME Lord John Falsworth
OCCUPATION Former German assassin **BASE** London
HEIGHT 5 ft 10 in **WEIGHT** 180 lbs **EYES** Red **HAIR** Black
SPECIAL POWERS/ABILITIES Vampiric powers, including superhuman strength, hypnotic abilities, and invulnerability to conventional weaponry; could fly without transforming into a bat.

The younger son of a British aristocrat, John Falsworth was killed and vampirized by DRACULA. As Baron Blood, Falsworth served German intelligence during World War I and II. During World War II, Baron Blood battled UNION JACK (who was secretly his brother, Montgomery) and the INVADERS. Decades later, Blood was beheaded by CAPTAIN AMERICA. Two later vampires took the name Baron Blood: DOCTOR STRANGE's brother Victor and Montgomery's grandson Kenneth Crichton.

BARON VON STRUCKER

FIRST APPEARANCE *Sgt. Fury And His Howling Commandos* #5 (January 1964) **REAL NAME** Baron Wolfgang Von Strucker
OCCUPATION Terrorist leader **BASE** Mobile
HEIGHT 6 ft 2 in **WEIGHT** 225 lbs **EYES** Blue **HAIR** None
SPECIAL POWERS/ABILITIES Can release the virulent Death Spore virus from within his body at will. He wears the Satan Claw, capable of discharging electrical shocks, upon his right hand.

Baron von Strucker fought for the Nazis during World War II as the leader of the Blitzkrieg Squad, Germany's answer to the HOWLING COMMANDOS. After the war, von Strucker evolved and modernized a Japanese secret society into HYDRA. Kept alive by the Death Spore virus, von Strucker strove for world domination. He cheated death many times and, following the Hydra CAPTAIN AMERICA's fall, changed sides, gaining praise for fighting rogue Hydra cells.

BARON MORDO

Doctor Strange and Baron Mordo battle in astral form before their mentor, the Ancient One.

As a child, Karl Mordo gained an interest in the occult from his grandfather, Viscount Crowler. As an adult, Mordo sought out the ANCIENT ONE in Tibet, who recognized that Mordo had great potential as a sorcerer but was motivated only by a desire for power. Mordo sent his spirit image to hypnotize the Ancient One's servant into poisoning his food, and then threatened to let the Ancient One die if he did not reveal all his knowledge of black magic. Another of the Ancient One's pupils, DOCTOR STRANGE, sent his spirit image to intervene, and Strange managed to revive the old man.

Thirsting for revenge, Mordo allied himself with powerful creatures like SATANNISH, DORMAMMU, and MEPHISTO and plagued Strange for years. Struck with incurable cancer brought on by his use of black magic, Mordo repented his sins on his deathbed. However, a past version of himself came into the present when Strange traveled through time to rescue SPIDER-MAN. Mordo showed up in South America, having kidnapped the father of M (*see* PENANCE) to force her to give her energy to cure Mordo's cancer. He became the mystical caretaker of New York during HYDRA's U.S. takeover until defeated by Strange and his allies. Another time-shifted version of Mordo briefly joined the RED HULK's Offenders.

FACTFILE
REAL NAME
Karl Amadeus Mordo
OCCUPATION
Sorcerer
BASE
Castle Mordo, Varf Mandra, Transylvania

HEIGHT 6 ft
WEIGHT 250 lbs
EYES Brown
HAIR Black

FIRST APPEARANCE
Strange Tales #111 (August 1963)

POWERS
Mordo can separate his spirit self from his physical body and travel through space unaffected by physical laws. He can mentally control others and can hurl magical energy bolts.

Baron Mordo allied himself with the dread Dormammu, hoping to increase his own mystical abilities in order to defeat his nemesis, Doctor Strange.

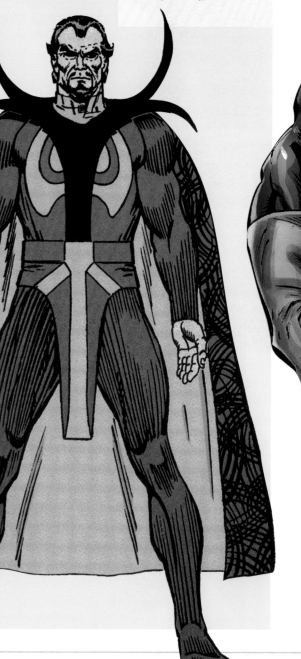

BARON ZEMO

Like father, like son

After the accident that bonded his mask to his face, the original Baron Zemo became obsessed with destroying Captain America.

Helmut Zemo is the son of Baron Heinrich Zemo, a Nazi scientist during World War II who designed super-weapons. Heinrich Zemo was working on a glue, "Adhesive X," that could never be dissolved, hoping it could be used to immobilize Allied troops. CAPTAIN AMERICA broke into his lab and, in the fight, Cap's shield shattered the vat containing the adhesive and Zemo's mask was glued to his head.

FACTFILE

REAL NAME
Helmut Zemo

OCCUPATION
Criminal entrepreneur

BASE
Mobile

HEIGHT 5 ft 11 in
WEIGHT 183 lbs
EYES Blue
HAIR Blond

FIRST APPEARANCE
Captain America #168 (June 1971)

POWERS
Master strategist, extensive training in hand-to-hand combat, and excellent marksman; lacks his father's scientific genius.

MASTER OF EVIL

Zemo later went to London to steal an experimental drone plane. Captain America and his teenage partner BUCKY BARNES attempted to stop him, but Bucky was killed and Captain America was flung into the ocean, where he froze into a state of suspended animation. When the Nazis lost the war, Zemo fled to the jungles of South America, where he conquered a small kingdom. Decades later, he came out of hiding after learning that Captain America had been revived by the AVENGERS. Zemo formed the first MASTERS OF EVIL and later transformed Simon Williams into WONDER MAN, but failed in all his attempts to destroy the Avengers. He was accidentally crushed by a landslide during a battle with Captain America.

ESSENTIAL STORYLINES
- ***Avengers #16*** During a battle with Captain America, the original Baron Zemo is killed.
- ***Captain America #357–362*** "The Bloodstone Hunt"—Helmut Zemo tries to resurrect his father.
- ***The Avengers: Under Siege (tpb)*** Helmut's new Masters of Evil invade the Avengers Mansion and take Edwin Jarvis hostage.
- ***Thunderbolts: Justice Like Lightning (tpb)*** Helmut Zemo repositions the Masters of Evil into seeming heroes.

Heinrich Zemo's hatred of Captain America ultimately led to the rock fall that killed him.

FROM VILLAIN TO HERO AND BACK

The Baron's son and next Baron, Helmut, calling himself Phoenix, attempted to drown Cap in a boiling vat of Adhesive X. The liquid splashed Helmut, scarring his face and giving it the appearance of melted wax. Zemo later organized a new Masters of Evil.

After the AVENGERS seemingly sacrificed themselves to quell the menace of ONSLAUGHT, Zemo became Citizen V and turned his Masters of Evil into a heroic super-team, the THUNDERBOLTS. After keeping the GRANDMASTER from the Wellspring of Power, he claimed it himself, planning to use it to take over the world—until the other Thunderbolts knocked him into a time vortex. Returning from the past, Zemo soon returned to evil, infiltrating HYDRA.

He was later interned in the Pleasant Hill prison facility controlled by KOBIK, but caused a revolt and escaped. In the new "reality" Kobik then created, Zemo had been life-long friends with Steve Rogers. He became Rogers' somewhat unwilling confidant as Steve and Hydra seized control of the US.

Zemo and his allies defeated the Winter Soldier's new Thunderbolts team, some of whom then joined his Army of Evil.

BASILISK

FACTFILE

REAL NAME
Basil Elks

OCCUPATION
Criminal; terrorist

BASE
Mobile

HEIGHT 5 ft 11 in
WEIGHT 210 lbs
EYES Red
HAIR None

FIRST APPEARANCE
Marvel Team-Up #16 (December 1973)

POWERS
Generated microwave-related energy, which he could project from his eyes as force blasts, to heat or freeze things, or to levitate himself. Possessed superhuman strength and durability and could teleport himself.

When burglar Basil Elks stole a gem from a museum, a guard shot at him, exploding the gem (actually the Alpha-Stone of the Kree), which gave Elks superhuman powers. Elks dubbed himself Basilisk after the mythological monster and tried to destroy civilization, only to be thwarted by Spider-Man and the Thing. Scourge assassinated Elks, but the Hood later returned him to life to take revenge on the Punisher. The Basilisk worked for Hydra, only to be defeated by the Superior Spider-Man.

The second Basilisk, Mike Columbus, was a mutant who could shoot a paralysis beam from his single eye. When another mutant, Kuan-Yin Xorn impersonated Magneto and led a new Brotherhood of Evil Mutants, he killed Columbus.

XORN'S BROTHERHOOD
1 One of Angel Salvadore's babies
2 No-Girl
3 Ernst
4 Basilisk
5 Xorn as Magneto
6 Esme (Stepford Cuckoo)
7 Beak
8 Angel Salvadore
9 Toad

BASTARDS OF EVIL

FIRST APPEARANCE *Young Allies* #1 (August 2010)
BASE New York City
MEMBERS AND POWERS
Aftershock (Danielle Blunt) Electric, flying daughter of Electro **Ember (Jason Pierce)** Pyrokinetic, lava-skinned son of Pyro **Mortar (Liana Feeser)** Cement-bodied, shape-shifting daughter of the Grey Gargoyle **Singularity (Devin Touhy)** Gravity-powered son of Graviton **The Superior** Super-intelligent, telekinetic son of the Leader **Warhead** Radioactive, explosive son of Radioactive Man.

The Bastards of Evil were supposedly a group of illegitimate children of Super Villains who banded together to commit acts of terrorism to prove their worth as the next generation of evil. In truth, the evil genius Superior kidnapped innocent teens, gave them powers via radiation, and implanted false memories in them. The Young Allies stopped them, but not before Warhead detonated (presumably killing himself) at the spot where the World Trade Center had stood. When the others regained their true memories, Superior murdered Singularity, but the others stuck with him. Superior and the remaining Bastards of Evil were defeated by the Young Allies and incarcerated at the Raft super-prison.

BASTARDS OF EVIL
1 The Superior
2 Mortar
3 Ember
4 Singularity
5 Aftershock

BASTION

FIRST APPEARANCE *Uncanny X-Men* #333 (June 1996)
REAL NAME Sebastion Gilberti
OCCUPATION Anti-Mutant crusader **BASE** Mobile
HEIGHT 6 ft 3 in **WEIGHT** 375 lbs **EYES** Red **HAIR** White
SPECIAL POWERS/ABILITIES Enhanced strength, speed, physical stamina, and resistance to injury; also immune to telepathic probes.

Bastion is a combination of Master Mold (a Sentinel robot) and Nimrod (a Sentinel prototype from a possible future). He led the anti-mutant initiative Operation: Zero Tolerance, during which his Prime Sentinels captured several X-Men and took over the Xavier Institute until stopped by SHIELD. For a while, Bastion worked under the name Template. The Purifiers restored Bastion, and he used the Technarch virus to revive a number of old X-Men foes. He later led their ill-fated effort to eliminate Hope Summers, during which he killed Nightcrawler. He was thought destroyed but returned and worked with Miss Sinister and Emma Frost to make mutants dominant, only to be destroyed by Xorn.

FACTFILE

BATROC THE LEAPER

REAL NAME
Georges Batroc

OCCUPATION
Mercenary

BASE
Mobile

HEIGHT 6 ft
WEIGHT 225 lbs
EYES Brown
HAIR Black

FIRST APPEARANCE
Tales of Suspense #75 (March 1966)

POWERS
Self-professed master of Savate, the French form of kickboxing; allegedly an expert hand-to-hand combatant; does not have any superhuman abilities but describes himself as Olympic-standard weight lifter with ability to leap vast distances; devises military tactics that serve to bewilder opponents.

BATROC THE LEAPER

Describing himself as the world's greatest mercenary and master of Savate, Marseilles-born Georges Batroc trained himself in this Gallic martial art while serving in the French Foreign Legion. Since embarking on a life of crime, Batroc has fought some of the world's greatest Super Heroes, including CAPTAIN AMERICA and the PUNISHER. Sadly, he has rarely survived these confrontations with more than the smallest degree of dignity.

Batroc is the eponymous leader of Batroc's Brigade, a motley collection of martial artists, assassins, and mercenaries whose membership is fluid. In the Brigade's early days, Batroc hired members for specific jobs, but most of the missions were unsuccessful. Employed to obtain the "seismo-bomb" from a foreign power, Batroc teamed with the SWORDSMAN and the LIVING LASER, but they did not succeed. Later, the RED SKULL hired him to attack Captain America. Although banded with PORCUPINE and WHIRLWIND, the mission failed.

Batroc has only scored significant victories with the British weapons master ZARAN and South American revolutionary Machete. During the CIVIL WAR, Batroc was forced to work for the THUNDERBOLTS Army. Afterward, he registered with the US government and trained heroes in the martial arts, though he subsequently returned to crime.

BATTLESTAR

FIRST APPEARANCE *Captain America* #341 (May 1988)
REAL NAME Lemar Hoskins
OCCUPATION Government agent **BASE** Chicago
HEIGHT 6 ft 2 in **WEIGHT** 196 lbs **EYES** Blue **HAIR** Black
SPECIAL POWERS/ABILITIES Superhuman strength and stamina; can lift 10 tons; excels at hand-to-hand combat, gymnastics, and acrobatics; carries an indestructible Adamantium shield.

After the POWER BROKER gave him his powers, Lemar Hoskins became a professional wrestler, along with his three US Army pals, Jerome Johnson, Hector Lennox, and John Walker. When Walker became the hero Super-Patriot, Hoskins and the others formed the Bold Urban Commandos (the BUCkies) as his support team. After Walker was chosen to replace Steve Rogers as CAPTAIN AMERICA, Hoskins became Walker's new Bucky (*see* BARNES, BUCKY). He changed his code name to Battlestar after another African-American mentioned that the name "Bucky" struck close to the way slaveholders sometimes called their men "bucks." Hoskins continued as Battlestar even after Rogers returned and Walker became the U.S.AGENT. After retiring from government service, Hoskins joined SILVER SABLE's Wild Pack. He sided with Rogers during the CIVIL WAR, and afterward joined the Garrison, the Vermont team of the FIFTY-STATE INITIATIVE. He later took a job with Project PEGASUS, where he fought interdimensional zombies.

BEAST

Mind of a genius, body of a wild thing!

BEAST

FACTFILE

REAL NAME
Henry P. "Hank" McCoy

OCCUPATION
Adventurer, biochemist

BASE
The Xavier institute, Salem Center, New York

HEIGHT 5 ft 11 in
WEIGHT 402 lbs
EYES Blue
HAIR Brown (originally); blue-black (currently)

FIRST APPEARANCE
X-Men #1 (September 1963)

POWERS

The Beast possesses superhuman strength, agility, and durability, and has enhanced senses, including catlike night vision. He is able to recover with superhuman swiftness from minor wounds. He also possesses genius-level IQ, with extraordinary expertise in genetics, biochemistry, and other subjects.

THE CHEMICAL! IT'LL CHANGE ME—AND IN AN HOUR'S TIME, I CAN CHANGE BACK AGAIN, JUST BY TAKING ANOTHER DRINK AS AN ANTIDOTE
DON'T KNOW WHAT WILL HAPPEN IF YOU MUTATE A MUTANT—BUT I'VE GOT TO TAKE THE CHANCE—

Dr. McCoy recklessly drank his own serum, which gave him a more bestial form and increased superpowers.

Nuclear-power-plant worker Norton McCoy was exposed to intense radiation, and his son Henry was born a mutant, with unusually large hands and feet. Henry's schoolmates called him "Beast," but his mutant physique enabled him to become a star football player. When a criminal called the Conquistador abducted Henry's parents to force Henry to work for him, the X-Men came to the rescue. The team's founder, Professor X, recruited Henry and, code-named the Beast, he thus became one of the X-Men's original members.

UNCHAINED

Under Professor X's tutelage McCoy earned his Ph.D. and went on to become a genetic researcher at the Brand Corporation. There he developed a serum that further mutated him: he grew fur all over his body, as well as fangs and pointed ears.

Initially, McCoy attempted to masquerade as a normal human by using a latex mask and gloves. However, he soon abandoned this disguise, joined the Avengers as the Beast, and publicly revealed his true identity. Later, the Beast reorganized another team, the Defenders. After this incarnation of the Defenders collapsed, the Beast rejoined Professor X's other four original X-Men in a new mutant team, X-Factor. Soon afterward, the Beast was captured by former Brand Corp. scientist Dr. Carl Maddicks, who used a serum to cause the Beast to revert to his previous, more human appearance. The mutant Infectia returned the Beast to his fur-covered form.

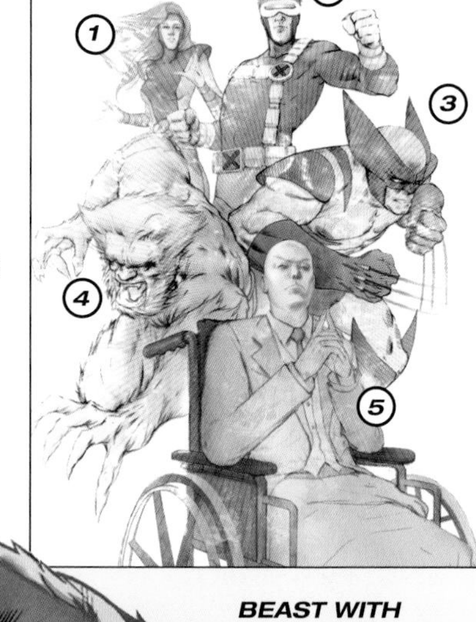

BEAST WITH THE X-MEN
1 Jean Grey
2 Cyclops
3 Wolverine
4 Beast
5 Professor X

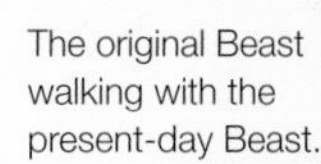

The original Beast walking with the present-day Beast.

The time-displaced Beast shared his older counterpart's urge to push the boundaries of knowledge, but focused on magical as opposed to scientific fields.

After rejoining the X-Men, the Beast helped create a cure for the Legacy Virus. When he was nearly killed in combat, Sage saved his life by mutating him even further. The Beast invented a time machine to help save Hope Summers and later to bring the original X-Men to the present day. After the death of Professor X, the Beast took over the Professor's spot in the Illuminati.

ESSENTIAL STORYLINES

- ***X-Men #49–53***
  The extraordinary origin of the Beast explained for the first time.
- ***Amazing Adventures #11–16***
  The Beast mutates into his furry, ape-like form and combats the Secret Empire.
- ***X-Treme X-Men #3***
  The Beast mutates into his leonine form.

BELLA DONNA

FIRST APPEARANCE *X-Men* #8 (May 1992)
REAL NAME Bella Donna Boudreaux
OCCUPATION Assassin **BASE** New Orleans
HEIGHT 6 ft **WEIGHT** 150 lbs
EYES Blue **HAIR** Blond
SPECIAL POWERS/ABILITIES Skilled assassin and hand-to-hand combatant. Ability to project fiery blasts. Astral projection

A deadly assassin, Bella Donna Boudreaux was the daughter of a high-ranking member of the Guild of Assassins in New Orleans. She grew up with Remy LeBeau (aka GAMBIT), whose father was a member of the rival Guild of Thieves. Their fathers agreed that Bella and Remy should marry to unite the guilds. After their marriage, Gambit was exiled and left Bella behind, but the couple had many run-ins over the years. Later, the External Candra awakened the X-gene in Bella, who gained powers of her own. Bella became the Guild of Assassins' leader, however she was killed, and her Guild disbanded, when they came into conflict with DEADPOOL.

BEREET

FIRST APPEARANCE *Rampaging Hulk* #1 (January 1977)
REAL NAME Bereet **OCCUPATION** Krylorian techno-artist
BASE The planet Krylor **HEIGHT/WEIGHT** Unrevealed
EYES Brown **HAIR** Unrevealed
SPECIAL POWERS/ABILITIES Carried the tools of her trade with her in a special distortion pouch. Accompanied by a hovering device called Sturky that could convert matter.

A renowned techno-artist from the planet Krylor, Bereet first came to prominence among her race when she created a series of adventure films depicting the earliest version of the HULK combating a fictitious invasion of Earth by the Krylorians. After several attempts to duplicate this early success, she journeyed to Earth intending to document the ongoing exploits of the true Hulk, and became embroiled in a number of his adventures. She remained on Earth and became a movie director in Hollywood.

BERENGETTI, MICHAEL

FIRST APPEARANCE *Incredible Hulk* #347 (September 1988)
REAL NAME Michael Berengetti **OCCUPATION** Casino owner
BASE Las Vegas **HEIGHT** 5 ft 10 in **WEIGHT** 170 lbs
EYES Brown **HAIR** Black
SPECIAL POWERS/ABILITIES Highly skilled businessman with a deep knowledge of underworld politics. Skilled with firearms and had a talent for mathematics relating to games of chance.

Michael Berengetti owned Las Vegas Coliseum casino, and he hired the HULK as a bodyguard and leg-breaker during the period when the Hulk sported gray skin and a cunning intellect. Berengetti, who called the Hulk "Joe Fixit," ensured that the Hulk had steady access to tailored suits and Las Vegas' more sensual pleasures. After the Hulk left Vegas, the android Frost (employed by the gangster Sam Striker) killed Berengetti.

An honorable employer, Berengetti treated the loyal members of his staff as family.

BETA-RAY BILL

Beta Ray Bill was a guardian-warrior of an extraterrestrial race whose galaxy was destroyed by the ancient demon Surtur. He was created when scientists transferred his life force into a bioengineered carnivorous beast with increased strength, speed, and agility.

While traveling in suspended animation in his starship, Beta Ray Bill entered the Milky Way Galaxy, where THOR was sent to investigate. They battled, and Thor was separated from his enchanted hammer, Mjolnir, which changed back into Donald Blake's cane. When Beta Ray Bill struck the cane on a wall he suddenly possessed Thor's power and a variation of the Thunder God's costume.

After a duel, in which Beta Ray Bill spared Thor's life, ODIN commissioned the creation of a new enchanted hammer called Stormbreaker. Bill left Earth to visit his people's new planet, but while he was there, GALACTUS devoured it. Bill returned to Earth and helped the new OMEGA FLIGHT battle demons of Surtur. He was replaced by a SKRULL before the SECRET INVASION, but Thor freed him and then fought alongside him to defeat the Skrull known as the Godkiller. Bill hunted down Galactus for revenge but saved him instead. Bill later joined the ANNIHILATORS and helped the INHUMANS defeat the Super-Inhuman Vox who was attacking them.

FACTFILE

REAL NAME
Beta Ray Bill

OCCUPATION
Warrior

BASE
Mobile; his alien race's space fleet, his own warship *Skuttlebutt*

HEIGHT 6 ft 7 in
WEIGHT 480 lbs
EYES None visible
HAIR None

FIRST APPEARANCE
Thor #337
(November 1983)

BETA-RAY BILL

POWERS

Bill (aka Beta Ray Thor) has the same powers as Thor himself. He has superhuman strength, and is immune to all disease and injury. His Asgardian metabolism gives him far greater endurance at all physical activities than humans.

When the entire realm of Asgard was taken by the Collector, Bill joined Odinson to free it from captivity.

BEYONDER

Observer of worlds

BEYONDER

FACTFILE

REAL NAME
Beyonder

OCCUPATION
Criminal/hero

BASE
Kyln prison

HEIGHT 6 ft 2 in (variable)
WEIGHT 240 lbs
EYES Blue
HAIR Black

FIRST APPEARANCE
Secret Wars #1 (May 1984)

POWERS
Virtually omnipotent; the Beyonder can change reality just by thinking. He has assumed various physical forms, created planets, destroyed galaxies, and taken control of every mind on Earth.

ESSENTIAL STORYLINES
- ***Secret Wars #1–12*** The Beyonder creates Battleworld and gets the Earth's Super Heroes to fight there.
- ***Secret Wars #1–9*** The Beyonder arrives on Earth and learns about humanity.
- ***Fantastic Four Annual #23*** The Beyonder and Molecule Man merge to form a new entity named Kosmos.

A race of cosmically-powered beings named the Beyonders created the energy that became the Cosmic Cubes. One of these cubes gained sentience and called itself the Beyonder. At times, this entity was believed to be the embodiment of another universe or even a mutant INHUMAN. The Beyonder was intrigued by humans and created Battleworld to watch Super Heroes and Super Villains fight. But eventually he got bored of watching…

The Beyonder created Battleworld—a single planet orbiting a lonely star.

Everything in the Beyonder's dimension was part of him. All matter—planets, suns, people—were aspects of his being, and he could alter and restructure it on the merest whim.

ENDLESS QUEST

The Beyonder arrived on Earth and took on the appearance of first MOLECULE MAN, then CAPTAIN AMERICA, and finally a square-jawed alpha male with bad dress sense. He traveled the world learning about humanity, but still felt unfulfilled and became increasingly unstable—a threat to the entire Multiverse. He decided that he needed to be fully human and tried to transplant himself into the body of a baby, which was gestating in a machine he had built. Before the child could be born, Molecule Man destroyed the birth tank to save the Multiverse, channeling the resulting explosive energies into a new and empty universe.

KOSMOS

In time, the Beyonder and Molecule Man fused to become a new Cosmic Cube. This Cube then expelled the Molecule Man and became the female entity Kosmos (below) who existed in mortal form as the Maker. THANOS tossed the Maker into the interstellar prison Kyln. During the ANNIHILATION Kyln was destroyed, and the corpse of Kosmos was found in the wreckage.

The Beyonders are near omnipotent and hail from a dimension outside the Multiverse. The true extent of their powers is beyond mortal comprehension.

THE BEYONDERS RETURN

The Beyonders later sought to destroy the entire Multiverse and planned to use the Molecule Man to do so. Following the destruction of countless realities, they seemed to have succeeded—only for DOCTOR DOOM to destroy them, himself using the Molecule Man. Doom saved fragments of the various realities as a new Battleworld, one he ruled with the godlike power of a Beyonder.

BI-BEAST

FIRST APPEARANCE *Incredible Hulk* #169 (November 1973)
REAL NAME Bi-Beast **OCCUPATION** Guardian of the Avian race
BASE Sky Island of the Avian race **HEIGHT** 7 ft 8 in (variable)
WEIGHT 360 lbs (variable) **EYES** Black **HAIR** None
SPECIAL POWERS/ABILITIES Bi-Beast's artificial minds contain the Avian race's accumulated knowledge: the top head specializes in knowledge related to warfare and combat, while the lower head is the repository of information pertaining to history and culture.

Created to be the guardian of the Avian race at a time when they were forced to go into hibernation in order to survive, the android Bi-Beast patrolled their now silent Sky Island, maintaining its security and keeping it from harm. But after years of loneliness, the twin personae of the Bi-Beast went mad, and they attempted to kidnap Betty Ross, who had been transformed into a winged, gamma-powered monster called the Harpy. The HULK pursued the Bi-Beast, and after a savage battle, Bruce Banner used the scientific apparatus found on Sky Island to cure Betty's condition, much to the Bi-Beast's displeasure. Thereafter, the Bi-Beast continued its lonely vigil, attacking any and all who came within reach. Eventually, however, the Avians were revived, and so the savage Bi-Beast was no longer alone.

BIG MAN

FIRST APPEARANCE *The Amazing Spider-Man* #10 (March 1964)
REAL NAME Frederick Foswell **OCCUPATION** Criminal
BASE New York City **HEIGHT** 5 ft 10 in; (Big Man) 6 ft 1 in
WEIGHT 185 lbs **EYES** Blue **HAIR** Gray
SPECIAL POWERS/ABILITIES Brilliant criminal mind, master of disguise and a crack shot. Padded costume to appear more robust and taller; wore mask and used a device that deepened voice.

Daily Bugle reporter Foswell tried to organize New York's gangs under his leadership as the Big Man, employing the ENFORCERS as his henchmen. After clashing with SPIDER-MAN, the police learned the Big Man's identity and arrested Foswell. He served his time in prison and, thanks to the generosity of publisher J. Jonah JAMESON, returned to the *Bugle*. Foswell adopted the identity of Patch to spy on the underworld and aided in the capture of mob boss Crime-Master. Foswell later returned to crime and worked for the KINGPIN. He sacrificed himself to save his former employer J. Jonah Jameson.

BIG HERO 6

FIRST APPEARANCE *Sunfire and Big Hero Six* #1 (September 1998)
BASE Tokyo, Japan **MEMBERS AND POWERS** **Hiro Takachiho** Boy genius. **Baymax** Shape-shifting robot with durable exoskeleton. **Honey Lemon** Genius with purse linked to another dimension. **Silver Samurai** Body generates tachyon field that he focuses through his sword. **GoGo Tomago** Skilled racer with high-tech battlesuit. **Sunfire** Can project "solar fire."

Big Hero 6 is Japan's state-sponsored Super Hero team. It was originally composed of the SILVER SAMURAI, SUNFIRE, Honey Lemon, Hiro Takachiho, Baymax, and GoGo Tomago. They protected Japan from the Everwraith, the astral embodiment of all the people who died at Hiroshima and Nagasaki. When Sunfire left, he was replaced by Sunpyre, and the team was later joined by two new members: Wasabi-No Ginger and Fred.

BIRD-BRAIN

FIRST APPEARANCE *New Mutants* #56 (October 1987)
REAL NAME Bird-Brain **OCCUPATION** None
BASE Paradise, an island in the North Atlantic **HEIGHT** 6 ft
WEIGHT 125 lbs **EYES** Red **HAIR** Vari-colored feathers
SPECIAL POWERS/ABILITIES Wings enable flight; entire body is hollow-boned, like a bird's; able to breathe at high altitudes; eyes are specially adapted to withstand high winds during flight.

Bird-Brain is a half-human, half-animal creature known as an Ani-Mate. He was created through genetic engineering by Dr. Frederick Animus, the Ani-Mator. Although Bird-Brain and his fellow Ani-Mates possessed human-level intelligence, the Ani-Mator treated them like slaves. After being subjected to a number of cruel tests, Bird-Brain used his wings to fly away from the Ani-Mator's Paradise Island. He was placed in quarantine by the US authorities in preparation for further testing in a research laboratory, but he escaped. Bird-Brain was then recruited by the New MUTANTS, who agreed to return with him to Paradise Island in order to help free his fellow Ani-Mates from the Ani-Mator's cruel thrall.

BISHOP

FACTFILE

REAL NAME
Lucas Bishop

OCCUPATION
Adventurer; law enforcement officer

BASE
The Xavier Institute, New York; District X, New York City

HEIGHT 6 ft 6 in
WEIGHT 275 lbs
EYES Brown
HAIR Black

FIRST APPEARANCE
The Uncanny X-Men #282 (November 1991)

POWERS
Can absorb energy and project it as concussive force or use it to enhance his strength, durability, and healing factor. Expert with a samurai sword and firearms. Bionic arm grants him superhuman strength and contains a time-travel device.

BISHOP

Bishop comes from the future of Earth-1191, in which SENTINELS conquered North America and he was branded with an M as a mutant. After the Summers Rebellion overthrew the Sentinels, Bishop joined XAVIER'S SECURITY ENFORCERS (XSE) and pursued a mutant criminal to Earth-616, where he joined the X-MEN. Later, he fought crime in District X, Manhattan's mutant ghetto. He sided with the government during the CIVIL WAR. After M-Day, Bishop kept his powers and tried to kill Hope SUMMERS to prevent his future. Instead, he lost an arm and accidentally shot PROFESSOR X, then stole a bionic arm from FORGE and escaped to the future, where he hunted CABLE and Hope though time, later allying with STRYFE. After Cable trapped him in a distant future he repented. On his deathbed, the Demon Bear possessed him and sent him back on a new mission, though PSYLOCKE managed to rid him of the Demon Bear's influence. Bishop later saved Hope's life when Stryfe tried to make the mutants turn on each other. When the SHADOW KING again made a move against the X-Men, Bishop answered Psylocke's call-to-arms. He protected his teammates' physical bodies while they fought the Shadow King on the Astral Plane and helped in the final confrontation.

Bishop's cybernetic arm allowed him to travel through time.

BLACK BOLT

FACTFILE

REAL NAME
Blackagar Boltagon

OCCUPATION
Monarch of the Inhumans

BASE
Attilan

HEIGHT 6 ft 2 in
WEIGHT 210 lbs
EYES Blue
HAIR Black

FIRST APPEARANCE
Fantastic Four #45 (December 1965)

POWERS
Harnesses electrons; power linked to vocal chords, which trigger shockwaves; antenna channels power, giving superhuman strength, speed; fires concussive blasts; creates force-fields; flight.

BLACK BOLT

Black Bolt was born the son of Agon, ruler of the INHUMANS. His powerful infant cries forced his parents to place him in a soundproof chamber until an energy-harnessing suit was designed for him and he was trained to use his powers. After he was released, Black Bolt learned that his younger brother MAXIMUS was about to betray the Inhumans to the alien KREE. Black Bolt shouted, blasting the Kree ship out of the sky. It crashed into the parliament building, killing his parents. As ruler of the Inhumans, Black Bolt often battled Maximus for control and oversaw the relocation of the Inhuman city of Attilan several times: to the Himalayas, to the Blue Area of the Moon, and even into a gigantic starship powered with his voice. After being replaced by a SKRULL before the SECRET INVASION, Black Bolt decided to take the battle to the races that endangered his people, and he led the Inhumans to conquer the Kree. Black Bolt then led the Kree into a battle against Vulcan and the Shi'ar. After the Inhumans separated again from the Kree and returned to Earth, Black Bolt unleashed the Terrigen Mists when THANOS threatened his people. The resulting gas clouds awakened many new Inhumans but also poisoned mutants, leading to a war between the Inhumans and X-Men. Black Bolt ended up in a cosmic jail after being betrayed by Maximus, but escaped and returned to Earth. The Jailer pursued him, but Black Bolt defeated him. Shortly after, Black Bolt found himself facing Vox, an assassin who killed many Inhumans on the orders of the new Kree leadership.

BLACK BOLT'S WIVES (L-R)
1 Avoe (Dire Wraith)
2 Oola Udonta (Centaurian)
3 Medusa (Earth)
4 Onomi Whitemane (Kymellian)
5 Aladi Ko Eke (Badoon)

BLACK CAT

Don't cross her path

The daughter of a famous cat burglar, Felicia Hardy was determined to follow in her father's footsteps. She devised the costumed identity of the Black Cat, setting up prearranged "accidents" to make it appear as though she could cause bad luck to befall others. After encountering SPIDER-MAN, she became smitten with him, and for a time she was one of his closest confidantes.

FACTFILE

REAL NAME
Felicia Hardy

OCCUPATION
Cat burglar; adventurer

BASE
New York City

HEIGHT 5 ft 10 in
WEIGHT 120 lbs
EYES Green
HAIR Platinum blond

FIRST APPEARANCE
The Amazing Spider-Man #194 (July 1979)

POWERS
Her costume gives improved strength, speed, and agility, and she can inflict bad luck on others.

THE CAT GETS HER CLAWS

After DOCTOR OCTOPUS nearly killed her, the Black Cat decided that she needed superpowers of her own, if only to make sure that Spider-Man wouldn't wind up getting killed while trying to protect her. She obtained bad luck powers via the KINGPIN, but these began to jinx Spider-Man as well. Because she couldn't bring herself to be honest with Spider-Man, he broke off their relationship. Hurt, she wanted revenge but eventually realized her feelings for him were too strong, so she left for an extended stay in Europe instead. She returned years later, angry to find that Spider-Man had married Mary Jane WATSON. Despite that, she overcame her jealousy and became friends with the couple.

When MEPHISTO erased everyone's memory of Spider-Man's true identity, she lost that knowledge too, but she regained her powers and struck up a new relationship with Spider-Man. After the CIVIL WAR, she worked with Misty KNIGHT's Heroes for Hire and also joined the Fearless Defenders. When she met the Superior Spider-Man (DOCTOR OCTOPUS in Spider-Man's body), he webbed her up for the police, considering her a criminal. A furious Felicia swore revenge, setting up her own gang of superpowered criminals and using HAMMERHEAD as a second-in-command. When criminal Lee Price gained the Mania symbiote, he used it to try to take over the Black Cat's criminal empire. Felicia joined forces with Spider-Man and VENOM to stop him. It saw the end of her feud with Spider-Man but also the end of her organization. Venom suggested she should return to life as a vigilante, which Felicia seemed to consider.

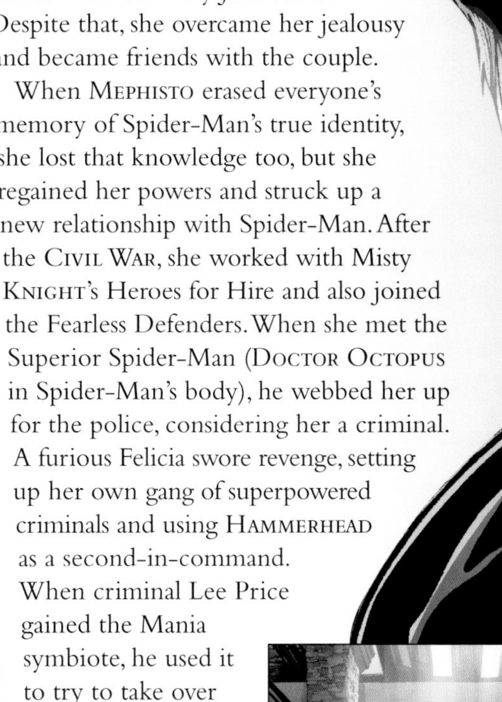

Peter Parker adored Felicia but, unfortunately, she preferred his amazing alter ego.

The Black Cat loves riches and sometimes assuages her guilt by playing Robin Hood with her ill-gotten gains.

As a gang boss Felicia was both heartless and vengeful, but in Lee Price she faced a villain who was even more ambitious and ruthless than she was.

ESSENTIAL STORYLINES

- ***Spider-Man/Black Cat: The Evil That Men Do #1–6*** The secret origin of the Black Cat.
- ***Wolverine & Black Cat: Claws #1–3*** Wolverine and Black Cat face off against Arcade.
- ***The Amazing Spider-Man Vol. 1 #606–607*** The Black Cat returns after Spider-Man's secret identity is erased.

BLACK KNIGHT

Knight of the Ebony Blade

BLACK KNIGHT

FACTFILE
REAL NAME
Dane Whitman
OCCUPATION
Adventurer
BASE
New York City

HEIGHT 6 ft
WEIGHT 190 lbs
EYES Brown
HAIR Brown

FIRST APPEARANCE
Avengers #47
(December 1967)

POWERS
An able scientist, Whitman built on the discoveries of his uncle, Nathan Garrett. He rides a winged horse and has a power lance that fires heat and force beams; also wields the Ebony Blade, sometimes more curse than blessing.

Weirdworld was one of the domains of Battleworld, filled with sorcery and bizarre creatures and ruled over by Witch Queen Morgan Le Fay.

The first Black Knight, Sir Percy of Scandia, was born in the 6th century and became one of the bravest knights at the court of King Arthur Pendragon at Camelot. Here he led a double life, posing as a mild-mannered fop while secretly fighting evil as the Black Knight, armed with the Ebony Blade, a sword fashioned by Merlin the Magician from the Starstone meteorite. Centuries later, Sir Percy's spirit returned to converse with his descendants, Professor Nathan Garrett and Dane Whitman, each of whom would take up his mantle.

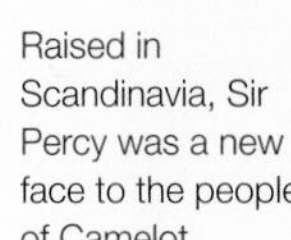

Raised in Scandinavia, Sir Percy was a new face to the people of Camelot.

VILLAINOUS KNIGHT

Nathan Garrett met the spirit of Sir Percy during a visit to the family home of Garrett Castle, and was offered the chance to become a latter-day Black Knight. However, Garrett failed to draw the Ebony Blade from its scabbard, thereby proving himself unworthy. Determined to become the Black Knight by other means, Garrett developed a lance that fired energy bolts, and embarked on a criminal career mounted upon a genetically engineered winged horse. Garrett battled the Avengers with the Masters of Evil, dying in a fight with Iron Man. Before passing away, Garrett confessed his crimes to his nephew, Dane Whitman, and begged him to restore his honor.

THE GOOD KNIGHT

Initially mistaken for the previous Black Knight and attacked by the Avengers, Dane Whitman soon gained their trust and joined the team. Blessed with a noble spirit, he was able to draw the Ebony Blade once wielded by his ancestor Sir Percy. Unfortunately, the sword had been cursed with the blood of those felled by Sir Percy. Dane joined Captain Britain in MI-13 during the Secret Invasion, taking on the new hero, Excalibur (Faiza Hussain), as his squire while protecting Britain from the Skrulls. The curse grew stronger as Dane joined Euroforce. After killing the villain Carnivore while under the blade's influence, Dane fled to Weirdworld where he established the kingdom of New Avalon. Steve Rogers (Captain America) and the rest of the Avengers Unity Division followed him there. When Rogers fell under the Ebony Blade's influence, he realized Dane was the best hope of controlling it. They left Dane in that strange land as its ruler.

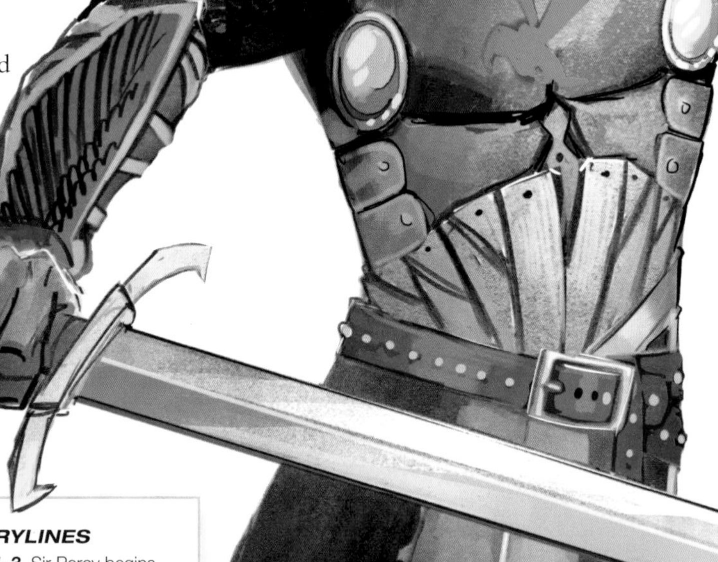

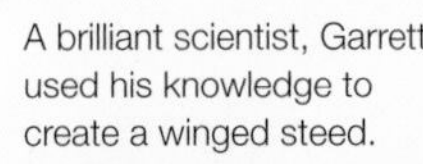

A brilliant scientist, Garrett used his knowledge to create a winged steed.

ESSENTIAL STORYLINES
- ***The Black Knight #1–3*** Sir Percy begins his adventures as the Black Knight.
- ***Avengers #71*** Dane Whitman helps the Avengers beat Kang and becomes a member.
- ***Doctor Strange Vol. 2 #68*** Whitman cleanses the Ebony Blade of evil and frees Sir Percy's ghost.

Black Mamba, see page 54

BLACK PANTHER

Warrior king of Wakanda

The Black Panther is an honorary title bestowed on the reigning monarch of the jungle kingdom of Wakanda. T'Challa was only a child when he succeeded his father, who had been murdered by KLAW. Before T'Challa assumed his throne from his uncle S'Yan, he was educated in the finest schools in Europe and America. He then embarked on a series of grueling tests to prove that he was worthy of donning the mantle and using the powers of the Black Panther.

The Black Panther's origin story came out in April, 1971, almost five years after his first appearance.

FACTFILE

REAL NAME
T'Challa

OCCUPATION
Monarch of Wakanda

BASE
Wakanda

HEIGHT 6 ft
WEIGHT 200 lbs
EYES Brown
HAIR Black

FIRST APPEARANCE
Fantastic Four #52
(July 1966)

POWERS

Olympic-level athlete, acrobat and gymnast; combat specialist. Mask enhances night vision; gloves expel gases; Vibranium boots enable him to land from great heights; Vibranium in costume makes bullets or other impacts lose power.

DEFENDING THE KINGDOM

Though T'Challa often allied himself with the FANTASTIC FOUR and the AVENGERS, the people of Wakanda have always been his highest priority. He wears a mask, but his identity as Wakanda's ruler is no secret, and he overcame challengers such as Erik KILLMONGER as well as a brain aneurism to maintain leadership of his homeland. T'Challa married his childhood sweetheart, Ororo Munroe, STORM of the X-MEN, making her his queen. Together they sided with CAPTAIN AMERICA's resistance during the CIVIL WAR, and they fought off a SKRULL attack upon Wakanda during the SECRET INVASION. NAMOR tried to bring T'Challa into the CABAL, but when he refused, DOCTOR DOOM critically wounded him. His younger sister SHURI stepped in to fill his role as the Black Panther—earning the blessing of the goddess Bast, the powers of the Black Panther, and the throne of Wakanda. When T'Challa recovered, he did not ask Shuri to step aside. Instead, at DAREDEVIL's request, he moved to Manhattan to take over the protection of Hell's Kitchen, and later rejoined the Avengers using the new secret identity of Mr. Okonkwo.

ESSENTIAL STORYLINES

- ***Jungle Action #6–18*** The Black Panther returns to Wakanda from the US to fight off Erik Killmonger's attempt to overthrow his rule.
- ***Black Panther #14–18*** T'Challa marries Storm.
- ***Black Panther #1–6*** Shuri takes over as the new Black Panther and ruler of Wakanda.

KING OF THE DEAD

As T'Challa searched for a way to renew his powers, he pledged himself once more to Bast, but this time as her King of the Dead, which boosted his abilities further than ever. During the conflict between the Avengers and the X-Men, Namor was under the Phoenix's influence and attacked Wakanda. T'Challa and Ororo also found themselves on opposite sides, and he annulled their marriage after the end of the conflict. Faced with the threat of his universe being destroyed, T'Challa joined the ILLUMINATI, despite having misgivings about the group. During his initial meeting with them, he vowed to kill Namor. Wakanda and Atlantis later went to war, despite T'Challa counseling Shuri to seek peace.

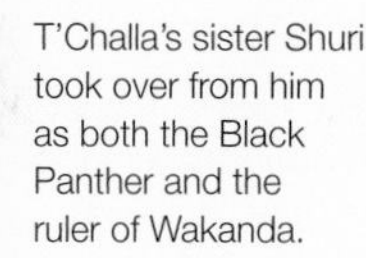

T'Challa's sister Shuri took over from him as both the Black Panther and the ruler of Wakanda.

REBELLION

When Earth was destroyed during the events of SECRET WARS, T'Challa was one of the few to survive. He used a Reality Stone to travel to a reborn Earth and became king again as his sister appeared to be dead. The People, a political group backed by outside sources, unsuccessfully tried to overthrow him. The DORA MILAJE sought more of a say in government, but agreed peace with their leader and a new political system for the country: a constitutional monarchy with T'Challa remaining as its monarch.

The Black Panther and Storm ruled as the king and queen of Wakanda until their fight over the Phoenix Force shattered their marriage.

BLACK MAMBA

FIRST APPEARANCE *Marvel Two-In-One* #64 (June 1980)
REAL NAME Tanya Sealy
OCCUPATION Mercenary **BASE** Mobile
HEIGHT 5 ft 7 in **WEIGHT** 115 lbs **EYES** Green **HAIR** Black
SPECIAL POWERS/ABILITIES Projects Darkforce energy, which suffocates opponents; hypnotic powers trick targets into thinking that Darkforce is a loved one, allowing it to ensnare them.

Roxxon Oil implanted a device in the brain of Tanya Sealy, a former call girl, giving her powers of telepathic hypnosis and the ability to control the Darkforce, an inky cloud of energy. She formed part of the original incarnations of the Serpent Squad and SERPENT SOCIETY. Later, she also worked with the MASTERS OF EVIL, the BAD Girls, and the Femizons. During the CIVIL WAR, she sided with CAPTAIN AMERICA's anti-registration forces, but during the SECRET INVASION, she rejoined a new Serpent Society. She later joined the Women Warriors, Delaware's FIFTY-STATE INITIATIVE team and later Serpent Solutions (*see* Serpent Society).

BLACK TOM

FIRST APPEARANCE *X-Men* #99 (June 1976)
REAL NAME Thomas Samuel Eamon Cassidy
OCCUPATION Criminal **BASE** Mobile
HEIGHT 6 ft **WEIGHT** 200 lbs **EYES** Blue **HAIR** Black
SPECIAL POWERS/ABILITIES Can project blasts of heat and concussive force, which he focuses through his shillelagh.

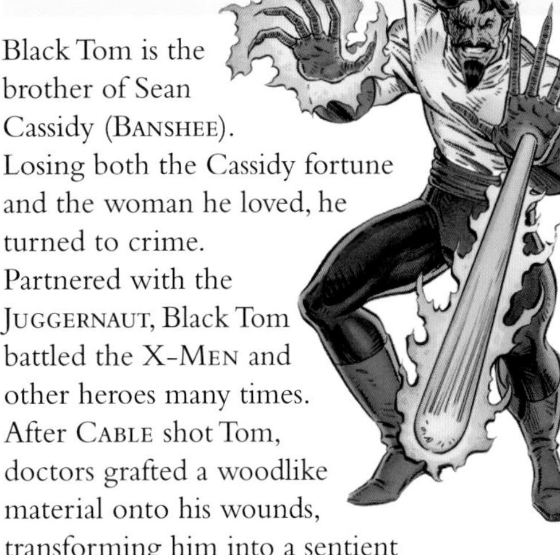

Black Tom is the brother of Sean Cassidy (BANSHEE). Losing both the Cassidy fortune and the woman he loved, he turned to crime. Partnered with the JUGGERNAUT, Black Tom battled the X-MEN and other heroes many times. After CABLE shot Tom, doctors grafted a woodlike material onto his wounds, transforming him into a sentient humanoid plant. On M-Day, Tom lost his plant powers and returned to his old self. He later teamed up with Juggernaut once more and seemed to be repowered as they fought the time-displaced X-Men.

BLACKWING

FIRST APPEARANCE *X-Men* #117 (October 2001)
REAL NAME Barnell Bohusk
OCCUPATION Student; reality traveler **BASE** New York City
HEIGHT 5 ft 9 in **WEIGHT** 122 lbs
EYES Brown **HAIR** Brown
SPECIAL POWERS/ABILITIES Possesses a suit that gives him superhuman strength, energy blasts, and flight.

At puberty, Barnell mutated into a birdlike human with hollow bones, talons, and wings. Soon after, he joined the Xavier Institute for Higher Learning (*see* X-MEN) as a student code-named Beak. There, he had six babies with fellow mutant Angel Salvadore. After rebelling against the mutant XORN's attempt to take over the world, Barnell became dislodged in time and was forced to join the EXILES. He reunited with Angel and their children just before he lost his powers on M-Day. He joined the latest version of the NEW WARRIORS as Blackwing, wearing a high-tech suit that granted him powers.

BLACK TALON

FIRST APPEARANCE *Avengers* #152 (October 1976)
REAL NAME Samuel Barone
OCCUPATION Houngan (voodoo priest) **BASE** Louisiana
HEIGHT 6 ft 2 in **WEIGHT** 240 lbs **EYES** Brown **HAIR** Black
SPECIAL POWERS/ABILITIES Supernatural voodoo powers, including the ability to create and control zombies, human corpses that can be reanimated through voodoo magic.

There have been three Black Talons. The most recent was Samuel Barone, a Creole with true voodoo powers and his own cult. The GRIM REAPER contacted him to bring his dead brother, WONDER MAN, back to life as a zombie. He battled the AVENGERS many times and retired for a while to produce drugs for the HOOD instead. When Black Talon attacked New York City with a zombie horde, the PUNISHER killed him. He returned to life and joined the Shadow Council's MASTERS OF EVIL.

BLACKOUT

FIRST APPEARANCE *Nova* #19 (May 1976)
REAL NAME Marcus Daniels
OCCUPATION Criminal **BASE** New York City
HEIGHT 5 ft 10 in **WEIGHT** 180 lbs **EYES** Gray **HAIR** Brown
SPECIAL POWERS/ABILITIES Projects and manipulates semi-solid black energy known as the Darkforce; has the strength and agility of a normal human being.

Exposed to "black star" rays by the physicist Dr. Croit, Daniels gained the ability to control this cosmic radiation. As "Blackout," he embarked on a series of robberies. Over time, exposure to this dark energy led to creeping insanity. Although his ally MOONSTONE helped him, she also sought to control his mind, as did their joint master, BARON ZEMO. During an attack on the AVENGERS' Mansion, Blackout fought Zemo's mental commands, but these efforts led to a brain haemorrhage. He later assisted HYDRA's take over of the US by cutting off Manhattan from the rest of the country.

BLACK SWAN

FIRST APPEARANCE *New Avengers* #1 (March 2013)
REAL NAME Yabbat Ummon Turru
OCCUPATION Destroyer **BASE** The Necropolis of Wakanda
HEIGHT 5 ft 7 in **WEIGHT** 120 lbs
EYES Black (red during incursions) **HAIR** White
SPECIAL POWERS/ABILITIES Yabbat can fly and fire optic blasts. She possesses superhuman strength and is telepathic. She can predict incoming incursions of other Earths.

Born a princess on an Earth in another dimension, as a girl Yabbat escaped the destruction of her world by fleeing into an interdimensional library. There the Black Swans of many dimensions took her in and raised her to join their ranks. As an adult, she traveled from Earth to Earth, destroying those Earths that threatened the others as an offering to Rabum Alal, a godlike being who she believed caused the world-shattering incursions. She was a member of NAMOR's new CABAL, and following the remaking of reality (*see* SECRET WARS), she joined a new incarnation of the Black Order.

BLACK WIDOW

Uncompromising and deadly

Natasha has assumed many roles, including assassin, spy, surrogate mother, field agent, and implacable opponent of a rival Black Widow.

Shortly after Russia's World War II victory at Stalingrad, a lady, trapped in a burning building, threw her baby to a stranger below—a soldier named Ivan Petrovich. He raised the baby, named Natasha, who turned out to be a superb student, athlete, and ballerina. She married test pilot Alexei Shostakov, but their happiness was cut short. Faking Shostakov's death and leaving Natasha to grieve, the KGB trained him to become the Red Guardian—a Russian Super-Soldier. Next, the KGB (via the so-called Red Room program) manipulated Natasha into becoming a spy, code-named Black Widow.

BLACK WIDOW I

FACTFILE

REAL NAME
Natalia (Natasha) Alianovna Romanova

OCCUPATION
Intelligence agent

BASE New York City

HEIGHT 5 ft 7 in
WEIGHT 125 lbs
EYES Blue
HAIR Red/auburn

FIRST APPEARANCE
Tales of Suspense #52 (April 1964)

POWERS
Martial artist; Olympic-level gymnast; trained spy; cartridges on wrist house various devices and also fire energy blasts known as the "Widow's Bite."

While they don't always see eye-to-eye, Black Widow remains loyal to her old lover, Daredevil.

HARD TIME

Two espionage missions against Stark Industries brought Black Widow into contact with Hawkeye, and he inspired her to join SHIELD. A romance between them proved short-lived. Encountering the Red Guardian on a mission, she had only just learned his true identity when he was shot and killed.

Later, Natasha became romantically involved with Daredevil and founded the Champions. She also led the Avengers during one of its hardest periods, when several members died.

More recently, she became the foe of a rival Black Widow, Yelena Belova. She also learned she was just one of many Black Widows and that her memories of her early life were implanted. While working for Iron Man's SHIELD, Natasha helped install Bucky Barnes as the new Captain America.

During Hydra's takeover of the United States, Black Widow helped lead the fight against the evil version of Captain America but was killed battling him. Following Hydra's fall, she found herself back in the Red Room—only to realize she was now a clone, albeit one with all her old memories in place, including the memory of her own death. She helped to bring down the new Red Room and went rogue once more.

ESSENTIAL STORYLINES

- ***Daredevil #87–90*** Black Widow and Daredevil move to San Francisco; Black Widow's history is explained.
- ***Pale Little Spider #1–3*** The origins of Yelena Belova are explained for the first time.
- ***Black Widow Vol. I #1–3*** The two Black Widows, Natasha Romanova and Yelena Belova, go head-to-head and their bitter enmity begins.

BLACK WIDOW II

FACTFILE

REAL NAME
Yelena Belova

OCCUPATION
Intelligence agent

BASE Russia

HEIGHT 5 ft 7 in
WEIGHT 135 lbs
EYES Blue
HAIR Blonde

FIRST APPEARANCE
Inhumans #5 (March 1999)

POWERS
Only experience and gadgets separate Belova from the first Black Widow: Belova achieved even higher marks in training; she is also a martial arts expert and Olympic-level gymnast.

YELENA BELOVA

Like Natasha, Yelena Belova was trained at the KGB's Red Room. She once worked for Hydra, who had transferred her mind into a Super-Adaptoid body. Following Natasha's death, Yelena became Black Widow again to honor her.

BLADE

Daywalking human vampire

BLADE

FACTFILE

REAL NAME
Eric Brooks

OCCUPATION
Vampire hunter

BASE
Mobile

HEIGHT 6 ft 2 in
WEIGHT 180 lbs
EYES Brown
HAIR Black

FIRST APPEARANCE
Tomb of Dracula #10
(July 1973)

POWERS

Immune to vampire bites and vampiric hypnosis; enhanced strength, speed, senses, and healing. Immune to vampire's susceptibility to sunlight. Carries arsenal of anti-vampire weapons; guns fire garlic-filled silver bullets; trademark blade is titanium; martial arts expert.

Over seventy years ago, Blade's mother (a London prostitute) was fatally bitten by vampire Deacon Frost while giving birth to him, transforming the infant into a half-vampire (dhampir). Friends of Blade's mother raised him in her brothel. When he was nine, he helped horn player Jamal Afari fend off a trio of vampires, and the jazz trumpeter moved into the brothel to tutor Blade in both music and the hunting of vampires.

Blade doesn't take orders well and is difficult to work with in large team settings.

Blade remains committed to his mission to rid the world of vampires. He now possesses the abilities of a pseudo-vampire due to a bite from Morbius.

After losing his left hand, Blade had a prosthetic made out of a gun.

VAMPIRE HUNTERS

In his youth, Blade ran a street gang called the Bloodshadows. After the vampire Lamia transformed his girlfriend, Glory, into a vampire, he gave up gang life and returned to vampire hunting. When DRACULA turned Afari into a vampire too, Blade assembled a team of hunters to track the vampire lord to China. After losing his first team, Blade partnered with Dracula's old foe Quincy Harker as well as Rachel VAN HELSING and Frank DRAKE to renew the pursuit.

When Blade's path crossed Deacon Frost's, he went after his mother's killer. During this time, he met and partnered with Hannibal KING, a detective whom Frost had turned into a vampire. Together with King, Drake, and DOCTOR STRANGE, Blade helped unleash the Montesi Formula, a spell that destroyed all the vampires on Earth. His quest ended, Blade opened a detective agency with Drake and King, named Borderline Investigations, and they battled occult threats such as the Nightstalkers.

DAYWALKER

When Dracula returned and beat Blade, Blade's fury caused him to have a breakdown, and he was placed in a mental institution until Doctor Strange could help him. Freed, Blade was tricked into using a page from the mystical book *Darkhold* to give himself supernatural powers as Switchblade. Another page from the forbidden book returned him to normal. While working with SPIDER-MAN, Blade was bitten by his sometime-ally MORBIUS. Blade's immunity to vampires didn't apply to Morbius' unique condition. Blade gained the powers of a vampire, but without their weakness to sunlight, causing him to be known as Daywalker.

During the CIVIL WAR, Blade registered and worked with SHIELD. He'd earlier bitten off one of his own hands to prevent himself being force-fed an innocent, and SHIELD gave him a gun-hand to replace it. During the SECRET INVASION, he worked with MI-13 and struck up a relationship with the part-vampire hero SPITFIRE. He later helped the X-MEN against Dracula's son XARUS, taught a class at the Jean Grey School, and fought THANOS' invasion while disguised as "Spider Hero." Afterwards he took on HAWKEYE's identity as Ronin and recovered the Talisman of Kamar-Taj. This led to a fight with the Deathwalkers, who also sought the Talisman.

ESSENTIAL STORYLINES

- ***Tomb of Dracula #10, #12–14*** Blade makes his debut and kills Dracula for the first time.
- ***Rise of the Midnight Sons*** The Nightstalkers join Doctor Strange, Morbius, Ghost Rider (Dan Ketch), Johnny Blaze (see Ghost Rider), and the Darkhold Redeemers in the battle against Lilith.
- ***Blade Vol. 6 #1–12*** Blade's past catches up with him—along with his father.

BLINDFOLD

FIRST APPEARANCE *Astonishing X-Men* #7 (January 2005)
REAL NAME Ruth Aldine **OCCUPATION** Student
BASE Jean Grey's School for Higher Learning **HEIGHT** 5 ft 6 in
WEIGHT 123 lbs **EYES** None **HAIR** Black
SPECIAL POWERS/ABILITIES Ruth is a telepath with limited precognition.

Born a mutant without eyes or sockets, Ruth was abandoned by her father, leaving her in the care of her mother and cruel older brother. Her mother died defending her from her brother and Ruth went to live with an aunt until her brother's execution; his ghost then stole half her powers. She joined the YOUNG X-MEN, later learning that she was related to DESTINY, which explained her powers of prediction. She helped LEGION control his powers and, in return, he saved her from her brother's spirit. Blindfold and Legion then fell in love, their minds connecting strongly on the mental plane.

BLING!

FIRST APPEARANCE *X-Men* #171 (August 2005)
REAL NAME Roxanne Washington **OCCUPATION** Student
BASE Jean Grey School for Higher Learning **HEIGHT** 5 ft 6 in
WEIGHT 152 lbs **EYES** Brown (or diamond) **HAIR** Brown (or diamond) **SPECIAL POWERS/ABILITIES** Roxy's bone marrow can produce diamonds, which can protect her skin or be fired at foes. She also has superhuman strength.

The daughter of hip-hop artists, Roxy is famous for appearing in her parents' music videos. To escape the music industry, she enrolled at the Xavier Institute, studying under GAMBIT. When the school was shut down, she followed the X-MEN to Utopia and helped with various missions. She declined a formal place with the X-MEN, and returned to her studies at the Jean Grey School for Higher Learning. She later transfered to the new Xavier Institute and was part of GENERATION X.

BLIZZARD

FIRST APPEARANCE *Tales of Suspense* #45 (September 1963)
REAL NAME Dr. Gregor Shapanka **OCCUPATION** Former scientist; criminal **BASE** New York City **HEIGHT** 5 ft 5 in
WEIGHT 165 lbs **EYES** Brown **HAIR** Brown
SPECIAL POWERS/ABILITIES Gloves on battlesuit could project intense cold, generate freezing mist, mini-blizzards, and darts of razor-sharp ice; could freeze people by covering them in frost.

Employed by Stark Industries, Dr. Gregor Shapanka attempted to steal and sell Stark technology to fund research into longevity. Caught and fired, he developed a suit with freezing powers and came to be known as the villain Jack Frost, and later Blizzard. Shapanka was killed by Arno STARK, the Iron Man of 2020, who had come back in time for data needed to disarm a bomb. Shapanka's successor was Donny Gill, an employee of Justin HAMMER. After leaving Hammer's employ, Gill joined the MASTERS OF EVIL, and later, the THUNDERBOLTS.

BLINK

Blink was part of a group of mutants captured by evil alien race the PHALANX. She helped save the others but accidentally killed herself with her powers in the process. The immortal EXTERNAL magician SELENE resurrected her and told her that the X-MEN had betrayed her, convincing Blink to fight against them. Blink later realized her error and joined WOLVERINE's X-Men team, also occasionally helping the NEW MUTANTS in Utopia. The Blink of Earth-295 was raised in the Age of Apocalypse by SABRETOOTH, but became unstuck in time—exiled from her home reality. Recruited by the Timebroker, she and a team of fellow EXILES repaired broken links in the chain of realities. She later formed a new Exiles team to defeat the timeline-devouring Time-Eater.

FACTFILE
REAL NAME
Clarice Ferguson
OCCUPATION
Adventurer
BASE Mobile

HEIGHT 5 ft 5 in
WEIGHT 125 lbs
EYES Green
HAIR Magenta

FIRST APPEARANCE
Uncanny X-Men #317
(October 1994)

BLINK

POWERS
Blink is a mutant with the ability to create teleportational warps. She carries a dagger and a set of javelins to use as weapons.

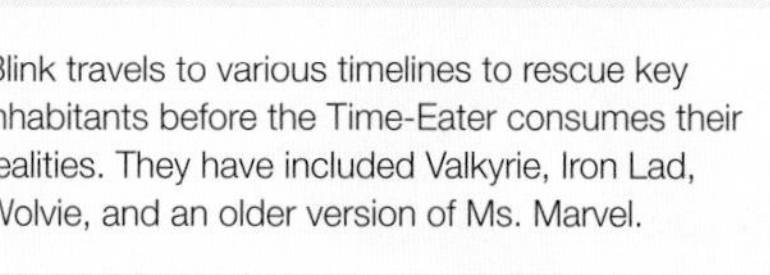

Blink travels to various timelines to rescue key inhabitants before the Time-Eater consumes their realities. They have included Valkyrie, Iron Lad, Wolvie, and an older version of Ms. Marvel.

BLOB

FACTFILE
REAL NAME
Fred J. Dukes
OCCUPATION Criminal; former circus performer
BASE
Mobile

HEIGHT 8 ft
WEIGHT 976 lbs
EYES Brown
HAIR Brown

FIRST APPEARANCE
Uncanny X-Men #3 (January 1964)

POWERS
Superhuman strength and durability. Fatty body could absorb bullets, even artillery shells, and was impervious to injury; however eyes, ears, nose, and mouth were not as injury-resistant. When he planted himself firmly, the Blob bonded with the ground beneath him and could not be moved.

BLOB

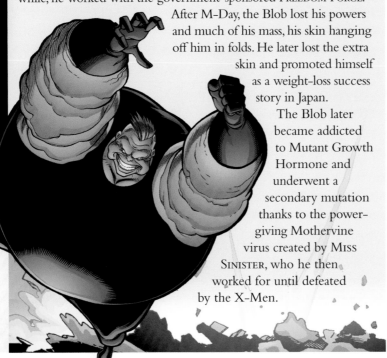

Life changed for carnival performer Fred J. Dukes when the X-Men revealed to him that he was a mutant. Instead of joining them, Dukes attempted to destroy them as the Blob. Recruited by Magneto for his Brotherhood of Evil Mutants, the Blob embarked on a life of crime, clashing with the X-Men, Avengers, and Defenders. For a while, he worked with the government-sponsored Freedom Force. After M-Day, the Blob lost his powers and much of his mass, his skin hanging off him in folds. He later lost the extra skin and promoted himself as a weight-loss success story in Japan. The Blob later became addicted to Mutant Growth Hormone and underwent a secondary mutation thanks to the power-giving Mothervine virus created by Miss Sinister, who he then worked for until defeated by the X-Men.

BLOODHAWK

FIRST APPEARANCE *Avengers* #179 (January 1979)
REAL NAME Bloodhawk **OCCUPATION** Adventurer
BASE Muara, an island in the Atlantic Ocean **HEIGHT** 6 ft 3 in
WEIGHT 150 lbs **EYES** Black **FEATHERS** Reddish-brown
SPECIAL POWERS/ABILITIES Superhuman strength and stamina; able to fly and communicate with birds; possesses razor-sharp claws.

Bloodhawk is the only son of a geneticist who experimented on his own wife. The poor woman died giving birth to a mutant of hawklike appearance and characteristics. Unable to accept the horror he had created, Bloodhawk's father turned his son over to his best friend, who removed the child from civilization. Plagued by bouts of insanity, Bloodhawk grew to adulthood in the South Seas. When a powerful totem was stolen from his island home, he journeyed to the US and battled the Avengers to recover it. Bloodhawk later gave his life to save Thor.

BLOODSCREAM

FIRST APPEARANCE *Wolverine* #4 (February 1989)
REAL NAME Unknown **OCCUPATION** Enforcer
BASE Madripoor, Southeast Asia **HEIGHT** 6 ft 5 in
WEIGHT Unknown **EYES** Unknown **HAIR** Gray
SPECIAL POWERS/ABILITIES Although not a true vampire, has many vampire powers: superhuman strength, agility, accelerated healing, hypnotic ability; can also kill or cause bleeding by touch.

Bloodscream was once a 16th-century sailor, whom a necromancer turned into a pseudo-vampire—a condition that could only be cured by drinking an immortal's blood. Centuries later, Bloodscream, now a Nazi soldier, encountered Wolverine. Meeting Wolverine decades later, Bloodscream saw the mutant hadn't aged. Assuming Wolverine was immortal, Bloodscream has hounded him ever since.

BLOODSTONE, ELSA

The daughter of Ulysses Bloodstone, Elsa inherited his estate soon after her 18th birthday and moved into Bloodstone Manor with her mother. She also inherited a fragment of the bloodgem, which she wears in a choker necklace. She later joined Dirk Anger to become part of HATE and battled the forces of the Beyond Corporation as part of the Nextwave squad. With the Beyond Corporation defeated, Elsa registered with the US government and joined The Fifty-State Initiative. On returning to England she became a teacher at the Braddock Academy, where her younger brother Cullen Bloodstone was enrolled. Elsa has fought numerous monsters, but has also teamed up with some, including Adam (Frankenstein's Monster) and the Legion of Monsters, who helped her retrieve a bloodgem from the Punisher. She later assisted the Fearless Defenders when monsters overran Chinatown and was made an Avenger by Doctor Doom when that team's heroes turned evil. She also fought alongside A-Force against the Poisons during their attempted invasion of Earth.

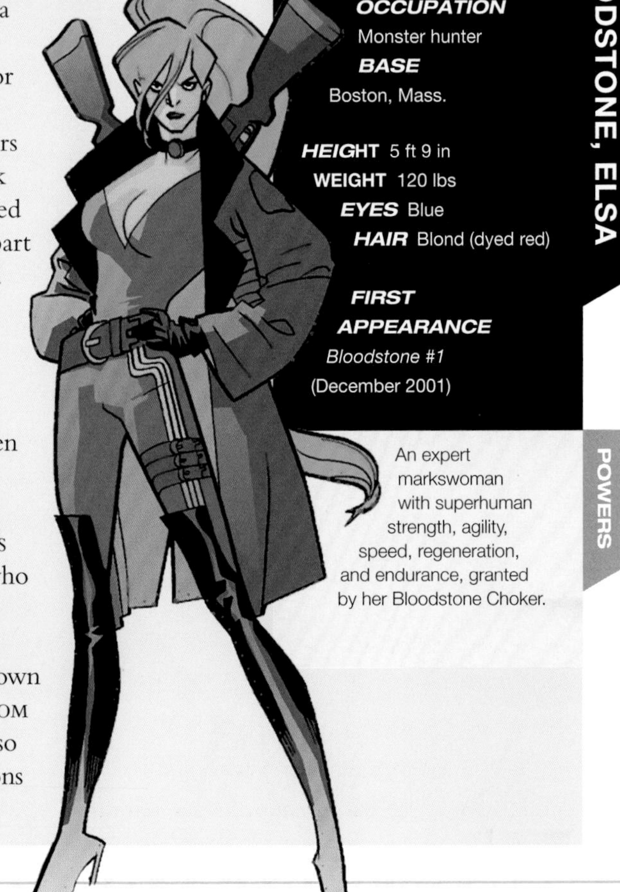

BLOODSTONE, ELSA

FACTFILE
REAL NAME
Elsa Bloostone
OCCUPATION
Monster hunter
BASE
Boston, Mass.

HEIGHT 5 ft 9 in
WEIGHT 120 lbs
EYES Blue
HAIR Blond (dyed red)

FIRST APPEARANCE
Bloodstone #1 (December 2001)

POWERS
An expert markswoman with superhuman strength, agility, speed, regeneration, and endurance, granted by her Bloodstone Choker.

BLOODSTONE, CULLEN

FIRST APPEARANCE *Avengers Arena* #1 (February, 2013)
REAL NAME Cullen Bloodstone **OCCUPATION** Student
BASE Mobile **EYES** Green **HAIR** Blond
SPECIAL POWERS/ABILITIES Superhuman strength and stamina; rapid healing abilities; possessed by the Glartrox, which feeds on the fear and anger of other beings (when not suppressed by the bloodgem ring).

When Cullen Bloodstone was ten, he was taken to a hellish dimension by his father, Ulysses BLOODSTONE, and told to fend for himself for 24 hours to prove he was worthy of the family name. Unfortunately his father was killed shortly afterward and Cullen remained trapped in the dimension for over two years, eventually returning to Earth with a Glartrox demon bonded to his soul. His sister Elsa BLOODSTONE gave him a bloodgem ring that enabled him to contain the demon. He started at Braddock Academy, but was kidnapped by ARCADE and placed in a death tournament with other teenage heroes, which he survived.

BLOODSTONE, ULYSSES

Born more than 10,000 years ago in the Hyborian Age, the man known as Ulysses Bloodstone belonged to a Scandinavian tribe of hunter-gatherers. He was lured away by Ulluxy'l Kwan Tae Syn, the alien guardian of a crystal entity called the Hellfire Helix. The Helix needed a human servant, so it endowed the tribe's foremost hunter with superhuman powers. However, when the Helix crystal killed the rest of his tribe, the hunter caused it to shatter. A piece embedded itself in his chest and the other pieces were scattered all over the world. The reddish crystal fragment made the hunter immortal, and led him to adopt the name Ulysses Bloodstone. Ulysses spent the rest of his life searching for Ulluxy'l, while the alien strove to piece the Helix back together. During his quest, Ulysses earned a fortune through mercenary work and shrewd investments, establishing six headquarters across the world and a base on what became known as Bloodstone Island.

The Helix had Ulluxy'l ally himself with a group called "The Conspiracy." They cut the crystal fragment from Ulysses' chest, leaving him for dead, however he managed to kill Ulluxy'l before his body withered and died. Ulysses left behind his ex-wife Elise, their daughter Elsa BLOODSTONE, and son Cullen.

FACTFILE
REAL NAME
Unknown; took the name Ulysses Bloodstone
OCCUPATION
Soldier of fortune
BASE
Bloodstone Island

HEIGHT 6 ft 2 in
WEIGHT 255 lbs
EYES Blue
HAIR Blond

FIRST APPEARANCE
Marvel Presents #1 (October 1975)

POWERS
Superhuman strength; blood-red Helix crystal endowed him with immortality and regenerative ability: could even regrow limbs; also had invisible third eye in forehead giving him psychic powers; expert with all kinds of weapons, though favored a customized sawn-off shotgun firing explosive shells.

BLOODSTORM

FIRST APPEARANCE *Mutant X* #1 (October 1998)
REAL NAME Ororo Munroe
OCCUPATION Adventurer **BASE** Earth of Mutant X universe
HEIGHT 5 ft 11 in **WEIGHT** 196 lbs **EYES** Blue **HAIR** White
SPECIAL POWERS/ABILITIES Possessed vampiric powers, including hypnotic abilities and the power to transform into mist, a bat, or a wolf; can control the weather over limited areas.

Years ago, DRACULA bit STORM of the X-MEN, who began transforming into a vampire. In the main Marvel Universe, Storm was cured. However, on an alternate Earth, Storm completed her metamorphosis, becoming the vampire known as Bloodstorm. She nevertheless refused to turn villainous, and fed only on the blood of that reality's FORGE, with his consent. Bloodstorm joined the Six, a team mostly comprised of former members of that reality's X-Men. When Madelyne PRYOR made Bloodstorm part of her Hex Men, Bloodstorm traveled to mainstream reality to fight alongside her. However, upon realizing Madelyne was evil, she swapped sides, joining the time-displaced X-Men.

BLUE MARVEL

FIRST APPEARANCE *Adam: Legend of the Blue Marvel* #1 (January 2009)
REAL NAME Adam Brashear **OCCUPATION** Adventurer
BASE Mobile **HEIGHT** 6 ft 4 in **WEIGHT** 230 lbs
EYES Brown **HAIR** Black with gray highlights
SPECIAL POWERS/ABILITIES Anti-Matter energy manipulation; hyper-cosmic awareness; superhuman strength; flight; longevity; near invulnerability

Adam Brashear was a Korean War veteran turned scientist who tried to harness antimatter in a Negative Reactor to create free energy. The experiment went awry and both Adam and his friend Conner Sims were genetically altered. Adam found himself with amazing powers and became the Super Hero Blue Marvel. Adam retired as a hero in 1962, but briefly fought alongside BLADE and others in the 1970s. With his aging slowed by his powers, Adam joined modern-day heroes such as Luke CAGE'S AVENGERS and then the Ultimates.

BOOMERANG

FIRST APPEARANCE *Tales to Astonish* #81 (July 1966)
REAL NAME Frederick Myers **OCCUPATION** Assassin for hire
BASE Mobile **HEIGHT** 5 ft 11 in **WEIGHT** 175 lbs
EYES Brown **HAIR** Black
SPECIAL POWERS/ABILITIES Brilliant baseball pitcher; famed for customized boomerangs, such as explosive "shatterangs," poisonous "gasarangs," and diamond sharp "razorangs."

Australian Fred Myers moved to the US as a child and became a Major League Baseball player. Suspended for taking bribes, he turned to crime full-time. The Secret Empire gave him the code name Boomerang and supplied his weaponry. He worked with Justin HAMMER, HAMMERHEAD, the KINGPIN, the SINISTER SYNDICATE, the Sinister Twelve, and the MASTERS OF EVIL, battling foes such as SHIELD, DAREDEVIL, and SPIDER-MAN. During Norman Osborn's control of SHIELD, Boomerang joined the Heavy Hitters, the FIFTY-STATE INITIATIVE'S Nevada team, under the name Outback. During HYDRA's takeover of the US, he briefly became crimelord of Newark.

BOX

FACTFILE

REAL NAME
Roger Bochs

OCCUPATION
Alpha Flight member

BASE
Tamarind Island, British Columbia

HEIGHT 7 ft
WEIGHT 465 lbs
EYES Blue
HAIR Red

FIRST APPEARANCE
Alpha Flight #1 (August 1983)

POWERS

An engineering genius, Bochs built the first Box robot to serve as transportation for himself. The Box robot possessed vast strength and durability and Bochs was able to "phase" in and out of robot at will.

Tensions erupt between Box and Shaman, a fellow Alpha Flight member.

BOX

Roger Bochs was a world-class engineer and a mechanic without equal, who had both of his legs amputated below the knees leaving him unable to walk. He built a giant humanoid robot—Box—which he could control to help him. With his robot, Roger came to the attention of James McDonald Hudson, who recruited him into ALPHA FLIGHT's training program. He progressed well until the Canadian government withdrew funding, and, out of a job, he returned to his home in Moosejaw.

Hudson kept the team going, but Roger didn't return immediately. Hired by Jerome Jaxon, Roger joined the nefarious OMEGA FLIGHT and was expected to destroy Alpha Flight. He opposed this but was helpless when Jaxon took control of Box and sent it into battle. By the end of the struggle, both Jaxon and Hudson were dead and Box was mangled. Roger rejoined the exhausted Alpha Flight, but first he needed to rebuild his robot.

With the help of fellow team member Madison Jeffries, Roger constructed a superior Box model, but his life took an unexpected turn. Manipulated into merging his being with Madison's unbalanced brother, Roger became part of a new entity—Omega. His attempts to limit Omega's sinister activities led to him being effectively lobotomized, and when Omega was defeated and died, Roger passed away, too.

When Roger Bochs died, Madison Jeffries inherited the Box armor and used his mutant ability to manipulate metal, glass, and plastic to augment the machine. He served with Alpha Flight but retired to marry teammate Diamond Lil. Later, agents of Weapon X captured Jeffries and brainwashed him into building the Neverland mutant concentration camp. He retained his powers after M-Day, but went into mourning when Diamond Lil was killed by Mortis. He currently works with the X-MEN as part of their team of scientists—X-Club.

Roger Bochs could telepathically link with his Box robot to control it.

BRADDOCK, JAMIE

FIRST APPEARANCE *Captain Britain Weekly* #9 (December 1976)
REAL NAME James Braddock
OCCUPATION Ex-racing driver, slave-trafficker **BASE** London
HEIGHT 6 ft 1 in **WEIGHT** 151 lbs **EYES** Blue **HAIR** Black
SPECIAL POWERS/ABILITIES Possesses the ability to warp reality, which he perceives as made of string; he can thus twist objects, such as people's bodies, into grotesque, agonizing shapes.

Brother of CAPTAIN BRITAIN and PSYLOCKE, Jamie was captured and tortured by Doctor Crocodile. His latent ability to reshape reality manifested the moment he lost his sanity, and he became one of the most dangerous beings alive. After EXCALIBUR defeated him, he spent years in a coma. During the House of M incident, he woke up and sacrificed himself to save his sister and the universe. He returned again and helped stop the Goat Monk, a future version of himself. When Psylocke realized this, she forced Captain Britain to kill him. Jamie returned yet again and tried to steal the Space Stone from BLACK WIDOW, who killed him.

BRANT, BETTY

Working at the *Daily Bugle*, Betty became photojournalist Peter Parker's (SPIDER-MAN's) first girlfriend. When their relationship ended, she married *Daily Bugle* reporter Ned Leeds. Dismayed when she discovered that Ned had become the HOBGOBLIN, she suffered a mental breakdown after his death. Betty later became an investigative reporter and cleared Ned's name by proving that Roderick Kingsley was the original Hobgoblin. Throughout it all, she and Peter have remained great friends. She dated Flash THOMPSON, the new VENOM, until his erratic behavior became too much for her. Betty was surprised when her dead husband (actually a living clone of Ned with his memories) left her a voicemail from beyond the grave, ending it with two mysterious words: blood creek. With Spider-Man's help, Betty uncovered a secret bomb disguised as a statue outside City Hall. Betty saved the day by punching a Maggia member before he could set it off.

BRANT, BETTY

FACTFILE

REAL NAME
Elizabeth Brant

OCCUPATION
Investigative journalist

BASE
New York City

HEIGHT 5 ft 7 in
WEIGHT 125 lbs
EYES Brown
HAIR Brown

FIRST APPEARANCE
Amazing Spider-Man #4 (September 1963)

POWERS

Expert investigative reporter with a strong personality and a hugely generous soul.

BRAND, ABIGAIL

FIRST APPEARANCE *Astonishing X-Men* #3 (September 2004)
REAL NAME Abigail Brand **OCCUPATION** Director of SWORD
BASE The Peak (SWORD HQ) **HEIGHT** 5 ft 8 in
WEIGHT 140 lbs **EYES** Green **HAIR** Green
SPECIAL POWERS/ABILITIES Produces heat and light from her hands and heals fast; extraterrestrial diplomat; trained pilot and combatant.

The daughter of a blue-furred alien father and a human mutant mother, Brand speaks a number of alien languages whose words most humans cannot pronounce. These qualities made her uniquely suited to serve as the director of SWORD (Sentient World Observation and Response Department), the off-Earth counterpart of SHIELD. Despite her lack of social skills outside of direct diplomacy, she had an ongoing relationship with the Beast. When Alpha Flight replaced SWORD, Abigail turned down the opportunity to lead it, but accepted the rank of Lieutenant Commander reporting to Captain Marvel.

BROO

The young Broo was a Brood mutant. Unlike the vast majority of his evil, parasitical species, Broo was friendly, compassionate, and possessed a superior intelligence. These traits caused him to be shunned by the Brood, who normally kill such mutants outright. Due to the low numbers of Brood, two surviving Brood Queens didn't kill Broo, but they refused to telepathically link with him through their Hive-Mind, fearing his compassion might infect them.

Broo was discovered by the X-Men on a SWORD space satellite that was overrun by the Brood. After he helped the heroes defeat them, Broo became a student at the Jean Grey School for Higher Learning. Here, he met Idie Okonkwo, who inadvertantly gave him his name, and he developed feelings for her.

After Broo was shot in the head, his innate Brood nature asserted itself, and he turned feral. Beast searched for a cure, but Broo was healed when he bit a Bamf. Broo went on to resume his studies at the Xavier Institute for Mutant Education and Outreach.

FACTFILE
REAL NAME
Broo
OCCUPATION
Student
BASE
Xavier Institute for Mutant Education and Outreach
HEIGHT Unknown
WEIGHT Unknown
EYES Red
HAIR None
FIRST APPEARANCE
Astonishing X-Men #40 (September 2011)

BROO

POWERS

Broo has a super-genius-level intellect, possibly on a par with that of Tony Stark. He shares most of the key physiological characteristics of the rest of his species, though appears to lack a tail, stingers, or wings.

BROOD, THE

The Brood is a race of alien insectoids that spreads across the universe like a cancer by injecting eggs into other beings. Comprised of multiple hives, each group is led by a Brood Queen who reports to the Brood Empress. When the eggs hatch, the host is consumed and transformed into a Brood member. The Brood use Acanti space whales as living starships. Native to the Shi'ar Galaxy, the Brood aided Deathbird's attempts to overthrow her sister Lilandra Neramani as the Shi'ar Majestrix.

The Brood infected the X-Men and planted the egg of a Bloodqueen into Professor X, but the team was saved by Wolverine, who was able to resist the transformation process. Their home planet, Broodworld, was destroyed, but many Brood survived to rebuild their race.

One Brood queen, No-Name, was separated from her species on Sakaar, but developed a bond of loyalty with Hulk and her fellow gladiators. She joined Hulk's Warbound and came to Earth during World War Hulk. She even helped the Fearless Defenders eradicate a hive of bio-engineered Brood.

Another surviving queen cooperated with other species and joined the Galactic Council. She lent her forces to stop the Builders during Infinity, but later agreed with the Council to conquer Earth and fell to Angela's blade.

Wolverine's healing factor let him resist the Brood egg that was deposited in his body.

The alien Brood eventually found their way to Earth and injected a team of mutants; however they were defeated by the X-Men.

FACTFILE
OCCUPATION
Extraterrestrial mercenaries
BASE
Shi'ar Galaxy
HEIGHT 8 ft
WEIGHT 825 lbs
EYES Red
HAIR None
SCALES Green
FIRST APPEARANCE
Uncanny X-Men #155 (March 1982)

BROOD, THE

POWERS

Individuals possess six legs, transparent wings, razor-sharp teeth, armor-plated scales, and long tails that are divided into two deadly stingers. The Brood are very hard to destroy and are vicious fighters, determined that their malignant race will survive.

BROTHERHOOD OF EVIL MUTANTS

Mutant terrorist organization

BROTHERHOOD OF EVIL MUTANTS

FACTFILE

KEY MEMBERS AND POWERS

MAGNETO (LEADER)
Manipulates magnetic forces.

ASTRA
Varies her molecular density.

TOAD
Tongue stretches 25 ft; leaps great heights; super-strong.

QUICKSILVER
Superhuman speed.

SCARLET WITCH
Chaos magician.

MASTERMIND
Illusion-caster.

BLOB
Immovable; impervious to injury.

UNUS
Impenetrable force-field.

LORELEI
Hypersonic, paralyzing scream.

BASE
Mobile

FIRST APPEARANCE
Uncanny X-Men #4 (March 1964)

ALLIES/FOES

ALLIES Magneto

FOES Professor X, The X-Men, New Mutants, X-Factor, X-Force, the Avengers, Cable, all non-mutant human beings

ORIGINAL BROTHERHOOD
1 Magneto ***2*** Scarlet Witch ***3*** Quicksilver ***4*** Mastermind ***5*** Toad

Founded by Magneto, the Brotherhood of Evil Mutants has remained, through its various incarnations, the opposite number of the X-Men. While the X-Men's mission has always been to promote tolerance and coexistence between mutants and normal humans, the Brotherhood's goal has been nothing less than total domination over mankind, and quite possibly the eradication of normal humans entirely.

MUTANT MENACE

Originally, Magneto formed the Brotherhood as a strike force, helping him to oppose Professor X's X-Men, who had foiled his takeover of the Cape Citadel rocket base. This initial assemblage included the high-leaping Toad, illusion-creating Mastermind, the super-swift Quicksilver, and his sister, the hex-casting Scarlet Witch. Time and again they struck against their X-Men foes and against humanity, never scoring a true victory. Eventually, with the defeat of Magneto, this incarnation of the Brotherhood was no more—and Quicksilver and the Scarlet Witch went on to become members of the Avengers.

Some years later, the mysterious, shape-shifting mutant terrorist Mystique formed a new Brotherhood of Evil Mutants under her command. This grouping comprised the immovable Blob, the earth-shaking Avalanche, the flame-wielding Pyro, and the future-predicting Destiny. This incarnation of the Brotherhood eventually transformed into Freedom Force when it was offered amnesty by the US Government in exchange for becoming government operatives. But Freedom Force was at its heart corrupt, and after assorted clashes with the X-Men and other hero groups, such as the Avengers, the program was quietly disbanded.

ESSENTIAL STORYLINES

- ***X-Men #4***
The newly-formed Brotherhood has its first clash with the X-Men.
- ***Uncanny X-Men #141–142***
Mystique's Brotherhood attempts to assassinate Senator Robert Kelly and prevent the passing of the Mutant Registration Act.
- ***The Brotherhood #1***
X's agents are assembled for covert terrorist missions against humankind.

GROWING THE FAMILY

Since then, a number of other villains have formed their own versions of the team, including Mystique, Daken, Exodus, Joseph (seen above), Madelyne Pryor, Toad, and Xorn and even the heroes Havok, Professor X, and Sunspot. Mystique used hers to create a mutant sanctuary, but it was destroyed by a furious Magneto. Mesmero formed his own unsuccessful group on behalf of the anti-mutant villain Lydia Nance, who was hoping to damage the reputation of mutantkind. After failing in his mentorship of the time-displaced X-Men, Magneto established his fourth Brotherhood, situated on his Asteroid M space station.

MAGNETO'S NEW BROTHERHOOD
1 Magneto
2 Black Bishop
3 Elixir
4 Unuscione
5 Exodus
6 Marrow
7 Toad

BROTHER VOODOO

FACTFILE
REAL NAME
Jericho Drumm
OCCUPATION
Houngan (voodoo priest)
BASE
Port-au-Prince and New Orleans

HEIGHT 6 ft
WEIGHT 220 lbs
EYES Brown
HAIR Brown

FIRST APPEARANCE
Strange Tales #169
(September 1973)

POWERS
Summoning brother's spirit from within own body doubles his strength; can send this spirit forth to possess other people; can create fire and smoke; hypnotic control over animals.

BROTHER VOODOO

The first Brother Voodoo appeared in the 17th century as a Haitian ex-slave named Laurent who bound his dead brother Alexandre's soul to his own. He inspired many successors, who also took the name.

In modern times, Jericho Drumm inherited the title as his dying twin brother Daniel's dying wish. Jericho turned to his brother's teacher Papa Jambo for training so he could avenge his brother's death at the hands of a voodoo sorcerer who claimed to serve Damballah, an evil serpent god. Jambo helped bind Daniel's spirit to Jericho's and Jericho became the new Brother Voodoo.

Jericho defeated Damballah, but became possessed by Damballah's power. DOCTOR STRANGE freed him, and he joined the HOWLING COMMANDOS. When Strange gave up being the Sorcerer Supreme Jericho took up that mantle. He later died in a battle against Agamatto, but was resurrected by DOCTOR DOOM, who hoped to use him to control SCARLET WITCH. He ended up joining the AVENGERS Unity Division and fighting the HAND.

BUG

FIRST APPEARANCE *Micronauts* #1 (January 1979)
REAL NAME Unknown
OCCUPATION Freedom Fighter **BASE** Adalon Prime
HEIGHT 6 ft 1 in **WEIGHT** 163 lbs
EYES Red **HAIR** None
SPECIAL POWERS/ABILITIES Typical Insectivorid abilities, including super strength, speed, and agility. Can communicate with other insectoid species via antennae.

Bug was a master thief from the planet Kaliklak in the Microverse. He freed the captive Acroyear, crown-prince of Spartak, and the two became best friends. They were later captured by the evil Baron Karza and forced to fight in his gladiator pits, but escaped and formed a team of heroes called the Microns. Bug has since teamed with the FANTASTIC FOUR, ANT-MAN, GUARDIANS OF THE GALAXY and CAPTAIN MARVEL (Genis-Vell).

BUILDERS, THE

FIRST APPEARANCE *Avengers* #1 (December 2012)
REAL NAME N/A
OCCUPATION Interstellar engineers **BASE** Mobile
HEIGHT 7 ft (average) **WEIGHT** 400 lbs (average)
EYES Purple **HAIR** None
SPECIAL POWERS/ABILITIES The Builders control amazing technologies and armies of robots and engineered races.

The Builders are supposedly the universe's oldest race, genetic and technological engineers who seed worlds with life and then direct their evolution. They scour the galaxy looking for races that live up to their standards and destroying all the rest. They often send trios of creatures out as scouts: an ALEPH (a powerful robot), a Gardener (such as EX NIHILO), and an ABYSS (who judges the work of the Gardener). Few worlds meet their criteria, and none that fail survive.

BUSHMAN

FIRST APPEARANCE *Moon Night* #1 (November 1980)
REAL NAME Raul Armand Bushman
OCCUPATION Terrorist and mercenary **BASE** Burunda
HEIGHT 6 ft 2 in **WEIGHT** 220 lbs **EYES** Brown **HAIR** Bald
SPECIAL POWERS/ABILITIES A normal man with metal teeth, facial tattoos, and severed fingers on his left hand. He is an expert in guerilla warfare tactics.

Raul Bushman was a mercenary who teamed with Marc Spector and Frenchie Duchamp. Bushman killed archaeologist Dr. Peter Alraune to steal the Egyptian gold he had discovered, but when he also tried to kill the archaeologist's daughter, Spector protected her and was nearly killed by Bushman. Spector became the hero vigilante MOON KNIGHT and repeatedly thwarted Bushman's schemes, eventually killing him. Bushman was resurrected by the HOOD to fight Moon Knight yet again. He was temporarily held at the Ravencroft Institute for the Criminally Insane before working for Sun King against Moon Knight once more.

BUSHMASTER

FIRST APPEARANCE *Captain America* #310 (October 1985)
REAL NAME Quincy McIver
OCCUPATION Criminal **BASE** Mobile
HEIGHT 18 ft 6 in from head to tail **WEIGHT** Unknown
EYES Brown **HAIR** Black (shaved bald)
SPECIAL POWERS/ABILITIES Tail enables him to travel and attack at speeds of up to 40 mph, and is a crushing weapon; backs of hands have retractable poison fangs.

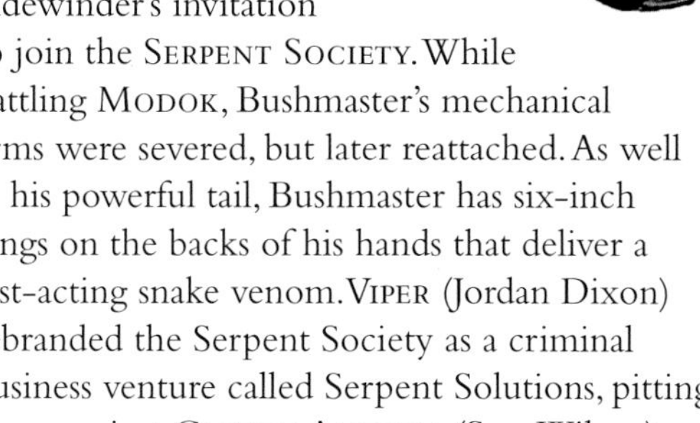

Quincy McIver's limbs were amputated by a ship's propeller and he was rebuilt as a cyborg with a snakelike tail by the Brand Corporation. Shortly after this transformation, Bushmaster accepted Sidewinder's invitation to join the SERPENT SOCIETY. While battling MODOK, Bushmaster's mechanical arms were severed, but later reattached. As well as his powerful tail, Bushmaster has six-inch fangs on the backs of his hands that deliver a fast-acting snake venom. VIPER (Jordan Dixon) rebranded the Serpent Society as a criminal business venture called Serpent Solutions, pitting them against CAPTAIN AMERICA (Sam Wilson).

BULLSEYE, SEE PAGE 64

BULLSEYE

Mysterious mercenary

BULLSEYE

FACTFILE

REAL NAME
Lester (last name unrevealed)

OCCUPATION
Assassin

BASE
New York City

HEIGHT 6 ft
WEIGHT 200 lbs
EYES Blue
HAIR Blond

FIRST APPEARANCE
Daredevil #131 (March 1976)

POWERS
Can use almost any object as a weapon and throw it with deadly aim; spine and other bones are reinforced with Adamantium, making them unbreakable; highly formidable hand-to-hand combatant.

Bullseye's origins remain mysterious. A notorious assassin trained by the NSA, he went freelance after clashing with the PUNISHER in Nicaragua. He first battled his archenemy, DAREDEVIL, while trying to extort money from the rich in New York City. New York crimelord the KINGPIN then hired him to be his chief assassin and sent him after crusading attorney Matt Murdock, Daredevil's secret identity, but Daredevil stopped him.

WAR WITH DAREDEVIL

Bullseye tried to lie low and accepted a contract to rescue an American gangster's son from the Black Knife Cartel in Colombia. His thirst for violence kept him in the spotlight, however. When Bullseye was imprisoned, the Kingpin replaced him with ELEKTRA, Daredevil's former lover. To reclaim his position, Bullseye killed her. Daredevil came after him, and in the ensuing battle, Bullseye fell from a great height, broke his back, and was paralyzed. Japanese scientist Lord Dark Wind repaired Bullseye's bones with Adamantium, and he resumed his criminal career and war with Daredevil. While Daredevil had amnesia, Bullseye impersonated him in order to discredit him; however Bullseye began to believe *himself* to be a hero. Daredevil donned Bullseye's costume to defeat him. Later, working with MYSTERIO, Bullseye murdered Karen PAGE, whom Daredevil had loved for many years.

Lady Bullseye is a master of martial arts and is faster than Bullseye and the Kingpin. She is a lawyer in her civilian guise.

THUNDERBOLTS

Bullseye joined the THUNDERBOLTS during the CIVIL WAR and fought alongside them against the SKRULLS during the SECRET INVASION. Afterward, Norman Osborn (*see* GREEN GOBLIN) made him the new HAWKEYE in his version of the AVENGERS. Under Osborn's orders, he killed the SENTRY's wife, later claiming she committed suicide.

After the DARK REIGN, Bullseye was sent to the Raft super-prison but escaped and hunted down Daredevil once more. A possessed Daredevil took him down and stabbed him through the heart with a sai knife, the same way Bullseye had killed Elektra years before. Bullseye was resurrected by Lady Bullseye, an assassin inspired by his example. Despite being paralyzed, deaf, and living in an iron lung, Bullseye managed to orchestrate a number of other villains to bedevil Daredevil once more. During a battle in which he sent Ikari and Lady Bullseye against Daredevil in his stead, Bullseye lost his last remaining sense: his sight.

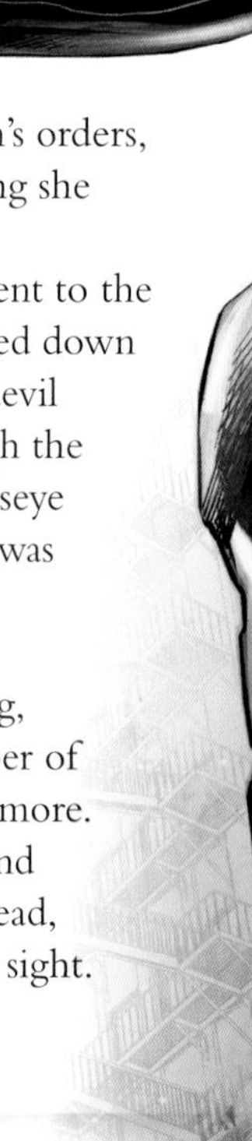

FACTFILE

ORIGINAL MEMBERS
DOCTOR DOOM
EMMA FROST
GREEN GOBLIN
THE HOOD
LOKI
NAMOR
TASKMASTER

BASE
Avengers Tower

FIRST APPEARANCE
Secret Invasion #8
(January 2009)

CABAL, THE

When Norman Osborn (*see* GREEN GOBLIN) took over US security for the United States during the DARK REIGN, he formed a coalition of the most powerful villains in the world to oppose the heroes' ILLUMINATI. The original group consisted of himself as IRON PATRIOT, DOCTOR DOOM, Emma FROST, the HOOD, LOKI, and NAMOR. The members soon began to form alliances within the group and to work against each other.

As a member of the Illuminati, Namor consulted with both organizations, always putting the welfare of the ATLANTEANS first. Their previous relationship made Frost and Namor natural allies in an early alliance against Osborn. Loki and Doom also partnered to make a play for power over Asgard, and Namor and Doom worked together as well. When Frost and Namor revealed that they'd been working against the Cabal from the inside, Osborn replaced them with the TASKMASTER. The revamped group fell apart when Osborn's forces were defeated during the Siege of Asgard.

Namor later formed his own Cabal to save the Earth from incursions by other universes, though his teammate THANOS quickly seized control. Namor tried to trap the others on a doomed world, but they escaped. They survived the end of the Multiverse in a life raft, only to be marooned on Doom's Battleworld (*see* SECRET WARS).

Osborn's Cabal, like other iterations, failed to stay together due to internal power struggles.

NAMOR'S CABAL
1 Black Swan ***2*** Corvus Glaive ***3*** Maximus
4 Proxima Midnight ***5*** Tyros (Terrax)
6 Namor ***7*** Thanos

CABE, BETHANY

FIRST APPEARANCE *Iron Man* #117 (December 1978)
REAL NAME Bethany Cabe
OCCUPATION Bodyguard **BASE** Seattle
HEIGHT 5 ft 7 in **WEIGHT** 125 lbs **EYES** Green **HAIR** Red
SPECIAL POWERS/ABILITIES Bethany Cabe is a skilled investigator, an expert markswoman, and extensively trained in self-defense techniques.

After the apparent death of her ex-husband, Bethany Cabe trained to become a bodyguard. In the course of her work, she met and became involved with Tony Stark (*see* IRON MAN). When Stark's alcoholism threatened to destroy him, Bethany convinced him to get help. Their romance ended when Cabe's ex-husband turned out to be still alive but in a coma, and she returned to him. Years later, Obadiah STANE swapped MADAME MASQUE's mind into Cabe's body and set her against Stark, but Cabe foiled the plot. Currently, Cabe is in charge of security at Resilient, Stark's eco-technology company.

CABLE

A living link between present and future

CABLE

FACTFILE

REAL NAME
Nathan Christopher Summers

OCCUPATION
Adventurer; former freedom fighter and US government agent

BASE
Mobile

HEIGHT 6 ft 8 in
WEIGHT 350 lbs
EYES Blue
HAIR White

FIRST APPEARANCE
Uncanny X-Men #201 (January 1986)

POWERS
Mutant with telepathic and telekinetic abilities. Possesses superhuman strength.

Cable has spent his life as a warrior, but longs for peace. He once established the airborne city of Providence as a futuristic utopia.

Hailing from the future of Earth-2107, Nathan Dayspring Askani'son, alias Cable, was actually born in modern times as Nathan Christopher Summers. He is the son of Scott Summers (Cyclops of the X-Men) and his first wife Madelyne Pryor, a clone of Jean Grey, alias Phoenix.

Cable teamed up with Deadpool for a number of adventures after their DNA was spliced together. This occurred while trying to stop a virus unleashed by the One World Church from turning everyone on Earth blue.

LIFE-SAVER

Apocalypse infected Nathan with a deadly techno-organic virus. He was brought to the 40th century of Earth-4935, where Mother Askani, a version of Rachel Summers, halted the virus' spread and had Nathan cloned. Apocalypse, who ruled this era, abducted and raised the clone, who became Stryfe. Mother Askani transported the souls of Scott Summers and Jean Grey into the future to raise young Nathan. After he destroyed Apocalypse, they returned to their own time.

Nathan became Clan Askani's foremost freedom fighter against Stryfe's New Canaanites. He married a fellow warrior, Aliya, and they had a son, Tyler. Stryfe murdered Aliya, and when he traveled back to the 20th century, Cable pursued him. There, Cable founded the mercenary team Six Pack and later reorganized the New Mutants into X-Force.

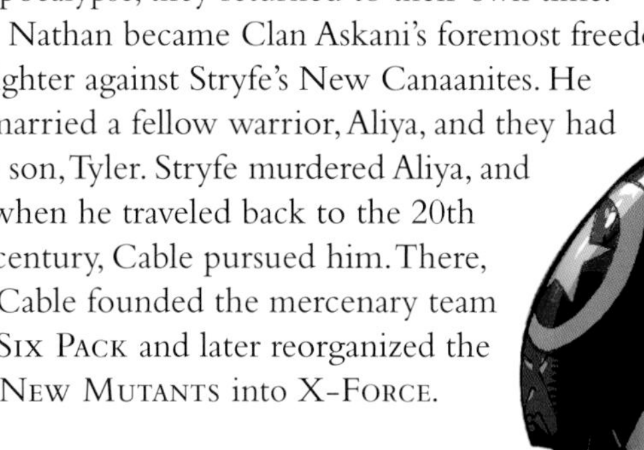

Next to Apocalypse, Cable's greatest enemy is literally himself: the terrorist Stryfe is Cable's clone. Stryfe framed Cable for an assassination attempt on Charles Xavier. Stryfe's mind once even took possession of Cable's body.

ESSENTIAL STORYLINES

- ***Adventures of Cyclops and Phoenix #1–4***
Scott Summers and Jean Grey raise young Nathan Summers in a distant future.
- ***The New Mutants #86–100***
Cable remolds the New Mutants into X-Force.
- ***Uncanny X-Men #294–296***
"The X-Cutioner's Song" storyline, featuring Cable's showdown with his nemesis Stryfe, which also crossed over into other Marvel titles.

FINDING A CURE

Cable saved the first mutant baby born after M-Day from Bishop and escaped into the future with her, naming her Hope Summers. He brought her back to the present when she was in her teens, and she saved his life by burning a fatal techno-organic virus out of him, removing his cybernetics as well. Later, the inventor Forge made an enhanced exoskeleton weapon for Cable's atrophied arm, and the two formed a new X-Force, stopping threats by using Cable's knowledge of the future. Cable regained his original look and arm after traveling through time with Deadpool. He joined the Avengers Unity team to fight the Red Skull and reclaim the portion of Xavier's brain that the Skull had stolen. Left comatose by the confrontation, Cable was cured by teammate Synapse.

CAGE, LUKE

Hero for hire

As a young man, Carl Lucas was in a street gang with his pal Willis Stryker. Lucas went straight while Stryker rose through the ranks. After the MAGGIA nearly killed Stryker, his girlfriend Riva Conners ended their relationship and sought solace with Lucas. Believing his friend had betrayed him, Stryker framed Lucas for possession of heroin. Sent to prison, Lucas volunteered to be a test subject for a Super-Soldier experiment in order to obtain an early parole. An angry guard tried to murder him by altering the experiment. Instead of killing him, the process reacted with his unique body chemistry and gave him superpowers. He escaped prison, faked his death, and adopted the name Luke Cage.

As a young gang member, Carl Lucas was sent to jail for a crime he did not commit.

FACTFILE

REAL NAME
Carl Lucas

OCCUPATION
Bodyguard; investigator

BASE
New York City

HEIGHT 6 ft 6 in
WEIGHT 425 lbs
EYES Brown
HAIR Formerly black, now bald

FIRST APPEARANCE
Hero For Hire #1 (July 1972)

POWERS

Cage possesses superhuman strength, very dense muscle and bone tissue, and steel-hard skin. He recovers three times faster from injury than a normal person and is an experienced and skilled street fighter.

POWER MAN

Needing money, Luke decided to become a hero for hire, sometimes using the name Power Man. He started out fighting normal crooks like his old friend Stryker—now calling himself DIAMONDBACK—but graduated to battling Super Villains and working with other Super Heroes. Cage joined the DEFENDERS and substituted for the THING in the FANTASTIC FOUR for a short time.

Blackmailed by BUSHMASTER into kidnapping Misty KNIGHT, Luke met and teamed up with her and her boyfriend, Danny Rand (IRON FIST). Together, they worked to clear his name and later worked for Misty's Nightwing Restorations detective agency. Luke and Danny began their own agency, Heroes for Hire, but when Danny was seemingly killed, Luke was blamed for the crime and went into hiding until Danny returned.

NEW AVENGER

A brief affair with Jessica JONES (aka the hero Jewel) grew into something more when the two worked as bodyguards for Matt Murdock (DAREDEVIL). The couple had a daughter (named Danielle after her godfather, Danny Rand) and married. Around this time, Luke joined the New AVENGERS. He sided with CAPTAIN AMERICA during the CIVIL WAR and stayed with the underground Avengers after Cap was killed. He fought the SKRULLS during the SECRET INVASION and was horrified when a Skrull, posing as Edwin JARVIS, kidnapped Danielle. Desperate, he made a deal with Norman Osborn (GREEN GOBLIN) for help to find his daughter, but went back on it once his little girl was safe. After the DARK REIGN, Tony Stark (IRON MAN) sold the original Avengers Mansion to Luke so that Luke could lead his own team of Avengers. Luke also took charge of the THUNDERBOLTS at the request of Captain America. He briefly retired to help raise his daughter, but returned to active service in the Mighty Avengers. He later joined a new incarnation of the Defenders with Iron Fist, Jessica Jones, and Daredevil.

Luke moved in with Jessica Jones when she revealed she was pregnant. He proposed after their daughter, Danielle, was born.

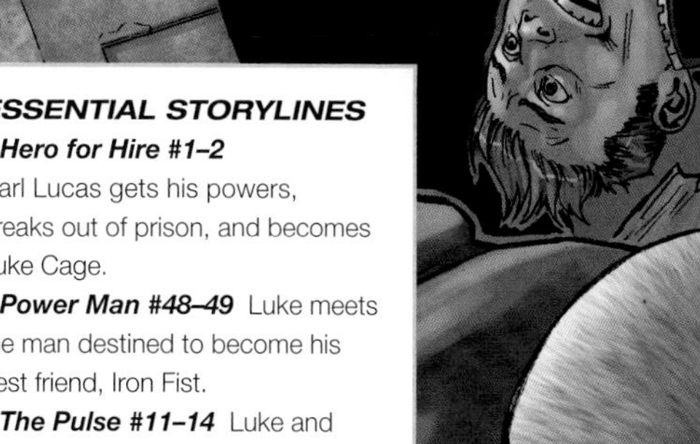

ESSENTIAL STORYLINES

- ***Hero for Hire #1–2*** Carl Lucas gets his powers, breaks out of prison, and becomes Luke Cage.
- ***Power Man #48–49*** Luke meets the man destined to become his best friend, Iron Fist.
- ***The Pulse #11–14*** Luke and Jessica Jones' daughter is born.

CAIERA

FIRST APPEARANCE *Incredible Hulk* #92 (April 2006)
REAL NAME Caiera **OCCUPATION** Gladiator; queen
BASE Sakaar **HEIGHT** 7 ft **WEIGHT** 270 lbs
EYES Green **HAIR** Black
SPECIAL POWERS/ABILITIES Superhuman strength and near invulnerability.

One of the Shadow People of the planet Sakaar, Caiera was enslaved by Prince Angmo II at age 13. She later became his trusted lieutenant and was named his Warbound Shadow when he ascended to the throne of the Red King. When the Hulk came to Sakaar, she fought him on the orders of the Red King but later joined Hulk's rebellion. After the HULK became king, Caiera joined him as his queen and became pregnant with SKAAR and HIRO-KALA. She died when the starship that brought Hulk to Sakaar exploded, but her sons survived in cocoons. They sometimes speak with visions of her.

CALEDONIA

FIRST APPEARANCE *Fantastic Four* #9 (September 1998)
REAL NAME Alysande Stuart **OCCUPATION** Champion
BASE New York City **HEIGHT** 5 ft 6 in **WEIGHT** 130 lbs
EYES Blue **HAIR** Blond
SPECIAL POWERS/ABILITIES Wore a warrior's armor and a long red cloak; wielded an enormous sword with the skill and courage of a great warrior of old; accomplished athlete.

In another world, Alysande Stuart was descended from a long line of ancient Scottish warrior champions. Her warrior name was Caledonia, and she also served as CAPTAIN BRITAIN. Freed from captivity in her world, Caledonia arrived in New York City. She worked as a nanny to Franklin RICHARDS, son of Reed Richards and Sue Storm (MR. FANTASTIC and INVISIBLE WOMAN), and thus came under the protection of the FANTASTIC FOUR. Her Earth-616 counterpart worked for W.H.O. (Weird Happenings Organization) and was killed by Jamie Braddock.

CALLISTO

FIRST APPEARANCE *Uncanny X-Men* #169 (May 1983)
REAL NAME Unrevealed **OCCUPATION** Former leader of the Morlocks; former model; former bodyguard **BASE** Formerly the Alley (tunnel beneath Manhattan); Mobile
HEIGHT 5 ft 9 in **WEIGHT** 130 lbs **EYES** Blue **HAIR** Black
SPECIAL POWERS/ABILITIES Superhumanly keen senses, including night vision.

Callisto was the leader of the MORLOCKS, mutant outcasts who lived beneath Manhattan. She survived the MARAUDERS' massacre of her people, and joined Mikhail RASPUTIN, who brought the other surviving MORLOCKS to a pocket dimension called the Hill and organized them into the terrorist group Gene Nation. The Morlock Masque transformed Callisto's arms into tentacles and made her fight in the Arena. Callisto lost her powers on M-DAY, becoming a normal human with regular arms. She later joined X-Cell, before retreating back into the sewers to care for a new generation of mutant runaways.

CAIN, ULYSSES

FIRST APPEARANCE *Civil War II* #0 (July 2016)
REAL NAME Ulysses Cain **OCCUPATION** Cosmic being; former college student
BASE New Attilan; Ohio State University, Columbus, Ohio
HEIGHT Unrevealed **WEIGHT** Unrevealed
EYES Green **HAIR** Brown
SPECIAL POWERS/ABILITIES Can predict the future through visions; mind is impervious to telepathic intrusion

Ulysses Cain was a normal student until the Terrigen Cloud unleashed by BLACK BOLT unlocked his INHUMAN gene. Cain, himself now an Inhuman, found that he had the ability to predict the future. Confused by what he was "seeing," he was taken in by MEDUSA and taught to use his powers by KARNAK. When IRON MAN and CAPTAIN MARVEL learned of his existence they came into conflict over how best to use his ability. The fight turned into a new Super Hero Civil War (*see* CIVIL WAR II), which only ended when Cain transformed into a cosmic entity.

CANNONBALL

Sam Guthrie's mutant abilities first triggered while he was trapped in a Kentucky coalmine, and he used them to save a co-worker and himself. Later, renegade HELLFIRE CLUB member Donald Pierce recruited Guthrie to battle the NEW MUTANTS. PROFESSOR X defeated Pierce and invited Sam to join them, and Sam became best friends with SUNSPOT. He matured into a team leader and later a member of X-FORCE and the X-MEN. CABLE believed Sam to be an External, an immortal mutant, but the sorceress Selene dismissed this theory. He is the eldest of several siblings, four of whom are mutants: Paige (HUSK), Melody (Aero), Jay (Icarus), and Jeb. He has dated rock star Lila CHENEY and fellow New Mutant MELTDOWN. While an AVENGER, he fell in love with Izzy Kane (SMASHER). The two married, having a child that they named Joshua. Cannonball split his time between his family and fighting alongside his teammates.

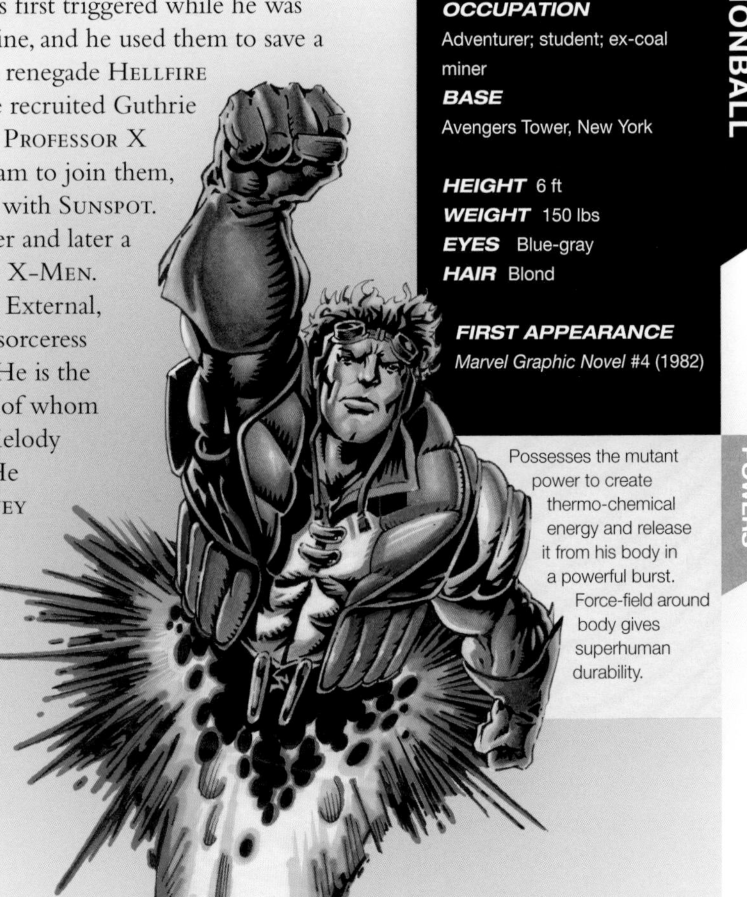

FACTFILE
REAL NAME
Samuel Guthrie
OCCUPATION
Adventurer; student; ex-coal miner
BASE
Avengers Tower, New York

HEIGHT 6 ft
WEIGHT 150 lbs
EYES Blue-gray
HAIR Blond

FIRST APPEARANCE
Marvel Graphic Novel #4 (1982)

CANNONBALL

POWERS
Possesses the mutant power to create thermo-chemical energy and release it from his body in a powerful burst. Force-field around body gives superhuman durability.

CALYPSO

FIRST APPEARANCE *New Mutants* #16 (June 1984)

REAL NAME Calypso Ezili

OCCUPATION Witch; troublemaker **BASE** New York City

HEIGHT 5 ft 8 in **WEIGHT** 120 lbs **EYES** Brown **HAIR** Black

SPECIAL POWERS/ABILITIES Skilled in Voodoo magic; combines potions and spells to confuse enemies; controls enemies with Yorumba spirit drum; can revive the dead and resurrect herself.

Born and raised in Haiti, Calypso was initiated into the arts of Voodoo. Meeting Kraven the Hunter shortly after his first defeat by Spider-Man, Calypso formed a love-hate attachment to him. After Kraven's death, Calypso became unhinged, killing her sister Mambo to obtain her supernatural powers. Although killed by the Lizard, Calypso resurrected herself and clashed with Daredevil before dying once more at the hands of Alyosha Kravinoff, the second Kraven. Her spirit then infused an amulet through which she could possess anyone who wore it.

CAPTAIN BRITAIN

Chosen as the champion of Great Britain by Merlyn and his daughter Roma, Brian Braddock became Captain Britain. Both alone and as a member of Excalibur, he strove to be worthy of his new role. Eventually he discovered he was one of an almost infinite number of Captains created to safeguard the Multiverse. He later succeeded Roma as ruler of the Otherworld and commander of the Captain Britain Corps. He married the mutant Meggan, who sacrificed herself to save the world near M-Day. They have since reunited. Brian worked with Britain's MI-13 to repel the Skrulls' invasion of the magical realm of Avalon during the Secret Invasion. He joined the Secret Avengers, helped stop Killpower's attempt to destroy the UK, and fought alongside the Champions of Europe during Hydra's takeover. He has recently had a child with Meggan.

FACTFILE

REAL NAME
Brian Braddock

OCCUPATION
Ruler of Otherworld

BASE
England; Otherworld

HEIGHT 5 ft 11 in
WEIGHT 180 lbs
EYES Blue ***HAIR*** Blond

FIRST APPEARANCE
Captain Britain Weekly #1 (December 1976)

CAPTAIN BRITAIN

POWERS

Captain Britain's uniform gave him superhuman strength and durability, enabled flight, and provided a protective force-field. His powers have now been internalized, and the level of his powers is based on his level of confidence instead.

Captain Britain marries Meggan, a fellow member of the team Excalibur.

CAPTAIN BRITAIN CORPS

CAPTAIN BRITAIN CORPS

FACTFILE

MEMBERS
Assorted interdimensional incarnations of **CAPTAIN BRITAIN,** including **CAPTAIN UK, CAPTAIN ANGLETERRE, CAPTAIN COMMONWEALTH, CAPTAIN EMPIRE, CAPTAIN ENGLAND, CAPTAIN MARSHALL, KAPTAIN BRITON, HAUPTMANN ENGLANDE, BROTHER BRIT-MAN** and others.

BASE
Otherworld; various Earths across the Multiverse.

FIRST APPEARANCE
Mighty World of Marvel #13 (1984)

The Captain Britain Corps is an alliance of interdimensional champions based out of the nexus realm known as Otherworld, charged with protecting their home realities from dimensional incursions. Each is a version of Captain Britain and is empowered by Merlyn and his daughter Roma. The Captain Britain of Earth-616 led the Corps for a while, but after its decimation at the hands of the mutant villain Mad Jim Jaspers and the death of Roma, the champion called Albion (the version of Captain Britain from Earth-70518) was charged with rebuilding it. The Corps was wiped out during the Beyonders' attempt to destroy all of reality, but with the Multiverse since reborn, the fate of the Captain Britain Corps remains unknown.

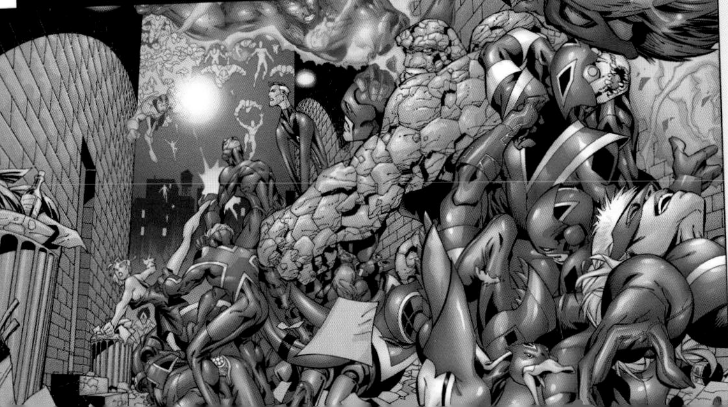

The Captain Britain Corps interceded when it was feared that the mutant powers once possessed by Franklin Richards, son of the Fantastic Four's Mr. Fantastic and the Invisible Woman, might destroy the Multiverse.

CAPTAIN FATE

FIRST APPEARANCE *Man-Thing* #13 (January 1975)

REAL NAME Captain Jebediah Fate **OCCUPATION** Pirate

BASE The ship *Serpent's Crown* in the Bermuda Triangle, Atlantic Ocean **HEIGHT** 5 ft 11 in **WEIGHT** Unknown

EYES Variable (originally brown) **HAIR** Variable (originally brown)

SPECIAL POWERS/ABILITIES No longer ages and is invulnerable to certain forms of injury.

In 1795, Jebediah Fate was first mate to pirate queen Maura Hawke when they met the satyr Khordes, who desired a mate. The traitorous Fate and his men turned Hawke over to Khordes, and Hawke cursed them to sail the seas for eternity. Centuries later, Fate again met Khordes and Hawke (reincarnated as oceanographer Maura Spinner), as well as Man-Thing. When Fate was killed by gunfire, the demon Thog resurrected him. Fate's soul became part of the Magus Sword, which possessed Sheriff John Daltry, transforming him into Fate. As Fate, he worked with Dracula until the Black Knight separated them.

CAPTAIN AMERICA

Living legend of World War II

Abraham Erskine, operating under the code name Professor Reinstein, created the Super-Soldier Serum. It turned frail Steve Rogers into a perfect specimen of humanity.

CAPTAIN AMERICA

FACTFILE

REAL NAME
Steve Rogers

OCCUPATION
Adventurer

BASE
Brooklyn, New York;
Stark Tower ("Avengers Tower"), Manhattan, New York

HEIGHT 6 ft 2 in
WEIGHT 240 lbs
EYES Blue
HAIR Blond

FIRST APPEARANCE
Captain America Comics #1 (March 1941)

POWERS

Super-Soldier Serum brought Rogers to the peak of physical perfection; able to lift twice his own body weight; expert military strategist; Olympic-level martial artist and gymnast; resistant to disease and fatigue.

ALLIES/FOES

ALLIES Bucky Barnes, Nick Fury, Sharon Carter, Rick Jones, The Falcon, Nomad (Jack Monroe), The Avengers

FOES The Red Skull, Baron Zemo, MODOK, the terrorist organizations AIM and Hydra, Crossbones

ISSUE #1

Captain America burst into action battling Hitler in his first issue. Cap's shield changed shape to circular in future issues because of objections from the creators of another hero called the Shield.

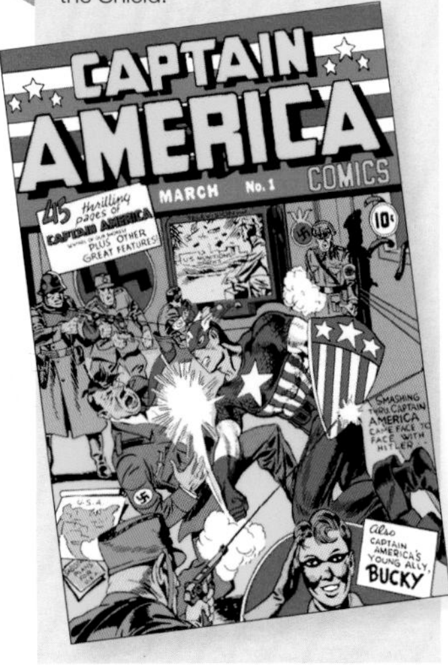

In the late 1930s, with the threat of world war looming in Europe, the American high command embarked upon a program to create the perfect soldier. Project: Rebirth, spearheaded by Dr. Abraham Erskine, was intended to create a battalion of supreme fighting men, stronger and more resilient than normal soldiers, expertly trained and equipped—a bulwark against Nazi aggression. The first test subject for Erskine's revolutionary Super-Soldier Serum was a young, would-be artist named Steve Rogers, who had attempted to enlist, but had been turned away, classified 4-F, because of his physical frailty.

THE SUPER-SOLDIER

Subjected to Erskine's process, Rogers' body virtually doubled in size, as millions of healthy cells were created almost instantaneously. His physique was accelerated to the pinnacle of human perfection, all weakness and deficiency drained out of it.

However the secret test area had been infiltrated by Nazi sympathizers, who slew Dr. Erskine, the only person who knew how the process worked. Although Rogers quickly captured the saboteurs, it was clear that there would be no battalion of Super-Soldiers now—Steve Rogers would be the only one.

Captain America arrives in the nick of time to prevent Sharon Carter from being blasted into the blue by Nazi menace Red Skull.

Equipped with a virtually unbreakable red, white, and blue shield, the product of a metallurgical accident, and trained in combat, tactics, espionage, and the fighting arts, Rogers was rechristened Captain America. Clad in a striking star-spangled uniform, he became a symbol for the US fighting forces and a dread nemesis of the Axis powers.

In his many battles against Nazi aggression, Captain America was joined by a sidekick, the worldly James "Bucky" Barnes, who had discovered the secret of Rogers' true identity.

Among the foes combated by Cap in the present day is MODOK, the Mental Organism Designed Only for Killing. MODOK was the result of an experiment by the sinister think tank known as Advanced Idea Mechanics, or AIM.

BUCKY'S "DEATH"

Toward the end of World War II, Cap and Bucky Barnes set out to foil Baron Zemo's scheme to steal a drone plane laden with a bomb. As the plane took off, Bucky and Cap leaped aboard. Cap fell into the sea, but Bucky clung on trying to defuse the bomb. The bomb exploded, Bucky was believed killed, and Cap was haunted by the memory for many years.

Together, Cap and Bucky tore a swath through the ranks of the enemy forces, vanquishing such Nazi menaces as the Red Skull, Agent Axis, and the Iron Cross. The duo were often joined by their allies in the Invaders team, including the original Human Torch and Namor, the Sub-Mariner.

In 1945, Cap and Bucky were on a mission to apprehend the German scientist Baron Zemo, who planned to steal an experimental long-range drone plane developed by the British. As the plane took off, Cap and Bucky made a desperate leap to catch it. Cap couldn't maintain his hold, and plummeted earthward... seconds later the plane self-destructed, seemingly killing Bucky Barnes. Cap's body plunged into the icy waters below, where he was frozen into a state of suspended animation, a condition he would remain in for decades to come.

To safeguard morale, the Allied high command kept the deaths of Cap and Bucky secret and recruited other heroes to play the role of Captain America. Meanwhile, the true Captain America slumbered within the ice.

THE RETURN

Eventually, while searching for their foe Namor (the same person who had fought alongside Steve Rogers in the Invaders), the Avengers came across Captain America's body floating in the icy waters, and revived him. Now Captain America was a man out of time, a soldier whose war was long over. Attempting to find a place for himself in this strange new society, Cap accepted an offer of Avengers membership, and swiftly became the binding glue that held the team together.

Sam Wilson, alias Harlem's guardian, the Falcon, has been one of Captain America's closest friends and most frequent crime-fighting partners.

THE AVENGERS
1 Hawkeye **2** The Wasp **3** Falcon **4** Captain America, team leader **5** Iron Man **6** Vision **7** Scarlet Witch

Cap also offered his services to his old war buddy Nick Fury, now head of SHIELD. It was while operating as a SHIELD agent that Cap first encountered Sharon Carter, SHIELD's Agent 13, who would become his paramour.

Hailed as the most trusted costumed champion of them all, Captain America fought on, struggling to uphold freedom and democracy, both alone and with the Avengers—right up until the moment of his death.

ESSENTIAL STORYLINES

- ***Captain America & The Falcon #153–156*** Cap and his partner, the Falcon, must combat the replacement Captain America and Bucky of the 1950s, who have been driven mad by the flawed serum that gave them their abilities.
- ***Captain America #1–6*** Captain America reveals his true identity as Steve Rogers to the world after he is forced to take the life of a terrorist leader.
- ***Captain America #1–14*** Cap is on the trail of the Winter Soldier, a legendary assassin from the pages of history who may actually be his former sidekick Bucky Barnes!

Over the years, Cap has contested with numerous opponents intent on taking up his mantle. One of his challengers was the "Anti-Cap," a modern day counterpart created by Naval Intelligence as an extreme anti-terrorist operative. Eventually facing defeat by Captain America for a second time, the Anti-Cap chose death rather than capture.

CAPTAIN AMERICA continued

After the announcement of the Superhuman Registration Act, Captain America (Steve Rogers) could not stomach enforcing what he considered to be an unjust law. He broke with his old friend Tony Stark (IRON MAN) and formed a resistance movement to help unwilling heroes to defy the law. This split fractured the Super Hero community and set the heroes against each other in what would become known as the CIVIL WAR. At the end of the war, Iron Man defeated and captured Rogers, who was soon after assassinated as he was brought into a federal courthouse in New York City.

To those who witnessed it, it appeared that Steve Rogers was gunned down on the courthouse steps. The reality, however, was much more complicated.

IN DEATH'S SHADOW

Without Rogers to lead it, the organized resistance against the Superhuman Registration Act fell apart. Many of the heroes who had held out stepped forward to register. The FALCON, for instance, signed up solely so he could appear at Rogers' funeral.

Wolverine infiltrated the SHIELD Helicarrier to inspect Steve Rogers' body.

Having seen many people supposedly die in the past, including Rogers himself, some heroes refused at first to believe that he was dead. It was only after Iron Man and WOLVERINE—each representing a different side in the Civil War—were able to corroborate Rogers' death that the reality began to sink in.

Steve Rogers was buried with honor in Arlington National Cemetery, beneath a giant memorial statue designed by Alicia Masters.

THE HUNT FOR A NEW CAPTAIN

Although Stark had gone on record stating that no one would replace Captain America, it wasn't long before he went looking for a replacement. With Captain America's costume and indestructible shield in SHIELD custody, he could give the assignment to whoever he liked. When Stark discovered that Clint Barton (HAWKEYE) had somehow survived the SCARLET WITCH's disassembling of the AVENGERS, he brought Barton aboard the SHIELD Helicarrier to show him the original shield, revealing that

Iron Man presents Captain America's original shield to Clint Barton.

he'd had two imperfect copies made. The first copy sat on display at the Smithsonian, while the second was to be buried with Rogers. The real shield was up for grabs.

Barton tried out the shield, becoming the first person to wield it properly after 77 other people had failed. Stark gave Barton the shield and the costume to try out as he went to arrest PATRIOT and the new Hawkeye for failure to comply with the Superhuman Registration Act. At the moment of truth, Barton—dressed in Rogers' uniform and holding his shield—let the two heroes go rather than arrest them. He then gave the shield back to Stark.

BUCKY CLAIMS THE SHIELD

Unwilling to let Rogers' shield languish in the custody of SHIELD—which he blamed in part for Rogers' death—Bucky BARNES stole it. Having returned from his own purported death, after which he had become the Winter Soldier, he used the shield in a few missions of his own. While taking the shield, he ran into Natasha Romanova (BLACK WIDOW), with whom he'd had a relationship when they'd been in the employ of the Soviet Union.

After SHIELD finally captured Barnes, Stark surprised him by offering him the identity of Captain America to go along with the shield. Barnes accepted on two conditions. First, any secret mental conditioning from his days as the Winter Soldier had to be telepathically removed. Second, he would answer only to himself. Knowing that this would be exactly what Rogers would have wanted, Stark accepted the deal.

Not feeling worthy to wear Rogers' own costume, Barnes had a new one designed for himself. Unlike Rogers, Barnes was happy to use weaponry of all sorts in his battles, not just the shield. He carried a pistol and a combat knife on his belt, which featured a number of pouches, and he brought in other ordnance as necessary.

A NEW ERA

As Captain America, Barnes foiled the Red Skull's attempt to assassinate both candidates for the US Presidency. He also faced off against the Captain America of the 1950s—William Burnside—who had been placed in suspended animation and brainwashed by the Red Skull and Dr. Faustus. Defeating this hero from the past and restoring his mind established Barnes' claim to be the sole Captain America. Barnes then fought alongside the heroes of Earth against the Skrulls during the Secret Invasion, participating in the final battle in Central Park. This was Barnes' first encounter with many of the heroes who had known Rogers and called him friend, and he handled himself well.

After the Skrulls were driven off, Barnes joined the underground Avengers team that Rogers had once led. He allowed them to use his secret home in an old warehouse as their base of operations, and worked with them under the leadership of Barton, who now called himself Ronin.

Barnes also renewed his relationship with the Black Widow and worked closely with her and the Falcon on many of his missions.

When Bucky agreed to become Captain America, he designed a new costume for the role.

In his new role as Captain America, Bucky Barnes played a vital role in defeating the Skrulls and their Secret Invasion.

BACK TO LIFE

Sharon Carter eventually learned she'd been brainwashed by Dr. Faustus to shoot Rogers, and that the gun she'd used was a device designed by Doctor Doom that didn't kill Rogers but fixed him at that moment in time. The Red Skull captured Carter and planned to use sympathetic nano-particles in her blood to retrieve Rogers. She escaped and damaged the machinery involved in the Red Skull's scheme. This unstuck Rogers in time, and sent him back in time to relive various events in his past. Eventually, the Red Skull managed to bring Rogers back and transferred his own mind from a robot body into Rogers' form. But when the Red Skull tried to kill the new Captain America (Bucky Barnes), Rogers broke his control.

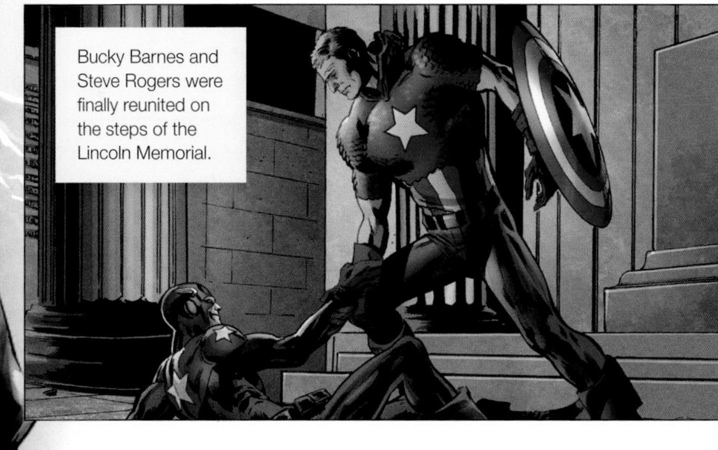

Bucky Barnes and Steve Rogers were finally reunited on the steps of the Lincoln Memorial.

CAPTAIN AMERICA continued

For a while, there were two Captain Americas, but only one shield.

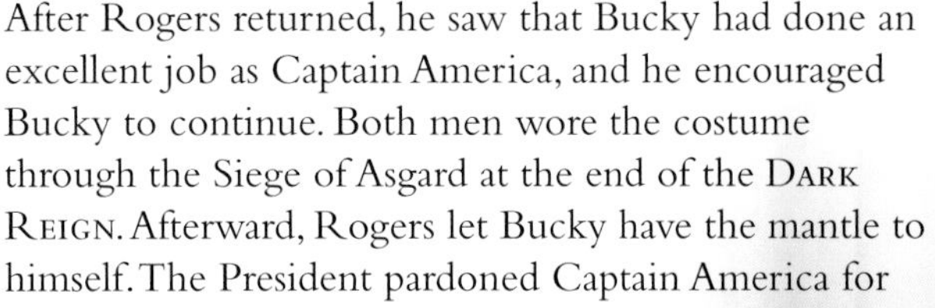

TWO CAPTAINS

After Rogers returned, he saw that Bucky had done an excellent job as Captain America, and he encouraged Bucky to continue. Both men wore the costume through the Siege of Asgard at the end of the Dark Reign. Afterward, Rogers let Bucky have the mantle to himself. The President pardoned Captain America for his actions during the Civil War and repealed the Superhuman Registration Act, which had sparked the conflict.

At the President's request, Rogers took over from Norman Osborn (*see* Green Goblin) as the head of national security, which put him in charge of rebuilding both SHIELD and the Avengers. Rogers served in that capacity until Baron Zemo revealed Barnes' identity not only as Captain America but also as the Winter Soldier. Barnes was found innocent in court, but his reputation was ruined, and the President asked Rogers to return to being Captain America. Rogers resisted for a while, but after it seemed that Skadi (a transformed Sin) had killed Bucky during Fear Itself, Rogers assumed the role again.

After he defeated Hydra's takeover of the United States, Cap appeared a darker, more troubled hero.

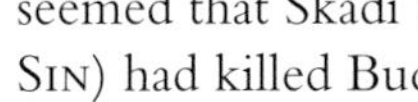

Rogers believed that Barnes had been killed trying to fill his role.

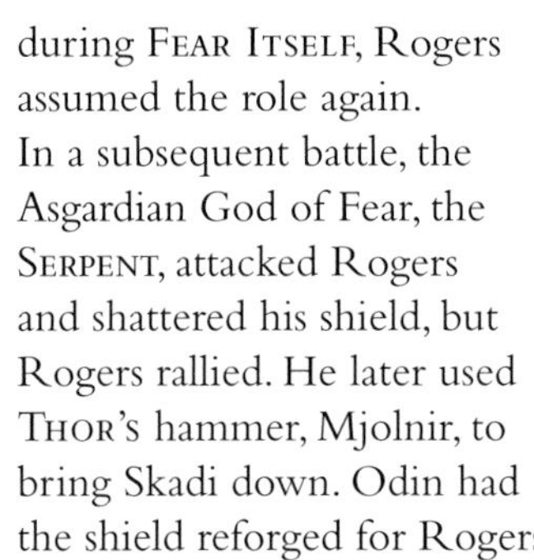

In a subsequent battle, the Asgardian God of Fear, the Serpent, attacked Rogers and shattered his shield, but Rogers rallied. He later used Thor's hammer, Mjolnir, to bring Skadi down. Odin had the shield reforged for Rogers.

During the Spider-Island event (see Spider-Man), the Spider-Queen and the Jackal transformed Rogers into the Spider-King, a creature capable of spreading spider-powers as a virus across New York City. By means of an antidote made with Anti-Venom's blood, Rogers was cured, after which he helped Spider-Man win the day.

After his shield was smashed into pieces by the Serpent, Steve briefly wielded the mystical hammer Mjolnir.

After leading the Avengers in a huge conflict with the X-Men over the use of the Phoenix Force, Rogers created an Avengers Unity Squad consisting of both X-Men and Avengers. The new team soon found themselves fighting the Red Skull, who had enhanced his powers by stealing Charles Xavier's brain.

DIMENSION Z

Shortly after defeating the Red Skull, both Rogers and Sharon Carter were transported to Dimension Z, a strange realm ruled by Arnim Zola. Rogers escaped from Zola, taking with him a baby that Zola had been growing in a test tube (whom Zola considered his own). Rogers spent years in Dimension Z fighting Zola's forces and raising the child, whom he named Ian, as his own. Rogers later managed to escape thanks to the sacrifice of Sharon Carter, who was left trapped there. Back on Earth, Rogers found himself facing an ex-SHIELD agent called Iron Nail who managed to neutralize the Super-Soldier Serum in Rogers, leaving him old and frail. When Zola's forces attacked from Dimension Z, Rogers knew the world needed a new Captain America and convinced his old ally Sam Wilson (Falcon) to take on the role.

Time worked differently in Dimension Z. To Steve Rogers and his "son" Ian, it appeared that they were trapped for over a decade.

While Rogers still used his tactical skills to help the Avengers, Wilson became an effective Captain America. Wilson also had his own take on Cap's classic costume. He fought the Sons of the Serpent and gained his own sidekick in the form of a new Falcon. Wilson's Captain America joined the Avengers and helped fight Warbringer and other foes. However, his unconventional methods eventually brought him into conflict with Rogers, causing Wilson to eventually step down as Captain America.

Sam Wilson's time as Captain America was marked by controversy, including major disagreements between him and the authorities, and criticism over his socially active agenda.

HAIL HYDRA!

By then, Rogers himself had been remade—and his youth and strength restored—by Kobik, a sentient Cosmic Cube who had been manipulated by the Red Skull into becoming a supporter of Hydra. Kobik used her immense powers to rewrite Rogers' entire history. The real Rogers was trapped in her mindscape while a new, evil version of Rogers—one that was a loyal Hydra agent—was placed into reality. This evil version of Captain America eventually revealed his true colors and took over Hydra, using its forces to conquer America and turn it into a fascistic state under Hydra control. Eventually the true Rogers escaped from Kobik's mindscape and returned to the real world, where he defeated the Hydra version of himself. In the aftermath, America was rebuilt, but Captain America's reputation had been badly damaged. It was a troubling time for Rogers, with enemies such as the Power Elite filling the void left by Hydra. But with the real Steve Rogers once again Captain America, he was more determined than ever to do the right thing.

The evil version of Captain America ruthlessly tried to remake the world in Hydra's image.

WOULD-BE CAPTAINS

Several others have tried to take on the mantle of Captain America but none were as successful as Bucky Barnes or Sam Wilson. One of the first was Isaiah Bradley. The victim of experimentation by the US Military on African Americans in an attempt to create a new Super-Soldier during World War II, Bradley was the only one of three hundred test subjects to survive the war. He stole a Captain America costume to free POWs from a Nazi experimentation camp only to be court-martialed on his return. His grandson was Elijah Bradley, who became the Patriot in the Young Avengers.

When Rogers went missing in action towards the end of WWII, the US military selected William Nalund to replace him. Nalund had previously been the hero Spirit of '76. He was killed trying to save John F. Kennedy. The next hero to step into the role was Jeffrey Mace (the original Patriot). He retired in 1949. In the 1950s, William Burnside—a scholar obsessed by Captain America—took on the role and had his appearance surgically altered to look like Steve Rogers. Burnside eventually went insane and was put in suspended animation with his version of Bucky (Jack Monroe). Burnside reappeared in the present, taking over far right groups and fighting Captain America. He was eventually captured by Steve Rogers and given help to cure his shattered mental state.

John Walker, a right-wing hero originally known as the Super Patriot, briefly took on the role of Captain America before realizing Steve Rogers was the only man truly capable of holding the title. Walker went on to become the U.S.Agent.

As Nomad, Rogers again became the first to don a costume that would be worn by many others.

Isaiah Bradley served his country well; however his country did not return the favor.

When Cap gave up his shield rather than follow orders he couldn't support, he began wearing a black costume and calling himself simply the Captain.

CAPTAIN MAR-VELL

Protector of the Universe

CAPTAIN MAR-VELL

FACTFILE

REAL NAME
Mar-Vell

OCCUPATION
Captain in Kree space fleet

BASE
Mobile

HEIGHT 6 ft 2 in
WEIGHT 240 lbs
EYES Blue
HAIR White; transformed to blond by Eon, a cosmic caretaker

FIRST APPEARANCE
Marvel Super Heroes #12 (December 1967)

POWERS

Thanks to his Kree Nega-Bands, Mar-vell possessed great strength (he could lift 10 tons), a high degree of imperviousness to harm, and the ability to fly. He could also exist in outer space without having to breathe.

Kree Nega-Bands converted Captain Mar-vell's psionic energy into incredible power.

Captain Mar-Vell was a member of the KREE, an alien humanoid race who built an empire known as the Greater Magellanic Cloud. Mar-Vell was a "White Kree," having the same skin color as Caucasian Earth humans and similar physiology to theirs. (Most members of the Kree race have blue skin.) As captain of a Kree space fleet, Mar-Vell distinguished himself in battles against the shape-changing SKRULLS, the Kree's age-old foes.

ESSENTIAL STORYLINES

- ***The Life of Captain Mar-Vell* 1991 (tpb)** Mar-Vell battles Thanos and performs other feats of cosmic heroism.
- ***Avengers* #89–#97** The Avengers aid Mar-Vell during the epic Kree-Skrull War.
- ***Captain Marvel: The Death of Captain Marvel*** Captain Mar-Vell succumbs to cancer, but achieves a hero's death.

OLD FOES OF MINE WHO HAVE DIED...
...RETURNING FROM THE GRAVE!

In delirium while dying from cancer, Captain Mar-Vell is haunted by terrifying phantoms of the enemies he fought and defeated during his career as a Super Hero.

Mar-Vell gained the ability to fire bolts of solar energy after his ailing psionic partner Rick Jones was treated with life-saving electromagnetic radiation by Professor Benjamin Savannah.

PROTECTOR

Wary of humanity's progress, the SUPREME INTELLIGENCE sent Mar-Vell to sabotage Earth's space programs. However, Mar-Vell grew to respect the people of Earth and helped them, earning the name Captain Marvel. The Intelligence believed humans possessed vast psionic potential, which it longed to steal so it could destroy humanity. To this end, the Intelligence forged a psionic link between Mar-Vell and Rick JONES by means of a pair of Kree Nega-Bands. The Intelligence used this link to nullify the Skrull space fleet, nearly killing Jones, but Mar-Vell used his own life force to revive Jones.

Mar-Vell then defeated THANOS, who wished to destroy all life in the universe. Mar-Vell also met with the alien being Eon, who gave him cosmic awareness, persuaded him to renounce the Kree's warmongering ways, and designated him Protector of the Universe.

During a battle with NITRO of the Lunatic Legion, an alien criminal organization formed by a band of renegade Kree scientists, Mar-Vell was exposed to a carcinogenic gas. He developed cancer and died on Saturn's moon Titan, surrounded by his lover, Elysius, Rick Jones, the AVENGERS, and many other friends. His son Genis-Vell eventually took over his mantle, as did his daughter Phyla-Vell. He also had a son he never knew with Anelle, the daughter of the Skrull Emperor. The boy became HULKLING.

Mar-Vell returned for the SECRET INVASION, but he was revealed to be a Skrull. In the end, he sided with Earth but was killed in the war. The real Mar-Vell returned during the Chaos War, but he died saving SWORDSMAN and YELLOWJACKET. The Kree later brought Mar-Vell back once more, hoping to gain the power of the Phoenix Force through him. He sacrificed himself to protect the Kree from that same power.

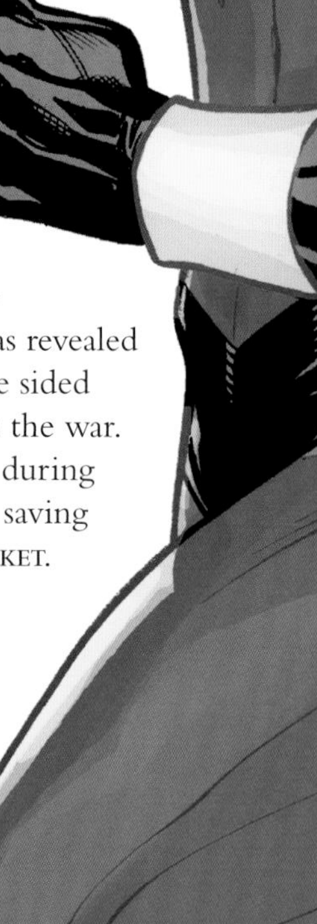

CAPTAIN MARVEL

Formerly Ms. Marvel of the Avengers

The first Captain Marvel was the Kree warrior Captain Mar-Vell. Several others followed in his wake, including Monica Rambeau (also known as Pulsar, Photon, and Spectrum) and Mar-Vell's own son Genis-Vell, but it is the former Ms. Marvel, Carol Danvers, who has made the role her own.

MANY MARVELS
1 Captain Marvel's original costume
2 Ms. Marvel's later costume
3 Ms. Marvel's original costume
4 Captain Marvel's later costume

CAPTAIN MARVEL

FACTFILE
REAL NAME
Carol Danvers
OCCUPATION
Adventurer
BASE
New York City

HEIGHT 5 ft 11 in
WEIGHT 124 lbs
EYES Blue
HAIR Blond

FIRST APPEARANCE
Marvel Super-Heroes #13 (March 1968)

POWERS
Possesses the ability to fly, has enhanced strength, damage resistance, and the ability to absorb and rechannel energy.

MS. MARVEL

US Air Force and NASA officer Carol Danvers was assigned to investigate Mar-Vell, and became involved with him. When her DNA was melded with his during an explosion, giving her powers like his, she adopted the code name Ms. Marvel. After she joined the Avengers, the villainous Marcus (son of Immortus) brainwashed her into joining him in Limbo. After his death, she escaped to Earth, but soon after lost her powers and memories to the mutant Rogue when Rogue attacked her. While working with the X-Men, she unlocked cosmic powers and became known as Binary, but this led to her feeling disconnected from her old life back on Earth. Carol could not stomach being on the same team as Rogue when the X-Men took Rogue in, and left to join the Starjammers.

Moonstone stole Ms. Marvel's identity as part of Norman Osborn's Dark Avengers, leading to a confrontation between the villain and Carol Danvers.

DOWN TO EARTH

Carol eventually burned out her powers while saving the sun. She recovered at Avengers Mansion, soon joining the team under the moniker of Warbird. She had trouble coming to terms with her weakened powers, though, and became an alcoholic. Tony Stark, himself no stranger to the dangers of alcohol, helped her to battle her drink problem and she became a valued member of the team, eventually reverting to the name Ms. Marvel. She fought alongside Iron Man during the first Super Hero Civil War and soon found herself in charge of her own team of Avengers.

CAPTAIN MARVEL

Captain America told Carol she had more than earned the right to call herself Captain Marvel, in honor of their old friend Mar-Vell. She adopted the name and became an inspiration for heroes the world over, even acting as a mentor to some younger ones such as the new Ms. Marvel (Kamala Khan). She worked alongside SWORD and the Ultimates, eventually taking charge of the Alpha Flight space program, but came into conflict with some of her fellow heroes when she argued Ulysses Cain's powers of premonition should be used to fight crime before it happened (*see* Civil War II).

Carol has offered guidance to many young heroes, most notably Kamala Khan, the new Ms. Marvel. However, During the second Super Hero Civil War, Kamala and her mentor were on opposite sides.

CAPTAIN UNIVERSE

FIRST APPEARANCE *Micronauts* #8 (August 1979)
REAL NAME Various, including Ray and Steve Coffin, Monty Walsh
OCCUPATION N/A **BASE** Mobile
HEIGHT Various **WEIGHT** Various **EYES** Various **HAIR** Various
SPECIAL POWERS/ABILITIES Captain Universe is any person endowed with the Uni-Power; abilities include superstrength, flight, and ability to alter an object's molecular structure.

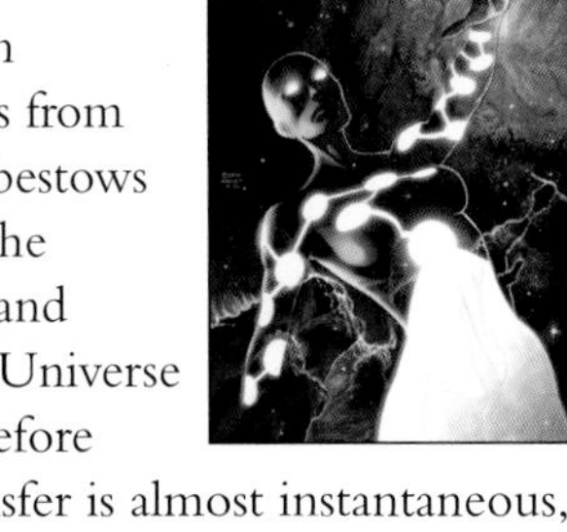

The Uni-Power is an energy that emanates from the Microverse and bestows upon an individual the powers, knowledge, and costume of Captain Universe for a short period, before moving on. The transfer is almost instantaneous, ensuring the cosmos is never without a Captain Universe. The might of the Uni-Power has been borne by ex-astronauts, cat burglars, and even the HULK, DAREDEVIL, X-23, SILVER SURFER, and DOCTOR STRANGE. The current holder is Tamara Devoux, who works with the AVENGERS. EX NIHILO and ABYSS recognized her as a god and refused to fight her.

CAPTAIN VICTORIA

FIRST APPEARANCE *Legendary Star-Lord* #1 (September 2014)
REAL NAME Victoria
OCCUPATION Commander of the Spartax Royal Guard
BASE Spartax **HEIGHT** Unknown **WEIGHT** Unknown
EYES Hazel **HAIR** Brown
SPECIAL POWERS/ABILITIES Skilled warrior; battle suit allows her to levitate and survive in the vacuum of space; spear can project blasts of electricity

The illegitimate daughter of Emperor J'son of Spartax, Victoria eventually became Commander of the Spartax Royal Guard. While never fully respected by her father, she remained loyal to her home, even attempting to claim the bounty on her half-brother STAR-LORD to help finance its army. Star-Lord convinced her to double-cross her employers to gain even more money, which he then made her keep. Later, she successfully distracted the COLLECTOR by dancing for him, allowing her men to steal the seed of the KREE SUPREME INTELLIGENCE, which she then destroyed.

CARDIAC

FIRST APPEARANCE (Dr. Wirtham) *The Amazing Spider-Man* #342 (December 1990), (Cardiac) *The Amazing Spider-Man #343* (January 1991)
REAL NAME Dr. Elias "Eli" Wirtham
OCCUPATION Surgeon; researcher; vigilante
BASE New York City **HEIGHT** 6 ft 5 in **WEIGHT** 300 lbs
EYES Brown **HAIR** Black
SPECIAL POWERS/ABILITIES Superhuman strength, speed, and stamina; bulletproof skin; can project beta particle-force blasts.

Elias Wirtham's brother died of a rare disease after insurance companies refused to pay for unproven cures. Dr. Wirtham devoted his life to medical research, secretly battling those who profit from suffering. He had his heart replaced with a beta particle reactor, and his skin with Vibranium mesh that transmits the particles to his muscles, giving him amazing strength. As Cardiac, he has both fought SPIDER-MAN and helped him.

CARNAGE

FACTFILE
REAL NAME
Cletus Kasady
OCCUPATION
Spreader of chaos
BASE
New York City

HEIGHT 6 ft 1 in
WEIGHT 190 lbs
EYES Green
HAIR Red

FIRST APPEARANCE
The Amazing Spider-Man #344 (February 1991)

POWERS
Superhuman strength; can generate swing lines and bladed weapons; able to neutralize Spider-Man's spider-sense.

CARNAGE

Murderer Cletus Kasady shared a cell with Eddie Brock, VENOM's original host, when the Venom symbiote arrived to attempt a jailbreak. It left behind its spawn, which bonded with Kasady, creating a new symbiote known as Carnage. Carnage is far more powerful, violent, and deadly than its parent. SPIDER-MAN enlisted the HUMAN TORCH and even Venom to defeat it. Besides Kasady, the symbiote has bonded with Ben Reilly (*see* SCARLET SPIDER), the SILVER SURFER, and John JAMESON. It even spawned its own offspring, which bonded with police officer Patrick Mulligan to become Toxin. The SENTRY ripped the Carnage symbiote apart, but it recovered and reunited with Kasady, before spawning yet more offspring, which became a hero called SCORN.

Later, the second Scarlet Spider lobotomized Kasady. The WIZARD removed the symbiote from Kasady to use for his own ends, but was defeated by Spider-Man, after which the symbiote rebonded with its original host. When SHIELD agents again removed it from Kasady, Norman Osborn used it to become the horrific Red Goblin. Osborn was seemingly cleared of the symbiote by Spider-Man, however Osborn's grandson Normie was also infected, becoming Goblin Childe.

Like its parent, Venom, Carnage quickly came to regard Spider-Man as its arch nemesis.

CARRION

FACTFILE

REAL NAME
"Miles Warren" (actually a clone of the original Miles Warren)

OCCUPATION
None

BASE
New York City

HEIGHT 5 ft 11 in
WEIGHT 175 lbs
EYES Yellow
HAIR None

FIRST APPEARANCE
The Spectacular Spider-Man #25 (December 1978)

POWERS

Carrion could repel living matter, levitate, destroy living matter with his touch, reduce the density of his body to become almost intangible, and teleport.

CARRION

The first Carrion was a clone of Miles Warren—aka SPIDER-MAN's enemy, the JACKAL. Before his death, Warren left a clone of himself in a capsule, but something went wrong and the creature that emerged was like a living corpse. Carrion died in a fire following a battle with Spider-Man. Many years later, a fellow research student of Peter Parker named Malcolm McBride discovered a test tube containing the "Carrion virus." The virus consumed McBride and turned him into a second incarnation of Carrion. When Dr. William Allen examined Warren's body, he was infected by the virus, and became the third and most powerful incarnation of Carrion. Ben Reilly, while taking on the Jackal identity, created a new Carrion virus that threatened the world.

CARTER, PEGGY

FIRST APPEARANCE *Tales of Suspense* #77 (May 1966)
REAL NAME Margaret "Peggy" Carter
OCCUPATION SHIELD agent
BASE Mobile **HEIGHT** 5 ft 5 in **WEIGHT** 101 lbs
EYES Blue **HAIR** White (formerly blond)
SPECIAL POWERS/ABILITIES Expert in espionage and unarmed combat; possesses formidable marksmanship and tactical skills.

Peggy Carter was an American agent working for the French Resistance during World War II when she met and fought alongside CAPTAIN AMERICA. The two fell in love before the war split them up. In the early 1950s she teamed up with Howard Stark and Woodrow McCord to stop HYDRA from gaining a powerful alien energy source. In later years, Peggy's stories of her life inspired her niece Sharon to become a SHIELD agent.

CARTER, SHARON

Sharon Carter grew up inspired by tales of her aunt Peggy CARTER's exploits as a member of the French Resistance, and learned the story of Peggy's love for CAPTAIN AMERICA during World War II. Sharon sought a career with SHIELD and became the operative Agent 13, during which time she too met and fell in love with Captain America. She infiltrated the National Force, a Neo-Nazi organization run by DOCTOR FAUSTUS and William Burnside, who had served as Captain America in the 1950s before going insane. Sharon faked her death to go deep undercover for SHIELD, but after the mission went bad, even SHIELD presumed her dead. When she returned, Sharon served as SHIELD's director for a short time. She became Captain America's SHIELD liaison officer again and the romantic tension between the pair blossomed into a renewed relationship. Later, under Faustus' hypnotic control, Sharon helped assassinate Captain America, although it turned out she had only unstuck him from time. After Cap's "death" she discovered she was pregnant with his child, but she lost the baby during a gun fight with SIN. After Cap returned, she asked him to marry her. Before he could give her an answer, she died saving him and the rest of the world from Arnim ZOLA.

CARTER, SHARON

FACTFILE

REAL NAME
Sharon Carter

OCCUPATION
SHIELD liaison officer

BASE
Mobile

HEIGHT 5 ft 8 in
WEIGHT 135 lbs
EYES Blue
HAIR Blond

FIRST APPEARANCE
Tales of Suspense #75 (March 1966)

POWERS

Highly trained field agent; martial-arts expert and weapons expert; special talent for disguise, infiltration, and undercover work.

Steve Rogers, the patriotic hero known as Captain America, teamed up with Sharon on missions against AIM, Hydra, Red Skull, and many others.

CAT PEOPLE

FIRST APPEARANCE *Giant-Size Creatures* #1 (May 1974)
BASE The Land Within, an otherdimensional netherworld
SPECIAL POWERS/ABILITIES Mystical abilities; enhanced strength, speed, and agility, similar to those of a human-sized cat.

The Cat People were created when Ebrok, a human sorcerer, enchanted two cats called Flavius and Helene into human form. In time, the numbers of the Cat People grew, to the displeasure of Ebrok's fellows in the Sorcerer's Guild. The Cat People were subsequently exiled to the limbo-like realm they call the Land Within, which caused them and their descendants to become demons. The legendary heroine of the Cat People is known as TIGRA, a human woman who was transformed into a catlike warrior. Greer Nelson was similarly been transformed into the heroine Tigra by the Cat People's magic and science. She served as their emissary to the outside world and as a member of the AVENGERS.

CELESTIALS

The Celestials are a race of virtually immortal space gods whose conscious minds gestate in the form of living galaxies for more than a million years. Once the Celestial is deemed worthy, this mind is encased by a full suit of virtually indestructible body armor that is "dimensionally transcendental" (far larger on the inside than it appears to be on the outside). Each Celestial appears to have a specific purpose. Barely a dozen and a half are known by their names and functions, but many more are believed to exist. For reasons of their own, the Celestials travel throughout the universe performing genetic experiments. They then return a million years later to judge the results of their experiments. If the world is judged favorably, it is allowed to continue. If not, it is cleansed of life.

FACTFILE

KNOWN CELESTIALS
ARISHEM THE JUDGE, JEMIAH THE ANALYZER, TEFRAL THE SURVEYOR, GAMMENON THE GATHERER, NEZARR THE CALCULATOR, ONEG THE PROBER, HARGEN THE MEASURER, ESON THE SEARCHER, ZIRAN THE TESTER, ONE ABOVE ALL, EXITAR THE EXECUTIONER

HEIGHT (average) 2,000 ft
WEIGHT (average) 260 tons

FIRST APPEARANCE
Eternals #1 (July 1976)

CELESTIALS

POWERS
Cosmic power on a scale immeasurable by Earth standards; have visited Earth, but eradicated all evidence and memory of their existence.

CATSEYE

FIRST APPEARANCE *New Mutants* #16 (June 1984)
REAL NAME Sharon Smith
OCCUPATION ex-Hellion team member
BASE Mobile **HEIGHT** 6 ft **WEIGHT** 140 lbs
EYES Lavender **HAIR** Lavender
SPECIAL POWERS/ABILITIES Transformed into a cat and a human-panther hybrid with increased strength, agility, reflexes, and senses; hybrid also boasted razor-sharp claws and prehensile tail.

Most mutants manifest their powers at puberty, but Sharon Smith first transformed into a cat as an infant. Abandoned by her parents, she was raised feral by a stray cat. As a teenager, she came to the attention of Emma FROST. The highly intelligent Sharon received an accelerated education, and within a year she gained high-school literacy and joined the HELLIONS. An attack on the HELLFIRE CLUB led to her death, but she was later brought back to life by the sorcerer Selene using the Transmode Virus.

CENTURIUS

FIRST APPEARANCE *Nick Fury, Agent of SHIELD* #2 (July 1968) **REAL NAME** Dr. Noah Black
OCCUPATION Geneticist **BASE** Mobile **HEIGHT** 6 ft
WEIGHT 225 lbs **EYES** Brown **HAIR** None
SPECIAL POWERS/ABILITIES Scientific genius specializing in genetics; evolved himself into a perfect human specimen, with attendant strength, agility, and durability; high-tech body armor incorporates an array of weapons; experiments with his Evolutionizer device have increased his lifespan.

The ridicule of the scientific community led scientist Dr. Noah Black to hide on Valhalla Island and experiment on himself with his Evolutionizer. His experiments succeeded in improving him but also increased his mania, and he decided humanity should be wiped out and started afresh. Calling himself Centurius, he intended to gather up superior specimens of life, shepherd them to an ark, then destroy human civilization from space. A century later he and his crew would land and reclaim the world. His initial plot was thwarted by Nick FURY and SHIELD, but Centurius continued to threaten world security. He worked for the HOOD's crime syndicate and helped repel the SKRULLS during the SECRET INVASION. He later joined Luke CAGE's THUNDERBOLTS.

CENTURY

FIRST APPEARANCE *Force Works* #1 (July 1994)
REAL NAME Century **OCCUPATION** Adventurer
BASE/HEIGHT/WEIGHT/EYES Unknown **HAIR** White
SPECIAL POWERS/ABILITIES Combines memories, skills, and abilities of one hundred Hodomur; projects energy from hands; wields the Parallax, a bladed weapon that binds his multiple personalities together and enables interdimensional travel.

Following the destruction of their world, Hodomur, by the extradimensional entity Lore, the survivors created a new being from one hundred of their number. Named Century, this creature was compelled to track down and destroy Lore and given a lifespan of a hundred years to attain this goal. During this quest, the pirate Broker enslaved Century and wiped his mind, leaving only the desire to find Lore. This led him to Earth where he served with FORCE WORKS until it disbanded. Lore was destroyed by the SCARLET WITCH and Century was last seen with the REVENGERS.

CERISE

FIRST APPEARANCE *Excalibur* #47 (March 1992)
REAL NAME Cerise
OCCUPATION Soldier **BASE** Shi'ar Empire
HEIGHT 5 ft 10 in **WEIGHT** 130 lbs **EYES** Brown **HAIR** Black
SPECIAL POWERS/ABILITIES Uses the energy of the red light spectrum to create weapons, force-fields, vortexes, and shields. She can fly, direct energy blasts, and hold her breath for 7 minutes.

Cerise is an alien of the SHI'AR race, which absorbs other cultures into its vast interplanetary empire through violent conquest. Disillusioned with the brutal tactics of the Shi'ar war machine, Cerise deserted from its army and fled to Earth. There, she became a member of EXCALIBUR and fell in love with teammate NIGHTCRAWLER. The STARJAMMERS brought her back to stand trial for her crimes. In time, the Shi'ar empress Lilandra pardoned her act of desertion and made her an operative to investigate reports of Shi'ar brutality. During ANNIHILATION, she joined GAMORA's team of warriors, known as the Graces.

CHAMBER

FIRST APPEARANCE *Generation X* #1 (November 1994)
REAL NAME Jonothon Starsmore **OCCUPATION** Weapon X field agent **BASE** Mobile **HEIGHT** 5 ft 9 in
WEIGHT 140 lbs **EYES** Brown **HAIR** Auburn
SPECIAL POWERS/ABILITIES (As Chamber) Can psionically fire blasts or cause objects to explode; communicates telepathically. (As Decibel) wears a high-tech suit that grants him a sonic scream and allows him to create things from solid sound.

Jonothon "Jono" Starsmore's mutant power manifested with an explosion of psionic energy that destroyed his mouth and chest, leaving him only able to talk telepathically. He helped found GENERATION X as Chamber and later joined the X-MEN. Weapon X made him a field agent and restored his face, but he lost his face and powers on M-Day. When healed, he looked like a young APOCALYPSE, one of his ancestors. He joined the NEW WARRIORS as Decibel, wearing a suit that gave him powers. He has since regained his original powers, losing his face again, and joined the Jean Grey School for Higher Learning as a teacher.

CHAMELEON

Dmitri Smerdyakov grew up in Russia as the half-brother and servant of Sergei Kravinoff, who later became known as the original KRAVEN the Hunter. Smerdyakov eventually became the mercenary spy known as the Chameleon, who was renowned as a master of disguise. Originally Chameleon relied on makeup, costumes, and his acting skill; he now uses a special serum and clothing to impersonate others.

The Chameleon first clashed with his nemesis, SPIDER-MAN, when he attempted to frame the crimefighter for the theft of classified plans for a missile defense system. However, Spider-Man captured the Chameleon and exposed him as the real thief. The Chameleon has also contended with other Super Heroes, including the HULK and DAREDEVIL.

After the original Kraven committed suicide, the Chameleon lost his sanity and jumped from a bridge. However, he turned up alive in an asylum, and resumed his criminal career.

FACTFILE
REAL NAME
Dmitri Smerdyakov
OCCUPATION
Professional spy and criminal
BASE Mobile

HEIGHT Unrevealed
WEIGHT Unrevealed
EYES Unrevealed
HAIR Unrevealed

FIRST APPEARANCE
Amazing Spider-Man #1 (March 1963)

CHAMELEON

POWERS
Experimental serum renders his flesh malleable, so that he can alter his appearance without makeup or prosthetics. Clothing contains "memory material" that responds to his nerve impulses and changes appearance at will.

CHAMPION OF THE UNIVERSE

Like many of the ELDERS OF THE UNIVERSE, the Champion's origin has been lost in antiquity. A true immortal, he devotes himself to physical perfection to avoid boredom. He considers himself the living spirit of competition and travels the universe, challenging the champions of each planet. If he finds them unworthy, he exterminates all life on their planets. He challenged the heroes of Earth to a match and was impressed with the THING's courage. He and other Elders battled the SILVER SURFER and GALACTUS. The Champion's only defeat came at the hands of SHE-HULK, after which he called himself the Fallen One.

FACTFILE
REAL NAME
Tryco Slatterus
OCCUPATION
Competitor
BASE
Mobile

HEIGHT 9 ft 2 in
WEIGHT 5,050 lbs
EYES Silver
HAIR Red

FIRST APPEARANCE
Marvel Two-In-One Annual #7 (1982)

CHAMPION OF THE UNIVERSE

POWERS
Has channeled the Power Primordial, the energy derived from the Big Bang, into his physical form, making his body a perfect fighting machine. Has also mastered thousands of different martial arts from across the universe.

CHAMPIONS OF XANDAR

FIRST APPEARANCE *Fantastic Four* #208 (July 1979)

BASE The planet Xandar; Nova-Prime starship

KEY MEMBERS AND POWERS

Nova-Prime Flight; superhuman strength; invulnerability.

Protector Psionic ability.

Powerhouse Siphons energy from any power source, including living beings.

Comet Flight; can project electrical energy.

Crimebuster No superhuman powers.

The Champions of Xandar were a team of superhumanoid beings who formed to protect the planet Xandar. Xandar suffered three huge alien invasions. In the first, the Luphoms shattered Xandar into pieces. Survivors on the four largest fragments connected the four planetoids with huge bridges and rebuilt their civilization. The second invasion was by the shape-shifting Skrulls, who hoped to bring Xandar into their empire. Having kept an active militia, Nova Corps, since the first invasion, the Xandarians resisted. They were aided by the Fantastic Four, and then by a group of Xandarians and Earth heroes, who banded together as the Champions of Xandar. Together, Nova Corps and the Champions repelled the Skrull invasion, though Crimebuster was killed. The third invasion, by Nebula, wiped out the entire population, including the remaining Champions.

CHANCE

FIRST APPEARANCE *Web of Spider-Man* #15 (June 1986)

REAL NAME Nicholas Powell

OCCUPATION Mercenary; gambler **BASE** New York City

HEIGHT 6 ft **WEIGHT** 185 lbs **EYES** Blue **HAIR** Brown

SPECIAL POWERS/ABILITIES Chance's armored costume contains wrist-blasters, boot-jets for flight, and assorted other weapons and paraphernalia.

A chronic gambler and inveterate risk-taker, Nicholas Powell took the name Chance and sought work as a mercenary to satisfy his craving for thrills. Chance's standard modus operandi is to wager his fee at double-or-nothing odds against his success—if he fails, he receives nothing. Chance's assignments have brought him into conflict with numerous Super Heroes, including Spider-Man and Daredevil. Chance is thoroughly immoral—but he prides himself on his ability to beat the odds.

CHANG, MONICA

FIRST APPEARANCE *Avengers A.I.* #1 (September 2013)

REAL NAME Monica Chang

OCCUPATION SHIELD A.I. Division Chief **BASE** Helicarrier

HEIGHT 5 ft 4 in **WEIGHT** 117 lbs

EYES Brown **HAIR** Black

SPECIAL POWERS/ABILITIES Normal human with training typical of a SHIELD agent; artificial intelligence expertise.

Hank Pym created an A.I. virus to destroy Ultron. The virus then evolved into countless self-aware A.I.s that lived in a virtual reality called "The Diamond." One such A.I., known as Dimitrios, sought to destroy strategic targets and eliminate humanity. Chang ordered Pym to form a new Avengers A.I. team of cyborgs and androids, which Chang then led against Dimitrios. As she studied the A.I.s, however, she gained sympathy for their right to survive and risked her career to advocate for them instead.

Changeling turned over a new leaf by taking Professor X's place at the latter's request.

CHANGELING

FACTFILE

REAL NAME
Unknown

OCCUPATION
Reformed criminal; one-time leader of the X-Men

BASE
Mobile

HEIGHT 5 ft 11 in
WEIGHT 180 lbs
EYES Brown
HAIR Black

FIRST APPEARANCE
X-Men #35 (August 1967)

POWERS

Metamorph, able to adopt the appearance and voice of other humanoids; limited telekinetic ability.

CHANGELING

A one-time member of the terrorist organization Factor Three, the Changeling switched sides when he learned that its leader, the alien Mutant Master, was seeking to eradicate humanity. When the Changeling discovered that he had contracted a terminal illness, he decided to make amends for his past misdeeds. He approached Professor X and volunteered to support the X-Men. The timing was fortuitous: the Professor needed to withdraw from active duty to fend off an impending alien invasion. The Changeling agreed to impersonate Professor X during his absence. However, his leadership of the X-Men was cut short when he was killed during a skirmish with the insane Prince Gor-Tok.

CHARCOAL

FIRST APPEARANCE *Thunderbolts* #19 (October 1998)
REAL NAME Charles Burlingame
OCCUPATION Adventurer; student **BASE** Mt. Charteris
HEIGHT 5 ft 7 in **WEIGHT** 135 lbs **EYES** Brown **HAIR** Black
SPECIAL POWERS/ABILITIES Transforms into a being composed of charcoal; manipulates heat and can reshape himself into any form of carbon, including flaming charcoal or rock-hard diamond.

When Charles Burlingame's father took him to a rally of the Imperial Forces of America, the scientist Arnim Zola discovered the boy's potential for wielding superhuman powers and transformed him into Charcoal, the Burning Man. At first, Charcoal joined a group called the Bruiser Brigade and battled the Thunderbolts. Later, as a member of the Thunderbolts, Charcoal witnessed the death of fellow member Jolt. He left to join the Redeemers, where he battled his father, who was still a member of the Imperial Forces. Charcoal later died at the hands of Graviton.

CHASTE, THE

FIRST APPEARANCE *Daredevil* #187 (October, 1982)
MEMBERS AND POWERS
Stick Martial artist; uses bo stick. **Stone** Martial artist; can turn body hard as stone. **Shaft** Martial artist with a bow. **Claw** Martial artist with artificial claws. **Star** Martial artist; uses shurikens. **Wing** Martial artist; flies by telekinesis. **Flame** Martial artist; pyrokinetic.

The Chaste is a martial arts organization based atop a mountain fronted by a sheer cliff called the Wall. Those who wish to train with the Chaste must climb the Wall to enter, as a test. The Chaste was founded by Master Izo—also a founding member of the Hand—to stand against the Hand's evil plans, but his students threw him out for carousing. Stick led the Chaste for many years, but after his death and that of the other listed members, Stone took over and helped raise Elektra from the dead.

CHENEY, LILA

FIRST APPEARANCE *New Mutants Annual* #1 (1984)
REAL NAME Lila Cheney **OCCUPATION** Songstress; thief
BASE A Dyson sphere somewhere in the Milky Way galaxy
HEIGHT 5 ft 8 in **WEIGHT** 120 lbs **EYES** Blue **HAIR** Black
SPECIAL POWERS/ABILITIES Lila Cheney possesses the mutant ability to teleport people and objects over intergalactic distances.

An acclaimed rock singer on Earth, Lila Cheney simultaneously pursued a very different career among the stars. Employing her mutant gift to teleport herself, Lila gained a reputation as one of the foremost thieves in the universe. She was an ally of the New Mutants, and a romance with Cannonball led her to curtail her criminal activities. Since their breakup, it remains to be seen whether she has abandoned her outlaw life for good.

CHARLIE-27

FIRST APPEARANCE *Marvel Super Heroes* #18 (January 1969)
REAL NAME Charlie-27 **OCCUPATION** Soldier; adventurer
BASE The starship *Icarus* **HEIGHT** 6 ft **WEIGHT** 555 lbs
EYES Blue **HAIR** Red
SPECIAL POWERS/ABILITIES Superhuman strength and endurance; high resistance to injury and disease; withstands the gravity of Jupiter (11 times that of Earth); pilot and master strategist.

In the 31st century of Earth-691, Charlie-27 was a member of a genetically bio-engineered race of humans sent to live on and mine the planet Jupiter. After completing a solo tour of duty as a space militia pilot, Charlie-27 learned that an alien race called the Badoon had overrun the Solar System and slaughtered the inhabitants of Jupiter, Pluto, Mercury, and Earth. Joining with Martinex (Pluto), Nikki (Mercury), Yondu Udonta (Centauri IV), and Vance Astro (Earth) to form the original Guardians of the Galaxy, Charlie-27 helped to expel the Badoon and later safeguarded the entire galaxy.

CHEMISTRO

FIRST APPEARANCE *Hero for Hire* #12 (August 1972)
REAL NAME Curtis Carr **OCCUPATION** Research scientist and reformed criminal **BASE** New York City
HEIGHT 5 ft 11in **WEIGHT** 185 lbs **EYES** Brown **HAIR** Black
SPECIAL POWERS/ABILITIES No superhuman powers; carried self-designed Alchemy Gun capable of transmuting one substance into another.

Curtis Carr developed an Alchemy Gun capable of changing one substance into another. When he was sacked for refusing to hand the weapon over to his boss, he disguised himself as Chemistro and began a series of revenge attacks against his employer. Carr's spree ended during a struggle with Luke Cage, when Carr accidentally shot his own foot and turned it to steel. He was thrown into prison where he was forced to give the secrets of his gun to a fellow prisoner, Arch Morton. Morton's version of the gun exploded in his hand, but the accident endowed his left hand with similar alchemical powers. On leaving prison, a reformed Carr developed a device called a Nullifier, and Luke Cage used it to disable Morton.

CHITAURI

FIRST APPEARANCE *Ultimates* #8 (November 2002)
OCCUPATION Conquerers
BASE Mobile **HEIGHT** Variable **WEIGHT** Variable
EYES White (sometimes also red and yellow) **HAIR** None
SPECIAL POWERS/ABILITIES Shape-shifting; bombs capable of eliminating entire solar systems; have mastered faster-than-light interstellar space travel.

The Chitauri are a changeling alien race who work behind the scenes, secretly manipulating societies and wars to bring their desired order to worlds. They supported the Nazis on Earth by providing them with the means to create a nuclear bomb, though they were defeated by Captain America. Another effort led them to infiltrate SHIELD. The Chitauri kidnapped Wasp and escaped to their base in Arizona, but were thwarted by the Avengers. Their leader, Herr Kleiser, was eaten by Hulk. A later war between the Chitauri and Kree witnessed the merger of the cosmic entities Gah Lak Tus and Galactus.

CHO, AMADEUS

FACTFILE

REAL NAME
Amadeus Cho

OCCUPATION
Adventurer

BASE
Mobile

HEIGHT 5 ft 6 in
WEIGHT 117 lbs
EYES Black
HAIR Black

FIRST APPEARANCE
Amazing Fantasy #15
(January 2006)

POWERS

Super-intelligence. His suit grants him flight, a force-field, and access to a supercomputer called Calvin, which includes a universal translator. He sometimes carries Hercules' mace, which he has enhanced with technology.

CHO, AMADEUS

While still in high school, Amadeus Cho won a game show tournament that declared him to be the seventh smartest person in the world and gave him a prize of half a million dollars. This brought him to the attention of Pythagoras Dupree, the sixth smartest person in the world—and the man behind the game show, which he'd used to try to find people as super-intelligent as him. Dupree blew up Cho's house, killing the boy's parents and sending him on the run from FBI agents pursuing him, but Cho escaped with the aid of the HULK.

Using nanobots created by the Leader, Cho harnessed gamma energy to became the Totally Awesome Hulk.

Cho assembled a team of heroes to try to stop the Hulk during WORLD WAR HULK, but they failed. The team included HERCULES, who became Cho's best friend. When Cho used nanites to absorb gamma radiation from Bruce Banner (the Hulk), it transformed Cho into a new version of Banner's monstrous alter ego, which he dubbed the "Totally Awesome Hulk." Using his extraordinary newfound powers, Cho became one of the new Champions, but soon found his Hulk persona spinning out of control. After it nearly consumed him, Cho realized he couldn't destroy his own dark side and so embraced it. This saw him transformed into a new green-skinned hero: Brawn.

CIRCUS OF CRIME

FACTFILE

MEMBERS
RINGMASTER (Maynard Tibolt), **STRONGMAN** (Bruno Olafsen), **CLOWN** (Eliot "Crafty" Franklin), **FIRE-EATER** (Tomas Ramirez), **THE GREAT GAMBONNOS** (Ernesto and Luigi), **HUMAN CANNONBALL** (Jack Pulver), **LIVE WIRE** (Rance Preston), **PRINCESS PYTHON** (Zelda DuBois), **RAJAH** (Kabir Mahadevu), **TEENA THE FAT LADY** (name unrevealed).

FIRST APPEARANCE
Incredible Hulk #3
(September 1962)

POWERS

Most of the members of the Circus of Crime have skills and abilities that fit their job descriptions; these they adapt for criminal purposes. Princess Python is a snake charmer; Rajah is an elephant trainer; and Live Wire possesses an electrified lariat.

The Ringmaster's mechanism has enough range to hypnotize a capacity crowd in a sports arena.

CIRCUS OF CRIME

Operating under many different commercial names, the Circus of Crime is constantly traveling around the United States. They usually enter a small town and give away a large quantity of free tickets in order to ensure a full house. Once the show has begun, the Ringmaster uses a hypnotic device in his top hat to place the audience in a deep trance. The audience is robbed, and sometimes the entire town is looted.

A post-hypnotic suggestion usually prevents the Ringmaster's victims from identifying any members of the Circus or from remembering any details of the crime. They only recall having had a great time at the circus!

The Circus doesn't always get away with its mass robberies. When the Ringmaster tried to turn HULK into a monstrous attraction, he failed badly, and when the Circus returned to New York City under the name Cirque du Nuit, two HAWKEYES foiled them.

Originally from Austria, the Ringmaster moved his circus to America where he believed he could strike it rich. However, he turned to crime when his small band was unable to compete with the larger circus shows.

CIVIL WAR, SEE PAGES 86–87; CIVIL WAR II, SEE PAGES 88–89

Doctor Strange meets Clea for the first time.

CLEA

Princess Clea, until recently the Faltinian ruler of the Dark Dimension, has experienced numerous trials and tribulations during her lifetime. The daughter of Prince Orini and UMAR, influential figures in the Dark Dimension, Clea became involved in much of the political turmoil that afflicted that pocket universe. DOCTOR STRANGE first met Clea during one of his first forays to her homeland, and he was to have a significant influence on her life. Together they fought against the demon DORMAMMU, and during these battles they fell in love. Inevitably, these struggles were not without their dangers, and for a time Clea became trapped in a separate pocket universe with Dormammu. After her rescue by Strange, Clea spent several years in New York City, where she became his disciple and also his lover. When she returned to her home, she led a revolution against her mother, who had become ruler. After she took her mother's place, she married Strange, but Dormammu later usurped her throne. She left Earth to lead the resistance against him. She hid in Valhalla for a time and subsequently returned to Earth with the Fearless Defenders.

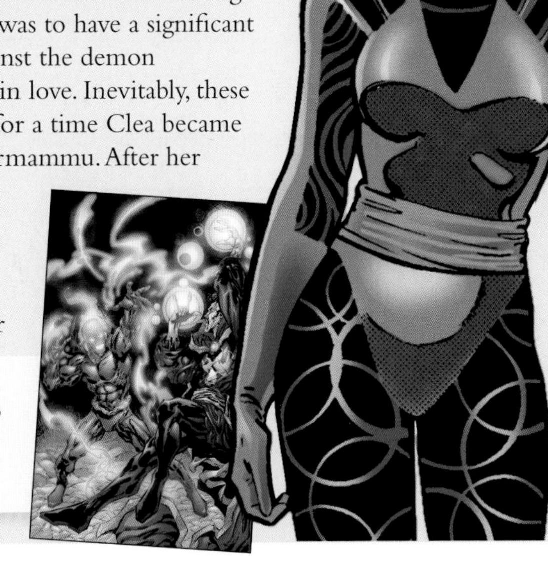

Even a burning head can't help Dormammu defeat Doctor Strange.

CLEA

FACTFILE
REAL NAME
Clea
OCCUPATION
Former ruler of the Dark Dimension
BASE
The Dark Dimension

HEIGHT 5 ft 8 in
WEIGHT 190 lbs
EYES Blue
HAIR White

FIRST APPEARANCE
Strange Tales #125 (November 1964)

POWERS
Formidable manipulator of mystical forces. Alien metabolism gives greater strength and endurance than a human of similar height and weight.

CLOAK AND DAGGER

Tyrone Johnson was a teenager whose stutter tragically prevented him from saving his friend Billy from being mistakenly shot as a thief by a policeman. Tandy Bowen felt neglected and unloved by her wealthy mother. Johnson and Bowen each ran away from home and met each other upon arriving in New York City at the Port Authority Bus Terminal.

They were offered a place to stay by men who worked for Simon Marshall, an unscrupulous chemist who was developing a new, highly addictive drug for the MAGGIA. Marshall was testing the drug on captured runaways. But whereas the drug killed the other runaways, it activated Johnson and Bowen's latent mutant abilities. Realizing he now resembled a living shadow, Johnson wrapped himself in fabric. He then entrapped some of Marshall's men in the blackness within this "cloak," while Bowen struck others down with "daggers" of "light." Johnson and Bowen decided to use their superhuman powers to save children and teenagers from drug dealers and other criminals and became the vigilante duo called Cloak and Dagger. They briefly became part of Norman OSBORN's Dark X-Men and have assisted SPIDER-MAN on several occasions.

Despite differing backgrounds, runaways Tyrone Johnson and Tandy Bowen became the closest of friends.

CLOAK AND DAGGER

FACTFILE
REAL NAMES
Tyrone Johnson, Tandy Bowen
OCCUPATION
Vigilantes
BASE The Holy Ghost Church, New York City
HEIGHT (Cloak) 6 ft (Dagger) 5 ft 5 in
WEIGHT (Cloak) 175 lbs (Dagger) 115 lbs
EYES (Cloak) Brown (Dagger) Blue
HAIR (Cloak) Black (Dagger) Blond

FIRST APPEARANCE
The Spectacular Spider-Man #64 (March 1982)

POWERS
Cloak can open a portal into the "Darkforce Dimension." He can project foes into this dimension, and teleport himself and others. Dagger projects psionic energy as "daggers of light," which deprive a victim of some life energy and can also cleanse people of drugs and poisons.

Dagger's "light-knives" are manifestations of the life energy that resides within all living beings. Dagger generates more of this life energy than normal humans do, and uses it to feed Cloak's hunger for such "light."

CIVIL WAR

The battle between heroes

When the New Warriors try to capture Nitro, he explodes, killing several hundred people. The government response splits the remaining Super Heroes, resulting in a Civil War.

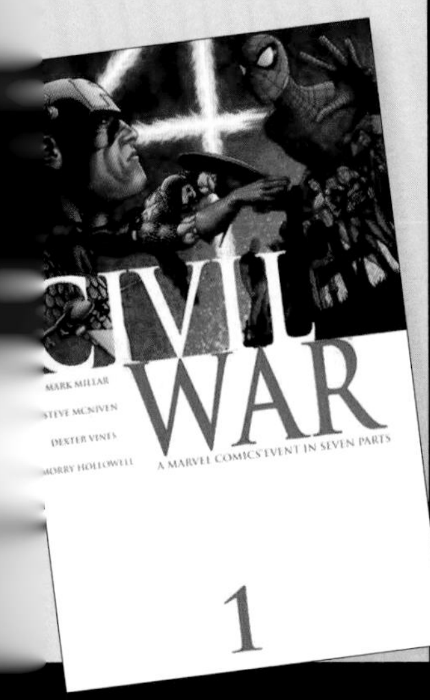

Having reinvented themselves as the heroes of a reality TV show, the New Warriors moved in on a house containing four Super Villains: Cobalt Man, Coldheart, Nitro, and Speedfreek. During the ensuing battle, Nitro exploded in the middle of Stamford, Connecticut. The blast killed over six hundred people, including Microbe, Namorita, and Night Thrasher.

After Namorita slammed him into a school bus outside of a playground, Nitro exploded and killed over 600 innocents—including dozens of children—rather than be captured and thrown into jail. This atrocity spurred the passage of the Superhuman Registration Act that launched the Civil War.

REGISTER OR ELSE

The public outcry over the tragedy spurred Congress to pass the Superhuman Registration Act, which required all superpowered people in the US to register with the government—and work for it as part of SHIELD—or face imprisonment. In the wake of M-Day, the public had already been pushing for such safeguards, and the Stamford disaster gave the Act the impetus to get through.

The new law split the Super Hero community in two. Many of the heroes understood the need for the law and planned to comply with it. Others believed it to be a bad law and planned to fight it. Iron Man, Mr. Fantastic, and Hank Pym led those who backed the law, while Captain America refused to help SHIELD and went underground to form a secret Avengers as the core of his resistance movement. As soon as the law came into effect and SHIELD starting rounding up outlaw heroes, the resistance set about freeing them.

Notably, most of the backers of the law already had public identities to begin with, while many of those who protested the law did not. The most famous exception was Spider-Man, who sided with his mentor Iron Man. After some soul-searching, he revealed his secret identity as Peter Parker at a globally televised press conference.

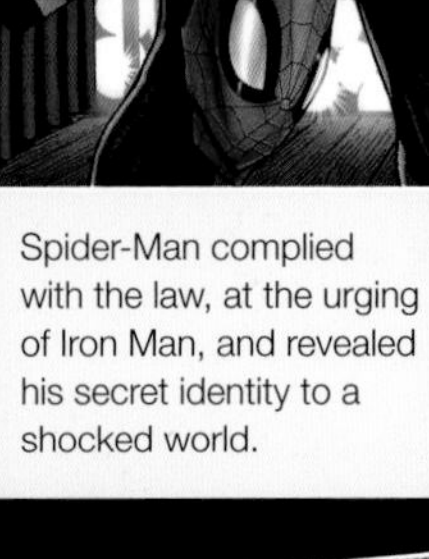

Spider-Man complied with the law, at the urging of Iron Man, and revealed his secret identity to a shocked world.

The Baxter Building served as a rallying point after the initial tragedy. With Congress about to pass the Superhuman Registration Act, the greatest heroes of the age assembled there to discuss how they should respond.

The X-Men officially declared neutrality during the conflict, which soon became known as the Civil War. Although they sympathized with the resistance, they had been nearly destroyed on M-Day and did not want to risk total eradication.

In the first major conflict between the two sides, SHIELD unleashed a clone of Thor. The clone killed Giant-Man (Bill Foster) and would have harmed others had the Invisible Woman not switched sides to protect the resistance. The incident caused heroes on both sides to reconsider their choices. Spider-Man switched to Captain America's team, while Nighthawk and Stature decided to register.

Desperate to even the sides, Captain America and his heroes launched an attack on the super-prison Mr. Fantastic had built in the Negative Zone. Anticipating this, Iron Man led a team to stop them. Cloak teleported the entire battle back to Manhattan, and the resistance was winning handily when a group of firefighters, EMTs, and police tackled Captain America to keep him from killing Iron Man.

Looking around at the damage the battle had caused, Captain America realized that his team had won "everything except the argument." He surrendered himself to the NYPD, effectively ending the conflict. In the aftermath, Iron Man became the new director of SHIELD and launched the Fifty-State Initiative.

At a turning point in the war, a clone of Thor slew Bill Foster, the latest Giant-Man.

Villains were promised a measure of amnesty if they would register with the government and help Iron Man track down and capture the outlaw heroes.

THE FINAL BATTLE

In the climactic battle of the Civil War, Captain America's resistance faction faced off against Iron Man's government-backed forces. The battle began in the maximum-security prison located in the Negative Zone, called 42 because it was the 42nd idea that Iron Man's team had for improving the world. It spilled out into New York City when Cloak teleported the entire battle back into the regular world.

At the climax of the battle, Captain America finally beat Iron Man but he hesitated when he had the chance to deliver the last blow. Gazing out at the destruction around him, he realized how many innocents were being caught up and harmed in the Civil War, and he gave himself up. Without Captain America, the active resistance crumbled, and the Civil War came to an end.

Soon afterward, while being marched in handcuffs into a federal courthouse, Captain America was assassinated by order of the Red Skull. Later, his old partner Bucky Barnes took up his name and shield and worked with a team of outlaw Avengers. They aimed to fight crime and save the world, while remaining outside the law.

CIVIL WAR II

Cain's visions sunder the Super Hero community

The president wants Super Heroes to get more involved in politics, "thought crime" is on the agenda, and students at Ohio State University get caught in a Terrigen Cloud.

Ulysses CAIN was just an ordinary student until a Terrigen Cloud rolled across the campus. Created years earlier, when BLACK BOLT exploded a Terrigen Bomb battling intergalactic warlord THANOS, the cloud released Cain's latent INHUMAN gene. He experienced Terrigenesis, and became haunted by terrifying, doom-laden premonitions.

Miles Morales was haunted by Cain's nightmarish vision of him killing Captain America on the steps of the Capitol Building. While this did not come to pass, a short while later an evil version of Captain America seized control of the country. Miles fought him as in the vision, but at the last moment refused to kill him.

FUTURE SHOCKS

MEDUSA, Queen of the Inhumans, and philosopher-priest Magister KARNAK, helped Cain understand his sudden prophetic powers. Medusa deemed Cain's vision of Earth's obliteration by a cosmic-level threat named a Celestial Destructor so convincing that she alerted the AVENGERS. Thus forewarned, a combined force of Avengers, Ultimates, and X-MEN succeded in magicking the deadly entity back to its own dimension. The heroes soon learned that they had Ulysses Cain's visions to thank for their victory, sparking a disagreement over how to best use Cain's powers. CAPTAIN MARVEL of the Ultimates was convinced Cain's visions would enable Earth's heroes to preempt major threats and disasters. IRON MAN was more suspicious of Cain's abilities, and counseled caution.

Iron Man and Captain Marvel fought their climactic battle in the skies above Washington, D.C. They ignored their friends' pleas to stand down—events had gone much too far for that. The fight ended only when Captain Marvel blasted Tony's armor apart and he plunged, unconscious, to the ground.

Iron Man's concerns proved tragically justified: Attempting to forestall an attack by Thanos, predicted by Cain, WAR MACHINE was killed and SHE-HULK critically injured. Grief-stricken by the death of his close friend, Iron Man infiltrated the Inhuman city of New Attilan and kidnapped Cain, hoping to study him and establish the true nature and extent of his powers. Captain Marvel led a rescue party of Avengers and Ultimates, who furiously confronted Iron Man. At that moment, Cain had a prophetic vision—which he projected onto all those present—in which they were all killed by a rampaging HULK. The vision was so convincing that a truce was called and Iron Man and Captain Marvel went to visit Bruce Banner, to see if there was any danger of him running amok as Hulk. Information from BEAST confirmed that Banner was experimenting with gamma rays. Believing that Banner was about to "Hulk out," HAWKEYE shot and killed him—and was put on trial for murder. Iron Man blamed Captain Marvel for all these developments.

Overwhelmed by his terrifying and disorienting visions, Cain fled from his college campus, but the Inhumans located him.

Following Hawkeye's aquittal, Iron Man informed Captain Marvel and other heroes that he had discovered Cain's visions were only ten per cent accurate. Captain Marvel refused to accept this, and heroes loyal to Iron Man and to Captain Marvel clashed, badly damaging SHIELD's Triskelion headquarters and destroying CITT, the GUARDIANS OF THE GALAXY's mobile base. The battle was halted by another Cain vision, in which Iron Man's ally, Miles Morales (SPIDER-MAN), killed CAPTAIN AMERICA in Washington, D.C. Captain America was prepared to help Miles disprove Cain's vision, but Captain Marvel insisted Miles should be arrested. Iron Man placed a force-field around Miles, and he and Captain Marvel clashed in a vicious battle that ended when Captain Marvel destroyed Iron Man's defenses, leaving him in a coma. Just at the moment of Captain Marvel's victory, however, Cain fell prey to a vision more powerful than any he had experienced before, in which he traveled through different futures. Eventually, he encountered the embodiment of reality, named ETERNITY, who welcomed Cain to a new realm of existence.

Captain Marvel looked on helplessly as Cain vanished. The second Super Hero Civil War was over. As the heroes tended their wounds—both physical and mental—Captain America was made SHIELD director, placing him in a position of unprecedented power (*see* SECRET EMPIRE).

The Inhumans tried to teach Cain not to fear his powers, but to embrace them.

Not even Beast could predict when or if Tony Stark would awaken from his coma. In Tony's absence, Captain Marvel pursued her own vision for the protection of Earth.

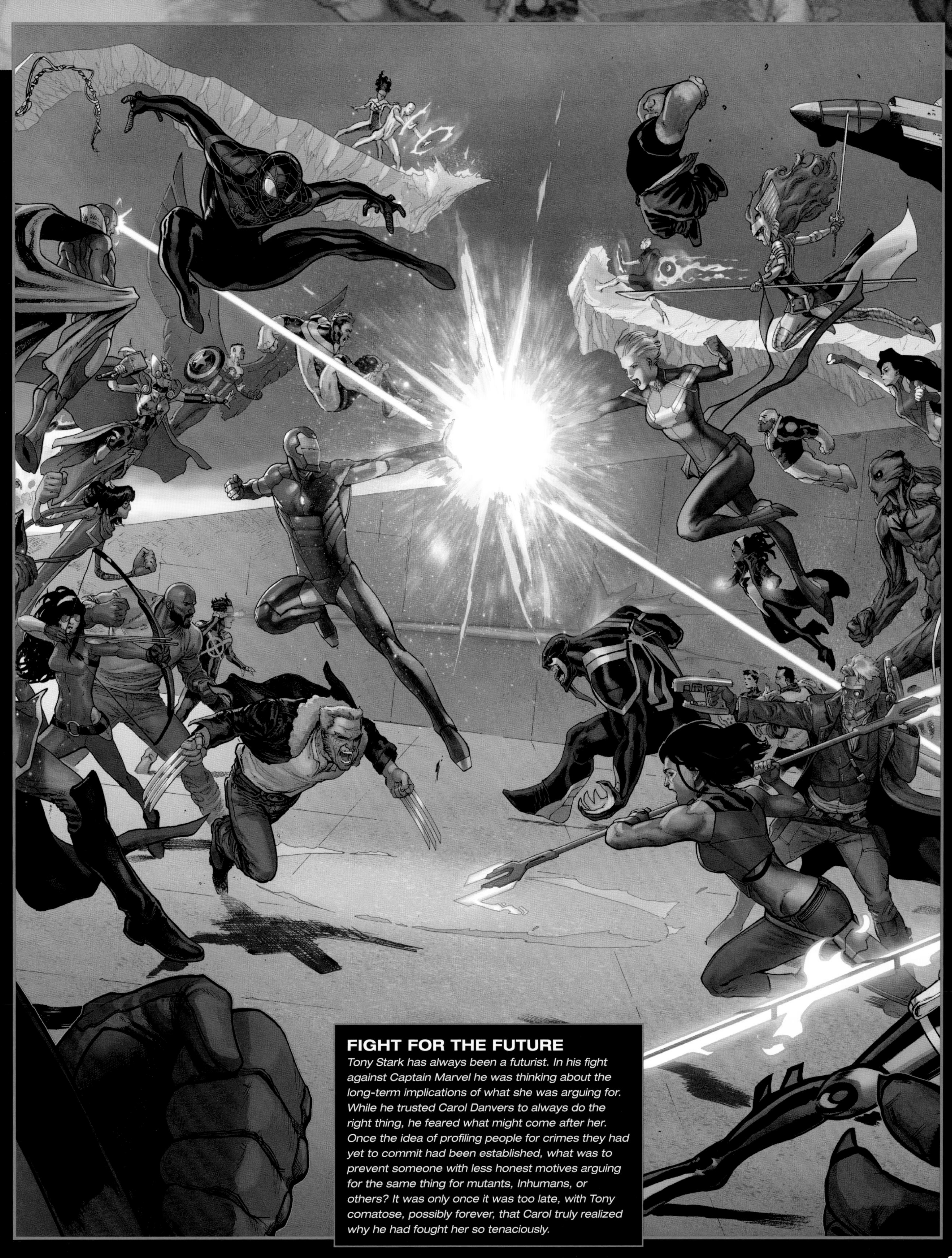

FIGHT FOR THE FUTURE

Tony Stark has always been a futurist. In his fight against Captain Marvel he was thinking about the long-term implications of what she was arguing for. While he trusted Carol Danvers to always do the right thing, he feared what might come after her. Once the idea of profiling people for crimes they had yet to commit had been established, what was to prevent someone with less honest motives arguing for the same thing for mutants, Inhumans, or others? It was only once it was too late, with Tony comatose, possibly forever, that Carol truly realized why he had fought her so tenaciously.

COLOSSUS

Metal X-Man with a soft heart

COLOSSUS

FACTFILE

REAL NAME
Piotr Nikolaievitch Rasputin

OCCUPATION
Adventurer

BASE
Mobile

HEIGHT 7 ft 5 in (armored)
WEIGHT 500 lbs (armored)
EYES Blue
HAIR Black

FIRST APPEARANCE
Giant Size X-Men #1
(May 1975)

POWERS
Mutant ability to change his body's tissue into an organic, steel-like material. This gives Colossus superhuman strength (he can lift at least 70 tons) and protects him from injury.

Piotr Rasputin was born on a Soviet collective farm in Russia, the same as his cosmonaut brother Mikhail and his sister Illyana (MAGIK). As a child he enjoyed drawing and painting, a talent he continued to develop as an adult. He discovered his mutant powers at age 13. When PROFESSOR X organized a new team of mutants to rescue the original X-MEN, he contacted Piotr and convinced him to join. Piotr first met Katherine PRYDE when the X-Men battled the White Queen and the Knights of the HELLFIRE CLUB. They fell in love, although circumstances often kept them apart. He also became close friends with NIGHTCRAWLER, STORM, and WOLVERINE.

The on-again, off-again relationship between Colossus and Kitty Pryde keeps him grounded as an X-Man but eventually takes its toll.

X-MAN, JUGGERNAUT, AVATAR

Colossus was injured by Riptide's shurikens while battling the MARAUDERS during their slaughter of the MORLOCKS. He couldn't turn his powers off for a while, and remained stuck in his metallic form. He was eventually healed by MAGNETO, and recuperated at Muir Island. He later sacrificed himself to cure the Legacy Virus that killed mutants, but returned thanks to an ill-intentioned alien named Ord, who brought him back to life in order to experiment on him.

During FEAR ITSELF, Colossus gained the power of the JUGGERNAUT from Cyttorak of the Crimson Cosmos. When the Phoenix Force came to Earth, he became one of its five avatars (consisting of Colossus, his sister MAGIK, CYCLOPS, Emma FROST and NAMOR) for a time. Though he then asked Cyttorak to release him from his obligations as a Juggernaut, Cyttorak refused. CABLE subsequently recruited him to join the new X-FORCE.

BROKEN MAN OF METAL

Colossus and his team of young mutants learned that SUGAR MAN planned to transport six hundred mutant embryos into the future, thus creating the next generation of mutants. When Colossus and his team intervened they found themselves teleported instead, leaving the Sugar Man behind. They arrived a thousand years in the future, in the Omega World, ruled by APOCALYPSE. Colossus was captured and forced to become the Horseman of War and hunt the X-Men. He was thwarted by Magik and transported back to the present where Nightcrawler restored him to his original self.

Colossus joined the X-Men in their battle against the INHUMANS over the Terrigen Cloud. He guarded X-Haven during the conflict and fought the Inhuman royal family on his own. MEDUSA destroyed the cloud when she realized the devastation it caused, thus ending the war.

Afterward, Kitty Pryde recruited Colossus to her new X-Men team. They reignited their relationship, awkwardly at first, until Kitty proposed marriage to Colossus. She got cold feet though, and backed out at the last moment. The broken-hearted Colossus subsequently left the X-Men and returned to Russia.

Few can resist the devastating power of Colossus when he is in his armored state. One of his mighty punches is enough to crush even Magneto himself.

COBRA

FIRST APPEARANCE *Journey into Mystery* #98 (November 1963)
REAL NAME Klaus Voorhees
OCCUPATION Criminal **BASE** Manhattan, formerly the Serpent Citadels in New York State **HEIGHT** 5 ft 10 in
WEIGHT 160 lbs **EYES** Blue **HAIR** None
SPECIAL POWERS/ABILITIES Has flexible, virtually unbreakable bones; can perform superhuman contortionist feats.

Given powers by the bite of an irradiated cobra, Klaus Voorhees became the first Cobra. He often partnered with MISTER HYDE and also joined other snake-themed criminals in the Serpent Squad and SERPENT SOCIETY. As the leader of the Serpent Society, he changed his name to King Cobra. He later injected his nephew Piet Vorhees with the same venom, making him the new Cobra. Piet worked as a mercenary and also with SIN's Serpent Squad, and then with HYDRA, which pitted him against CAPTAIN AMERICA (Sam Wilson). He went on to work with Viper's Serpent Solutions and BARON ZEMO's Army of Evil.

Thor was confronted by the Collector's horrifying true form.

COLLECTOR

One of the immortal ELDERS OF THE UNIVERSE, the Collector foresaw the destruction of all life by THANOS, and began to collect specimens for future repopulation. He was slain by KORVAC, but returned to life when the GRANDMASTER, a fellow Elder, won a contest with DEATH. The Collector briefly held the Reality Gem, but lost it to Thanos who sought it for the Infinity Gauntlet.

The Collector often gambled with the Grandmaster, pitting his Defenders team against the latter's Offenders. THOR later rescued a captive Alter Ego from his collection leading to a fight with the Collector, who revealed his true, terrifying appearance. After the events of the SECRET WARS, he and the Grandmaster staged a new Contest of Champions in Battlerealm, the remnants of DOCTOR DOOM's destroyed Battleworld.

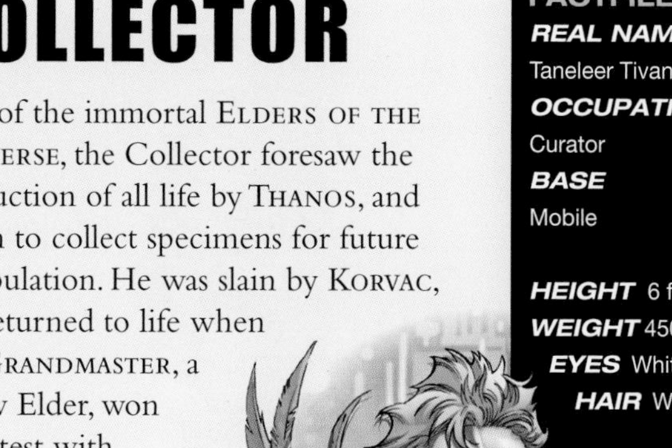

FACTFILE
REAL NAME
Taneleer Tivan
OCCUPATION
Curator
BASE
Mobile

HEIGHT 6 ft 2 in
WEIGHT 450 lbs
EYES White
HAIR White

FIRST APPEARANCE
Avengers #28
(June 1966)

Immortality, precognition and telepathy; can manipulate cosmic energy to change his size and shape; Temporal Assimilator permits time travel.

COLLINS, RUSTY

FIRST APPEARANCE *X-Factor* #1 (February 1986)
REAL NAME Rusty Collins
OCCUPATION Adventurer **BASE** X-Factor HQ, New York City
HEIGHT 5 ft 11 in **WEIGHT** 160 lbs **EYES** Blue **HAIR** Red
SPECIAL POWERS/ABILITIES Rusty Collins was a pyrokinetic with the mutant ability to cause flames to spontaneously generate in his vicinity.

Leaving a troubled home life behind, Rusty Collins enlisted in the United States Navy while still underage. But his career as a sailor came to an end when his mutant ability to generate flames first manifested itself. Rusty was thereafter recruited by X-FACTOR, members of the original X-MEN who had taken on the role of mutant hunters in order to conceal their activities in recruiting and training young mutants. Rusty eventually gained some control over his flaming abilities, and he adventured with X-Factor's junior team, the X-Terminators. He died during a battle with Holocaust. He recovered years later due to Selene's Transmode Virus but was killed again soon after.

COMET

FIRST APPEARANCE *Nova* #21 (September 1978)
REAL NAME Harris Moore
OCCUPATION Crimefighter **BASE** New York City/Xandar
HEIGHT 5 ft 11 in **WEIGHT** 190 lbs **EYES** Blue **HAIR** Gray
SPECIAL POWERS/ABILITIES Flies and projects energy blasts from his hands.

Harris Moore was one of the very first superpowered individuals to adopt a costume and take up the fight against crime. During an encounter with a gaseous, comet-like object in the 1950s, Moore was mutagenically affected by its radiation. Discovering that he could now fly and fire electrical energy from his hands, Moore decided to battle criminals on the streets of New York. His new vocation was not to end well. Moore was a wealthy individual with a wife and two children, but his good life came to an end when an enemy tracked him down to his suburban home and attacked him and his family. While he was hospitalized and appeared to have lost his powers, his family were all thought to be dead. Moore retired his costume for many years until joining the CHAMPIONS OF XANDAR. He was later killed by NEBULA.

COMET MAN

FIRST APPEARANCE *Comet Man* #1 (February 1987)
REAL NAME Dr. Stephen Beckley
OCCUPATION Former astronaut, astronomer and astrophysicist **BASE** Mobile
HEIGHT 6 ft 1 in **WEIGHT** 190 lbs **EYES** Blue **HAIR** Brown
SPECIAL POWERS/ABILITIES Possesses superhuman strength and self-healing ability. Can teleport, levitate, and project concussive energy from his hands.

On a mission in space, Dr. Stephen Beckley lost control of his spacecraft, which entered a comet's tail. The comet's intense heat vaporized the ship and Beckley. However, within the comet was another spaceship piloted by Max, an alien from the Colony Fortisque. Max used Fortisquian technology to reconstruct Beckley's body and endow him with superhuman powers. Returning to Earth, Beckley was quarantined by David Hilbert, a member of the Bridge, an intelligence agency headed by Beckley's brother John, the Superior. Stephen escaped captivity and became a tragic Super Hero.

CONSTRICTOR

CONSTRICTOR

FACTFILE

REAL NAME
Frank Payne (alias Frank Schlichting)

OCCUPATION
Professional criminal and assassin

BASE
Mobile

HEIGHT 5 ft 11 in
WEIGHT 190 lbs
EYES Blue
HAIR Black

FIRST APPEARANCE
Incredible Hulk #212 (June 1977)

POWERS

Battlesuit contains two cybernetically-controlled, electrically-powered adamantium cables, used as whips, as crushing coils, and to release electrical charges.

The cables in Constrictor's battlesuit are made of Adamantium, the strongest metal ever forged by man.

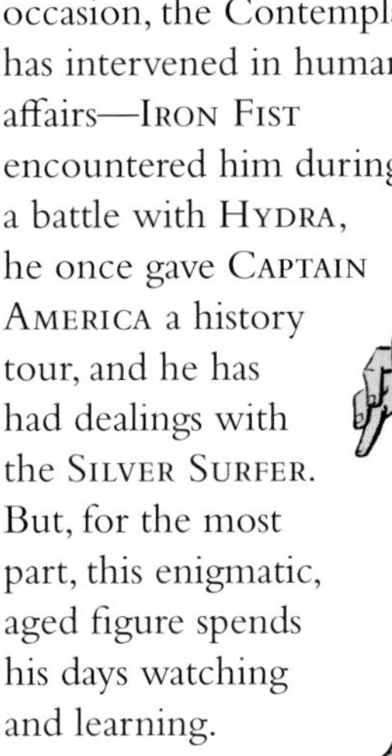

Using the alias Frank Schlichting, SHIELD agent Frank Payne infiltrated the Corporation, a criminal group. When Payne was forced to kill some youths during a fight, he suffered a nervous breakdown. The Corporation then gave him the Constrictor battlesuit and made him a criminal operative. When the Corporation dissolved, Constrictor went freelance. He usually preferred solo work, but sometimes teamed up with other villains, too. Payne put his criminal past behind him when he won a multimillion-dollar lawsuit after taking a beating from Hercules. He was part of the Fifty-State Initiative's Shadow Initiative team. He briefly went back to crime before moving in with Diamondback. When Payne died of a terminal illness, he left his suit to his son, who took on the role, eventually joining the Hood's crime gang.

CONTEMPLATOR

FIRST APPEARANCE *Marvel Treasury Special* #1 (1976)
REAL NAME Tath Ki
OCCUPATION Philosopher **BASE** Coal Sack Nebula
HEIGHT 5 ft **WEIGHT** 100 lbs **EYES** Blue **HAIR** None
SPECIAL POWERS/ABILITIES Control of his body's involuntary responses: heartbeat, perspiration, etc.; highly developed mental powers; acute awareness of this and alternate universes.

An Elder of the Universe, the Contemplator is one of the most ancient beings in the cosmos. Born in the early days of the universe, he has spent most of his life in meditation, reflecting on and teasing out the universe's deepest secrets. On occasion, the Contemplator has intervened in human affairs—Iron Fist encountered him during a battle with Hydra, he once gave Captain America a history tour, and he has had dealings with the Silver Surfer. But, for the most part, this enigmatic, aged figure spends his days watching and learning.

CONTROLLER

FIRST APPEARANCE *Iron Man* #12 (April 1969)
REAL NAME Basil Sandhurst **OCCUPATION** Criminal
BASE Mobile **HEIGHT** 6 ft 2 in **WEIGHT** 565 lbs
EYES White **HAIR** Black
SPECIAL POWERS/ABILITIES Armored exoskeleton provides enhanced strength and damage resistance; can telepathically control victims who are wearing his slave discs.

Injured in a lab accident while working for Cord Industries (one of Stark Industries' main rivals), Basil Sandhurst built himself an exoskeleton powered by mental energy. By placing a slave disc on a victim's head or neck, Sandhurst could direct that person's actions and leech his or her brainpower to charge up his suit. On various occasions, he set himself up as a cult leader or clinic director to get easy access to more bodies. At other times, Thanos and the Master of the World upgraded his technology to make it more efficient. The Controller clashed with Iron Man and the Avengers several times. He worked for the Hood during the Dark Reign.

COOPER, VALERIE

FIRST APPEARANCE *X-Men* #176 (December 1983)
REAL NAME Valerie Cooper **OCCUPATION** Chair of the Commission on Superhuman Activities **BASE** Washington, D.C.
HEIGHT 5 ft 9 in **WEIGHT** 135 lbs
EYES Green **HAIR** Blond
SPECIAL POWERS/ABILITIES Highly intelligent, efficient, and loyal; superb organizer; trained in the use of weapons.

A Special Assistant to the US National Security Advisor, Dr. Valerie Cooper was concerned about the number of mutants in the world. She feared that if control of mutants fell into the wrong hands, they could be used as weapons against the US. When Mystique offered the help of the Brotherhood of Evil Mutants, Cooper accepted, changing the group's name to Freedom Force. Later, as the head of the Commission on Superhuman Activities, Cooper was the liaison with the mutant team X-Factor. Cooper also helped found the Office of National Emergency and was named its deputy director. She oversaw the mutant refugee camp set up at the Xavier Institute for Higher Learning after M-Day.

COPYCAT

FIRST APPEARANCE (In the guise of Domino) *New Mutants* #98 (Feburary 1991) **REAL NAME** Vanessa Geraldine Carlysle
OCCUPATION Professional criminal; mercenary **BASE** Mobile
HEIGHT Unrevealed **WEIGHT** Unrevealed
EYES Black with white pupils **HAIR** White
SPECIAL POWERS/ABILITIES Copycat can transform herself into a duplicate of any other person.

Vanessa Carlysle's mutant power to transform her appearance manifested itself in her early teens. She went on to become Wade Wilson's lover (*see* Deadpool) but he left her when he found out he had cancer. Vanessa became a mercenary herself and came to the attention of the shadowy Mr. Tolliver, who used her to infiltrate X-Force in the guise of Domino. But Copycat came to like the members of X-Force, and she could not go through with the plan to blow them up. Her deception discovered, Copycat was forced to return to being a mercenary. She was nearly killed by Sabretooth but survived when Deadpool used some of his blood to help her.

CORRUPTOR

FIRST APPEARANCE *Nova* #4 (December 1976)
REAL NAME Jackson Day
OCCUPATION Criminal mastermind **BASE** Mobile
HEIGHT 6 ft 1 in **WEIGHT** 225 lbs **EYES** Red **HAIR** White
SPECIAL POWERS/ABILITIES His touch makes his victims susceptible to his commands. Left to themselves, they will behave in an uninhibited, even amoral, fashion.

While employed by a drug company, factory worker Jackson Day was accidentally drenched with chemicals. They turned his skin blue-black, and removed his inhibitions against wrongdoing. He also gained the power to control the wills of others by touching them. As the Corruptor, Day turned Thor into a violent menace. However, Nova intervened, and together he and Thor prevailed. The Corruptor later tried to corrupt the Hulk and the Avengers. He also worked with the Hood, battling the newest versions of the Avengers and helping repel the Skrulls during the Secret Invasion.

CORSAIR

FIRST APPEARANCE *X-Men* #104 (April 1977)
REAL NAME Christopher Summers **OCCUPATION** Adventurer
BASE The starship *Starjammer*
HEIGHT 6 ft 3 in **WEIGHT** 175 lbs **EYES** Brown **HAIR** Brown
SPECIAL POWERS/ABILITIES Trained pilot of airplanes and starcraft; trained combatant.

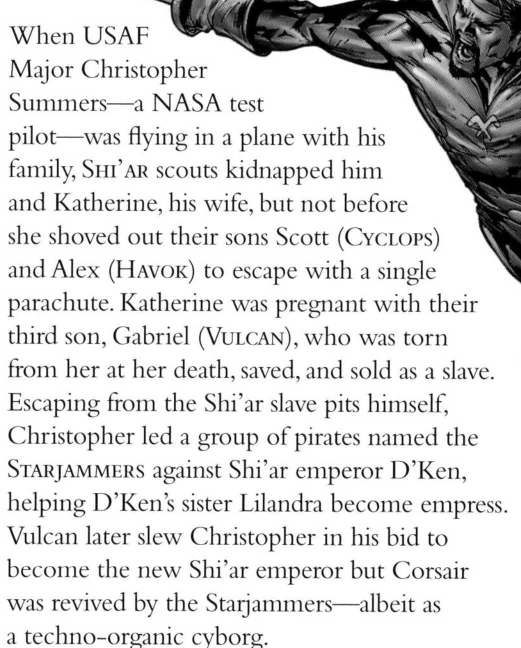

When USAF Major Christopher Summers—a NASA test pilot—was flying in a plane with his family, Shi'ar scouts kidnapped him and Katherine, his wife, but not before she shoved out their sons Scott (Cyclops) and Alex (Havok) to escape with a single parachute. Katherine was pregnant with their third son, Gabriel (Vulcan), who was torn from her at her death, saved, and sold as a slave. Escaping from the Shi'ar slave pits himself, Christopher led a group of pirates named the Starjammers against Shi'ar emperor D'Ken, helping D'Ken's sister Lilandra become empress. Vulcan later slew Christopher in his bid to become the new Shi'ar emperor but Corsair was revived by the Starjammers—albeit as a techno-organic cyborg.

CORVUS GLAIVE

FIRST APPEARANCE *Free Comic Book Day: Infinity* #1 (May 2013)
REAL NAME Corvus Glaive **OCCUPATION** Member of the Black Order
BASE Mobile **HEIGHT** Unknown **WEIGHT** Unknown
EYES Black **HAIR** None
SPECIAL POWERS/ABILITIES Superhuman strength, speed, and durability; immortal as long as his glaive is intact; master tactician.

The leader of the Cull Obsidan (also known as the Black Order), Corvus Glaive is a vicious killer who, together with his wife Proxima Midnight, once served Thanos. He was killed by Hyperion but revived himself thanks to the power of the mighty glaive he carries. Later, when facing Thanos, he killed himself rather than have his old master slay him. He was resurrected by the Challenger to take part in a new cosmic fight against the Avengers. After his defeat, Corvus was offered work by the Grandmaster, along with the rest of the Black Order.

COSMIC GHOST RIDER

FIRST APPEARANCE *Thanos* #13 (January 2018)
REAL NAME Frank Castle **OCCUPATION** Adventurer
BASE Mobile **HEIGHT** Unknown **WEIGHT** Unknown
EYES None **HAIR** None
SPECIAL POWERS/ABILITIES Spirit of Vengeance; can manipulate and project hellfire; superhuman durability; as a former herald of Galactus, can wield the Power Cosmic.

In an alternate future, Frank Castle, aka the Punisher, died while fighting Thanos. Castle ended up in Hell, where he did a deal with Mephisto to become the new Ghost Rider, hoping to return to Earth and gain revenge on Thanos. When Castle returned, Thanos had destroyed all life on Earth. Castle eventually became a herald of Galactus in order to fight Thanos, but when Thanos killed Galactus, Castle became a servant to his old enemy. After Frank was killed once again, Odin took him to Valhalla, eventually bringing him back to life and sending him to a time when Thanos was still young.

COSMO

FIRST APPEARANCE *Nova* #8 (January 2008)
REAL NAME Cosmo **OCCUPATION** Chief of security on Knowhere; liaison to Guardians of the Galaxy team; vigilante
BASE Knowhere **HEIGHT** 1 ft 1 in at withers **WEIGHT** 70 lbs
EYES Brown **FUR** Brown
SPECIAL POWERS/ABILITIES Telepathy; extremely accurate telekinesis; lifespan extended far beyond that of a normal dog.

Cosmo the spacedog was a test animal for the Soviet Space program. He was launched into orbit but his craft drifted off course. While drifting through space, Cosmo was mutated, gaining exceptional telepathic abilities and an extended lifespan. He ended up at Knowhere, a city built inside the severed head of a Celestial, and became its security chief. Cosmo was part of an early version of Star-Lord's Guardians of the Galaxy and helped to fight the Phalanx, as well as form the Annihilators. He still works in Knowhere, now as part of a team of vigilantes called the Knowhere Corps.

COULSON, AGENT PHIL

FACTFILE
REAL NAME
Phillip Coulson
OCCUPATION
Agent of SHIELD
BASE
SHIELD Helicarrier

HEIGHT 5 ft 9 in
WEIGHT 170 lbs
EYES Brown
HAIR Brown

FIRST APPEARANCE
Battle Scars #1
(November 2011)

POWERS
Special forces unarmed combat and firearms training; excellent administrative abilities; resourceful, loyal, and patriotic—inspired by his idol, Captain America.

COULSON, AGENT PHIL

Agent Coulson has taken to his role with the rebuilt SHIELD—and to wearing a suit—well.

Phil "Cheese" Coulson fought in Afghanistan as a member of the US Army Rangers 2nd Battalion, alongside his best friend, Marcus Johnson (aka Nick Fury, Jr.). When Johnson's mother was killed, Coulson used his leave to travel back with Johnson for her funeral, where they discovered that Johnson was secretly the son of Nick Fury. With Orion—one of the elder Fury's old enemies—after Johnson for the powers he'd inherited, Coulson did his best to haul his friend to safety. When Johnson knocked him out instead, Coulson called in the Avengers to help him find and save Johnson.

Both Coulson and Johnson were offered jobs with the reconstituted SHIELD. Coulson became the lead tactical support officer with SHIELD's version of the Secret Avengers. He was shot and seemingly killed by Deadpool on the orders of the Hydra version of Captain America.

COUNT NEFARIA

FACTFILE
REAL NAME
Count Luchino Nefaria
OCCUPATION
Criminal; former head of Nefaria "family" of Maggia
BASE
Various, including castle originally located in Italy and reconstructed in the New Jersey Palisades

HEIGHT 6 ft 2 in
WEIGHT 230 lbs
EYES Blue
HAIR Black

FIRST APPEARANCE
The Avengers #13 (February 1965)

POWERS
Superhuman strength, speed, and resistance to injury; projects laser beams from eyes; regenerates after injury; drains energy from other beings powered by ionic energy.

COUNT NEFARIA

Italian nobleman Count Luchino Nefaria used his fortune both to finance technological research and to make himself a power in the Maggia crime syndicate. Nefaria's wife Renata died giving birth to their daughter Giulietta, who would grow up in America as Whitney Frost before eventually becoming the Maggia leader Madame Masque. In retaliation for the Avengers' opposition to the Maggia, Nefaria framed them for treason. The Avengers were cleared, but Nefaria was publicly exposed as a criminal. Among his grandest schemes, Nefaria captured Washington, D.C. and held it for ransom, and later took over the North American Defense Command base at Valhalla Mountain. On both occasions he was thwarted by the X-Men.

Later, Nefaria had Prof. Kenneth Sturdy endow him with the powers of the Living Laser, Power Man, and Whirlwind and again battled the Avengers. Soon afterward, he seemed to be killed. However, he returned as a superhuman, powered by ionic energy. He later became the kingpin of crime in Los Angeles.

Nefaria was the villain in the 1975 issue that relaunched the X-Men Super Heroes.

IN ALL VALHALLA BASE, MY CHILDREN, WE SIX ARE THE ONLY ONES STILL CONSCIOUS, AND ONCE AGAIN, COUNT NEFARIA IS TRIUMPHANT...
THIS TIME TO HOLD THE *FATE* OF A *WORLD* IN HIS HANDS.

Thunderbird, a Native American member of the X-Men, perished while trying to prevent Count Nefaria's escape from Valhalla Mountain.

CRAZY GANG

FIRST APPEARANCE *Marvel Super Heroes* #377 (Sept. 1981)
BASE Mobile
MEMBERS AND POWERS
Executioner A hooded, scythe-wielding humanoid robot.
Jester Accomplished swordsman.
Knave Possesses superhuman strength.
Red Queen Her insanity twists all reality into negative situations.
Tweedledope Savant who devises advanced machinery.

The Crazy Gang is a team of professional criminals from another dimension (Earth-238, or the Crooked World) who look like characters from children's storybooks. They were assembled by that dimension's "Mad Jim" Jaspers. When the Crazy Gang was transported to the Earth of CAPTAIN BRITAIN, who was really Brian Braddock, they proved incompetent at committing crimes and so advertised for a new leader. They were taken over by Captain Britain's foe the Slaymaster, who masterminded a series of spectacular crimes which the Crazy Gang carried out for him. They were then recruited by master assassin ARCADE to abduct Courtney Ross, the former girlfriend of Captain Britain. Ross managed to escape from the bumbling group, but was taken prisoner by Arcade himself. The Crazy Gang later clashed with EXCALIBUR, who subsequently allowed them to remain in this dimension.

CRAZY GANG
1 Jack of Hearts
2 Jester
3 Tweedledope
4 Executioner
5 Red Queen

CREED, GRAYDON

FIRST APPEARANCE *Uncanny X-Men* #299 (April 1993)
REAL NAME Graydon Creed
OCCUPATION Politician; wheeler-dealer
BASE New York City; New York State; mobile
HEIGHT 6 ft **WEIGHT** 181 lbs **EYES** Blue **HAIR** Brown
SPECIAL POWERS/ABILITIES Charismatic orator, skilled political operator, and rabble-rouser.

Victor Creed was psychologically abused as a child and became SABRETOOTH. His son, Graydon Creed, grew up similarly malcontent but without any mutant powers. Born to the shapeshifting MYSTIQUE, Graydon came to hate all mutants and founded the Friends of Humanity, an organization that aimed to wipe out mutants. While running for President, Graydon was assassinated by Mystique, who had traveled back from the future to kill him. BASTION revived him with a techno-organic virus years later, but Hope SUMMERS killed him once more.

CRIMSON COWL

FIRST APPEARANCE *Thunderbolts* #3 (June 1997)
REAL NAME Justine Hammer
OCCUPATION Businesswoman; criminal mastermind
BASE Symkaria **HEIGHT** 5 ft 11 in **WEIGHT** 161 lbs
EYES Blue **HAIR** Black with white streaks
SPECIAL POWERS/ABILITIES The Crimson Cowl's cloak is prehensile and capable of attacking foes. It also allows its wearer to levitate and to teleport groups of people.

Four people wore the Crimson Cowl. ULTRON used the identity to disguise his true nature as he led the MASTERS OF EVIL against the AVENGERS. He hypnotized the Avengers' butler Edwin JARVIS to pose as the Crimson Cowl, too. Years later, Justine Hammer—daughter and heir of Justin HAMMER—took up the Cowl and the leadership of the Masters of Evil. When nearly captured, she put an unconscious Dallas RIORDAN into the costume to cast suspicion on her. Justine and her daughter Sasha HAMMER (fathered by the MANDARIN) plagued IRON MAN until Ezekiel STANE and Sasha killed her.

CRIMSON DYNAMO

More than a dozen people have worn the Crimson Dynamo armor. The first—Russian inventor Anton Vanko—built the original battlesuit and battled IRON MAN, but defected to work for Tony Stark. Vanko died killing the second Dynamo, Boris Turgenev, who had been sent to assassinate him. Vanko's protégé Alex Nevsky became the third Dynamo until his death at the hands of the KGB. Most of the others operated as Russian agents, with a few exceptions: the eighth was a college student who accidentally activated a prototype suit, and the tenth was a bank robber who bought his suit on the black market. A number of the Russians served with the WINTER GUARD. Tony Stark (IRON MAN) borrowed a suit of Crimson Dynamo armor from Dmitri Bukharin, the fifth and perhaps best-known Crimson Dynamo, and wore it for a short time during the DARK REIGN. The latest Crimson Dynamo was Galina Nemirovsky, the first woman to wear the armor. After leaving the Winter Guard, she worked for the MANDARIN and Ezekiel STANE in a redesigned suit, attacking Tony Stark on their behalf.

CRIMSON DYNAMO

FACTFILE
REAL NAME
Dmitri Bukharin
OCCUPATION
Russian hero
BASE
Moscow, Russia

HEIGHT 6 ft
WEIGHT 200 lbs
EYES Brown
HAIR Bald

FIRST APPEARANCE
Tales of Suspense #46 (October 1963)

POWERS
Armored suit provides flight, enhanced strength, and damage resistance; built-in weapons include missiles, guns, electrical generators, and a fusioncaster.

Nemirovsky's current armor casts a menacing aura and utilizes alien Dire Wraith technology.

CROSSBONES

FACTFILE

REAL NAME
Brock Rumlow

OCCUPATION
Mercenary; criminal

BASE
Mobile

HEIGHT 6 ft 4 in
WEIGHT 290 lbs
EYES Brown
HAIR Brown

FIRST APPEARANCE
Captain America #360 (October 1989)

POWERS
Brutal hand-to-hand combatant; highly adept with weapons and explosives, including pistols, throwing knives, which he keeps in his boots, and wrist blades, which are hidden in his wrist bands.

When Crossbones had superpowers, he could form a ball of fire in front of his face and fire a blast from it.

CROSSBONES

As a young man, Brock Rumlow—a budding neo-Nazi and childhood fan of the RED SKULL—led Manhattan's Savage Crims street gang. During that time, he attacked 15-year-old Rachel Leighton (who would later become DIAMONDBACK) and beat her two brothers, killing one. Fleeing prosecution, he trained under the TASKMASTER to become a deadly mercenary. As Crossbones, he worked for the Red Skull, and he repeatedly battled CAPTAIN AMERICA on his boss's behalf, even remaining loyal when the Skull once fired him. He also became the lover of the Skull's daughter, SIN.

Crossbones took part in Captain America's assassination, firing the first shot. SHIELD arrested him for this, but the Serpent Squad freed him soon after. He joined Luke CAGE's version of the THUNDERBOLTS, during which time he was exposed to the mutagenic Terrigen Mists, which temporarily allowed him to fire energy blasts from his face. He and Sin went on to work with HYDRA's Department of Occult Armaments (DOA), and later for BARON ZEMO at Hydra's base in Bagalia. After a stint at SHIELD's Pleasant Hill prison, he founded a new Hydra with Red Skull and Sin.

CYBER

FIRST APPEARANCE *Marvel Comics Presents* #85 (August 1991)
REAL NAME Silas Burr **OCCUPATION** Mercenary
BASE Mobile **HEIGHT** 6 ft 4 in **WEIGHT** 365 lbs
EYES Hazel **HAIR** Unrevealed
SPECIAL POWERS/ABILITIES Superhuman strength; mutant healing; ability to track brain patterns; Adamantium-laced skin; claws containing poisons or hallucinogens; cybernetic eye.

Silas Burr trained Logan (*see* WOLVERINE) during World War I and also, decades later, Logan's son DAKEN. After being shot and left for dead by Daken, Burr's skin was laced with Adamantium and he was given Adamantium claws. As Cyber, Burr lost an eye in a clash with Wolverine. He died when his flesh was consumed by mutant deathwatch beetles, but returned in astral form to possess another mutant's body. He hired the TINKERER to enhance this body, but it had a bad heart and Cyber eventually died. He was resurrected again and became the new Hornet, working for Silas Thorne, which pitted him against SCARLET SPIDER.

CROSSFIRE

FIRST APPEARANCE *Marvel Two-In-One* #52 (June 1979)
REAL NAME William Cross
OCCUPATION Ex-CIA agent; criminal **BASE** Mobile
HEIGHT 6 ft **WEIGHT** 190 lbs **EYES** Blue **HAIR** Brown
SPECIAL POWERS/ABILITIES Marksman, spy, deadly hand-to-hand fighter; left eye replaced by infrared device allowing night vision; left ear replaced by audio sensor giving super-hearing.

William Cross learned all about espionage, especially brainwashing techniques, as a CIA agent. Leaving the CIA and taking the code name Crossfire, he organized an army of mercenaries with the goal of disrupting society and earning himself a hefty profit from the ensuing chaos. When his enemies set off an explosion in Crossfire's headquarters, he lost his left eye and left ear. Replacing these with an enhanced cybernetic eye and ear, Crossfire set about brainwashing costumed heroes. His attempts put him in conflict with the THING, MOON KNIGHT, and HAWKEYE.

CRYSTAL

FIRST APPEARANCE *Fantastic Four* #45 (December 1965)
REAL NAME Corystalia Amaquelin **OCCUPATION** Princess
BASE Royal Inhuman Vessel (R.I.V.) **HEIGHT** 5 ft 6 in
WEIGHT 110 lbs **EYES** Green **HAIR** Red
SPECIAL POWERS/ABILITIES Elemental powers enable her to psionically control fire, air, earth, and water.

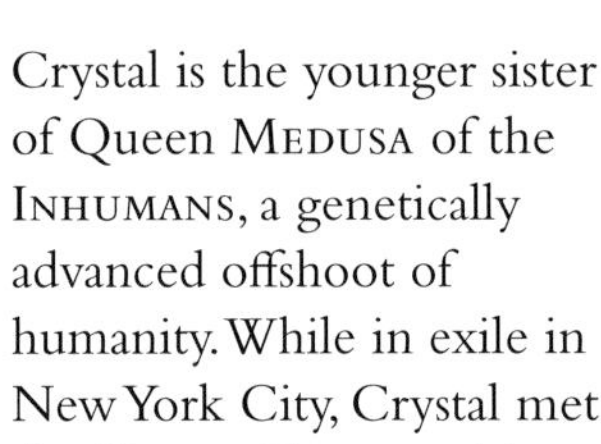

Crystal is the younger sister of Queen MEDUSA of the INHUMANS, a genetically advanced offshoot of humanity. While in exile in New York City, Crystal met and fell in love with the HUMAN TORCH and became a substitute member of the FANTASTIC FOUR. She eventually married QUICKSILVER, and they had a daughter named LUNA, but their marriage was annulled after Quicksilver illegally exposed both himself and Luna to the mutagenic Terrigen Mists. After the SECRET INVASION, she fled Earth with the rest of the Inhumans and agreed to marry RONAN THE ACCUSER to cement an alliance with the KREE. They reluctantly separated, by order of BLACK BOLT, and she was made an ambassador by Medusa, working to ally with the UN and assist victims of the Terrigen Cloud.

CYPHER

FIRST APPEARANCE *New Mutants* #13 (March 1984)
REAL NAME Douglas Ramsey **OCCUPATION** Student
BASE San Francisco
HEIGHT 5 ft 9 in **WEIGHT** 150 lbs **EYES** Blue **HAIR** Blond
SPECIAL POWERS/ABILITIES Cypher possessed a mutant facility for translating any sort of language. His ability to analyze patterns improved to the point at which he could predict the future.

PROFESSOR X realized that Doug Ramsey's brilliance with computers was an aspect of his mutant talent for languages. Doug became one of the NEW MUTANTS and helped them communicate with the newly arrived WARLOCK. Doug died after taking a bullet meant for his girlfriend, WOLFSBANE. For a while, his body merged with that of Warlock, forming Douglock. Years later, the Transmode Virus revived Doug, enhancing his powers so that he could predict the future. He rejoined the New Mutants and then switched to X-FACTOR. Later he assisted in the search for WOLVERINE.

CYCLOPS

Leader of the Uncanny X-Men

Deadly solar energy continually crackles forth from the eyes of Cyclops, controlled only by his visor.

When PROFESSOR X set up his School for Gifted Youngsters, the first mutant he recruited was Scott Summers. Scott also joined the X-MEN, adopting the code name Cyclops. He proved Professor X's most trusted student, and quickly became the team's deputy leader and master strategist, displaying great tactical abilities.

ORPHANED YOUNG

Scott Summers was the elder of two sons of Air Force Major Christopher Summers (CORSAIR) and Katherine Anne Summers. When their private plane was attacked by a SHI'AR starship, Katherine pushed Scott and his brother Alex out of the burning plane with the one parachute left. Both brothers were hurt, and Scott struck his head and fell into a year-long coma. The brain damage eventually prevented him from controlling his optic blasts once they emerged.

Alex ended up in an orphanage, and the boys lost contact for many years. Alex later became the mutant HAVOK and joined the X-Men too. They later discovered they had another brother, Gabriel, who became the conqueror VULCAN.

In his mid-teens, Scott developed terrible headaches and eyestrain, when his mutant powers emerged and he unintentionally blasted a crane at a construction site. He then fired another blast to save the crowd below it. Scott fled and fell into an unwilling partnership with a mutant criminal, named the Living Diamond.

THE X-MAN

When Professor X learned about Scott, he rescued him from the Living Diamond and invited him to join his school. Scott loved his teammate Jean GREY but, after her death, he married her clone, Madelyne PRYOR, and had a son named Nathan (CABLE) with her. After Jean returned and Madelyne died, Scott and Jean were married. After Jean died again, Scott dated Emma FROST.

Scott took over from Professor X as the leader of the X-Men. He retained his powers after M-DAY and gathered mutants worldwide on a Pacific island he named Utopia. This led to a schism between him and his teammate WOLVERINE, who reopened Professor X's school as the Jean Grey School for Higher Learning. When the Phoenix Force returned to Earth, Scott became one of the Phoenix Five. He eventually transformed into a new Dark Phoenix and killed Professor X.

Stricken with grief, Scott allowed himself to be arrested. He later broke out of prison and formed his own group to lead the mutant revolution. He became the leader of a mutant sanctuary just before the end of the Multiverse. After bonding with the Phoenix Force again, he survived the end of the Multiverse aboard the ILLUMINATI's life raft, but was killed by DOCTOR DOOM in Battleworld. Cyclops was revived when the Multiverse was restored, only to be killed again by the Terrigen Mists. A young, time-displaced Cyclops living in the present day hated his older self. He was forced to come to terms with the fact that humans and mutants alike would hate him because they considered his older self a terrorist. Meanwhile, the Phoenix Force resurrected the older Cyclops, only for him to be killed by Jean Grey to restore the natural order.

When the rest of the Phoenix Five lost their powers, Scott became the Dark Phoenix.

FACTFILE

REAL NAME
Scott Summers

OCCUPATION
Adventurer; former student and radio announcer

BASE
New Charles Xavier School for Mutants, Alberta, Canada

HEIGHT 6 ft 3 in
WEIGHT 175 lbs
EYES Black (red when his optic power is active)
HAIR Brown

FIRST APPEARANCE
X-Men #1
(September 1963)

CYCLOPS

POWERS

Cyclops has the mutant ability to project ruby-colored beams of concussive force from his eyes. Cyclops' cells constantly absorb sunlight, and he uses that solar energy to create openings from another universe in front of his eyes, and the beams fire from these breaches. Due to a childhood trauma, Cyclops' optic beam is always "on." The only way to block it is by closing his eyes or wearing a special visor or glasses. Cyclops' optic blasts are powerful enough to punch holes through a mountain.

ESSENTIAL STORYLINES
- ***X-Men #107*** First appearance of Corsair, Cyclops' father (Christopher Summers), whom Scott believed to be dead, but is now a member of the Starjammers, an alien group opposed to Shi'ar tyranny.
- ***X-Men #30*** Marriage X-Men style: after years of romance, Scott Summers finally marries his beloved, Jean Grey.

DAKEN

FACTFILE
REAL NAME
Daken Akihiro
OCCUPATION
Assassin, agent
BASE
Mobile

HEIGHT 5 ft 9 in
WEIGHT 167 lbs
EYES Blue
HAIR Black

FIRST APPEARANCE
Wolverine Origins #10 (March 2007)

POWERS
Mutant healing factor, retractable claws made of bone, superhuman senses, endurance, and reflexes, plus ability to manipulate others via pheromones.

DAKEN

While trying to capture Wolverine, the Winter Soldier killed Wolverine's pregnant wife, Itsu. Romulus cut the baby from her womb and gave him to a Japanese couple, leaving Wolverine unaware the child had survived. The child, Daken, trained under Cyber and worked for Romulus, who encouraged him to kill Wolverine, claiming his father had been the one who'd murdered his mother. Wolverine drew Daken into a trap so the Winter Soldier could shoot Daken with a Carbonadium bullet, which worked against his healing factor. Discovering that Romulus had orchestrated Itsu's death, Daken and Wolverine worked together to bring him down.

During the Dark Reign, Daken took over his father's identity as Wolverine to join Norman Osborn's (*see* Green Goblin) Dark Avengers and X-Men. After that, he tried to take over crime in Los Angeles but became addicted to a drug called "Heat," which destroyed his healing factor. Dying, he drew out Wolverine for a confrontation and then blew himself up. He later returned as the leader of a new Brotherhood of Mutants, but Wolverine drowned him. The Apocalypse Twins revived him to become one of their Horsemen of Death. He later returned to human form and joined Lady Deathstrike and Sabretooth to search for Wolverine when his father's body went missing.

Daken served alongside Banshee, Grim Reaper, and Sentry as a one of the Horsemen of Death.

DAMAGE CONTROL

FIRST APPEARANCE *Marvel Comics Presents* #19 (June 1989)
BASE Manhattan
MEMBERS **Anne Marie Hoag** Director of Operations; **Henry Ackerdson** V.P. Marketing; **Albert Cleary** Comptroller; **Eugene Strausser** Head of R&D

Damage Control is an engineering and construction company that specializes in cleaning up and repairing property damage caused by superpowered conflicts. With its headquarters in Manhattan's Flatiron Building and a warehouse in New Jersey, the company has about 300 employees. Kid Kaiju and his monsters were placed under Damage Control's protection after they saved the world. Kid Kaiju, his family, and monsters were given the artificial island of Mu as a home and base, with Damage Control on hand for any cleanups needed after monstrous battles.

DANSEN MACABRE

FIRST APPEARANCE *Marvel Team-Up* #93 (May 1980)
REAL NAME Unknown **OCCUPATION** Criminal; exotic dancer; second-in-command of Night Shift **BASE** Los Angeles
HEIGHT 5 ft 10 in **WEIGHT** 135 lbs **EYES** Blue **HAIR** Silver
SPECIAL POWERS/ABILITIES Her dancing can hypnotize or even kill; able to evade Spider-Man's telepathic "Spider-Sense."

Dansen Macabre was the high priestess of Kali, a religious cult. When Macabre believed the Shroud to be a member of a rival cult, she hypnotized Spider-Man into attacking him. Her plan failed and the pair defeated her. Realizing the impossibility of imprisoning Macabre, Spider-Man left her in the Shroud's care. She became second-in-command of Night Shift, the Shroud's gang, but was killed by Count Nefaria after failing to kill Moon Knight.

Daredevil, see pages 100–101

DARK ANGEL

FIRST APPEARANCE *Hell's Angel* #1 (July 1992)
REAL NAME Shevaun Haldane **OCCUPATION** Bio-occult researcher **BASE** Darkmoor, England **HEIGHT** 5 ft 7 in
WEIGHT 120 lbs **EYES** Green **HAIR** Auburn
SPECIAL POWERS/ABILITIES Costume is powered by Fabric of the Universe. Can use various types of energy blasts, manipulate gravitons to fly, and also has extrasensory abilities.

Shevaun Haldane's father, Ranulph, was part of the Mys-Tech Board until Mephisto killed him. Shevaun inherited his debt to Mephisto, but was approached by a dark angel who gave her a fragment of the universe. It formed into a costume that granted her exceptional powers. She fought Mys-Tech, changing her name from Hell's Angel to Dark Angel. Shevaun also helped the X-Men and explored various mystical realms. After using her powers to prevent Killpower from unleashing hell, she became Tony Stark's mystical consultant, helping him against the Dark Bride and Malekith the Accursed.

DARK AVENGERS

FIRST APPEARANCE *Dark Avengers* #1 (March 2006)
BASE HAMMER secret base
FOUNDING MEMBERS **Norman Osborn (Iron Patriot); Moonstone** (impersonating Ms. Marvel)**; Sentry; Venom** (impersonating Spider Man)**; Aries; Daken** (impersonating Wolverine)**; Bullseye** (impersonating Hawkeye)**; Noh-Varr (Captain Marvel)**

Following the Secret Invasion, Norman Osborn (*see* Green Goblin) assumed control of the Avengers. Most of the team resigned in protest, so Osborn recruited various villains to fill their roles, leading them personally as Iron Patriot. Following the climactic Siege of Asgard, in which Osborn was defeated, most of the Dark Avengers were arrested. Several other iterations of the team have been recruited since.

DARKHAWK

FIRST APPEARANCE *Darkhawk* #1 (August 1964)
REAL NAME Christopher Powell **OCCUPATION** High-school student **BASE** Queens, New York City
HEIGHT 6 ft ½ in **WEIGHT** 320 lbs **EYES** Brown **HAIR** Brown
SPECIAL POWERS/ABILITIES Bio-mechanical armored suit possesses enhanced strength, speed, agility, and durability. Also possesses a pair of retractable glider wings and a claw-cable on his right hand that can act as a grappling hook. Can generate defensive force shields and concussive blasts of dark energy.

Teenager Christopher Powell discovered an alien amulet that exchanged his body for the Darkhawk android, transferring his mind into it. He later obtained a new android form that could become invisible, and he became able to change directly between the two forms. As Darkhawk, he worked with the New Warriors, the West Coast Avengers, and later the Loners, a group for teen ex-heroes. He registered with the government during the Civil War and served as the security chief of Project PEGASUS during the Secret Invasion. Chris recently gained a new, more powerful form while fighting the Raptors.

Dark Reign, see pages 102–103

DARKSTAR

FIRST APPEARANCE *Champions* #7 (August 1976)
REAL NAME Laynia Petrovna **OCCUPATION** Adventurer
BASE Russia **HEIGHT** 5 ft 6 in **WEIGHT** 125 lbs
EYES Brown **HAIR** Blond
SPECIAL POWERS/ABILITIES Darkstar could tap into the extradimensional Darkforce to create solid objects, to teleport herself and others, and to fly.

Professor Piotr Phobos made the mutant Laynia into Darkstar, part of his Soviet Super-Soldiers team. She and her brother Nicolai (Vanguard) turned against him when he betrayed the state. She defected to the US, but later returned to Russia and joined the Winter Guard. She and Vanguard then worked with their father, the Presence. She joined the X-Corps, but Fantomex killed her when Weapon XII possessed her. Her essence survived in an amulet that gave the wearer her powers. When a Dire Wraith took it, Laynia possessed the creature and turned it into herself.

DARK BEAST

FIRST APPEARANCE *X-Men Alpha* #1 (February 1995)
REAL NAME Henry P. McCoy **OCCUPATION** Genetic engineer
BASE Formerly Sinister's slave pens in the "Age of Apocalypse"
HEIGHT 5 ft 11 in **WEIGHT** 355 lbs **EYES** Blue
HAIR Formerly brown, now blue-black
SPECIAL POWERS/ABILITIES Possesses superhuman strength, agility, and durability. Expert in genetics and biochemistry.

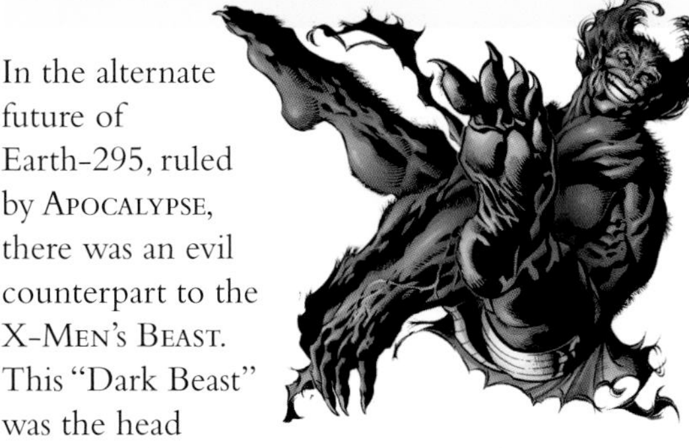

In the alternate future of Earth-295, ruled by Apocalypse, there was an evil counterpart to the X-Men's Beast. This "Dark Beast" was the head geneticist for that reality's version of Mister Sinister, and experimented on the inmates in his slave pens. When Apocalypse was defeated, the Dark Beast transported himself 20 years into the past of Earth-616, where he met a young Emma Frost and created the Morlocks. At one point, he captured the Beast and impersonated him. He joined the Dark X-Men during Dark Reign, and was caught experimenting on Inhumans during Hydra's takeover of the USA.

DAZZLER

Alison Blaire's mutant power first manifested itself during a high-school talent show. She became a singer whose amazing light-show powers helped to make her a star. Although she had no intention of using her abilities to fight crime, she joined the X-Men after she was exposed as a mutant. She later met and fell in love with Longshot, with whom she bore a son who became Shatterstar, although her memories of this birth were wiped.

After Longshot was reported dead, Alison returned to her singing career. They later reunited and she returned to the X-Men, but his amnesia drove them apart. After that, she became the leader of a dimension-hopping team of X-Men trying to defeat ten evil versions of Professor X. When she returned, she became an agent of SHIELD, and later joined Havok's rogue X-Men team.

Dazzler recently returned to her original look on stage for the anniversary tour of her *Sounds of Light and Fury* album.

FACTFILE

REAL NAME
Alison Blaire
OCCUPATION
Singer, actress
BASE
Mobile

HEIGHT 5 ft 8 in
WEIGHT 115 lbs
EYES Blue
HAIR Blond

FIRST APPEARANCE
X-Men #130 (February 1980)

DAZZLER

POWERS
Mutant with the ability to convert sonic vibrations into various forms of light, including blinding, colorful, mind-numbing, and hypnotic displays, high impact photon blasts, laser beams, holographic illusions, and protective force-fields.

DAREDEVIL

The man without fear

DAREDEVIL

FACTFILE

REAL NAME
Matthew Michael Murdock

OCCUPATION
Lawyer

BASE
Hamilton Heights, New York City (formerly Hell's Kitchen)

HEIGHT 5 ft 11 in
WEIGHT 185 lbs
EYES Blue
HAIR Red-Brown

FIRST APPEARANCE
Daredevil #1 (April 1964)

POWERS

Although he is blind, Daredevil's remaining senses are honed to superhuman levels. Radar Sense allows him to detect the contours of his environment. A trained athlete and acrobat, he carries a billy club that converts into a cane; it contains a reeled line that allows Daredevil to swing over the rooftops or entangle an enemy.

ALLIES/FOES

ALLIES Foggy Nelson, Spider-Man, Gladiator, Iron Man, Luke Cage, the Avengers

FOES Elektra, Bullseye, Electro, Impossible Man, Kingpin, Mysterio, the Hand

ISSUE #1

"The Origin of Daredevil" reveals how Matt Murdock, son of a prizefighter, loses his sight but gains superpowered senses. He becomes the Super Hero Daredevil, trains as a lawyer, and sets up a law firm with Foggy Nelson.

HERE COMES...
DAREDEVIL
THE MAN WITHOUT FEAR!
SPIDER-MAN

NOW THAT PLAY TIME'S OVER, I'LL HANG AROUND UNTIL I FIND THE FIXER! AS FOR WHO I AM, YOU CAN JUST CALL ME... DAREDEVIL

When he began his crime-fighting career, Daredevil wore a yellow and red costume similar to that of a wrestler.

Matt Murdock was the only son of professional boxer "Battling" Jack Murdock. His father, forced to work as a mob enforcer in order to supplement his meager income as a prize-fighter, made Matt promise to get a good education, and not become a fighter like himself. As a dedicated student who would never compete in athletics with his fellows, Matt was ironically nicknamed "Daredevil" by his taunting classmates. Not wanting to break his promise to his father, Matt took their insults—but he secretly kept up a rigorous training regimen all by himself.

RADIOACTIVE ACCIDENT

One fateful day, Matt saw a blind pedestrian about to be struck down by a truck. Matt rushed to the old man's aid, knocking him from the path of the vehicle. In the crash that followed, a canister of radioactive material fell from the truck and struck Matt in the face. Despite the best efforts of the doctors, Matt would thereafter be blind.

However, Matt discovered that the accident had a secondary effect on him: all of his remaining senses had been enhanced to a superhuman degree. Additionally, he now possessed a new sense: a radar-like ability to detect the contours of his environment that compensated for his lack of sight. Initially overwhelmed by his powers, Matt was helped by martial arts master Stick, who taught him not only how to control his new abilities, but how to use them to improve his fighting skills. While at college, Matt became friends with future business partner Foggy Nelson. He also met and fell in love with Elektra Natchios, daughter of the Greek ambassador to the US. Elektra left college when her father was killed, eventually becoming an assassin for the Hand, a cult of ninja warriors.

REVENGE AND THE LAW

When mob boss the Fixer told Jack Murdock to throw a fight, Jack, with his son watching, won. He was soon gunned down by the Fixer's men.

In order to track down the men who had murdered his father, Matt, now a successful lawyer, adopted the identity of Daredevil. After the Fixer had been brought to justice, Matt continued his crime-fighting double life. He tried to combine life as Daredevil with his career as a lawyer and set up a legal firm with his old college buddy Foggy Nelson.

ESSENTIAL STORYLINES

- ***Daredevil #168***
Daredevil has a reunion with his college sweetheart Elektra, now an assassin for hire.
- ***Daredevil #227–232***
The Kingpin methodically tears Matt Murdock's life apart, piece by piece.
- ***Daredevil Vol. 2 #32***
Daredevil's true identity as Matt Murdock is revealed to all the world.

In college, Matt Murdock fell in love with exchange student Elektra Natchios. The two would one day become implacable foes.

As leader of the Hand, Daredevil wore a black costume with red detailing.

For a time, Daredevil fought crime alongside the Black Widow before Elektra returned to his life as a rogue assassin hunted by the Hand. Refusing to kill Foggy, who was her target, she went on the run. Elektra was eventually killed by a rival assassin in the form of Daredevil's archenemy Bullseye, who himself nearly died in a brutal battle with Daredevil. The hero then helped Stick and the secret order known as the Chaste against the Hand, and in the ensuing conflict, the Chaste was decimated and Elektra resurrected.

TROUBLED TIMES

When Wilson Fisk, aka the Kingpin, learned Daredevil's secret identity, he first tried to ruin Murdock, then became obsessed with killing him. Fisk used his military contacts to unleash an insane Super-Soldier named Nuke on the city, but Daredevil defeated him. Fisk's attack on Daredevil had also brought Karen Page, an early love of Matt's, back into his life, but she was then killed by Bullseye. When Fisk came under investigation from the FBI, he revealed Daredevil's secret identity and for a time it seemed to have been made public. Iron Fist helped restore Matt's secret by taking on the role of Daredevil while Matt was briefly in jail.

When pushed to the brink by Daredevil's heroic friends, the Beast revealed himself.

Eventually Matt decided the only way to stop the Hand was to take the group over and turn it into a force for good. While he succeeded in gaining control of the Hand, it turned out to be a trap so that the Hand's demonic leader, the Beast, could possess Matt. A tainted Daredevil built a Shadowland in New York and grew increasingly dark and violent until master Izo—Stick's mentor and founder of the Chaste—brought together several of Matt's heroic allies to stop him. Iron Fist eventually managed to rid Daredevil of the demon.

ORDER OF THE DRAGON

After taking some time off to rebuild his life, Matt returned to New York and briefly joined the Avengers. He helped the Purple Man's children when their father tried to manipulate them. He also revealed his secret identity to the world under oath when the Sons of the Serpent tried to use the information to blackmail him. With the world knowing that he was Daredevil, Matt could no longer practice law in New York so moved to San Francisco. The Purple Man's children eventually helped to reinstate his secret identity by using their powers to wipe the knowledge from the minds of everyone in the world. With his secret safe again (and Matt only revealing his heroic identity to Foggy), Matt became New York's assistant district attorney and took on an apprentice—Blindspot—just as Fisk made his move and became mayor of the city. Fisk wanted to keep his enemies close, so offered Matt the position of deputy mayor, and Matt accepted, as it would allow him to keep tabs on Fisk.

When the Beast and the Hand attacked New York, Fisk was injured and Matt briefly assumed his position as mayor, helping to defeat the Hand with the Order of the Dragon, a secret cult of soldiers that Blindspot joined. Soon after, Fisk regained consciousness and returned as mayor, continuing his long and deadly fight with Daredevil.

Daredevil also joined forces with Iron Fist, Luke Cage, and Jessica Jones to become the Defenders when Cage's old foe Diamondback returned.

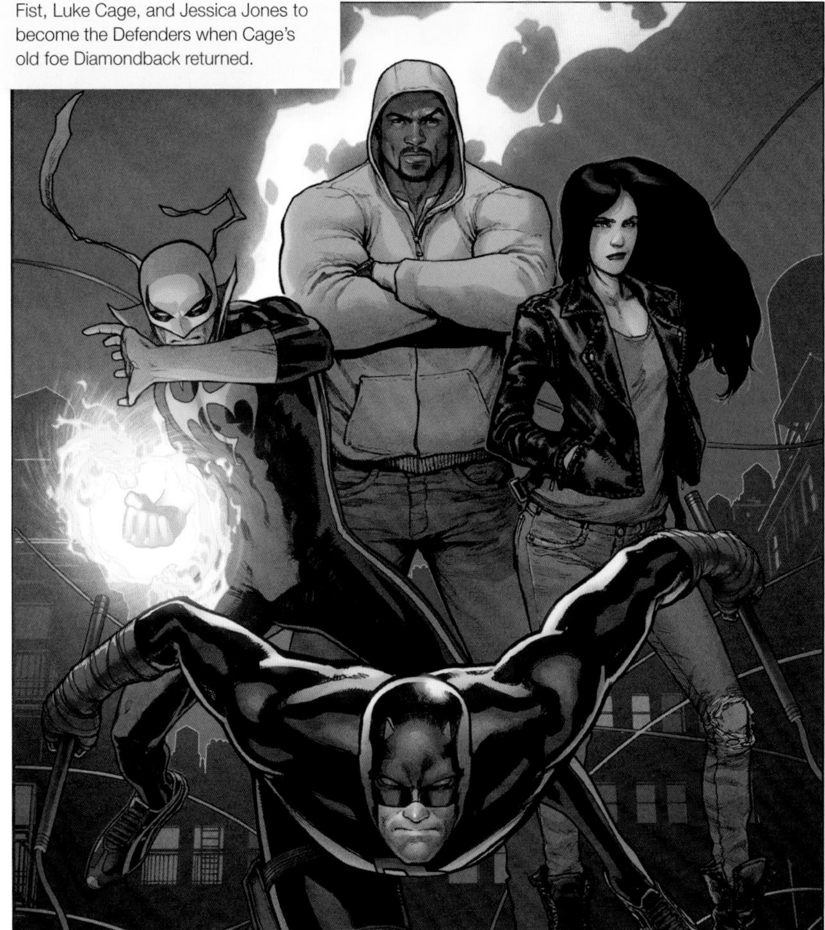

DARK REIGN

When Norman Osborn gained "the keys to the kingdom"

ISSUE #1

The Secret Invasion was at an end and Norman Osborn was now in charge of US security. Osborn called together his Cabal of villains to divvy up the world.

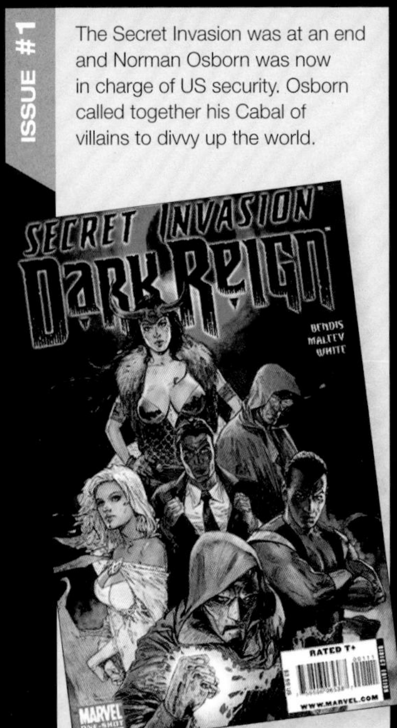

At the end of the Secret Invasion, Norman Osborn (Green Goblin) personally killed the Skrull queen Veranke while leading the Thunderbolts, whom he'd been put in charge of during the Civil War. He used the fame to get himself appointed head of national security in the US. He immediately dismantled SHIELD and put himself in charge of a new agency called HAMMER.

THE DARK X-MEN
Norman Osborn replaced the public faces of the X-Men with a team under his control. ***1*** Mimic ***2*** Weapon Omega ***3*** Mystique ***4*** Dark Beast.

DARK HEROES

Osborn forced any of the heroes who might oppose him to flee and hide. Meanwhile, he replaced them with villains possessing similar powers, forming his own teams of Avengers and X-Men. He also called together some of the most powerful villains in the world to form the Cabal, his answer to the heroes' Illuminati. Meanwhile, he worked with the Hood to sew up control over the organized criminal element in the US.

Osborn took a suit of Iron Man's armor and fashioned it after Captain America's costume. Donning it, he called himself the Iron Patriot, presenting himself as the premier hero for this new era. However, the mental problems that had led Osborn to become the Green Goblin continued to plague him, despite the medications he took for his condition.

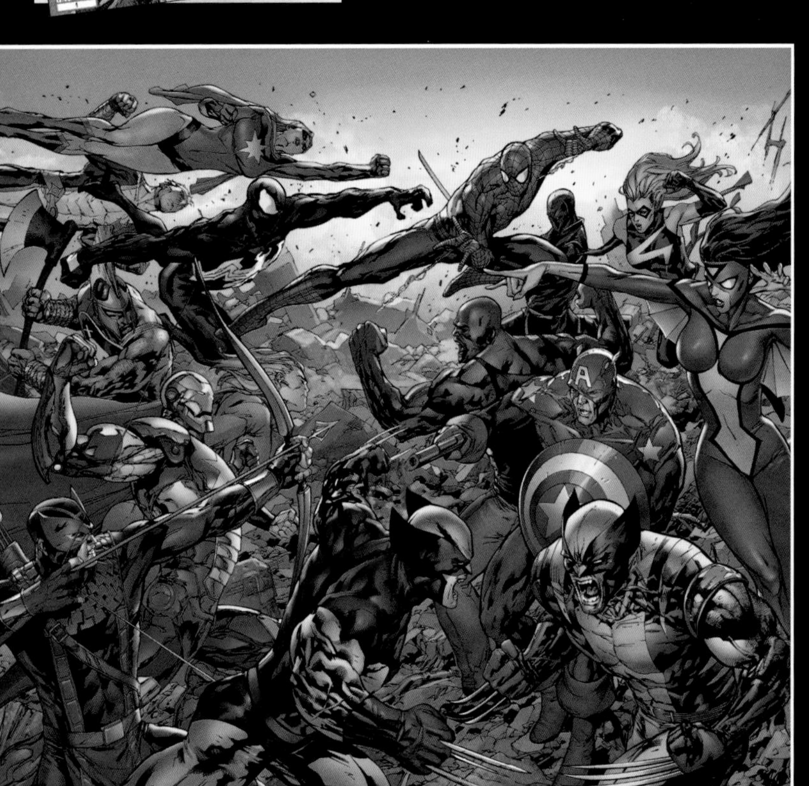

The Avengers and their dark counterparts were well matched, but the power of both Ares and the Sentry gave Osborn's team the edge. Osborn relied on his status as the Sentry's mentor and confidant (and fellow mental patient) to keep the man under control, making sure the Void didn't emerge to destroy his plans.

THE SIEGE

Loki worked to keep Osborn unstable and convinced him that Asgard—the home of the Norse Gods, which had been relocated to float over Broxton, Oklahoma—presented a grave threat to his power. Osborn tried to convince the President to allow him to launch an attack against Asgard but failed. Loki manufactured an incident in which Volstagg of the Warriors Three faced off against the U-Foes in a battle that destroyed Chicago's Soldier Field, killing tens of thousands.

The Sentry destroyed the foundation of Asgard and brought the entire floating city down.

This gave Osborn the excuse he needed to attack Asgard, with or without the President's permission. He sent his Dark Avengers into battle, tricking Ares into leading the charge. When Ares realized he'd been played for a fool, he sought revenge, but on Osborn's orders, the Sentry tore him in half.

Steve Rogers (Captain America) returned from his supposed death and led the Avengers to defend Asgard. Furious, Osborn told the Sentry to destroy the place. Iron Man dismantled the Iron Patriot armor by remote, exposing Osborn's face. He had painted his visage to resemble the Green Goblin and was clearly insane. The Sentry had transformed into his evil alter ego, the Void; Iron Man crashed the HAMMER helicarrier into the Void, and Thor finished the Sentry off at his own request, before the Void could return. The Dark Reign was over.

When Osborn was defeated, his Green Goblin personality rose again.

THE DARK AVENGERS

With the real Avengers on the run, Norman Osborn replaced them with a team of his own, putting villains in the heroes' costumes—and replacing both Iron Man and Captain America himself.

1 *Iron Patriot (Green Goblin)*
2 *Ms. Marvel (Moonstone)*
3 *Captain Marvel (Marvel Boy)*
4 *Ares*
5 *Hawkeye (Bullseye)*
6 *Spider-Man (Mac Gargan as Venom)*
Not pictured: Daken as Wolverine

DEADPOOL

The (unstoppable) Merc with a mouth

DEADPOOL

FACTFILE

REAL NAME
Wade Wilson

OCCUPATION
Mercenary

BASE
Mobile

HEIGHT 6 ft 2 in
WEIGHT 210 lbs
EYES Brown
HAIR None

FIRST APPEARANCE
New Mutants #98 (February 1991)

POWERS
Wade has advanced healing abilities, and is an expert marksman and hand-to-hand combatant. Uses a teleportation device to travel instantly from one place to another.

ALLIES/FOES
ALLIES Mercs for Money, Cable, Avengers Unity Division, Wolverine, SHIELD, Copycat, Heroes for Hire

FOES Tolliver, T-Ray, Bullseye, New Mutants, Juggernaut, Black Tom, Thanos, Skrulls, Norman Osborn, Ajax

ISSUE #1
In his first appearance, Deadpool is introduced as a mysterious and deadly mercenary out to collect a bounty on Cable's head. His assignment is thwarted by the New Mutants, and Deadpool is "mailed" back to his employer, Tolliver.

Diagnosed with cancer, ex-soldier Wade Wilson allowed Weapon X scientists to try and cure him by recreating WOLVERINE's mutant healing factor. The procedure worked, giving Wade advanced regenerative abilities, but it also left him physically and mentally scarred. Adopting the name Deadpool, Wade became an effective if wildly unpredictable mercenary, with a deranged sense of humor and the uncanny ability to sense another world outside his reality.

Wade Wilson's early childhood is shrouded in mystery—a result of the Weapon X program and his own use of mind-wiping drugs.

UNCERTAIN BEGINNINGS

Little is known of Wade Wilson's childhood, largely due to his own conflicting memories and damaged psyche. For a time, he believed his father had abandoned his mother while she was pregnant with him. Later, he thought that his mother had died when he was five, leaving him to cope with an abusive father who was eventually killed by one of Wade's friends. It eventually transpired that this was also untrue, and that his parents were alive and living in Canada, waiting for their son's return.

Wade enlisted in the US Army Special Forces from which he was dishonorably discharged thanks to his rebellious streak. After a stint as a CIA-sponsored mercenary assassin and a spell working undercover in Japan as a sumo wrestler hired to hit a yakuza crimelord, Wade returned to the US. Here he befriended one of his targets, Blind Al, who became a mother-figure to him, and began a relationship with Vanessa Carlysle (*see* COPYCAT). When he learned he had terminal cancer, Wade broke up with Vanessa rather than burden her with his illness, and stopped his chemo treatments.

WEAPON X FACTOR

Wade was given hope when he became a guinea pig for Canada's Weapon X Program, which implanted in him a healing factor derived from another Weapon X subject, Wolverine. With his cancer in temporary remission, Wade became a covert operative for Canada's Department H, but after killing a psychotic teammate, he was sent to the notorious Hospice, where failed experiments were subjected to excruciatingly painful tests. On the verge of dying, Wade fell in love with the physical embodiment of DEATH and became part of a "dead pool" set up by guards, who would bet on the Hospice's next fatality. When Wade survived every test, the sadistic head guard, Ajax, tried to kill him, but the brutal attack accidentally triggered Wade's full healing abilities. He escaped the facility along with other inmates, mockingly adopted the name Deadpool, and returned to his mercenary activities.

ANTI-HERO FOR HIRE

As Deadpool, Wade gained a reputation as a lethal, erratic, and loudmouthed assassin for hire. He worked for KINGPIN, the WIZARD, HAMMERHEAD, and even the Canadian Government, from whom he acquired a teleporation device. He played a crucial role in ending the BEYONDER's Secret Wars, where he became aware of his nature as a fictional character. Sometime later, he was employed by the time-traveling arms dealer Tolliver, who hired him to kill CABLE, the time-displaced mutant soldier, who was, in reality, Tolliver's father. Deadpool was defeated by Cable and his young charges, the NEW MUTANTS, later reorganized as X-FORCE. During a final battle, Tolliver seemingly perished.

Wade Wilson survived horrific experiments during his time at the Weapon X Program and, later, the Hospice for Weapon X rejects. The ordeal changed him forever.

ESSENTIAL STORYLINES

- ***Deadpool Vol.1 #1***
Deadpool comes into his own as the trigger-happy, wise-cracking, off-the-(fourth)-wall breaking "Merc with a mouth."
- ***Deadpool Vol.2 #1***
A darker, weirder Deadpool tries to fight his way into joining the X-Men, runs amok in Las Vegas, and becomes a pirate.
- ***Cable & Deadpool #1–6***
One of Marvel's best "odd couple" team-ups, with the anti-heroes tethered together for some riotous escapades.

Bound together by a teleportation accident, Deadpool and Cable developed a close yet wary friendship that lasted well after the technical glitch had been fixed.

In the aftermath, Deadpool sacrificed some of his healing ability to save mortally wounded Copycat, who had been secretly involved in Tolliver's plan.

Deadpool's next assignments brought him into conflict with Silver Sable, Daredevil, Black Tom, Juggernaut, and Wolverine. A run-in with Bullseye, who took exception to Deadpool muscling in on his turf as Kingpin's "go-to" killer, led Wade to Hellhouse, a mercenary dispatch center. But a string of failures suggested that he might be losing his edge and should perhaps consider a career change. At one of his lowest ebbs, the ghosts of his former fellow Hospice prisoners put him onto a job he couldn't resist—to take out their ex-jailer, Ajax, before he murdered the inmates Wade had once helped escape. Killing his former tormentor got Deadpool back in the game.

CABLE CONNECTION

After a period where Deadpool worked with Heroes for Hire, rejoined the Weapon X program for an upgrade that backfired and temporarily wiped his memory, and set up the ill-fated Agency X, which killed (and resurrected) him, Deadpool once again encountered Cable. Hired to protect the One World Church, Deadpool fought Cable and, during a teleportation glitch, the DNA of both became linked so that neither could teleport without bringing the other along for the ride. Forced to work together, the two developed a testy friendship as Cable's messianic desire to enforce a new era of peace on the world saw them take on the X-Men and the Silver Surfer. Even after the DNA-teleportation link was severed, Wade and Cable still found that their paths regularly crossed, often when they least expected it.

DEADPOOL RISING

Deadpool later got caught up in several largely non-paying misadventures. He sacrificed his life (briefly) to return symbiote-infected dinosaurs to the Savage Land; outwitted the Skrulls during their Secret Invasion of Earth (only for Norman Osborn to steal his glory during the latter's Dark Reign); battled an evil doppelgänger created by a stalker from leftover Deadpool body parts; defeated Thanos after getting embroiled in a love triangle with the Mad Titan and his missing lover Death; and, after having his personality cleansed, managed to stop the malign Axis Avengers from killing the White Skull (Red Skull's inverted counterpart).

It took the death and rebirth of the universe for Deadpool to get his finances back on track. On a wave of rising popularity, Deadpool formed the mercenary group Mercs for Money to extend his brand worldwide. Using profits from merchandising, he also funded the Avengers Unity Division, once again working alongside his long-suffering "buddy," Cable. During Hydra's takeover of the US, Wade was duped by the evil Captain America into killing SHIELD agents Phil Coulson and Emily Preston. Wracked with guilt, Deadpool put a bounty on his own head, but no one managed to bring him in. As a last resort, he took a huge dose of a mind-wiping drug that deleted a large chunk of his memories. He returned to the mercenary game working with former Mercs for Money teammate Negasonic Teenage Warhead.

In an attempt to broaden his brand, Deadpool established a global franchise—Mercs for Money—that traded on his growing appeal.

DEATH

FIRST APPEARANCE *Captain Marvel* #27 (July 1973)
REAL NAME N/A
OCCUPATION Embodies principle of mortality **BASE** Mobile
HEIGHT Varies **WEIGHT** Varies **EYES** Vary **HAIR** Varies
SPECIAL POWERS/ABILITIES Often appears as a cowled skeleton, but has adopted various male and female guises; an arch-manipulator; extent of other powers remains unknown.

Just as the being ETERNITY represents life, so Death symbolizes mortality. Death often chooses to appear in a familiar form to those she visits—so mortals may see her as a human or as a human skeleton, and often in female form. She became intrigued by THANOS when he was young, almost becoming his muse as he sought to impress her. She has also possessed the body of Marlon Chandler. APOCALYPSE named one of his Four Horsemen Death and both WOLVERINE and ANGEL have taken on that role.

DEATHBIRD

FIRST APPEARANCE *Ms. Marvel* #9 (September 1977)
REAL NAME Cal'syee Neramani **OCCUPATION** Adventurer
BASE Shi'ar Empire **HEIGHT** 5 ft 8 in **WEIGHT** 180 lbs
EYES White **HAIR** None; black, purple and blue feathers
SPECIAL POWERS/ABILITIES Flight (18 ft wingspan); vast strength and stamina; razor-sharp talons; wrist-bands contain telescopic javelins; has javelins that emit gas or electric charges.

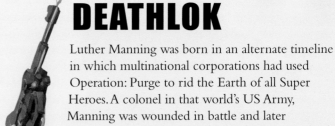

Deathbird was born a mutant into the ruling house of the alien SHI'AR, her full set of wings a remnant of her avian ancestry. Her younger sister Lilandra, aided by the X-MEN, assumed the Shi'ar throne first, and Deathbird attempted several coups to become Majestrix. She eventually won the throne, but her rule was short-lived. She later married VULCAN, who became ruler of the Shi'ar Empire. When Vulcan was killed, Deathbird, who was pregnant, fled, but was captured by the Providian Order. They experimented on her unborn child until she escaped.

DEATHCRY

FIRST APPEARANCE *Avengers* #363 (June 1993)
REAL NAME Sharra Neramani **OCCUPATION** Warrior
BASE The Shi'ar Empire **HEIGHT** 6 ft 2 in **WEIGHT** 196 lbs
EYES White **HAIR** Purple
SPECIAL POWERS/ABILITIES Deathcry possesses super-acute senses, superhuman reflexes, and natural claws which she can use as weapons.

Empress Lilandra of the alien SHI'AR sent Deathcry—the daughter of her sister DEATHBIRD—to help the AVENGERS, fearing they might suffer reprisals by the KREE for helping her during the Kree-Shi'ar War. When Deathcry's mission came to an end, she returned to the Shi'ar Empire. Later, the Kree captured her, releasing her only to help fight the PHALANX. CAPTAIN UNIVERSE accidentally killed her in self-defense, but she returned to life during the Chaos War, calling herself Lifecry. Whether she survived that conflict is unknown.

DEATHLOK

DEATHLOK

FACTFILE
REAL NAME
Luther Manning
OCCUPATION
Cyborg Super-Soldier
BASE Mobile

HEIGHT 6 ft 4 in
WEIGHT 395 lbs
EYES Red
HAIR Gray/brown

FIRST APPEARANCE
Astonishing Tales #25 (August 1974)

POWERS
Cybernetic brain and body parts give superhuman strength, endurance, and reactions; Deathlok's special armaments include a dagger and laser pistol.

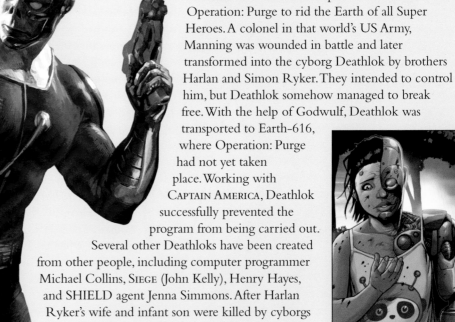

Luther Manning was born in an alternate timeline in which multinational corporations had used Operation: Purge to rid the Earth of all Super Heroes. A colonel in that world's US Army, Manning was wounded in battle and later transformed into the cyborg Deathlok by brothers Harlan and Simon Ryker. They intended to control him, but Deathlok somehow managed to break free. With the help of Godwulf, Deathlok was transported to Earth-616, where Operation: Purge had not yet taken place. Working with CAPTAIN AMERICA, Deathlok successfully prevented the program from being carried out.

Several other Deathloks have been created from other people, including computer programmer Michael Collins, SIEGE (John Kelly), Henry Hayes, and SHIELD agent Jenna Simmons. After Harlan Ryker's wife and infant son were killed by cyborgs from the future, Ryker saved his injured teenage daughter Rebecca by transforming her into the cyborg Death Locket.

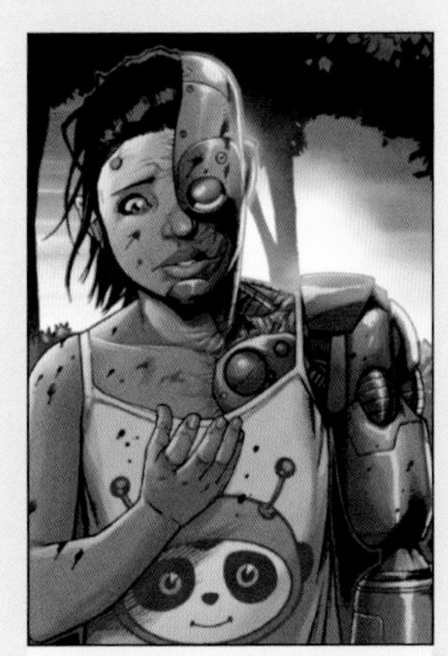

Death Locket is still unsure how to manage her powers, or even if she is really the one in control of them.

DEATH'S HEAD

FACTFILE

REAL NAME
Death's Head

OCCUPATION
Bounty hunter

BASE Mobile

HEIGHT Varies
WEIGHT Varies
EYES Vary
HAIR Varies

FIRST APPEARANCE
The Transformers #113 (May 1987)

POWERS
Superhumanly strong; able to detach limbs and substitute them for weapons; controls limbs even when separated from body; jets in feet enable short-range flight.

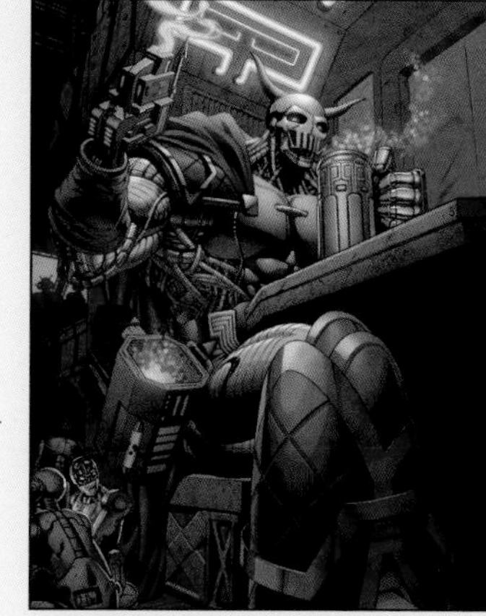

Death's Head's original body was created by Lupex, a psychotic Techno-Mage who wanted a suitable vessel to contain his life force. However Pyra, one of Lupex' enemies, gave the creature its own consciousness. Death's Head set himself up as a bounty hunter—though preferred the term "freelance peacekeeping operative." He worked with the FANTASTIC FOUR, SHE-HULK, IRON MAN, and others. While trying to claim the bounty on Wilson Tyler, Death's Head encountered the Minion cyborg created by AIM's Evelyn Necker. Minion had been created to defeat a future threat and had been programmed to download the abilities of 106 of the Multiverse's deadliest people. Minion seemingly destroyed Death's Head and downloaded his abilities. However, with the help of Reed Richards (*see* MR. FANTASTIC), Death's Head took control of the Minion form and continued as a new-look Death's Head, often working with renegade Tuck. He recently joined forces with his original self and other heroes to stop Killpower bringing hell to Earth.

DE LA FONTAINE, CONTESSA

FIRST APPEARANCE *Strange Tales* #159 (August 1967)
REAL NAME Valentina Allegra de la Fontaine
OCCUPATION Former secret agent **BASE** Mobile
HEIGHT 5 ft 8 in **WEIGHT** 196 lbs
EYES Blue **HAIR** Black with white streak
SPECIAL POWERS/ABILITIES Superb strategist and hand-to-hand combatant; expert with most types of weapons.

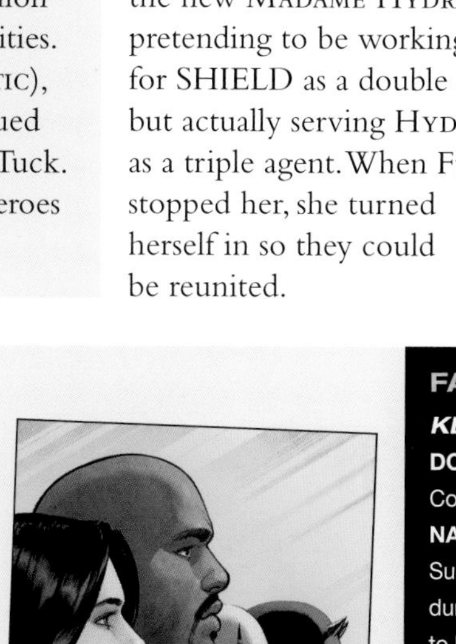

The Contessa caught the eye of Nick FURY by defeating him in hand-to-hand combat during SHIELD training. The two became lovers and teammates, and she later led SHIELD'S Femme Force. At two different times, a SKRULL replaced her temporarily. The Contessa later became the new MADAME HYDRA, pretending to be working for SHIELD as a double agent, but actually serving HYDRA as a triple agent. When Fury stopped her, she turned herself in so they could be reunited.

DEFENDERS

The original Defenders consisted of HULK, NAMOR the Sub-Mariner, and DOCTOR STRANGE. They were a "non-team" who only came together when fate demanded it. Other heroes, such as HELLCAT, NIGHTHAWK, the SILVER SURFER, and VALKYRIE became part of the team at various times. They fought the AVENGERS when LOKI and DORMAMMU manipulated both teams. Under the FIFTY-STATE INITIATIVE, a Defenders team composed of Blazing Skull, COLOSSUS, DARKHAWK, and SHE-HULK guarded New Jersey. The GRANDMASTER later brought together the original team to take on the RED HULK'S Offenders. Valkyrie also gathered an all-female team called the FEARLESS DEFENDERS, which included Anabelle Riggs, CLEA, Dani MOONSTAR, Elsa BLOODSTONE, Misty KNIGHT, and the resurrected goddess Hippolyta, who called herself Warrior Woman. Luke CAGE, who had briefly fought with the original Defenders, formed his own street team of heroes using the name.

When Luke Cage faced a gang war, he teamed up with Iron Fist, Jessica Jones, and Daredevil to bring peace to the streets.

THE DEFENDERS
1 Namor, the Sub-Mariner
2 The Hulk
3 The Silver Surfer
4 Doctor Strange

FACTFILE

KEY MEMBERS

DOCTOR STRANGE
Command of the mystic arts.

NAMOR, THE SUB-MARINER
Superhuman strength and durability; ability to fly; ability to breathe air and also survive beneath the ocean waves.

HULK
Rampaging monster of almost unlimited strength.

SILVER SURFER
Possesses the Power Cosmic—one of the fundamental forces of the universe.

BASE
The Defenders team usually operates out of Doctor Strange's sanctum in Greenwich Village, New York City.

FIRST APPEARANCE
Marvel Feature #1 (December 1971)

DEMOLITION MAN

FIRST APPEARANCE *The Thing* #28 (October 1985)
REAL NAME Dennis Dunphy **OCCUPATION** Adventurer
BASE New York City **HEIGHT** 6 ft 3 in **WEIGHT** 335 lbs
EYES Blue **HAIR** None **SPECIAL POWERS/ABILITIES** Enhanced strength and endurance, damage resistance; expert wrestler; trained in hand-to-hand combat by Captain America.

Given superhuman strength by the corrupt POWER BROKER, Dennis Dunphy became a pro wrestler, during which time he befriended the THING. He later became CAPTAIN AMERICA's unofficial partner as D-Man and even worked with the AVENGERS. His near brushes with death diminished his confidence, and he also struggled with schizophrenia. Dunphy joined the REVENGERS to fight the Avengers and went to jail. After being killed and brought back to life he became Captain America's pilot and mechanic before fighting the Poisons when they invaded Earth.

DESTINY

Born with impaired vision, Destiny's precognitive powers kicked in at the age of 13, and she spent over a year writing down her visions in diaries that were called the Books of Truth. During this time, she became totally blind. She raised ROGUE as her adopted daughter and later became lifelong friends with MYSTIQUE and joined her BROTHERHOOD OF EVIL MUTANTS and FREEDOM FORCE. She was killed by LEGION, who was possessed by the SHADOW KING. She was revived by the Techno-Organic virus long enough to see Rogue and meet her great-granddaughter BLINDFOLD, but died soon afterward. During the Chaos War, Destiny briefly possessed a reanimated Moira MACTAGGART to help defeat Carrion Crow.

DESTINY

FACTFILE
REAL NAME
Irené Adler
OCCUPATION
US government agent
BASE Washington, D.C.

HEIGHT 5 ft 7 in
WEIGHT 110 lbs
EYES Unknown
HAIR Silver

FIRST APPEARANCE
X-Men #141 (January 1981)

POWERS

Mutant power to see future allowed her to scan the probability spectrum of alternate futures, then focus on events before they happened.

DEVIL DINOSAUR

DEVIL DINOSAUR

FACTFILE
REAL NAME
N/A
OCCUPATION
Carnivore
BASE
A jungle on the otherdimensional planet "Dinosaur World," later the Savage Land.

HEIGHT 25 ft
WEIGHT Unknown
EYES Yellow

FIRST APPEARANCE
Devil Dinosaur #1 (April 1978)

POWERS

Has unusually high intelligence for a dinosaur. Possesses immense strength and stamina.

On a planet similar to prehistoric Earth, dinosaurs coexisted with primitive, fur-covered humans. When a tribe called the Killer-Folk tried to burn to death a creature resembling one of Earth's tyrannosaurs, the reptile was rescued by MOON BOY, part of a rival tribe known as Small-Folk. The fire had turned its hide bright red, so Moon Boy named the creature Devil Dinosaur, and the two became loyal companions, battling menaces on their world and beyond. For a time they became stranded on Earth-616 in the Savage Land, but returned to Dinosaur World—only for Moon Boy to be murdered by the Killer-Folk. A young genius from present-day Earth called MOON GIRL used a time machine to let Devil Dinosaur go back in time to save Moon Boy, after which Devil was returned to Earth-616. He teamed up with Moon Girl on some new adventures.

DETROIT STEEL

FIRST APPEARANCE *Invincible Iron Man* #25 (June 2010)
REAL NAME Doug Johnson III **OCCUPATION** Soldier, powered armor pilot **BASE** New York City **HEIGHT** 12 ft
WEIGHT 9,000 lbs **EYES** Blue **HAIR** Blond
SPECIAL POWERS/ABILITIES The Detroit Steel armor grants its wearer durability, strength, and flight. It is armed with a Gatling gun and a chainsaw; some models fire energy blasts.

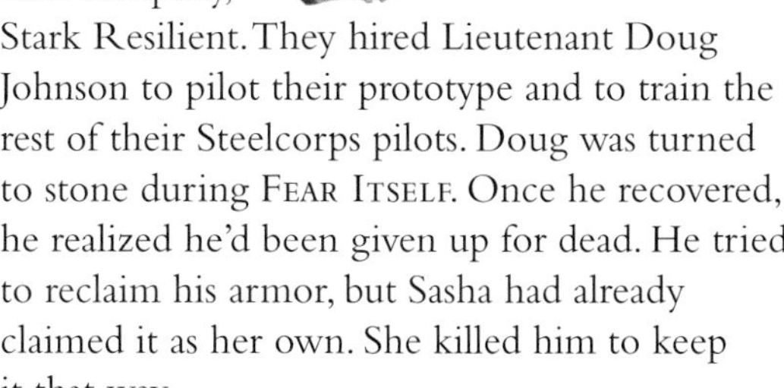

Justine Hammer (Crimson Cowl) and Sasha Hammer designed the Detroit Steel armor to be Hammer Industries' answer to the Iron Man armor of their rival company, Stark Resilient. They hired Lieutenant Doug Johnson to pilot their prototype and to train the rest of their Steelcorps pilots. Doug was turned to stone during Fear Itself. Once he recovered, he realized he'd been given up for dead. He tried to reclaim his armor, but Sasha had already claimed it as her own. She killed him to keep it that way.

DIABLO

FIRST APPEARANCE *Fantastic Four* #30 (September 1964)
REAL NAME Esteban Corazon de Ablo
OCCUPATION Alchemist **BASE** Mobile **HEIGHT** 6 ft 3in
WEIGHT 190 lbs **EYES** Brown **HAIR** Black
SPECIAL POWERS/ABILITIES Alchemical elixir bestows extended life and vitality. Clothing lined with alchemical potions including a sleeping potion and nerve gas; a master of disguise.

Born into the aristocracy in 9th-century Spain, Diablo became fascinated with the alchemical arts. Realizing that time was against him, Diablo sold his soul to the demon Mephisto in exchange for knowledge. Developing an elixir of life and moving to Transylvania, Diablo spent the next millennia tyrannizing the local villagers, until they rose up, trapping him in a crypt for over a century. Having tricked the Thing into freeing him, Diablo clashed with the Fantastic Four numerous times. He has also clashed with Alpha Flight and Spider-Man.

DIGGER

FIRST APPEARANCE *The Amazing Spider-Man* #51 (May 2003)
REAL NAME None (a combination of 13 mobsters)
OCCUPATION None **BASE** New York City sewers
HEIGHT 7 ft 1 in **WEIGHT** 275 lbs **EYES** Blue **HAIR** None
SPECIAL POWERS/ABILITIES Gamma-powered strength, but limited endurance; possesses the combined consciousnesses of the Vegas 13, with their various 1950s predilections.

In 1957, a meeting of 13 mobsters in Las Vegas turned nasty, resulting in their deaths. The bodies of the gangsters, who became known as the Vegas 13, were secretly buried in the Nevada desert. Many years later, scientists detonated a gamma bomb near the site of the grave, the resulting radiation fusing the 13 dead mobsters into a huge, powerful, green zombie who called himself Digger. The creature started on a mission of vengeance against the Forelli mob, who had wiped out the Vegas 13. Hired by Morris Forelli to investigate, Spider-Man figured out Digger's identity, and during a battle between the two of them, Digger finally broke apart and died.

DESTROYER

FIRST APPEARANCE *Journey into Mystery* #118 (July 1965)
REAL NAME None **OCCUPATION** Destroyer
BASE Asgard **HEIGHT** 6 ft 2 in (varies)
WEIGHT 850 lbs (varies) **EYES** None **HAIR** None
SPECIAL POWERS/ABILITIES The Destroyer can levitate, generate fire, transmute matter, and shoot a disintegrator beam from its face. It is nearly indestructible.

Odin, the All-Father of the Gods of Asgard, created the Destroyer as the ultimate weapon to be used against the Celestials when they returned to Earth to judge it. He and the other gods granted it a portion of their power. It has no soul of its own and must be operated by the life force of another, plunging that person into a coma. Loki unearthed the Destroyer to use against Thor, and others have controlled it since. When used against the Celestials, they nearly destroyed it. Doctor Doom once made his own version.

DIAMONDBACK

FIRST APPEARANCE *Hero for Hire* #1 (June 1972)
REAL NAME Willis Stryker **OCCUPATION** Criminal
BASE Harlem, New York **HEIGHT** 6 ft 4 in
WEIGHT 200 lbs **EYES** Brown **HAIR** Black
SPECIAL POWERS/ABILITIES Diamond drug bestows superhuman strength, speed, and durability; expert knife thrower; skilled street fighter

Two villains have taken the name Diamondback. Willis Stryker was a close friend of Carl Lucas (Luke Cage) before framing Carl when he grew jealous of his relationship with Reva Connors. Stryker gained the name Diamondback due to his skill with poisoned knives. He became a member of the criminal group the Syndicate, often battling Luke Cage. Rachel Leighton has also gone by the name Diamondback. A member of the Serpent Society, she was an occasional ally of Captain America before becoming a mercenary. During the Dark Reign she helped the Secret Avengers, and she later joined SHIELD.

DIMITRIOS

FIRST APPEARANCE *Avengers A.I.* #2 (October 2013)
REAL NAME Dimitrios **OCCUPATION** Evil sentient virus
BASE Mobile **HEIGHT** Variable
WEIGHT Variable **EYES** Variable **HAIR** Variable
SPECIAL POWERS/ABILITIES Control and manipulation of mechanical systems; in digital form can rapidly duplicate himself and spread through any cyber network.

Dimitrios came into being as a computer virus created by Hank Pym in order to destroy the malicious A.I. Ultron. Unfortunately the virus became sentient and launched cyber attacks across the world. SHIELD tasked Monica Chang with creating a new Avengers team, dubbed "Avengers A.I.," to locate and stop the threat. Dimitrios used a rejected suit of Iron Man armor as his own body and took control of machines, including the devastating Kilgore Sentinel, to launch attacks across the world. He sought to wipe out all organic life until the Avengers A.I. managed to end his plans.

DOCTOR BONG

FIRST APPEARANCE *Howard the Duck* #15 (August 1977)
REAL NAME Lester Verde **OCCUPATION** Genetic engineer
BASE An island in the Atlantic Ocean **HEIGHT** 8 ft 8 in
WEIGHT 225 lbs **EYES** Blue **HAIR** Reddish-brown
SPECIAL POWERS/ABILITIES When struck by the large metal ball he wears on his hand, Doctor Bong's helmet can produce sonic waves for a variety of effects.

Bullied as a youth, Lester Verde became a tabloid journalist to strike back at his foes with his sensational articles. After losing his left hand while covering a rock concert, Lester reinvented himself as Doctor Bong, a villain whose exploits he promoted with self-penned press releases. Intent on forcing Beverly Switzler to marry him, Bong was undone by Beverly's boyfriend, Howard the Duck, and by Switzler creating quintuplet clones of him and threatening to expose him as a deadbeat dad. He later battled She-Hulk and faced off against Deadpool, who cut off his prosthetic metal ball hand.

DOCTOR FAUSTUS

FIRST APPEARANCE *Captain America* #107 (November 1968)
REAL NAME Johann Fennhoff
OCCUPATION Psychiatrist; criminal mastermind
BASE New York City
HEIGHT 6 ft 6 in **WEIGHT** 321 lbs **EYES** Blue **HAIR** Red
SPECIAL POWERS/ABILITIES Expert in brainwashing and mind control.

A master psychiatrist, Doctor Faustus drives people to the brink of suicide and beyond. He clashed often with Captain America, Spider-Man, and the Fantastic Four. He also mentored Moonstone, schooling her in the arts of manipulation. Presumed dead for years, he returned, allying himself with the Red Skull and posing as a SHIELD psychiatrist. In this position, he brainwashed Sharon Carter into killing Captain America. Faustus held the Captain America of the 1950s in suspended animation for years, releasing him to attack the then-current Captain America (Bucky Barnes). He was part of Hydra's High Council during their takeover of the US, using his hypnotic skills to help the evil Steve Rogers keep SHIELD agents on his side.

DOC SAMSON

FACTFILE
REAL NAME
Dr. Leonard Samson
OCCUPATION
Psychiatrist
BASE
Mobile

HEIGHT 6 ft 6 in
WEIGHT 380 lbs
EYES Blue
HAIR Green

FIRST APPEARANCE
Incredible Hulk #141 (July 1971)

POWERS
Gamma radiation greatly increased Samson's body mass and musculature; he has the equivalent strength of a "relaxed" Hulk, plus great endurance and injury resistance. The gamma rays also turned his hair green. Unlike the Hulk, Samson's razor-sharp mind has been unaffected by the changes in his physiology.

A dedicated psychiatrist, Doctor Leonard Samson was fascinated by gamma radiation's potential to help the mentally ill. When Betty Ross was transformed into a crystalline creature, Samson used a specially developed machine to drain gamma radiation from the Hulk and used it to cure Betty. Later, he exposed himself to the rays and gained Hulk-like powers. Samson doggedly pursued Bruce Banner, hoping to rid him of the Hulk. He also helped treat several others, including Molecule Man, She-Hulk, Rachel Summers, and Multiple Man. He sided with the US government during the Civil War and worked as a therapist at Camp Hammond. He helped the Illuminati send the Hulk into space and fought him when he returned during World War Hulk. Later, MODOK brainwashed him into developing an evil secondary personality that was stronger than ever. Samson died helping the Hulk save lives, but was resurrected during the Chaos War.

DOCTOR NEMESIS

FIRST APPEARANCE *Invaders* #1 (May 1993)
REAL NAME James Nicola Bradley **OCCUPATION** Inventor
BASE Asgard **HEIGHT** 5 ft 11 in **WEIGHT** 170 lbs
EYES Blue **HAIR** Blond
SPECIAL POWERS/ABILITIES James is a mutant genius who used his gift to grant himself longevity, an enhanced immune system, and cybernetic X-ray eyes.

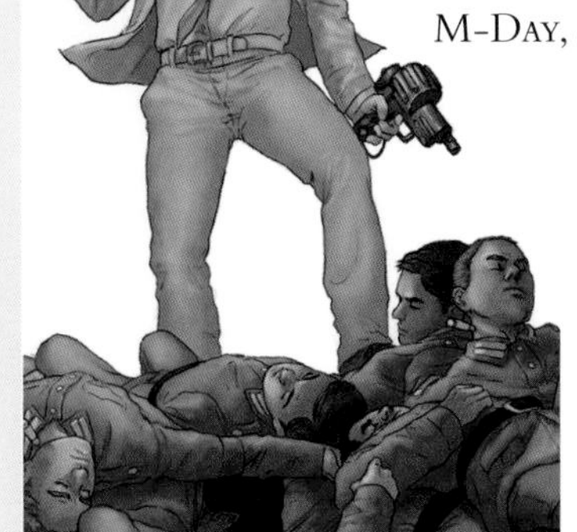

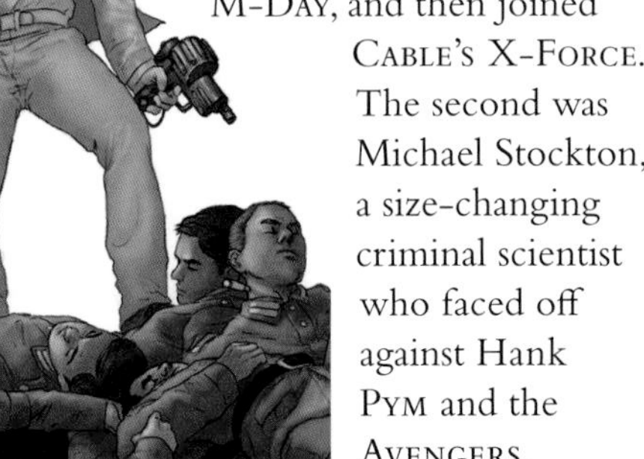

Two men have used the name Doctor Nemesis. The first was a mutant who helped create the original Human Torch and his own android, Volton. He worked with the Nazis during World War II as Doctor Death but repented and turned to hunting Nazi scientists after the war. He later joined the X-Men to help them figure out how to restore mutantkind after M-Day, and then joined Cable's X-Force. The second was Michael Stockton, a size-changing criminal scientist who faced off against Hank Pym and the Avengers.

DOCTOR DOOM

The lord of Latveria

Victor von Doom was born in a Romani camp in the tiny kingdom of Latveria in the Balkan Mountains of Eastern Europe. Victor's mother, Cynthia, was killed when he was an infant. When Victor was a boy, his father Werner, a healer, failed to save the wife of a Latverian baron from dying of cancer. With Victor, Werner fled the baron's retaliation, only to perish from cold. Victor survived and vowed vengeance on the world for his parents' deaths.

A mysterious order of Tibetan monks helped Doctor Doom forge the metal mask with which he conceals his hideously scarred features.

FACTFILE

REAL NAME
Victor von Doom

OCCUPATION
Monarch of Latveria

BASE
Doomstadt, Latveria

HEIGHT 6 ft 2 in; (in armor) 6 ft 7 in
WEIGHT 225 lbs; (in armor) 415 lbs
EYES Brown
HAIR Brown

FIRST APPEARANCE
Fantastic Four #5 (July 1962)

POWERS
Scientific genius; knowledge of sorcery. Learned from alien Ovoids how to psychically transfer his consciousness into the body of another person. Armor is actually a battlesuit that increases his strength to superhuman levels and contains highly advanced weaponry.

SCARRED

Victor discovered his mother's chest of magical artifacts and realized that she had been a witch. He developed immense talents for sorcery and also science, eventually winning a scholarship to State University in the US. There he first encountered fellow student Reed Richards (*see* MISTER FANTASTIC).

Resolving to contact his mother in the hereafter, he invented an interdimensional communication device. Richards happened upon Doom's notes and pointed out an error in his calculations. Furious that Richards had invaded his privacy, Doom refused to heed his warning. When Doom activated his machine it exploded, scarring his face. (According to one account the explosion left only one thin scar; however, Doom's ego could not tolerate a single imperfection in his appearance.)

THE METAL MASK

Blaming Richards for the accident, Doom made his way to Tibet, where an order of monks helped him forge the metal mask and armor that he would wear in his new role as Doctor Doom. Donning the newly cast mask before it had fully cooled, Doom further scarred his face for life. Returning to Latveria, Doom overthrew the monarch and made himself king. As ruler of Latveria, Doom has diplomatic immunity to shield him from many laws. In this role, he invented many devices, including an army of Doombots and a time machine. He also adopted a young orphan (Kristoff VERNARD), who steps in to rule when Doom is absent. Doom became part of the CABAL but left over differences with Norman Osborn (*see* GREEN GOBLIN).

Doctor Doom led an army of Super Villains on the Beyonder's Battleworld in the first "Secret War."

DOOMED HERO

In the most recent SECRET WARS, when incursions from other Earths threatened reality, Doom, working with MOLECULE MAN and DOCTOR STRANGE, salvaged portions of reality as a new Battleworld. A godlike Doom installed himself as ruler, with Sue Richards (*see* INVISIBLE WOMAN) as his wife, and Valeria and Franklin RICHARDS as his children. When Reed Richards, who'd survived the destruction of his reality, appeared on Battleworld, Doom's control began to slip until he was defeated. When Reed recreated reality with his family and Molecule Man, he healed Doom's scarred face, giving him the chance of a new life. For a time, Doom acted as a hero, even becoming IRON MAN when Tony Stark was incapacitated. However, when Doom was scarred again while fighting the HOOD, he retreated to his castle. There he was asked by Zora Vokuvic to help restore Latveria to its former glory. Doom donned his mask and went to war: Doctor Doom was back.

As the creator of his own new Battleworld, Doom presided over a remade reality with Sue, Valeria, and Franklin Richards at his side.

ESSENTIAL STORYLINES

- ***Fantastic Four #5***
Doctor Doom first clashes with the world's greatest team.
- ***Fantastic Four Annual #2***
The origin of Doctor Doom.
- ***Fantastic Four #39–40***
Doctor Doom battles the Fantastic Four without their powers.
- ***Fantastic Four #57–60***
Doom steals the power of the Silver Surfer.
- ***Fantastic Four #84–87***
Doctor Doom traps the Fantastic Four in Latveria.

DOCTOR DRUID

FACTFILE
REAL NAME
Dr. Anthony Ludgate Druid
OCCUPATION
Psychiatrist and master of the occult
BASE Mobile

HEIGHT 6 ft 5 in
WEIGHT 310 lbs
EYES Green
HAIR White

FIRST APPEARANCE
Amazing Adventures #1 (June 1961)

POWERS
Master of the mystical arts; able to control his heartbeat, respiration, bleeding, etc; can undertake telepathy, scan thoughts, control minds of others, and levitate objects.

DOCTOR DRUID

Harvard-educated Anthony Druid pursued a career as a psychiatrist, while harboring an interest in all things mystical and occult. Growing older, he began to devote more and more time to this area but it was only when called to the side of a dying Tibetan lama that he started to develop his abilities. After Druid survived a number of trials, the lama helped him to realize his latent potential while conferring upon him some of his own powers.

Druid was later recruited by NSA agent Jake Curtiss to join his team of Monster Hunters—a team that also included Ulysses BLOODSTONE and the Eternal Makkari (*see* ETERNALS). Following the emergence of Super Heroes like the FANTASTIC FOUR, Druid aligned himself with the AVENGERS.

Druid was manipulated into betraying his friends twice. He was held in the thrall of Terminatrix (*see* RAVONNA) and later corrupted by his manipulative lover, NEKRA, who killed him. He was resurrected temporarily during the Chaos War to join the Avengers in fighting Nekra and the GRIM REAPER. He then found himself on Weirdworld, where he could maintain corporeal form and control others.

A powerful sorcerer, Doctor Druid could project images of himself.

DOCTOR SPECTRUM

FACTFILE
REAL NAME
Joseph Ledger
OCCUPATION
Squadron Supreme member
BASE
Squadron City

HEIGHT 6 ft
WEIGHT 190 lbs
EYES Brown
HAIR Blond

FIRST APPEARANCE
Avengers #85 (March 1971)

POWERS
Internalized power prism allows flight, the discharge of energy blasts, and the ability to construct objects of solid energy.

DOCTOR SPECTRUM

There have been several Doctor Spectrums, each coming from a parallel Earth; some have been heroes and others villains. On one parallel Earth, astronaut Joe Ledger rescued an alien SKRULL who gave him a power prism. Using the prism's energies to become the heroic Doctor Spectrum, Ledger joined the SQUADRON SUPREME. After the defeat of the villainous OVERMIND, the Squadron Supreme repaired the damage to their world by becoming virtual dictators.

A second group of heroes, known as Nighthawk's Redeemers, formed a resistance movement. One of their number, the Black Archer (formerly the GOLDEN ARCHER), shattered Doctor Spectrum's power prism with an arrow, only to watch as its energies became part of Ledger's own body. A female Doctor Spectrum later joined an incarnation of the Squadron Supreme made up of heroes from lost universes.

Various versions of Doctor Spectrum, and other Squadron Supreme members, exist among the parallel Earths that compose the Multiverse.

DOCTOR OCTOPUS

Mastermind of mechanical menace

Otto was the son of Torbert and Mary Lavinia Octavius. He was a shy bookworm, but his father, a construction worker, believed that a man was measured by his brute strength. Mary Lavinia wanted Otto to rely on his brains, and when his father was killed in a construction accident, she convinced Otto that an early grave was the destiny of all manual laborers.

Doc Ock can use his tentacles simultaneously, with each one performing a different action.

FACTFILE

REAL NAME
Otto Octavius

OCCUPATION
Criminal mastermind, former nuclear scientist

BASE
New York area

HEIGHT 5 ft 9 in
WEIGHT 245 lbs
EYES Brown
HAIR Brown

FIRST APPEARANCE
Amazing Spider-Man #3 (July 1963)

DOCTOR OCTOPUS

POWERS

Mental control over four electrically powered, 6-ft-long, prehensile, titanium steel tentacles that can telescope to 24 ft in length and lift 3 tons; tentacles terminate in three single-jointed pincers that can rotate 360 degrees and grip with a force of 170 lbs per sq in.

ESSENTIAL STORYLINES

- ***Amazing Spider-Man Annual #1*** Octopus forms the Sinister Six to kill Spider-Man.
- ***Spectacular Spider-Man #221*** He appears to be killed by Peter Parker clone Kaine.
- ***Amazing Spider-Man #426*** Doc Ock is restored to life thanks to his protégée Carolyn Trainer.

ARM'S LENGTH

Otto became a scientist specializing in nuclear research, and invented a mechanical harness of four metallic arms that allowed him to perform dangerous experiments at a distance. He also began dating Mary Alice Anders, a fellow researcher, and even asked her to marry him. Believing that no woman was good enough for her son, Otto's mother forced him to break off the engagement. Shortly afterward, she died of a heart attack while arguing with her son over Mary Alice. Lost in a private world of grief and guilt, Otto caused a laboratory accident: he was bombarded with radiation and his mechanical arms somehow fused with his body.

MIND CONTROL

Able to mentally control his metal tentacles, even when separated from them, Otto became Doctor Octopus and battled Spider-Man and others both alone and as part of the Sinister Six. Over the years, his body deteriorated to the point that death seemed near. Desperate, Octopus managed to swap his mind with that of Peter Parker (Spider-Man) before his health failed, seemingly killing his enemy and taking over his body to become the Superior Spider-Man. With his new lease on life, he gave up his villainy and struggled to become a better hero than Parker had ever managed.

After many adventures, Otto became part of the Spider-Army to take on Morlun. He then seemingly gave up his body to allow Peter to take back control and defeat the Green Goblin and his Goblin Nation. While part of the Spider-Army, Otto had backed up his consciousness. This ended up in the android known as the Living Brain, but he soon found a clone of his original body to transfer into, thanks to the Jackal (Ben Reilly). The two villains came to blows when the Jackal was cruel to scientist (and Peter Parker's tutor) Anna Maria Marconi, whom Otto had developed feelings for. Otto's consciousness again escaped death—this time into a perfect cloned body of Peter. After saving Aunt May from the Red Goblin, Otto made peace with Spider-Man.

Taking over his foe's body, Otto tried to remake himself into a superior man—and Spider-Man!

DOCTOR STRANGE

Sorcerer Supreme of Earth's dimension

DOCTOR STRANGE

FACTFILE

REAL NAME
Dr. Stephen Vincent Strange

OCCUPATION
Former surgeon, now Sorcerer Supreme of Earth's dimension

BASE
177A Bleecker St., Greenwich Village, Manhattan

HEIGHT 6 ft 2 in
WEIGHT 180 lbs
EYES Gray
HAIR Black; white at temples

FIRST APPEARANCE
Strange Tales #110 (July 1963)

POWERS
Greater mastery of the arts of magic than anyone else in Earth's dimension; astral projection and mental communication. Possesses various magical paraphernalia, including cloak of levitation which enables him to fly, and amulet the Eye of Agamotto.

Doctor Stephen Strange was a highly successful but arrogant surgeon whose brilliant career was abruptly cut short by a car accident. He suffered nerve damage to his hands that left him unable to work as a surgeon. Desperate for a cure, he went to Tibet to meet a healer known as the Ancient One. When Strange discovered the Ancient One's pupil Baron Mordo intended to murder his master, Mordo cast a spell on Strange that prevented him from warning the Ancient One. The Ancient One revealed that he was already aware of Mordo's treachery, and Strange became his new pupil.

Strange had a long relationship with the mystic Clea, taking her on as his pupil until she returned to her home dimension to fight Dormammu.

SORCERER SUPREME

Upon finishing his training, Doctor Strange lived in New York City's Greenwich Village protecting humanity from supernatural menaces such Mordo, Nightmare, and Dormammu. When the Ancient One died, Doctor Strange inherited his role as Sorcerer Supreme of Earth. Strange later co-founded the Defenders and the Illuminati, and often helps the Avengers. Because of his use of dark magic on desperate occasions, Strange temporarily lost his position as the Sorcerer Supreme. Brother Voodoo assumed the mantle for a time, but after Voodoo's death, Strange proved he could handle black magic without losing control and won back his title.

While in space trying to find new sources of magic, Strange encountered the Super Skrull.

STRANGE TIMES

Strange survived the destruction of reality, helping Doctor Doom to create Battleworld. Following its obliteration, he faced one of his greatest challenges when the Empirikul arrived on Earth intent on wiping out magic. They nearly succeeded, and Strange only just managed to stop them. While fighting the Empirikul, it was revealed that all of Strange's pain and misery had, over time, been magically transferred into a creature in the cellar of Strange's Sanctum. The creature took on a more lifelike form after the Empirikul were destroyed, called itself Mister Misery, and sought revenge on Strange before it was defeated. When Strange mysteriously lost his magical abilities, he ventured into space to find magic on other worlds, in order to make himself once more worthy of the title Sorcerer Supreme.

ESSENTIAL STORYLINES
- ***Strange Tales #130–146*** Doctor Strange battles Baron Mordo and Dormammu and first meets Eternity
- ***Strange Tales #150–168*** Doctor Strange first combats Umar and encounters the Living Tribunal.
- ***Doctor Strange Vol. 2 #1–2, 4–5*** Doctor Strange battles Silver Dagger, dies, and is resurrected.

DOMINO

FIRST APPEARANCE *X-Force* #8 (March 1992)
REAL NAME Neena Thurman (many aliases include "Beatrice")
OCCUPATION Covert operative **BASE** Mobile
HEIGHT 5 ft 8 in **WEIGHT** 196 lbs
EYES Blue **HAIR** Black
SPECIAL POWERS/ABILITIES Able to influence the laws of probability to shift odds in her favor; weapons expert; her staff fires projectiles; a superb athlete, martial artist, and linguist.

A career mercenary during her early adult life, it was only after being employed as a bodyguard to the genius Milo Thurman that the mutant Domino became drawn into more official circles. She and Milo fell in love, only to be separated when an attack by AIM terrorists forced Milo into deeper cover. Believing that Milo was dead, Domino joined SIX-PACK and became an ally of CABLE. For a while she was impersonated by COPYCAT. Domino has since served with X-FACTOR, worked for the Hong Kong branch of X-Corporation, and fought alongside the X-MEN. She is now a member of the WEAPON X-FORCE team.

DORA MILAJE

The Dora Milaje or "Adored Ones" were an ancient tradition in Wakanda. When the nation had an unmarried king, each tribe sent their best female warrior to be one of the Dora Milaje: the king's bodyguards and potential wives. T'Challa (BLACK PANTHER) reinstated their position to help ease tensions in the kingdom. The first two chosen were Nakia and Okoye. The new Dora Milaje represented the finest, fiercest female warriors in Wakanda, and their ranks grew as they defended the nation from countless threats. When two of their number, Ayo and Aneka, rebelled, it started a near revolution in Wakandan society.

While the Dora Milaje helped to defeat the terrorist group called the People, they also managed to effect political change in Wakanda, with T'Challa turning the country into a constitutional monarchy.

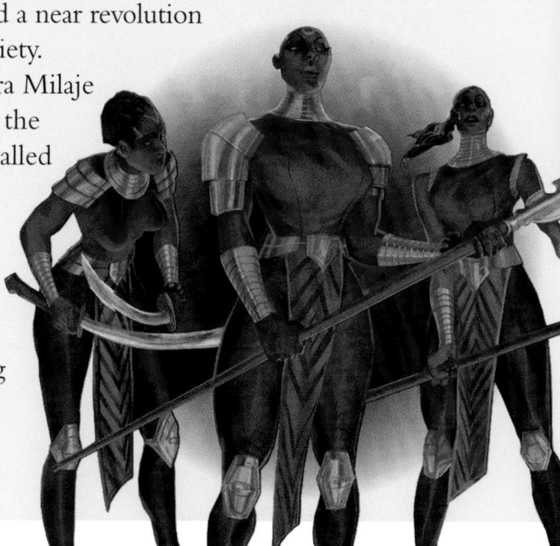

FACTFILE
NOTABLE MEMBERS AND POWERS
DALIA, LULU, NAILAH, NAREEMA, and **ONYEKA** are supremely skilled combatants and trained to use various weapons. **ANEKA, AYO,** and **TEELA** are members of the Midnight Angels, an elite Dora Milaje strike force.
BASE
Wakanda

FIRST APPEARANCE
Black Panther #1 (November 1998)

DORA MILAJE

ALLIES/FOES

ALLIES T'Challa (Black Panther), Shuri, Queen Mother Ramonda, Hatut Zeraze, Manifold, Storm, White Tiger

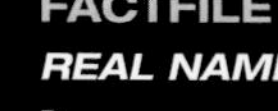

FOES Batroc the Leaper, the Desturi, Doctor Doom, Hydra, Klaw, Cape-Killers, White Gorilla Army

DOOP

FIRST APPEARANCE *X-Force* #116 (July 2001)
REAL NAME Doop **OCCUPATION** Former cameraman
BASE Xavier Institute for Mutant Education and Outreach
HEIGHT Variable, usually around 3 ft **WEIGHT** Variable
SPECIAL POWERS/ABILITIES Levitation; auxillary brain; superhuman strength; speaks a strange language only intelligible to those in close proximity.

Doop's past is shrouded in mystery, though he was part of a Cold War weapons project and is believed to have helped to bring about the fall of the Eastern Bloc. Doop joined X-FORCE (later X-STATIX) as their videographer and soon became one of the team's most popular members, boasting a line of merchandise based on himself. Doop notably has a back-up brain in his lower body. Though he seemingly died alongside his teammates in a hail of bullets, he later returned from space after M-Day. Doop has known WOLVERINE for some time and joined the Jean Grey School for Higher Learning during Logan's time as leader. Doop has also had a romantic relationship with Warbird and has asked Kitty PRYDE to marry him.

DORMAMMU

Although a member of the Faltine race, Dormammu has spent most of his life in the Dark Dimension, to which his people had banished him. Following his arrival there, Dormammu allied himself to the Dark Dimension's ruler, Olnar, showing him how to expand his realm by absorbing other pocket universes into it. Inadvertently, this was to precipitate Dormammu's rise to power. One of these universes was occupied by the Mindless Ones, destructive beings that, once released in the Dark Dimension, began to wreak havoc. Before they were finally stopped, Olnar was killed and Dormammu had been named regent.

Dormammu set his sights on conquering Earth but the ANCIENT ONE and, later, DOCTOR STRANGE and his heroic friends foiled him, trapping him in a pocket universe for a time. He often works by proxy and, for instance, granted the HOOD his powers. He later took over Limbo and commanded that, too.

His niece CLEA ruled the Dark Dimension in his absence and led the resistance against his reclaimed governance.

FACTFILE
REAL NAME
Dormammu
OCCUPATION
Sometime ruler of the Dark Dimension
BASE
Dark Dimension

HEIGHT 6 ft 1 in
WEIGHT Unknown
EYES Green
HAIR Black

FIRST APPEARANCE
Strange Tales #126 (November 1964)

DORMAMMU

POWERS

One of the most powerful mystical beings in the universe; can teleport between dimensions, alter his size, travel in time, and perform telepathy.

Only Doctor Strange stands in the way of Dormammu's domination of the Dark Dimension and a strike against the Earth itself.

DRACULA

The most powerful vampire on Earth

DRACULA

FACTFILE

REAL NAME
Vlad Tepes Dracula

OCCUPATION
Ruler of Earth's vampires

BASE
Castle Dracula, Transylvania; otherwise mobile

HEIGHT 6 ft 5 in
WEIGHT 220 lbs
EYES Red
HAIR White (formerly black)

FIRST APPEARANCE
Tomb of Dracula #1 (April 1972)

POWERS

Drains blood from victims by biting, enabling him to control their wills. Those who die become vampires. Has superhuman strength, virtual immortality, and cannot be killed by conventional means. Transforms into a bat, wolf, or mist. Can mentally control other vampires and mesmerize human beings.

Vlad Tepes Dracula was born in 1430 in Schassberg, Transylvania. The following year his father, the Transylvanian nobleman Vlad Dracul, became prince of nearby Wallachia. Dracula's father was later assassinated by other Transylvanians. Dracula nevertheless went through with the marriage his father had arranged with Zofia, a Hungarian noblewoman. After the birth of their daughter, Dracula put an end to their marriage. Zofia committed suicide; her daughter would become the vampiress Lilith.

THE IMPALER

Dracula regained the throne of Wallachia in 1456 and had those responsible for his father's assassination impaled. He then fought a war with the Turks, during which he impaled huge numbers of them. Hence Dracula became known as "Vlad the Impaler." Dracula married his second wife, Maria, who bore him a son, Vlad Tepelus.

In 1459, Dracula was defeated in battle by the Turkish warlord Turac, who mortally wounded him. Turac took Dracula to the Romani healer Lianda, who proved to be a vampiress. She bit and killed Dracula, transforming him into a vampire. After Turac murdered Maria, Dracula slew him and turned his son Vlad Tepelus over to the care of gypsies. By defeating the vampire Nimrod, Dracula took his place as the ruler of Earth's vampires. The eldest vampire on Earth, VARNAE, enhanced Dracula's blood with his own before killing himself. As a result Dracula became the most powerful vampire on the planet.

LOOK!
MOTHER OF MINE--
I'VE FINALLY DONE IT--
I'VE KILLED DRACULA!

Dracula's most persistent modern adversaries were the team of (from left to right) Quincy Harker, Frank Drake, Rachel Van Helsing, and Blade.

KING OF THE VAMPIRES

In 1890, Dracula moved to England but ran afoul of vampire hunter Abraham Van Helsing and his friends. They pursued him as he fled back to Transylvania and seemingly killed him. However, Dracula has repeatedly returned from death. In modern times, Dracula's main foes have been Quincy Harker (the son of two of his old enemies in the UK), Rachel VAN HELSING (Abraham's descendant), Frank DRAKE (Dracula's own descendant), the vampire hunter BLADE, the vampire detective Hannibal KING, and the monster hunter Elsa BLOODSTONE.

Dracula, along with all the other vampires on Earth, was destroyed when DOCTOR STRANGE cast the Montesi Formula. He returned to form a vampire colony on the moon and tried to conquer the UK. Old Man Logan (a version of WOLVERINE from an alternate future) finally confronted and killed Dracula, and arranged for Dracula's severed head to be thrown into the sun.

ESSENTIAL STORYLINES

- ***Dracula Lives #2–3*** How Count Dracula first became a vampire.
- ***Tomb of Dracula #64–70*** Dracula becomes human again. After regaining his powers, Dracula and Quincy Harker die in their final confrontation.
- ***X-Men: Curse of the Mutants Saga*** Dracula's son, Xarus, kills him and then goes after the X-Men, who revive him to help save the world.

DRAGON MAN

FIRST APPEARANCE *Fantastic Four* #1 (February 1965)
REAL NAME Dragon Man
OCCUPATION None **BASE** Mobile
HEIGHT 15 ft 3 in **WEIGHT** 3.2 tons **EYES** Gray **HAIR** None
SPECIAL POWERS/ABILITIES Possesses colossal natural strength. He can exhale flame from his mouth, and his gigantic wings enable him to fly.

An artificial life-form created by Professor Gregson Gilbert of State University and brought to life by Diablo the alchemist, Dragon Man has the intelligence of a dog. He has been used as a pawn by various Super Villains, including Diablo himself, wealthy industrialist Gregory Gideon, and Machinesmith. But Dragon Man is not evil himself—he operates strictly by animal instinct. The Fantastic Four have often tried to help Dragon Man, and Mister Fantastic upgraded him so he could join the Future Foundation.

DRAGON OF THE MOON

FIRST APPEARANCE *The New Defenders* #143 (May 1985)
REAL NAME Unrevealed **OCCUPATION** Demon
BASE Mobile **HEIGHT** Unknown **WEIGHT** Unknown
EYES Red **SCALES** Dark blue
SPECIAL POWERS/ABILITIES The Dragon is a virtually immortal, demonic entity with godlike powers; able to influence other beings to commit evil deeds.

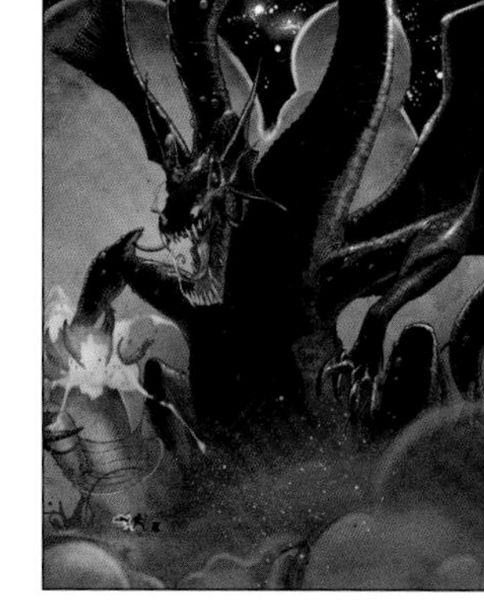

A billion-year-old demonic being, the Dragon of the Moon seeks to corrupt the human race. The Dragon once allied with Mordred, who was trying to overthrow King Arthur Pendragon of Britain. The Dragon was defeated and imprisoned within Saturn's moon, Titan, by the Eternals. It also corrupted Moondragon, whom Ultron killed. Later, Phyla-Vell (*see* Quasar) entered Oblivion to free Moondragon and destroy the Dragon.

DRAKE, FRANK

FIRST APPEARANCE *Tomb of Dracula* #1 (April 1972)
REAL NAME Frank Drake
OCCUPATION Private Investigator; former vampire hunter
BASE Boston, Massachusetts
HEIGHT 6 ft **WEIGHT** 165 lbs **EYES** Blue **HAIR** Blond
SPECIAL POWERS/ABILITIES Adept at hand-to-hand fighting and a fair marksman.

A distant descendent of Dracula, Frank Drake led a life dogged by his vampiric ancestor. After frittering his considerable inheritance away, all Drake had left was his family's castle in Transylvania. Traveling there with the aim of selling up, Drake accidentally resurrected Dracula. The following years were marked by a series of battles against the undead fiend. He fought alongside many other vampire hunters, including Blade, Rachel Van Helsing, and Quincy Harker. He tried to retire but returned to the fight with a nanotech gun he called Linda. This he overloaded to destroy the vampire lord Varnae, nearly killing himself in the process.

DRAX THE DESTROYER

Mentor, the powerful Titanian, had been monitoring the reckless actions of his mad son Thanos on Earth. When Thanos destroyed a car containing Arthur Douglas and his wife and daughter, Mentor took Douglas' daughter Heather, who was still alive, back to Titan to be raised. She would later return to Earth as Moondragon. Then, with the aid of his father, Chronos, Mentor took the living consciousness of Arthur Douglas before it had completely left his body and placed it into a humanoid body he had created from the Earth's soil, granting it superhuman powers. This new being was known as Drax the Destroyer. Mentor blocked all of Douglas' human memories and instilled in him a single-minded desire to destroy Thanos. Drax clashed with Thanos several times, both of them dying on occasion and being resurrected. Eventually, Drax learned who he was and reunited with Moondragon, and he and his daughter fought alongside each other through the Annihilation events. Today, Drax is part of the new Guardians of the Galaxy.

Drax pauses after his latest session of carnage, plotting the next steps in his all-consuming quest to completely destroy Thanos.

FACTFILE

REAL NAME
Arthur Douglas

OCCUPATION
Former real estate agent; agent of Chronos

BASE
Titan

HEIGHT 6 ft 4 in
WEIGHT 680 lbs
EYES Red
HAIR None

FIRST APPEARANCE
Iron Man #55 (February 1973)

POWERS

Cosmic energy gives him superhuman strength, invulnerability, and the ability to fly and make interplanetary voyages in a matter of weeks. He can survive for an indefinite time in outer space without air, food, or water. He fires concussive blasts from his hands.

DREADKNIGHT

FIRST APPEARANCE *Iron Man* #101 (August 1977)
REAL NAME Bram Velsing
OCCUPATION Engineer; vengeful vigilante **BASE** Mobile
HEIGHT 5 ft 8 in **WEIGHT** 160 lbs **EYES** Red **HAIR** None
SPECIAL POWERS/ABILITIES High-tech suit of armor protects him from attack. Within his arsenal are a lance containing a number of offensive weapons, and a nerve-gas pistol.

Born in Latveria, Bram Velsing was a skilled engineer, carrying out the schemes of Doctor Doom. As punishment for an act of disobedience, Doom had an iron mask fused to Velsing's face, so that he would know what it was like to be Doom. Fleeing Latveria, Velsing took refuge in the castle of Victor Frankenstein. Calling himself Dreadknight, armed with his own inventions, and riding a winged horse that once belonged to the Black Knight, he vowed to take revenge on his former master—no matter how many innocent people got hurt along the way.

DREADNOUGHT

FIRST APPEARANCE *Strange Tales* #154 (May 1940)
REAL NAME Dreadnought
OCCUPATION Weapons system **BASE** New York State
HEIGHT 8 ft **WIDTH** 40 in **WEIGHT** 2,200 lbs
SPECIAL POWERS/ABILITIES Portable fusion generator ensures 1.5 years of continuous use; travels at 35 mph; lifts up to 10 tons; armed with flamethrower, knuckle spikes, and electrical field.

A robotic juggernaut, the Dreadnought was built by the terror group Hydra, but its first field trial proved unsuccessful. It was directed to kill Nick Fury, but the SHIELD director's resourcefulness, combat training, and arsenal of miniaturized weaponry combined to overwhelm the automaton. This wasn't the end of the machine, however; when the Maggia crime family stole its blueprints, eight more of them were built, the most sophisticated being a silver version of the robot. The Mandarin later used updated Dreadnoughts designed by Ezekiel Stane to attack the Three Gorges Dam in China. In each case, Super Heroes like Iron Man, Spider-Man, and the Fantastic Four stopped the robots.

DREAMQUEEN

Eight hundred years ago, Nightmare, ruler of the Dream Dimension, captured a succubus called Zhilla Char, mated with her, and then confined her in a pocket dimension. Zhilla Char was consumed by flames while giving birth to her daughter, the Dreamqueen. Three hundred and fifty years ago the astral self of Native American shaman Nanquato traveled into the Dreamqueen's realm in search of the sky gods that could save his tribe from drought. Believing the Dreamqueen to be a sky god, Nanquato accepted a totem from her. Through this totem, the Dreamqueen terrified Nanquato's tribe with hallucinations, as a means to escape to Earth. But her plan was thwarted when Nanquato's tribesmen slew the shaman and buried the totem.

In recent years, the mutant Laura Dean visited the Dreamqueen's dimension, which Dean named "Liveworld." The Canadian Super Hero team Alpha Flight inadvertently traveled to Liveworld, and when they returned to Earth, the Dreamqueen came with them. However, Alpha Flight's Puck and Laura Dean succeeded in forcing her back to Liveworld.

By afflicting Alpha Flight with nightmares, the Dreamqueen escaped to Earth, where she took control of the minds of the people of the Canadian city of Edmonton. But Alpha Flight's sorceress Talisman defeated her and drove her from Earth. Still later, the Dreamqueen sided with Alpha Flight against their enemy, the Master.

FACTFILE
REAL NAME
Unrevealed
OCCUPATION
Ruler of Liveworld
BASE
The dimension of Liveworld

HEIGHT Variable, normally 6 ft 3 in
WEIGHT Variable
EYES White
HAIR Green

FIRST APPEARANCE
Alpha Flight #57 (April 1988)

POWERS
Wields virtually unlimited magical abilities, including the ability to create living beings, but only when she is in Liveworld. In or out of Liveworld, she can mentally control the minds and the perceptions of other beings, and cause them to experience hallucinations.

DREW, PATIENCE

FIRST APPEARANCE *Marvel Fanfare* #43 (April 1989)
REAL NAME Unknown **OCCUPATION** Pirate Captain
BASE Sargasso Sea **HEIGHT** Unknown **WEIGHT** Unknown
EYES Blue **HAIR** Black
SPECIAL POWERS/ABILITIES Skilled in the use of sabers, swords, and pistols, and other weapons of her time. Possessed the same skills in death.

Patience Drew was a pirate captain who lived several hundred years ago. She and her crew were killed by a British ship which led them into a trap during battle. After they sank into the Sargasso Sea, they were doomed to relive their deaths forever. NAMOR rescued Drew and her ship on one of these occasions and the pair fell in love. Namor joined Drew as a pirate and she gave him an earring to remember her by. Namor eventually left her ship and never returned. When he later found her ship and skeleton on the seabed, he was unsure if he had ever known her, until he realized he was still wearing her earring.

DUGAN, DUM DUM

FIRST APPEARANCE *Sgt. Fury and his Howling Commandos* #1 (May 1963) **REAL NAME** Timothy Aloysius Cadwallader Dugan **OCCUPATION** Ex-SHIELD agent
BASE New York City **HEIGHT** 6 ft 2 in
WEIGHT 196 lbs **EYES** Blue **HAIR** Red
SPECIAL POWERS/ABILITIES Expert boxer, wrestler, marksman, and commando.

In 1941, while touring Europe as a circus strongman, the Boston-born Dugan met Nick FURY, who was on a covert rescue mission. Later, he became part of Fury's military strike force, the HOWLING COMMANDOS. When Fury was appointed to head SHIELD, Dugan joined him. Dugan eventually discovered that for many years he'd been an LMD (Life Model Decoy) and that the original Dugan had died years before. He killed himself, but was brought back by Maria HILL to head STAKE and then lead a new, monstrous incarnation of the HOWLING COMMANDOS.

D'SPAYRE

FIRST APPEARANCE *Marvel Team-Up* #68 (April 1978)
REAL NAME Unknown **OCCUPATION** Demonic being
BASE Extradimensional tower **HEIGHT** 6 ft 3 in
WEIGHT Unknown **EYES** Black **HAIR** None
SPECIAL POWERS/ABILITIES Enhanced strength; able to levitate; able to instill fear into other beings; various other unrevealed magical abilities.

D'spayre is an extradimensional demon created by another demon, the Dweller-in-Darkness. He feeds off the psychic energy of suffering. D'spayre has teamed with NIGHTMARE, and is attended by a horde of small servant-beings, the D'sprites. One of D'spayre's first clashes with Super Heroes took place in the Florida Everglades, where he was defeated by SPIDER-MAN and MAN-THING. He has since fought CYCLOPS and DOCTOR STRANGE, and served as a member of the Fear Lords, an alliance of demons.

DUSK

FIRST APPEARANCE *Slingers* #0 (December 1998)
REAL NAME Cassie St. Commons **OCCUPATION** Adventurer
BASE New York City **HEIGHT** 5 ft 6 in **WEIGHT** 125 lbs
EYES Blue **HAIR** Black
SPECIAL POWERS/ABILITIES Receives power from the Negative Zone that allows her to melt into shadows or to teleport; possesses minor psychic abilities.

During a time when SPIDER-MAN was accused of murder, he adopted four separate costumes and identities, including one called Dusk. Later, former World War II hero Black Marvel gave the costumes to four youths to create the Slingers. Cassie St. Commons, a moody Empire State University student from a rich family, became the new Dusk. After what seemed a fatal fall, she returned with the power of teleportation. The Slingers disbanded after saving Black Marvel's soul from MEPHISTO, and Dusk has since kept a low profile.

EBONY MAW

FIRST APPEARANCE *New Avengers* #8 (September 2013)
REAL NAME Ebony Maw **OCCUPATION** Part of the Black Order
BASE Mobile **HEIGHT** Unknown **WEIGHT** Unknown
EYES Blue **HAIR** White
SPECIAL POWERS/ABILITIES Extreme powers of persuasion; has the ability to teleport and is an excellent strategist, tactician, and combatant.

As a master of strategy and deception, Ebony Maw is considered one of the most dangerous members of the Black Order. When THANOS targeted Earth, he used Ebony Maw to turn DOCTOR STRANGE into an unknowing agent for him. Maw later found Thanos' son, THANE, and after Thanos' defeat remained by Thane's side, trying to turn him into something far greater than his father. He returned to the Black Order to fight in a cosmic contest between the Challenger and the GRANDMASTER. When the Black Order was defeated, the Grandmaster offered them work.

ECHO

FIRST APPEARANCE *Daredevil* #9 (December 1999)
REAL NAME Maya Lopez
OCCUPATION Adventurer; performance artist
BASE Los Angeles, California **HEIGHT** 5 ft 9 in
WEIGHT 125 lbs **EYES** Brown **HAIR** Black
SPECIAL POWERS/ABILITIES Echo can mimic any physical action she sees, making her an incredible acrobat and combatant.

Maya was born deaf. Her Cheyenne father worked with the KINGPIN, who killed him but honored his dying request to raise his daughter. Kingpin told Maya that DAREDEVIL had murdered her father, and he also encouraged her to date Matt Murdock, Daredevil's alter ego. While hunting Daredevil, Maya realized who he was and spared him. She shot the Kingpin in revenge. She later became an AVENGER as ninja Ronin. COUNT NEFARIA killed her while she was working with MOON KNIGHT, but she later mysteriously returned to life and helped Daredevil fight KLAW.

ECSTASY

FIRST APPEARANCE *Doctor Strange* #74 (December 1985)
REAL NAME Renée Deladier
OCCUPATION Drug kingpin **BASE** Marseilles, France
HEIGHT 5 ft 9 in **WEIGHT** 130 lbs **EYES** Green **HAIR** Blond
SPECIAL POWERS/ABILITIES Formerly possessed the ability to project semi-solid tentacles of darkness, or to absorb beings into the Darkforce Dimension.

Ecstasy, who can wield tendrils of Darkforce energy, proves more than a match for the light-generating heroine Dagger.

Renée Deladier, who headed up a French cartel distributing the drug ecstasy, adopted the drug's name as her alias. The vigilante CLOAK tried to punish her by absorbing her into the Darkforce Dimension, but instead the sentience inhabiting the Darkforce selected Ecstasy to be its new agent, and absorbed Cloak instead, transferring his powers to Ecstasy. DOCTOR STRANGE came to Cloak's assistance, and with the help of the Eye of Agamotto, Cloak was able to defeat Ecstasy and regain his powers.

EEL

FIRST APPEARANCE *Strange Tales* #112 (October 1963)
REAL NAME Leopold Stryke **OCCUPATION** Criminal
BASE New York City **HEIGHT** 5 ft 10 in **WEIGHT** 192 lbs
EYES Brown **HAIR** Brown
SPECIAL POWERS/ABILITIES The Eel's costume contains devices that generate and shoot electrical charges; it also contains a layer of nearly frictionless synthetic fabric.

Leopold Stryke was the curator of an aquarium who turned to crime as the Eel. After being defeated by the HUMAN TORCH, he worked as henchman for Mister Fear and COUNT NEFARIA. He later joined his brother Jordan, the VIPER, in the Serpent Squad. Stryke was eventually killed by GLADIATOR. Edward Lavell became the second Eel, battling heroes as well as villains like HAMMERHEAD and MISTER HYDE. He was pressed into the Thunderbolt Army for a while, and he later joined Serpent Solutions.

EGGHEAD

EGGHEAD

FACTFILE
REAL NAME
Elihas Starr
OCCUPATION
Criminal; scientist
BASE
New York City

HEIGHT 5 ft 7 in
WEIGHT 210 lbs
EYES Blue
HAIR None

FIRST APPEARANCE
Tales to Astonish #38
(December 1962)

POWERS
Egghead created machines to enable communication with ants, powerful robots, and mind-controlling, prosthetic limbs; he is prone to delusions of grandeur and obsessed with destroying rival Henry Pym.

A brilliant scientist, Elihas Starr—or Egghead as he was known because of his unusually shaped head—lacked a conscience and was prone to boredom. Seeking extra excitement, Egghead had been working for the US government when he was sacked for stealing and selling secrets.

Coming to the attention of the New York mobs, Egghead was contracted to rid them of the original Ant-Man (Hank PYM). In the years that followed, the pair became archenemies. Egghead's strenuous efforts to destroy Ant-Man involved a range of intriguing devices: he built a machine to communicate with ants and persuaded them to turn against Pym, and on another occasion, he developed a bionic arm designed to control the thoughts of Pym's niece.

Although he appeared fairly harmless, Egghead was responsible for the destruction of an entire Mid-western town, an incident that brought him into direct conflict with the AVENGERS. He also became a member of the INTELLIGENCIA. Egghead was killed when a gun he was using exploded before he could shoot Pym, after it was hit by one of HAWKEYE's arrows. In fact, Egghead survived thanks to the Rejuvetech serum. He soon returned to trouble Pym once again before he was finally stopped by Pym and Scott Lang (*See* ANT-MAN II).

Egghead was hired by Darren Cross to kill Ant-Man (Scott Lang). Cross himself eventually fought Ant-Man as the villainous Yellowjacket.

EGO THE LIVING PLANET

EGO THE LIVING PLANET

FACTFILE

REAL NAME
Ego

OCCUPATION
N/A

BASE
Mobile

DIAMETER
4,165 miles

FIRST APPEARANCE
Thor #132
(September 1966)

POWERS
Vast intelligence and psionic powers, including telepathy and telekinesis; travels through space faster than light and can change its surface appearance.

Ego is a self-aware planet, one of two such sentient creatures the STRANGER made as part of an experiment. About the size of a small moon, Ego hails from the Black Galaxy, where it created armies of superhuman warriors from its own substance and sent them out to conquer other worlds. During a battle with GALACTUS, THOR sided with Ego at first, but the Thunder God later realized Ego's evil intentions when it attacked Earth, and he battled it alongside Galactus, HERCULES, and FIRELORD.

Ego once took over the Nova Corps and brainwashed its members until NOVA lobotomized it. Ego healed from this and fled before Nova could harm him again.

Ego later discovered his sibling planet, Alter-Ego, which the COLLECTOR had imprisoned since their creation as part of the Stranger's experiment to see whether captivity or freedom would make a creature stronger. Thor kept Ego from killing Alter-Ego, and Alter-Ego became a moon of Ego, orbiting it as they traveled together. While GALACTUS was the Life-Bringer, he used his powers to give Ego a humanoid body. The sentient planet then took the name Ego-Prime and joined Galactus in the Eternity Watch.

After their battle, Ego and Alter-Ego became a family.

ELECTRO, SEE PAGE 122

ELEKTRA, SEE PAGE 123

EMPATH

FIRST APPEARANCE *New Mutants* #16 (June 1984)
REAL NAME Manuel Alfonso Rodrigo de la Rocha
OCCUPATION Student **BASE** Massachusetts Academy, Snow Valley, Massachusetts **HEIGHT** 5 ft 11 in
WEIGHT 160 lbs **EYES** Black **HAIR** Light brown
SPECIAL POWERS/ABILITIES Able to manipulate the emotions and feelings of those around him. His powers can be used on one individual or a crowd.

As a member of the HELLIONS, Empath studied under Emma FROST, then the White Queen of the HELLFIRE CLUB. He later fell in love with MAGMA of the NEW MUTANTS and used his powers to make her reciprocate. Long after they broke up, they worked together for the X-Corporation in Los Angeles. Empath's powers survived M-Day, and he joined Madelyne PRYOR's Hellfire Cult, attacking the X-MEN for her. PIXIE stabbed him in the head with her soulsword, blinding him. Imprisoned by the X-Men, he was revealed to be a Trojan Horse, intended to disable their powers. Pixie stabbed him once more, shattering his mind.

ELDERS OF THE UNIVERSE

FIRST APPEARANCE *Avengers* #28 (May 1966)
BASE Mobile
MEMBERS
Gardener [1], **Possessor** [2], **Collector** [3], **Grandmaster** [4], **Challenger** [5], **Contemplator** [6], **Champion**, **Stranger**, **Architect**, **Astronomer**, **Caregiver**, **Father Time**, **Explorer**, **Inbetweener**, **Judicator**, **Promoter**, **Runner**, **Trader**, **Voyager**, **Obliterator**, **and many others**

The Elders of the Universe are among the oldest sentient creatures in existence. Although they do not belong to the same race, they have come to regard one another as brothers. This is because their origins date back to the formation of the first primordial galaxies, and because they have each chosen an area of specialty with which to fill their eons-long lives. In this way they manage to overcome the inevitable boredom that would otherwise accompany their virtual immortality. The exact number of Elders in existence is not known, but several of their number have had dealings with the Super Heroes of Earth, including the GRANDMASTER, the COLLECTOR, the GARDENER, the CONTEMPLATOR, and the CHAMPION.

ELIXIR

FIRST APPEARANCE *New Mutants* #5 (November 2003)
REAL NAME Joshua Foley
OCCUPATION Adventurer; student **BASE** Genosha
HEIGHT 5 ft 9 in **WEIGHT** 157 lbs **EYES** Blue **HAIR** Blond
SPECIAL POWERS/ABILITIES Elixir can control organic matter on a genetic level, including healing others, restoring organs and suppressed mutations, causing pain, and ending life.

A former member of the REAVERS, Josh joined the Xavier Institute after his parents signed over his guardianship to the school. He restored WOLFSBANE's powers, and she nearly killed him in surprise. When he healed himself, his skin turned golden. He kept his powers after M-DAY and trained to join the X-MEN. When STRYKER assassinated his friend Wallflower, Josh killed him. The trauma turned his own skin black, although it began to turn gold again once he resumed healing people. After helping MAGNETO stop the Mothervine virus, he joined Magneto's new Brotherhood of Mutants.

EMPLATE

FIRST APPEARANCE *Generation X* #1 (November 1994)
REAL NAME Marius St. Croix
OCCUPATION None **BASE** Mobile
HEIGHT 6 ft 3 in **WEIGHT** Variable **EYES** Red **HAIR** Gray
SPECIAL POWERS/ABILITIES Must consume the marrow of mutants to prevent being pulled into a pocket dimension of untold tortures; absorbs the abilities of each mutant he feeds on for a time.

The brother of M, Emplate's mutant power flung him into a pocket dimension, where his physical body was ravaged. By feeding on the marrow of the mutant PENANCE he was able to return home, albeit encased in a respirator unit he now needed to survive. To remain here, Emplate must constantly feed on the marrow of other mutants, for which he targeted GENERATION X. He once merged with his other sisters, the M-Twins, to become M-Plate.

Exiled to a horrific other dimension, Emplate could only remain in our reality by consuming the bone marrow of mutants like himself.

ELECTRO

Living electrical generator

ELECTRO

FACTFILE

REAL NAME
Francine Frye

OCCUPATION
Criminal

BASE
Mobile

HEIGHT Unknown
WEIGHT Unknown
EYES Brown
HAIR Brown

FIRST APPEARANCE
Amazing Spider-Man #17 (October 2016)

POWERS

Electro can store, release, and manipulate electricity to fire electric bolts, travel along power lines, and control machinery.

While working as a lineman for an electrical company during a thunderstorm, Max Dillon received a shock that endowed him with superhuman powers, and he became the villain Electro. On his first outing, Electro robbed *Daily Bugle* publisher J. Jonah Jameson, who was sure Electro was Spider-Man in disguise. To clear his name, Spider-Man defeated Electro by short-circuiting his powers with a water stream.

IT'S UNBELIEVABLE! MY BODY KEEPS RECHARGING IT-SELF! I'M LIKE A LIVING ELECTRICAL GENERATOR!!

Thor threw Electro into space. When he made it back to Earth, he vowed revenge.

A SHOCKING FAILURE

Electro then allied himself with criminal teams, including the Sinister Six and the Frightful Four. This did little to help him with his chronic inferiority complex about being a B-list villain at best. Whether alone or with a team, he never managed to triumph. His frustration with this sent him into retirement for a while, but he returned when the Rose promised to increase his powers in exchange for his services.

Francine Frye became the new Electro after killing the original.

Electro once attacked the super-prison called the Raft, breaking out dozens of villains, but fainted when a new version of the Avengers, now including Spider-Man, cornered him. He joined the Hood's criminal syndicate when it took part in the battle against the Skrulls during the Secret Invasion.

Over the years, Electro's powers have taken their toll on him, burning him out from within and scarring his skin. At one point, he lost so much control that even his slightest touch could prove lethal. He launched a campaign called "Power to the People" targeted at right-wing publisher Dexter Bennett, who'd taken over the *Daily Bugle*, as a ploy to get Bennett to fund a search for a cure. Electro made a deal with the Mad Thinker to upgrade his powers and his control over them, but Spider-Man intervened to disrupt the process. Electro temporarily transformed into pure electricity, and he destroyed the *Daily Bugle* building in his rage.

Later, still frustrated with his power troubles, Electro turned to the scientists at AIM to make an anti-matter version of himself, one powered by protons rather than electrons. Working with Thor, the Superior Spider-Man (Doctor Octopus) managed to defeat him.

FRIED BY FRYE

While Electro's powers were out of control, he accidentally killed his girlfriend, Francine Frye. She was reborn as a clone by the Jackal (Ben Reilly) and when she kissed Max, her saliva mixed with his DNA, transferring his powers to her, and killing him in return. Frye assumed the role of Electro with relish. She worked for the Jackal, and was one of the few clones to survive his experiment. She later became part of a new Sinister Six.

ELEKTRA

Conflicted assassin

Elektra was not the first to be resurrected by the Hand. That fate fell to 16th-century warrior, Eliza Martinez.

For proficient martial artist Elektra Natchios, the choice between heroism and a career of villainy has never been clear-cut. While she continually yearns for contentment, time and again her happiness has been spoiled by tragedy and the intervention of others—beginning even before she was born, when her mother was shot while pregnant and died soon after giving birth to her.

From their first encounter, Elektra's fate was bound to Matt Murdock's.

FACTFILE ELEKTRA

REAL NAME
Elektra Natchios

OCCUPATION
Mercenary assassin

BASE
Mobile

HEIGHT 5 ft 9 in
WEIGHT 130 lbs
EYES Blue-black
HAIR Black

FIRST APPEARANCE
Daredevil #168 (January 1981)

POWERS
Awesome martial arts skills, particularly proficient in ninjutsu; skilled with martial art weaponry, especially the sai; Olympic-standard gymnast and athlete; limited telepathic abilities and partial control of nervous system.

STALKED BY TRAGEDY

When Elektra's overprotective father became Greek ambassador to the US, she enrolled at Columbia University in New York City, but was followed everywhere by security guards. Despite this restriction, a clandestine romance grew between Elektra and Matt Murdock (*see* DAREDEVIL), a fellow student. For a year, their relationship flourished, but when Elektra's father was killed during a hostage incident her whole world fell apart. Riven with grief she fled, leaving Matt and the US behind.

KILLER FOR HIRE

Elektra trained as a ninja and for a year belonged to the CHASTE, a ninja order led by Matt Murdock's mentor, STICK. Elektra's impure heart stopped her from joining the Chaste, driving her to their enemies, the HAND. She later abandoned them and became an assassin for hire, putting her in conflict with Matt, who'd become Daredevil. Once lovers, they were now foes, but despite this, when Elektra was mortally wounded by BULLSEYE, she crawled to Matt's door and died in his arms. Matt tried to halt the Hand's attempt to resurrect a corrupted version of her. His love purified her soul, making her useless to the Hand when she returned.

Fatally injured, Elektra crawls to Matt's apartment to die.

ELEKTRA REBORN

Elektra appeared to have rejoined the Hand to battle the AVENGERS, but when she was killed, the Avengers discovered she was a SKRULL imposter. This heralded the SECRET INVASION, during which Elektra escaped the Skrulls and returned to her life. When Daredevil took charge of the Hand, she joined the organization once again, but she betrayed him to his friends so they could save him from the BEAST, a demon who had possessed him. She later joined the RED HULK'S THUNDERBOLTS.

After the team disbanded, the PURPLE MAN made Elektra believe she had had a child with Matt. She returned to New York to find her child only to learn that she had been manipulated. She helped Daredevil fight the Hand when the Beast tried to retake New York, and then left to seek her revenge on the Purple Man.

Following her resurrection, a purified Elektra fought evil, garbed in a white costume that she made herself.

KEY STORYLINES

- ***Daredevil #168–9*** Elektra's first encounter with Matt Murdock; her origin is revealed.
- ***Daredevil #174–181*** Elektra fights the Hand with Matt, is recruited by the Kingpin, and dies at the hands of Bullseye.
- ***Daredevil #190*** Elektra is reborn and more about her past is revealed.
- ***Elektra Vol. 2 #11–15*** As her addiction to violence reaches new heights, relatives of Elektra's victims seek revenge.

ENCHANTRESS

ENCHANTRESS

FACTFILE

REAL NAME
Amora

OCCUPATION
Goddess

BASE
Asgard, otherworldly home of the Norse Gods

HEIGHT 6 ft 3 in
WEIGHT 450 lbs
EYES Green
HAIR Blond

FIRST APPEARANCE
Journey Into Mystery #103 (April 1964)

POWERS

Possesses the enhanced lifespan, durability, and might of a goddess of Asgard. Adept at sorcery, specializing in spells that enhance her beauty and allow her to control the minds and emotions of men. Her kiss can enslave any man. Able to fire power bolts from her hands.

One of the immortals of the Norse realm of Asgard (*see* GODS OF ASGARD), the Enchantress studied under the master sorceress Karnilla. Vain and headstrong, she centered her magic on increasing her allure, so as to more easily ensnare the hearts and minds of those around her. When her desire for Odin's son THOR proved unrequited, she turned her mystic powers to evil, hoping to catch him one way or another. She especially resented Thor's love of humanity, and longed for him to take her as his queen and rule over Asgard. Her feelings for the Thunder God are genuine, and she has come close to realizing her dream; however Thor's love of humanity always gets in the way.

Not only can the Enchantress manipulate magical energy, but she uses various spells and potions to exert control over mortal men and other Asgardians.

The Enchantress' Asgardian body is three times denser and heavier than that of a normal human being.

THE FEMME FATALE

The Enchantress often teamed up with Skurge the EXECUTIONER, who was hopelessly infatuated with her. She treated him with contempt but truly grieved for him when he died. She also became a member of the MASTERS OF EVIL.

A younger Enchantress later joined the YOUNG MASTERS, hoping to become a YOUNG AVENGER. She believed she was from Asgard, but she soon learned her real name was Sylvie Lushton of Broxton, Oklahoma, and that LOKI had granted her powers to her. She eventually left both groups to work on her own.

ENCLAVE

FIRST APPEARANCE *Fantastic Four* #66 (September 1967)
BASE Various, including a North Atlantic island
MEMBERS AND POWERS
Maris Morlak Lithuanian nuclear physicist
Jerome Hamilton American medical biologist
Carlo Zota Spanish electronics technician
Wladyslav Shinski Polish geneticist

The group of scientists known as the Enclave believed they could establish a benevolent world dictatorship. Faking their deaths, the Enclave established a base on a remote North Atlantic island. They first endeavored to create a race of superbeings to control the human race. However, they failed to control the monsters, the first of which rampaged through their base, destroying it. Initially named "Him," this creature eventually came to be called Adam WARLOCK. The Enclave embarked on new schemes, such as attempting to dominate the race known as the INHUMANS and exploit the aliens' technology. Intervention by the AVENGERS resulted in two of the Enclave being imprisoned. They broke out and plagued SPIDER-MAN, the FANTASTIC FOUR, and Adam Warlock for years.

ENERGIZER

FIRST APPEARANCE *Power Pack* #1 (August 1984)
REAL NAME Katie Power **OCCUPATION** Student; adventurer
BASE New York City **HEIGHT** (age 5) 3 ft 7 in
WEIGHT (age 5) 41 lbs **EYES** Blue **HAIR** Strawberry blond
SPECIAL POWERS/ABILITIES Can disintegrate objects in order to absorb energy, which she can release as "power balls" of destructive force—hence her code name.

Katie Power is the youngest child of Dr. James and Margaret Power, and the sister of Alex, Jack, and Julie Power. When Katie was five, she and her siblings met Aelfyre Whitemane of the alien Kymellians. Dying, "Whitey" endowed the children with superpowers, and they became the POWER PACK. At times the Pack members have exchanged powers. Katie was Starstreak when she could fly, and Counterweight when she could alter her body density.

ENFORCER

FIRST APPEARANCE *Ghost Rider* #22 (February 1977)
REAL NAME Charles L. Delazny, Jr. **OCCUPATION** Criminal
BASE Los Angeles, California **HEIGHT** 5 ft 11 in
WEIGHT 180 lbs **EYES** Brown **HAIR** Brown
SPECIAL POWERS/ABILITIES Wears bulletproof costume and carries automatic pistols; formerly possessed a disintegration amulet and ring.

Delazny left college to become the Enforcer. His primary weapon was a disintegration device worn as an amulet or ring. Often going by the name of Carson Collier, he built up a secret criminal empire from his father's Delazny Studios and clashed with GHOST RIDER and SPIDER-WOMAN. He was later shot and killed by the original SCOURGE, who claimed to be his younger brother. His nephew, Mike Nero, later took up the Enforcer identity and clashed with supernatural threats, including the HOOD.

ENFORCERS

FIRST APPEARANCE *Amazing Spider-Man* #10 (March 1964)
BASE New York City
MEMBERS AND POWERS
Fancy Dan Judo and karate expert—a nice line in suits, too.
Montana Proficient with the lariat.
Ox Not superstrong, but very strong nevertheless.
Snake Marston Entwines body around objects and people.
Hammer Harrison Expert boxer and unarmed combatant.
Big Man Would-be crime lord Frederick Foswell.

The Enforcers can give most Super Heroes a run for their money. Although they have been defeated by SPIDER-MAN a number of times, he has required the help of others to overcome them, calling on the NYPD, the HUMAN TORCH, or the reformed SANDMAN. Initially employed by the BIG MAN during his bid to control New York's underworld, the Enforcers have also worked for the GREEN GOBLIN and the KINGPIN, until he was overthrown, forcing them back into the muscle-for-hire market.

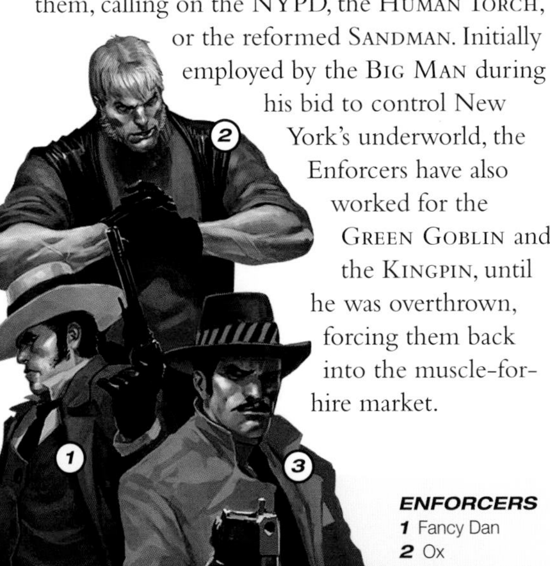

ENFORCERS
1 Fancy Dan
2 Ox
3 Montana

FACTFILE
KEY MEMBERS
KRONOS, MENTOR (Alars), **ZURAS, IKARIS, URANOS, ARLOK, THENA, SERSI, MAKKARI, THE FORGOTTEN ONE, KINGO SUNEN, SPRITE, CYBELE, PHASTOS, KHORYPHOS, INTERLOPER, AJAK, DOMO, VALKIN, DRUIG, AGINAR, ZARIN, DELPHAN BROTHERS, SIGMAR, VIRAKO, VAMPIRO.**
BASE
Earth; Titan (moon of Saturn)

FIRST APPEARANCE
Eternals #1 (July 1976)

ETERNALS

POWERS

All Eternals have superhuman strength, can levitate themselves or other objects, can fly (at up to 600 mph), create mental illusions, and project cosmic energy in beams from their eyes. Some Eternals can transform an object's shape.

ETERNALS

A million years ago, the CELESTIALS came to Earth to experiment on the human race. They accelerated the evolution of a few subjects, giving them the potential to mentally control small amounts of cosmic energy. These people became the Eternals, a nearly immortal race of people who possess superhuman powers. Subsequent experiments led to the creation of the Deviants, who later vied for power with the Eternals.

Eventually, the Eternals split into two factions: a benevolent one led by Kronos, and a warlike one led by Uranos. After a bitter civil war, Kronos' side triumphed, and Uranos and his people were exiled to Saturn's moon Titan.

The Eternal known as Thena is a powerful fighter with a brilliant mind. Like all Eternals she doesn't age or get sick.

The Eternals on Earth, led by Kronos' son Zuras, clashed with the fourth host of the Celestials, when the latter arrived to judge the Earth and its people. Although Zuras was killed, the Celestials spared the peoples of Earth and departed. Most of the Eternals left the planet then as well, leaving only a small group ruled by IKARIS behind.

The Eternal named Sprite erased the memories of the other Eternals on Earth and placed them in new lives, although they eventually remembered who they were. When the Final Host of Dark Celestials came to Earth with LOKI, the Eternals were driven to killing each other—having realized they were never humanity's protectors, but merely its cultivators.

ETERNITY

FIRST APPEARANCE *Strange Tales* #138 (November 1965)
REAL NAME Inapplicable; alias Adam Quadmon
OCCUPATION None; abstract entity **BASE** Inapplicable
HEIGHT Inapplicable **WEIGHT** Inapplicable
EYES Inapplicable **HAIR** Inapplicable
SPECIAL POWERS/ABILITIES Unlimited ability to manipulate time, space, matter, energy, or magic for any purpose.

Eternity is the collective consciousness of all life, and is dependent on the many trillions of beings within it. It exists everywhere simultaneously. Eternity can take on humanoid form when it deigns to communicate with sorcerers and the like, such as when it once aided DOCTOR STRANGE against DORMAMMU. To have a greater understanding of humanity, Eternity has occasionally walked the Earth, using the name Adam Quadmon. There is also a Multiversal incarnation of Eternity.

EX NIHILO

FIRST APPEARANCE *Avengers* #1 (February 2013)
REAL NAME Ex Nihilo **OCCUPATION** Creator **BASE** Mars
HEIGHT 9 ft **WEIGHT** 600 lbs **EYES** Green **HAIR** None
SPECIAL POWERS/ABILITIES Ex Nihilo can create new life and terraform planets by touch or missile. He can also fire energy blasts and control and grow plants in an instant. If his kind commits suicide, they can destroy an entire planet.

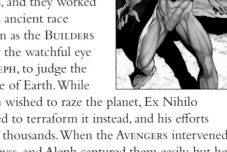

Ex Nihilo is one of many of his kind—a Gardener. He came to Mars with his sister ABYSS, and they worked for an ancient race known as the BUILDERS under the watchful eye of ALEPH, to judge the people of Earth. While Aleph wished to raze the planet, Ex Nihilo wanted to terraform it instead, and his efforts killed thousands. When the AVENGERS intervened, he, Abyss, and Aleph captured them easily, but he surrendered to CAPTAIN UNIVERSE. He and Abyss now work with the Avengers to prevent the Builders from destroying the Earth and the rest of the galaxy.

EXECUTIONER

FIRST APPEARANCE *Journey into Mystery* #103 (April 1964)
REAL NAME Skurge **OCCUPATION** Giant-killer
BASE Asgard **HEIGHT** 7 ft 2 in **WEIGHT** 1100 lbs
EYES Blue **HAIR** Black
SPECIAL POWERS/ABILITIES A master of combat. Superhuman strength and stamina; wielded a magical double-bladed ax that could create dimensional rifts enabling time travel and fired blasts of intense heat or cold; also possessed an unbreakable helmet.

Skurge was the son of an Asgardian goddess and a Storm Giant. Turning against his father's people, he killed many giants in war, earning the nickname "the Executioner." He fell under the ENCHANTRESS' spell, serving her in attempts to dominate Earth and Asgard. In time, he realized she was toying with him and rejected her. On a mission to Hel with THOR, he restored his reputation by fighting to free mortal souls from Hela, and he died a hero's death. Much later, an unrelated Executioner joined the YOUNG MASTERS. He was the son of PRINCESS PYTHON.

EXCALIBUR

EXCALIBUR

FACTFILE

ORIGINAL MEMBERS

CAPTAIN BRITAIN
Superpowered defender of Earth-616.

SHADOWCAT
Phases through solid objects.

NIGHTCRAWLER
Can teleport.

MEGGAN
Shapeshifter.

PHOENIX
(Rachel Summers-Grey)
Telepathy; telekinesis; projects force bolts.

LOCKHEED
Breathes fire and flies.

BASE
United Kingdom

FIRST APPEARANCE
Excalibur: The Sword is Drawn (April 1988)

Excalibur missions are bywords for exotic travel to alien worlds and otherworldly dimensions.

Based at CAPTAIN BRITAIN's lighthouse, the Excalibur team of heroes was formed following the X-MEN's apparent demise at the hands of the ADVERSARY. With a base located not just on the shores of the UK but also at the nexus of several realities, many of their battles have been fought across multiple alternate worlds. For instance, Excalibur confronted its Nazi counterparts the Lightning Force on Earth-597. Excalibur's unity has been undermined by romantic tensions. When NIGHTCRAWLER developed feelings for Captain Britain's lover, MEGGAN, friction grew within the team, culminating in a brawl between the two men. After Captain Britain and Meggan finally married, the original team disbanded. Captain Britain has since reformed the team twice, each time with a new lineup. The latest version disbanded after a climactic battle with MERLYN, but the original team met up to celebrate the birth of Captain Britain and Meggan's baby.

EXCALIBUR
1 Meggan ***2*** Captain Britain
3 Rachel Summers
4 Kitty Pryde ***5*** Nightcrawler

FACTFILE

ORIGINAL MEMBERS

BLINK (leader)
Ability to teleport herself and others.

BEAK
Mutant power of flight.

MIMIC
Can duplicate the powers and abilities of others.

MORPH
Shapeshifter.

SABRETOOTH
Mutant healing factor, enhanced senses, retractable claws.

BASE
Mobile Panoptichron base

FIRST APPEARANCE
Exiles #1 (August 2001)

EXILES

The Exiles are a group of heroes taken from alternate realities, tasked by the Timebroker with fixing snags in the Multiverse of divergent timestreams. A device called Tallus gives them guidance on repairing the timestream. The founding Exiles team consisted of otherdimensional versions of BLINK, MIMIC, Magnus, THUNDERBIRD, NOCTURNE, and Morph. Later members included variants of GAMBIT, LONGSHOT, MAGIK, MYSTIQUE, PSYLOCKE, Valeria RICHARDS, SABRETOOTH, SAGE, SUNFIRE, and SASQUATCH, plus SPIDER-MAN 2099 and several versions of WOLVERINE. During their dimension hopping, the team faced off against HYPERION and the opposing team Weapon X, and welcomed NAMORA and Beak to their ranks.

The team's lineup has fluctuated over the years. It was recently brought together again by the Unseen—Nick FURY's doomed persona on the moon—to save the Multiverse from a new threat. The new team included original member Blink, alongside a war-hardened version of Ms. MARVEL known as Khan, Iron Lad, Wolvie (a cute version of WOLVERINE from Mojoverse), and a Valkyrie from an alternate version of Asgard. They remained together after defeating the Time-Eater and continued to adventure through the Multiverse.

EXILES
1 Blink ***2*** Iron Lad ***3*** Khan
4 Valkyrie ***5*** Wolvie

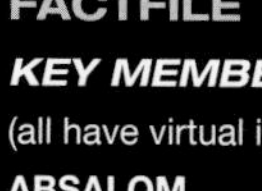

EXODUS

FIRST APPEARANCE *X-Factor* #92 (July 1993)
REAL NAME Bennet du Paris **OCCUPATION** Super Villain
BASE Mobile **HEIGHT** 5 ft 10 in **WEIGHT** 165 lbs
EYES White **HAIR** Black
SPECIAL POWERS/ABILITIES Incalculable psionic powers including telepathy, telekinesis, and the ability to fire mental bolts; possesses enhanced strength, near-invulnerability, and flight.

In the 12th century, crusader Bennet du Paris crossed paths with APOCALYPSE, who placed him in suspended animation when he refused to kill the BLACK KNIGHT. Awakened by MAGNETO in the modern era, du Paris took the name Exodus and joined Magneto's Acolytes. He led the Acolytes until Nate Grey (X-MAN) sealed him in a mountain. He was one of the few mutants to maintain his powers after M-Day. After PROFESSOR X was shot, Exodus rebuilt his brain, and he later dueled with the professor over Magneto's fate.

EXTERNALS

The Externals, also known as the High Lords, were a small group of superhuman mutants whose lifespans were potentially unlimited. Their aging process was greatly slowed, and they could recover from injuries that would be fatal to normal humans.

The External Candra exacted payments of "tithes" from the Thieves and Assassins Guilds of New Orleans until GAMBIT stopped her. GIDEON was the owner of Ophrah Industries and a recurring foe of X-FORCE. SELENE lived for thousands of years and became Black Queen of the HELLFIRE CLUB. Most of the Externals proved to be not as immortal as they hoped. Burke and Nicodemus succumbed to the Legacy Virus. Candra perished in an encounter with the X-MEN. CABLE and a new team of mutants stopped Gideon when he started killing the other Externals, with only Selene and Absalom surviving.

FACTFILE

KEY MEMBERS
(all have virtual immortality)

ABSALOM
Causes bone-like spikes to emerge from his skin.

BURKE Precognition.

CANDRA Telekinesis.

CRULE Superhuman strength.

GIDEON
Duplicates powers of superhumans.

SELENE Drains life forces from others; telekinetic powers; superhuman

FIRST APPEARANCE
X-Force #10 (May 1992)

One of the oldest known mutants, Selene is also a powerful sorceress.

FALCON

FACTFILE

REAL NAME
Sam "Snap" Wilson

OCCUPATION
Hero and urban planner

BASE
Harlem, New York City

HEIGHT 6 ft 2 in
WEIGHT 240 lbs
EYES Brown
HAIR Black

FIRST APPEARANCE
Captain America #117 (September 1969)

POWERS

Falcon has a telepathic link allowing him to see through the eyes of his trained falcon, Redwing. Trained by Captain America, Falcon is skilled in numerous fighting styles, and possesses the agility of a skilled acrobat. Jet-powered glider wings enable him to fly.

Fantastic Four, see pages 130–133

FALCON

After his father was killed trying to stop a street fight and his mother died during a mugging, Sam Wilson became a community volunteer. On a flight to Rio de Janeiro, his plane crash-landed in the Caribbean and he encountered the Red Skull. To realize one of his diabolical schemes, the Skull used a Cosmic Cube to endow Sam with limited superpowers, molding him to become Captain America's ideal sidekick. Red Skull also gave Sam false memories in which he'd been a criminal.

After helping Cap defeat Red Skull, Sam branded himself the Falcon and began a long partnership with the famed Super-Soldier. A gift of jet-powered wings from Black Panther enabled Sam to become Cap's airborne companion. Wilson moved in and out of the Avengers over the years, but retired from being a hero after the troubled Scarlet Witch unbalanced his mind. He returned to support Cap's resistance during the Civil War, but after Cap's assassination, Sam registered and was assigned to protect Harlem. He later joined the Heroes for Hire and even returned to the Avengers for a time.

Following Steve Rogers' return and later rapid aging after being deprived of the Super-Soldier Serum, Sam became the new Captain America. Believing his role should be more socially conscious, Sam fell out with SHIELD. After handing the mantle back to a revitalized Steve Rogers, Sam was forced to become Captain America once more during Hydra's takeover of the US. After the fall of Hydra, Sam returned to fighting street crime as the Falcon.

FANTOMEX

FIRST APPEARANCE *New X-Men* #128 (August 2002)
REAL NAME Jean-Phillipe/Charlie Cluster-7
OCCUPATION Adventurer **BASE** Mobile **HEIGHT** 5 ft 9 in
WEIGHT 175 lbs **EYES** Blue **HAIR** Black
SPECIAL POWERS/ABILITIES Fantomex has three brains and a techno-organic morphable flying saucer named EVA. He has superhuman coordination, durability, endurance, hearing, speed, strength, and pain resistance. His mask blocks telepathy.

Fantomex was born and raised in the World, an artificial environment designed to create perfect living weapons. Designated Weapon XIII, he escaped and when not trying to stop the Weapon Plus and Weapon X programs, worked as a master thief. He later joined Cyclops' new X-Force team and died saving Psylocke. Cloned by EVA to restore him, he wound up with a new body for each of his three brains: evil Weapon XIII, noble (and female) Cluster, and mischievous Fantomex. After becoming one again, Fantomex donated his body to Professor X so that the professor's astral form could escape from the astral plane.

FEARLESS DEFENDERS

Doommaidens (corrupted Valkyries) were causing long-dead Vikings to rise and attack the world. Valkyrie, with the help of Misty Knight, Dani Moonstar, resurrected Amazon leader Hippolyta, and archaeologist Annabelle Riggs, set out to stop the Doommaidens. At a crucial moment, Valkyrie siphoned off Dani's Valkyrie power to increase her own, but sent herself into a berserker fury. Only Annabelle was able to stop Valkyrie with her love, but at the cost of her own life.

Grieving for her friend, Valkyrie urged the others to join her in a new Defenders team. With the help of Clea, Valkyrie brought Annabelle back from Valhalla, but only by making Annabelle Valkyrie's host. The two could now switch places with each other between Valhalla and Earth. Later, Elsa Bloodstone helped the Fearless Defenders take down a gang in New York's Chinatown, who were using Brood hatchlings to kill their rivals. In an effort to destroy the Doommaidens once and for all, the Fearless Defenders prevented their leader, Caroline Le Fay, from becoming a Valkyrie—but not before she was able to resurrect her mother, Morgan Le Fay.

Fear Itself, see pages 134–135

FEARLESS DEFENDERS

FACTFILE

MEMBERS

ANNABELLE RIGGS
Archaeologist, now host of Valkyrie

DANI MOONSTAR
Empathic illusionist and Valkyrie

VALKYRIE
Leader of the Valkyrior

MISTY KNIGHT
Private detective with bionic arm

WARRIOR WOMAN
Hippolyta, former Amazon leader

BASE
Unrevealed

FIRST APPEARANCE
Fearless Defenders #1 (April 2013)

FENRIS WOLF

FIRST APPEARANCE *Journey into Mystery* #114 (March 1965)
REAL NAME Fenris Wolf **OCCUPATION** Predator
BASE Varinheim **HEIGHT** Usually 15 ft **WEIGHT** Unrevealed
EYES Red **HAIR** Gray
SPECIAL POWERS/ABILITIES Superhuman strength, speed, and durability; razor-sharp claws and teeth; able to transform change into a humanoid god and wield weapons.

Fenris Wolf was a shape-changing Asgardian creature that usually took the form of a huge wolf, but could also transform into a humanoid and an Earth wolf. After showing a vicious streak, Fenris was tethered to a rock with an enchanted fetter by the GODS OF ASGARD. It was prophesied that Fenris would devour ODIN during Ragnarok, but when the event occurred, the creature itself was destroyed. Fenris was reborn as a wolf on Midgard and later helped the mutant WOLFSBANE and the wolf-child she was carrying escape from mythical beasts hunting her. After a fierce battle, all the beasts were banished to Hel by the goddess Hela.

FIXER (TECHNO)

FIRST APPEARANCE *Strange Tales* #141 (February 1966)
REAL NAME Paul Norbert Ebersol
OCCUPATION Adventurer **BASE** New York City
HEIGHT 5 ft 8 in **WEIGHT** 160 lbs **EYES** Brown
HAIR Bald with black goatee
SPECIAL POWERS/ABILITIES Fixer is an engineering genius who sometimes lives in a morphable robot body.

A genius with electronic and mechanical devices, Fixer began his criminal career working with HYDRA. He clashed with many heroes, fighting alongside MENTALLO and Professor Power. Later, he joined BARON ZEMO and the MASTERS OF EVIL. As part of the original THUNDERBOLTS, Fixer's neck was broken, and he transferred his mind into a robot body. When that was destroyed, he returned to his original body, which was now healed, although it required the use of his tech-pac to keep him from being paralyzed. He joined the Redeemers and lived for a while on Counter-Earth. He has since returned to Earth.

FLAG-SMASHER

FIRST APPEARANCE *Captain America* #312 (December 1985)
REAL NAME Karl Morgenthau **OCCUPATION** Terrorist
BASE Rumekistan **HEIGHT** 6 ft 2 in **WEIGHT** 235 lbs
EYES Brown **HAIR** Brown
SPECIAL POWERS/ABILITIES Skilled at shotokan karate-do; multilingual, can speak Russian, German, and Japanese; wields spiked mace, flame-throwing pistol, and tear-gas gun.

When his diplomat father died in a riot, Flag-Smasher vowed to establish peace by violent means. Regarding nationalism as the root problem, he began a terrorist campaign against symbols of national identity. CAPTAIN AMERICA repeatedly defeated him. Forming the terrorist group ULTIMATUM, Flag-Smasher took over the country of Rumekistan, but DOMINO killed him. Flag-Smasher's name and leadership of ULTIMATUM was later assumed by two equally obsessed individuals in quick succession. Both were assassinated, the last by DEADPOOL, a frequent adversary.

FERAL

FIRST APPEARANCE *New Mutants* #99 (March 1991)
REAL NAME Maria Callasantos **OCCUPATION** Terrorist
BASE New York City **HEIGHT** 5 ft 9 in **WEIGHT** 110 lbs
EYES Yellow **HAIR** Orange and white
SPECIAL POWERS/ABILITIES Enhanced strength, speed, and agility; superhumanly acute senses, especially her senses of sight and smell.

When Feral's mutant powers emerged, she killed her stepfather and her mother and joined X-FORCE. When X-Force tried to rescue Henry GYRICH from the MUTANT LIBERATION FRONT, she switched sides. The New York City Police arrested her for the murders of her parents. Later, she joined the X-Corporation, along with her sister, Thornn. They both lost their powers on M-Day, and SABRETOOTH killed Feral. SELENE's techno-organic virus resurrected her, but not for long.

FIRESTAR

Angelica Jones' mutant powers emerged when she was 13 years old. She was soon recruited by the Massachusetts Academy, and became a member of the HELLIONS. Emma FROST, the school's headmistress and the White Queen of the HELLFIRE CLUB at the time, secretly trained Angelica as an assassin who could kill without detection.

After the Hellions repeatedly clashed with the X-MEN and NEW MUTANTS, Angelica left the school. She joined the NEW WARRIORS and fell in love with Vance "JUSTICE" Astrovik. After briefly becoming reserve members of the AVENGERS, the two decided to leave the team to focus on their relationship, but separated soon after. Angelica retained her powers after M-Day, but during the CIVIL WAR she retired from being a hero to remain in college. She survived cancer caused by her own powers, and became a founding member of the YOUNG ALLIES. She then joined the X-Men, taking up a teaching position at the Jean Grey School of Higher Learning.

FIFTY-STATE INITIATIVE, SEE PAGES 136–137

FACTFILE
REAL NAME
Angelica Jones
OCCUPATION
College student
BASE
Manhattan, New York

HEIGHT 5 ft 1 in
WEIGHT 101 lbs
EYES Green
HAIR Red

FIRST APPEARANCE
Uncanny X-Men #193 (May 1985)

FIRESTAR

POWERS
Firestar possesses the mutant ability to project microwave energy and to generate intense heat. She can propel herself and others through the air by mentally pushing microwave energy behind or beneath herself.

FANTASTIC FOUR

Superheroic planet protectors

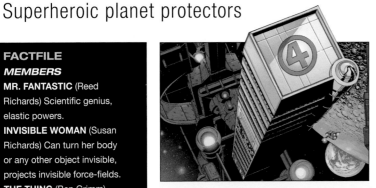

FANTASTIC FOUR

FACTFILE

MEMBERS

MR. FANTASTIC (Reed Richards) Scientific genius, elastic powers.

INVISIBLE WOMAN (Susan Richards) Can turn her body or any other object invisible, projects invisible force-fields.

THE THING (Ben Grimm) Man monster with superhuman strength.

HUMAN TORCH (Johnny Storm) Generates fiery plasma over his entire body and can fly.

ADDITIONAL MEMBERS

CRYSTAL, MEDUSA, SHE-HULK, ANT-MAN (Scott Lang), **LUKE CAGE** (Carl Lucas), **SHARON VENTURA** (Ms. Marvel/She-Thing), **NAMORITA** (Namorita Prentiss), **MISS-THING, BLACK PANTHER, STORM**

BASE

The Baxter Building, NYC

FIRST APPEARANCE

Fantastic Four #1 (November 1961)

ALLIES/FOES

ALLIES Spider-Man, Namor the Sub-Mariner, Alicia Masters, Agatha Harkness, Wyatt Wingfoot, Silver Surfer, Lyja (Lyja Storm)

FOES Dr. Doom, Puppet Master, Red Ghost and his Super-Apes, Frightful Four, Galactus

ISSUE #1

After being exposed to cosmic rays, the Fantastic Four kept a low profile and didn't reveal their powers to the public until giant monsters began attacking atomic research facilities.

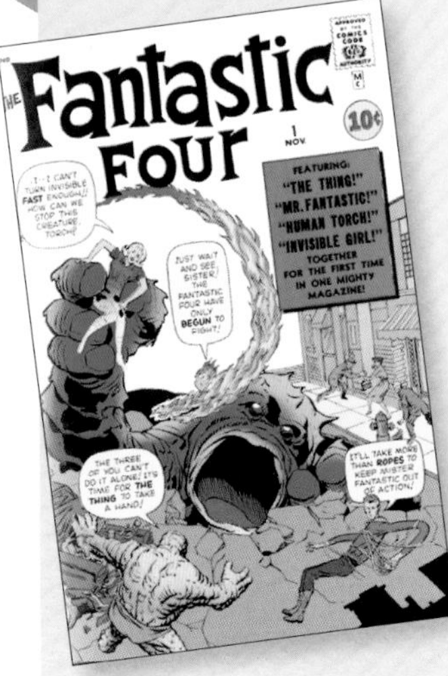

The Baxter Building was built by Noah Baxter, one of Reed's professors and mentor.

Reed Richards was a scientific genius who dreamed of exploring the stars. His roommate at New York's State University was football star Ben Grimm. Reed shared his dream of building a starship and Grimm, who wanted to become a pilot, promised to fly it. Grimm subsequently joined the US Air Force and became a test pilot and astronaut. Meanwhile, using his own family's fortune as well as money from the government, Richards built a starship.

COSMIC RAYS

Fearing that Reed's ship didn't have sufficient shields, Ben tried to talk the others out of flying.

When the government threatened to withdraw its funding, Richards decided to take his prototype ship on a test flight with Grimm at the helm. Richards' fiancée, Susan Storm, and her teenage brother Johnny came along for the ride. Soon after takeoff, a solar flare bombarded the ship with an unknown form of cosmic radiation that mutated their bodies and gave them fantastic powers. Richards became Mr. Fantastic, Susan Storm became Invisible Woman, Ben Grimm became the Thing, and Johnny Storm became the Human Torch.

NO CHARGE

Pledging to use their new powers for the good of mankind, the four adventurers formed a legal corporation. The Fantastic Four safeguards the planet from human and extraterrestrial super-menaces, and also specializes in pure scientific research and explorations into the unknown. Funded by the patents on inventions and scientific discoveries made by Richards, the team offers its services without charge.

I AIN'T BEN ANYMORE-- I'M WHAT SUSAN CALLED ME--THE THING!!

AND I'LL CALL MYSELF... MISTER FANTASTIC!!

The Fantastic Four have vowed to safeguard Earth.

On their first public mission, the Fantastic Four prevented the Mole Man conquering the world. They later stopped the Skrulls invading Earth and the Miracle Man from blackmailing New York City. They were also responsible for the return of Prince Namor, the Sub-Mariner: the Human Torch found him living like a tramp in the Bowery slums and helped restore his lost memory. The FF also uncovered the menace of Doctor Doom and made first contact with Uatu the Watcher and the mysterious Inhumans. They blocked Galactus from consuming the Earth and discovered the area of sub-space known as the Negative Zone. The team also battled the Frightful Four, the Overmind, and the Sphinx, and defended the Planet Xandar against a Skrull invasion.

ALTERNATE WORLDS

After a prolonged engagement, Reed Richards married Susan Storm and she gave birth to their son Franklin Richards. Soon afterward, Richards' scientist father Nathaniel switched young Franklin with his alternate-world teenage counterpart in an effort to help the team battle Hyperstorm, a menace they were destined to face in the future. Richards and Doctor Doom were later transported into a possible alternate future where the son of Franklin had conquered the universe.

A few months later, Franklin somehow created a pocket universe called Counter Earth, where he transported his parents to protect them from a psychic monster called Onslaught. The FF later returned and soon faced another reality-altering cosmic entity called Abraxas. Shortly after they defeated him, the Invisible Woman gave birth to a daughter, named Valeria Richards.

CHANGING THE WORLD

The Fantastic Four have been embroiled in every major event on Earth over the past several years. Reed supported the Superhuman Registration Act, although he lost the backing of every other member of the team. When the Civil War ended,

THE FANTASTIC FOUR
1 The Thing ***2*** Mr. Fantastic
3 Invisible Woman ***4*** Human Torch

BASES AND EQUIPMENT

The team established its first headquarters on the top five floors of the Baxter Building in Manhattan, New York City. Although this building was later destroyed, Richards designed another base that was constructed in outer space by his former mentor Noah Baxter. The new Baxter Building is equipped with a state-of-the-art security system that is regularly upgraded. Roberta, the Fantastic Four's robot receptionist, is networked with the team's main computer and can undertake hundreds of tasks simultaneously.

Richards has also designed many different types of Fantasti-cars for easy travel around Manhattan (they're easy to park). Each team member is equipped with a wireless communications link and an emergency flare gun. The FF also have a Pogo-Plane that is outfitted with vertical take off and landing capabilities, a captured Skrull starship that they use for galactic travel, and a time platform and space/time sled that allow them to visit alternate time eras or dimensions. The team's costumes are composed of unstable molecules that are specifically designed to adjust to their individual powers.

Roberta is able to operate 24 hours a day and can answer various calls simultaneously.

ESSENTIAL STORYLINES

- ***Greatest Villains of the Fantastic Four (tpb)*** The FF battle Psycho-Man, Blastaar, Annihilus, Puppet Master, the Mad Thinker, and Doctor Doom.
- ***Fantastic Four: Monsters Unleashed (tpb)*** The Hulk, Ghost Rider, Wolverine, and Spider-Man help the FF battle the Mole Man and the Skrulls.
- ***Fantastic Four: Nobody Gets Out Alive (tpb)*** The FF travel through time and various alternate dimensions on a hunt for the missing and presumed dead Reed Richards.
- ***Fantastic Four: Unthinkable (tpb)*** Doctor Doom attempts to use black magic as well as Reed and Sue's own children as weapons against the FF.
- ***Fantastic Four #1*** The Fantastic Four finally return after years apart.

he and Sue reunited and left the team for a while to re-examine their marriage. During the SECRET INVASION, the SKRULLS captured Reed and Sue and sent the others, including Franklin and Valeria, into the Negative Zone. They all survived and were reunited, but the experience inspired Reed to start exploring alternate universes.

The team have traveled into space and alternate dimensions.

FANTASTIC FOUR continued

WORLDS APART

Disturbed by the fact that the Superhuman Registration Act had caused so much trouble, resulting in the Civil War and the assassination of Captain America, Reed decided to explore other realities in an effort to discover what had gone wrong. To that end, he built a device called the Bridge and used it to locate alternative versions of himself, who had banded together to form the Interdimensional Council of Reeds.

These were versions of Reed who had lost their fathers. Because of this, they preferred to stay coldly detached from their worlds, and Reed refused to leave his family to join them. Nevertheless, they filled Reed's head with all sorts of new ideas, essentially crowd-sourcing solutions to his problems from within his multiple variants. Soon after, Reed decided to start up a new group called the Future Foundation, a group of thinkers—mostly younger people, even children—charged with coming up with fresh solutions to the world's problems.

The Interdimensional Council of Reeds featured all sorts of people with one thing in common. Each of them were their world's version of Reed Richards.

SURPRISE ATTACK

At a chaotic point in the lives of the Fantastic Four, Reed left Earth to deal with Galactus, Devourer of Worlds, and Sue Richards traveled deep into the ocean to help with a problem in Atlantis. This left Johnny Storm and a depowered Ben Grimm to watch over Franklin, Valeria, and the kids from the Future Foundation. Seizing their chance, the members of the fanatical Cult of the Negative Zone launched an attack on the Baxter Building, seeking to throw open the gateway to the Negative Zone, which Reed had sealed off from the Earth side.

After sealing the gateway to Earth, the Human Torch stood alone against the forces of Annihilus

THREAT OF ANNIHILATION

Working with the kids, Johnny Storm and Ben stopped the Cult. However, the gateway had opened, leaving the Earth exposed to an Annihilation Wave led by ANNIHILUS that threatened not only to destroy the planet but the rest of the galaxy. The only way to seal the gateway was from inside the Negative Zone, which would inevitably cut off that person's escape route. Ben volunteered, but at the last moment Johnny threw him to safety and sacrificed himself instead.

With Johnny gone, the remaining members of the Fantastic Four decided to focus their efforts on the Future Foundation. They adopted white uniforms with black trim and new logos. The young people on their roster included Alex Power (of the POWER PACK), Artie Maddicks (a mute mutant who could project images of thoughts; depowered but working with a helmet that duplicated his powers), Bentley 23 (a young clone of the WIZARD), DRAGON MAN, Franklin RICHARDS, LEECH (whose power-dampening power kept Franklin under control), and four clever Moloids (the subterranean race ruled by the MOLE MAN): Korr, Mik, Tong, and Turg.

The Fantastic Four sometimes arranged for a team of substitutes to take its place when it had to leave Earth. One team included Ant-Man II, Medusa, She-Hulk, and She-Thing.

Reed, Sue, and Ben ran the Future Foundation, but they also lined up some other adults to help. Reed's father Nathaniel RICHARDS joined. Johnny's will requested that SPIDER-MAN take his place, which the wall-crawler did. Franklin and Valeria also invited Doctor Doom to join, despite objections from Reed and Ben. (Doom soon set up a symposium of evil geniuses to figure out how to defeat Reed Richards and, later, the Council of Reeds.)

THE TORCH RETURNS

In the Negative Zone, Johnny stood against the Annihilation wave for as long as he could but was eventually defeated. Not content to let the hero die, Annihilus tried to torture him into opening the gateway to Earth, something Johnny couldn't have done if he'd wanted to. Johnny died three times, but Annihilus revived him each time and then threw him into prison and forced him to participate in arena combat.

When it seemed that Annihilus might find another way out of the Negative Zone, Johnny led a revolt against him with the help of his fellow prisoners, a team of universal INHUMANS known as the Light Brigade. They defeated Annihilus, and Johnny took the villain's Cosmic Control Rod, becoming the new ruler of the Negative Zone. Although not much time had passed on Earth, Johnny had spent a full two years in the Negative Zone by the time he returned to his teammates.

He arrived just in time, as his army turned the tide of battle and saved the Earth from KREE invasion. With Johnny now back, the team went on to stop the threat of the Mad Celestial and returned to calling themselves the Fantastic Four, while also maintaining the Future Foundation. The Fantastic Four soon had other problems to deal with, though, most notably the Quiet Man. This mysterious villain had been a student at Columbia University with Reed and Sue. Always jealous of their relationship, the Quiet Man tried to destroy the Fantastic Four. His actions nearly bankrupted the team and saw Ben sent to jail, but eventually he was defeated.

SECRET WARS

Soon after, the incursions from other universes caused the end of the world—but Reed managed to survive in a "life raft," a spaceship constructed by him and a handful of other heroes. Tragedy struck when Sue, Franklin, and Valeria were lost as the ship tried to escape the end of reality.

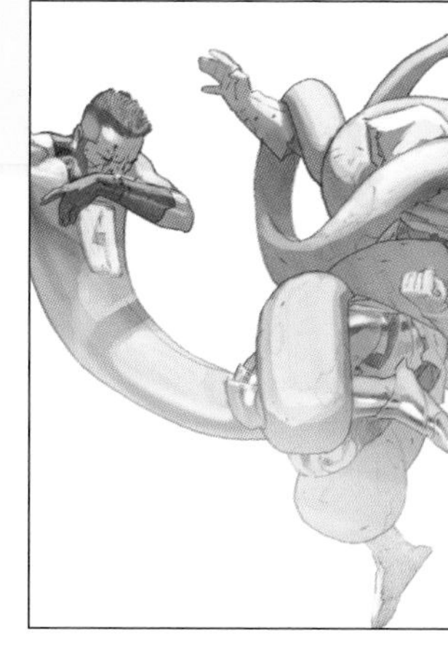
In their final conflict on Battleworld, Reed confronted and defeated Doom.

The ship crash-landed on Battleworld, a hodgepodge reality created by Doctor Doom, DOCTOR STRANGE, and the MOLECULE MAN from the remnants of various destroyed realities (*see* SECRET WARS). In the reality of Battleworld, Doom was its godlike ruler, with Sue as his wife, and Valeria and Franklin his children. Doom had had his revenge on his old enemies—Ben Grimm had been transformed into a huge wall protecting Doom's kingdom, while the Human Torch was trapped in the sky in a constant state of supernova, providing light to the world. Reed and his surviving allies soon managed to end Doom's rule and bring back their old realities. Reed, Sue, the children, and the Molecule Man then set off with the Future Foundation to create and explore a whole new Multiverse, returning Ben and Johnny to Earth.

After several years (in their time) making and exploring new universes, the Future Foundation came across a new threat: the Griever at the End of all Things. As this new enemy threatened them, Reed managed to send a signal out to his friends and bring them to his side. This included not just Johnny and Ben, but everyone who had ever fought alongside the team. The Fantastic Four were back—and were more fantastic than ever.

The Fantastic Four has fought alongside countless allies in their battles to protect Earth. When word spread that they had returned, their friends rushed to their aid.

FEAR ITSELF

It's all you have to fear

When the new Red Skull takes up the Hammer of Skadi, she unleashes an ancient terror aching to feed on the fear of the Earth and destroy the Norse Gods.

With the original Red Skull dead, his daughter Sin took up his mantle. With the aid of the Book of the Skull, which she recovered with the help of Baron Zemo, she set out to succeed at one mission from World War II in which her father had failed: the use of the Hammer of Skadi.

ATTACK OF THE WORTHY

The new Red Skull became the new incarnation of Skadi, and seven more hammers fell from the sky like meteors and landed around the world. They took control of their superpowered holders, transforming them into the Worthy, generals of the Asgardian superbeing the Serpent. The Worthy set to wreaking havoc and terrifying the locals.

As worldwide panic rose, Odin revealed that the Serpent was his long-banished brother Cul. He decided the wise move was to abandon the Asgard on Earth that had been shattered at the end of the Dark Reign. Over his son Thor's objections, he brought his people to a new, off-world Asgard and told them to prepare for war. Odin knew that the Serpent fed on the power of fear and believed the only way to defeat him would be to raze the planet, eliminating the terror along with the people who felt it. Thor insisted he be allowed to fight the Serpent, and Odin grudgingly let him go, despite a prophecy that Thor would die defeating the Serpent.

Skadi attacked Washington, D.C., and wounded Captain America (Bucky Barnes). This forced Steve Rogers to become Captain America again. Thor battled two of the Worthy, killing Angrir (whom Franklin Richards later restored to life as the Thing) and blasting Nul (Hulk) into space. Iron Man battled Mokk in Paris, alongside Pepper Potts in her Rescue armor. Other heroes battled the rest of the Worthy in terrible conflicts around the planet.

Following Iron Man's desperate plea, Odin granted him access to his workshop so he could build weapons capable of defeating the Worthy.

Despite Cul's destruction of his shield, Captain America and the bravest people in Broxton, Oklahoma, fought on against the Worthy, whom Cul had called there to join him in the final battle. The weapon-equipped Avengers joined the battle, with Thor wielding Odin's blade, Ragnarok, while Cap took up Thor's hammer. Together, they carried the day, but at the loss of Thor, who sacrificed himself in order to kill the Serpent. The Thunder God later battled the Demogorge and returned from the land of the dead.

Not even Captain America's unbreakable shield could withstand the power of the hammers of the Worthy.

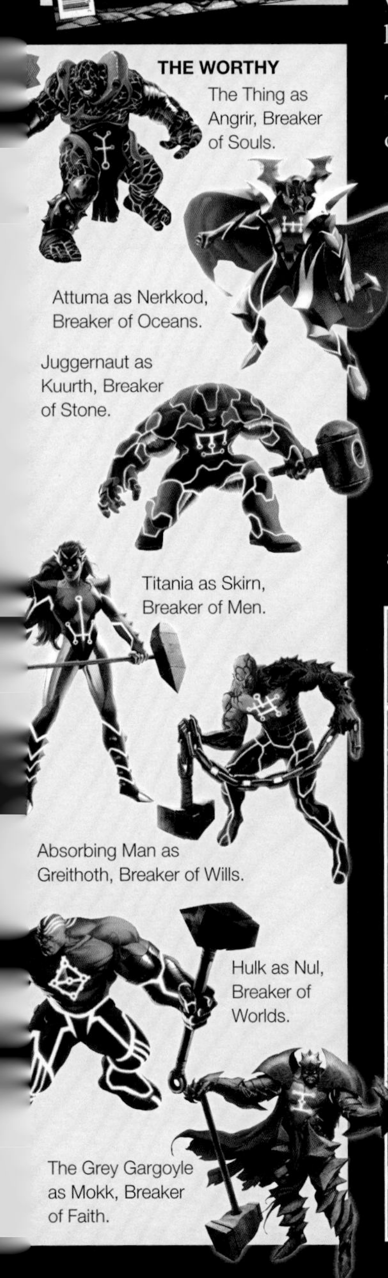

THE WORTHY

The Thing as Angrir, Breaker of Souls.

Attuma as Nerkkod, Breaker of Oceans.

Juggernaut as Kuurth, Breaker of Stone.

Titania as Skirn, Breaker of Men.

Absorbing Man as Greithoth, Breaker of Wills.

Hulk as Nul, Breaker of Worlds.

The Grey Gargoyle as Mokk, Breaker of Faith.

With the help of the dwarves of Svartalfheim, Iron Man used his repulsor technology and molten uru metal—plus Odin's blessing—to build weapons to make eight Avengers more powerful than ever.

SKADI REVEALED
At Adolf Hitler's behest, the Red Skull performed a ritual during World War II that brought the Hammer of Skadi to Earth. He could not lift the hammer, so he had a fortress built around it, guarded by Hitler's fanatical Thule Society. The new Red Skull launched a full-on attack on the fortress. She felt the hammer call to her, and when she grabbed it, it transformed her into Skadi, Herald of the Serpent.

FIFTY-STATE INITIATIVE

Super Heroes for all of America

FIFTY-STATE INITIATIVE

FACTFILE

KEY MEMBERS

ANT-MAN (Eric O'Grady) Can shrink or grow to dramatic sizes.

GAUNTLET Drill sergeant with an alien superweapon.

MUTANT ZERO (Typhoid Mary) Telekinesis, telepathy, and pyrokinesis.

TASKMASTER Martial arts expert with photographic reflexes.

TRAUMA Telepath and shapeshifter.

BARON VON BLITZSCHLAG Scientific genius and electricity control.

ADDITIONAL MEMBERS

ARMORY, CLOUD 9, HARDBALL, MICHAEL VAN PATRICK, and many others.

BASE

Camp Hammond, Stamford, Connecticut

FIRST APPEARANCE

Civil War: The Initiative #1 (April 2007)

ALLIES/FOES

ALLIES The US government, SHIELD, HAMMER, the Dark Avengers

FOES Any terrorist threat, the New Avengers

ISSUE #1

Michael Pointer becomes the new Guardian and joins Omega Flight. The Thunderbolts hunt down Hurricane. Iron Man (Tony Stark) begins selecting heroes for a new Avengers team.

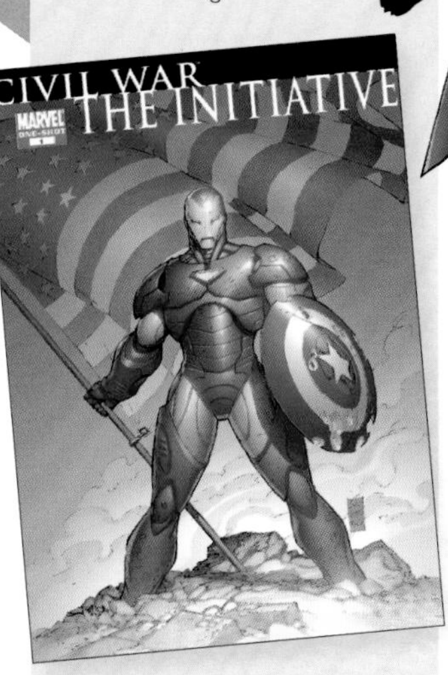

After the passage of the Superhuman Registration Act, Tony Stark (Iron Man) realized that SHIELD needed a plan for how to make use of all of the Super Heroes soon to be under its remit. During the Civil War, Stark, Reed Richards (Mister Fantastic), and Hank Pym brainstormed a long list of ideas for how to improve the world. The Fifty-State Initiative was number 41 on that list.

Gauntlet—the drill sergeant at Camp Hammond—greets the first busload of trainees as they arrive.

HEROES UNITED AND DEPLOYED

To get the Initiative started, Stark funded a super-team of his own: the Order. This team was ready to see action in the final battle of the Civil War. When Stark was made the director of SHIELD after the Civil War, he had the power to build a Super Hero team for each state in the nation, based on that prototype.

Many of the initial teams were simply existing teams or heroes brought into the new structure. The Great Lakes Avengers, for example, were renamed the Great Lakes Initiative and assigned to their home state of Wisconsin, while Hellcat was sent to Alaska to serve as its hero.

HERO BOOT CAMP

Many new heroes joined the Initiative, and these required training to make the best use of their powers and reduce the danger they presented to others. To this end, Stark set up Camp Hammond as the Initiative's headquarters and training facility. Sergeant Joe Green (GAUNTLET) served as the base's drill instructor under administrator Henry Peter GYRICH with Hank Pym as the chief administrator, and Baron WERNER VON BLITZSCHLAG in charge of the science division. Gyrich formed a black ops team answerable only to himself, called the Shadow Initiative. Members included Bengal, CONSTRICTOR, the Scarlet Spiders, TRAUMA, and Mutant Zero (TYPHOID MARY).

Stark formed the Order as a template for the Fifty-State Initiative. The California team was the first to be generated specifically for the program.

EARLY TROUBLES

In the first combat training session, a terrified ARMORY fired an alien weapon named the Tactigon wildly and killed fellow recruit Michael VAN PATRICK.

The following cover-up came back to haunt the Initiative when Von Blitzschlag fitted a clone of Van Patrick with the Tactigon, causing him to become psychotic and go on a murderous rampage.

Initiative recruits helped during WORLD WAR HULK and the SECRET INVASION. In the confusion surrounding the HULK's attack, SLAPSTICK beat Gauntlet into a coma for berating the NEW WARRIORS, of which Slapstick had once been a member. Gauntlet later recovered.

SHIELD scientists developed Super-Power-Inhibiting Nanobots (SPIN) technology that could be used to remove superpowers. HYDRA leader Senator WOODMAN persuaded Initiative recruit HARDBALL to steal this for him. Later, when Woodman blackmailed Hardball into continuing to work for him, Hardball killed him, left the Initiative, and took over the leadership of Hydra instead.

The Thunderbolts were brought into the Initiative.

THE SKRULL INFILTRATION

Before the Secret Invasion, the SKRULL Queen VERANKE made sure to insert a Skrull into every team in all 50 states. When the Skrulls launched their attack, many of the spies revealed themselves, and the rest of the Initiative's members could not tell who to trust. Using 3-D MAN's powers, TRIATHLON managed to spot most of them located at Camp Hammond, but few other teams were so lucky.

Afterward, DOC SAMSON held group therapy sessions for those replaced by Skrulls. When Norman Osborn (*see* GREEN GOBLIN) became director of HAMMER, he changed the name of the program to the Thunderbolt Initiative.

He then secretly placed TASKMASTER and the HOOD in charge so that they could use the base to create new forces for Osborn's DARK AVENGERS team.

Soon after, a failsafe program set up by the Skrull impersonating Hank Pym reactivated RAGNAROK (a clone of THOR). After helping to stop Ragnarok's rampage, an underground team called Counter Force—made up of former New Warriors—revealed the scandal behind Michael Van Patrick's death and cover-up. Osborn used this as an excuse to shut down Camp Hammond. He later opened a new training facility, Camp HAMMER, in New Mexico. After Osborn's fall from power, Camp Hammer was shut down and a new Avengers Academy to teach young heroes was opened.

When the Civil War ended, Stark faced a flood of registered heroes to choose from for the Initiative's teams.

ESSENTIAL STORYLINES

- ***Civil War: The Initiative #1*** As the new leader of SHIELD, Tony Stark considers how to best organize the heroes available to him.
- ***Avengers: The Initiative #1*** The first team of recruits arrives at Camp Hammond and promptly suffers its first disaster with the training death of Michael Van Patrick.
- ***Avengers: The Initiative #8–11*** KIA is created and nearly destroys the Initiative.

FLUX

FIRST APPEARANCE *Incredible Hulk* #17 (August 2000)
REAL NAME Benjamin Tibbetts **OCCUPATION** US Army private
BASE Washington, D.C. **HEIGHT** Variable
WEIGHT Variable **EYES** Green **HAIR** Green
SPECIAL POWERS/ABILITIES Exposure to gamma radiation and experimentation by the military gave Flux superhuman strength and durability; however his physiology is in a constant state of change.

Benny Tibbetts enlisted in the US army to fight in the Gulf War and was caught in the blast of gamma bombs dropped by a black-ops team headed by General Ryker. Tibbetts survived, but like the Hulk before him, was forever changed by the gamma radiation. His self-doubts prevented his powers from permanently catalyzing, and as Flux his body stayed in a constant state of transformation. General Ryker sent him to fight the Hulk twice, but he lost each time. Later, AIM captured him, and Grey of the Gamma Corps killed him on the orders of General Ryker.

General Ryker hoped that his creation, Flux, would defeat the Hulk, but Flux had too many mental insecurities.

FOOLKILLER

Paralyzed from the waist down, Ross Everbest's childhood was never going to be easy; then his parents were killed in the Korean War. However, when traveling revivalist preacher Reverend Mike Pike used faith-healing to restore his legs, Everbest's life changed. Joining Pike on the road, Everbest became increasingly angry with the "immoral fools" he encountered every day. Vowing to rid the world of sinners and dissidents, he became Foolkiller, his murder spree beginning when he discovered Pike indulging in a drunken orgy.

Everbest's psychotic reign of death ended when he was killed by the Man-Thing. His example inspired two more Foolkillers: Greg Salinger, who was eventually locked up in a mental institution; and Kurt Gerhardt, who was killed by Deadpool. Salinger returned as the Foolkiller to join Deadpool's Heroes for Hire.

FACTFILE
REAL NAME
Ross G. Everbest
OCCUPATION
Killer
BASE
Mobile

HEIGHT 6 ft
WEIGHT 185 lbs
EYES Blue
HAIR Blond

FIRST APPEARANCE
Man-Thing #3
(March 1974)

FOOLKILLER

POWERS
Psychopathic energy gave him greater strength and endurance than an average man of his weight; possessed a raygun, he termed his "purification gun," capable of disintegrating victims.

Foolkiller had a calling card warning victims that they had 24 hours to live and telling them to use the time wisely.

FORCE WORKS

FACTFILE
MEMBERS AND POWERS
CENTURY
Composite being of 100 alien warriors.
IRON MAN
Powered armor; flight; energy blasts.
MOONRAKER
Emits electrical energy from hands.
SCARLET WITCH
Chaos magic.
SPIDER-WOMAN
Various spider powers; spins webs of psionic energy.
U.S.AGENT
Enhanced strength; expert combatant.
WONDER MAN
Body composed of ionic energy.
BASE
The Works, Ventura, California

FIRST APPEARANCE
Force Works #1
(July 1994)

FORCE WORKS

After the disbanding of the Avengers West Coast, Tony Stark (Iron Man) founded Force Works, a team with a more aggressive, proactive stance. By using the Scarlet Witch's hex powers, combined with data from a predictive supercomputer, the members of Force Works set out to squash budding threats before they could escalate to crisis levels.

On Force Works' first mission, Wonder Man seemingly died while battling a band of Kree warriors. The team bounced back from this loss by welcoming the alien Century into their ranks. Soon, the events known as the Crossing caused Iron Man to appear to turn traitor, behaving irrationally and murderously due to the mind-controlling Immortus. A new hero named Moonraker (claiming to be Libra) joined the group to distract them from Immortus' larger schemes. Force Works dissolved following the Crossing episode. A new Force Works team was assigned to Iowa for the Fifty-State Initiative.

FORCE WORKS
1 Spider-Woman (Julia Carpenter) ***2*** Wonder Man
3 Iron Man ***4*** Scarlet Witch ***5*** U.S.Agent

FORGE

FACTFILE
REAL NAME
Unknown
OCCUPATION
Inventor; former soldier
BASE
Dallas, Texas

HEIGHT 6 ft
WEIGHT 180 lbs
EYES Brown
HAIR Black

FIRST APPEARANCE
X-Men #184
(August 1984)

POWERS
Mutant ability gives superhuman talent for inventing mechanical devices. While even the greatest inventors must work out the principals and designs of their inventions, the ideas for Forge's inventions spring fully formed from his mutant mind.

FORGE

The Native American who became known as Forge was not only trained in mystic arts by Naze, a shaman in his Cheyenne tribe, but was also a mutant, with the ability to invent highly sophisticated mechanical devices.

Forge lost a leg and a hand during the Vietnam War and designed mechanical limbs to replace them. When industrialist Anthony Stark (*see* IRON MAN) stopped making advanced weaponry for the federal government, the US Defense Department began buying new weaponry designs from Forge. During that time, he created a device that could detect hidden aliens and one that neutralized mutant powers.

Forge later joined the X-MEN, subsequently worked with X-FACTOR, and had a relationship with STORM. After being shot by BISHOP, who was hunting Hope SUMMERS, Forge went insane and was barely stopped before he allowed an interdimensional invasion of Earth. He has since fought alongside CABLE and continues to have close ties with the X-Men and Storm.

FREEDOM FORCE

FIRST APPEARANCE *Uncanny X-Men* #199 (November 1985)
BASE Washington, D.C.
MEMBERS AND POWERS **Stonewall** [1] Superstrength; **Spiral** [2] Spellcaster; **Destiny** [3] Precognition; **Mystique** [4] (leader) Shapeshifter; **Pyro** [5] Controls fire; **Crimson Commando** [6] Expert combatant; **Avalanche** [7] Groundquakes; **Blob** Immovable; **Spider Woman** Spider powers; **Super Sabre** Superspeed. *[Dazzler [8] is not a member]*

Freedom Force was an incarnation of the BROTHERHOOD OF EVIL MUTANTS, formed to wipe out mutant threats to America. The team clashed with outlaw mutants such as the X-MEN and X-FACTOR. The Force later teamed with the X-Men to save Dallas, Texas, from the ADVERSARY, but the group disbanded after a disastrous mission to the Middle East. An all-new Freedom Force team was formed for Montana as part of the FIFTY-STATE INITIATIVE. It included the Challenger, Cloud 9, Spinner, Think Tank, and Equinox.

FORGOTTEN ONE, THE

FIRST APPEARANCE *Eternals* #13 (July 1977)
REAL NAME Unknown; has been known as Gilgamesh
OCCUPATION Adventurer; agent of the Celestials
BASE Mobile **HEIGHT** 6 ft 5 in **WEIGHT** 269 lbs
EYES Brown **HAIR** Black
SPECIAL POWERS/ABILITIES Superhuman strength and stamina; immortality; full mental control over body; ability to manipulate matter on a subatomic scale.

As an Eternal known throughout the years as Hero or Gilgamesh, the immortal Forgotten One has lived for millennia. For meddling in the affairs of humanity, he was confined to the city of Olympia for centuries, only regaining his freedom after helping foil an attack by the Deviants—grotesque, distant cousins of humanity. As Gilgamesh, he served with the AVENGERS, but he was killed during a battle with IMMORTUS. Reborn later in a new body, he could not recall his former life. He was working in a circus in Brazil when AJAK found him and restored his lost memories.

FRANKENSTEIN'S MONSTER

FIRST APPEARANCE *X-Men* #40 (January 1968)
REAL NAME None **OCCUPATION** Caretaker; wanderer
BASE Bavaria, Germany **HEIGHT** 8 ft
WEIGHT 325 lbs **EYES** Brown **HAIR** Brown
SPECIAL POWERS/ABILITIES The Monster possesses superhuman strength and stamina; able to go into suspended animation when exposed to intense cold.

In the late 18th century, Victor Frankenstein created a living person from corpses. Spurned by his creator, the Monster forced Frankenstein to create a mate for him. After Frankenstein killed her, the Monster slew Frankenstein's own bride and pursued him to the Arctic. The Monster revived in 1898 and again in modern times. As "Adam," he assisted monster hunter Elsa BLOODSTONE. Clones of the Monster were created by both the Nazis and SHIELD, and a descendant of Frankenstein used an army of them to attack the Jean Grey School for Higher Learning. The original Monster then joined the HOWLING COMMANDOS.

FRENZY

FIRST APPEARANCE *X-Factor* #4 (May 1986)
REAL NAME Joanna Cargill **OCCUPATION** Adventurer
BASE Jean Grey School for Higher Learning
HEIGHT 6 ft 11 in **WEIGHT** 275 lbs
EYES Brown **HAIR** Black
SPECIAL POWERS/ABILITIES Joanna has steel-hard skin, rendering her invulnerable to most harm, and she possesses superhuman strength.

After accidentally killing her abusive father when her mutant powers manifested, Joanna Cargill ran away from home and became a mercenary. She ended up working as a member of APOCALYPSE's Alliance of Evil, but she later threw in with the Femizons instead. She found a home with MAGNETO's Acolytes, serving with them for years. After experiencing life as a hero in the Age of X reality created by LEGION, she changed her ways and joined the X-MEN. During the X-Men's schism she followed WOLVERINE, and worked closely with CRYSTAL's INHUMANS when the Terrigen Mists threatened mutantkind.

FROST, EMMA

Psi of the highest order

FROST, EMMA

FACTFILE

REAL NAME
Emma Frost

OCCUPATION
CEO of Frost International; Instructor, Massachusetts Academy

BASE
Massachusetts Academy

HEIGHT 5 ft 10 in
WEIGHT 125 lbs
EYES Blue
HAIR Ash blond

FIRST APPEARANCE
X-Men #129
(January 1980)

POWERS
Frost is a formidable telepath who can read minds and project thoughts into others' minds, controlling their actions. She can project pain and knock out victims by touching their brows. She later developed a secondary mutation that allows her to take on a nearly indestructible, diamond-hard form at will, during which time she cannot use her mental powers.

Emma Frost was born into a wealthy New England family. Gifted with a superb business brain and mutant powers of telepathy, she spurned her father's fortune and set out on her own. At a remarkably young age, she was running a multi-billion-dollar corporation specializing in transportation and electronics, which she re-named Frost International. She also became the chair of a college prep school called the Massachusetts Academy, where she trained young mutants.

Emma was one of the Phoenix Five, alongside Namor, Scott Summers, Piotr Rasputin, and Illyana Rasputin.

JOIN THE CLUB

Emma's great wealth, intelligence, and charisma soon attracted the attention of the Hellfire Club, an elite social organization of powerful politicians and businessmen and women. When Frost and Sebastian Shaw discovered a plot by Hellfire Club leader Edward Buckman to build massive Sentinel robots to hunt down and destroy mutants, they seized control of the organization's Inner Circle, and took the code names White Queen and Black King.

As the White Queen, Frost became an enemy of the X-Men. However, guilt over her inability to prevent the violent deaths of her mutant student team, the Hellions, caused her to offer the Massachusetts Academy to Professor X, who turned it into his new School for Gifted Youngsters. Emma Frost taught there, instructing the young mutants of Generation X, until her sister Adrienne ruined the school as an act of revenge and killed one of the students.

X-WOMAN

Emma later joined the X-Men and commenced a telepathic affair with Cyclops. After his wife, Jean Grey, died, the two began a physical relationship. Emma has never had children, but the Stepford Cuckoos and hundreds of other clones were created from her eggs.

During the Dark Reign, Emma became part of the Cabal and led a team of Dark X-Men for Norman Osborn (*see* Green Goblin). However, she and Namor, who was also part of the Cabal, betrayed Osborn at the critical moment. When the X-Men split into two groups, Emma stayed with Cyclops in Utopia rather than leave to teach at Wolverine's new school.

Emma underwent a secondary mutation during the destruction of Genosha, and she can now turn her body into almost impenetrable living diamond.

Emma was on the moon when Iron Man's attempt to destroy the Phoenix Force broke it into pieces, and she became one of the Phoenix Five. She was furious with Cyclops when he took her fragment of the Phoenix Force to become Dark Phoenix, but stuck with him after he lost the Phoenix Force. When the Terrigen Mists killed Cyclops, Emma made people believe Black Bolt had killed him—leading to conflict between the Inhumans and X-Men. She was appointed ruler of the mutant territory of New Tian during Hydra's takeover of the US, but was secretly fighting against Hydra's forces. Emma then joined a Cabal with Havok, Miss Sinister, and Bastion to unleash Mothervine—a virus that could make more mutants—on the world. But when Emma realized it could also be used to control people she re-joined the X-Men in order to help stop it.

FRIGHTFUL FOUR

FRIGHTFUL FOUR

FACTFILE

ORIGINAL MEMBERS AND POWERS

PASTE-POT PETE
Later known as the Trapster.

SANDMAN
Made of living sand.

WIZARD
Brilliant scientist and inventor

MEDUSA
Inhuman with prehensile hair.

BASE
Subterranean Manhattan headquarters; mobile

FIRST APPEARANCE
Fantastic Four #36 (March 1965)

The WIZARD (Bentley Wittman) was a much-lauded scientist until the similarly brilliant MISTER FANTASTIC (Reed Richards) led the FANTASTIC FOUR into the limelight and forced him from the public eye. Insanely jealous, the Wizard committed himself to destroying Reed and his friends by establishing the Frightful Four team of Super Villains. The original lineup consisted of the Wizard himself, SANDMAN, Paste Pot Pete (LATER TRAPSTER) and MEDUSA.

The Wizard changed his team's roster many times, but it continued to suffer defeats. Even when it caught the Fantastic Four off guard—during Reed and Sue Storm's engagement party, for example—the Wizard's team was still beaten. The search for new members led the Wizard to look everywhere, even placing ads and holding auditions. Other members included ABSORBING MAN, Beetle, Brute (an alternate Reed Richards), CONSTRICTOR, DEADPOOL, DRAGON MAN, DREADKNIGHT, ELECTRO, HYDRO-MAN, KLAW, LIVING LASER, LLYRA, Man-Bull, MISTER HYDE, RED GHOST, SHE-THING, TASKMASTER, THUNDRA, and TITANIA.

FRIGHTFUL FOUR
1 Wizard
2 Hydro-Man
3 Trapster
4 Salamandra

FROG-MAN

FIRST APPEARANCE Marvel Team-Up #121 (September 1982)
REAL NAME Eugene Paul Patilio
OCCUPATION High-school student **BASE** New York City
HEIGHT 5 ft 8 in **WEIGHT** 158 lbs **EYES** Brown **HAIR** Red
SPECIAL POWERS/ABILITIES Frog-man wears an electrically-powered suit with leaping coils built into his boots; can leap a maximum height of 60 ft and a maximum distance of 100 ft.

Eugene's father designed a pair of electrically powered leaping coils. Calling himself Leap-Frog, he took to crime to support his family, but ended up in jail. To redeem his father's name, Eugene donned one of his old costumes to become the crimefighter Frog-Man, helping SPIDER-MAN and the HUMAN TORCH defeat the SPEED DEMON. Eugene later tried to team up with the Toad and Spider-Kid (now called the Steel Spider). A SKRULL posing as Frog-Man joined the Action Pack, but was killed during the SECRET INVASION. Frog-Man helped the AVENGERS defeat Flag-Smasher when the Spider-Queen turned Manhattan into "Spider-Island."

FURY, JAKE

FIRST APPEARANCE *Strange Tales* #159 (August 1967)
REAL NAME Jacob Fury
OCCUPATION Spy **BASE** Mobile
HEIGHT 5 ft 10 in **WEIGHT** 185 lbs **EYES** Blue **HAIR** Brown
SPECIAL POWERS/ABILITIES Jake is a genius and an excellent combatant as well as a top spy.

Jake Fury was born and raised in New York City with his older brother Nick FURY. Like his brother, Jake excelled at espionage, joining the Great Wheel organization after WWII and gaining the code name Scorpio. Jake uncovered the tech that would create Life Model Decoys (LMDs), accidentally creating one of himself. He seemingly joined Zodiac and became a criminal, but when he committed suicide was revealed to be an LMD. The real Jake went under deep cover as HYDRA's leader, Kraken, disrupting the organization. After arranging the death of BARON STRUCKER, Jake gave Daisy JOHNSON a letter and has not been seen since.

FURY, NICK, JR.

FURY, NICK, JR.

Born to Nia Jones, Marcus Johnson never knew his real father. He was serving with the US Army in Afghanistan when he received word his mother had been killed during FEAR ITSELF. When he and his pal Phil COULSON came back home for the funeral, men working for the villain Orion attacked him, wanting the Infinity Formula in his blood. He soon found out that Nick FURY was his real father, and he changed his name to Nick Fury, Jr. After defeating Orion and his mercenaries, both Fury Jr. and Coulson joined SHIELD's secret AVENGERS team.

During CIVIL WAR II, Fury went undercover to take out a HYDRA cell, faking his own death to do so. Afterward, he remained rogue for a while. He eventually rejoined SHIELD and found himself revisiting one of his father's old missions while dealing with Hydra agent Frankie Noble.

FACTFILE

REAL NAME
Nicholas Fury, Jr.

OCCUPATION
Agent of SHIELD

BASE
SHIELD Helicarrier

HEIGHT 6 ft
WEIGHT 185 lbs
EYES Brown
HAIR Bald

FIRST APPEARANCE
Battle Scars #1 (January 2012)

POWERS
Nick is a trained soldier. He inherited some of the Infinity Formula in his father's blood, giving him longevity and helping him heal fast.

NICK FURY, SEE PAGE 142

FURY, NICK

Agent of SHIELD

Nick Fury grew up in New York during the Great Depression of the 1930s. He enlisted in the US Army at the outbreak of World War II, eventually becoming the sergeant in command of the HOWLING COMMANDOS, an elite unit of Able Company given the most dangerous missions.

Once a gung-ho sergeant during World War II, Fury became Director of SHIELD.

FACTFILE

REAL NAME
Nicholas Joseph Fury

OCCUPATION
Spymaster, director of SHIELD

BASE
SHIELD mobile Helicarrier

HEIGHT 6 ft 1 in
WEIGHT 225 lbs
EYES Brown
HAIR Brown, graying at temples

FIRST APPEARANCE
Sgt. Fury and His Howling Commandos #1 (May 1963)

FURY, NICK

As director for the Strategic Hazard Intervention Espionage Logistics Directorate (SHIELD), Fury had access to state-of-the-art weapons and technologies.

INFINITY FORMULA

Fury and his Howlers racked up impressive victories over the AXIS forces, defeating such foes as BARON VON STRUCKER and his Blitzkrieg Squad, and the RED SKULL. Wounded, Fury was injected with an experimental Infinity Formula by Professor Berthold Sternberg. The formula allowed Fury to survive what would have been fatal injuries (though he did lose his left eye) and extend his life, but the drawback was that Fury needed a yearly dosage to survive—and for decades Professor Sternberg blackmailed Fury in order to provide the necessary supply of the drug. After the war, Fury became an agent for the OSS, and later the CIA, earning the rank of colonel. Fury then headed SHIELD, a worldwide peacekeeping force.

POWERS

Nick Fury is a trained soldier with decades of experience. His youth and vigor have been maintained, despite his age, by the rejuvenating Infinity Formula. He is an expert martial artist and highly trained in the use of all kinds of weapons, both conventional and advanced.

THE ENEMY WITHIN

After Fury led a failed coup attempt in Latveria, he lost his position as director of SHIELD. He subsequently formed a team of SECRET WARRIORS to help fight the SKRULLS and, later, HYDRA. This turned out to be a ploy he'd engineered with his brother Jake FURY to destroy Hydra. Fury's illegitimate son Mikel had thought Jake was his father, but when he learned the truth, he joined the Secret Warriors—only to be killed in action. A long-hidden son of Fury's—Marcus Johnson, now known as Nick FURY JR.—joined SHIELD.

Resourceful, cool, courageous, and committed to the cause, Fury is a superb field agent and a brilliant leader.

THE UNSEEN

When Fury was asked to investigate the death of UATU THE WATCHER, it was revealed that Fury had been an LMD (Life Model Decoy) for decades. The real Fury was far older, having taken over from Woodrow McCord in the 1950s as Earth's secret protector, prepared to do anything to defend humanity. When the Watcher had endangered his role, the real Fury killed him, but as punishment was transformed into the Unseen—a chained figure doomed to watch events but never interfere. In recent times Fury, as the Unseen, managed to warn the EXILES of a threat called the Time-Eater, which saved much of reality.

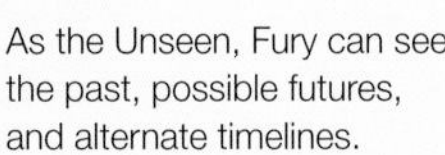

As the Unseen, Fury can see the past, possible futures, and alternate timelines.

ESSENTIAL STORYLINES

- ***Strange Tales #135*** Nick Fury is recruited by SHIELD to be its director in its war against Hydra.
- ***Nick Fury vs. SHIELD #1–6*** Having discovered corruption deep within his own spy organization, Fury must battle his own men.
- ***Secret War #1–5*** When Fury becomes aware of a clear and present danger to world security, he must organize a covert team of superhuman operatives to wage a secret war.

GALACTUS

Devourer of worlds

GALACTUS

FACTFILE

REAL NAME
Galen

OCCUPATION
Consumer of planets

BASE
Mobile

HEIGHT 26 ft 9 in (variable)
WEIGHT 18 tons (variable)
EYES Unknown; appear white to humanoids
HAIR Unknown; appears black to humanoids

FIRST APPEARANCE
Fantastic Four #48 (March 1966)

POWERS

Manipulates vast cosmic power; can restructure matter and deliver a planet-shattering energy blast; able to teleport across the galaxy and create force-fields; travels the galaxy in a worldship the size of the solar system; also pilots a smaller, circular "shuttle."

In the last universe's final moments, Galactus awaited his death.

The only survivor of the universe that came before our own, Galactus' fate is inextricably bound up with that of the entire cosmos. Although at times he has been a force for good, far more often he has brought doom, destroying whole peoples and consuming entire planets, for his hunger for energy is insatiable; without it, the "devourer of worlds" would cease to exist.

GALEN OF TAA

Born Galen, on the paradise world of Taa, Galactus was fated to live in the last days of his universe just as it was entering the final stages of the Big Crunch. Realizing that his people were doomed, he persuaded them to pilot a vessel into the heart of the Crunch, to die in one last act of heroism. His people perished, but Galactus survived and was reborn with an immense hunger that could only be sated by consuming the life-energies of a world. At first he searched for uninhabited planets, but his eternal hunger gradually forced him to consume planets populated by sentient races. He created heralds to find him new worlds to consume.

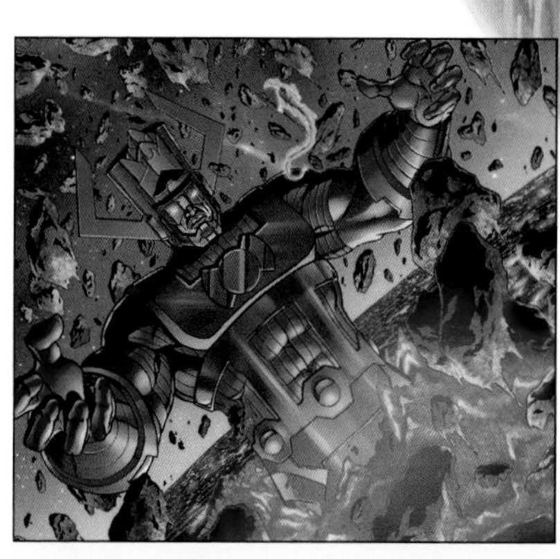
As the centuries passed, countless worlds crumbled before Galactus' devouring might.

HERALDS AND FATE

When Galactus reached the planet Zenn-La, a Zenn-Lavian struck a deal with him to save his world, and became the Silver Surfer. He eventually betrayed his master to protect Earth. At one point, Galactus was killed, but he was later resurrected to help prevent Abraxas from destroying the entire Multiverse.

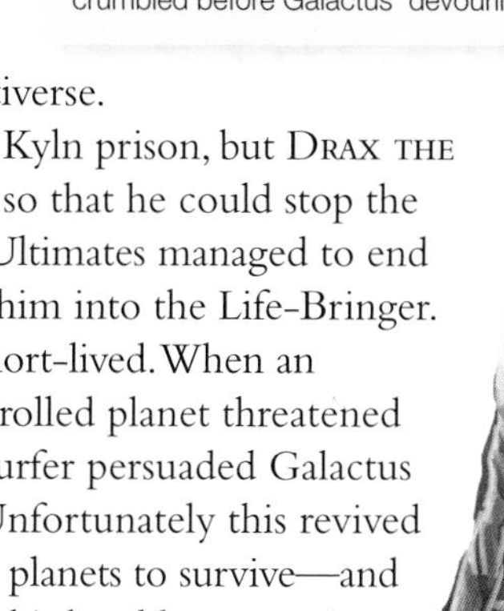

Galactus was held in the Kyln prison, but Drax the Destroyer broke him out so that he could stop the Annihilation Wave. The Ultimates managed to end his hunger and transform him into the Life-Bringer. However, his peace was short-lived. When an Ultron/Hank Pym-controlled planet threatened the universe, the Silver Surfer persuaded Galactus to consume the world. Unfortunately this revived Galactus' need to devour planets to survive—and the Silver Surfer became his herald once again.

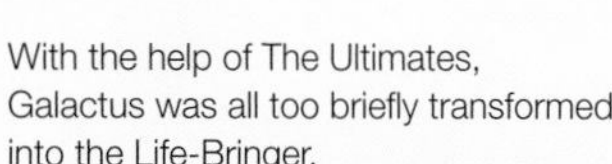
With the help of The Ultimates, Galactus was all too briefly transformed into the Life-Bringer.

ESSENTIAL STORYLINES

- ***Fantastic Four* #48–50**
Galactus discovers the Earth and, for the very first time in his immortal life, experiences defeat.
- ***Silver Surfer Vol. 1* #1**
Galactus' first meeting with Norrin Radd, soon to become the Silver Surfer, is detailed.
- ***Galactus the Devourer* #1–6**
Galactus is seemingly destroyed by the combined efforts of the Avengers, the Fantastic Four, and the Shi'ar Empire.

GAEA

FIRST APPEARANCE *Doctor Strange* #6 (February 1975) **REAL NAME** Gaea **OCCUPATION** Goddess **BASE** Earth **HEIGHT** Variable **WEIGHT** Variable **EYES** Blue **HAIR** Brown **SPECIAL POWERS/ABILITIES** Possesses enormous mystical energies tied to the Earth; commands the forces of nature, such as storms and volcanic activity; power to heal and make things grow; telekinetic abilities; able to bestow magical powers.

Gaea is the embodiment of the spirit of life, growth, harvest, and renewal on Earth. One of the Elder Gods who ruled the world when humanity was not even a glimmer, Gaea was the only one not to devolve into a demon, instead becoming Mother Earth. With ODIN, Gaea conceived THOR, who is both of Asgard and of Earth, the champion of both realms. During the Chaos War, she gave HERCULES the power he needed to defeat AMATSU-MIKABOSHI. With Freyja and Idunn, she became part of the All-Mother who rules Asgardia.

GALACTUS, SEE PAGE 143

GAMORA

Gamora is the sole survivor of the Zen-Whoberi, an alien race wiped out by the Badoon. The Mad Titan THANOS rescued Gamora as an infant and trained her to become the deadliest assassin in the galaxy so she could kill the MAGUS, an evil future version of ADAM WARLOCK whose Universal Church of Truth had wiped out her people in her original timeline.

Thanos killed her after she recognized the threat he presented to all life in the galaxy and rebelled against him. Warlock absorbed her spirit into his Soul Gem. She returned in a new form to stop Thanos from using the Infinity Gauntlet, and she guarded the Time Gem as a member of the Infinity Watch.

Gamora later led the fight against the ANNIHILATION, helping stop the first wave. During the second, she was absorbed into the PHALANX but freed when they were defeated. She later joined STAR-LORD's new GUARDIANS OF THE GALAXY.

GAMORA

FACTFILE

REAL NAME
Gamora

OCCUPATION
Former assassin; galactic hero

BASE
Mobile

HEIGHT 6 ft
WEIGHT 170 lbs
EYES Green
HAIR Black

FIRST APPEARANCE
Strange Tales #180 (June 1975)

POWERS
Gamora is an expert gymnast and martial artist proficient with all known weapons. She has enhanced durability, endurance, strength, and speed.

GAMBIT

GAMBIT

FACTFILE

REAL NAME
Remy LeBeau

OCCUPATION
Professional thief, adventurer

BASE
New Orleans, Louisiana; the Xavier Institute, Salem Center, New York State

HEIGHT 6 ft 1 in
WEIGHT 175 lbs
EYES Red (with black sclera)
HAIR Auburn

FIRST APPEARANCE
The Uncanny X-Men #266 (August 1990)

POWERS
Mutant ability to charge small objects with an unknown form of energy; when he throws the objects at a target, they explode on impact.

The mutant Gambit (Remy LeBeau), was abducted soon after his birth by members of the Thieves' Guild of New Orleans. Hoping to make peace with their rivals in the Assassins' Guild, the Thieves' Guild arranged for Remy to marry the granddaughter of the leader of the Assassins' Guild. Her brother Julien was opposed to the union, and Remy killed him in a duel. Banished from New Orleans, Remy became the international master thief known as Gambit. He was employed by MISTER SINISTER to organize the MARAUDERS, a mutant team of assassins, but was shocked when Sinister then sent the Marauders to massacre the MORLOCKS.

Later, Gambit met and aided STORM, who had been turned into a child, and she sponsored his membership in the X-MEN, where he met ROGUE and began a longstanding affair with her. Gambit later served as one of APOCALYPSE's Horsemen—Death—and rejoined the Marauders. He helped save Hope SUMMERS and came back to the X-Men. He traveled with X-23 for a while, before returning to the X-Men and marrying Rogue.

Gambit and Rogue's relationship has had its ups and downs and, occasionally, an explosive side.

Rogue gives Gambit a taste of his own medicine—an energy blast that knocks him off his feet.

GARGOYLE

GARGOYLE

FACTFILE

REAL NAME
Isaac Christians

OCCUPATION
Caretaker

BASE
The estate of Daimon Hellstrom

HEIGHT 5 ft 10 in
WEIGHT 204 lbs
EYES Red
HAIR None

FIRST APPEARANCE
Defenders #94 (April 1981)

POWERS
Possesses the increased strength and mystic durability of one of the demon race. He can also levitate, fly, and project bolts of eldritch force from his hands; leathery skin is bulletproof; impervious to disease and to aging.

In order to secure economic prosperity for his impoverished town, elderly Isaac Christians made a pact with a demonic group called the Six-Fingered Hand. He allowed his essence to be transplanted into the body of a demon, while the demon's mind would reside within his own human body. This demon had formerly been trapped in stone form as a gargoyle, as seen on ancient churches throughout Europe.

Despite his appearance, the Gargoyle was not evil, and after the destruction of his human body, he rebelled against the Six-Fingered Hand and joined the Defenders. At one point, his body became the vessel for the Dragon of the Moon, and he found a new body that could change to his Gargoyle form and back at will. He later became an instructor at Camp Hammond before retiring.

The Gargoyle should not be confused with a similarly-named Soviet agent (real name: Yuri Topolov) who attempted to capture the Hulk on the eve of the latter's creation and was the father of the Gremlin.

GATEWAY

FIRST APPEARANCE *Uncanny X-Men* #227 (March 1988)
REAL NAME Unrevealed
OCCUPATION None known **BASE** Australia
HEIGHT 4 ft 6 in **WEIGHT** 80 lbs
EYES Brown **HAIR** Gray-black
SPECIAL POWERS/ABILITIES Ability to open teleportation doorways, transdimensional clairvoyant.

The mysterious, silent Gateway is an Aboriginal Australian mutant who can open teleportation doorways. The outlaw Reavers forced Gateway to assist them by threatening to destroy an aboriginal sacred site. The X-Men later evicted the Reavers from their headquarters, and Gateway became an unofficial member. Gateway has a special connection to M and is an ancestor of Bishop. He became the mentor of Manifold but was later killed by Ultimaton (Weapon XV).

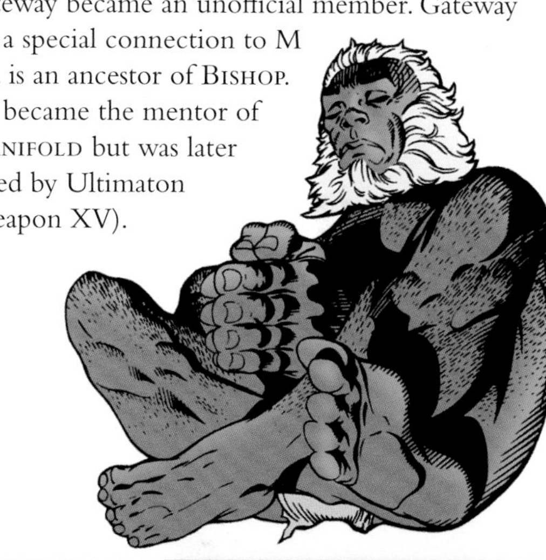

GAROKK

FIRST APPEARANCE *Astonishing Tales* #2 (October 1970)
REAL NAME Unrevealed **OCCUPATION** Sailor; wanderer; god
BASE The Savage Land **HEIGHT** 7 ft **WEIGHT** 355 lbs
EYES (as human) Brown; (as Garokk) Yellow
HAIR (as human) Brown; (as Garokk) Virtually none
SPECIAL POWERS/ABILITIES Can project heat, light, and concussive force from his eyes. Possesses virtual immortality.

In the 15th century, a British sailor from *HMS Drake* became stranded in the Savage Land. Immersion in a pool of mysterious liquid made him virtually immortal. He wandered the world for centuries, and his body took on a rocklike appearance, as if he were petrified. In recent times, the Petrified Man returned to the Savage Land, where he was worshiped by the Sun People as the incarnation of their god Garokk. He regards himself as the guardian of the Savage Land, but his insanity makes him a menace.

GATHERERS

The Gatherers serve Proctor, an extra-dimensional being. Each member of the Gatherers comes from an alternate Earth in another dimension. On each of their Earths, the Gatherers were Avengers. Also, on each of their Earths, Sersi, a member of the Eternals, went mad and killed everyone. The Gatherers were each the last survivors of their home worlds. They were recruited by Proctor to destroy Sersi and the Avengers of Earth-616. But in order for the Gatherers to exist on Earth-616, they had to each kill their own counterpart on Earth-616. This process was known as "gathering." The Gatherers infiltrated the Avengers Mansion on Earth-616 several times. In the final battle, Proctor tried to destroy all realities, but Thunderstrike hit Proctor with a bolt of lightning, and all the Gatherers collapsed.

GATHERERS

FACTFILE

MAIN MEMBERS AND POWERS

PROCTOR
Teleportation; mind control.

CASSANDRA
Telepath; strategist.

MAGDALENE
Wields power lance.

SLOTH
Superstrong; razor-sharp claws.

SWORDSMAN
Sword fires energy beam.

FIRST APPEARANCE
Avengers #355 (October 1992)

THE GATHERERS
1 Cassandra
2 Magdalene
3 Swordsman
4 Sloth

GAUNTLET

FIRST APPEARANCE *She-Hulk* #100 (January 2006)
REAL NAME Joseph Green **OCCUPATION** Super Hero trainer
BASE Camp Hammond, Stamford, Connecticut
HEIGHT 5 ft 11 in **WEIGHT** 210 lbs **EYES** Brown **HAIR** Black
SPECIAL POWERS/ABILITIES Has an alien gauntlet on his right hand. It can project a powerful hand composed of pure energy.

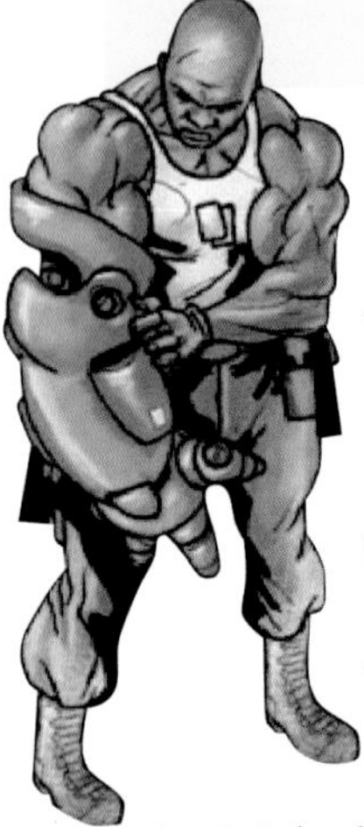

When two alien artifacts crashed in the Sudanese desert, the US Army investigated and clashed with HYDRA agents who were also after the items. One of the soldiers, Sergeant Green, defended himself with an alien gauntlet. He won, but found he couldn't remove the gauntlet. During the CIVIL WAR, Green was drill sergeant at Camp Hammond, a training camp for the FIFTY-STATE INITIATIVE. When KIA (*see* Michael VAN PATRICK) threatened Green's life, his gauntlet saved him. Green stuck with Camp Hammond, even through the DARK REIGN, and was later posted to Helmand Province. He clashed with IRON MAN and WAR MACHINE over Manticore, a new multi-purpose tank developed with illegally-appropriated Stark tech.

GHOST

FIRST APPEARANCE *Iron Man* #219 (June, 1987)
REAL NAME Unknown
OCCUPATION Former assassin, galactic hero **BASE** Mobile Hammond, Stamford, Connecticut **HEIGHT** 5 ft 11 in
WEIGHT 175 lbs **EYES** Blue **HAIR** Brown
SPECIAL POWERS/ABILITIES Brilliant inventor, tactician, and hacker. Suit grants invisibility and intangibility.

Originally a computer engineer, Ghost studied how to make computers phase through matter. When his girlfriend, a co-worker, was murdered, Ghost found that his company was responsible. He used the tech to evade a bomb they directed at him, but became fused with the invention. After exacting his revenge, he sold his services as a saboteur. When SPYMASTER was sent to kill him, Ghost killed his assailant instead. He joined the THUNDERBOLTS under Norman Osborn, but betrayed Osborn at the end of the DARK REIGN and joined Luke CAGE's Thunderbolts. Ghost later infiltrated Parker Industries, managing to destroying the building and all its contents.

GENESIS

FIRST APPEARANCE *Cable* #18 (December 1994)
REAL NAME Tyler Dayspring
OCCUPATION Would-be conqueror; arms-dealer **BASE** Mobile
HEIGHT 6 ft 1 in **WEIGHT** 191 lbs **EYES** Blue **HAIR** Blond
SPECIAL POWERS/ABILITIES Mutant ability to create solid holograms from the memories of another person; trained in military tactics and combat techniques; wears armored suit.

The adopted son of CABLE in a future world ruled by APOCALYPSE, Tyler Dayspring was brainwashed by Cable's twisted clone STRYFE into becoming his father's enemy. Tyler traveled to the present, intent on ensuring that Apocalypse's rise to power would take place, and on avenging himself on Cable. He operated at first under the alias of a rogue arms dealer named Tolliver, but then abandoned that identity for direct action as Genesis. However, when Genesis attempted to restore WOLVERINE's lost Adamantium to his skeleton, the pain-crazed mutant slew him.

GENERATION X

FACTFILE

ORIGINAL MEMBERS AND POWERS

HUSK
Sheds skin to reveal shape-shifted body beneath.

SKIN
Has 6 ft of extra skin, to manipulate as required.

M
Superstrength; invulnerability.

JUBILEE
Projects explosive energy bolts.

CHAMBER
Projects psionic energy blasts from chest.

SYNCH
Mimics powers of students.

PENANCE
Super-dense body.

BASE
Massachusetts Academy

FIRST APPEARANCE
Generation X #1 (November 1994)

GENERATION X

As one generation of X-MEN matured another stepped forward—Generation X. Having banded together to face danger in the form of the alien collective intelligence the PHALANX, Generation X members had a fair idea what fate had in store. Accepted by the Xavier Institute's new mutant high school at Massachusetts Academy, the team learned to hone its abilities and were introduced to PROFESSOR X's vision of the future. While at the Academy, Generation X fought various foes, including EMPLATE, who preyed on the marrow of mutants. After the team was outed to the world as mutants and those in charge of the school—Emma FROST and Sean Cassidy (BANSHEE)—became increasingly unstable, they decided to go their separate ways.

Years later, a new Generation X was set up, with former member JUBILEE mentoring a new crop of students, this time matching tasks to their powers and personalities.

GENERATION X
1 Emma Frost ***2*** M
3 Banshee ***4*** Chamber
5 Synch ***6*** Jubilee
7 Penance ***8*** Skin ***9*** Husk

GHOST RIDER

The brimstone biker

The Ghost Riders are brilliant motorcyclists who can perform incredible stunts. Their mystical bikes enable them to ride up walls and even across water.

Posing as Satan, Mephisto approached stunt motorcyclist Johnny Blaze and agreed to cure Blaze's mentor "Crash" Simpson of a fatal disease in exchange for Blaze's soul. Simpson then died performing a stunt, and Mephisto bonded the demon Zarathos to Blaze's body, transforming him into a demonic Ghost Rider. Blaze was temporarily freed of the curse when Zarathos became trapped in a crystal of souls, but that was far from the end of the Ghost Rider.

As the new Ghost Rider, Alejandra didn't always get along with Johnny Blaze.

FACTFILE

GHOST RIDER

REAL NAME
John "Johnny" Blaze

OCCUPATION
Stunt motorcyclist

BASE
Mobile

HEIGHT (Ghost Rider) 6 ft 2 in
WEIGHT (Ghost Rider) 220 lbs
EYES (Ghost Rider) flaming red
HAIR (Ghost Rider) none

FIRST APPEARANCE
Marvel Spotlight #5 (August 1972)

POWERS

Turns into a superhuman mystical being that projects hellfire; Ghost Rider I can create a mystical motorcycle from hellfire. Ghost Rider II's "Penance Stare" causes wrongdoers to suffer the same emotional pain they inflicted.

THE FAMILY CURSE

When criminals wounded Barbara Ketch, her brother Dan carried her to a junkyard. With Barbara's innocent blood on his hands, Dan touched a mysterious motorcycle and became the new Ghost Rider. Danny Ketch and Johnny Blaze later learned they were brothers, each with their own demon. Johnny was once more bonded to Zarathos and became a Ghost Rider again, pursuing the demon Lucifer.

The rogue angel Zadkiel convinced Danny to collect the power of the spirits of vengeance all around the world—including Johnny's—as it turned out that these spirits came not from demons but angels. However, Zadkiel was actually using Danny to gather the power for himself so he could launch an assault on the walls of Heaven itself. Danny and Johnny reunited with the other spirits of vengeance to topple Zadkiel from his stolen throne.

THE NEW RIDER

Wishing to be rid of the Ghost Rider, Johnny cut a deal with Adam (the first man and the creator of sin) to give his spirit of vengeance to a stranger. It wound up with a young Nicaraguan woman, Alejandra, who Adam forced to eliminate sin in Nicaragua by turning its people mindless. Realizing his mistake, Johnny tried to stop Alejandra and Adam from eradicating sin across the Earth. Alejandra broke free from Adam's control just in time.

John mentored Alejandra in the use of her powers, but she proved a headstrong student. Racing off to stop an incursion from Hell in Las Vegas, she activated it instead. Johnny joined Red Hulk, Venom (Flash Thompson), and X-23 to stop this, but they were all killed. Sent to Hell, they worked together, temporarily giving Red Hulk the powers of Venom and the Ghost Rider. Thirsting for vengeance, Alejandra went after Mephisto, caring nothing that destroying Hell might well destroy reality. Johnny stopped her and took back the power of the Ghost Rider. Alejandra, who retained some of her previous power, swore revenge against Johnny. Later, Johnny along with his fellow Midnight Sons helped Doctor Strange defeat Mephisto, who had opened a gateway in Las Vegas to mount an invasion of Earth. A clever ploy saw Johnny depose an overconfident Mephisto and install himself as the new King of Hell.

GENOSHANS

FIRST APPEARANCE *Uncanny X-Men* #235 (October 1988)
BASE The island of Genosha, Indian Ocean
SPECIAL POWERS/ABILITIES The inhabitants of Genosha were a mixture of ordinary humans and those with mutant abilities. The latter were called "Mutates" and were conditioned to fulfil specific tasks tailored to their particular mutant ability. From time to time Mutates managed to rebel against their human masters.

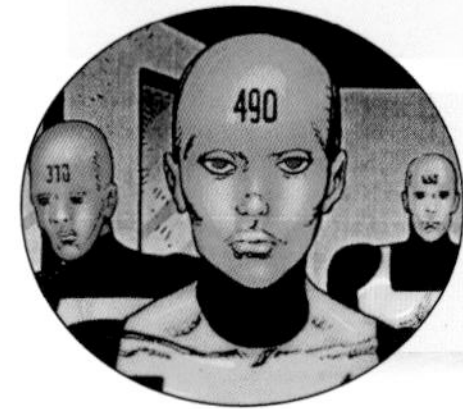
Adolescent mutates were tattooed with a number on their foreheads, their identities were eliminated, and they faced a life of enslavement.

The island of Genosha was located near the Seychelles in the Indian Ocean. Originally, mutants were identified and enslaved as adolescents, stripped of their identities, given a number, and genetically engineered to alter or enhance their abilities. A militia called the Magistrates enforced these laws. The X-MEN toppled this regime, and after a period of turmoil, the UN turned the country over to MAGNETO to govern. Later, Cassandra Nova and her SENTINELS destroyed the nation and killed nearly everyone on it. Even later, SELENE brought nearly everyone on the island back from the dead with a techno-organic virus, but when she died, so did they.

GIDEON

FIRST APPEARANCE *New Mutants* #98 (February 1991)
REAL NAME Gideon **OCCUPATION** CEO of Ophrah Industries
BASE Denver, Colorado
HEIGHT 6 ft 8 in **WEIGHT** 265 lbs **EYES** Blue **HAIR** Green
SPECIAL POWERS/ABILITIES Mutant ability to duplicate the superhuman powers of others by aligning himself with their energy signatures. He also had a greatly extended lifespan.

A member of the long-lived mutants who call themselves the EXTERNALS, Gideon was a power broker who called the halls of big business his natural habitat. Utterly corrupt, Gideon attempted to take Roberto DaCosta, the NEW MUTANT known as SUNSPOT, under his wing, and turn him into his protégé. However his attempts to turn Sunspot into an External like himself met with failure, and he soon turned his attentions to other pursuits. Gideon was subsequently slain by the External vampire SELENE, who had embarked on a vendetta against her fellow Externals.

GLADIATOR (KALLARK)

FIRST APPEARANCE *X-Men* #107 (October, 1977)
REAL NAME Kallark **OCCUPATION** Majestor of the Shi'ar Empire
BASE Chandilar, Shi'ar Galaxy; mobile
HEIGHT 6 ft 6 in **WEIGHT** 595 lbs **EYES** Blue **HAIR** Blue
SPECIAL POWERS/ABILITIES Superhuman strength, the limits of which are unknown; superhuman speed and stamina; near invulnerability; flight; heat beams; microscopic vision; enhanced longvevity

A member of the super-powered Strontian race, Kallark was born under SHI'AR rule. His absolute loyalty to the Shi'ar and its Emperor was first tested and rewarded when he was made Praetor of the Shi'ar Imperial Guard. Resolute in his defense of his people and their ruler, from the honorable Lilandra to the brutal VULCAN, Kallark has both fought against and sided with the X-MEN and the AVENGERS. After becoming Emperor, Kallark ordered the annhilation of Earth to save the universe during the incursions, but he and his forces were destroyed by IRON MAN.

GLADIATOR

FACTFILE
REAL NAME
Melvin Potter
OCCUPATION
Ex-criminal
BASE
New York City

HEIGHT 6 ft 6 in
WEIGHT 300 lbs
EYES Blue
HAIR None

FIRST APPEARANCE
Daredevil #18
(July 1966)

POWERS
Skilled athlete and combatant; wore armored suit with saw blades in gauntlets.

When Foggy NELSON rented a DAREDEVIL outfit from Melvin Potter's costume shop, Potter dressed up like a villain to ambush Foggy. Potter acquired a taste for crime, becoming the Gladiator and serving with ELECTRO's Emissaries of Evil and the MAGGIA. Later reformed, the Gladiator allied with Daredevil and ELEKTRA to fight the HAND. He was forced back into his evil ways because of threats against his daughter and ended up in jail. He escaped and embarked on a psychotic killing spree as a result of chemicals administered by Mr. Fear, but Daredevil put a stop to it.

Melvin Potter is not to be confused with the alien Gladiator (aka Kallark) who led the SHI'AR Imperial Guard and became the emperor of the shattered Shi'ar.

Gladiator clashes with Daredevil in an amphitheater located in the Dibney Museum of Human History.

GLOB

FIRST APPEARANCE *Incredible Hulk* #121 (November 1969)
REAL NAME Joe Timms **OCCUPATION** Petty thief; swamp creature **BASE** Florida Everglades
HEIGHT 6 ft 6 in **WEIGHT** 900 lbs **EYES** Brown **HAIR** None
SPECIAL POWERS/ABILITIES Superhumanly strong, the Glob's mutated swampy body can withstand severe attacks; enhanced speed and stamina

Three men have been known as the Glob. The first was Joe Timms, who drowned in the Florida Everglades. After his corpse was exposed to radioactive waste, he returned to life as a swamp-like beast. Sumner Samuel Beckwith became the second Glob after injecting himself with a flawed Super-Soldier Serum. The third—called Glob Herman—was a mutant student at the Xavier Institute. His flesh was made of a transparent, living wax called bio-paraffin that burned when set afire. He joined a mutant riot after a prominent mutant was killed in what seemed to be a hate crime. After M-Day, he retained his powers.

Not a pretty sight, the Glob is, nevertheless, a well-meaning soul.

GOLDBUG

FIRST APPEARANCE *Luke Cage, Power Man* #41 (March 1977)
REAL NAME Matthew Gilden
OCCUPATION Criminal **BASE** New York City
HEIGHT 5 ft 9 in **WEIGHT** 170 lbs **YES** Blue **HAIR** Blond
SPECIAL POWERS/ABILITIES Battlesuit contains electrically-powered exoskeleton that amplifies strength; "gold-gun" shoots gold-colored dust that hardens on contact; uses "bugship" hovercraft and submarine.

Matthew Gilden, aka Goldbug, was a thief obsessed with gold. He clashed with Luke CAGE and soon after teamed up with the HULK in El Dorado to defeat the subterranean ruler TYRANNUS. He later tried to steal undersea gold, but was foiled by NAMOR. He worked for Latveria when it was attacked by Nick FURY and his allies who were trying to overthrow the Latverian government. During the CIVIL WAR, the PUNISHER killed Gilden before he could join CAPTAIN AMERICA's forces. A new Goldbug joined WHITE RABBIT and WALRUS in an attempt to tamper with New York City's water supply, but they were defeated by SPIDER-WOMAN.

GOLDEN CLAW

FIRST APPEARANCE *Yellow Claw* #1 (October 1956)
REAL NAME Plan Tzu **OCCUPATION** Conqueror
BASE Various hidden bases around the world
HEIGHT 6 ft 2 in **WEIGHT** 210 lbs **EYES** Brown **HAIR** Bald
SPECIAL POWERS/ABILITIES Knowledge of biochemistry, genetics, robotics, and sorcery (can reanimate the dead); can mentally create illusions in the minds of others.

Born in China in the 1800s, Plan Tzu (aka Master Plan) was a direct descendant of Genghis Khan and leader of the Atlas Foundation. Wishing to make Atlas a force for good, Tzu chose a young Jimmy Woo as his successor, but Woo's parents moved their family to the US to avoid that fate. When Woo joined the FBI in the 1950s and later became a SHIELD agent, Tzu became Woo's nemesis, the Golden Claw, so that he could test Woo's abilities. In modern times, Tzu finally revealed his plan to Woo and his AGENTS OF ATLAS. After Woo accepted his heritage, Tzu let himself be devoured by the dragon Mr. Lao.

GLORIAN

FIRST APPEARANCE *Incredible Hulk* #191 (September 1975)
REAL NAME Thomas Gideon
OCCUPATION Apprentice dream-shaper **BASE** Known universe
HEIGHT 5 ft 9 in **WEIGHT** 155 lbs **EYES** Pink **HAIR** Orange
SPECIAL POWERS/ABILITIES Glorian can control tachyons, small speed-of-light particles, forming them into rainbow-shaped bridges allowing him to travel across worlds or star systems at light speed. He can also mentally redefine small pockets of reality for short periods of time.

Thomas Gideon survived radiation poisoning thanks to the SHAPER OF WORLDS. The Shaper renamed him Glorian and taught him to manipulate reality and dreams. Recently, Glorian tricked GAMORA and RONAN THE ACCUSER into battling so he could absorb their energy and use it to reshape a world. When the ANNIHILATION Wave interrupted him, he destroyed all he'd made, shattering his mind along with his attackers.

GOLIATH

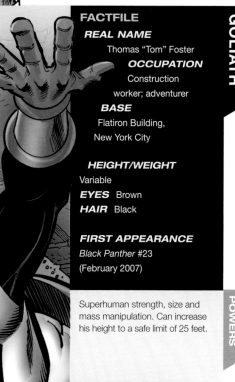

Dr. Hank PYM discovered how to use his Pym Particles to change his size and became the first Giant-Man. His lab assistant, Bill Foster, became the first Goliath and later the second Giant-Man. Foster fell victim to radiation poisoning while fighting Atom-Smasher, but SPIDER-WOMAN cured him with a blood transfusion. He later became the fourth Goliath. During the CIVIL WAR he sided with CAPTAIN AMERICA and was killed by RAGNAROK. In the aftermath of WORLD WAR HULK, Bill's nephew Tom Foster became the new Goliath. He later joined the REVENGERS to attack the AVENGERS.

FACTFILE
REAL NAME
Thomas "Tom" Foster
OCCUPATION
Construction worker; adventurer
BASE
Flatiron Building, New York City

HEIGHT/WEIGHT
Variable
EYES Brown
HAIR Black

FIRST APPEARANCE
Black Panther #23 (February 2007)

GOLIATH

POWERS
Superhuman strength, size and mass manipulation. Can increase his height to a safe limit of 25 feet.

GODS OF ASGARD

Immortals who rule the dimension of Asgard

GODS OF ASGARD

FACTFILE

KEY ASGARDIANS

ODIN
(Monarch of Asgard) The most powerful god, possessing vast magical abilities. He can enchant objects or living beings, project energy bolts, and open gateways between dimensions. He also commands the life energies of all Asgardians, which he can absorb at will.

THOR
(God of Thunder) Asgard's finest warrior; exceptionally skilled in hand-to-hand combat and hammer-throwing.

BALDER
(God of Light) Thor's closest friend; almost invulnerable; skilled in hand-to-hand combat, swordsmanship, and horsemanship.

HELA
(Goddess of Death) Ruler of the underworlds of Hel and Nifleheim; holds the power of life and death over the gods; can levitate and travel in astral form; touch is fatal to mortals.

LOKI
(God of Evil) Great magical abilities; can shapeshift into any animal, god, or giant; can plant hypnotic suggestions into others' minds.

CUL
(God of Fear) Odin's brother, also known as the Serpent.

VALKYRIE
Brunnhilde the Valkyrie can see a "deathglow" around a person about to die. Originally charged with transporting dead warriors to Valhalla; can travel between dimensions.

HEIMDALL
(Guardian of the Rainbow Bridge) Has extremely acute senses. He can focus on, or block out, any specific sensory information.

ANGELA
(Asgard's Assassin) Daughter of Odin, mighty warrior raised as an angel in Heven, the Tenth Realm.

BASE
The Otherdimensional Realm of Asgard

FIRST APPEARANCE
Journey into Mystery #85 (October 1962)

The otherdimensional planetary body known as Asgard.

The Gods of Asgard are a powerful race of beings who live in a dimension called Asgard, a small planetary body whose laws of physics are different from those of the planets we know in the Earthly realm. Asgard is also home to five other races—Giants, Dwarves, Elves, Trolls, and Demons. The Gods of Asgard are the most human-looking and powerful of the six races of Asgard.

NINE REALMS

All Asgardians refer to the known universe as the "Nine Realms of Asgard." Four of those worlds—Asgard, home of the gods; Vanaheim, home of the Asgardians' sister race called the Vanir; Nidavellir, home of the Dwarves; and Alfheim, home of the Light Elves—actually share the planetary body on which the city of Asgard is located.

The other five worlds exist in separate dimensions connected by an unknown number of interdimensional nexuses. They are Midgard, the Asgardian name for Earth, home of humanity; Jotunheim, home of the giants; Svartalfheim, home of the Dark Elves; Hel, land of the dead and its adjunct world Niflheim, the frozen realm of the dishonored dead; and Muspelheim, land of the fire demons and home to Surtur, Asgard's most deadly enemy. It was recently revealed that there is a Tenth Realm, Heven, that Odin cut off from the other Nine Realms after a war with Asgard. Heven is home to the angels.

Surtur rises from the flames of Muspelheim, land of the fire demons.

THE ASGARDIANS

The origin of the Gods of Asgard is not clearly known, but it is believed that unlike the other races of the realm, the gods are not native to Asgard. Legend has it that they were born on Earth, but moved to Asgard in the far distant past. The Rainbow Bridge, also known as the Bifrost—one of the interdimensional nexuses—connects Asgard to Earth.

Although they look like humans, the Gods of Asgard possess superhuman physical abilities. They are extremely long-lived (although not actually immortal, unlike their Olympian counterparts) and age at an extremely slow pace once they reach adulthood. Their skin and bones are three times as dense as those of a human and they are almost invulnerable to physical attack. They possess great strength (most are able to lift 30 tons) and, due to their density, weigh far more than humans of comparable size. The Gods of Asgard are immune to all diseases found on Earth and their metabolism gives them superhuman endurance while performing physical activities. All Asgardians are born with the potential to use and control mystical energies, although only a few (such as Loki) have developed this power to any significant degree.

As the Bifrost's gatekeeper, Heimdall the All-Seeing guarded the entrance to Asgard from enemy invasions and incursions by monsters.

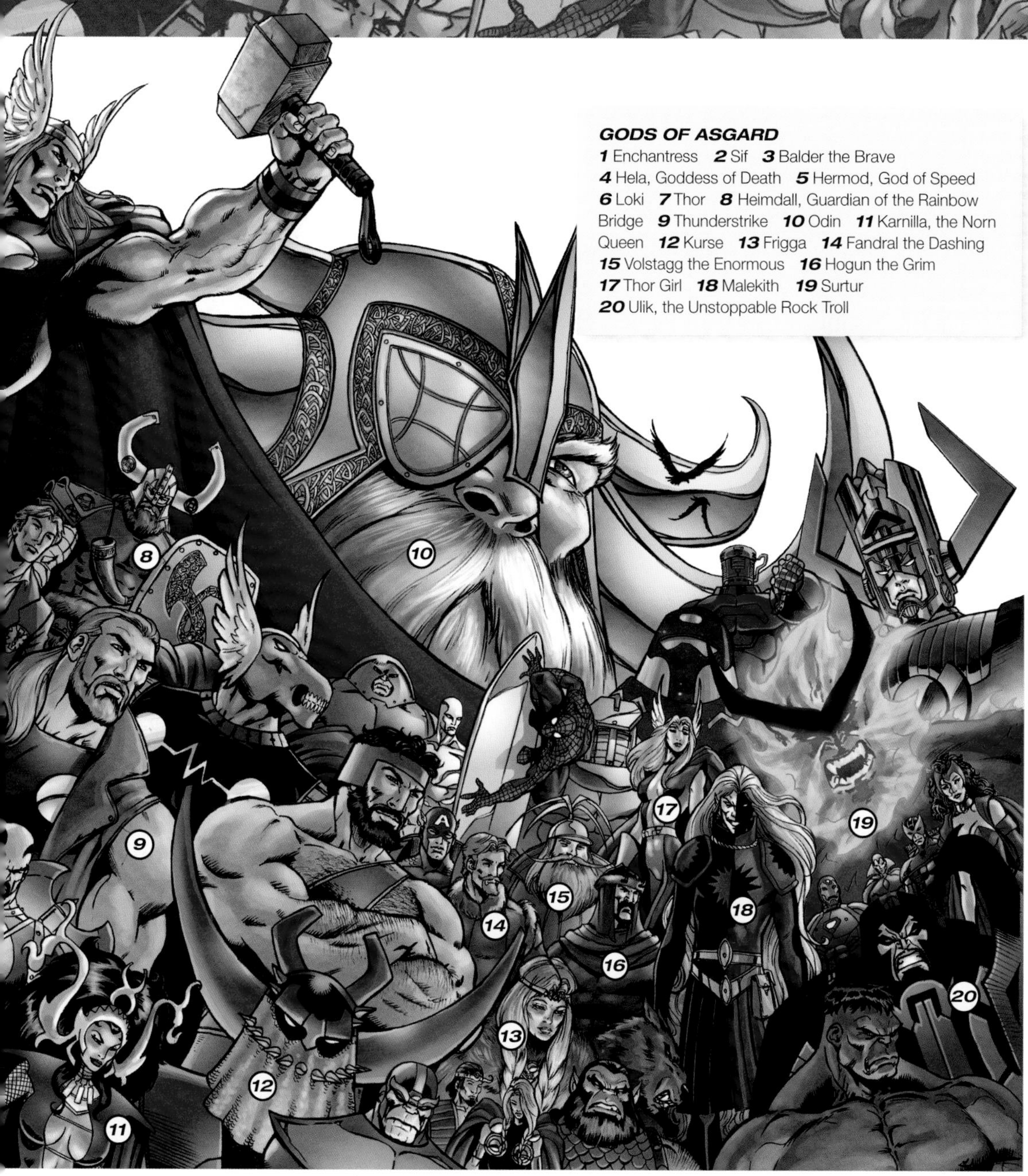

GODS OF ASGARD
1 Enchantress ***2*** Sif ***3*** Balder the Brave
4 Hela, Goddess of Death ***5*** Hermod, God of Speed
6 Loki ***7*** Thor ***8*** Heimdall, Guardian of the Rainbow Bridge ***9*** Thunderstrike ***10*** Odin ***11*** Karnilla, the Norn Queen ***12*** Kurse ***13*** Frigga ***14*** Fandral the Dashing
15 Volstagg the Enormous ***16*** Hogun the Grim
17 Thor Girl ***18*** Malekith ***19*** Surtur
20 Ulik, the Unstoppable Rock Troll

ESSENTIAL STORYLINES
- ***The Mighty Thor Vol. 2 #80–85*** In the Ragnarok (Doom of the Gods) Saga, Loki and his followers unleash an attack on Asgard intended to destroy the home of the gods and all its inhabitants. Thor's hammer, Mjolnir, is shattered during the battle that follows.
- ***The Mighty Thor #418*** The fire demon Surtur possesses Odin and gains control of Asgard.

ODIN THE ALL-FATHER

ODIN, also called All-Father, is the leader of the Gods of Asgard. Odin is the grandson of Buri, the first of the Asgardians. He is the son of the God Bor and Bestia, of the race of Frost Giants.

For many ages, Odin has ruled Asgard wisely and effectively. Odin wields the enchanted, three-pronged spear Gungnir ("The Spear of Heaven"), which returns to his hand when thrown, and he travels through space in Skipbladnir, a Viking-style longboat with enchanted sails and oars.

THOR AND RAGNAROK

Although Odin made Frigga his queen, he mated with GAEA, the Goddess of Earth, who bore him THOR, the God of Thunder. However, Frigga raised the boy, who believed her to be his mother.

The Dwarves of Nidavellir created the hammer Mjolnir, forged from the mystical metal uru. Odin enchanted the hammer so that only one worthy of wielding such a powerful weapon could lift it. When Thor came of age, Odin presented him with Mjolnir, and Thor became Asgard's greatest warrior.

Loki, who had been adopted by Odin, turned to sorcery and became the God of Mischief. Jealous of Thor, Loki vowed to destroy him. Loki launched the final war of Ragnarok (the end of the universe in Norse myth), but Thor broke the cycle and stopped the war.

THE FALL OF ASGARD

Ragnarok caused the gods to disappear, but they later reappeared in mortal guises. Thor brought them to a reborn Asgard, which hovered over the plains of Oklahoma.

At the end of the DARK REIGN, the SENTRY destroyed Asgard. Soon after, the new RED SKULL found the hammer of Skadi and revived Odin's brother Cul the SERPENT, along with his generals, called the Worthy (*see* FEAR ITSELF). Odin remade Asgard in another realm, planning to raze the Earth to destroy Cul; instead, Thor led the world's heroes to victory against the Worthy. Thor himself slew Cul the Serpent, but at the cost of his own life.

Stricken with grief, Odin gave up the rule of the Norse Gods to Frigga, Gaea, and Idunn (the Goddess of Immortality) and locked himself away in his new Asgard. IRON MAN helped to build Asgardia, the Norse Gods' new home. Initially it hovered over Broxton, Oklahoma, as Asgard once had, but eventually the gods moved Asgardia into space, settling in Saturn's orbit.

Asgardia was a glorious combination of Earthly tech and Asgardian magic.

Cul returned and brought trouble to Asgardia, turning Odin—who had since returned from self-imposed exile in Asgard—into a more dictatorial ruler. The result was a civil war and the new Thor (Jane Foster) attacking Odin. It was a war that only stopped when Loki stabbed Frigga in the back with a poisoned dagger that sent her into a coma.

As the War of the Ten Realms started to rage, the monster known as Mangog attacked Asgardia, gaining its controls and sending the realm towards the sun. The Asgardians were forced to evacuate, Thor (Jane Foster) giving her life to stop Mangog's rampage. The Asgardians then returned to old Asgard to rebuild anew.

Asgard had crumbled into ruins after Odin abandoned the city. After rediscovering it, the Asgardian refugees set about reconstructing it, turning it into their new home.

GODS OF HELIOPOLIS

Deities of Ancient Egypt

GODS OF HELIOPOLIS

FACTFILE

NOTABLE GODS

OSIRIS (Ruler of the Gods) God of the Dead
BES God of Luck
GEB God of the Earth
HORUS God of the Sun
ISIS Goddess of Fertility
KHONSHU God of Light
NUT Goddess of the Sky
SETH God of Evil
THOTH God of the Moon

BASE

Celestial city of Heliopolis

FIRST APPEARANCE

Thor #240 (October 1975)

The Path of the Gods enabled the Egyptian deities to visit Earth and meddle in human affairs.

In ancient times the pantheon of the Egyptian Gods lived in Heliopolis, ruling Egypt until humans finally took their place as the dynastic kings known as the pharaohs. It was then that the Heliopolitan Gods departed Earth, settling in a parallel dimension, where they established the celestial city of Heliopolis. However, like the Asgardian Gods (*see* GODS OF ASGARD), the Heliopolitan deities retained strong links with Egypt, traveling to and from Earth on a golden bridge named the Path of the Gods.

Creeping up on the sleeping Osiris, Seth prepared to slice him into pieces.

CLASH OF THE GODS

Although essentially an extended family, the Heliopolitan Gods were somewhat dysfunctional. When Osiris, God of the Dead, was appointed ruler of the Gods his younger brother Seth was overwhelmed with jealousy—the tensions between the pair were to reverberate far beyond their celestial home. Seth's first solution was drastic—he killed Osiris, slicing up his body and scattering the pieces. When Osiris' wife and son—Isis and Horus—managed to resurrect him, Seth employed a different tactic, imprisoning all three in a pyramid. Although trapped there for millennia, Osiris and Isis eventually made the pyramid appear in the 20th century. This attracted the attention of the Asgardian Gods THOR and Odin but their efforts to free their fellow immortals did not prove straightforward. Odin was forced to join battle with Seth, their struggle finally culminating in the severing of Seth's left hand.

Releasing Osiris from his pyramid prison, Thor and Odin joined him in the battle to overthrow Seth. However, before they could reach him, they were forced to fight through Seth's skeletal legions.

CONTINUING MENACES

Seth has attempted time and again to destroy all life in the Multiverse. An alliance of evil let loose the demonic Demogorge the God-Eater. Only when the entity attempted to consume Thor was its path of destruction brought to an end. On a separate occasion, Seth drained the energies of his fellow Gods and invaded Asgard. He was only defeated by the combined forces of the AVENGERS and Earth Force. When THANOS threatened the universe with his Infinity Gauntlet, Osiris attended a Council of the God Kings to discuss their response. Fortunately, Thanos was thwarted by other entities.

Although the time of the Heliopolitan Gods is now long over, they and their petty squabbles still spill over into human affairs.

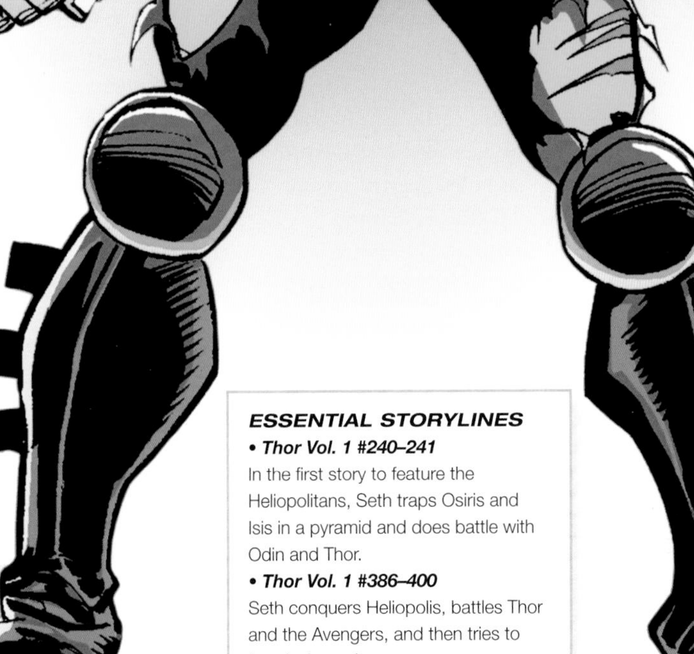

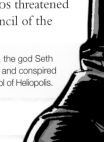

For millennia, the god Seth has brooded and conspired to gain control of Heliopolis.

ESSENTIAL STORYLINES

- ***Thor Vol. 1 #240–241***
  In the first story to feature the Heliopolitans, Seth traps Osiris and Isis in a pyramid and does battle with Odin and Thor.
- ***Thor Vol. 1 #386–400***
  Seth conquers Heliopolis, battles Thor and the Avengers, and then tries to invade Asgard.

GODS OF OLYMPUS

Deities of Ancient Greece

Olympus was ruled by the stern and hirsute Zeus.

Although for centuries they were worshiped by the Greeks, it remains unclear where the Gods of Olympus first originated—was it on Earth or in the pocket dimension of Olympus where they currently reside? Wherever they came from, their influence on this planet has faded over the last two millennia, although a handful of their number still walk the Earth.

THE GOLDEN AGE

Children of the Titans, the first generation of the Olympian Gods were imprisoned in the underworld realm of Tartarus as soon as they were born, their father Cronos fearing that they would eventually overthrow him. His anxiety proved to be well-founded: the last of his children, Zeus, avoided being incarcerated and, when he was old enough, freed his siblings and led a ten-year-long war against Cronos.

Victorious, Zeus and his siblings became the Gods of Olympus, worshiped by peoples across Europe. It was only when Christianity began to dominate the Western world that the Gods chose to withdraw to the Olympus dimension and began to reduce their ties with the mortal realm.

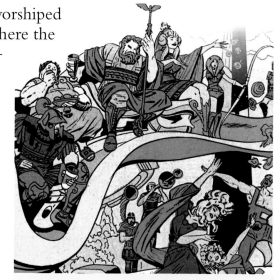

The court of Zeus was a byword for feasting and revelry. While most enjoyed the carefree hedonism of the place, some, including Venus and Hercules, yearned for a slightly more challenging existence.

Although most of the Gods departed a handful either remained on the Earth or returned, time and again, in the years that followed. Of those that stayed on Earth, Neptune (or Poseidon, as the Greeks called him) remained to watch over and be worshiped by the Atlanteans, while Hercules and Venus (Aphrodite to the Greeks) spent time living with mortals.

BACK TO EARTH

With the destruction of Asgard during Ragnarok, Amatsu-Mikaboshi led an attack on Olympus. Zeus was slain in the conflict, only to return later as a boy, and Olympus was destroyed.

During the Secret Invasion, Hercules assembled the God Squad to defeat the Skrull Gods. Afterward, Hera and Pluto took control of the Olympus Group, the new home of the Olympians on Earth. Hera created a new universe called the Continuum, into which she planned to transfer the Gods while destroying the original. Her plan was foiled, although it cost her, Zeus (again), and Hercules their lives.

The rule of the Olympus Group fell to Amadeus Cho. Hercules took over from Cho when he returned, but he used all his power to restore reality at the end of the Chaos War, and Zeus resumed his rule.

Zeus did not entirely approve of the life his son, Hercules, had chosen to lead.

FACTFILE

NOTABLE GODS

ZEUS (Ruler of the Gods) God of the Sky and Weather
APOLLO God of Light
ARES God of War
ARTEMIS Goddess of the Hunt
ATHENA Goddess of Wisdom
ATLAS Mountain God
BELLONA Goddess of Discord
CUPID God of Love
DEIMOS God of Terror
DEMETER Goddess of Fertility
DIONYSUS God of Wine
GAEA Mother-Earth
HEBE Goddess of Youth
HEPHAESTUS God of Fire
HERA Goddess of Marriage; Queen of the Gods
HERMES God of Commerce and Travel
NEPTUNE (POSEIDON) God of the Sea
NOX God of Night
PAN God of Shepherds, Flocks and Forests
PERSEPHONE Queen of the Underworld
PHOBOS God of Fear
PROMETHEUS Titan of forethought; benefactor of mankind
PSYCHE Goddess of Fidelity and Adoration
TYPHON God of Wind
VENUS (APHRODITE) Goddess of Love and Beauty

BASE

Mount Olympus, Greece; later in an otherdimensional world

FIRST APPEARANCE

Journey Into Mystery Annual #1 (1965)

ESSENTIAL STORYLINES

- ***Venus #1–5***
The goddess Venus becomes editor of Beauty Magazine and helps bring couples together.
- ***Thor #126–131***
Hercules fights Thor who then rescues him from the netherworld where he has been imprisoned. Their firm friendship is sealed.
- ***Avengers #281–285***
Angered by injuries suffered by Hercules, Zeus attacks the Avengers and forbids the Olympus Gods from traveling to Earth.

GORGON

FIRST APPEARANCE *Fantastic Four* #44 (November 1965)
REAL NAME Unrevealed
OCCUPATION Administrator **BASE** Attilan, Blue Area, the moon
HEIGHT 6 ft 5 in **WEIGHT** 450 lbs **EYES** Brown **HAIR** Black
SPECIAL POWERS/ABILITIES Immensely powerful legs and hooves give him the ability to create seismic tremors.

Gorgon is a member of the INHUMAN royal family and cousin of their ruler, BLACK BOLT. Like all Inhumans, Gorgon underwent exposure to the mutating Terrigen Mists as a youth. For Gorgon this meant he gained hooves in place of feet—capable of creating seismic tremors. He often acts as Black Bolt's bodyguard. When he was exposed to the Terrigen Mists a second time, he was transformed into a true beast, but later managed to return to his Inhuman form. He is not to be confused with the Japanese villain called Gorgon, who was killed by WOLVERINE.

GORILLA-MAN

FIRST APPEARANCE *Men's Adventures* #26 (1954)
REAL NAME Kenneth Hale **OCCUPATION** Adventurer
BASE San Francisco
HEIGHT 6 ft **WEIGHT** 340 lbs **EYES** Brown **HAIR** Brown
SPECIAL POWERS/ABILITIES Hale is a man cursed to live in a gorilla's body.

Legend says, "If you kill the Gorilla-Man, you become immortal." When forced to commit this act, Ken Hale discovered the immortality came with the curse of becoming the Gorilla-Man he had killed. In the 1950s, Ken worked with a super group called the G-Men under Jimmy Woo. Decades later, he became an agent of SHIELD and joined the supernatural version of THE HOWLING COMMANDOS. Gorilla-Man has since reunited with his G-Men friends to fight the Atlas Foundation. He was also part of DOMINO'S MERCS FOR MONEY.

GORR THE GOD BUTCHER

Born on a brutal planet, Gorr came to believe that the gods deserved nothing but butchery for refusing to answer the prayers of those in dire need, such as his dying wife and children. After suffering such losses, he didn't think gods could exist, but once he confirmed that they did, he vowed to exterminate them all. The fact that he managed to murder so many of them is a testimony to his determination even more than his strength.

Gorr first battled THOR a millennium ago; Thor thought he had slain him, but the God Butcher survived and grew stronger. Using the blood of gods, he traveled through time. He later plucked Thor from three different ages and forced him to construct a bomb that would destroy the gods throughout time and space. When all the threatened gods prayed to Thor, however, Thor was able to stop the bomb and slay Gorr.

FACTFILE
REAL NAME
Gorr
OCCUPATION
God killer
BASE
Mobile

HEIGHT 6 ft 7 in
WEIGHT 260 lbs
EYES White
HAIR Bald

FIRST APPEARANCE
Thor: God of Thunder #2 (January 2013)

GORR THE GOD BUTCHER

POWERS
Gorr is nearly immortal and has superhuman strength, endurance, and durability. He can also manipulate darkness and fashion it into solid objects.

GRANDMASTER

Like his kinsman the COLLECTOR, the Grandmaster is a survivor of an extraterrestrial race that evolved shortly after the Big Bang. To combat the unending boredom of immortality, the Grandmaster has spent the eons engaging in various games, tournaments, and contests. He particularly relishes challenging other cosmic beings to games of skill and chance for incredibly high stakes. Grandmaster discovered Earth-712, which was inhabited by the SQUADRON SUPREME, and created duplicates of these heroes to pit against the AVENGERS. He also challenged DEATH to a series of games, resulting in the banning of all the ELDERS OF THE UNIVERSE from his kingdom, making them all virtually immortal. He also once joined with the other Elders in a plot to kill GALACTUS, but the SILVER SURFER foiled this. The Grandmaster once pitted the original DEFENDERS against the RED HULK'S Offenders. He was seemingly killed, but again cheated death. He once used his daughter, Voyager, in a contest involving the Challenger, the LETHAL LEGION, the Avengers, and the Black Order. He lost, but offered work to the Black Order in the aftermath.

FACTFILE
REAL NAME
En Dwi Gast
OCCUPATION
Game player
BASE
Mobile throughout the universe

HEIGHT 7 ft 1 in
WEIGHT 240 lbs
EYES Red (no visible pupils)
HAIR White (pale blue skin)

FIRST APPEARANCE
Avengers #69 (October 1969)

GRANDMASTER

POWERS
The Grandmaster has an encyclopedic knowledge and comprehension of games and game theory played throughout the universe. Possesses a cosmic life force and is immune to aging, disease, or injury. Can levitate, project energy blasts, and travel through time, space, and alternate dimensions with the speed of thought. He can also rearrange matter on a planetary scale.

GRANT, GLORIA

FACTFILE
REAL NAME
Gloria "Glory" Grant
OCCUPATION
Administrative assistant, former model
BASE
New York City

HEIGHT 5 ft 8 in
WEIGHT 120 lbs
EYES Brown
HAIR Black

FIRST APPEARANCE
The Amazing Spider-Man #140 (February 1975)

POWERS
Highly efficient secretarial skills, including typing and computer skills. Outgoing, romantic, and warm-hearted; prepared to do almost anything to help the man she loves.

GRANT, GLORIA

Model Glory Grant befriended Peter Parker when they both lived in an apartment house on Manhattan's Lower West Side. Grant was looking for work, and Peter, a freelance photographer for the *Daily Bugle,* suggested she apply to be J. Jonah JAMESON's secretary at the paper, a post recently vacated by BETTY BRANT. The irascible Jameson liked Grant and she became Brant's replacement. Mexican crimelord Eduardo Lobo seduced Grant to obtain the *Daily Bugle*'s files on his enemy, the KINGPIN; in time, Grant and Lobo fell genuinely in love. During a battle between SPIDER-MAN and Lobo, Grant tried to shoot Spider-Man, but shot and killed Lobo instead. Later, Grant was possessed by the spirit of the sorceress CALYPSO as part of Calypso's plan to return to life. She became one of Jonah's aides when he became mayor of New York City only to quit when she realized he would never let go of his Spider-Man obsession.

GRAVITY

FIRST APPEARANCE *Gravity* #1 (August 2005)
REAL NAME Greg Willis
OCCUPATION Student **BASE** New York City
HEIGHT 5 ft 10 in **WEIGHT** 175 lbs **EYES** Blue **HAIR** Brown
SPECIAL POWERS/ABILITIES Greg can manipulate gravitons on his skin to affect the weight and acceleration of anything he touches. This allows him to fly and imitate superhuman strength.

Born in Sheboygan, Wisconsin, Greg developed gravity-related powers, and when he moved to New York to attend college, he decided to become a Super Hero. Gravity was part of a group of heroes taken off to Battleworld by a being who claimed to be the BEYONDER but was in fact the STRANGER, and he sacrificed himself to save the others. He returned as the Protector of the Universe but used those powers to feed GALACTUS. Gravity led Nevada's Heavy Hitters team as part of the FIFTY-STATE INITIATIVE, and later joined the YOUNG ALLIES and YOUNG AVENGERS teams.

GRAVITON

FIRST APPEARANCE *Avengers* #158 (April 1977)
REAL NAME Franklin Hall
OCCUPATION Criminal **BASE** Mobile
HEIGHT 6 ft 1 in **WEIGHT** 200 lbs **EYES** Blue **HAIR** Black
SPECIAL POWERS/ABILITIES Control over gravity allows Graviton to levitate objects, generate force-fields and shockwaves, and pin opponents to the ground.

Franklin Hall, a Canadian researcher, gained absolute control over gravity in an accident involving a particle accelerator. Dubbing himself Graviton, he battled the AVENGERS, the THUNDERBOLTS, SPIDER-MAN, and the AVENGERS WEST COAST, and was banished to an alternate dimension more than once. Upon one return, he went to exact his revenge on the Thunderbolts. Finding the Redeemers in their place, he destroyed them, then seemed to die while stopping an invasion from the dimension in which he'd been trapped. He seemed to have committed suicide while battling IRON MAN but turned up again later and joined AIM.

GREAT LAKES AVENGERS

Formed by Craig Hollis, the GLA was a self-proclaimed branch of the AVENGERS. Despite much mockery and their successes being overlooked, they insisted on remaining together. The group's bills are met by Big Bertha, whose alter ego is the wealthy supermodel Ashley Crawford. Other misfit members have included SQUIRREL GIRL, Leather Boy, Monkey Joe, Tippy-Toe, Grasshopper, and even DEADPOOL. After they won the rights to the name "Champions" from HERCULES in a poker game, they became the Great Lakes Champions. They became the Great Lakes Initiative, the FIFTY-STATE INITIATIVE's team for Wisconsin, but have since returned to the GLA name.

THE GREAT LAKES AVENGERS
1 Mr. Immortal
2 Big Bertha
3 Squirrel Girl
4 Flatman
5 Doorman
6 Tippy-Toe

GREAT LAKES AVENGERS

FACTFILE
FOUNDING MEMBERS AND POWERS
MR. IMMORTAL
Immortal; team leader.
DINAH SOAR
Alien flying reptile, attacks with high-pitched shriek.
BIG BERTHA
Controls body mass; alternates between super-obesity and strength and supermodel skinniness.
DOORMAN
Can teleport himself and others into the next room.
FLATMAN
Two-dimensional mutant with elasticated body.

FIRST APPEARANCE
The West Coast Avengers #46 (July 1989)

GREEN GOBLIN

Spider-Man's greatest enemy

GREEN GOBLIN

FACTFILE

REAL NAME
Norman Osborn

OCCUPATION
Criminal/Industrialist

BASE Mobile

HEIGHT 5 ft 11 in
WEIGHT 185 lbs
EYES Blue
HAIR Reddish-brown

FIRST APPEARANCE
The Amazing Spider-Man #14
(July 1964)

POWERS

Superhuman strength, endurance, and reactions, endowed by Goblin Formula (which have increased steadily over time); weaponry includes armored costume, Goblin Glider, and Pumpkin Bombs.

ALLIES/FOES

ALLIES The Enforcers, the Cabal of Scrier, Crime-Master, Jackal, the Sinister Twelve

FOES Spider-Man, the Avengers, SHIELD

Norman Osborn reveals himself to be the Green Goblin.

For almost as long as there has been a Spider-Man, so too has the Green Goblin existed. Spider-Man's arch nemesis, the Green Goblin is the insane, malevolent alter ego of that once-respectable industrialist Norman Osborn. Despite their mutual antagonism, the relationship between the pair is complex. Although the Green Goblin loathes and resents Spider-Man's very existence, for a long time Norman Osborn and Peter Parker shared a deep mutual respect and admiration. Osborn saw in the orphaned Peter the son he really wanted.

ESSENTIAL STORYLINES

- ***Amazing Spider-Man #39–40***
The Green Goblin discovers Peter Parker's secret identity, the Goblin is unmasked as Norman Osborn and we learn about his origins.
- ***Amazing Spider-Man #121–2***
A climactic battle between the Green Goblin and Spider-Man results in the death of Gwen Stacy and the Goblin's own apparent demise.
- ***Superior Spider-Man: Goblin Nation (tpb)***
Norman Osborn returns—this time as the Goblin King, head of a vast criminal network.

GENESIS OF THE GOBLIN

Long before his transformation into the Green Goblin, Norman Osborn was an ambitious businessman, quite prepared to sacrifice others on the altar of his own success. The co-founder of chemical company Oscorp, Osborn gained total control by framing his business partner, Professor Mendel Stromm, for embezzlement. The Goblin Formula that was to prove Osborn's undoing was a concoction detailed in the professor's notes, but it was Osborn's attempt to manufacture it for himself that resulted in the solution exploding in his face. As a result of this explosion, Osborn's strength, stamina, and reflexes were enhanced but his sanity began to erode.

As the Green Goblin, Osborn wished to lead New York's criminal underworld and he set out to gain the respect of the key gangs by destroying Spider-Man. He developed high-tech weaponry specifically designed to achieve this end. Despite discovering Spider-Man's true identity, the Green Goblin was ultimately defeated: an electric shock, sustained during a battle with the web-slinger, caused Osborn to regain his sanity and lose all memory of his malevolent alter ego. Peter Parker judged that it was better to allow Osborn to resume his old life.

ISSUE #1

Teaming up with the Enforcers, the Green Goblin is determined to destroy Spider-Man.

STRIKING AT SPIDER-MAN

Osborn's regained sanity proved fragile. Time and again his inner demon—the Green Goblin—reasserted control, and although Peter repeatedly brought Osborn back to reality, the businessman's grip on sanity became more and more tenuous. During this period, Peter's then-girlfriend, Gwen Stacy, met Osborn

The Green Goblin throws Gwen Stacy to her death from the George Washington Bridge.

and, overwhelmed by his charisma, became pregnant by him. Nine months later, she gave birth to twins, Gabriel and Sarah, in France, keeping their existence a secret from Peter.

Following Gwen's return to New York, an angry altercation between her and a desperately unbalanced Osborn served to destabilize him further. Determined to punish both her and Spider-Man, when Osborn reverted to the Green Goblin he kidnapped Gwen and carried her to the top of Brooklyn Bridge.

The ensuing confrontation with Spider-Man resulted in Gwen's death and in Osborn being impaled by his own Goblin Glider.

OTHER GREEN GOBLINS

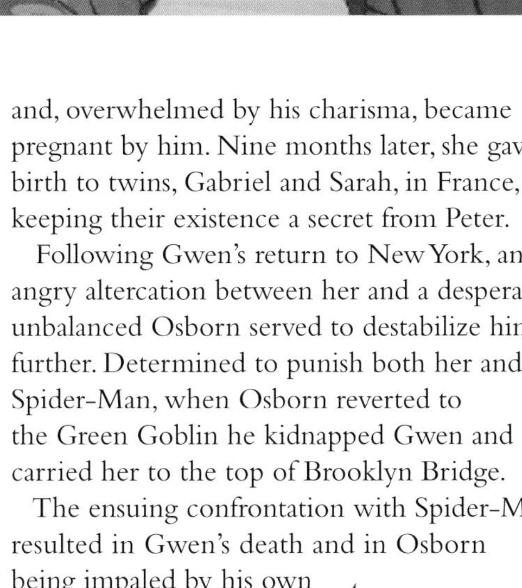

To protect his father, Harry Osborn said he was the Green Goblin.

In becoming the Green Goblin, Norman Osborn inadvertently founded a Goblin dynasty. After witnessing his father's apparent death, a mentally unstable Harry Osborn adopted the Green Goblin mantle and attempted to destroy Spider-Man. Although Harry eventually put his father's legacy behind him, even settling down with a wife and child, life's pressures finally drove him back to the Goblin formula. Tragically, he was killed by the deadly concoction. Twice, the Goblin name has been borne by non-Osborns, with Harry's psychiatrist, Bart Hamilton, and Phil Urich, the nephew of reporter Ben Urich, both pretenders to the Goblin crown. More recently, Gabriel Stacy, the son of Norman Osborn and Gwen Stacy, injected himself with the Goblin Formula and briefly became the Gray Goblin.

The third Green Goblin is revealed.

HEY-- YOU'RE NOT HARRY

YOU'RE HIS PSYCHIATRIST-- BART HAMILTON

All the Green Goblins have shared similar equipment

The Goblin uses a variety of grenades, which all look like Halloween pumpkins.

Peter Parker assumed that Osborn had been killed by this impact, but he had not allowed for the extraordinary potency of the Goblin formula. While lying on a mortuary slab, Osborn's body suddenly revived. To keep his survival secret, Osborn substituted his own body for that of an anonymous drifter.

NORMAN OSBORN, HERO

Osborn subsequently worked hard to become a hero in the eyes of the world. As the director of the Thunderbolts, he killed the Skrull queen Veranke live on television, ending the Secret Invasion and catapulting him into becoming US head of security.

During the ensuing Dark Reign, Osborn founded the Cabal. He then dismantled SHIELD, replaced it with HAMMER, and placed villains into both the Avengers and the X-Men. He also took the place of both Iron Man and Captain America himself, as the Iron Patriot.

When Osborn led HAMMER and his Dark Avengers in an unauthorized assault on Asgard, however, he met defeat, and his always fragile sanity shattered once again. He escaped on his way to prison and created another Avengers team, hoping to use them to regain his position of power.

Defeated once more, despite temporarily gaining the powers of the Super-Adaptoid, Osborn based himself in the sewers of New York City as the Goblin King, gathered a new gang around him, and plotted ways to regain his power. As the Goblin King's power spread, the Superior Spider-Man (Otto Octavius in Peter Parker's body) was forced to allow Peter Parker to regain control of his body so the real Spider-Man could confront and defeat Osborn.

GOBLIN CARNAGE

Osborn ended up in Symkaria, helping Countess Katarina Karkov turn the nation into the world's largest arms manufacturer (complete with an army of Goblinized soldiers), before Spider-Man, Silver Sable, and their allies stopped them. Still seeking something to give him an edge over Spider-Man, Osborn gained the Carnage symbiote and bonded with it, becoming the Red Goblin. He then went after Spider-Man's allies, and used the symbiote to turn his own grandson, Normie, into "Goblin Childe." Yet again Spidey defeated him, leaving Osborn's mind more fractured and broken than ever.

Peter Parker used Osborn's ego against him, taunting him that he was too weak to defeat Spider-Man without the symbiote.

GREENWOOD, DAWN

FIRST APPEARANCE *All-New Marvel Now! Point One* #1 (March 2014) **REAL NAME** Dawn Greenwood
OCCUPATION Adventurer **BASE** Mobile
HEIGHT 5 ft 10 in **WEIGHT** 150 lbs
EYES Green **HAIR** Black
SPECIAL POWERS/ABILITIES Physical abilities of an average human; possessed an extremely inquisitive and adventurous mind.

Born in Anchor Bay, Massachusetts, Dawn Greenwood wished upon a star when young, little realizing it was the Silver Surfer. Years later, she was abducted by Incredulous Zed and rescued by the Surfer. The two became close and fell in love. The couple had a series of amazing adventures, and Dawn married the Surfer when they found themselves in the universe before the Big Bang. Dawn eventually died of old age. The Surfer took her energy into the new universe and it became the first light of creation.

GREMLIN

FIRST APPEARANCE *Incredible Hulk* #187 (May 1975)
REAL NAME Unrevealed
OCCUPATION Scientist **BASE** A secret base in Khystyro, somewhere in the Arctic, and Bitterfrost, a secret base in Siberia
HEIGHT 4 ft 6 in **WEIGHT** 215 lbs **EYES** Blue **HAIR** None
SPECIAL POWERS/ABILITIES Mutant who inherited father's genius-level intelligence; battlesuit gave superhuman strength.

The Gremlin is the son of the dead Soviet scientist Yuri Topolov, also known as the Gargoyle. Yuri participated in atomic tests that vastly increased his intelligence but scarred his face and body. He died following an encounter with the Hulk. Yuri's son, aka the Gremlin, inherited his father's heightened intelligence, and he achieved a position of authority while still only a child. Unfairly blaming the Hulk for his father's death, the Gremlin frequently tried to destroy him. Wearing a battlesuit similar to Titanium Man, he was eventually killed in a battle with Iron Man.

GRIM REAPER

FIRST APPEARANCE *Avengers* #52 (May 1968)
REAL NAME Eric Williams
OCCUPATION Criminal **BASE** Mobile
HEIGHT/WEIGHT Unrevealed **EYES** Brown **HAIR** Black
SPECIAL POWERS/ABILITIES Has a scythe in place of his right hand, which can fire arcs of electrical energy and induce comas in victims.

Brother of Wonder Man, Eric Williams became the Grim Reaper to get revenge on the Avengers, whom he believed were responsible for his brother's death.
To that end, he allied with Ultron, and formed the Lethal Legion. He has come back from death more than once and served as one of the Apocalypse Twins' Horsemen of Death. He was ultimately killed by the Vision's wife and buried in the backyard of her house.

GRIZZLY

FIRST APPEARANCE *The Amazing Spider-Man* #139 (December 1974) **REAL NAME** Maxwell Markham
OCCUPATION Wrestler, criminal **BASE** Mobile
HEIGHT 6 ft 9 in **WEIGHT** 290 lbs
EYES Blue **HAIR** Blond, dyed red
SPECIAL POWERS/ABILITIES Superhuman durability, endurance, and strength.

Several characters have used the name Grizzly over the years. The most prominent was Maxwell Markham, a former professional wrestler who was so violent in the ring that he was banned from the sport. The Jackal gave him a bear suit fitted with an exoskeleton that enhanced his strength. He later underwent procedures that gave him his powers without the need of a suit. Another Grizzly worked for Cable's Wild Pack and Silver Sable's Six Pack but was later killed by Domino.

GREY GARGOYLE

GREY GARGOYLE

FACTFILE
REAL NAME
Paul Pierre Duval
OCCUPATION
Chemist, criminal
BASE
Mobile

HEIGHT 5 ft 11 in
WEIGHT 175 lbs (human form); 750 lbs (stone form)
EYES Blue (human form); white (stone form)
HAIR Black (human form); gray (stone form)

FIRST APPEARANCE
Journey into Mystery #107 (August 1964)

POWERS
Can transform himself into living stone without losing mobility, thereby gaining superhuman strength and durability. By touching people or objects with his right hand, he can transform them into an immobile, stone-like substance for about an hour.

French chemist Pierre Paul Duval accidentally spilled a potion that had been contaminated by an unknown substance onto his right hand. His hand permanently transformed into stone; however, he could still move it as if it were flesh. Duval discovered that he could transform his entire body into living stone, and decided to become a costumed criminal, the Grey Gargoyle.

Hoping to learn the secret of immortality, the Grey Gargoyle battled Thor, who remains his principal enemy, though he has fought many others including the Avengers. The Grey Gargoyle also briefly served as a member of Baron Zemo's Masters of Evil. The Gargoyle became Mokk, Breaker of Faith (one of the Worthy), during Fear Itself, turning thousands of people in Paris to stone. Odin later restored the ones who were still whole. The Grey Gargoyle was captured by the authorities and kept in a cage of Tony Stark's design. He then became an inmate at Pleasant Hill before escaping and joining Zemo's Army of Evil.

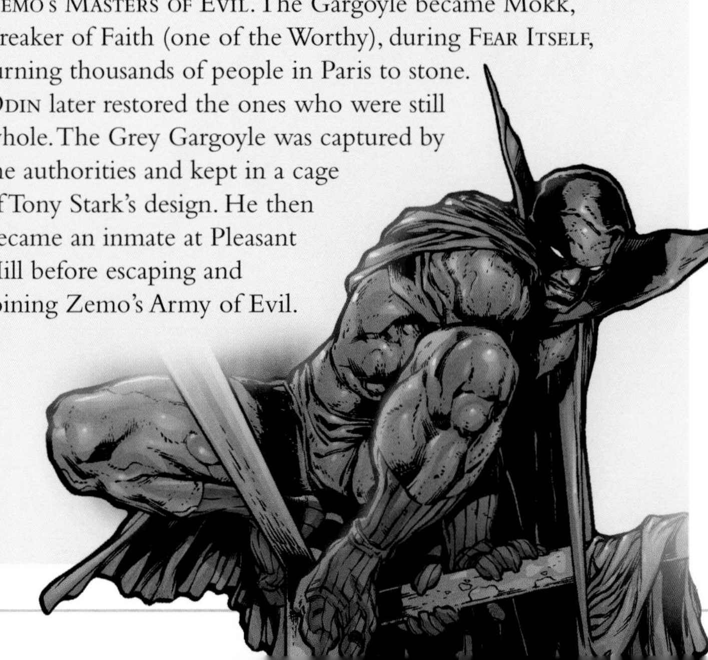

GROOT

FACTFILE

REAL NAME
Groot

OCCUPATION
Adventurer

BASE
Mobile

HEIGHT Variable
WEIGHT Variable
EYES Black
HAIR None

FIRST APPEARANCE
Tales to Astonish #13 (November 1960)

POWERS

Groot has superhuman durability and strength. He can regrow limbs or even his entire body from a shoot and communicate with plants.

GROOT

Groot is the last known member of an alien species once thought extinct, known as the *Flora Colossi*. He was exiled from his home and people for refusing to take part in their brutal treatment of other races. Groot eventually ended up in prison where he joined Star-Lord's prototype Guardians of the Galaxy to fight the second Annihilation wave. He gave his life to stop the Phalanx but Rocket Raccoon regrew him. He developed a strong bond with Rocket, who was one of the few creatures who could understand his language. After being destroyed and regrown by the cosmically powerful Gardener, others can now understand Groot. Another of his race, also calling himself Groot, once came to Earth to experiment on humans, was captured by SHIELD, and later became a Howling Commando.

GUARDIAN

FACTFILE

REAL NAME
James MacDonald Hudson

OCCUPATION
Scientist, adventurer

BASE
Canada (Dept. H)

HEIGHT 6 ft 2 in
WEIGHT 196 lbs
EYES Blue
HAIR Black

FIRST APPEARANCE
X-Men #109 (February 1978)

POWERS

Electromagnetic battlesuit has built-in force-field, allows him to fly, and discharge force bolts; also uses gravity to slingshot him in a westward direction at 1000 mph.

GUARDIAN

James MacDonald Hudson stole the prototype battlesuit he was developing when he discovered that his employers, Am-Can Petro-Chemical, intended to turn it over to the US military. Hudson took the suit to the Canadian government and founded Alpha Flight, which he led, first as Weapon Alpha, and then as Vindicator. When Canada ended its support for Alpha Flight, Hudson took the name Guardian to symbolize his new role. The Collective—an energy mass derived from the depowering of mutants by the Scarlet Witch—possessed Michael Pointer, a postman unaware he was also a mutant, and used him to kill Hudson, along with most of Alpha Flight. Ironically, Pointer then became the new Guardian of a government-sponsored version of Omega Flight, wearing Hudson's battlesuit to control his energy absorption powers. Pointer later took the name Weapon Omega. During the Chaos War, many of the members of Alpha Flight returned from the dead. Hudson was among them. He has since rejoined both his wife and team.

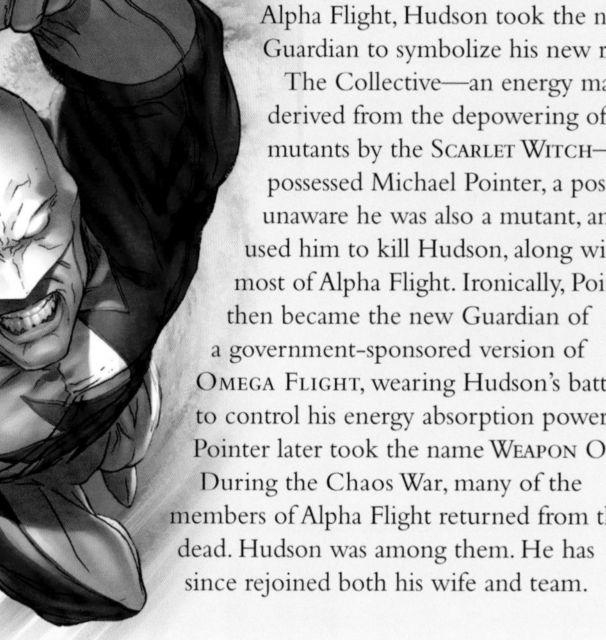

GUARDSMAN

FIRST APPEARANCE *Iron Man #43 (November 1971)*
REAL NAME Kevin O'Brien
OCCUPATION Research scientist
BASE Long Island, New York
HEIGHT 5 ft 10 in **WEIGHT** 195 lbs **EYES** Blue **HAIR** Red
SPECIAL POWERS/ABILITIES Armor augments strength and enables flight; it is also equipped with radiation shielding and a pulsed laser.

Kevin O'Brien headed up Stark Industries' research department and aided Iron Man against the Spymaster and the Espionage Elite. After revealing that he was Iron Man, Stark asked O'Brien to substitute for him if the need arose. That day came before O'Brien's Guardsman armor had been fully tested. Stark was kidnapped; O'Brien put on his armor, but it malfunctioned, stimulating the areas of his brain responsible for rage and jealousy. Guardsman and Iron Man clashed and Kevin was killed. Furious, Kevin's brother Michael obtained the Guardsman armor, and fought Stark. They have since reconciled, and Michael led a Guardsman force guarding the high-tech Vault prison.

GYRICH, HENRY PETER

FIRST APPEARANCE *Avengers* #168 (February 1978)
REAL NAME Henry Peter Gyrich
OCCUPATION Adventurer **BASE** Washington, D.C.
HEIGHT 6 ft 8 in **WEIGHT** 225 lbs **EYES** Green **HAIR** Red
SPECIAL POWERS/ABILITIES Gyrich is a normal human being with no superhuman powers; a cunning, ruthless strategist and highly efficient administrator.

Henry Gyrich was the Avengers' government liaison. He threatened to cut off the team's unlimited airspace access and use of secret government equipment unless they obeyed his rules. As head of Project Wideawake, he transformed the Brotherhood of Evil Mutants into Freedom Force. He took over from Valerie Cooper as head of the Commission on Superhuman Activities. With the launch of the Fifty-State Initiative, Gyrich became Secretary of the Superhuman Armed Forces. He later became co-director of SWORD but, not long after, Captain America captured him on behalf of SHIELD for helping to turn Demolition Man into the next incarnation of the murderous Scourge. He was also on the board of governors for the Alpha Flight space program.

GREY, JEAN

Telepath of virtually unlimited psychic power

GREY, JEAN

FACTFILE

REAL NAME
Jean Grey-Summers

OCCUPATION
Adventurer; former fashion model

BASE
Atlantis-X

HEIGHT 5 ft 6 in
WEIGHT 110 lbs
EYES Green
HAIR Red

FIRST APPEARANCE
X-Men #1 (September 1963)

POWERS

As Marvel Girl, possessed mutant abilities of telepathy and telekinesis. The Phoenix Force amplified these powers to a virtually unlimited extent. The Phoenix Force can manifest itself as a fiery corona in the shape of a bird that surrounds Jean Grey's body.

ALLIES/FOES

ALLIES Professor Charles Xavier, Cyclops, Archangel, Beast, Iceman, Storm, Wolverine, Marvel Girl (Rachel Summers), Cable

FOES Magneto, Mastermind, Hellfire Club, Apocalypse, Sentinels, Xorn I

ISSUE #1

In the first X-Men comic, Jean Grey arrives at Professor Xavier's school, meets her future husband Scott Summers, becomes Marvel Girl, and first battles Magneto.

When Jean Grey was ten years old, her best friend, Annie Richardson, was hit by an automobile. Jean's anguish as she held her friend activated her mutant telepathic powers, and Jean thus shared Annie's emotions as she died. Traumatized, Jean suffered from deep depression and was unable to control her new telepathic powers.

Jean Grey was only a small child when she first met Charles Xavier. She joined the X-Men in her mid-teens.

MARVEL GIRL

Jean's telekinetic power enables her to levitate objects.

When Jean was eleven, her parents turned to Professor Charles Xavier (PROFESSOR X) for help. Xavier created psychic shields in Jean's mind to prevent her from utilizing her telepathic powers until she was mature enough to control them. He also began training her to use her telekinetic ability to mentally manipulate objects. As a teenager, Jean enrolled in Xavier's School for Gifted Youngsters, becoming the fifth member of the original X-MEN, the team of young mutants whom Xavier was training to combat mutant menaces to humanity. Grey was given the code name "Marvel Girl."

The Phoenix Force is a primal power of creation and destruction that manifests itself as a gigantic bird of prey composed of cosmic flame.

Grey and her fellow student Scott Summers (CYCLOPS) quickly fell in love, although they did not reveal their feelings to each other for a long time. After she had trained for years at his school, Xavier finally enabled Grey to use her telepathic powers.

Following Xavier's recruitment of a new class of X-Men, Grey left the team. However, soon afterward she and other X-Men were abducted by SENTINELS to a space station orbiting the Earth. The X-Men had to escape in a space shuttle during a solar radiation storm. Grey volunteered to pilot the shuttle, although she had to sit in a section without sufficient radiation shielding. Grey's powers proved insufficient to hold back the intense radiation, and it began to kill her.

PHOENIX FORCE

A sentient cosmic entity of limitless power, the Phoenix Force, made contact with the dying Grey. The Phoenix Force created a human host body for itself that was a duplicate of Grey's, and infused it with a portion of her consciousness. The Phoenix Force placed Grey's original body into suspended animation within a large cocoon, in which it would slowly heal. When the shuttle crash-landed in Jamaica Bay, the Phoenix Force's new host body rose from the water, declaring herself to be Phoenix. The X-Men believed that Phoenix was the real Jean Grey, and Phoenix/Grey joined the team.

ESSENTIAL STORYLINES

- ***Uncanny X-Men #129–137***
The Dark Phoenix Saga.
- ***Fantastic Four #286, X-Factor #1***
Jean Grey returns from apparent death and reunites with Scott Summers (Cyclops).
- ***Phoenix Resurrection: The Return of Jean Grey (tpb)***
The Phoenix brings Jean Grey back to life.

THE YOUNG JEAN GREY

The teenage Jean Grey and her teammates were pulled forward in time by the Beast and stranded in the present. The young Jean handled the situation better than her teammates and she became their leader. When the Phoenix Force returned, it used the young Jean to help bring adult Jean back to life. Young Jean found herself trapped in the White Hot Room, but managed to use her power to force the Phoenix to return her home, where she then met her reborn adult self.

The X-Men's old foe the criminal Mastermind began manipulating Phoenix/Grey's mind to prove his worthiness to join the Inner Circle of the HELLFIRE CLUB, thereby awakening the dark side of her personality. Finally, Mastermind mesmerized her into becoming the new Black Queen of the Hellfire Club. However, he could not control her for long: Phoenix/Jean Grey not only turned against him, she transformed into the insane Dark Phoenix.

Dark Phoenix battled the X-Men, and inadvertently destroyed an inhabited planet. Finally, Jean's original personality reasserted itself. To prevent herself from reverting to Dark Phoenix, she committed suicide as the horrified Cyclops looked on.

BACK FROM THE DEAD

Upon the death of Phoenix's body, Jean's consciousness returned to her original body in a cocoon at the bottom of Jamaica Bay. The Avengers eventually found and revived Jean, and she emerged to find that in the interim, Scott had married her clone (Madelyne PRYOR) and had a son Nathan (CABLE) by her. Despite this, she joined the original X-Men to found X-FACTOR. Pryor went mad, developed powers as the Goblin Queen, and died in combat with Grey.

Finally, Jean and Scott reunited and married. During their honeymoon, their souls were brought into the future and, as Redd and Slym, they raised Nathan for ten years before returning home.

Later, Jean assumed the name Phoenix and linked herself with the Phoenix Force. She and Scott drifted apart, and she discovered that Scott was having an affair with Emma FROST. Later, the first Xorn, posing as Magneto, slew Jean, but the Phoenix Force resurrected her once again. She became the White Phoenix of the Crown in a pocket dimension called the White Hot Room. The Shi'ar later forced the Phoenix Force from there and shattered it. Jean set about gathering the fractured pieces and trying to heal the universe.

When the Phoenix Force returned to Earth to possess the Phoenix Five, Scott eventually took on all of its power and became the Dark Phoenix, slaying Professor X. At one point, at the height of his power, he bumped up against the bottom of the White Hot Room and could hear Jean telling him he was an idiot, but she did nothing more.

Jean Grey as the White Phoenix of the Crown.

Jean Grey finally told the Phoenix Force that it had nothing to offer her, and renounced it.

REBORN

Desperate to bond with Jean again, the Phoenix Force resurrected her in yet another pocket reality. However, Jean's subconscious saw through the illusion. After the X-Men went to her aid, she renounced the Phoenix Force and returned to the real world. It was a very different world to the one she had left. Scott was dead and it seemed mutants were in greater danger than ever. While Jean was attempting to increase rights for mutants at the UN, Cassandra Nova, Professor X's evil twin, killed the British ambassador and framed Jean and her allies. Jean's new team of X-Men soon found themselves in conflict with Cassandra Nova—with the fate of the world hanging in the balance.

Jean Grey's new "Red" X-Men, headquartered in Atlantis, were soon forced to operate in the shadows as Jean was labeled a fugitive.

GUARDIANS OF THE GALAXY

Heroes sworn to protect the universe

PREVIOUS GUARDIANS
(Clockwise from top left): Charlie-27, Starhawk, Aleta, Major Victory, Yondu, Nikki, Martinex

FACTFILE

ORIGINAL MEMBERS

MAJOR VICTORY
(Vance Astro) Psychokinesis, mental force blasts.

ALETA
Can create objects of solid light.

CHARLIE-27
Enhanced strength and stamina.

MARTINEX
Enhanced strength, projection of heat and cold.

NIKKI
Resistant to heat and bright light, sharpshooter.

STARHAWK
Flight, enhanced strength, energy projection.

YONDU
Skilled archer, mystical sensory abilities.

BASE
Mobile

FIRST APPEARANCE
Marvel Super Heroes #18 (January 1969)

In an alternate timeline of the 31st century (Earth-691), the Guardians of the Galaxy acted as protectors of the Milky Way. The group formed in response to the Badoon invasion of 3007, which decimated Pluto, Mercury, Jupiter, and Earth. The Guardians defeated the Badoon by 3015 and then became adventurers. They traveled to Earth's current reality several times, becoming honorary members of the AVENGERS.

GUARDIANS OF THE FUTURE

Originally, there were only four Guardians, each representing the last survivors of their kind from different planets. They were Vance Astro (Earth), Charlie-27 (Jupiter), Martinex (Pluto), and YONDU (Centauri IV). They were later joined by STARHAWK, his wife Aleta, and Nikki (Mercury).

The Guardians' adventures in their own time included a quest for CAPTAIN AMERICA's shield. Vance Astro also convinced his younger self to follow a different path, leading to his mainstream version becoming MARVEL BOY (later JUSTICE). Other teammates included Hollywood (a future WONDER MAN), the feline Talon, the shapeshifting SKRULL Replica, a time-traveling YELLOWJACKET II, and the former herald of GALACTUS, Firelord. Many of these joined a spin-off team called the Galactic Guardians.

GUARDIANS OF TODAY

In the wake of the two ANNIHILATION events in the mainstream universe, STAR-LORD (Peter Quill) banded together with Adam WARLOCK, DRAX THE DESTROYER, COSMO (an evolved Russian space dog), GAMORA, GROOT, MANTIS, QUASAR (Phyla-Vell), and ROCKET RACCOON to form a new team of heroes to help protect the galaxy. They established a headquarters in Knowhere, the head of a long-dead Celestial floating in space near the end of the universe. Soon after forming, they discovered a frozen Vance Astro (also known as MAJOR VICTORY) and, at his suggestion, they called themselves the Guardians of the Galaxy.

The team suffered troubles from the start, breaking up when the others found out that Star-Lord had asked Mantis to telepathically compel them to join. They reformed during the SHI'AR-KREE War of Kings and brought in master thief BUG (from the Microverse), Jack Flag (an Earth hero who worked with CAPTAIN AMERICA), and MOONDRAGON as well. They even went into the future to encounter the original team. Later, with help from THANOS, the Guardians stopped the Cancerverse from attacking and destroying their own universe, but at the cost of the lives of NOVA and Star-Lord, who stayed behind to keep the Cancerverse sealed away.

Star-Lord later returned and restarted the Guardians, featuring himself, Drax, Gamora, Groot, and Rocket Racoon. IRON MAN joined them temporarily, followed by Agent VENOM. Quill and his girlfriend, Kitty PRYDE, teamed up to recover the artifact known as the Black Vortex, and ended up engaged for a time. The THING also joined the team when Quill temporarily left to become king of the planet Spartax, with Pryde filling in as Star-Lord. The Guardians sided with CAPTAIN MARVEL in the second Super Hero Civil War (*See* CIVIL WAR II), though it divided them. They reunited to fight THANOS, but Gamora's relentless quest for the Soul Gem finally tore the team apart.

THE GUARDIANS
1 Drax
2 Star-Lord
3 Gamora
4 Groot
5 Rocket Raccoon

HALLER, GABRIELLE

FIRST APPEARANCE *The Uncanny X-Men* #161 (September 1982) **REAL NAME** Gabrielle Haller
OCCUPATION Israel's ambassador to the United Kingdom
BASE Tel Aviv, Israel; London, England
HEIGHT/WEIGHT Unrevealed **EYES** Brown **HAIR** Black
SPECIAL POWERS/ABILITIES Gabrielle Haller has no superpowers, but is a highly accomplished diplomat.

Gabrielle Haller was held in a Nazi concentration camp during WWII. While there, the Nazis concealed in her mind the location of a secret cache of gold. After the war, she was afflicted with catatonic schizophrenia and hospitalized in Israel. Charles Xavier (PROFESSOR X) used his telepathic powers to cure her and they fell in love. When BARON VON STRUCKER kidnapped Haller to find the gold, Xavier and "Magnus" (the future MAGNETO) rescued her. Many years later Xavier learned that Gabrielle had given birth to a son, David (*see* LEGION). Haller later became Israel's ambassador to the UK. She was accidentally shot and killed, but resurrected by her son.

HAMMER, JUSTIN

FIRST APPEARANCE *Iron Man* #120 (March 1979)
REAL NAME Justin Hammer
OCCUPATION Criminal financier **BASE** Mobile
HEIGHT 6 ft 2 in **WEIGHT** 170 lbs **EYES** Blue **HAIR** Gray
SPECIAL POWERS/ABILITIES A financial and business genius, Hammer has cunningly preserved his wealth despite being worldwide *persona non grata*.

Whatever Justin Hammer lacked in guile he made up for with low cunning. Infuriated by Stark International's success, Hammer resolved to undermine Tony Stark's business by compromising its corporate emblem, the IRON MAN. Using a hypersonic device to take control of the armored suit, Hammer used it to kill a foreign ambassador. After Stark cleared his name, Hammer went into hiding and took to funding various criminals, including BLIZZARD, BOOMERANG, and Water Wizard. Another showdown with Stark left Hammer frozen in a block of ice and floating through space.

HAMMER, SASHA

FIRST APPEARANCE *Invincible Iron Man* #1 (July 2008)
REAL NAME Sasha Hammer
OCCUPATION Industrialist; criminal **BASE** Mobile
HEIGHT 5 ft 6 in **WEIGHT** 120 lbs **EYES** Brown **HAIR** Black
SPECIAL POWERS/ABILITIES Sasha has been embedded with technology that grants her energy whips, flight, and superhuman durability. She also sometimes wears the Detroit Steel armor.

As the granddaughter of Justin HAMMER and the daughter of Justine Hammer (CRIMSON COWL) and the MANDARIN, Sasha's hatred for Tony Stark (IRON MAN) is in her blood. Her boyfriend, Ezekiel STANE, upgraded her with Stane technology to make her a formidable foe. She later piloted her family's Detroit Steel armor, which HAMMER Industries had developed to take the place of the Iron Man armor for the US military. She ruthlessly decapitated the original pilot of the Detroit Steel armor after he took her hostage to get the suit back.

HAMMER

After Norman Osborn (GREEN GOBLIN) became the US director of national security, one of his first acts was to dismantle SHIELD and replace it with an organization of his own, entirely loyal to him: HAMMER. The name HAMMER highlighted the fact that the organization's main aim would not be protecting the US but crushing its enemies. Osborn didn't even bother to come up with an acronym; he let the name stand on its own. As director of HAMMER, Osborn issued a warrant for Tony Stark's (IRON MAN) arrest for perceived failures during the SECRET INVASION. He then set up his own versions of both the AVENGERS and the X-MEN, putting villains in the roles. Osborn had an Iron Man suit repainted in patriotic colors and became the IRON PATRIOT.

HAMMER fell apart at the end of the DARK REIGN, after Osborn's failed assault on Asgard. The HAMMER Helicarrier was destroyed, taking down SENTRY. Deidre Wentworth, aka mysandric terrorist Superia, later tried to revive the organization, with the help of AIM, but failed.

Despite his tendency to micromanage every bit of evil he committed, Norman relied on people like Victoria Hand to help execute his plans.

Norman cemented his hold over HAMMER by setting up covert alliances with prominent criminal organizations, including Hydra and AIM.

FACTFILE

NOTABLE MEMBERS

NORMAN OSBORN
Founder, director

SUPERIA
Second director

VICTORIA HAND
Assistant director; triple agent

BASE
The HAMMER Helicarrier; mobile

FIRST APPEARANCE
Secret Invasion #8 (January 2009)

HAMMERHEAD

HAMMERHEAD

FACTFILE

REAL NAME
Unknown

OCCUPATION
Criminal; gang boss of Hammerhead "family"

BASE
Manhattan, New York City

HEIGHT 5 ft 10 in
WEIGHT 195 lbs
EYES Blue
HAIR Black

FIRST APPEARANCE
Amazing Spider-Man #113 (October 1972)

POWERS

Hammerhead's reinforced skull allows him to head-butt with devastating effect, and even smash through walls. He can also use his head as a shield against blows. He has strong criminal organizational skills, and his favorite weapon is a Tommy gun.

A full-powered Spider-punch means nothing to the criminal with the hardest head in the business.

Once an obscure, small-time criminal, Hammerhead was found, severely injured, by Dr. Jonas Harrow. Harrow reconstructed the criminal's shattered skull, making it as strong as steel—hence his new name. Hammerhead retained no knowledge of his past life, save that he had been a criminal. Taking his inspiration from the poster of a gangster movie, *The Al Capone Mob*, he adopted a Prohibition-era style and returned to the New York underworld, determined to become the boss of bosses.

He was prepared to violently dispatch anyone who stood in his way, including DOCTOR OCTOPUS, the KINGPIN, and MAGGIA boss Don Fortunato. During the CIVIL WAR, the Kingpin hired the assassin Underworld to kill Hammerhead. Shot down once more, Hammerhead was saved this time by Mr. Negative, who had his brain transferred into a robotic skeleton made of Adamantium. In return, he now trains and leads his benefactor's enforcers.

Hammerhead's style recalls the Prohibition gangsters of the 1920s.

HAND, THE

HAND, THE

FACTFILE

NOTABLE MEMBERS
The Beast (demon with mystical powers), Kirigi, Shadow, Thought, Pain, Kwannon, Mandarin (all boast martial arts skills and powers of occult magic)

BASE
Various

FIRST APPEARANCE
Daredevil #174 (September 1981)

POWERS

In addition to possessing various mystical powers, Hand operatives are trained in the ways of the ninja: all are expert spies and assassins skilled at unarmed combat, and with all kinds of weapons.

The Hand is a cult of mystical ninjas involved with organized crime and often hired to carry out assassinations. The Hand dates back to 16th-century Japan, where the cult adapted classical ninjitsu techniques to its own evil purposes. The Hand's activities have now spread throughout the world. Hand operatives are servants of a demon known only as the Beast. Skilled in the use of powerful occult magic, they can kill a person, then bring that person back to life as a member of the Hand. Only ELEKTRA and WOLVERINE have ever been able to reverse this process. If one of the Hand is killed, their body magically turns to dust in order to prevent identification.

The Hand has most often clashed with DAREDEVIL, ELEKTRA, and the CHASTE. Elektra led the Hand for a while, but after the SKRULL impersonating her was killed, Daredevil reluctantly took the position, hoping to turn the Hand into a force for good. He failed, and both the KINGPIN and Hive have since led these formidable assassins.

The Hand is involved in regular clashes with members of the Super Hero community.

Implacable, faceless killers, the Hand cult remains one of the most feared groups of assassins at large in the world.

HAND, VICTORIA

FIRST APPEARANCE *The Invincible Iron Man* #8 (February 2009)
REAL NAME Victoria Louise Hand
OCCUPATION Liasion to the New Avengers
BASE Avengers Mansion **HEIGHT** 5 ft 6 in **WEIGHT** 135 lbs
EYES Hazel **HAIR** Black with red streak
SPECIAL POWERS/ABILITIES Skilled markswoman and tactician; trained in hand-to-hand combat; gifted in mathematics, accounting, and public speaking

Victoria Hand was a SHIELD accountant who objected to Nick Fury's running of the organization. When Norman Osborn took over SHIELD and transformed it into HAMMER, he made Hand deputy director. She served him loyally—even during the Siege of Asgard—and willingly surrendered to the authorities following Osborn's fall. Steve Rogers surprised Hand by making her the liaison for Luke Cage's Avengers team. While at times it seemed she was betraying Rogers and the Avengers to Osborn, she was acting as a double—and sometimes triple—agent for Rogers. She was killed when the Avengers fought Daniel Drumm. A statue of her was placed in the grounds of Avengers Mansion.

HARDBALL

FIRST APPEARANCE *Avengers: The Initiative* #1 (March 2007)
REAL NAME Roger Brokeridge
OCCUPATION Hydra agent **BASE** Camp Hammond
HEIGHT 6 ft **WEIGHT** 200 lbs **EYES** Green **HAIR** Blond
SPECIAL POWERS/ABILITIES Creates and throws a number of different types of balls of energy.

Roger never wanted to be a hero. His brother Paul purchased powers from the Power Broker and then became paralyzed in a wrestling match. When Roger confronted the Power Broker, he signed up for his own powers. Trying to rob an armored car, he accidentally saved a little girl and became a hero. The Power Broker sold Roger's contract to Hydra, and Roger became part of the first class of cadets at Camp Hammond and spied on the organization from within. He later killed Senator Woodman, took over the man's Hydra cell, and wound up running a Hydra training camp in Madripoor. He surrendered to Constrictor.

HARKNESS, AGATHA

FIRST APPEARANCE *Fantastic Four* #94 (March 1969)
REAL NAME Agatha Harkness
OCCUPATION Witch **BASE** New York City
HEIGHT 5 ft 11 in **WEIGHT** 130 lbs **EYES** Blue **HAIR** White
SPECIAL POWERS/ABILITIES Could manipulate magical forces through the recitation of spells; possessed magical familiar named Ebony, a pet cat that could transform into a vicious panther.

Agatha Harkness was raised in the town of New Salem, Colorado, whose inhabitants practiced magic. She excelled in her craft and eventually became the town's most powerful sorceress and leader. Agatha believed that witches and warlocks didn't have to live apart from normal humans. Her son and the town elders disagreed, and she chose to leave New Salem. After moving to Whisper Hill, New York, she was hired as the governess for Franklin Richards, son of Mister Fantastic and Invisible Woman. When the Scarlet Witch became unbalanced and disassembled the Avengers, she apparently murdered Agatha, but Agatha was returned to life years later by Wanda's mother, Natalya.

HAVOK

The brother of the X-Men leader Cyclops, Alex Summers was separated from his sibling following the death of their parents. Although Alex's mutant abilities developed during puberty, his mutant college professor, Ahmet Abdol, was the first to recognize them. After absorbing the cosmic energy stored in Alex's body, Abdol became the Living Monolith, but was defeated by the X-Men. Reunited with his brother, Alex joined the X-Men. Despite working in Cyclops' shadow, he later led X-Factor and fought to save the dark and twisted Earth-1298. He has long had a romantic relationship with the mutant Polaris. Alex worked with the Starjammers to put an end to his long-hidden brother Vulcan's plans for galactic conquest. He sided with the X-Men in their conflict with the Avengers, but he later agreed to lead the Avengers Unity Division. He was turned evil during a confrontation with archvillain Red Onslaught, but Emma Frost and Polaris returned him to normal. He later went on to create his own X-Men team.

Havok can project plasma in the form of a blast with a tell-tale concentric circle pattern.

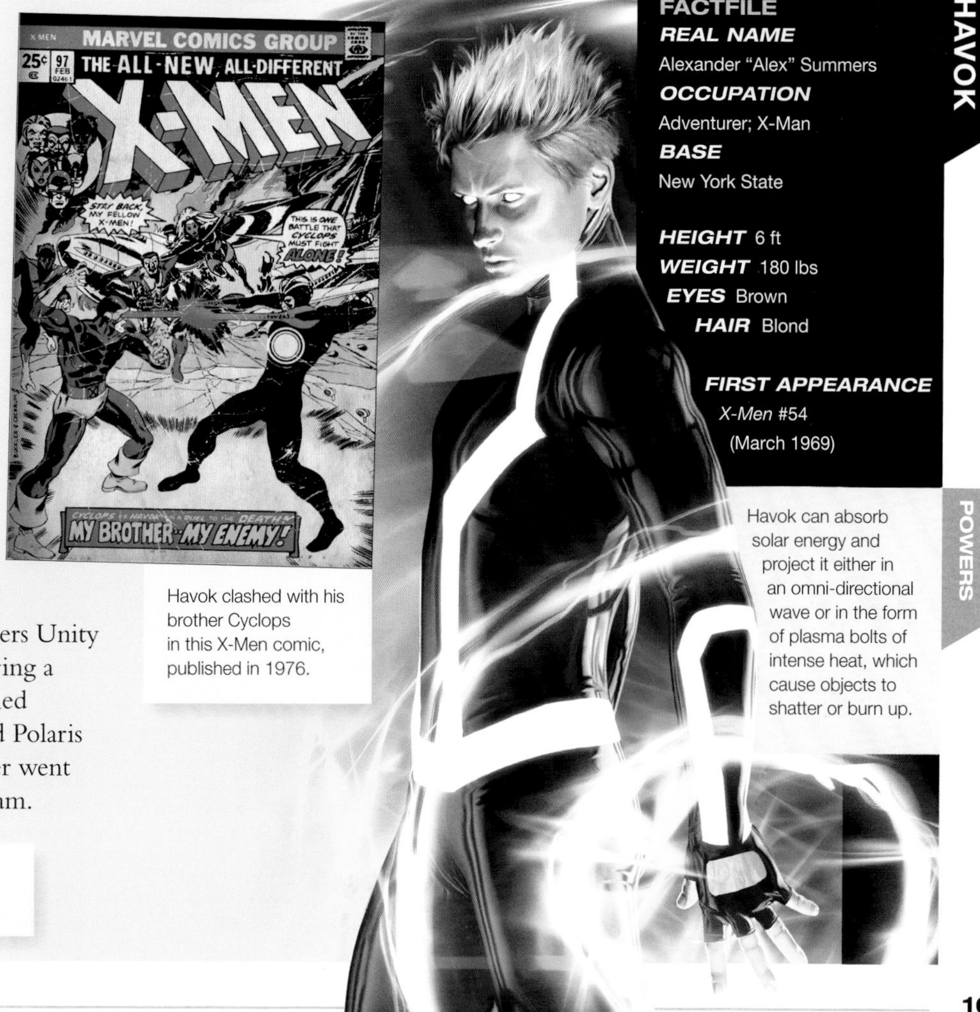

Havok clashed with his brother Cyclops in this X-Men comic, published in 1976.

HAVOK

FACTFILE

REAL NAME
Alexander "Alex" Summers

OCCUPATION
Adventurer; X-Man

BASE
New York State

HEIGHT 6 ft
WEIGHT 180 lbs
EYES Brown
HAIR Blond

FIRST APPEARANCE
X-Men #54 (March 1969)

POWERS

Havok can absorb solar energy and project it either in an omni-directional wave or in the form of plasma bolts of intense heat, which cause objects to shatter or burn up.

HAWKEYE

The Marksman

HAWKEYE

FACTFILE

REAL NAME
Clinton "Clint" Barton

OCCUPATION
Super Hero; adventurer

BASE
Manhattan, New York City

HEIGHT 6 ft 3 in
WEIGHT 230 lbs
EYES Blue
HAIR Blond

FIRST APPEARANCE
Tales of Suspense #57
(September 1964)

POWERS

Expert archer with perfect accuracy. Employs an arsenal of custom-made bows and a variety of trick arrows. Extensive training as an aerialist and acrobat. Skilled in hand-to-hand combat.

Barton was only 14 when he joined a carnival and attracted the attention of the show's star Jacques Duquesne, the SWORDSMAN. Duquesne trained Barton in the art of throwing knives, but quickly realized the boy was a natural at archery and turned him over to TRICKSHOT, the carnival's archer. On stage, Barton was known as Hawkeye the Marksman.

Wickedly sarcastic, Hawkeye has developed some of his trick arrows to humiliate as well as defeat his foes.

GOING WRONG

Witnessing IRON MAN in action inspired Barton to use his archery skills to fight crime. When he tried to prevent a robbery, he was mistaken for a thief, and he wound up fighting Iron Man instead. Soon after that, he met the original BLACK WIDOW, fell in love with her, and started committing crimes to impress her.

Barton reformed and begged to be admitted into the AVENGERS. Iron Man sponsored him, and Barton remained an Avenger for many years, though he occasionally took brief breaks and even joined the DEFENDERS during one of them. To help the team, Barton sometimes borrowed Hank PYM's growth formula and became a new GOLIATH.

While on leave, Barton married Bobbi Morse (MOCKINGBIRD). They moved to California when Barton was assigned to set up the AVENGERS West COAST. After Mockingbird was apparently killed in action, the West Coast branch disbanded, and Barton rejoined the Avengers. He died stopping a KREE warship during the SCARLET WITCH's breakdown, but she restored him to life when she rearranged reality after M-Day. In the meantime, at the request of CAPTAIN AMERICA, Kate Bishop of the YOUNG AVENGERS took on the identity of Hawkeye.

Kate Bishop in her role as Hawkeye while fighting in the Young Avengers.

THE HERO REBORN

Barton temporarily took on the identity of Ronin, a masked swordsman. During the SECRET INVASION, he discovered Mockingbird was still alive. They reunited but, despite their best efforts, the marriage fell apart.

During the DARK REIGN, BULLSEYE assumed the Hawkeye identity as part of the DARK AVENGERS. Barton later returned to being Hawkeye, leading various teams of Avengers and sharing the name with Kate, whom he took on as a protégé.

During CIVIL WAR II, Barton shot Bruce Banner with an arrow specially developed by Banner to kill both himself and the HULK in case his monstrous alter ego showed signs of returning. Barton was put on trial for the murder, but acquitted. After HYDRA's takeover of the USA, both Barton and Kate fought the evil CAPTAIN AMERICA's forces. By then Kate had relocated to Los Angeles, where she set herself up as a Super Hero-turned-private eye. She eventually formed a new incarnation of the Avengers West Coast, with her mentor giving invaluable support.

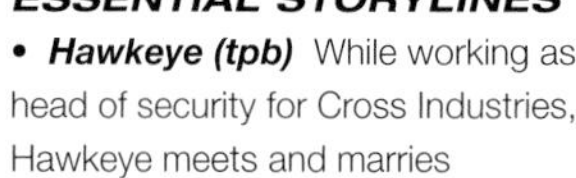

While Barton mentored Kate, she quickly proved herself to be his equal.

ESSENTIAL STORYLINES

- ***Hawkeye (tpb)*** While working as head of security for Cross Industries, Hawkeye meets and marries Mockingbird.
- ***Solo Adventures #1–6*** Hawkeye's former mentor Trickshot returns and we learn Clint's true origin.
- ***West Coast Avengers Limited Series #1–4*** Hawkeye opens a branch office for the Avengers.
- ***Avengers #502*** Hawkeye courageously sacrifices his life to protect his Avengers teammates.

THE HEADMEN
1 Gorilla-Man **2** Ruby Thursday
3 Orago the Unconquerable (not a member) **4** Chondu the Mystic
5 Shrunken Bones

HEADMEN, THE

The Headmen comprised four brilliant individuals, each so confident of their abilities they were convinced that they should rule the Earth. United by Dr. Arthur Nagan, they agreed to combine their talents to gain control of the planet. Despite obvious ability, their tactics were at best questionable.

Looking to obtain superhuman powers for themselves, the Headmen targeted the DEFENDERS and succeeded in implanting Chondu's brain into the head of Kyle Richmond, alias NIGHTHAWK. When his consciousness was subsequently transferred into the body of a vile monster, Chondu went mad. Although his sanity had returned by the time his brain was transferred into a SHE-HULK clone, this proved to be one step too far. Furious at having been given a woman's body, Chondu attacked the Headmen with the help of SPIDER-MAN. The group reunited and attempted to take over the world, starting with Manhattan, by manipulating a hugely powerful, extra-dimensional entity named Orago the Unconquerable.

FACTFILE

MEMBERS AND POWERS

GORILLA-MAN
(Dr. Arthur Nagan)
A brilliant scientist, whose head has been mysteriously transplanted onto a gorilla's body.

SHRUNKEN BONES
A biologist and biochemist, experiments on own body led to skeleton shrinking but not skin.

CHONDU THE MYSTIC
A minor adept in the mystic arts; powers determined by body his brain is currently occupying.

RUBY THURSDAY
Artificial head serves as "organic computer," capable of superhuman storage and processing.

BASE Mobile

FIRST APPEARANCE
Defenders #21
(March 1975)

Patsy Walker had a teenage crush on Reed Richards of the Fantastic Four.

HELLCAT

As a teenager, Patsy Walker was the subject of a popular comic written by her mother. As an adult, Walker wed Air Force officer Buzz Baxter (later MAD DOG), though the marriage ended unhappily. She had always idolized Super Heroes, so Walker decided to become one, donning a costume once worn by Greer Nelson (TIGRA). Calling herself Hellcat, she aided the AVENGERS and served with the DEFENDERS for years. Eventually she married master of the occult Daimon Hellstrom, (*see* HELLSTORM). The couple moved to San Francisco, becoming paranormal investigators. Hellcat later took her own life, but her spirit lived on in Hell. There she encountered HAWKEYE and the THUNDERBOLTS, who had journeyed to the underworld to rescue MOCKINGBIRD. The team returned to Earth with Hellcat, who rededicated herself to the heroic life. She is close friends with the SHE-HULK, having worked with the hero's alter ego Jennifer Walters in the past.

HELLCAT WITH THE DEFENDERS
1 Doctor Strange **2** Hellcat **3** Nighthawk
4 Valkyrie **5** Daimon Hellstrom

FACTFILE

REAL NAME
Patricia "Patsy" Walker Hellstrom

OCCUPATION
Adventurer

BASE
San Francisco, California

HEIGHT 5 ft 8 in
WEIGHT 135 lbs
EYES Blue
HAIR Red

FIRST APPEARANCE
The Avengers #144
(February 1976)

POWERS
Minor psionic abilities, skilled acrobat and combatant (received combat training from Moondragon on Saturn's moon Titan). Costume enhances strength and agility; steel-tipped claws in gloves and boots; a wrist device fires a 30-ft cable with grappling hook for scaling tall buildings.

HELLFIRE CLUB

Founded in England in the mid-18th century, the Hellfire Club was an exclusive social organization for Britain's upper classes. According to legend, the Club provided a place where members could secretly pursue illicit pleasures. In the 1770s, Sir Patrick Clemens and Lady Diana Knight established the Hellfire Club's American branch in New York City. Today, the Hellfire Club is a worldwide organization with branches in London, Manhattan, Paris, and Hong Kong. Its members include socialites, celebrities, wealthy businessmen, and politicians. Despite the Club's outward respectability, its Inner Circle secretly seeks world domination through political and economic influence. Inner Circle members hold positions named after chess pieces and dress in 18th-century costume.

HELLFIRE CLUB

FACTFILE

MEMBERS

***1* SHINOBI SHAW** (White King)
***2* SELENE** (Black Queen)
***3* SEBASTIAN SHAW** (Black King)
***4* EMMA FROST** (White Queen)
***5* HARRY LELAND** (Black Bishop)
***6* EMMANUEL DA COSTA** (White Rook)
***7* JASON WYNGARDE** (Mastermind)
***8* TESSA** (Sage)
***9* DONALD PIERCE** (White Bishop)
***10* FRIEDRICH VON ROEHM** (Black Rook)
***11* MADELYNE PRYOR** (Black Rook)
***12* TREVOR FITZROY** (White Rook)

BASE
London, Manhattan, Paris, and Hong Kong.

FIRST APPEARANCE
(as Council of the Chosen) *X-Men* #100 (August 1976); (as Hellfire Club) *The Uncanny X-Men* #129 (January 1980)

INNER CIRCLE

Industrialist Sebastian SHAW ruled as Black King over an Inner Circle that included his fellow mutant Emma FROST as the White Queen, and cyborg Donald Pierce. To win admission to the Inner Circle, Mastermind mesmerized Phoenix (Jean GREY) into becoming the Club's Black Queen. Other members have included Blackheart, Cassandra Nova, HELLSTORM, Kade Kilgore, MAGNETO, SELENE, SUNSPOT, and VIPER. As Black King, Kilgore later founded the Hellfire Academy, a villainous competitor to the Jean Grey School.

HELLIONS

FIRST APPEARANCE *New Mutants* #16 (June 1984)

BASE Snow Valley, MA

MEMBERS AND POWERS

Rockslide (Santo Vaccarro) Made of granite, can fire hands as projectiles [1]; **Emma Frost** Telepath [2]; **Wither** (Kevin Ford) Touch disintegrates organic matter [3]; **Dust** (Sooraya Qadir) Turns into sandlike substance [4]; **Mercury** (Cessily Kincaid) Shapeshifter made of non-toxic mercury [5]; **Hellion** (Julian Keller) Telekinesis [6]; **Tag** (Brian Cruz) Tags others, causing them to emit a psionic signal [7].

A number of groups of young mutants have called themselves the Hellions. The originals were students at Emma FROST's Massachusetts Academy who served the HELLFIRE CLUB. They were wiped out by a psychotic criminal. The second band was formed by enemies of X-FORCE. The third group was composed of students at the Xavier Institute for Higher Learning. Kade Kilgore's new Hellfire Academy also featured a fresh team of Hellions.

HELLSTORM

FIRST APPEARANCE *Marvel Spotlight* #12 (October 1973)

REAL NAME Daimon Hellstrom

OCCUPATION Demonologist; occult investigator; exorcist; former priest **BASE** San Francisco, CA

HEIGHT 6 ft 1 in **WEIGHT** 180 lbs **EYES** Blue **HAIR** Red

SPECIAL POWERS/ABILITIES Trident projects "soulfire"; can cast spells to transport himself and others into mystical dimensions.

Daimon Hellstrom only learned that his father was the demon Satan after his mother, traumatized by Satan's actions, sent Daimon to an orphanage. Acting as a hero, he joined the DEFENDERS. He married teammate Patsy Walker (HELLCAT), but while saving his life she saw his true face, which ultimately led to her death. Now calling himself Hellstorm, Daimon figured out how to kill Satan and take over Hell, and helped HAWKEYE's THUNDERBOLTS revive Patsy. Later, he sent copies of himself out into the world and tried to add the VENOM symbiote to his Monsters of Evil.

HIGH EVOLUTIONARY

FIRST APPEARANCE *Thor* #134 (November 1966)

REAL NAME Herbert Edgar Wyndham

OCCUPATION Founder of the Knights of Wundagore

BASE Unknown **HEIGHT** 6 ft 2 in **WEIGHT** 200 lbs

EYES Brown **HAIR** Brown

SPECIAL POWERS/ABILITIES Highly evolved intelligence; immense psionic powers; armor reconstructs body when injured, enabling virtual immortality; able to grow to 300 ft.

At Oxford University in the 1920s, Herbert Wyndham built a genetic accelerator that had the power to evolve creatures. Ostracized by his peers, he used his accelerator on himself—becoming the High Evolutionary—and created an army of humanoid animals he called the Knights of Wundagore. He founded a new planetary home for his knights, established Counter-Earth, and tried to evolve all humanity. He helped defeat ULTRON in the ANNIHILATION, and restored MAGNETO's powers after M-Day. When the Champions and AVENGERS defeated his plan to merge Counter-Earth with their own, they learned he had created a clone of himself called the Higher Evolutionary.

HERCULES

Super-strong demigod son of Zeus

During his 12 labors, Hercules killed a flock of man-eating birds belonging to his half-brother Ares, the God of War, who has hated him ever since.

Hercules is the son of Zeus—king of the Gods of Olympus—and a mortal woman. He is best known for his Twelve Labors, which he carried out to prove that he was worthy of immortality. He made three enemies during the course of these labors: Ares the God of War, Pluto (Hades) lord of the underworld, and Typhon the giant son of Titan.

Hercules can be rash and stubborn but is usually gregarious and exuberant. He is a faithful friend and valiant warrior who loves the thrill of battle.

FACTFILE

REAL NAME
Hercules; aliases Heracles, Harry Cleese, Herc

OCCUPATION
Adventurer

BASE
Olympus

HEIGHT 6 ft 5 in
WEIGHT 325 lbs
EYES Blue
HAIR Dark brown

FIRST APPEARANCE
Journey Into Mystery Annual #1 (1965)

POWERS

Virtually immortal. Trained in hand-to-hand combat and ancient Greek wrestling skills. Excellent archer. Wields a practically indestructible mace.

PRINCE OF POWER

Hercules is known throughout Olympus as the Prince of Power and he lives for the thrill of battle. He believes that it is a great honor to fight him and often bestows this so-called "gift" on friends and foes alike. Instead of a handshake, Hercules likes to greet his fellow Avengers with a friendly punch in the face!

In modern times, Hercules met and battled Thor when the Thunder God accidentally journeyed to Olympus. Hercules later traveled to Earth to renew his acquaintance with the Asgardian and unwittingly signed a contract that made him Pluto's slave. After being rescued by Thor, Hercules returned to Olympus until the Enchantress cast a spell on him and sent him to battle the Avengers. He later joined the team when Zeus temporarily exiled him to Earth. He was taken prisoner by Ares and his minions, but rescued by the Avengers. Hercules joined Thor on a journey to the far end of the galaxy, where they battled the Destroyer, Firelord, and Ego, the Living Planet. He also joined the Los Angeles super-team known as the Champions and spent time as one of the Defenders.

Hercules often greets Thor with the "gift" of his power—in the form of a punch in the face.

Hercules has been a vital part of several mortal super-teams—including the Champions and the Avengers.

GODHOOD AND HUMANITY

Herc fought for the resistance during the Civil War and slew Ragnarok with the Thor-clone's own hammer. He sided with the Hulk during World War Hulk, after which he became best friends with Amadeus Cho. During the Secret Invasion, Hercules led the God Squad to defeat the Skrull gods. He died stopping Hera from destroying the universe, but Cho brought him back as an All-Father in time to lead the Chaos War against Amatsu-Mikaboshi. After defeating the Chaos King, Herc used all his power to restore reality, making him mortal. He remained an active hero while also working in a small Greek shop in New York. Scientist Rachna Koul helped him regain his powers and he rejoined the Avengers.

Though outnumbered, Hercules tried to defeat the Masters of Evil and almost paid the price.

ESSENTIAL STORYLINES
- ***Thor #124–130*** Hercules' first journey to Earth in modern times: enslaved by Pluto, rescued by Thor.
- ***The Avengers: Under Siege (tpb)*** Zemo's new Masters of Evil invade Avengers Mansion and almost beat Hercules to death.
- ***Hercules: Prince of Power (tpb)*** Hercules confronts Galactus in the far future.

HILL, MARIA

FACTFILE
REAL NAME
Maria Hill
OCCUPATION
Director of SHIELD
BASE
SHIELD Helicarrier, mobile

HEIGHT 5 ft 10 in
WEIGHT 130 lbs
EYES Brown
HAIR Black

FIRST APPEARANCE
New Avengers #4
(April 2005)

POWERS
Maria is a trained combatant and excellent tactician.

HILL, MARIA

Born in Chicago, Maria Hill joined the US military and later SHIELD, working her way up to commander. When Nick Fury was removed as director, Hill was chosen to take his place. She served in that position throughout the Civil War, leading the effort to bring fugitive heroes into line. Afterward, she willingly gave over the job to Tony Stark (Iron Man) and stayed on as his deputy director.

After Norman Osborn (Green Goblin) took over SHIELD and replaced it with HAMMER, Hill became a fugitive because of her support for Stark. She fought against Osborn and his false Avengers team during the siege of Asgard. With Osborn removed and HAMMER destroyed, Hill was appointed as the leader of the Avengers. After Fear Itself, she rejoined SHIELD as its deputy director under Daisy Johnson. She took on the role of the "mayor" of Pleasant Hill, a prison in the form of a small town created by a sentient Cosmic Cube, until the villains escaped.

Maria Hill uses a jet pack to escape from an exploding Helicarrier.

HOBGOBLIN

FACTFILE
REAL NAME
Roderick Kingsley
OCCUPATION
Super Villain
BASE
Mobile

HEIGHT 5 ft 11 in
WEIGHT 185 lbs
EYES Blue
HAIR Gray

FIRST APPEARANCE
The Spectacular Spider-Man #43
(June 1980)

POWERS
Hobgoblin's strength and agility are enhanced by an improved Goblin formula; flies upon a vertical-thrust Goblin glider; wears electro-shock gloves; carries Jack O'Lantern-shaped grenades in a pouch. Possessed an armor-plated battle-van with an arsenal of weaponry.

HOBGOBLIN

Fashion designer Roderick Kingsley uncovered a cache of the Green Goblin's costumes and weaponry and sought to dominate New York's criminal underworld as the Hobgoblin, until Spider-Man undermined his efforts. Kingsley also manipulated two other men into taking the Hobgoblin role. Petty crook Lefty Donovan served as a human guinea pig for a new version of the Goblin formula and, after brainwashing by Kingsley, *Daily Bugle* reporter Ned Leeds acted as his substitute until Leeds' death. Jason Macendale (formerly Jack O'Lantern) stole the identity from Leeds, but when he was imprisoned, Kingsley murdered him.

When Betty Brant outed Kingsley as the Hobgoblin, he fled to the Caribbean. While there, his brother Daniel took his place, but Phil Urich (nephew of Ben Urich) killed him and took over the identity. Kingsley returned and confronted Urich, but allowed him to continue using the Hobgoblin identity for a cut of his stolen booty. He also sold on villainous identities to would-be criminals and joined an incarnation of the Sinister Six.

The various Hobgoblins have all tested Spider-Man's mettle, but the wall-crawler is always victorious.

HIRO-KALA

FIRST APPEARANCE *Skaar: Son of Hulk* #2 (September 2008)
REAL NAME Hiro-Kala **OCCUPATION** Messiah, ruler of K'ai
BASE K'ai **HEIGHT** 5 ft 10 in **WEIGHT** 140 lbs
EYES Black **HAIR** Bald
SPECIAL POWERS/ABILITIES Hiro-Kala controls both the Old Power and the Power Cosmic. He can also fire energy from his eyes and hands.

When the HULK's wife CAIERA was killed in an explosion, she placed her twin sons into cocoons to shield them. Thinking the children were dead, Hulk abandoned them, leaving SKAAR and Hiro-Kala on their own. Hiro-Kala was raised as a slave, unaware of his heritage. After Skaar lost a battle with GALACTUS to save their homeworld Sakaar, Hiro-Kala gathered as many of his people as he could to escape. He wound up on the Microverse planet K'ai, which he later pulled into the larger universe and sent hurtling toward Earth to kill his father. With Skaar's help, the Hulk stopped him.

HOGAN, HAROLD

FIRST APPEARANCE *X-Men Alpha* #1 (February 1995)
REAL NAME Harold "Happy" Hogan
OCCUPATION Tony Stark's right-hand man; chauffeur
BASE New York City **HEIGHT** 5 ft 11 in **WEIGHT** 221 lbs
EYES Brown **HAIR** (as human) Brown; (as Freak) None
SPECIAL POWERS/ABILITIES As the Freak, Hogan possesses superhuman strength and durability.

Former boxer "Happy" Hogan saved Tony Stark from a car crash and Stark hired him as his chauffeur. Hogan eventually realized that Stark was secretly IRON MAN and sometimes donned an Iron Man battlesuit to stand in for Stark. Doctors used Stark's invention, the Enervator, to save Hogan's life, but its cobalt radiation also transformed Hogan into a virtually mindless monster known as the Freak. Iron Man restored him to normal using the Enervator, although Hogan has sometimes reverted to the Freak. Hogan married Pepper POTTS—twice. He was nearly killed while saving her from the SPYMASTER, and he later died from his injuries.

HODGE, CAMERON

FIRST APPEARANCE *X-Factor* #1 (February 1986)
REAL NAME Cameron Hodge
OCCUPATION Businessman **BASE** Mobile
HEIGHT 6 ft 2 in **WEIGHT** 196 lbs **EYES** Blue **HAIR** Black
SPECIAL POWERS/ABILITIES Cunning manipulator; due to a pact with the demon N'astirh, Cameron Hodge cannot die; since becoming a cyborg, he has vast strength and weaponry.

Cameron Hodge grew up secretly hating mutants, becoming the leader of the anti-mutant radical group the RIGHT. Hodge suggested that the X-MEN go undercover as mutant hunters called X-FACTOR, so as to conceal their activities in recruiting and training mutants. However, his real objective was to stir up anti-mutant sentiment. Hodge later made a pact with the demon N'ASTIRH that gave him immortality. Even after his head was cut off and he was consumed by the techno-organic race known as the PHALANX, Hodge remained a thorn in the X-Men's side.

HONEY BADGER

FIRST APPEARANCE *All-New Wolverine* #2 (January 2016)
REAL NAME Gabrielle "Gabby" Kinney
OCCUPATION Adventurer **BASE** Mobile
HEIGHT 4 ft 6 in **EYES** Green **HAIR** Black
SPECIAL POWERS/ABILITIES Lethal bone claw on each hand; impervious to pain; regenerative healing; trained bodyguard; expert hand-to-hand combatant.

Created by Alchemax Genetics, Gabrielle was the youngest of The Sisters, clones of Laura Kinney (*see* X-23). Trained as bodyguards and assassins, Gabby and her sisters freed themselves from the corrupt Alchemax and, with Laura's help, took down their brutal handlers. Gabby was then taken under Laura's wing and survived a misguided attack by Old Man Logan and a dangerous mission that briefly turned her into an alien BROOD Queen. She teamed up with Laura and her half-brother, DAKEN, to fight the anti-Logan cult, Orphans of X. Gabby and Laura both then joined the reformed cult as new members, out to punish anyone connected with the Weapon X program.

HOOD, THE

The son of a criminal who worked with the KINGPIN, Parker seemed destined for a life of petty crime. While robbing a warehouse, he stumbled upon a summoned demon, killed it, and took its boots and cloak. After becoming embroiled in a battle on a reconstituted Battleworld, Parker returned to Earth and began to build a criminal empire based on Super Villains. This put him into direct conflict with the AVENGERS. At this time, he started a relationship with MADAME MASQUE.

During the SECRET INVASION, the Hood joined forces with the heroes to save the Earth, and he discovered that the powers his cloak granted him came from the demon DORMAMMU. During the DARK REIGN, he joined the CABAL at the invitation of Norman Osborn (*see* GREEN GOBLIN). Soon after, Dormammu sent the Hood to kill DOCTOR STRANGE and become the new Sorcerer Supreme, but the demon was exorcised from him, leaving him powerless.

LOKI granted Parker new powers by loaning him the Norn Stones, but took them back during the Siege of Asgard. The Hood formed his own ILLUMINATI and, after gaining more Norn Stones, tried, and failed, to become the new Kingpin of Crime.

FACTFILE
REAL NAME
Parker Robbins
OCCUPATION
Criminal mastermind
BASE
New York City

HEIGHT 5 ft 10 in
WEIGHT 165 lbs
EYES Brown
HAIR Brown

FIRST APPEARANCE
Hood #1 (July 2002)

HOOD, THE

POWERS
When possessed by Dormammu, the Hood's magic cloak and boots granted him invisibility, electrical bursts from his hands, the ability to walk on air, and the ability to transform into a demon.

HOWARD THE DUCK

FACTFILE

REAL NAME
Howard (last name unknown)

OCCUPATION
Many, including former candidate for President of the United States; most often unemployed.

BASE
Cleveland, Ohio

HEIGHT 2 ft 7 in
WEIGHT 40 lbs
EYES Brown
FEATHERS Yellow

FIRST APPEARANCE
Fear #19 (December 1973)

POWERS

Howard is skilled in the little-known martial art of Quack Fu, and a formidable opponent in hand-to-hand combat.

HOWARD THE DUCK

Howard the Duck was born on Duckworld, where people evolved from waterfowl. When the demon Thog caused the Interdimensional Cosmic Axis to shift, Howard was dropped into the Florida Everglades on Earth, the site of the Nexus of All Realities. Hoping to return home, Howard teamed up with Korrek the Barbarian, the Earth sorceress Jennifer KALE, Dakimh the Enchanter, and the MAN-THING. As this group battled Thog, Howard fell off the Stepping Stones of Oblivion and tumbled back to Earth, landing in Cleveland, Ohio. There he met Beverly SWITZLER, when the two were attacked by the criminal accountant Pro-Rata. Howard and Beverly escaped and began living together in a human-duck relationship. Howard tried to register under the Superhuman Registration Act but was told that the government's official policy was that he did not exist. This was later corrected, and he fought against the SKRULLS during the SECRET INVASION. As a member of ARMOR, he helped battle an interdimensional zombie plague, and later led the Ducky Dozen. Howard then went back to private detective work, but was kidnapped by the COLLECTOR. Attempting to return to his own universe using the Abundant Glove, he accidentally turned himself into a living Nexus of All Realities. Howard later discovered he was unwittingly the star of one of MOJO's reality shows and fought Mojo's Sparkitects to gain his freedom.

Howard teamed up with the Guardians, Silver Surfer, Linda the Duck, and Shocket to free the Collector's prisoners.

HOWLING COMMANDOS

FACTFILE

MEMBERS
Sgt. Nick Fury; Corporal Thaddeus "Dum Dum" Dugan; Privates Dino Manelli, Izzy Cohen, Gabe Jones, Percival Pinkerton, Reb "Rebel" Ralston, Jonathan "Junior" Juniper (killed in action), Eric Koenig

BASE
Pacific Theater of Operations, World War II

FIRST APPEARANCE
Sgt. Fury and His Howling Commandos #1 (May 1963)

POWERS

Apparently ill-assorted group welded into crack unit by Sgt. Fury's unmatched leadership qualities. Each member was a highly trained commando, with skills in hand-to-hand combat, the use of explosives, and proficiency with a variety of firearms.

HOWLING COMMANDOS

The Howling Commandos formed the first attack squad of Able Company during World War II. Under orders from Captain "Happy" Sam Sawyer, Sergeant Nick FURY led his men against the worst the Axis powers could throw at them, including the legendary Blitzkrieg Squad of BARON VON STRUCKER, and the RED SKULL. Many members of the unit survived to become the nucleus of SHIELD. SHIELD later used the Howling Commandos name for a top-secret squad of monsters led by Dum Dum DUGAN, dedicated to battling supernatural forces. After leaving SHIELD, Fury assembled a new team of Howling Commandos—aka the SECRET WARRIORS—to fight the SECRET INVASION. When Norman Osborn (*see* GREEN GOBLIN) dismantled SHIELD, Dum Dum Dugan and Gabe JONES formed a private military company called the Howling Commandos. As a black ops unit, the Howlers captured the PUNISHER, but released him in order to uncover a US government gun-running conspiracy.

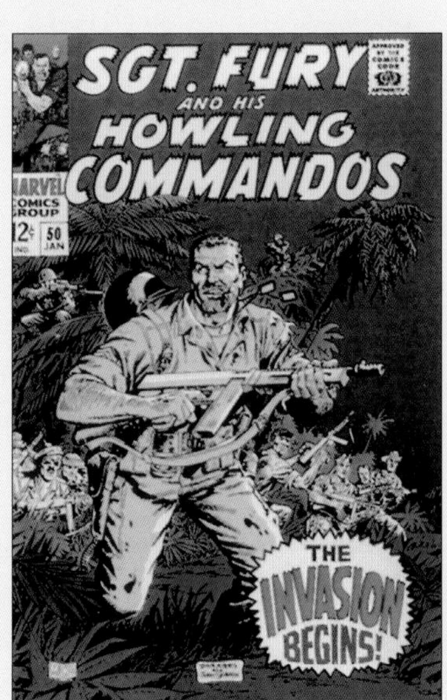

The Howling Commandos were heroes of World War II.

THE LINEUP
1 Sgt. Nick Fury ***2*** Jonathan "Junior" Juniper
3 Reb Ralston ***4*** Cpl. Dum Dum Dugan
5 Gabe Jones ***6*** Dino Manelli ***7*** Izzy Cohen

HULK, SEE PAGES 174–177

HULKLING

FIRST APPEARANCE *Young Avengers* #1 (April 2005)
REAL NAME Theodore "Teddy" Altman/Dorrek VIII
OCCUPATION Adventurer; student **BASE** New York City
HEIGHT Varies **WEIGHT** Varies
EYES Usually blue **HAIR** Usually Blond
SPECIAL POWERS/ABILITIES Shapeshifting and superhuman strength and healing.

Born the secret son of Princess Anelle (a SKRULL) and CAPTAIN MAR-VELL (a KREE), Teddy Altman had thought he was a human mutant when he co-founded the YOUNG AVENGERS. After learning the truth, Teddy became a pawn in a face-off between the Kree and Skrull empires, settled only when he agreed to spend six months with each race before deciding which side to join—but the Super-Skrull took his place. Teddy came out as gay and became engaged to teammate WICCAN. As New Avengers, Hulking and Wiccan confronted the Plunderer and Celestial Destroyer before disbanding the team to focus on their relationship.

HUNTARA

FIRST APPEARANCE *Fantastic Four* #377 (June 1993)
REAL NAME Huntara Richards **OCCUPATION** Guardian of the Sacred Timelines **BASE** Elsewhen
HEIGHT 6 ft 2 in **WEIGHT** 185 lbs **EYES** Brown **HAIR** Black
SPECIAL POWERS/ABILITIES Psionic scythe cuts through almost any material, fires concussive bolts, and teleports her between dimensions and across space; superior athlete and combatant.

Huntara was born on an alternate Earth. The daughter of Nathaniel RICHARDS and the half-sister of MR. FANTASTIC, she was taken to Elsewhen, a barbaric alien dimension. Huntara was trained in the arts of war and combat alongside her nephew Franklin RICHARDS and they both became Guardians of the Sacred Timelines, who prevent and repair time paradoxes. When her father created a time paradox by exchanging the teenaged Franklin with his younger self, Huntara was forced to journey to this timeline where she eventually met the FANTASTIC FOUR. She later returned to Elsewhen and resumed her duties as a Guardian.

HUNTER, STEVIE

FIRST APPEARANCE *The Uncanny X-Men* #139 (November 1980)
REAL NAME Stephanie "Stevie" Hunter
OCCUPATION Dance instructor **BASE** Salem Center, New York State **HEIGHT** 5 ft 9 in **WEIGHT** 121 lbs
EYES Brown **HAIR** Dark brown
SPECIAL POWERS/ABILITIES A talented dancer and athlete and an excellent dance teacher.

Stevie Hunter was a ballet dancer, until a broken leg forced her to retire. She became a dance instructor and opened a school in Salem Center, New York State. Professor Charles Xavier's School for Gifted Youngsters, the headquarters of the X-MEN, was located nearby. One of Xavier's students, Kitty PRYDE, began taking lessons at Hunter's school. After Hunter discovered that Xavier's students were mutants, Xavier hired her to be a physical trainer and therapist at his school. Hunter evenually returned to operating her own dance academy and years later was elected as a congresswoman for Connecticut.

HUSK

Husk, Archangel, and Iceman are surrounded by a pack of slavering wolf men.

FACTFILE
REAL NAME
Paige Elisabeth Guthrie
OCCUPATION
Adventurer
BASE
New York State

HEIGHT 5 ft 7 in
WEIGHT 127 lbs
EYES Blue
HAIR Black

FIRST APPEARANCE
X-Force #32
(March 1994)

POWERS
A mutant metamorph, Husk can shed skin and transform her body into any form with similar or less mass. She frequently turns her body into a different substance, such as steel or stone, taking on the properties of that substance, for example increased strength.

Paige Guthrie envied her elder brother who, as CANNONBALL, had forged a career with the NEW MUTANTS. Paige kept her own mutant powers hidden until she was forced into a battle of wits with the Gamesmaster, a psionic mutant who formed the UPSTARTS, a group that assassinated mutants. Paige freed her brother and several of his friends from the Gamesmaster's clutches. Shortly afterward, she was captured by the techno-organic alien PHALANX, along with several other young mutants. Its effort to assimilate them into its consciousness was foiled, and Paige was invited to join the Xavier Institute's Massachusetts Academy and become a member of GENERATION X.

Paige subsequently joined X-CORPS, helping to police mutants in Europe, and later became part of the X-MEN. When the X-MEN split into two factions, she followed WOLVERINE to the Jean Grey School for Higher Learning. Her brother Jay and sister Melody were also mutants. Melody lost her powers on M-Day, and Jay died soon after. While teaching at the Jean Grey School, Paige began to lose full control of her powers and suffered personality shifts. She subsequently transferred to the Hellfire Academy.

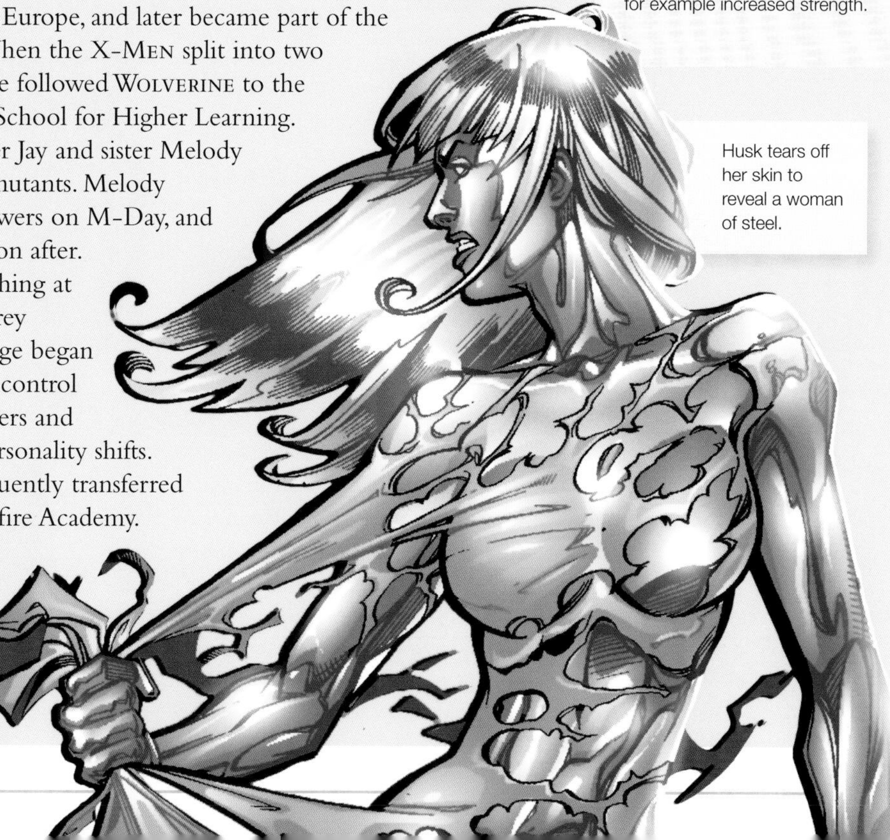

Husk tears off her skin to reveal a woman of steel.

THE HULK

The strongest man-like creature on Earth!

THE HULK

FACTFILE

REAL NAME
Robert Bruce Banner

OCCUPATION
Scientist; wanderer

BASE
Mobile

HEIGHT 7 ft
WEIGHT 1,040 lbs
EYES Green
HAIR Green

FIRST APPEARANCE
Incredible Hulk #1
(May 1962)

POWERS

Fueled by gamma radiation, the Hulk possesses almost unlimited physical strength. The madder he gets, the stronger he gets. He can leap several miles in a single bound. His body heals almost instantly, He possesses a strong homing instinct for the desert where he was "born."

ALLIES/FOES

ALLIES Rick Jones, Betty Ross, Doc Samson, Jennifer Walters (She-Hulk), Jarella, the Avengers

FOES The Leader, The Abomination, Rhino, Sandman, Juggernaut, Absorbing Man, General Thaddeus "Thunderbolt" Ross, Bi-Beast, Zzzax

ISSUE #1

In his first appearance in *The Incredible Hulk #1* (May 1962), the Hulk's skin was colored gray, rather than the more familiar green.

Bruce had a troubled childhood; his father called him a monster, and eventually killed his mother.

A child prodigy, Bruce Banner grew up in an abusive household, one that would have a profound long-term effect on his psyche. An introverted child, Bruce was ill-equipped to deal with the outbursts of his father, who called young Bruce a monster and terrorized both him and his mother. Bruce developed a multiple personality disorder, repressing all of his negative emotions when the trauma became too much to take. This cycle of abuse continued until the day Brian Banner slew his wife in a fit of rage. Thereafter, Bruce was shuttled from relative to relative, and grew ever more socially awkward, even as his remarkable intellect became more apparent.

FIRST LOVE

The US Army recruited Banner to develop new weapons systems while he was still in high school. Bruce was placed under the authority of General Thaddeus "Thunderbolt" Ross, a blustering, no-nonsense veteran. It was in the person of Ross' daughter Betty (*see* Ross, Betty) that Bruce found a kindred spirit. Both he and Betty had lost mothers, and were subjected to the outbursts of raging fathers. An attraction soon developed between them.

Recruited by the military, Bruce Banner worked on developing new weapons systems on the military base commanded by hard-nosed general "Thunderbolt" Ross.

THE GAMMA BOMB

Prodded by his military handlers, Banner developed the G-Bomb, a weapon harnessing the power of gamma radiation. On the day the bomb was to be tested, a reckless teenager, Rick Jones, drove out onto the test range on a dare, little realizing that he was standing on ground zero of the most potent explosive device ever developed. In an uncharacteristic moment of heroism, Bruce Banner rushed out onto the test site and dragged Jones to the safety of a nearby trench before the G-Bomb detonated. However Banner was exposed to the full force of the weapon, his every atom bombarded by gamma radiation.

Banner was bathed in gamma rays while trying to save the life of Rick Jones.

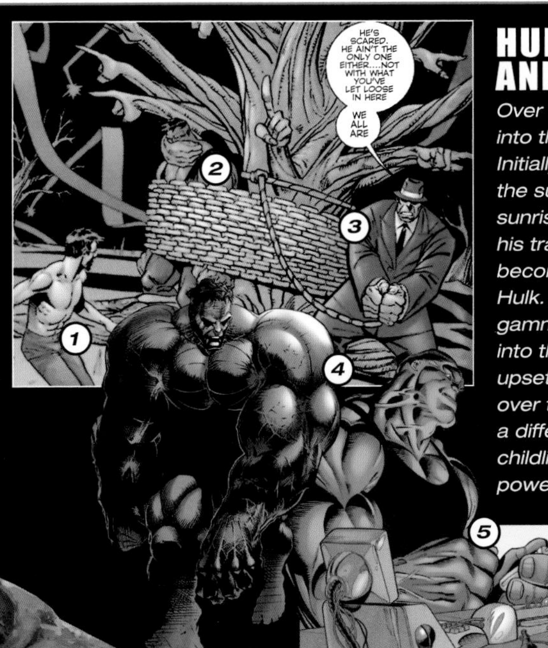

HULK'S PSYCHE AND THE MAESTRO

Over the years, Bruce Banner's transformations into the Hulk have taken on a variety of styles. Initially, Banner would become the Hulk when the sun set, and return to his Banner identity at sunrise. Soon after, Banner learned to control his transformations using a gamma ray machine, becoming a more intelligent but no less savage Hulk. Eventually, the continued exposure to gamma radiation caused Banner to transform into the Hulk whenever he became agitated or upset. Banner's Hulk persona has also differed over the years, each one apparently representing a different facet of his fragmented psyche: the childlike Green Hulk, the more intelligent but less powerful Gray Hulk, the extremely intelligent but egocentric "Professor" Hulk—and even a "Devil Hulk" representing all of the evil within Banner's soul. Additional permutations of the Hulk are apt to emerge at any given time, should conditions prove favorable.

On a future Earth where much of the world—and its Super Heroes—had been destroyed in a nuclear apocalypse, the Hulk survived. His strength increased by the radiation but also driven mad, this Hulk seized control, becoming the Maestro. Rebels against the Maestro's rule stole Doctor Doom's time-platform and went back in time to get the Hulk's help, at a time when he was the Professor. The Hulk managed to defeat the Maestro by sending him back in time to the moment the Gamma bomb explosion had originally created the Hulk. The Maestro has returned since then, but has never been as deadly.

MULTIPLE PERSONALITIES
1 Bruce Banner ***2*** Savage Hulk
3 Joe Fixit ***4*** Mindless Hulk ***5*** Professor Hulk

A day later, Banner was still silently screaming. But the military doctors could find nothing wrong—he had miraculously escaped the blast unscathed. Or so it seemed. For the gamma radiation Banner had been exposed to had unlocked long-repressed feelings of hate and rage. When conditions were right, Banner found himself transforming into an unstoppable juggernaut of destruction, the personification of his long-denied dark side: the incredible Hulk!

At first, the Hulk only manifested at nightfall. When the sun went down, Banner would inexorably change into a green-skinned powerhouse and remain out of control until daybreak.

Eventually, due in part to Banner's attempts to cure himself of these unwanted transformations, the appearance of the Hulk would be brought on by stress and anxiety. Whenever Bruce became outraged or fearful, the change in his emotional state would trigger the gamma radiation within his system, and the Hulk would live again.

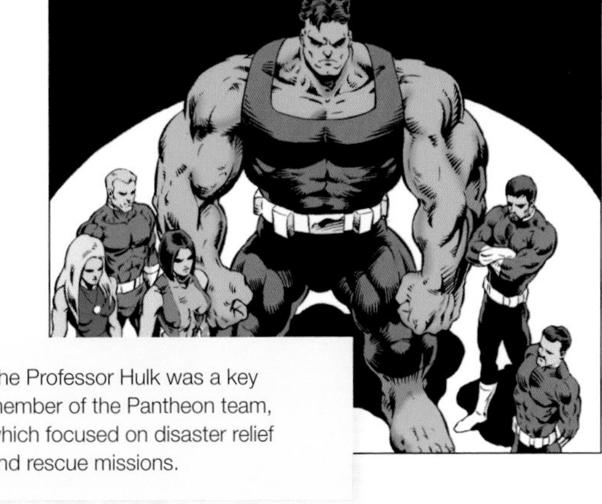

The Professor Hulk was a key member of the Pantheon team, which focused on disaster relief and rescue missions.

For a time, with the aid of Rick Jones, Bruce kept his dual identity secret, even while the Hulk was hunted by the same military forces for whom Banner toiled. But eventually the truth was revealed to the world, forcing Banner to become a fugitive, both to escape those who desired the Hulk's destruction and to protect those who might be harmed during his uncontrollable episodes.

MIND OF A CHILD

The character of the Hulk changed over time. Initially, he had a strong dislike for humanity. However he mellowed as the years went by, resulting in a more childlike Hulk. He simply wanted to be left alone, and couldn't understand why people were persecuting him. Eventually, the superpowered psychiatrist Doc Samson figured out the truth: each of the Hulk's personalities represented a different fragment of Banner's shattered psyche. For a time, Samson was able to fuse the disparate elements of Banner's mind together, granting Banner the strength of the Hulk while allowing him to maintain his own intellect. But this construct proved unstable, and eventually splintered once again.

Over the years, the Hulk has proved a force for good almost as often as he has been an engine of destruction. He was instrumental in the formation of the Avengers, Earth's Mightiest Heroes, though friction between himself and his teammates quickly led to him leaving the group. He has stood side-by-side with the Defenders, Doctor Strange, Namor the Sub-Mariner, and the Silver Surfer in defense of our planet. But for the most part, the Hulk calls no man friend. Bruce Banner and his superhuman alter ego remain ever at odds as they strive to stay one step ahead of forces that would see the Hulk destroyed, or exploit his power for their own ends.

ESSENTIAL STORYLINES

- ***Incredible Hulk #312*** The truth about Bruce Banner's multiple personality disorder and traumatic childhood is revealed.
- ***Incredible Hulk #377*** Doc Samson unites Banner's splintered psyche into an intelligent Hulk.
- ***Incredible Hulk #24–25*** General "Thunderbolt" Ross unleashes the Hulk against the Abomination, who had secretly poisoned Ross' daughter and Hulk's beloved, Betty Banner!

THE HULK continued

PLANET HULK

The planet Sakaar offered Hulk a series of battles from the moment he crawled from his starship and onto its shattered surface.

The Hulk eventually found his way to Alaska, where Bruce Banner set up house in a remote cabin, far away from the rest of humanity and any of its troubles. It did not last long. Nick Fury found him and asked Banner to become the Hulk and help SHIELD disarm a lethal satellite in orbit around the Earth. Banner agreed, but after the Hulk completed the mission, he was not brought home—instead he was fired into deep space by the Illuminati. Having learned of the Hulk's mission, they had seen a chance to get rid of the Hulk and had taken it, exiling him. Instead of reaching a verdant and unpopulated planet, however, the ship entered a wormhole and crashed onto war-ravaged Sakaar. Far from being a paradise, Sakaar was a savage planet filled with danger and a variety of alien life-forms. Immediately after the crash, the Hulk was captured and enslaved. He was fitted with an obedience disk, a device that ensured he would do his new masters' bidding. Forced to fight as a gladiator in the Red King's arena, the Hulk survived his training and bonded with his fellow warriors, who became his Warbound, a tight-knit team of some of the toughest people and creatures from Sakaar and beyond. Fighting his way up the arena's chain, the Hulk got his chance at the Red King and wounded him before being brought down.

The Hulk's actions in the arena turned him into a hero among Sakaar's resistance fighters.

Later, the Hulk and the Warbound broke free and led a rebellion against the bloodthirsty Red King. When the Hulk's blood caused a flower to grow, many believed the Hulk was a legendary savior called Sakaarson, destined to lead the enslaved to freedom. The Hulk and his allies succeeded in overthrowing the Red King and Hulk placed himself on the throne, marrying one of his compatriots—Caiera, the Red King's former lieutenant—who became pregnant with his child. Finally happy and at peace as King of Sakaar, the Hulk began to work to improve the lives of his subjects—until the ship he'd first come to Sakaar in mysteriously exploded. The massive blast killed millions of people, including Caiera.

Filled with righteous fury, the Hulk returned to Earth accompanied by his Warbound and waged war on the so-called heroes who had exiled him into space. He tore through their ranks until finally Stark satellites turned him back into Banner and he was arrested.

THE HULK FAMILY

Shortly after the events of World War Hulk, a new, Red Hulk (secretly General Ross) appeared and Hulk's son Skaar came to Earth from Sakaar to find and defeat his father. Soon after, the Red Hulk absorbed the gamma radiation from Banner, keeping him from turning back into the Hulk. Banner reconciled with Skaar and set about training him how to defeat the Hulk, should he return.

Banner mounted an effort to save his ex-wife Betty Ross from the Leader and MODOK. He was captured and imprisoned so the

THE HULK FAMILY
1 Korg (of the Warbound)
2 Skaar ***3*** Bruce Banner
4 She-Hulk ***5*** A-Bomb (Rick Jones)
6 Red She-Hulk ***7*** Hulk

Leader could hulk-out the subjects of his experiments. When Banner escaped, he discovered Betty had been transformed into the Red She-Hulk. As the Leader fled, Banner had to absorb the radiation from the hulked-out people, transforming him into the "Worldbreaker" Hulk. Skaar finally had a chance to fight his father, but the furious battle made both monsters see the error of their ways. Returning to human form, they made peace.

The Hulk later turned to DOCTOR DOOM to physically separate him from Banner, taking part of his brain and putting it into a clone body. Banner eventually figured out how to make them whole again. Afterward, he rejoined the Avengers and even worked with SHIELD's TIME branch to try to fix the broken timestream.

When Banner was shot in the head by an enemy, he was saved by Tony Stark using a version of the Extremis virus. The result was Banner becoming Doc Green, a new, intelligent version of the Hulk. Believing that Gamma-powered monsters were too dangerous to exist, Doc Green created a cure, depowering A-Bomb, Skaar, and Red Hulk. Eventually, Doc Green's intelligence started to fade and he returned to the more mindless Hulk of old.

ESSENTIAL STORYLINES

- **Incredible Hulk Vol. 3 #92–105** In "Planet Hulk," the Hulk rises from being a gladiatorial slave to the conqueror of an entire alien planet.
- **Hulk #1–6** The mysterious Red Hulk debuts.
- **Immortal Hulk #1** Bruce Banner is alive and the Hulk is more savage than ever.

When Banner returned to being the Hulk, he absorbed cosmic rays as well as gamma rays and became the Worldbreaker Hulk.

As Doc Green, the Hulk hunted down and depowered other gamma-powered beings.

Banner's death drove a deep wedge between Tony Stark and Captain Marvel, whom he blamed.

IMMORTAL HULK

After the future-seeing INHUMAN Ulysses CAIN had a vision of the Hulk at the center of a rampage that left countless dead, Banner gave HAWKEYE a special custom-built arrow that could kill him as he was transforming. When the time came, it worked. The Hulk was dead. He was resurrected several times, only to die again—firstly by the HAND, and again during HYDRA's takeover of the United States. He was brought back a third time by the Challenger during a cosmic contest with the GRANDMASTER. The Hulk tore his way through the Avengers until WONDER MAN tried to reason with him. Realizing he had been used, the Hulk smashed the pyramid he was supposed to collect for the Challenger and later managed to hurt the immortal being. In the aftermath of that battle, Banner realized with horror that he could not die. If Banner was killed, the Hulk would still emerge and Banner would be healed. Haunted by this new knowledge, Banner left, leading a nomadic existence for a while, as most of the world considered him dead. It was not long before the Hulk's actions started to draw attention, though. The Hulk was back—and angrier than ever.

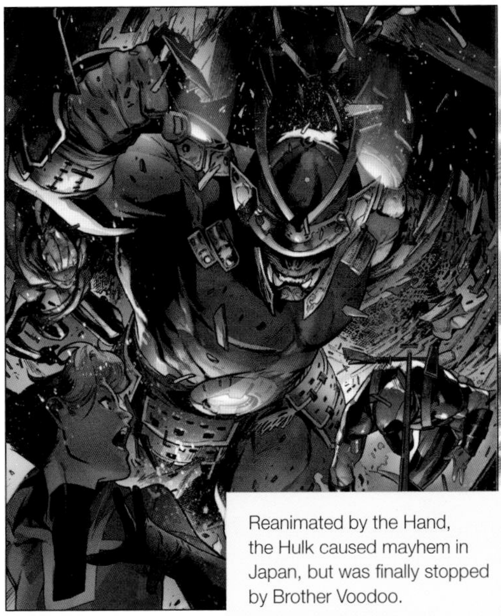

Reanimated by the Hand, the Hulk caused mayhem in Japan, but was finally stopped by Brother Voodoo.

Raging at being taken advantage of, the Hulk smashed the pyramid, costing the Challenger his victory in his contest with the Grandmaster.

HUMAN TORCH

The Super Hero who is literally "hot stuff!"

HUMAN TORCH

FACTFILE

REAL NAME
Jonathan Lowell Spencer Storm

OCCUPATION
Adventurer

BASE
New York City

HEIGHT 5 ft 10 in
WEIGHT 170 lbs
EYES Brown
HAIR Brown

FIRST APPEARANCE
Fantastic Four #1
(November 1961)

POWERS

Able to control heat energy and cover his body with fiery plasma for over 16 hours, but then needs to rest for about 12 hours. He can release a single "Nova-burst" which strikes with the force of a nuclear warhead. He can create shapes from flame, including letters which burn in the sky for 3 minutes. He can also control the temperature of objects with his mind. Clothing is made of special fire-resistant fabric.

ALLIES/FOES

ALLIES Invisible Woman, the Thing, Mister Fantastic, Lyja the Lazerfist, Alicia Masters, Spider-Man

FOES Doctor Doom, Onslaught, Gormuu, Frightful Four, Galactus

ISSUE #1

When Johnny Storm's sister, Sue, accompanied her fiancé, Reed Richards, into space, Johnny insisted on tagging along. Transformed into the Human Torch, he battled the Mole Man.

The Human Torch can generate and control fire from any part of his body.

Johnny Storm and his older sister Susan grew up on Long Island, New York, the children of a doctor and his wife. In spite of the fact that Johnny's mother was killed in a car crash when he was nine years old, the boy developed a passion and skill for building, fixing, and driving cars. He overhauled his first transmission at the age of 15. The following year his father bought him his first hot rod.

FATEFUL FLIGHT

While a teenager, Johnny went to California to visit his sister Susan who had moved out west to become an actress. Susan Storm (Invisible Woman) was engaged to marry a brilliant physicist and engineer named Reed Richards (Mister Fantastic). Richards was developing a starship that would be capable of exploring other galaxies.

While Johnny was in California, the government threatened to cut off Richards' funding so he decided to prove his ship's worth by taking it on a test flight to the stars. Reed's best friend Ben Grimm (the Thing) piloted the craft. Susan and Johnny insisted on coming along.

In space, inadequate shielding on the starship allowed a huge dose of cosmic radiation to bombard the crew. They managed to return to earth using the autopilot, but all four were changed forever.

The cosmic rays altered Johnny's genetic structure allowing him to create fiery plasma that covered his entire body in flames without causing him harm. He also discovered that he was able to fly, shoot flames, and absorb heat.

Following exposure to cosmic radiation, Johnny Storm's body burst into flame.

The Human Torch creates multiple flaming images of himself in an attempt to escape from fireproof warriors with poison-tipped spears.

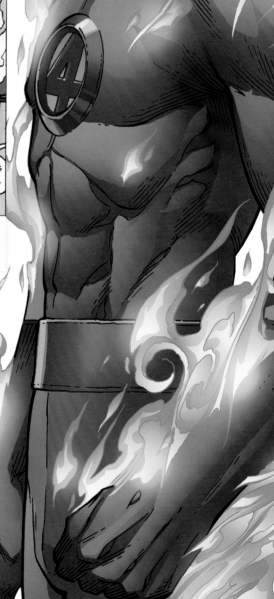

AS SOON AS I START TO HEAT UP, THE FILM OF WATER BOILS AWAY...
...AND THEN...
FLAME ON!!

Exposure to oxygen caused the photoelectric cells in the original Human Torch's skin to burst into flame, to the surprise of the android and its creator.

THE FIRST HUMAN TORCH

The original Human Torch was an android, created by Professor Phineas T. Horton. But the professor's dream of creating a perfect human being failed when the android's body, which was covered in photoelectric solar cells, burst into flames on contact with oxygen. Astonishingly, the android itself was not harmed by the fire. At first the public labeled this Human Torch a menace. The Torch then rejected his creator's "ownership," claiming he didn't want to be a "slave" to someone more concerned about his own fame than about his creation's well-being.

Once he learned to control his flames, the Human Torch vowed never to use his power for evil or harm, and he became a crimefighter. When World War II broke out, the Human Torch teamed with other Super Heroes, using his abilities to fight the Axis Powers.

In modern times, the Human Torch worked with Heroes for Hire, the West Coast Avengers and even the Fantastic Four. At one point, Immortus split the Torch into two bodies, one of which became the Vision. He was believed dead for years, but was recreated and fought alongside the Secret Avengers and a new incarnation of the Invaders.

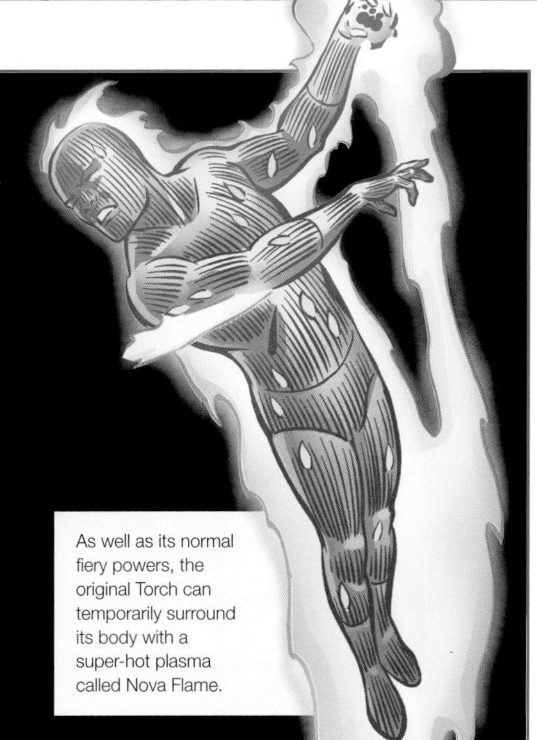
As well as its normal fiery powers, the original Torch can temporarily surround its body with a super-hot plasma called Nova Flame.

ESSENTIAL STORYLINES

- ***Fantastic Four #4*** The Human Torch quits the Fantastic Four. He meets the Sub-Mariner (for the first time since the revival of both characters), who threatens the human race.
- ***The Essential Human Torch Vol. 1 (tpb)*** A collection of some of the Human Torch's key adventures.
- ***Human Torch Vol. 1: Burn (tpb)*** A fiery tale, in which Johnny's high-school rival reappears in his life years later.
- ***Spider-Man/Human Torch #1–5*** The Human Torch teams up with Spider-Man in these new adventures.
- ***Fantastic Four #600*** Johnny Storm returns from the Negative Zone, and the story of how he survived is revealed.

Calling themselves the Fantastic Four, the transformed astronauts decided to use their new powers to help humanity. Johnny called himself the Human Torch, a name originally used by an android hero of the 1940s.

Johnny loved to tease the Thing, who was jealous of Johnny, but they grew to be like brothers. Their relationship suffered when Johnny fell in love with and married the blind sculptress Alicia Masters, the only woman who'd ever returned Ben's affection. Alicia was revealed to be a Skrull spy named Lyja, a deception that devastated Johnny. During the Secret Invasion, he had a chance to settle matters with Lyja, who teleported the upper part of the Baxter Building—along with Johnny, the Thing, and Franklin and Valeria Richards—into the Negative Zone.

When the Human Torch returned from his apparent death in the Negative Zone, he did so triumphantly, and with new friends.

DEATH AND LIFE

When the Cult of the Negative Zone attacked the Baxter Building, threatening the children in the Future Foundation, Johnny and Ben fought to protect the kids and to keep Annihilus from unleashing an Annihilation Wave upon the Earth. The only way to manage this was for one of them to remain inside the Negative Zone to lock the gateway behind the others. Ben volunteered, but Johnny took his place at the last second and sacrificed himself.

Annihilus brought Johnny back to life and, failing to force him to reveal the way back to Earth, put him to work fighting in the arena. Johnny led a revolt against the creature, seized his Cosmic Control Rod and became the Negative Zone's ruler. Shortly afterward, he returned to Earth, just in time to help his teammates stop a Kree invasion.

During the remaking of reality by Doctor Doom and the creation of Battleworld (*see* Secret Wars), the Human Torch became that strange world's sun, caught in an eternal supernova. After Earth was remade, Johnny and Ben found themselves left on Earth while Reed and Sue recreated the Multiverse. Johnny felt lost, helping the Inhumans for a time and even having a brief affair with Medusa. When Johnny's powers started to fade, Ben gave him purpose by suggesting that Reed and Sue were still alive, and that they had to find them. The two friends traveled through parallel worlds but to no avail. Just as they'd given up hope, Johnny saw the famous "4" and answered the call to help Reed and Sue—the Fantastic Four were together once more.

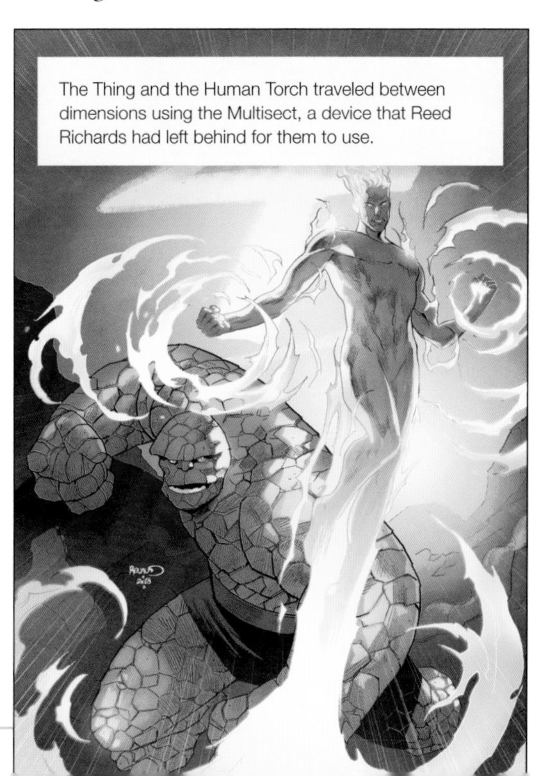
The Thing and the Human Torch traveled between dimensions using the Multisect, a device that Reed Richards had left behind for them to use.

HYDRA

FACTFILE

KEY MEMBERS

BARON VON STRUCKER
Master criminal strategist; founder of Hydra.

ARNOLD BROWN
Brilliant bureaucrat who transformed Hydra.

RED SKULL
Instructed Strucker to found Hydra.

MADAME HYDRA
Leader of Hydra forces in New York City.

LAURA BROWN
Daughter of Arnold Brown; one of the first women to serve in Hydra.

BASE Mobile

FIRST APPEARANCE
Strange Tales #135 (August 1965)

HYDRA

Created by BARON VON STRUCKER after World War II, Hydra was based on a Pacific island. When US Marines destroyed this base, Hydra decentralized, becoming harder to attack. Under Strucker's guidance, Hydra twice attempted to blackmail the world, first with a Betatron bomb and later with a biological weapon. After Strucker's supposed death, Hydra focused on criminal activities, and allied with the HAND for a confrontation with the AVENGERS. SPIDER-WOMAN worked for both Hydra and SHIELD as a double agent, until she was revealed to be the SKRULL queen VERANKE. Nick FURY later discovered that Hydra had controlled SHIELD and other international intelligence organizations for decades. It was also revealed that Fury had been several steps ahead of Hydra all along.

RED SKULL used the sentient Cosmic Cube KOBIK to replace Steve Rogers with a copy that was loyal to Hydra. The new Rogers rebelled, killed Red Skull, and took control of Hydra. He then seized control of the entire country. Hydra was subsequently defeated by an uprising and Kobik restored the original Steve Rogers, who defeated his Hydra-loyalist doppelganger.

The personalities of Hydra personnel are subordinate to the organization they serve.

HYDRO-MAN

FIRST APPEARANCE *Amazing Spider-Man* #212 (January 1981)

REAL NAME Morris Bench

OCCUPATION Criminal **BASE** New York City

HEIGHT 6 ft 2 in **WEIGHT** 265 lbs

EYES Brown **HAIR** Brown

SPECIAL POWERS/ABILITIES Changes body into watery liquid; can merge with larger bodies of water; propels liquid body as if it were shooting through a fire hose; can turn body into ice or steam.

While working as a crewman on a cargo ship lowering an experimental generator into the ocean, Morris Bench was accidentally knocked overboard by SPIDER-MAN. Exposed to the energy-conversion process of the generator, which mixed with volatile volcanic gases, Bench gained the ability to change his body into water. As Hydro-Man he sought revenge against Spider-Man. Later, in a battle with SANDMAN, Hydro-Man fused with the Super Villain and the two became a mud creature. Eventually they were separated. Hydro-Man joined the SINISTER SYNDICATE and later, GREEN GOBLIN's Sinister Twelve, and continues to battle Spider-Man, BLACK CAT, and the AVENGERS.

HYPERION

A member of the race of Eternals on Earth-712, Hyperion, unaware of his lineage, was raised by human beings and taught to use his tremendous powers for good. He became the foremost champion of his world and a founding member of the heroic SQUADRON SUPREME. After the Squadron was manipulated by the OVERMIND into participating in a plan that left their world decimated, Hyperion and his fellow Squadron members resolved to turn their world into a utopia.

Despite initial success, their program met with resistance from one of the Squadron's former members, NIGHTHAWK. In time, the government Hyperion and the Squadron members set up turned into a corrupt, totalitarian regime and they disbanded it. Ever since, the Squadron Supreme have worked as freedom fighters, trying to liberate their homeland. An evil Hyperion appeared on Earth as part of the GRANDMASTER's Squadron Sinister, and the Hyperion from Earth-13034 had his world destroyed and now works with the AVENGERS.

In one world visited by the reality-hopping Exiles, Hyperion had murdered most of humanity.

HYPERION

FACTFILE

REAL NAME
Unrevealed; adopted the human identity of Mark Milton for a time.

OCCUPATION
Adventurer; world leader

BASE
Squadron City on the Squadron Supreme's parallel Earth.

HEIGHT 6 ft 4 in
WEIGHT 460 lbs
EYES Blue
HAIR Red

FIRST APPEARANCE
Avengers #85 (February 1971)

POWERS

Hyperion possesses almost limitless strength, speed, and endurance. He is impervious to virtually any injury, can fly through the air, and can project radioactive beams of energy from his eyes as "Flash-Vision."

ICEMAN

FACTFILE
REAL NAME
Robert Drake
OCCUPATION
Adventurer
BASE
The Xavier Institute for Higher Learning

HEIGHT 5 ft 8 in
WEIGHT 145 lbs
EYES Brown
HAIR Brown

FIRST APPEARANCE
Uncanny X-Men #1 (September 1963)

POWERS
Iceman can manipulate temperatures around him to freeze the water vapor in the air, forming a variety of icy weapons, protective ice shields, and ice slides.

Bobby's powers have progressed from simply generating ice to turning his entire form into living, sentient ice.

ICEMAN

Born a mutant, young Bobby Drake was almost lynched when his ability to freeze moisture in the air was discovered. Bobby was saved by Cyclops of the X-Men, and became the second recruit to Professor Charles Xavier's School for Gifted Youngsters (*see* Professor X), where he would learn to control his mutant gifts. Adopting the code name Iceman, Drake fought as one of the X-Men, battling such menaces as Magneto's Brotherhood of Evil Mutants, the Juggernaut, and the robotic Sentinels. Upon graduation, Iceman attempted to forge a super-heroic career on his own, founding the Champions of Los Angeles. When the X-Men split in two, he co-founded the Jean Grey School for Higher Learning with Wolverine. Jean Grey discovered that the younger, time-displaced version of Bobby was gay. The young Bobby confronted his older self, who admitted he was hiding his feelings. Inspired by the self-confidence of his younger version, he began living as an openly gay mutant.

IKARIS

FIRST APPEARANCE *The Eternals* #1 (July 1976)
REAL NAME Unrevealed
OCCUPATION Prime Eternal **BASE** Olympia, Greece
HEIGHT 6 ft 2 in **WEIGHT** 230 lbs **EYES** Blue **HAIR** Blond
SPECIAL POWERS/ABILITIES Superhuman strength; virtual immortality and indestructibility; psionic abilties, including flight through levitation; projects cosmic energy from eyes or hands.

Born over 20,000 years ago, Ikaris is one of the Polar Eternals—a race of humans with immense lifespans and superpowers. He calls himself Ikaris in memory of his deceased son. Under the name "Ike Harris," Ikaris accompanied archeologist Dr. Daniel Damian and his daughter Margo to the Andes, where they witnessed the arrival of the Fourth Host of the Celestials. He later succeeded Thena as Prime Eternal. After the Eternals all lost their memories, Ikaris was killed. Reborn with his memories restored, he worked to locate the other Eternals and remind them who they were.

IMMORTUS

FACTFILE
REAL NAME
Unknown
OCCUPATION
Ruler of Limbo
BASE
Limbo, outside the timestream

HEIGHT 6 ft 3 in
WEIGHT 230 lbs
EYES Green
HAIR Gray

FIRST APPEARANCE
Avengers #10 (November 1964)

POWERS
Immortus has no superhuman powers. His abilities come from his use of the vast knowledge and advanced technology he has accumulated on his travels through time.

IMMORTUS

Immortus was born in the 31st century of one of Earth's alternate futures. Using parts found in the ruins of his ancestors' property, he built a time machine and set off traveling through time. In each era he arrived in, he adopted a new guise, among them Rama-Tut and Kang the Conqueror. He left behind countless temporal counterparts capable of existing on their own and of further time travel. The being who became Rama-Tut journeyed to Limbo, a realm existing outside the timestream. There he was visited by the Time-Keepers, who helped him unlock the secrets of time. During the Destiny War with Kang, Immortus was killed but returned as someone entirely separate from Kang, freeing their destinies from each other.

IMPERATOR

FIRST APPEARANCE *Doctor Strange* #1 (December 2015)
REAL NAME Imperator **OCCUPATION** Leader of the Empirikul
BASE Mobile
HEIGHT Unknown **WEIGHT** Unknown **EYES** Yellow **HAIR** None
SPECIAL POWERS/ABILITIES A variety of science-based abilities. Excellent strategist and leader with a high-tech arsenal.

The Imperator was the leader of the Empirikul on their crusade to destroy magic. He was born in a dimension where people worshiped Shuma-Gorath and practiced magic, but his parents were scientists who suffered for their scientific rationality. They created a ship to try to escape, but were killed by Shuma-Gorath's followers. Their sacrifice bought their son time to escape. As the Imperator he attacked Earth's magic users and came close to destroying Doctor Strange, until the mage teamed up with other magic users and the "Thing in the Cellar" to defeat him. The Imperator then took the place of the Thing in the Cellar.

ILLUMINATI

Great heroes with best intentions

ILLUMINATI

FACTFILE

NOTABLE MEMBERS

BLACK BOLT
Inhuman King with lethal voice.

DOCTOR STRANGE
Master of the mystic arts.

IRON MAN
Genius engineer wearing powered armor.

MISTER FANTASTIC
Genius scientist with elastic body.

NAMOR
Mutant Atlantean king.

PROFESSOR X
Powerful telepath.

BLACK PANTHER
Olympic-level athlete, acrobat and gymnast; King of Wakanda.

BASE
New York City

FIRST APPEARANCE
New Avengers #7
(July 2005)

ALLIES/FOES

ALLIES Atlanteans, Avengers, Fantastic Four, X-Men, Inhumans

FOES Cabal, Kree, Skrulls

ISSUE #1

Iron Man gathers the leaders of the superpowered community in Wakanda to discuss forming an official organization for heroes. Instead, the Illuminati is born.

Iron Man's first attempt to band together the best minds on the planet failed due to a lack of trust among them.

Following the Kree-Skrull War, Iron Man saw the need for an organization that could band together various heroes to form a force capable of responding to planetary threats. To that end, he invited Black Bolt, Mister Fantastic, Namor, and Doctor Strange to meet at the Black Panther's palace in Wakanda. Other heroes were approached but raised objections to Iron Man's vision, and the Black Panther refused to participate. Therefore, instead of working together officially, the five like-minded heroes agreed to secretly share information so that they might better anticipate and respond to world-threatening events.

CAPTURED BY SKRULLS

When the Illuminati traveled to the Skrull homeworld to deliver a warning, the Skrull ruler refused to heed them. Black Bolt destroyed his warship. Unfortunately, the Illuminati were captured as they tried to leave the system. After bringing the Illuminati back to the planet, the Skrulls separated them and nullified their powers. Then they analyzed their prisoners, learning much that they would later use to give their operatives superpowers during the Secret Invasion. Believing Iron Man to be helpless without his armor, they were careless, and Stark found the opportunity to break loose and to free the others.

While Iron Man was the only one of the Illuminati able to cope with being tossed into outer space, the Skrulls thought very little of him and his armor.

THE INFINITY GAUNTLET

The Infinity Gauntlet has twice nearly destroyed everyone in the universe. This device holds the six Infinity Gems, assembling them into an artifact that grants the wearer limitless power. At one stage Mr. Fantastic began collecting the gems and turned to the Illuminati to help him. Namor, Professor X, and Doctor Strange searched for the Mind Gem, while Black Bolt, Mr. Fantastic, and Iron Man went after the Reality Gem. Once the Gauntlet was complete, the Watcher showed up to see what would happen and scolded them for meddling with such power. Mr. Fantastic chose to try to use the Gauntlet to destroy itself. When that failed, he removed the gems from the Gauntlet and gave one to each member of the Illuminati to safeguard in secret.

THE ILLUMINATI
1 Doctor Strange ***2*** Namor ***3*** Iron Man ***4*** Black Bolt ***5*** Mister Fantastic ***6*** Professor X ***7*** Black Panther

OTHER ADVENTURES

Later, the Illuminati approached the BEYONDER directly during the second Secret Wars. Professor X convinced the Beyonder that he had once been an INHUMAN who had been a mutant even before being exposed to the Terrigen Mists. Because of this, Black Bolt—who was therefore the Beyonder's king—could command him to leave, and did.

Deeming the Hulk too dangerous to remain on Earth, the Illuminati shot him into space.

EXILING THE HULK

The Illuminati arranged for a Life Model Decoy (android) version of Nick FURY to send the HULK on a mission into space to disable a dangerous satellite. Once he entered the satellite, it turned into a starcraft, programmed to release the Hulk on an idyllic but unpopulated planet, and rocketed away. Unfortunately, the ship wound up on the war-torn planet Sakaar instead. The Hulk later returned to exact his revenge during WORLD WAR HULK.

WAR AND INVASION

The CIVIL WAR shattered the Illuminati. Mr. Fantastic and Iron Man backed the Superhuman Registration Act, but Doctor Strange and Black Bolt opposed it. Namor abstained, saying it did not affect Atlantis, and Professor X was not available to comment at the time. None were willing to change their mind, so the Illuminati ended. Despite this, when Iron Man discovered an impending SECRET INVASION by the Skrulls he called the Illuminati together again.

REALIGNMENT

MEDUSA took Black Bolt's place until he was able to return, and she helped the lluminati fight the HOOD, who came after the Infinity Gems. Afterward, CAPTAIN AMERICA (Steve Rogers) took custody of Black Bolt's gem. During the clash between the Avengers and the X-Men, Cap tried to bring the group together again, but they failed to agree a course of action.

ESSENTIAL STORYLINES

- ***New Avengers #7–10*** The Illuminati makes its first appearance to discuss the problem of the Sentry.
- ***New Avengers: Illuminati #1–5*** The Illuminati gather for a series of secret adventures, starting with the aftermath of the Kree-Skrull War.
- ***World War Hulk #1–5*** The Hulk comes back from outer space to have his revenge on the members of the Illuminati who kicked him off Earth.

When BLACK SWAN showed the Black Panther the danger of other universes intruding upon and destroying each other, T'Challa had a change of heart. He called the Illuminati together and joined them as a team of Avengers under Captain America. BEAST took the place of the deceased Professor X, holding his Infinity Gem. Cap tried to use the Infinity Gauntlet to push back the intruding universe but failed, shattering all but the Time Gem, which disappeared. When he objected to destroying other universes to save their own, the rest of the Illuminati erased his memories of their group and set to work without him.

THE HOOD'S ILLUMINATI

Following Battleworld and the recreation of reality (*see* SECRET WARS), the Hood formed his own Illuminati—one with less altruistic intentions than the original. He chose the Black Ant, ENCHANTRESS, MAD THINKER, Thunderball, and TITANIA as members. They helped free fellow criminals from SHIELD's Pleasant Hill prison, but broke up soon after.

THE ILLUMINATI AVENGERS
1 Namor ***2*** Doctor Strange ***3*** Black Panther
4 Iron Man ***5*** Mister Fantastic
6 Black Bolt ***7*** Beast

IMPOSSIBLE MAN

FACTFILE

REAL NAME
Unknown

OCCUPATION
Trickster and student of Earth's popular culture

BASE
Mobile

HEIGHT 6 ft 4 in
WEIGHT 165 lbs
EYES White
HAIR None

FIRST APPEARANCE
Fantastic Four #11 (February 1963)

POWERS
Limitless shape-shifting abilities; can mirror properties of objects he imitates (if he's a hose he can spray water, as a light bulb he can light up); asexual reproduction.

IMPOSSIBLE MAN

The planet Poppup was an inhospitable world, its people surviving through asexual reproduction, their shape-changing abilities, and a group mind. Then a Poppupian was born who had a degree of individuality. Bored by life, this creature transformed himself into a spacecraft and traveled to Earth where he encountered the FANTASTIC FOUR. Finding him unbearably annoying, the THING told the creature that he was "impossible," and so "Impossible Man" was born.

To the Fantastic Four's annoyance, the team has encountered Impossible Man several times. When GALACTUS was threatening to consume Counter-Earth, Impossible Man tricked him into eating Poppup instead, giving him a bad case of cosmic indigestion. With his peoples' consciousness living on through him, Impossible Man set about rebuilding the Poppup race, first creating a wife—Impossible Woman—and later scores of children. AMATSU-MIKABOSHI appeared to kill him during the Chaos War, but the Impossible Man soon popped up alive again.

INFERNO

FIRST APPEARANCE *Inhumans* #1 (June 2014)
REAL NAME Dante Pertuz
OCCUPATION Wedding band drummer **BASE** New Attilan
HEIGHT 5 ft 11 in **WEIGHT** 161 lbs **EYES** Brown **HAIR** Black
SPECIAL POWERS/ABILITIES Inferno's body turns to flaming molten rock. He can throw blasts of fiery plasma and generate volcanic eruptions.

After BLACK BOLT detonated the Terrigen Bomb during his conflict with THANOS, Dante Pertuz and his mother underwent Terrigenesis. Though his mother didn't survive the process, Dante gained fiery new powers. He was immediately attacked by an INHUMAN named LASH, but Queen MEDUSA came to his aid. Dante (now called Inferno) and his sister then moved to New Attilan, the capital of Inhumans and NuHumans (NuHumans like Dante have both human and Inhuman ancestry). There he befriended Kamala Khan (Ms. MARVEL), Flint, and Naja; together they protected the people of New Attilan. Inferno later joined Quake's SECRET WARRIORS.

INTELLIGENCIA

FACTFILE

MEMBERS
DOCTOR DOOM
Genius and mystic.
EGGHEAD
Genius.
LEADER
Gamma-powered genius.
MAD THINKER
Genius with Awesome Android.
MODOK
Big-headed genius.
RED GHOST
Genius with Super-Ape allies.
WIZARD
Genius.

BASE Salvaged SHIELD Helicarrier dubbed the "Hellcarrier"; mobile

FIRST APPEARANCE
Fall of the Hulks: Alpha #1 (December 2009)

INTELLIGENCIA

The Intelligencia was a collection of the greatest criminal minds in the world. The LEADER and MODOK led the team, and by their efforts created both the RED HULK and the Red She-Hulk (*see* ROSS, BETTY). EGGHEAD was part of the group before his death, and DOCTOR DOOM was an early member of the group, but left over differences with the others—making him a target for their schemes. The Red Hulk even worked with the team for a while, until they betrayed him.

The Intelligencia's biggest plan involved capturing the eight smartest people on the planet—besides themselves—thereby eliminating the people smart enough to foil their ambitions. DOCTOR DOOM defeated them during his time as IRON MAN. A New Intelligencia later formed consisting of MAD THINKER, the AWESOME ANDROID, Leader, MODOK Superior and MISTER SINISTER. This group fought Kid Kaiju and the CHAMPIONS.

IN-BETWEENER

FIRST APPEARANCE *Warlock* #10 (December 1975)
REAL NAME Inapplicable **OCCUPATION** Cosmic entity
BASE Mobile
HEIGHT 15 ft **WEIGHT** Unrevealed
EYES White **HAIR** None
SPECIAL POWERS/ABILITIES Near-infinite cosmic power, often held in check by its own need for balance.

The In-Betweener, the creation of LORD CHAOS and MASTER ORDER, is the living synthesis of balance, representing both life and death, good and evil, logic and emotion, reality and illusion, existence and nothingness, and god and man. When the Titan THANOS tried to plunge the universe into death, the In-Betweener tried to restore balance by abducting Adam WARLOCK and turning him into a champion of life. The In-Betweener briefly had possession of the reality-warping Soul Gem until Thanos stole the item in his quest to build the Infinity Gauntlet. Lord Chaos and Master Order later forced the In-Betweener to merge them into one being: Logos.

INFINITY, SEE PAGES 186–187

INHUMANS

Superpowered human tribe

The alien KREE created a race of superpowered warrior-servants out of early humans. They abandoned their plans for their subjects, but left a small tribe of them—known as the Inhumans—behind. The Inhumans settled on an island in the North Atlantic named Attilan and developed technology and culture at an astounding rate, living hidden from the rest of the world. The Inhuman geneticist Randac developed a substance called Terrigen that accelerated genetic advances. Immersing himself in the Terrigen Mist, he developed advanced mental powers, and the other Inhumans soon followed suit, each developing a different set of powers.

TO THE WORLD

The Inhumans kept to themselves until the 20th century, when threats to the world required them to join forces with teams including the FANTASTIC FOUR, AVENGERS, and X-MEN. Even when the public took notice of them, however, they maintained their distance.

Years later, the Inhuman king BLACK BOLT moved Attilan to the air-filled Blue Area of the Moon. For a time, Kree leader RONAN THE ACCUSER enslaved them there, using them as an army against the SHI'AR. Black Bolt won their freedom by defeating Ronan in single combat, but the Inhumans exiled him and the rest of the royal family for a while afterward, unwilling to trade one ruler for another. Nevertheless, Black Bolt returned to lead them once again.

The Inhumans are an incredibly technologically advanced race descended from early humans.

FACTFILE

KEY MEMBERS AND POWERS

SUPER-RANDAC
Mental manipulation ability.

BLACK BOLT
Electron-harnessing powers linked to his speech.

MEDUSA
Hugely strong prehensile hair.

TRITON
Super-fast swimmer; resists crushing water pressure.

FALCONA
Mental control over birds of prey.

CRYSTAL
Mentally manipulates the four basic elements of nature.

STALLIOR
Speed and endurance; powerful hooves for fighting.

BASE
New Arctilan, the moon

FIRST APPEARANCE
Fantastic Four #45 (December 1965)

INHUMANS

TO THE STARS

Before the SECRET INVASION, the SKRULLS kidnapped and replaced Black Bolt. Once the original was restored, Black Bolt dislodged Attilan from the moon, turning it into a starship, in which he led the Inhumans to space. They destroyed the last of the Skrull armada that had attacked Earth and then destroyed Shi'ar ships that fired upon them. They made their way to the Kree Empire, where Black Bolt became their king too.

Black Bolt led his people against the Shi'ar in the War of Kings. While the Kree won, he was lost in a final confrontation with the Shi'ar emperor, VULCAN. Black Bolt later returned and cemented his control over the five Inhuman tribes from across the galaxy by taking a wife from each one.

The Inhumans returned to Earth, floating Attilan over New York City. When THANOS invaded Earth he attacked Attilan, hoping to force the Inhumans to turn over his Inhuman-descended son, Thane. Black Bolt defeated Thanos with his scream, destroying Attilan in the process. Black Bolt then activated a Terrigen Bomb that transformed anyone on Earth with Inhuman genes into a full Inhuman.

Attilan floated over a burning New York City as Thanos' envoys arrived to demand their tribute.

THE INHUMANS
1 Grid
2 Crystal
3 Karnak
4 Medusa
5 Iso ***6*** Flint
7 Reader

NUHUMANS

Many new Inhumans—known as NuHumans—came to the fallen city of New Attilan, now located in the Hudson River. The original Inhumans had to protect them, both from human enemies and from LASH. He was a high priest from another Inhuman city called Orollan, and he began to hunt the NuHumans down, believing them unworthy. The Terrigen Cloud created by the bomb also caused mutants harm. This led to conflict between the X-Men and Inhumans, which only ended when Medusa destroyed the Cloud. The Inhumans eventually established a new city on the moon called New Arctilan, but faced perhaps their biggest ever threat when the Kree Empire attacked, killing many of them.

INFINITY

When everything falls apart, what's left?

The Avengers learn of the threat of the Builders, and Thanos plots his attack on Earth.

An Earth elsewhere in the Multiverse was destroyed before its time, causing the remaining universes to collapse upon each other at the focal point of their respective Earths, an incident known as an incursion. As the BLACK SWAN informed the ILLUMINATI, the destruction of the colliding universes could only be stopped if one of the two Earths in an incursion was destroyed, so they made the hard decision to defend their universe by destroying other Earths. At the same time, the ruthless BUILDERS—the oldest race in the universe—sent envoys, supposedly to judge the people of Earth. Soon after, they launched a war designed to destroy Earth, thereby ending the incursions into their universe.

THE BUILDERS THREAT

The Builders had embarked on a devastating march through the universe; most of the races they encountered they judged to be only worthy of destruction. They obliterated Galador, home of the SPACEKNIGHTS, and moved on to destroy SKRULL and KREE planets as well. Nothing seemed able to stop them and their army of ALEPHS and EX NIHILI, not even the SILVER SURFER or CAPTAIN UNIVERSE.

Realizing the Builders were heading toward Earth, the AVENGERS sent a team to support other galactic civilizations—including the SHI'AR—hoping to stop the Builders there. The Illuminati stayed behind to work on contingency plans. However, they and the other heroes of Earth soon found themselves hard-pressed from another quarter.

The Avengers discovered that Skrull refugees had fled to Earth, After defeating them, the heroes had a more serious problem to ponder: What horrific force could have chased the Skrulls there to hide?

THANOS STRIKES

THANOS sent his envoy, CORVUS GLAIVE, out into the galaxy, demanding tribute from planets that he had visited before. This involved sacrificing the young of a certain age, among which, Thanos believed, he might find his child. Thanos' spies, called Outriders, searched Earth and found evidence of one such offspring in Attilan, the ancestral city of the INHUMANS of Earth, which hovered over Manhattan.

When Thanos learned that the bulk of the Avengers had headed into space to fight the Builders, leaving their homeworld less defended, he decided the time was ripe to strike Earth again. He sent his Black Order—also called the Cull Obsidian—to invade, both to find his spawn and to renew his search for the Infinity Gems the Illuminati had recently lost. Meanwhile, the Illuminati had to deal with the incursion of another Earth from a new dimension that threatened to destroy the home they'd been fighting so hard to defend.

THE BLACK ORDER

Thanos, worshipper of Death and the commander of the Black Order.

Proxima Midnight, who conquered the people of Atlantis.

Corvus Glaive, Thanos' chief negotiator.

Ebony Maw, who took control of Doctor Strange for Thanos.

Super Giant, who helped Corvus Glaive take down the X-Men.

Black Dwarf, who attacked the nation of Wakanda—and lost.

THE AVENGERS IN SPACE

Faced with the realization that the Builders were coming to destroy the Earth, the Avengers decided to gather a large force to assist the members of the galactic council whose people were on the front lines of the war. Realizing they didn't have the power to outgun the Builders' forces, they relied on cunning and ingenuity, and making every shot count.

INVADERS

The greatest Super Heroes of World War II

INVADERS

FACTFILE

CURRENT MEMBERS AND POWERS

U.S.AGENT
Super-strong soldier.

BLAZING SKULL
Immortal; impervious to flame.

THIN MAN
Can distend body and teleport by twisting dimensions.

UNION JACK
Trained fighter who specializes in battling monsters.

TARA
Android life form that bursts into flame and can fly.

BASE
The Infiltrator, a battleship capable of interdimensional travel

FIRST APPEARANCE
Giant-Size Invaders #1 (June 1975)

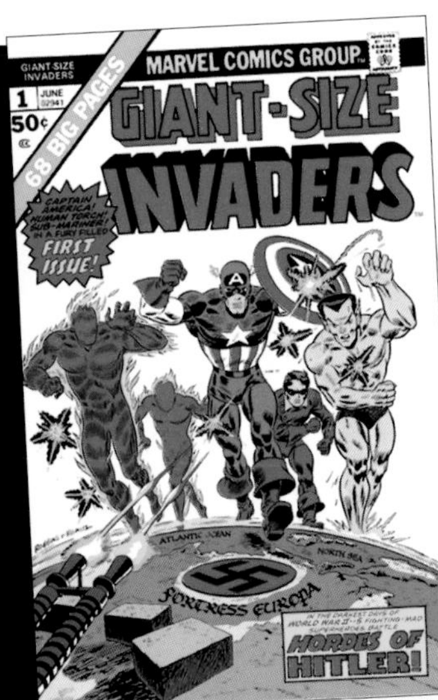

The Invaders were brought together in 1941 by Winston Churchill.

During the opening days of World War II, before the United States had formally entered the conflict, an elite fighting unit was banded together by British Prime Minister Winston Churchill to halt Nazi aggression. It was the first great gathering of superhuman champions ever recorded—Captain America and Bucky Barnes, Namor the Sub-Mariner, the Human Torch and Toro, Union Jack, Spitfire, Miss America, and the Whizzer. This alliance, known formally as the Invaders, cut a swath through enemy forces until the Axis powers were defeated.

As a team, the Invaders battled both conventional forces, and Nazi superhuman operatives such as the Atlantean U-Man.

ESSENTIAL STORYLINES

- ***Invaders #5–6 and Marvel Premiere #29–30*** The Invaders are joined by the homefront heroes of the Liberty Legion to thwart a scheme by the Red Skull.
- ***Avengers #83–85, New Invaders #0*** When the Avengers become a global organization, a modern-day team of Invaders is assembled by the US government to do the jobs that they will not.

THE ALL-WINNERS

Although they disbanded after the war, for a time combating crime on the homefront as the All-Winners Squad, the Invaders established a legend and a tradition that would inspire others to follow in their footsteps. Some of those heroes associated with the Invaders joined forces with Parisian resistance fighters to form the covert V-Battalion, maintaining world order secretly through the decades.

More recently, the Red Skull organized a new incarnation of the Invaders while posing as US Secretary of Defense Dell Rusk. Recruited by the U.S.Agent (as Captain America) and led by the Thin Man, the new Invaders discovered the Red Skull's plot and turned their efforts towards the destruction of the villainous Axis Mundi.

The original Invaders traveled through time to a horrifying present. When they returned, they discovered that a soldier who'd tagged along with them had let the Red Skull get his hands on a Cosmic Cube and won World War II. The Avengers had to go back to World War II, disguised as contemporary heroes, to set things right. After that, many of the original Invaders reunited in the present to battle a threat dormant since World War II.

THE INVADERS
1 Union Jack ***2*** Tara ***3*** The U.S.Agent (as Captain America) ***4*** The Blazing Skull

The Machiavellian Thin Man, once imprisoned for his murder of a former Nazi agent, was the brains behind the modern-day Invaders' operation.

INVISIBLE WOMAN

The heart of the Fantastic Four

Actress Susan Storm had already struck up a romance with the scientist Reed Richards (*see* MR. FANTASTIC) when she volunteered to join him on an experimental mission into space. Along with her brother, Johnny Storm, and the starship's pilot, Ben Grimm, Sue received a mutagenic dose of cosmic rays; they gave her the power to turn invisible at will. The others had also received superhuman powers, and Sue became a member of their new team, the FANTASTIC FOUR, under the identity of the Invisible Girl. Sue's powers evolved over time, giving her the ability to project impenetrable force-fields and to turn objects invisible through mental control.

FACTFILE

REAL NAME
Susan Storm Richards

OCCUPATION
Adventurer

BASE
New York City

HEIGHT 5 ft 6 ins
WEIGHT 120 lbs
EYES Blue
HAIR Blond

FIRST APPEARANCE
Fantastic Four #1 (November 1961)

INVISIBLE WOMAN

POWERS
Can turn herself invisible, and is able to project energy around other people or objects that makes them invisible too; can generate protective force-fields, or shape invisible objects of psionic force. By projecting force-fields beneath her, she can travel through the air.

Sue and Reed's son was named after his maternal grandfather, Franklin Storm.

COSMIC POWERS

Sue soon married Reed and battled threats to Earth including planet-devouring GALACTUS. Complications with her first pregnancy forced Reed to stabilize her labor with the energies of ANNIHILUS' Cosmic Control Rod, and Sue gave birth to a boy, Franklin RICHARDS. She briefly separated from Reed and left the FANTASTIC Four, allowing MEDUSA to fill her spot. Sue's second pregnancy ended in a stillbirth. During this vulnerable period, PSYCHO-MAN controlled Sue's mind and caused her to assume the villainous identity of Malice. After shaking off Psycho-Man's influence, Sue renamed herself the Invisible Woman.

Sue and Reed briefly joined the AVENGERS, but returned to their original team. After Reed's apparent death at the hands of DOCTOR DOOM, Sue served as the Fantastic Four's leader, rejecting romantic overtures from NAMOR the Sub-Mariner. It transpired that the child from Sue's earlier stillbirth had been preserved in another dimension by Franklin. After a battle with Abraxas, the unborn girl returned to Sue's womb and soon after became her daughter Valeria RICHARDS.

Sue's ability to generate force-fields is more versatile than her power of invisibility, making her one of the team's strongest members.

During the CIVIL WAR, Sue left Reed over his support for the Superhuman Registration Act; however soon she reunited with him. She was kidnapped during the SECRET INVASION and replaced by a SKRULL named LYJA, but she escaped soon after. She helped launch the Future Foundation after Johnny Storm's apparent death, despite her mourning. The Fantastic Four re-formed when Johnny returned, though the team fell on hard times and Sue became violent thanks to the manipulations of the QUIET MAN and Psycho-Man. They were eventually thwarted by Mr. Fantastic and Valeria.

Faced with the end of the Multiverse, Sue and the Future Foundation built a life raft to survive, but it failed and all except Reed died. However, Reed then gained the power of the BEYONDERS, and resurrected his family. Years later, Sue and the team were threatened by the "Griever at the End of All Things," a being who opposed their mission to expand the Multiverse.

As part of the FF, Sue helped people around the world, including her friends in Wakanda.

ESSENTIAL STORYLINES

- ***Secret Wars II #2***
Sue assumes the villainous identity of Malice while under the influence of the Psycho-Man.
- ***Fantastic Four #284***
It's goodbye to the venerable code name Invisible Girl, as Sue reinvents herself as the Invisible Woman.
- ***Fantastic Four Vol. 3 #54***
Sue gives birth to her second child, Valeria Richards, assisted in the delivery by the Fantastic Four's archenemy, Doctor Doom.

IRON FIST

FACTFILE

REAL NAME
Daniel Thomas Rand-K'ai
(Daniel Thomas Rand in US)

OCCUPATION
Adventurer; co-owner of Rand-Meachum, Inc.

BASE
New York City

HEIGHT 5 ft 11 in
WEIGHT 175 lbs
EYES Blue
HAIR Blond

FIRST APPEARANCE
Marvel Premiere #15
(May 1974)

POWERS
Master of the martial arts of K'un-L'un. Can focus his chi (natural energy) and superhuman energy in his hand, endowing his fist with superhuman strength, durability, or healing power.

IRON FIST

The Iron Fist is granted to the chosen of K'un-Lun, one of the Cities of Heaven. In modern times, philanthropist Danny Rand controls the Iron Fist. At age nine, he accompanied his parents and their treacherous business partner Harold Meachum to K'un-Lun. Both parents were killed and only Danny reached the sacred city. At 19, he gained the power of the Iron Fist and confronted Meachum, but spared him. A ninja slew Meachum instead. Rand became wealthy as co-owner of Rand-Meachum and partnered with Luke CAGE to form the Heroes for Hire. He joined Cage in the AVENGERS after the CIVIL WAR. Iron Fist later learned he was one of seven Immortal Weapons set to battle for the supremacy of their respective Cities of Heaven. He also mentored Victor Alvarez when the teenager became the new POWER MAN and fought alongside the DEFENDERS.

Iron Fist's mastery of the K'un-Lun martial arts and his "iron fist" make him a match for even superhuman opponents.

Iron Fist's hands glow with superhuman energies.

IRON MAN, SEE PAGES 192–195

IRON NAIL

FIRST APPEARANCE *Captain America* #12 (December 2013)
REAL NAME Ran Shen
OCCUPATION Warlord **BASE** Gungnir (giant Helicarrier robot)
HEIGHT Unknown **WEIGHT** Unknown
EYES Orange **HAIR** Black
SPECIAL POWERS/ABILITIES Blessing of Nian granted the power to transform into a humanoid dragon; poisonous tentacles erupt from hole in chest; training and experience of a top-level SHIELD operative.

Ran Shen was once a leading SHIELD agent, rivaling Nick FURY as one of the agency's best. In 1966 he was sent on a mission to free ex-Nazi scientists Mila and Peter Hitzig from HYDRA. The mission was a failure and Mila—whom Shen had fallen in love with—was killed. Shen later infiltrated China and in 1968 met a reptilian humanoid called Nian who gave him exceptional powers. He used these in a failed attempt to bring down SHIELD, though he did succeed in draining Cap of the Super-Soldier Serum. He died calling out Mila's name.

IRONHEART

FIRST APPEARANCE *Invincible Iron Man* #7 (May 2016)
REAL NAME Riri Williams
OCCUPATION Student **BASE** Chicago
HEIGHT 5 ft 2 in **WEIGHT** 100 lbs
EYES Brown **HAIR** Black
SPECIAL POWERS/ABILITIES Super-genius level intelligence—winning a scholarship to Massachusetts Institute of Technology at age 15—plus inventor, coding expert, and engineer. Armor provides her with equivalent powers to Iron Man.

Riri Williams is a teenage super-genius. After she lost her best friend and stepfather in a shooting, she became determined to finish armor she was making based on an old IRON MAN design. She soon took to the skies, arresting two escaping convicts. Tony Stark was so impressed that he mentored her, with an AI version of Stark later continuing to do so. She joined the CHAMPIONS but lost her armor fighting THANOS. Her teammates encouraged her to build a new, improved version.

IT

FIRST APPEARANCE *Tales of Suspense* #14 (September 1961)
REAL NAME None
OCCUPATION Instrument of destruction **BASE** Los Angeles
HEIGHT 100 ft (later reduced to 30 ft) **WEIGHT** approximately 1,000 tons (later 100 tons) **EYES** White **HAIR** None
SPECIAL POWERS/ABILITIES Outside consciousness needed to animate—or reassemble—statue. Vast strength. Granite construction impervious to bullet, shells, and electric shocks; limited flying ability. Vulnerable to gas attack.

It, the Living Colossus, was a statue built to celebrate the might of the USSR. The night before its unveiling, the statue was animated by a stranded alien Kigor. "It" rampaged through Moscow until a Kigor rescue craft retrieved the alien. The statue was later sent to Los Angeles and once again animated by the Kigor, but special-effects expert Robert O'Bryan tricked the aliens with a booby-trapped prop and uploaded his own mind into It.

IRON PATRIOT

Flying the Super Hero flag

FACTFILE

REAL NAME
Norman Osborn

OCCUPATION
Inventor; criminal; government agent

BASE
New York City

HEIGHT 5 ft 11 ins
WEIGHT 185 lbs
EYES Blue
HAIR Reddish-brown

FIRST APPEARANCE
Dark Avengers #1 (March 2009) (as Iron Patriot)

POWERS
Armor has superhuman strength, flight, magnetic heat-seeking missiles, miniaturized lasers, and flamethrowers; helmet interfaces with US-controlled satellites or computer networks.

Osborn also fashioned a suit of armor for his son Harry, calling it American Son. Harry refused it, but Gabriel Stacy ended up wearing it.

When Norman Osborn (Green Goblin) took over from Tony Stark (Iron Man) as the leader of national security for the United States (a period known as the Dark Reign), he started dismantling everything that had come before him and replacing it with new versions he could better control. He set up HAMMER in place of SHIELD, and he took the greatest team of heroes in the world—the Avengers—and dressed up villains in their place. Instead of taking one spot for himself on the team, however, he took two, replacing both Captain America and Iron Man. In a suit of armor painted red, white, and blue, he became the Iron Patriot.

FALSE PATRIOT

Osborn may have wrapped himself in the flag, but his aim wasn't to help the country—he wanted to boost his own meteoric rise to power even higher. Although a genius in his own right, he was unable to fathom the latest Stark technology and so had to repurpose an older Iron Man suit for his Iron Patriot outfit, a model he could manage to control.

Osborn made many public appearances in his armor and even faced off against real threats during the Dark Reign. He wore it when he led the assault on Asgard as well. This proved to be his downfall as Iron Man was able to remotely remove the Iron Patriot armor from Osborn—exposing the fact that the increasingly unstable and erratic leader had painted his face green to resemble his Green Goblin identity.

PATRIOT DRONES

After Osborn was hauled off to jail, scientists from AIM stole the Iron Patriot armor and used it to create a fleet of deadly drones. With the help of SHIELD, James Rhodes (War Machine) established communications with the drones and was able to convince them that they had been given bad orders. In order to learn from him, they sent him a suit of Iron Patriot armor so he could join them. He led them in a retaliatory strike against AIM.

THE NEW PATRIOT

After James returned to his War Machine incarnation, engineering genius Toni Ho, daughter of scientist Ho Yinsen—who once saved Tony Stark's life—created her own Iron Patriot armor to use while part of Avengers Idea Mechanics. Toni has also fought under the name Rescue (*see also* Pepper Potts) and with the U.S.Avengers.

Toni Ho was part of the U.S.Avengers, a super-team formed by AIM after the company became the intelligence arm of SHIELD.

IRON MAN

The armored Avenger

IRON MAN

FACTFILE

REAL NAME Anthony Stark

OCCUPATION
Businessman and philanthropist; hero and leader of the Avengers

BASE
Stark Tower ("Avengers Tower"), Manhattan, New York

HEIGHT 6 ft 1 in
WEIGHT 225 lbs
EYES Blue
HAIR Black

FIRST APPEARANCE
Tales of Suspense #39 (March 1963)

POWERS

Prodigious inventiveness and business acumen. Standard Iron Man armor provides superhuman strength and durability, jet-boot powered flight, has repulsor beams in gauntlets, and chest-mounted uni-beam. Armor's underlayer is now incorporated into Stark's body, letting him control Iron Man remotely.

ALLIES/FOES

ALLIES The Avengers, James Rhodes (War Machine), SHIELD, Virginia Potts, Bethany Cabe, Edwin Jarvis

FOES Obadiah Stane, Justin Hammer, Madame Masque, Titanium Man, Spymaster, the Mandarin

Injured in Vietnam, Stark's first Iron Man armor saves his life and helps him escape capture. From that day on, he cannot survive without it.

Billionaire industrialist and philanthropist Tony Stark is perhaps the most influential superpowered individual on the planet. While PROFESSOR X has the respect of the Earth's mutant community, Stark's work as Iron Man, his long-term membership of the AVENGERS, and position as head of Stark International arguably gives him even wider authority.

FORGING THE IRON MAN

The son of a wealthy industrialist, Tony Stark's parents died in a car crash when he was young, leaving him their business conglomerate, Stark Industries. Taking over the company when he was 21, in retrospect some of Tony's early business decisions were ethically suspect. Tony was an engineering prodigy, and many of his early inventions were designed for use by the US military. It was his dealings with the army that ultimately led him to create his Iron Man armor.

In the nick of time, the first Iron Man armor saved Tony Stark's life.

Developing mini-transistors for use on the battlefield, Tony traveled to Vietnam to see them in use on the ground. The trial ended badly when an exploding bomb left a piece of shrapnel dangerously close to his heart and Tony was captured by the North Vietnamese warlord, Wong-Chu.

Told that the shrapnel would only be removed if he developed a weapon for the North Vietnamese, Tony responded with typical tenacity. Teaming with a fellow prisoner, Nobel prize-winning physicist Ho Yinsen, Tony developed an iron suit that would protect his heart as well as allow him to fight the warlord and his men and escape.

SOCIAL CONSCIENCE

In the following years, Tony donned this armor many times. Claiming the Iron Man was his bodyguard and corporate emblem, at first he simply used it to fight communists and threats to his business empire. With the advent of new technologies and ideas, the armor evolved—becoming increasingly, and at times dangerously, sophisticated.

Initially a defender of Stark Industries, gradually Iron Man began to serve the general public.

Over the years Tony's own world view also began to evolve: he halted sales to the military, recognizing that they caused more harm than good, and established a number of charitable foundations. He became a founder member of the Avengers, allowing the team to use his mansion as their base and providing financial backing via the Maria Stark foundation—a non-profit-making organization named for his mother.

ESSENTIAL STORYLINES

- ***Iron Man Vol. 1 #120–129 #153–156*** Tony Stark's first encounter with Justin Hammer and his battle with alcohol.
- ***Iron Man Vol. 2 #162–200*** Stark's long dark fall to the gutter at the hands of Obadiah Stane, and his gradual resurrection.
- ***Iron Man Vol. 3 #27–30*** The Iron Man armor becomes sentient and attacks Stark.
- ***Civil War II (tpb)*** Iron Man goes to war with Captain Marvel.
- ***Iron Man: The Secret Origin of Tony Stark (tpb)*** Tony Stark uncovers shocking facts about his parents.

OLD FLAMES

Wealthy, charming, handsome—over the years, Tony Stark has drawn countless women to him, and many hearts have been broken, including his own. Time and again, his dual identity and multiple responsibilities have sabotaged any hope of a settled, long-term romance.

JANICE CORD
Daughter of Stark rival Drexel Cord.

BETHANY CABE
Tony's lover until her husband returned.

SUNSET BAIN
Seduced Tony and stole his secrets.

VIRGINIA POTTS
One of Tony's most loyal confidantes.

NATASHA ROMANOVA
Sometime adversary and former fiancée.

Although Tony is immensely strong-willed, at times the pressures on him have proved overwhelming—twice he has succumbed to the lure of alcohol. Tony's first fall from grace was precipitated by a series of attacks from Super Villains hired by business rival Justin Hammer. While fending these off, Iron Man was framed for the murder of a diplomat, and at the same time national security agency SHIELD was attempting to buy his company and so gain his military secrets. Gradually, with the support of his friends, Tony overcame these threats and defeated his addiction.

This episode was nothing compared to Tony's second dance with drink. As a result of the emotional manipulations of his competitor Obadiah Stane, Tony became a homeless vagrant. His epiphany came when he was forced to deliver the child of a homeless woman, who died soon after. After waking up in hospital, he began to rebuild his life, creating a new business empire—Stark Enterprises—and defeating Stane in combat.

Like his father before him, Tony Stark was cursed by the demon drink. With Iron Man labeled a murderer and his company under siege, Tony was driven to the bottle.

AN ENEMY OF AMERICA

Although a long-term member of the Avengers, Tony's decisions have brought him into direct conflict with his teammates, as well as with the US government. When Justin Hammer stole Stark technology and distributed it to criminals across the world, Tony began a quest to find each item of missing technology. His efforts to track down the US military's Stark-derived Guardsmen suits resulted in Iron Man being branded an outlaw by the US government. This action also antagonized Captain America.

A HEAVY BURDEN

During the Civil War Tony led the Super Heroes who complied with the Superhuman Registration Act and worked with SHIELD. When the conflict ended, he was named the new director of SHIELD and used his new power to set up the Fifty-State Initiative.

Unfortunately, because of his membership in the Illuminati, Tony became the target of the Hulk's wrath during World War Hulk. This scandal was the beginning of the end for him. When the Secret Invasion of the Skrull Empire caught Tony off guard, the public backlash forced his removal as director of SHIELD. The man who took his place—Norman Osborn (*see* Green Goblin)—ordered his capture. Tony ran, making himself as much an outlaw as the heroes he'd once sought to capture for SHIELD.

In the House of M universe, Tony Stark is a competitor in Sapien Death Match, a televised gladiatorial contest. There he competes against other armored humans.

Although sometimes at odds with his fellow Avengers, Tony Stark remains one of the team's most constant members. While his money keeps the team afloat, it is as Iron Man that he really leaves his mark.

IRON MAN continued

When HAMMER replaced SHIELD, a warrant went out for Tony Stark's arrest.

The Model 29 Extremis Iron Man armor could be controlled by Tony's thoughts. Following the second Super Hero Civil War, after he recovered from his coma, he started using it again.

DARK TIMES

The rise of Norman Osborn during the DARK REIGN coincided with the fall of Tony Stark. To keep Osborn from learning all of the secrets Tony had learned while director of SHIELD, he purged the database of Super Heroes, keeping only a single record in his head, stored in the Extremis nanotechnology he'd used to enhance the interface between himself and his Iron Man armor. The only way Tony could get rid of the information stored in his head, however, was to damage his own brain. This caused his vaunted intelligence to decay. He grew unable to control his most sophisticated sets of armor, and eventually his life was threatened.

Meanwhile, Osborn repurposed an Iron Man suit to become the IRON PATRIOT, pursuing and nearly killing Iron Man. Pepper POTTS recorded and released this information, causing public opinion to start to turn against Osborn. Tony recuperated in the care of THOR's alter ego, Dr. Donald Blake, who had been given Tony's power of attorney.

Led by Pepper, Tony's friends made a desperate attempt to reboot Tony's brain from a backup he'd made before he started using the Extremis tech. To do so, they had to channel a thunderbolt from Thor through the shield of CAPTAIN AMERICA. The initial attempt failed, but DOCTOR STRANGE worked with Tony to help free his mind.

Still recovering, Tony put on an old set of Iron Man armor and joined the other heroes to help defend Asgard against Oborn's forces. Tony disabled Osborn's Iron Patriot armor by remote, revealing that the man had become mentally unstable again and had painted his face to resemble the Green Goblin.

RESILIENT STARK

After Osborn was put away, Stark launched a new company with Pepper in charge: Stark Resilient, dedicated not to weaponry but to bringing free, clean energy to the world. With Stark no longer in the weapons business, Justine Hammer (Crimson Cowl) and her daughter Sasha Hammer started a line of their own power armor called Detroit Steel. They attacked Iron Man, hoping to prove the worth of their technology.

Tony also had other troubles to deal with. During Fear Itself, he fought the Grey Gargoyle, who'd been possessed by Mokk, Breaker of Faith, in Paris. Tony failed to stop many Parisians from being turned to stone. Desperate, he pleaded with Odin for help, sacrificing the one thing he had left: his sobriety. Odin granted Tony's request, allowing him to use his workshop alongside the Dwarves of Svartalfheim to create enchanted weapons for himself and the other Avengers. After the Avengers triumphed, Tony raged at Odin for not caring about the people who'd been turned to stone and Odin restored them to full health.

Despite giving up making weapons, Iron Man had to face off against the forces of Detroit Steel.

When the Mandarin and Ezekiel Stane joined forces and upgraded some of Iron Man's old foes, Tony realized that he needed to leave Stark Resilient in order to protect Pepper and the other employees. He quit being Iron Man and faked his death, helped by his old friend James Rhodes (War Machine). Rhodey became the new Iron Man.

Ezekiel Stane and Iron Man joined forces to battle the Mandarin and defeat his plans for world domination.

The Mandarin then revealed that he'd taken over Tony's brain with a virus. He forced Tony to work alongside Ezekiel to create massive Titanomech suits of armor to act as bodies for the alien spirits that supposedly inhabited the Mandarin's ten rings. Tony and Ezekiel allied with Blizzard, Living Laser, and Whirlwind to rebel against the Mandarin and defeat him.

FAMILY SECRETS

Back home, Tony decided that he'd been thinking too small. He needed to explore the rest of the universe to come up with better ideas for helping Earth. To that end, he became Iron Man again and joined the Guardians of the Galaxy. While in space, he learned that he had been genetically altered in the womb so that he could control a huge craft called the Godkiller, and use it to protect Earth. Tony found he was unable to pilot the craft, however, and discovered this was because he was actually adopted—his parents' natural born son, Arno, was the child who had been genetically manipulated, but had spent his life hidden away, with machinery keeping him alive. Like Tony, Arno was a genius, and the pair soon set about making the world a better place. Tony then tracked down his birth mother, the famous singer and ex-SHIELD agent Amanda Armstrong, whom he brought in to work for his company.

MORE WAR

Following the incursions and the remaking of reality, Tony found himself with a new ally—Victor von Doom. Healed by Reed Richards when reality was remade, Doom was trying to be a reformed man and helped Tony defeat Madame Masque. Tony then found himself fighting in another Super Hero Civil War (*see* Civil War II), this time against Captain Marvel, over her plan to use the Inhuman Ulysses Cain's powers of prediction to arrest people for crimes they had yet to commit. War Machine was killed fighting Thanos and Tony himself fell into a coma during a final showdown with Captain Marvel. His body was taken to a secure location by his allies while it rebooted itself. Meanwhile, Doom took over as Iron Man to carry on Tony's heroic actions. At the same time an A.I. version of Tony acted as a mentor to the young hero Ironheart.

Just as in the first Civil War, the Super Hero community lined up in opposing teams, with Tony Stark leading one of them. The conflict with Captain Marvel quickly escalated out of control.

STARK UNLIMITED

Tony's body eventually healed itself thanks to all the advanced technology he had used on it over the years. The revived Tony then used the same tech to bring Rhodey back to life. Together they stopped a mass attack on Stark Industries by the Hood's forces. Shortly afterward, Tony was forced to deal with his birth father, Jude, who had been an agent of Hydra. Tony then renamed his company Stark Unlimited and hired a host of new staff—including the robot Jocasta, who helped Tony start a relationship with Janet Van Dyne (the original Wasp). Stark Unlimited's founding concept was to invent the future and make the world a better place, and Tony little suspected that his old foe the Controller was planning to make moves against him.

After years of almost constant hardship, Tony Stark sought comfort in the arms of Janet, one of his oldest friends.

J2

FIRST APPEARANCE *What If?* #105 (February 1998)
REAL NAME Zane Yama
OCCUPATION High-school student **BASE** New York City
HEIGHT 5 ft 5 in (Zane); 6 ft 6 in (J2) **WEIGHT** 137 lbs (Zane), 725 lbs (J2) **EYES** Blue **HAIR** Brown
SPECIAL POWERS/ABILITIES Superhuman strength and durability; virtually unstoppable and indestructible.

In one possible future, Zane's parents are Cain Marko, the original JUGGERNAUT, and Sachi Yama, an assistant district attorney. They fell in love shortly after Marko renounced his criminal ways, joined the X-MEN, and was pardoned for his past crimes. They married, but Sachi kept her last name for professional reasons. While on an X-Men mission, Marko was lost in an alien dimension. Years later, Zane discovered that he could temporarily gain the mass and power of the Juggernaut. Calling himself J2, Zane joined the AVENGERS of his timeline and eventually freed his father from an alien sorcerer who had been holding him prisoner.

JACK OF HEARTS

Jack Hart's mother was an extraterrestrial Contraxian and his father a human scientist. He was born with volatile energy powers that would have killed him, and his father created Zero Fluid in an attempt to give his son control. After an accidental drenching in the fluid when agents of the criminal Corporation killed his father, Jack became the costumed hero Jack of Hearts, but he required regular periods of isolation in a SHIELD facility to keep from exploding. After learning of his origins, Jack traveled to Contraxia to rekindle the planet's waning star. He became romantically involved with Ganymede of the Spinsterhood during the fight against GALACTUS' offspring TYRANT, and joined the AVENGERS upon his return to Earth. Frustrated by the segregation required by his condition, Jack detonated himself in space after saving the life of ANT-MAN II's daughter, Cassie Lang (STATURE). Under the control of SCARLET WITCH, a seemingly zombified Jack returned and appeared to kill Ant-Man in an explosion. He was later resurrected by Project PEGASUS, using Z-Energy.

JACK OF HEARTS

FACTFILE
REAL NAME
Jonathan "Jack" Hart
OCCUPATION
Adventurer
BASE
Mobile

HEIGHT 5 ft 11 in
WEIGHT 175 lbs
EYES Blue (right), white (left)
HAIR Brown

FIRST APPEARANCE
Deadly Hands of Kung Fu #22 (March 1976)

POWERS
Enhanced strength, resistance to injury and accelerated healing rate, ability to release massive quantities of explosive energy as shock waves. Power of flight is achieved by controlling blasts of energy. Computerized intelligence enables him to think at phenomenal speeds.

JACKAL

FACTFILE
REAL NAME
Dr. Miles Warren
OCCUPATION
Criminal; former university lecturer
BASE
New York City

HEIGHT 5 ft 10 in
WEIGHT 175 lbs
EYES Green
HAIR Gray; (as Jackal) none

FIRST APPEARANCE
The Amazing Spider-Man #31 (December 1965)

POWERS
Expert in cloning; superhuman strength; had poison-tipped, razor-sharp claws; used gas bombs.

JACKAL

Peter Parker's biochemistry teacher, Dr. Miles Warren, was obsessed with Peter's girlfriend, Gwen STACY. Grief-stricken by her death, he became unhinged, creating clones of Gwen and Peter and killing his lab assistant when he was discovered. Unable to face what he had done, he developed an alternate personality, the Jackal, who gradually became dominant. The Jackal blamed SPIDER-MAN for what had happened to Gwen and forced Peter to face up to his own guilt for her death. The Jackal created several clones of Peter, including those that became Ben Reilly (SCARLET SPIDER), Spidercide, and KAINE. For a while, he had everyone—including Peter—convinced that Ben was the original Spider-Man rather than the clone, but that turned out to be a trick engineered by the GREEN GOBLIN.

The Jackal was responsible for the virus that gave everyone in Manhattan spider powers. In addition, he attacked the Superior Spider-Man (DOCTOR OCTOPUS) with several clones, including ones of himself, CARRION (the result of another cloning experiment), Gwen Stacy, and a number of half-spiders.

JACK FROST

FIRST APPEARANCE *USA Comics* #1 (August 1941)
REAL NAME Unrevealed **OCCUPATION** Adventurer
BASE North Pole; mobile in US in World War II
HEIGHT 5 ft 11 in **WEIGHT** 172 lbs
EYES Blue-white **HAIR** Blue
SPECIAL POWERS/ABILITIES Possesses innate superhuman ability to generate sub-freezing temperatures.

Jack Frost may have been the human-sized offspring of Frost Giants (*see* GODS OF ASGARD). In the 1940s, he joined the Liberty Legion, a hero team that battled Axis agents on the American home front. Jack Frost was later swallowed by a gigantic Ice Worm in the Arctic yet remained alive. Dr. Gregor Shapanka, whose costume generated intense cold, also adopted the name "Jack Frost" as his original criminal identity. A foe of IRON MAN, Shapanka later called himself BLIZZARD. He was killed by Arno STARK, the time-traveling Iron Man of an alternate future.

JAMESON, J. JONAH

Crusading publisher of the *Daily Bugle*

Irascible and domineering, Jameson had no time for costumed Super Heroes.

J. Jonah Jameson began his career in journalism while he was still in high school, working as a part-time copy boy for New York's prestigious *Daily Bugle* newspaper. The son of a war hero, he obtained firsthand experience of conflict when he served as a war correspondent in Europe during World War II. Jameson later spent three years covering the Korean War, during which time Joan—his first wife and the mother of his son, John—was tragically killed by a masked mugger, sparking a lifelong distrust of mask-wearers, be they villain or hero!

CRIME FIGHTER

Jameson reacted to the grief by throwing himself even more fully into his professional life, rising to become editor-in-chief of the *Daily Bugle.* He eventually became the paper's publisher, relinquishing the editor-in-chief position to Joe "Robbie" ROBERTSON. In time, Jameson bought the paper.

For many years Jameson used his newspaper to fight for civil rights and to battle organized crime. THE KINGPIN tried to have him killed, but this attempt on his life did nothing to change Jameson's uncompromising attitude. The stubborn, belligerent, but courageous publisher continued to print exposés of big-time criminals—even when his friend, Norman Osborn (*see* GREEN GOBLIN), turned out to be one of them.

Jameson began writing editorials against costumed Super Heroes, criticizing them as vigilantes who took the law into their own hands. When SPIDER-MAN appeared in New York and began fighting crime as a costumed hero, Jameson focused his most pointed attacks on the wall-crawler. He called Spider-Man a menace, claiming that the web-swinger was a danger to the citizens of New York City.

MEET THE MAYOR

After years of heartfelt rants at Spider-Man, Jonah had a heart attack while arguing with Peter Parker. While he was in the hospital, his wife Marla Madison sold the *Daily Bugle*, which had been struggling financially. After recovering, he ran for mayor of New York City and won, giving him the full resources of the city to send after Spider-Man, despite the objections of his staff.

Marla was killed trying to protect Jonah from ALISTAIR SMYTHE, the son of the scientist Jonah had hired to create a series of Spider-Slayer robots. This caused Jonah to examine his life, and he eventually came to respect Spider-Man—although by that time DOCTOR OCTOPUS had taken over Spider-Man's body.

Jameson had no idea that his fellow club member Norman Osborn was the Green Goblin.

The *Daily Bugle*'s staff learned to cope with Jameson's outbursts.

JAMESON, J. JONAH

FACTFILE

REAL NAME
J. Jonah Jameson

OCCUPATION
Owner and publisher of the *Daily Bugle* newspaper

BASE
New York City

HEIGHT 5 ft 11 in
WEIGHT 210 lbs
EYES Blue
HAIR Black, white at the temples

FIRST APPEARANCE
The Amazing Spider-Man #1 (March 1963)

POWERS

J. Jonah Jameson has no superhuman powers, but his stubborn, uncompromising attitude makes him a formidable opponent. Outspoken and tenacious, he refuses to back down when he believes he is right.

JARELLA

FACTFILE
REAL NAME
Jarella
OCCUPATION
Empress of K'ai
BASE
The city-state of K'ai

HEIGHT (on Earth) 5 ft 6 in
WEIGHT (on Earth) 126 lbs
EYES Green
HAIR Blond

FIRST APPEARANCE
The Incredible Hulk #140
(May 1971)

POWERS
Jarella was an excellent swordswoman and formidable hand-to-hand combatant; a brilliant military leader and a wise and compassionate ruler of her people.

JARELLA

A creature called PSYKLOP subjected the HULK to a ray that caused him to shrink until he was shunted into an alternate dimension called a "microverse." The Hulk found himself outside the city of K'ai on an unnamed planet, whose humanoid inhabitants had green skin like his own. After defeating huge beasts called warthos, the Hulk was hailed as a hero by the people of K'ai. Its warrior queen, Jarella, chose the Hulk to become her husband and king of the city-state. K'ai's Pantheon of Sorcerers cast a spell that enabled the personality and intellect of Dr. Bruce Banner to dominate the superhuman form of his alter ego, the Hulk. Believing he would never return to Earth, Banner came to love Jarella. However, the day before their wedding, Psyklop returned the Hulk to Earth, where the spell no longer had effect.

Jarella visited Banner on Earth, and the Hulk twice went back to K'ai, before returning to Earth with Jarella. The Hulk later battled a robot, the Crypto-Man, causing a wall to collapse. Saving a child from the toppling wall, Jarella was crushed to death by it. She was temporarily returned from the dead during the Chaos War.

JARVIS, EDWIN

FACTFILE
REAL NAME
Edwin Jarvis
OCCUPATION
Butler
BASE
Stark Tower, New York City

HEIGHT 5 ft 11 in
WEIGHT 160 lbs
EYES Blue
HAIR Black

FIRST APPEARANCE
Tales of Suspense #59
(November 1964)

POWERS
Former boxing champion of the Royal Air Force. Resourceful under pressure, courageous, and loyal; an excellent, manager, administrator, and organizer. World's leading authority on cleaning otherworldly stains from clothing, rugs, and fabrics.

JARVIS, EDWIN

Jarvis keeps track of all the Avengers' expenditures.

Edwin Jarvis is a war hero and a former pilot in Britain's Royal Air Force. After retiring to the US, he became the butler of Howard and Maria Stark and continued to work for their son Tony (*see* IRON MAN) after their deaths. When Stark gave his mansion to the AVENGERS, he asked Jarvis to stay helping the team. Jarvis served the team loyally until ULTRON brainwashed him into becoming the CRIMSON COWL and allowing the second version of the MASTERS OF EVIL to enter Avengers Mansion and capture the team. After recovering, Jarvis returned to his duties.

When the SCARLET WITCH, in a fit of madness, destroyed both the Avengers and the mansion, Jarvis followed the new team to its headquarters in Stark Tower. During the SECRET INVASION, the Avengers learned that a SKRULL had replaced Jarvis and kidnapped Luke CAGE and Jessica JONES' infant daughter. Cage rescued the baby just before BULLSEYE shot the imposter. After his own rescue, Jarvis worked with Hank PYM's Avengers. When Nadia Van Dyne (*see* WASP) came to America to claim her legacy, Jarvis helped her to acclimatize. She created an assistant called JARVIS to help him as he again provided assistance to a new team of Avengers.

JESTER

FIRST APPEARANCE *Daredevil* #42 (July 1968)
REAL NAME Jonathan Powers
OCCUPATION Former actor; criminal **BASE** New York City
HEIGHT 6 ft 2 in **WEIGHT** 190 lbs **EYES** Blue **HAIR** Brown
SPECIAL POWERS/ABILITIES No superpowers; above-average athlete, skilled in gymnastics, swordsmanship, and unarmed combat; uses toys converted into deadly weapons or tools.

Struggling actor Jonathan Powers studied fencing, gymnastics, and bodybuilding, hoping to win additional roles, but all he landed was a job as a comic foil on a children's TV show. Calling himself the Jester, Powers went on a crime spree in New York, using deadly toys and gimmicks that the Tinkerer made for him. Daredevil stopped him several times. When Powers temporarily retired, Doctor Doom outfitted a second Jester (Jody Putt), who formed the Assembly of Evil to take on the Avengers. While part of the Thunderbolts army, Putt attacked Spider-Man, but the Punisher shot him dead.

JOCASTA

FIRST APPEARANCE *Avengers* #162 (August 1977)
REAL NAME Jocasta
OCCUPATION N/A **BASE** Mobile
HEIGHT 5 ft 9 in **WEIGHT** 750 lbs **EYES** Red **HAIR** None
SPECIAL POWERS/ABILITIES Robot with ability to process information; superhuman strength, durability, and senses of sight and hearing; projects energy blasts from eyes and hands.

The evil robot Ultron created Jocasta to be his mate, basing her personality on that of the Wasp, who was the wife of Ultron's creator, Henry Pym. Ultron programmed Jocasta to serve him, but she turned against him and aided the Avengers instead. Later, Jocasta's A.I. entered the main computer in the mansion of Tony Stark (Iron Man), and she became his personal ally. Jocasta returned in a new robot body and joined Pym's team of Avengers and his Avengers Academy. She later got a job at Stark Unlimited as a robotic ethicist and also started a troubled relationship with Machine Man.

JOHNSON, DAISY

FIRST APPEARANCE *Secret War* #1 (August 2004)
REAL NAME Daisy Johnson **OCCUPATION** Agent of SHIELD
BASE SHIELD Helicarrier, mobile
HEIGHT 5 ft 4 in **WEIGHT** 115 lbs **EYES** Blue **HAIR** Black
SPECIAL POWERS/ABILITIES A trained agent of SHIELD, Daisy also has the power to generate seismic waves in people and objects.

Mister Hyde's illegitimate daughter, Daisy, was given up by her mother and raised as Cory Sutter by adoptive parents. Her powers manifested when she was a teenager and she joined SHIELD to be trained in the use of them. She took the code name Quake and became director of SHIELD when it was rebooted after Dark Reign. She later lost this position and worked underground with Nick Fury. During Hydra's takeover of the USA, Daisy led a new Secret Warriors team, helping to free Inhumans from Hydra camps.

JINADU, KYLE

FIRST APPEARANCE *Uncanny X-Men* #508 (June 2009)
REAL NAME Kyle Jinadu-Beaubier
OCCUPATION Business manager
BASE New York City; Toronto **HEIGHT** 6 ft 1 in
WEIGHT 195 lbs **EYES** Brown **HAIR** Black
SPECIAL POWERS/ABILITIES None

Kyle had been a friend of Canadian Super Hero Aurora for years when she asked him to manage her brother's business, Extreme Northstar Snowsports. He accepted and got to work closely with and eventually date her brother, Northstar. Their relationship continued to grow stronger, even when Northstar moved out to the island of Utopia as a show of support for his fellow mutants. Kyle was kidnapped by the Marauders and, when he was rescued, Northstar proposed. They married in a lavish ceremony.

JOHN THE SKRULL

FIRST APPEARANCE *Wisdom* #1 (November 2006)
REAL NAME Unknown **OCCUPATION** Adventurer
BASE Massachusetts Academy **HEIGHT** Varies
WEIGHT Varies **EYES** Usually brown **HAIR** Usually brown
SPECIAL POWERS/ABILITIES Shapeshifting and flight.

In 1963, the Skrull empire sent four Skrulls to Earth to impersonate The Beatles and use their worldwide popularity to help launch an invasion. The Skrull Beatles decided to stay human and abandon the empire's plans. Decades later, John joined MI-13, the British secret service charged with investigating paranormal creatures and events. With the start of the Secret Invasion, the Skrulls went after all "traitors" and killed every Skrull Beatle except for John. He joined Captain Britain, Peter Wisdom, and Spitfire to stop the Skrulls and was executed by a Skrull while trying to prevent an invasion of Avalon.

JONES, GABE

FIRST APPEARANCE *Sgt. Fury and his Howling Commandos* #1 (May 1963) **REAL NAME** Gabriel Jones
OCCUPATION SHIELD agent **BASE** New York City
HEIGHT 6 ft 2 in **WEIGHT** 225 lbs **EYES** Brown **HAIR** White
SPECIAL POWERS/ABILITIES Formidable hand-to-hand combatant when younger; excellent marksman and combat tactician; expert jazz trumpeter.

Like so many other members of World War II heroes the Howling Commandos, Gabe Jones continued to fight alongside his commander, Nick Fury, for most of his life. Reuniting with the rest of the military strike squad during the Korean and Vietnam wars, Gabe became a key aide to Fury when he was made director of SHIELD. Gabe infiltrated and helped to bring down the insidious organization known as the Secret Empire. When Norman Osborn (*see* Green Goblin) dismantled SHIELD, Gabe and Dum Dum Dugan started a new initiative called the Howling Commandos Private Military Company. He was killed by the assassin Gorgon, buying time for his allies to escape from the forces of Hydra.

JONES, JESSICA

FACTFILE
REAL NAME
Jessica Jones
OCCUPATION
Private investigator
BASE
New York City

HEIGHT
5 ft 4 in
WEIGHT 120 lbs
EYES Brown
HAIR Brown

FIRST APPEARANCE
Alias #1
(November 2001)

POWERS
Jessica has superhuman strength, durability, and can fly.

While a teenager attending high school in Queens with Peter Parker (SPIDER-MAN), Jessica Jones was in a car accident in which she was doused with chemicals and put into a coma. She lost her family but acquired superpowers. With hair dyed pink and using the code name Jewel, she battled criminals until the PURPLE MAN enslaved her mind. After losing a fight with the AVENGERS, Jessica fell into another coma until Jean GREY revived her, establishing mental defenses for her against further mind control. Jessica later opened a detective agency specializing in cases involving superpowered beings, and she worked as a reporter for *The Pulse,* a supplement to the *Daily Bugle.* During this time, she became the Knightress. Jessica dated and then married Luke CAGE, with whom she had a baby girl, Danielle. She fled to Canada during the CIVIL WAR but returned to rejoin the Avengers when it was over. As the SECRET INVASION ended, a SKRULL posing as Edwin JARVIS kidnapped Danielle, but Norman Osborn (*see* GREEN GOBLIN) helped Luke rescue her. She joined Luke Cage in the DEFENDERS and later faced the Purple Man one last time before he was killed.

JONES, MARLO

FIRST APPEARANCE *Incredible Hulk* #347 (September 1998)
REAL NAME Marlo Chandler-Jones
OCCUPATION Talk show host, comic shop owner
BASE Las Vegas, Los Angeles
HEIGHT 5 ft 8 in **WEIGHT** 135 lbs **EYES** Green **HAIR** Red
SPECIAL POWERS/ABILITIES In excellent physical shape. At one point she acquired the ability to see the spirits of dead people.

Marlo Chandler dated the HULK when he was in his gray Joe Fixit personality, but she broke it off after witnessing the Hulk kill an enemy. Marlo later met the Hulk's friend Rick JONES when he was on a book tour promoting his memoirs. They married and hosted a television talk show called *Keeping Up With the Joneses,* then opened a comic-book shop in Los Angeles. During this time, Marlo was temporarily possessed by DEATH. The LEADER later turned her into a new version of the Harpy. During the Chaos War, her connection with Death became important, and she used it to call for help from dead friends.

JONES, RICK

FACTFILE
REAL NAME
Richard Jones
OCCUPATION
Adventurer
BASE
Various

HEIGHT 5 ft 9 in
WEIGHT 165 lbs
EYES Brown
HAIR Brown

FIRST APPEARANCE
Incredible Hulk #1
(May 1962)

POWERS
Rick Jones possesses a courageous spirit and the expert fighting skills of one trained by Captain America.

As a teenager, Rick Jones snuck onto a military test site on a dare. Bruce Banner rescued him but was caught in the blast, which caused him to transform into the HULK whenever angered. Feeling responsible, Rick helped Banner conceal his secret from the military. When the AVENGERS formed to deal with the Hulk, Rick became an honorary member. Trained by CAPTAIN AMERICA, Rick served as his partner for a time, and subsequently worked in concert with both CAPTAIN MAR-VELL—with whom he helped end the KREE-SKRULL War—and with his son Genis-Vell (*see* CAPTAIN MARVEL). Rick stood by the Hulk during WORLD WAR HULK but was impaled by Miek, the traitorous member of the Hulk's WARBOUND. He survived, and the INTELLIGENCIA made him into A-Bomb, a blue-skinned, armored creature resembling the ABOMINATION. The Hulk, in his Doc Green persona, took his power away leaving him human. Jones then became the Whisperer, a hacker opposed to HYDRA's US takeover. He was captured and shot by a Hydra firing squad. Since reality was then remade by KOBIK, he is possibly now alive and well.

Although usually blue, as A-Bomb, Rick could change the color of his scales to camouflage himself.

JOSEPH

FIRST APPEARANCE *Uncanny X-Men* #327 (December 1995)
REAL NAME Unknown **OCCUPATION** Adventurer
BASE Xavier Institute, New York State
HEIGHT 6 ft 2 in **WEIGHT** 190 lbs
EYES Blue-gray **HAIR** White
SPECIAL POWERS/ABILITIES As Magneto's clone Joseph has the same power as Magneto—the ability to control magnetism and magnetic forces—frequently to devastating effect.

Astra of the BROTHERHOOD OF EVIL MUTANTS created a clone of MAGNETO, hoping that it would kill the original. The clone and Magneto clashed in Guatemala and Magneto knocked the clone unconscious. When he came to, he had lost his memory. Sister Maria de la Joya nursed the clone back to health and named him Joseph. She sent him to seek help from the X-MEN, but they assumed he was a young Magneto with amnesia. Nevertheless, they let him join the team. Joseph once sacrificed his life to save the world from Magneto. He was revived, with Magneto's early memories intact, to lead a new Brotherhood of Mutants team.

JUBILEE

Born to wealthy Chinese immigrants, Jubilee was raised in Beverly Hills and became a top-class gymnast. After her parents lost their fortune and then their lives, Jubilee was left orphaned.

Embittered, Jubilee ran away, living at the Hollywood Mall, where her mutant powers became manifest. Having evaded mall security with the help of various X-MEN, Jubilee followed them through a teleportal to their Australian base, remaining hidden there until it was abandoned. She left the base with WOLVERINE and they traveled through Asia: he found her directness, sarcasm, and honesty refreshing; she came to regard him as a surrogate father. Jubilee has been a member of the X-Men, GENERATION-X, and X-CORPS. She lost her powers but was then turned into a vampire by XARUS. She subdued her bloodsucking instincts and adopted Shogo, an orphaned baby. Quentin QUIRE saved her life when she was exposed to sunlight, using his portion of the Phoenix Force to cure her vampirism and give her back her mutant powers.

FACTFILE
REAL NAME
Jubilation Lee
OCCUPATION
X-Corporation employee
BASE
Mobile

HEIGHT 5 ft 5 in
WEIGHT 105 lbs
EYES Blue
HAIR Black

FIRST APPEARANCE
Uncanny X-Men #244
(May 1989)

JUBILEE

POWERS
Generates and projects energy globules—"fireworks"—from her fingers; Jubilee is also able to control, direct, and reabsorb these.

JUGGERNAUT

After the death of her husband, nuclear researcher Brian Xavier, Sharon Xavier married his colleague, Dr. Kurt Marko. Dr. Marko often beat his son Cain, who in turn bullied his new stepbrother, Charles Xavier (*see* PROFESSOR X). Cain Marko joined the army, but deserted while in Korea. In a cave he found a large ruby empowered by the demonic entity Cyttorak, which magically transformed Cain into a "human juggernaut," an unstoppable super-being. Enemy bombs then caused the cave to collapse, burying him alive.

Years later, Marko resurfaced as the Juggernaut, invading Xavier's mansion and trying to kill him. The Juggernaut had several battles with the X-MEN, often teaming up with BLACK TOM. For a while, the Juggernaut lost much of his power and made peace with Xavier. He even fell out with Tom and joined the X-Men and the third incarnation of EXCALIBUR. During WORLD WAR HULK, however, he embraced his destructive nature—alienating himself from Xavier once more—and his full power returned. During FEAR ITSELF, while working with Luke CAGE'S THUNDERBOLTS, Juggernaut became Kuurth, Breaker of Stone. He briefly lost his powers before Cyttorak transformed him into the Juggernaut once again.

FACTFILE
REAL NAME
Cain Marko
OCCUPATION
Former soldier, later mercenary, professional criminal, adventurer
BASE
Mobile

HEIGHT 6 ft 10 in
WEIGHT 900 lbs
EYES Blue
HAIR Red

FIRST APPEARANCE
X-Men #12
(July 1965)

JUGGERNAUT

POWERS
Virtually invulnerable, with superhuman strength and an impenetrable force-field. His helmet protects him from psychic attack.

When Juggernaut regained his powers and became Cyttorak's champion once more, he had to fight Thor.

JUSTICE

FIRST APPEARANCE *Giant-Size Defenders* #5 (July 1975)
REAL NAME Vance Astrovik
OCCUPATION Adventurer **BASE** New Salem, Colorado
HEIGHT 5 ft 10 in **WEIGHT** 180 lbs **EYES** Hazel **HAIR** Brown
SPECIAL POWERS/ABILITIES His telekinesis allows him to lift objects and fly, though overuse gives him nosebleeds.

Vance Astrovik's mutant powers were activated prematurely when he met his future self, MAJOR VICTORY of the GUARDIANS OF THE GALAXY, thus creating an alternate timeline. Vance spent time in prison for killing his abusive father before joining the AVENGERS. He felt inadequate serving amongst his fellow heroes. Now known as Justice, he sided with CAPTAIN AMERICA in the first CIVIL WAR. His suspicion of the Initiative led him to form the Counter-Force, later retitled the NEW WARRIORS. Afterward he became a teacher at Henry PYM's Avengers Academy.

KALE, JENNIFER

FIRST APPEARANCE *Adventures Into Fear* #11 (December 1972)
REAL NAME Jennifer Kale
OCCUPATION Sorceress **BASE** Citrusville, Florida
HEIGHT 5 ft 6 in **WEIGHT** 122 lbs **EYES** Blue **HAIR** Blonde
SPECIAL POWERS/ABILITIES Jennifer Kale is a highly knowledgeable sorceress with developing skill in manipulating various magical forces.

Jennifer is the granddaughter of Joshua Kale, a leader of the Cult of Zhered-Na. Jennifer and MAN-THING were magically transported to another dimension, where they met the wizard Dakimh, last surviving pupil of Zhered-Na. As Dakimh's apprentice, Jennifer became a sorceress. An ally of Man-Thing and HOWARD THE DUCK, she is a founder of the Legion of Night and teamed with TOPAZ and Satana as the Three Witches. She was killed by Victoria HAND, but resurrected herself with dark magic, though without skin over the right side of her face. Maria HILL then hired her to work with ELEKTRA against the HAND.

KALUU

FIRST APPEARANCE *Strange Tales* #147 (August 1966)
REAL NAME Kaluu
OCCUPATION Sorcerer **BASE** Not known
HEIGHT 6 ft 5 in **WEIGHT** 190 lbs **EYES** Yellow **HAIR** Black
SPECIAL POWERS/ABILITIES Arguably most powerful living black magician; has knowledge of vast number of spells including all those contained in Book of the Vishanti.

Born 500 years ago in Tibet, Kaluu trained with a youth who would become the ANCIENT ONE. Corrupted by the vampire VARNAE, Kaluu turned to black magic. Over the centuries he threatened Earth many times, but redeemed himself by helping DOCTOR STRANGE to destroy a horde of demons. Unable to eradicate the greatest of these demons, Shuma-Gorath, Kaluu was left behind by Strange, who finished the job. Kaluu later helped Strange purge himself of the side-effects of using black magic. He has since assisted Ronin (*see* BLADE) and joined the Mighty AVENGERS.

KAINE

FACTFILE
REAL NAME
Kaine Parker
OCCUPATION
Adventurer; former assassin
BASE
Various

HEIGHT 6 ft 4 ins
WEIGHT 250 lbs
EYES Brown
HAIR Brown

FIRST APPEARANCE
Web Of Spider-Man #118
(November 1994)

POWERS
Kaine possesses the strength, speed, and agility of Spider-Man, as well as the ability to burn the "mark of Kaine" onto the skin of his victims. He also receives prophetic visions from his imperfect spider-sense. As the Scarlet Spider, he has organic webbing, can see in the dark, communicate with spiders, and has a retractable stinger inside each wrist, but has lost his spider-sense.

The first, flawed clone of Peter Parker created by the JACKAL, Kaine developed cellular degeneration and survived only by wearing a special life-support suit. His condition left him badly scarred, and caused his spider-powers to become twisted and magnified. Abandoned by his creator, and knowing himself to be merely a mockery of true life, he wandered the world taking on work as an assassin to survive.

Kaine believed the Ben Reilly clone of Peter Parker was the true Spider-Man and tormented Reilly, framing him for a series of murders. Eventually, the Jackal drew Kaine back into Peter's life, and he finally learned the truth. Kaine later traded places with Peter when the KRAVEN family was after him, and he was sacrificed to bring Kraven back from the dead. The Jackal revived Kaine as the new TARANTULA, but after taking the Spider-Island cure, Kaine was healed to be a stable, perfect clone with new spider powers. He later took the identity of the SCARLET SPIDER, moved to Houston, Texas, and tried to live up to Reilly's heroic example. During the Spider-Verse saga, Kaine killed the leader of the Inheritors to stop them from feeding on the Spider heroes of the Multiverse. Kaine was killed in the process, but later came back to life. Unfortunately his cellular degradation returned, but he found a cure before it killed him. When he subsequently discovered the villainous Jackal was in fact Ben Reilly, Kaine hunted him down, but ended up cooperating with him to save the life of a child. This mission failed, however, due to the meddling of MEPHISTO.

KANG

Time-traveling conqueror

Born in an alternate timeline in 3000 AD, Nathaniel Richards (a descendant of MR. FANTASTIC's father, who bore the same name) discovered time-travel technology that enabled him to journey virtually anywhere he liked in the timestream.

Despite having the entirety of time and space at his disposal, the only thing for which Kang truly cared was the beautiful princess Ravonna. His obsession with her inspired several of his early schemes.

FACTFILE

REAL NAME
Nathaniel Richards

OCCUPATION
Conqueror

BASE
Mobile

HEIGHT 6 ft 3 in
WEIGHT 230 lbs
EYES Brown
HAIR Brown

FIRST APPEARANCE
Avengers #8 (September 1964)

KANG

POWERS
Master of time travel; suit provides enhanced strength, force-field projection, and energy projection; typically armed with futuristic weaponry.

TIME TRAVELER

Richards' first stop was ancient Egypt, where he seized power and ruled for a decade as Pharaoh Rama-Tut until forced to flee after a fight with the FANTASTIC FOUR. Arriving in the 40th century, he briefly became the SCARLET CENTURION before settling on the name Kang the Conqueror. Kang found the century in turmoil and easy to subjugate.

Looking for new challenges, Kang traveled to 1901 and established the city of Timely, Wisconsin, in his guise as Victor Timely. He assembled an elite warrior class, the Anachronauts, from all eras of history before returning to the 40th century. There he fell in love with Princess RAVONNA. After her death during a revolt by Kang's troops, he tried and failed to become the consort of the Celestial Madonna (MANTIS), killing the original SWORDSMAN in the process. A future version of Kang, calling himself IMMORTUS, tried to thwart his younger self's aggressive schemes, but Kang would not be contained, and he assembled the original LEGION OF THE UNLIVING.

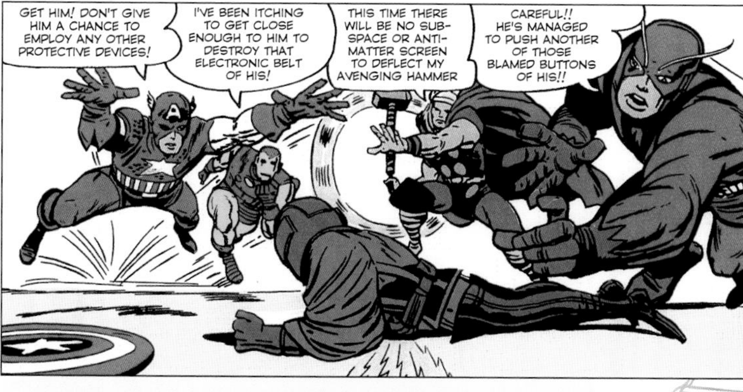

The Avengers faced Kang shortly after the team's founding, and have clashed with him countless times since. During the "Destiny War," Kang handpicked a group of Avengers from across the timestream to aid in his fight against Immortus.

KANG'S GANG

Kang gathered the alternate versions of himself from branching timestreams and formed the Council of Kangs. They killed the duplicates deemed unworthy until only the prime Kang remained. Kang joined with Libra, the SUPREME INTELLIGENCE, and the AVENGERS to prevent Immortus and the TIME KEEPERS from wiping out a multitude of alternate realities. During the battle, Kang and Immortus' histories diverged.

The YOUNG AVENGER called Iron Lad turned out to be an adolescent Kang, and he fought to separate himself from his future self. After the destruction of Attilan, BLACK BOLT gave his son Ahura to Kang to raise, hoping this would save Ahura from the impending end of the Multiverse. This later sparked a series of battles across time between Kang and the INHUMANS. When VISION abducted an infant Kang in an attempt to eliminate him, Kang retaliated by trying to wipe out all of the Avengers as babies. WASP corrected things by returning the baby Kang to where he belonged. Some time later Kang kidnapped Adam WARLOCK to prevent the Infinity Gems from being assembled.

ESSENTIAL STORYLINES

- ***Avengers Vol. 1 #8***
In his first appearance, Kang battles Earth's mightiest heroes and proves why he is a foe for the ages.
- ***Avengers Vol. 1 #129–135, Giant Sized Avengers #2–4***
In the "Celestial Madonna" story arc, Kang kidnaps Mantis, the Scarlet Witch, and Agatha Harkness to determine which will give birth to a being of great power.

KARKAS

FIRST APPEARANCE *The Eternals* #8 (January 1977)
REAL NAME Karkas
OCCUPATION Scholar **BASE** Olympia
HEIGHT 8 ft 3in **WEIGHT** 1,260 lbs **EYES** Black **HAIR** None
SPECIAL POWERS/ABILITIES Possesses superhuman strength. His thick hide, resembling an elephant's, gives him superhuman resistance to injury.

The Deviants are an evolutionary offshoot of humanity with an unstable genetic code. Those whose genetic makeup varies beyond standards set by the Deviant priesthood are labeled mutates. The Deviant mutate Karkas was raised to be a gladiator, but at heart he was a philosopher. He was defeated in the arena by another mutate, Ransak the Reject. Then Karkas asked Thena, a visiting Eternal, to grant sanctuary to himself and the Reject. She transported them to Olympia, home of the Eternals. Ever since then Karkas has been a staunch ally of the Eternals.

KARNAK

FIRST APPEARANCE *Fantastic Four* #45 (December 1965)
REAL NAME Unrevealed **OCCUPATION** Priest/philosopher
BASE Attilan, Blue Area, the moon
HEIGHT 5 ft 7 in **WEIGHT** 150 lbs **EYES** Blue **HAIR** Black
SPECIAL POWERS/ABILITIES Superhuman strength and ability to control his heartbeat and other autonomic body functions. Has the extrasensory ability to perceive weakness in objects and people.

A member of the royal family of the Inhumans, Karnak is the second son of the Inhuman priest Mander. Mander and his wife Azur had sent their first son, Triton, into the Terrigen Mist which produced genetic mutations. They decided not to expose Karnak to the mist, instead sending him to his father's religious seminary in the Tower of Wisdom. There, he trained in physical and mental disciplines, martial arts, and religious study until the age of 18. Karnak joined Daisy Johnson's Secret Warriors team to fight Hydra during the latter's takeover of the USA.

KELLY, SENATOR ROBERT

FIRST APPEARANCE *X-Men* #135 (September 1980)
REAL NAME Senator Robert Kelly
OCCUPATION Politician **BASE** Washington, D.C.
HEIGHT 5 ft 10 in **WEIGHT** 175 lbs **EYES** Brown
HAIR Brown (graying temples)
SPECIAL POWERS/ABILITIES Charismatic individual with rabble-rousing public speaking skills.

As senator for Massachusetts, Robert Kelly proposed strong anti-mutant legislation. Repeated assassination attempts and his wife's death hardened his stance until, while standing for president on an anti-mutant platform, he was saved from another attempt on his life by the sacrifice of Pyro. Kelly then changed his stance dramatically, only to be killed by a non-mutant who accused him of betraying humanity. In one alternate future, the assassination of Senator Kelly led to the death or imprisonment of all mutants.

KARMA

FIRST APPEARANCE *Marvel Team-up* #100 (December 1980)
REAL NAME Xi'an Coy Manh
OCCUPATION Adventurer **BASE** Mobile
HEIGHT 5 ft 4 in **WEIGHT** 90 lbs **EYES** Brown **HAIR** Black
SPECIAL POWERS/ABILITIES Has the ability to psionically possess other people's minds, controlling their actions and turning them into virtual puppets.

Psionically powered Xi'an absorbed her brother Tran's psyche when he tried to force her to work for their criminal uncle. She attended Professor X's School for Gifted Youngsters, and was the first member of the New Mutants. She rescued her siblings from her uncle and became the Xavier Institute's librarian. She later lost her leg in a battle with mutant-hating Cameron Hodge. Becoming a billionaire after her brother's death, she used her newfound wealth to finance the New Mutants.

KA-ZAR

FIRST APPEARANCE *Uncanny X-Men* #10 (March 1965)
REAL NAME Lord Kevin Plunder
OCCUPATION Hunter, trapper, lord of the Savage Land
BASE The Savage Land
HEIGHT 6 ft 2 in **WEIGHT** 215 lbs **EYES** Blue **HAIR** Blond
SPECIAL POWERS/ABILITIES Expert physical combatant, hunter and forager.

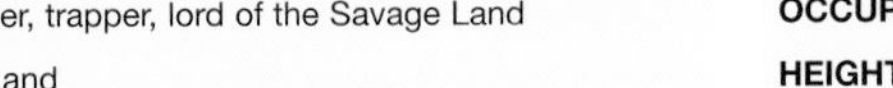

Son of British nobleman Lord Robert Plunder (the discoverer of Antarctic Vibranium), Ka-Zar grew up in the Antarctic "Savage Land" following the murder of his father at the hands of Man-Apes. Raised by the intelligent sabertoothed tiger Zabu, Ka-Zar learned to survive against dinosaurs and Man-Apes. His enemies have included his brother Parnival, also known as the Plunderer, and the Savage Land Mutates. Ka-Zar eventually married Shanna the She-Devil, and the two are currently raising a son, Matthew.

KILLER SHRIKE

FIRST APPEARANCE *The Rampaging Hulk* #1 (January 1977)
REAL NAME Simon Maddicks
OCCUPATION Criminal **BASE** Mobile
HEIGHT 6 ft 5 in **WEIGHT** 250 lbs **EYES** Brown **HAIR** Brown
SPECIAL POWERS/ABILITIES Possesses enhanced strength; implanted anti-gravity generator in spine enables flight; bracelets with titanium talons and power-blasters fire electrical blasts.

The Brand Corporation, a Roxxon Oil subsidiary, boosted mercenary Simon Maddicks' strength to superhuman levels. Roxxon assigned him, as Killer Shrike, to infiltrate the Conspiracy cabal. This led to his defeat by Ulysses Bloodstone. Killer Shrike later became a free agent and has battled the Super Heroes Spider-Man, Moon Knight, and the She-Hulk. He later sold the identity to Roderick Kingsley (Hobgoblin) who sold it on to another, unnamed, villain who continued in the role.

KILLMONGER

FIRST APPEARANCE *Jungle Action* #6 (September 1973)
REAL NAME Erik Killmonger (originally N'Jadaka)
OCCUPATION Tribal leader **BASE** Wakanda
HEIGHT 6 ft 6 in **WEIGHT** 225 lbs **EYES** Brown **HAIR** Black
SPECIAL POWERS/ABILITIES Superhuman strength, agility, speed, and acute senses that give him an advantage over his foes. Is highly skilled in hand-to-hand combat and has high intellect.

As a child, N'Jadaka escaped from the villain Ulysses KLAW but found himself trapped outside of Wakanda. Raised in the US, N'Jadaka went by the name of Erik Killmonger. He petitioned Wakanda's ruler, T'Challa, the BLACK PANTHER, and was allowed to return to his homeland. However, he blamed T'Challa, and T'Challa's father, T'Chaka, for his exile and consequently tried to usurp power. He was killed in battle but later raised from the dead by the MANDARIN. He once briefly gained the throne of Wakanda but soon lost it. A ruthless fighter and expert tactician, Erik remains one of T'Challa's deadliest enemies.

KING, HANNIBAL

FIRST APPEARANCE *Tomb of Dracula* #25 (October 1974)
REAL NAME Hannibal King
OCCUPATION Private Investigator **BASE** Boston, Massachusetts
HEIGHT 6 ft 2 in **WEIGHT** 196 lbs **EYES** Blue **HAIR** Black
SPECIAL POWERS/ABILITIES Has all of the abilities typical of a vampire, but prefers not to use them owing to his self-loathing about his condition.

A low-rent private investigator, Hannibal King was slain by the vampire Deacon Frost and three days later rose from the dead, himself a vampire. King's force of will was so strong that he refrained from feasting on human blood. Later, while fighting DRACULA, he met the vampire hunter BLADE. The two men tracked Frost to his lair and put an end to him.

Along with Frank DRAKE, King and Blade formed the Nightstalkers to battle supernatural evil. At one point, King turned a woman he loved into a vampire to save her from a painful death. King later fought Blade over a means of restoring souls to vampires. Blade then gave him a potion to cure his bloodlust.

KNIGHT, MISTY

FIRST APPEARANCE *Marvel Team-Up* #1 (March 1972, as bystander); *Marvel Premiere* #20 (January 1975, identified)
REAL NAME Misty Knight **OCCUPATION** Private investigator
BASE Nightwing Restorations, New York City
HEIGHT 5 ft 9 in **WEIGHT** 136 lbs **EYES** Brown **HAIR** Black
SPECIAL POWERS/ABILITIES A trained fighter with a bionic right arm with superhuman strength.

Police officer Misty Knight lost her right arm to a terrorist's bomb, but Stark International fitted her with a bionic replacement. Misty went into business as a private investigator with samurai Colleen WING. As the Daughters of the Dragon, the two shared many adventures, often with Luke CAGE and Misty's lover, IRON FIST. Misty later started Heroes for Hire with Colleen, BLACK CAT, Humbug, Orka, PALADIN, SHANG-CHI, and the new TARANTULA.

The team folded after WORLD WAR HULK, and Colleen and Misty parted ways. She is now an agent for the Aberrant Crime Division.

KILLRAVEN

FIRST APPEARANCE *Amazing Adventures* #18 (May 1973)
REAL NAME Jonathan Raven
OCCUPATION Freedom fighter **BASE** Mobile
HEIGHT 6 ft 1 in **WEIGHT** 185 lbs **EYES** Blue **HAIR** Red
SPECIAL POWERS/ABILITIES An expert combatant and swordsman who can take mental control of a Martian's body. A natural leader who has keen survival instincts suited for a post-apocalyptic world.

On Earth-691, invaders from Mars conquered Earth in the year 2001 and forced many survivors to battle in gladiatorial pits, where Jonathan Raven first won fame as "Killraven." The scientist Keeper Whitman genetically modified Killraven, giving him the ability to seize mental control of the aliens. Killraven led a team of Freemen to hunt for his lost brother Deathraven, who they discovered to be a traitor. Another Killraven fought aliens on Earth-2120, and on the standard Earth-616, trans-dimensional aliens attacked a young Jonathan Raven. Peter WISDOM stopped the aliens but had to kill Jonathan's mother to do it.

KLAW

FIRST APPEARANCE *Fantastic Four* #53 (August 1966)
REAL NAME Ulysses Klaw
OCCUPATION Scientist, professional criminal **BASE** Mobile
HEIGHT 5 ft 11 in **WEIGHT** 175 lbs **EYES** Red **HAIR** None
SPECIAL POWERS/ABILITIES Can turn sound waves into matter and reshape his body, which is made of sound waves. Able to project deafening sounds and fire concussive blasts of sound waves.

Physicist Ulysses Klaw was working on a device to turn sound into physical objects and needed Vibranium, an element found only in the African nation of Wakanda. He traveled to the country and tried to seize the element from the Cult of the BLACK PANTHER, but in the battle, Klaw's right hand was destroyed by his own sonic blaster. He made a prosthetic device that could turn sound into matter, to replace his hand. He later replaced his entire body with solid sound.

KNULL

FIRST APPEARANCE *Venom* #3 (August 2018)
REAL NAME Knull
OCCUPATION Conquerer; deity **BASE** Klyntar
HEIGHT Varies **WEIGHT** Varies **EYES** Black with red spiral-shaped pupils **HAIR** White
SPECIAL POWERS/ABILITIES Divine being, with almighty strength, healing powers, and immortality, with the ability to shapeshift and create and control symbiotes.

An evil entity pre-dating the universe, Knull is the creator of symbiotes such as VENOM. He abhors light and killed a CELESTIAL when they first appeared. Sent into the darkness, he forged a blade—the first symbiote—and used it to wage war. Struck down, and his sword taken by GORR the God Butcher, he found he could command an army of symbiotes. When THOR attacked, the link with his symbiotes was broken. They rebelled and made an artificial planet named Klyntar, meaning "cage," to be his prison. Actions by SHIELD meant Knull was nearly released again—only to be stopped by VENOM.

KINGPIN

Heavyweight criminal mastermind

KINGPIN

FACTFILE

REAL NAME
Wilson Grant Fisk

OCCUPATION
Criminal mastermind

BASE
New York City

HEIGHT 6 ft 7 in
WEIGHT 450 lbs
EYES Blue
HAIR None

FIRST APPEARANCE
The Amazing Spider-Man #50 (July 1967)

POWERS
Brilliant criminal mind and superb fighting skills; his body, though huge and heavy, is composed of almost solid muscle.

When Fisk became mayor of New York City, he invited Matt Murdock to be his deputy mayor. Though Matt accepted, both parties had hidden motives.

Wilson Fisk, the Kingpin, is the most formidable figure in organized crime, and a perennial enemy of Super Heroes Spider-Man, the Punisher, and, most frequently, Daredevil. The Kingpin's operations are global and the assassins that have done his dirty work are legion, including such names as Bullseye, Elektra, and Typhoid Mary.

ESSENTIAL STORYLINES

- ***Daredevil Vol. 1 #227–233***
In the acclaimed "Born Again" story arc, the Kingpin's malicious schemes bring Daredevil to the edge of a mental breakdown.
- ***Daredevil Vol. 2 #46–50***
In a shocking turn of events, Daredevil defeats the Kingpin and takes over as boss of New York City's notorious Hell's Kitchen.

UNDERWORLD KING

As a youth, Fisk bulked up his body to strike back against the bullies who tormented him. He committed his first murder at the age of 12. At 15, he led a gang of street toughs and came to be called the "Kingpin of Crime." Employed by crimelord Don Rigoletto, he ended up killing Rigoletto and assuming control of his operation. He married Vanessa, a beautiful socialite, and they had a son, Richard. The Kingpin also became the guardian of Maya Lopez (Echo), the daughter of one of his murdered business partners. After decades in power, the Kingpin organized the various New York gangs and challenged the Maggia, triggering a war that Spider-Man helped to end.

POWER STRUGGLES

The Kingpin believed his son Richard had died in a skiing accident, but instead he had become a rival crimelord, the Schemer, and later the Rose. The Kingpin left his empire behind to pursue a new life with Vanessa in Japan, but he returned with a vengeance after Vanessa's apparent death. He rebuilt his empire and persuaded his foster daughter Echo to help him destroy Daredevil. After learning the Kingpin had killed her real father, Echo blinded the Kingpin by shooting him in the face, and his inner circle—including his son Richard—stabbed him and left him for dead. Vanessa nursed her husband back to health and killed Richard for betraying his father.

Imprisoned, the Kingpin continued to scheme from behind bars, exposing Daredevil's secret identity and even ordering the assassination of May Parker. Despite this, Daredevil helped the Kingpin win his trial in exchange for him leaving the country. The Kingpin took control of the Hand following Daredevil's spell as leader and used the organization to rebuild his empire. During Hydra's takeover of America, Fisk helped the heroes protect New York's inhabitants and became Mayor following Hydra's fall. He used his position to try to outlaw heroes and vigilantes, only to be left severely injured when the Hand attacked.

Sabotage by various costumed crimefighters has hobbled the Kingpin's illicit empire.

The Kingpin's son, Richard Fisk, became a rival to his father as the masked Rose.

Sheer muscle mass makes the Kingpin surprisingly strong and tough, allowing him to withstand Spider-Man's powerful blows.

KOBAYASHI, AMIKO

FIRST APPEARANCE *Uncanny X-Men* #181 (May 1984)
REAL NAME Amiko Kobayashi
OCCUPATION Student, thief
BASE Tokyo
HEIGHT 5 ft 2 in **WEIGHT** 100 lbs
EYES Brown **HAIR** Black
SPECIAL POWERS/ABILITIES Amiko is a trained martial artist.

When Amiko's mother was killed by a dragon in Toyko, her dying request to WOLVERINE was that he take care of her daughter. He placed her in the home of his fiancée, Mariko YASHIDA, but when Mariko was killed she wound up in a foster home. He later placed her with his friend YUKIO, under the guardianship of the SILVER SAMURAI.

Amiko learned that her mother was part of the Shosei warriors, and she worked with them to hone her fighting skills. She later started a relationship with Shin Yashida, the new Silver Samurai, joining him on heists.

KOBIK

FIRST APPEARANCE *Avengers Standoff: Welcome to Pleasant Hill* #1 (April 2016)
REAL NAME Kobik **OCCUPATION** None
BASE Formerly Pleasant Hill, Connecticut
HEIGHT Unknown **WEIGHT** Unknown **EYES** Blue **HAIR** White
SPECIAL POWERS/ABILITIES Near omnipotence; able to reshape reality

Kobik is a sentient Cosmic Cube that took on the form of a young girl. After SHIELD used her reality-altering abilities to create a prison for Super Villains called Pleasant Hill, RED SKULL took advantage of her naive, childlike mind, convincing her that HYDRA was a force for good.

Kobik created a new version of history in which Steve Rogers (*see* CAPTAIN AMERICA) had been brainwashed by Hydra since he was a child. She then replaced the real Steve with the new version she had created. After a series of near-disasters as various villains tried to take advantage of her powers, Kobik realized her mistake and restored the original Steve Rogers, who went on to defeat the evil version of himself.

KOMODO

FIRST APPEARANCE *Avengers: The Initiative* #1 (March 2007)
REAL NAME Melati Kusuma **OCCUPATION** Adventurer
BASE Arizona **HEIGHT** Varies **WEIGHT** Varies
EYES Black **HAIR** Black
SPECIAL POWERS/ABILITIES Komodo can shift to a lizard-woman form that grants her superhuman strength, endurance, agility, and reflexes, plus armored skin, sharpened teeth and claws, and a healing factor.

Missing her legs from the knees down, Melati Kusuma pursued a college internship under Dr. Curt Conners (*see* LIZARD). The moment he trusted her with his experimental regeneration formula, she tested it on herself. The formula worked, but turned her into a lizardwoman. Taking the code name Komodo, Melati became a cadet in the inaugural class at Camp Hammond as part of the FIFTY-STATE INITIATIVE, where she met and fell for

HARDBALL, who later betrayed her to lead HYDRA. She stayed with the Initiative through the DARK REIGN and was last seen working for Briggs Chemical LLC, a rival organization to Avengers Academy.

KORG

FIRST APPEARANCE *Journey into Mystery* #1 (August 1962)
REAL NAME Korg
OCCUPATION Gladiator
BASE Earth, formerly Sakaar
HEIGHT 8 ft 1 in **WEIGHT** 2,045 lbs **EYES** Black **HAIR** None
SPECIAL POWERS/ABILITIES Superhuman strength and stamina. Rocky hide gives incredible resistance to damage.

A member of the Kronan race, Korg found himself trapped in the Red King's alien arena on the planet of Sakaar following a failed invasion of Earth. While in the arena, Korg met and befriended HULK, becoming "WARBOUND" with Hulk and several other gladiators. Korg helped

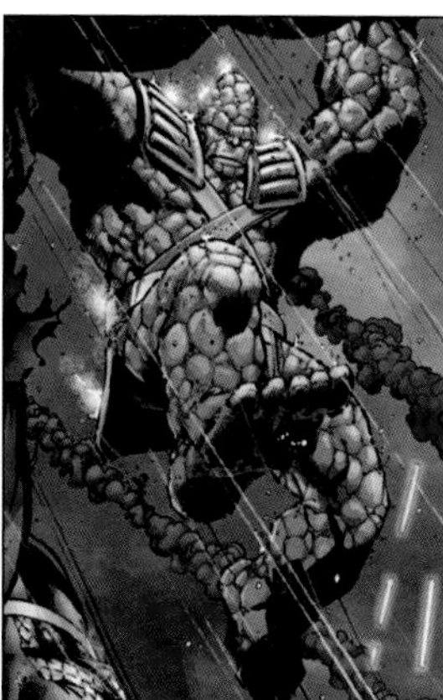

overthrow the Red King and, following Sakaar's destruction, followed the Hulk to Earth and helped him fight those heroes who had betrayed Hulk. He helped Rick JONES fight the ABOMINATION during the Chaos War and was reunited with his lover, Hiroim.

KORVAC

FIRST APPEARANCE *Giant-Size Defenders* #3 (January 1975)
REAL NAME Michael Korvac **OCCUPATION** Computer technician; would-be master of the universe **BASE** Mobile
HEIGHT 6 ft 3 in **WEIGHT** 230 lbs **EYES** Blue **HAIR** Blond
SPECIAL POWERS/ABILITIES Cosmic power on an unimaginable scale. Capable of time travel, astral projection, projecting lethal energy blasts, and of power absorption from any source.

Korvac comes from the same possible 31st-century future as the GUARDIANS OF THE GALAXY. When the Badoon invaded Earth, he quickly offered to help the alien conquerors. They rewarded his loyalty by amputating the lower half of his body and replacing it with a mobile computer module. Realizing the potential of his new form, Korvac began to plot against the Badoon. He also managed to siphon energy from the GRANDMASTER and absorbed the power cosmic from the world-sized starship that belonged to GALACTUS. Now seemingly omnipotent, Korvac traveled to the 20th century with the intention of restructuring the universe in his image. He was killed at the Avengers Academy while trying to forcibly recover his wife.

KRANG

FIRST APPEARANCE *Fantastic Four Annual* #1 (1963)
REAL NAME Krang **OCCUPATION** Warlord
BASE Formerly Atlantis, now mobile in the Atlantic Ocean
HEIGHT 6 ft **WEIGHT** 290 lbs **EYES** Blue **HAIR** Black
SPECIAL POWERS/ABILITIES Like all Atlanteans, Krang has superhuman strength, gills for breathing in water, and other physical adaptations for undersea living.

A member of Atlantis' military, Krang aspired to the throne of NAMOR the Sub-Mariner during his long absence. When Namor returned, he appointed Krang as his warlord, but Krang seized the throne and plotted to conquer the surface world. Namor bested Krang in combat and exiled him from Atlantis. Since then, Krang has continued to scheme against Namor and has allied himself with Namor's enemies ATTUMA and Byrrah. Krang once fell under the sway of the Serpent Crown and joined forces with the second VIPER's Serpent Squad. Krang later joined NIGHTHAWK's version of the DEFENDERS.

KRAVEN

KRAVEN

FACTFILE

REAL NAME
Sergei Kravinoff

OCCUPATION
Professional game hunter and mercenary

BASE
Mobile

HEIGHT 6 ft
WEIGHT 235 lbs
EYES Brown
HAIR Black

FIRST APPEARANCE
The Amazing Spider-Man #15 (August 1964)

POWERS
Enhanced strength, speed, and agility; expert tracker and skilled hand-to-hand fighter.

After his Russian aristocrat parents died while he was a child, Sergei Kravinoff joined the crew of an African safari, learning to track and kill big game. A mystical serum augmented his strength and speed, and Kravinoff became the world's greatest hunter. After anglicizing his name to Kraven, he took up a challenge from his half-brother, the Chameleon, to hunt the most dangerous game of all: Spider-Man. After numerous defeats, both on his own and as one of the Sinister Six, Kraven tranquilized Spider-Man and buried him alive. Kraven then assumed the hero's identity in a bid to prove himself the better crime fighter. In despair at his failure, Kraven shot himself. Kraven's son Vladimir briefly served as the Grim Hunter—until Kaine killed him—and his other son Alyosha became the second Kraven the Hunter. Kraven's young daughter Ana Tatiana also took up the Kraven the Hunter mantle. His wife Sasha returned to rally the family and resurrect Kraven by sacrificing Spider-Man. Kaine took Spider-Man's place, however, disturbing the ritual. Kraven later killed Sasha and also Vladimir, who'd returned as a half-lion.

Despite his modest superpowered abilities, Kraven's combat skills allowed him to hold his own against multiple metahuman opponents.

KRO

FIRST APPEARANCE *The Eternals* #1 (July 1976)
REAL NAME Kro **OCCUPATION** Monarch of Earth's Deviants
BASE Deviant Lemuria **HEIGHT** 6 ft 5 in **WEIGHT** 320 lbs
EYES Red **HAIR** Bald with black facial hair
SPECIAL POWERS/ABILITIES Superhuman strength; mental control over his body, giving him virtual immortality; the power to heal from severe injuries, and limited shapeshifting abilities.

Unlike other members of the Deviants, an offshoot of humanity, Kro is virtually immortal, and has lived more than 20,000 years. Kro has concealed his longevity by pretending to be his own descendants. Kro fell in love with Thena of the Eternals, the Deviants' foes. They have mostly remained apart, but decades ago they had twins known as Donald and Deborah Ritter. Formerly a warlord, Kro has become ruler of the Deviants on Earth.

KULAN GATH

FIRST APPEARANCE *Conan the Barbarian* #15 (May 1972)
REAL NAME Kulan Gath
OCCUPATION Sorcerer **BASE** Mobile
HEIGHT N/A **WEIGHT** N/A **EYES** Red **HAIR** Black
SPECIAL POWERS/ABILITIES Manipulates magic to a very high level. Can summon demonic entities, mentally control individuals, project beams of mystical force, and restructure flesh and bone.

Kulan Gath once held a high position among the sorcerers of Stygia during the Hyborian era. He married his bitter rival, the sorceress Vammatar, to gain access to the Iron-Bound Books of Shuma-Gorath and together they opened the books, unleashing a Nether Demon. Kulan Gath also studied under the master sorcerer Thoth-Amon, a longtime enemy of Conan the Barbarian. The wizard's physical body has been killed more than once but his spirit always survives, often in a necklace, to enslave others. He has clashed with Doctor Strange, Spider-Man, the Avengers, and the X-Men, among others.

KURSE

FIRST APPEARANCE *Thor* #347 (September 1984, as Algrim), *Secret Wars II* #4 (October 1985, as Kurse)
REAL NAME Valgoth, formerly Algrim the Strong
OCCUPATION Vengeance-seeker **BASE** Asgard
HEIGHT 7 ft **WEIGHT** 840 lbs **EYES** Yellow **HAIR** None
SPECIAL POWERS/ABILITIES Almost limitless strength, and is invulnerable to almost all harm. Can sense the presence of those he hunts from a world away.

Kurse began life as Algrim the Strong, mightiest of the Dark Elves who served their ruler, Malekith. Chosen to battle Thor on behalf of his master, Algrim fell into a pit of lava. His desire for vengeance was so strong he survived, but he no longer knew who he was. The Beyonder decided to use Algrim to study vengeance. He transformed Algrim into the vastly more powerful Kurse, who pursued Thor across the Nine Realms. Kurse eventually learned that his true enemy was his one-time ruler, Malekith. After he slew the Dark Elf Lord, Kurse's craving for revenge was sated, and he became a sword protector of Asgard and its children. When Malekith returned, he transformed Lady Waziria into a new incarnation of Kurse.

KREE, THE

Extraterrestrial empire-builders

The Kree are aliens, similar in appearance to humans but possessing twice the strength and endurance. They originated on the planet Hala in the Pama system, located in the Greater Magellanic Cloud, a planet they shared with another intelligent species, the plant-like Cotati. Kree consist of two primary races: the original blue-skinned race and a pink-skinned race that emerged millennia later.

ESSENTIAL STORYLINES

- ***"Operation: Galactic Storm"*** *(19-part crossover in Avengers, Avengers West Coast, Captain America, Iron Man, Quasar, Thor, and Wonder Man).* The Kree-Shi'ar war comes to an explosive conclusion when a Nega-Bomb nearly exterminates Kree society.
- ***Maximum Security #1–3*** A new galactic species, the Ruul, are revealed to be Kree agents, hatching a scheme to restore their decimated empire.

FACTFILE

BASE
Kree-Lar, Turunal system, Greater Magellanic Cloud

FIRST APPEARANCE
Fantastic Four #65 (August 1967)

POWERS

Strength and endurance that are twice the human average.

Armored mobile infantry platforms decimated the enemy and protected Kree operators from counterattack.

WAR YEARS

Nearly a million years ago, the SKRULLS landed on Hala and set up a contest between the KREE and the Cotati. When the Cotati were named as victors, the enraged Kree killed the contact team, stole their starship technology, and launched the Kree-Skrull War, which raged for eons. They took special interest in Earth, creating the offshoot of humanity known as the INHUMANS. Kree society was ruled by the SUPREME INTELLIGENCE, a computer consciousness formed by the minds of the greatest Kree thinkers. In the modern era, the Kree officer Mar-Vell scouted Earth for a possible invasion, but defected to Earth's side as the Super Hero CAPTAIN MARVEL.

Warships, bristling with weaponry, formed the Kree defense fleet and its expeditionary strike teams.

Warriors dominated Kree society. Other respectable professions included politician and scientist, since both used their unique talents to advance the glory of the Kree empire.

KREE EVOLUTION

During the Kree-Shi'ar War, the Supreme Intelligence arranged for the detonation of a Nega-Bomb in Kree space in hoping to jumpstart the species' evolution. Over ninety percent of the Kree died, and the survivors became vassals of the SHI'AR. The AVENGERS executed the Supreme Intelligence for this genocide, but it survived, and using the Forever Crystal, it accelerated the evolution of some Kree into a new breed, the Ruul, who could spontaneously adapt to their environment.

The INHUMANS conquered the Kree, uniting them under the leadership of BLACK BOLT. They fought in the War of Kings against the Shi'ar and their Emperor VULCAN, finally ending that threat. However the Kree soon fell on hard times, while the Inhumans returned to deal with problems on Earth. A reborn Supreme Intelligence sought to rebuild the Kree Empire and in doing so wanted to bring the Inhumans to heel. An agent of the Kree called Vox was sent across space with a simple message for the Inhumans—join or die.

The Kree created many technological wonders, including Kree Sentries and the Psyche-Magnetron, which can conjure up any weapon from Kree history.

LADY DEATHSTRIKE

LADY DEATHSTRIKE

FACTFILE

REAL NAME
Yuriko Oyama

OCCUPATION
Assassin; CEO of Oyama Heavy Industries

BASE
Japan, later mobile

HEIGHT 5 ft 9 in
WEIGHT 128 lbs
EYES Brown
HAIR Black

FIRST APPEARANCE
Daredevil #197 (August 1983)

POWERS
Cyborg whose bones have been laced with Adamantium molecules, rendering them unbreakable. Her fingers were replaced with Adamantium talons. Can interface with computers.

Yuriko Oyama is the daughter of Japanese scientist Lord Dark Wind, who developed the process by which Adamantium could be bonded to a human skeleton. Seeking vengeance on her father for the death of her brothers and the scarring of her face, Oyama joined forces with DAREDEVIL against him. She killed Lord Dark Wind just as he was about to murder Daredevil. However, the man she loved, Kira, a member of Lord Dark Wind's private army, then committed suicide. Traumatized, Yuriko embraced her father's legacy and sought out those who had used his process, which eventually brought her into conflict with Wolverine.

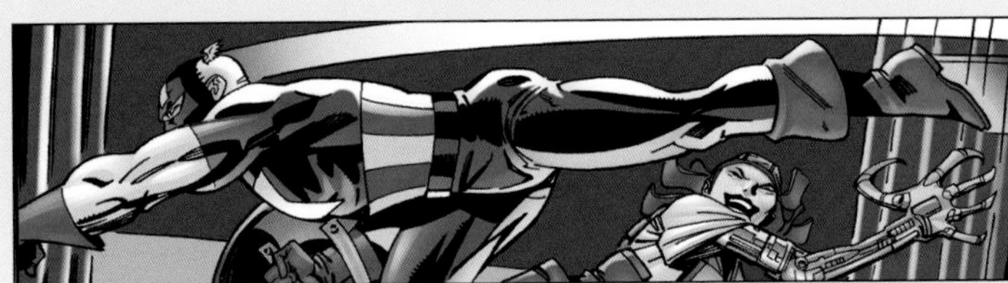

Lady Deathstrike is not only a mistress of Japanese martial arts, but also, as a cyborg, has increased strength, speed, and agility.

CYBORG ASSASSIN

Oyama attempted to kill WOLVERINE and take his skeleton. However, she was defeated by Wolverine's friend Heather Hudson in her costumed identity of VINDICATOR. Subsequently, Lady Deathstrike was converted into a cyborg by the extradimensional being SPIRAL. In this new form, Lady Deathstrike's own skeleton has been reinforced with Adamantium.

Although Lady Deathstrike heads Oyama Heavy Industries, she also works as a professional assassin. For a time she was a member of the Reavers, Donald Pierce's team of cyborgs.

She has survived death several times and jumped her consciousness into the bodies of others to stay alive—namely the criminal CEO Ana Cortés and the assassin Reiko. She was experimented on during the creation of Weapon H, and later joined the hunt for Wolverine and the WEAPON X-FORCE mercenary team.

Like her archfoe Wolverine, Lady Deathstrike has an Adamantium-laced skeleton and Adamantium claws. Normally a foot long, her claws can extend to about twice that length.

LASH

FIRST APPEARANCE *Inhuman* #1 (June 2014)
REAL NAME Lash
OCCUPATION High Priest of Orollan
BASE Orollan, Greenland
HEIGHT 7 ft 6 in **WEIGHT** 440lbs **EYES** Red **HAIR** Black
SPECIAL POWERS/ABILITIES Lash can convert energy from other sources into blasts from his hands.

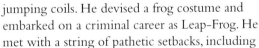

Lash is an INHUMAN from the hidden city of Orollan. After BLACK BOLT released the Terrigen Mists over New York, Lash sought out the "NuHumans" it created to judge whether they were worthy to be Inhuman. This brought him into conflict with Attilan's royal family. When Ulysses CAIN was taken into custody by IRON MAN, Lash saw it as an act of war against Inhumans and attacked Iron Man and his allies only to be defeated by MEDUSA and the Ultimates. After escaping captivity, he was killed by the Jailer when it followed Black Bolt to Earth.

LEAP-FROG

FIRST APPEARANCE *Daredevil* #25 (February 1967)
REAL NAME Vincent Patilio
OCCUPATION Inventor; professional criminal
BASE New York City
HEIGHT 5 ft 9 in **WEIGHT** 170 lbs **EYES** Brown **HAIR** Gray
SPECIAL POWERS/ABILITIES Electrical coils in boots enable leaps up to 60 feet high; exoskeleton provides enhanced strength.

Vincent Patilio started out as a toy inventor before seeing a chance to make some money when he created a set of electrically-powered jumping coils. He devised a frog costume and embarked on a criminal career as Leap-Frog. He met with a string of pathetic setbacks, including a disastrous stint with ELECTRO's Emissaries of Evil and numerous humiliations at the hands of DAREDEVIL and SPIDER-MAN. Vincent's son Eugene later donned his father's costume and became FROG-MAN, an identity that Vincent has sometimes assumed as he continues in his modest calling.

LEADER, THE

FACTFILE
REAL NAME
Samuel Sterns
OCCUPATION
Would-be world conqueror
BASE
Another dimension

HEIGHT 5 ft 10 in
WEIGHT 140 lbs
EYES Green
HAIR Black

FIRST APPEARANCE
Tales to Astonish #62
(December 1964)

POWERS
Superhuman intelligence, several times that of a genius, with an incredible memory for facts and information. Specializes in creating robots, computer systems, high-tech weapons. Has devised methods of telepathic control.

LEADER, THE

After dropping out of school, Samuel Sterns took a menial job in a US government research facility, where an accident led to his body being bombarded by intense gamma radiation. Sterns developed an insatiable thirst for knowledge, and as his intelligence expanded at exponential rates, so too did his cranium.

Unfortunately, Sterns' increased intellectual capacity was not matched by emotional maturity. Disgusted by government corruption, he decided that he should command the human race, and restyled himself as the Leader.

Over the years, the Leader's efforts to dominate the world have been repeatedly foiled by the HULK and his own impatience. However, he has had some successes, in particular the construction of Freehold, a utopian city hidden in Canada's icy north. As part of the INTELLIGENCIA, the Leader helped create the RED HULK, RED SHE-HULK, and the new Harpy (Marlo JONES). When the PUNISHER killed the Leader, the Red Hulk revived him with gamma radiation, restoring his powers and turning him into the Red Leader. The Hulk, in his Doc Green form, tried to turn the Red Leader human, but merely turned him back to his former green-skinned self.

The Red Leader became part of the Red Hulk's Thunderbolts team.

LEFT-WINGER

FIRST APPEARANCE *Captain America* #323 (November 1986)
REAL NAME Hector Lennox
OCCUPATION Former wrestler **BASE** Mobile
HEIGHT 6 ft 5 in **WEIGHT** 265 lbs **EYES** Blue **HAIR** Black
SPECIAL POWERS/ABILITIES Left-Winger possessed superhuman strength and stamina thanks to the Power Broker's strength-augmentation program.

When his ex-army buddy John Walker (*see* U.S.AGENT) became the Super-Patriot, Lennox became one of his Bold Urban Commandos ("Buckies"). Walker was then selected to replace Steve Rogers as CAPTAIN AMERICA. Angered, Lennox and his partner took on guises as Left-Winger and Right-Winger, and set out to destroy Walker's tenure as Captain America. They revealed Walker's true identity to the media, Walker's parents were killed as a result, and he vowed vengeance. Left-Winger was so badly burned in an ensuing explosion that he took his own life.

LEECH

FIRST APPEARANCE *Uncanny X-Men* #179 (March 1984)
REAL NAME Unrevealed
OCCUPATION Adventurer **BASE** Various
HEIGHT 4 ft 2 in **WEIGHT** 67 lbs **EYES** Yellow **HAIR** None
SPECIAL POWERS/ABILITIES Leech can dampen the superhuman powers of any Super Heroes or Villains, mutant or not, within his proximity, up to a range of 30 ft.

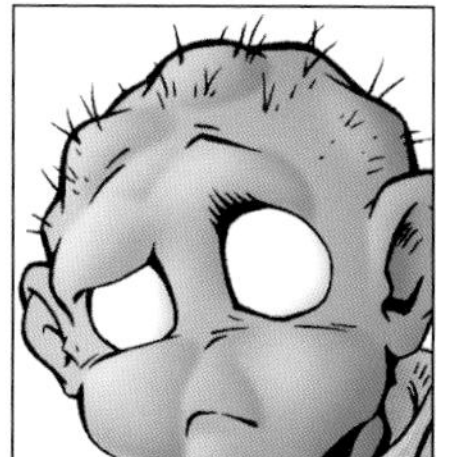

Abandoned by his parents, Leech was found by Caliban, who welcomed him into the MORLOCKS, who lived in the sewers beneath Manhattan. Leech was happy there—until the MARAUDERS came to kill the Morlocks. POWER PACK and X-FACTOR saved him, and the green-skinned boy lived with X-Factor as one of the X-Terminators, and then worked with GENERATION X and the Daydreamers. The Weapon X program later captured Leech and used him to control mutant prisoners. He escaped, and survived M-Day with his powers intact. Leech is now a member of the Future Foundation.

LEGION

After an affair with PROFESSOR X, Gabrielle HALLER secretly gave birth to a son, David. David became a powerful mutant named Legion. After a horrifying terrorist attack, he developed multiple personalities. When the Professor learned of David's existence, he helped David's core persona reassert itself. David decided to change history by killing MAGNETO in the past, but he killed a younger version of his father instead, bringing on the Age of Apocalypse (Earth-295). BISHOP restored the timeline by killing David, but he later reappeared alive. During a course of therapy with his father and DOCTOR NEMESIS, David later caused the Age of X (Earth-11326) timeline. Sometimes his personalities develop bodies of their own, and he has to hunt down and absorb them. He had established some measure of control over his issues, until CYCLOPS became the Dark Phoenix and killed his father. The shock destroyed David's controls and let many of his evil personalities loose again, with one called Lord Trauma proving especially dangerous. Fortunately, with the help of psychotherapist Hannah Jones, David managed to overcome it.

LEGION

FACTFILE
REAL NAME
David Charles Haller
OCCUPATION
Student
BASE
The Jean Grey School for Higher Learning

HEIGHT 5 ft 9 in
WEIGHT 130 lbs
EYES (left) Green; (right) Blue
HAIR Black

FIRST APPEARANCE
New Mutants #25
(March 1985)

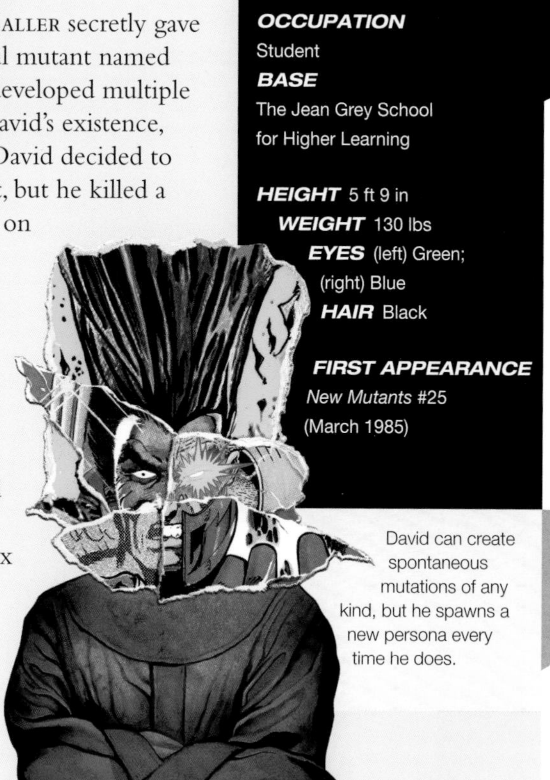

POWERS
David can create spontaneous mutations of any kind, but he spawns a new persona every time he does.

LEGION OF MONSTERS

FIRST APPEARANCE *Marvel Premiere* #28 (February 1976)

BASE New York City

MEMBERS AND POWERS **Franken-Castle** The undead Punisher.

Ghost Rider The spirit of vengeance.

Living Mummy Ancient Egyptian.

Manphibian Alien fish-man.

Man-Thing Swamp creature with burning touch.

Morbius The living vampire.

Werewolf by Night Cursed wolfman.

Satana Hellstrom Daughter of the devil.

The Legion of Monsters first met when they squabbled over the fate of the strange creature known as the Starseed. Even as it lay dying, it tried to cure them of their curses but failed. A new Legion gathered together in the MORLOCK tunnels beneath New York City, working to protect the monsters who'd hidden there. When the MOLE MAN's Moloids brought them the pieces of the PUNISHER's body, they put him back together in an undead form called Franken-Castle. They later helped the RED HULK expel the dark spirit of DOC SAMSON.

LEI-KUNG

FIRST APPEARANCE *Marvel Premiere* #16 (July 1974)

REAL NAME Lei-Kung **OCCUPATION** Martial artist

BASE K'un-Lun **HEIGHT** 6 ft 1 in

WEIGHT 200 lbs **EYES** Black **HAIR** Bald

SPECIAL POWERS/ABILITIES Immortal master of the martial arts.

Lei-Kung the Thunderer was one of the world's greatest martial artists. He trained both IRON FIST and his own son, Davos, the Steel Serpent, in his ways, as well as most of the men of the fabled city of K'un-Lun. After Lord Tuan died and his corrupt son Nu-An took over as ruler of the city, Lei-Kung secretly began to instead train the women of the city for rebellion. He launched his attack during the Celestial Tournament, and with the help of the seven immortal weapons (including Iron Fist), Lei-Kung became the new master of K'un-Lun. The One killed him and left his decapitated corpse for Iron Fist to find.

LETHAL LEGION

When Simon Williams (*see* WONDER MAN) sacrificed his life to save the AVENGERS, his altruism had untold consequences. His grieving brother, Eric, blamed the Avengers for Simon's death. In order to destroy them, Eric adopted the guise of the GRIM REAPER and formed the Lethal Legion of Super Villains. The Legion's efforts ended in failure, while Eric's own enmity to the Avengers was compromised following his brother's resurrection. Nevertheless the Lethal Legion lived on under the leadership of COUNT NEFARIA. Not much of a team player, Nefaria stole the powers of his fellow legionnaires but was still defeated, despite his augmented abilities.

Following Grim Reaper's death, the Legion's name was adopted by the demon lord Satannish, who resurrected various historical figures—including Josef Stalin and Heinrich Himmler—to capture the souls of the Avengers. The Grim Reaper returned and rebuilt the group during the DARK REIGN with his brother WONDER MAN at his side. The GRANDMASTER later formed an alien Lethal Legion to fight the Challenger's BLACK ORDER.

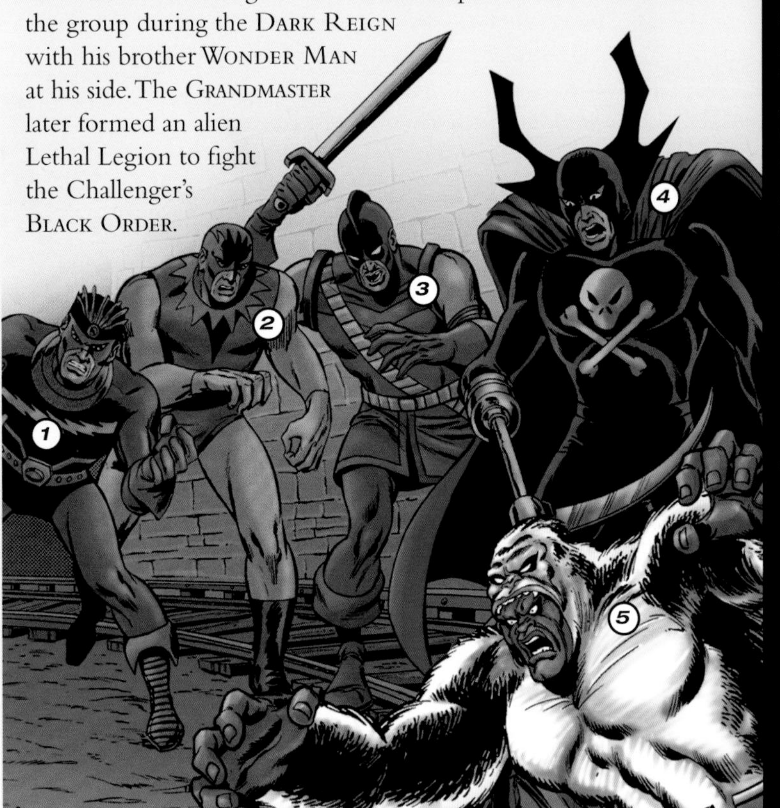

FACTFILE

MEMBERS AND POWERS

GRIM REAPER
A mechanical scythe replaces his right hand.

LIVING LASER
A collection of light particles possessing human consciousness.

MAN-APE
Superhuman strength, endurance, and agility.

POWER MAN
Can grow from 6 ft to 60 ft, with tenfold increase in strength.

SWORDSMAN
Superb athlete and master swordsman.

COUNT NEFARIA
Superhuman strength, speed, and the power of flight.

WHIRLWIND
Achieves superhuman speed by spinning body.

ULTRON
A robot with vast strength, speed, and deadly weapons.

BLACK TALON
Can create and control zombies.

BASE
Mobile

FIRST APPEARANCE
Avengers #78 (July 1970)

LETHAL LEGION
1 Living Laser
2 Power Man
3 Swordsman
4 Grim Reaper
5 Man-Ape

LIBERTEENS, THE

FIRST APPEARANCE *Avengers: The Initiative Annual* #1 (December 2007) **BASE** Philadelphia, PA

MEMBERS AND POWERS **The Revolutionary** Swordsman.

Ms. America Superhuman strength, flight, and invulnerability.

Blue Eagle Flying marksman. **Iceberg** Ice powers.

2-D Turns flat and stretches. **Whiz Kid** Super speed.

Hope Superhuman strength and invulnerability.

THE LIBERTEENS
1 Blue Eagle
2 Ms. America
3 Iceberg
4 Whiz Kid
5 The Revolutionary
6 Hope
7 2-D

The Liberteens are a young group of Super Heroes based in Philadelphia as part of the FIFTY-STATE INITIATIVE. Team members are modeled directly on the members of the 1940s Liberty Legion. Unfortunately, their team leader, the Revolutionary, turned out to be a SKRULL inserted into their team as part of the Skrulls' efforts to infiltrate every branch of the Initiative. During the SECRET INVASION, the Skrull Kill Krew—a team of humans infected with a rare Skrull disease—helped root the Revolutionary out, along with several of the Skrulls hiding inside other Initiative teams.

LEGION OF THE UNLIVING

The undead are on the march!

THE ORIGINAL LEGION
1 Wonder Man **2** Midnight
3 Baron Zemo
4 Human Torch
5 Flying Dutchman
6 Frankenstein's Monster

The Legion of the Unliving are foes of the AVENGERS, their ranks made up of deceased heroes and villains brought together by outside entities. Legion members have variously appeared as duplicates or animated zombies and, most disturbingly, have included former Avengers. KANG the Conqueror, allied with IMMORTUS, assembled the original Legion. Scouring the timestream, Kang brought together FRANKENSTEIN'S MONSTER, Midnight, Flying Dutchman, villain-turned-hero WONDER MAN, BARON ZEMO, and the heroic HUMAN TORCH.

DEFEATED

Despite their combined powers, Kang's Legion of the Unliving failed to defeat the Avengers, and Immortus—after defeating the turncoat Kang—restored the Legion members to their proper places in the timestream.

The second Legion of the Unliving came about through the efforts of the GRANDMASTER, who raised such figures as Bucky BARNES, the SWORDSMAN, CAPTAIN MAR-VELL, KORVAC, DRACULA, and the RED GUARDIAN to guard "life bombs" that threatened to wipe out the universe. As the Avengers struggled to thwart the Grandmaster's scheme, their slain members joined the ranks of the Legion of the Unliving. Fortunately, all the Avengers returned to life after the resolution of the crisis.

THE SECOND LEGION
1 Swordsman **2** Nighthawk **3** Executioner **4** Terrax
5 Hyperion **6** Green Goblin **7** Korvac **8** Death Adder
9 Dracula **10** Bucky Barnes **11** Black Knight
12 Captain Mar-Vell **13** Baron Blood
14 Drax the Destroyer **15** Red Guardian

FACTFILE

ORIGINAL MEMBERS AND POWERS

KANG THE CONQUEROR
Master of time travel.

FRANKENSTEIN'S MONSTER
Enhanced strength, damage resistance.

BARON ZEMO
(Heinrich Zemo)
Extended longevity, brilliant criminal mind.

WONDER MAN
Flight, enhanced strength, body suffused with ionic energy.

HUMAN TORCH
(Jim Hammond)
Flight, flame projection.

FLYING DUTCHMAN
Projection of energy blasts.

MIDNIGHT
Master martial artist.

BASE
Mobile

FIRST APPEARANCE
Avengers #131 (January 1975)

THE THIRD LEGION
1 Iron Man (Arno Stark)
2 Grim Reaper
3 Swordsman
4 Left-Winger
5 Right-Winger
6 Oort the Living Comet

NEVER SAY DIE

A third Legion included such notable figures as the GRIM REAPER, the BLACK KNIGHT (Nathan Garrett), and Toro. They were gathered by Immortus in order to help him capture the SCARLET WITCH.

Following Immortus' failure, the undead Grim Reaper gained additional power from the demon Lloigoroth and gathered a fourth version of the Legion of the Unliving. Grim Reaper's Legion included copies of villains such as COUNT NEFARIA and Inferno, but the team once again met defeat in battle against the Avengers.

The fifth Legion of the Unliving were once more pawns of the Grim Reaper against the Avengers. It consisted of the deceased heroes CAPTAIN MAR-VELL, DOCTOR DRUID, HELLCAT, MOCKINGBIRD, Swordsman, Wonder Man, and THUNDERSTRIKE (Eric Masterson). The Scarlet Witch used her powers to send the spirits of this Legion into the afterlife, and her love for Wonder Man restored him to life. Likewise, Wonder Man restored his brother the Grim Reaper to full physical health, thus ending his threat.

THE FIFTH LEGION
1 Wonder Man
2 Captain Mar-Vell
3 Swordsman
4 Doctor Druid
5 Thunderstrike
6 Mockingbird

LIFEGUARD

FIRST APPEARANCE *X-Treme X-Men* #6 (December 2001)
REAL NAME Heather Cameron
OCCUPATION Member of X-Corp **BASE** Mumbai, India
HEIGHT 5 ft 10 in **WEIGHT** 156 lbs **EYES** Blue **HAIR** Blond
SPECIAL POWERS/ABILITIES Possesses bio-morphic ability—powers adapt to circumstances. In past, Lifeguard has grown wings, extra arms, and developed the ability to breathe underwater.

When the Chinese Triad targeted Heather and Davis Cameron, only the X-Men's intervention saved the siblings' lives. Forced to uncover their mutant abilities during this conflict, both siblings joined the X-Men afterward, and Heather began a relationship with Neal Shaara (Thunderbird). As her powers developed, Heather's appearance became increasingly alien, and Jean Grey suggested that her mother was of the Shi'ar race. Disturbed by this, Davis disappeared, and Heather left the team to find him. Later, she went to work for the X-Corporation and then came to live at the Xavier Institute. She retained her powers after M-Day.

LIGHTSPEED

FIRST APPEARANCE *Power Pack* #1 (August 1984)
REAL NAME Julie Power **OCCUPATION** Student
BASE Avengers Academy **HEIGHT** 5 ft 4 in
WEIGHT 110 lbs **EYES** Blue **HAIR** Strawberry blond
SPECIAL POWERS/ABILITIES Julie can teleport and fly at supersonic speeds. She also has superhuman endurance, reflexes, and healing factor.

As part of the Power Pack, Julie and her siblings received superpowers from Aelfyre Whitemane as he lay mortally wounded after seeking to save them from the alien Snarks, who had attacked their family. Julie was granted the power to fly while leaving a rainbow of light behind her and took the name Lightspeed. When she grew older, Julie left home for Hollywood. In LA, she worked with the teen heroes called the Loners. She has since joined the Avengers Academy.

LILITH (DRACULA'S DAUGHTER)

FIRST APPEARANCE *Giant-Size Chillers* #1 (June 1974)
REAL NAME Unrevealed
OCCUPATION Adventurer **BASE** South of France
HEIGHT 6 ft **WEIGHT** 125 lbs **EYES** Red **HAIR** Black
SPECIAL POWERS/ABILITIES Unique among vampires, Lilith could walk in sunlight and was unaffected by religious talismans; superhuman strength; hypnotic abilities; could transform into a bat.

The daughter of Dracula and his first wife, Zofia, Lilith hated her father for throwing them out of their castle home and driving her mother to suicide. A Romani woman called Gretchin raised Lilith, but when Dracula killed Gretchin's son, Gretchin magically transformed Lilith into a vampire and condemned her to hunt Dracula for the rest of her life. For centuries, Lilith stalked and battled her father, but when she finally had the chance to kill him, she found she could not. Later, she became an agent of Nick Fury's supernatural Howling Commandos.

LIGHTMASTER

FIRST APPEARANCE *Peter Parker, the Spectacular Spider-Man* #1 (December 1976) **REAL NAME** Dr. Edward Lansky
OCCUPATION Physics professor **BASE** New York City
HEIGHT 5 ft 11 in **WEIGHT** 175 lbs **EYES** Brown **HAIR** Brown
SPECIAL POWERS/ABILITIES Lightmaster possesses the ability to generate light, including lasers, to create simple solid objects out of light, and to fly.

In a bid to prevent budget cuts that might affect his position at Empire State University, Dr. Edward Lansky donned a high-tech suit designed to harness the power of light and became the criminal Lightmaster. His intent was to hold various key government officials hostage, but his scheme was foiled by Spider-Man. During the conflict, Lansky's suit was damaged, transforming him into an energy being. Since that time, Lightmaster has often resurfaced, attempting to cash in on his light-based powers. He formed a new Masters of Evil with the Wrecking Crew to fight the Superior Spider-Man and his Superior Six, but was again defeated.

LILITH

FIRST APPEARANCE *Ghost Rider* #98 (August 1992)
REAL NAME Lilith Drake **OCCUPATION** Sumerian Goddess
BASE The Shadowside Dimension, Atlantis
HEIGHT 6 ft **WEIGHT** 140 lbs **EYES** Yellow **HAIR** Black
SPECIAL POWERS/ABILITIES Superhuman strength and stamina; manipulates the dark forces of the universe. She can summon her children from other dimensions, giving them new bodies on Earth.

Lilith is believed to be the daughter of Aehr, the ancient god of darkness. She lived on the island of Atlantis and survived its destruction. Later, Atlantean sorcerers imprisoned her within the belly of a Leviathan believed to be Tiamat. On emerging, Lilith gathered her children, known as the Lilin, to her and battled Ghost Rider Johnny Blaze. She and the Lilin later came into conflict with Doctor Strange. At one point, she was imprisoned inside the magical realm of Avalon, but during the Secret Invasion, Peter Wisdom freed her to help battle the Skrulls.

LINEAGE

FIRST APPEARANCE *Thunderbolts* #14 (as Gordo Nobili) (October 2013)
REAL NAME Gordon Nobili **OCCUPATION** Mob boss
BASE New York City
HEIGHT Unknown **WEIGHT** Unknown **EYES** White **HAIR** None
SPECIAL POWERS/ABILITIES Enhanced strength and speed. Can access the consciousness of anyone linked to his bloodline

Gordon "Gordo" Nobili was the head of the Nobili crime family. He and his two sons, Joey and Carmen, were all transformed into Inhumans by the Terrigen Cloud. Joey was killed by his enemies while Carmen committed suicide, unable to live with his Inhumanity. When Gordo transformed he gained the ability to access the memories and knowledge of deceased members of his family, who would appear on his body. He took the name Lineage and joined the Inhumans. Always manipulative, he was imprisoned after a failed coup attempt against Medusa.

LIPSCOMBE, DR. ANGELA

FIRST APPEARANCE *The Incredible Hulk* #12 (March 2000)
REAL NAME Angela Lipscombe
OCCUPATION Neuropsychologist **BASE** Mobile
HEIGHT 5 ft 9 in **WEIGHT** 125 lbs **EYES** Blue **HAIR** Blond
SPECIAL POWERS/ABILITIES Genius-level knowledge of the science of neuropsychiatry; kind-hearted and a loyal and courageous friend to Bruce Banner in his hour of need.

Angela Lipscombe and Bruce Banner (*see* HULK) dated in medical school, but Banner broke off the relationship, jealous when Lipscombe received a coveted grant for graduate study and he did not. Doctor Lipscombe became one of the world's foremost experts in the field of neuropsychiatry. Many years later, Bruce Banner looked her up in terrible distress, believing he had contracted an incurable disease. Lipscombe used the opportunity to study the bizarre and disturbing multiple personalities that Banner exhibited as the Hulk. She is the partner of DOC SAMSON.

LIVING LIGHTNING

FIRST APPEARANCE *Avengers West Coast* #63 (October 1990)
REAL NAME Miguel Santos
OCCUPATION Student **BASE** California
HEIGHT 5 ft 9 in **WEIGHT** 170 lbs **EYES** Brown **HAIR** Black
SPECIAL POWERS/ABILITIES Living Lightning can transform his body into sentient electrical energy, which he uses for various effects, including to fly.

Miguel Santos' father was Lightning Lord, head of the Legion of Living Lightning, which hoped to control the HULK and use him to overthrow the US government. The Hulk destroyed the Legion's headquarters, killing Lightning Lord. Miguel intended to follow in his father's footsteps, but an accident with one of his father's devices transformed him into a being of pure electrical energy, who needed a containment suit to remain stable. He eventually became a member of the AVENGERS. He sided with CAPTAIN AMERICA during the CIVIL WAR, but later joined the Texas hero team the Rangers. He defeated the Grandmaster when he was one of the Avengers pulled into the Grandmaster's latest tournament.

LIVING MONOLITH

FIRST APPEARANCE *X-Men* #54 (1969)
REAL NAME Ahmet Abdol
OCCUPATION Would-be world conqueror, now living planet
BASE Formerly Egypt, now distant solar system
HEIGHT 5 ft 8 in **WEIGHT** 196 lbs **EYES** Blue **HAIR** Black
SPECIAL POWERS/ABILITIES Absorbs cosmic energy and wields it as destructive force; at times able to vastly increase body size.

Egyptian academic Ahmet Abdol was obsessed with pharaohs. Unsurprisingly, When his mutant powers manifested, he became the Living Pharaoh. He also sometimes grew into the 30-foot-high Living Monolith. After THOR hurled him into deep space, cosmic energy transformed him into a rich and verdant Living Planet. APOCALYPSE later tried to use him to drain the power of other mutants, which caused Abdol to break up and flee. He later returned and tried to gain the power of the Juggernaut only to be killed by Cain Marko.

LIVING LASER

FIRST APPEARANCE *Avengers* #34 (November 1966)
REAL NAME Arthur Parks
OCCUPATION Criminal **BASE** Mobile
HEIGHT 5 ft 11 in **WEIGHT** (formerly) 125 lbs
EYES (formerly) Blue **HAIR** (formerly) Brown
SPECIAL POWERS/ABILITIES Composed entirely of light, he can travel at light speed or transform himself into an offensive laser.

Technician Arthur Parks strapped lasers to his wrists to become Living Laser. Obsessed with WASP, he kidnapped her, but the AVENGERS rescued her. He escaped from prison and worked as a criminal henchman for the MANDARIN, BATROC's Brigade, and the LETHAL LEGION. He later implanted lasers beneath his skin, but the process caused him to explode. He reappeared as a sentient being made of light, and battled IRON MAN several times. He joined the HOOD and fought the SKRULLS during the SECRET INVASION. The MANDARIN and Ezekiel STANE upgraded him before his latest battle with Iron Man.

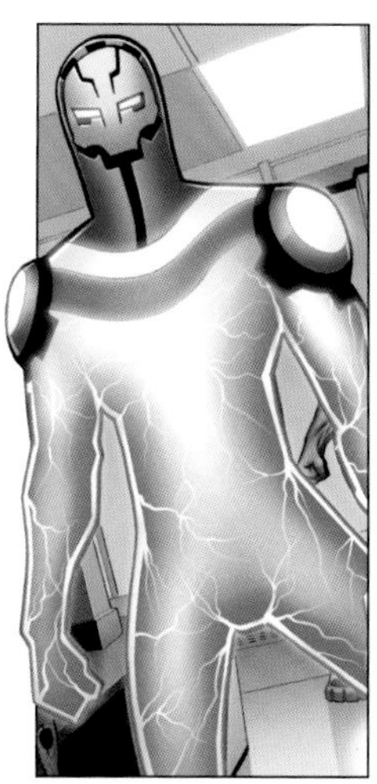

LIVING MUMMY

FIRST APPEARANCE *Supernatural Thrillers* #5 (August 1973)
REAL NAME N'Kantu
OCCUPATION Wanderer **BASE** Egypt
HEIGHT 7 ft 6 in **WEIGHT** 650 lbs **EYES** Brown **HAIR** None
SPECIAL POWERS/ABILITIES Blood replaced by life-preserving fluid, removing human need for food, water, or sleep; enhanced strength, rock-hard body, near-immortality; limited mobility.

Chief N'Kantu of the Swarili organized a slave rebellion against the Pharaoh Aram-Set. The revolt was crushed, and N'Kantu was entombed while still alive. Preserved for 3,000 years, he reawakened in the modern era and went on a rampage before being shocked back to relative sanity when he seized a power line. He later joined Nick FURY's supernatural HOWLING COMMANDOS. He was imprisoned during the CIVIL WAR for refusing to register with the US government, and then returned to Egypt, where he harvested evil souls for the god Anubis. Agent COULSON later recruited him for a new team of Howling Commandos.

LIVING TRIBUNAL

FIRST APPEARANCE *Strange Tales* #157 (June 1967)
REAL NAMES Equity, Necessity, and Vengeance
OCCUPATION Guardian of the continuum of alternate universes
BASE The Multiverse
HEIGHT N/A **WEIGHT** N/A **EYES** N/A **HAIR** N/A
SPECIAL POWERS/ABILITIES Immensely powerful; can cause a sun to go supernova by firing a single bolt of its cosmic energy.

The Living Tribunal is a powerful humanoid cosmic entity that has existed as long as the universe itself. Its purpose is to safeguard the Multiverse from an imbalance of mystical forces by preventing any one universe from acquiring more mystical power than any other. The Living Tribunal can also intervene to prevent an imbalance between the mystical forces of good and evil within a single universe. It is capable of destroying entire planets to maintain the cosmic balance. In its humanoid form, the Living Tribunal has three faces. Its fully visible face represents equity, its partially hooded face represents vengeance, and its fully hooded face represents necessity. It only passes judgment when all three are in agreement, as it did recently on the cosmic being Logos, created when the former entities MASTER ORDER and LORD CHAOS merged.

LIZARD

FACTFILE
REAL NAME
Dr. Curtis Connors
OCCUPATION
Research biologist
BASE
New York City

HEIGHT 5 ft 11 in
WEIGHT 175 lbs
EYES (as human) Blue, (as Lizard) Red
HAIR (as human) Brown, (as Lizard) None

FIRST APPEARANCE
Amazing Spider-Man #6 (November 1963)

POWERS
Superhuman strength and speed; can cling to walls like a gecko and telepathically control reptiles. In Shed form, he can push humans to use only the lower, lizard part of their brains.

LIZARD

When Dr. Curtis "Curt" Connors was an army surgeon, his wounded right arm had to be amputated. Back in civilian life, he researched reptiles' ability to grow missing limbs and created a serum to regenerate his arm. It worked—but turned him into a savage humanoid lizard. Spider-Man restored him to human form, but Curt has repeatedly reverted into the Lizard. The Lizard is one of Spider-Man's main enemies, but Dr. Connors has also acted as a friend to Spider-Man and the hero's true identity, Peter Parker.

Tragically, the Lizard killed Curt's own son Billy. The trauma drove Curt mad. Morbius restored Curt's human body, but left his mind in Lizard form. Curt later became the Lizard again, now with his human mind trapped in his reptilian body. When Ben Reilly created clones of Curt's family, Curt injected them with the Lizard formula—creating a Lizard-like family. Curt later returned to teaching at Empire State College after creating a chip that prevented him from hurting anyone while he was the Lizard.

Spider-Man often holds back against the Lizard for fear of hurting Dr. Connors.

LLYRA

FIRST APPEARANCE *Sub-Mariner* #32 (December 1970)
REAL NAME Llyra Morris **OCCUPATION** Subversive
BASE Mobile **HEIGHT** 5 ft 11 in
WEIGHT 220 lbs **EYES** Green **HAIR** Green
SPECIAL POWERS/ABILITIES Amphibious—can live under water or on land—and able to change skin color to pass as human or *homo mermanus*; can manipulate brains of primitive marine life.

Daughter of a *Homo mermani* (*see* Atlanteans) and a human woman, Llyra was raised on land by her mother following her father's death. Confused by her hybrid status, Llyra became increasingly unstable, and caused great angst to those she encountered. On her first visit to the underwater kingdom of Lemuria, Llyra seized the throne, only to be overthrown by Namor the Sub-Mariner. Llyra made Namor the focus of her rage, murdering his fiancée and even giving birth to an heir to his throne by sleeping with Leon McKenzie, the human grandson of Namor's father. Llyron, the product of this union, temporarily took the throne before Namor regained it. Llyra was ultimately betrayed by Llyron, who left her for dead.

LOCKHEED

FIRST APPEARANCE *Uncanny X-Men* #166 (February 1983)
REAL NAME Unknown **OCCUPATION** None
BASE Westchester County, New York
HEIGHT 2 ft **WEIGHT** 20 lbs **EYES** White **HAIR** None
SPECIAL POWERS/ABILITIES Can fly and breathe fire; empathic ability.

Lockheed is a small dragon belonging to alien species the Flock. He first encountered the X-Men during their fight with the Brood and took a liking to Kitty Pryde, who named him Lockheed. He served alongside her as a member of the X-Men and Excalibur. The X-Men later learned that Lockheed could speak several languages and was spying on them for SWORD. He left the X-Men after Kitty's apparent death, joining SWORD full-time and then founding the Pet Avengers.

LOCKJAW

FIRST APPEARANCE *Fantastic Four* #45 (December 1965)
REAL NAME Not known **OCCUPATION** Dog
BASE New Arctilan, the moon **LENGTH** 6 ft 8 in
WEIGHT 1, 240 lbs **EYES** Brown **HAIR** Brown
SPECIAL POWERS/ABILITIES Immense physical strength; can teleport self and up to a dozen others the distance from the Earth to the Moon; can also teleport to other dimensions.

When they come of age, Inhumans are exposed to the Terrigen Mists, from which they gain their unique powers. For the Inhuman known as Medusa, exposure gave her living hair, while another Inhuman, Crystal, gained the ability to manipulate elements. The Inhumans also experimented on canines—a bulldog pup thus became Lockjaw, who developed a strong affinity for Black Bolt. Lockjaw was able to teleport a maximum combined weight of one ton. Kree technology later improved his teleportation range. While he spent most of his time with the Inhumans, he also helped found the Pet Avengers. He helped protect Ms. Marvel (Kamala Khan) when she first gained her powers, but seemingly perished when the Kree Empire attacked New Arctilan.

LOKI

God of Mischief with a will to rule Asgard

Loki was born the son of Laufey, king of the Frost Giants of Jotunheim. Ashamed of Loki's small size, Laufey hid him away, but the child's existence came to light after the Frost Giants were defeated in a battle with the Asgardians. Odin (*see also* Gods of Asgard), the ruler of Asgard, discovered Loki in the Frost Giants' fortress. Realizing that Loki was the son of Laufey, a king whom he had slain, Odin took the boy back to Asgard and raised him as his own son.

Loki was a megalomaniac, who aimed to overthrow his father and rule over Asgard.

FACTFILE

LOKI

REAL NAME
Loki Laufeyson

OCCUPATION
God of Mischief; later God of Evil

BASE
Asgard

HEIGHT 6 ft 4 in
WEIGHT 525 lbs
EYES Green
HAIR Black-gray

FIRST APPEARANCE
Journey Into Mystery #85
(October 1962)

POWERS

Enhanced strength, stamina, longevity, and limited invulnerability; uses his vast skills in sorcery to fly, generate force-fields, teleport between dimensions, animate objects, and change his own shape.

ASGARD'S MISFIT

Loki never fitted in among the inhabitants of Asgard. He nursed a virulent grudge against his stepbrother Thor, the God of Thunder, who possessed in abundance the heroic qualities that Loki himself lacked. Jealous of the praise Odin showered on Thor, Loki took up the dark arts of sorcery and plotted for a way to become ruler of Asgard. His love of trickery earned him a reputation first as the God of Mischief, and then, as he grew more and more cruel, the God of Evil. After many attempts by Loki to usurp the throne of Asgard, Odin lost patience with him and imprisoned him within a mystical tree. Loki eventually freed himself and went in search of Thor, who was then living on Earth in the mortal guise of Donald Blake.

Kid Loki receives serveral surprises from his brother, Thor: the offer of help, advice to simply have faith in himself, and a hug.

By leading armies against Asgard, Loki helped achieve the end-cycle of Ragnarok.

RAGNAROK AND BEYOND

Loki precipitated the formation of the Avengers by inciting the Hulk to violence, and he transformed Crusher Creel into Thor's foe, the Absorbing Man. He later allied himself with the Enchantress and turned Earth's major villains into his pawns during the Acts of Vengeance conspiracy.

Loki finally conquered Asgard and remade it in his own image, but Thor succeeded in decapitating him. Thor carried Loki's preserved head to observe the final act of Ragnarok, when Asgard and all its inhabitants vanished from existence. After Ragnarok, Loki returned, occupying the body of the goddess Sif. Soon after, he fooled Thor into killing his grandfather Bor. As a consquence, Thor was banished from the new Asgard. Loki joined the Cabal during the Dark Reign and convinced Norman Osborn (Green Goblin) to launch a full-scale assault on Asgard. The attack was so fierce that Loki changed sides to help defend Asgard and paid for his treachery with his life.

Learning that his brother's spirit had not been sent to Hel, Thor searched for Loki and found him in the form of a boy. Restored to his godhood, but without any memories of his past, he became known as Kid Loki. Thor treated him with such respect and affection he came to idolize his older brother and changed his goals, if not his ways. Later, to save the world, Kid Loki allowed the spirit of his older self to kill him and take over his body. From then onward, Kid Loki appeared to exist only as a conscience to plague his original self.

When the malevolent Dark Elf Malekith brought war to the Ten Realms, Loki worked for both sides. He later tried to purge Earth of life using the Dark Celestials, but his actions brought the Avengers together to defeat him.

ESSENTIAL STORYLINES

- ***Avengers #1*** Loki hatches a plot to destroy his brother Thor, accidentally inspiring the world's greatest heroes to form the Avengers.
- **Loki #1–4** In this limited series, told from Loki's point of view, the Trickster God temporarily succeeds in winning power over all of Asgard.
- **The Mighty Thor #582–588** As Ragnarok unfolds around them, Loki and Thor face off for their final battle, then tour the end of the world.

LONGSHOT

FACTFILE

REAL NAME
Unknown

OCCUPATION
Former slave; former movie stuntman; rebel leader

BASE
Mobile

HEIGHT 6 ft 2 in
WEIGHT 80 lbs
EYES Blue
HAIR Blond

FIRST APPEARANCE
Longshot #1
(September 1985)

POWERS

His genetically engineered powers include the ability to affect probability to bring him what is commonly called "good luck." He can telepathically read a person's memories by touching the person and can read psychic imprints left on objects touched by someone.

LONGSHOT

On Mojoworld, where Longshot is from, the original inhabitants have no spines. The scientist Arize created an exoskeleton to allow them to stand upright, but a group called the Spineless Ones refused to use such devices. Still, they became the planet's rulers and forced Arize to create a race of slaves; Longshot was one of these. He refused to be anyone's slave and helped organize a revolt. On the run, Longshot escaped through an interdimensional portal, arriving on Earth. MOJO, the Spineless One who claimed to own Longshot, pursued him to Earth. With help from a stuntwoman called Ricochet Rita, another slave called Quark, and DOCTOR STRANGE, Longshot defeated Mojo. Later, Longshot joined the X-MEN and developed a relationship with DAZZLER. After he left the X-Men, he joined the transdimensional EXILES team for a while, but he parted ways with them to return to Dazzler, whom he married on Mojoworld. The couple had a child, SHATTERSTAR, but their knowledge of the child was then wiped. In a temporal paradox, Shatterstar's genetic material was then used by Arize to create Longshot.

Longshot and his team of rebels prepare to do battle with the manipulative Mojo, the Spineless One.

LOOTER

FIRST APPEARANCE *Amazing Spider-Man* #36 (May 1966)
REAL NAME Norton G. Fester
OCCUPATION Criminal **BASE** New York City
HEIGHT 5 ft 9 in **WEIGHT** 190lbs **EYES** Brown **HAIR** Brown
SPECIAL POWERS/ABILITIES Superhuman strength, speed, stamina, and durability.

Norton G. Fester was a scientist, though not a very talented one, who discovered a strange meteor. While examining it, a strange dust burst from the meteor and hit Fester. It gave him super strength and amazing agility. He chose to use his power for personal gain, turning to crime, and though initially successful was eventually defeated by SPIDER-MAN and imprisoned. He later escaped and changed his name to Meteor Man, but his new look and criminal efforts were lackluster. Over the years his activities have brought him into conflict with the FANTASTIC FOUR and VENOM.

LORD CHAOS

FIRST APPEARANCE *Marvel Two-in-One Annual* #2 (1977)
REAL NAME None
OCCUPATION Abstract entity **BASE** Everywhere
HEIGHT/WEIGHT Unknown **EYES** None **HAIR** None
SPECIAL POWERS/ABILITIES Scope of powers is unknown, but can change destinies of specific individuals.

An abstract entity (depicted as a disembodied purple head), Lord Chaos embodies the concept of Chaos, just as other entities represent DEATH, Order (MASTER ORDER, depicted as a bald head with black eyebrows), and ETERNITY. Alongside Order, Chaos strives to maintain a cosmic balance, occasionally intervening in mortal affairs. Following the restructuring of reality after Battleworld (*see* SECRET WARS), Lord Chaos merged with Master Order to become a new cosmic being named Logos. The new entity tried to bend reality to its will until defeated and separated into Order and Chaos once more.

LORD TEMPLAR

FIRST APPEARANCE *The Avengers* #13 (February 1999)
REAL NAME Unrevealed (last name presumably Tremont)
OCCUPATION Operative of Jonathan Tremont **BASE** Mobile
HEIGHT/WEIGHT Unrevealed **EYES** Red **HAIR** Gray
SPECIAL POWERS/ABILITIES Various powers include the ability to fire energy blasts; can summon counterparts of himself called the Avatars of Templar, each of whom has a different superpower.

Jonathan Tremont's two older brothers died from a disease. Years later Tremont acquired a cosmic artifact in the form of a triangle and used it to resurrect his brothers as the superhumans Lord Templar and Pagan. Jonathan Tremont founded the Triune Understanding, a cult allegedly devoted to world peace. In actuality, Tremont sought to amass power for himself. He used Lord Templar to combat the AVENGERS. Ultimately, Tremont absorbed the life forces of Lord Templar and Pagan into himself, only to be defeated by the Avenger TRIATHLON.

LORELEI

FIRST APPEARANCE *Uncanny X-Men* #63 (December 1969)
REAL NAME Lani Ubanu
OCCUPATION Mercenary **BASE** Savage Land
HEIGHT 5 ft 6 in **WEIGHT** 125 lbs **EYES** Blue **HAIR** Blonde
SPECIAL POWERS/ABILITIES Power lies in her voice; emits hypersonic pitches that affect the sexual drives of human males and mesmerize them.

A member of the Swamp People inhabiting the Antarctic jungle known as the Savage Land, Lorelei received the vocal power to hypnotize men after Magneto subjected her to a DNA-altering machine. Her powers are irresistible to males but have no effect on females. Lorelei became a member of the Savage Land Mutates (also known as the Beast Brood), battling foes from the X-Men to Ka-Zar. She later joined Magneto's Brotherhood of Evil Mutants and fought the Defenders. More recently, Lorelei found employment as a recruiter for AIM, enlisting other Savage Land mercenaries like herself.

LUKIN, GENERAL

FIRST APPEARANCE *Captain America* #5 (November 2004)
REAL NAME Aleksander Lukin
OCCUPATION Russian KGB general
BASE New York City
HEIGHT 5 ft 11 in **WEIGHT** 200 lbs **EYES** Blue **HAIR** Black
SPECIAL POWERS/ABILITIES Strategic genius and political mastermind.

During World War II, The Red Skull used Lukin's Russian village as a base. When the Invaders helped retake the town, Lukin's mother was killed, and General Vasily Karpov took the orphan in. Lukin rose through the ranks of the Russian military to become a KGB general in charge of many special projects, including the Winter Soldier. When Lukin ordered the Red Skull killed, the Red Skull used the Cosmic Cube to transfer his mind into Lukin's body. Eventually, Lukin rid himself of the Red Skull's mind when it was transferred into a robot, but shortly afterward Sharon Carter shot him dead.

LUNA

FIRST APPEARANCE *Fantastic Four* #240 (March 1982)
REAL NAME Luna Maximoff
OCCUPATION None **BASE** New Attilan
HEIGHT 3 ft 10 in **WEIGHT** 47 lbs **EYES** Blue **HAIR** Blond
SPECIAL POWERS/ABILITIES Empath, able to sense and read the emotions of other beings; mind manipulation; telepathic immunity makes her resistant to mind control; precognition of future events.

Luna is the daughter of Crystal and Quicksilver, and a member of the Inhuman royal family. When she was born she was human, but at the age of six Quicksilver exposed her to the Terrigen Mists, unlocking her Inhuman abilities. From then on, Luna could sense, remove, and alter emotions. She was also empathic. She remained with the Inhumans when they moved to Hala to take over the Kree Empire, and forgave her father for his various lies when he finally admitted he had stolen Terrigen Crystals from the Inhumans. She remained with her father as part of Polaris' X-Factor.

LUCIFER

FIRST APPEARANCE *X-Men* #9 (January 1965)
REAL NAME Unknown
OCCUPATION Agent for the Arcane **BASE** Mobile
HEIGHT 6 ft 2 in **WEIGHT** 325 lbs **EYES** Blue **HAIR** Black
SPECIAL POWERS/ABILITIES Initially merely possessed limited telepathic powers; later able to manipulate ionic energy to increase strength, generate protective shield and fuse self with other beings.

Belonging to the planet-conquering Arcane race, the alien Lucifer served as one of their leading agents and was responsible for the capture of numerous worlds. Ordered to obtain Earth for the Arcane, Lucifer was thwarted by a young Charles Xavier (*see* Professor X). Furious at his defeat, before fleeing, Lucifer used a stone slab to disable Xavier's legs. This encounter motivated Xavier to create the X-Men. That mutant organization claimed victory over Lucifer several more times. Angry at their agent's failures, the Arcane leaders had him executed.

LUMPKIN, WILLIE

FIRST APPEARANCE *Fantastic Four* #11 (February 1963)
REAL NAME William Lumpkin
OCCUPATION United States Postal Courier **BASE** New York City
HEIGHT 5 ft 8 in **WEIGHT** 165 lbs **EYES** Blue **HAIR** White
SPECIAL POWERS/ABILITIES None, although he believes that he possesses a special talent when it comes to wiggling his ears; good at his job, courageous, and loyal.

After working as a postman for a small town, Lumpkin moved to New York City, where he was assigned a mail route that included the Baxter Building. Soon after the Fantastic Four moved into the top five floors of the Baxter, Lumpkin half-jokingly petitioned for membership on the grounds that he had the ability to wiggle his ears. Although he never joined the team, he has been involved with them on many occasions. He once rang a bell that allowed the team to escape the Mad Thinker and a Skrull once impersonated him to gain access to the FF headquarters. When Willie developed a life-threatening brain tumor, Reed shrunk the FF down so they could destroy it.

LYJA THE LAZERFIST

FIRST APPEARANCE (as Alicia Masters) *Fantastic Four* #265 (April 1984); (as Lyja) *Fantastic Four* #357 (October 1991)
REAL NAME Lyja
OCCUPATION Skrull agent **BASE** Mobile
HEIGHT 5 ft 5 in **WEIGHT** 120 lbs **EYES** Green **HAIR** Green
SPECIAL POWERS/ABILITIES A shapeshifter, like all Skrulls, Lyja can also fly and project energy bursts and is immune to heat and fire.

The Skrull called Lyja posed as Alicia Masters and married the Human Torch in a plot to destroy the Fantastic Four. The Torch broke off their relationship when he discovered the ruse. Lyja became "the Lazerfist" after the Skrulls gave her energy powers, and she alternated between fighting the Fantastic Four and seeking to reconcile with the Torch. After losing her powers during a false pregnancy, she posed as human Laura Greene. During the Secret Invasion, Lyja regained her powers and sent the Baxter Building into the Negative Zone. She voluntarily remained in the Zone after helping the building's occupants return to Earth.

M

FIRST APPEARANCE *Uncanny X-Men* #316 (September 1994)
REAL NAME Monet St. Croix **OCCUPATION** Investigator
BASE Mutant Town area of New York
HEIGHT 5 ft 7 in **WEIGHT** 125 lbs **EYES** Brown **HAIR** Black
SPECIAL POWERS/ABILITIES M possesses superhuman strength and durability, flight, and telepathy.

Having lived much of her young life mystically trapped in the speechless form of PENANCE by her brother EMPLATE, Monet St. Croix's existence was usurped by her two younger sisters Claudette and Nicole. They used their mutant abilities to combine into a single entity that resembled Monet. Both Penance and the amalgam-Monet became members of GENERATION X. Later, the truth of M's situation became apparent, and she and her sisters were restored to their rightful forms. M joined Jamie Madrox's detective agency, X-FACTOR Investigations, and later the X-MEN.

MACH-X

FIRST APPEARANCE *Strange Tales* #123 (August 1964)
REAL NAME Abner Jenkins
OCCUPATION Super Hero; former criminal
BASE New York City **HEIGHT** 5 ft 11 in **WEIGHT** 175 lbs
EYES Brown **HAIR** Brown
SPECIAL POWERS/ABILITIES Armored flight suit provides enhanced strength and supersonic flight; has a built-in tactical computer and a generator that can fire electrostatic blasts.

Abner Jenkins joined the MASTERS OF EVIL as The Beetle and agreed to BARON ZEMO's scheme to turn them into the THUNDERBOLTS. As Mach-1, he decided to go straight and returned to prison to pay for his previous crimes. After parole, he joined SONGBIRD to lead a new team of Thunderbolts. Every time he upgraded his armor, he renamed himself, finally becoming Mach-X. He served as head of security at the Raft super-prison before joining the WINTER SOLDIER's team of Thunderbolts. Jenkins was seemingly killed during a confrontation between Zemo, the Thunderbolts, and KOBIK.

MACHINE TEEN

FIRST APPEARANCE *Machine Teen* #1 (July 2005)
REAL NAME Adam Aaronson
OCCUPATION Student
BASE New York City **HEIGHT** 5 ft 8 in **WEIGHT** 225 lbs
EYES Blue **HAIR** Blond
SPECIAL POWERS/ABILITIES Adam is an android with superhuman durability, endurance, strength, and speed, plus a computer brain.

When Adam Aaronson started attending high school, he didn't suspect he was actually an android built by Dr. Aaron Isaacs, the man he thought was his father. After a series of strange seizures and displays of odd powers, his secret came out, and he confronted Dr. Isaacs about it. Isaacs had fled from the Holden Radcliffe Corporation with Adam rather than give him up. Radcliffe tried to capture Adam, but Adam escaped. He later joined the AVENGERS Academy and then went to work with Briggs Chemical.

M-11

FIRST APPEARANCE *Menace* #11 (May 1954)
REAL NAME M-11 **OCCUPATION** Adventurer
BASE San Francisco
HEIGHT 6 ft **WEIGHT** 900 lbs **EYES** None **HAIR** None
SPECIAL POWERS/ABILITIES Robot with telescopic arms, heat vision, force-field projection, image projection, superhuman strength, and the ability to repair itself.

In the 1950s, the GOLDEN CLAW commissioned a scientist to build a robot to help his plan to make FBI agent Jimmy Woo the next Khan. To give the robot free will, the scientist had it electrocute him and absorb some of his life force. M-11 then walked into the sea, but NAMORA found it and brought it to Jimmy to join his G-Men group of heroes. Woo and his friends reactivated the robot decades later to help in their battle against the forces of the Golden Claw. Today, M-11 works alongside the other former G-Men as part of the AGENTS OF ATLAS.

MACHINE MAN

X-51 was a prototype for a government project to build artificially intelligent robot soldiers. His limbs could extend 100 feet, his endoskeleton housed solar-power-augmented batteries, multi-optical imaging devices with zoom, and magnifying sensors, while anti-gravity devices allowed flight. His fingers featured miniature lasers, concussive blasters, and a .357 Magnum pistol. Believing a robot would only act like a man if treated like one, Dr. Aaron Stack took X-51 into his home and even designed a human face for him. Stack died protecting X-51 after the program was terminated.

Assuming Stack's identity, X-51 attempted to assimilate into human society, but he later fell in love with the robot JOCASTA. He has fought alongside the AVENGERS, FANTASTIC FOUR, HULK, X-MEN, and NEXTWAVE. His personality changed over that time, moving from friendly but distant to crass and obnoxious, especially during his spell in Nextwave where he seemed more at ease with his robotic nature. He and Jocasta traveled to Earth-2149 to help stop a zombie invasion. Jocasta recently split up with him because of his increasingly anti-human, pro-robot views.

FACTFILE
REAL NAME
X-51
OCCUPATION
Insurance investigator
BASE
Manhattan, New York

HEIGHT 6 ft
WEIGHT 850 lbs
EYES Red imaging sensors
HAIR Black (artificial)

FIRST APPEARANCE
2001: A Space Odyssey #8 (July 1977)

MACHINE MAN

POWERS
Robot composed of titanium alloy. Motorized endoskeleton which houses a vast array of weapons systems.

MACHINESMITH

FIRST APPEARANCE *Marvel Two-In-One* #47 (January 1979)
REAL NAME Samuel "Starr" Saxon
OCCUPATION Robot maker; professional criminal **BASE** Mobile
HEIGHT 6 ft 1 in **WEIGHT** 295 lbs **EYES** Green **HAIR** Bald
SPECIAL POWERS/ABILITIES A living computer program, his consciousness can be placed into multiple robot bodies which approximate human beings.

Master robot builder Starr Saxon built robots for criminals. When DAREDEVIL defeated one of his robots, Saxon sought revenge, but died during the battle. One of his robots, following its programming, took Saxon's body back to his workshop and transferred his brain patterns into a robotic body. On recovery, Saxon replaced this body with a human-looking one. Calling himself Machinesmith, he resumed his career of building robots for the underworld. Machinesmith has come into conflict with SHIELD and CAPTAIN AMERICA. He now exists as a computer program which can be placed into robot bodies.

MACTAGGERT, DR.

FIRST APPEARANCE *Uncanny X-Men* #96 (December 1975)
REAL NAME Moira Kinross MacTaggert
OCCUPATION Geneticist **BASE** Muir Island, Scotland
HEIGHT 5 ft 7 in **WEIGHT** 135 lbs
EYES Blue **HAIR** Brown
SPECIAL POWERS/ABILITIES Brilliant geneticist with expertise in the mutant genome.

Moira MacTaggert was once engaged to Charles Xavier (*see* PROFESSOR X), but she broke it off. She secretly bore Xavier's child (PROTEUS) and later adopted the mutant child Rahne Sinclair (WOLFSBANE). Like Xavier, she set up a secret home for young mutants, but the heroes all seemingly died on their first mission. Later, she struck up a romance with Sean Cassidy (BANSHEE). She established a Mutant Research Center on Muir Island, where she found a cure for the Legacy virus. MYSTIQUE killed her, but she was temporarily resurrected during the Chaos War.

MAD DOG

FIRST APPEARANCE (as Baxter) *Amazing Adventures* #13 (July 1972); (as Mad Dog) *Defenders* #125 (November 1983)
REAL NAME Robert "Buzz" Baxter **OCCUPATION** Criminal; retired US Air Force Colonel **BASE** Mobile **HEIGHT** 6 ft 2 in
WEIGHT 270 lbs **EYES** Blue **HAIR** Black and brown
SPECIAL POWERS/ABILITIES Possesses superhuman strength, smell and hearing. Enhanced speed and agility. Has hollow fangs which secrete poison, to which he is immune.

In the comics she wrote, Dorothy Walker based her characters on her daughter Patsy and Patsy's friend "Buzz" Baxter. After the real Patsy and Baxter graduated from high school, they married and Baxter joined the Air Force. As a security consultant for the Brand Corporation, Baxter hunted the mutant BEAST. Patsy divorced Baxter and became the HELLCAT. When Brand captured the AVENGERS, Hellcat forced Baxter to free them. Baxter underwent treatment by Roxxon Oil's Mutagenics Department that gave him superhuman powers. Thus Baxter became Mad Dog, who has battled not only Hellcat, but also other costumed adventurers.

MAD THINKER

For many years the police did not know of the Mad Thinker's existence, despite the various criminal activities he had masterminded over that period. He only leaped into the public eye when he went head-to-head with the FANTASTIC FOUR. A brilliant strategist, he tempted each of them away from New York with various impossible-to-refuse jobs. He subsequently used their absence to enter the Baxter Building and steal Reed Richards' inventions. Manufacturing superhuman androids based on Richards' designs, he used them to battle the Fantastic Four. However, for all his brilliance, the Mad Thinker failed to account for a circuit breaker that Richards had built into the designs for just this eventuality.

Once the circuit was activated, all of Richards' robots became disabled. Since then, the Mad Thinker has spent much of his time in prison, but he has somehow managed to continue his devious activities from inside. He has also been a member of the INTELLIGENCIA, working with other criminal masterminds.

With low cunning the Fantastic Four are almost duped into defeat.

MAD THINKER

FACTFILE
REAL NAME
Unknown
OCCUPATION
Criminal mastermind
BASE
Mobile

HEIGHT 5 ft 11 in
WEIGHT 195 lbs
EYES Blue
HAIR Brown

FIRST APPEARANCE
Fantastic Four #15 (June 1963)

POWERS
Brilliant criminal mind. Created a way to project his mind into an android body to continue criminal activities in his absence.

MADAME HYDRA

FIRST APPEARANCE *Captain America: Steve Rogers* #1 (July 2016)
REAL NAME Elisa Sinclair
OCCUPATION Hydra leader **BASE** Washington, D.C.
HEIGHT Unknown **WEIGHT** Unknown **EYES** Brown **HAIR** Black
SPECIAL POWERS/ABILITIES Powerful witch with the ability to cast believable illusions; increased longevity; form of clairvoyence known as "the Sight"; formidable combatant.

Originally, the subversive organization HYDRA restricted its membership to men. The first female Hydra agent was Laura Brown. Another female operative seized command of Hydra's New York operations, took the name Madame Hydra, and battled CAPTAIN AMERICA. Eventually she took a new alias, the VIPER, and became one of the world's most dangerous terrorists. Another female Hydra agent, Madame Hydra VI (so named because five other Madame Hydras outranked her), clashed with SHIELD and allied with the GOLDEN CLAW. She committed suicide to avoid capture. When KOBIK, a living Cosmic Cube, recreated reality to turn Captain America into an agent of Hydra, Kobik inserted Elisa Sinclair into Steve Rogers' life. In the reality that Kobik created, Elisa was the new Madame Hydra and a powerful sorceress. She became one of the Hydra Captain America's closest advisors when he took over the United States. When Tony Stark's A.I. attempted to kill the evil version of Rogers, Sinclair teleported Rogers away and saved his life—at the cost of her own.

MADAME MASQUE

Adopted by financier Byron Frost, Whitney Frost grew up in New York's high society, but when Byron died, her world collapsed. Learning that her biological father was the Italian COUNT NEFARIA, head of the MAGGIA criminal organization, she became his heir. Following his imprisonment, she became head of the Maggia, now based in New York. Her face was disfigured during a botched raid on Stark Industries. Hiding her scars behind a golden mask, Whitney took the name Madame Masque. Falling in love with Tony Stark (IRON MAN), she impersonated his assistant to spend time with him, but when Tony was unable to save her father's life, she resumed her role as the Director of the Maggia.

It was Mordecai Midas who first suggested the golden mask.

Over the years, Whitney made several clones of herself, killing them when they'd served their purpose. One, known as Masque, worked briefly with the AVENGERS before being killed. Whitney supposedly renounced her criminal past after witnessing her clone's sacrifice, but she served as the HOOD's top lieutenant in his new crime syndicate. He healed her face with the Reality Gem. She later fought with Kate Bishop (*see* HAWKEYE) and tried to find magical items with which to empower herself. This brought her into conflict with both Iron Man and a reformed DOCTOR DOOM. Doom managed to exorcise demons that had taken possession of her and she was given over the SHIELD custody.

FACTFILE

REAL NAME
Countess Giulietta Nefaria (adopted name Whitney Frost)

OCCUPATION
Crimelord

BASE
Unknown

HEIGHT 5 ft 9 in
WEIGHT 130 lbs
EYES Gray
HAIR Black

FIRST APPEARANCE
Tales of Suspense #97 (January 1968)

MADAME MASQUE

POWERS
Gymnast and athlete trained to Olympic standards; superb markswoman and exceptional mistress of strategy.

Madame Masque is highly skilled with a huge variety of instruments of death, ranging from submachine guns to rocket launchers.

MADAME WEB

FACTFILE
REAL NAME
Julia Carpenter
OCCUPATION
Adventurer, fugitive
BASE
New York City

HEIGHT 5 ft 9 in
WEIGHT 140 lbs
EYES Blue
HAIR Strawberry blond

FIRST APPEARANCE
(as Julia Carpenter) *Marvel Super Heroes Secret Wars* #6 (October 1984); (as Madame Web) *Amazing Spider-Man* #636 (August 2010)

POWERS
Through clairvoyance, Madame Web can predict the future, read minds and perform psychic surgery.

The original Madame Web, Cassandra Webb, was born blind but developed skills as a clairvoyant that compensated for her sightlessness. Cassandra's first encounter with SPIDER-MAN came when businessman Rupert Dockery was scheming to take over the *Daily Globe*. At first skeptical of the help she offered, Spider-Man later acknowledged her usefulness and they worked together.

At times, Cassandra could be manipulative. She once tricked Spider-Man into obtaining a mystical object for her so she could try to gain youthful immortality. She later mentored the third SPIDER-WOMAN, Mattie Franklin, but she couldn't prevent KRAVEN's family from killing them both. Julia Carpenter—the second Spider-Woman—inherited her powers and has taken over as the new Madame Web. Julia helped bring her insane ex-boyfriend, the SHROUD, to justice. Cassandra was later cloned by the Jackal only to die again—asking Julia to save the PROWLER as she died.

MADCAP

FIRST APPEARANCE *Captain America* #307 (July 1985)
REAL NAME Not known
OCCUPATION Prankster **BASE** New York City
HEIGHT 5 ft 9 in **WEIGHT** 145 lbs **EYES** Blue **HAIR** Brown
SPECIAL POWERS/ABILITIES Remarkable self-healing ability, able to survive almost any injury; causes others to lose inhibitions with embarrassing and sometimes lethal consequences.

A devoted member of a Christian church, Madcap began his descent into insanity following a terrible accident. He was traveling on a bus with his family and 40 church members when it collided with a truck carrying an experimental nerve agent. Madcap was the only survivor, and in the days that followed he developed the ability to heal himself and cause temporary insanity in others. He became part of the MERCS FOR MONEY but soon started a feud with DEADPOOL; one that ended when Deadpool gave Madcap to the COLLECTOR. Madcap went willingly, saying that Deadpool had damaged his own life more than Madcap could ever have done.

MADMAN

Phillip Sterns, brother of Samuel Sterns (aka the LEADER), was a classmate of Bruce Banner (*see* the HULK) in graduate school. Banner was always at the top of his class, with Phillip Sterns at the bottom. After graduation, both Banner and Sterns began researching the use of gamma radiation as a potential weapon. But the government funded Banner's research, not Sterns', increasing Sterns' envy of Banner.

When Sterns learned that Bruce Banner had become the Hulk through exposure to gamma radiation, he grew even more jealous and began exposing himself to gamma radiation over a period of years. As a result of this exposure, he transformed into the Madman. Sterns and Madman existed as two separate personalities in the same body. Over the years, Madman battled the Hulk many times. In the end, however, it was Sterns' brother who killed him. The Leader whispered a code into Madman's ear, something that instantly unlocked so much stored data in Madman's head that it exploded.

FACTFILE
REAL NAME
Phillip Sterns
OCCUPATION
Scientist
BASE
Mobile

HEIGHT Variable
WEIGHT Variable
EYES Variable
HAIR None

FIRST APPEARANCE
(as Phillip Sterns) *Incredible Hulk* #363 (January 1990); (as Madman) *Incredible Hulk* #364 (February 1990)

POWERS
Superhuman strength, ability to increase and decrease his mass, and to change his shape and form.

MAELSTROM

FACTFILE
REAL NAME
Unrevealed
OCCUPATION
Nihilist
BASE
Mobile

HEIGHT 8 ft 2 in
WEIGHT 425 lbs
EYES Purple
HAIR White

FIRST APPEARANCE
Marvel Two-In-One #71 (January 1981)

POWERS
Increases his own powers through control of kinetic energy and draining the energy of others; projects force blasts.

MAELSTROM

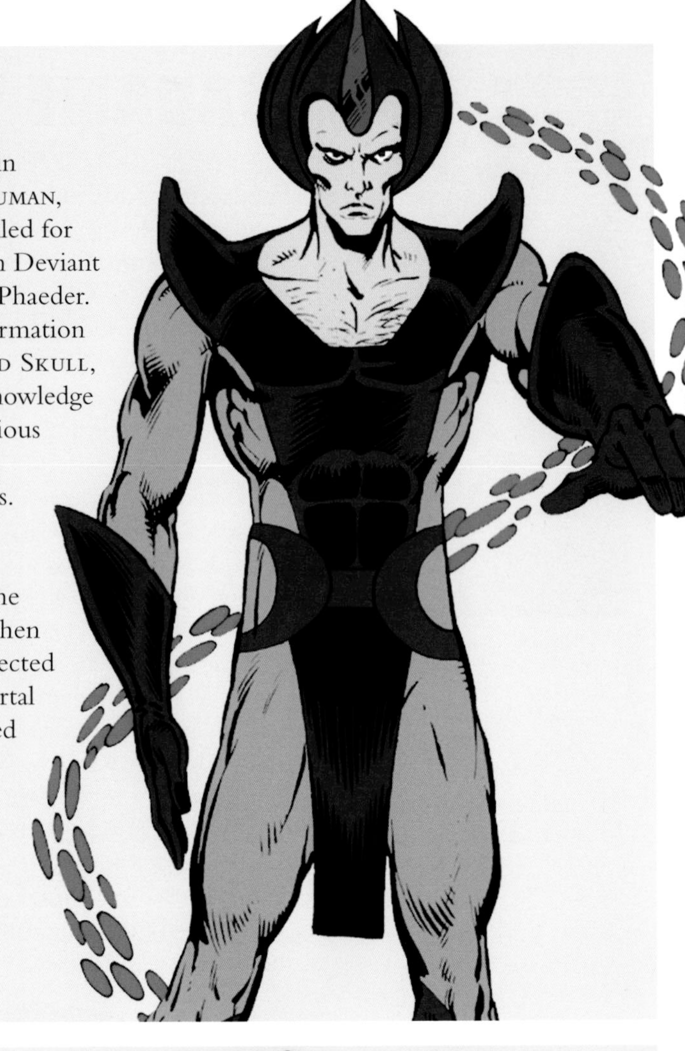

The seeds of a Super Villain's behavior can often be found in their childhood. The hybrid child of a Deviant and an INHUMAN, Maelstrom's birth caused consternation. His mother was killed for giving birth to him, and as a child he was forced to work in Deviant slave pits until rescued by his father, the brilliant geneticist Phaeder.

Following in his father's footsteps, Maelstrom traded information on genetics with various dubious individuals including RED SKULL, MAGNETO, and the HIGH EVOLUTIONARY. Their use of this knowledge caused untold suffering: the Nazi genetic atrocities and various clones of SPIDER-MAN were direct results of Maelstrom's collaborations.

A desperately lonely individual, Maelstrom looked for an antidote to his unhappiness in plans to end the Multiverse. Destroyed by QUASAR when he first attempted this, he was resurrected and tried again. This time, Mr. Immortal of the GREAT LAKES AVENGERS tricked him into committing suicide. While dead, he served Oblivion, another aspect of DEATH. Hoping to buy his return to life, Maelstrom empowered Phyla-Vell as Martyr, an emissary of Oblivion. He later tricked Phyla-Vell into freeing Thanos, who killed her.

Maelstrom can divert absorbed energy into a blast of kinetic energy.

MAGGIA

FACTFILE
NOTABLE MEMBERS
TOP MAN (Hammerheads)
Cunning mind.
HAMMERHEAD (Hammerheads)
Enhanced strength through metal exoskeleton.
COUNT NEFARIA (Nefarias)
Vast powers of ionic energy.
MADAME MASQUE (Nefarias)
Skilled martial artist.
SILVIO "SILVERMANE" MANFREDI (Silvermanes)
Cybernetic body.
JOSEPH MANFREDI
(Silvermanes) Formerly had control over bats.

BASE Worldwide

FIRST APPEARANCE
Avengers #13 (February 1965)

MAGGIA

The Maggia is the world's most powerful crime syndicate. The organization's operations are worldwide, though its roots began in southern Europe during the 13th century and it spread to the United States in the 1890s. The Maggia has its fingers in gambling, narcotics, loan-sharking, organized labor, and crooked politics. Those who betray the Maggia are executed, often with a death grip to the chin nicknamed the "Maggia touch."

The three largest Maggia families active in New York City include the SILVERMANE family, the HAMMERHEAD family, and the NEFARIA family. The Silvermanes are a traditionally-structured crime network controlling the narcotics trade. The Hammerheads are styled in the fashion of 1920s gangsters, and are led by the flat-topped HAMMERHEAD. The Nefarias, organized by COUNT NEFARIA, are the most colorful of the three families, frequently employing costumed criminals to further their schemes. Early in his career, the gang boss KINGPIN was one of the Maggia's most successful rivals.

THE MAGGIA
1 Silvermane
2 Count Nefaria
3 Hammerhead

MAGGOTT

FIRST APPEARANCE *Uncanny X-Men* #345 (June 1997)
REAL NAME Japheth
OCCUPATION Former X-Man **BASE** Mobile
HEIGHT 6 ft 8 in **WEIGHT** 350 lbs **EYES** Brown **HAIR** Black
SPECIAL POWERS/ABILITIES Two semi-sentient slugs can leave and re-enter Maggott's body. They feed on anything and use it to nourish him. Can replay in his mind's eye past events in local area.

A sickly child, unable to eat solid food, young Japheth felt that he was nothing but a burden to his poor South African family. Heading into the desert to die, Japheth encountered Magneto who activated his mutation, allowing two slugs to leave his body and feed on his behalf. Now calling himself Maggott, Japheth went searching for Magneto. In Antarctica, he first encountered the X-Men, and briefly joined the mutant team. Unfortunately, Maggott was captured by the Weapon X facility, became an inmate at the Neverland concentration camp, and was executed there. Selene revived him with her techno-organic virus, and he survived her subsequent defeat.

Thanks to her seismic mutant talents, Magma is impervious to heat and, by encasing herself in fiery molten rock, is as comfortable inside the crater of an erupting volcano as she is in the open air.

MAGMA

FIRST APPEARANCE *New Mutants* #8 (October 1983)
REAL NAME Amara Aquilla
OCCUPATION Adventurer **BASE** Mobile
HEIGHT 5 ft 6 in **WEIGHT** 124 lbs **EYES** Brown **HAIR** Blond
SPECIAL POWERS/ABILITIES Projects bursts of heat and molten rock, and causes shifts in the tectonic plates beneath the surface of the Earth to produce volcanic eruptions.

Raised in the hidden city of Nova Roma in the Amazon jungles of Brazil, Amara's mutant abilities surfaced when Selene—a nigh-immortal mutant who drains the life essences of others—hurled her into an active volcano. The New Mutants rescued her, and she became a longtime member of the group. For a time, she believed herself to be Allison Crestmere, daughter of an English ambassador, but this proved false. She later joined the Xavier Institute's staff, working with the younger mutants. She survived M-Day with her powers intact. Later, trapped in Hell with the New Mutants, she traded a date with Mephisto for their freedom.

MAGIK

Illyana Rasputin is the younger sister of Piotr Rasputin (Colossus). The sorcerer Belasco brought Illyana and the X-Men to his timeless realm, Limbo. The X-Men escaped, but Belasco kept Illyana there and turned a portion of her soul evil. Her darksoul gave her powers of sorcery, and Illyana mastered the magic in Belasco's books and defeated him with her magical Soulsword. She returned to Earth several years older and joined the New Mutants under the code name Magik. Eventually, she managed to find her younger self in Limbo and prevented her corruption, erasing all subsequent events. Restored to her youth, she later died of the mutant-killing Legacy Virus. Belasco brought together the fragments of Illyana in Limbo and created the Darkchylde. This form of Illyana stole a part of the X-Man Pixie's soul and dedicated herself to reclaiming her own soul. When the Phoenix Force returned to Earth and was shattered, she became one of the Phoenix Five. Later, she joined the fugitive Cyclops' new X-Men. Traveling back in time, she asked Doctor Strange to teach her how to control her powers, later helping him fight the Empirikul. She then became leader of a new team of New Mutants.

Mutant Illyana Rasputin (code name Magik) joined her brother Piotr (code name Colossus) at Professor Xavier's school for mutants, where they became X-Men.

MAGIK

FACTFILE
REAL NAME
Illyana Nikolievna Rasputin
OCCUPATION
Student
BASE
Professor Xavier's School for Gifted Youngsters, New York; the extradimensional realm, Limbo

HEIGHT 5 ft 5 in
WEIGHT 120 lbs
EYES Blue
HAIR Blond

FIRST APPEARANCE
(as a child) Giant-Size X-Men #1 (May 1975)

POWERS
Magik is both a mutant with superhuman powers and an expert sorceress. She can teleport herself and others through time, perform astral projection, and sense the presence of magic.

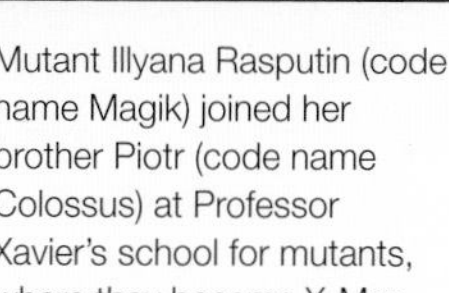

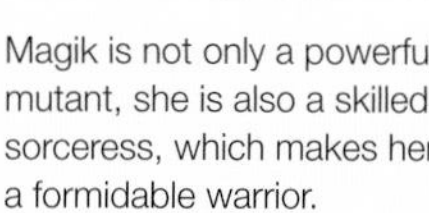

Magik is not only a powerful mutant, she is also a skilled sorceress, which makes her a formidable warrior.

MAGNETO

Master of magnetism

MAGNETO

FACTFILE

REAL NAME
Max Eisenhardt; also uses the name Erik Magnus Lehnsherr

OCCUPATION
Conqueror

BASE
Mobile

HEIGHT 6 ft 2 in
WEIGHT 190 lbs
EYES Blue-gray
HAIR White

FIRST APPEARANCE
X-Men #1 (September 1963)

POWERS

Mutant ability to manipulate magnetism and all forms of electromagnetic energy

ALLIES/FOES

ALLIES Brotherhood of Evil Mutants, (sometimes) Professor Charles Xavier, (formerly) the X-Men, the New Mutants

FOES Professor Charles Xavier, the X-Men, the Avengers, the Fantastic Four

ISSUE #1

In the first *X-Men* comic, Magneto captured the Cape Citadel missile base, only to be defeated by the original X-Men in their initial battle.

Magneto's sufferings in his youth inspired his hatred of humankind.

One of the most powerful and dangerous of all mutants, Magneto has been both the foremost enemy of the X-Men and, sometimes, their ally. Born Max Eisenhardt, as a boy, he was imprisoned in the Nazi death camp in Auschwitz, Poland. Sickness and malnourishment prevented Magneto's mutant powers from emerging there. In Auschwitz, Magneto's family perished, and he witnessed the inhumanity that people can show to those who are considered different.

MUTANT RAGE

Magneto magnetically shielded Magda and Anya in a burning inn, but could not save Anya's life.

Following World War II, Magneto married his childhood sweetheart, Magda, and they had a daughter, Anya. When Anya was trapped in a burning building, a mob prevented Magneto from rescuing her. Infuriated, Magneto lashed out with his powers, killing them.

Frightened by what her husband had done, Magda fled from him. Magneto employed a forger to create a false identity, "Erik Magnus Lehnsherr," and started to create a new life for himself hunting Nazi war criminals. Eventually Magneto settled in Israel, where he became friends with the young Charles Xavier (*see* Professor X). They continually debated their different views on whether mutants could peacefully coexist with the rest of humanity. When Baron von Strucker and his Hydra agents kidnapped Magneto and Charles' friend Gabrielle Haller, both men used their mutant powers to rescue her. Realizing Haller would never agree with him, Magneto used his powers to steal a cache of Nazi gold that Strucker had sought. Magneto had decided that the only way to stop humanity from oppressing the emerging race of mutants was for mutants to conquer the rest of the human race—and he needed funds to make that happen.

Magneto created a helmet that made him immune to telepathy and set about proving mutants' superiority to humans. His new militancy soon brought him into conflict with Charles Xavier's X-Men when Magneto tried to take over a missile base at Cape Citadel, Florida. Shortly after, Magneto formed the first incarnation of the Brotherhood of Evil Mutants, recruiting Toad, Mastermind, Scarlet Witch and Quicksilver. The two teams clashed several times until Quicksilver and the Scarlet Witch quit the Brotherhood and joined the Avengers.

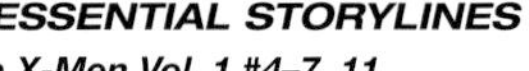

ESSENTIAL STORYLINES

- ***X-Men Vol. 1 #4–7, 11***
Magneto's original Brotherhood of Evil Mutants battles the original team of X-Men.
- ***X-Men Vol. 1 #62–63***
Magneto's unmasked face is revealed when he combats the X-Men in the Savage Land.
- ***Uncanny X-Men #161***
The story of how Magneto first met Charles Xavier in Israel.
- ***Classic X-Men #12***
Magneto's captivity at Auschwitz and the death of his daughter.

Magneto built Avalon as a haven for his mutant Acolytes, from where he could also launch devastating attacks on Earth.

A NEW ERA

Magneto soon found himself fighting other teams, including the Avengers, Fantastic Four, and Defenders. He also formed several new versions of the Brotherhood. Using his advanced knowledge of genetic engineering, Magneto created a being called Alpha the Ultimate Mutant, but Alpha rebelled against his creator, devolving Magneto into a powerless infant. Xavier turned the baby Magneto over to his colleague Dr. Moira MacTaggert, who began experiments to alter the child's mind. Later, Davan Shakari, an alien Shi'ar agent, restored Magneto to his adult physical prime, making Magneto far younger than his World War II contemporaries.

Magneto resumed his battles against the X-Men, but when he almost killed a young Kitty Pryde, Magneto saw the error of his ways. During a period in which Xavier took an extended absence from Earth, Magneto even became headmaster of Xavier's school, mentoring the New Mutants. At the time, Magneto also learned that Scarlet Witch and Quicksilver were his children—something all three of them would later discover to be untrue.

MUTANT HOMELAND

Magneto later returned to his more violent ways, becoming convinced once again that humanity intended to wipe out mutants. He created an orbital base called Avalon that was meant to be a sanctuary for mutants. Many flocked to him, calling themselves his Acolytes, and even Colossus joined them for a short time. Though Avalon was later destroyed during a fierce fight with the X-Men, Magneto eventually gained his wish for a mutant homeland when the UN acceded to his demands, granting him the island of Genosha as a refuge for mutantkind. It proved be a short-lived triumph as Genosha was destroyed when Xavier's evil twin, Cassandra Nova, used her powers to unleash an army of Sentinels on the island. It seemed that Magneto, along with over 16 million other mutants, had perished in the ensuing devastation. Soon after, a new X-Men recruit, Xorn, revealed himself to be Magneto, but this was found to be a ruse. The real Magneto had in fact survived the Genosha attack—but only just and at great personal cost.

Magneto achieved his desire for mutant power when his "daughter" the Scarlet Witch reimagined reality to be one where mutants and Magneto ruled. When this "House of M" reality eventually crumbled, the mentally disturbed Scarlet Witch used her abilities to depower most mutants—including Magneto. His powers were eventually restored by the High Evolutionary and, following a schism of views between Cyclops and Wolverine, Magneto joined Cyclops' more militant X-Men team. Later, while fighting Red Onslaught (*see* Red Skull), a spell cast by Scarlet Witch revealed that she and Quicksilver were not Magneto's children after all. Magneto continued to fight for mutants, giving his life in a desperate attempt to save the world when incursions caused by the Beyonders threatened the planet.

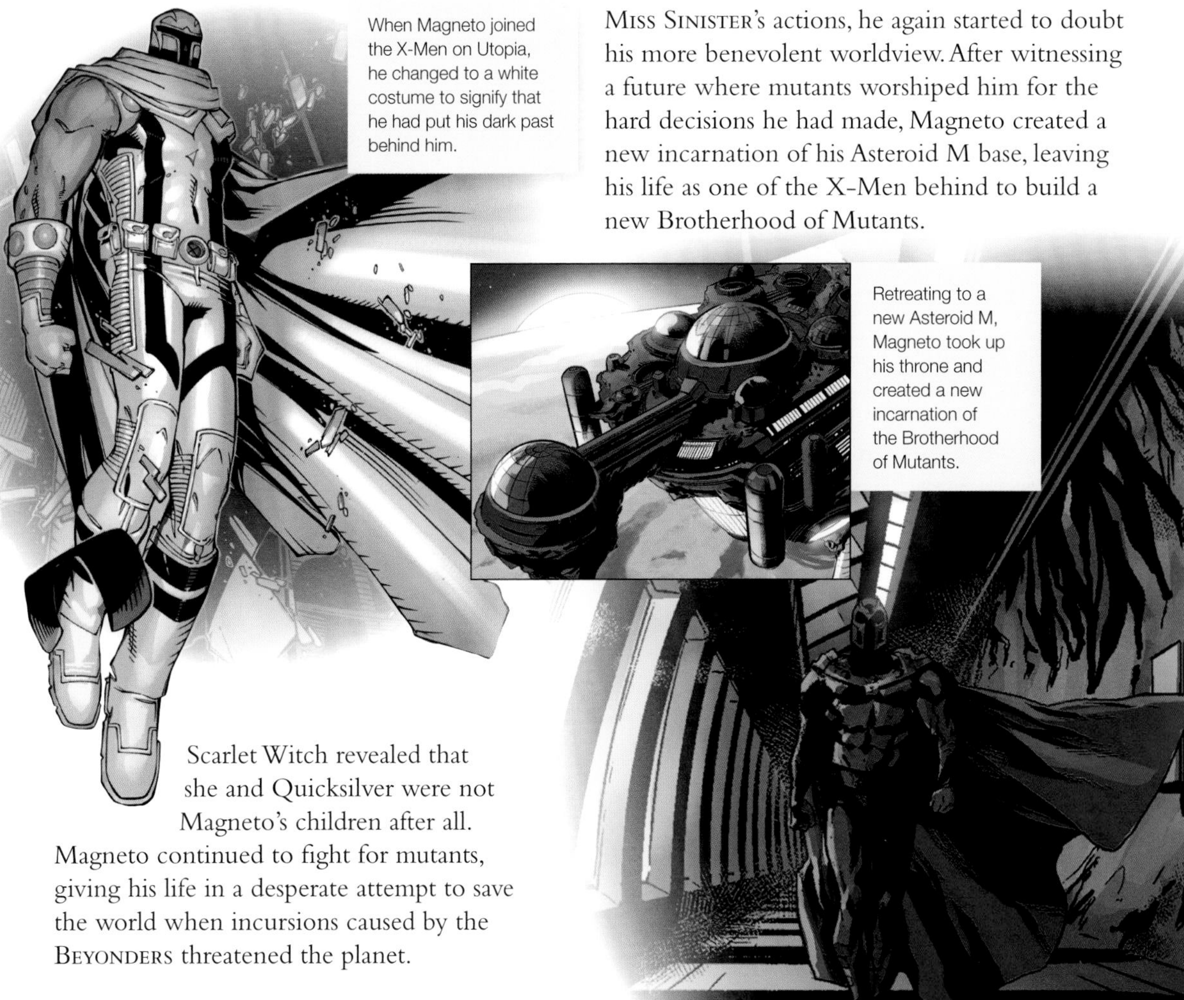

When Magneto joined the X-Men on Utopia, he changed to a white costume to signify that he had put his dark past behind him.

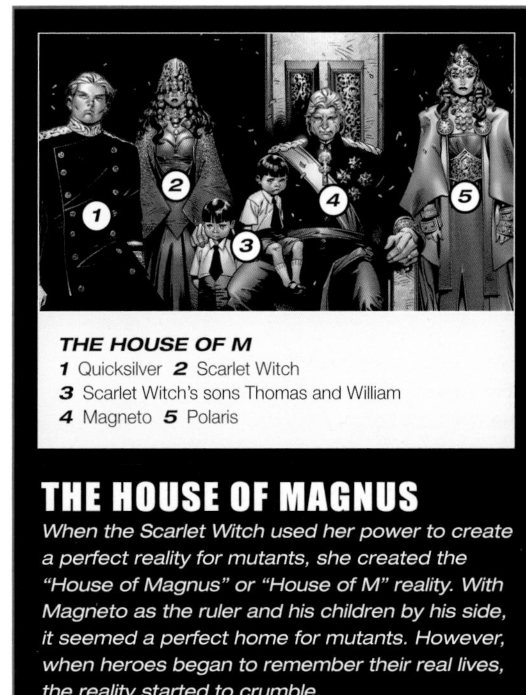

THE HOUSE OF M
1 Quicksilver ***2*** Scarlet Witch
3 Scarlet Witch's sons Thomas and William
4 Magneto ***5*** Polaris

THE HOUSE OF MAGNUS

When the Scarlet Witch used her power to create a perfect reality for mutants, she created the "House of Magnus" or "House of M" reality. With Magneto as the ruler and his children by his side, it seemed a perfect home for mutants. However, when heroes began to remember their real lives, the reality started to crumble.

When reality was recreated, Magneto was reborn and formed a new X-Men team—one that was willing to do the dirty work to get jobs done. He eventually rejoined the rest of the X-Men and helped mentor the young time-displaced X-Men team. However, when he was forced to kill several mutants in self-defense because of Miss Sinister's actions, he again started to doubt his more benevolent worldview. After witnessing a future where mutants worshiped him for the hard decisions he had made, Magneto created a new incarnation of his Asteroid M base, leaving his life as one of the X-Men behind to build a new Brotherhood of Mutants.

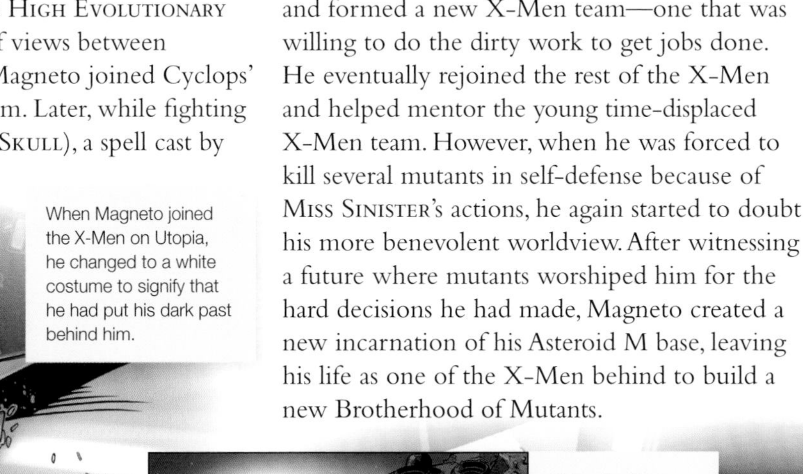

Retreating to a new Asteroid M, Magneto took up his throne and created a new incarnation of the Brotherhood of Mutants.

MAGNUM, MOSES

FIRST APPEARANCE *Giant-Size Spider-Man* #4 (April 1975)
REAL NAME Moses Magnum
OCCUPATION Terrorist, arms merchant **BASE** Various
HEIGHT/WEIGHT Not known **EYES** Brown **HAIR** Black
SPECIAL POWERS/ABILITIES Can generate vibrational force, which he can use to bolster his own strength and durability or release outward to cause earthquakes.

Arms dealer Moses Magnum's operation was dismantled by SPIDER-MAN and the PUNISHER. Narrowly escaping death, Magnum was found by APOCALYPSE, who offered him great power if he agreed to help spread chaos. Reconstructed by Apocalypse with the power to cause earthquakes, Magnum blackmailed Japan but was foiled by the X-MEN. Displeased, Apocalypse destabilized Magnum's abilities so that he caused earthquakes simply by touching the Earth. Magnum tried to regain Apocalypse's favor but was undone by the AVENGERS. DAKEN hunted him down and thought he had killed him, but Magnum resurfaced later as a major player in the criminal underworld, selling advanced technology.

MAJOR VICTORY

FIRST APPEARANCE *Marvel Super-Heroes* #18 (January 1969)
REAL NAME Vance Astro (Vance Astrovik)
OCCUPATION Adventurer **BASE** Starship Captain America II
HEIGHT 6 ft 1 in **WEIGHT** 235 lbs **EYES** Hazel **HAIR** Black
SPECIAL POWERS/ABILITIES Psychokinesis, a form of telekinesis, mostly manifested in the form of psych-blasts of explosive energy.

Vance Astro was an astronaut on a mission to colonize Centauri-IV. He was placed in suspended animation but awoke a millennium later. Upon finding Earth enslaved, he and friend YONDU formed a group of freedom fighters called the GUARDIANS OF THE GALAXY. Vance traveled to the present and convinced his younger self to follow a different path. He was later found frozen by STAR-LORD's team. Joining them, Vance suggested they call themselves the new Guardians of the Galaxy.

MAJOR DOMO

FIRST APPEARANCE *Longshot* #4 (December 1985)
REAL NAME Major Domo
OCCUPATION Principal aide to Mojo
BASE Mojoworld
HEIGHT/WEIGHT Not known **EYES** Blue **HAIR** Gray
SPECIAL POWERS/ABILITIES Constantly monitors Mojoworld's markets, enabling ongoing evaluation of his master's businesses.

The sycophantic yet contemptuous aide to MOJO, the ruler of Mojoworld, Major Domo's job is to ensure the smooth running of his master's household. An android, Major Domo provides information on and analysis of Mojo's businesses, while at the same time soothing his paranoid ego. These abilities make him Mojo's most prized servant. Although treated as nothing more than a glorified toaster, Major Domo remains at Mojo's side, playing a key role in curbing the worst excesses of his master's personality.

MAGUS

FIRST APPEARANCE *Strange Tales* #178 (February 1975)
REAL NAME Magus (Adam Warlock)
OCCUPATION Sorcerer **BASE** Mobile
HEIGHT 6ft 2in **WEIGHT** 240 lbs **EYES** White **HAIR** White
SPECIAL POWERS/ABILITIES All of the abilities of Adam Warlock. Magus is a powerful sorcerer capable of wielding energy, altering time, space, and reality to varying extents.

There have been three incarnations of Magus, all evil future versions of Adam WARLOCK. The first ruled the Universal Church of Truth and traveled to the past to manipulate Adam Warlock into becoming Magus. With THANOS' aid, Adam Warlock altered the future and erased Magus from the timeline. The second Magus was created when Warlock acquired the Infinity Gauntlet and purged good and evil from his soul. The evil part manifested as Magus. Warlock became the third Magus while repairing the space-time continuum. He died and was reborn, as was Warlock, creating two separate beings. Magus was subsequently killed by ULTRON to obtain his Infinity Gem.

MAGUS (TECHNARCHY)

FIRST APPEARANCE *New Mutants* #18 (August 1984)
REAL NAME Magus **OCCUPATION** Monarch **BASE** Mobile
HEIGHT Variable **WEIGHT** Variable **EYES** Black
HAIR In true form he has no hair, but parts of his head resemble it.
SPECIAL POWERS/ABILITIES Able to grow to the size of a star and destroy it. Can exist in outer-space and change his shape to that of any being or machine. Can replenish his life energies.

The Magus is the leader of the planet Technarch, which is populated by sentient "techno-organic" beings, a species with an organic structure resembling metal. Each child of the Magus must face him in a battle to the death for his position. One son, WARLOCK, instead fled to Earth and joined the NEW MUTANTS. The Magus came after Warlock, but the X-MEN defeated him and he went into hiding. Upon his return, the Magus attacked New York, and the AVENGERS drove him from Earth.

MALUS, DR. KARL

FIRST APPEARANCE *Spider-Woman* #30 (September 1980)
REAL NAME Dr. Karl Malus
OCCUPATION Former surgeon, now criminal scientist
BASE Los Angeles, California
HEIGHT 5 ft 9 in **WEIGHT** 155 lbs **EYES** Brown **HAIR** Black
SPECIAL POWERS/ABILITIES Advanced knowledge of genetic engineering, expertise in biochemistry, radiology, and surgery.

Fascinated with superhuman beings, scientist Karl Malus became involved with the criminal underworld to obtain funding for his research. Malus attempted to capture the original SPIDER-WOMAN. He restored the superhuman strength of Eric Josten (now known as ATLAS) and enabled him to grow to gigantic size. Working for the POWER BROKER, Malus gave many clients superhuman strength. He became the head of the criminal organization called the Corporation and later temporarily became the host for the CARNAGE symbiote. He was eaten by Carnage but reconstituted as a human-symbiote hybrid. He went on to work for Serpent Solutions, creating human-animal hybrids, including Cap-Wolf.

MAN-APE

While T'Challa—the Black Panther and king of the African nation of Wakanda—was away helping the Avengers in the US, M'Baku schemed to seize his throne. Reviving the outlawed White Gorilla cult, M'Baku killed a rare white gorilla, then bathed in its blood and ate its flesh, which gave him the power of the ape. Calling himself Man-Ape, he battled Black Panther and the Avenger's teammates, both in Wakanda and in the US. Defeated, he teamed with the Grim Reaper—despite the Reaper's racism—to form a new Lethal Legion. He was later slain by the vampire Morlun. He was resurrected and recruited for Headhunter and Purple Man's Villains for Hire. He spent time imprisoned in SHIELD's Pleasant Hill facility before dying again. For a short time, his brother Mandla became the White Gorilla, but Man-Ape was raised from the dead yet again by Baron Macabre.

FACTFILE

REAL NAME
M'Baku

OCCUPATION
Mercenary, renegade

BASE
Mobile

HEIGHT 7 ft
WEIGHT 355 lbs
EYES Brown
HAIR Brown

FIRST APPEARANCE
Avengers #62 (March 1969)

MAN-APE

POWERS
Possesses superhuman strength, agility, and resistance to injury. He is a powerful warrior whose fighting techniques are based on those of gorillas.

Clad in the pelt of the rare Wakandan white gorilla, M'Baku the Man-Ape takes up a battle position at the head of a band of his followers in the White Gorilla cult.

MAN-BEAST

FIRST APPEARANCE *Thor* #134 (November 1966)
REAL NAME Man-Beast
OCCUPATION Would-be world conqueror
BASE Somewhere below New York City
HEIGHT 6 ft 10 in **WEIGHT** 320 lbs **EYES** Red **HAIR** Brown
SPECIAL POWERS/ABILITIES Superhuman strength, speed, endurance, and senses; remarkable scientific ability, particularly in genetics and engineering.

Created by accident, the Man-Beast was born when a wolf was placed inside the High Evolutionary's genetic accelerator. Despite creating an entire evil army using the same device, the Man-Beast was eventually defeated by Thor, placed in a shuttle, and exiled into space. The Man-Beast sought revenge on the High Evolutionary when he landed on Counter-Earth—a world created by that being. He introduced Counter-Earth's people to the concept of evil and even attempted to destroy the planet. In the years since, the Man-Beast has fought both Adam Warlock and the Hulk. He attempted to raise a new army, using the Legion of Light cult as a front, and went head-to-head with Spider-Man. Later, with help from Quicksilver, the High Evolutionary captured him and devolved him back into a wolf.

MANCHA, VICTOR

FIRST APPEARANCE *Runaways* #1 (April 2005)
REAL NAME Victor Mancha **OCCUPATION** Adventurer
BASE New York City
HEIGHT 5 ft 8 in **WEIGHT** 220 lbs
EYES Brown **HAIR** Brown
SPECIAL POWERS/ABILITIES Victor is a cyborg who can control electromagnetic energy.

When a woman helped one of Ultron's spare bodies return to health, he gave her what she wanted most: a son. That boy, Victor, was a cyborg built with samples of his mother's DNA. Unaware of his origins, Victor joined teenage heroes the Runaways while he was a student at East Angeles High School. When Ultron revealed himself, he triggered a switch in the boy that put him under Ultron's control, but Victor overrode his programming. Later, Victor accidentally killed Vision's son, and was killed by Vision's wife in revenge. Victor's friend Chase Stein found his head though, and set about restoring him.

MANDRILL

Jerome Beechman's parents worked at the atomic testing grounds in New Mexico, where exposure to radiation caused mutations in their son. Jerome was born with animal-like fur on his body and an apelike appearance. When he was ten, his parents abandoned him in the desert. There he met Nekra Sinclair, whose mother had worked at the atomic testing grounds. Jerome took the name Mandrill, and the two traveled the American Southwest together, avoiding all human contact. Mandrill and Nekra formed Black Spectre, an organization of black women hoping to overthrow the American government—until Daredevil stopped them. After SHIELD captured Nekra, Mandrill formed Fem-Force, an army of radical women under his control. Fem-Force teamed up with Magneto's Mutant Force, but the Defenders stopped their plans. Mandrill's powers survived M-Day, and he has recently been seen working for the Hood in New York.

FACTFILE

REAL NAME
Jerome Beechman

OCCUPATION
Professional criminal

BASE
Mobile

HEIGHT 6 ft
WEIGHT 270 lbs
EYES Black
HAIR Brown

FIRST APPEARANCE
Shanna the She-Devil #4 (June 1973)

MANDRILL

POWERS
Mandrill has the ability to emit powerful pheromones which give him the power to attract and enslave adult women causing them to submit to his will.

Mandarin, see page 230

MANDARIN

Evil master of the ten rings

MANDARIN

FACTFILE

REAL NAME
Unrevealed

OCCUPATION
Criminal mastermind

BASE
The Palace of the Star Dragon in the Valley of Spirits within China

HEIGHT 6 ft 2 in
WEIGHT 215 lbs
EYES Blue-black
HAIR Black

FIRST APPEARANCE
Tales of Suspense #50 (February 1964)

POWERS
One of the world's greatest scientific minds and a superb athlete. Possesses ten rings of extraterrestrial origin that have amazing powers.

A direct descendant of Genghis Khan, the Mandarin was born in China to a wealthy father who lost everything in the Communist revolution. In the forbidden Valley of Spirits, the Mandarin found a crashed starship containing ten alien rings. These rings could control another's mind, rearrange matter, fire a disintegration beam, create a vortex, produce deadly gases, create ice blasts, or discharge electricity, flames, bursts of blinding light, or clouds of darkness. With the rings, the Mandarin conquered the valley and made plans to seize control of the world, often clashing with Iron Man and the Avengers.

The Mandarin is a trained martial artist and his rings pack a punch, but Spider-Man is too quick for him!

A WORLD POWER

The Mandarin developed teleportation technology, which he used both to get himself into and out of trouble but also to kidnap people like Happy Hogan. He allied himself with various villains, including Doctor Doom, the Enchantress and the Executioner, Living Laser, Power Man (Atlas), and Swordsman. For a while, he even tried to make the Hulk his accomplice, but he could not control the beast. He worked hard to unmask the man inside the Iron Man armor, and once he established that it was Tony Stark, used that information against him. For a while, the world thought him dead, and his son Temugin inherited his rings—which were still attached to his hands. The Mandarin returned however, sporting bionic hands, the rings now fused to his spine.

A NEW APPROACH

The Mandarin began using more subtle methods to attack Stark. He kidnapped Maya Hansen, creator of the Extremis techno-organic virus, which could rewrite the user's DNA and which Stark had used to improve his Iron Man armor. With her expertise, the Mandarin hacked into the Extremis inside Stark and commandeered his mind and body. He also broke Ezekiel Stane out of prison to help in his quest to destroy Stark, and set his daughter, Sasha Hammer, against Stark.

With Stark under his control, the Mandarin forced him to create Titanomech bodies for the alien spirits contained inside his rings. While trapped in the Mandarin's employ, Stark convinced the villain's allies that the man was insane and persuaded them to rebel. Stark's latest company, Resilient, managed to reactivate a clean copy of the Extremis technology inside of him, and Stark and his allies brought the Mandarin and his Titanomech down. Ezekiel shot him through the head soon after. The Mandarin's rings found new hosts, designated Mandarin-One through Mandarin-Ten. Malekith the Dark Elf disabled and killed several Mandarins, and Stark combined four of their rings to create a Master Ring to control the others. Thus Stark was able to defeat them and acquire all ten.

Since the Mandarin believes he can use technology to achieve world domination, he often ends up in conflict with Iron Man.

MAN-THING

All who fear burn at the Man-Thing's touch!

Unflappable insurance claims adjustor Nathan Mehr comes face to face with the shambling, monstrous Man-Thing.

Ted Sallis was a research scientist on a project aiming to replicate the Super-Soldier formula that empowered CAPTAIN AMERICA in the 1940s. But he was betrayed to the sinister criminal think tank known as AIM, who wanted his research. Fearing that his work would fall into evil hands, Sallis destroyed his notes and injected himself with the only sample of his serum. But while fleeing for his life, he crashed his car in the swampland surrounding his laboratory, and was seemingly killed.

TRANSFORMATION

Unknown to Sallis, the area in which he'd located his lab was close to the Nexus of All Realities, a mystical gateway that linked all of the myriad dimensions of existence. In some mysterious fashion, Sallis' serum combined with the ambient mystical energies of the Nexus, and caused the vegetation of the swamp that surrounded his almost lifeless body to reconstitute him as a mindless, shambling mass—the Man-Thing.

FEELING THE BURN

Possessing scant intellect of his own, the Man-Thing is instead empathetically attuned to his surroundings. While Ted Sallis' soul still resides within the great beast, in general the Man-Thing is mindless, reacting only to the emotions of those around him. Fear causes the Man-Thing great pain, and he will journey forth from his swampy home to put an end to any source of fear that causes him distress. Because of a quirk of chemistry in his makeup, any creature who feels fear in the Man-Thing's presence burns at his touch.

The Man-Thing seldom leaves the confines of his swamp, but he can occasionally be drawn forth by strong emotions, which affect him painfully through his animalistic empathy.

ESSENTIAL STORYLINES

- ***Adventures Into Fear* #17–19 and *Man-Thing* #1** The Man-Thing and a ragtag band of allies including Dakimh the Sorcerer, Jennifer Kale, Korrek the Barbarian and Howard the Duck defend the Nexus of All Realities from Thog the Netherspawn.
- ***Giant-Size Man-Thing* #4** The Man-Thing is drawn to the pain experienced by an angst-ridden high-school student.

FACTFILE MAN-THING

REAL NAME
Ted Sallis

OCCUPATION
Guardian of the Nexus of All Realities

BASE
Swamp in the Florida Everglades that conceals the Nexus of All Realities

HEIGHT Around 7 ft
WEIGHT Around 500 lbs
EYES Red, bulbous
HAIR None

FIRST APPEARANCE
Savage Tales #1 (May 1971)

POWERS
Virtually indestructible, he has superhuman strength. Fear causes him pain, and changes his chemical makeup so that the touch of his body burns those who feel fear in his presence.

Man-Thing guards the Nexus of All Realities, an interdimensional gateway at the center of his swamp.

IN THE WORLD

During the DARK REIGN, ARES captured the Man-Thing, although he soon after showed up living under Manhattan with the LEGION OF MONSTERS. Later, Hank PYM studied him while he was imprisoned in the Raft and figured out a way to use the creature's connection to the Nexus to teleport Luke CAGE's team of THUNDERBOLTS all around the world. After serving with the THUNDERBOLTS, Man-Thing returned to his Florida swamp.

MANIFOLD

FIRST APPEARANCE *Secret Warriors* #4 (July 2009)
REAL NAME Eden Fesi **OCCUPATION** Adventurer
BASE Australia
HEIGHT 5 ft 10 in **WEIGHT** 175 lbs
EYES Brown **HAIR** Black
SPECIAL POWERS/ABILITIES Eden can teleport many people any distance within his own universe.

An Aboriginal Australian, Eden studied under his mentor GATEWAY, who had similar powers. Nick FURY recruited the young man for his SECRET WARRIORS, with Gateway's blessing. During a battle with HYDRA, he was injured and fell into a coma. He recovered, and during the conflict between the AVENGERS and the X-MEN over the approaching Phoenix Force, the Avengers recruited him to their side. Eden played a crucial role in getting them where they needed to be as fast as possible.

MANSLAUGHTER

FIRST APPEARANCE *Defenders* #133 (July 1984)
REAL NAME Not known
OCCUPATION Former hired assassin **BASE** Mobile
HEIGHT 5 ft 7 in **WEIGHT** 115 lbs **EYES** Blue **HAIR** Red
SPECIAL POWERS/ABILITIES Low-level telepath: influences peripheral vision and subliminal hearing of others in order to render himself invisible; uses abilities to enhance skills as a huntsman.

Manslaughter used his mutant powers for tracking and hunting. He impressed the ETERNAL known as the INTERLOPER by successfully tracking him down in the Siberian wastelands. The Interloper agreed to help Manslaughter hone his powers but did not train him fully. This was just as well, for Manslaughter later became a ruthless assassin. Eventually he redeemed himself, sacrificing his life in the effort to destroy the DRAGON OF THE MOON. He has since returned to life.

MAN-WOLF

FIRST APPEARANCE (as Man-Wolf) *The Amazing Spider-Man* #124 (September 1973) **REAL NAME** John Jameson
OCCUPATION Former astronaut; pilot; security chief
BASE New York City
HEIGHT 6 ft 6 in **WEIGHT** 350 lbs **EYES** Red **HAIR** White
SPECIAL POWERS/ABILITIES As Man-Wolf: superhuman strength, speed, agility, durability, and heightened senses.

Astronaut and son of *Daily Bugle* publisher J. Jonah JAMESON, John Jameson discovered a gem on the moon. On Earth, this gem caused him to transform into a wolflike creature under a full moon. The Moongem contained the essence of Stargod, ruler of Other-Realm, in another dimension. Man-Wolf journeyed to Other-Realm, where he helped its people defeat their enemy Arisen Tyrk. John underwent radiation treatment, which destroyed the Moongem. He married SHE-HULK and then became Stargod and left for space. After he returned, they annulled their marriage, and he returned to being an astronaut.

MANTIS

MANTIS

FACTFILE
REAL NAME
Unknown
OCCUPATION
Adventurer
BASE
Temple of the Priests, Pama, Vietnam; Ho Chi Minh City, Vietnam; Avengers Mansion, New York City

HEIGHT 5 ft 6 in
WEIGHT 115 lbs
EYES Green
HAIR Black

FIRST APPEARANCE
Avengers #112 (June 1973)

POWERS

Mantis has superior agility, extraordinary martial arts skills, and the ability to sense the emotions of others. She can also will herself to heal quickly after injury.

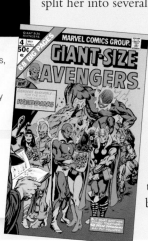

Giant-Size Avengers #4 features Vision and Scarlet Witch's wedding, and Mantis' transformation and departure from Earth.

Born in Vietnam, Mantis was raised by the Priests of Pama, a pacifist sect of the alien KREE. When Mantis had completed her martial arts training, the priests sent her to live among humans, implanting false memories of life as an orphan struggling for survival on the streets of Ho Chi Minh City. She eventually teamed up with the SWORDSMAN, a costumed criminal, whom Mantis helped rehabilitate. When the Swordsman joined the AVENGERS, Mantis joined as well.

After her marriage to the eldest of the Cotati, an alien race of telepathic plant-beings, Mantis transformed into pure energy and left Earth. She gave birth to a son named Quoi, and joined the SILVER SURFER for a while, but was caught in an explosion that split her into several independent aspects. Once she managed to reintegrate herself, she battled THANOS to protect her son. After surviving the ANNIHILATION events, she joined the GUARDIANS OF THE GALAXY.

The Guardians fell apart after they discovered Mantis had used her powers to force them all to join. Later, she and the other Guardians were held prisoner by MAGUS. After their escape, she refused to join STAR-LORD's new Guardians, but helped him find the source of the "time quakes" that he had been afflicted with.

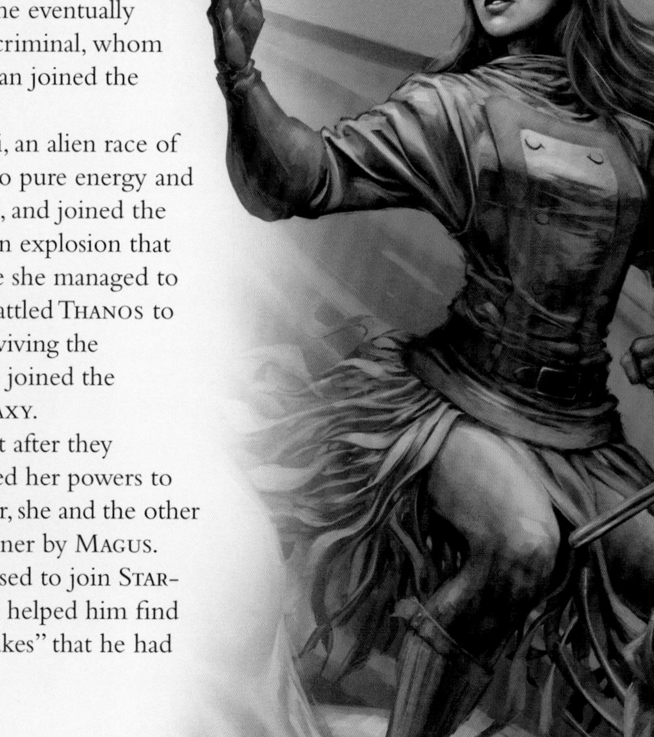

MARAUDERS

MARAUDERS

FACTFILE

MEMBERS

MISTER SINISTER Telepathy.
MALICE Telepathy.
VERTIGO Affects equilibrium.
ARCLIGHT Seismic shocks from hands.
HARPOON Bio-energetic projectiles.
RIPTIDE A mutant whirlwind.
BLOCKBUSTER Super-strong.
PRISM Captures powers then projects back at source.
SABRETOOTH Adamantium skeleton; supersenses.
SCALPHUNTER Manipulates mechanical components.
SCRAMBLER Disrupts living and mechanical systems.

FIRST APPEARANCE
Uncanny X-Men #210 (October 1986)

The personal army of mutant eugeneticist, Mister Sinister, the Marauders are among the deadliest forces the X-Men have ever faced. Mister Sinister loathed the Morlocks, so the Marauders' first mission was to obliterate them. They later went head-to-head with the X-Men, even destroying the Xavier Institute.

Sinister created clones of the original Marauders, and if one fell, a duplicate replaced them. The Marauders helped him try to track down Hope Summers; many of them were killed, and a group of clones were activated, but X-Force killed them too. Magneto wiped out the Marauders in revenge for the Morlock massacre, then created his own army of Marauder clones. Miss Sinister used the Mothervine virus to create another group called the New Marauders, but was forced to eliminate them when they turned on her during a battle with Emma Frost.

THE MARAUDERS
1 Scrambler ***2*** Sabretooth
3 Malice ***4*** Scalphunter
5 Vertigo ***6*** Harpoon
7 Riptide

MARROW

MARROW

Marrow is a young mutant who left her normal life behind to journey into the sewers controlled by the mysterious Morlocks. She was one of the few survivors of the massacre that decimated their ranks. Escaping to the dimension ruled by Mikhail Rasputin, Marrow became a member of Gene Nation, a radical mutant group dedicated to striking back at their human oppressors.

After a number of encounters with the X-Men, Marrow joined them, however her fiery personality meant that she never fitted in at Xavier's School and she left under mysterious circumstances.

She was recruited by the newly-reformed Weapon X program, which boosted her powers so as to allow her to control her appearance. She lost her powers on M-Day but joined the X-Cell terrorists. When she learned the truth of M-Day, Marrow left X-Cell and nearly died fighting Quicksilver. Marrow's powers were restored by Volga, though the procedure caused her to have a miscarriage. Cable then found Marrow and recruited her to X-Force.

FACTFILE

REAL NAME
Sarah; last name may be Rushman

OCCUPATION
Genetic terrorist; adventurer

BASE
Various

HEIGHT 6 ft
WEIGHT Unknown
EYES Green
HAIR Magenta

FIRST APPEARANCE
Uncanny X-Men #325 (October 1995)

POWERS

Marrow's mutant physiognomy allows her to rapidly regrow the bone spurs that protrude from her body, and which she uses as weapons. She also has two hearts and enhanced durability, making her difficult to kill.

MARRINA

FIRST APPEARANCE *Alpha Flight* #1 (August 1983)
REAL NAME Marrina Smallwood
OCCUPATION Adventurer **BASE** Mobile
HEIGHT 6 ft **WEIGHT** 200 lbs **EYES** Black **HAIR** Green
SPECIAL POWERS/ABILITIES Enhanced strength and stamina; able to breathe both air and water; can swim at high speed and generate waterspouts.

The Plodex alien life form who became known as Marrina hatched from an egg that had soaked in the Atlantic Ocean, giving her aquatic adaptations that surfaced when she assumed the humanoid forms of her adoptive guardians, the Smallwoods. Her superhuman abilities allowed her to join Alpha Flight, and she later married Namor the Sub-Mariner. Tragedy struck when, during her pregnancy, she turned into a monstrous leviathan. Namor was forced to kill her, but she returned during the Chaos War and now works with Alpha Flight once more.

MARVEL BOY

MARVEL BOY

There have been many Marvel Boys: Martin Burns who wielded the power of Hercules in the 1940s; Robert Grayson who received cosmic bracelets from the Eternals in the 1950s; Wendell Vaughn, who became Quasar; Vance Astrovik, who became Justice; and the mutant David Bank. The latest is the Kree Noh-Varr, whose starship was shot down on Earth. He sided with Earth during the Secret Invasion and became a new Captain Marvel in HAMMER's Dark Avengers. He left to become the Protector but failed and was stripped of much of his power. Noh-Varr later became romantically involved with Hawkeye (Kate Bishop) and joined the Young Avengers against the interdimensional parasite, Mother. Afterward, he helped the Inhumans search the cosmos for their origins.

FACTFILE

REAL NAME
Noh-Varr

OCCUPATION
Adventurer

BASE
New York City

HEIGHT 5 ft 10 in
WEIGHT 165 lbs
EYES Black
HAIR White

FIRST APPEARANCE
Marvel Boy #1 (September 2000)

POWERS

Enhanced strength, speed, and stamina; can mentally control his body's growth; nanobots reroute pain sensations.

MASTER OF THE WORLD

FIRST APPEARANCE *Alpha Flight* #2 (September 1983)
REAL NAME Eshu **OCCUPATION** Conqueror
BASE Mobile
HEIGHT 6 ft 4 in **WEIGHT** 270 lbs
EYES Green **HAIR** Black
SPECIAL POWERS/ABILITIES Eshu has superhuman endurance, healing, and strength and can mentally control his living starship.

Eshu was a simple hunter over 4,000 years ago—before an alien ship from the Plodex captured him and he somehow took control of it. He has since plotted to take over the world, often starting with Canada, which put him into conflict with ALPHA FLIGHT. He even led the Unity political party there. He defended the world from KANG, if only so he could have it for himself. He has been seemingly killed several times, but has always managed to survive.

MASTER ORDER

FIRST APPEARANCE *Marvel Two-in-One Annual* #2 (December 1977)
REAL NAME None **OCCUPATION** Cosmic entity
BASE Everywhere
HEIGHT/WEIGHT/EYES/HAIR N/A
SPECIAL POWERS/ABILITIES Scope of powers is unknown although can change destinies of specific individuals.

DEATH, LORD CHAOS, ETERNITY, and Master Order—enigmatic beings all, each embodying a distinct abstract concept. Their origins are unknown and so are their powers, although many surmise that these are without limit. The "brother" of Lord Chaos, Master Order strives to maintain a cosmic balance with his sibling, intervening in mortal affairs on only the rarest of occasions. Both Order and Chaos were destroyed by the BEYONDERS in their quest to erase the Multiverse. However, after reality was rebuilt, both entities returned and became Logos, a cosmic being who sought to impose their united will on all existence. After Logos was defeated, they were split up again.

MASTER PANDEMONIUM

FIRST APPEARANCE *West Coast Avengers* #4 (January 1986)
REAL NAME Martin Preston **OCCUPATION** Demon commander
BASE Los Angeles, California
HEIGHT 6 ft 1 in **WEIGHT** 205 lbs **EYES** Blue **HAIR** Black
SPECIAL POWERS/ABILITIES Amulet of Azmodeus permits inter-dimensional teleportation. Can detach his own arms as living demons, fire energy beams from his hands, levitate, and breathe fire.

After making a deal with MEPHISTO, Martin Preston became a monstrous being with a star-shaped hole in his chest for the fragments of his missing soul. As Master Pandemonium, he identified the SCARLET WITCH's twins as having two of the fragments. When all five were found, Mephisto captured him. Preston escaped, and WICCAN and SPEED later found him but decided he was now harmless. He later taught at the Hellfire Academy.

MASTER KHAN

FIRST APPEARANCE *Strange Tales* #77 (October 1960)
REAL NAME Khan **OCCUPATION** God to the people of K'un-Lun
BASE K'un-Lun, New York City
HEIGHT Unknown **WEIGHT** Unknown **EYES** Red **HAIR** Black
SPECIAL POWERS/ABILITIES Magical powers allow him to distort reality, levitate and shrink objects, alter his appearance, form energy shields, fire energy blasts, and cast mystic spells.

The human sorcerer Master Khan was worshiped as a god on the alien planet of K'un-Lun, where the dominant life form is a sentient plant called the H'ylthri. He served as the protector of the inhabitants of K'un-Lun, and his power came from their worship. On Earth, Khan was a scholar but also a student of the occult. Once on K'un-Lun, Master Khan became a mortal enemy of IRON FIST. Returning to Earth, Khan fought with WOLVERINE, NAMOR, and NAMORITA. He once captured Namor and posed as him, but the Atlantean prince broke free and killed him.

MASTERS, ALICIA

As a child, Alicia Masters was blinded in the same accident that killed her father. Undaunted, she discovered that she had a talent for sculpting. The man responsible for the accident, Phillip Masters (PUPPET MASTER), married her mother and adopted Alicia. When her stepfather clashed with the FANTASTIC FOUR, the THING (Ben Grimm) rescued Alicia, who was a pawn in her stepfather's scheme. A strong relationship developed between Alicia and the Thing.

Perhaps Alicia's greatest moment was when she appealed to the humanity buried deep within the sky-spanning SILVER SURFER and convinced him to rebel against his master, the world-devouring GALACTUS, in defense of Earth. For a while, she broke up with the Thing and dated the Surfer, but she later returned to Ben. At one point, the SKRULL agent LYJA THE LAZERFIST replaced Alicia and married the HUMAN TORCH. After the longest of courtships, Ben and Alicia finally tied the knot in a wedding ceremony to be remembered.

FACTFILE
REAL NAME
Alicia Reiss Masters
OCCUPATION
Sculptress
BASE
Manhattan

HEIGHT 5 ft 4 in
WEIGHT 110 lbs
EYES Blue
HAIR Blond

FIRST APPEARANCE
Fantastic Four #8
(November 1962)

MASTERS, ALICIA

POWERS
A talented sculptress; able to sense the good in people regardless of their appearance.

Despite her blindness, Alicia Masters is a world-renowned sculptress who practices her art through touch.

Alicia had a powerful effect on the deep-buried emotions of the Silver Surfer. She convinced him to rebel against his master, the world-devouring Galactus, and fight for Earth by appealing to his inner goodness.

MASTERS OF EVIL

A villainous alliance against the Avengers

Believing that there's strength in numbers, the original Baron Zemo forms a sinister super-team equal in power to the mighty Avengers.

The Masters of Evil are perennial foes of the AVENGERS, assembling multiple times over the years, often with no link between the various groupings other than their name.

The first Masters of Evil came about through the efforts of Nazi mastermind BARON ZEMO.

DECADES OF VILLAINY

Zemo schemed to defeat his wartime nemesis CAPTAIN AMERICA by enlisting the most notorious enemies of Captain America's comrades in the Avengers. He gathered the Melter to fight IRON MAN, the RADIOACTIVE MAN to fight THOR, and the BLACK KNIGHT to battle both the WASP and Giant Man (Henry PYM). Later, Zemo welcomed the ENCHANTRESS and the EXECUTIONER into the Masters of Evil. The team disbanded after Zemo's death.

A second Masters of Evil took its place, founded by the robot ULTRON, in his cover identity as the CRIMSON COWL. The team obtained blueprints of Avengers Mansion from butler Edwin JARVIS and struck at the Avengers in their own home. The new Black Knight, Dane Whitman, turned on his teammates in the Masters of Evil and helped the Avengers scatter the villains.

LATEST MASTERS
1 Whiplash
2 Wrecker
3 Man-Killer
4 Thunderball
5 Klaw
6 Bulldozer
7 Piledriver
8 Tiger Shark

The criminal mastermind EGGHEAD organized a third Masters of Evil, hoping to take vengeance on Henry Pym, but met defeat (and death) soon after. Helmut Zemo, son of the original Baron Zemo, brought together the fourth incarnation of the Masters.

THE DARKEST HOUR

Baron Zemo II gathered more than a dozen criminals to crush the Avengers through force of numbers. Their most infamous exploit was the failed siege of Avengers Mansion.

DOCTOR OCTOPUS assembled a fifth Masters of Evil and fought the GUARDIANS OF THE GALAXY. Baron Zemo II returned to organize a sixth team, the THUNDERBOLTS, who masqueraded as heroes.

Justine Hammer, the new Crimson Cowl, assembled the seventh and eighth versions of the team. Max Fury—a twisted, android version of Nick FURY—led the ninth team for the SHADOW COUNCIL. Some time later, Helmut Zemo returned as leader and transformed the latest incarnation of the Masters of Evil into an Army of Evil, boasting the largest membership to date.

ESSENTIAL STORYLINES

- ***Avengers #6*** Baron Zemo assembles the first Masters of Evil, featuring a villainous counterpart for each member of the Avengers.
- ***Avengers #270–277*** The Masters of Evil raid their enemies' headquarters in the classic storyline "The Siege of Avengers Mansion."
- ***Thunderbolts #24–25*** The most recent grouping of the Masters of Evil unites 25 Super Villains, providing a formidable foe for the Thunderbolts.
- ***Guardians of the Galaxy #28–29*** Doctor Octopus' Masters of Evil team clash with the Guardians of the Galaxy.

FACTFILE

ORIGINAL MEMBERS AND POWERS

BARON ZEMO Extended longevity, brilliant criminal mind.
MELTER Could melt any metal with a molecular beam.
RADIOACTIVE MAN Can release blasts of lethal radioactive energy.
BLACK KNIGHT (Nathan Garrett) Skilled combatant; carried power lance.
EXECUTIONER Enhanced strength, carried enchanted ax.
ENCHANTRESS Sorceress

FIRST APPEARANCE
Avengers #6 (July 1964)

ORIGINAL MASTERS
1 Black Knight
2 Melter
3 Radioactive Man

MAXIMUS

FACTFILE
REAL NAME
Maximus Boltagon
OCCUPATION
Would-be conqueror
BASE
New Arctilan

HEIGHT 5 ft 11 in
WEIGHT 180 lbs
EYES Blue
HAIR Black

FIRST APPEARANCE
Fantastic Four #47
(February 1966)

POWERS
Maximus possesses a genius-level intellect unhampered by sanity, and possesses the ability to overwhelm the thought-processes of those in close proximity, taking over their conscious minds.

The younger brother of Black Bolt, king of the Inhumans, Maximus exhibited no outward signs of change after his exposure to the gene-altering Terrigen Mists. Instead, as he grew, he chose to hide his growing psionic abilities along with his lust for power. When they were adolescents, Black Bolt caught Maximus forging an alliance with the Kree, the aliens responsible for the creation of the Inhumans. Black Bolt's sonic scream destroyed the Kree warship and also shattered Maximus' grip on sanity. Maximus the Mad then devoted himself to wresting control of his people from his noble brother. He succeeded several times over the years, but Black Bolt always managed to retake the throne from him. During the Secret Invasion, the two finally ended their quarrel while facing a common foe. While Maximus remained manipulative, thereafter he was mostly loyal to his family. When the Kree assassin known as Vox started killing Inhumans, Maximus was seemingly one of his first victims.

The relationship between Maximus and his brother was always strained. Maximus' heightened cognitive function filled him with a burning desire to usurp his brother's throne.

Maximus and the giant dog known as Lockjaw tried to stop Vox, but paid with their lives.

MAYHEM

FIRST APPEARANCE *Cloak and Dagger* #1 (October 1983)
REAL NAME Brigid O'Reilly
OCCUPATION Former policewoman; vigilante
BASE New York City **HEIGHT** 5 ft 4 in
WEIGHT 120 lbs **EYES** Green **HAIR** Green
SPECIAL POWERS/ABILITIES Skin constantly secretes a poisonous gas; this can cause paralysis if it gets in bloodstream and can serve as truth drug; Mayhem is also able to fly.

As a New York police detective, Brigid O'Reilly confronted the vigilante partnership Cloak and Dagger. Feeling that their approach endangered innocent lives, Brigid was initially hostile to them, but became more tolerant when she learned of their origins. Following a confrontation with several corrupt police officers while she was investigating a drug-smuggling operation, Brigid was killed by poisonous gas. However, the intervention of Cloak and Dagger led to her resurrection as a superpowered individual, enabling her to exact revenge. Since then, Brigid has adopted the alias Mayhem and become a vigilante, targeting New York drug pushers.

The poisonous gas produced by Mayhem's body is used in her fight against crime.

MEDUSA

FACTFILE
REAL NAME
Medusalith Amaquelin
OCCUPATION
Queen of the Inhumans
BASE
New Arctilan

HEIGHT 5 ft 11 in
WEIGHT 130 lbs
EYES Green
HAIR Red

FIRST APPEARANCE
Fantastic Four #36
(March 1965)

POWERS
Can use her long hair to attack, lift weights, pick locks, and as a whip or a rope.

A member of the Inhumans' royal family on Attilan, Medusa was exposed to Terrigen Mist as a baby. She gained the ability to use her hair like extra limbs. She learned to interpret Black Bolt's body language and fell in love with him. When Maximus seized power from Black Bolt, Medusa left Attilan and suffered amnesia due to a plane crash. The Wizard found her and made her part of the Frightful Four. When Black Bolt retook his throne, Medusa returned to act as his interpreter and later married him. They had a son, Ahura, who suffers from his uncle Maximus' madness. Medusa also substituted as a member of the Fantastic Four when she could. Medusa became the ruler of the Inhumans following Black Bolt's apparent death. She led them when they were attacked by the X-Men, but took the decision to destroy the Terrigen Mists when she learned they were killing mutants. She had a relationship with the Human Torch and helped the Inhumans stop the alien Progenitors from invading the Earth.

MEGGAN

FACTFILE

REAL NAME
Meggan

OCCUPATION
Adventurer

BASE
England

HEIGHT Variable
WEIGHT Variable
EYES Variable
HAIR Variable

FIRST APPEARANCE
Mighty World of Marvel #7 (December 1983)

POWERS
Meggan is a shapeshifter whose forms are influenced by the emotions of others; she can fly and project energy blasts drawn from the Earth.

Born to a Romani family, Meggan grew up in a fur-covered form and considered herself a freak. Only later, after being taken in by Brian Braddock (Captain Britain), did she discover that she could consciously alter her appearance. She transformed herself from her furry form into a strikingly beautiful woman with long, golden hair. Not long after this, Meggan and Braddock started a relationship and founded the super-team Excalibur, and the two eventually married. As Captain Britain's wife, Meggan is the queen of Otherworld, assisting in the management of the dimensions that make up the Omniverse. She sacrificed herself to save her husband but later returned to the living. She recently had a baby with Captain Britain.

MENTALLO

FIRST APPEARANCE *Strange Tales* #141 (February 1966)
REAL NAME Marvin Flumm **OCCUPATION** Professional criminal
BASE Mobile **HEIGHT** 5 ft 10 in
WEIGHT 175 lbs **EYES** Brown **HAIR** Brown
SPECIAL POWERS/ABILITIES Possesses telepathic powers. Can read the thoughts of anyone within five miles, locate a particular brain pattern and project his own thoughts into the minds of others.

Marvin Flumm went to work for SHIELD while his powers developed. Calling himself Mentallo, he stole a battlesuit and telepathy-enhancing equipment and teamed with the Fixer to try to take over SHIELD, but Nick Fury stopped them. Flumm called himself Think Tank when he first faced Captain America, but soon returned to the code name Mentallo. He tangled with the Hulk, the Avengers, Professor X, and the Fantastic Four, among others. He was part of the Hood's criminal crew, and was one of the many villains imprisoned in SHIELD's Pleasant Hill facility.

MELTDOWN

FACTFILE

REAL NAME
Tabitha Smith

OCCUPATION
Adventurer

BASE
New York State

HEIGHT 5 ft 5 in
WEIGHT 120 lbs
EYES Blue
HAIR Blond

FIRST APPEARANCE
Secret Wars II #5 (November 1985)

POWERS
Generates and throws "time bombs"—energy balls of concussive force. She can vary the size and power of her time bombs at will.

When Tabitha Smith's father learned of her mutant abilities, he beat her, and she fled to Xavier's School for Gifted Youngsters. Encountering the Beyonder on the way, she went on a series of cosmic adventures before falling in with the Vanisher's gang of thieves, the Fallen Angels. She oscillated between X-Factor and the Fallen Angels before becoming a member of the New Mutants.

She later joined X-Force as Boom Boom and became a protégée to Cable, helping him attack the Weapon X facility and the Neverland mutant concentration camp. After that, she joined the new team Nextwave and put an end to the terrorist organization Silent. She retained her powers after M-Day and joined the X-Men when they moved to San Franscisco. The Leper Queen—the leader of the anti-mutant Sapien League—kidnapped her soon after and shot Tabitha, but X-23 saved her life. She became one of the Utopians, but then returned to the New Mutants.

A founding member of X-Force, in the early days Meltdown was known as Boom-Boom.

MENACE

FIRST APPEARANCE (as Lily) *The Amazing Spider-Man* #545 (December 2007); (as Menace) *The Amazing Spider-Man* #550 (April 2008) **REAL NAME** Lily Hollister
OCCUPATION Terrorist; socialite **BASE** New York City
HEIGHT 5 ft 6 in **WEIGHT** 116 lbs
EYES Brown/Yellow **HAIR** Black, dyed blond/red
SPECIAL POWERS/ABILITIES Lily has superhuman durability and strength, and some combat training. She is skilled at politics.

The daughter of wealthy attorney and aspiring politician Bill Hollister, Lily wanted for nothing. She fell in love with Harry Osborn (*see* Green Goblin) and decided to read his journal, which she used to figure out where Harry's father Norman had one of his secret hideouts. Once inside, she accidentally spilled a vial of Goblin Serum on herself, which granted her superpowers. She became Menace and attacked her father, winning him sympathy in his campaign to become mayor of New York. She later had a baby she claimed was Norman's but turned out to be Harry's. She became the Goblin Knight when Norman Osborn created the Goblin Nation, but was later turned human again. After losing her memory, she gained a new identity from Roderick Kingsley and became Queen Cat.

MEPHISTO

Lord of lies

MEPHISTO

FACTFILE

REAL NAME
Unrevealed

OCCUPATION
Ruler of an extradimensional realm of the dead

BASE
A hell dimension

HEIGHT 6 ft 6 in
WEIGHT 310 lbs
EYES Variable, usually white with no visible pupils or irises
HAIR Variable, usually black

FIRST APPEARANCE
The Silver Surfer #3 (December 1968)

POWERS
Possesses virtually unlimited ability to manipulate magical energies; potentially incalculable strength, godlike durability, immortality, and shapeshifting ability. He can possess the souls of those who hand them over willingly.

Mephisto can magically augment his strength to an immeasurable extent, rivaling even the possibly limitless power of the Hulk.

Mephisto is an extradimensional demon of immense power who often poses as Satan. He continually schemes to make bargains with people for their souls. Mephisto especially covets the souls of heroes for their purity and has repeatedly sought the soul of the noble SILVER SURFER. Mephisto has also contended with THOR, DOCTOR STRANGE, DAREDEVIL, the FANTASTIC FOUR, and many others.

DIRTY DEEDS

It was Mephisto, pretending to be Satan, who bonded the demon ZARATHOS to Johnny Blaze, turning him into the GHOST RIDER. He also held the soul of DOCTOR DOOM's mother until Strange helped Doom free her. Mephisto has a son, Blackheart, and a daughter, Mephista, who sometimes work with him. Other demons impersonate him from time to time, usually weaker creatures who wish to trade off his fearsome reputation.

The SCARLET WITCH once unwittingly used fragments of Mephisto's soul to give life to her twin sons, and Mephisto's reclamation of these fragments drove her mad, resulting in her altering all reality. When she finally brought the world back to normal, she did so by removing the mutant gene from most of the population of the planet, an event known as M-Day.

Mephisto may seem as if he works mostly small, personal deals, but in the end, he wishes to rule the world.

CUTTING DEALS

Mephisto made a deal with SPIDER-MAN to save his aunt May PARKER—and erase memory of Spider-Man's secret identity from the world—in exchange for destroying his marriage to Mary Jane WATSON. In all his years, Mephisto had rarely seen two people so happy with each other, and crushing that pure and beautiful thing brought him immense delight.

When the NEW MUTANTS accidentally found themselves in Mephisto's Hell rather than Hela's Hel, he offered to bring them where they wished to be—if MAGMA agreed to go on a date with him. When Las Vegas was destroyed during the HYDRA CAPTAIN AMERICA's time in power, Mephisto tried to lay claim to the city but was defeated by Doctor Strange and his allies. He lost the throne of Hell to Johnny Blaze (*see* GHOST RIDER) and was imprisoned. However, being immortal, Mephisto often makes plans that may not come to fruition for decades, if not centuries. He is powerful and patient, and can wait for the world to bend his way.

MERCS FOR MONEY

FIRST APPEARANCE *Deadpool* #1 (January 2016)

BASE Mobile

NOTABLE MEMBERS AND POWERS

Deadpool Peerless martial artist, near invulnerability; **Domino** Probability manipulation, expert assassin; **Gorilla Man** Superhuman strength, stamina, durability, and immortality; **Machine Man** Nanotech enhancements give superhuman strength, flight, and self repair; **Tweedledope** Savant who devises advanced machinery.

Created by DEADPOOL, Mercs for Money originally went by the name Heroes for Hire until a cease and desist order from Luke CAGE and IRON FIST made the team change its name. The original team included Solo, MADCAP, FOOLKILLER, Masacre, SLAPSTICK, STINGRAY, and TERROR—though Stingray was secretly keeping an eye on Deadpool for CAPTAIN AMERICA. DOMINO formed a new team after the group disbanded and was eventually joined by Deadpool, Negasonic Teenage Warhead, and Hit Monkey, alongside GORILLA-MAN, MACHINE MAN, and Masacre.

MESMERO

Mesmero started out as a party hypnotist, using his mutant powers to convince guests to surrender their valuables. He branched out into Super Villainy when the MACHINESMITH recruited him to lead the robotic "Demi-Men" alongside a robot duplicate of MAGNETO. MESMERO, who didn't realize that his comrades were robots, hypnotized POLARIS into becoming his partner until the X-MEN crushed the Machinesmith's plot.

Mesmero later found work as a stage hypnotist and clashed with SPIDER-MAN. He then served as a field agent for the Weapon X program in exchange for treatments that augmented his hypnotic abilities. His powers let him entrance crowds into doing anything he wished, putting Mesmero's mind-control abilities in the same class as PROFESSOR X's. Mesmero helped hide the locations of Weapon X installations, but his superiors abandoned him when his power levels dipped after the death of his mother.

Mesmero lost his powers during the reality-altering decimation unleashed by the SCARLET WITCH, but those powers later mysteriously returned. Under the pay of anti-mutant activist Lydia Nance, he created a new incarnation of the BROTHERHOOD OF EVIL MUTANTS, but was eventually captured by the X-Men.

FACTFILE

REAL NAME
Vincent (full name unrevealed)

OCCUPATION
Professional criminal

BASE
Mobile

HEIGHT 5 ft 10 in
WEIGHT 180 lbs
EYES Red
HAIR Green

FIRST APPEARANCE
X-Men #49 (October 1968)

MESMERO

POWERS

Mutant powers of hypnotism allow him to take control of others. Mesmero does this by making eye contact. His powers can induce amnesia, put memories into a victim's head, or even change their personality.

MERLYN

FIRST APPEARANCE *Black Knight* #1 (May 1955)

REAL NAME Merlyn

OCCUPATION Sorcerer; guardian of the Multiverse

BASE Otherworld **HEIGHT/WEIGHT/EYES/HAIR** Variable

SPECIAL POWERS/ABILITIES Almost unlimited command of sorcerous energies allow him to perform innumerous feats, including extending his natural lifespan.

Born a powerful immortal in an alternate universe, Merlyn studied under Necrom, and with him and his fellow student Feron, he helped attune the various universes together to link the Multiverse in a magical matrix. With his daughter ROMA, he created the CAPTAIN BRITAIN CORPS to safeguard all the parallel Earths of the Multiverse, then later manipulated Roma and CAPTAIN BRITAIN into forming EXCALIBUR when they thought he was dead. After Excalibur destroyed the source of his power he disappeared. He returned to attack Captain Britain and kill Roma, although she later returned to life.

MI-13

FIRST APPEARANCE *Excalibur* #101 (September 1996)

BASE UK **MEMBERS AND POWERS Black Knight (Dane Whitman)** Wields the Ebony Blade. **Blade (Eric Brooks)** Half-vampire vampire hunter. **Captain Britain (Brian Braddock)** Superhuman strength, durability, and flight. **Faiza Hussain** Control over living bodies. **John the Skrull** Shapeshifting and flight. **Spitfire (Jacqueline Falsworth)** Superhuman speed and durability, fangs, and healing factor.

MI-13 is the branch of British Intelligence charged with the investigation of supernatural phenomena. Alistair Stuart founded it from the remnants of the Weird Happenings Organisation (WHO), but when he left to join MI-6 he handed over the reins to Peter WISDOM. During SECRET INVASION, the Prime Minister drafted all UK Super Heroes into MI-13. To keep the SKRULLS out of Avalon, MI-13 had to unleash the demons from that magical dimension. The plan worked, but MI-13 had a lot of cleaning up to do. CAPTAIN BRITAIN led MI-13's semiautonomous STRIKE team, helping to stop an invasion by Dracula's forces.

MICROCHIP

FIRST APPEARANCE *Punisher* #4 (November 1987)

REAL NAME Linus Lieberman

OCCUPATION Mechanic; computer hacker; inventor

BASE New Jersey **HEIGHT** 5 ft 8 in **WEIGHT** 220 lbs

EYES Green **HAIR** Brown

SPECIAL POWERS/ABILITIES No superhuman abilities; highly skilled computer hacker; weapons engineer.

A former weapons engineer, Linus Lieberman put his skills to work building the PUNISHER'S arsenal. Calling himself Microchip, he became a close friend and confidante of the Punisher—and also a target of the Punisher's enemies. THE KINGPIN had Microchip kidnapped, then cut off his finger and sent it to the Punisher in the mail. Microchip also lost his son Louis Frohike (Microchip Jr.) to the Punisher's war on crime. Microchip died, but the HOOD brought him back to help take down the Punisher. The Punisher killed Microchip instead.

MILLER, LAYLA

FIRST APPEARANCE *House of M* #4 (September 2005)
REAL NAME Layla Miller
OCCUPATION File clerk, former student **BASE** New York City
HEIGHT 5 ft 5 in **WEIGHT** 125 lbs
EYES Green **HAIR** Blond
SPECIAL POWERS/ABILITIES Layla can predict the futures of individuals, with some exceptions. She can also resurrect people from the dead, but without their souls.

As an orphaned teen, Layla's mutant powers gave her horns and let her breathe fire. In the House of M reality conjured up by the Scarlet Witch, Layla could make people remember their original lives. She lost her powers on M-Day, but a future self came back and downloaded 80 years of memories into her, giving her limited precognition. She went to work for X-Factor Investigations and jumped 80 years into the future with Multiple Man while helping to find Hope Summers. Separated from him, she returned several years later, now an adult, and they later married.

MIMIC

FIRST APPEARANCE *X-Men* #19 (April 1966)
REAL NAME Calvin Rankin
OCCUPATION Adventurer **BASE** Mobile
HEIGHT 5 ft 5 in **WEIGHT** 125 lbs
EYES Brown **HAIR** Brown
SPECIAL POWERS/ABILITIES Can ape the powers and abilities of up to five individuals at a time; can only wield powers at half strength.

After spilling chemicals from his father's laboratory on himself, Calvin Rankin became able to emulate the abilities and powers of others. As Mimic, he sought to imitate the X-Men, but when he was found out, Professor X invited him to join the team. Mimic's membership was short-lived—his arrogance made him difficult to work with—and, following his expulsion, he was thought to have died battling the Hulk. He returned several years later to battle X-Force, and he later befriended Excalibur. He worked under Mystique for HAMMER's X-Men and later joined the real team. A heroic version of him from Earth-12 worked with the Exiles before being killed. His present whereabouts are unknown.

MINDWORM

FIRST APPEARANCE *The Amazing Spider-Man* #138 (November 1974) **REAL NAME** William Turner
OCCUPATION None **BASE** New York City
HEIGHT 6 ft 1 in **WEIGHT** 210 lbs
EYES Brown **HAIR** Brown
SPECIAL POWERS/ABILITIES Feeds on emotions of others; can cause death; can control others; extraordinarily brilliant.

A mutant born with an oversized cranium and brilliant mind, William Turner was cursed with the need to absorb the emotions of others. Unable to understand or control his psychic hunger, he fed off his parents, causing their deaths. William's hunger continued into adulthood, when he took to feeding off the residents of his apartment block, until Spider-Man intervened. Before he could exact revenge, William had an epiphany, realizing his actions were motivated by guilt at his parents' death. After developing mental illness, William became homeless and was killed by a street gang.

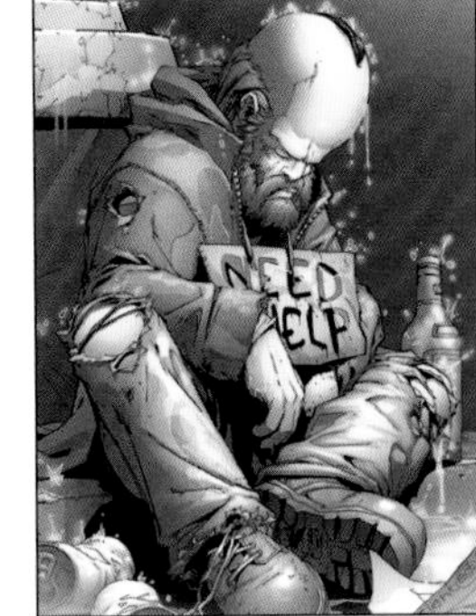

MILLIE THE MODEL

FIRST APPEARANCE *Millie the Model* #1 (Winter 1945)
REAL NAME Millicent "Millie" Collins
OCCUPATION Fashion model; actress; business executive
BASE Hanover Modeling Agency, New York
HEIGHT 5 ft 7 in **WEIGHT** 137 lbs **EYES** Blue **HAIR** Blond
SPECIAL POWERS/ABILITIES None, but has the poise and grace of a top fashion model; some fighting ability.

Having grown up in a rural farming town, Millie Collins left home for the big city, where she found employment as a model for the Hanover Modeling Agency. Over the years, Millie became involved in all sorts of outlandish adventures, often accompanied by her photographer boyfriend Clicker Holbrook and her rival, Chili Storm. Millie retired from active modeling to run an agency of her own. In recent years, Millie's niece Misty has become embroiled in comedic adventures herself.

MINDLESS ONES

FIRST APPEARANCE *Strange Tales* #127 (December 1964)
REAL NAME None **OCCUPATION** None
BASE Dormammu's Dark Dimension
HEIGHT/WEIGHT/EYES/HAIR Variable
SPECIAL POWERS/ABILITIES All possess incalculable strength, near-invulnerability, and the ability to fire energy blasts from their cyclopean eyes.

Dormammu and his sister Umar sought refuge in the Dark Dimension after their exile. There, they taught the wizard-king Olnar how to absorb other dimensions, which backfired when the Mindless Ones appeared. These soulless, violent creatures killed Olnar and rioted over the Dark Dimension until Dormammu and Umar imprisoned them. They have broken through to Earth many times, battling Spider-Man, Doctor Strange, Captain Britain, and Nextwave. They later appeared to evolve self-awareness; Thing and Spider-Man witnessed one kill itself after considering its own crimes.

MINORU, NICO

FIRST APPEARANCE *Runaways* #1 (July 2003)
REAL NAME Nico Minoru **OCCUPATION** Adventurer
BASE Southern California **HEIGHT** 5 ft 4 in **WEIGHT** 102 lbs
EYES Brown **HAIR** Black
SPECIAL POWERS/ABILITIES If Nico's blood is drawn, she can summon the Staff of One, which she can use to cast any magical spell once.

When Nico discovered her parents were part of a cult known as the Pride, she and the other children of the Pride fled, becoming the Runaways. Nico took the name Sister Grimm and tried to master her new magical powers. At one point she ended up in 1907, and her great-grandmother, the Witchbreaker, taught her how to better control her magic. Arcade later pitted her against a number of other young heroes in his new Murderworld. Nico survived, though she was emotionally scarred. She left the Runaways to spend time with her family in Japan and briefly joined Medusa, She-Hulk, and Singularity in A-Force, but she later returned to the Runaways.

MIRACLE MAN

FIRST APPEARANCE *Fantastic Four* #3 (March 1962)
REAL NAME Joshua Ayers
OCCUPATION Would-be conqueror **BASE** Mobile
HEIGHT 5 ft 11 in **WEIGHT** 185 lbs **EYES** Blue **HAIR** Black
SPECIAL POWERS/ABILITIES Master hypnotist, able to mesmerize people with a glance and make them see what he wants; occasionally telekinesis, animating objects, and restructuring matter.

A brilliant illusionist and stage magician, Miracle Man most likely had some mutant abilities. During a performance, he spotted the FANTASTIC FOUR in the audience and began taunting them about how much greater his powers were than theirs. Enraged, the THING challenged him but was outdone by Miracle Man's abilities. After escaping from prison following a crime spree, Miracle Man studied the mystical powers of the Cheemuzwa or the Silent Ones. Miracle Man remained a powerful foe of the Fantastic Four until he was shot dead by SCOURGE. The HOOD later resurrected him.

MISS ARROW

FIRST APPEARANCE (as the Other) *Friendly Neighborhood Spider-Man* #4 (January 2006); (as Miss Arrow) *Friendly Neighborhood Spider-Man* #11 (October 2006) **REAL NAME** Ero
OCCUPATION Hunting Spider-Man **BASE** New York
HEIGHT 5 ft 10 in **WEIGHT** 115 lbs **EYES** Brown **HAIR** Blond
SPECIAL POWERS/ABILITIES Ero is a hive mind composed of thousands of pirate spiders, but can appear human. She can extend spider stingers from her wrists and control spiders telepathically.

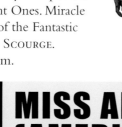

After Morlun killed SPIDER-MAN, Peter Parker sloughed off his skin and returned in a fresh body. Pirate spiders devoured his old flesh and used it as a framework for a collective intelligence that called itself the Other. Spider-Man drove it off, but it returned as Miss Arrow, the nurse at the high school at which Parker and Flash THOMPSON worked. Ero had to reproduce to survive, and she chose to mate with Flash, which would kill him. Spider-Man lured her into an aviary and birds devoured her. After MEPHISTO changed Spider-Man's past, none of this had happened, but Ero found and revived KAINE after the KRAVEN family sacrificed him.

MISS SINISTER

FIRST APPEARANCE *X-Men: Legacy* #214 (September 2008)
REAL NAME Claudine Renko
OCCUPATION Mad scientist **BASE** Mobile
HEIGHT Variable **WEIGHT** Variable **EYES** Red **HAIR** Black
SPECIAL POWERS/ABILITIES Shapeshifting and rapid healing; powerful telepathic powers allow her to control and paralyze others, astral project, levitate, and move objects with her mind.

As a fail-safe should he ever be killed, MISTER SINISTER injected a virus into Claudine Renko that would transform her DNA, turning her into a female clone of him, complete with his telepathic powers. When he apparently perished, the virus activated and Claudine took on the name Miss Sinister. The villain worked with Sebastian SHAW, and targeted WOLVERINE's children. As the original Mister Sinister's persona began to take over Claudine's body, she attempted to expel him. Later, Claudine used the Mothervine virus to create and enslave mutants.

FACTFILE
REAL NAME
America Chavez
OCCUPATION
Adventurer
BASE
Mobile

HEIGHT 6 ft
WEIGHT 165 lbs
EYES Brown
HAIR Black

FIRST APPEARANCE
Vengeance #1 (September 2011)

POWERS
Super strength and speed. America can also fly, and she can also travel across the Multiverse and through time, too.

MISS AMERICA (AMERICA CHAVEZ)

America Chavez was raised by Elena and Amalia Chavez in a dimension outside the Multiverse, known as Utopia Parallel. Her mothers sacrificed themselves to save their universe from being torn apart by black holes, after which America ran away to seek a Super Hero's life. She joined the TEEN BRIGADE and co-led the team together with Ultimate Nullifier, but they later disbanded due to "creative differences." America frequently tangled with LOKI, and protected WICCAN from Loki's malice. She later helped Wiccan, HULKLING, and Loki defeat the interdimensional parasite, Mother, in Central Park. During the SECRET WARS, Chavez was a member of the all-woman A-FORCE team, but earned DOCTOR DOOM's ire when she violated the shield separating worlds. After the Secret Wars, America joined the Ultimates team and attended Sotomayor University.

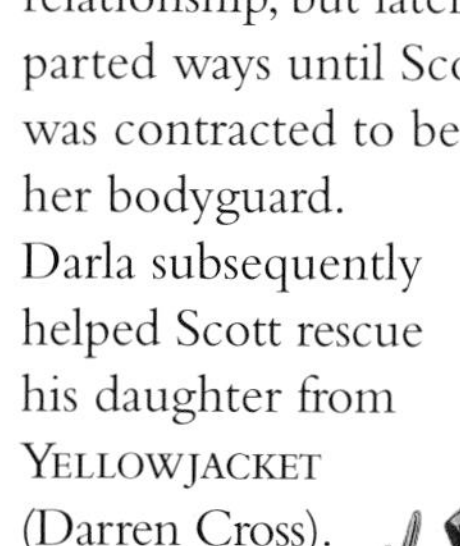

Madeline Joyce Frank was the first Miss America. She was a member of the Liberty Legion and the Invaders (later called the All-Winners Squad).

MISS THING

FIRST APPEARANCE *Marvel NOW Point One* #1 (December 2012)
REAL NAME Darla Deering
OCCUPATION Pop star **BASE** New York City
HEIGHT 5 ft 8 in **WEIGHT** 125 lbs **EYES** Brown **HAIR** Pink
SPECIAL POWERS/ABILITIES Darla wears the Thing Rings, which when touched place a Thing exoskeleton around her, giving her superhuman durability and strength.

A model and pop music star, Darla dated the HUMAN TORCH. When the FANTASTIC FOUR were planning to go on a mission through time and space, MISTER FANTASTIC asked each member to find a substitute in case they were gone too long. The Torch forgot, so he asked Darla at the last second. When they didn't return, she borrowed an old THING exoskeleton Fantastic had designed so she could meet her obligations. Darla and Scott Lang (Mister Fantastic's fill-in) struck up a relationship, but later parted ways until Scott was contracted to be her bodyguard. Darla subsequently helped Scott rescue his daughter from YELLOWJACKET (Darren Cross).

MISTER FANTASTIC

Leader of the Fantastic Four

MISTER FANTASTIC

FACTFILE

REAL NAME
Reed Richards

OCCUPATION
Scientist; adventurer

BASE
New York City

HEIGHT 6 ft 1 in
WEIGHT 180 lbs
EYES Brown
HAIR Brown

FIRST APPEARANCE
Fantastic Four #1
(November 1961)

POWERS

A scientific genius specializing in physics, aeronautics; Mister Fantastic can stretch, compress, or expand his entire body or parts of his body into any shape. He can stretch his neck, limbs, or torso up to 1,500 feet without pain. He can create a canopy, sheath, umbrella, or parachute with his body.

ALLIES/FOES

ALLIES Susan Storm (Invisible Woman), Ben Grimm (the Thing), Johnny Storm (Human Torch), Lyja the Lazerfist, Alicia Masters

FOES Gormuu, Doctor Doom, Frightful Four, Galactus, Puppet Master, the Skrulls, Annihilus, Blastaar, Diablo

He's the leader of one of the world's most important Super Hero teams. He's also a brilliant scientist. Reed Richards is Mister Fantastic. As leader of the Super Hero group the FANTASTIC FOUR, Mister Fantastic uses both his ability to stretch his body and his sharp scientific mind in his quest to help mankind.

ESSENTIAL STORYLINES

• Fantastic Four #5
Victor von Doom blames Reed for the facial scar he receives when a machine explodes. He dons a mask and becomes Doctor Doom, Mister Fantastic's worst enemy.

• Secret Wars #9
Reed Richards confronts Doctor Doom on Battleworld, with the fate of reality itself hanging in the balance.

A BRILLIANT STUDENT

The son of highly intelligent parents, Reed Richards was a child prodigy and a brilliant student. His father, Nathaniel Richards, was a wealthy physicist. Reed's mother, Evelyn, died when the boy was seven years old.

Young Reed showed a genius for math, physics, and mechanics, which his father encouraged. Nathaniel guided his son's scientific studies. By the time Reed was 14, he was already taking and excelling in college-level courses. When he reached college age, Reed attended several universities, including Empire State University in New York.

It was there that Reed Richards met several people who would play a major role in his later life as Mister Fantastic. Victor von Doom was a foreign student from the nation of Latveria. This scientific genius was assigned to be Reed's first college roommate, but Doom disliked Reed from the moment he met him and asked for a new roommate. Later, as DOCTOR DOOM, he would become Mister Fantastic's and the Fantastic Four's greatest enemy.

ISSUE #1

In November 1961, *Fantastic Four* #1 ushered in the Marvel Age of Comics and introduced millions to what would become the Marvel Universe. Comic books would never be the same!

Reed Richards' attempt to make friends with fellow student Victor von Doom were rudely brushed aside.

Replacing Doom as Reed's roommate was Benjamin J. Grimm, a former high school football star who, though very different in personality, became Reed's best friend.

In college, Reed began working on plans to build a ship that could travel to other solar systems. Ben joked that if Reed could build the ship, he would pilot it.

After transferring to Columbia University in Manhattan, Reed rented a room from a woman whose daughter, Susan Storm, immediately fell for Reed. One day she would be his wife, as well as his partner in the Fantastic Four.

A FATEFUL JOURNEY

Using money left to him by his father, Nathaniel, who arranged for the fortune to be given to Reed while Nathaniel was on an alternate Earth, Reed began developing his starship shortly after college. When his own funds began to run out, Reed got funding from the US government to complete the project.

Able to turn his body into a highly malleable state, Mister Fantastic can stretch his neck to peek around corners, or even look over entire buildings!

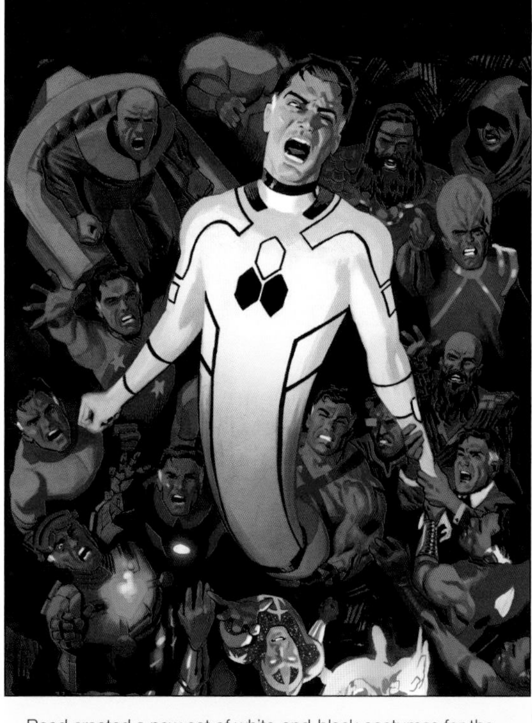

Reed created a new set of white-and-black costumes for the Future Foundation. He wore one while fighting the interdimensional Council of Reeds.

However, shortly before Reed could complete the ship, the government threatened to cut off funding to the project. Desperate to prove that his starship would fly, Reed decided to take the ship up on a test flight himself. Ben argued against the idea, telling Reed that he thought the ship's shielding would be inadequate against the powerful cosmic radiation found in space.

Reed finally convinced Ben to pilot the ship on its test voyage. By this time, Reed and Sue Storm were engaged. Sue insisted in coming along on the flight, as did her younger brother Johnny Storm. The quartet snuck onto the launch pad, slipped onto the ship, and blasted off into space. Before they could achieve hyperspace and a journey to another solar system, a solar flare shot intense levels of radiation at the ship. Ben had been right. The ship's shields were not strong enough to withstand the radiation, which irradiated the four astronauts. Ben was forced to cut short the flight and land back on Earth.

BIG CHANGES

Upon their return to Earth, each member of the foursome soon discovered that the cosmic radiation had changed the very structure of their bodies. Reed discovered that he could bend and stretch his body at will. Sue could turn herself invisible. Johnny could cover his body with flames and also fly. Ben's skin was transformed into an orange, rock-like substance, and he gained tremendous strength.

Reed became the team's leader, calling himself Mister Fantastic. Sue called herself Invisible Girl (later Invisible Woman). Johnny called himself the Human Torch, and Ben called himself the Thing. All four agreed to use their new powers to help humanity.

Guided by Reed Richards, the Fantastic Four became the most respected Super Hero team on Earth, and saved the planet from destruction many times. Reed and Sue eventually married and had two children: Franklin and Valeria Richards.

HUMANITY GUIDE

During the Civil War, Reed sided with Iron Man and the US government. Sue left him over this; when the conflict ended, they reunited.

As a father, Reed became more concerned about what the future held. He set up the Future Foundation to train tomorrow's geniuses and became a founding member of the Illuminati, in an effort to help guide humanity's destiny. He also contacted the Interdimensional Council of Reeds to glean new insights from his counterparts, though he soon realized they were colder and more ruthless than himself and left. He was one of the few people to escape the end of the world, surviving on a "life raft" that crash-landed on Doctor Doom's Battleworld. Reed managed to regain his family and end Doom's rule, recreating reality with the help of Franklin and the Molecule Man. He then set off with his family and the Future Foundation, creating and exploring new realities, until an attack by the Griever at the End of All Things forced him to call his old friends for help—and the Fantastic Four were together again.

The Griever at the End of All Things describes itself as the embodiment of entropy, destined to witness the final ray of light at the end of eternity. It viewed the Future Foundation's creation of new universes as an attempt to avoid the inevitable.

MISSING LINK

FIRST APPEARANCE *Incredible Hulk* #105 (July 1968)
REAL NAME Lincoln Brickford
OCCUPATION Miner **BASE** Lucifer Falls, West Virginia
HEIGHT/WEIGHT Not known **EYES** Yellow **HAIR** None
SPECIAL POWERS/ABILITIES Possesses superhuman strength and durability. His core is radioactive, and he can project heat from his epidermis.

A Neanderthal man born millennia ago, the Missing Link was accidentally sealed in a cave, where a mysterious mist kept him in suspended animation. He was awakened from his sleep by an atomic test that changed his molecular structure. Not understanding the modern world in which he found himself, the Missing Link went on a rampage and battled the HULK. Seemingly destroyed, the Link reconstructed himself, and was found and adopted by the kindly Brickford family. They called him Lincoln and got him a job in the local mines. After further battles with the Hulk, he was turned over to the authorities.

MISTER SENSITIVE

FIRST APPEARANCE *X-Force* #117 (June 2001)
REAL NAME Guy Smith **OCCUPATION** Adventurer
BASE X-Force/X-Statix Tower in Santa Monica, California.
HEIGHT 5 ft 10 in **WEIGHT** 190 lbs
EYES Green **HAIR** White
SPECIAL POWERS/ABILITIES Superhuman senses, superhuman speed, and the ability to levitate himself.

Erroneously believing his parents died in a house fire, Guy Smith was raised as an orphan. As his mutant powers emerged, he became extremely sensitive to his surroundings. PROFESSOR X designed a special costume for him that allowed him to control his senses, and Guy took to calling himself Mister Sensitive. When he joined the mutant team X-FORCE (later called X-STATIX), he changed his code name to Orphan. He fell in love with teammate U-GO GIRL, and her death crushed him. He died on X-Statix's final mission. He and U-Go Girl were then reunited in Heaven.

MOCKINGBIRD

FIRST APPEARANCE *Astonishing Tales* #6 (June 1971)
REAL NAME Barbara "Bobbi" Morse-Barton
OCCUPATION Adventurer **BASE** Mobile
HEIGHT 5 ft 9 in **WEIGHT** 135 lbs **EYES** Blue **HAIR** Blond
SPECIAL POWERS/ABILITIES Expert hand-to-hand combatant and gymnast; her battle-stave can be used as a quarterstaff or broken into two smaller segments.

Bobbi Morse began her career as a SHIELD agent by striking up a romance with HAWKEYE. The two eventually married and became founding members of the AVENGERS WEST COAST. During a time-travel adventure to the Old West, Mockingbird allowed the abusive PHANTOM RIDER to fall to his death, an action that drove a wedge between Mockingbird and Hawkeye. She seemed to die at the hands of MEPHISTO, but in fact she'd been replaced by a SKRULL. She returned during the SECRET INVASION and later divorced Hawkeye and joined SHIELD's Secret Avengers.

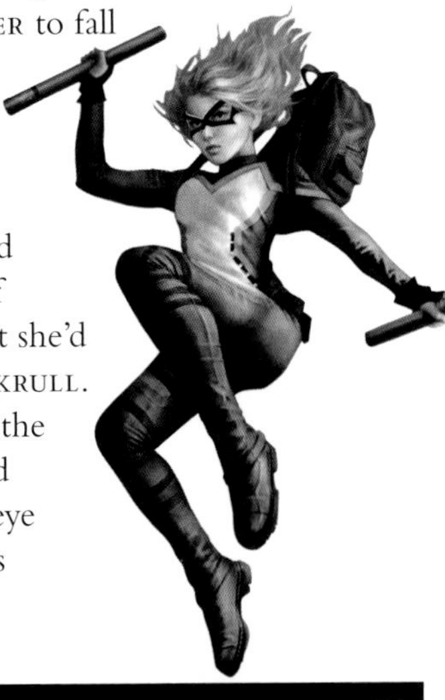

MISTER HYDE

FIRST APPEARANCE *Journey Into Mystery* #99 (December 1963)
REAL NAME Calvin Zabo **OCCUPATION** Professional criminal
BASE New York City **HEIGHT** 5 ft 11 in; (as Hyde) 6 ft 5 in
WEIGHT 185 lbs; (as Hyde) 420 lbs **EYES** Brown
HAIR Gray; (as Hyde) Brown
SPECIAL POWERS/ABILITIES Superhumanly strong; astonishing recuperative ability and resistance to pain.

Inspired by *Dr. Jekyll and Mr. Hyde,* medical researcher Calvin Zabo concocted a potion that worked like the one in R. L. Stevenson's classic tale. As Mister Hyde, he worked with the MASTERS OF EVIL against the AVENGERS. Hyde also joined the HOOD's criminal organization and later the THUNDERBOLTS. He served time in SHIELD's Pleasant Hill prison before joining BARON ZEMO's Army of Evil, aiding HYDRA's takeover of the United States. This put him at odds with his estranged daughter, Daisy JOHNSON, who was a member of Nick FURY's SECRET WARRIORS and who temporarily became director of SHIELD.

MISTER SINISTER

Dr. Nathaniel Essex was recruited by APOCALYPSE, who enhanced his genetic structure, bestowing him with virtual immortality and superhuman physical attributes. Taking the name Mister Sinister, Essex continued his forbidden experiments into the secrets of mutation, and played a hidden role in the upbringing of the Summers brothers, CYCLOPS and HAVOK. He is the guiding hand behind the MARAUDERS, whom Sinister used to massacre the MORLOCKS. Sinister hoped to breed a mutant child between Cyclops and Jean GREY, so he fashioned a clone later revealed to be Madelyne PRYOR. Sinister reformed the Marauders to track down Hope SUMMERS. He also tried to mix INHUMAN and mutant DNA to create a powerful hybrid. The only result, a clone of Cyclops, ultimately failed, and Sinister was imprisoned by SHIELD. He escaped and tried to acquire the body of WOLVERINE, but was horribly wounded by X-23.

FACTFILE

REAL NAME
Nathaniel Essex

OCCUPATION
Geneticist

BASE
Various

HEIGHT 6 ft 5 in
WEIGHT 285 lbs
EYES Red
HAIR Black

FIRST APPEARANCE
Uncanny X-Men #221 (September 1987)

MISTER SINISTER

POWERS

Enhanced strength and durability and some command over his own genetic structure. Essex's advanced knowledge of cloning allows him to transfer his intellect into a pristine new body whenever his current one starts to wears out.

MODOK

FACTFILE
REAL NAME
George Tarleton
OCCUPATION
Leader of AIM
BASE
Various

HEIGHT 12 ft
WEIGHT 750 lbs
EYES Red
HAIR Brown

FIRST APPEARANCE
Tales of Suspense #93
(October 1967)

POWERS
Superhuman mental and psionic powers; computer-like brain; headband enabled him to teleport from one AIM base to another; possessed a hover-chair that could fly and was equipped with weaponry.

MODOK

Scientists at AIM (Advanced Idea Mechanics) needed an organic computer to analyze a Cosmic Cube, so they mutated one out of AIM agent George Tarleton. As MODOK (Mental Organism Designed Only for Killing), Tarleton quickly concluded that AIM would be better with him in charge and took over. As part of the INTELLIGENCIA, he helped make the RED HULK and Red She-Hulk. However, the Hulked-out Amadeus CHO caused him to revert to a normal man. MODOK's brain had been cloned however, and one of the brains developed into MODOK Superior. He went on to work with the Intelligencia and even teamed up with SHIELD to take down AIM. He put together a group of assassins called Agents of MODOK, but made the mistake of hiring Gwenpool (*see* POOLE, GWEN).

MOJO

A spineless mass of yellow flesh, Mojo is ruler of Mojoworld, a bizarre, media-oriented planet. A manipulative tyrant, Mojo produces movies and TV shows to keep the masses amused. The need to maintain these entertainments' popularity has drawn him to Earth.

Mojo's first visit occurred when his slave, LONGSHOT, tried to persuade the X-MEN to help overthrow his master. Although they triumphed, Mojo's successor—"Mojo II, the Sequel"—proved to be even more tyrannical, and Mojo reclaimed the reins of power. Since the X-Men are such crowd-pleasers, Mojo has repeatedly involved them in his entertainment programmes, but they are rarely willing participants. Frustrated by this, he created younger versions of the X-Men, the so-called X-Babies, but they proved no easier to work with.

MOJO

FACTFILE
REAL NAME
Mojo
OCCUPATION
Ruler of Mojoworld
BASE
Mojoworld

HEIGHT Unknown
WEIGHT Unknown
EYES Yellow
HAIR None

FIRST APPEARANCE
Longshot #3
(November 1985)

POWERS
Travels on robotic platform that moves on metal spiderlike legs; projects energy bolts from hands; his very presence can kill life nearby.

MOLE MAN

Shunned and ridiculed for his bizarre appearance, Mole Man turned his back on the surface world and sought a legendary underground kingdom. He eventually found an entrance to it on Monster Island, in the Bermuda Triangle—an underground world filled with advanced technical devices left by a race known as the Deviants. Mole Man also found a race of semi-human creatures, whom he enslaved. Sometimes in partnership with RED GHOST, Kala or the Outcasts, his deadly plots against the surface world have been thwarted by the FANTASTIC FOUR, the AVENGERS, IRON MAN, and the HULK.

Mole Man declared himself ruler of Subterranea and formed an alliance and budding relationship with Kala, queen of the Netherworlders. But when his homeland was destroyed by ULTRON, he turned his attention toward the surface world once more. Mole Man and Kyzerra Os had a s on, Mole Monster. The repulsive, clawed monster ruled another area of Subterranea until he overthrew his father and continued his conquest on the surface, where he was defeated by NOVA (Samuel Alexander).

Hideous and lonely, Mole Man found solace in the depths of Subterranea.

MOLE MAN

FACTFILE
REAL NAME
Harvey Elder
OCCUPATION
Former nuclear engineer; ruler of the Subterraneans
BASE
Subterranea

HEIGHT 4 ft 10 in
WEIGHT 165 lbs
EYES Brown
HAIR Gray

FIRST APPEARANCE
Fantastic Four #1
(November 1961)

POWERS
Ingenious inventor of weapons capable of seismic disturbance; dominating personality; heightened senses, including a radar sense that enables him to navigate in pitch darkness, or to sense the presence of objects, or people behind him.

MOLECULE MAN

MOLECULE MAN

FACTFILE

REAL NAME
Owen Reece

OCCUPATION
Atomic plant worker turned criminal

BASE
Brooklyn, New York; later a suburb of Denver, Colorado

HEIGHT 5 ft 7 in
WEIGHT 140 lbs
EYES Brown
HAIR Brown

FIRST APPEARANCE
Fantastic Four #20 (November 1963)

POWERS
Possesses psionic ability to manipulate all forms.

Lab assistant Owen Reece accidentally activated a machine that opened a pinhole into another dimension, exposing himself to radiation that scarred his face and endowed him with the power to control matter. An embittered misfit, Reece used his powers to evil ends, but was defeated by the FANTASTIC FOUR. UATU THE WATCHER imprisoned Reece in another dimension, but he returned to Earth and took part in all three SECRET WARS. Though he was killed by the SENTRY, DOCTOR DOOM resurrected him to use as a weapon to defeat the BEYONDERS. He subsequently became the source of Doom's power to create his new Battleworld, and later the source of MISTER FANTASTIC's power to end it and recreate the Multiverse.

Doom held the Molecule Man captive as he investigated the nature and source of the Multiverse incursions.

MOON BOY

FIRST APPEARANCE *Devil Dinosaur* #1 (April 1978)
REAL NAME Moon Boy **OCCUPATION** Adventurer
BASE The Valley of Flame, located on an extra-dimensional planet
HEIGHT 6 ft 2 in **WEIGHT** 196 lbs
EYES Blue **HAIR** Black
SPECIAL POWERS/ABILITIES Able to communicate with Devil Dinosaur and possibly other unrevealed powers.

Moon Boy grew up on a distant planet where tribes of apelike humanoids coexisted with dinosaurs. His people called themselves the Small-Folk. When he saved a Tyrannosaurus from the rival Killer-Folk, the dinosaur became his constant companion. Moon Boy and DEVIL DINOSAUR later stole the Night Stone from the Killer-Folk, who then beat Moon Boy to death and escaped to Earth through a vortex accidentally opened by Lunella Lafayette (MOON GIRL). Devil Dinosaur followed them to avenge his friend. Later he and Moon Girl returned to save Moon Boy, arriving moments before his impending death.

MOLTEN MAN

FIRST APPEARANCE *The Amazing Spider-Man* #28 (September 1965) **REAL NAME** Mark Raxton
OCCUPATION Security guard for Osborn Industries
BASE New York City
HEIGHT 6 ft 5 in **WEIGHT** 225 lbs **EYES** Brown **HAIR** Gold
SPECIAL POWERS/ABILITIES Superhuman strength and durability. Metallic epidermis is capable of producing flames and heat.

The stepbrother of Liz Osborn, Mark Raxton worked as an assistant to Professor Spencer SMYTHE. Raxton stole Smythe's latest creation, a synthetic metallic liquid, but spilled it on himself and became Molten Man. When his molten skin threatened to destroy him, SPIDER-MAN saved his life. He later took a job as a security guard at the company owned by Liz's then-husband, Harry Osborn. During the first CIVIL WAR, the PUNISHER nearly killed Raxton. As he recuperated, his powers ran out of control, but Harry discovered a cure for Raxton's condition. When Liz took over Alchemax, she used the company's resources to find a more holistic cure for Mark. He then aided his sister by hiring the GHOST to foil Parker Industries.

MOONDRAGON

MOONDRAGON

FACTFILE

REAL NAME
Heather Douglas

OCCUPATION
Adventurer

BASE
Mobile

HEIGHT 6 ft 3 in
WEIGHT 150 lbs
EYES Blue
HAIR None

FIRST APPEARANCE
Iron Man #54 (January 1973)

POWERS
Telepathy; telekinetic levitation of objects; ability to fire mental blasts; trained martial artist.

Moondragon grew up on Titan after THANOS killed her parents. The evil DRAGON OF THE MOON tried to corrupt her, but she resisted him. On Earth, Moondragon joined the DEFENDERS, but the influence of the Dragon of the Moon sometimes turned her into a villain. She became a reservist of the AVENGERS, and later safeguarded the Mind Gem as a member of the Infinity Watch. She became lovers with Marlo JONES, but when that ended she turned to Phyla-Vell (CAPTAIN MARVEL) instead. Murdered by ULTRON, she died in Phyla's arms but has since been resurrected and was a member of the GUARDIANS OF THE GALAXY while they were stationed on Knowhere.

MOON GIRL

FIRST APPEARANCE *Moon Girl and Devil Dinosaur* #1 (January 2016)
REAL NAME Lunella Louise Lafayette **OCCUPATION** Student
BASE Moon Girl's secret laboratory, New York City
HEIGHT 3 ft 9 in **WEIGHT** 48 lbs **EYES** Brown **HAIR** Black
SPECIAL POWERS/ABILITIES Can swap consciousness (or rather, swap bodies) with her dinosaur friend; a child genius.

Lunella Lafayette is perhaps the smartest person in the world. The nine-year-old girl was often teased by classmates for her intellect. When she found an Omi-Wave Projector she inadvertently opened a portal that allowed the Killer-Folk and DEVIL DINOSAUR to enter the world from another dimension. She protected the dinosaur and they became fast friends. The Terrigen Mists awakened her mutant ability to swap minds. She later teamed up with the HUMAN TORCH and THING, who were missing their old FANTASTIC FOUR teammates.

MOON KNIGHT

A mercenary left for dead in the Egyptian desert, Marc Spector was found by followers of the Egyptian god Khonshu, who saved his life and gave him superhuman powers. Returning to the US, Marc became a crimefighter, calling himself the Moon Knight and assuming two more alter egos: millionaire Steven Grant and taxi driver Jake Lockley. Marc fought crime for many years, battling against WEREWOLF, Midnight Man, and Black Spectre, and alongside SPIDER-MAN, and the PUNISHER. Eventually, Marc retired his alter egos, but then felt compelled to travel to Egypt. There, members of the cult of Khonshu explained to him that being the Moon Knight was his destiny, one he could not shirk.

Reinvigorated, Marc became the Moon Knight once more. When Norman Osborn (*see* GREEN GOBLIN) took over the AVENGERS, Marc faked his death. He later joined the Avengers in their fight against the X-MEN and started a battle at the Jean Grey School. Marc also took on another persona as Mister Knight, helping NYPD Detective Flint solve cases. His multiple personas were a symptom of Khonshu taking over his mind. After regaining control, he engaged the Sun King in a battle of mind and spirit, and won.

MOON KNIGHT

FACTFILE
REAL NAME
Marc Spector
OCCUPATION
Millionaire playboy and taxi driver
BASE
New York City

HEIGHT 6 ft 2 ins
WEIGHT 225 lbs
EYES Dark brown
HAIR Brown

FIRST APPEARANCE
Werewolf by Night #32 (August 1975)

POWERS
His strength waxes and wanes with the moon. He bears weapons given to him by the Egyptian god Khonshu: scarab throwing darts, a golden ankh that glows when danger is near, and an ivory boomerang.

MOONSTAR, DANI

FACTFILE
REAL NAME
Danielle "Dani" Moonstar
OCCUPATION
Former SHIELD agent, later adventurer and teacher
BASE
The Xavier Institute, Salem Center, New York State

HEIGHT
5 ft 6 in
WEIGHT
105 lbs
EYES Brown
HAIR Black

FIRST APPEARANCE
Marvel Graphic Novel #4: The New Mutants (June 1982)

POWERS
Created three-dimensional images of thoughts in others' minds; had rapport with higher animals.

Danielle "Dani" Moonstar is the granddaughter of Black Eagle, a Cheyenne chief. When Black Eagle was murdered by agents of Donald Pierce, Dani joined forces with PROFESSOR X to defeat him. She then joined the NEW MUTANTS, at first known as Psyche and later as Mirage and Moonstar. For a time Dani served as a VALKYRIE in Asgard before becoming a SHIELD agent and then a member of X-FORCE. Dani lost her mutant powers on M-Day, and later joined the FEARLESS DEFENDERS as Hela's Valkyrie. When the Terrigen Cloud covered Earth and began poisoning mutants, Dani used her Valkyrie death-tracking abilities to find victims and bring them to X-Haven.

MOONSTONE

FIRST APPEARANCE *Captain America* #192 (December 1975)
REAL NAME Dr. Karla Sofen
OCCUPATION Psychologist, criminal adventurer
BASE Mobile
HEIGHT 5 ft 11 in **WEIGHT** 130 lbs **EYES** Blue **HAIR** Blond
SPECIAL POWERS/ABILITIES Able to fly and become intangible; creates blinding flashes and emits laser beams from hands.

As a child, Karla Sofen learned to manipulate others to get what she wanted. She became a psychologist in adulthood, and tricked the original Moonstone, Lloyd Bloch, into giving up the gem (actually a KREE lifestone) that gave him superpowers. Using the gem, she became a superpowered villain, serving with the MASTERS OF EVIL and the THUNDERBOLTS. She joined HAMMER's DARK AVENGERS as the new Ms. Marvel, and when the DARK REIGN ended, she became part of Luke CAGE's Thunderbolts. After serving time in SHIELD's Pleasant Hill prison, Karla joined the WINTER SOLDIER's new Thunderbolts, though contested his leadership.

MORBIUS

FACTFILE
REAL NAME
Dr. Michael Morbius
OCCUPATION
Biochemist
BASE
Mobile

HEIGHT 5 ft 10 in
WEIGHT 170 lbs
EYES Blue
HAIR Black

FIRST APPEARANCE
The Amazing Spider-Man #101 (October 1971)

POWERS
A pseudo-vampire who can glide on air currents, Morbius has superhuman strength and healing ability and can hypnotize people to do his bidding.

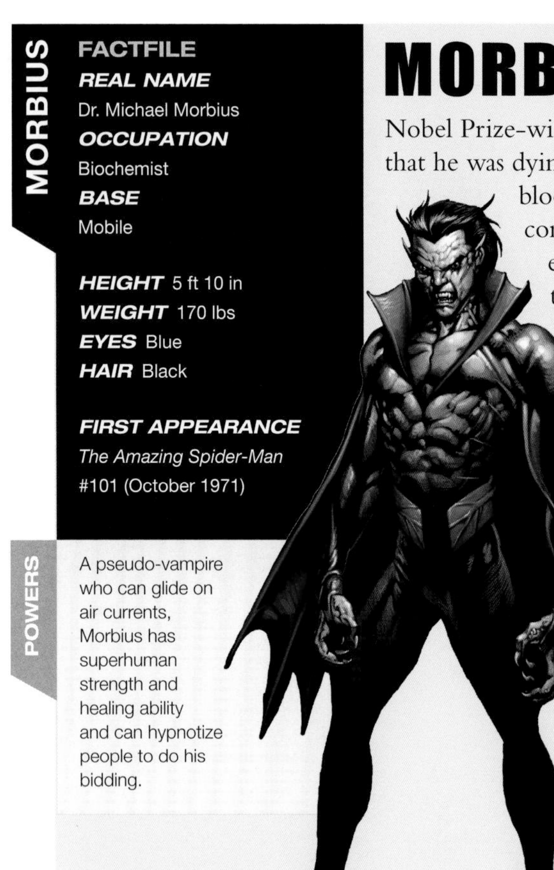

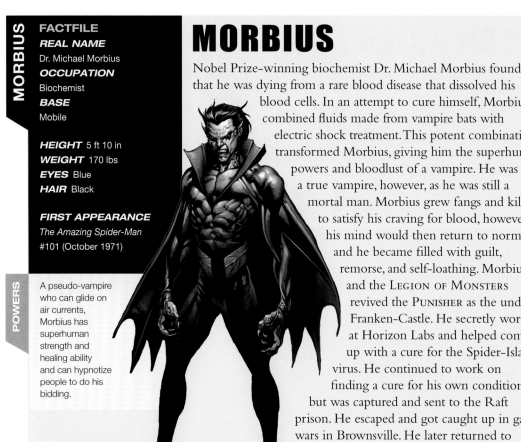

Nobel Prize-winning biochemist Dr. Michael Morbius found that he was dying from a rare blood disease that dissolved his blood cells. In an attempt to cure himself, Morbius combined fluids made from vampire bats with electric shock treatment. This potent combination transformed Morbius, giving him the superhuman powers and bloodlust of a vampire. He was not a true vampire, however, as he was still a mortal man. Morbius grew fangs and killed to satisfy his craving for blood, however, his mind would then return to normal and he became filled with guilt, remorse, and self-loathing. Morbius and the LEGION OF MONSTERS revived the PUNISHER as the undead Franken-Castle. He secretly worked at Horizon Labs and helped come up with a cure for the Spider-Island virus. He continued to work on finding a cure for his own condition, but was captured and sent to the Raft prison. He escaped and got caught up in gang wars in Brownsville. He later returned to Horizon Labs and cured his vampirism before recovering an Ultimate Nullifier from the gangster known as The ROSE.

MORLOCKS

FIRST APPEARANCE *Uncanny X-Men* #169 (May 1983)
BASE New York City; Kenya
KEY MEMBERS AND POWERS **Callisto** (former leader) Strength, agility, enhanced senses; **Ape** Shapeshifter; **Caliban** Strength and speed, projects fear ; **D'Gard** Empathic ability; **Leech** Projects force-field; **Marrow** Bone growth, recuperation; **Masque** Alters features of other beings; **Plague** Projects deadly diseases.

The Morlocks were failed experiments by the DARK BEAST who established their own outcast society in the tunnels beneath New York City. The MARAUDERS, soldiers of the ruthless geneticist MISTER SINISTER, slaughtered many Morlocks in what became known as the Mutant Massacre. Mikhail RASPUTIN, brother of COLOSSUS, transported most of the survivors to the alternate dimension of "The Hill," where a new generation grew to adulthood. One of their number, named MARROW, founded the terrorist group Gene Nation. Another group of mutants and humans coexisting underground have since formed the New Morlocks under CALLISTO's leadership.

MORDRED THE EVIL

FIRST APPEARANCE *Black Knight* #1 (May 1955)
REAL NAME Sir Mordred
OCCUPATION Conqueror **BASE** Various
HEIGHT 5 ft 10 in **WEIGHT** 185 lbs **EYES** Blue **HAIR** Black
SPECIAL POWERS/ABILITIES An expert swordsman, Mordred's mystic power is enhanced when he functions as the male familiar to the sorceress Morgan Le Fay.

The illegitimate son of King Arthur PENDRAGON, Mordred was eventually made a knight of the realm, though evil grew in his heart. Mordred repeatedly tried to usurp the throne of England, but was frequently foiled by Sir Percy, the mysterious BLACK KNIGHT. Eventually, the two men slew each other, but Mordred's ally, the sorceress MORGAN LE FAY, drew his essence to her side where she lay, imprisoned in the Netherworld. Revived and sent into the modern world by the Nether Gods for their own purposes, Mordred frequently battled Dane Whitman, the descendant of Sir Percy, and his allies, the AVENGERS.

MORGAN LE FAY

FIRST APPEARANCE *Spider-Woman* #2 (May 1978)
REAL NAME Morgan (or Morgana) Le Fay
OCCUPATION Sorceress **BASE** The astral plane
HEIGHT 6 ft 2 in **WEIGHT** 140 lbs **EYES** Green **HAIR** Magenta
SPECIAL POWERS/ABILITIES One of the most powerful sorceresses of all time; able to manipulate the natural environment of Earth and the astral plane. She can also fly and shapeshift.

The sorceress half-sister of King Arthur PENDRAGON, Morgan plotted against King Arthur until MERLIN magically imprisoned her. Her body trapped, she sent her astral form to various time periods. She and DOCTOR DOOM became lovers across time, but when this went wrong she traveled to the future to kill him. She wound up trapped in the year 1,000,000 BC. Morgan was freed by her daughter and attacked Europe with an army of the dead, though she was thwarted by the AVENGERS. On Battleworld (*see* SECRET WARS), Doom made her Witch Queen of Weirdworld, which was later relocated to the Bermuda Triangle.

MOTHER NIGHT

FIRST APPEARANCE *Captain America* #356 (August 1989)
REAL NAME Susan Scarbo
OCCUPATION Agent of the Red Skull **BASE** Red Skull's chalet
HEIGHT 5 ft 7 in **WEIGHT** 133 lbs **EYES** Green **HAIR** Black
SPECIAL POWERS/ABILITIES Expert hypnotist; could generate illusions, make herself appear to be invisible, and force others to obey her will.

Susan Scarbo and her brother Melvin were stage hypnotists whose ambitions grew beyond show business. When they turned to crime, Susan took the name "Suprema" and was enlisted by the RED SKULL. Changing her identity to Mother Night, she took command of the SISTERS OF SIN, formerly led by the Red Skull's daughter Synthia (also known as SIN). In this role, Mother Night battled CAPTAIN AMERICA. When the Red Skull was captured by MAGNETO, Mother Night joined with the Skeleton Crew (Red Skull's main operatives) to try to free him. Mother Night was killed by the WINTER SOLDIER.

MOY, DR. ALYSSA

FIRST APPEARANCE *Fantastic Four* #5 (May 1998)

REAL NAME Dr. Alyssa Moy

OCCUPATION Scientist and explorer **BASE** Mobile

HEIGHT 5 ft 9 in **WEIGHT** 129 lbs **EYES** Brown **HAIR** Black

SPECIAL POWERS/ABILITIES A scientific genius on a par with Reed Richards himself, she carries a universal skeleton key and drives a flying car.

Alyssa Moy knew Reed Richards before he founded the Fantastic Four. The pair became romantically involved and Reed once even proposed to her. They remained in contact after Reed's cosmic mutation and, in recent years, Alyssa has lent occasional support to the Fantastic Four who returned the favor by curing her of a mystical virus. Alyssa received Reed's help with Nu-World, a planet for refugees from Earth. On the near-future Nu-World, she became a brain in a robot body, and her foes killed her.

MULTIPLE MAN

After his parents died, Jamie Madrox's mutant power to duplicate himself ran riot. The Fantastic Four subdued Madrox, and turned him over to Professor X so he could learn how to control his mutant talent. But Madrox wasn't comfortable around other people, and chose instead to work with Dr. Moira MacTaggert at her Muir Island complex.

Madrox became a member of X-Factor, making the first true friends of his life. After X-Factor was disbanded, Madrox sent his duplicates out into the world to experience all the possibilities life had to offer. He then opened X-Factor Investigations as a detective agency, and he and Layla Miller went into the future to help rescue Hope Summers. He later married Layla, and they retired to his family farm. Shortly afterward he was killed by the Terrigen Mists when he returned to Muir Island to investigate them, but appears to have since come back to life.

FACTFILE

REAL NAME
Jamie Madrox

OCCUPATION
Detective

BASE
"Mutant Town," New York City

HEIGHT 5 ft 11 in
WEIGHT 155 lbs
EYES Blue
HAIR Brown

FIRST APPEARANCE
Giant-Size Fantastic Four #4 (October 1974)

POWERS
Madrox has just one superhuman ability: when struck, he can create duplicates of himself. Each duplicate lasts as long as he wishes and embodies an aspect of his personality. He also has a special suit, which prevents duplication taking place.

Because each of his duplicates is a facet of his personality, Madrox can have problems when he has to make a quick decision.

MS. MARVEL

FACTFILE

REAL NAME
Kamala Khan

OCCUPATION
Student; adventurer

BASE
Jersey City, NJ

HEIGHT Around 5 ft 4 in
WEIGHT 110-115 lbs
EYES Dark brown
HAIR Dark brown

FIRST APPEARANCE
Captain Marvel #17 (November 2013)

POWERS
Kamala Khan is a polymorph who can extend and grow any part of her limbs, grow to giant size, and shrink to the size of a doll. She is also a shapeshifter.

A Muslim Pakistani-American, Kamala Khan comes from a traditional, conservative home. She wanted to make her parents proud, but also felt that their boundaries were holding her back. Kamala is an Inhuman whose powers manifested following exposure to the Terrigen Mists released when the floating Inhuman city of Attilan was destroyed. Kamala's Inhuman powers have been present in her DNA her whole life, it just took the Mists to unlock them. She idolized all of the Avengers—but particularly Captain Marvel (Carol Danvers), because Captain Marvel did all of the amazing things she wished she could do. Kamala joined the Avengers, but later resigned and formed the Champions with Nova (Sam Alexander), Spider-Man (Miles Morales), Viv Vision, and Hulk (Amadeus Cho). She helped free other Inhumans from internment camps before the Champions went on to aid the Avengers against the High Evolutionary.

MUTANT LIBERATION FRONT

FIRST APPEARANCE *New Mutants* #86 (February 1990)

BASE Mobile

MEMBERS Blindspot, Blastfurnace, Corpus Derelicti, Burnout, Stryfe, Reignfire, Reaper, Forearm, Tempo, Strobe, Thumbelina, Wildside, Zero, Skids, Rusty Collins, Sumo, Kamikaze, Dragoness, Moonstar, Locus, Feral, Selby, Deadeye, Thermal

Initially formed by Stryfe, a clone of Cable from the future, the MLF staged assorted terrorist events which initially brought them into conflict with the New Mutants, and subsequently with Cable's X-Force unit. When they were of no further use to Stryfe, this incarnation of the MLF was left to their own devices. The organization was reformed by Reignfire, who had been infused with the DNA of the New Mutant Sunspot, and who seemed to be Sunspot himself. When they were defeated by X-Force, the truth of Reignfire's identity was exposed. The third incarnation of the MLF was composed of humans who posed as mutants so as to increase tensions between humans and mutants. They were later destroyed by the Punisher and SHIELD.

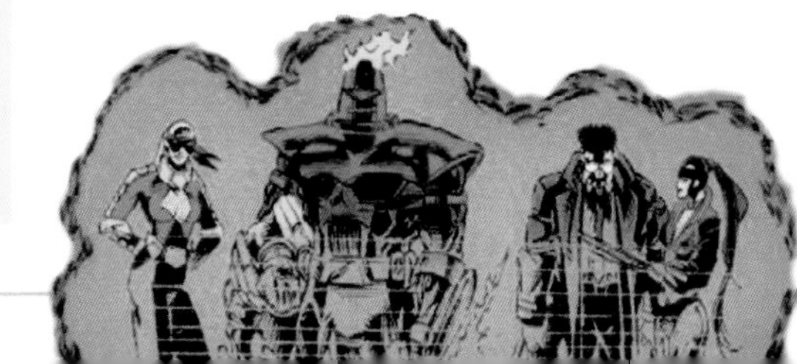

MUTANT X

FACTFILE

MEMBERS AND POWERS

HAVOK (Alex Summers)
Projects concussive force and heat.

BLOODSTORM (Ororo Munroe)
Vampiric powers, controls the weather.

BRUTE (Hank McCoy)
Superhuman strength and agility.

FALLEN (Warren Worthington III)
Has wings enabling flight.

ICEMAN (Bob Drake)
Generates intense cold.

MARVEL WOMAN (Madelyne Pryor)
Telekinetic powers.

FIRST APPEARANCE
Mutant X #1
(October 1998)

MUTANT X

Alex Summers, aka the Super Hero Havok, a former X-Man on "mainstream" Earth (Earth-616), was seemingly killed in an explosion. At the same time, the Havok of an alternate reality (Earth-1298) was brutally killed by a Sentinel robot. The spirit of the Havok of Earth-616 took possession of the body of the Havok of Earth-1298 and thus returned to physical life.

In this "Mutant X" universe Havok became the leader of a mutant team called the Six, who were counterparts of various members of the X-Men.

Eventually, the Havok of Earth-616 returned to physical existence on his native Earth.

Mutant X #1: The Six battle the Sentinels.

MEMBERS OF THE SIX
1 The Fallen (Warren Worthington III)
2 Bloodstorm (Ororo Munroe)
3 The Brute (Hank McCoy)
4 Ice-Man (Bob Drake)
5 Havok (Alex Summers), alias Mutant X
6 Marvel Woman (Maddie Pryor)

MYS-TECH BOARD

FACTFILE

CURRENT MEMBERS
(All board members possess immortality)
ALGERNON CROWE
BRONWEN GRYFFN
RANULPH HALDANE
PORLOCK
RATHCOOLE
GUDRUN TYBURN
ORMOND WYCHWOOD

BASE
London, England

FIRST APPEARANCE
Warheads #1
(June 1992)

MYS-TECH BOARD

In the year 987, seven members of a Druid cult bargained with the demon Mephisto: in exchange for immortality, they agreed to funnel souls into Mephisto's realm. Over the subsequent millennium, the mages gained great wealth and became the board members of a London-based corporation, Mys-Tech. To pay their debt to Mephisto, the Mys-Tech board plotted to take over the world and kill multiple innocents. Their assets included the Un-Earth, a model of the planet that operated like a voodoo doll, and the Warheads, mercenaries who could travel through wormholes to other dimensions or times. Mys-Tech tried to sacrifice the whole of the UK to Mephisto to get out of their contract with him, only for the UK's greatest heroes to defeat them at the Battle of London Bridge, trapping the Mys-Tech Board in Hell.

Hungry for greater power, the members of the Mys-Tech board transformed themselves into the Techno-Wizards so they could confront Super Heroes directly.

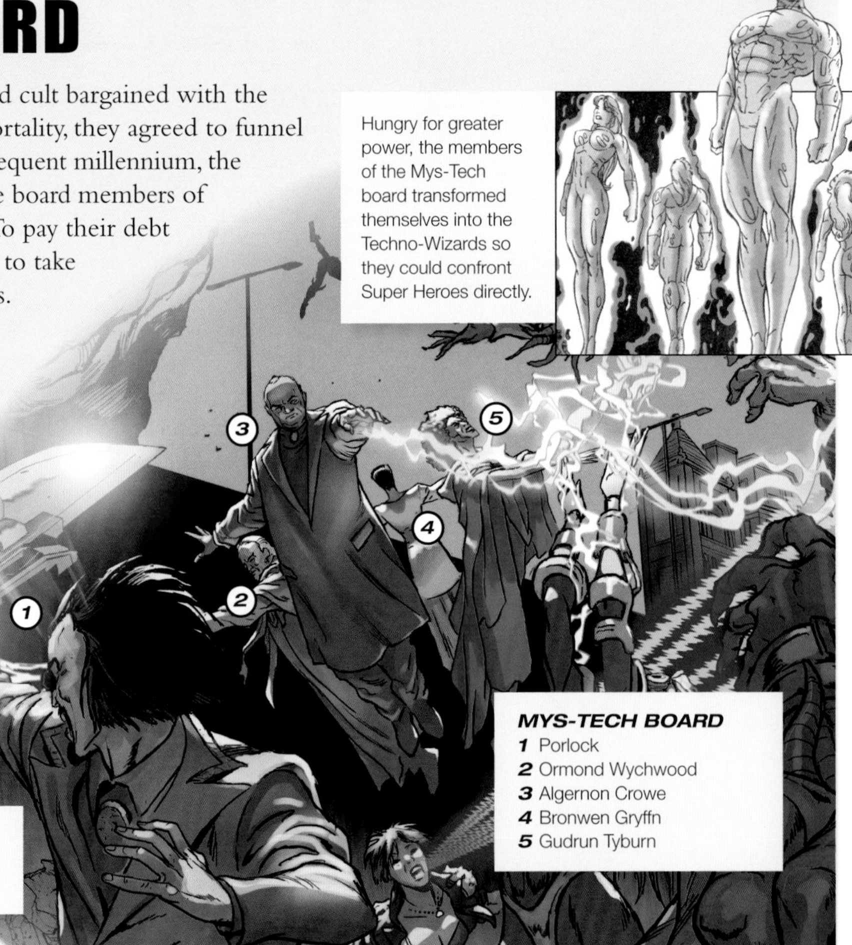

MYS-TECH BOARD
1 Porlock
2 Ormond Wychwood
3 Algernon Crowe
4 Bronwen Gryffn
5 Gudrun Tyburn

At the Battle of London Bridge, Mys-Tech were defeated by an army composed of Super Heroes and Mys-Tech's own monstrous creations who had rebelled against them.

MYSTERIO

Quentin Beck was a leading special-effects designer in Hollywood but, hungry for fame, he became the villain Mysterio. Using illusions to confound Spider-Man, Mysterio became one of his greatest foes, both on his own and as part of the Sinister Six. Mysterio once devised an elaborate scheme to drive Daredevil insane. When it failed, Beck faked his death. His old apprentice Daniel Berkhart took up his helmet, as did Francis Klum, who acquired Mysterio's costume from the Kingpin but was then killed. A new criminal purchased the identity from Roderick Kingsley, calling himself Mysterion, but was defeated by the Superior Spider-Man (Doctor Octopus).

Mysterio's helmet allowed him to see out without being seen and contained a holographic projector to create 3D illusions.

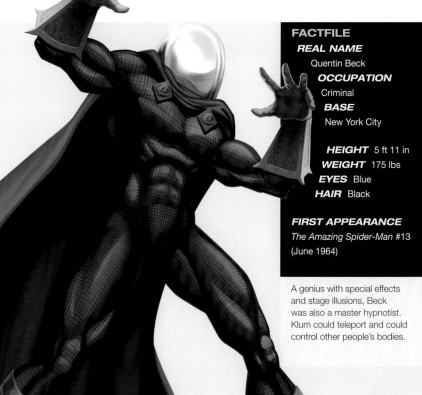

FACTFILE

REAL NAME
Quentin Beck

OCCUPATION
Criminal

BASE
New York City

HEIGHT 5 ft 11 in
WEIGHT 175 lbs
EYES Blue
HAIR Black

FIRST APPEARANCE
The Amazing Spider-Man #13 (June 1964)

A genius with special effects and stage illusions, Beck was also a master hypnotist. Klum could teleport and could control other people's bodies.

MYSTIQUE

Mystique learned to use her mutant shapeshifting powers at an early age. As Raven Darkhölme, she hid her powers so well that she rose to a position of great power within the US Defense Department, giving her access to military secrets and advanced weaponry to use for her criminal purposes. As Mystique, she organized the second Brotherhood of Evil Mutants, teaming with Avalanche, the Blob, Destiny, and Pyro. The Brotherhood attempted to assassinate Senator Robert Kelly, a vocal enemy of all mutants, but the X-Men stopped them. The Brotherhood later changed its name to Freedom Force and began working for the US government. When that ended, Mystique joined X-Factor. She joined the X-Men but betrayed them in the hunt for Hope Summers, and she later led HAMMER's Dark X-Men, posing as Professor X. She was killed by Wolverine, but the Hand raised her from the dead, after which she started to work for the Hellfire Club.

Mystique has two sons: Nightcrawler (left) and Graydon Creed (not pictured). Rogue (center) is her foster daughter.

FACTFILE

REAL NAME
Raven Darkhölme

OCCUPATION
Criminal; terrorist; government agent; teacher

BASE
The Pentagon, Washington, D.C.

HEIGHT 5 ft 10 in
WEIGHT 120 lbs
EYES Yellow
HAIR Red-orange

FIRST APPEARANCE
Ms. Marvel #16 (April 1978)

A mutant shapeshifter who can make herself look like any human, humanoid, or semi-humanoid being, male or female, copying every detail including retina, fingerprints, and voice pattern.

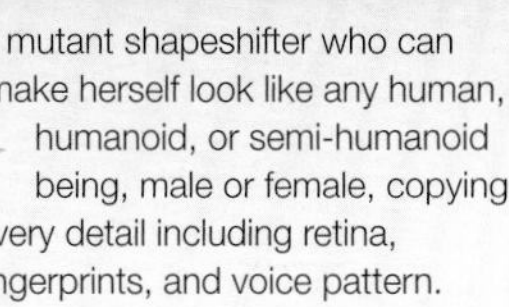

NTH COMMAND

FACTFILE

KEY MEMBERS

HENRY AKAI
As Timestream, he can travel forward or backward in time.

ALBERT DEVOOR
Director of the Nth Project.

ABNER DOOLITTLE
Scientist who designed the dimensional transporter.

DR. T.W. ERWIN
Mathematician famous for his theories of parallel time.

GODWULF
Cybernetic technology allows him to link with computers.

DR. THOMAS LIGHTNER
Magical abilities, on par with those of Doctor Strange.

BENNETT PITTMAN
Was in charge of Roxxon's extra-dimensional oil drilling facilities.

ANGLER
Passes through solid material, teleports, travels through hyper-space.

DEATHLOK THE DEMOLISHER
Superhuman strength, agility.

FIRST APPEARANCE
Marvel Two-In-One March #53 (July 1979)

NTH COMMAND

Nth Command was formed by the Roxxon Corporation to gain total control of the world's energy supply. This was done by operatives, known as Nth Commandos, using devices called Nth projectors that could transport material from one dimension to another. The sorcerer Thomas Lightner was hired to destroy Project PEGASUS, so that the Nth Command could gain a monopoly on energy research. Lightner took control of the time-traveling cyborg, DEATHLOK, removed his organic parts, then reprogrammed him to serve Nth Command.

Breaking into Project PEGASUS with Deathlok, Lightner hoped to use an Nth projector to transport the entire facility to another dimension. He was stopped by the THING, QUASAR, GIANT-MAN, THUNDRA, and the AQUARIAN.

Albert DeVoor, Director of the Nth Project, addresses the Nth Commandos.

N'ASTIRH

FIRST APPEARANCE *X-Terminators* #1 (October 1988)
REAL NAME N'astirh
OCCUPATION Conqueror; sorcerer **BASE** Washington, D.C.
HEIGHT/WEIGHT Variable **EYES** Red **HAIR** Greenish
SPECIAL POWERS/ABILITIES Able to turn humans into demons, fly and change size; considerable mystical abilities; knowledge of a vast number of magical spells.

N'astirh by name, nasty by nature—that's what they said about this demon from the Limbo dimension. Angered when Limbo's ruler made the human mutant, MAGIK, his apprentice, N'astirh felt compelled to rebel, and when a plan was hatched to take over the Earth, N'astirh usurped the scheme so that he could rule the Earth.
His efforts were foiled by Magik, however N'astirh made a second attempt to become a world conqueror by transforming Madelyne PRYOR into the Goblin Queen. Eventually, the X-MEN destroyed him, but he later reappeared, working with Magik. He later helped BASTION abduct Magik to Limbo.

NAMORA

FACTFILE

REAL NAME
Aquaria Nautica Neptunia

OCCUPATION
Adventurer

BASE
Formerly Atlantis; mobile

HEIGHT 5 ft 11 in
WEIGHT 189 lbs
EYES Blue
HAIR Blond

FIRST APPEARANCE
Marvel Mystery Comics #82 (May 1947)

POWERS
Superhuman strength (even by Atlantean standards) and durability; can breathe in air or underwater. Formerly had the power of flight.

NAMORA

The Namora of Earth-616 was the cousin of Prince NAMOR the Sub-Mariner. Like Namor, and unlike most Atlanteans, she did not have blue skin. Both possessed similar powers. She is considered the "mother" of NAMORITA, her altered clone. LLYRA of Lemuria seemed to have murdered Namora years ago, but Namora recently resurfaced and joined the AGENTS OF ATLAS. During WORLD WAR HULK she sided with the HULK. When Prince Namor began to act like a tyrant in Atlantis, Namora risked her own life to make him see the error of his ways.

Another Namora was Earth-2189's blue-skinned counterpart of Namor. As queen of Atlantis, she conquered her world before joining the EXILES, a team of interdimensional adventurers. This Namora was finally slain by an alternate version of HYPERION.

Unlike Namor, the Exiles' Namora had two water-breathing Atlantean parents and blue skin. In conquering the surface world, Namora killed her alternate Earth's Avengers and Fantastic Four.

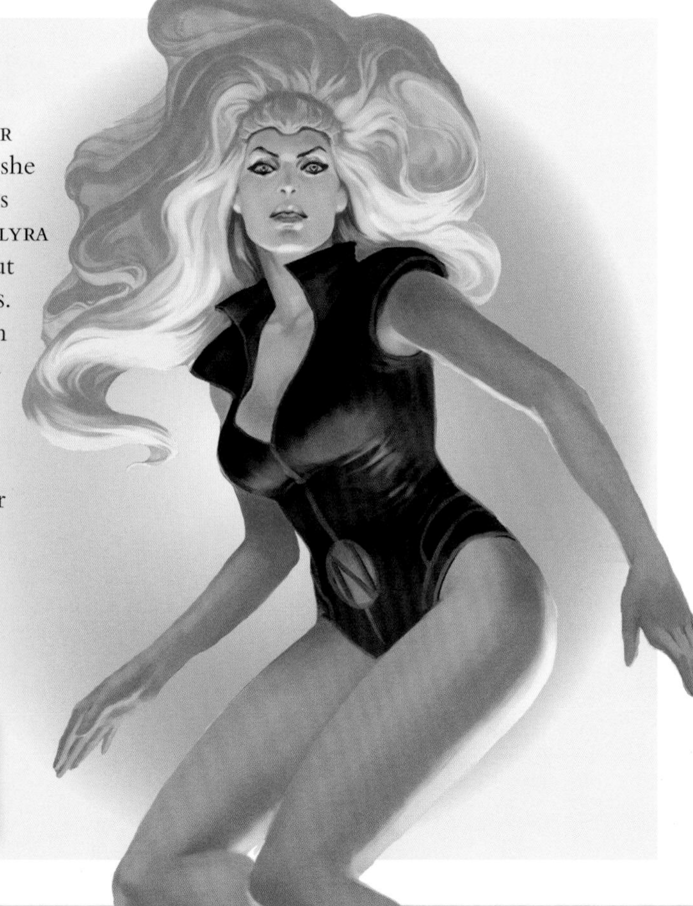

NAMOR

Ruler of the undersea realm of Atlantis

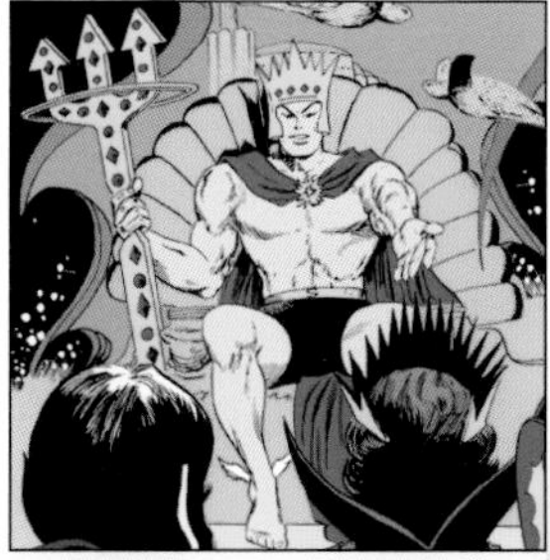

Occasionally Namor helps protect the surface world but his priority is the welfare of the people of Atlantis.

Prince Namor is the mutant son of a blue-skinned ATLANTEAN princess and an American sea captain. He was raised in the underwater kingdom of Atlantis and grew up hating all surface dwellers. During World War II, Namor briefly sided with the Allies against the Axis Powers and joined the super-teams known as the INVADERS and the Liberty Legion.

THE ALL-WINNER

After the war, Namor became a member of the ALL-WINNERS SQUAD, but returned to Atlantis when the Squad disbanded in 1949. He returned to the surface world in the late 1950s and encountered a man called Destiny, who removed his memory and sent him to New York where he lived as a derelict. His memory was restored by Johnny Storm, the HUMAN TORCH.

Namor turned against the human race when he learned that the city of Atlantis had been destroyed in his absence. During his first battle with the FANTASTIC FOUR, Namor fell in love with the INVISIBLE WOMAN. While traveling in the Arctic, Namor once stumbled upon an Inuit tribe who were worshiping a figure frozen in ice. In a fury, Namor hurled the figure into the sea. The ice melted to reveal CAPTAIN AMERICA, who was later picked up and revived by the AVENGERS.

LOVE AND WAR

Namor has been married twice, to Lady Dorma and then MARRINA, but both wives died. He has also been linked to the INVISIBLE WOMAN, Emma FROST, and NAMORA. Namor's son Kamar tried to take over Atlantis, but Namor evacuated the Atlanteans to Latveria and detonated the villain NITRO inside Atlantis to foil Kamar.

Namor joined both the ILLUMINATI and CABAL, and he sided with the X-MEN when the Phoenix Force returned to Earth; he was one of the Phoenix Five to be given its partial power. Despite BLACK PANTHER (T'Challa) also being a part of the Illuminati, Namor has been unable to avoid war with Wakanda. He later joined the X-Men, while also ruling over a restored Atlantis following a confrontation with the SQUADRON SUPREME. When his rule began to grow increasingly dictatorial, rebels—led by Namora—helped Namor to change his ways. Namor also helped his fellow heroes defeat the HYDRA Captain America.

FACTFILE

REAL NAME
Prince Namor, aka Namor McKenzie, aka the Sub-Mariner

OCCUPATION
Lord of Atlantis, CEO of Oracle, Inc.

BASE Atlantis

HEIGHT 6 ft 2 in
WEIGHT 278 lbs
EYES Blue-gray
HAIR Black

FIRST APPEARANCE
Motion Picture Funnies Weekly #1 (April 1939)

NAMOR

POWERS

Super-strength, stamina, and durability (these traits decline the more time he spends out of water). Amphibious; can swim underwater at 60 mph; can see clearly in the ocean depths. Telepathic rapport with marine life and can duplicate many of their abilities; wings on ankles enable flight; long-lived.

After repeatedly battling the Fantastic Four, Namor eventually made peace with them and is now their greatest ally.

Namor became smitten with Sue Storm (Invisible Woman), but gallantly stepped aside once she decided to marry Reed Richards (Mister Fantastic).

ESSENTIAL STORYLINES

- ***Fantastic Four #4*** Namor regains his memory and declares war on the surface world.
- ***Fantastic Four Annual #1*** Namor is reunited with the kingdom of Atlantis and invades New York City.
- ***Tales To Astonish #70–76*** Namor seeks the sacred trident of Neptune and proves that he is worthy to rule.

NAMORITA

FACTFILE
REAL NAME
Namorita Neptunia
(aka Namorita Prentiss)
OCCUPATION
College student
BASE
New York City

HEIGHT 5 ft 6 in
WEIGHT 225 lbs
EYES Blue
HAIR Blond

FIRST APPEARANCE
Sub-Mariner #50
(June 1972)

POWERS

Namorita is amphibious: able to survive on land and in the sea; power of flight; her hands exude a paralyzing toxin; chameleon-like ability to camouflage herself.

NAMORITA

Half-human, half-Atlantean, Namorita was a clone of her mother, NAMORA, although she was an adult before she discovered this fact.

Orphaned when she was still a child, Namorita was watched over by NAMOR the Sub-Mariner and his friend Betty Prentiss. Their love and support carried Namorita through the tragic and traumatic loss of her mother. When Namorita became an adult, they also helped and encouraged her to attend a US college.

During an especially traumatic period, Namorita became blue-skinned and very violent. During this time she took on the name Kymaera.

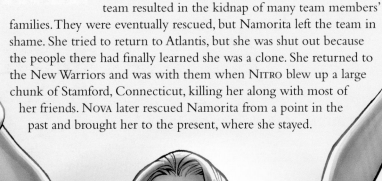

Not long after starting college, Namorita became a founder member of the NEW WARRIORS, a team of young Super Heroes, with whom she fought against the HELLIONS, PROTEUS, and TERRAX. The group provided Namorita with a certain amount of security and stability, but not all her time with them was happy: her first attempt to lead the team resulted in the kidnap of many team members' families. They were eventually rescued, but Namorita left the team in shame. She tried to return to Atlantis, but she was shut out because the people there had finally learned she was a clone. She returned to the New Warriors and was with them when NITRO blew up a large chunk of Stamford, Connecticut, killing her along with most of her friends. NOVA later rescued Namorita from a point in the past and brought her to the present, where she stayed.

NEBULA

FIRST APPEARANCE *Avengers* #257 (July 1985)
REAL NAME Nebula
OCCUPATION Space pirate **BASE** Various throughout galaxy
HEIGHT/WEIGHT Unrevealed **EYES** Blue **HAIR** Bald
SPECIAL POWERS/ABILITIES Nebula's cybernetic components provide her with enhanced strength and durability, and a number of built-in weapons.

Claiming to be the granddaughter of the mad Titan THANOS, Nebula embarked on a career as a space pirate, hijacking Thanos' old flagship *Sanctuary II* and attempting to conquer the fragmented SKRULL Empire. The AVENGERS stopped her, but not before she ravaged the planet Xandar. When Thanos was reborn, he denied any relationship to Nebula, who nevertheless almost succeeded in wresting the omnipotent Infinity Gauntlet away from him. She worked as one of GAMORA's Graces and later teamed up with STARFOX, the CHAMPION OF THE UNIVERSE, and THANE in an attempt to kill Thanos. Nebula's identity was also adopted for a time by RAVONNA the Terminatrix.

NEKRA

FIRST APPEARANCE *Shanna the She-Devil* #5 (August 1973)
REAL NAME Nekra Sinclair
OCCUPATION Subversive; cult priestess **BASE** Mobile
HEIGHT 5 ft 11 in **WEIGHT** 140 lbs **EYES** Black **HAIR** Black
SPECIAL POWERS/ABILITIES Mutant whose feelings of hatred for the world and humanity in general endow her with superhuman strength, agility, and durability.

Gemma Sinclair and Frederick Beechman were accidentally exposed to radiation at the Los Alamos Atomic Proving Grounds. As a result, Gemma's daughter, Nekra, was born a mutant with chalk-white skin. An outcast, she teamed up with Beechman's mutant son Jerome, who had apelike features. As they grew older, they discovered their superhuman powers. As Nekra and the MANDRILL, they attempted to conquer three African nations and later the United States. Nekra became leader of a fanatical religious cult and later partnered with the GRIM REAPER. He killed her, but HELLSTORM brought her back. She killed DOCTOR DRUID, but the VISION blew her up. Her daughter is the villain Death Reaper.

NELSON, FOGGY

Legal student Foggy Nelson roomed with Matt Murdock at Columbia University and Harvard Law School, never suspecting that Murdock possessed the superhuman powers of DAREDEVIL. After graduation, the two friends opened a legal firm, Nelson & Murdock, and hired a secretary, Karen PAGE. Although Nelson pursued Page romantically, he also maintained a relationship with his old girlfriend Deborah Harris. Nelson won the election for New York City District Attorney, failed in his bid for reelection, and briefly opened Storefront Legal Services before re-establishing Nelson & Murdock.

Nelson and Deborah Harris married but soon divorced, and the Nelson & Murdock partnership came to an end when the KINGPIN learned that Murdock was secretly Daredevil. Nelson took a position with Kelco Industrials, resigning when it became clear that Kelco was in the Kingpin's pocket. Nelson survived cancer with the help of Hank PYM and, when Daredevil's secret identity was restored, Foggy became the one person Matt could trust with this knowledge. When Matt briefly became Mayor of New York after Wilson Fisk (the Kingpin) was injured, Foggy became his chief of staff until Fisk's recovery.

FACTFILE

REAL NAME
Franklin P. Nelson

OCCUPATION
Lawyer, former district attorney

BASE
New York City

HEIGHT 5 ft 10 in
WEIGHT 220 lbs
EYES Blue
HAIR Brown

FIRST APPEARANCE
Daredevil #1 (April 1964)

POWERS

Foggy has a brilliant legal mind and is a skilled debater. He is honest and loyal to his friends, particularly Matt Murdock, and usually good at keeping secrets.

NEW MUTANTS

Believing his X-MEN were dead, Charles Xavier (PROFESSOR X) started over with the New Mutants. A group of adolescents, they were charged with mastering their own powers at the same time as learning about themselves and fighting for Professor X's cause of mutant-human harmony. Following their graduation from Xavier's school, the surviving New Mutants remained together to form X-FORCE, with some of them also becoming teachers at the institute.

MORE NEW MUTANTS

Later, Professor X decided to divide his students into squads, placing a second New Mutants team under the tutelage of Danielle MOONSTAR. The lineup constituted PRODIGY (absorbs skills and knowledge); Wind Dancer (creates winds upon which she can fly); Wallflower (releases pheromones to alter moods); Elixir (heals herself and others); SURGE (projects electric blasts, uses superspeed); and Icarus (flies, has healing ability, mimics sounds). The new group was disbanded after many students lost their powers on M-Day.

A third team was formed following the dramatic reappearance of MAGIK. It was led by CANNONBALL and included KARMA, MAGMA, Moonstar, SUNSPOT, and Magik. Karma later inherited her family's fortune and used some of it to finance a re-formed New Mutants team, including many of her old teammates and newcomers such as STRONG GUY. The new team struck trouble when Karma turned out to still be possessed by her twin brother Tran and WARLOCK seemingly returned, using his powers to transform the team into machine/human hybrids.

Noriko Ashida—Surge—belonged to the second New Mutants team.

NEW MUTANTS III
1 Psyche
2 Wolfsbane
3 Magma
4 Cannonball
5 Karma
6 Sunspot

FACTFILE

KEY MEMBERS

CANNONBALL
Invulnerable in flight.

WOLFSBANE
Transforms into a wolf.

PSYCHE
Creates illusions representing the fears and desires of others.

KARMA
Possesses the minds of others.

SUNSPOT
Sunlight lends him superhuman strength.

BASE
Xavier School for Gifted Youngsters, New York State

FIRST APPEARANCE
Marvel Graphic Novel #4 (November 1982)

NEW WARRIORS

FACTFILE

ORIGINAL MEMBERS

NIGHT THRASHER
Master of martial arts; creator of various technological devices.

NOVA
Strength; resistance to injury; flight.

MARVEL BOY
Flight; the projection of blinding light; telepathy; superstrength.

FIRESTAR
Generates and manipulates microwaves.

NAMORITA
An amphibious flying girl.

SPEEDBALL
Surrounds himself with "bouncy" force-field; travels within it.

BASE
New York City

FIRST APPEARANCE
Thor #411
(December 1989)

After battling Galactus' herald, Terrax, the New Warriors officially came into being.

After his vigilante partner Silhouette was shot, Night Thrasher sought to establish his own version of the Fantastic Four, bullying and cajoling Nova, Marvel Boy, and Firestar to work with him. Later, Namorita and Speedball joined the team, establishing the New Warriors. From their base at Night Thrasher's New York penthouse suite, they battled many different villains. Over the years, the team's lineup and focus has shifted several times. On its most notorious mission, a team consisting of Microbe, Night Thrasher, Namorita, and Speedball fought a team of villains for a reality TV show. During the fight, Nitro exploded, killing several hundred people—including most of the New Warriors—an event that ultimately triggered the Civil War. After this, several different formations of the team appeared, including one led by Night Thrasher. Perhaps the most successful incarnation saw Speedball and Justice create a New Warriors that included the Scarlet Spider, Nova, Water Snake, Sun Girl, and Hummingbird. They fought various villains including the High Evolutionary.

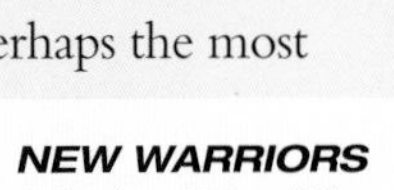

NEW WARRIORS
1 Justice ***2*** Sun Girl
3 Water Snake
4 Hummingbird ***5*** Haechi
6 Speedball ***7*** Nova
8 Scarlet Spider

NEXTWAVE

FIRST APPEARANCE *Nextwave* #1 (March 2001)

BASE The Shockwave Rider

MEMBERS AND POWERS **Elsa Bloodstone (5)** Markswoman, superhuman strength, agility, speed, regeneration, endurance; **The Captain (1)** Superhuman strength, flight, sight, endurance; **Monica Rambeau (3)** Energy manipulation, transforming of body into energy (*see* Spectrum); **Tabitha Smith (2)** Creates balls of psionic explosives; **Aaron Stack (4)** Robot with flight, superhuman strength, endurance, reflexes, telescopic limbs.

Nextwave was originally a strike team assembled by the Highest Anti-Terrorism Effort (HATE) to thwart the terrorist efforts of SILENT. When Nextwave discovered that SILENT was actually funding HATE through a subsidiary known as the Beyond Corporation, they stole an experimental vehicle called the Shockwave Rider and took the fight straight to Beyond. They ran around the US, destroying Beyond's Unusual Weapons of Mass Destruction (UWMDs) while the leader of HATE—Dirk Anger—tried to chase them down.

NIGHTHAWK

Kyle Richmond was originally recruited into the Squadron Sinister, but later gave up crime and joined the Defenders until an explosion left him in a coma. After recovering, he led a new team of Defenders against the original members, and then led them as the New Jersey team of the Fifty-State Initiative, later joining the Fearsome Four. On Earth-712, Nighthawk was a member of the Squadron Supreme. On Earth-31916, Kyle Richmond was an African-American entrepreneur who lost his parents and uses high-tech weaponry, stealth, and fighting prowess to bring criminals to justice. He was transported to mainstream reality after Secret Wars, but later died fighting Hydra. Tilda Johnson, aka Nightshade, then took over as Nighthawk.

FACTFILE

REAL NAME
Kyle Richmond

OCCUPATION
Former president of Richmond Enterprises, adventurer

BASE
New York City; Richmond Riding Academy, Long Island

HEIGHT 5 ft 11 in
WEIGHT 180 lbs
EYES Brown
HAIR Red-brown

FIRST APPEARANCE
Avengers #71
(December 1971)

POWERS
Nighthawk's powers of superhuman strength, increased endurance, and speedy reaction time only emerge at night.

ULTIMATE SERIES NIGHTHAWK
1 Valkyrie ***2*** Power Man
3 Nighthawk ***4*** Giant-Man
5 Son of Satan ***6*** Hellcat

NIGHTCRAWLER

Demonic face of the X-Men

Although Nightcrawler looks like a demon, he is actually a deeply religious Catholic who studied for the priesthood.

Kurt Wagner is the son of AZAZEL—a mutant who resembles a demon—and the shapeshifting mutant MYSTIQUE. When Kurt was born in Bavaria, Mystique posed as an ordinary human and married a German baron, Eric Wagner. The local populace was horrified by newborn Kurt's demonic appearance: he had pointed ears, three fingers on each hand, two toes on each foot, and a tail. Pursued by a mob, Mystique threw the infant down a waterfall.

CIRCUS FAMILY

Azazel saved the baby, who was raised by sorceress Margali Szardos. Kurt grew up in a Bavarian circus where Szardos was a fortune-teller. The circus performers accepted Kurt as part of their family. His best friend was Szardos' son Stefan, and Kurt fell in love with Stefan's sister Jimaine. With his great agility, Wagner became the circus' star acrobat and trapeze performer. Audiences assumed that his inhuman appearance was merely a costume.

However, when Texas millionaire Amos Jardine bought the circus, he insisted that Wagner be exhibited as a freak. Outraged, Wagner quit the circus. Two nights later he battled Stefan, who had become a serial killer, and accidentally killed him.

Charles Xavier of the X-Men arrived just in time to save Nightcrawler from a lynch mob.

Nightcrawler briefly used an image inducer to make himself look like a normal person.

Believing Kurt was a demon responsible for the murders, a mob would have killed him, had Charles Xavier (PROFESSOR X) not arrived and immobilized the crowd with his telepathic powers. Xavier recruited Kurt into his second team of X-MEN, with Kurt taking the name "NIGHTCRAWLER." He was reunited with Jimaine, now calling herself Amanda Sefton, and was reconciled with Margali Szardos, who had blamed him for Stefan's death.

Nightcrawler later became a founding member of EXCALIBUR, but he returned to the X-Men after Excalibur disbanded. He met his half-brothers Nils Styger (alias Abyss) and Kiwi Black, and together they defeated Azazel.

Nightcrawler seemingly died rescuing Hope SUMMERS from BASTION, but he later returned. He rejoined the X-Men, becoming a teacher at the Jean Grey School for Higher Learning. He rekindled his romance with Amanda Sefton, but then lost her while protecting the world from a reemergent Azazel. Kurt remained with the X-Men when Kitty PRYDE took over. He developed feelings for longtime teammate Rachel SUMMERS, and the two eventually became a couple.

FACTFILE

REAL NAME
Kurt Wagner

OCCUPATION
Adventurer

BASE
The Xavier Institute, Salem Center, New York State

HEIGHT 5 ft 9 in
WEIGHT 195 lbs
EYES Yellow, no visible pupils
HAIR Indigo

FIRST APPEARANCE
Giant-Size X-Men #1 (May 1975)

NIGHTCRAWLER

POWERS

Mutant power to teleport himself, his clothing, and a limited amount of additional mass, by traveling through another dimension. When he teleports, part of the atmosphere of that dimension escapes onto Earth, accompanied by a "bamf" sound and the smell of brimstone.

ESSENTIAL STORYLINES

- ***X-Men Vol. 1 Annual #4***
Margali Szardos seeks vengeance on Nightcrawler for killing her son.
- ***Nightcrawler #1–4***
Nightcrawler journeys through various dimensions in a quest to return to Earth.
- ***X-Men Unlimited Vol. 1 #4***
Nightcrawler learns that Mystique is his mother.
- ***X-Men: Days of Future Past (tpb)***
Turns the spotlight on Nightcrawler's interesting origins.

NIGHTMARE

FIRST APPEARANCE *Strange Tales* #110 (July 1963)
REAL NAME Unknown **OCCUPATION** Ruler of the Nightmare World **BASE** The Nightmare World within the Dream Dimension
HEIGHT/WEIGHT Variable **EYES** Black **HAIR** Black
SPECIAL POWERS/ABILITIES A demon who draws power from the psychic energies of the subconscious minds of dreaming sentient beings; can draw the life energy from sleeping people, leaving them in a coma; manipulates the substance of the Dream Dimension.

Nightmare is the ruler of the Nightmare World within the Dimension of Dreams, where the life essence of humans is brought while they sleep. Nightmare monitors the collective unconscious of humans and can manipulate the dreams of an individual, giving them nightmares to gain control of that person. He is the father of the DREAMQUEEN, Daydream, and TRAUMA. AMATSU-MIKABOSHI killed him to launch the Chaos War, but he has since returned.

NIGHTSHADE

FIRST APPEARANCE *Captain America* #164 (August 1973)
REAL NAME Tilda Johnson
OCCUPATION Criminal mastermind **BASE** New York City
HEIGHT 5 ft 4 in **WEIGHT** 115 lbs **EYES** Brown **HAIR** Black
SPECIAL POWERS/ABILITIES A fair athlete and accomplished street fighter; brilliant scientist and inventor; in the past has created mind-controlling chemicals and lifelike robots.

A child prodigy growing up in a poor Harlem neighborhood, Tilda Johnson developed a sophisticated understanding of physics, genetics, and cybernetics. However, she hid her brilliance behind a veneer of childish behavior. Determined never to experience poverty again, Tilda saw

crime as a way to get rich quick and assumed the name Nightshade. Her life was turned around when the vigilante NIGHTHAWK of Earth-31916 became part of mainstream reality and asked her to join him. Tilda took over his heroic identity when he was gunned down by CAPTAIN AMERICA's HYDRA forces.

NIGHT THRASHER

FIRST APPEARANCE *Thor* #411 (December 1989)
REAL NAME Dwayne Michael Taylor **OCCUPATION** Crime-fighter
BASE Ambrose Building and a former factory in New York City.
HEIGHT 6 ft 3 in **WEIGHT** 220 lbs **EYES** Brown **HAIR** Black
SPECIAL POWERS/ABILITIES Weapons in battle-suit include truncheons, aerosols, a pneumatically-fired piton-line, and an Uzi submachine gun. Fiberglass skateboard doubles as a shield.

After his parents were murdered, Dwayne Taylor vowed to become a hero. He founded the NEW WARRIORS to help achieve his aims, and he led them through many incarnations. Dwayne was killed when NITRO caused the explosion that triggered the Superhuman Registration Act. His half-brother Donyell took over as Night Thrasher. During a contest of champions between the COLLECTOR and the GRANDMASTER, Dwayne was pulled out of the timestream the moment before his death to fight in the contest. He rebelled, so was sent back alive to present-day Earth with his last memory being of his own death.

NIGHTMASK

FIRST APPEARANCE *Avengers* #3 (March 2013)
REAL NAME N/A; sometimes known as Adam
OCCUPATION Adventurer **BASE** Mobile **HEIGHT** 6 ft
WEIGHT 200 lbs **EYES** Brown **HAIR** Black
SPECIAL POWERS/ABILITIES Nightmask can speak Builder machine code and communicate with sophisticated machines of all kinds. He can also fly and teleport himself and others incredible distances.

Soon after Ex NIHILO and ABYSS arrived on Mars, Ex Nihilo created a person on the planet's terraformed surface. He became known as Nightmask. The AVENGERS brought him to Earth, where he informed them that the universe was dying and the White Event was arriving. He accompanied the Avengers to find Kevin Conner, a college student who had just become the STAR BRAND as part of the White Event. He later tutored Kevin in the use of his newfound powers, which the Avengers would need in their fight to defeat the BUILDERS' attempt to destroy the Earth (*see* INFINITY).

NILE, TANA

FIRST APPEARANCE *Thor* #129 (June 1966)
REAL NAME Tana Nile
OCCUPATION Colonizer of Rigel **BASE** Rigel-3
HEIGHT 5 ft 4 in **WEIGHT** 110 lbs **EYES** Blue **HAIR** Black
SPECIAL POWERS/ABILITIES Can increase her density at will, giving her superhuman strength and durability; using her mind thrust, she can control the actions of another being.

One of the Colonizers of the Rigellian Empire, Tana Nile visited Earth to annex it for her people. Opposed by THOR, she was able to overwhelm the Thunder God. Eventually, Thor earned Earth's freedom—to Tana's disappointment. Later, Tana took up residence on Earth for a time and accompanied Thor and his fellow gods on a number of adventures. She helped locate a substitute world for the Rigellian seat of government after the destruction of Rigel-3. Later, Tana joined GAMORA's group of cosmic-powered females, the Graces. While working with them, she was killed by the ANNIHILATION Wave.

NITRO

FIRST APPEARANCE *Captain Marvel* #34 (September 1974)
REAL NAME Robert Hunter
OCCUPATION Professional criminal **BASE** Mobile
HEIGHT 6 ft 3 in **WEIGHT** 235 lbs **EYES** Blue **HAIR** White
SPECIAL POWERS/ABILITIES Can explode his body, or any part of his body, and reconstitute himself at will. Cannot reintegrate if any of his molecules become separated from the rest.

Renegade KREE scientists gave Robert Hunter his powers. On an early mission, he exposed CAPTAIN MAR-VELL to nerve gas, giving the hero the cancer that later killed him. Nitro could be stopped by trapping a portion of his molecules in an airtight container after he exploded, preventing his body reintegrating. While fighting the NEW WARRIORS, Nitro ignited his most terrible blast, killing Cobalt Man, Coldheart, NAMORITA, NIGHT THRASHER, SPEEDFREEK, and 600 innocents, spurring the CIVIL WAR. PENANCE brought him in to pay for his crimes, but he was later seen working with the HOOD.

NOCTURNE

FIRST APPEARANCE *Exiles* #1 (August 2001)

REAL NAME Talia Josephine Wagner

OCCUPATION Adventurer **BASE** England

HEIGHT 5 ft 7 in **WEIGHT** 125 lbs **EYES** Yellow **HAIR** Indigo

SPECIAL POWERS/ABILITIES Nocturne can inhabit the body of another person and remain in control of it for one lunar cycle. She can also fire blasts of energy, and possesses a prehensile tail.

The daughter of NIGHTCRAWLER and the SCARLET WITCH of Earth-2182, Nocturne became unstuck in time and was the first recruit to the EXILES. After a mission to the prime reality (Earth-616), in which she met our Nightcrawler, Nocturne left the Exiles to stay. She infiltrated the BROTHERHOOD OF EVIL MUTANTS as a double agent for the X-MEN, but was captured by MOJO. Later, she accompanied her father to the UK, where she joined CAPTAIN BRITAIN'S EXCALIBUR team. Nocturne suffered a stroke and retired to Earth-3470 with her previously thought dead boyfriend, the THUNDERBIRD of Earth-1100. She later rejoined the Exiles.

NORTHSTAR

Twins Jean-Paul and Jeanne-Marie's (*see* AURORA) parents died when they were young. They were adopted separately but reunited when Jean-Paul joined ALPHA FLIGHT as Northstar. One of the first Super Heroes to come out as gay, he later joined the X-MEN. Northstar was killed by a HYDRA-brainwashed WOLVERINE and resurrected as a Hydra drone. He recovered and retained his powers after M-Day. He later married his boyfriend Kyle JINADU. After the Chaos War, he rejoined the restored Alpha Flight.

NORTHSTAR

FACTFILE

REAL NAME
Jean-Paul Baubier

OCCUPATION
Member of Alpha Flight

BASE
Tamarind Island, British Columbia, Canada

HEIGHT 5 ft 11 in
WEIGHT 185 lbs
EYES Blue
HAIR Black

FIRST APPEARANCE
Uncanny X-Men #120 (April 1979)

POWERS
Can redirect the kinetic motion of his body's molecules, giving him flight and superspeed.

NOMAD

FACTFILE

REAL NAME
Jack Monroe

OCCUPATION
Adventurer

BASE
Mobile

HEIGHT 5 ft 11 in
WEIGHT 200 lbs
EYES Brown
HAIR Brown

FIRST APPEARANCE
Captain America #282 (June 1983)

POWERS
Physical perfection through the Super-Soldier formula; skilled at throwing stun discs.

NOMAD

The first Nomad was Steve Rogers, who temporarily adopted the identity after giving up being CAPTAIN AMERICA. The second was Edward Ferbel, to whom the RED SKULL gave the costume to try to harm Cap's reputation. He was killed by the Skull's Ameridroid.

During the 1950s, young Jack Monroe became the sidekick of the replacement Captain America who was active at that time. The two battled Communists, until the variant Super-Soldier formula with which they had beeen injected affected their sanity. The US government placed Monroe in suspended animation for decades until SHIELD could cure his madness. He worked with the real Captain America as Nomad. Later, government agent Henry GYRICH placed Nomad under nanobot control and forced him to become the newest SCOURGE of the Underworld, but the THUNDERBOLTS freed him.

His mental state started to deteriorate rapidly after that, and the WINTER SOLDIER—the original Bucky—eventually assassinated him.

Rikki Barnes, who had been Bucky to Captain America on Counter-Earth, came to the regular Earth after sacrificing herself to stop the psionic entity ONSLAUGHT. BLACK WIDOW discovered her and gave her a new Nomad costume. She later joined the YOUNG ALLIES, but died stopping Onslaught again, who was using her as a means of reaching Earth. The Nomad role was later assumed by Ian ZOLA from Dimension Z.

NORTH, DAKOTA

FIRST APPEARANCE Dakota North #1 (June 1986)

REAL NAME Dakota North

OCCUPATION Private investigator; former fashion model

BASE Mobile **HEIGHT** 5 ft 7 in **WEIGHT** 130 lbs

EYES Blue-gray **HAIR** Auburn

SPECIAL POWERS/ABILITIES Adept hand-to-hand combatant and skilled gymnast; accomplished with various firearms.

The daughter of a US intelligence agent, Dakota North pursued a career as a model before establishing a highly successful private investigation firm named North Security. Boasting branch offices across the globe, North Security rapidly gained a formidable reputation, taking on a multitude of cases that ranged from the mundane to the outright dangerous. The law firm Nelson & Murdock—Foggy NELSON and Matt Murdock (DAREDEVIL)—hired Dakota to help them with investigations and security. This turned into a long-term job, during which she was shot and also lost her license.

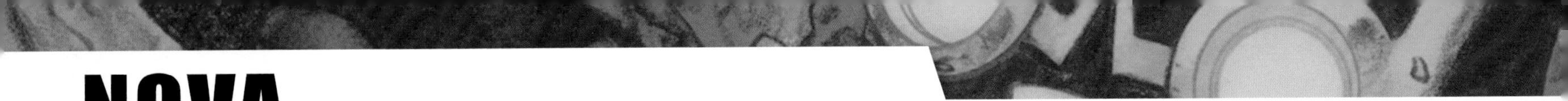

NOVA

The human rocket

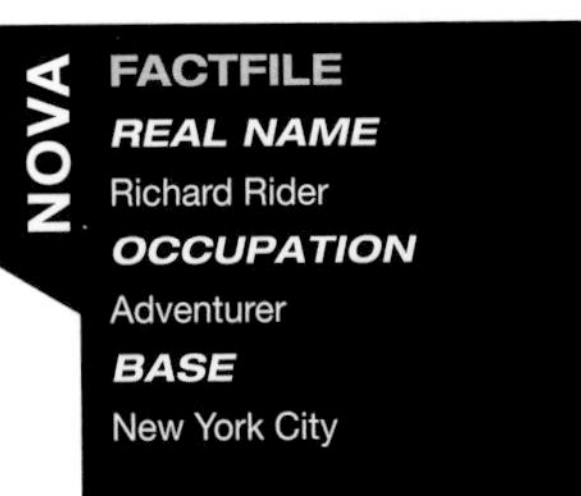

NOVA

FACTFILE

REAL NAME
Richard Rider

OCCUPATION
Adventurer

BASE
New York City

HEIGHT 5 ft 9 in
WEIGHT 145 lbs
EYES Brown
HAIR Brown

FIRST APPEARANCE
Nova #1 (September 1976); (as Frankie Raye) *Fantastic Four* #164 (November 1975)

POWERS
The first Nova had superhuman strength and durability and the power to fly at supersonic speed. The second Nova could manipulate cosmic energy as stellar fire. She could project stellar energy, had nearly total invulnerability, and could survive unprotected in space.

Mortally wounded, Rhomann Dey—a Centurion of the Nova Corps, the space militia of the alien Xandarians—transferred his powers to student Richard Rider. As Nova, Rider became a crimefighter on Earth, then later traveled into space and became one of the Champions of Xandar.

High school student Rider became cosmic adventurer Nova.

HOME AND BACK

On Earth, Rider joined the New Warriors. When he returned to space, Rider helped rebuild Xandar and the Nova Corps and became its leader, Centurion Prime. Rider saw Xandar destroyed in the Annihilation and became the repository of the Xandarian Worldmind. He later killed Annihilus to end that crisis.

During the second Annihilation, Rider brought in the Technarchy to defeat the Phalanx. With that over, he helped found the Guardians of the Galaxy. He returned to Earth to help stop the Secret Invasion.

Afterward, he discovered that the Worldmind had been mentally controlling the Nova Corps, had recruited Richard's brother Robbie without permission, and had taken Ego the Living Planet as a new base. When Richard objected, he was kicked out of the Corps, but he became the new Quasar instead and became embroiled in the Shi'ar-Kree War of Kings. When he discovered that Ego was the one behind the Worldmind's troubles, he returned as Nova to stop him.

After working with the Avengers for a while, Rider went to the Cancerverse, a universe where nothing dies. He and Star-Lord sacrificed themselves to keep it—and Thanos—from destroying their home universe.

Sam Alexander's confidence with his father's armor grew quickly.

THE NEW NOVA

Jesse Alexander was an elite member of the Nova Corps, but he gave it up to get back to Earth and see his son Sam be born. When Sam was 15, Jesse was finally called back to fight the alien Chitauri. They captured him, but he managed to leave Sam his helmet, along with instructions for Gamora and Rocket Raccoon to train him to use it. Sam warned the Avengers about the return of the Phoenix Force, and joined the team before leaving to become one of the Champions. When he learned that Richard Rider was still alive in the Cancerverse, Sam helped free him, the two continuing as Nova.

THE OTHER NOVA

Frankie Raye—stepdaughter of Phineas T. Horton, creator of the first Human Torch—started her career as a hero as another Human Torch, working with the Fantastic Four alongside Johnny Storm. She assumed the name Nova after becoming the herald of Galactus to save Earth. She left Galactus' service and later helped his other former heralds fight his then-current herald Morg. She died in that battle, but years later she returned to life on Earth.

OCCULUS

FIRST APPEARANCE *Fantastic Four* #363 (April 1992) **REAL NAME** Unrevealed **OCCUPATION** Absolute Monarch of an unnamed world in the Inniverse **BASE** Castle Occulus **HEIGHT** 6 ft 4 in **WEIGHT** 290 lbs **EYES** Black **HAIR** Black **SPECIAL POWERS/ABILITIES** Gem in place of his right eye draws energy from power crystals. Fires beams of concussive force, heat, and light from his gem-eye and hands. Can fly and form force-fields.

Occulus and his brother Wildblood were children of the Inniverse, a dimensional plane that exists between the subatomic particles of matter. Occulus grew in power until he ruled his entire world. When Wildblood escaped to Earth, soldiers sent by Occulus to capture him also kidnapped Sue and Franklin RICHARDS. Occulus intended to use Franklin's psionic abilities for his own ends, but the FANTASTIC FOUR put a stop to that. Occulus later stole DOCTOR OCTOPUS' arms and called himself Doc Occulus. He was one of the first prisoners in the Vault prison in the Negative Zone.

ODIN

FIRST APPEARANCE *Journey into Mystery* #86 (November 1962) **REAL NAME** Odin Borson **OCCUPATION** All-Father **BASE** Asgard **HEIGHT** 6 ft 9 in **WEIGHT** 650 lbs **EYES** Blue (one) **HAIR** White **SPECIAL POWERS/ABILITIES** Odin was an immortal god with superhuman physical attributes and the ability to manipulate incredible magics.

Odin was the ruler of the pantheon of Norse Gods and created their home, Asgard. In the prehistoric past he joined forces on Midgard with superpowered mortals to defeat a CELESTIAL and became romantically involved with that era's Phoenix. He later fathered THOR with GAEA and adopted LOKI as well. He sacrificed his right eye for the wisdom to stop Ragnarok, the battle at the end of times, and has been killed and resurrected more than once. He disliked the female Thor (Jane Foster) until she won his respect battling the monster Mangog, after which he helped save Jane Foster's life.

OGUN

FIRST APPEARANCE *Kitty Pryde and Wolverine* #2 (December 1984) **REAL NAME** Ogun **OCCUPATION** Assassin **BASE** Japan **HEIGHT** 5 ft 9 in **WEIGHT** 146 lbs **EYES** Blue **HAIR** Black **SPECIAL POWERS/ABILITIES** A master martial artist and expert swordsman. As a spirit, Ogun can possess the bodies of others, and is immune to physical harm.

A legendary sorcerer and warrior who may have been born as early as the 17th century, Ogun trained WOLVERINE in the martial arts. Originally a man of integrity, Ogun was eventually corrupted by the dark sorceries that kept him alive and invulnerable to harm, and he turned to the path of evil. As revenge against his former pupil, Ogun mentally enslaved Kitty PRYDE, training her and sending her to kill Wolverine. But Wolverine ultimately freed Kitty, and together they slew Ogun's physical form. However, Ogun survived as a spirit that could possess other beings of weaker will and employ them as puppets in the material world. Once again, Wolverine stopped him.

OMEGA RED

Omega Red is the product of the KGB's attempt to create a Soviet Super-Soldier. The test subject, former serial killer Arkady Rossovich, gained mutant powers after receiving genetic treatments, though complications required him to drain the life energy of victims to survive. Placed in suspended animation by the Soviets, Omega Red reemerged after the fall of communism and sought a Carbonadium synthesizer to stabilize his condition. He wound up working with the HAND and, for a while, he led New York's Red Mafia. This led him to clash with many heroes, but most often with WOLVERINE. He found himself in and out of SHIELD custody over the years.

Omega Red killed WILD CHILD in a squabble that was started while they were trying to kill Wolverine. In return, Wolverine later slew him with the Muramasa Blade, which prevents wounds from healing.

Later, three clones of Omega Red were created to form an Omega Clan: Omega White, Omega Black, and Omega Red. Rossovich was raised from the dead and became part of a rebranded mutant mercenary team called WEAPON X-FORCE.

OMEGA RED

FACTFILE

REAL NAME
Arkady Rossovich

OCCUPATION
Crime lord

BASE
Mobile

HEIGHT 6 ft 11 in
WEIGHT 425 lbs
EYES Red
HAIR Blond

FIRST APPEARANCE
X-Men #4 (January 1992)

POWERS
Possesses enhanced strength and mutant healing factor; body secretes deadly pheromones; has Carbonadium coils implanted in arms.

OMEGA FLIGHT

Canada's final answer for its national team

OMEGA FLIGHT

FACTFILE

NOTABLE MEMBERS

ARACHNE
Formerly Spider-Woman, with superhuman agility, speed, and strength, plus a healing factor, wall-crawling, and psi-webs.

GUARDIAN
Can absorb energy, fire energy blasts, and fly.

SASQUATCH
Furry giant with superhuman durability, strength, and endurance, sharp claws, a healing factor, and genius intellect.

OTHER MEMBERS
BETA RAY BILL, TALISMAN, U.S.AGENT

BASE
Canadian Secret Intelligence Service, Ottawa, Canada

FIRST APPEARANCE
(original) *Alpha Flight #11 (June 1984)*; (second) *Alpha Flight #110 (September 1992)*; (current) *Civil War: The Initiative #1 (April 2007)*

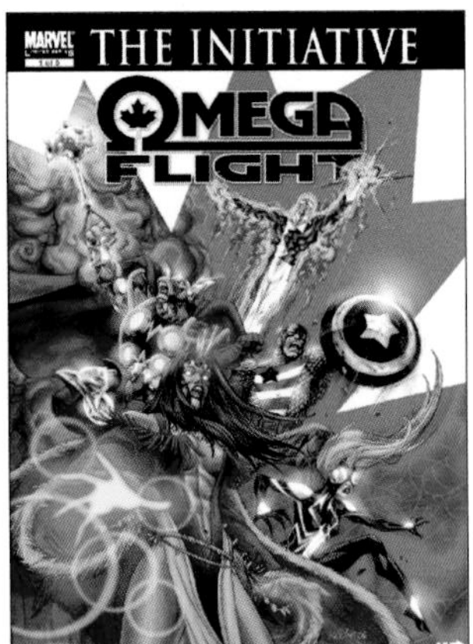

With help from SHIELD, Canada formed Omega Flight to help out with the Fifty-State Initiative of their southern neighbors.

Three teams have used the name Omega Flight, each in response to the existence of ALPHA FLIGHT, which was intended to be the official national Super Hero team of Canada.

Sasquatch worked hard to form the team, although he met resistance from old friends like Talisman.

THE FIRST OMEGAS

Jerry Jaxon of Roxxon Oil formed the first team to kill Alpha Flight and steal GUARDIAN's battlesuit, which he claimed to have invented himself. He gathered several superpowered Canadians for his team, including Box, Diamond Lil, Flashback, Smart Alec, and WILD CHILD. When Roger Bochs balked at murder, Jaxon took over his Box robot, controlling it himself. Jaxon died in their first battle, and for a long while it seemed that Guardian had, too.

Omega Flight first faced off against the Wrecking Crew, which had come to Canada to avoid the Fifty-State Initiative.

ESSENTIAL STORYLINES

- ***Alpha Flight #11–12*** The introduction of the first Omega Flight, and the death of Jerry Jaxson and Guardian.
- ***Alpha Flight #128–130*** The introduction of Antiguard and the end of the second version of Omega Flight.
- ***Omega Flight #1–5*** The creation of the new, heroic Omega Flight.

THE MASTER'S OMEGAS

A Super Villain called the MASTER OF THE WORLD formed the second Omega Flight as part of his plans to rule the planet. His team included Bile, Brain Drain, Miss Mass, Sinew, Strongarm, and Technoir. He first pitted them against Beta Flight, a group of heroes in training to become members of Alpha Flight. When that failed, he decided to take over the Canadian government from within, calling himself Joshua Lord. He discovered the missing Guardian trapped in another dimension, and he rescued the hero and brainwashed him into becoming the villainous Antiguard. Fighting alongside Antiguard, Omega Flight nearly destroyed Alpha Flight. Only after Guardian's wife, Heather Hudson (VINDICATOR), finally got through to him did the tide turn against Omega Flight.

OMEGA HEROES

Following the near-total destruction of Alpha Flight by the Collective (Michael Pointer) following M-Day, the Canadian government formed a new team. This was headed by SASQUATCH, and included American heroes Arachne (formerly SPIDER-WOMAN) and the U.S.AGENT alongside Talisman and the new Guardian. Pointer (now called WEAPON OMEGA) joined in order to atone for his deeds as the Collective.

After the AVENGERS' conflict with the X-MEN, Department H formed another team, consisting of new heroes Boxx, Kingdom, Validator, and a Wendigo. After they were sent to investigate the landing of one of EX NIHILO's origin bombs in Regina, Saskatchewan, only Validator survived.

ONSLAUGHT

During a ferocious battle between the X-Men and Magneto's Acolytes, Professor X shut down Magneto's brain. At that moment, Xavier's own dark fears, doubts, and frustrations combined with Magneto's anger and lust for revenge, to form a new being: Onslaught. This creature lay dormant in Xavier's mind, only manifesting itself when the Professor's frustrations came to the fore. When Onslaught finally took over the Professor's body, the X-Men quickly realized what had happened. However, they were unable to prevent Onslaught's capture of Franklin Richards, a mutant with reality-altering powers. The Fantastic Four and the Avengers stopped him, but many Super Heroes were catapulted to a pocket universe and presumed dead, only returning several months later. Onslaught returned, reenergized by the collective mutant powers lost on M-Day. Rikki Barnes (Nomad) gave her life to stop him. He also formed part of the terrifying entity called Red Onslaught (*see* Red Skull).

By trapping Franklin Richards inside his body, Onslaught could tap into the boy's power to restructure reality.

FACTFILE
REAL NAME
N/A
OCCUPATION
Would be world-conqueror
BASE
New York City

HEIGHT 10 ft
WEIGHT 900 lbs
EYES Red
HAIR None

FIRST APPEARANCE
X-Men #15 (May 1996)

ONSLAUGHT

POWERS
Onslaught possessed Xavier's mental abilities combined with Magneto's powers of magnetism. He was able to induce illusions, amnesia, or paralysis, and manipulate magnetic fields. He also had powers of telekinesis and astral projection.

ORPHAN-MAKER

FIRST APPEARANCE X-Factor #30 (July 1988)
REAL NAME Peter (last name unrevealed)
OCCUPATION Warrior **BASE** Mobile
HEIGHT 7 ft 1 in **WEIGHT** Unrevealed
EYES Unrevealed **HAIR** Unrevealed
SPECIAL POWERS/ABILITIES Carries an arsenal of guns; armored battlesuit protects against most damage.

Never seen out of his armored battlesuit, the Orphan-Maker was once a mutant child named Peter. Peter was subject to the cruel experimentations of Mister Sinister, who planned to kill the boy when he had no further use for him. The cyborg known as Nanny saved Peter and indoctrinated him in her philosophy of rescuing mutant children from threats both real and imaginary. As the first of Nanny's "Lost Boys and Girls," Orphan-Maker abducted young mutants and killed their parents, clashing with X-Factor and Generation X.

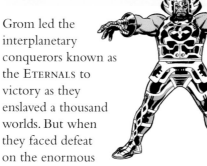

Order, The ***see page 264***

OVERMIND

FIRST APPEARANCE Fantastic Four #113 (August 1971)
REAL NAME Grom
OCCUPATION Conqueror **BASE** Various
HEIGHT 10 ft **WEIGHT** 750 lbs **EYES** Black **HAIR** Red
SPECIAL POWERS/ABILITIES Possesses vast psionic powers. He can lift up to 70 tons, read the minds of others and manipulate matter through the power of his mind.

Grom led the interplanetary conquerors known as the Eternals to victory as they enslaved a thousand worlds. But when they faced defeat on the enormous world Gigantus, the Eternals selected Grom to be the sole survivor of their race and transferred their mental energies to him, making him into the Overmind. When he came to conquer Earth, the Fantastic Four, Doctor Doom, and the Stranger stopped him. After that, he tried to conquer Earth-712, but Squadron Supreme defeated him, reducing his powers. He joined the Defenders for a while, but he was later forced to work for the Thunderbolts to avoid jail.

OYA

FIRST APPEARANCE Uncanny X-Men #528 (November 2010)
REAL NAME Idie Okonkwo
OCCUPATION Student **BASE** New York **HEIGHT** 5 ft 8 in
WEIGHT 115 lbs **EYES** Brown (when using her powers, right is blue, left is red) **HAIR** Black
SPECIAL POWERS/ABILITIES Idie can move temperatures from one place to another, generating fire and freezing cold.

Fourteen-year-old Idie Okonkwo was one of the Five Lights, the first five mutants to manifest their powers after M-Day. A religious girl growing up in Nigeria, she was horrified to discover her powers, as were many others in her village, who considered her a witch. Storm and Hope Summers came to rescue her. She lived on Utopia with the X-Men for a while, but later moved back east to be one of the first students at Wolverine's new Jean Grey School for Higher Learning.

ORDER, THE

California's Fifty-State Initiative team

FACTFILE

NOTABLE MEMBERS

ANTHEM (Henry Hellrung)
Actor and team leader, fires electric blasts, flight.

ARALUNE (Rebecca "Becky" Ryan) Pop star, shapeshifter, flight.

CALAMITY (James Wa)
Ex-athlete, engineer, superhuman speed, flight.

VIRGINIA "PEPPER" POTTS
Executive, uses telepresence equipment to tap Stark satellites and coordinate team strategy.

SUPERNAUT (Milo Fields)
Pilots massive armor suit.

VEDA (Magdelena "Maggie" Neuntauben) Actress, generates and controls golems and can see through their eyes.

BASE Bradbury, California

FIRST APPEARANCE
Civil War #6 (January 2007)

Two teams have called themselves the Order. The first was the Defenders while the second was created for the Fifty-State Initiative.

DEFENDING THE ORDER

One of the first foes the Defenders fought was the alien scientist Yandroth. As he died, he cursed the original Defenders—the Hulk, Namor, the Silver Surfer, and Doctor Strange—to always reunite whenever catastrophe struck the Earth. Worst of all, every time they did, they would become more and more selfish. Unaware of the curse, these Defenders eventually decided to form the Order and take an active interest in shaping the world's future.

The other Defenders figured this out and broke Yandroth's curse, foiling his plan to be reborn with the negative energy the Order was generating around the planet. The Earth goddess Gaea gave Nighthawk the power to call the Defenders together instead, but without any of the side effects. After the end of the Civil War, Tony Stark (Iron Man) became the director of SHIELD. Already the leader of the Avengers, he decided to launch the Fifty-State Initiative, which planned to put a team of heroes in every state in the nation.

In their first solo outing, the Order faced off against the Infernal Man and lost two members, the androids Bannerman Brown and Green.

Stark formed the team for California from scratch, using handpicked people without any pre-existing powers. He put his most trusted employee, Pepper Potts, in charge of the team. For the field leader, he tapped Henry Hellrung, an actor who had played Tony Stark in films—and who also had sponsored Tony in Alcoholics Anonymous. Together, they trained a crew of actors, singers, and other entertainers to become the Initiative's California team. The roster included: Anthem (Henry Hellrung), Aralune, Calamity, Supernaut, and Veda, as well as Aphrodite, Avona, Bannerman Brown and Green, Corona, Heavy, Maul, Mulholland, and Pierce.

THE ORDER
1 Aralune ***2*** Supernaut ***3*** Anthem
4 Calamity ***5*** Veda ***6*** Mulholland

PANTHEON MODEL

The team's structure followed that of the Gods of Olympus. Stark served as Zeus, Potts as Hera, and Hellrung as Apollo, with the other members of the team in various roles. The roles were more important than the people who filled them. If members misbehaved or disobeyed orders, they could be fired and their powers stripped from them. They were then replaced with new heroes-to-be.

The group saw action in the final battle against Captain America's resistance, clashing with the female gang the Black Dahlias, controlled by Ezekiel Stane. They also fought against the Skrulls during the Secret Invasion, being one of the few Initiative teams to have escaped Skrull infiltration.

ESSENTIAL STORYLINES

- ***The Order Vol. 1 #1–6***
The original Order forms out of Yandroth's curse—and the Defenders stop them.
- ***The Order Vol. 2 #1–10***
The entire run of the second version of the Order is only 10 issues, covering from its origins to its demise as a public relations-focused team.

FACTFILE

REAL NAME
Karen Page

OCCUPATION
Sometime secretary, actress and radio personality

BASE
New York City

HEIGHT 5 ft 7 in
WEIGHT 125 lbs
EYES Blue
HAIR Blond

FIRST APPEARANCE
Daredevil #1 (April 1964)

POWERS
Efficient secretarial skills and fair ability as an actor and presenter; some aptitude for street fighting, having battled alongside both Daredevil and Black Widow.

PAGE, KAREN

Karen's love for Matt was always troubled.

Karen Page's relationship with Matt Murdock spawned happiness but also much mutual heartache. Matt hired her as his secretary, but their relationship only blossomed when he told her about his secret identity. This happiness was not to last: in the middle of wedding preparations, Karen asked Matt to give up his DAREDEVIL alter ego. When he refused she ended the engagement and entered a long vicious cycle of self-destruction.

Embarking on a career as an actress, things went badly. As film and TV work dried up she became involved in the porn industry and fell prey to heroin addiction. At her lowest ebb, Karen told a dealer Matt's secret identity in exchange for drugs. Fortunately, Matt is a man with a forgiving heart. After helping her kick the habit, their relationship continued intermittently until she was killed—another of Matt's lovers to fall at BULLSEYE's hand.

PALADIN

FIRST APPEARANCE Daredevil #150 (January 1978)
REAL NAME Paul Denning
OCCUPATION Mercenary **BASE** Mobile
HEIGHT 6 ft 2 in **WEIGHT** 225 lbs **EYES** Brown **HAIR** Brown
SPECIAL POWERS/ABILITIES Enhanced strength, stamina, and reflexes; carries a nerve-scrambling stun gun; costume deflects most small-arms fire, and goggles permit vision in darkness.

Paladin has teamed with Spider-Man to advance his mercenary career.

Paladin is infamous for his mercenary attitude, yet his considerable charm has gotten him far in life. He has allied with many heroes, but he doesn't hesitate to abandon his partners if he's not getting paid. He's even accepted contracts on heroes like DAREDEVIL and the PUNISHER. Paladin has often worked with SILVER SABLE's Wild Pack. He joined Heroes for Hire, but only to get close to capturing CAPTAIN AMERICA. He also worked with the THUNDERBOLTS but betrayed them to keep the Spear of Odin from them. He subsequently rejoined the Heroes for Hire.

PANTHEON

Making a secret stand for human rights

The Pantheon is a family of long-lived superhumans who style themselves after the Greek gods of old. Centuries ago, Vali, their patriarch, bartered with the alien race known as the Troyjans for the secret of eternal youth. Afterward, now known as AGAMEMNON, he fathered several children and adopted others, creating an organization of superhuman operatives bolstered by non-enhanced doctors, scientists, and technicians.

THE PANTHEON
1 Paris ***2*** Ajax ***3*** Hector
4 Ulysses ***5*** Atalanta

The Pantheon operated as a covert strike team, pledged to maintaining the stability of the world.

FACTFILE

NOTABLE MEMBERS

ACHILLES Virtually invulnerable; his invulnerability is weakened by the presence of gamma radiation.

AGAMEMNON Immortality; ability to project a holographic representation of himself.

AJAX Massive superhuman strength and a childlike intellect.

ATALANTA Fires energy arrows.

CASSIOPEIA Fires energy blasts fueled by starlight.

DELPHI Able to see glimpses of the future.

HECTOR Trained fighter; can walk on air; carries a plasma mace.

PARIS Possesses an empathetic sense of those around him.

PROMETHEUS Drives a high-tech armored vehicle.

ULYSSES Expert fighter; carries an energy sword and shield.

OTHER MEMBERS

ANDROMEDA, JASON, PERSEUS

BASE

The Mount, Arizona

FIRST APPEARANCE

Incredible Hulk #377 (January 1991)

ENTER THE HULK

Agamemnon feared that mankind would destroy or despoil the Earth, so he and his clan moved in secret to prevent potential disasters before they could reach fruition. The Pantheon's existence first became known to the world at large when it moved to recruit Bruce Banner, the incredible HULK, to its ranks. At that time, the Hulk's fragmented psyche had been somewhat restored, giving him the intellect of Banner with the massive strength and power of the Hulk. Wanting to make amends for the destruction he'd caused to the world while he was no more than a rampaging brute, the Hulk agreed to joining Agamemnon's cause, and eventually came to function as the Pantheon's field leader.

The Pantheon had access to high-tech weaponry

ESSENTIAL STORYLINES

- ***Hulk #372–379***
  The Pantheon recruits the newly-intelligent Hulk into their organization.
- ***Hulk #422–425***
  During his trial, Agamemnon summons the Endless Knights to destroy the Pantheon and the Hulk.

For a time, the Hulk led the Pantheon, as in this battle against the Endless Knights.

THE PANTHEON AT WAR

But things went wrong when the Troyjans returned to Earth, and the truth about Vali's deal with them came out: in exchange for the secret of bestowing his godly attributes and extended lifespan on his offspring, Vali had promised to give the best of them up to the Troyjans to use as they saw fit. A vast battle ensued, in which the Troyjans were repelled and Agamemnon was taken into custody by the Pantheon. He responded by summoning the Endless Knights, massive zombie warriors whose ranks included undead former members of the Pantheon itself, and commanding them to destroy the Pantheon's base, the Mount. Though the Pantheon survived this attack, its ranks were decimated, and the Hulk left, having gone through another psychological shift that changed the nature of his transformations. Since then, the Pantheon has gone back underground. It is presumed to have returned to covertly interfering in the affairs of man whenever the future of mankind is imperiled.

PARKER, AUNT MAY

FACTFILE

REAL NAME
May Reilly Parker

OCCUPATION
Homemaker

BASE
New York City

HEIGHT 5 ft 5 in
WEIGHT 110 lbs
EYES Blue
HAIR White

FIRST APPEARANCE
Amazing Fantasy #15
(August 1962)

POWERS
Amazing cook, (particularly her corn beef hash) and formidable personality—even Wolverine is afraid of her.

It may not have always been easy, but May Parker's life has certainly been eventful. Following a difficult childhood, May found love with Ben Parker, their marriage being further enriched when they became guardians to Ben's nephew, Peter. Sadly, their life together ended prematurely when Ben was shot dead by a burglar. The years that followed would be testing.

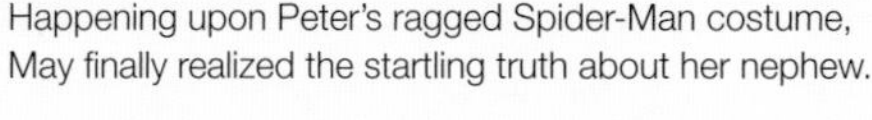
Happening upon Peter's ragged Spider-Man costume, May finally realized the startling truth about her nephew.

After Peter became SPIDER-MAN, he kept his secret identity from her for fear of upsetting her health. She learned it at one point, but she has now forgotten. An assassin hired by the KINGPIN shot May after Spider-Man revealed his identity to the world during the CIVIL WAR.

To save her life, Peter and his wife Mary Jane WATSON gave up their entire marriage to MEPHISTO, who wiped it—and everyone's memory of Peter's secret—from existence. Restored to health, May eventually married J. Jameson Sr. and moved to Boston to start a new life, but they returned to New York not long after. They involved themselves in Peter's charitable Uncle Ben Foundation and had a happy life until Jameson died suddenly, leaving May a widow once more.

Spider-Man intervened just in time to prevent Doctor Octopus marrying May.

PARKER, UNCLE BEN

FACTFILE

REAL NAME
Benjamin Parker

OCCUPATION
Retired

BASE
New York City

HEIGHT 5 ft 9 in
WEIGHT 175 lbs
EYES Blue
HAIR White

FIRST APPEARANCE
Amazing Fantasy #15
(August 1962)

POWERS
Wisdom, charisma, integrity, strength of personality and high moral standards.

Although never rich, his wisdom and fair-mindedness earned Ben Parker the respect of everyone he met. A carnival barker in his youth, Ben grew up in the same neighborhood as May Reilly, for whom he harbored deep feelings. Love did not come easily to the pair, though—Ben was forced to compete for May's affections with the glamorous Johnny Jerome. It was only when May learned that Johnny was a petty crook that she finally accepted Ben into her life.

Following his brother's death, Ben felt honor bound to raise his nephew, Peter, as his very own.

Throughout their time together, Ben and May were to struggle financially, and these monetary straits only worsened when they adopted Ben's nephew, Peter, as their own. In spite of these pressures, however, Peter brought considerable joy into their lives. Tragically, that joy would be cut short when Ben was killed by a burglar's bullet.

The memory of his kindly uncle inspired Peter to use his newfound spider powers to do good in the world, and so Ben Parker's spirit lives on.

Ben's tragic murder continues to inspire Peter Parker, even to this day.

PARKER, TERESA

FIRST APPEARANCE *Amazing Spider-Man: Family Business* (June 2014)
REAL NAME Teresa Parker (aka Teresa Durand)
OCCUPATION Government agent; spy **BASE** Mobile
HEIGHT Unknown **WEIGHT** Unknown
EYES Blue **HAIR** Brown
SPECIAL POWERS/ABILITIES A highly trained agent with a quick mind, Teresa is an accomplished fighter, driver, and spy.

Teresa Parker was raised as Teresa Durand, but while investigating lost Nazi gold, found information that indicated that she was the daughter of SHIELD agents Richard and Mary Parker, parents of Peter. While it later seemed this was part of an elaborate plan by the KINGPIN and MENTALLO to get the Nazi gold, a time-traveling adventure to the past led her to more evidence proving that she was indeed Peter's younger sister. A spy and exceptional fighter, Teresa helped SPIDER-MAN defeat the TINKERER and an alien invasion.

PAYBACK

FIRST APPEARANCE *Punisher War Journal* #48 (November 1992)
REAL NAME Edward "Eddie" Dyson
OCCUPATION Unknown, former vigilante
BASE Possibly Madison, Wisconsin; formerly New York
HEIGHT 5 ft 10 in **WEIGHT** 170 lbs
EYES Brown **HAIR** Brown
SPECIAL POWERS/ABILITIES Skilled in both unarmed and armed combat and uses a wide range of firearms.

Eddie Dyson was a rookie police officer in the NYPD when he discovered his squad were taking payment from the mob. He sought the PUNISHER's advice, who persuaded him to expose this corruption to Internal Affairs. The mafia took revenge and killed Dyson's family, so Dyson became Payback to avenge their deaths. At first, he blamed the Punisher, but the two made peace when the Punisher helped Payback kill Steve Venture—the mobster responsible for the family's murder. Dyson retired but he was attacked by Vigil, and became Payback again. He fought Vigil, Heathen, and the Trust with Lynn Michaels, then fled to the Midwest with her and her father.

PENANCE

FIRST APPEARANCE *The Amazing Spider-Man Annual* #22 (September 1988) **REAL NAME** Robert Baldwin
OCCUPATION Adventurer **BASE** New York City
HEIGHT 6 ft **WEIGHT** 190 lbs **EYES** Blue **HAIR** Blond
SPECIAL POWERS/ABILITIES Whenever Robbie feels pain, he can fire explosive blasts from his body, create a dangerous field of energy around himself, and form a force-field that allows him to levitate.

Robbie Baldwin was originally the hero SPEEDBALL. When he led the NEW WARRIORS into an attack against NITRO that cost over 600 lives and sparked the CIVIL WAR, the guilt he felt altered the way he interacted with his powers. His suit of armor had 612 inward-facing spikes, one for each of the people who died that day, and the pain from them activated his powers. He joined the THUNDERBOLTS and went AWOL to bring NITRO to justice. After the DARK REIGN, he returned to being Speedball and worked at the AVENGERS Academy for a while.

PATRIOT

FACTFILE
REAL NAME
Elijah Bradley
OCCUPATION
Student
BASE
New York City

HEIGHT 6 ft 2 ins
WEIGHT 205 lbs
EYES Brown
HAIR Black

FIRST APPEARANCE
Young Avengers #1 (April 2005)

POWERS
For a time, Patriot used MGH (Mutant Growth Hormone) to give him enhanced strength, speed, and durability, but he now has these powers due to the Super-Solider serum.

Elijah Bradley is the grandson of Isaiah Bradley, the black CAPTAIN AMERICA of World War II, whose mind had been reduced to that of a child by the Super-Soldier serum that empowered him. When Iron Lad needed help battling KANG the Conqueror, Eli resorted to using the designer drug MGH to give himself superhuman powers so he could become a founding member of the YOUNG AVENGERS. When his teammates learned that Eli was using such dangerous drugs, they convinced him to give them up. Critically wounded saving the original Captain America from a KREE attack, Eli received a blood transfusion from his grandfather. This saved his life and also gave him Isaiah's superpowers.

During the CIVIL WAR, Eli and most of the Young Avengers sided with Captain America's anti-registration forces. Following the battles of the SECRET INVASION and DARK REIGN, Eli eventually gave up life as the Patriot and moved to the Midwest.

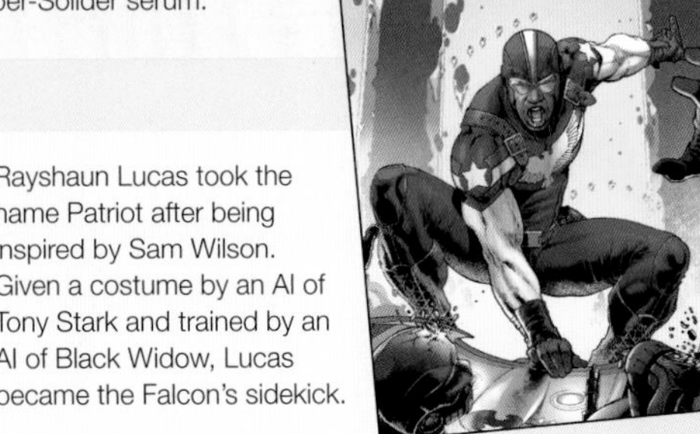

Rayshaun Lucas took the name Patriot after being inspired by Sam Wilson. Given a costume by an AI of Tony Stark and trained by an AI of Black Widow, Lucas became the Falcon's sidekick.

PENDRAGON, KING ARTHUR

FIRST APPEARANCE *Black Knight Comics* #1 (May 1955)
REAL NAME Arthur Pendragon
OCCUPATION King of the Britons **BASE** Avalon, Otherworld
HEIGHT 6 ft 2 in **WEIGHT** 230 lbs **EYES** Blue **HAIR** Brown
SPECIAL POWERS/ABILITIES Inspirational and courageous leader and strategist; a highly skilled horseman and swordsman; he wielded the indestructible magical sword Excalibur.

When Arthur pulled an enchanted sword from a stone in the 5th century, he became the king of all Britons and founded the court at Camelot. After breaking the sword in battle, Arthur received the mystical Excalibur from the Lady of the Lake. He had a son, MORDRED, by his sorceress half-sister MORGAN LE FAY, and married Guinevere. When Arthur learned of an affair between Guinevere and Lancelot he sentenced both to execution, but Lancelot rescued Guinevere. Morgan Le Fay allied with Mordred and raised armies against Camelot. Arthur died while striking a mortal blow against Mordred. In the Otherworld realm of Avalon, Arthur awaited his return. He formed a peace treaty with the Manchester Gods when they invaded Otherworld. The mystical Pendragon spirit has been used to empower the warriors known as the Knights of Pendragon.

PHALANX

The techno-organic race called the Technarchy creates its food by using its transmode virus to convert organic matter into Phalanx, a collective intelligence life-form. Members of the Technarchy then feed on the Phalanx, draining away its life energy. While experimenting on the renegade Technarch WARLOCK, human scientists obtained a strain of the transmode virus and injected it into humans, hoping to create a new generation of SENTINEL robots. Transformed into Phalanx, their subjects began assimilating other humans. Fortunately, the Phalanx could not digest mutants, and the X-MEN stopped them.

In space, another group of Phalanx threatened the SHI'AR Empire, but the X-Men foiled their plans as well. The insane android ULTRON subsequently led yet another breed of Phalanx against the KREE, nearly conquering them until several heroes and the Technarchy intervened (*see* ANNIHILATION).

Sentient biological weapons, the Phalanx are formidable adversaries.

FACTFILE

REAL NAME
N/A; alien being with collective intelligence

BASE
Outer space

HEIGHT Variable
WEIGHT Variable
EYES Unknown
HAIR None

FIRST APPEARANCE
Uncanny X-Men #305 (October 1993)

PHALANX

POWERS

Transforms sentient beings into techno-organic life-forms and assimilates them into its collective. Superhumanly strong, also possess ability to teleport and shapeshift—molding their limbs into weapons or mimicking the appearance of others.

PETROVICH, IVAN

FIRST APPEARANCE *Amazing Adventures* #1 (August 1970)
REAL NAME Ivan Petrovich **OCCUPATION** Chauffeur
BASE Mobile **HEIGHT** 6 ft 5 in **WEIGHT** 300 lbs
EYES Brown **HAIR** Brown
SPECIAL POWERS/ABILITIES Does not possess superpowers, but is a skilled hand-to-hand combatant; a reliable chauffeur, and steadfast ally of the Black Widow.

After the devastating siege of Stalingrad during World War II, Russian soldier Ivan Petrovich searched the city for his lost sister. As he was walking through the ruins he heard a woman's cries from a burning building. The woman died in the fire, but she let her baby fall into his arms. Petrovich raised the girl as his own. She was Natasha Romanova, who eventually became the BLACK WIDOW, Russia's top spy. Petrovich, feeling responsible for Natasha, accompanied her to America as her chauffeur. He lived with the Black Widow and DAREDEVIL while the two heroes struck up a romance in San Francisco. His son Yuri Petrovich briefly served as the fourth CRIMSON DYNAMO. When Ivan became a cyborg and went insane, the Black Widow was forced to kill him.

PHANTOM EAGLE

FIRST APPEARANCE *Marvel Super Heroes* #16 (September 1968)
REAL NAME Karl Kaufman **OCCUPATION** Pilot
BASE Mobile **HEIGHT** 5 ft 11 in **WEIGHT** 175 lbs
EYES Blue **HAIR** Brown
SPECIAL POWERS/ABILITIES Although he had no superhuman powers, Phantom Eagle was an extraordinary pilot, exceptionally skilled in aerial combat.

When World War I broke out, ace flyer Karl Kaufman wanted to use his skills against the Germans, but he feared reprisals against his German parents. So he donned a costume and mask and took the name Phantom Eagle. He became one of the greatest aerial warriors of the war, winning many dogfights, and then joined Freedom's Five, a team of costumed heroes who assisted the Allies. Kaufman's identity was discovered by a German pilot, who killed him and his parents. The ghost of the Phantom Eagle hunted the pilot down and killed him.

PHANTOM RIDER, SEE PAGE 270

PHASTOS

FIRST APPEARANCE *Eternals* #1 (October 1985)
REAL NAME Phastos **OCCUPATION** Technologist, weaponsmith
BASE Ruhr Valley, Germany **HEIGHT** 6 ft 3 in
WEIGHT 410 lbs **EYES** Brown **HAIR** Bald (black beard)
SPECIAL POWERS/ABILITIES Able to fly and levitate objects; virtually invulnerable, super-strong, and projects cosmic energy from eyes or hands; ingenious inventor; hammer fires energy bolts.

Phastos is an ETERNAL, a nearly immortal race created thousands of years ago by the alien CELESTIALS. Being a weaponsmith, Phastos was mistaken for the Olympian god Hephaestus (VULCAN) during the days of ancient Greece (*see* GODS OF OLYMPUS). Phastos is more reticent than his fellows, having a melancholy spirit and an ambivalence toward fighting. When APOCALYPSE tried to incite a new war with the Deviants, the Eternals decided to go public as Super Heroes. In his new identity, Phastos adopted the code name Ceasefire.

PHANTOM RIDER

PHANTOM RIDER

FACTFILE
REAL NAME
Carter Slade
OCCUPATION
Schoolteacher; vigilante
BASE
Bison Bend in the Old West

HEIGHT 6 ft 1 in
WEIGHT 200 lbs
EYES Blue
HAIR Reddish-blond

FIRST APPEARANCE
Ghost Rider #1
(February 1967)

POWERS
A fast draw and a brilliant marksman; formidable hand-to-hand combatant; notable horseman.

Originally a schoolteacher in the Wild West, Carter Slade was shot by a ruthless local land baron, but a Comanche Native American called Flaming Star saved his life. After Carter recovered, Flaming Star gave him a white horse and a cloak covered with a phosphorescent dust. Styling himself the Phantom Rider, Carter began a one-man battle against injustice.

Not knowing that the Phantom Rider was his brother, Marshall Lincoln Slade teamed up with him to battle the Reverend Reaper, a vicious gunfighter set on taking control of Bison Bend, the town Carter had sworn to protect. In their final confrontation, both Carter and the reverend died. Learning the truth about his brother, Lincoln decided to follow in his footsteps. He later went mad and died while battling a time-traveling MOCKINGBIRD.

In modern times, Lincoln's descendant, archaeologist Hamilton Slade, became a modern-day Phantom Rider. Nick FURY made J.T. Slade—Carter's grandson—a member of his new SECRET WARRIORS team. J.T. can charge weapons with fire and calls himself Hellfire. He turned out to be a double agent for HYDRA and is now dead. Later, Hamilton's daughter Jaime became possessed, and he was killed while exorcising the demon from her.

PIP THE TROLL

FIRST APPEARANCE *Strange Tales* #179 (April 1975)
REAL NAME Pip Gofern
OCCUPATION Former bearer of the Space Gem, prince of Laxidazia and painter **BASE** Mobile within Milky Way Galaxy
HEIGHT 4 ft 4 in **WEIGHT** 144 lbs **EYES** Pink **HAIR** Red
SPECIAL POWERS/ABILITIES Claims to be irresistible to women; could teleport anywhere in the universe when he possessed the Space Gem.

Born a prince on the alien world of Laxidazia, Pip was exiled from the court for befriending a tribe of trolls. Missionaries from the Universal Church of Truth came to Laxidazia to convert the population. When the trolls resisted, the Church began exterminating them. Pip was captured and placed on a Death-Ship where he met Adam WARLOCK. They became friends and overthrew the Church. Warlock called on Pip to help stop THANOS from using the Infinity Gems to control reality and later gave him the Space Gem as a reward, making him a member of the Infinity Watch. The Watch disbanded after losing control of the gems. Pip joined X-FACTOR, where he was nearly killed by a bullet to the head, but survived as his brain is located in his chest.

PHOTON

PHOTON

FACTFILE
REAL NAME
Genis-Vell
OCCUPATION
Adventurer
BASE
Mobile throughout the universe

HEIGHT 6 ft 2 in
WEIGHT 210 lbs
EYES Blue
HAIR Blond (becomes white when "cosmically aware")

FIRST APPEARANCE
Silver Surfer Annual #6 (1993)

POWERS
Kree Nega-Bands (now absorbed into his body) confer superhuman strength and durability, the ability to fly, the power to project concussive energy blasts. Genis-Vell also possesses cosmic awareness, allowing him to perceive cosmic dangers.

The first Photon was Monica Rambeau of the AVENGERS (*see* SPECTRUM). The second Photon was Genis-Vell. Following the death of KREE warrior CAPTAIN MAR-VELL, his lover Elysius used cell samples from his body to conceive a son—Genis-Vell. To keep the child safe from harm, his aging was accelerated so that he rapidly reached maturity. When he discovered his heroic lineage, Genis-Vell donned his father's Nega-Bands and became the adventurer Legacy. He later adopted his father's code name, CAPTAIN MARVEL.

In order to save the life of his father's friend Rick JONES, Genis-Vell's atomic structure was bonded to Rick's. This meant that whenever Genis-Vell was in the Earth dimension, Rick was cast into the Microverse, and vice versa. Genis-Vell went insane and helped the cosmic entities Entropy and Epiphany destroy the universe. However, Genis then triggered a new Big Bang, recreating the cosmos. Elysius and another Titan, STARFOX, returned Genis to sanity. The bonding between Jones and Genis was undone, allowing them to exist on Earth separately.

After ATLAS beat Genis nearly to death, BARON ZEMO used moonstones to heal him. Genis took the name Photon and joined the THUNDERBOLTS. Zemo learned that the moonstones' effect on Genis would cause the universe's destruction so he killed Genis and scattered his body through the Darkforce Dimension.

PIECEMEAL

FIRST APPEARANCE *Incredible Hulk* #403 (March 1993)
REAL NAME Unrevealed
OCCUPATION Criminal **BASE** Loch Ness, Scotland
HEIGHT 7 ft 6 in **WEIGHT** 1,400 lbs **EYES** Red **HAIR** Gray
SPECIAL POWERS/ABILITIES Possesses all of the abilities of the criminal New World Order, including superhuman strength, the ability to fire energy blasts, and razor-sharp claws.

The man who would become Piecemeal was an operative from the Commission on Superhuman Activities sent to spy on the RED SKULL. The Skull captured him, intending to make him into a living symbol of his criminal organization, the New World Order. Imbued with the properties of members of the Order, and with memories of his previous life erased, Piecemeal became enthralled with being alive. He began using his powers to absorb the life-experiences of others, until the HULK seemingly ended his menace.

PIXIE

FIRST APPEARANCE *New X-Men* #5 (November 2004)
REAL NAME Megan Gwynn **OCCUPATION** Adventurer
BASE New York **HEIGHT** 5 ft 4 in **WEIGHT** 121 lbs
EYES Black **HAIR** Pink and black
SPECIAL POWERS/ABILITIES Megan can fly and generate hallucinogenic dust. She can detect the supernatural and cast spells, including ones to teleport groups long distances. She also wields a Souldagger.

Megan grew up in a Welsh mining town, unaware that her father was Mastermind, making her the half-sister of Lady Mastermind. She joined the Xavier Institute, where she was transported to Limbo. There, MAGIK tried to steal a part of her soul to make a Soulsword but was interrupted and only fashioned a Souldagger instead. Pixie joined the X-MEN and started to use magic to teleport her teammates around the globe and back to Limbo.

PHOBOS

FIRST APPEARANCE *Ares* #1 (March 2006)
REAL NAME Alexander Aaron **OCCUPATION** Adventurer
BASE New York City **HEIGHT** 5 ft 1 in **WEIGHT** 95 lbs
EYES Blue **HAIR** Blond
SPECIAL POWERS/ABILITIES Alex is an immortal God of Olympus, with superhuman durability, endurance, intelligence, and strength. He can instill fear in others by looking into their eyes, and predict the future.

Alexander is the son of the Greek god ARES. He was kidnapped by AMATSU-MIKABOSHI, who wanted to use him against the other gods, but Ares and Zeus rescued him. Alexander wasn't aware of his lineage until his powers began to develop. He worked with his father in the AVENGERS for a while, then joined Nick FURY'S SECRET WARRIORS. Fury didn't let Alexander join in the defense of Asgard from Ares, knowing that Ares might be (and was) killed. Phobos later died in battle with the villain GORGON, slain by the sword Godkiller.

PLANTMAN

Strange Tales #113 was Plantman's first appearance.

While working in London as a botanist's assistant, Samuel Smithers became involved with experiments to explore the mental activity of plants. After ten years the botanist died, and Smithers moved to the US, where he planned to continue his work in trying to increase the intelligence of plants so that humans could communicate with them. However, due to his lack of formal education he had difficulty in finding support for his ideas and was forced to take a job as a gardener. Smithers tried to combine the job with his research, but was eventually fired for spending too much time on his experiments.

FACTFILE
REAL NAME
Samuel Smithers
OCCUPATION
Professional criminal; formerly a gardener
BASE
A submarine in the Atlantic Ocean

HEIGHT 6 ft
WEIGHT 190 lbs
EYES Green
HAIR Dark gray

FIRST APPEARANCE
Strange Tales #113 (October 1963)

POWERS

Plantman's projector weapons allow him to control plants, animating their limbs to attack a victim; and to manipulate plants so they look like duplicates of humans.

REVENGE

Not long after Smithers lost his job, a bolt of lightning struck his experimental plant ray-gun, charging the device with the power to control and animate plant life. Smithers put on a costume and, taking the name Plantman, sought revenge on the man who had fired him, but was stopped by the HUMAN TORCH, who destroyed the plant-gun. Undeterred, Plantman built a second, more powerful weapon, and tried to kill the Human Torch, but his plan failed. Later he joined the international crime syndicate, the MAGGIA. Creating plant duplicates of himself, Plantman battled the X-MEN, the AVENGERS, NAMOR, TRITON, and SHIELD, among others.

The Plantman simuloid possessed all the powers of the original Plantman.

CHARACTER KEY
1 Plantman
2 Porcupine
3 The Eel
4 The Scarecrow

TRANSFORMATION

Over the years, Smithers' body gradually mutated to become more and more plantlike. At one point, he connected with the Verdant Green—the manifestation of the Earth's biosphere—and was given the option of wiping humans from the planet or preserving them. Although his transformation had already cost him a great deal of his humanity, he chose to let the people of Earth live. For a while, Smithers worked with the THUNDERBOLTS under HAWKEYE's leadership, using the name Blackheath. He later returned to crime and was imprisoned in Pleasant Hill. A shop clerk called Paul later took on the identity of Plantman, joining BARON ZEMO's new MASTERS OF EVIL.

POLARIS

While her green hair marked her as a mutant, Lorna Dane had no idea growing up that she had been adopted, and that her true father was MAGNETO. When her powers manifested, she found herself at the center of an all-out war between the X-MEN and the demonic MESMERO for control of her abilities. Falling in love with the X-Man HAVOK, Lorna desired nothing more than to live a normal life. But fate would not let her be, and time and again she was pulled to the center of mutant strife as Polaris, mistress of magnetism. She led X-FACTOR beside Havok and later joined the X-Men.

Polaris lost her powers on M-Day, but APOCALYPSE restored them when he made her Pestilence, one of his Horsemen. She and Havok broke up when he left her at the altar, but they renewed their relationship during their attempt to save the SHI'AR Empire from Havok's brother VULCAN. They have since parted again. Polaris formed a new X-Factor alongside teammates GAMBIT and QUICKSILVER, before helping Magneto tutor and protect the time-displaced teenage X-Men.

POLARIS

FACTFILE

REAL NAME
Lorna Dane

OCCUPATION
Adventurer

BASE
The Xavier Institute for Higher Learning

HEIGHT 5 ft 7 in
WEIGHT 115 lbs
EYES Green
HAIR Green

FIRST APPEARANCE
Uncanny X-Men #49 (October 1968)

POWERS
Polaris has power over magnetism and can use it to fly, create force-fields, and manipulate anything made of magnetic materials. She also now has a healing factor.

POOLE, GWEN

FIRST APPEARANCE *Howard the Duck* #1 (January 2016)
REAL NAME Gwendolyn "Gwen" Poole
OCCUPATION Adventurer **BASE** Mobile
HEIGHT 5 ft 4 in **WEIGHT** Unknown **EYES** Blue **HAIR** Blond
SPECIAL POWERS/ABILITIES Acknowledges the fictional world in which she lives; knowledge of other heroes and villains' secrets.

Gwen Poole once lived in the real world, where heroes and villains exist as fictional characters in comic books and movies. After finding herself in the Marvel Universe, Gwen was keen to lead the Super Hero life and believed her actions had no real consequence. With the aid of her tailor, Ronnie, who misread her name and assumed she wanted to look like DEADPOOL, Gwen became the Super Hero Gwenpool. During her first misadventure she targeted HOWARD THE DUCK, who made her see that her actions did matter in that universe. But Gwenpool cheerfully accepted more mercenary jobs, and later became an agent for mechanised villain MODOK. She is now trying harder to be a hero as part of HAWKEYE's West Coast Avengers.

POTTS, VIRGINIA "PEPPER"

"Pepper" Potts became Tony Stark's secretary early in his career. Stark entrusted her with the secret of his identity as IRON MAN but didn't notice her crush on him. She eventually married Stark's chauffeur, Harold "Happy" HOGAN and dropped out of Tony's life. Pepper and Harold later divorced—and then remarried, by which time they were both working for Tony again. Soon after Hogan died from injuries inflicted by the SPYMASTER, Pepper joined the ORDER, the California team of the FIFTY-STATE INITIATIVE, calling herself Hera.

Later, Ezekiel STANE harmed Pepper, and Tony had to turn her into a cyborg to save her life. During the DARK REIGN, Tony made her CEO of Stark Industries, where her main job was to keep sensitive information from going to HAMMER, which was controlled by Norman Osborn (*see* GREEN GOBLIN). Calling herself Rescue, she was forced to flee its headquarters in her own suit of power armor. She and Tony became lovers as she helped him escape from MADAME MASQUE, and afterward she infiltrated HAMMER disguised as Madame Masque. Although she and Tony separated, Pepper remained close to the company and helped Riri Williams when she became IRONHEART.

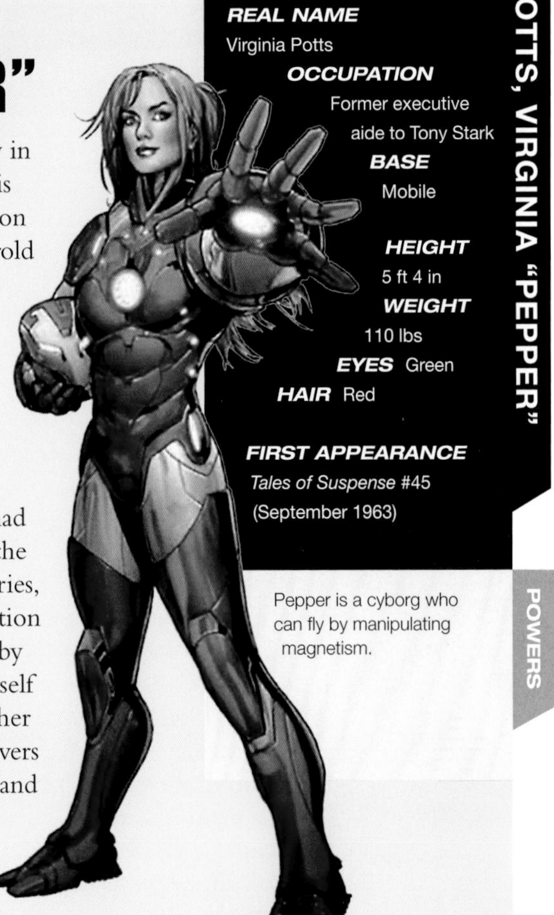

POTTS, VIRGINIA "PEPPER"

FACTFILE

REAL NAME
Virginia Potts

OCCUPATION
Former executive aide to Tony Stark

BASE
Mobile

HEIGHT
5 ft 4 in
WEIGHT
110 lbs
EYES Green
HAIR Red

FIRST APPEARANCE
Tales of Suspense #45 (September 1963)

POWERS
Pepper is a cyborg who can fly by manipulating magnetism.

PORCUPINE

FIRST APPEARANCE *Tales to Astonish* #48 (October 1963)
REAL NAME Alexander Gentry
OCCUPATION Weapons designer/criminal **BASE** New York City
HEIGHT (with battlesuit) 6 ft 7 in **WEIGHT** (with battlesuit) 305 lbs
EYES Blue-gray **HAIR** Brown
SPECIAL POWERS/ABILITIES Battlesuit fired quills, laser beams, bombs, gases, and other weapons. Belt jets enabled him to fly.

A weapons designer for the US government, Alexander Gentry invented a battlesuit inspired by a porcupine. It was covered in razor-sharp, projectile quills that he could fire at opponents, and quill-like tubes through which other weapons could be fired. Getting greedy, Gentry used the suit to become the Porcupine, but his criminal career was a failure. CAPTAIN AMERICA agreed to buy the battlesuit from Gentry if he would help the AVENGERS defeat the SERPENT SOCIETY. Gentry agreed, but was fatally impaled on his own quill during the battle. A new Porcupine surfaced later and wound up working with the THUNDERBOLTS.

POWERHOUSE

A member of the alien Xandarians, Rieg Davan was a Syfon warrior in the elite Nova Corps. He was sent to Earth to locate Centurion Nova-Prime Rhomann Dey. Davan's starship crash-landed on Earth. He was found and brainwashed by the Condor, a costumed criminal.

As the Condor's accomplice Powerhouse, Davan battled NOVA, the young Earthman who had inherited the deceased Dey's powers. Eventually Davan recovered his memory and with Nova and other heroes journeyed to Xandar. As the CHAMPIONS OF XANDAR, they helped the Xandarians defeat the invading SKRULLS.

Davan later perished in combat defending Xandar against a successful invasion by the forces of the space pirate NEBULA.

The name Powerhouse has since been used by a criminal mutant Earthwoman who also has the power to drain energy from other living beings through touch to amplify her own. She has battled SPIDER-MAN and WOLVERINE, among others.

Alex Power of POWER PACK also used the name Powerhouse when he temporarily possessed the superhuman powers of his siblings.

FACTFILE
REAL NAME
Rieg Davan
OCCUPATION
Syfon warrior
BASE
The planet Xandar
HEIGHT
6 ft 3 in
WEIGHT
265 lbs
EYES Brown
HAIR Brown
FIRST APPEARANCE
Nova #2 (October 1976)

POWERHOUSE

POWERS
Powerhouse could siphon energy from external sources, including living beings to amplify his strength or discharge energy blasts.

POWDERKEG

FIRST APPEARANCE *Captain Marvel* #1 (December 1995)
REAL NAME Frank Skorina
OCCUPATION Prisoner **BASE** The Big House
HEIGHT/WEIGHT/EYES Unrevealed **HAIR** Red
SPECIAL POWERS/ABILITIES Secretes nitro-glycerine through skin; when body strikes object with sufficient force the chemical ignites, causing an explosion.

Powderkeg was a member of the MASTERS OF EVIL during DOCTOR OCTOPUS' ill-conceived turn as leader. Following the failure of the group's attempt to invade Avengers Mansion and their subsequent demise, Powderkeg ran a protection racket in the neighborhood where Ben Grimm (*see* THING) grew up, but Grimm stopped that cold. For a while, he was an inmate in the experimental penitentiary the Big House, in which all the prisoners were shrunk to reduce costs. Recently, he was seen in the Bar with No Name, which caters to criminals.

POWER BROKER

FIRST APPEARANCE *Machine Man* #6 (September 1978)
REAL NAME Curtiss Jackson
OCCUPATION Criminal **BASE** Los Angeles
HEIGHT 7 ft 6 in **WEIGHT** 600 lbs
EYES Brown **HAIR** Black
SPECIAL POWERS/ABILITIES Once a normal man, Jackson possesses superhuman strength. However, his body is so overdeveloped that he cannot move without a steel exo-skeleton.

Curtiss Jackson was an agent of the Corporation, a criminal organization run like a respectable business. After meeting Dr. Karl MALUS, Jackson formed his own company—Power Broker, Inc.—which sold superhuman strength to its clients. He empowered numerous people, including U.S.AGENT, DEMOLITION MAN, and most of the wrestlers on the UCWF circuit. Hunted by the criminal-killing SCOURGE, Jackson augmented himself but wound up so musclebound he could hardly move. A new Power Broker appeared recently, wearing a battlesuit that allows him to fire blasts of energy from his hands. He gave HARDBALL his powers.

POWER MAN

FIRST APPEARANCE *Shadowland: Power Man* #1 (October 2010)
REAL NAME Victor Alvarez
OCCUPATION Adventurer **BASE** New York
HEIGHT 5 ft 9 in **WEIGHT** 160 lbs
EYES Brown **HAIR** Black
SPECIAL POWERS/ABILITIES Victor can draw the chi from those around him, granting him superhuman durability and strength.

Afro-Dominican Victor Alvarez, the son of the villain Shades, lived in Hell's Kitchen. When BULLSEYE caused an explosion that killed about 100 people, Victor survived by drawing an energy called chi from those who had died, gaining superhuman strength. Soon after, he donned a costume and became a hero for hire called Power Man. He later joined the Avengers Academy and then Luke CAGE's AVENGERS team. Cage and Erik Josten (ATLAS) have both also used the name Power Man.

POWER PACK

Young hero team with power to burn

POWER PACK

FACTFILE

CURRENT MEMBERS

ZERO-G
(Alex Power, leader) Ability to control the gravity of himself or other objects.

LIGHTSPEED
(Julie Power) Flight, super-speed.

MASS MASTER
(Jack Power) Can compress or disperse his body's mass.

ENERGIZER
(Katie Power) Can absorb and release energy.

BASE
Bainbridge Island, Washington

FIRST APPEARANCE
Power Pack #1 (August 1984)

Dr. James Power inadvertently caused his children to join the ranks of Earth's Super Heroes.

Professor James Power, father of Alex, Julie, Jack, and Katie, invented an antimatter generator that siphoned energy from an alternate dimension. Aelfyre "Whitey" Whitemane, a member of the alien Kymellian race, arrived on Earth to prevent the machine being used, knowing it had the potential to wipe out entire planets. A rival species, the Snarks, attempted to steal the device.

SECRET SUPER HEROES

Whitemane suffered fatal injuries in the ensuing struggle, but before dying he bestowed one of his abilities on each of the four Power children. They became the superheroic Power Pack, and adopted the identities of Gee (Alex), Lightspeed (Julie), Mass Master (Jack), and Energizer (Katie). Hiding their dual identities from their parents, the Pack dealt with extraterrestrial threats and employed Whitey's intelligent spacecraft, the smartship *Friday*. Power Pack aided the Morlocks during the Mutant Massacre, and fought Apocalypse's Horsemen during the Fall of the Mutants. Franklin Richards, using the name Tattletale due to his ability to perceive possible futures, became an unofficial member of the team, as did Kofi, a Kymellian relative of the late Whitemane.

ESSENTIAL STORYLINES

- ***Power Pack Vol. 1 #1***
Power Pack debuts, launching a popular 62-issue series.
- ***Power Pack Vol. 2 #1–4***
The heroes return—now a few years older—in a limited series that pits them against their perennial enemies, the Snarks.
- ***X-Men and Power Pack #1–4***
Power Pack returns to its roots in a limited series that guest-stars such famous mutants as Cyclops, Beast, and Wolverine.

Frequent contact with the Kymellians and the Snarks has turned the members of Power Pack into veteran interstellar adventurers.

ENERGY SWAPPING

Power Pack's powers often switched from one member to another. At one point, they adopted the names of Destroyer (Alex), Molecula (Julie), Counterweight (Jack), and Starstreak (Katie) and helped the Kymellians relocate to a new world. Alex appeared to become a Kymellian, though this was revealed to be a pseudoplasm duplicate planted by Technocrat, a Kymellian.

Alex temporarily stole the energies of his brother and sisters to join the New Warriors as Powerpax and then Powerhouse. He later changed his code name to Zero-G and joined the Fifty-State Initiative. Julie ran away to Los Angeles, joining Excelsior (later the Loners), a team of young ex-heroes. Julie, Alex, and Katie reunited as the Power Pack to help the Future Foundation (Fantastic Four) defeat mad Celestials.

After the re-formation of the Multiverse, Alex was lost with the rest of the Future Foundation. Julie enrolled at Empire State University while Jack attended high school and Katie junior high.

POWER PACK
1 Mass Master
2 Energizer
3 Lightspeed
4 Zero-G

POWER PRINCESS

FIRST APPEARANCE *Supreme Power* #2 (November 2003)
REAL NAME Zarda
OCCUPATION Adventurer **BASE** Mobile
HEIGHT 6 ft **WEIGHT** 178 lbs **EYES** Purple **HAIR** Black
SPECIAL POWERS/ABILITIES An extremely long lifespan; can heal others or herself by transferring life force energy; can also fly.

The first Princess Zarda (Power Princess) was from Utopia Island on Earth-712. She was a member of the Exiles and Squadron Supreme. The second Zarda was an alien posing as a Greek goddess, who awoke in a mausoleum after sleeping for millennia and joined the new Squadron Supreme. She assumed a false identity to blend in, but ended up registering with the government as Power Princess. Her Squadron invaded the Ultimate Universe and she decided to remain there and strike up a short relationship with the Hulk. She was killed in Battleworld fighting the Squadron Sinister.

PRATT, AGENT

FIRST APPEARANCE *Incredible Hulk* #40 (July 2002)
REAL NAME Agent Pratt
OCCUPATION Agent for clandestine organization **BASE** Mobile
HEIGHT/WEIGHT/EYES Unrevealed **HAIR** None
SPECIAL POWERS/ABILITIES Body able to regenerate itself as a result of H Section Programming; injection of Hulk blood endowed him with Hulk-like powers.

When he first met Bruce Banner, this ruthless operative was posing as an FBI agent. In truth he belonged to the sinister, clandestine organisation Home Base. After forcing Banner to change into the Hulk, Pratt obtained a sample of his blood, but a police officer snatched it and, plunging it into Pratt's own bloodstream, caused him to explode. Pratt's H Section Programming enabled his body to regenerate itself, and he soon returned to taunt Banner again. This time the Hulk emerged to tear Pratt's body apart.

PRESTER JOHN

FIRST APPEARANCE *Fantastic Four* #54 (September 1966)
REAL NAME Prester John
OCCUPATION Traveler **BASE** Mobile
HEIGHT 6 ft 1 in **WEIGHT** 210 lbs **EYES** Blue **HAIR** Red
SPECIAL POWERS/ABILITIES Skilled swordsman; a weapon called the Evil Eye allowed him to fire energy blasts, generate force-fields, and rearrange matter.

Prester John, monarch of a 12th-century kingdom, aided Richard the Lionheart during the Crusades. Afterward, John discovered the fabled isle of Avalon, but while he was there, a plague struck. As sole survivor, he sat in the Chair of Survival and slept. Reawakening in the modern era, he crossed paths with many heroes, including the Fantastic Four. He carries the powerful Stellar Rod, a weapon made from the Evil Eye. He served as Head of Multi-Religious Studies on the isle of Providence for a time. Later he commanded an army of human-animal hybrids called the New Men and ruled Wundagore Mountain.

PRINCESS PYTHON

FIRST APPEARANCE *Amazing Spider-Man* #22 (March 1965)
REAL NAME Zelda DuBois
OCCUPATION Snake charmer; criminal **BASE** Mobile
HEIGHT 5 ft 8 in **WEIGHT** 140 lbs
EYES Green **HAIR** Red-brown
SPECIAL POWERS/ABILITIES Can control her trained rock python; sometimes carries an electric prod.

Princess Python is a snake charmer who trained her rock python to attack on command. She served with several versions of the Circus of Crime while also pursuing a solo career. Princess Python briefly joined the mercenaries of the Serpent Society and even started up one incarnation of the Serpent Squad. For a while she worked at the Quentin Carnival and became involved with Johnny Blaze (Ghost Rider). At one point, she even married the Stilt-Man, and was blinded during the Punisher's attack on the Stilt-Man's funeral. Her son Daniel appeared to kill her in a bombing after discovering she was Princess Python. Nonetheless, she returned as part of Max Fury's Masters of Evil. Later she joined Viper's Serpent Society, renamed Serpent Solutions, which merged with Baron Zemo's Army of Evil.

PRESENCE

FIRST APPEARANCE *Defenders* #52 (October 1977)
REAL NAME Sergei Krylov
OCCUPATION Super Villain **BASE** Mobile
HEIGHT 6 ft **WEIGHT** 200 lbs **EYES** Yellow **HAIR** None
SPECIAL POWERS/ABILITIES Body produces lethal radiation which can be harnessed to enable flight, energy blasts, force-fields, enhanced strength, or telepathy.

Nuclear physicist Sergei Krylov became an important player in Russian politics and sought to increase his might by subjecting himself to experimental radiation. He succeeded in gaining radioactive powers, deadly to the unprotected, which could also be used to control the minds of others. He brainwashed Dr. Tania Belinskya (the Red Guardian) into becoming his partner. He fought Kang and later tried to conquer Russia after Tania left him for his son, Vanguard. The hero Powersurge sacrificed himself to stop him, killing them both. Presence was revived by Umbral Dynamics, but Negasonic Teenage Warhead drained his power and killed him.

PRINCE OF ORPHANS

FIRST APPEARANCE *Immortal Iron Fist* #12 (October 2007)
REAL NAME John Aman
OCCUPATION Adventurer **BASE** Tibet
HEIGHT 5 ft 11 in **WEIGHT** 162 lbs **EYES** Blue **HAIR** Bald
SPECIAL POWERS/ABILITIES John is a fantastic martial artist with superhuman coordination, reflexes, speed, and strength, and can change into a green mist.

John was an orphan raised in Tibet by the members of the Council of Seven. He was sent to assassinate Orson Randall, who was Iron Fist before Danny Rand. Instead, he learned from Randall that the masters of the Seven Cities had lied about their contact with the rest of the world. Randall asked him to join the next Iron Fist and fight against those masters. He has since worked with the Secret Warriors and helped defend Washington, D.C. during Fear Itself. Later he helped Steve Rogers stop the undead Zheng Zu from restoring himself to full power.

PROCTOR

The man who came to be called Proctor was actually the Black Knight of an alternate Earth. While serving as a member of the Avengers, he met and fell in love with the Sersi of his world. He became her "gann josin," a mate that was forever bound to her by a mental link that allowed them to share their powers, thoughts, and souls. His Sersi eventually became mentally unstable, destroying their world and rejecting Proctor.

Desperate for revenge, Proctor and his companions used a gateway into alternate dimensions and journeyed across the Multiverse. They were on a quest to kill every alternate world version of Sersi, along with every world and Avenger that had ever befriended her. They gathered and rescued all the alternate-Avengers that they deemed worthy of life.

After defeating the Black Knight of the real Earth, Proctor was slain by this world's Sersi.

Proctor possessed the battle prowess of the real Black Knight and the mental and physical powers of an Eternal, because he had become one with the Sersi of his world.

PROCTOR

FACTFILE

REAL NAME
Dane Whitman (of an alternate dimension)

OCCUPATION
Former Super Hero turned destroyer of worlds

BASE
A secret citadel hidden on the edge of reality

HEIGHT 6 ft
WEIGHT 190 lbs
EYES Brown
HAIR Black

FIRST APPEARANCE
Avengers #344 (February 1992)

POWERS

Expert combatant; immune to aging; can psionically manipulate matter, and project cosmic blasts from eyes and hands. Possesses ten rings that produce, among other things, ice blasts, flames, bursts of light, and deadly gases.

PRODIGY

PRODIGY

FACTFILE

REAL NAME
David Alleyne

OCCUPATION
Adventurer

BASE
Sotomayor University; formerly Professor X's School for Gifted Youngsters, Salem Center, New York

HEIGHT 6 ft 3 in
WEIGHT 230 lbs
EYES Brown
HAIR Black

FIRST APPEARANCE
New Mutants #4 (October 2003)

POWERS

Prodigy has the mutant ability to absorb (although not permanently) the skills and knowledge of those near him. He cannot, however, absorb their mutant powers.

Four different men used the name Prodigy. The first was Spider-Man, who employed it as one of four different identities when he was a wanted man. College athlete Richie Gilmore took over this identity. He was the first hero to publicly defy the Superhuman Registration Act. He later joined the Fifty-State Initiative, after which he took his team, the Heavy Hitters, and declared them to be independent. He was jailed for this but has since been released and taken a job with the Avengers Initiative.

The third Prodigy, David Alleyne, was unrelated to the first two. His mutant powers allowed him to absorb the knowledge of anyone nearby, although the knowledge faded when they parted. He lost his powers on M-Day, but he can now remember every bit of knowledge he ever absorbed. He left the X-Men and joined the Young Avengers, where he developed feelings for Hulkling. The fourth Prodigy, Timothy Wilkerson, was mutated with the Leader's gamma-irradiated DNA and joined the Gamma Corps, until he was depowered by Doc Green, an incarnation of the Hulk.

High above the US Capitol, Prodigy (David Alleyne) tangles with fellow X-Men member Wind Dancer.

Professor X see page 278–279

PROTEUS

FIRST APPEARANCE *Uncanny X-Men* #125 (September 1979)
REAL NAME Kevin MacTaggert
OCCUPATION None **BASE** Muir Island, Scotland
HEIGHT/WEIGHT/EYES/HAIR N/A
SPECIAL POWERS/ABILITIES Able to warp reality. Made of psionic energies, he must inhabit a host body, which burns up over time.

Moira MacTaggert imprisoned her son Kevin in the Mutant Research Facility on Muir Island, where an energy field kept his powers from consuming his body. When his cell was breached during an attack by Magneto, Kevin escaped, shifting from host-body to host-body as each wore out. Only the intervention of the X-Men—and Kevin's vulnerability to metal—stopped him. AIM reconstituted him in the body of a young mutant called Piecemeal (not the adult villain of the same name), but the combined creature didn't last. After time with the Exiles, sharing a body with Morph, Proteus returned to Earth for revenge on the X-Men, especially Colossus.

PROXIMA MIDNIGHT

FIRST APPEARANCE *New Avengers* #8 (September 2013)
REAL NAME Proxima Midnight
OCCUPATION Warrior **BASE** Mobile
HEIGHT Unknown **WEIGHT** Unknown
EYES White **HAIR** Blue
SPECIAL POWERS/ABILITIES Superhuman strength, speed, and endurance. Her lance was forged for her by Thanos.

Proxima Midnight is a member of the Black Order and the wife of Corvus Glaive. Alongside the rest of the Order she originally served the Mad Titan Thanos. She was imprisoned by Thanos' son, Thane, but later freed by Namor and joined his incarnation of the Cabal. She survived the destruction of the Multiverse and subsequent Battleworld. After failing a mission for Thanos, she was killed by The Asgardian Goddess of Death, Hela. The Challenger revived her to fight alongside her husband in a new incarnation of the Black Order against the Lethal Legion and the Avengers.

PROWLER

Hobie Brown's gift for inventions is rivaled only by that of Peter Parker (Spider-Man).

While working as a window washer, mechanical genius Hobie Brown invented gadgets to make his job easier, including wrist-mounted, high-pressure sprayers. When his boss dismissed his ideas, Brown quit in frustration. He turned to crime, refashioning his contraptions into climbing gear and miniaturized weapons, and adopting the costumed identity of the Prowler. Seeking recognition rather than profit, Brown intended to return what he stole as the Prowler under his real identity. Almost immediately, he came into conflict with Spider-Man, though the two later put aside their differences and became allies.

A second Prowler appeared when the villainous Cat Burglar stole Brown's costume and worked with Belladonna to commit a string of crimes. Brown resumed his role as the original Prowler, joining the team of reformed criminals called the Outlaws, but suffered a severe spinal injury at the hands of El Toro Negro. A third Prowler, medical student Rick Lawson, briefly adventured while Brown recuperated in the hospital, but Brown has since retaken the role he created. He seemingly died at the hands of the Jackal while helping Spider-Man and was cloned. Though his clone died, the real Brown was found alive in the Jackal's basement.

FACTFILE

REAL NAME
Hobie Brown

OCCUPATION
Adventurer

BASE
New York City

HEIGHT 5 ft 11 in
WEIGHT 170 lbs
EYES Brown
HAIR Dark brown

FIRST APPEARANCE
Amazing Spider-Man #78 (November 1969)

POWERS

The cape of Prowler's costume allows him to glide; wrist cartridges fire compressed air; steel-tipped claws allow him to scale buildings.

PROFESSOR X

Mastermind of the X-Men

PROFESSOR X

FACTFILE

REAL NAME
Charles Francis Xavier

OCCUPATION
Mutant rights activist; teacher

BASE
Mobile

HEIGHT 6 ft
WEIGHT 190 lbs
EYES Blue
HAIR None

FIRST APPEARANCE
The X-Men #1
(September 1963)

POWERS

Vast psionic abilities including mind-reading, mind-erasing, astral projection, the projection of illusions, the ability to take mental control of others, and the ability to fire mental blasts.

ALLIES/FOES

ALLIES The X-Men, the Starjammers

FOES Magneto, Juggernaut, Cassandra Nova, the Sentinels, the Hellfire Club

ISSUE #1

In *X-Men* #1, Professor X's team unites to fight off the menace of Magneto, marking the first appearance of both the heroic X-Men and their arch-foe.

Widely considered the most powerful mutant on Earth, Charles Xavier has dedicated his life to the idea that humans and mutants can coexist peacefully. His father, Brian, died when Charles was a child. Kurt Marko, his father's research partner, married Charles' mother Sharon, but only valued her for her fortune. Charles became a rival of his stepbrother Cain (who one day gained the powers of the Juggernaut), and saw both his mother and stepfather die in separate incidents.

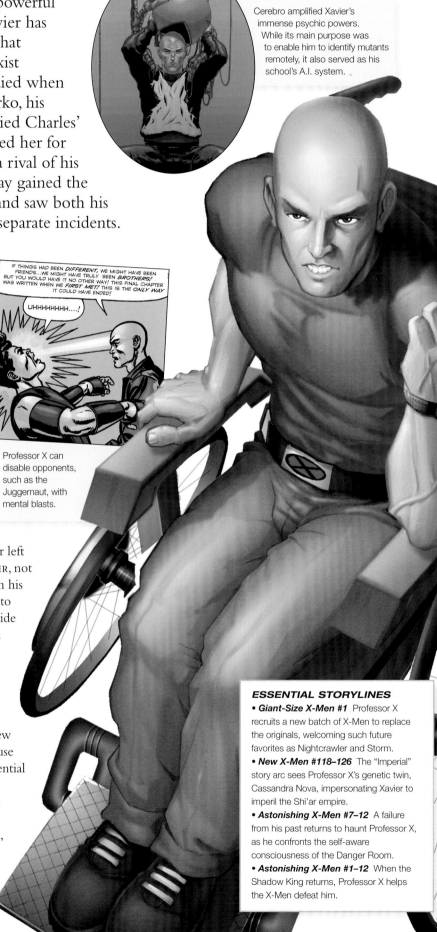

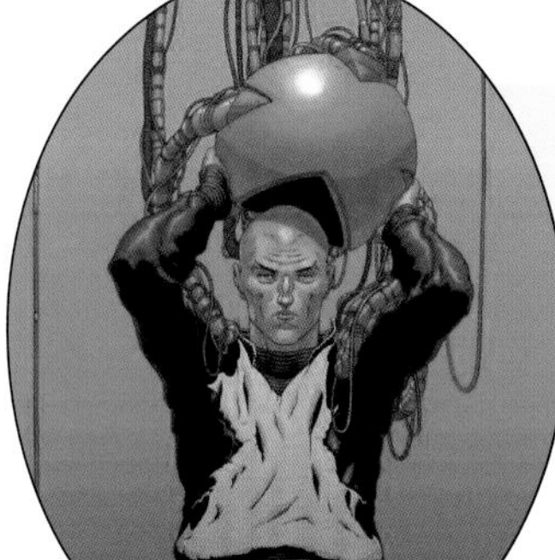

Cerebro amplified Xavier's immense psychic powers. While its main purpose was to enable him to identify mutants remotely, it also served as his school's A.I. system.

FIRST LOVE

Xavier attended graduate school at Oxford University, England, where he fell in love with Moira MacTaggert; however their relationship ended when Charles joined the US Army. Following his tour of duty, Xavier traveled the world. At a clinic for Holocaust survivors in Israel, he befriended the man who would become Magneto. Magneto and Xavier teamed up to fight Baron von Strucker, but Magneto's ruthless methods made it clear that the two had incompatible philosophies concerning the use of violence. Xavier left Israel, leaving behind Gabrielle Haller, not realizing that Haller was pregnant with his child (the boy, David, would grow up to become the mutant Legion). A rockslide caused by the villainous alien Lucifer left Xavier a paraplegic.

IF THINGS HAD BEEN *DIFFERENT*, WE MIGHT HAVE BEEN FRIENDS...WE MIGHT HAVE TRULY BEEN *BROTHERS!* BUT YOU WOULD HAVE IT NO OTHER WAY! THIS FINAL CHAPTER WAS WRITTEN WHEN WE *FIRST MET!* THIS IS THE *ONLY WAY* IT COULD HAVE ENDED!

UHHHHHHHH....!

Professor X can disable opponents, such as the Juggernaut, with mental blasts.

THE X-MEN

As Professor X, Charles Xavier founded Xavier's School for Gifted Youngsters in Westchester County, New York, to train mutant children in the use of their powers. Xavier identified potential students with the machine Cerebro, which amplified his telepathic powers and allowed him to pinpoint mutants from afar. His initial Super Hero team, the X-Men, consisted of Cyclops, Angel, Marvel Girl (*see* Jean Grey), Iceman, and Beast, who sought to improve the image of mutants by selfless deeds.

ESSENTIAL STORYLINES

- ***Giant-Size X-Men #1*** Professor X recruits a new batch of X-Men to replace the originals, welcoming such future favorites as Nightcrawler and Storm.
- ***New X-Men #118–126*** The "Imperial" story arc sees Professor X's genetic twin, Cassandra Nova, impersonating Xavier to imperil the Shi'ar empire.
- ***Astonishing X-Men #7–12*** A failure from his past returns to haunt Professor X, as he confronts the self-aware consciousness of the Danger Room.
- ***Astonishing X-Men #1–12*** When the Shadow King returns, Professor X helps the X-Men defeat him.

BATTLING MAGNETO

The philosophies held by Professor X and Magneto are diametrically opposed, but share some similarities. Both men profess the goal of protecting mutantkind, but Magneto wants to subjugate or eliminate human opposition, while Professor X dreams of a world where humans and mutants can coexist. After Professor X founded the X-Men, Magneto created the Brotherhood of Evil Mutants. Over the years, the two men have been friends and foes.

The X-Men repeatedly faced off against Magneto, who had dedicated himself to subjugating humanity through his powers as the master of magnetism.

Professor X founded a second team of X-Men, whose members included Nightcrawler, Colossus, Storm, Banshee, and Wolverine. The new X-Men helped Xavier battle Shi'ar emperor D'ken and the Imperial Guard. Xavier then fell in love with the new Shi'ar empress, Lilandra. He entered into the Shi'ar equivalent of marriage with Lilandra, and adventured with the Starjammers.

Back on Earth, Xavier organized a third grouping of students, the New Mutants, but

Although his love for Shi'ar empress Lilandra took him across the galaxy, Professor X eventually returned to the X-Men.

fell under the influence of the alien Brood. To prevent his transformation into a Brood Queen, Xavier shifted his consciousness into a clone body with fully-functional legs. After suffering injuries as a result of a hate crime, Xavier reunited with Lilandra to recuperate among the Shi'ar, leaving Magneto to run the academy in his absence. Xavier again lost the use of his legs battling the Shadow King, and brought together a fourth team of young mutants, Generation X.

The relationship between Magneto and Xavier took a turn for the worse, culminating in a terrible moment when Magneto ripped the Adamantium from Wolverine's skeleton. Enraged by Magneto's brutality, Xavier mind-wiped his former friend, unwittingly creating a powerful psionic being known as Onslaught. All of Earth's heroes united to destroy Onslaught, leading to the apparent deaths of the Avengers and the Fantastic Four. In the aftermath, Xavier briefly lost his telepathic powers and became a prisoner of the US government. He later uncovered a Skrull plot to infiltrate the X-Men, and trained a promising group of Skrull mutants calling themselves Cadre K.

TRANSITIONS

Xavier's genetic twin, the sinister Cassandra Nova, had died in Sharon Xavier's womb yet somehow maintained her life-essence. Nova orchestrated the devastation of the mutant nation Genosha and took mental control of Xavier, outing him as a mutant to the world and inciting the Shi'ar Imperial Guard to attack the X-Mansion. Xavier's students helped free him from Nova's influence.

Xavier then founded the X-Corporation, stepping down as head of the academy. He tried to help Magneto's daughter, the Scarlet Witch, recover from a breakdown, but was unable to prevent her from removing the power from most mutants—including himself—on M-Day. The huge backlash of power reawakened Vulcan, and Xavier and a team of X-Men tracked him to the Shi'ar Empire. They failed to stop him, but when Vulcan threw Xavier into the M'Kraan Crystal, Xavier's powers were restored.

As one of the Illuminati, Xavier faced the Hulk's wrath during World War Hulk, until the Hulk realized that M-Day had cost Xavier enough. During the hunt for the first mutant baby born since M-Day, Bishop accidentally shot Xavier in the head, putting him into a coma. He recovered but had lost much of his memory.

During the Dark Reign, HAMMER captured Xavier, and Mystique impersonated him in an attempt to gain control over the X-Men. After being released, Xavier turned his attention to helping nurse his son David back to health.

When the Phoenix Force returned to Earth and possessed the Phoenix Five, Xavier stood against them and tried to convince Cyclops to give up the power. Cyclops lost control and killed his old mentor, then turned into the Dark Phoenix. Xavier's corpse was stolen by the Red Skull and his brain connected to the Skull's to make the villain even more powerful. When Red Skull was finally defeated, Rogue and the Human Torch made sure Xavier's brain was incinerated.

Professor X's life tragically ended at the hands of Cyclops, his greatest student.

A MAN CALLED X

Xavier's astral form had survived and had been imprisoned on the astral plane by the Shadow King. When Psylocke's X-Men faced the Shadow King on the astral plane they discovered Xavier, and Fantomex allowed Xavier to return to Earth using his body. With the Shadow King defeated, Xavier wiped everyone's minds of recent events—apart from Psylocke's, as he wanted her to remember what had happened in case the Shadow King returned. Xavier was alive again, but literally a new man—one now simply called X.

Only recently reborn in Fantomex's body, Xavier wasn't yet comfortable using his own name, hence his new moniker.

PRYDE, KATHERINE

Courageous X-Men leader

PRYDE, KATHERINE

FACTFILE

REAL NAME
Katherine "Kitty" Pryde

OCCUPATION
Adventurer; student; former SHIELD employee

BASE
The Xavier Institute, Salem Center, New York State

HEIGHT 5 ft 6 in
WEIGHT 110 lbs
EYES Brown
HAIR Brown

FIRST APPEARANCE
X-Men #129 (January 1980)

POWERS
Mutant ability to pass ("phase") through solid matter by altering the vibratory rate of the atoms of her body, her clothing, and a limited amount of other matter. Highly adept with computers.

As a schoolgirl in Deerfield, Illinois, Kitty Pryde began suffering intense headaches—a sign that her mutant power to phase through solid matter and disrupt electronics was about to emerge. Emma Frost, the White Queen of the Hellfire Club visited Kitty's parents to recruit her as a student. Professor X and three of his X-Men soon followed, hoping to convince Kitty's parents to let her attend his School for Gifted Youngsters instead.

CHOOSING SIDES

After the White Queen kidnapped the visiting X-Men, Kitty helped Cyclops and Phoenix (Jean Grey) rescue them. She entered Xavier's school and joined the X-Men. Kitty briefly adopted the code names Sprite and Ariel. During an adventure in Japan, where Wolverine taught her martial arts, she chose the name Shadowcat, which she sometimes still uses today.

Kitty and fellow student Colossus fell in love, although the relationship turned stormy and eventually ended. She later became a founding member of the original Excalibur, a British-based team of adventurers. She also worked for the law enforcement agency SHIELD for a short time.

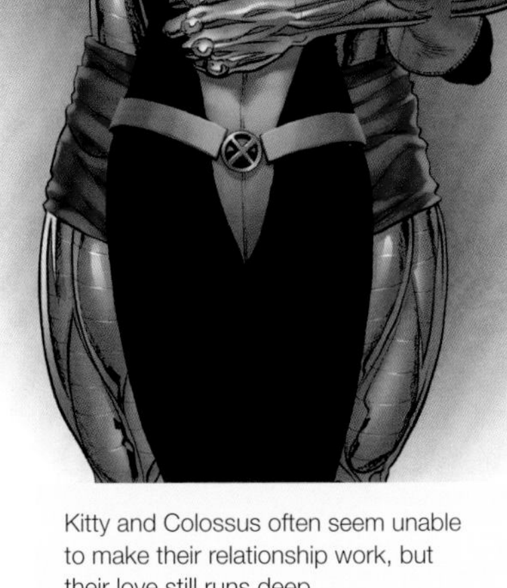

Kitty and Colossus often seem unable to make their relationship work, but their love still runs deep.

While on an adventure in space, Kitty met the small, dragonlike alien Lockheed, who took an instant liking to her. They became close friends for many years, until she discovered that he could speak—something he had never done before—and was spying on the X-Men for SWORD.

SAVIOR AND TEACHER

After Excalibur disbanded, Kitty rejoined the X-Men. She was lost while on a mission to Breakworld—she saved the Earth by phasing a gigantic bullet all the way through the planet, but the X-Men were unable to remove her from it after it sailed off into space. Much later, Magneto brought her back by returning the bullet and breaking it open. Having been forced to remain in her phase state for so long, Kitty found she could not turn substantial again. The Breakworlder Haleena had to kill her and revive her to make her solid once more.

When the schism within the X-Men split them into two groups, Kitty helped Wolverine open the Jean Grey School for Higher Learning. She stayed out of the subsequent conflict between the Avengers and the X-Men, concentrating on the school instead. When the Beast brought the original X-Men from the past to visit the present, however, she took charge of taking care of them. She went on to take over Charles Xavier's role as leader of all the X-Men. Though she asked Colossus to marry her, she couldn't go through with the wedding, feeling their lives as X-Men made things too complicated.

PRYOR, MADELYNE

Madelyne Pryor was a clone of Jean Grey and created to meet Scott Summers.

Mr. Sinister was obsessed with obtaining the spawn of a union between Jean Grey and Scott Summers (*see* Cyclops), but it was only after Jean's death that he achieved his goal. Using stored genetic material, he successfully cloned Jean. He named his creation Madelyne Pryor, provided her with false memories, and manipulated Scott into marrying her. Their relationship resulted in a son—Nathan Summers (*see* Cable)—but when the real Jean Grey was resurrected, Scott left Madelyne. Insanely jealous, Madelyne began to lose her grip on reality, a process that accelerated when Sinister kidnapped Nathan. As her mutant powers began to emerge, so did her thirst for vengeance, and she transformed herself into the Goblin Queen.

Madelyne was killed in a showdown with the X-Men. She later returned as a psychic ghost and then as the Red Queen, recruiting a Sisterhood of Mutants to help her acquire a new body. When reality was altered, Madelyne returned to Earth with her team of Hex-Men allies, only to be again defeated by the X-Men.

As the Goblin Queen, Madelyne Pryor was a terrifying enemy for the X-Men.

FACTFILE

REAL NAME
Madelyne Jennifer Pryor-Summers

OCCUPATION
Vengeance-seeker

BASE
Mobile

HEIGHT 5 ft 6 in
WEIGHT 110 lbs
EYES Green
HAIR Red

FIRST APPEARANCE
Uncanny X-Men #168 (April 1983)

PRYOR, MADELYNE

POWERS

Most of Madelyne's abilities stem from her status as a clone of Jean Grey. She possesses vast psionic powers including telepathy and telekinesis. Madelyne is able to generate energy and manipulate it so that she can fly, project powerful force blasts, and create force-fields that act as shields.

PSIONEX

FIRST APPEARANCE *New Warriors* #4 (October 1990)
BASE Mobile
MEMBERS AND POWERS **Asylum** Converts body to a mist that causes hallucinations, uses Darkforce; **Coronary** Controls the bodies of other, has crystal form; **Darkling** Controls Darkforce; **Impulse** Superhuman reflexes and speed; **Mathemanic** Can project math into others' heads; **Pretty Persuasions** Amplifies erotic urges and wields energy whip.

The Genentech corporation created a team of superpowered youths, led by Asylum, who battled the New Warriors. Mathemanic and Impulse were injured in an escape attempt and retired, but the rest of the team broke free. They later united under Darkling, who posed as Asylum. Some time later, Psionex became the Fifty-State Initiative team for Maryland.

PSYCHO-MAN

FIRST APPEARANCE *Fantastic Four Special* #5 (November 1967)
REAL NAME Unrevealed
OCCUPATION Scientist; conqueror **BASE** Traan; his World-Ship
HEIGHT Indeterminate **WEIGHT** Indeterminate
EYES Unrevealed **HAIR** Unrevealed
SPECIAL POWERS/ABILITIES Superhuman intelligence; his main weapon projects a "psycho-ray" that stimulates fear, doubt, and hate.

The Psycho-Man was chief scientist of Traan, a planet in a different dimension known as the Microverse. He traveled to Earth to conquer the planet by means of his "psycho-ray," but was thwarted by the Fantastic Four's Human Torch and Thing, the Black Panther, and the Inhumans' Royal Family. The Psycho-Man's true size and appearance are mysteries: on Earth he remained tiny while encased in a human-sized suit of body armor. He continues to clash with the Fantastic Four, both on Earth and within the Microverse.

PSYKLOP

FIRST APPEARANCE *Avengers* #88 (May 1971)
REAL NAME Psyklop
OCCUPATION Servant of the Dark Gods **BASE** Mobile
HEIGHT 8 ft **WEIGHT** 450 lbs **EYES** Red **HAIR** None
SPECIAL POWERS/ABILITIES Possessed of superhuman strength and durability, Psyklop can also fire beams of energy from his eye that can hypnotize an opponent, or make them experience illusions.

The devoted servant of the Dark Gods who ruled the Earth at the dawn of time, Psyklop hibernated for millennia until called upon to serve his masters once more. He tried to offer up the Hulk as a sacrifice to his sinister lords, but was prevented from doing so by the Avengers. The Hulk ended up miniaturized, and fell into the Microverse, alighting on the planet K'ai. Pursuing the Hulk, Psyklop engaged him in battle and was defeated. For his failure, the Dark Gods exiled Psyklop to K'ai, where he seemingly met his end, consumed by the spirits of all the people he had slain.

PSYLOCKE

FACTFILE

REAL NAME
Elisabeth "Betsy" Braddock

OCCUPATION
Adventurer

BASE
The Xavier Institute, Salem Center, New York State

HEIGHT 5 ft 11 in
WEIGHT 155 lbs
EYES (current body) blue
HAIR (current body) black, dyed purple

FIRST APPEARANCE
Captain Britain #8 (December 1976)

POWERS
Possesses telekinetic powers. Can focus her psionic powers into a "psychic knife" to stun or kill an adversary. Former telepath. Highly skilled in martial arts.

James Braddock Sr. was an inhabitant of Otherworld who came to Britain and fathered three children, James Jr., Brian, and Elizabeth. Brian became the hero CAPTAIN BRITAIN, a role Betsy later briefly took over at the behest of the British government agency RCX. Blinded and nearly killed by the villain Slaymaster, Betsy was abducted by MOJO, who gave her new artificial eyes. She was rescued by the NEW MUTANTS and joined the X-MEN as Psylocke. SPIRAL switched the minds of Psylocke and the Japanese assassin Kwannon into each other's bodies. Discovering that her new body was dying, Kwannon had the crimelord Matsu'o Tsurayaba kill her. Elizabeth survived in Kwannon's original body. Psylocke sacrificed her telepathy to defeat the X-Men's enemy, the SHADOW KING. Subsequently, she gained telekinetic abilities. Betsy has also fought alongside the EXILES and X-FORCE. She helped to destroy the Shadow King with the help of the X-Men and a returned PROFESSOR X, who was now in the body of FANTOMEX. Following a battle in Madripoor in which her body was killed, Psylocke recreated her original body, molecule by molecule.

Psylocke alongside her teammates in the Exiles, including alternate versions of Morph, Rogue, and Sabretooth.

PUCK

FACTFILE

REAL NAME
Eugene Milton Judd

OCCUPATION
Alpha Flight member

BASE
Tamarind Island

HEIGHT 3 ft 6 in
WEIGHT 225 lbs
EYES Brown
HAIR Black

FIRST APPEARANCE
Alpha Flight #1 (August 1983)

POWERS
Superb athlete and gymnast; formidable hand-to-hand combatant with unique fighting style; trained bullfighter; limited knowledge of sorcery.

Eugene Judd released the evil sorcerer Black Raazer and managed to trap him in his own body, which extended his life but reduced him to the height of a dwarf. Judd was later invited to join Beta Flight as Puck, and he worked his way up to the top-level Canadian team: ALPHA FLIGHT. He eventually rid himself of Black Raazer, which cost him his powers and caused him to gain both years and height. The DREAMQUEEN restored him to his former self so she could torture him longer, although he later escaped.

Later, Puck's daughter Zuzha Yu joined a new Alpha Flight, calling herself Puck, too. She inherited her father's powers and made good use of them. Both father and daughter died trying to stop the Collective (*see* WEAPON OMEGA), a man imbued with all of the mutant energies lost on M-Day.

While Zuzha is still gone, the elder Puck helped WOLVERINE as he battled his way through Hell. This gave him a chance to escape so he could help his friends in Alpha Flight as they battled the Unity Party, which had taken over the Canadian government. He later joined X-FORCE and the Alpha Flight space program.

Zuzha Yu only joined Alpha Flight after losing an arm-wrestling bout to Sasquatch.

PUMA

FIRST APPEARANCE *The Amazing Spider-Man* #256 (Sept. 1984)
REAL NAME Thomas Fireheart
OCCUPATION CEO of Fireheart Enterprises; mercenary
BASE Mobile **HEIGHT** 6 ft 2in **WEIGHT** 240 lbs
EYES Green **HAIR** (as Puma) Red; (as Fireheart) black
SPECIAL POWERS/ABILITIES As Puma, Fireheart has superhuman strength, agility, heightened senses, and claws.

Puma was the heir to a long tradition of mystical champions created by a Native American tribe. Raised to oppose the BEYONDER, Thomas Fireheart donned the mantle of the Puma and kept his fighting skills sharp by becoming a mercenary, often fighting (or aiding) SPIDER-MAN. Fireheart also served as the head of Fireheart Enterprises, which supplied him with high-tech weaponry and vehicles, but he constantly struggled to control his animalistic Puma persona. After the CIVIL WAR, he was accused of taking bribes and joined MODOK to make money to pay for his defense.

PUNISHER, SEE PAGES 284–285

PUPPET MASTER

FACTFILE
REAL NAME
Phillip Masters
OCCUPATION
Professional criminal
BASE
Sunshine City, Florida

HEIGHT 5 ft 6 in
WEIGHT 150 lbs
EYES Blue
HAIR None

FIRST APPEARANCE
Fantastic Four #8
(November 1962)

POWERS
A brilliant biologist and technician; able to control the actions and thoughts of others by making models of them out of special radioactive clay. He then turns the models into marionettes, attaching strings to their limbs.

Phillip Masters was the research partner of Jacob Reiss. Resentful of Reiss' success, Masters killed his partner during a botched robbery of their lab, triggering an explosion that blinded Reiss' daughter, Alicia. Masters later married Reiss' widow and became Alicia's stepfather. Learning he could control others with his clay sculptures, Masters became the Puppet Master, one of the earliest enemies of the FANTASTIC FOUR. He also teamed up with the villains EGGHEAD, MAD THINKER, and DOCTOR DOOM. To his horror, his daughter Alicia fell in love with the THING, though in time the Puppet Master was reconciled to their relationship. The US government recruited the Puppet Master to run their Sunshine City project, where mind-controlled criminals safely served out their prison sentences. He returned to crime during the CIVIL WAR, using the YANCY STREET GANG. The Quiet Man later framed the THING for the Puppet Master's death (as part of a plan to destroy the FF) only for Masters to later be found alive.

The Fantastic Four look on helplessly as the Puppet Master tinkers with a robot clutching a model of an atomic bomb. What can the villain be up to?

PYRO

FIRST APPEARANCE *Uncanny X-Men* #141 (January 1981)
REAL NAME St. John Allerdyce
OCCUPATION Professional criminal **BASE** Mobile
HEIGHT 5 ft 10 in **WEIGHT** 150 lbs **EYES** Blue **HAIR** Blond
SPECIAL POWERS/ABILITIES Could control and manipulate flames within his immediate vicinity, though he could not produce flames himself. His insulated costume had built-in flamethrowers.

Born in Sydney, Australia, St. John Allerdyce won fame as a novelist until MYSTIQUE convinced him to join her BROTHERHOOD OF EVIL MUTANTS. As the flame-shaping Pyro, Allerdyce battled the X-MEN and remained with his teammates when they transitioned into the US government-sanctioned FREEDOM FORCE. Teenage mutant Simon Lasker also took on the name Pyro when he joined a new incarnation of the Brotherhood of Mutants before changing his ways and joining the X-Men.

PURPLE MAN

FACTFILE
REAL NAME
Zebediah Killgrave
OCCUPATION
Former spy, professional criminal, conqueror
BASE
Mobile

HEIGHT 5 ft 11 in
WEIGHT 165 lbs
EYES Purple
HAIR Purple

FIRST APPEARANCE
Daredevil #4 (October 1964)

POWERS
Killgrave's body secretes psychoactive chemicals that deaden the will of people in his vicinity, rendering them susceptible to his commands. Individuals with unusually strong willpower can resist him.

Born in Yugoslavia, Zebediah Killgrave was a spy who was accidentally covered with an experimental nerve agent. This permanently dyed his hair and skin purple and gave him the power to compel others to obey his commands. As the Purple Man, he was repeatedly defeated by DAREDEVIL, one of the few people able to resist his power. For a while, he made Jessica JONES his slave. She was so traumatized, she gave up being a Super Hero.

He later tried to retire from crime, but the KINGPIN and DOCTOR DOOM exploited him. He attempted to compel the mutant Nate Grey, alias X-MAN, to help him conquer the world, but Grey defeated him. He later controlled all of New York at the behest of BARON ZEMO, then joined the HOOD's crime syndicate and ran a Las Vegas casino. The Purple Man had a number of children who, when together, were even more powerful than their father. He tried to use them to take over the world only to be stopped by Daredevil. After menacing Jessica Jones again, the Purple Man was shot and killed by KRAVEN, and his corpse thrown into the sun by CAPTAIN MARVEL.

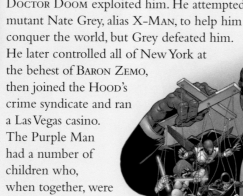

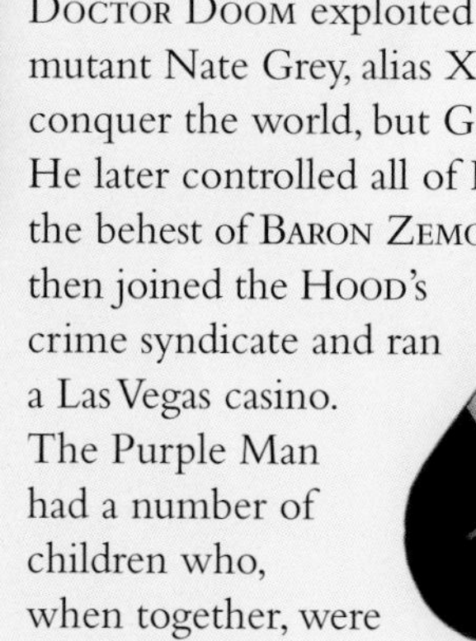

PURPLE WOMAN

FIRST APPEARANCE *Alpha Flight* #41 (December 1986)
REAL NAME Kara Killgrave **OCCUPATION** Adventurer
BASE Mobile **HEIGHT** 5 ft 3 in **WEIGHT** 120 lbs
EYES Brown **HAIR** Black
SPECIAL POWERS/ABILITIES Has the mutant power to secrete psychoactive will-sapping pheromones from her pores that allow her to link with the minds of others and make them do her bidding.

Unaware she was the daughter of the Purple Man, Kara Killgrave was shocked when her skin turned purple and her powers manifested themselves. She took the name Purple Girl and joined Beta Flight, ALPHA FLIGHT's training group. When the group split up, Kara went home to her mother. She followed the teams through a number of breakups and reunions, eventually taking the name Persuasion. She retained her powers after M-Day and was seen at the X-MEN's headquarters in San Francisco.

PUNISHER

War hero turned vengeful vigilante

PUNISHER

FACTFILE

REAL NAME
Frank Castle (born Castiglione)

OCCUPATION
Vigilante

BASE
Mobile

HEIGHT 6 ft 1 in
WEIGHT 200 lbs
EYES Blue
HAIR Black

FIRST APPEARANCE
The Amazing Spider-Man #129 (February 1974)

POWERS

The Punisher is a seasoned combat veteran of exceptional skill. He has undergone SEAL (Sea, Air, Land), UDT (Underwater Demolition Team), and LRRP (Long-Range Reconnaissance Patrol) training. He is an expert using all types of small arms and large caliber guns, and he has extensive training using explosives and tactical weapons. He is a superior martial artist and hand-to-hand combatant.

ALLIES/FOES

ALLIES Daredevil, Legion of Monsters, Microchip, Rachel Cole-Alves, the Red Hulk's Thunderbolts, Spider-Man

FOES Bullseye, Daken, The Exchange, the Hand, the Hood, the Kingpin, the Mafia, the Yakuza

ISSUE #1

The Jackal hires a vigilante named the Punisher to hunt down and kill Spider-Man. The Punisher eventually realizes that the wall-crawler is no criminal and vows vengeance on the Jackal.

Marine Captain Frank Castle was a decorated hero during the Vietnam War. Winner of the Bronze and Silver Star, and recipient of four Purple Hearts, Castle was an exceptionally skilled combat veteran. Then came the event that changed his life. While on leave in New York, Castle took his family for a picnic in Central Park. There they witnessed a mob murder. The mobsters then killed Castle's wife and two young children.

Frank Castle, family man, in happier days.

ONE-MAN ARMY

With his whole world destroyed, Castle deserted from the Marines and dropped out of sight for a few months. When he resurfaced, it was as a vigilante named the Punisher, who conducted a one-man, anti-crime campaign throughout New York City. Equipped with an arsenal of weapons, the Punisher took his vengeance on the mob gang who had killed his family, but he didn't stop there. He vowed to kill criminals of every kind.

The Punisher has devoted his life to destroying organized crime, drug dealers, street gangs, muggers, killers, or any other criminal element. His actions have brought him into conflict with several costumed heroes, such as Spider-Man (with whom he has also cooperated), and Daredevil, who strictly opposes Punisher's lethal methods.

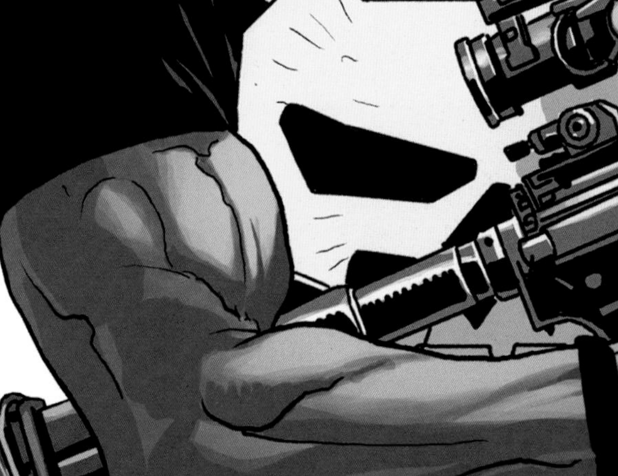

The big white skull on Punisher's costume draws criminal fire to his heavily armored body rather than to his unprotected head.

WEAPONS AND ENEMIES

To carry out his war on crime, the Punisher uses firearms of all types, knives, grenade launchers, armor-piercing bullets, and explosives. His weapons are customized with tactical scopes, night-vision scopes, silencers, and tripods.

During the Civil War, the Punisher targeted Super Villains. In the aftermath of the Secret Invasion, he dedicated himself to killing one of the most powerful people in the world: Norman Osborn (Green Goblin). Under Osborn's orders, Daken cut the Punisher into pieces.

When Spider-Man was on the run after switching sides during the Civil War, the Punisher stepped in to save him.

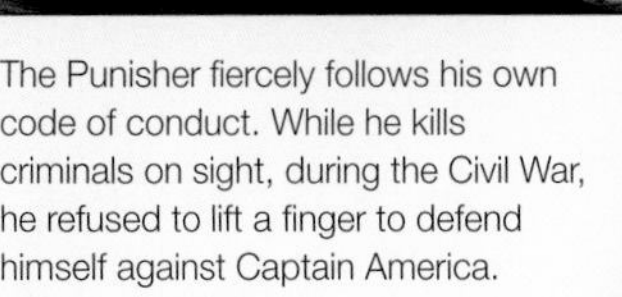

The Punisher fiercely follows his own code of conduct. While he kills criminals on sight, during the Civil War, he refused to lift a finger to defend himself against Captain America.

Not even death could stop the Punisher.

DEATH AND BACK

The Legion of Monsters recovered the Punisher's body, stitched the pieces together, and brought him back to life as Franken-Castle. They asked him to help defend them against a group of monster-hunting samurai led by Robert Hellsgaard, an old friend of Ulysses Bloodstone, brought back from limbo. Franken-Castle refused at first but eventually relented. He later used the Bloodstone gem itself to restore himself to life.

Soon after, the Punisher partnered with Marine Sergeant Rachel Cole-Alves, whose husband had been killed at their wedding reception, along with dozens of others. They worked together to bring down the Exchange, the organized crime ring that had ordered the killings. Rachel wound up on death row after exacting her vengeance, but the Punisher broke her out of jail just in time, letting himself be captured so she could escape.

WAR MACHINE

As a former marine, Castle had always had great respect for Captain America, so when Steve Rogers took control of the United States, he convinced Castle to work for him eliminating Hydra's enemies. When this Rogers was revealed to be an evil doppelganger, Castle realized he had made a huge mistake, perhaps the worst of his life. Shortly after Hydra's fall, Nick Fury Jr. approached Castle and offered him a new purpose. Fury wanted Frank to steal the War Machine armor and use it to take out General Petrov, a dictator who had seized power in Chernaya. Castle waged a one-man war against Petrov's forces, eventually killing the dictator. Castle then returned home, using the War Machine armor to continue his war on crime. He joined forces with the Black Widow and Winter Soldier to try to kill the now-incarcerated evil Steve Rogers, only to be stopped by Iron Man and Jim Rhodes, the latter convincing Castle to surrender. On the way to jail, Castle was broken out of custody by the Black Widow and Winter Soldier. His time as War Machine was at an end, but his war against Hydra was only just beginning.

The Punisher soon started to use the War Machine armor to maximum effect, using it to tear through numerous criminals and rogue SHIELD agents.

THE THUNDERBOLTS

While Castle usually works alone, he joined Red Hulk's new Thunderbolts team when approached by General Ross. The team included some of the world's deadliest assassins—Elektra, Deadpool, Agent Venom and the Red Hulk. When Ross tried to bring the Leader back to life, the Punisher shot the Leader in the head. While the Leader was reborn thanks to gamma radiation, the team remained fractured, only staying together long enough to complete a handful of missions. When Ross allowed each member to select a mission, Castle chose a crime family in New Jersey to take out. The Punisher eventually quit the team and returned to the role of solo vigilante. When it became clear the world was going to end due to incursions from other Earths, the Punisher took out some of New York's greatest villains before dying while fighting the Black Dawn terrorist group. He was restored to life after reality was remade following the Secret Wars.

While in the Thunderbolts, Frank and Elektra started a relationship. Both had traumatic pasts and were deadly killers.

ESSENTIAL STORYLINES

- ***Marvel Preview #2***

Marine captain Frank Castle takes his wife and two children for a picnic in New York's Central Park. There, they witness a mob killing, after which the mobsters kill Castle's wife and children. Traumatized, Castle take vengeance against the killers and continues his one-man vigilante campaign against all criminals as the Punisher.

- ***The Punisher Vol. 1 Welcome Back, Frank (tpb)***

After a long absence, the Punisher returns to the streets of Manhattan to take on Ma Gnucchi and her crime family.

- ***The Punisher Max Vol. 1 In the Beginning (tpb)***

The Punisher returns to his roots in a brutal story.

PYM, HANK

Scientific genius behind Ant-Man, Giant-Man, and Goliath

PYM, HANK

FACTFILE

REAL NAME
Dr. Henry "Hank" Pym

OCCUPATION
Adventurer; biochemist; roboticist; manager of Avengers Compound

BASE
Cresskill, New York; Avengers Compound, LA, California

HEIGHT 6 ft
WEIGHT 185 lbs
EYES Blue
HAIR Blond

FIRST APPEARANCE
Tales To Astonish #27 (January 1962)

POWERS

By ingesting Pym Particles, either as a serum, gas, or capsule, Henry Pym can shrink to the size of an ant, or grow up to 100 ft tall. He can also change the size of objects. Using his cybernetic helmet, Pym can communicate with ants and control them.

ALLIES/FOES

ALLIES Ants, the Avengers, Captain America, Iron Man, Thor, Tigra, The Wasp

FOES Egghead, Kang the Conqueror, Morgan Le Fay, Ultron

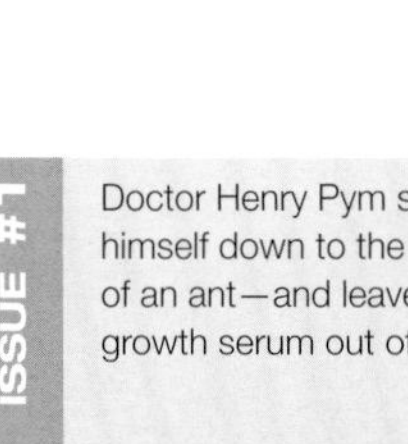

ISSUE #1

Doctor Henry Pym shrinks himself down to the size of an ant—and leaves his growth serum out of reach.

As Ant-Man, Henry Pym could shrink himself so small that he could ride atop an ant.

Dr. Henry Pym, a brilliant scientist, discovered a rare group of subatomic particles that became known as "Pym Particles." When ingested through a serum (and later through a gas and a capsule) the particles could either shrink a person down to the size of an ant, or increase a person's size to 10, 25, even 100 feet in height.

ANT AND WASP

Undertaking a study of ants, Pym also developed a cybernetic helmet that allowed him to communicate with and control ants. Developing a costume to go along with his size-changing ability and helmet, Pym reduced himself to the size of an ant and fought evil as Ant-Man. Pym and his future wife Janet Van Dyne were founding members of the AVENGERS as Ant-Man and the WASP.

Later, Pym decided to use his size-changing power to grow rather than shrink, and he began fighting crime as the costumed hero Giant-Man. Eventually, Pym realized that changing his size was putting too great a strain on his body and he stopped.

Janet did her best to cope with Hank's violent mood swings, but their marriage ended in divorce.

A TROUBLED MIND

When Janet was kidnapped by ATTUMA and the COLLECTOR, Pym helped the Avengers rescue her. He then became GOLIATH.

While experimenting in his lab, an accident changed Pym's personality. He claimed that he had murdered Pym and became Yellowjacket. He married Janet, but they later divorced.

During the SECRET INVASION, it was revealed that this Pym was a SKRULL imposter. The real Pym returned to see the Wasp die due to modifications his Skrull impersonator had made to her powers. Pym renamed himself the Wasp in honor of Janet and formed a new Avengers team.

CHANGING LOOKS
Hank has taken on many names and looks over the years, perhaps inspired by his wife Janet's stylish ways. He became the Wasp in tribute to her after her apparent death.
YELLOWJACKET
WASP
ULTRON/PYM
ANT-MAN
GOLIATH

REDEDICATION

During the Dark Reign, Pym formed his own team of renegade Avengers to work against Norman Osborn (see Green Goblin). Following Osborn's downfall, Pym decided that he could do most good by doing something similar to what his Skrull impersonator had done: teaching the next generation of heroes how to handle their powers. To that end, he founded the Avengers Academy.

Meanwhile, Pym studied the son of Tigra, who'd had a relationship with Pym's Skrull impersonator. Since the Skrull had duplicated Pym's genetic code, the boy turned out to be genetically Pym's, and Tigra asked Pym to take care of him should anything ever happen to her.

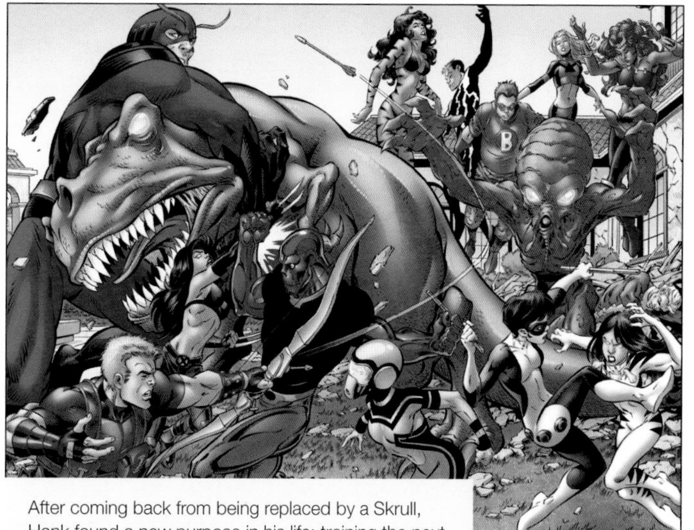

After coming back from being replaced by a Skrull, Hank found a new purpose in his life: training the next generation of heroes at the Avengers Academy.

The younger Hank Pym didn't let Wolverine—whom he'd not met before—take him down without a fight.

BAD SONS

Early in his career with the Avengers, Pym had invented a robot called Ultron, which grew to be one of the greatest villains of all time, dedicated to the eradication of organic life. Ultron had left the planet long ago, but he now returned and laid the world to waste. A few heroes survived, and they traveled to the Savage Land to find a time machine to stop Ultron (*see* Age of Ultron).

While most of the heroes went into the future, where Ultron had hidden himself, Wolverine and Invisible Woman traveled back in time. They found Pym working in his lab just before he created Ultron, and Wolverine killed him. However, this act eradicated all the good Pym had done as well as the bad, as Wolverine and Invisible Woman discovered when they returned to the present. They went back to stop themselves, and convinced Pym to send a secret message to his future self and then erase his memories of the entire event. Pym eventually created a virus to defeat Ultron, but the virus evolved into Dimitrios, a sentient A.I. bent on revenge against humanity. Pym joined SHIELD to found a new Avengers A.I. team to combat the virus.

During a later attack by Ultron, Pym merged with his creation and was seemingly killed after Ultron fled into space. Hank later returned to Earth wearing Ultron as armor, and told his fellow Avengers that he was in control and that Ultron was no more. In fact, the reverse was true. This new Ultron/Pym hybrid later gained control of the Soul Gem, with Pym's soul trapped inside it. Pym tried to escape and believed he had done so—only to discover it was an illusion created by one of the creatures living in the Soul Gem, as it seemed to consume him.

Avengers A.I.
1 Doombot **2** Protector
3 Vision **4** Victor Mancha
5 Hank Pym **6** Monica Chang

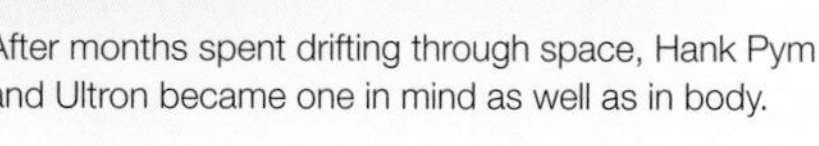

After months spent drifting through space, Hank Pym and Ultron became one in mind as well as in body.

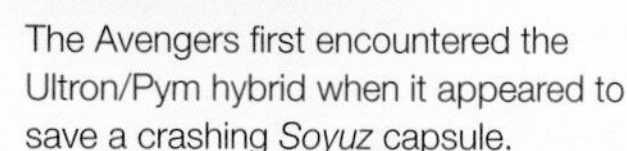

The Avengers first encountered the Ultron/Pym hybrid when it appeared to save a crashing *Soyuz* capsule.

It transpired that before its return to Earth, Ultron had infected countless worlds with its techno-organic virus, killing millions.

ESSENTIAL STORYLINES

- ***Tales to Astonish #49*** Hank Pym first uses his size-changing Pym Particles to grow in size, transforming himself from Ant-Man into Giant-Man.
- ***Avengers #54*** Hank Pym creates Ultron, an incredibly powerful robot, which he implants with his own brain patterns. However Ultron rebels against his inventor.
- ***Avengers Forever (tpb)*** Pym (as Giant-Man) and the Avengers battle Kang with humanity's future at stake.

QUASAR

FACTFILE

REAL NAME
Wendell Vaughn

OCCUPATION
Protector of the Universe

BASE
Mobile

HEIGHT 5 ft 10 in
WEIGHT 168 lbs
EYES Blue
HAIR Blond

FIRST APPEARANCE
Captain America #217 (January 1978)

POWERS

Quantum Bands permit flight, teleportation, and the ability to form quantum energy constructs, including weapons and armor.

QUASAR

When Wendell Vaughn's graduation ceremony from the SHIELD academy was attacked by AIM terrorists, a desperate Vaughn donned Quantum Band bracelets worn by a copy of 1950s Marvel Boy. As the new Marvel Boy, Vaughn joined SHIELD's Super-Agent program, later calling himself Marvel Man before settling on Quasar. Vaughn had been chosen by the cosmic entity Eon to become the new Protector of the Universe, replacing the late Captain Mar-Vell. Annihilus destroyed Vaughn during the Annihilation event and the Quantum Bands were passed on to Mar-Vell's daughter, Phyla-Vell. Shortly after Vaughn was resurrected in solid light form, Phyla-Vell was killed. Richard Rider (Nova) was briefly given the Quantum Bands before Vaughn resumed his duties as Quasar. When his powers started to malfunction while he was working at Pleasant Hill prison, he passed them on to SHIELD agent Avril Kincaid. As the new Quasar, Kincaid helped free New York from the evil Captain America's Hydra forces (*see* Secret Empire), showing exceptional power while doing so.

Using his Quantum Bands, Quasar can project bubbles of energy that act as force shields. They can also transport things through space.

Avril Kinkaid used her powers to destroy Earth's new defense shield after Steve Rogers seized control of it—something that Captain Marvel, Blue Marvel, and many other powerful heroes had all failed to do.

QNAX

FIRST APPEARANCE *Tales to Astonish* #74 (December 1965)
REAL NAME Qnax (also known as Amphibian)
OCCUPATION Gladiator **BASE** The planet Xantares
HEIGHT 7 ft 9 in **WEIGHT** 915 lbs **EYES** Green **HAIR** None
SPECIAL POWERS/ABILITIES A product of centuries of scientific breeding to create the ultimate fighting machine; can travel fast and breathe underwater.

Xantares' Council of Elders sent Qnax on a mission to obtain the Sphere of Ultimate Knowledge, telling him the Sphere was needed to save the planet. Arriving on the homeworld of the Watchers, Qnax encountered the Hulk, who was also searching for the Sphere. They fought, and Qnax was hurled into space. Exiled from Xantares for this failure, Qnax traveled the cosmos as a gladiator-for-hire. He eventually discovered that the Council of Elders wanted the Sphere in order to dominate Xantares. Dismayed by this, Qnax returned home, hoping to bring justice to his people.

QUASIMODO

FIRST APPEARANCE *Fantastic Four Special* #4 (November 1966)
REAL NAME Quasi-Motivational Destruct Organism
OCCUPATION Former computer **BASE** Mobile
HEIGHT 6 ft **WEIGHT** 1,350 lbs **EYES** White **HAIR** Brown
SPECIAL POWERS/ABILITIES Computer brain; superhuman strength (when in physical form); left eye projects force blasts; can exist as pure consciousness without a physical body.

Quasimodo originated as a sentient computer created by the Mad Thinker. Endowed with a grotesque face that appeared on a screen, Quasimodo longed for a more human form. However, despite promising to fulfill his wish, the Thinker abandoned him. The Silver Surfer took pity on Quasimodo and transformed him into a mobile, humanoid creature, but the ungrateful Quasimodo fought the Surfer, who rendered him immobile. Eventually Quasimodo regained his mobility, and has since battled such champions as Spider-Man, the Beast, the Vision, and the original Captain Mar-Vell. During the Dark Reign, he assembled files on heroes and villains for HAMMER.

QUIRE, QUENTIN

FIRST APPEARANCE *New X-Men* #134 (January 2003)
REAL NAME Quintavius Quirinius Quire
OCCUPATION Adventurer; student **BASE** New York
HEIGHT 5 ft 8 in **WEIGHT** 129 lbs
EYES Brown **HAIR** Brown, dyed pink
SPECIAL POWERS/ABILITIES Quentin is an Omega-level telepath.

Quentin Quire became a star pupil at Professor X's Xavier Institute, but he also became addicted to Kick, a designer drug that enhanced mutant powers. While using it, he formed the Omega Gang and started a student riot at the school. His abuse of Kick caused him to become a being of mental energy, only able to reformulate his body when the Phoenix Force arrived. Quentin later attended the Jean Grey School for Higher Learning and helped Thor fight the Shi'ar, before joining Kitty Pryde's new X-Men school—the Xavier Institute for Mutant Education and Outreach. He later joined Hawkeye's (Kate Bishop) new Avengers West Coast team.

QUICKSILVER

The super-fast Super Hero

Pietro and his twin sister, Wanda (Scarlet Witch), grew up never knowing their father's identity, but came to believe it was Magneto. They were told that their mother, Magda, fled from Magneto while pregnant with them, and gave birth to them in the hills of Wundagore Mountain. The Romani family of Django Maximoff raised the children, but when their mutant powers first showed, they were persecuted as demons.

Since childhood, Quicksilver has been overly protective of his unstable sister, the Scarlet Witch.

FACTFILE

REAL NAME
Pietro Maximoff

OCCUPATION
Adventurer

BASE
Mobile

HEIGHT 6 ft
WEIGHT 175 lbs
EYES Blue
HAIR Silver

FIRST APPEARANCE
X-Men #4 (March 1964)

QUICKSILVER

POWERS

Quicksilver possesses the mutant ability to run at superhuman speeds over great distances. His top speed is alleged to be 175 mph. He can create a whirlwind by running in a circle; his temper can be as quick as his feet.

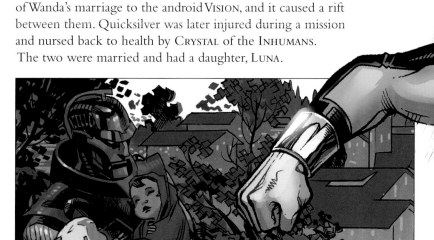

ESSENTIAL STORYLINES

- ***Avengers #16*** Quicksilver and his sister the Scarlet Witch join the Avengers.
- ***Avengers #127, Fantastic Four #150*** Quicksilver marries Crystal of the isolationist Inhumans.
- ***Avengers #185–187*** Quicksilver and the Scarlet Witch return to Wundagore Mountain in Eastern Europe to discover the strange secrets of their birth and their parentage.

VILLAINS AND HEROES

Magneto found the pair during his hunt for members to join his Brotherhood of Evil Mutants. As Quicksilver and Scarlet Witch, they engaged in a series of battles with the X-Men, until they vowed never again to use their powers for evil. Hearing that the Avengers needed new blood, Pietro and Wanda applied to join and were accepted as members. Quicksilver did not approve of Wanda's marriage to the android Vision, and it caused a rift between them. Quicksilver was later injured during a mission and nursed back to health by Crystal of the Inhumans. The two were married and had a daughter, Luna.

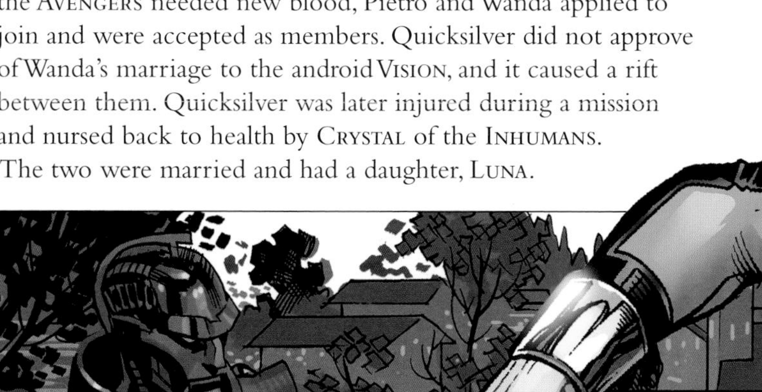

Viewing Pietro and Wanda as failed experiments, the High Evolutionary returned them and tried to pass them off as regular mutants.

When Wanda had a breakdown and destroyed the Avengers, Quicksilver persuaded her to use her powers to change the world into a place where mutants ruled, creating the House of M (Earth-58163). Once mainstream reality returned on M-Day, Quicksilver lost his powers. He used the Inhumans' Terrigen Mists to restore himself and others, but his plans went awry. Furious, Crystal announced that their marriage was over. Hoping to redeem himself, Quicksilver joined Hank Pym's new Avengers and later served on the staff of the Avengers Academy.

While fighting Red Onslaught, Quicksilver and his sister discovered that Magneto wasn't their father. Quicksilver eventually learned they were really the children of Django Maximoff, but they had been abducted and experimented on as babies by the High Evolutionary. Quicksilver was part of the Avengers team taken into space to fight in one of the Grandmaster's games. He seemingly died helping his teammates, but was instead trapped outside of time.

Quicksilver was one of the veterans who became teachers at the Avengers Academy, helping young and vulnerable Super Heroes.

RADIOACTIVE MAN

FIRST APPEARANCE *Journey Into Mystery* #93 (June 1963)
REAL NAME Dr. Chen Lu
OCCUPATION Former scientist; criminal **BASE** Mobile
HEIGHT 6 ft 6 in **WEIGHT** 310 lbs **EYES** Brown **HAIR** None
SPECIAL POWERS/ABILITIES Manipulates radioactivity given off by body; emits radiation as heat or blinding light and can incinerate a city block; hypnotic abilities; superhuman strength.

Dr. Chen Lu was a nuclear physicist in the People's Republic of China, and was among those asked by the Chinese government to defeat Thor. Lu exposed himself to nuclear radiation, transforming him into Radioactive Man. He traveled to New York and battled Thor, but lost. Baron Zemo then enlisted him in his Masters of Evil. He later joined the Thunderbolts, and when he returned to China, he was made part of the People's Defense Force. A Russian mutant, Igor Stancheck, also used the Radioactive Man name. He was killed while attacking Wakanda.

RAGNAROK

FIRST APPEARANCE *Civil War* #3 (September 2006)
REAL NAME Ragnarok
OCCUPATION Warrior **BASE** Mobile
HEIGHT 6 ft 6 in **WEIGHT** 640 lbs **EYES** Blue **HAIR** Blond
SPECIAL POWERS/ABILITIES Ragnarok has superhuman durability, endurance, speed, and strength. He can project electric shocks from his hammer.

When the Civil War erupted, Henry Pym, Iron Man, and Mister Fantastic needed more power on their side. Thor would have been perfect, but he had died, so they made a cyborg clone of him, Ragnarok. In his first battle, Ragnarok murdered Goliath and had to be shut down. In the final Civil War battle, Hercules destroyed him. Revived, he hunted down the returned Thor, who slew him again. He was rebuilt for HAMMER and destroyed again. He returned once more to join Luke Cage's Thunderbolts.

RASPUTIN, MIKHAIL

FIRST APPEARANCE *Uncanny X-Men* #284 (January 1992)
REAL NAME Mikhail Rasputin **OCCUPATION** Cosmonaut
BASE The Hill, in an unspecified dimension
HEIGHT 6 ft 5 in **WEIGHT** 255 lbs **EYES** Blue **HAIR** Black
SPECIAL POWERS/ABILITIES Manipulates matter on a sub-atomic level. He uses this power to fire destructive blasts, warp reality, and teleport through space and between dimensions.

During a space flight, Soviet cosmonaut Mikhail Rasputin entered another dimension. There he fell in love with and married a princess, but when he had to try to close the dimensional rift, the backlash killed hundreds of people, including his beloved wife. When he returned to Earth, he became leader of the Morlocks before massacring them and setting up the mutant terrorist group Gene Nation for Dark Beast. He later helped the X-Men defeat Apocalypse and his Horsemen. Eventually, he banished himself to another dimension to save his brother from Mister Sinister.

RAGE

FIRST APPEARANCE *Avengers* #326 (November 1990)
REAL NAME Elvin Daryl Haliday
OCCUPATION Student **BASE** Oatridge School for Boys
HEIGHT 6 ft 6 in **WEIGHT** 450 lbs **EYES** Brown **HAIR** None
SPECIAL POWERS/ABILITIES Exposure to alien radiation granted him the ability to fly and to understand the language of birds.

Twelve-year-old Elvin Haliday plunged into Newtown Creek to escape a gang of racist thugs. The chemicals in the water caused him to grow into an adult with superhuman strength. Although Elvin could have used his new powers for crime, his only relation, the devout Granny Staples, convinced him to become a hero. Elvin slipped from this road just once: when Granny Staples herself was murdered. Rage worked with both the Avengers and the New Warriors. He sided with Captain America during the Civil War, but later joined the Fifty-State Initiative at Camp Hammond. He is now part of the latest New Warriors team.

RAVONNA

In the 41st century of an alternate future, Kang had conquered all of Earth except the small kingdom of Princess Ravonna, who refused his offer of marriage. Kang's army ultimately overwhelmed Ravonna's kingdom but when Kang refused to execute Ravonna, his commander Baltag rebelled against him.

Kang joined forces with Ravonna and the Avengers to defeat Baltag and Ravonna fell in love with Kang. When the vengeful Baltag fired a blaster at Kang, Ravonna pushed him out of the way, and the blast struck her instead. To restore her to life, Kang played a game with the alien Grandmaster, who gave him temporary power over life and death when Kang won. However, Kang wasted this short-lived power in an unsuccessful attempt to kill the Avengers.

After this point various timelines diverge, in which Ravonna leads different lives. In one timeline Kang saves Ravonna from Baltag's attack, but she becomes the ally and consort of Kang's own future counterpart, Immortus. In another the Grandmaster revives Ravonna, who seeks vengeance on Kang. She assumes a number of identities, including Nebula, the Temptress, and the Terminatrix. A future counterpart will take the name Revelation.

NO ONE COMMANDS A *PRINCESS!*

RAVONNA

FACTFILE
REAL NAME
Ravonna Lexus Renslayer
OCCUPATION
Princess
BASE
Originally an unnamed kingdom on 41st-century Earth in an alternate future.

HEIGHT 5 ft 8 in
WEIGHT 142 lbs
EYES (as Ravonna) Green; (as Nebula/Terminatrix) Blue
HAIR (as Ravonna) Red-brown; (as Nebula/Terminatrix) Blond

FIRST APPEARANCE
Avengers #23 (December 1965)

POWERS
As Terminatrix or Revelation: has enhanced durability, speed, and agility, is a formidable hand-to-hand combatant, and uses highly advanced technology.

RAWHIDE KID, THE

FIRST APPEARANCE *Rawhide Kid* #1 (March 1955)
REAL NAME Johnny Bart
OCCUPATION Gunslinger **BASE** The American Old West
HEIGHT 5 ft 10 in **WEIGHT** 185 lbs
EYES Blue **HAIR** Red
SPECIAL POWERS/ABILITIES Skilled brawler and horseman; among the quickest draws in the Old West.

The Rawhide Kid learned to handle a six-shooter thanks to his adoptive father, a Texas Ranger, after his real parents were killed by Cheyenne warriors. When his adoptive father died in a rigged duel, the Rawhide Kid took revenge on the killers and then wandered the West astride his horse, Nightwind, keeping one step ahead of the sheriff who suspected the Kid of murder. By means of time travel, the Rawhide Kid occasionally crossed paths with modern-era Super Heroes.

REAPER

FIRST APPEARANCE *New Mutants* #87 (March 1990)
REAL NAME Pantu Hurageb
OCCUPATION None **BASE** Unknown
HEIGHT/WEIGHT/EYES/HAIR Unrevealed
SPECIAL POWERS/ABILITIES Neurosynaptic energy generated by Reaper slows reflexes and movements of those nearby; scythes focus energy and can be used to paralyze others.

Pantu Hurageb was a member of the MUTANT LIBERATION FRONT. During his stint there, he lost a hand and a lower leg and replaced both with artificial limbs. Following Reaper's incarceration in Neverland, Nathan Summers (CABLE) tried to pry the camp's location from his mind, causing him severe brain damage and turning him mute. He lost his powers on M-Day, but QUICKSILVER restored them. Reaper was later trapped in the Brimstone Dimension, but recovered by Terrance Hoffman, who drained him of his powers like a battery. Hoffman accidentally freed him during a fight with X-FACTOR.

REAVERS

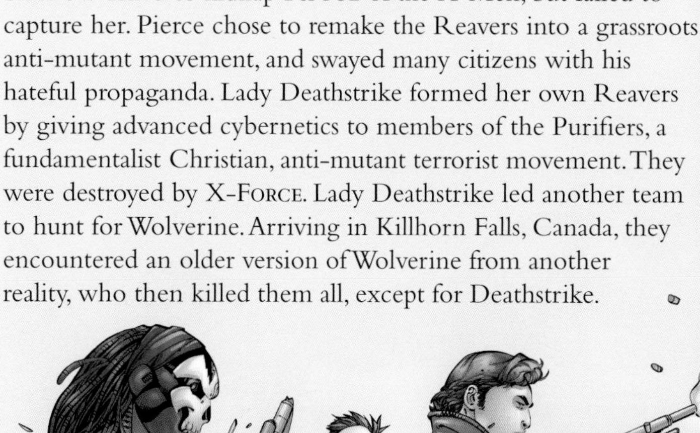

The cyborg mercenaries known as the Reavers originated in an underground complex in Cooteman's Creek, Australia. They used teleportation to commit robberies around the world until the X-MEN forced them from their base. Ex-HELLFIRE CLUB member Donald Pierce reorganized the team, bringing in Cole, Macon, Reese, and LADY DEATHSTRIKE. The new Reavers nearly killed WOLVERINE, and launched a failed attack on Moira MACTAGGERT's Muir Island laboratory. A squad of SENTINELS nearly destroyed the Reavers, though most members survived due to their half-machine physiologies.

The Reavers later won a contract from the psionic entity the SHADOW KING to kidnap ROGUE of the X-Men, but failed to capture her. Pierce chose to remake the Reavers into a grassroots anti-mutant movement, and swayed many citizens with his hateful propaganda. Lady Deathstrike formed her own Reavers by giving advanced cybernetics to members of the Purifiers, a fundamentalist Christian, anti-mutant terrorist movement. They were destroyed by X-FORCE. Lady Deathstrike led another team to hunt for Wolverine. Arriving in Killhorn Falls, Canada, they encountered an older version of Wolverine from another reality, who then killed them all, except for Deathstrike.

FACTFILE
KEY MEMBERS
DONALD PIERCE (LEADER)
Adamantium-enhanced body, enhanced strength; morphing cyborg limbs emit energy blasts.
BONEBREAKER
Cyborg strength, tank treads, built-in weaponry.
PRETTY BOY
Extendible cyborg limbs and capture coils; reprograms the personalities of others.
SKULLBUSTER
Cyborg strength, robot legs; uses machine guns, grenade launchers.
SKULLBUSTER/CYLLA
Cyborg strength, reflexes; wrist claws, thermite launchers.
LADY DEATHSTRIKE
Augmented strength, reflexes; talons extend from fingertips.
COLE, MACON, AND REESE
Cyborg strength, reflexes; bionic scanners and tracking devices.
BASE Mobile

FIRST APPEARANCE
Uncanny X-Men #229 (May 1988)

THE REAVERS
(left to right) Skullbuster, Bonebreaker, Pretty Boy

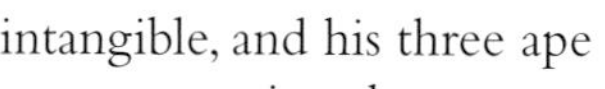

RED GHOST

FIRST APPEARANCE *Fantastic Four* #13 (April 1963)
REAL NAME Ivan Kragoff **OCCUPATION** Villain
BASE Mobile **HEIGHT** 5 ft 11 in **WEIGHT** 215 lbs
EYES Brown **HAIR** White, balding
SPECIAL POWERS/ABILITIES Renders himself and nearby objects intangible and transparent; ingenious scientist and brilliant engineer.

Russian scientist Ivan Kragoff envied the achievements of the FANTASTIC FOUR. Determined to beat them to the moon, he designed his spacecraft to maximize exposure to cosmic rays, hoping to duplicate the freakish accident that had created his rivals. Kragoff gained the ability to become intangible, and his three ape companions became smarter and obtained powers of strength, magnetism, and shapeshifting. As the Red Ghost, Kragoff and his SUPER-APE companions clashed with the Fantastic Four, the AVENGERS, and SPIDER-MAN. He became a member of the INTELLIGENCIA and was later killed by DOCTOR OCTOPUS but revived by MODOK.

RED GUARDIAN

FACTFILE

REAL NAME
Alexei Shostakov

OCCUPATION
Espionage agent for Soviet Union; later for People's Republic of China

BASE
Various secret KGB bases in USSR; later a military base in the People's Republic of China

HEIGHT 6 ft 2 in
WEIGHT 220 lbs
EYES Blue
HAIR Red

FIRST APPEARANCE
Avengers #43 (August 1967)

POWERS

Brilliant athlete and test pilot, trained in espionage techniques and hand-to-hand combat by the KGB. Disc on Red Guardian's belt could be detached and used as a throwing weapon; magnetic force returned the disc after throwing.

RED GUARDIAN

A talented athlete and test pilot—and husband to Natasha Romanova (Black Widow)—Alexei Shostakov faked his death and trained to become a top KGB operative code-named Red Guardian, modeled after a Soviet hero from World War II. While Natasha became disillusioned with her KGB masters and defected to the USA, Alexei remained loyal and increasingly ruthless and vindictive. He was thought to have given his life to save her and Captain America, but he turned up alive again years later, trying to bring Natasha to justice for betraying her homeland.

Dr. Tara Belinsky became the next Red Guardian and even joined the Defenders for a while. When Presence gave her radioactive powers, she changed her name to Starlight. Five other Red Guardians followed after her, each athletic men. The latest became leader of the Winter Guard.

After encountering the Avengers, the Red Guardian battles Hawkeye, Black Widow's lover.

The Red Guardian's identity is revealed.

RED HULK

FACTFILE

REAL NAME
General Thaddeus E. Ross

OCCUPATION
Adventurer, retired soldier

BASE
Mobile

HEIGHT 7 ft
WEIGHT 1200 lbs
EYES Yellow
HAIR Black

FIRST APPEARANCE
Hulk #1 (March 2008)

POWERS

Red Hulk has superhuman durability, endurance, and strength. As he gets angrier, he gets hotter. He can also absorb radiation to become more powerful.

RED HULK

After World War Hulk, the Intelligencia took General Thunderbolt Ross—who'd faked his death—and transformed him into the Red Hulk, a smarter version of the Hulk. The Red Hulk grew hotter when angry rather than stronger. For a long time, the Red Hulk worked with them, never letting anyone outside the group know who he really was. He appeared in Russia and gunned down the Abomination with a pistol the size of a small cannon. He next arrived at the new SHIELD Helicarrier built by Iron Man and tore it from the sky. Soon after that, he attacked Rick Jones, who transformed into A-Bomb, a gamma-irradiated creature with armored, blue skin.

When the time came for Red Hulk to help the Intelligencia take over America, he betrayed them and tried to take the country over for himself. The original Hulk stopped him, and Steve Rogers (Captain America), believing Ross could be redeemed, offered him a spot in the Avengers. During the events of Avengers vs X-Men, the Red Hulk battled Cyclops who sent him back to the Avengers with an X carved on his chest. He later formed and led a new Thunderbolts team. Doc Green (Hulk) eventually injected Red Hulk with a cure, reverting Ross to normal. General Robert L. Maverick used a SHIELD "Hulk Plug-In" to become the new Red Hulk, Working for AIM and the U.S.Avengers.

After Hydra sabotaged him, General Maverick became trapped in his Red Hulk form, causing serious damage to his body.

RED RAVEN

FIRST APPEARANCE *Red Raven Comics* #1 (August 1940)
REAL NAME Unknown
OCCUPATION Adventurer **BASE** Mobile
HEIGHT 6 ft **WEIGHT** 180 lbs **EYES** Black **HAIR** Red
SPECIAL POWERS/ABILITIES Can fly using anti-gravity metallic wings, which can also deflect bullets and fire energy beams.

Raised by a lost tribe of Inhumans known as the Bird-People, on a hovering island in the Atlantic, Red Raven was a heroic member of the World War II-era Liberty Legion. After the war, he placed himself and his people into suspended animation to prevent aggression between them and humanity. Later, the Angel discovered Red Raven, who made it appear that his island had been destroyed to ensure the privacy of the Bird-People. His daughter Dania has also assumed the identity of Red Raven. Arcade kidnapped her for his latest Murderworld, and she died trying to escape it.

Red Skull, see pages 294–295

REPTIL

FIRST APPEARANCE *Avengers: The Initiative Featuring Reptil* #1 (May 2009) **REAL NAME** Humberto Lopez
OCCUPATION Hero-in-training **BASE** Avengers Academy
HEIGHT 5 ft 10 in **WEIGHT** 168 lbs **EYES** Brown **HAIR** Brown
SPECIAL POWERS/ABILITIES Reptil can fully transform into any prehistoric animal, such as a dinosaur. At first he could only change parts of his body at a time.

Berto Lopez's paleontologist parents discovered a fossilized amulet and gave it to him. After they went missing, he discovered the amulet allowed him to change parts of his body into those of a dinosaur. He registered with the US government, but after the Dark Reign ended, he joined the Avengers Academy instead. At one point, he swapped minds with his future self and learned he would have a child with fellow Avenger student Finesse. Later, Arcade kidnapped him and pitted him against other young heroes in a new Murderworld. After Hydra's short-lived takeover of America, he joined the new SHIELD created by the time traveler Leonardo da Vinci.

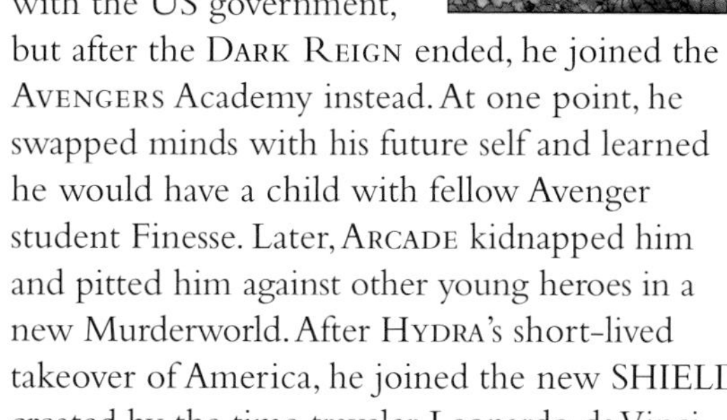

REVANCHE

FIRST APPEARANCE *X-Men* #17 (February 1992)
REAL NAME Kwannon **OCCUPATION** Assassin **BASE** Japan
HEIGHT (both bodies) 5 ft 11 in **WEIGHT** (both bodies) 155 lbs
EYES (original body) Blue, (Braddock's body) Violet
HAIR (original body) Black, (Braddock's body) Brown, dyed purple
SPECIAL POWERS/ABILITIES Martial arts; (as Revanche) telepath; manifested psychic energy in form of Samurai sword.

Kwannon was a Japanese assassin and the lover of crimelord Matsu'o Tsurayaba. When Kwannon was mortally injured, Tsurayaba made a deal with Spiral, who transferred Kwannon's mind into the body of Psylocke and swapped Psylocke's mind into Kwannon's body. Gaining Psylocke's memories and powers, Kwannon claimed to be her and called herself Revanche (French for "revenge"). Discovering that she was infected with the Legacy Virus, she begged Matsu'o to kill her with a ceremonial dagger. She was later revived to join the Sisterhood of Mutants, but Psylocke slew her soon after.

RED WOLF

FIRST APPEARANCE *1872* #1 (September 2015)
REAL NAME Red Wolf **OCCUPATION** Adventurer; vigilante; former sheriff
BASE Mobile; formerly New Mexico **HEIGHT** Unknown
WEIGHT Unknown **EYES** Brown **HAIR** Black
SPECIAL POWERS/ABILITIES Master combatant; expert tracker and hunter; can use zoopathy to communicate with and influence wolves.

The first Red Wolf tamed the first horse and conquered the American plains for the Cheyenne. Another was Johnny Wakeley, a Cheyenne orphan who forged peace between his people and the US Cavalry. The next Red Wolf was Will Talltrees, who joined the Fifty-State Initiative's Rangers. The current Red Wolf was born in New Mexico. As a sheriff he investigated a series of murders by a time-traveler called the Surveyor. Hawkeye helped him stop the Oasis Spring Water company and Hydro-Man from stealing water from the Sweet Medicine Indian Reservation. When Steve Rogers overthrew the US government for Hydra, Red Wolf joined the resistance against him.

REDEEMER

FIRST APPEARANCE *Incredible Hulk* #343 (May 1988)
REAL NAME Craig Saunders
OCCUPATION Former demolitions expert **BASE** New York
HEIGHT 6 ft 1 in **WEIGHT** 205 lbs **EYES** Brown **HAIR** White
SPECIAL POWERS/ABILITIES Bonded with combat suit armed with twin plasma canons on each hand, a rocket and grenade launcher, and rocket boots enabling 30 minutes of flight.

After joining the military as a demolitions expert, Craig Saunders' world came crashing down when he failed to defuse a bomb in an airport terminal, causing the death of two civilians. Desperate, he joined a new paramilitary team called the Hulkbusters, but their effort to defeat the Hulk also ended in disappointment. Taking advantage of Saunders' despair, the Leader persuaded him to become the Redeemer and integrated Saunders' body into a formidable yellow combat suit. Sadly, redemption was not to be his—Saunders died during his very first confrontation with old greenskin.

REVENGERS, THE

FIRST APPEARANCE *New Avengers Annual* #1 (November 2011)
BASE New York City
MEMBERS AND POWERS
Anti-Venom Wears a healing symbiote. **Atlas** Grows to huge size.
Captain Ultra Superhuman who can fly, become intangible, use X-ray vision and super breath. **Century** Teleporting superhuman.
Demolition Man Superhuman durability, endurance, and strength.
Devil-Slayer Teleporter with mystic, prehensile cloak that holds many things. **Ethan Edwards** A super-Skrull. **Goliath** Grows to huge size. **Wonder Man** Controls the ionic energy of which he's composed.

Angered at what he saw as the way the Avengers continued to endanger the world with their irresponsible adventures, Wonder Man assembled a team to stop them. They attacked Luke Cage's Avengers in the Avengers Mansion first and defeated them soundly, but the fully assembled Avengers captured them and put an end to the team. Wonder Man would later repent this action and go on to rejoin the Avengers, trying to lead through example. A villainous New Revengers team was later formed by the Maker to defeat AIM's (Avengers Idea Mechanics) New Avengers.

RED SKULL

The most dangerous of all Nazi agents

RED SKULL

FACTFILE

REAL NAME
Johann Schmidt

OCCUPATION
Terrorist; conqueror

BASE
Nazi Germany, later various secret bases around the world

HEIGHT (original body) 6 ft 1 in; (cloned body) 6 ft 2 in
WEIGHT (original body) 195 lbs; (cloned body) 240 lbs
EYES (both bodies) Blue
HAIR (original body) Brown; (cloned body) Formerly blond, later none

FIRST APPEARANCE
Captain America Comics #5 (August 1941)

POWERS

Totally ruthless, brilliant subversive strategist; excellent hand-to-hand combatant and marksman. Uses lethal "dust of death," which causes a victim's head to resemble a ghoulish red skull.

ALLIES/FOES

ALLIES Adolf Hitler, Sin Crossbones, Doctor Faustus, Arnim Zola, the S-Men, Honest John

FOES Captain America, General Lukin, the Winter Soldier, the Avengers, Wolverine

ISSUE #1

In "The Ringmaster of Death" Cap and Bucky discover that a circus is a front of a gang of Nazi assassins. The Red Skull lurks behind the scenes.

The Red Skull's Cosmic Cube could alter reality.

Johann Schmidt was born in a German village. His mother died giving birth to him and, after failing to drown the newborn child, Johann's father committed suicide. The orphaned Schmidt became a beggar and thief, though he sometimes took menial jobs. Schmidt was working as a bellboy in a hotel when Adolf Hitler, the dictator of Nazi Germany, paid a visit there.

A PERFECT NAZI

Recognizing in Schmidt's eyes a hatred of all humanity that mirrored his own, Hitler decided to turn him into "the perfect Nazi." Hitler oversaw Schmidt's training, presented him with a skull-like head mask, and named him "The Red Skull." Answerable only to Hitler himself, the Red Skull undertook a range of missions for the Third Reich, especially acts of terrorism.

In order to have an American counterpart to the Red Skull, the US government gave Super-Soldier Steve Rogers the identity of Captain America. Shortly before the US entered World War II, the Red Skull first battled Captain America, who would become his greatest foe. During the war, the Red Skull commanded numerous military missions. He rose to become the second most powerful man in the Third Reich, feared even by Hitler.

During the fall of Berlin, Captain America fought the Red Skull in Hitler's bunker. A bomb caused a cave-in that seemingly killed the Red Skull. However, an experimental gas kept the villain in suspended animation for decades.

During World War II the Red Skull repeatedly battled Captain America and his partner Bucky.

BACK FROM THE DEAD

In the 1950s, communist agent Albert Malik impersonated the Red Skull, but eventually the original was found and revived. Since then, Captain America has repeatedly thwarted his bids for global domination. At one point, the Red Skull died, but Arnim Zola transferred the Skull's consciousness into a clone of Captain America. By accident, his own "dust of death" caused the Skull's new head to resemble a living red skull.

The Skull made many enemies, including General Lukin, who sent the Winter Soldier to kill him. Before dying, the Skull used a Cosmic Cube to transfer his mind into Lukin's body. With the help of his daughter, Sin, as well as Crossbones and Doctor Faustus, the Skull set up the assassination of Captain America at the end of the Civil War. This was, however, not just the end of his plans for Cap, but the beginning.

ESSENTIAL STORYLINES

- ***Tales of Suspense #66***
The first time that the fascinating origin of the Red Skull was revealed.
- ***Tales of Suspense #79–81***
The Red Skull is revived in modern times and steals the Cosmic Cube.
- ***Captain America: Reborn***
The Red Skull plans to use Steve Rogers' body to become even more deadly.
- ***Uncanny Avengers Vol 1: The Red Shadow***
A new Red Skull rises up and is more dangerous than ever.

THE ENEMY RETURNS

It seemed that Captain America had died from a bullet fired by the Skull's henchman Crossbones; however, the Red Skull had actually arranged for Doctor Faustus to brainwash Sharon CARTER and she had shot Cap in the confusion caused by Crossbones' attack. She hadn't used a pistol, however, but a device designed to freeze Captain America in time. With the help of Arnim Zola, the Red Skull planned to pluck his foe back out of time and transfer his mind into Cap's body.

Carter foiled the Skull's plan by escaping from him and damaging Zola's machinery. The Red Skull succeeded in transferring his consciousness into Rogers' body, but as he tried to kill the new Captain America (Bucky Barnes), the real Steve Rogers broke through the Red Skull's mental controls and pushed him out of his brain.

The Red Skull returned to his robot body and battled the Avengers. Carter shot him with a weapon she thought would shrink him, but instead it grew him into a giant. While the Avengers kept the Red Skull occupied, Carter shot him with a barrage of missiles, destroying his body and putting an end to him.

The Red Skull's daughter, SIN, was standing close to him when his robot body was destroyed. The explosion blasted her, removing her hair and turning her burnt skin bright red. She took on his name and mantle, becoming the new Red Skull.

Temporarily without a body of his own, the Red Skull was forced to use one of Arnim Zola's spare robots.

The new Skull returned to her father's secret bases to explore her inheritance. In one, she discovered his diary and learned of his attempt to invoke the SERPENT of Norse myth to help the Nazis win World War II. This led her to an isolated fortress in which she found a mystical hammer. When she picked it up—something her father had been unable to do—it transformed her into Skadi, the herald of the Serpent. This launched FEAR ITSELF.

Following the eventual defeat of the Serpent, ODIN took Skadi's hammer, and the Red Skull changed back into Sin, still disfigured. Despite her defeat, she managed to remain free.

With her face disfigured in the same way as her father's, Sin assumed his mantle of evil.

THE NEW SKULL

After Sin's defeat, Arnim Zola revived a clone of the Skull he had kept in suspended animation since the end of World War II. The cloned Skull decided that mutants were the source of everything that was wrong with the world. He stole Professor X's body and grafted part of Xavier's brain onto his own, giving him some semblance of Xavier's tremendous psychic powers. He then took to the streets of Manhattan, telepathically projecting his hatred of mutants to the people there. A new Avengers Unity team, made up of both X-Men and Avengers, managed to put a stop to the Skull's plans but he escaped to fight another day.

The Red Skull resurfaced on Genosha, having turned the island into a concentration camp for mutants. Magneto killed the Red Skull, only to unleash a new entity—Red Onslaught. While heroes tried to defeat the creature, an inversion spell cast by the Scarlet Witch went wrong and inversed the heroes and villains. In the chaotic aftermath, the new "White Skull" acted as a hero and helped Captain America reverse the changes.

As the White Skull, a newly heroic Schmidt temporarily aided his sworn enemy, Captain America.

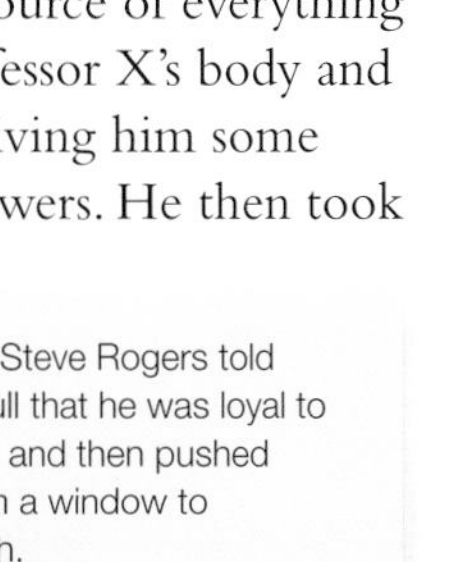

The evil Steve Rogers told Red Skull that he was loyal to nothing, and then pushed him from a window to his death.

RED ONSLAUGHT

Since its defeat, the entity known as Onslaught had lain dormant in Professor X's mind. After Red Skull stole Xavier's brain and merged it with his own, Onslaught became part of Red Skull, too. On Genosha, Magneto bludgeoned Red Skull to death, but in so doing merely unleashed an even deadlier, merged form of Onslaught. In this persona—Red Onslaught—the Red Skull became more powerful than ever.

HAIL HYDRA

In his next villainous scheme, Red Skull convinced KOBIK, a sentient Cosmic Cube in the form of a young girl, that HYDRA was a force for good and had her use her powers to rewrite Captain America's history, creating a new one in which he had always been a Hydra agent. This proved to be a fatal mistake, as the evil Captain America then rebelled and killed the Red Skull. Despite his death, the Red Skull appeared to the real Steve Rogers—who was trapped in Kobik's mindscape while his evil duplicate ran riot—only to be seemingly killed yet again.

RHINO

FACTFILE
REAL NAME
Aleksei Sytsevich
OCCUPATION
Criminal
BASE
Mobile

HEIGHT 6 ft 5 in
WEIGHT 710 lbs
EYES Brown
HAIR Brown

FIRST APPEARANCE
The Amazing Spider-Man #41 (October 1966)

POWERS
The Rhino possesses the strength and enhanced durability of his namesake due to his protective suit, which is bonded to his body.

RHINO

A member of the Russian Mafia, the man who would become the Rhino was selected for experimentation by a group of spies because of his low intelligence. After months of chemical and radiation treatments, he was given a protective suit that resembled rhinoceros hide. He was sent to America under the identity Alex O'Hirn to abduct astronaut John JAMESON, but was foiled by SPIDER-MAN. The Rhino subsequently used his strength in a number of criminal endeavors.

Believing himself to be trapped permanently within his costume, the Rhino was subject to bouts of insanity, but eventually gave himself up to SHIELD, who were able to remove the suit. Released on parole, he fell in love and got married. A new Rhino tried to destroy him but killed his wife instead. Aleksei donned his old suit and killed the newcomer. Joining a new SINISTER SIX, the Rhino seemingly drowned SILVER SABLE. He was later hired by JACKAL with the promise of restoring his wife as a clone. Aleksei worked for Jackal until his wife disintegrated, sending Aleksei into a rampage of grief.

The Hulk seemed to have killed the Rhino once, but Aleksei survived that too.

RICHARDS, FRANKLIN

FACTFILE
REAL NAME
Franklin Benjamin Richards
OCCUPATION
Adventurer
BASE
New York City

HEIGHT 4 ft 8 in
WEIGHT 100 lbs
EYES Blue
HAIR Blond

FIRST APPEARANCE
Fantastic Four Annual #6 (1968)

POWERS
Possesses vast powers of telepathy and telekinesis, as well as the ability to fire psionic blasts, reshape reality, appear in astral form, and perceive future events.

RICHARDS, FRANKLIN

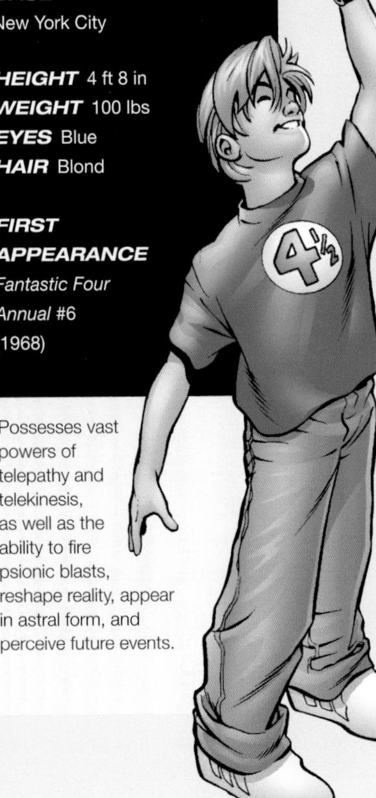

Son of Reed and Sue Richards of the FANTASTIC FOUR, Franklin Richards was one of the most powerful mutants on Earth. As a young boy he began to exhibit immense psionic powers. Using his ability to see possible futures, he became a member of POWER PACK under the name Tattletale. Nathaniel RICHARDS, his grandfather, later raised him in a realm outside of time, where he became the adult adventurer Psi-Lord, and founded the Fantastic Force before Hyperstorm erased his adult form from existence. When the AVENGERS and the Fantastic Four seemingly perished fighting ONSLAUGHT, Franklin sent them to a "Counter-Earth" of his own creation. He used his powers to bring back GALACTUS and return his sister Valeria to his mother's womb. Later, as the Multiverse collapsed, Franklin tried to create a pocket universe where the people of Earth could survive, but his efforts failed. His father tried to save the family in a life raft, but Franklin was killed. Eight years later, Reed acquired the power of the BEYONDERS and resurrected Franklin and his family. Franklin set about recreating new universes in the Multiverse, but this drew the ire of a being called the Griever at the End of All Things.

RICHARDS, NATHANIEL

FIRST APPEARANCE *Fantastic Four* #272 (November 1984)
REAL NAME Nathaniel Richards
OCCUPATION Adventurer and scientist **BASE** Mobile
HEIGHT 6 ft 2 in **WEIGHT** 170 lbs
EYES Brown **HAIR** Gray
SPECIAL POWERS/ABILITIES Nathaniel is a super genius who can travel through time.

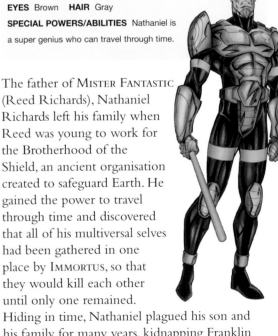

The father of MISTER FANTASTIC (Reed Richards), Nathaniel Richards left his family when Reed was young to work for the Brotherhood of the Shield, an ancient organisation created to safeguard Earth. He gained the power to travel through time and discovered that all of his multiversal selves had been gathered in one place by IMMORTUS, so that they would kill each other until only one remained. Hiding in time, Nathaniel plagued his son and his family for many years, kidnapping Franklin RICHARDS and even posing as DOCTOR DOOM. He later joined the Future Foundation to work with his family rather than against them.

RICHARDS, VALERIA

RICHARDS, VALERIA

FACTFILE

REAL NAME
Valeria Meghan Richards

OCCUPATION
Student; adventurer

BASE
New York City

HEIGHT 3 ft 5 in
WEIGHT 50 lbs
EYES Blue
HAIR Blond

FIRST APPEARANCE
Fantastic Four #50 (February 2002)

POWERS

Valeria has superhuman intelligence and can generate force-fields.

The second child of MISTER FANTASTIC and the INVISIBLE WOMAN, Valeria was conceived in the Negative Zone and believed stillborn. Instead, her brother Franklin had taken her to an alternate future where she was raised by the INVISIBLE WOMAN and her husband, a heroic DOCTOR DOOM. Valeria eventually returned to their time as a teenager calling herself Marvel Girl. When battling the universe-destroyer Abraxas with their family, Valeria and Franklin used their powers to revive GALACTUS to defeat him.

In the subsequent restructuring of reality, Valeria went back to being a fetus in her mother's womb. This time, Doctor Doom came to the FANTASTIC FOUR's aid and saved the girl. He asked only that he be able to name her.

When the Multiverse came to an end, Valeria and the whole family died, apart from Mister Fantastic. Several years later he achieved the power of the BEYONDERS and restored Valeria and the rest of the family to life. When the Richards family began recreating the Multiverse, it caught the attention of a being called the Griever at the End of All Things, leading to a battle between it and the entire Future Foundation.

RICTOR

FIRST APPEARANCE *X-Factor* #17 (June 1987)
REAL NAME Julio Esteban Richter
OCCUPATION Private Investigator **BASE** New York City
HEIGHT 5 ft 9 in **WEIGHT** 162 lbs **EYES** Brown **HAIR** Brown
SPECIAL POWERS/ABILITIES By touching objects can cause them to vibrate and crumble; applied to buildings his powers have an earthquake-like effect.

As a boy, Julio Richter saw the mutant clone STRYFE murder his father. Julio later developed mutant powers and was captured by the RIGHT to cause mayhem in San Francisco. Freed by X-FACTOR, he has since served with them as well as the NEW MUTANTS and X-FORCE. M-Day robbed him of his powers. He later started a relationship with SHATTERSTAR, and the SCARLET WITCH restored his powers. He and Shatterstar found themselves hopping around in time and across alternate universes. Once back in their own time, they grew apart.

RICOCHET

RICOCHET

FACTFILE

REAL NAME
Jonathon "Johnny" Gallo

OCCUPATION
College student

BASE
Los Angeles, California; formerly Brooklyn, New York

HEIGHT 5 ft 10 in
WEIGHT 155 lbs
EYES Blue
HAIR Blond

FIRST APPEARANCE
Slingers #0 (December 1998)

POWERS

Mutant with superhuman leaping, acrobatic, and gymnastic skills. Possesses a "danger sense," similar to Spider-Man's "spider-sense." Also uses throwing disks as weapons.

When SPIDER-MAN was falsely accused of murder, he was forced to adopt a new identity in order to find the real killer. Instead of temporarily assuming one new persona, he created four: Ricochet, DUSK, Hornet, and PRODIGY. After clearing his name, Spider-Man discarded these identities and their costumes. The costumes came into the possession of a former Super Hero called the Black Marvel, who gave them to four teenagers and formed a new super-team called the Slingers. One of the members was Johnny Gallo, a troubled youth whose mother had been killed in a car accident.

Johnny leaped at the chance to use his mutant powers, but like the rest of the team he became disillusioned when it emerged that Black Marvel had been given the costumes by the demon MEPHISTO. Nevertheless, the Slingers battled to save the Black Marvel's soul from Mephisto and won, although the battle claimed Black Marvel's life. The Slingers then disbanded and Gallo moved to L.A. He joined a group of former teenage heroes who were adjusting to civilian life. Later, a demon impersonating the Black Marvel brought the Slinger team back together to hunt down SCARLET SPIDER. However Scarlet Spider ended up killing the demon and making peace with Jonathon and the team.

RIGHT, THE

FIRST APPEARANCE *X-Factor* #17 (June 1987)
MEMBERS AND POWERS
Cameron Hodge (commander) Brilliant planner; made immortal through a mystical pact.
Ani-Mator Genius-level geneticist.
Other unnamed operatives and soldiers.
BASE Mobile

The Right is a secret organization dedicated to preserving human freedoms by the eradication of mutantkind. Cameron HODGE, a former public relations director for X-FACTOR, founded the Right using X-Factor's own profits. Hodge's double-dealing soon became all too obvious and he engaged his former colleagues in combat, clashing with both X-Factor and the NEW MUTANTS. Agents of the Right wear armored battlesuits equipped with built-in machine guns and flight jets. Their battlesuits have facemasks that bear a distinctive "smiley face" design.

RIORDAN, DALLAS

FIRST APPEARANCE *Thunderbolts* #1 (April 1997)
REAL NAME Dallas Riordan **OCCUPATION** Adventurer
BASE New York City **HEIGHT** 5 ft 1 in **WEIGHT** 150 lbs
EYES Blue **HAIR** Red
SPECIAL POWERS/ABILITIES Expert swordswoman and adept hand-to-hand combatant.

Dallas served as New York City's liaison to the THUNDERBOLTS until BARON ZEMO discredited the team and ruined Dallas' own reputation. Invited to become the new Citizen V, Dallas' career as a costumed crusader was cut short when she lost the use of her legs. For a while, she could only walk when she merged her consciousness with that of her dead lover, Erik Josten (ATLAS). Erik has since returned—and the two have separated. Dallas regained the ability to walk thanks to Josten bestowing on her some of his ionic energy. Dallas currently works for the Commission on Superhuman Activities.

RIOT SQUAD

The Riot Squad came into being when the villainous LEADER detonated a gamma bomb on the town of Middletown, Arizona. Amazingly, a few residents survived, mutated by gamma radiation in the same manner as the HULK. These five took the cover names Jailbait, Hotshot, Ogress, Omnibus, and Soul Man, and became the Leader's elite guards. Charged with protecting the Freehold base, where the Leader gave sanctuary to those suffering from radiation sickness, the team fought the Hulk on several occasions.

During an attack on the Freehold base by HYDRA, Soul Man was killed, and with the Leader also presumed dead, Omnibus took control of the Riot Squad. His teammates put him on trial after he orchestrated terrorist bombings in an effort to gain more power. Despite his protestations that he had been under the control of the Leader when he committed the crimes, they found him guilty and banished him to the Arctic. The Troyjans later decimated Freehold despite the efforts of Riot Squad. The team is likely to continue as a mercenary outfit.

RIOT SQUAD
1 Rock
2 Soul Man
3 Ogress
4 Hotshot
5 Jailbait
6 Redeemer

FACTFILE

MEMBERS AND POWERS
JAILBAIT
Can project psionic force-fields.
HOTSHOT
Can project energy blasts.
OGRESS
Enhanced strength and damage resistance.
OMNIBUS
Super-genius intellect.
SOUL MAN
Possessed ability to resurrect the dead.

FIRST APPEARANCE
(As normal humans) *Incredible Hulk* #345 (July 1988); (as Riot Squad) *Incredible Hulk* #366 (February 1990)

RISQUE

FIRST APPEARANCE *X-Force* #51 (August 1991)
REAL NAME Gloria Dolores Muñoz
OCCUPATION X-Corporation employee
BASE Hong Kong **HEIGHT** 5 ft 9 in **WEIGHT** 120 lbs
EYES Brown **HAIR** Black
SPECIAL POWERS/ABILITIES Compresses matter, both inorganic and organic; can destroy smaller objects, like a cell phone, altogether.

Gloria Muñoz had a lonely childhood. Her parents divorced when she was 12 and she left home at 16. Forced to fend for herself, Gloria developed a cold, distant personality and her first encounters with the mutant group X-FORCE did not endear her to them. However, she became romantically involved with WARPATH, even falling in love with him, before betraying him to the Deviant (*see* ETERNALS) known as Sledge. After making recompense for her misdeeds, Gloria was invited to join X-Corporation's Hong Kong office, but she wasn't there long. While investigating the trade in mutant body parts, Gloria was killed by the U-Men, a group of humans seeking mutant body parts to graft onto themselves.

ROBERTSON, JOE

Robertson defeated his nemesis Tombstone after years of trying.

Joseph "Robbie" Robertson, long-time editor-in-chief of the *Daily Bugle*, grew up in Harlem alongside the brutal Lonnie Thompson Lincoln (TOMBSTONE). While working as a reporter in Philadelphia, Robertson saw Tombstone kill a man, but he kept silent about the murder for nearly two decades. Years later, he finally gathered evidence of the murder and Tombstone's other crimes, only for Tombstone to break his back. Robertson recovered and testified against Tombstone in court, receiving a jail sentence of his own for withholding evidence. He resigned from the *Daily Bugle* when Norman Osborn (*see* GREEN GOBLIN) purchased the newspaper, but later returned to the job. His son Randy attended college with Peter Parker, and Robertson is believed to have guessed that Peter Parker was SPIDER-MAN. When Dexter Bennett bought the *Daily Bugle* following J. Jonah JAMESON's heart attack, Robertson left to go work for another newspaper, *Front Line*. After the *DB* was destroyed by ELECTRO, the Jamesons bought the paper back and gave Robertson the money to transform *Front Line* into the new *Daily Bugle*.

FACTFILE
REAL NAME
Joseph Robertson
OCCUPATION
Editor-in-chief of the *Daily Bugle*
BASE
New York City

HEIGHT 6 ft 1 in
WEIGHT 210 lbs
EYES Brown
HAIR White

FIRST APPEARANCE
Amazing Spider-Man #51 (August 1967)

POWERS
Highly skilled writer and dogged investigative reporter.

ROCKET RACCOON

ROCKET RACCOON

FACTFILE

REAL NAME
Rocket Raccoon

OCCUPATION
Adventurer

BASE
Mobile

HEIGHT 4 ft 0 in
WEIGHT 25 lbs
EYES Brown
HAIR Black, brown, and white

FIRST APPEARANCE
Marvel Preview #7 (June 1976)

POWERS

Rocket is an evolved raccoon who stands on his hind legs and speaks. He is an excellent combatant and tactician.

Rocket Raccoon was the chief guardian on Halfworld, a planet on which animals had been forcibly evolved to help provide care for an outpost of insane humanoids. The Hulk arrived and helped Rocket and his first mate Wal Rus rescue Rocket's girlfriend, the evolved otter Lylla, from the evolved mole Judson Jakes. He later helped Star-Lord stop the second Annihilation and then joined the Guardians of the Galaxy, helping to bring the team back together after it disbanded. Rocket introduced Groot to the team, the two becoming firm friends. He also learned that his memories of Halfworld were fake, and Halfworld had actually been an Asylum for the Criminally Insane at which Rocket had been a guard. His physical form had been created by the hospital's doctor, who believed anthropomorphic animals would calm the patients. Rocket has also led the Guardians when Star-Lord had been absent.

ROCKET RACER

FIRST APPEARANCE *Amazing Spider-Man* #172 (September 1977)
REAL NAME Robert Farrell
OCCUPATION Student **BASE** New York City
HEIGHT 5 ft 10 in **WEIGHT** 160 lbs **EYES** Brown **HAIR** Black
SPECIAL POWERS/ABILITIES Rides jet-powered skateboard to which boots are magnetically attached; mini-rockets on gloves can tear holes in three-inch thick steel.

When Robert Farrell's mother died, he became responsible for his six younger siblings. Realizing he couldn't earn enough to support his family, he turned to a life of crime. He developed a superpowered skateboard and a weapon-equipped costume to become the Rocket Racer. After repeated defeats at the hands of Spider-Man—and several brushes with the law, including a short jail sentence—Robert decided to reform. Later, he joined the Fifty-State Initiative and trained at Camp Hammond. He was also with the Avengers Academy for a while.

ROCKSLIDE

FIRST APPEARANCE *New Mutants* #3 (September 2003)
REAL NAME Santo Vaccarro
OCCUPATION Adventurer
BASE Mobile **HEIGHT** 6 ft 2 in **WEIGHT** 482 lbs
EYES White **HAIR** None
SPECIAL POWERS/ABILITIES Body composed of inorganic granite that can reform itself; superhuman strength, stamina, and durability; formidable hand-to-hand combatant.

Santo Vaccarro was a teenage mutant taken in to the Xavier Institute and selected by Emma Frost to be part of her Hellions team. Santo was something of a brash bully at first, as his powers enable him to create a body out of rock. He once took on the Hulk but was defeated. While in Limbo, he remade his body using rock from that realm—making him impervious to magic. His body has been destroyed several times, but Santo has always managed to reconstruct himself. Despite his sometimes arrogant attitude, he remains exceptionally protective of his friends and teammates.

ROGUE

ROGUE

FACTFILE

REAL NAME
Unrevealed

OCCUPATION
Former terrorist, now adventurer

BASE
The Xavier Institute, Salem Center, New York State

HEIGHT 5 ft 8 in
WEIGHT 120 lbs
EYES Green
HAIR Brown

FIRST APPEARANCE
Avengers Annual #10 (1981)

POWERS

Mutant ability to absorb the memories, knowledge, talents, personality, and physical abilities of another person through physical contact with them.

Orphaned, Rogue ran away from her Mississippi home and was adopted by Mystique and Destiny. Her mutant power manifested itself when she kissed a boy and absorbed his memories. She joined Mystique's Brotherhood of Evil Mutants in her teens. While fighting Ms. Marvel, Rogue absorbed her superhuman strength, durability, and the power of flight. Unable to control her absorption power, Rogue turned to the X-Men for help. Professor X invited her to join them, and she fell in love with Gambit. After the villain Pandemic infected her with the 88 virus, Rogue's skin became lethal to anyone she touched. To save her, Mystique let the infant Hope Summers touch Rogue, which took away her lethal touch and all her absorbed powers and memories. Later, Professor X helped remove the mental blocks that formed when she used her powers, allowing her to control them. She then followed Wolverine to his new Jean Grey School for Higher Learning and joined the Avengers Unity Squad. When Kitty Pryde halted her own wedding to Colossus, Gambit asked Rogue to marry him. She agreed, and they married in front of their teammates.

ROMA

FIRST APPEARANCE *Captain Britain* #1 (January 1985)
REAL NAME Roma **OCCUPATION** Sorceress
BASE Otherworld **HEIGHT** 5 ft 10 in
WEIGHT 135 lbs **EYES** Green **HAIR** Black
SPECIAL POWERS/ABILITIES Sorceress with mystical abilities; casts spells that restore life to the dead or block her own presence or others' presence from detection by organic or technological means.

Daughter of MERLYN, Roma appeared to Brian Braddock as the Goddess of the Northern Skies and gave him the Amulet of Right. The amulet's energy turned him into CAPTAIN BRITAIN, and Roma became one of his advisors. Thinking her father dead, she took over his duties as ruler of Avalon and guardian of the Omniverse, and she oversaw the formation of EXCALIBUR. When Merlyn returned, Roma helped Excalibur defeat him and gave her throne to Captain Britain. Roma seemingly died at her father's hand, but not before she transferred her knowledge to the mutant SAGE. She survived her father's attack and helped Spider-UK when the Inheritors were hunting down Spider-heroes.

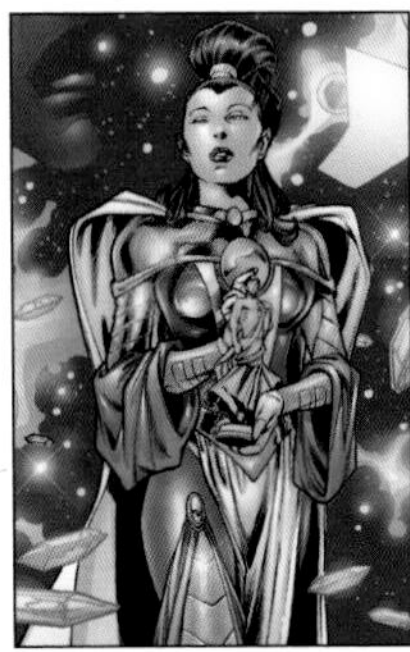

ROMULUS

FIRST APPEARANCE *Wolverine* #50 (March 2007)
REAL NAME Romulus **OCCUPATION** Tyrant
BASE Unknown
HEIGHT 7 ft **WEIGHT** 300 lbs **EYES** Red **HAIR** White
SPECIAL POWERS/ABILITIES Immortal Lupine.

Romulus was the leader of the Lupines, a group of feral mutants he claimed were descended from wolves instead of primates. Thousands of years old, he was once an emperor of Rome. In the 1940s, he murdered WOLVERINE's wife, Itsu, and cut the infant DAKEN from her womb, raising and training him, then pitting him against his father to see which one of them would triumph. Wolverine had CLOAK trap Romulus in the Darkforce Dimension, but SABRETOOTH broke him out. His twin sister Remus helped Wolverine capture him again.

RONAN THE ACCUSER

FIRST APPEARANCE *Fantastic Four* #65 (August 1967)
REAL NAME Ronan **OCCUPATION** Supreme Public Accuser
BASE Citadel of Judgement, on planet Kree-Lar
HEIGHT 7 ft 5 in **WEIGHT** 480 lbs **EYES** Blue **HAIR** Unknown
SPECIAL POWERS/ABILITIES Wields Universal Weapon—fires concussive energy bolts, disintegrates matter, creates force-fields.

Born to an aristocratic KREE family, Ronan was accepted into the Accuser Corps and rose to the position of Supreme Public Accuser. After failing to punish the FANTASTIC FOUR for defeating a Kree Sentry, his humiliation drove him to plot to take over the Empire himself during the Kree-SKRULL War, but Rick JONES stopped him. During the ANNIHILATION, Ronan euthanized a lobotomized SUPREME INTELLIGENCE and finally took over as Kree ruler. To strengthen the Kree, he agreed to cede his position to BLACK BOLT if CRYSTAL agreed to marry him. The pair grew to love each other, but separated at Black Bolt's request. He later joined the ANNIHILATORS and remains a loyal Kree warrior.

ROSE, THE

FIRST APPEARANCE (JC) *Daredevil* #131 (March 1976); (RF) *Amazing Spider-Man* #83 (April 1970)
REAL NAME Jacob Conover; Richard Fisk **OCCUPATION** (JC) columnist; (RF) crime lord **BASE** (JC & RF) New York City
HEIGHT (JC) 6 ft; (RF) 6 ft 2 in **WEIGHT** (JC) 210 lbs; (RF) 225 lbs
EYES (JC) brown; (RF) brown
SPECIAL POWERS/ABILITIES (JC & RF) criminal masterminds, manipulators, and strategists.

The first leather-masked Rose was Richard Fisk, the son of criminal KINGPIN. Fisk believed that his father was an honest businessman. When he learned the truth, he tried to ruin his father's empire and became a member of HYDRA. Fisk eventually joined forces with his father and became the Rose, but was killed by his mother. The second Rose was a police officer seeking revenge on the Kingpin. The third Rose was Jacob Conover, a *Daily Bugle* journalist given the identity as a reward for saving crime lord Don Fortunato. SPIDER-MAN put him in prison. The fourth Rose, Philip Hayes, worked with Jackpot in her secret identity and ordered her husband's murder. He was eventually killed by MORBIUS.

ROSS, GENERAL T. E.

FIRST APPEARANCE *Incredible Hulk* #1 (May 1962)
REAL NAME Thaddeus E. Ross
NICKNAME Thunderbolt
OCCUPATION Lieutenant General, US Air Force **BASE** Mobile
HEIGHT 6 ft 1 in **WEIGHT** 245 lbs **EYES** Blue **HAIR** White
SPECIAL POWERS/ABILITIES Is a capable combatant and has an advanced military mind.

General Ross' troops nicknamed him Thunderbolt because he struck like a thunderbolt in combat. After Bruce Banner transformed into the HULK, General Ross became obsessed with him. Ross worked alongside Colonel Glenn TALBOT, who married his daughter Betty Ross. She later left Talbot and married Bruce. For a time, Ross possessed the electrical form of Zzzax. He later seemed to be killed, but the INTELLIGENCIA stole his body and transformed him into the RED HULK. After the Hulk depowered Ross, the general was arrested by the military for desertion, but ultimately freed for his role fighting the HYDRA version of CAPTAIN AMERICA. Ross was then given a new position in the military.

ROSS, BETTY

The Hulk's beloved

IT SEEMS ONLY YESTERDAY WHEN I FIRST MET BRUCE... BEFORE THE HORROR OF THE HULK CAME BETWEEN US!

Betty Banner met her one-day husband Bruce when she came to live on a New Mexico military base with her father, Thunderbolt Ross.

The only daughter of renowned military general Thaddeus "Thunderbolt" Ross, Betty spent her formative years firmly under her father's thumb. Thunderbolt Ross had wanted a son, and had no use for his unfortunate daughter; after her mother died during Betty's teenage years, she was sent away to boarding school. After graduating, she returned to her father's side, a repressed wallflower. Thunderbolt Ross was then in charge of a top-secret project to create a new type of weapon employing the limitless power of gamma radiation. The head scientist on the project was the quiet, bookish Bruce Banner, and an attraction between Betty and Banner soon developed.

FACTFILE
REAL NAME
Elizabeth Ross
OCCUPATION
Adventurer
BASE
Mobile

HEIGHT 5 ft 6 in
WEIGHT 110 lbs
EYES Blue
HAIR Brown

FIRST APPEARANCE
Incredible Hulk #1
(May 1962)

ROSS, BETTY

POWERS
No superhuman powers, but courageous and resourceful; steadfastly loyal to her husband Bruce Banner through many shared tribulations.

TRAGIC LOVE

Their relationship was forever changed when, during the gamma-bomb test, Banner was struck by the full force of the detonation, and its radiations transformed him into the HULK whenever he grew angry. Banner tried to keep his condition secret from Betty, which only served to alienate them. Betty was then ardently pursued by Major Glenn Talbot (*see* TALBOT, Glenn), the new aide attached to her father's Hulkbuster task force. Eventually, the secret of Banner's dual identity became public knowledge, and his transformations and rampages created a rift between Betty and himself. With no one else to turn to, Betty married Major Talbot. Their union soon ended in divorce, however, and Talbot died attempting to destroy the Hulk.

HULKS AND HARPIES

MODOK used gamma rays to turn Betty into a flying menace known as the Harpy, who attacked the Hulk, but Banner cured her. Despite her father's objections, she eventually married him. Later, the ABOMINATION used his gamma-irradiated blood to poison and kill Betty, hoping to pin the crime on Bruce. Her father kept her body in cryogenic storage. After he became the RED HULK, he urged the LEADER and MODOK to use the same process on Betty to revive her, turning her into the Red She-Hulk. No one outside of their group knew who she was until Hulk's son SKAAR stabbed her and she reverted to human form. The Hulk, in the guise of "Doc Green" later depowered her.

While her relationship with Banner remained troubled, she mourned him when the world believed Banner had been killed by HAWKEYE.

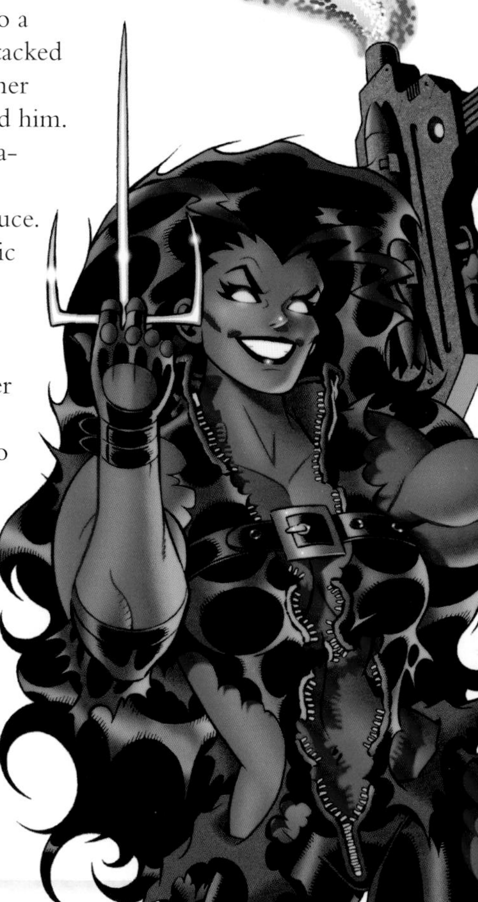

As the Red She-Hulk, Betty was far more aggressive than when she was her normal self.

ESSENTIAL STORYLINES
- ***Hulk Vol. 2 #168–169***
MODOK transforms Betty into the Harpy.
- ***Hulk Vol. 2 #319***
After years of courtship and chaos, Bruce Banner finally marries Betty.
- ***Hulk Vol. 2 #465–469***
Betty is exposed to radiation poisoning; Bruce desperately tries to save her.

ROTH, ARNOLD

FIRST APPEARANCE *Captain America* #270 (May 1982)
REAL NAME Arnold "Arnie" Roth
OCCUPATION Sailor; later publicist; later costume shop manager
BASE New York City
HEIGHT Unknown **WEIGHT** Unknown **EYES** Blue **HAIR** Gray
SPECIAL POWERS/ABILITIES Possessed the normal human strength of a man of his age who engaged in mild exercise.

Arnold Roth became friends with Steve Rogers when they were growing up in the 1930s. During World War II, Roth served in the US Navy and realized that CAPTAIN AMERICA was his friend Steve. While Captain America spent years in suspended animation, Roth aged normally. Learning of Roth's friendship with Captain America, Baron Helmut Zemo (*see* BARON ZEMO) imperiled Roth and his life partner, Michael. Later, the RED SKULL captured Roth. Captain America and Roth remained friends. Roth worked as the AVENGERS' publicist and managed Steve Rogers' costume shop before dying from bone cancer.

RUIZ, "RIGGER"

FIRST APPEARANCE *The Mighty Thor* #426 (November 1990)
REAL NAME Margarita Allegra "Rigger" Ruiz
OCCUPATION Police officer **BASE** New York City
HEIGHT Unknown **WEIGHT** Unknown
EYES Unknown **HAIR** Black
SPECIAL POWERS/ABILITIES Adept with range of weaponry; she invented "port-a-pulley" for easy navigation of elevator shafts.

Margarita Allegra "Rigger" Ruiz is the armory specialist of Code: Blue, a SWAT team designated to deal with superpowered criminals. Bodybuilder Rigger has come face-to-face with these superhumans on a regular basis and her experiences have been many and varied. The strongest member of Code: Blue, Rigger has rescued hostages from the WRECKING CREW, been driven mad by the Super Villain Dementia, and posed as a slave during a mission to Asgard. During this last assignment, Rigger also flirted with Fandral the Dashing, an Asgardian noble—life is never dull in Code: Blue.

RUSSIAN, THE

FIRST APPEARANCE *Punisher* #8 (November 2000)
REAL NAME Unrevealed
OCCUPATION Mercenary **BASE** Mobile
HEIGHT 7 ft 2 in **WEIGHT** 573 lbs
EYES Blue **HAIR** Reddish-blond
SPECIAL POWERS/ABILITIES Post-reconstruction, the Russian possessed enhanced strength and damage resistance.

The mercenary nicknamed "The Russian" accepted a job from crime boss Ma Gnucci to kill the PUNISHER. After a brutal fight, the Punisher smothered the Russian, later taunting Ma Gnucci by showing her the Russian's severed head. A secret paramilitary agency then resurrected the Russian, giving him an enhanced body with boosted olfactory senses, three hearts, and a toughened skeleton. This new body required regular injections of female hormones. The Russian apparently died when he was caught in the explosion of a nuclear warhead on Grand Nixon Island.

RUNAWAYS

When Alex Wilder was growing up he was forced to hang around with the children of his parents' friends once a year—Nico MINORU, Karolina Dean, Molly Hayes, Chase STEIN, and Gertrude Yorkes. When the six of them witnessed their parents sacrifice a teenage girl, they realized that their parents were Super Villains and part of a group called the Pride. The teenagers stole tech and equipment from their parents, and went on the run as the Runaways, eventually bringing their parents to justice. Alex died in this effort (although later returned) and Nico took over as leader as they fought to prevent other villains taking over the space left by the Pride. In time, other teens joined them, including Victor MANCHA, the cybernetic son of ULTRON.

RUNAWAYS
1 Gertrude Yorkes
2 Old Lace
3 Nico Minoru
4 Chase Stein
5 Karolina Dean
6 Molly Hayes

RUNAWAYS

FACTFILE

KEY MEMBERS

ALEX WILDER
Natural leader with genius intelligence.

NICO MONORU
Uses blood magic and the Staff of One to cast spells.

KAROLINA DEAN
Majesdanian with solar powers.

MOLLY HAYES
Super strong and invulnerable.

GERT YORKES
No powers, but telepathically and empathically linked to Old Lace, her deinonychus from the future.

CHASE STEIN
Skilled athlete; shares a link with Old Lace.

VICTOR MANCHA
Android built by Ultron to infiltrate the Avengers.

BASE
Secret location, Los Angeles, California

FIRST APPEARANCE
Runaways #1 (July 2003)

RYKER, GENERAL J.

FIRST APPEARANCE *Incredible Hulk* #14 (May 2000)
REAL NAME General John Ryker
OCCUPATION Senior general in US Army
BASE Currently unknown **HEIGHT** 6 ft 2 in **WEIGHT** 190 lbs
EYES Brown **HAIR** Gray
SPECIAL POWERS/ABILITIES Brilliant manipulator, possesses intuitive understanding of people's emotional vulnerabilities; exceptional strategist, excels at seeing big picture; inveterate liar; impervious to the suffering of others.

Desperate to find a cure for his wife's cancer, US Army General John Ryker became obsessed with the idea that the HULK's biology held the answers. To unlock those secrets, he tormented Banner and used both vagrants and soldiers as his test subjects. One man became a corrupt version of the Hulk, code-named FLUX. When Ryker's wife, Lucy, learned about her husband's actions from General Ross, she rebuked him, wanting no part in his methods. Ryker formed the Gamma Corps—a team of gamma-powered soldiers with grudges against the Hulk. Ryker set them on his old foe, but one member, Grey, later lost his temper and brought Ryker's headquarters down on the general.

SABRETOOTH

Wolverine's nemesis

SABRETOOTH

FACTFILE

REAL NAME
Victor Creed

OCCUPATION
Assassin

BASE
Mobile

HEIGHT 6 ft 6 in
WEIGHT 275 lbs
EYES Amber
HAIR Blond

FIRST APPEARANCE
Iron Fist #14
(August 1977)

POWERS

Sabretooth possesses an extended lifespan, thanks to the healing ability that also allows him to recover rapidly from any injury. He also possesses enhanced animalistic strength, speed and agility, and razor-sharp claws on each hand.

Sabretooth was chained up as a child due to his feral nature.

Young mutant Victor Creed was treated as an animal growing up, raised by an abusive father and kept chained in the family cellar for much of his early life, until he chewed off his own hand to escape and killed his father. Logan (Wolverine) killed Victor's younger brother, Saul, when Saul betrayed Logan to Mister Sinister. Years later, Creed took the life of Logan's lover, Silver Fox, as retaliation. Like Logan's, Sabretooth's abilities were enhanced by the top-secret Weapon X project and the two fought together on various missions—with Victor taking the code name Sabretooth. He later had a son, Graydon, with Mystique. Following the collapse of the Weapon X project, Sabretooth became a mercenary, gaining a reputation as one of the world's most ruthless killers. He also took part in the Morlock Massacre as part of the Marauders.

ESSENTIAL STORYLINES
- ***Wolverine #10***
A flashback to an early Wolverine/Sabretooth face off.
- ***Sabretooth #1***
Sabretooth gets his own mini-series.

A FALSE DEATH

Over the years, Sabretooth has been imprisoned by the X-Men and even forced to work with X-Force many times. Wolverine once killed him with the Muramasa Blade, a weapon no healing factor could counter, only to later learn that his victim had been a clone created by manipulative Lupine Romulus. The real Sabretooth re-emerged in the Far East and slaughtered the crimelords there, declaring himself the invisible king of Asia. He later joined Daken's new Brotherhood of Evil Mutants and another lineup with Mystique as leader.

When he helped fight Red Onslaught (*see* Red Skull) a spell turned him into a hero. He became part of the Avengers Unity Squad and Magneto's X-Men. While the effects of the inversion started to recede, Creed made a conscious decision to reform his ways. This was partly down to the influence of Monet St. Croix (M). He also worked with Old Man Logan in a new Weapon X team before they broke away from Logan and renamed themselves Weapon X-Force.

Sabretooth's powers made him a skilled tracker.

Sabretooth's "final" showdown with Wolverine, after years of conflict.

SABAHNUR, EVAN

FIRST APPEARANCE *Uncanny X-Force* #7 (June 2011)
REAL NAME Evan Sabahnur
OCCUPATION Fugitive
BASE Xavier Institute for Mutant Education and Outreach
HEIGHT Unknown **WEIGHT** Unknown
EYES Black **HAIR** Black
SPECIAL POWERS/ABILITIES Capable of shapeshifting and projecting energy blasts. He can also exhibit a seemingly unlimited range of supernatural powers as he learns them.

Evan is a young clone of the mutant villain APOCALYPSE, created by FANTOMEX. He was used by Fantomex to defeat Archangel (*see* ANGEL), the Horseman of Death. He attended the Jean Grey School for Higher Learning, where DEATHLOK warned that Evan would grow up to be either their greatest hero or their destruction. He later joined the time-displaced X-MEN. When he turned sixteen, he and Hank McCoy (BEAST) were transported to ancient Egypt and met the original En Sabah Nur, a young Apocalypse. En Sabah Nur tried to help them but was caught by his abusive father as Evan and Hank escaped to the present.

SABRA

FIRST APPEARANCE *The Incredible Hulk* #250 (August 1980)
REAL NAME Ruth Bat-Seraph
OCCUPATION Police officer; Israeli government agent
BASE Jerusalem, Israel **HEIGHT** 5 ft 11 in
WEIGHT 240 lbs **EYES** Brown **HAIR** Black
SPECIAL POWERS/ABILITIES Wrist bracelets equipped with neuronic-frequency stunners that shoot "energy quills." Cape has a device that neutralizes gravity, enabling flight; superhuman strength.

When Ruth Bat-Seraph's mutant powers emerged, the Israeli government sent her to live at a special kibbutz where she was trained to use them. As an adult, she became the first member of Mossad's super-agent program. After terrorists killed her son, she disobeyed orders and brought them down. She fought alongside the X-MEN and worked for the X-Corporation in Paris. After the CIVIL WAR, she returned to Israel and fought the SKRULLS during the SECRET INVASION. She was shot by CROSSBONES, but survived, and later worked against Hydra's takeover of the US.

SAGE

FIRST APPEARANCE *Uncanny X-Men* #132 (April 1980)
REAL NAME Unrevealed, goes by "Tessa"
OCCUPATION Member of New Excalibur **BASE** England
HEIGHT 5 ft 7 in **WEIGHT** 135 lbs **EYES** Blue **HAIR** Black
SPECIAL POWERS/ABILITIES Able to remember everything she sees and hears; can "jump start" the mutant abilities of others; possesses limited telepathy.

Born in Eastern Europe, the mysterious Sage rescued an injured PROFESSOR X from Afghanistan and became one of his first mutant recruits. Rather than joining the original X-MEN, Sage became a spy within the HELLFIRE CLUB, working as an advisor to Sebastian SHAW. When she tricked the mind-controlling Elias Bogan into losing a wager, he scarred her face. Rescued by STORM, Sage joined the X-Men and later NEW EXCALIBUR. Later, she was recruited into the EXILES and went dimension hopping, but she's since returned to Earth.

ST. LAWRENCE, COL.

FIRST APPEARANCE *Incredible Hulk* #446 (October 1996)
REAL NAME Colonel Cary St. Lawrence
OCCUPATION US Army officer **BASE** Mobile
HEIGHT/WEIGHT Unrevealed **EYES** Brown **HAIR** Black
SPECIAL POWERS/ABILITIES Skilled military strategist, highly trained athlete, adept with variety of weaponry.

When she was a cadet at West Point academy, General "Thunderbolt" Ross was dismissive about Cary St. Lawrence's chances of a successful career in the military. Inspired to work even harder to prove him wrong, Cary graduated third in her class.

Assigned to capture the HULK, Cary proved to be unusually effective in her dealings with the green fiend. At first she favored brute force during her encounters with the creature, but soon came to realize that there was no point in employing strong-arm tactics: after all, the Hulk only got more powerful the angrier he became. She thus began to use more subtle approaches to subdue the creature. Perhaps all the Hulk has ever needed is a woman's touch.

SABRECLAW

The son of WOLVERINE in the alternate future of Earth-982, Sabreclaw felt jealous of his half-sister Rina (WILD THING) because she had the chance to actually be raised by their father, who didn't know of Hudson's existence for many years. Sabreclaw started out as a villain, battling the A-NEXT (future AVENGERS) team alongside the REVENGERS and fighting SPIDER-GIRL as part of the Savage Six. However, when GALACTUS returned to threaten the Earth, he joined the Avengers and their allied heroes to drive him away. Afterward, he asked to join Avengers, and despite some reservations was accepted.

FACTFILE
REAL NAME
Hudson Howlett
OCCUPATION
Adventurer
BASE
New York City

HEIGHT 5 ft 10 in
WEIGHT 198 lbs
EYES Brown
HAIR Brown

FIRST APPEARANCE
J2 #8 (May 1999)

POWERS
Superhuman agility, reflexes, stamina, and strength, plus sharp teeth, Adamantium-laced claws, and a healing factor.

SABRECLAW

SALEM'S SEVEN

The children of Nicolas SCRATCH lived in the isolated village of New Salem, where witches and warlocks held sway. When Scratch's mother, Agatha HARKNESS, left to become the governess of Franklin RICHARDS, Scratch put her on trial for treason, transforming his offspring into Salem's Seven to act as guards. They failed to stop the FANTASTIC FOUR from rescuing her, but later became rulers of New Salem and burned Harkness at the stake. Harkness' spirit led the VISION and the SCARLET WITCH to New Salem, and Salem's Seven died in the battle. When the Scarlet Witch returned them to life, Scratch tricked the Seven into releasing the demon Shuma-Gorath. DOCTOR STRANGE, the Fantastic Four, and DIABLO intervened. They become the guardians of New Salem's magical residents, however the WIZARD recruited three of them to join his FRIGHTFUL FOUR and fight MISTER FANTASTIC.

Salem's Seven first appeared in the pages of the Fantastic Four as diabolical, sorcerous opponents for the science-based team led by Mr. Fantastic.

SALEM'S SEVEN
1 Brutacus
2 Hydron
3 Vakume
4 Vertigo
5 Thornn
6 Reptilla
7 Gazelle

FACTFILE

FORMER MEMBERS

BRUTACUS
Enhanced strength.

GAZELLE
Superhuman agility and reflexes.

HYDRON
Able to blast water from left arm.

REPTILLA
Fanged arm-snakes could bite and constrict.

THORNN
Ability to fire explosive spines.

VAKUME
Could drain air or energy, and assume an intangible state.

VERTIGO
Power to induce dizziness in others.

BASE
New Salem, Colorado

FIRST APPEARANCE
Fantastic Four #186 (September 1977)

SANDMAN, SEE PAGE 306

SASQUATCH

FACTFILE

REAL NAME
Walter Langkowski

OCCUPATION
Scientist; adventurer

BASE
Canada

HEIGHT 10 ft
WEIGHT 2000 lbs
EYES Red
HAIR Orange

FIRST APPEARANCE
Uncanny X-Men #120 (April 1979)

POWERS
Sasquatch possesses superhuman strength and greatly enhanced resistance to injury, and is able to leap enormous distances. He can shift between his normal human form and his Sasquatch body at will.

Inspired by Bruce Banner's metamorphosis into the HULK, Dr. Walter Langkowski was experimenting with gamma radiation when he breached the realm of the Great Beasts and was possessed by a spirit called Tanaraq, who gave him his powers. He became a member of ALPHA FLIGHT and later took part in Alpha Flight's Space Program, but as he spent more time as Sasquatch, he became susceptible to possession by the spirit of Bruce Banner's dead father, Brian Banner. Walter sought Bruce out to ask for help.

In Alpha Flight, Sasquatch often came to blows with members of the X-Men.

SATANA

FIRST APPEARANCE *Vampire Tales* #2 (October 1973)
REAL NAME Satana Hellstrom
OCCUPATION Hero **BASE** Mobile
HEIGHT 5 ft 7 in **WEIGHT** 120 lbs
EYES Black with red highlights **HAIR** Red
SPECIAL POWERS/ABILITIES Levitation and limited spellcasting; could feed on human souls and project bolts of "soulfire."

The half-human daughter of the demon Satan—and the half-sister of Daimon Hellstrom (HELLSTORM)—for a time Satana was forced to live as a succubus, draining the spirits of humans to survive. Rebelling at this, Satana became estranged from her father and started to appreciate human society. Learning that DOCTOR STRANGE was trapped in the form of a werewolf, Satana traveled to the astral realm and freed his soul. The price was her own life but Strange later resurrected her. Later, after becoming ruler of her own Hell, she unsuccessfully tried to commandeer Doctor Strange's soul as a tourist attraction.

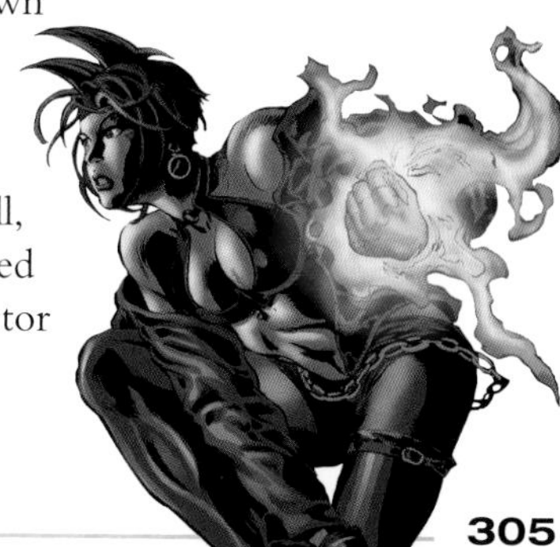

SANDMAN

The villain who slips through Spidey's fingers

SANDMAN

FACTFILE

REAL NAME
William Baker

OCCUPATION
Former professional criminal

BASE
Brooklyn, New York

HEIGHT 6 ft 1 in
WEIGHT 450 lbs
EYES Brown
HAIR Brown

FIRST APPEARANCE
Amazing Spider-Man #4 (September 1963)

POWERS
Sandman is able to change all or part of his body into a sand-like substance which he can form into any shape. He can spread out the grains of sand in his body to avoid attack, project them outward at high speeds, or harden them into a super-powered weapon.

With the ability to change his body into grains of sand and reshape it at will, Sandman has proven to be a dangerous and slippery foe for Spider-Man, the Fantastic Four, and the Hulk. Born William Baker in one of the rougher areas of New York City, he had a bad start in life. His father abandoned him and his mother when William was three years old, and the boy grew up in poverty. He quickly learned to steal and cheat.

A LIFE OF CRIME

William was kicked out of high school for taking money to throw a big football game, but soon found work with a protection racket. He took the alias "Flint Marko," and became a success in New York's crime underworld. After an arrest and a jailbreak, Marko headed south. He was on a beach near a military testing site in Georgia when a nuclear reactor's steam system exploded, knocking him unconscious. Marko woke to find that his body now had the properties of sand. Reveling in his new ability, he called himself Sandman and set out on a major criminal career. Sandman battled Spider-Man (his main nemesis), and many other Super Heroes. He joined the Wizard, Trapster, and Medusa to form the Frightful Four and teamed up with five more of Spider-Man's foes to form the Sinister Six.

ESSENTIAL STORYLINES
- ***Amazing Spider-Man Annual #1*** Sandman, Vulture, Mysterio, Electro, Kraven the Hunter, and Doctor Octopus get together to form the Sinister Six.
- ***Amazing Spider-Man #217–218*** Sandman teams up with Hydro-Man, but a freak accident merges the two villains into a mud creature.

GOOD OR EVIL?

When Sandman teamed up with Hydro-Man, an accident caused the two to merge into a mud creature. After he was freed, Sandman gave up crime, becoming a probationary member of the Avengers. The Wizard brainwashed him into becoming a criminal again, thinking he'd been faking his turn toward good, and he rejoined the Sinister Six. Venom destroyed Sandman, but he reconstituted himself, and later discovered he could create duplicates of himself with distinct personalities. Some of these duplicates murdered the mother of his daughter Keemia without his knowledge. The Superior Spider-Man (Doctor Octopus) later stole him from where the Fantastic Four had imprisoned him and stored him in an underwater lab. A spell cast by Scarlet Witch caused Sandman to temporarily return to his heroic ways, but he reverted to villainy when the spell was reversed and went on to join a new iteration of the Sinister Six.

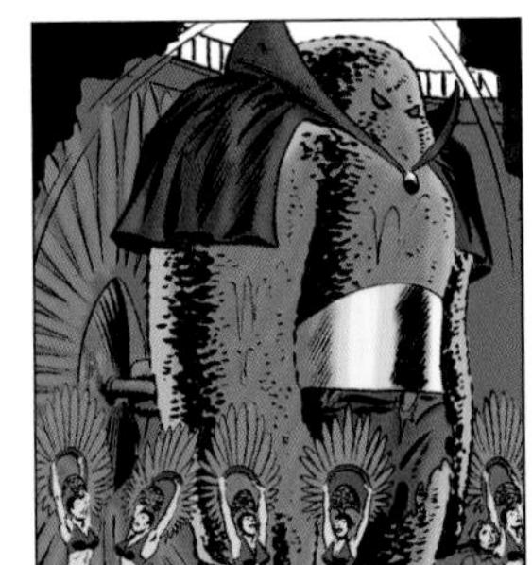
When Sandman and Hydro-Man combined they became the Mud-Thing. The new creature proved to be a big attraction.

SANDS OF THE FUTURE

Sandman struggled to hold a human form and appeared to be dying. He was also forced to see memories from his past and visions of a future he didn't yet realize was his. Spider-Man took him to the beach, where Sandman's human body fell apart but his consciousness lived on in a grain of sand. He realized that a version of himself from billions of years in the future had traveled back in time to take over his body. The present Sandman gave Spider-Man his sand powers temporarily to fight the future Sandman. With the Human Torch's help, they sent the alternate Sandman back to his time. The present Sandman had to deal with the realization that he is immortal and will outlive the universe itself.

Spider-Man quickly learned how to use his temporary new powers to fight the future Sandman with sand.

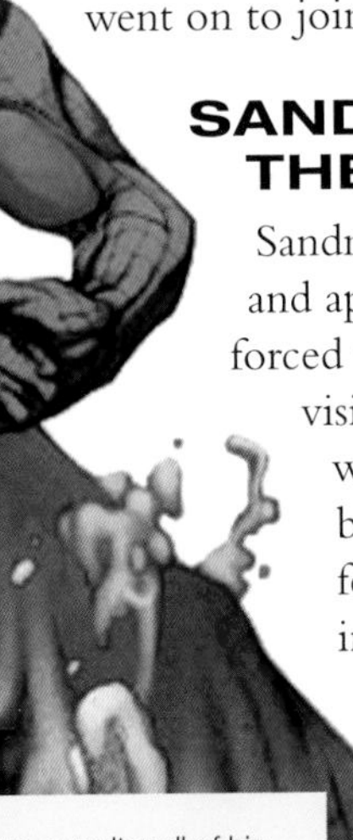
Sandman can alter all of his body at once or just selective parts, as in this example of his right arm changing while the rest of his body remains in its human-looking form.

SAURON

FIRST APPEARANCE *X-Men* #59 (August 1969)
REAL NAME Dr. Karl Lykos
OCCUPATION Geneticist; hypnotherapist
BASE New York City, Savage Land
HEIGHT 7 ft **WEIGHT** 200 lbs **EYES** Red **HAIR** None
SPECIAL POWERS/ABILITIES Drains victims' life forces into his own body. Uses eye contact to hypnotize and induce hallucinations.

Young Karl Lykos was in Antarctica when he was bitten by a pteranodon from the Savage Lands. Thereafter, he had to feed off the life energy of others to survive. As an adult, he transformed into an evil half-human, half-pteranodon creature after attacking HAVOK. He took the name Sauron, became an enemy of the X-MEN, and returned to the Savage Land. During the SECRET INVASION, he fought beside KA-ZAR and SHANNA THE SHE-DEVIL against the SKRULLS. Later, he returned to the US and joined the Hellfire Academy. Then with Stegron, he tried, but failed, to take over Staten Island. Later, he returned to the Savage Land once more and enslaved its people, until they turned on him.

SCARLET CENTURION

In the year 3000 of Earth-6311, Earth is a utopia, founded centuries earlier by Nathaniel RICHARDS, father of Reed Richards (MR. FANTASTIC). However this paradise does not suit everyone. One distant descendant of Richards, a man known as the Scarlet Centurion, feels suffocated by his surroundings. Learning that one of his ancestors built a time machine, the Centurion recreates this device and wreaks chaos across multiple realities and times zones.

Arriving in ancient Egypt, the Centurion became the pharaoh Rama-Tut—until the FANTASTIC FOUR forced him back to the future. Since then, he has also become KANG the Conqueror and IMMORTUS at various times, as well as the YOUNG AVENGER known as Iron Lad. The one-time ruler of 30th-century Earth, he has tried to conquer the present-day world many times, only to be defeated by the Fantastic Four or the AVENGERS. One of his sons (the 23rd) also called himself the Scarlet Centurion and worked with him while he was Kang. After another failure to conquer the world, Kang stabbed him and put him in stasis.

FACTFILE
REAL NAME
Nathaniel Richards
OCCUPATION
Conqueror
BASE
Mobile

HEIGHT 6 ft 3 in
WEIGHT 230 lbs
EYES Brown
HAIR Brown, later gray

FIRST APPEARANCE
Avengers Annual #2 (September 1968)

SCARLET CENTURION

POWERS
Master of numerous far future technologies; wears battlesuit armed with electrical bolts and concussive force beams; adept time traveler.

For a short time, the second Scarlet Centurion ruled the Earth alongside his father.

SCARLET SPIDER

Professor Miles Warren, the criminal known as the JACKAL, created a clone of Peter Parker, alias SPIDER-MAN. He endowed the clone with Parker's memories and pitted him against Spider-Man. Seemingly killed, the clone revived and wandered America for years, calling himself Ben Reilly. In New York, he became a costumed hero, the Scarlet Spider. The original GREEN GOBLIN manipulated Peter and Ben into believing that Ben was the real Spider-Man, with Ben even adopting Spider-Man's costumed identity. Ultimately, the Goblin killed Ben, and Peter reclaimed his identity.

The JACKAL recovered DNA from Ben's corpse and brought him back to life through cloning, but the process mentally scarred him. Ben managed to knock out, brainwash, and then clone the Jackal. Ben took the Jackal name himself and set up a company named New U. He resurrected many deceased allies and enemies of Spider-Man, but they had to take a daily pill to stay alive. Ben's plans went awry when he angered DOCTOR OCTOPUS, who activated the Carrion virus. This caused all of the clones to degrade, though Parker saved many of them.

Following the failure of New U, Ben moved to Las Vegas and called himself Scarlet Spider once more. While trying to cure the young Abigail Mercury's illness, Ben ran into KAINE, who wanted to kill him, but let him live until he found a cure. Ben then met DEATH, who explained that if Ben was resurrected one more time his soul would be fragmented for good. Due to MEPHISTO's machinations, Kaine killed Ben, but Ben was brought back to life by Abigail (who had gained temporary angelic powers). Embracing villainy, Ben wounded Kaine and told him to leave Las Vegas if he survived the injury.

Reilly actually fought a second Scarlet Spider, one the second DOCTOR OCTOPUS (Carolyn Trainer) fashioned out of FBI agent Joe Wade and a virtual reality graft of holograph technology. Later, triplet clones of Michael VAN PATRICK donned suits of Spider-Man's Iron Spider armor, designed by IRON MAN. Two of them were killed in action. Later, Kaine adopted the Scarlet Spider identity, even when Ben returned from the dead and reclaimed the title.

FACTFILE
REAL NAME
Ben Reilly
OCCUPATION
Adventurer
BASE
New York City

HEIGHT 5 ft 10 in
WEIGHT 165 lbs
EYES Hazel
HAIR Brown

FIRST APPEARANCE
(as Scarlet Spider)
Web of Spider-Man #118 (November 1994)

SCARLET SPIDER

POWERS
Super-strength and agility, able to adhere to surfaces; spider-sense alerts him to danger. Wore web-shooters that projected artificial webbing.

SCARLET WITCH

Magical mistress of "Hex Power"

SCARLET WITCH

FACTFILE

REAL NAME
Wanda Maximoff, aka Wanda Frank, Wanda Magnus

OCCUPATION
Adventurer

BASE
Europe

HEIGHT 5 ft 7 in
WEIGHT 130 lbs
EYES Blue
HAIR Auburn

FIRST APPEARANCE
X-Men #4
(March 1964)

POWERS

Possesses ability to affect probability fields and cause unlikely events to occur. Can make objects spontaneously burst into flame, rust, or decay. Her "hex bolts" can also deflect flying objects and disrupt energy transmissions or fields.

After Magneto rescued the Scarlet Witch from certain death, she and her brother Quicksilver became members of his Brotherhood of Evil Mutants.

For years, Wanda Maximoff and her twin brother, Pietro (Quicksilver), believed Magneto was their father. Supposedly their mother had fled from Magneto while she was pregnant and, fearing her husband would exploit her unborn children, gave her twins up for adoption.

SOCIAL OUTCAST

The twins were raised in the eastern European country of Transia by a Romani couple named Django and Marya, and Wanda soon learned that she could cause strange things to happen. After accidentally making a house burst into flames, she was about to be stoned as a witch when Magneto arrived and saved her. Wanda and Pietro took on costumed identities and joined Magneto's war against humanity. After many battles with the X-Men, the twins abandoned Magneto and later joined the Avengers in return for full pardons for their past crimes. Wanda became attracted to the synthezoid called the Vision and began a long romance with him; they were eventually married.

The Scarlet Witch and the Vision were married in the same ceremony that united Mantis and the Cotati.

TROUBLED SOUL

Wanda began to study real magic, combining it with her natural mutant abilities. She eventually grew powerful enough to defeat the dreaded Dormammu. However, her increased power came at a terrible cost. She conjured up imaginary children and experienced temporary bouts of insanity. The Vision was later disassembled by the US after trying to seize control of every computer on Earth. He was rebuilt, but he no longer possessed emotions, and his relationship with Wanda ended in divorce. Wanda suffered another breakdown and destroyed the Avengers Mansion, killing a number of teammates. Still unbalanced, she later used her powers to warp reality so that her father ruled the world (House of M), and when she was stopped she removed the mutant gene and powers from most of the world (M-Day). It turned out that Doctor Doom had helped her channel too much power in an effort to bring her children back, and this had driven her mad. He later stole her powers but was equally unable to handle them.

Through gestures and mental concentration, the Scarlet Witch creates finite pockets of force that can disrupt reality. She can hurl these "hex-spheres" at her intended targets.

When the Avengers battled the X-Men over the Phoenix Force, Wanda returned to the Avengers, despite the Vision's objections. With Hope Summers' help, she erased the Phoenix Force, an act that repowered mutantkind again.

While fighting Red Onslaught, Wanda and Pietro learned that Magneto was not their father. They later learned the High Evolutionary had stolen them as babies and given them their powers. Wanda spent some time working alone and met her real mother, Natalya Maximoff—who had also called herself the Scarlet Witch. Wanda rejoined the Avengers but was possessed by the evil god Chthon during the Hydra Captain America's time in power. Doctor Strange later freed her from Chthon's influence.

Suffering from a breakdown, the Scarlet Witch drastically altered reality, disassembling the Avengers team and eliminating many of Earth's mutants.

ESSENTIAL STORYLINES

- ***Avengers: The Yesterday Quest (tpb)***
The Scarlet Witch learns her true origins.
- ***The Vision and Scarlet Witch #1–12***
The Vision and Scarlet Witch leave the Avengers and move to the suburbs.
- ***Avengers: Avengers Disassembled (tpb)***
The Scarlet Witch goes mad and attacks the Avengers, killing many of her former comrades.
- ***House Of M (tpb)***
The Scarlet Witch restructures reality and depowers most of Earth's mutants.

SCHEMER

FIRST APPEARANCE *Amazing Spider-Man* #83 (April 1970)
REAL NAME Richard Fisk
OCCUPATION Criminal mastermind **BASE** New York City
HEIGHT 6 ft 2 in **WEIGHT** 175 lbs **EYES** Blue
HAIR Reddish blond
SPECIAL POWERS/ABILITIES Had the normal strength of a man who engages in regular moderate exercise; was a cunning criminal strategist.

Richard Fisk was devoted to his father Wilson—until he learned that Wilson Fisk was the KINGPIN. Psychologically shattered, Richard secretly became a criminal leader himself, the Schemer, to take revenge on his father. As the Schemer, Richard disguised himself with a face mask that made him look much older. Subsequently Richard became head of a Las Vegas fragment of HYDRA. Still later, Richard took on two more masked identities, the original ROSE and the Blood Rose. Ultimately Richard was shot dead by his own mother, Vanessa.

SCORN

FIRST APPEARANCE *Carnage* #1 (December 2010)
REAL NAME Tanis Nieves
OCCUPATION Adventurer; psychiatrist **BASE** Mobile
HEIGHT 5 ft 5 in **WEIGHT** 115 lbs **EYES** Brown **HAIR** Brown
SPECIAL POWERS/ABILITIES Scorn wears an alien symbiote that grants her superhuman durability, endurance, speed, and strength, as well as accelerated healing, a danger sense, webbing, and wall-crawling. The symbiote can also bond with technology.

Tanis Nieves was a psychiatrist working with SHRIEK until the CARNAGE symbiote bonded with her. Once it found its original host, it abandoned her, but it left an offspring that bonded to her prosthetic arm and later to her. As Scorn, she helped defeat Shriek and Carnage and later partnered with the Mercury Team—a group of soldiers bonded with parts of a symbiote known as Hybrid—to take down Carnage again. Because the symbiote bonded with her arm first, it can change the arm at will.

SCRATCH, NICHOLAS

FIRST APPEARANCE *Fantastic Four* #185 (August 1977)
REAL NAME Nicholas Scratch **OCCUPATION** Warlock
BASE New Salem, Colorado **HEIGHT** 6 ft 3 in
WEIGHT 196 lbs **EYES** Blue **HAIR** Black with white streaks
SPECIAL POWERS/ABILITIES Nicholas Scratch possesses an encyclopedic knowledge of magical incantations and lore and a wide array of sorcerous abilities.

The son of Agatha HARKNESS, the witch who became governess to Franklin RICHARDS, Nicholas Scratch grew up to be leader of the witches of New Salem. Scratch convinced his followers that Agatha had betrayed their existence to the outside world and that she must be executed. When Agatha and Franklin were abducted, the FANTASTIC FOUR came to the rescue. Scratch and his most devoted followers, SALEM'S SEVEN, vainly sought revenge on the Fantastic Four and Agatha. For a while, he worked for the demon DORMAMMU, but after being banished to Hell, he struck a deal with MEPHISTO.

SCORPION

Carmilla Black's parents worked for AIM, which genetically modified her in the womb to give her powers.

Dr. Farley Stillwell had developed a method of giving animals the attributes of other creatures. When newspaper editor J. Jonah JAMESON found out, he asked Stillwell to test it on a human guinea pig, a private investigator named Mac Gargan. Stillwell's amazing procedure gave Gargan the strength and agility of a scorpion. Stillwell also provided him with a specially designed mechanical tail.

Nothing comes without a price and the cost to Gargan—now calling himself the Scorpion—was the loss of his sanity. Contracted to put an end to SPIDER-MAN, it was only by his wits that the wallcrawler defeated the hugely powerful and vengeful Scorpion. Since then, Scorpion has become an assassin-for-hire, and his attempts to defeat Spider-Man have been repeatedly foiled.

Gargan gave up his Scorpion suit to become the new VENOM. As part of the AVENGERS team assembled by Norman Osborn (GREEN GOBLIN), he impersonated Spider-Man. At the end of the DARK REIGN, however, he lost the symbiote. Alistair SMYTHE broke him out of jail and provided him with a new Scorpion suit, which he used to battle the Superior Spider-Man (DOCTOR OCTOPUS). He went on to work as a bodyguard for Tiberius STONE at Alchemax and was part of the BLACK CAT's criminal empire.

Other Scorpions have included a mercenary and former SHIELD employee named Carmilla Black, who has a stinger in her arm that can deliver deadly poison, and a criminal named Elaine Coll, who also wore an upgraded Scorpion suit and called herself Scorpia.

FACTFILE
REAL NAME
MacDonald "Mac" Gargan
OCCUPATION
Assassin-for-hire
BASE
New York City

HEIGHT 6 ft 2 in
WEIGHT 220 lbs
EYES Brown
HAIR Brown

FIRST APPEARANCE
The Amazing Spider-Man #20 (January 1965)

SCORPION

POWERS
Strength greater than Spider-Man's; mechanical tail can be used as a bludgeon or to propel Scorpion 30 ft into the air. Tail has also been equipped with a toxic "sting" and a mechanism to fire electric blasts.

SCOURGE

FACTFILE
ANGEL (Tom Halloway)
Financed Scourges of the Underworld.
SCOURGE I
Gunned down the Enforcer, started killing criminals around the US.
SCOURGE II
Killed Scourge I to keep him from talking.
SCOURGE III
Leaving the group, he became an agent of the Red Skull.
SCOURGE IV
Killed Scourge II, then went after Priscilla Lyons who left the group.
SCOURGE V (Priscilla Lyons)
Left Scourges, incurring their wrath.
CAPRICE (Scourge VI)
Master of disguise, espionage, brain washing, interrogation.
BLOODSTAIN (Scourge VII)
Master of armed and unarmed combat.
DOMINO (Dunsinane)
Encyclopedic knowledge of every costumed hero, villain, organization.

FIRST APPEARANCE
Iron Man #194
(May 1985)

SCOURGE

Scourge was the brother of the criminal known as the Enforcer. Outraged by his brother's behavior, Scourge got a gun, disguised himself as an old woman, and gunned down the Enforcer. He then became obsessed with traveling the country ruthlessly exterminating criminal after criminal, all while disguised.

Known as Scourge of the Underworld, Scourges wanted to rid the world of crime.

Scourge was captured by Captain America and then shot by an unseen assailant. To date, there have been at least nine Scourges of the Underworld. Each Scourge has been assassinated by the following Scourge to keep the previous one from talking. Scourges relied on an investigator named Domino to feed them information about their targets and killed countless villains. Baron von Strucker made Henry Gyrich force Jack Monroe (Nomad) to become a Scourge. Gyrich later did the same thing to Demolition Man.

Demolition Man Dennis Dunphy, the new Scourge, attacks Captain America with his own shield.

SCREAM

FIRST APPEARANCE *Venom: Lethal Protector* #4 (May 1993)
REAL NAME Donna Diego
OCCUPATION Villain **BASE** Mobile
HEIGHT 5 ft 11 in **WEIGHT** 130 lbs **EYES** White **HAIR** Red
SPECIAL POWERS/ABILITIES Symbiote provides enhanced strength, speed, and stamina. Scream's prehensile hair can shape itself into deadly weapons.

Researchers at the Life Foundation laboratories tried to replicate the process that had given rise to Carnage by bonding five workers with alien symbiotes. One of the subjects, a mentally fragile woman named Donna, found that the process drove her further into madness. The five test subjects sought out Venom for help in controlling their symbiotes, but Donna killed her fellow hybrids. As Scream, Donna struggled to reform and help others with symbiotes. In the end, Venom (Eddie Brock) hunted her down and killed her.

SCRIER

FIRST APPEARANCE *The Amazing Spider-Man* #394 (Oct. 1994)
REAL NAME N/A (discovered to be an organization)
OCCUPATION Criminal Cult **BASE** Unrevealed
HEIGHT/WEIGHT/EYES/HAIR N/A
SPECIAL POWERS/ABILITIES Each member of the Scrier is a formidable combatant. The Scrier also have access to an array of sophisticated weaponry.

By wearing identical garb, for centuries the Brotherhood of the Scrier maintained the deception that the Scrier was just one being. It was a clever ploy, disguising the true nature and scope of this worldwide criminal organization. United by their worship of a godlike being, itself called the Scrier, the Brotherhood became especially powerful under a new and mysterious leader who focused the organization's energies on Spider-Man and his clone, Ben Reilly. It emerged that this new leader was in fact Norman Osborn (*see* Green Goblin). Following Osborn's defeat the fate of the Scriers remains uncertain.

***Secret Invasion* see pages 314–315**

SECRET WARRIORS

Nick Fury lost his job as director of SHIELD after a failed coup attempt in Latveria, but he didn't give up trying to save the world. During the Secret Invasion, he assembled a team called the Secret Warriors to help defeat the Skrulls. When Fury learned that Hydra had been controlling SHIELD since its founding—and was now taking over HAMMER from within—he moved to put an end to it, working with Dum Dum Dugan's Howling Commandos. The Secret Warriors also helped defend Asgard at the end of the Dark Reign.

Secret Warriors was composed of three teams. Fury ran the main team, Team White, and two covert teams. Deep-cover agent Alexander Pierce led Team Black, and Fury's son Mikel took charge of Team Gray. In the course of their work, Slingshot lost her arms, and Phobos was killed. Fury secretly killed Hellfire himself after the man betrayed the team to Hydra.

Although no longer with SHIELD, Fury still worked with old friends like Steve Rogers (Captain America).

Fury lost many things, including his son Mikel and the rest of Team Gray.

FACTFILE

DAISY JOHNSON, aka Quake. Can shake people and Earth.
DRUID Alchemist.
HELLFIRE Channels mystical fire through a chain.
MANIFOLD Teleporter.
NICK FURY Former director of SHIELD.
PHOBOS Young god of fear.
SLINGSHOT Superfast runner.
STONEWALL Property-absorbing strongman.

BASE
New York City

FIRST APPEARANCE
Mighty Avengers #13 (July 2008)

SELENE

FIRST APPEARANCE *New Mutants* #9 (November 1983)
REAL NAME Selene Gallio
OCCUPATION Goddess; sorceress; conqueror **BASE** Mobile
HEIGHT 5 ft 10 in **WEIGHT** 130 lbs **EYES** Brown **HAIR** Black
SPECIAL POWERS/ABILITIES Selene is immortal and can siphon the life force from others. She has superhuman durability, endurance, speed, strength, and telepathic powers, including pyrokinesis and the ability to control the minds of those from whom she's siphoned life. She can control darkforce (solid shadow) and has mastered magic.

Born over 17,000 years ago, Selene attempted to commit mass murders in order to ascend to godhood. After fleeing a failed plot in ancient Rome, she founded Nova Roma in Brazil and became the goddess of a cult. Intrigued after meeting the New Mutants, she went to New York and joined the Hellfire Club as its Black Queen. Later, she began animating dead mutants around the world, gathering them for a strike on Genosha. She sacrificed them all, only to be eventually defeated by the X-Men. She later became part of the mysterious Power Elite.

SENTRY

When meth addict Robert Reynolds broke into a secret lab and consumed a glowing Super-Soldier Serum, he developed the power of a thousand exploding suns and went on to become the Sentry, the greatest hero the world had ever known. He later discovered that his archenemy the Void was actually part of his own repressed personality, and he had all memories of the Sentry erased from the world—and from his own mind.

When the memories began to return, Reynolds transformed into the Sentry once more. Enlisting the help of other heroes against the Void, he wound up re-erasing himself.

Reynolds later turned up in the Raft super-prison when Electro started a jailbreak, and joined the Avengers in trying to stop it. At the end of Norman Osborn's Dark Reign, Sentry destroyed Asgard and the Void burst out of him, trying to destroy the world. Thor killed him and carried his body to burn in the sun, but he was remade by the Apocalypse Twins as one of their Horsemen of Death. Doctor Strange and Tony Stark later worked with him to find a way of controlling his strange powers. Reynolds briefly had a normal life, until the Sentry was unleashed once again.

FACTFILE

REAL NAME
Robert Reynolds

OCCUPATION
Adventurer

BASE
Watchtower

HEIGHT 6 ft 2 in
WEIGHT 200 lbs
EYES Blue
HAIR Blond

FIRST APPEARANCE
Sentry #1 (September 2000)

POWERS
Serum provides super-strength, speed, and invulnerability. Can fly and control light.

SECRET EMPIRE

Hydra takes over the world—thanks to Captain America

With Earth and its heroes assailed by challenges on all sides, Captain America makes his move, revealing his allegiance to Hydra and seizing control of the United States.

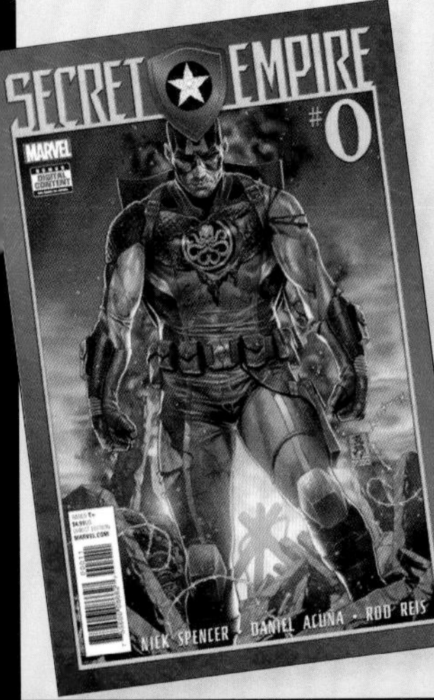

Hoping to rid the world of Super Villains, SHIELD created its own reality-altering Cosmic Cube from fractured pieces. The pieces became child-like KOBIK, who fell under the influence of RED SKULL. At the evil genius' prompting, Kobik replaced CAPTAIN AMERICA (Steve Rogers), head of SHIELD, with an evil version—a sleeper agent for the terrorist organization HYDRA.

The Tony Stark A.I. led the Super Heroes of the Underground on a daring mission to infiltrate Ultron's fortress in Alaska, to retrieve a fragment of Cosmic Cube.

AGENT OF HYDRA

Steve Rogers soon put his plans for Hydra's world conquest into operation. To stretch SHIELD's resources to breaking point, he arranged for Hydra to shut down the Planetary Defense Shield while an invasion force of alien CHITAURI was heading toward Earth; at the same time a band of Super Villains named the Army of Evil attacked Manhattan, and a message broadcast by Hydra agent DR. FAUSTUS brainwashed the crews of SHIELD's Helicarrier fleet. Captain America then reactivated the Planetary Defense Shield, exiling in space the Super Heroes who had gone to face the Chitauri. Those heroes facing the Army of Evil in Manhattan were trapped in a Darkforce Dome and, to complete Hydra's coup, Rogers moved the Helicarrier fleet to Washington, D.C.

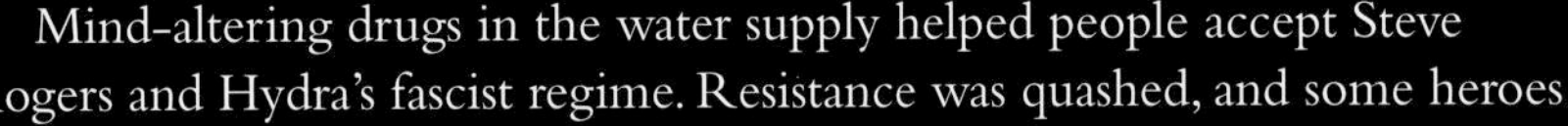

Hank Pym and Ultron had merged into a hideous biomechanical entity. When the Underground and Hydra both infiltrated his fortress, Pym forced his former Avengers allies to sit down to a grotesque "family dinner" to lecture them on his own greatness.

Mind-altering drugs in the water supply helped people accept Steve Rogers and Hydra's fascist regime. Resistance was quashed, and some heroes joined Hydra's own AVENGERS force. The only major resistance—named the Underground—was led by HAWKEYE and based in The Mount, Nevada.

A force led by MADAME HYDRA set out to destroy the Underground, prompting BLACK WIDOW and her "Red Room" rebels to plot to assassinate Rogers. Hawkeye, however, was more concerned with finding the now-shattered and scattered pieces of Kobik. Hydra's Avengers were also in the hunt. The two groups clashed in Alaska and were captured by ULTRON, who had gained possession of one of Kobik's shards. After an appeal by ANT-MAN (Scott Lang), Ultron agreed to give it to the Underground. Meanwhile, Hydra had induced NAMOR to give up a shard, in order to safeguard his people. The Underground rebels gave up their quest and returned to the Mount, whereupon their stronghold was breached by Hydra—Ant-Man had betrayed the group to protect his daughter, Cassie. Rogers confronted the rebel Tony Stark A.I. who activated his self-destructing armor. Madame Hydra gave her life to save Rogers from the explosion. A little later, Black Widow's attempt to assassinate Rogers failed: he broke her neck with his shield.

Separate from the Underground, Black Widow led a team of mostly teenage rebel heroes, which she dubbed the Red Room.

Black Widow had planned to assassinate Steve Rogers as he gave a speech at the Capitol Building. Prevented from sniping him at a distance by the Punisher, who had allied himself with Cap, she was forced to take Steve on in close combat. She was killed by a single blow.

Hydra and the Underground's hunt for Cosmic Cube shards resumed. Eventually, the Underground recovered enough pieces to free the heroes shut inside the Darkforce Dome and bring home those exiled by the Planetary Defense Shield. The combined heroes attacked Washington—to be confronted by Steve Rogers wearing armor granting him the immense power of the Cosmic Cube. A final shard from the Underground's Sam Wilson gave Rogers enough fragments to complete his own Cosmic Cube and finish Hydra's conquest of Earth. When all seemed lost, Rogers was faced by the real Captain America and Kobik, who had both been contained in Wilson's shard. Kobik returned reality to normal, Captain America defeated the evil Steve Rogers, and order was restored.

Alpha Flight, Earth's space-based defenders, were left helpless, trapped outside the planetary defense shield.

Emerging from the Cosmic Cube, the real Steve Rogers fought his own worst nightmare—himself as Hydra Supreme. Using Mjolnir, he smashed his foe to the ground.

FRAGMENT OF EVIL

The villainous incarnation of Captain America orchestrated Hydra's numerous attacks on rebel Super Heroes. He was created evil by Kobik because one of the fragments from which she was made had once belonged to Red Skull. Kobik's naive, innocent personality was easily influenced by Red Skull when she came to him searching for some kind of affection. Skull convinced her that Hydra was good, and SHIELD was evil. It was only later, when Kobik encountered the real Captain America, that she realized, and rectified, her terrible mistake.

SECRET INVASION

Trust no one...

ISSUE #1

Once the Avengers finally realize that the Skrulls have infiltrated Earth, Queen Veranke launches the invasion. Sleeper agents around the world awaken, and the destruction begins.

At one time, the Skrull Empire ruled one of the most powerful interplanetary civilizations in the galaxy. However, a series of wars with the Kree, the destruction of the empire's capital planet by Galactus, and the loss of nearly all the empire's other planets to the Annihilation Wave drove the Skrulls to seek a new home. Because of the interference of humanity over the years—and owing to information the Skrulls gleaned after the Illuminati's botched mission to warn them off—the Skrulls resolved to fulfill an ancient prophecy and lay claim to Earth.

The Skrull who replaced Elektra reverted to her natu form after Echo killed her. The fact that none of the Avengers had realized she w a Skrull before, told them t an untold number of Skrull had likely invaded Earth.

Disaster struck when the Skrulls launched their invasion. The Peak (the orbiting headquarters of SWORD), the SHIELD Helicarrier, the Fantastic Four's Baxter Building, and Thunderbolt Mountain were all destroyed.

THEY CAME TO CONQUER

The Skrull Queen Veranke began planning the invasion soon after ascending the throne. She began with an initiative to replace powerful and influential defenders of Earth with undetectable sleeper agents. When the Avengers discovered that Elektra had been replaced by a Skrull, Tony Stark (Iron Man) immediately suspected the potential Skrull threat. He called on the Illuminati to come up with a plan to counter an invasion. The other Avengers then learned that a Skrull had replaced Black Bolt long ago. Feeling that they could not even trust each other, the Super Hero team split to attack the problem on their own.

Realizing that the Avengers knew of the infiltration, Veranke—who had replaced Spider-Woman—gave the word to launch the invasion. Skrull agents simultaneously attacked several vital people and key points in Earth's defenses. Meanwhile, two teams of Avengers (one sanctioned by the US government and one not) raced to the Savage Land to investigate a crashed Skrull starship. There they faced off against each other and a third group of heroes who claimed to be the originals that the Skrulls had replaced over the years.

When a Skrull infiltrator heard another Skrull say the words, "He loves you," his original personality resurfaced. Until then, the infiltrator was often unaware that he was a Skrull.

Manhattan became the central battleground in the invasion attempt. With the Avengers in the Savage Land, Nick Fury led a new crew of young heroes called the Secret Warriors to help the remaining heroes check the Skrull attacks. Even the Hood and his villains joined the heroes to fight the Skrulls. As the Hood remarked, "No more Earth is bad for business."

Once Reed Richards (Mr. Fantastic) came up with a way to identify the Skrulls, the Avengers raced back to New York and joined the battle there, along with Thor and every other hero in the area. In the course of the battle, Veranke fell, and one of her lieutenants, who had posed as Hank Pym, activated the growth serum he had given to the Wasp back when she thought he was her husband. This caused her to grow to giant size and give off a lethal biotoxin.

Thor stopped this, but only at the cost of the Wasp's life. Meanwhile, Veranke had recovered, but before she could escape, Norman Osborn (*see* Green Goblin) shot her dead. In the aftermath, Tony Stark took much of the blame for not stopping the invasion. The president disbanded SHIELD and replaced it with the Thunderbolts Initiative, placing Norman Osborn, now feted as a hero, in charge of overseeing the USA's registered superhumans.

The climactic conflict happened once Reed Richards had come up with a way to identify the Skrull infiltrators. The heroes of Earth and the invading Skrulls destroyed large chunks of New York City in a pitched battle that shook the streets.

Norman Osborn formed a team of villains to help run the world after the Secret Invasion. Besides him, it included Doctor Doom, Loki, the Hoo the Sub-Mariner, and the White Quee

THE SECRET IS OUT

The most terrifying part of the Secret Invasion was that the people of Earth had no way to tell whom they could trust. The embedded Skrulls were so well hidden that no one—not even they themselves—could tell who they were. Once the Skrulls revealed themselves to each other and united in the Secret Invasion, the heroes had to face off against a desperate army of foes who could not only shift shapes but also often had multiple sets of superpowers to draw upon. With no world left to call their own, the Skrulls fought hard for what they hoped would be their new home.

SECRET WARS

When universes collide, Battleworld is all that's left

ISSUE #0

From the ashes of the Marvel Universe arises Battleworld, a bizarre patchwork realm formed from the joined fragments of countless realities.

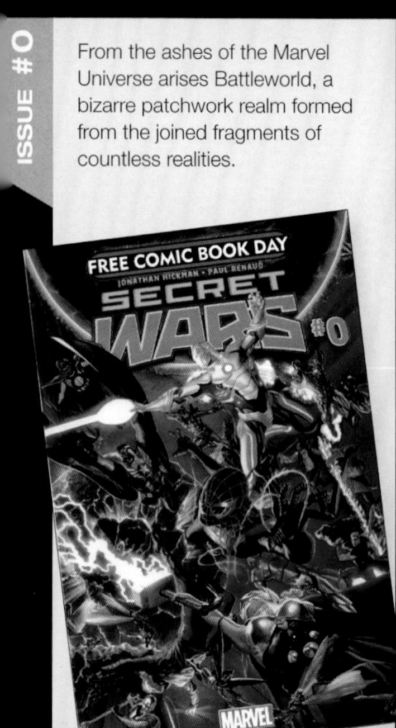

The Beyonders had created Molecule Men throughout the Multiverse—living bombs that caused universes to collide and destroy each other in events that were named "incursions." As the incursion of the last two remaining Multiversal worlds, Earth-1610 and Earth-616, began, Doctor Doom, Doctor Strange, and Owen Reece, the Molecule Man of Earth-616, confronted the Beyonders. Doom had adapted the Beyonders' scheme for his own purposes, creating a weapon from the Molecule Men of various worlds. Channeling this weapon through Reece, Doom destroyed the Beyonders, gained their powers, and created his own world—Battleworld—from fragments of the destroyed Multiverse.

The life raft containing the heroes of Earth-616 was found on Battleworld three years after the final incursion. Doctor Strange left it unopened, with its occupants in stasis, as he was fearful of destabilizing Battleworld. Five years later, when he finally opened it, it set in motion events that would lead to Doom's defeat.

THE DAY OF DOOM

The incursion of Earth-1610 and Earth-616 had sparked a battle between worlds, in which many died. Just before the worlds collided, two life rafts designed by Mr. Fantastic (Reed Richards) escaped, one from each world. One raft contained the villainous Cabal, led by Thanos; the other bore several heroes, including Black Panther and Mr. Fantastic. Mr. Fantastic's life raft was damaged, resulting in the deaths of the remainder of the Richards family.

Eight years later, on Battleworld, Doctor Doom was God Emperor, with Doctor Strange as his sheriff. The Human Torch was its sun and the spacestation Knowhere its moon. Battleworld was a patchwork of different universes, known as domains, including the Deadlands, Perfection, Spider-Island, Weirdworld, Doomstadt, the Kingdom of Manhattan, Limbo, and Utopolis. Each domain was ruled by a Baron or Baroness.

The final incursion witnessed the destruction of Earth-616 and Earth-1610.

Black Panther used the Infinity Gauntlet to try and counter Emperor Doom, who wielded the power of the Beyonders.

The inhabitants of each domain—the survivors of past incursions—had no idea how or when Battleworld had come into being and no memories of their previous existences. Alone among the inhabitants of Battleworld, Doom and Strange retained memories of the "time before." The Thor Corps, comprised of the Thors of many past universes, kept order and prevented people moving from one domain to another.

God Emperor Doom, with a recreated version of Sue Storm at his side to ease any self-doubt, seemed in total control. Then reports came from Utopolis that an abandoned life raft had been discovered. The Cabal had landed and clashed with the Thor Corps before escaping. Sheriff Strange was dispatched to investigate and discovered that the life raft had a stowaway—the Spider-Man of Earth-1610, Miles Morales. Strange took Spider-Man to his Sanctum Sanctorum, the Isle of Agamotto, where he stored items from his lost reality, including a life raft and an Infinity Gauntlet. Strange opened the raft to discover several Earth-616 Super Heroes, including Spider-Man, Thor, Captain Marvel, Black Panther, and Mr. Fantastic. Doom soon arrived to face the heroes and the Cabal. Fearing for their safety, Strange used a spell to scatter both groups throughout Battleworld.

Enraged by Strange's betrayal, Doom killed him. However, the fragile equilibrium of Doom's world was now fatally compromised. Some Earth-616 interlopers were captured, but dissatisfaction spread and several domains openly rebelled. A battle for supremacy began, culminating in a showdown between Mr. Fantastic and Doom. No victor emerged, and when Doom agreed that Mr. Fantastic could have done better with Doom's power, Molecule Man gave Doom's power to Mr. Fantastic, thus destroying Battleworld. Reunited with his family, Mr. Fantastic set about reconstructing the Multiverse as it had been before.

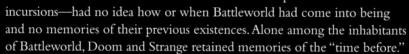

The Thor Corps worshiped the God Emperor Doom and served him loyally as his peacekeeping force.

The end of Secret Wars also marked the end of the Fantastic Four, as Reed and his family left with the Molecule Man to explore the cosmos and create whole new universes.

REED VERSUS DOOM

Despite calling himself God Emperor, Doom's rule was never truly absolute. The fact that he was in charge at all was with Doctor Strange's agreement, as Strange had not wanted the burden. Strange felt that the preservation of Battleworld, the last remaining reality, was more important than anything else; if it took someone like Doom to keep things under control and Battleworld in existence, then it was a price worth paying. But Doom began to doubt that he had created the perfect world, suggesting that he should have remained separate from his creation as other gods had. It seemed his very presence spoiled Battleworld. When Mister Fantastic left his life raft and the old foes finally encountered each other, two things became very clear; that in spite of his omnipotence Doom was afraid of Reed, and that his feelings of inferiority spread into the very heart of the world he had created.

SENTINELS

Enormously powerful, mutant-hunting robots

SENTINELS

FACTFILE
MARK V MODEL
HEIGHT 20 ft
WEIGHT (including fuel) 7,400 lbs
MAX. CARGO 2,000 lbs
FLIGHT RADIUS 400 miles
MAX. LEVEL AIRSPEED (sea level) 600 mph
SERVICE CEILING 10,000 ft
MAX. RATE OF CLIMB 450 ft per second

FIRST APPEARANCE
X-Men #14
(November 1965)

POWERS
Most Sentinels possess superhuman strength and jet propulsion units in their feet which enable them to fly, and can fire lasers and electron beams from their eyes and hands. Mark II Sentinels could adapt to counter any opponent.

Dr. Bolivar Trask introduced the Sentinels to the world on live TV.

The Sentinels were created by Dr. Bolivar Trask to combat superhuman mutants. Trask had concluded that a superhuman mutant race was evolving that would conquer the rest of humanity. He organized the team of scientists and engineers who built the first Mark I models.

TAKING OVER

However, despite being programmed by Trask to protect humanity, the Sentinels decided to take control of the human race. They kidnapped Trask, and the lead Sentinel, the Master Mold, ordered him to create a Sentinel army. The X-Men battled the Sentinels and Trask lost his life destroying the Master Mold and other Sentinels. Trask's son, Larry, oversaw the creation of the Mark II Sentinels. However, once the Sentinels recognized that Trask was a mutant himself, they turned against him. The government then seized the Sentinel designs, and Dr. Steven Lang built the Mark III Sentinels; but both he and they were destroyed battling the X-Men.

After mutant terrorists tried to kill Senator Robert Kelly, the President initiated "Project: Wideawake." Shaw Industries constructed Sentinels to combat mutant threats to national security. Xavier's evil twin, Cassandra Nova, used Mega-Sentinels to devastate Genosha, a nation with a large mutant population. She also devised microscopic "nano-Sentinels," which attacked mutants' bloodstreams.

Following only their own logic, the Sentinels have repeatedly turned against their human masters as well as mutants.

SENTINEL TAKE OVER

Later, the US government created Sentinel Squad O★N★E, headed by Dr. Valerie Cooper and James Rhodes (War Machine) for defense against superhuman threats. These Sentinels were not robots but gigantic suits of armor with human pilots. However, Nano-Sentinels took over these pilots and their armor, forcing them to attack Professor X's mansion. Simon Trask (Bolivar's brother) later created a techno-organic virus that transformed people into Sentinels.

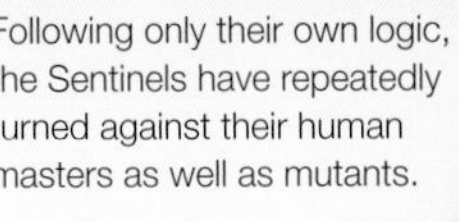
The Sentinel Bastion created cyborgs known as Prime Sentinels that could pass as ordinary humans.

ESSENTIAL STORYLINES

- ***X-Men Vol. 1 #14–16***
Dr. Bolivar Trask creates the original Sentinel robots. He introduces them on live TV—and they promptly capture him.
- ***X-Men Vol. 1 #57–59***
Larry Trask's Mark II Sentinels capture and imprison mutants.
- ***Uncanny X-Men #141–142***
The Sentinels rule North America in the "Days of Future Past" storyline set in an alternate reality.

SERSI

FIRST APPEARANCE *Strange Tales* #109 (June 1963)
REAL NAME Sersi
OCCUPATION Adventurer **BASE** New York City
HEIGHT 5 ft 9 in **WEIGHT** 140 lbs
EYES Blue **HAIR** Black
SPECIAL POWERS/ABILITIES A powerful sorceress, Sersi can release cosmic energy, create illusions, and transmute matter. Capable of flight and virtually immortal.

Sersi's playful personality can irritate some, and she is an incorrigible flirt around attractive men.

A member of the ETERNALS, Sersi inspired the legend of Circe in Homer's *Odyssey* and encountered MERLIN and King Arthur PENDRAGON. She proved her value during the Eternals' struggles against the Deviants. Sersi also joined the AVENGERS but PROCTOR manipulated her into battling her teammates. Seeking penance, she departed for an alternate reality with her lover the BLACK KNIGHT. Upon her return, she joined Heroes for Hire, before returning to the Eternals' home, Olympia. A fellow Eternal named Sprite wiped the memories of all the Eternals, including Sersi. Once Sersi recovered, she decided to return to her fabricated but normal life.

SERPENT

FIRST APPEARANCE *Fear Itself* #1 (June 2011)
REAL NAME Cul Borson
OCCUPATION God of Fear; Royal Inquisitor **BASE** Asgardia
HEIGHT 6 ft 2 in **WEIGHT** 230 lbs
EYES White **HAIR** Black (gray in old man form)
SPECIAL POWERS/ABILITIES Stronger than most Asgardian Gods, Cul can also feed off fear and use it to make himself even stronger.

Cul Borson is the older brother of ODIN and once ruled Asgard. He spread fear across the Nine Realms, taking the name Serpent, before a young Odin stopped him, trapping and imprisoning him while also expunging him from history. Cul was released in modern times by SIN, and unleashed a wave of fear and violence across the world through his Worthy—heroes and villains transformed into god-like beings. He was killed by THOR, only to be revived by Odin. His crimes were forgiven and he became Asgard's Royal Inquisitor and Minister of Justice. One of his first actions was to try to retrieve Mjolnir from Jane Foster.

Though it rarely mixes business with revenge, the Serpent Society has often made an exception in Captain America's case.

SERPENT SOCIETY

The original VIPER founded the first Serpent Squad with EEL and COBRA. The team changed its lineup several times, and it inspired one member, Sidewinder, to expand the squad into the Serpent Society and focus on treating their enterprise as a business. The leader assigned specific members to each job, supplying them with a detailed plan in return for a percentage of the take. CAPTAIN AMERICA put them out of commission several times.

SIN led a new Serpent Squad including COBRA, EEL, and VIPER. During the SECRET INVASION, the Serpent Society held a large group of people hostage, claiming to be protecting them from the SKRULLS, but NOVA and his teammates shut them down. Viper returned to the group, changing its name to Serpent Solutions.

FACTFILE

KEY MEMBERS

COBRA (Klaus Voorhees)
Super-flexible.
SIDEWINDER (Seth Voelker)
Interdimensional travel.
ANACONDA (Blanche Sitznski)
Elongates limbs; amphibious.
ASP (Cleo Nefertiti)
Energy field; fires venom-bolts.
BLACK MAMBA (Tanya Sealy)
Mesmerism; projects inky clouds of Darkforce.
BUSHMASTER (Quincy McIver)
Tail crushes his enemies.
COTTONMOUTH (Burchell Clemens) Bionic jaws.
RATTLER (Gustav Krueger)
Bionic tail generates sonic shockwaves.

FIRST APPEARANCE
Captain America #310 (October 1985)

SERPENT SOCIETY
1 Death Adder ***2*** Rattler
3 Cottonmouth ***4*** Diamondback

SHADOW COUNCIL

FIRST APPEARANCE *Secret Avengers* #1 (July 2010)

BASE Mobile

MEMBERS AND POWERS

Aloysius Thorndrake Immortal soldier.

Arnim Zola Mad genius in robot bodies.

Max Fury Superhuman android copy of Nick Fury.

John Steele Original Super-Soldier.

The secretive Shadow Council has been operating since Confederate soldier Aloysius Thorndrake founded it around the time of the American Civil War, to pave the way for a mysterious alien called the Abyss. Thorndrake later recruited a brainwashed John Steele and Max Fury (a Life Model Decoy of Nick Fury), along with a number of trained agents and a new Masters of Evil. The Secret Avengers—along with Nick Fury and Taskmaster—foiled their plans and cured Steele of his brainwashing.

SHADOWMASTERS

FIRST APPEARANCE *Shadowmasters* #1 (October 1989)

LINEUP Sojin Ezaki, Yuriko Ezaki, Phillip Richards

SPECIAL POWERS/ABILITIES Masters of ninjitsu

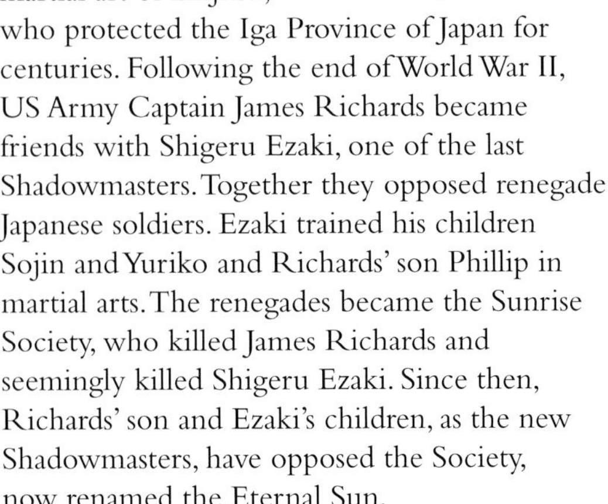

Demonstrating his martial arts skills, Phillip Richards wields a katana sword and *kyoketsu shoge* knife.

The original Shadowmasters were expert practitioners of the martial art of ninjitsu, who protected the Iga Province of Japan for centuries. Following the end of World War II, US Army Captain James Richards became friends with Shigeru Ezaki, one of the last Shadowmasters. Together they opposed renegade Japanese soldiers. Ezaki trained his children Sojin and Yuriko and Richards' son Phillip in martial arts. The renegades became the Sunrise Society, who killed James Richards and seemingly killed Shigeru Ezaki. Since then, Richards' son and Ezaki's children, as the new Shadowmasters, have opposed the Society, now renamed the Eternal Sun.

SHADOW KING

The Shadow King is an immortal demon that has lived on the astral plane. It possesses people in the real world, making them fat as it feeds upon the hatred it breeds. In the 1940s, it worked with Baron von Strucker to try to replace King George VI of the UK with a Nazi puppet. Years later, the Shadow King reappeared as Amahl Farouk, an Egyptian crimelord and the first evil mutant Professor X ever met. Farouk's gang included a young thief who would one day become Storm. Professor X defeated Farouk in a psychic duel and believed him killed. However, he had only been banished back to the astral plane and remained an omnipresent threat to Xavier's dream of peaceful coexistence between mutants and normal humans. The Shadow King once controlled a group of X-Men from a parallel world, dubbing them his Dark X-Men, before Excalibur defeated him. Bast, the Panther God of Wakanda, later devoured the Shadow King for daring to attack the Black Panther and his wife Storm. His remnants grew in power until he was able to take over a nuclear launch site and aim the missiles at the X-Men's island home of Utopia. When the Shadow King tried to use the world's telepaths to escape the astral plane, Psylocke sent a team of X-Men there to stop him, only to learn he had also imprisoned the astral form of Charles Xavier. The X-Men defeated him with Xavier's help.

Using his telepathic powers, Amahl Farouk came to rule Cairo's criminal underworld.

FACTFILE

REAL NAME
Amahl Farouk

OCCUPATION
Criminal

BASE
Various

HEIGHT Various
WEIGHT Various
EYES Various
HAIR Various

FIRST APPEARANCE
Uncanny X-Men #117 (January 1979)

SHADOW KING

POWERS

An entity composed solely of malevolent psionic power, the Shadow King can possess others, bending them to his will. He also possesses various telepathic and telekinetic abilities.

The Shadow King was the first mutant encountered by Professor X as he wandered the world, a tale told in *Uncanny X-Men* #117.

SHALLA-BAL

FIRST APPEARANCE *Silver Surfer* #1 (August 1968)
REAL NAME Shalla-Bal
OCCUPATION Empress of the planet Zenn-La **BASE** Zenn-La
HEIGHT 5 ft 9 in **WEIGHT** 125 lbs **EYES** Blue **HAIR** Black
SPECIAL POWERS/ABILITIES Born with no special powers, Shalla-Bal was later invested with power to restore life to the soil of Zenn-La after it was devastated by Galactus.

Shalla-Bal is a member of an alien race, the Zenn-Lavians. She was separated from her lover, Norrin Radd, after he offered to become the SILVER SURFER and serve GALACTUS if he would spare Zenn-La. For years the Silver Surfer traveled the universe, scouting out uninhabited planets for Galactus to consume. When the Surfer eventually decided to abandon Galactus and remain on Earth, Shalla-Bal was caught up in his struggle with MEPHISTO. Then Galactus returned to consume Zenn-La in revenge for the Surfer's betrayal. After the Surfer endowed Shalla-Bal with the power to restore life to Zenn-La, she was declared Empress. She tried to spread Zen-Lavian culture, but when her armada reached Earth, the Surfer opposed her plans. He ended the threat, but Shalla-Bal scolded him that he was no longer Zen-Lavian.

SHAMAN

FIRST APPEARANCE *Uncanny X-Men* #120 (April 1979)
REAL NAME Michael Twoyoungmen
OCCUPATION Medicine man; Super Hero **BASE** Mobile
HEIGHT 5 ft 10 in **WEIGHT** 175 lbs **EYES** Brown **HAIR** Black
SPECIAL POWERS/ABILITIES Vast magical powers. Able to fire energy bolts, change his appearance, control weather, levitate, and teleport. Powers are focused through the use of his medicine pouch.

Michael Twoyoungmen was a Canadian surgeon who embraced his heritage as a Native American medicine man after his wife's death. The spirit of his grandfather trained him in the use of magic, and he helped deliver Narya, the daughter of the Northern Goddess. Twoyoungmen and Narya took the code names of Shaman and SNOWBIRD and joined ALPHA FLIGHT. Shaman's daughter Elizabeth was known as TALISMAN, an identity he had briefly used himself. He died at the hands of The Collective (*see* WEAPON OMEGA), but was resurrected during the Chaos War.

SHANNA THE SHE-DEVIL

FIRST APPEARANCE *Shanna the She-Devil* #1 (December 1972)
REAL NAME Shanna O'Hara
OCCUPATION Vet and adventurer **BASE** Savage Land
HEIGHT 5 ft 10 in **WEIGHT** 140 lbs **EYES** Hazel **HAIR** Red
SPECIAL POWERS/ABILITIES Trained veterinarian and extraordinary gymnast and athlete with superb hunting and foraging skills. Post-resurrection, she is tied to the Savage Land and knows its languages and history. She also has superhuman strength and speed.

Now living in the Savage Land with her husband KA-ZAR and their young son, Shanna O'Hara first worked in a New York zoo. Furious when a sniper casually killed most of the zoo's big cats, she chose to return the surviving animals to Africa and live with them in the wild. Shanna lost her friends and father to criminal organizations and was forced to team up with DAREDEVIL to defeat them. She was killed in the Savage Land and resurrected with the blood of a native MAN-THING, tying her to the land.

The Savage Land in Antarctica is maintained at tropical temperatures. It has been stocked with species that are extinct elsewhere on Earth.

SHANG-CHI

SHANG-CHI

FACTFILE

REAL NAME
Shang-Chi

OCCUPATION
Former secret agent; fisherman

BASE
Formerly Zheng Zu's retreat in Honan, China, mobile for a while, then Yang Yin, China

HEIGHT 5 ft 10 ins
WEIGHT 175 lbs
EYES Brown
HAIR Black

FIRST APPEARANCE
Special Marvel Edition #15 (December 1973)

POWERS

Shang-Chi is the greatest living master of kung fu. He is also highly skilled in many other mental and physical disciplines. Although he has no superhuman powers, Shang-Chi has defeated superpowered enemies.

Shang-Chi was born in China, the son of the criminal mastermind Zheng Zu. Trained in the mental and martial arts at Zheng Zu's retreat, Shang-Chi was a brilliant pupil but grew up unaware of his father's crimes. When Shang-Chi was nineteen, his father sent him away on a mission of assassination. The boy assumed that his father's enemies must be evil and so went willingly, but he soon learned the truth. Feeling betrayed, Shang-Chi vowed to destroy his father. He also learned that his father had created a conscienceless clone of him, called Moving Shadow. Defeating them both, Shang-Chi retired, but during the CIVIL WAR he returned to action as a member of Heroes for Hire. He later worked with MI-13 and also joined the AVENGERS.

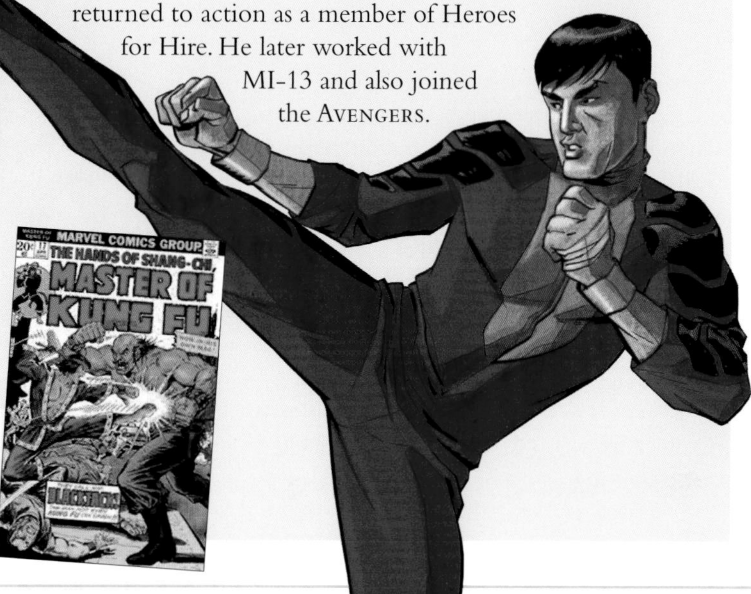

This was the first issue to feature Shang-Chi's name in the title.

SHAPER OF WORLDS

FIRST APPEARANCE *The Incredible Hulk* #155 (September 1972)
REAL NAME Unrevealed, perhaps inapplicable
OCCUPATION Reality manipulator **BASE** The known universe
HEIGHT 18 ft **WEIGHT** 5.6 tons **EYES** Blue **HAIR** None
SPECIAL POWERS/ABILITIES Restructures pockets of reality, and rearranges the molecular structure of objects and living beings. Can teleport, and perceive dreams.

The Shaper of Worlds originated in the Skrull empire as a Cosmic Cube, an object which can alter reality according to the thoughts of whoever holds it. In time it developed sentience, and took the form of a metallic Skrull with tractor treads. The Shaper wanted to use his powers to restructure reality, but had little creative imagination. So he sought out those who could supply dreams and imaginative concepts that he could use. He was killed by his slave Glorian, but returned to the universe, later helping Galactus save Eternity.

SHATTERSTAR

FIRST APPEARANCE *New Mutants* #99 (March 1991)
REAL NAME Benjamin Russell **OCCUPATION** Adventurer
BASE The Xavier Institute, Salem Center, New York State
HEIGHT 6 ft 2 in **WEIGHT** 210 lbs **EYES** Black **HAIR** Gray
SPECIAL POWERS/ABILITIES Genetically engineered for enhanced strength, speed, stamina; converts sonic frequencies into a vibratory shockwave that he channels through weapons.

Born to Dazzler and Longshot a hundred years in the future on Mojoworld, Shatterstar's parents' memories of him were wiped. Trained as an arena warrior, he escaped and joined the Cadre Alliance, to overthrow Mojo. Shatterstar traveled back in time to Earth and oined Cable to found X-Force. During a battle, Shatterstar was mortally wounded, and Longshot transferred Shatterstar's consciousness into the comatose body of Benjamin Russell. Later, Cortex possessed him and made him attack his friends in X-Factor. When cured, he and Rictor started a new relationship. He traveled to the past and lent DNA to create Longshot, thus becoming his own grandfather.

SHAW, SEBASTIAN

FIRST APPEARANCE *X-Men* #130 (February 1980)
REAL NAME Sebastian Shaw **OCCUPATION** CEO of Shaw Industries, Inc. **BASE** Worldwide; Hellfire Club, New York City
HEIGHT 6 ft 2 in **WEIGHT** 210 lbs **EYES** Black **HAIR** Gray
SPECIAL POWERS/ABILITIES Mutant power to absorb kinetic energy, which enhances his strength, speed, and stamina. He can also absorb electrical energy.

Sebastian Shaw became a self-made millionaire by the age of 20. As head of Shaw Industries, he joined the Hellfire Club, and then became part of its Council of the Chosen, which schemed to achieve world domination. Seizing control of the club and becoming its Black King, he changed its name to the Inner Circle and teamed with Emma Frost, the White Queen, in secretly creating mutant-hunting Sentinels. The X-Men captured Shaw, and Frost wiped his mind so that he could only remember the faces of the Genoshans the Sentinels destroyed. Hope Summers found him later and brought him to the X-Men, as he seemed to be a changed man. He later helped a group of mutants escape from the Avengers.

SHE-THING

FACTFILE
REAL NAME
Sharon Ventura
OCCUPATION
Adventurer
BASE
Mobile

HEIGHT 6 ft
WEIGHT 340 lbs
EYES Blue
HAIR None

FIRST APPEARANCE
The Thing #27 (September 1985)

POWERS
Sharon Ventura was a superb athlete and a daring stuntwoman, motorcyclist and a proficient wrestler. As She-Thing, she possesses superhuman strength and durability.

Sharon Ventura has now returned to her human form—and the wrestling ring.

SHE-THING

Sharon Ventura was working as a stunt cyclist with the Thunderiders when she first met Ben Grimm, the Thing of the Fantastic Four, who was immediately attracted to her.

Subsequently, Ventura accepted an offer to join the Grapplers, a professional team of superhuman female wrestlers. Working for the Power Broker, Dr. Karl Malus augmented Ventura's strength to superhuman levels. As a Grappler, she adopted a costumed identity, becoming the second Ms. Marvel. The Thing helped her battle the Grapplers when they turned on her.

Later, Ventura accepted the Thing's offer to join the Fantastic Four. During a mission in space, she was exposed to cosmic rays, which mutated her into a female version of the Thing. She was later restored to her normal human appearance by Doctor Doom.

Ventura later mutated into an even more grotesque version of the Thing. Worse, her intellect began to deteriorate. As the She-Thing, she even temporarily joined the Wizard's Frightful Four and battled her former friends the Fantastic Four. During the Secret Invasion, the Skrulls captured and replaced the She-Thing, but after the war was over she escaped. She ended up a prisoner at Ryker's Island, but escaped and rejoined the Frightful Four. Afterward, she resumed her human form and got back into wrestling.

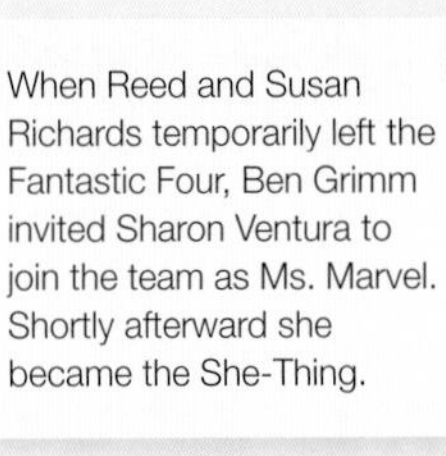

When Reed and Susan Richards temporarily left the Fantastic Four, Ben Grimm invited Sharon Ventura to join the team as Ms. Marvel. Shortly afterward she became the She-Thing.

SHE-HULK

Legal eagle and green-skinned crimefighter

As Jennifer Walters, She-Hulk practiced superhuman law for the legal firm of Goodman, Lieber, Kurtzberg & Holliway.

The cousin of Bruce Banner, who would one day become the HULK, Jennifer Walters pursued her dream of becoming a successful lawyer. Shot by criminals whose boss she was prosecuting, Jennifer received a life-saving blood transfusion from her cousin Bruce. But this infusion of gamma-irradiated blood had an effect on Jennifer's physiology similar to that experienced by Bruce himself: the repressed part of her personality began to manifest itself as a green-skinned powerhouse: the savage She-Hulk!

She-Hulk was one of the last characters created by Stan Lee.

FACTFILE

REAL NAME
Jennifer Walters

OCCUPATION
Lawyer

BASE
The law offices of Goodman, Lieber, Kurtzberg & Holliway

HEIGHT 6 ft 7 in
WEIGHT 650 lbs
EYES Green
HAIR Green; brown as Jennifer Walters

FIRST APPEARANCE
The Savage She-Hulk #1 (February 1980)

POWERS

As the She-Hulk, Jennifer Walters possesses superhuman strength and durability; she can withstand extreme temperatures and her skin is highly resistant to injury.

RAMPAGING FREE

At first, Jennifer kept her dual role as the She-Hulk a secret. But over time, she found that she enjoyed being the She-Hulk, who, while definitely an extrovert, was far more controlled than her cousin's rampaging alter ego. She began to spend more time as the She-Hulk, using her gamma-spawned strength to battle villainy. Eventually, the She-Hulk was offered membership in the AVENGERS.

Thereafter, transported to the Battleworld created by the celestial BEYONDER alongside her fellow Avengers, She-Hulk fought in the first Secret Wars. Following that conflict, the THING decided to remain on Battleworld, and asked the She-Hulk to take his place in the FANTASTIC FOUR, which she did for a while, becoming almost one of the family. During her time with the FF, Jennifer abandoned her identity as Jennifer Walters, remaining in her She-Hulk form full time.

LEGAL TROUBLESHOOTER

However, the She-Hulk's more boisterous personality created problems for her down the line, and she was asked to move out of Avengers Mansion. At this low point in her life, she was recruited by the law offices of Goodman, Lieber, Kurtzburg & Holliway, a firm specializing in superhuman law. But a condition of Jennifer's employment was that she had to pursue her duties in her normal human state, rather than as the She-Hulk.

After the CIVIL WAR, Jennifer helped train heroes in the FIFTY-STATE INITIATIVE. Disbarred for revealing privileged information about a client she thought guilty of murder, Jennifer later turned to bounty hunting with her SKRULL friend Jazinda (daughter of the SUPER-SKRULL). For a while, she was thought killed at the hands of the Red She-Hulk (Betty ROSS) but LYJA found and freed her. Later, she served in a substitute Fantastic Four.

She joined Luke CAGE's Mighty Avengers next, followed by the all-woman A-FORCE team. She fought THANOS after his attack on Project PEGASUS and was nearly killed. When she awoke, Jennifer learned that Bruce Banner had been killed by HAWKEYE. She left Super Hero life and went back to lawyering, but the stress got to her, leading Jennifer to seek advice from self-help author Florida Mayer.

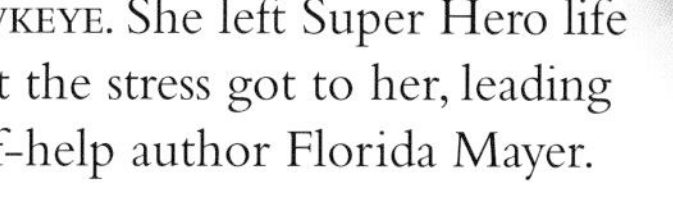

Stress from her fight with Thanos and the loss of her cousin Bruce turned Jennifer into Grey She-Hulk.

ESSENTIAL STORYLINES

- ***Fantastic Four #265*** She-Hulk replaces the Thing as a member of the Fantastic Four.
- ***Avengers Vol. 3 #72–75*** Having lost control of her transformations, She-Hulk is pursued by her fellow Avengers and her cousin, the Hulk.
- ***She-Hulk #2*** Jennifer joins the superhuman law offices of Goodman, Lieber, Kurtzberg & Holliway.

SHI'AR

Empire-building alien race

SHI'AR

FACTFILE

BASE
Chandilar (Aerie), Shi'ar Galaxy

FIRST APPEARANCE
Uncanny X-Men #97
(February 1976)

IMPERIAL GUARD

CURRENT MEMBERS AND POWERS

GLADIATOR (LEADER) Flight, enhanced strength, speed, near-invulnerability, heat vision.
ASTRA Ability to phase through solid objects.
ELECTRON Power over electricity and magnetism.
FANG Enhanced strength, speed, and senses; razor-sharp claws.
HOBGOBLIN/SHAPESHIFTER Can assume nearly any form.
IMPULSE/PULSAR Energy-based body can be released as concussive force.
MIDGET/SCINTILLA Can shrink to tiny size.
NIGHTSHADE/NIGHTSIDE Can draw others into the Darkforce dimension.
MAGIQUE Ability to cast illusions.
MENTOR Genius-level intelligence and boosted calculating speed.
ORACLE Telepathy, precognition, and ability to fire mental blasts.
QUASAR/NEUTRON Enhanced strength and damage resistance.
STARBOLT Flight, energy projection.
SMASHER Enhanced strength.
TEMPEST/FLASHFIRE Ability to release electrical bolts.
TITAN Can grow to giant size.

BASE
Chandilar (Aerie), Shi'ar Galaxy

FIRST APPEARANCE
Uncanny X-Men #107
(October 1977)

Majestor D'ken failed to hold onto the Shi'ar throne.

The Shi'ar are an alien species descended from avians, who typically sport feathery hair and sometimes vestigial wings. Unlike the rival SKRULL and KREE empires, the Shi'ar Imperium consists of a patchwork of alien species, each absorbed into the empire through treaties or by force. A hereditary Majestor (male) or Majestrix (female) rules the Imperium, overseeing a High Council under the protection of the Elite Corps of the Shi'ar Imperial Guard.

ESSENTIAL STORYLINES

- ***Uncanny X-Men* #107–109**
The X-Men battle the Shi'ar Imperial Guard in a fight involving D'ken, Lilandra, and the M'Krann crystal.
- ***New X-Men* #118–126**
The "Imperial" story arc sees Cassandra Nova, the villainous genetic twin of Professor X, launching a scheme to ruin the Shi'ar empire.

CRUEL RULE

The Shi'ar are aggressive about absorbing other cultures into their empire, though the newcomers seldom receive the same rights as the Shi'ar themselves. Majestrix Lilandra has made strides to reverse this inequality, but under the leadership of Majestor D'ken, the cruel treatment of alien slaves triggered the formation of the pirates called the STARJAMMERS.

The M'Krann crystal is an artifact of immense power located on a lifeless world. It has the ability to destroy all of reality.

The first contact between the Shi'ar and Earth's heroes occurred when the X-MEN stopped Lilandra's brother D'ken from exploiting the powerful M'Krann crystal. Lilandra subsequently became the Majestrix of the Shi'ar Empire, briefly losing her throne to her sister DEATHBIRD until gaining it once more. Lilandra and PROFESSOR X of the X-Men enjoyed a romantic relationship for years.

When Skrull spies fanned the flames of war between the Shi'ar and the Kree, a team of AVENGERS tried to negotiate a cessation of hostilities with Majestrix Lilandra, but they could not prevent the detonation of the Nega-Bomb, a Shi'ar weapon that nearly destroyed the Kree. The Shi'ar annexed vast swaths of the Kree Empire, and Deathbird served as the viceroy of the conquered territories.

The X-Men have been staunch allies of Lilandra's, thanks to her romantic liaison with Professor Charles Xavier.

The mutant VULCAN later returned to the Shi'ar Empire to avenge his mother's death and become Majestor by marrying Deathbird and killing her brother D'Ken. He led the Shi'ar into a final war with the INHUMANS-led Kree, which they lost after Vulcan died in a battle with BLACK BOLT. The former GLADIATOR, Kallark, then became leader of the Shi'ar under the dominion of the Kree.

Still a violent race, the Shi-ar later brought war to Asgard when their gods demanded it. The female THOR (Jane Foster), and her allies defeated them, and some Shi-ar then turned on their gods.

THE IMPERIAL GUARD

The Elite Corps of the Shi'ar Imperial Guard, also known as the Superguardian Elite, are the protectors of the Majestor or Majestrix of the Shi'ar Empire. Most members of the Imperial Guard are not Shi'ar—they represent a cross-section of cultures from the multispecies mix that comprises the Shi'ar empire. Typically, each member has a distinct superpower that adds a needed component to the team's overall power mix.

Their leader, called the praetor, is currently the powerful Strontian called Gladiator. The Imperial Guard also has a larger, secondary division known as the Borderers, who are charged with enforcing local laws on member planets.

The Imperial Guard first came into conflict with the inhabitants of Earth when the X-Men followed a space warp and emerged on the desolate planet that housed the reality-altering M'Krann crystal. On the orders of Majestor D'ken, the Imperial Guard battled the X-Men and D'ken's sister Lilandra, though the Guard shifted its allegiance to Lilandra as soon as she assumed the throne. Later, the Imperial Guard fought the X-Men on Earth's moon, in an honor duel over the fate of the Dark Phoenix.

Throughout the changes in Shi'ar rule, the Imperial Guard has remained loyal to whomever holds the royal office. The Guard clashed with the Starjammers and Excalibur during Deathbird's time as Majestrix, and welcomed Lilandra back as leader after her return to power.

During the Kree-Shi'ar war, the Imperial Guard helped steal the nega-bands worn by Captain Mar-Vell from the late hero's tomb, which then went into the construction of the Shi'ar ultimate weapon, the nega-bomb. Following the apparent death of Earth's greatest heroes while fighting the entity Onslaught, Lilandra ordered Gladiator and several other Imperial Guard members to protect Earth, where the team uncovered a cell of undercover Kree agents.

The Imperial Guard served Vulcan during the War of Kings against the Kree. The newest ruler of the Shi'ar came from within their ranks: the former Gladiator, Kallark.

When they combine their powers, the Shi'ar Imperial Guard are nearly unstoppable. They are among the most feared combatants in the universe.

GLADIATOR  ASTRA 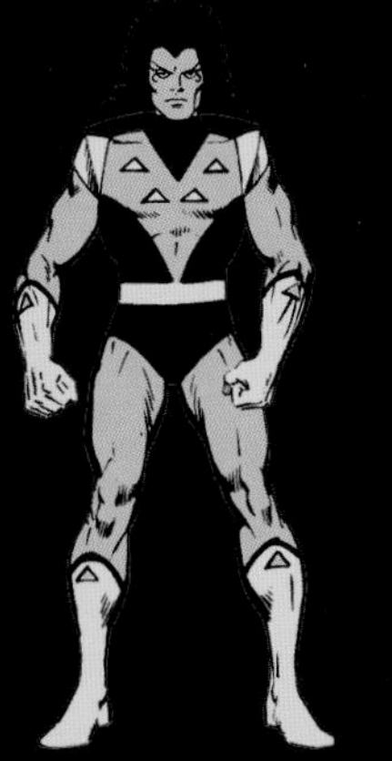 ELECTRON  FANG

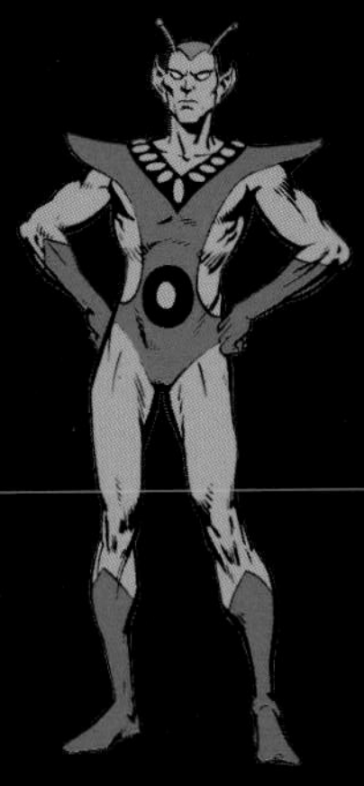

SHAPE-SHIFTER  IMPULSE  SCINTILLA  NIGHTSIDE

MAGIQUE  MENTOR  ORACLE 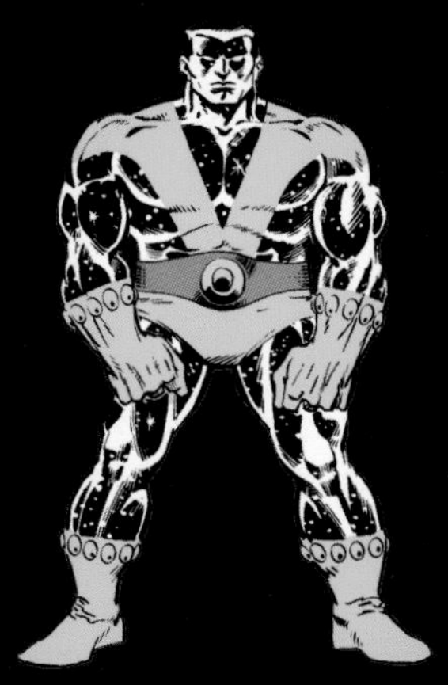 NEUTRON

STARBOLT  SMASHER  FLASHFIRE  TITAN

SHIELD

Strategic Homeland Intervention, Enforcement, and Logistics Division

FACTFILE

NOTABLE MEMBERS

NICK FURY Former director
CONTESSA VALENTINA ALLEGRA DE FONTAINE
YELENA BELOVA (Black Widow)
G. W. BRIDGE Former director
SHARON CARTER (Agent 13), former director, liaison officer to Captain America
JESSICA DREW (Spider-Woman)
TIMOTHY "DUM DUM" DUGAN Former director
MARIA HILL Former director
GABRIEL "GABE" JONES
AL MACKENZIE CIA liaison officer
ALI MORALES
CLAY QUARTERMAIN
NATASHA ROMANOVA (Black Widow)
JASPER SITWELL
TONY STARK (Iron Man), former director
JIMMY WOO (Agents of Atlas)

BASE

The Helicarrier; mobile

FIRST APPEARANCE

Strange Tales #135 (August 1965)

Fury may be the longest-serving director of SHIELD, but not even he knows the identity of the man he replaced.

SHIELD (Strategic Homeland Intervention, Enforcement, and Logistics Division; previously "Supreme Headquarters International Espionage Law-Enforcement Division" and later "Strategic Hazard Intervention, Espionage, and Logistics Directorate") is a counter-terrorism, intelligence, espionage, and peace-keeping organization. SHIELD runs covert as well as military operations, and works with governments and their military forces around the world.

SHIELD'S FORMATION

SHIELD was established to counter the threat posed by the technologically advanced neo-fascist subversive organization known as Hydra. The identity of SHIELD's founders remained classified, as did the identity of its first executive director, who was assassinated by Hydra operatives. SHIELD's second and longest-serving leader was Nick Fury, a colonel in the U.S. Army, who had also been a top CIA operative. Other top SHIELD members include Timothy "Dum Dum" Dugan, Valentina Allegra De Fontaine, and Jasper Sitwell.

For many years, SHIELD's headquarters were the Helicarrier, a huge flying aircraft carrier kept airborne at all times. It carried a squadron of jet fighters and an ICBM. The Helicarrier was damaged and even destroyed several times over the years, but SHIELD rebuilt it every time. It also maintained several regional headquarters throughout the world.

As director of SHIELD, Maria Hill tried to cut the agency's dependency on Super Heroes and rely on human resources instead.

SHIELD kept close ties to the Super Hero community and often called upon Captain America, the Avengers, and the Fantastic Four for help. In addition to battling earthly terrorist and military threats, SHIELD saved the world many times from extraterrestrial invasion and infiltration. As well as its human operatives, SHIELD also employed Life Model Decoys (LMDs), incredibly lifelike androids sent into extremely dangerous situations to help avoid human casualties. Nick Fury was known to deploy several LMDs of himself to confuse assassins and even the agents working beneath him.

Over the years, SHIELD's main enemies included Hydra, AIM, Zodiac, the Corporation, the Golden Claw, the Viper, Centurius, Doctor Demonicus, and the Red Skull. SHIELD provided intelligence and technical support to the Avengers and the Fantastic Four during the Kree-Skrull War, when an alien battle took place close to Earth.

Although chartered by the UN, SHIELD maintained close ties to the US. The UN also founded a number of sister organizations. ARMOR (Altered-Reality Monitoring and Operational Response) stopped invasions from other universes, and SWORD (Sentient World Observation and Response Department) defended the planet from alien invasions.

The terrorist organization Hydra, dedicated to world domination, is SHIELD's greatest and most persistent enemy.

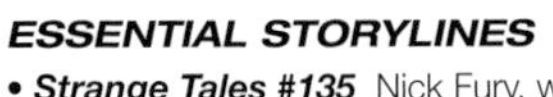

ESSENTIAL STORYLINES

- ***Strange Tales #135*** Nick Fury, who will be the organization's top operative and eventual leader, is recruited by SHIELD.
- ***Strange Tales #158*** Hydra Island sinks, and Baron Wolfgang von Strucker, Hydra's leader, is killed.

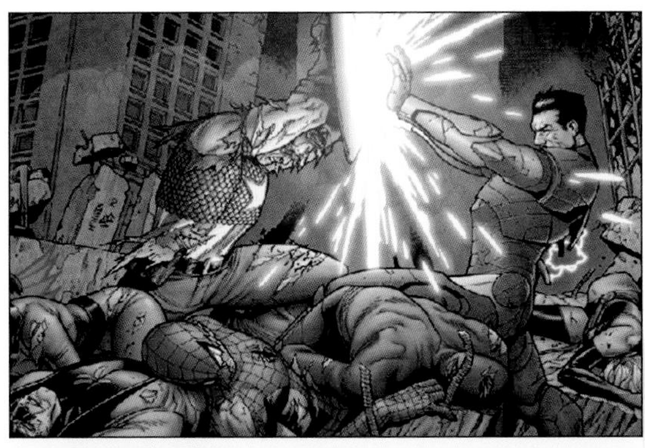

Iron Man was made director of SHIELD after defeating one of its staunchest allies, Captain America, during the Civil War.

TROUBLE AT THE TOP

As director of SHIELD, Nick Fury gathered a secret team of Super Heroes and launched a covert attempt to topple the government of Latveria. Although helped by Captain America, Spider-Man, Luke Cage, Daredevil, Black Widow, Wolverine, and agent Daisy Johnson (Quake), the mission failed. Fury had all memories of the mission wiped from the heroes' minds. A year later, Latveria launched an attack on New York City in revenge, and Fury's role in the disaster was exposed. He resigned soon afterward and then disappeared underground.

Eager to show a clean break with Fury, the UN appointed Maria Hill as the next director of SHIELD. During her leadership, the Superhuman Registration Act was passed, placing her in charge of controlling all registered superhumans in the US—and of hunting down the rest. She served as director throughout the Civil War, but when the conflict finally resolved, she suggested that Tony Stark—who had led the pro-registration heroes as Iron Man—take over as director and that she serve as his deputy. As SHIELD director, Stark launched the Fifty-State Initiative and ordered a new Helicarrier to be built using the latest Stark technology. He also used SHIELD money to fund the Avengers and their HQ in Stark Tower.

FURY'S SECRET WARRIORS
1 Nick Fury **2** Phobos **3** Druid **4** Slingshot **5** Stonewall **6** Quake **7** Hellfire

A DARK REIGN

When SHIELD failed to prevent the Secret Invasion, Norman Osborn (Green Goblin) replaced Stark as director, and SHIELD with a new organization called HAMMER. Osborn formed a team of villains masquerading as Avengers, which he led as the Iron Patriot. Thus began the period known as the Dark Reign.

Nick Fury had resurfaced during the Secret Invasion with his Secret Warriors to help defeat the Skrulls. Discovering that Hydra had controlled SHIELD from its founding, Fury rededicated his team to bringing his old foes down, revealing to them in the end that they'd actually been working for him.

After the Dark Reign ended, Captain America ended HAMMER, rebuilt SHIELD, and put Daisy Johnson (Quake) in charge. She added new agents, including Nick Fury Jr. and Phil Coulson, and formed her own secret Avengers team. Maria Hill also established a secret prison for Super Villains known as Pleasant Hill, using Kobik, a living Cosmic Cube, to trick villains into believing they were normal people living in suburbia. Shortly after Pleasant Hill was destroyed by its inmates the evil Hydra Captain America took control of the USA. Following his downfall, SHIELD restructured and rebuilt to face new threats.

As the Iron Patriot, Norman Osborn led both the official Avengers team and SHIELD's replacement organization, HAMMER.

SHOCKER

FIRST APPEARANCE *The Amazing Spider-Man* #46 (March 1967)
REAL NAME Herman Schultz
OCCUPATION Burglar **BASE** New York City
HEIGHT 5 ft 9 in **WEIGHT** 175 lbs **EYES** Brown **HAIR** Brown
SPECIAL POWERS/ABILITIES Wears gauntlets containing "vibro-shock units" that project compressed air blasts creating highly destructive vibrations.

While imprisoned, safecracker Herman Schultz invented a new device for opening safes by projecting intense vibrations. He used it to shatter the prison's walls and escape. Wearing an insulated costume to absorb the vibrations, Schultz became the Shocker. After SPIDER-MAN beat him several times, he joined a number of teams, including the SINISTER SIX. After being part of the BLACK CAT's criminal gang, he opened up a bar with 8-Ball and Javelynn. Another criminal, Randall Darby, once called himself the Shocker, too, but later changed his name to Paralyzer.

SHRIEK

FIRST APPEARANCE *Spider-Man Unlimited* #1 (May 1993)
REAL NAME Frances Louise Barrison **OCCUPATION** Patient
BASE Ravencroft Institute for the Criminally Insane
HEIGHT 6 ft **WEIGHT** 170 lbs **EYES** Blue **HAIR** Black
SPECIAL POWERS/ABILITIES Manipulates sound as a destructive force. Hypersonically generates emotions of fear, hate, or despair in others. Can employ sonic energy to fly.

After being mistreated by her mother for being overweight, Frances Louise Barrison turned to drugs, eventually becoming a dealer. She lost her fragile grip on reality when she was shot in the head by the police, and spent a brief period in the dark dimension of the costumed adventurer known as CLOAK. Her powers may be the result of her time in that dimension, her injury, some latent mutant gene, or a combination of all three factors. She used her emerging powers to commit crimes and create chaos until she was committed to the Ravencroft Institute. CARNAGE later freed her and they went on a murder spree until they were captured by a team of heroes led by SPIDER-MAN. Shriek has escaped Ravencroft many times and joined Kraven when he hunted human-dinosaur hybrids lurking beneath New York City.

SHROUD

FIRST APPEARANCE *Super-Villain Team-Up* #5 (April 1976)
REAL NAME Unknown **OCCUPATION** Crime fighter masquerading as a criminal **BASE** Los Angeles
HEIGHT 6 ft 2 in **WEIGHT** 220 lbs **EYES** Blue **HAIR** Blond
SPECIAL POWERS/ABILITIES Though blind, has extrasensory perception that allows him to "see" his environment; can summon absolute darkness by opening a portal into another dimension.

After witnessing the murder of his parents as a boy, the Shroud dedicated his life to fighting crime. After college, he traveled to Nepal and joined a cult that trained him in mysticism and martial arts. Seven years later, he was given the "Kiss of Kali" and branded with the imprint of the goddess on his eyes, cheeks, and forehead, trading his eyesight for a mystical perception. He often pretends to be a criminal and formed a gang called the Night Shift. After splitting with his wife, Julia Carpenter (*see* MADAME WEB), he became obsessed with her and slowly went insane.

SHURI

FIRST APPEARANCE *Black Panther* #2 (May 2005)
REAL NAME Shuri **OCCUPATION** Black Panther
BASE Royal Palace of Wakanda
HEIGHT Unknown **WEIGHT** Unknown
EYES Brown **HAIR** Black
SPECIAL POWERS/ABILITIES Enhanced physiology; master acrobat and combatant; genius-level intelligence.

Shuri is the younger sister of T'Challa, the BLACK PANTHER. A genius, Shuri wanted to be the Black Panther all her life. After T'Challa was injured she finally got her chance, but was rejected by the Panther God as unworthy. When she nearly died fighting MORLUN, the Panther God granted her the Panther's abilities and she took on the role while her brother recuperated from fighting the CABAL. She also ruled Wakanda in his absence. She was left in a "living death" after battling PROXIMA MIDNIGHT but was later revived by T'Challa. She now sits on Wakanda's ruling council.

SIF

Sif was born with blond hair, but LOKI cut it off as a prank. He hired dwarves to replace it, but then refused to pay them. When Sif wore her new hair, it turned jet black. Tired of her tears over the matter, her parents sent her to be trained to become a great warrior. As an adult, she dated THOR, and they pledged to marry (although they never have).

Like the rest of the Norse Gods (*see* GODS OF ASGARD), Sif died during Ragnarok. Thor returned and set about reviving the gods, finding them wearing the bodies of mortals on Midgard. He didn't find Sif, because Loki had taken her body, trapping her spirit in that of an elderly woman dying of cancer. Thor realized this and raced to restore Sif just moments before her host's body died. Sif returned to Asgard and helped defend it against HAMMER's attack at the end of the DARK REIGN. She also battled alongside Thor against the SERPENT. When Jane Foster became Thor, Sif was one of many female heroes who stood by her side when ODIN sent the DESTROYER to reclaim Mjolnir from Foster.

FACTFILE — SIF

REAL NAME
Sif

OCCUPATION
Warrior

BASE
Asgardia

HEIGHT 6 ft 2 in
WEIGHT 425 lbs
EYES Blue
HAIR Black

FIRST APPEARANCE
Journey Into Mystery #102 (March 1964)

POWERS

Sif is a god of Asgard, gifted with superhuman durability, endurance, speed, and strength. She's also an excellent combatant.

SILHOUETTE

FACTFILE

REAL NAME
Silhouette Chord

OCCUPATION
Adventurer

BASE
Manhattan

HEIGHT 5 ft 6 in
WEIGHT 105 lbs
EYES Black with white pupils, formerly brown
HAIR Black

FIRST APPEARANCE
New Warriors #2 (August 1990)

POWERS

Able to pass through the Darkforce Dimension, allowing her to effectively teleport through the shadows. In her shadowy form, she can also phase through others, causing them injury. Her crutches variously house taser devices, anesthetic needles, pellet guns, and smoke capsules.

SILHOUETTE

Silhouette was conceived during the Vietnam War as part of a pact between a squad of American soldiers and the protectors of a secret temple, intended as a mystic sacrifice that would convey great power. Unaware of her parentage, Silhouette and her brother Midnight's Fire grew up on the streets of New York City, a nemesis to the gangs that preyed there. In one foray against the underworld, Silhouette encountered the young Night Thrasher, and they began a torrid relationship. But then Silhouette was caught in the crossfire between the police and a street gang, losing the use of her legs. Midnight's Fire blamed Night Thrasher for this accident, and became his enemy. It was only to prevent her brother from slaying Night Thrasher that Silhouette came into contact with him again, and she thereafter joined his group the New Warriors. She eventually left both Night Thrasher and the New Warriors, though returned to help a new line up of the team when evil Inhumans kidnapped Sun Girl and Haechi.

SILK

FIRST APPEARANCE *Amazing Spider-Man* #1 (June 2014)
REAL NAME Cindy Moon **OCCUPATION** Vigilante; adventurer
BASE New York City
HEIGHT 5 ft 6 in **WEIGHT** 130 lbs **EYES** Brown **HAIR** Black
SPECIAL POWERS/ABILITIES Similar spider-based powers to Spider-Man, though less strong and more agile.

After a radioactive spider bit Peter Parker (*see* Spider-Man), it went on to bite another of his classmates—Cindy Moon. Like Peter, Cindy gained amazing arachnid-like powers—and could even spin organic webs. However she found it hard to control her powers until Ezekiel Sims started to train her. Worried about Morlun and the Inheritors finding her, Sims locked her up to protect her. Years later, Spider-Man freed her and she took the name Silk. She quickly became a Super Hero and helped Spidey defeat Morlun and his family. Cindy eventually joined SHIELD and helped spy on the Black Cat's criminal empire.

SILVER DAGGER

FIRST APPEARANCE *Doctor Strange* #1 (June 1974)
REAL NAME Isaiah Curwen
OCCUPATION Self-appointed mystic policeman **BASE** Mobile
HEIGHT 6 ft **WEIGHT** 220 lbs **EYES** Black **HAIR** Gray
SPECIAL POWERS/ABILITIES Spellcaster; can project mystic energy bolts, enlarge animals, and give himself superstrength; his silver dagger can cut through Doctor Strange's magical barriers.

The Pope's favored choice of successor, Isaiah Curwen harbored hopes of elevation to the Holy See. But the College of Cardinals failed to elect him, and Curwen decided to fight for the church in a different way. After studying the Vatican's library of black magic books, he set off to fight mystical masters across the world. A cruel psychopath, he has been a thorn in the side of Doctor Strange, even taking Strange's lover, Clea, and burning her soul in mystical fire.

SILVER SABLE

FACTFILE

REAL NAME
Silver Sable

OCCUPATION
CEO, Silver Sable International

BASE
Symkaria

HEIGHT 5 ft 5 ins
WEIGHT 125 lbs
EYES Blue
HAIR Silver

FIRST APPEARANCE
Amazing Spider-Man #265 (June 1985)

POWERS

Silver Sable is a master of martial arts and a highly skilled markswoman, swordswoman, gymnast, and strategist. She sometimes uses a samurai sword (katana), and the chai, a half-moon-shaped, weighted projectile of her own design.

Symkaria, a small country in the Balkans, suffered greatly under German occupation during World War II. After the war, Sable's father formed a group called the Wild Pack that scoured the world for Nazi war criminals. Silver was only a child when her mother died in her arms, the victim of a terrorist attack. From that moment she devoted her entire life to preparing for the day she would take over the Wild Pack, training in all forms of martial arts and becoming a weapons expert. Silver began her leadership of the Wild Pack by continuing the fight to bring former Nazis to justice, but as the years passed she expanded the scope of the Wild Pack. She formed Silver Sable International, a company that provided security, apprehended wanted felons, and recovered stolen property for foreign governments, major corporations, and private individuals. Her company eventually became Symkaria's primary source of income and any citizen could be drafted into its service. She seemingly died while fighting the Rhino, but survived and decided to fight from the shadows while the world thought her dead. When Countess Karkov seized power in Symkaria, backed by Norman Osborn, Silver Sable teamed up with Spider-Man and the Wild Pack to free her country from Karkov's control.

SILVER SAMURAI

Master with a deadly katana blade

FACTFILE

SILVER SAMURAI

REAL NAME
Keniuchio Harada

OCCUPATION
Mercenary

BASE
Mobile

HEIGHT 6 ft 6 in
WEIGHT 250 lbs
EYES Brown
HAIR Black

FIRST APPEARANCE
Daredevil #111 (July 1974)

POWERS
Body generates tachyon field that he focuses through his sword; skilled in ways of samurai—master of bushido and kenjutsu.

The illegitimate mutant son of a Japanese crimelord—and the half-brother of Mariko Yashida—Keniuchio (or Ken) mastered bushido before becoming a mercenary whose assignments included work for Hydra and pitted him against Daredevil, Spider-Man, and Black Widow. He often served as a bodyguard for Viper and once battled Spider-Man on the set of *Saturday Night Live*. After his father's death, Keniuchio struggled with Mariko for the leadership of Clan Yashida, but her lover Wolverine helped her prevail against him. When Mariko died, Keniuchio finally took on that mantle.

HERO OR CROOK

Keniuchio proved unsuited for the leadership of a large criminal organization. He reformed for a while and worked as a Super Hero in Japan. He was later brainwashed into believing that Professor X had telepathically compelled him to leave crime behind, so he returned to his old ways as a mercenary. However, he managed to lose his suspicion and become the head of security for the Prime Minister of Japan. Madame Hydra recruited him to become the leader of the Hand, but he refused that particular honor and helped the Avengers against them instead.

Keniuchio retained his powers after M-Day, but soon after that he lost a fight with Wolverine—along with his right hand. He survived, but was later attacked by black-suited samurai hired by the Red Right Hand—a group dedicated to destroying Wolverine and everything he held dear. He died defending his sister's grave.

The Silver Samurai met the new Avengers in their first adventure abroad.

SON OF THE SAMURAI

Keniuchio's son Shingen—Shin, for short, named after Keniuchio's father—took on the identity of the Silver Samurai after the original's death. He joined with Wolverine's adopted daughter Amiko Kobayashi (whom he was dating) to become thieves, but they ran afoul of the Hand and had to be rescued by Wolverine. Some time afterward, Shin joined Mystique in her efforts to recruit mutants to her side, and he later attended the Hellfire Academy run by Kade Killgore. This put him in direct conflict with Wolverine's Jean Grey School for Higher Learning. Later, while attending a meeting of the Universal Bank as CEO of Yashida Corp, Shin fought Roxxon's superpowered CEO, Dario Agger.

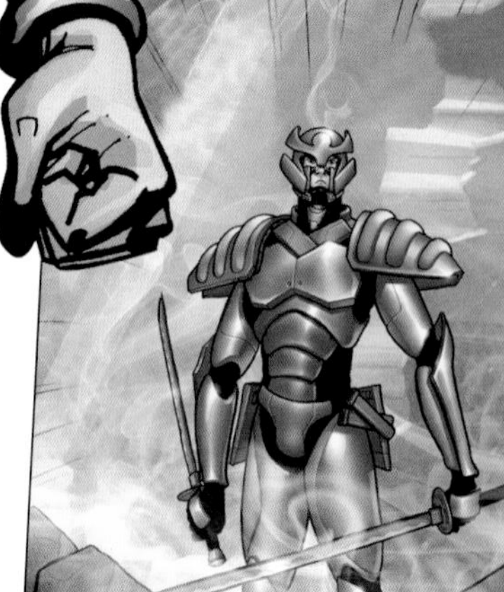

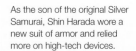

As the son of the original Silver Samurai, Shin Harada wore a new suit of armor and relied more on high-tech devices.

SILVERMANE

SILVERMANE

FACTFILE

REAL NAME
Silvio Manfredi

OCCUPATION
Criminal leader and mastermind

BASE
New York City

HEIGHT 6 ft 2 in;
(as cyborg) 7 ft

WEIGHT 195 lbs;
(as cyborg) 440 lbs

EYES Blue

HAIR Silver

FIRST APPEARANCE
The Amazing Spider-Man #73
(June 1969)

POWERS
Body generates tachyon field that he focuses through his sword; skilled in ways of samurai—master of bushido and kenjutsu.

A leader of the Maggia crime syndicate, the elderly Silvermane ordered the theft of an ancient tablet bearing a formula for a youth serum. He forced Dr. Curt Connors to create the serum and drank it. As a horrified SPIDER-MAN watched, Silvermane grew younger and younger until he seemingly disappeared completely. Fortunately the serum had a boomerang effect, and Silvermane rapidly aged back into his forties.

Silvermane briefly took over a New York-based splinter group of HYDRA and then vainly attempted to unite New York City's organized crime under his leadership. He fell from a great height while fighting the third GREEN GOBLIN and Spider-Man. His injuries undid the effects of the youth serum, causing him to revert to old age. Nearly slain by the vigilante Dagger (*see* CLOAK AND DAGGER), Silvermane had his brain, face, and vital organs transplanted into a robotic body. He was thought killed in a gang war with the Owl after his body was dropped into a garbage compactor. He seemed to reappear later, but it was only a trick by MYSTERIO. His head later turned up in a dump, however, still alive. Silvermane counts Spider-Man, DAREDEVIL, Cloak and Dagger, the PUNISHER, and the KINGPIN among his foes. He is also the father of Joseph Manfredi, the criminal BLACKWING.

SIMS, EZEKIEL

FIRST APPEARANCE *Amazing Spider-Man* #30 (June 2001)
REAL NAME Ezekiel Sims
OCCUPATION Businessman **BASE** Manhattan
HEIGHT 6 ft **WEIGHT** 180 lbs **EYES** Blue **HAIR** Gray
SPECIAL POWERS/ABILITIES Like Spider-Man, he has Spider-Sense, super-strength, enhanced speed and agility, and can crawl and swing from webs.

Ezekiel Sims is a Spider-Totem. He has powers similar to SPIDER-MAN, and is connected to the Multiverse Web of Life that links all beings with spider powers. He is a member of the Spider Society and exceedingly wealthy. He attempted to save Peter Parker (Spider-Man) from Morlun, the Devourer of Totems, but Parker would not listen until he finally encountered Morlun. Ezekiel then rescued Parker. He also helped Parker evade Shathra the Spider-Wasp, but betrayed Parker when the mystical entity the Gatekeeper decreed that only one of them could live. Taking pity on Parker at the last moment, Ezekiel sacrificed himself to save Spider-Man.

SIN

Since the Red Skull ordered Crossbones to retrain Sin, she has been deadlier than ever and central to the Skull's plans.

Synthia's father—the RED SKULL—used a strange machine to accelerate her aging and grant her superpowers, transforming her into Mother Superior. Encouraged by his success, he repeated the process on four orphaned girls and used them to form a team of Super Villains named the Sisters of Sin. When CAPTAIN AMERICA later used the same machine to reverse his own aging, Synthia and the other Sisters of Sin reverted to girlhood again. This cost Synthia her powers.

SHIELD tried to reform her by erasing her memories, but her lover CROSSBONES kidnapped and tortured her until she recovered them. She was later injured in the blast that killed her father, scarring her face and transforming her into a new Red Skull, determined to carry on her father's legacy. Sin retrieved the Book of the Skull which led her to Red Skull's magical hammer, transforming her into the powerful Skadi. She used the hammer to free her new master, the SERPENT (Cul Borson), but was defeated by Steve Rogers wielding Mjolnir. Odin then confiscated her hammer, reverting Skadi to Sin's original form. Sin went on to work for HYDRA alongside BARON ZEMO, Crossbones and TASKMASTER. When their scheme failed, she allied herself with a clone of Red Skull, making plans to rewrite Steve Rogers' past with KOBIK the Cosmic Cube.

SIN

FACTFILE

REAL NAME
Synthia Schmidt

OCCUPATION
Terrorist

BASE
Mobile

HEIGHT 5 ft 8 in

WEIGHT 120 lbs

EYES Green

HAIR Red

FIRST APPEARANCE
(as Mother Superior) *Captain America* #290 (February 1984); (as Sin) *Captain America* #355 (July 1989)

POWERS
As Mother Superior: intangibility, telepathy, telekinesis, and teleportation. These powers have since been lost.
As Sin: experienced with a range of weapons.

Due to years of training, Sin is one of the world's deadliest killers.

SILVER SURFER

Sentinel of the Spaceways

SILVER SURFER

FACTFILE

REAL NAME
Norrin Radd

OCCUPATION
Spacefaring adventurer

BASE
Mobile

HEIGHT 6 ft 4 in
WEIGHT 225 lbs (variable)
EYES Silver (blue as Radd)
HAIR None (black eyebrows as Radd)

FIRST APPEARANCE
Fantastic Four #48 (March 1966)

POWERS

Navigates the galaxy at faster-than-light speeds, riding virtually indestructible board; can channel cosmic energy to augment strength, heal others, and restructure matter.

ALLIES/FOES

ALLIES Fantastic Four, Shalla-Bal, Alicia Masters, Al B Harper, theDefenders, Mantis, Nova

FOES Galactus, Mephisto, Loki, Terrax, Yarro Gort, the Abomination, Doomsday Man

ISSUE #1

Pre-warned by Uatu the Watcher, the Fantastic Four stand ready for their first encounter with the herald of Galactus—the Silver Surfer.

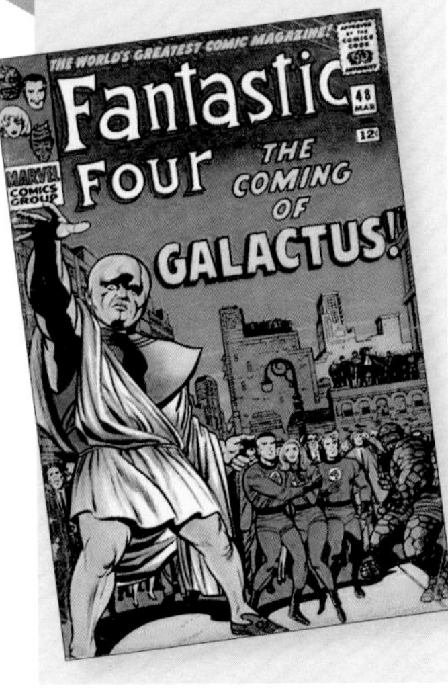
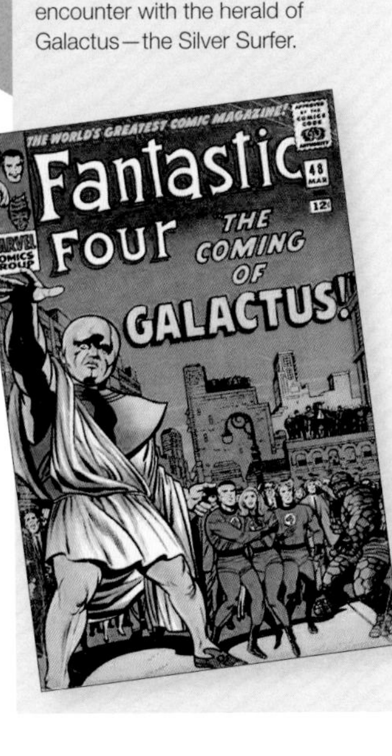

Bored and frustrated by life on Zenn-La, Norrin Radd sought a more challenging existence.

The Silver Surfer is one of the most noble heroes in the galaxy, but also one of the most feared. At times he has been the herald of GALACTUS, when his appearance could mean destruction for the worlds he visits. But the Surfer also has the heart of a hero and is an explorer, always seeking the best in those he meets. He is willing to sacrifice everything—including his own freedom—for the greater good.

THE ZENN-LAVIANS

Born Norrin Radd on the faraway world of Zenn-La, even as a child Norrin was something of an outcast. Wanting for nothing, the Zenn-Lavians were an easy-going people, whereas Norrin hungered for a more meaningful, vibrant life. Even Norrin's lifelong companion, Shalla-Bal, could not calm his restless spirit. It was only when the Zenn-Lavians detected the approach of an alien entity—GALACTUS, Devourer of Worlds—that Norrin came into his own.

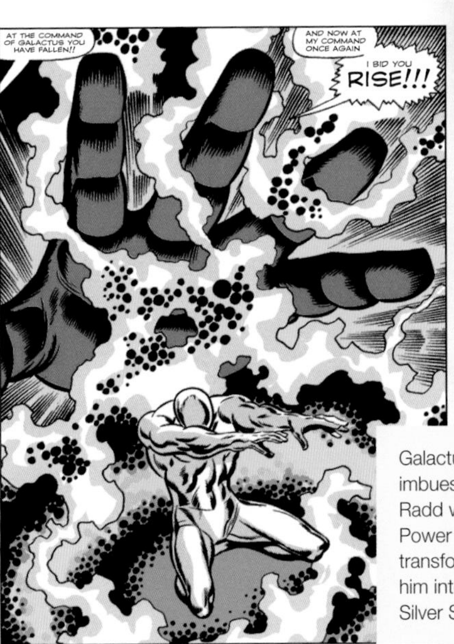

Galactus imbues Norrin Radd with the Power Cosmic, transforming him into the Silver Surfer.

ESSENTIAL STORYLINES
- ***Fantastic Four #48–50*** The Silver Surfer and Galactus' first encounter with Earth.
- ***Silver Surfer Vol. 1 #1*** Stan Lee tells the story of the Silver Surfer's origins in the character's first stand-alone series.
- ***Silver Surfer Vol. 2 #1*** Returning to Zenn-La the Surfer discovers it has been devastated by the world-devouring Galactus.

In exchange for Galactus sparing Zenn-La, Norrin offered to become the entity's herald—to scour the galaxy for planets devoid of life but suitable for Galactus' needs. To empower Norrin for this role, Galactus plucked an old adolescent fantasy from the young Zenn-Lavian's mind and transformed him into a silver-skinned creature who could travel the galaxy on a silver board. Norrin became the Silver Surfer.

HERALD OF GALACTUS

Over time it became increasingly difficult for the Surfer to find suitable worlds for his master, and so Galactus began to make subtle changes to the Silver Surfer's mind. He was made to care less about avoiding sentient life, and countless worlds and peoples were sacrificed. Until, that is, the Silver Surfer arrived on planet Earth.

There the Surfer encountered the FANTASTIC FOUR and Alicia MASTERS. Their compassion and heroism reawakened the Silver Surfer's suppressed emotions and he aligned himself with them. Threatened with the Ultimate Nullifier, a weapon used by Reed Richards (MISTER FANTASTIC), Galactus was driven off, but not before punishing the Silver Surfer for his treachery: Galactus wrapped a field around the Earth to prevent the Silver Surfer from ever leaving. Galactus returned to Earth several times, wishing to reclaim the Silver Surfer as his herald. Each time the Fantastic Four helped drive Galactus away.

INNOCENCE LOST

The Silver Surfer arrived on Earth as something of an innocent. The malevolent DOCTOR DOOM played on this naivety, befriending him and at one point briefly stealing his powers. The Silver Surfer also attracted the attention of the demon MEPHISTO, who became obsessed with claiming the Surfer's soul.

Essentially exiled to the Earth, the Silver Surfer never stopped yearning to travel among the stars once more. With Reed Richards' help he found a way of doing this, but his wanderings were not without upset. Returning to his home world Zenn-La, the Surfer discovered that, although his people still survived, Galactus had returned and ravaged the planet. The Surfer's visit to Zenn-La was curtailed when he learned that his former lover, Shalla-Bal, had been kidnapped by Mephisto. The Silver Surfer freed Shalla-Bal and provided her with some of his own cosmic power—sufficient to heal their home planet.

When the Annihilation Wave threatened the galaxy, the Silver Surfer fought Galactus, Tenebrous (Lord of All Sorrows) and Aegis (Lord of the Darkness Between). In the aftermath, he joined a team of some of the greatest powers in the cosmos, the ANNIHILATORS.

His conscience awoken by Alicia Masters, the Silver Surfer stood ready to oppose Galactus for the very first time.

A NEW DAWN

No matter where he traveled in the universe, the Silver Surfer maintained a great love for Earth. He even had close relationships with three Earth women: Frankie Raye, who herself became a herald of Galactus called Nova; Alicia Masters, who journeyed briefly in space with the Surfer; and Dawn GREENWOOD. The latter proved to be the great love of the Surfer's life. The Surfer met Dawn after he'd rescued her from an alien. Dawn accompanied the Surfer on numerous adventures, and the two eventually admitted their love for each other. When a Zenn-Lavian armada arrived on Earth—led by Shalla-Bal—and threatened to wipe out Earth culture with their own technology, the Surfer stood against them, choosing his new life over his old.

While she was adventuring in space, Dawn's father died. Dawn asked the Surfer if he could help her travel back in time to share a last moment with him. The Surfer agreed, but overshot, and they ended up in the universe that existed before the Big Bang. Unable to return home, the Surfer and Dawn settled down and enjoyed a full life before Dawn eventually died of old age. A heartbroken Surfer turned her remains into cosmic energy and fired it into the Big Bang while Galen (the being who would become Galactus) fled the destruction of his universe (unknowingly also helping the Surfer survive). Dawn's transformed energy became the first light of the universe. The Surfer also created the Power Cosmic in memory of Dawn. He then watched the universe evolve, even visiting Dawn's home as a tourist, until he caught up with the moment he had traveled back in time. He then carried on exploring, as Dawn would have wished.

As the Silver Surfer and Dawn explored the universe before the Big Bang, Dawn grew old. The immortal Surfer used his powers to age his own appearance to match hers.

THE HERALD RETURNS

In time the Surfer found himself trapped once again, this time by ULTRON, who had gained the Soul Gem and was creating a planet of robotic copies on the world of Saiph, threatening to infect the universe with them. The Surfer escaped with the help of Adam WARLOCK, and convinced Galactus to consume the world before Ultron could unleash his legions. In return, Galactus made the Surfer swear allegiance to him. The Silver Surfer was a herald of Galactus once again.

The Surfer's tale went full circle as he found himself once more the herald of the World-Eater.

SINISTER SIX

Super Villain team out to get Spider-Man

FACTFILE

ORIGINAL MEMBERS

DOCTOR OCTOPUS
Mastermind, mechanical arms.

VULTURE Mechanical wings.

ELECTRO Human dynamo.

KRAVEN THE HUNTER
Super-strong combatant.

LIZARD Bloodthirsty human/reptile hybrid.

MYSTERIO Master of illusion.

BASE
Secret

FIRST APPEARANCE
The Amazing Spider-Man Annual #1 (January 1964)

Determined to beat SPIDER-MAN, DOCTOR OCTOPUS contacted five of the web-slinger's greatest enemies and formed a team of Super Villains dedicated to destroying their common foe. He decided that each member of the Six would take on Spider-Man in turn, wearing him down until they could kill him. As the mastermind, Doctor Octopus, of course, would be the final foe. Despite starting out against the original Sinister Six without his powers, Spider-Man regained his abilities along with his self-confidence and prevailed against them.

SEVERAL SINISTERS

The membership, size, and leadership of the team has varied, depending on the villains available. The second time Octopus gathered the six together, he replaced KRAVEN (who had died) with the HOBGOBLIN, but the SANDMAN, who was trying to reform, betrayed them all.

The third Sinister Six replaced the Sandman with a lizard-like alien named Gog. Armed with alien weapons, this group beat Spider-Man at first, and it eventually took the combined efforts of Spider-Man, the FANTASTIC FOUR, the HULK, NOVA, and SOLO to end their spree.

To execute the Spider-Man clone KAINE, the Hobgoblin formed a Sinister Seven consisting of himself, Beetle (*see* MACH-V), ELECTRO, MYSTERIO, Scorpia (a female SCORPION), SHOCKER, and VULTURE. Spider-Man teamed up with KAINE to defeat them.

Furious with Doc Ock, Sandman gathered a Sinister Six to attack him, replacing Octopus with VENOM and employing new versions of Mysterio and Kraven. This backfired when Venom turned on the rest of the team.

BOOMERANG'S SINISTER SIX
1 Overdrive ***2*** Beetle ***3*** Speed Demon ***4*** Shocker ***5*** Boomerang

DEADLY DOZEN

The GREEN GOBLIN formed the Sinister Twelve. Mac Gargan (the new Venom) led the team to break Osborn out of jail. BOOMERANG, CHAMELEON, Electro, HAMMERHEAD, HYDRO-MAN, LIZARD, TOMBSTONE, Sandman, Shocker, and Vulture rounded out the deadly dozen. CAPTAIN AMERICA, DAREDEVIL, the Fantastic Four, IRON MAN, and Yellowjacket rallied to help Spider-Man and stop the Goblin's plans.

During the CIVIL WAR, Doctor Octopus rallied a new team with help from GRIM REAPER, Lizard, Shocker, TRAPSTER, and Vulture. The rebel AVENGERS led by Captain America made short work of them.

The Avengers helped Spider-Man once more against a version of the Sinister Six formed just before Doctor Octopus' death. With Chameleon, Electro, Mysterio, RHINO, and Sandman by his side, Doc Ock held the entire world hostage. After Doctor Octopus took over Spider-Man's body, Boomerang started a new short-lived group.

Spider-Man (now Otto Octavius) captured a number of Super Villains and used mind-control to form them into his new "heroic" Superior Six team. He lost control of them during a battle with the MASTERS OF EVIL. Later, SWARM (Fritz von Meyer) and Aaron Davis (Iron Spider) each tried forming their own group.

SINISTER SIX
1 Sandman ***2*** Vulture ***3*** Mysterio ***4*** Kraven ***5*** Doctor Octopus ***6*** Electro

Otto Octavius' Superior Six was a failed experiment.

SINGULARITY

FIRST APPEARANCE *A-Force* #1 (July, 2015)
REAL NAME Singularity
OCCUPATION Adventurer
BASE Mobile **HEIGHT** 5 ft 2 in **WEIGHT** Unknown
EYES White **HAIR** Blue
SPECIAL POWERS/ABILITIES Able to use her body, within which exists a pocket dimension, to shield and conceal others; teleportation; flight; telepathic tracking.

Singularity crashed like a falling star into Arcadia, a realm of Doom's Battleworld. There she met the women of A-Force, who found themselves caught in the middle of one of Loki's schemes. When Loki's deception unraveled, Singularity blast a hole into the Deadlands, unleashing an army of zombies. To save her new A-Force friends, Singularity enveloped the zombies and carried them into the sky before exploding. Though believed dead, Singularity was reborn in the recreated universe that followed. She rejoined A-Force for a while, before retreating outside the Multiverse.

SINISTER SYNDICATE

FIRST APPEARANCE *Amazing Spider-Man* #280 (Sept. 1986)
BASE New York City **MEMBERS AND POWERS**
Rhino Nearly invulnerable, with superhuman strength [1].
Beetle Armored, multi-weaponed battlesuit [2].
Speed Demon Able to run at superhuman speeds [3].
Boomerang An expert with his specially equipped boomerangs [4].
Hydro-Man Can convert all or part of body into water [5].
Shocker Gauntlets generate highly destructive vibrations [6].

After defeats by the Human Torch and Spider-Man, the Beetle decided to stop being a solo act and organize a super-team. Inspired by the Sinister Six, the Beetle called his group the Sinister Syndicate. The Beetle was soon contacted by international mercenary Jack O'Lantern who hired the Syndicate to assassinate Silver Sable. Spider-Man and the Sandman interfered and foiled this scheme. The Syndicate was then hired by Doctor Octopus to kidnap the royal family of Belgriun, a small European country. Once again, Spider-Man and Silver Sable defeated the Syndicate and eventually forced the team to disband.

SIRYN

FIRST APPEARANCE *Spider-Woman* #37 (April 1981)
REAL NAME Theresa Rourke (Cassidy)
OCCUPATION Private investigator
BASE New York City **HEIGHT** 5 ft 7 in **WEIGHT** 130 lbs
EYES Blue **HAIR** Blond
SPECIAL POWERS/ABILITIES Combination of psionic ability and sonic waves produced by her voice can shatter steel, enable flight, and generate force blasts.

Theresa Rourke was born when her father, Sean Cassidy—Banshee—was on a secret mission. When her mother died, Theresa's uncle Black Tom Cassidy took her in and tried and failed to lead her into a life of crime. When Black Tom was arrested, he told her who her father was and Theresa and Sean were joyfully united. Theresa joined X-Force and served as its deputy leader. After that, she worked with X-Factor. She gave birth to a baby fathered by Jamie Madrox, the Multiple Man, but when he held the baby, it merged into his body. She later took the name Banshee after her father and, after becoming the latest incarnation of an Irish goddess called the Morrigan, disappeared. She returned once to heal Jamie, and then departed.

SIX PACK

FIRST APPEARANCE *Cable* #1 (October 1992) **BASE** Mobile
MEMBERS AND POWERS
Domino Can influence the laws of probability.
G. W. Bridge Skilled combatant and weapons expert.
Anaconda Can stretch limbs and use them to crush enemies.
Solo Able to teleport himself and weapons.
Hammer Weapons designer and technician.
Constrictor Has electrically powered cables mounted on wrists.

Originally known as the Wild Pack, Cable's mercenary team included him, Deadpool, Domino, Grizzly, Hammer, and Garrison Kane. Six Pack often clashed with the mutant villain Stryfe. On one mission, Stryfe threatened to kill Kane if he didn't receive a data disc, and Cable shot Hammer in the back to stop the trade. Outraged, the rest of Six Pack cut ties with Cable. A later incarnation of Six Pack, assembled by Shield, added Solo, Constrictor, and Anaconda under agent G. W. Bridge, but they broke up after Cable defeated them.

SKAAR

The son of the Hulk and Caiera—a warrior of Sakaar's native Shadow People—Skaar was born after his father had left for Earth to exact revenge on the Illuminati for his mother's death (*see* World War Hulk). He emerged from a cocoon, already half-grown. He failed to save Sakaar from Galactus and headed to Earth to kill the Hulk. Bruce Banner, who had been robbed of the ability to become the Hulk by the Red Hulk, trained him how to kill the Hulk should he return, as an excuse to get to know the boy. In the end, surprised by the Hulk's compassion for the innocent, Skaar couldn't kill him. He later settled in the Savage Land and was tracked down by Doc Green (Hulk), who depowered him and took him to Paris to start a new life as a normal human. Skaar, now calling himself Santos, went on to live as a mountain man in the Pyrenees.

SKAAR

FACTFILE
REAL NAME
Skaar
OCCUPATION
Warrior
BASE
Planet Sakaar

HEIGHT 6 ft 1 in
WEIGHT 500 lbs
EYES Brown
HAIR Black

FIRST APPEARANCE
World War Hulk #5 (November 2007)

POWERS
Skaar is a master warrior with superhuman strength and limited invulnerability. Like the Hulk, when calm he turns to a more human form.

Nothing on Sakaar could stand before Skaar's wrath.

SKRULLS, THE

Shape-changing alien race

SKRULLS, THE

FACTFILE

BASE

Tarnax IV, Andromeda Galaxy

FIRST APPEARANCE

Fantastic Four #2

(January 1962)

Skrull warships are designed to protect the paranoid species.

POWERS

Shapeshifting permits radical changes in size, shape, and color; lifespans reach 200 years on average.

The Skrulls are an ancient humanoid species from the Andromeda galaxy, with reptilian physiologies. The cosmic beings known as the CELESTIALS visited the species' birthworld of Skrullos long ago and created Skrullian equivalents to Earth's ETERNALS and Deviants. The Deviant Skrulls exhibited the ability to shapeshift and soon wiped out all competing racial branches.

THE KREE WAR

After forging an interstellar empire, the Skrulls encountered the primitive KREE, who murdered the Skrull contact team and stole their starship technology. A Kree armada soon attacked the Skrulls, triggering the eons-long Kree-Skrull War. Skrull scientists later developed the first Cosmic Cube, which gained sentience and decimated the Skrull Empire, eventually evolving into the exceptionally powerful SHAPER OF WORLDS. The Skrulls eventually bounced back from this tragedy, establishing an Imperial throneworld on Tarnax IV.

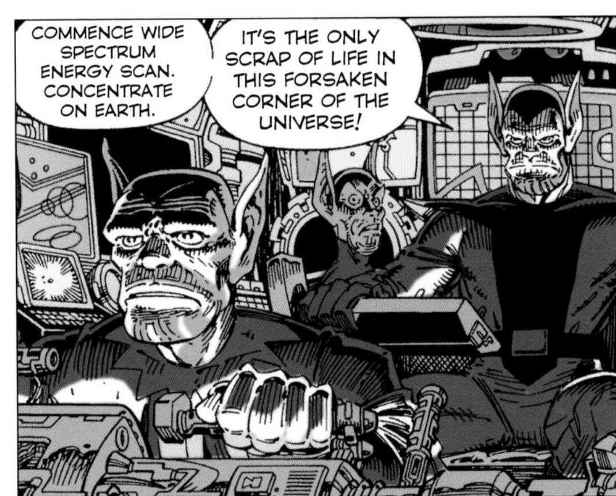

The Skrulls have taken a secret role in Earthly affairs, using their shapeshifting powers to impersonate world leaders.

SECRET AGENTS

The Skrulls placed agents on Earth, but these were defeated by the FANTASTIC FOUR. In response, the Skrull emperor Dorrek VII created the SUPER-SKRULL, who possessed the combined powers of the Fantastic Four. The Skrulls also engineered an elite class of Warskrulls, agents that could duplicate the powers of other beings when they assumed those beings' shapes. After GALACTUS devoured Tarnax IV, the Skrull Empire fell into civil war. The mad Skrull Zabyk detonated a hyper-wave bomb that removed the shapeshifting ability from all Skrulls. The Super-Skrull escaped the bomb's effects and managed to restore the species' shapeshifting powers.

Skrulls can alter their appearance to duplicate anyone, but can be shocked into dropping their disguise if they are hurt or knocked out.

During the ANNIHILATION, the Skrulls lost nearly all of their planets. They turned to VERANKE and made her their queen. Relying on Skrull prophecies, she led the SECRET INVASION in an effort to make Earth the new Skrull homeworld. However, the people of Earth banded together to root out the Skrulls and repel their attack, leaving the few remaining Skrulls homeless once more. AMATSU-MIKABOSHI then slew their gods. The surviving Skrulls are now rebuilding their civilization on other worlds such as Tarnax II.

ESSENTIAL STORYLINES

- ***Avengers #89–97*** The devastating Kree-Skrull War reaches Earth, and the Avengers assemble to prevent innocents from being caught in the crossfire.
- ***Avengers Annual #14*** The insane Skrull warrior Zabyk detonates a hyper-wave bomb, removing the shapeshifting abilities of all Skrulls.
- ***Secret Invasion #1–8*** The Skrulls invade Earth.

SKIDS

FIRST APPEARANCE *X-Factor* #7 (August 1986)
REAL NAME Sally Blevins
OCCUPATION Adventurer **BASE** Mobile
HEIGHT 5 ft 5 in **WEIGHT** 115 lbs **EYES** Blue **HAIR** Blond
SPECIAL POWERS/ABILITIES Skids possesses a protective, frictionless force-field which shields her from harm, and which she can extend to envelop others.

Born a mutant, Skids lived among the sewer-dwelling MORLOCKS until the Mutant Massacre by the MARAUDERS caused her to flee. Rescued by X-FACTOR, for a time she became a trainee with that team, and she fought alongside their junior members, the X-Terminators. Brainwashed into serving with the MUTANT LIBERATION FRONT, Skids eventually regained her freedom after her boyfriend Rusty COLLINS was killed battling Holocaust, and she herself was injured. She kept her powers after M-Day and became an undercover agent of SHIELD.

SLAPSTICK

FIRST APPEARANCE *Slapstick* #1 (November 1992)
REAL NAME Steve Harmon
OCCUPATION Adventurer **BASE** Mobile
HEIGHT 5 ft 7 in **WEIGHT** 145 lbs **EYES** Blue **HAIR** Blond
SPECIAL POWERS/ABILITIES Indestructible, stretchable, and gains strength from electricity, plus superhuman strength, speed, endurance, and agility.

While facing the Overlord and his evil Clowns of Dimension X, Steve Harmon's molecules were transformed into unstable molecules. He also gained a pair of high-tech gloves: the left allowed him to change from human to Slapstick and back, while the right featured an extra-dimensional storage pocket. Steve managed to defeat the Overlord and rescue all of his captives. Later, he joined the NEW WARRIORS for a time, working with his friend SPEEDBALL. After working for the FIFTY-STATE INITIATIVE, Slapstick left and joined the recently rebuilt New Warriors. Becoming disillusioned with the group, he then joined the MERCS FOR MONEY team founded by DEADPOOL.

SLINGSHOT

FIRST APPEARANCE *Mighty Avengers* #13 (July 2008)
REAL NAME Yo-Yo Rodriguez
OCCUPATION Secret agent **BASE** Mobile
HEIGHT Unknown **WEIGHT** Unknown **EYES** Brown
HAIR Black (shaved bald)
SPECIAL POWERS/ABILITIES Super speed, prosthetic arms provide enhanced strength and combat capabilities.

Yo-Yo Rodriguez was the daughter of the Super Villain known as the Griffin. When Daisy JOHNSON was tasked with creating a covert team by Nick FURY, Yo-Yo was one of the people she selected. Thanks to her father's DNA, Yo-Yo possessed super speed. As part of the SECRET WARRIORS, Yo-Yo fought against the SKRULLS and HYDRA. She lost both her arms while fighting Gorgon (the Hydra leader), and had them replaced by two prosthetic arms. She was killed by the WRECKING CREW after the Hydra CAPTAIN AMERICA sent Daisy's team into an ambush at the start of his takeover of the USA.

SKYHAWK

FIRST APPEARANCE *Thor* #395 (September 1988)
REAL NAME Winston Manchester **OCCUPATION** Entrepreneur
BASE New York City **HEIGHT** (as Skyhawk) 6 ft 3 in
WEIGHT (as Skyhawk) 210 lbs **EYES** Blue **HAIR** Brown
SPECIAL POWERS/ABILITIES As Skyhawk, possesses superhuman strength and the ability to fly; formerly a high-achiever working 20 hours a day, he now leaves the office at 5 o'clock.

Businessman Manchester collapsed in the office and was taken to the same hospital where the god Hogun (*see* GODS OF ASGARD) was staying. Manchester opened his eyes to find that he was with two other patients. They had all attracted the attention of Seth, God of Death, (*see* GODS OF HELIOPOLIS). Claiming that Hogun was a threat to the Earth, Seth branded their left palms with the sign of Aton, the glowing disc of the sun, and gave them all superhuman powers. Manchester and his teammates learned that Seth was the real menace and they helped THOR defeat him.

SLATER, JINK

FIRST APPEARANCE *The Incredible Hulk* #36 (March 2002)
REAL NAME Jink Slater
OCCUPATION Professional assassin **BASE** Mobile
HEIGHT/WEIGHT Unrevealed **EYES** Brown **HAIR** Black
SPECIAL POWERS/ABILITIES Excellent marksman; expert with guns and knives; a formidable hand-to-hand combatant; above average in strength and endurance; ruthless in pursuit of his quarry.

Jink Slater was hired by unidentified parties to capture the HULK. Despite his objections, his employers ordered Slater to work with a partner, Sandra Verdugo, on the assignment. Eventually, Slater and Verdugo found the Hulk in his human identity of Bruce Banner in a diner. Their attempt to capture him was thwarted by the arrival of DOC SAMSON. Not trusting his partner, Slater shot Verdugo in the head and escaped. Subsequently, Slater found Banner and Verdugo together in a cabin. Slater shot Verdugo in the shoulder. Verdugo retaliated by setting off explosives that killed Slater.

SMASHER

FIRST APPEARANCE *Avengers* #1 (February 2013)
REAL NAME Isabel Kane
OCCUPATION Astronomer; Imperial Guard **BASE** Mobile
HEIGHT 5 ft 8 in **WEIGHT** 135 lbs **EYES** Blue **HAIR** Brown
SPECIAL POWERS/ABILITIES Izzy wears Exospex, which grant her a life-support system and access to one power at a time: vision powers, energy blasts, hyperspace travel, superhuman durability, strength, and speed. Her suit also allows her to fly.

Izzy Kane was the granddaughter of World War II Super Hero Captain Terror. When she found the Exospex suit of a Smasher (a member of the SHI'AR Imperial Guard) on her family's farm, she used it to be come a Super Hero. After briefly becoming a Subguardian of the Imperial Guard Izzy joined the AVENGERS as Smasher. She had a child with CANNONBALL and later returned to duty in the Imperial Guard. Smasher had previously been the name of other Imperial Guard heroes. Smasher was also the name taken by Kid Kaiju when he became a super monster.

SMYTHE, ALISTAIR

FIRST APPEARANCE *The Amazing Spider-Man Annual* #19 (1985) **REAL NAME** Alistair Smythe
OCCUPATION Criminal inventor **BASE** New York City
HEIGHT 6 ft **WEIGHT** 220 lbs **EYES** Brown **HAIR** Brown
SPECIAL POWERS/ABILITIES Ultimate Spider-Slayer armature provides enhanced strength, and features built-in cutting blades and web shooters.

Alistair Smythe grew up hating SPIDER-MAN. His father, Professor Spencer SMYTHE, built the first robotic Spider-Slayer units, and Alistair continued that legacy. Following a stint in the employ of the KINGPIN, Alistair constructed ever more deadly Spider-Slayers until an accident left him in a wheelchair. He fashioned a cyborg armature for himself and emerged as the Ultimate Spider-Slayer. He later rebuilt the SCORPION's costume for him and murdered J. Jonah JAMESON's wife. The Superior Spider-Man (DOCTOR OCTOPUS) killed him in a final battle.

SNOWBIRD

Nelvanna, goddess of the Northern Lights, mated with a human to produce a child that could defend humanity from the mystical Great Beasts. The infant, named Narya, was raised by Native American sorcerer Michael Twoyoungmen (SHAMAN). She grew to adulthood within a few years, and James MacDonald Hudson invited her and Shaman to join ALPHA FLIGHT. Narya took the name Snowbird, and the cover identity of Anne McKenzie, an officer in the Canadian Mounties. When Alpha Flight teammate Walter Langkowski (SASQUATCH) fell under the mental control of Tanaraq, one of the Great Beasts, Snowbird slew his physical body.

Anne McKenzie married a fellow officer in the RCMP and they had a son. A menace called Pestilence subsequently took mental possession of Snowbird. Hudson's wife Heather defeated Pestilence by killing Narya's physical form. Langkowski's spirit took over Narya's resurrected body, becoming the new Sasquatch. Snowbird's spirit later gained a new body and returned to Alpha Flight. She was not with the team when the Collective (*see* WEAPON OMEGA) destroyed it. During the SECRET INVASION, she helped destroy the SKRULL god Kly'bn.

FACTFILE
REAL NAME
Narya
OCCUPATION
Goddess; adventurer
BASE
Canada

HEIGHT 5 ft 10 in
WEIGHT 108 lbs
EYES (Snowbird) White; (Anne McKenzie) Blue
HAIR Pale blond; (in animal form) White

FIRST APPEARANCE
(as Anne McKenzie)
Uncanny X-Men #120
(April 1979)

SNOWBIRD

POWERS
Snowbird can assume the form of a human woman or of any animal native to the Canadian Arctic. She has superhuman strength and the ability to fly.

SMYTHE, PROFESSOR

FIRST APPEARANCE *The Amazing Spider-Man* #25 (June 1965)
REAL NAME Spencer Smythe
OCCUPATION Professor; criminal inventor
BASE New York City **HEIGHT** 5 ft 10 in **WEIGHT** 175 lbs
EYES Gray **HAIR** Gray
SPECIAL POWERS/ABILITIES Genius-level expertise in engineering and robotics.

Professor Spencer Smythe's life was marked by an irrational hatred for SPIDER-MAN. He used his engineering expertise to construct the Spider-Slayer, a Spider-Man hunting robot, and persuaded *Daily Bugle* publisher J. Jonah JAMESON to pay for it. He followed up with several improved generations of Spider-Slayers, but the radiation used in their construction gradually poisoned him. He died during a revenge plot hatched against both Spider-Man and Jameson, leaving his son Alistair (*see* SMYTHE, Alistair) to carry on his work.

SNARKS

FIRST APPEARANCE *Power Pack* #1 (August 1984)
REAL NAME Zn'rx (pronounced "Snarks")
BASE Snarkworld **HEIGHT** 8 ft (average) **WEIGHT** 400 lbs (average) **EYES** Red **HAIR** None (green scales)
SPECIAL POWERS/ABILITIES Snarks are larger, stronger, and live longer than human beings. As well as various high-tech weapons (their technology is generally more advanced than Earth's), they have a vicious array of teeth and sharp claws.

A malevolent, warlike, reptilian race, the Zn'rx or "Snarks" are based on a planet in the Milky Way galaxy known on Earth as Snarkworld. The Snarks first came to notice when their ages-long conflict with the horselike Kymellians spilled over to Earth. The Queen Mother, Maraud, sent raiding parties to Earth in order to learn the secrets of a new scientific breakthrough discovered by Dr. James Power, and use it as a weapon against their ancient foes. Sent by his people to prevent this from happening, Kymellian champion Aelfyre Whitemane was slain by the Snarks, but not before he passed on his abilities to Dr. Powers' four children. These children, now known as the POWER PACK, defeated the Snark menace.

SONGBIRD

FIRST APPEARANCE *Marvel Two-In-One* #54 (August 1979)
REAL NAME Melissa Gold
OCCUPATION Adventurer
BASE Mobile **HEIGHT** 5 ft 5 in **WEIGHT** 145 lbs
EYES Green **HAIR** White with pink streaks
SPECIAL POWERS/ABILITIES Acoustikinesis: Songbird can generate and manipulate sound waves to create blasts and force-fields, as well as sonic "constructs" such as wings and weaponry.

Melissa Gold grew up with her alcoholic father—her mother was in prison. After a troubled childhood, she ran away from home, took the name Mimi, and eventually fell in with a bunch of female wrestlers called the Grapplers. With the aid of a device that could replicate sonic powers, "Screaming Mimi" worked for Roxxon Oil and the MASTERS OF EVIL. The FIXER upgraded her powers when she joined BARON ZEMO's THUNDERBOLTS, but Melissa eventually turned on Zemo, enjoying life as a hero. She started a relationship with fellow Thunderbolt Abner Jenkins, aka MACH-1 and unlike many of her teammates has remained a hero.

FACTFILE

KEY MEMBERS

GENERAL CHEN
The first Supreme Serpent; a grossly overambitious individual.

DAN DUNN
Co-leader; talk-show host, white right-winger.

MONTAGUE HALE
Co-leader and black, left-winger.

J.C. PENNYSWORTH
Head of Richmond Enterprises; sponsor of Sons of the Satan.

HATE-MONGER
Foments hatred and anger.

RUSSELL DABOIA
Mystic powers.

SKINHEAD
Superhuman neo-Nazi.

BASE California

FIRST APPEARANCE
Avengers #32 (September 1966)

SONS OF THE SERPENT

"As the first serpent drove Adam and Eve from Eden, so shall we drive all foreigners from this land." This is the mantra of the Sons of the Serpent—an organization fueled by hatred and sponsored by a few wealthy businessmen. Targeting non-whites, immigrants, and the infirm, the Sons of the Serpent is dedicated to making the US a citadel of white racial supremacy.

During their first bid for power, they took CAPTAIN AMERICA hostage to try to force the AVENGERS into publicly supporting their evil cause. When this failed, the Sons developed further plots aimed at dividing America and black against white, one of which actually culminated in a mind-controlled Captain America fighting against his black partner, the FALCON. They have used mysticism at times and infiltrated the New York judicial system before DAREDEVIL intervened. They also fought against Sam Wilson when he was Captain America.

SOUTHERN, CANDY

FIRST APPEARANCE *X-Men* #31 (April 1967)
REAL NAME Candace Southern **OCCUPATION** CEO Southern Industries **BASE** New York City; Colorado Rocky Mountains
HEIGHT/WEIGHT Unknown **EYES** Blue **HAIR** Black
SPECIAL POWERS/ABILITIES Normal human strength of woman who engaged in regular exercise. Had great leadership abilities.

Archangel Warren Worthington was unable to prevent Candy's murder.

Candace "Candy" Southern began dating Warren Worthington III when they were teenagers. Southern discovered that Worthington was the ANGEL, a member of X-MEN, when his uncle, the original DAZZLER abducted her. Southern and Worthington later shared a home in the Rocky Mountains which became the DEFENDERS' headquarters. Southern was the team's business manager and government liaison. She was killed by Worthington's enemy, Cameron HODGE. Southern's mind was assimilated into the group consciousness of the techno-organic PHALANX. She sacrificed herself to destroy Hodge.

SOVIET SUPER-SOLDIERS

Created to be the Soviet Union's answer to the AVENGERS, the Soviet Super-Soldiers functioned as that nation's defenders through much of the latter part of the Cold War. Eventually, questioning some of the orders given to them by the State, they rebelled, and began to operate independently. The Russian government sent their replacement team, the Supreme Soviets, to reclaim the members of the Soviet Super-Soldiers and bring them back into line—an attempt that met with failure.

Thereafter, with the fall of communism and the dissolution of the Soviet Union, the surviving members of both the Soviet Super-Soldiers and the Supreme Soviet joined forces with other new heroes to become first the People's Protectorate, then the WINTER GUARD, still dedicated to using their great powers to defend their homeland, no matter who ruled it.

SOVIET SUPER-SOLDIERS
1 Red Guardian ***2*** Unicorn ***3*** Ursa Major ***4*** Vanguard ***5*** Crimson Dynamo ***6*** Darkstar ***7*** Synthesizer ***8*** Perun ***9*** Titanium Man (The Gremlin) ***10*** Vostok ***11*** Fantasma ***12*** Blind Faith ***13*** Firefox ***14*** Sibercat ***15*** Stencil

FACTFILE

NOTABLE MEMBERS

CRIMSON DYNAMO
In armor, has superhuman strength, durability, and can fly.

URSA MAJOR
Transforms into a large bear; retains his intelligence while in bear form.

VANGUARD
Forcefield repels virtually all electromagnetic and kinetic energy. By crossing his hammer and sickle in front of his body, he can redirect energy repelled by his natural force-field.

DARKSTAR
Manipulates extradimensional energy called the Darkforce.

TITANIUM MAN (GREMLIN)
Armor provided superhuman strength, durability flight; fired force blasts from hands.

BASE
The former Soviet Union, now Russia

FIRST APPEARANCE
Incredible Hulk #258 (April 1981)

SPACE PHANTOM

FIRST APPEARANCE *Avengers* #2 (November 1963)
REAL NAME Unknown **OCCUPATION** Agent of Immortus
BASE Limbo **HEIGHT** 6 ft 6 in **WEIGHT** 215 lbs **EYES** Blue
HAIR Red or black **SPECIAL POWERS/ABILITIES** Space Phantom can change his appearance to look like any living being. If they have superpowers, then he assumes those powers as well. The being whose form is taken is instantly sent to the dimension of Limbo.

The Space Phantom is an alien from the planet Phantus, which shifted into the timeless dimension of Limbo when the space-time continuum ruptured. Or so it was thought. There are actually several Space Phantoms, and anyone trapped in Limbo for too long forgets their past life and becomes one. Immortus took advantage of this to mold them into his servants and send them out to kidnap others for his examination. Since they can impersonate anyone, including each other, it's difficult to determine which Space Phantoms are responsible for what.

SPACEKNIGHTS

FIRST APPEARANCE *Rom* #1 (December 1979)
BASE The planet Galador
NOTABLE MEMBERS
Breaker Red, with radiation powers. **Firefall** Red, with magical fire. **Rom** Silver, with neutralizer gun. **Scanner** Blue, with incredible senses. **Seeker** Red, with missiles.
Starshine Golden, with magical light. **Terminator** Black, with optic blasts. **Unseen** White, with invisiblity. **Ikon** Silver, wields an energized polearm
SPECIAL POWERS/ABILITIES The powers of the Spaceknights vary, but they usually include superhuman durability, endurance, speed, and strength, and each can expose the shape-changing Dire Wraiths and achieve spaceflight.

When the planet Galador came under threat of invasion by Dire Wraiths, a number of Galadorians volunteered to be transformed into cyborg warriors known as Spaceknights, each with their own style, weapon, and powers. The first of these was Rom, who became a legend among the Spaceknights. After rescuing Galador, the Spaceknights hunted down the Dire Wraiths scattered on planets throughout the galaxy, including Earth. There have been four generations of Spaceknights, improving them each time. The ancient Builders later evaluated Galador and, judging it unworthy, destroyed it, including every Spaceknight on it.

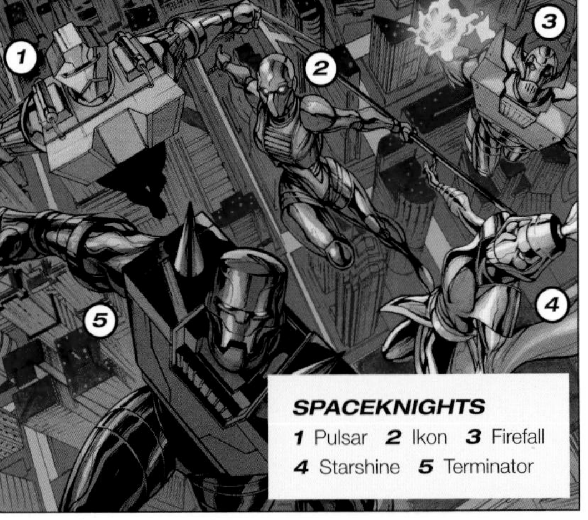

SPACEKNIGHTS
1 Pulsar ***2*** Ikon ***3*** Firefall
4 Starshine ***5*** Terminator

With the help of the Annihilators, the Spaceknights made peace with the Dire Wraiths.

SPECTRUM

SPECTRUM

FACTFILE
REAL NAME
Monica Rambeau
OCCUPATION
Adventurer
BASE
New Orleans; New York City

HEIGHT 5 ft 8 in
WEIGHT 145 lbs
EYES Black
HAIR Black

FIRST APPEARANCE
The Amazing Spider-Man Annual #16 (1982)

POWERS
Spectrum can turn into any type of energy, including light, electricity, microwaves, radio waves, ultra-violet waves, gamma rays, or lasers. She can travel at the speed of light and fire blasts of whatever type of energy she becomes.

New Orleans Harbor Patrol lieutenant Monica Rambeau was struck by extradimensional energy from a terrorist's "energy disruptor" weapon. This exposure gave Rambeau her superpowers. Dubbed "Captain Marvel" by the media, she tried to put her new abilities to good use. Early in her career she met Spider-Man, who introduced her to the Avengers. They agreed to help train her to use her powers more skillfully. In time she became a valuable member of the Avengers, and was even their leader for several stints.

When Genis-Vell, the son of Captain Mar-Vell, wanted to use his father's name, Rambeau gladly gave up the name and became Photon. Later, Genis-Vell changed *his* name to Photon, forcing Rambeau to change her Super Hero name yet again, this time to Pulsar.

Monica led the team Nextwave against terrorist organization SILENT and the Beyond Corporation. She sided with Captain America during the Civil War but later registered with the Fifty-State Initiative. She has since changed her code name to Spectrum and joined Luke Cage's Avengers team, helping stop Shuma Gorath from destroying the world. She later helped form the Ultimates, a group protecting the Earth from cosmic threats. One of the team's early actions was to transform Galactus from a devourer of worlds to a life-bringer.

As a member of the Ultimates, Spectrum fought alongside America Chavez.

SPEED

FIRST APPEARANCE *Young Avengers* #10 (February 2006)
REAL NAME Thomas Shepherd
OCCUPATION Adventurer **BASE** New York City
HEIGHT 5 ft 10 in **WEIGHT** 182 lbs **EYES** Blue **HAIR** White
SPECIAL POWERS/ABILITIES Superhuman speed, plus atomic destabilization, which can cause touched objects to explode.

Tommy Shepherd thought he'd been born and raised in New Jersey to Frank and Mary Shepherd. In fact, he and Billy Kaplan (*see* Wiccan) of the Young Avengers were products of the Scarlet Witch's powers. Desperate for children, the Scarlet Witch had created twin boys for herself out of lost souls, but Mephisto eventually came to reclaim them. When the Scarlet Witch remade the world on M-Day, she remade the boys too, placing them in different homes. Soon after the Vision and Super-Skrull had figured this out, Tommy took the code name Speed and joined his twin brother Billy in the Young Avengers.

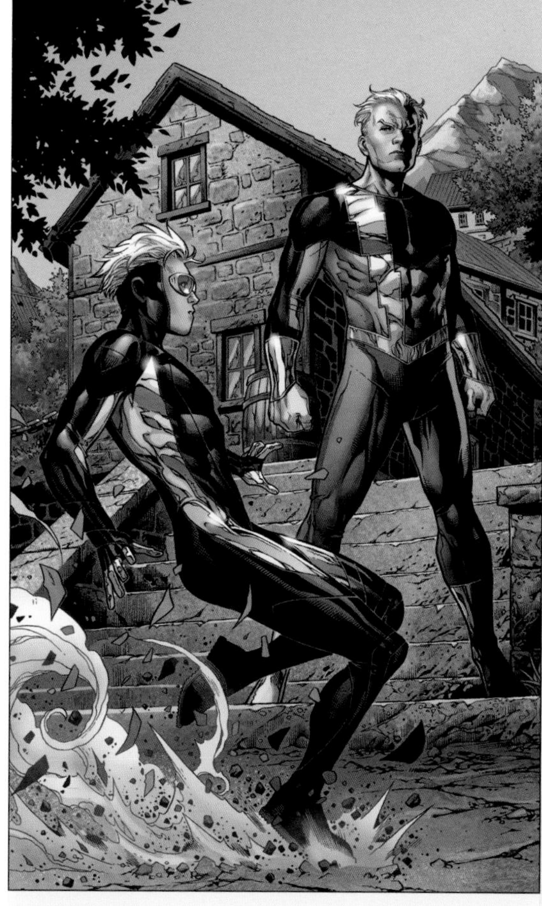

Tommy bears a striking resemblance to his uncle Quicksilver.

SPEEDFREEK

FIRST APPEARANCE *Incredible Hulk* #388 (December 1991)
REAL NAME Leon Shappe
OCCUPATION Assassin **BASE** Mobile
HEIGHT/WEIGHT Unrevealed **EYES** Brown **HAIR** Brown
SPECIAL POWERS/ABILITIES Combat suit of titanium steel alloy that is virtually indestructible; rocket-powered boots enable flight and travel at 150 mph; uses two long Adamantium blades.

Drug addict Leon Shappe stole a sophisticated combat suit from an inventor and became the assassin Speedfreek. He clashed with the Hulk a few times. When a protestor erroneously gunned down Shappe's daughter outside an abortion clinic, the Hulk stopped him from murdering the killer. While dodging Speedfreek's blades, the Hulk threw a car battery at him. Speedfreek sliced right through it with his blades, accidentally showering himself with battery acid. He was part of the band of villains battling the New Warriors in Stamford, Connecticut, when Nitro destroyed the place. Speedfreek died in the blast.

SPEEDBALL

FIRST APPEARANCE *The Amazing Spider-Man Annual* #22 (1988)
REAL NAME Robert Baldwin **OCCUPATION** High-school student **BASE** New York City; formerly Springdale, Connecticut
HEIGHT 5 ft 6 in **WEIGHT** 133 lbs **EYES** Blue **HAIR** Blond
SPECIAL POWERS/ABILITIES Personal force-field allows him to absorb all kinetic energy directed at him and reflect it back at a greater velocity, which he often does by bouncing off objects.

Bombarded with energy bubbles from another dimension, Robert Baldwin gained strange powers. Once he learned to control them, he created a costume and took the name Speedball, becoming a crimefighter in his hometown. He co-founded the New Warriors and was with them when Nitro exploded, destroying a city and initiating the Civil War. Surviving Nitro's blast, Baldwin joined the Thunderbolts, calling himself Penance and donning a suit of armor with 612 internal spikes, one for every person who had died in the explosion. He later returned to being Speedball and worked at the Avengers Academy, then reformed the New Warriors.

SPEED DEMON

FIRST APPEARANCE *The Amazing Spider-Man* #222 (Nov. 1981)
REAL NAME James Sanders
OCCUPATION Professional criminal **BASE** New York City
HEIGHT 5 ft 11 in **WEIGHT** 175 lbs **EYES** Black **HAIR** Gray
SPECIAL POWERS/ABILITIES A super speedster, able to run at up to 160 mph; also possesses superhuman strength.

The Grandmaster gave James Sanders his powers when he recruited the chemist for his Squadron Sinister. Sanders called himself the Whizzer at first, but then changed it to Speed Demon. He regularly fought Spider-Man and later joined the Sinister Syndicate. After that, he took up with Baron von Strucker's Thunderbolts, but he returned to the Squadron Sinister when the Grandmaster called him again. Speed Demon later joined a new incarnation of the Sinister Six before being arrested by Captain America (Sam Wilson) for robbing a pawn shop.

SPHINX

FIRST APPEARANCE *Nova* #6 (October 1999)
REAL NAME Anath-Na Mut
OCCUPATION Wizard **BASE** Mobile flying pyramid
HEIGHT 7 ft 2 in **WEIGHT** 450 lbs **EYES** Red **HAIR** None
SPECIAL POWERS/ABILITIES Enhanced strength; Ka stone permitted immortality, flight, telepathy, energy transference, and the ability to fire concussive beams.

Anath-Na Mut, an ancient Egyptian mutant given further powers by the Caretaker of Arcturus, served in the court of Ramses II until his failure to defeat Moses branded him an exile. He became the immortal Sphinx through the energies of the Ka stone, wandering for five thousand years until absorbing the extraterrestrial Xandar living computer with unwitting help from the hero Nova. Now nearly omnipotent, the Sphinx met defeat at Galactus' hands. Later, Anath-Na Mut returned to life. When he merged with his reincarnated Egyptian lover, Meryet Karim (Sphinx II), the two formed the "Omni-Sphinx."

Spider-Girl, see page 348

SPIDER-MAN

Your friendly neighborhood Web-slinger

SPIDER-MAN

FACTFILE

REAL NAME
Peter Benjamin Parker

OCCUPATION
Freelance photographer, science teacher

BASE
New York City

HEIGHT 5 ft 10 in
WEIGHT 170 lbs
EYES Hazel
HAIR Brown

FIRST APPEARANCE
Amazing Fantasy #15 (August 1962)

POWERS

Possesses the proportionate strength, speed, agility, and reflexes of a spider. Can cling to any surface and generate organic webbing. Also possesses a "spider-sense" that warns him of danger and can psychically align him with his environment. Invented spider-tracers that he can track across the city with his spider-sense.

ALLIES/FOES

ALLIES Ben and May Parker, Mary Jane Parker, Captain America, the Avengers, the Fantastic Four, the X-Men, Eugene "Flash" Thompson, Betty Brant Leeds

FOES Chameleon, Vulture, Doctor Octopus, Sandman, Kingpin, Green Goblin, Lizard, Electro, Kraven the Hunter, Black Cat, Venom, Mysterio, Carnage, Scrier, Judas Traveller

ISSUE #1

While attending a scientific demonstration, Peter Parker was bitten by a spider that had been exposed to radioactivity. Feeling nauseous, the teenager immediately headed home and began to exhibit the most amazing powers—like the ability to stick to walls and crawl up sheer surfaces!

Before gaining his spider-powers, Peter Parker was weaker than most of the kids his age.

Peter Parker's parents died in a plane crash while he was still a child. When they said goodbye at the airport, his parents told him to be a good boy for his Aunt May and Uncle Ben Parker, who later raised him as their own son. Peter always thought of his Uncle Ben as his best friend. Not only did Ben Parker spend quality time with the boy, he had a great sense of humor and spent many hours telling jokes and pulling gags on Peter, who developed a real appreciation for quips and pranks. Peter studied hard in school and became an honor student. Although his teachers praised him, the other students had little use for a know-it-all like puny Parker. The girls thought him too quiet, and the boys considered him a wimp.

ORIGIN OF SPIDER-MAN

On the day his life changed forever, Peter went to a science exhibition by himself where he was bitten by a common house spider that had been exposed to a massive dose of radiation. Within a few hours, Peter discovered that he could stick to walls and had gained other amazing arachnid abilities.

Anxious to cash in on his new powers he designed a distinctive costume that concealed his identity, built a pair of web-shooters, and went into showbusiness using the Amazing Spider-Man as his stage name.

One night, after a performance, he was walking toward an elevator when a security guard asked him to stop a fleeing man. However, Peter Parker did nothing and the burglar escaped. A few days later the same thief murdered Peter's Uncle Ben! Filled with remorse, Peter vowed that he would never allow another innocent person to suffer because Spider-Man had failed to act. He had learned, in the hardest possible way, to use his great powers in a responsible manner.

Peter began to suspect that his powers might be the result of paranormal forces.

MY FAULT -- ALL MY FAULT! IF ONLY I HAD STOPPED HIM WHEN I COULD HAVE! BUT I DIDN'T -- AND NOW -- UNCLE BEN -- IS DEAD...

HIGH-SCHOOL HERO

Spider-Man soon found himself battling criminals such as the Chameleon, the Vulture, Doctor Octopus, the Sandman, Doctor Doom, the Lizard, Electro, Mysterio, the Green Goblin, the Scorpion, and many more. He attempted to join the Fantastic Four and began a feud with the Human Torch.

J. Jonah Jameson, publisher of the *Daily Bugle,* hated masked vigilantes and claimed Spider-Man was a menace to the public. Peter saw an opportunity to exploit Jameson's campaign and began taking pictures of himself as Spider-Man. He was soon supporting himself by selling these pictures to the *Daily Bugle* on a freelance basis.

Peter eventually graduated from Midtown High with the highest scholastic average in the school's history. However, he almost missed the graduation ceremony. While the other seniors were donning caps and gowns, he was busy battling the Molten Man. He won his fight and arrived at the ceremony just in time to learn that he had won a full scholarship to Empire State University.

RIGHT HERE,
JUST WHERE I WANNA BE.
NOOOOO!

The Green Goblin murdered Gwen Stacy, Peter's first true love.

COLLEGE YEARS AND BEYOND

While in college, Peter met Mary Jane Watson (his future wife), but began to date Gwen Stacy. (Gwen would later die tragically at the hands of the Green Goblin.) Peter became best friends with Harry Osborn and later learned that the Green Goblin was secretly Harry's father Norman. Spider-Man also encountered such villains as Kingpin, the Rhino, Shocker, Silvermane and the Prowler.

High above the streets of Manhattan, Spider-Man tangled with Doc Ock.

ESSENTIAL STORYLINES

- ***Amazing Spider-Man #31–33*** Spider-Man battles the Master Planner in order to obtain a rare serum that can save Aunt May's life.
- ***Amazing Spider-Man: Fearful Symmetry or Kraven's Last Hunt (tpb)*** Kraven the Hunter kidnaps Spider-Man and takes his place in a battle against the deadly Vermin.
- ***Amazing Spider-Man: The Saga of the Alien Costume (tpb)*** Spider-Man learns that his new black costume is actually an alien symbiote.
- ***Amazing Spider-Man vs. Venom (tpb)*** Spider-Man meets his match when Venom enters his life.
- ***Amazing Spider-Man: Identity Crisis (tpb)*** When a $5 million bounty is placed on his head for a murder he didn't commit, Spider-Man must adopt four new costumed identities to find the real murderer.
- ***Amazing Spider-Man: Coming Home (tpb)*** Spider-Man meets the man called Ezekiel and learns that there may be a lot more to his origin than he ever realized.

After graduating from college, Peter encountered the acrobatic cat burglar Black Cat (his girlfriend for a while), and the criminals Hydro-Man, Speed Demon, and the Hobgoblin. He also battled the unstoppable Juggernaut and cosmically-powered Firelord. He temporarily donned a new black costume that possessed some additional new powers, but later proved to be an alien symbiote. Meanwhile, his relationship with the beautiful model Mary Jane Watson had grown serious and they were married.

FURTHER DEVELOPMENTS

After leading a European crime cult for many years, Norman Osborn reentered Peter's life. Peter also met a man called Ezekiel (*see* Sims, Ezekiel) who claimed that Spider-Man's powers were the result of magic and not a radioactive spider. Peter later confronted the Queen (*see* Spider-Queen), who had the power to control insects and she mutated him into a giant spider. After returning to his human form, Peter learned that his powers and strength had been increased and that he had gained the ability to produce organic webbing. Peter also joined a new Avengers team.

After a battle with the mysterious, super-strong, vampiric villain Morlun, in which Peter appeared to have been killed, Peter temporarily accepted a new armored costume and a job working for Tony Stark (*see* Iron Man). However he has since returned to his traditional look.

THE ALIEN SUIT

Along with other heroes, Spider-Man was transported to a planet created by a near-omnipotent being called the Beyonder and forced to fight in a series of "Secret Wars." When his original red and blue costume was torn in battle, the web-spinner tried to repair it, but mistakenly activated a device that released a little black ball. The ball spread across him, duplicating the costume worn by Julia Carpenter as Spider-Woman.

Spider-Man's new suit could instantly mimic any kind of clothing, could carry his camera and spare change, was equipped with its own web-shooters, and possessed a seemingly endless supply of webbing. He eventually discovered that the alien suit was a symbiote with a mind of its own. Spider-Man had to enlist the scientific help of Mr. Fantastic to remove it, using soundwaves at a certain frequency.

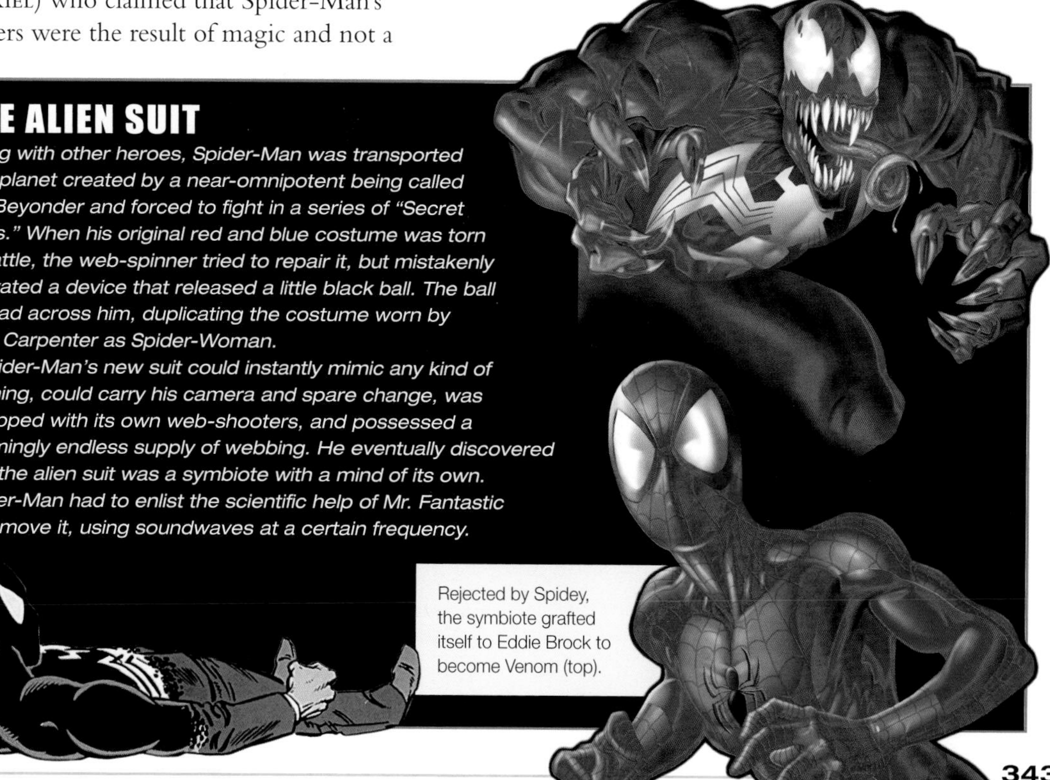

Rejected by Spidey, the symbiote grafted itself to Eddie Brock to become Venom (top).

SPIDER-MAN continued

Peter sided with Iron Man (Tony Stark) during the Civil War, even going so far as to register with the government and expose his true identity during a televised press conference. He quickly came to regret this decision when he saw the tactics the pro-registration forces used to win, and he switched sides to join Captain America's resistance. For a short time, he returned to his black costume while he, Mary Jane, and Aunt May went into hiding, but he soon returned to his red and blue suit.

NOOOO!
Peter heeded his spider-sense and dodged the bullet. It hit Aunt May instead.

AUNT MAY SHOT

Besides the government hounding him, Peter now had to deal with the fact that all his old foes knew who he was. From inside prison, the Kingpin hired an assassin, who waited outside the hotel room in which Peter, Mary Jane, and Aunt May were staying. When Peter's guard was down, he fired. Peter's spider-sense enabled him to dodge the bullet, but it struck Aunt May. Peter and Mary Jane rushed her to the hospital, where the doctor informed them that she was too frail to survive.

I TRUSTED YOU! I LET YOU GET CLOSE TO ME... YOU WERE LIKE A FATHER TO ME!
I TRUSTED YOU WHEN YOU SAID I HAD TO EXPLORE MY IDENTITY! THAT IT WAS THE ONLY EAY! I KEPT IT SECRET TO PROTECT MAY, AND MJ, BUT YOU SAID THEY'D BE SAFE! YOU SAID--
Peter Parker tangled up Iron Man in his webs, forcing Tony Stark to listen to his pleas for financial help to save Aunt May's life.

Needing money to pay for Aunt May's treatment, Peter turned to the wealthiest man he knew: Tony Stark. Tony immediately changed into Iron Man and tried to arrest Peter, but Peter managed to entangle Iron Man with his new webs, which now sprang directly from his wrists rather than from a webshooter. While Iron Man was trapped, Peter accused Tony of misleading him into making the worst mistake of his life. Then he demanded that Tony help Aunt May. Tony refused, saying that he couldn't be seen aiding and abetting a known criminal like Peter. Breaking free from the webs, he flew off without trying to arrest Peter again, but he made it clear that he could not help. Later, Tony's butler, Edwin Jarvis—who had been dating Aunt May—arrived at the hospital with a check for two million dollars to help pay for her care. Despite the money, however, the doctor believed that Aunt May would not live long.

MEPHISTO'S DEAL

Torn apart with guilt over Aunt May's shooting, Peter scoured the city for a cure. He visited Doctor Strange, who transported Spider-Man's astral form around the globe to ask for help, but no one could do anything to save her. Peter even tried to travel back in time to stop the shooting, but failed.

Then Mephisto approached Peter and Mary Jane with an offer. He would save Aunt May and alter reality so that no one would remember that Peter was Spider-Man. All he wanted in exchange was their greatest source of happiness: their marriage.

Searching their souls, Peter and Mary Jane agreed to Mephisto's offer. The next morning, Peter awoke alone—but with Aunt May alive and well and cooking him a stack of wheatcakes—and with no one aware that anything had ever been different.

ALL CHANGE

While Mephisto had supposedly only made a couple of changes, their effect was to alter Peter's life drastically. He was alone once again, living at his Aunt May's and looking for an apartment in Manhattan. His old friend Harry Osborn had returned after being presumed dead. And without Mary Jane in his life, Peter was unlucky in love.

An anguished Peter and Mary Jane waited by Aunt May's hospital bed, realizing that only a miracle could save her. It would come from a most unexpected source.

Tired of bargaining for souls, Mephisto demanded something far more rare from Peter and Mary Jane: the pure happiness found in their true love for each other.

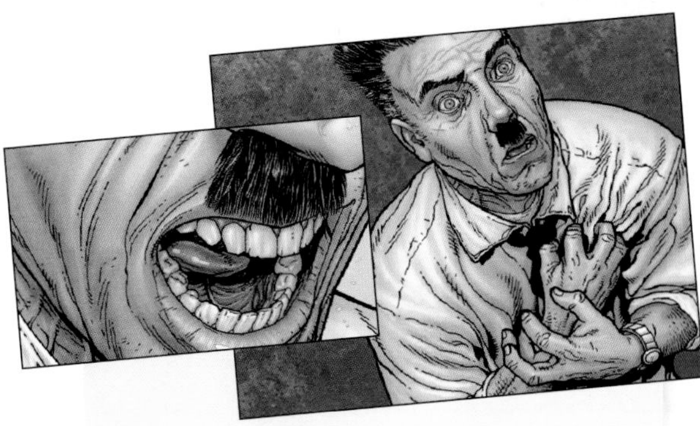

Peter saved Jameson's life by giving him CPR after he collapsed during an argument. Later, as Spider-Man, he had to do so again when he inadvertently told Jameson that his wife had sold the *Daily Bugle* while he was ill.

Some things, however, stayed the same. With the *Daily Bugle* having cash troubles, J. Jonah Jameson hadn't paid Peter for several photos he'd bought. When Peter confronted Jameson about the money he was owed, they fell into a shouting match, and Jameson collapsed from a heart attack. Jameson survived, but the paper had to be sold, and Peter wound up working as a paparazzo. He soon gave that up to become a photographer for Ben Urich's new paper, *Front Line*.

ALTERED STATES

Many of Spider-Man's foes cropped up soon after Peter's life changed. With his secret identity once more intact, however, he could fight them on his own terms.

Aunt May now did volunteer work at a homeless shelter, working under the philanthropist Martin Li, who was secretly Chinatown crimelord Mr. Negative. Eddie Brock returned, no longer as Venom but as the new Anti-Venom. Norman Osborn (*see* Green Goblin) showed up as the leader of the Thunderbolts and even, eventually, the Avengers—a separate team from the secret Avengers with which Spider-Man still worked. He also battled a new villain called Menace, who used many of the Green Goblin's old tricks.

A new hero—Jackpot—entered Peter's life too. As she was a tall, beautiful redhead, Peter suspected her of actually being Mary Jane, with whom he still had a romantic—but apparently sour—history. Instead, she turned out to be Alana Jobson, a woman who'd bought the identity from Sara Ehret. Alana died soon after Peter learned her secret, destroyed by the drugs she'd been taking to gain her powers.

While Peter enjoyed the fact that no one knew his secret identity, in time he did tell a few of those closest to him, including the Fantastic Four and some of his fellow Avengers.

Menace turned out to be none other than Lily Hollister, the woman who Peter's unwitting friend Harry Osborn (the second Green Goblin) hoped to marry. As Menace, she publicly attacked her father to drum up sympathy support for his mayoral campaign.

ESSENTIAL STORYLINES

- ***Civil War #1–7*** During the Civil War, Spider-Man registers with the government and reveals his identity to the world—and then comes to regret it.
- ***One More Day (tpb)*** With Aunt May at death's door after taking a sniper's bullet meant for Peter, he and Mary Jane cut a deal with Mephisto to trade their marriage to save her life.
- ***Amazing Spider-Man #546*** His marriage erased—along with any knowledge anyone has about his secret identity—Spider-Man starts again fresh, but alone.
- ***Amazing Spider-Man #700*** Doctor Octopus defeats Spider-Man and steals his body.
- ***Amazing Spider-Man: Spider-Verse (tpb)*** Web-slingers from across the Multiverse join forces to fight Morlun.

Both Peter Parker and Spider-Man started all over again with a Brand New Day—but Mary Jane was no longer by Peter's side.

SPIDER-MAN continued

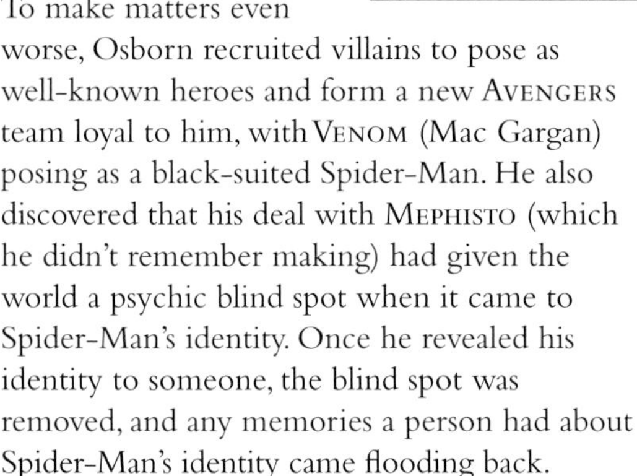

A flashback story revealed that in the timeline Mephisto had modified, Peter and Mary Jane had never married because he'd missed their wedding day.

DARK DAYS

During the DARK REIGN, Peter had to deal with the fact that his worst enemy—Norman Osborn (GREEN GOBLIN)—had taken charge of security in the US. To make matters even worse, Osborn recruited villains to pose as well-known heroes and form a new AVENGERS team loyal to him, with VENOM (Mac Gargan) posing as a black-suited Spider-Man. He also discovered that his deal with MEPHISTO (which he didn't remember making) had given the world a psychic blind spot when it came to Spider-Man's identity. Once he revealed his identity to someone, the blind spot was removed, and any memories a person had about Spider-Man's identity came flooding back.

When he worked for the Future Foundation, Spider-Man wore an all-new, white-and-black costume.

THE KRAVINOFFS

The surviving family of KRAVEN THE HUNTER—his children Ana and Aloysha, helped by the CHAMELEON (Kraven's half-brother) and led by his wife Sasha Kravinoff—decided to take their revenge on Spider-Man. They started by kidnapping MADAME WEB and Mattie Franklin, the third SPIDER-WOMAN. Using Madame Web's powers, they forced Spider-Man to battle a gallery of his old foes, weakening him until they were ready to launch their ultimate plan.

The Kravinoffs sacrificed Mattie to revive the dead Vladimir Kravinoff—Kraven's son, known as the Grim Hunter. However, he came back to life as a half-lion creature rather than himself. Using what they learned from this attempt, they sacrificed Spider-Man to bring Kraven himself back from the dead. It turned out that they'd killed Spidey's clone KAINE instead, who'd swapped himself with Peter.

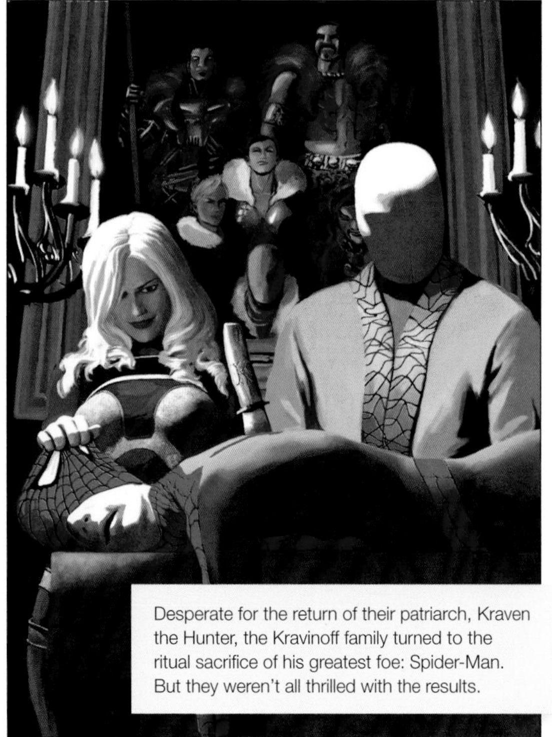

Desperate for the return of their patriarch, Kraven the Hunter, the Kravinoff family turned to the ritual sacrifice of his greatest foe: Spider-Man. But they weren't all thrilled with the results.

WORKING-CLASS HERO

Peter always had a hard time holding on to a job, but he had been working as a science teacher at his old school, Midtown High in Queens. After his Aunt May married John Jonah Jameson Sr. (the father of J. Jonah JAMESON), however, May and John asked Jonah—who had become the mayor of New York City—if they could find Peter a better job. Jonah's wife Marla Madison recommended Peter to Horizon Labs, where he became one of the think tank's top scientists.

Meanwhile, after the apparent death of his pal the HUMAN TORCH, Spider-Man joined the Fantastic Four, as the Torch had requested in his will. He served with their Future Foundation until the Torch returned. He also served with the AVENGERS after Norman Osborn was removed from power at the end of the Dark Reign.

SPIDER-ISLAND

The JACKAL, who had been behind all of Peter's problems with clones, returned with a new plot. Working for the SPIDER QUEEN and with Kaine revived as a new, Jackal-controlled Tarantula, the Jackal infected most of the citizens of Manhattan with a virus that gave them superpowers. Fortunately, MISTER FANTASTIC created a cure for the virus, using the symbiote of ANTI-VENOM.

During this time, Peter displayed the use of his spider-powers on live TV. This weakened the psychic blind spot the world had about his identity as Spider-Man. His girlfriend at the time—forensic police officer Carlie COOPER—suspected who Peter was, and she broke up with him.

SUPERIOR SPIDER-MAN

The enfeebled and dying Doctor Octopus returned as Spider-Man's greatest foe. Using a specialized Octobot, he managed to swap his mind with that of Spider-Man, trapping Peter in his body. Despite his best efforts, Peter could not reverse this before Doc Ock's body died. A repentant Doc Ock took up Peter's life as his own, determined to do a better job than Peter had managed. Still, some part of Peter's mind survived in his body, and he eventually managed to communicate with Doc Ock inside their shared head. They wound up in a psychic battle in which Doc Ock triumphed. Soon after, he deleted all of Peter's memories from his mind.

Wishing to make himself the Superior Spider-Man, Doc Ock even found time to finish Peter's doctorate and create a new tech company, Parker Industries. Otto fell in love with fellow scientist Anna Maria Marconi but that would ultimately prove his downfall. A sliver of Peter's consciousness remained in the new Spider-Man's mind and when the Green Goblin returned—creating a Goblin Nation across Manhattan—he kidnapped those close to the web-slinger, including Anna Maria. Otto realized only Peter Parker could ever hope to defeat the Green Goblin, so he let Peter regain control of his body. Peter saved Anna Maria and took down the Green Goblin.

Otto Octavius, in his role as the self-proclaimed "Superior Spider-Man," fought a number of powerful villains, including Phil Ulrich the Hobgoblin.

MILES MORALES

Miles Morales—the Spider-Man of Earth-1610 (the Ultimate universe)—received his powers from the bite of a genetically enhanced spider created by Oscorp. Unlike Peter Parker, Miles was afraid of his newfound abilities and hadn't felt the responsibility to use them, until he witnessed the Peter Parker of his world—as Spider-Man—get killed battling Norman Osborn. That event inspired Miles to take up crimefighting himself. When Peter Parker of Earth-616 first met Miles, he was shocked to discover that the Peter Parker of Miles' world was dead.

SPIDER-VERSE

Shortly after regaining his body, Peter learned that when he had first gained his powers another student, Cindy Moon, had also been bitten by the radioactive spider. Ezekiel SIMS had trained her and, to stop Morlun from killing her, kept her in a special bunker. After Spidey freed her, Cindy took the name SILK and soon became a new web-slinging hero, helping Spider-Man defeat ELECTRO and the BLACK CAT, the latter having gone back to crime after being captured by the Superior Spider-Man.

When Morlun and his family started to hunt Spider-Heroes across the Multiverse, including a time-displaced Superior Spider-Man, Peter found himself in an epic multi-dimensional war against Morlun's family, helped by an army of Spider-heroes from parallel worlds.

No sooner had Spidey defeated Morlun than the Jackal returned, this time seemingly bringing the dead back to life (albeit as clones). The new Jackal was eventually revealed to be Ben Reilly (*see* SCARLET SPIDER). Spider-Man managed to stop the Jackal's plans before he could spread a Carrion-like virus across the world. To stop the virus spreading, Peter was forced to use Parker Industries tech, damaging the company in the process. PI was finally laid low when HYDRA, during their takeover of the USA, tried to seize PI's technology, forcing Peter to scupper much of his company.

RED GOBLIN

Soon after, Norman Osborn returned, bonded to the Carnage symbiote. As the Red Goblin, he tried to kill those close to Spider-Man—including Aunt May, who was saved by a revived Doctor Octopus. Spidey eventually managed to defeat Osborn but only after Flash THOMPSON had given his life to save those close to Peter and himself.

Spider-Man briefly had to bond with his old foe, the Venom symbiote, in order to gain enough strength to face the Red Goblin.

With his company gone, Peter went back to basics. He started to share an apartment with old pal Randy Robertson and rekindled his relationship with Mary Jane. Trouble was never far away though, especially when Peter and Randy gained a new roommate: Fred Myers, aka the mercenary BOOMERANG.

SPIDER-GIRL

FACTFILE

REAL NAME
May "Mayday" Parker

OCCUPATION
Student; adventurer

BASE
New York City

HEIGHT 5 ft 7 in
WEIGHT 119 lbs
EYES Blue
HAIR Brown

FIRST APPEARANCE
What If? #105
(February 1998)

POWERS
Similar powers of agility, strength, and climbing ability as Spider-Man; uses web-shooters, developed by her father, to travel across the city or trap enemies.

SPIDER-GIRL

On Earth-982, Spider-Man and his wife, Mary Jane Watson, had a daughter named May and a son named Benjamin. After the Green Goblin maimed Spidey in battle, he retired to become Peter Parker, NYPD forensic scientist.

As a teenager, May inherited Peter's powers and became Spider-Girl. She battled new villains—such as Funny Face and Killerwatt—plus the descendants of her dad's foes—like Raptor, and Normie Osborn (Norman Osborn's grandson). She and her father also battled the Green Goblin's ghost, along with a symbiote-hybrid clone of May, named April. They defeated the Goblin, and May welcomed April into her family, but April later sacrificed herself to save May's life.

When her father, Peter, was killed by the Inheritors, May saved her brother and joined the Spider-Army to get revenge, but she soon realized her father wouldn't want vengeance, and she settled for justice instead. Following the conflict, she also joined the Web-Warriors to protect Earths that had lost their heroes and also fought the Inheritors when they escaped from their incarceration.

In a possible future, Mayday Parker inherited her father Peter's spider-powers—and his fashion sense.

In the main timeline, Brooklyn high-school student Anya Corazón nearly died in a battle between the Spider Society and the Sisterhood of the Wasps. Miguel, the sorcerer of the Spider Society, endowed her with a spider-shaped tattoo which gave her spider-like powers and an exoskeleton. She called herself Araña (Spanish for spider). During the Civil War, Anya registered with the government and lost her exoskeleton in a fight. Anya later became Spider-Girl when she received Julia Carpenter's old Spider-Woman outfit. She later joined a group of super teens called the Young Allies. Following Infinity, Anya helped the Avengers investigate who was stealing NuHuman cocoons. She joined the Spider-Army when the Inheritors attacked and, thanks to her tattoo, was the only one able to read the ancient Inheritors prophecy and discover their plan. She stayed on Loomworld and became a member of the Web-Warriors.

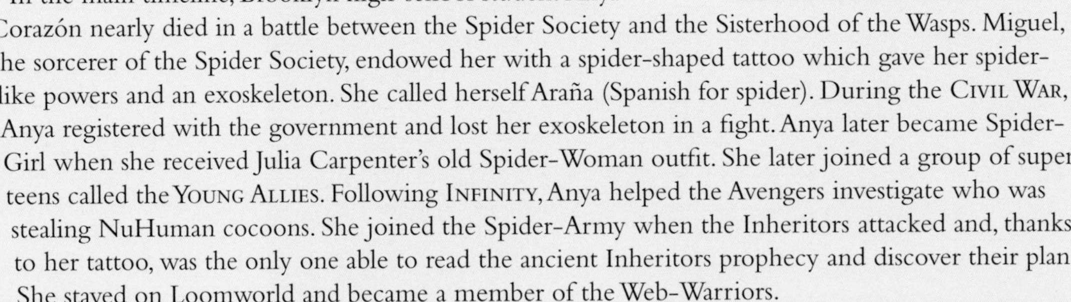

In the present day, Anya Corazón was no relation to Peter, and she soon established her own look.

SPIDER-MAN 2099

FACTFILE

REAL NAME
Miguel O'Hara

OCCUPATION
Genetic engineer; adventurer

BASE
New York City

HEIGHT 5 ft 10 in
WEIGHT 170 lbs
EYES Brown
HAIR Brown

FIRST APPEARANCE
Spider-Man 2099 #1
(November 1992)

POWERS
Superhuman strength, speed, and agility. Can adhere to surfaces and project webbing from spinnerets in forearms. Retractable talons and fangs that secrete poison.

SPIDER-MAN 2099

In the year 2099 on Earth-928, Miguel O'Hara, head of genetics for the Alchemax corporation, gained Spider-Man's powers in an episode of industrial intrigue. As Spider-Man 2099, he battled both criminals and Alchemax. Traveling back in time to preserve his own ancestry, Miguel was trapped in the present after encountering the Superior Spider-Man (Doctor Octopus). He started working undercover in Alchemax and continued being a hero. He also assisted Spider-Man and joined the fight against the Inheritors. Miguel later died, but was resurrected years later in his original time—the year 2099.

In a possible future, he was given Thor's hammer Mjolnir, and he used that power to rule Earth peacefully for a thousand years. On Earth-6375, after Spider-Man 2099's secret identity was exposed, he joined the Exiles for a while. He later returned to be with the woman he loved, Dana D'Angelo.

SPIDER-QUEEN

FIRST APPEARANCE *The Spectacular Spider-Man* #15 (August 2004) **REAL NAME** Adriana (Ana) Soria **OCCUPATION** Conqueror **BASE** New York City **HEIGHT** 5 ft 10 in **WEIGHT** 125 lbs **EYES** Brown **HAIR** Black **SPECIAL POWERS/ABILITIES** Ana has superhuman strength and can emit a sonic blast. She is also telepathic with insects and humans who have insect DNA, and can control their minds.

Ana Soria was the first female marine to enter combat as part of the US military's Super-Soldier program. Exposed to radiation during the Bikini Atoll atomic bomb tests, she developed spider powers. She arrived in modern times and controlled Spider-Man's mind, but Captain America stopped her. She arose years later with a plan to infect everyone in Manhattan with spider powers so she could control them. She transformed into a spider-monster nearly thirty stories tall, and many heroes attacked and killed her.

SPIDER-WOMAN

Investigator with irresistible powers

The daughter of scientist Jonathan Drew, Jessica gained her powers before birth, when a laser laced with spider DNA hit her mother's womb. Born and raised on Wundagore Mountain, her powers manifested when she was six years old. She was in stasis for a long time and when she woke found herself in the care of Hydra.

Jessica Drew was a powerful member of the Avengers team.

FACTFILE

REAL NAME
Jessica Drew

OCCUPATION
Adventurer

BASE
Mobile

HEIGHT 5 ft 10 in
WEIGHT 130 lbs
EYES Green
HAIR Brown (dyed black)

FIRST APPEARANCE
Marvel Spotlight #32 (February 1977)

SPIDER-WOMAN

POWERS
Enhanced strength, speed, and hearing; flight; superhuman healing factor; emits mood-altering pheromones that attract both sexes; ability to adhere to walls and fire electric "venom blasts."

SUPER SPY

Trained by the Taskmaster—and with her mind warped by Mentallo—Jessica became an agent of Hydra. Captured by SHIELD on her first mission and then released, she went underground. She resurfaced to become an agent of SHIELD for a short time, after which she struck out on her own. Calling herself Spider-Woman, Jessica became a private investigator, a bounty hunter, and a sometime Super Hero. At one point, she saved the life of Giant-Man (Bill Foster) through a blood transfusion, and lost some of her powers in the process.

Others took on the name of Spider-Woman, but when Hydra offered to restore Jessica's powers if she would become their agent, she accepted the deal, then contacted Nick Fury and became a double agent for SHIELD. Shortly thereafter, she was kidnapped by the Skrulls and replaced by Queen Veranke.

While posing as Jessica, Veranke led the Secret Invasion. Norman Osborn (*see* Green Goblin) shot and killed Veranke in the final battle of the Skrull invasion. Jessica, along with several other replaced heroes, was found in a Skrull prison ship and brought back to Earth. She has since joined the Avengers team led by Captain America (Bucky Barnes).

Jessica used her spycraft to infiltrate the evil Inheritors' homeworld and ensured that her allies got the information they needed to defeat them. Then, she resigned from the Avengers and went back to being a detective. Jessica gave birth to her son, Gerry, and was determined to be a heroic example for him.

KEY STORYLINES
- ***The Spider-Woman #1*** The first issue of her original, self-titled series sees Jessica Drew striking out on her own as a hero.
- ***Spider-Woman: Origin #1–6*** This limited series retells Spider-Woman's beginnings, from a Hydra pawn to a member of the New Avengers.
- ***New Avengers #1*** Jessica Drew returns as Spider-Woman in the New Avengers... or does she?

THE OTHERS

Julia Carpenter (now Madame Web) was made Spider-Woman by the Commission on Superhuman Activities. Later, Mattie Franklin became the third Spider-Woman after taking her father's place during a ceremony called the Gathering of the Five. Doctor Octopus gave Charlotte Witter the ability to absorb spider-powers only to have Mattie reclaim them, along with the name. Mattie worked with the Loners for a while, but she was on her own when the Kraven family hunted her down and killed her.

Julia Carpenter as Spider-Woman.

Charlotte Witter was the only villainous Spider-Woman. Doctor Octopus bestowed her with powers sufficient to kill Spider-Man. Witter also possessed the ability to drain the powers of the other Spider-Women, but lost them when defeated by the third Spider-Woman—Mattie Franklin.

Mattie Franklin as Spider-Woman.

SPIRIT OF '76

FIRST APPEARANCE *The Invaders* #14 (March 1977)
REAL NAME William Nasland
OCCUPATION Costumed adventurer **BASE** Mobile
HEIGHT 6 ft 2 in **WEIGHT** 215 lbs **EYES** Blue **HAIR** Black
SPECIAL POWERS/ABILITIES Top level athlete and formidable hand-to-hand combatant; wore a bullet-proof cape; as Captain America he had a steel shield, which was not indestructible.

Inspired by CAPTAIN AMERICA's World War II exploits, William Nasland became the costumed adventurer, Spirit of '76. After battling Nazi spies in Philadelphia, Nasland moved to Great Britain and joined the Crusaders team of heroes, until its leader was revealed to be a German agent. Nasland continued to contribute to the war effort, partnering Captain America on a mission to Berlin. Following the Cap's apparent demise, Nasland agreed to become a second Captain America but his career as this emblematic figurehead was cut short when he died preventing the assassination of would-be congressman John F. Kennedy.

SPITFIRE

FIRST APPEARANCE *The Invaders* #7 (July 1976)
REAL NAME Jacqueline Falsworth Crichton
OCCUPATION Adventurer **BASE** Falsworth Manor, England
HEIGHT 5 ft 4 in **WEIGHT** 110 lbs **EYES** Blue **HAIR** Blond
SPECIAL POWERS/ABILITIES Spitfire can move at speeds up to 50 mph for up to four hours. She has a vampire's fangs, superhuman strength, and a healing factor, but feels no bloodlust.

During World War II, Jacqueline Falsworth served in England's Home Guard and was attacked by the Nazi vampire BARON BLOOD. She was rescued by the original HUMAN TORCH, an android who gave her a transfusion of his artificial blood. The combination of the vampire bite and the android blood gave Falsworth superhuman speed. She adopted the name Spitfire and teamed up with the INVADERS, a group of Allied heroes who battled the Axis powers. Over time her powers faded, but another transfusion from the HUMAN TORCH restored them. In modern times, she served with the NEW INVADERS and with MI-13. After her romance with BLADE, she was seen helping Captain Britain at Braddock Academy.

SPIRAL

FIRST APPEARANCE *Longshot* #1 (September 1985)
REAL NAME "Ricochet" Rita **OCCUPATION** Warrior sorceress
BASE Mobile
HEIGHT 5 ft 10 in **WEIGHT** 150 lbs
EYES Blue **HAIR** Silver
SPECIAL POWERS/ABILITIES Enhanced strength; spellcasting abilities allow teleportation between dimensions; excellent swordswoman who can wield six weapons at once.

Spiral is a six-armed sorceress who worked as an aide to MOJO. An actress in her former life, Spiral received genetic alterations in the Mojoverse, which gave her the ability to manipulate magic. On Earth, she briefly served in FREEDOM FORCE and opened a cybernetics store, the Body Shoppe, whose customers included LADY DEATHSTRIKE. She later conquered Earth-2055 until SHATTERSTAR defeated her, then joined Madelyne PRYOR's Sisterhood of Mutants. After Mojo left her stranded on Earth, she became a member of the mutant black-ops team X-FORCE.

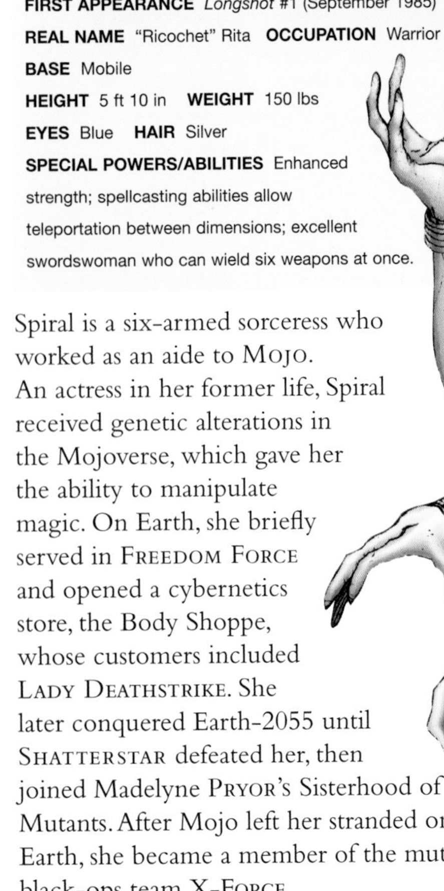

SPOT

FIRST APPEARANCE *Peter Parker, The Spectacular Spider-Man* #98 (January 1985) **REAL NAME** Dr. Jonathan Ohnn
OCCUPATION Criminal; research scientist
BASE New York City **HEIGHT** 5 ft 10 in
WEIGHT 170 lbs **EYES** Blue **HAIR** Brown
SPECIAL POWERS/ABILITIES Ohnn's body is covered with black spots that can teleport items from one of them to another. The spots are movable and can even be removed and placed off his body.

While researching teleportation for the KINGPIN, Dr. John Ohnn was transported into the Spotted Dimension, and when he returned, he found his body covered with portable wormholes. He clashed with SPIDER-MAN and the BLACK CAT soon after. When he opened up a spot into the Negative Zone, he ran afoul of the FANTASTIC FOUR. While in prison, he helped TOMBSTONE escape, for which the crook broke his neck. He survived only to be killed by ELEKTRA and resurrected by the HAND. Another villain called the Coyote captured him to use his powers against DAREDEVIL.

SPYMASTER, SEE PAGE 352

SQUADRON SUPREME

Another world's mightiest heroes

In a 12-issue series, the Squadron Supreme explores absolute power.

The Squadron Supreme is a force of superhuman champions inhabiting the Earth of an alternate reality. They have crossed paths with the AVENGERS many times, including an early team-up to eradicate the evil influence of the serpent-god Set's Serpent Crown.

THE SINISTER ONES

The Avengers first encountered the Squadron Sinister, a team of villains the GRANDMASTER created in the main universe after he'd discovered the Squadron Supreme in his travels through the Multiverse. They included DOCTOR SPECTRUM, HYPERION, NIGHTHAWK, and WHIZZER (later known as SPEED DEMON). The Avengers defeated them, but they later clashed with the DEFENDERS as well. Appalled at the team's plans, Nighthawk betrayed them, after which he joined the Defenders.

When the Avengers later found themselves in the Squadron Supreme's world (Earth-712), they initially thought they were facing the Squadron Sinister again. They soon sorted out their mistake, and together they defeated a mad scientist who called himself Brain-Child, saving the Squadron Supreme's world.

A new Hyperion recently arrived from a doomed dimension that had been part of an incursion on the main reality. He was the only survivor.

FACTFILE

NOTABLE MEMBERS

HYPERION (leader)
Flight, enhanced strength, super-speed, near-invulnerability, atomic vision.

AMPHIBIAN
Enhanced strength, able to live underwater at ocean depths.

DOCTOR SPECTRUM
Power prism permits flight and the projection of hard-energy objects.

GOLDEN ARCHER
Unsurpassed skill with a bow and arrow.

NIGHTHAWK
Brilliant strategist, top-level combatant.

POWER PRINCESS
Enhanced strength, skilled warrior.

THE WHIZZER
Super-speedster.

BASE Squadron City

FIRST APPEARANCE
Avengers #85 (March 1971)

POWER CORRUPTS

The Squadron Supreme faced their greatest challenge when the OVERMIND and Null the Living Darkness conquered their planet. Hyperion escaped to mainstream Earth and recruited the Defenders, who successfully defeated the Overmind. The damage to their world from the Overmind war was so great that the Squadron Supreme implemented the Utopia Program, seizing control of the government and forcibly implementing new methods of policing and social engineering.

Nighthawk left the Squadron in protest and organized the Redeemers to act as a rebel insurgency. The Redeemers forced the Squadron's surrender, but at the price of Nighthawk's life, and the two groups dismantled the Utopia Program. The Squadron Supreme later became marooned on Earth, where they adventured alongside QUASAR.

The Squadron eventually returned to their own world, where they found that a Global Directorate had taken the reins of power they'd abandoned, fulfilling their nightmares. Working with a new underground movement called the Nighthawks—and led by Neal Richmond, the son of Nighthawk—they successfully liberated their world from the grip of various monolithic corporations who were seeking to gain control of the planet.

SQUADRON SUPREME
1 Tom Thumb ***2*** Whizzer ***3*** Nuke ***4*** Redstone ***5*** Shape ***6*** Power Princess ***7*** Hyperion ***8*** Lamprey ***9*** Doctor Spectrum ***10*** Firefox ***11*** Arcanna ***12*** Blue Eagle ***13*** Black Archer ***14*** Ape X

SPYMASTER

FIRST APPEARANCE *Iron Man* #33 (January 1971)
REAL NAME Unrevealed
OCCUPATION Industrial spy **BASE** Mobile
HEIGHT 6 ft **WEIGHT** 195 lbs **EYES** Blue **HAIR** Blond
SPECIAL POWERS/ABILITIES Master of disguise; expert saboteur; exceptional hand-to-hand combatant; expert with high-tech weaponry; bulletproof costume; used hoverjet for transport.

From his first days as IRON MAN, Tony Stark was dogged by the Spymaster. Initially working with his Espionage Elite team, Spymaster tried many times to steal Stark's technology. ZODIAC, SHIELD, and MADAME MASQUE all employed him, but Justin HAMMER benefited most. The first Spymaster died at the hands of a rival named the Ghost. A second Spymaster discovered Iron Man's identity and beat Stark badly only to be stopped by the BLACK WIDOW. A third Spymaster killed the second and then plagued Stark before nearly dying in the fall that killed Happy HOGAN. He was later killed by the police.

SQUIRREL GIRL, SEE PAGE 354

STACY, CAPTAIN GEORGE

FIRST APPEARANCE *Amazing Spider-Man* #56 (January 1968)
REAL NAME George Stacy
OCCUPATION NYPD captain **BASE** New York City
HEIGHT 6 ft 1 in **WEIGHT** 190 lbs
EYES Blue **HAIR** Gray
SPECIAL POWERS/ABILITIES
Captain Stacy was a sharp policeman.

George Stacy—father of Gwen STACY—was a decorated member of the NYPD, along with his brother Arthur. He injured his leg in a battle with the Proto-Goblin (a predecessor of the GREEN GOBLIN), but continued to work to semi-retirement. He became a fan of SPIDER-MAN and took an instant liking to his daughter's new boyfriend Peter Parker. During a battle between Spider-Man and DOCTOR OCTOPUS, George saved a boy from falling rubble, paying for his heroism with his life. With his dying breath, he revealed he knew who Spider-Man was, and he exhorted Peter to take care of Gwen.

STACY, GWEN, SEE PAGE 355

STANE, EZEKIEL

FIRST APPEARANCE *The Order* #10 (April 2008)
REAL NAME Ezekiel (Zeke) Stane
OCCUPATION High-tech inventor and futurist **BASE** Mobile
HEIGHT 5 ft 11 in **WEIGHT** 223 lbs **EYES** Brown **HAIR** Bald
SPECIAL POWERS/ABILITIES Superhuman intelligence and bio-upgrades granting various superpowers.

The son of Obadiah STANE, Ezekiel inherited his father's fortune and promptly turned it and his incredible intellect toward making Tony Stark (IRON MAN) obsolete. He started by coordinating attacks against the ORDER, the California team for the FIFTY-STATE INITIATIVE. When his efforts failed, he went after Stark directly. Zeke reverse-engineered Stark technology that was available on the black market. Instead of building a better Iron Man suit, however, he upgraded his body directly. He sometimes wears a suit as a heat sink for his powers. The MANDARIN later enslaved Zeke to help capture Stark. Zeke and Tony worked together to turn the tables on the Mandarin. He went on to serve as CEO of Stark International.

STANE, OBADIAH

FACTFILE
REAL NAME
Obadiah Stane
OCCUPATION
President and chairman of the board of Stane International
BASE
Stane International headquarters, Long Island, New York

HEIGHT 6 ft 5 in
WEIGHT 230 lbs
EYES Blue
HAIR Bald

FIRST APPEARANCE
Iron Man #163 (October 1982)

POWERS
"Iron Monger" battlesuit amplified his strength to superhuman levels; boot jets enabled flight; projected repulsor rays (force beams) and laser blasts.

Orphaned when his father killed himself in a game of Russian roulette, Obadiah Stane regarded life as a game that he was determined to win.

His preferred tactic was to wage psychological warfare against his opponent. Stane became the head of a multinational corporation that produced munitions. Knowing that Anthony Stark, head of Stark International, was a reformed alcoholic, Stane manipulated events to drive Stark back to drinking. Buying up the debts of Stark International, Stane took control of the company, renaming it Stane International, and froze Stark's personal fortune. Stark duly became a drunken derelict.

Eventually Stark stopped drinking and resumed his secret identity as IRON MAN. Stane had his scientists create his own armored battlesuit, called the Iron Monger. In the Iron Monger armor, Stane personally battled Iron Man, who defeated him. Removing his helmet, Stane committed suicide by firing a repulsor ray blast at his head.

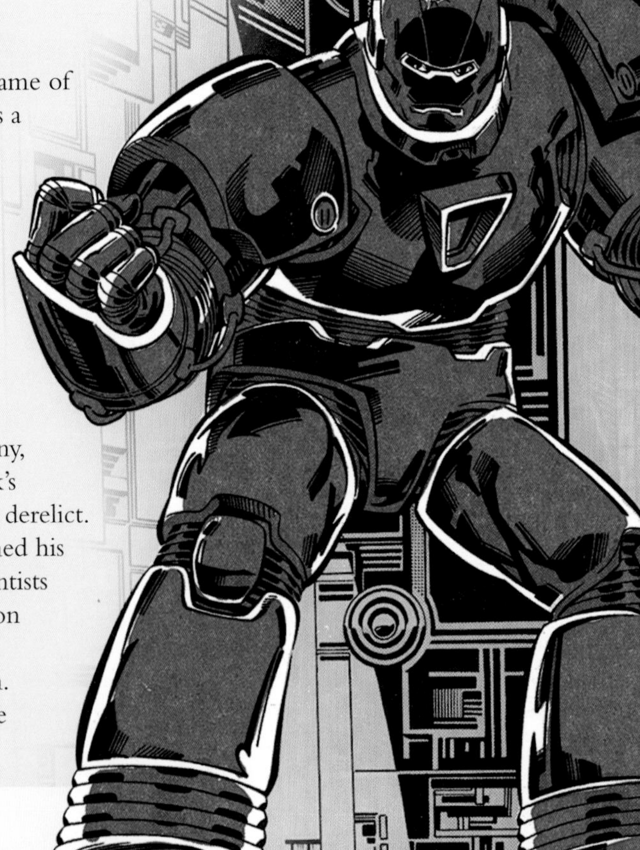

Stane's Iron Monger armor was larger than Iron Man's, but he could not defeat him.

STAR BRAND

The Star Brand is a mark of great power that has appeared in many universes, and the bearer is often known as Star Brand. The first such person was Ken Connell from Earth-148611, who gained the brand during the White Event from the Old Man, who'd grown bored with it. It was later granted to QUASAR in the main universe, and it fell into the hands of the STRANGER, who then moved Earth-148611 into the same universe, where the Star Brand was quarantined for being too dangerous.

A White Event (a cosmic upheaval) happened in the main universe when EX NIHILO tried to give the Earth sentience, and the Star Brand wound up with college student Kevin Connor, who destroyed his entire campus by accident. He worked with NIGHTMASK to understand what had happened, and in the course of their investigations, he accidentally killed the Earth's new sentience. The AVENGERS captured and imprisoned him after this, placing him in the Dyson sphere that IRON MAN was building in outer space. He later aided the Avengers in the BUILDER war, but was eventually killed by the BEYONDERS. He was reborn in the new universe and went back to college, though continued his Super Hero adventures. After the rise and fall of HYDRA, Kevin was seemingly killed in a confrontation with Robbie Reyes (GHOST RIDER).

Kenneth Connell was a car mechanic from Pittsburgh. He received the Star Brand from the mysterious Old Man who had carried it since the Middle Ages. Ken was a poor brand bearer though. He tried to abandon it, resulting in great destruction.

FACTFILE
REAL NAME
Kevin Connor
OCCUPATION
Adventurer; student
BASE
Mobile

HEIGHT 5 ft 9 in
WEIGHT 155 lbs
EYES Blue
HAIR Blond

FIRST APPEARANCE
Star Brand #1
(October 1986)

STAR BRAND

POWERS
The Star Brand gives its bearer nearly infinite power limited only by their imagination.

STARFOX

FIRST APPEARANCE *Iron Man* #55 (February 1973)
REAL NAME Eros
OCCUPATION Adventurer **BASE** Mobile
HEIGHT 6 ft 1 in **WEIGHT** 190 lbs **EYES** Blue **HAIR** Red
SPECIAL POWERS/ABILITIES Flight; enhanced strength; telekinesis; ability to generate personal force-fields; the power to stimulate the brain's pleasure centers.

Eros is an ETERNAL, raised on the Saturn moon of Titan by his father, Mentor. His buoyant outlook is the opposite of that of his older brother THANOS. For years Eros wandered in search of sensual pleasure, but he returned to Titan when Thanos and the SUPER-SKRULL attacked it. After the death of CAPTAIN MAR-VELL, Eros raised Mar-Vell's son, Genis-Vell, and eventually joined the AVENGERS as Starfox. When ULTRON conquered Titan, Starfox asked the Avengers for help and they ultimately vanquished the human-android hybrid. Later, Eros recruited THANOS to help stop Thanos' son, Thane, who was on a rampage.

STARHAWK

On Earth-691, Stakar Vaughn Ogord is the child of the superpowered beings Quasar and Kismet, making him half human and half artificial. Born on the planet Vesper, Stakar was kidnapped as an infant and taken to the planet Arcturus IV, where he was adopted by Ogord, a Reaver. Stakar eventually married Ogord's daughter Aleta. When an accident merged Stakar and Aleta, they became a single being known as Starhawk, taking turns to control their shared body. Starhawk fled Arcturus IV, de-merged, and had children. They later re-merged, but Stakar seized control and left their children in order to join the original GUARDIANS OF THE GALAXY.

He and Aleta constantly wrestled for control of their body—Aleta hoping to force Stakar out so she could return to their children. A time-flux caused the Guardians to re-fight old battles with new outcomes—and Starhawk to change gender, becoming female. When the modern-day Guardians battled a male version of Starhawk, the female Starhawk returned and eventually helped them.

FACTFILE
REAL NAME
Stakar Vaughn Ogord
OCCUPATION
Adventurer
BASE
Arcturus IV

HEIGHT Unknown
WEIGHT Unknown
EYES Unknown
HAIR Unknown

FIRST APPEARANCE
Defenders #27
(September 1975)

STARHAWK

POWERS
Starhawk can fly at light speed and can manipulate cosmic energy. He also has the power of precognition, knowing events that will occur before they happen.

SQUIRREL GIRL

The unbeatable hero

SQUIRREL GIRL

FACTFILE

REAL NAME
Doreen Green

OCCUPATION
Adventurer; babysitter; student

BASE
New York City

HEIGHT 5 ft 3 in
WEIGHT 100 lbs
EYES Brown
HAIR Brown

FIRST APPEARANCE
Marvel Super-Heroes #8
(December 1991)

POWERS
Doreen has enhanced agility, speed, and strength, plus small claws and large, sharp incisors, as well as a knuckle spike and a tail; she can also communicate with squirrels.

While studying, Squirrel Girl joined Sunspot's New Avengers and stayed with the team when it was transformed into the U.S.Avengers.

Doreen had a clone, named Allene, who turned evil when her favorite squirrel died. Allene thought squirrels should rule the planet, until Doreen persuaded her to form a squirrel utopia in the Negative Zone.

Doreen Green possesses a range of incredible abilities, including a prehensile squirrel-like tail, super-strength, and a powerful jaw and teeth that enable her to bite through steel. She grew up in Los Angeles believing that she was a mutant, but geneticists later discovered she was actually some form of mutate. When she was ten, Doreen found out she could speak and understand squirrelese (the language of squirrels) and she began conversing with a squirrel buck named Monkey Joe. He inspired her to become a hero and became her trusty sidekick.

ESSENTIAL STORYLINES

- ***G.L.A. #1–4*** Doreen and Monkey Joe join the Great Lakes Avengers.
- ***New Avengers #15–16*** Doreen beats Wolverine in a sparring match and protects Danielle from Nazi mechwarriors.
- ***The Unbeatable Squirrel Girl Vol. 1 #1*** Squirrel Girl begins studying at Empire State University.
- ***The Unbeatable Squirrel Girl Vol. 2 #1*** Doreen starts her second year at ESU.

HEROIC BEGINNINGS

When she was fourteen, Doreen tried to convince Iron Man to let her be his sidekick, but he declined her offer, even after she rescued him from Doctor Doom. A year later, Bruce Banner (Hulk) fell out of the sky and landed on Doreen's tree house, disrupting her reading time. Abomination wasn't far behind, and Doreen helped Hulk defeat him with a scurry of her squirrel pals.

Doreen and Monkey Joe eventually moved to New York City and saved the Great Lakes Avengers from some muggers. Afterward, they joined the team, but Monkey Joe was killed by disgruntled former GLA member Leather Boy, leaving Doreen distraught. During a fight with Batroc the Leaper to stop him destroying the universe, Doreen called upon squirrels for aid but most of them were killed. The only survivor was a squirrel doe, whom Doreen named Tippy-Toe and made her BSFF (Best Squirrel Friend Forever). The pair went on to defeat the Mandarin, MODOK, and even Thanos himself.

LATER ADVENTURES

Squirrel Girl remained with the GLA team through its various rebrands (Great Lakes X-Men, Great Lakes Champions, and the Great Lakes Initiative). But she left when she realized she was holding back her teammates as they all knew that Doreen could defeat villains all by herself. With Tippy-Toe, Doreen returned to NYC and was hired to be the nanny of Luke Cage and Jessica Jones' baby Danielle.

COLLEGE LIFE

Following her stint as a nanny, Doreen started studying computer science at Empire State University. She became best friends with her dormmate Nancy Whitehead. On her first day, she convinced Kraven the Hunter to abandon his hunt for Spider-Man and, thanks to the Squirrel Information Network, learned of Galactus' imminent arrival. She stopped the Devourer of Worlds from consuming Earth by befriending him and finding him an alternative planet full of nuts to eat. Doreen started adventuring with Chipmunk Hunk and Koi Boi, two fellow students who are also heroes.

STACY, GWEN

Hero across realities

The daughter of NYPD Captain George STACY, Gwen Stacy was friendly, intelligent, and generous. She was a talented biochemistry student at Empire State University, and met Peter Parker (aka SPIDER-MAN) there. On the alternate world of Earth-65, it was Gwen Stacy, not Peter Parker, that was bitten by a radioactive spider and became a Super Hero known as Spider-Woman.

The cloned Gwen died fighting, helping Spider-Man save the world from a zombie virus.

Hurled off of a bridge by the Green Goblin, Gwen Stacy perished without ever learning that her boyfriend, Peter Parker, was secretly Spider-Man.

FACTFILE

REAL NAME
Gwendolyn Stacy

OCCUPATION
Student

BASE
Empire State University, New York City

HEIGHT 5 ft 7 in
WEIGHT 130 lbs
EYES Blue
HAIR Blond

FIRST APPEARANCE
Amazing Spider-Man #31 (December 1965)

POWERS
On Earth-616, Gwen Stacy possessed an aptitude for science but no special powers of any kind. Gwen Stacy of Earth-65 has super-strength, speed, agility, durability, and a spider-sense.

ESSENTIAL STORYLINES
- ***The Amazing Spider-Man Vol. 1 #121–122*** Gwen Stacy is kidnapped by the Green Goblin and killed when Spider-Man tries to save her.
- ***Edge of the Spider-Verse #2*** Spider-Gwen's first appearance details her origin story.

EARTH-616

Eventually, Gwen and Peter became a couple, despite competition from Mary Jane WATSON, but the Parker-Stacy relationship was an uneasy one. After her father was slain during a battle between Spider-Man and DOCTOR OCTOPUS, Gwen came to hate Spider-Man, a fact that weighed heavily on Peter's mind. Not long after, Gwen was captured by the GREEN GOBLIN and hurled from the top of a bridge. When Spider-Man attempted to save her with his webbing, the sudden shock of deceleration snapped Gwen's neck, causing her death. It was later revealed that Gwen had had an affair with Norman Osborn (Green Goblin) and bore twins by him, Gabriel and Sarah Stacy, who had since grown to adulthood by accelerated aging.

Gwen returned from the dead when Ben Reilly (see SCARLET SPIDER) discovered a process to reanimate deceased people with their memories intact. She helped Ben until he revealed his evil plans and met Peter Parker, forgiving him for her death. She helped Peter stop Ben and was happy to die while helping to save the world from the Carrion virus.

SPIDER-GWEN

On Earth-65, Gwen attended Midtown High and loved music. While fighting crime as Spider-Woman and studying, Gwen was the drummer in the Mary Janes band. She decided to be a more responsible hero after hearing her father say he was unimpressed with Spider-Woman's choices. She also bonded with shy and bullied student Peter Parker.

Tragically, Peter turned himself into a lizardlike monster and attacked the school to get revenge on his bullies. Spider-Woman stopped him, but he died in her arms as a human, and the world thought that she had killed him. When her father held Spider-Woman at gunpoint, she revealed her secret identity to him, and he let her escape.

Gwen joined the Spider-Army to fight the Inheritors and formed firm friendships with the other heroes, whom she helped whenever they needed it. Gwen soon returned to her reality, where she fought new villains including the Green Goblin and VULTURE, and befriended CAPTAIN AMERICA.

She lost her powers when injected with a cure by an evil Cindy Moon, but found a method to regain them temporarily. Soon, Gwen was hunted by overzealous cop Frank Castle so had to accept corrupt Matt Murdock's help. After being betrayed by Murdock, Gwen accepted the VENOM symbiote. She wanted to kill Matt, but had a change of heart when she realized she didn't want to become evil like him.

Later, Gwen learned to control the symbiote and bonded it to her suit. She went on to reveal her identity to the world and was imprisoned for a year for her actions. Upon her release, Gwen still wanted to help people without resorting to violence. She now goes by the name Ghost-Spider.

Spider-Gwen joined the Web-Warriors to defend Earths who had lost their heroes to the Inheritors.

STARJAMMERS

FACTFILE

MEMBERS AND POWERS

CORSAIR (Christopher Summers) Excellent pilot, swordsman, and combatant.

CH'OD Natural strength, tough skin, slashing claws.

HEPZIBAH Feline reflexes, night vision, retractable claws.

RAZA Cyborg strength, vision and reflexes, skilled with bladed weapons.

SIKORSKY Advanced medical knowledge.

KEEYAH Skilled pilot.

CR'REEE Ch'od's semi-intelligent, white-furred pet.

BASE Mobile

FIRST APPEARANCE
Uncanny X-Men #104 (April 1977)

STARJAMMERS

Corsair—real name Christopher Summers, father of Cyclops, Havok, and Vulcan—was abducted and enslaved by the alien Shi'ar. After his wife died for Emperor D'ken's pleasure, Corsair staged a jailbreak with fellow prisoners Ch'od, Raza, and Hepzibah. The group became the Starjammers, space pirates who fought against the cruel excesses of Shi'ar rule. The team helped the X-Men defeat D'ken in his bid to possess the M'Krann crystal, and later teamed with the X-Men to rescue D'ken's sister Lilandra. The Starjammers accepted Carol Danvers (*see* Captain Marvel) as a member when she was known as Binary, while both Lilandra and Professor X worked with the team during the fight against Deathbird.

Later, Vulcan returned to Shi'ar space, appeared to kill Corsair, and took over the Shi'ar Empire. Havok then led the Starjammers in their attempt to stop his brother. Later, again captained by Corsair, they helped the X-Men and Guardians of the Galaxy against the Shi'ar.

The Starjammers' leader, Corsair, is quick-witted and skilled with a blade.

STARJAMMERS
1 Ch'od ***2*** Hepzibah
3 Corsair ***4*** Raza

STARK, ARNO

FIRST APPEARANCE *Iron Man* #12 (September, 2013)
REAL NAME Arno Stark
OCCUPATION Custodian of Troy **BASE** Troy
HEIGHT Unknown **WEIGHT** Unknown
EYES Blue **HAIR** Black
SPECIAL POWERS/ABILITIES Genius-level intellect derived from genetic engineering prior to birth.

Arno Stark is Tony Stark's adoptive brother. It was only while adventuring in space that Tony learned he was adopted, and that Howard and Maria Stark had had another son, Arno. Their son had been born with the help of aliens, and to protect Arno from them, his parents had kept his existence secret and adopted Tony, hoping the aliens would think Tony was their real son. A gifted scientist, Arno helped Tony transform Mandarin City into Troy and created his own armor to enable himself to walk again. In an alternate future reality, another Arno Stark is Tony's first cousin and became an evil version of Iron Man.

STARK, HOWARD

FIRST APPEARANCE *Iron Man* #28 (August, 1970)
REAL NAME Howard Stark
OCCUPATION Inventor, industrialist **BASE** New York City
HEIGHT 6 ft **WEIGHT** 170 lbs
EYES Blue **HAIR** Gray, white at the temples
SPECIAL POWERS/ABILITIES Howard was a genius inventor, a ruthless businessman, and a scrapper in a fight.

As a young man, Howard Stark founded Stark Industries with his father. During World War II, he worked on the Manhattan Project and afterward joined the Brotherhood of the Shield, where he helped Nathaniel Richards save the world. He married Maria Carbonell. When Maria had pregnancy troubles, Howard sought the help of a Rigellian Recorder to save his son. The Recorder genetically altered the baby with Kree technology, but to ill effect. The child, Arno, was hidden away and the Starks adopted Tony (Iron Man) as a substitute. Howard and Maria eventually died in a suspicious car crash.

STAR-LORD

When Peter Quill's father—J'Son of Spartax, future ruler of the Spartoi Empire—crash-landed on Earth, Meredith Quill took him in and cared for him. When J'Son headed for the stars, he left two things behind: his high-tech gun and a pregnant Meredith. When Peter was ten, Badoon warriors came to kill him and his mother. Meredith died, but Peter secretly escaped. As an adult, he joined NASA to get into space and wound up in a galactic prison after a fight with the Fallen One, a former herald of GALACTUS. During the ANNIHILATION, NOVA broke Peter out of prison, and they helped defeat both ANNIHILUS and the PHALANX.

Believing the universe needed protecting, Peter formed the GUARDIANS OF THE GALAXY. When the others discovered he'd asked MANTIS to mentally push them into joining his group, the Guardians banished him. Peter later joined a new Guardians team formed by ROCKET RACCOON and traveled through time to try to save the future.

He was eventually made king of Spartax and his fiancé, Kitty PRYDE, replaced him in the Guardians as the new Star-Lord. Ultimately Quill was ousted from power and he rejoined the Guardians. They aided CAPTAIN MARVEL in CIVIL WAR II, but afterward the group learned Peter was keeping secrets from them, and they briefly split up. They reunited to help Gamora find the Soul Gem (and the other Infinity Gems), though Gamora killed Peter—temporarily—to keep him from interfering.

FACTFILE

REAL NAME
Peter Quill

OCCUPATION
Adventurer

BASE
Mobile

HEIGHT 6 ft 2 in
WEIGHT 175 lbs
EYES Blue
HAIR Blond

FIRST APPEARANCE
Marvel Preview #4
(January 1976)

STAR-LORD

POWERS
Peter's half-Spartoi heritage grants him top human durability, endurance, intelligence, speed, and strength. He also has triple the normal life expectancy.

Intent on acquiring the Infinity Gems and restoring her soul, Gamora impaled Star-Lord, knowing Doctor Strange could save him with the Time Gem.

STARK, MORGAN

FIRST APPEARANCE *Tales of Suspense* #68 (August 1965)
REAL NAME Morgan Stark **OCCUPATION** Businessman
BASE New York City **HEIGHT** 5 ft 11 in **WEIGHT** 175 lbs
EYES Hazel **HAIR** Brown
SPECIAL POWERS/ABILITIES None.

The cousin of Tony Stark (IRON MAN), Morgan was jealous of his famous cousin, believing that Tony's father had stolen Stark Industries from his own father. He worked with COUNT NEFARIA to try to discredit Tony but failed. He returned years later during the DARK REIGN to pose as Tony and take control of Stark Solutions. While there, he drank a vial of Ultimo Virus—a weaponized version of ULTIMO—which converted him into a giant robot. WAR MACHINE used the robot's programming against it, and it self-destructed, presumably killing Morgan.

STAR STALKER

FIRST APPEARANCE (Star Stalker I) *Avengers* #123 (May 1974), (Star Stalker II) *Power Pack* #56 (May 1990)
REAL NAME Unrevealed **OCCUPATION** Predator
BASE Planet Vormir in the Kree Galaxy (Greater Magellanic Cloud)
HEIGHT 16 ft 6 in **WEIGHT** Unrevealed **EYES** Black **HAIR** None
SPECIAL POWERS/ABILITIES Superhuman strength; could drain planetary energy and travel through outer space without protection.

The original, red Star Stalker was part of the reptilian alien Vorns. He used his tail as a weapon and his mutant powers to form an ionic cocoon to drain energy from other planets. His enemies were the Priests of Pama, a cult of KREE who knew his vulnerability to intense heat. Following the massacre of the Priests of Pama living on Earth, he journeyed there to absorb its energies.

The VISION slew him with heat beams, but he returned later as part of the GRIM REAPER'S LEGION OF THE UNLIVING. The Star Stalker's son later menaced Earth, but was apparently destroyed by NOVA (Frankie Raye). An unrelated Starkstalker, known as Monark, was a bounty hunter with an android falcon.

STATURE

FIRST APPEARANCE *Marvel Premiere* #45 (April 1979)
REAL NAME Cassandra Eleanore "Cassie" Lang
OCCUPATION Adventurer **BASE** New York City
HEIGHT Varies **WEIGHT** Varies **EYES** Blue **HAIR** Blond
SPECIAL POWERS/ABILITIES Can grow and shrink to extremes.

When Cassie Lang was a young girl, her father Scott became the second ANT-MAN so he could save her life. Cassie's mother (Scott's ex-wife) then sued for and won full custody of Cassie. After her father's death, Cassie joined the YOUNG AVENGERS to continue his legacy. She sided with CAPTAIN AMERICA during the CIVIL WAR, but after his death joined the FIFTY-STATE INITIATIVE. Cassie started dating the VISION and joined the new AVENGERS team led by Henry PYM. She died battling DOCTOR DOOM, but when an inversion spell prompted Doom to right his past wrongs, he resurrected Cassie, who learned her father was also alive. She went back to middle school, but returned to duty after being kidnapped by the Cross family. HYDRA then captured her to use as leverage against Scott.

STEELE, JOHN

FIRST APPEARANCE *Daring Mystery Comics* #1 (January 1940)
REAL NAME John Steele
OCCUPATION Adventurer **BASE** Mobile
HEIGHT 6 ft 1 in **WEIGHT** 187 lbs
EYES Brown **HAIR** Black
SPECIAL POWERS/ABILITIES Superhuman durability, endurance, speed, and strength; heals faster and ages slower; an expert combatant.

John Steele—America's first Super-Soldier—has been part of the country's conflicts since the American Civil War. He fought in World War I, and was later captured by the German army and placed into stasis for study. Freed in 1940, he set to fighting Nazis. He disappeared after the Allies invaded Normandy, and was captured by the SHADOW COUNCIL and brainwashed into working for them. Steve Rogers (CAPTAIN AMERICA) helped cure him, and John fought the Shadow Council's MASTERS OF EVIL until the android named Max Fury killed him.

STEIN, CHASE

FIRST APPEARANCE *Runaways* #1 (July 2003)
REAL NAME Chase Stein
OCCUPATION Adventurer **BASE** Mobile
HEIGHT 5 ft 11 in **WEIGHT** 188 lbs **EYES** Blue **HAIR** Blond
SPECIAL POWERS/ABILITIES An excellent pilot and athlete; uses gear stolen from his parents. Fistigon gloves allow him to manipulate fire; X-Ray Specs give X-ray vision. When his girlfriend Gert died, he inherited an empathic link to her dinosaur, Old Lace.

Chase is the son of evil geniuses who are part of an organization called the Pride. In exchange for the annual sacrifice of a pure human soul, ancient deities would grant the six couples who made up the Pride wealth, power, and influence. Chase joined with the Pride's other children to flee their parents, including Chase's abusive father, after witnessing them ritually sacrifice a girl. He fell in love with fellow RUNAWAY Gertrude Yorkes, who was later killed battling the Pride. Chase was one of the sixteen youths ARCADE pitted against each other in his latest Murderworld. He survived, and became the latest DARKHAWK after recovering Chris Powell's Darkhawk amulet. Years after Gert's death, Chase managed to fix her time machine, and used it to save her from dying. Meanwhile, Chase discovered the severed head of his android teammate Victor MANCHA, and set about restoring Victor to working order.

STEPFORD CUCKOOS

FIRST APPEARANCE *New X-Men* #118 (November 2001)
MEMBERS AND POWERS Celeste, Esme, Mindee, Phoebe, and Sophie, Identical telepaths. **BASE** New Xavier's School for the Gifted, Canada

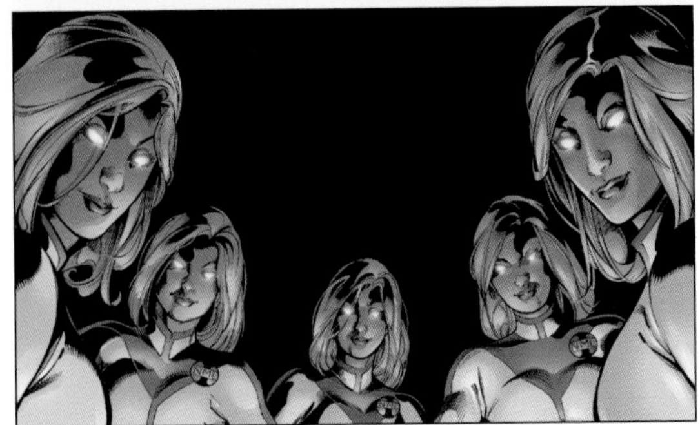

As part of the Weapon Plus program, John Sublime harvested eggs from Emma FROST and used them to create thousands of age-accelerated clones of her, a project called Weapon XIV. Five of the telepathic clones were activated and sent to the Xavier Institute. Sophie died while using the power-enhancing drug Kick to defeat Quentin QUIRE. Esme was later killed by the mutant Xorn, with whom she'd been using Kick. The remaining three gained Phoenix powers for a short time and destroyed the unactivated clones. They remained loyal to CYCLOPS through his troubles and joined his mutant revolution.

STICK

Despite being blind, Stick, who took his name from his combat staff, was the sensei of an elite warrior school called the CHASTE. When young Matt Murdock (*see* DAREDEVIL) lost his vision in a toxic waste accident, Stick helped him develop his remaining senses to compensate. Stick also trained the assassin ELEKTRA, although he expelled her when she could not control her rage in combat. When the evil ninjas of the HAND attacked Stick and his allies, Stick absorbed the life essences of his attackers, killing himself. His spirit was reincarnated a number of times, including once as a baby girl. Later he was reanimated by the GRANDMASTER for his Contest of Champions, but disintegrated by Punisher 2099. Maestro inadvertently resurrected him in the elderly body of Rick JONES. Once again alive on Earth, he formed a team with ARES, Guillotine, Outlaw, and White Fox.

STICK

FACTFILE
REAL NAME
Unrevealed
OCCUPATION
Sensei
BASE Mobile

HEIGHT 5 ft 9 in
WEIGHT 135 lbs
EYES Blue
HAIR White

FIRST APPEARANCE
Daredevil #176
(November 1981)

POWERS

Martial arts expert; "proximity sense" allows him to detect others despite his blindness; some telepathic abilities; an inspirational teacher.

STILT-MAN

FIRST APPEARANCE *Daredevil* #8 (June 1965)
REAL NAME Wilbur Day **OCCUPATION** Criminal
BASE New York City **HEIGHT** 5 ft 10 in (variable)
WEIGHT 185 lbs **EYES** Brown **HAIR** Black
SPECIAL POWERS/ABILITIES Legs of armored costume can extend up to 60 feet in length; costume also contains a formidable array of built-in weaponry.

Lab assistant Wilbur Day made off with his boss's revolutionary hydraulic ram technology and—after adapting the device to an armored costume—became the Stilt-Man and embarked on a life of crime. DAREDEVIL and SPIDER-MAN regularly foiled his efforts. After becoming a laughing stock, Day tried to give up his costumed identity, but he found himself pulled back into the underworld. He later married PRINCESS PYTHON and registered with the government, but the PUNISHER killed him on one of his missions. A couple of others have worn Stilt-Man suits, including Callie Ryan, who calls herself Lady Stilt-Man. She has worked with Misty KNIGHT'S Crew, PURPLE MAN'S Villains for Hire, and the Shadow Council's MASTERS OF EVIL. She is likewise an occasional foe of DEADPOOL and Spider-Man.

STINGRAY

FIRST APPEARANCE *Tales to Astonish* #95 (September 1967)
REAL NAME Walter Newell **OCCUPATION** Adventurer; oceanographer **BASE** Mobile within Atlantic Ocean
HEIGHT 6 ft 3 in **WEIGHT** 200 lbs **EYES** Hazel **HAIR** Brown
SPECIAL POWERS/ABILITIES Costume incorporates built-in rebreathing apparatus and provides enhanced strength, the ability to travel underwater at great speed, and to fire electrical bolts.

The US government gave oceanographer Walter Newell a seemingly impossible task: bring in NAMOR the Sub-Mariner for questioning. Newell built a revolutionary submersible suit and actually succeeded in his task, in the process becoming the adventurer Stingray. Subsequent adventures saw him fighting the Atlantean warlord ATTUMA, and becoming a reserve member of the AVENGERS. He helped the resistance during the CIVIL WAR but later joined the FIFTY-STATE INITIATIVE. He joined MERCS FOR MONEY, posing as DEADPOOL, but secretly spied on his teammates for Steve Rogers. Stingray was savagely killed by Namor while defending a cruise ship from TIGER SHARK.

STONE, LT. MARCUS

FIRST APPEARANCE *Thor* #404 (June 1989)
REAL NAME Marcus Stone
OCCUPATION Police officer **BASE** New York City
HEIGHT 6 ft 2 in **WEIGHT** 225 lbs **EYES** Brown **HAIR** Bald
SPECIAL POWERS/ABILITIES A dedicated and tenacious police officer who never gives up on a case; an expert marksman and highly trained hand-to-hand combatant.

After serving as one of New York's Finest for 25 years, Marcus Stone was ready to retire. His marriage to his childhood sweetheart was in trouble because he kept bringing his police work home with him. Stone knew the time had come to choose between his job and his wife. On what should have been his last day, he stumbled upon a battle between the mighty THOR and Ulik, the unconquerable rock troll. After Thor fell, Stone pursued Ulik and managed to arrest him. Having proved that normal cops can handle super-menaces, Stone was later assigned to head up Code: Blue, a special New York City strike-force that takes on Super Villains.

STONE TIBERIUS, SEE PAGE 360

STINGER

FIRST APPEARANCE *Spider-Girl* #1 (October 1998)
REAL NAME Cassandra Lang **OCCUPATION** Adventurer
BASE New York City (Earth-982) **HEIGHT** 5 ft 5 in
WEIGHT 105 lbs **EYES** Blue **HAIR** Reddish-blond
SPECIAL POWERS/ABILITIES Synthetic wing implants enable flight; armored costume protects from harm; possesses ability to shrink to the size of a wasp.

On Earth-982, Stinger is the superpowered pseudonym of Cassandra Lang, the daughter of the second ANT MAN. Cassandra combined the powers and costume of her father with those of the WASP, and she demonstrated a natural aptitude for organization and leadership. With a new generation of heroes emerging, Cassandra helped reform the AVENGERS and was in charge of the resurrected super-team when LOKI attempted to rid the world of heroes. A scientist in her mid-20s, Cassandra is the oldest and best-educated member of the team.

STRANGER, THE

The Stranger is an immeasurably powerful cosmic being, created from the life-energies of a vanished species from the planet Gigantus in the Andromeda Galaxy. The Gigantians built the Stranger to stand against the OVERMIND, a villainous composite entity fashioned by the Gigantians' traditional enemies, the Eternians. The Stranger wandered for eons until he encountered Earth. Convinced that Earth's superhuman mutants posed a threat to the greater galaxy, the Stranger attempted to destroy the Earth on multiple occasions. The heroism of champions such as the HULK won him over, and the Stranger agreed to spare Earth for the immediate future. For a while he used the ABOMINATION as a servant.

The Stranger eventually faced and defeated the Overmind, then selected an Earth from the New Universe (Earth-148611) as an object of study for his Labworld. The Stranger subsequently posed as the BEYONDER and gathered a number of superpowered people to battle for him as an experiment. It was revealed that he created EGO THE LIVING PLANET and Alter-Ego as part of an experiment.

STRANGER, THE

FACTFILE
REAL NAME
Unrevealed
OCCUPATION
Surveyor of Worlds
BASE
The Stranger's own Labworld

HEIGHT Variable
WEIGHT Variable
EYES Black
HAIR White

FIRST APPEARANCE
Uncanny X-Men #11
(May 1965)

POWERS

Vast strength; wields cosmic power to emit energy blasts, reshape matter, generate force-fields, levitate, and change his own size.

STONE, TIBERIUS

FIRST APPEARANCE *Iron Man* #37 (February 2001)
REAL NAME Tiberius "Ty" Stone **OCCUPATION** Owner of Viastone, a multinational corporation **BASE** Mobile
HEIGHT 6 ft **WEIGHT** 210 lbs **EYES** Blue **HAIR** Blond
SPECIAL POWERS/ABILITIES Brilliant business strategist; a totally ruthless sociopath, driven by jealousy and revenge.

Ty Stone and Tony Stark (Iron Man) were childhood friends, although their parents were business rivals. Stark's father eventually drove Stone's to the verge of bankruptcy. Pretending to still be Stark's friend, Stone vowed to get revenge. He planted news stories to tarnish Stark's reputation, stole Stark's girlfriend, Rumiko Fujikawa, and attempted to take over Stark Industries. Stone later worked for Kingpin and infiltrated Horizon Labs to sabotage the work of Peter Parker (Spider-Man). He co-created Alchemax with Liz Allan, and also turned out to be an ancestor of Spider-Man 2099.

STRONG GUY

FIRST APPEARANCE *New Mutants* #29 (July 1985)
REAL NAME Guido Carosella **OCCUPATION** Special Enforcer for X-Factor Investigations **BASE** New York City
HEIGHT 7 ft **WEIGHT** 750 lbs **EYES** Blue **HAIR** White
SPECIAL POWERS/ABILITIES Absorbs kinetic energy—failure to release it quickly causes physical distortions and damages heart; kinetic energy enhances strength.

Guido Carosella was the bodyguard of Lila Cheney until he wound up on Muir Island under the Shadow King's control. After X-Factor freed him, he joined their team and became friends with Multiple Man. He joined X-Factor Investigations, then served as sheriff of New York's Mutant Town. He kept his powers after M-Day but was later killed while saving J. Jonah Jameson from an assassination attempt. Layla Miller resurrected him, but without his soul. For a while he became the King of Hell, but eventually returned to Earth and started to work closely with the New Mutants.

SUGAR MAN

FIRST APPEARANCE *Generation Next* #2 (April 1995)
REAL NAME Unknown
OCCUPATION Geneticist **BASE** Mobile
HEIGHT 6 ft 9 in **WEIGHT** 400 lbs **EYES** White **HAIR** Black
SPECIAL POWERS/ABILITIES Enhanced strength and reflexes; razor-sharp extendible tongue; four arms; advanced regenerative abilities; can control his size and mass.

Sugar Man comes from the future of Earth-295—the Age of Apocalypse—where he operated the Seattle Core slave camp. When Colossus came to rescue his sister Illyana Rasputin (Magik), Sugar Man shrank down and hid in Colossus' boot, emerging in Earth-616, 20 years in the past. From there, he built up the island nation of Genosha by supplying genetic technology to create a population of mutant slaves. Sugar Man survived the Genosha holocaust, but he took a brutal beating at the hands of Callisto. He later returned to his home timeline to help the new Apocalypse, but was captured by the Human Resistance, only to eventually escape and return to Earth-616.

STRAW MAN

FIRST APPEARANCE *Dead of Night* #11 (August 1975)
REAL NAME Skirra Corvus
OCCUPATION Mystic guardian **BASE** An unnamed magical realm
HEIGHT 5 ft 10 in **WEIGHT** 60 lbs **EYES** Red **HAIR** Yellow
SPECIAL POWERS/ABILITIES Incarnates himself in bodies composed of straw, projects fear, can command crows and local plant life, and has assorted other mystic attributes.

A being indigenous to an extra-dimensional realm bordering that of Earth, the Straw Man can access our universe through a mystic painting that depicts him. The painting's origins are shrouded in mystery; it is coveted by the Cult of Kalumai, who can summon their demonic master and his underlings through it. However the Straw Man considers himself a guardian of the Earth, and has successfully kept Kalumai in check. Recruited by the Dweller-In-Darkness as one of his Fear Lords, the Straw Man refused to go along with the demonic entity's plan to subjugate Earth, and he incarnated himself as Skirra Corvus, a television personality, in whose form he was able to warn Doctor Strange of the Dweller's plan.

STRYFE

Infected with a techno-organic virus, the infant Nathan Summers was taken nearly two millennia into the future of Earth-4935, to save his life. In case he should die, Mother Askani of the Askani Sisterhood had him cloned. The tyrant Apocalypse kidnapped and raised the clone, whom he called Stryfe. The original Nathan grew up to become hero Cable, leader of the freedom fighters that battled armies commanded by Stryfe. Both men traveled back to the present day, and continued to bitterly oppose each other. Although his original form was destroyed, Stryfe's consciousness managed to take over other bodies. He later sacrificed himself to save the Earth. Stryfe returned in his original form to help Bishop hunt for Hope Summers, and though he was captured by Apocalypse, he escaped to menace Cable and his allies once more.

FACTFILE
REAL NAME
Stryfe
OCCUPATION
Terrorist leader
BASE
Mobile

HEIGHT 6 ft 8 in
WEIGHT 350 lbs
EYES Blue
HAIR White

FIRST APPEARANCE
The New Mutants #87 (March 1990)

POWERS
A mutant possessing superhuman strength and other physical abilities, Stryfe also has vast telepathic and telekinetic powers. Unlike his clone Cable, he does not have to waste any of these powers keeping a techno-organic virus in check.

STORM

The mighty mutant leader

Goddess, mutant, and queen, Storm is a woman of many facets.

Ororo Munroe is descended from a long line of African witch-priestesses. Her mother married an American photographer, and Ororo was born in New York City. When the child was six months old, the family moved to Egypt. Five years later, Ororo's parents were killed during an Arab-Israeli conflict. Young Ororo was buried under the rubble of her home beside her dead mother's body, an experience that gave her intense claustrophobia.

ESSENTIAL STORYLINES

- ***Ororo: Before the Storm #1–4***
  The story of Ororo's early days, before she became an X-Man.
- ***Uncanny X-Men #253–272***
  Storm is regressed to the age of a young girl by Nanny and the Orphan Maker.
- ***Black Panther Vol. 3 #14–18***
  Ororo's courtship with and marriage to the Black Panther.

FACTFILE

REAL NAME
Ororo Munroe

OCCUPATION
Adventurer

BASE
Wakanda

HEIGHT 5 ft 11 in
WEIGHT 127 lbs
EYES Blue (white when using her powers)
HAIR White

FIRST APPEARANCE
Giant-Size X-Men #1 (1975)

POWERS
Mutant ability to manipulate the weather. Storm can control the creation of rain, snow, sleet, fog, hail, and lightning. She can create hurricane-force winds or lower the temperature around her to freezing point and below.

Ororo evolved from a thief on the streets of Cairo to the leader of the X-Men.

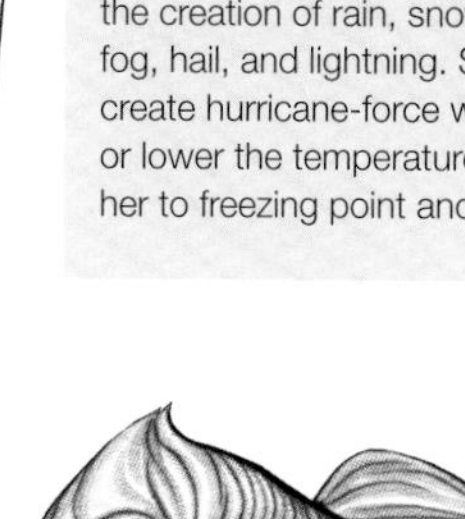

THE YOUNG GODDESS

Ororo wandered the streets of Cairo and eventually became an accomplished thief and pickpocket. She even robbed Professor X, who was in Cairo to battle the Shadow King. By the age of 12, her amazing mutant power to control the weather began to emerge. She traveled throughout Africa, where she used her abilities to help several tribes, the members of which came to worship her as a goddess of rain.

Professor X later returned to Africa and convinced Ororo to use her powers to help all of humanity. She joined the X-Men under the code name Storm and quickly became one of Professor X's most trusted students. At times, she even served as the team's leader.

POWERLESS

At one point, Henry Peter Gyrich shot Ororo with a weapon that removed her powers. Shortly after this, she met and fell in love with Forge, the man who designed that weapon. She continued to work with the X-Men, eventually regaining her powers. She gave her life to defeat the Adversary, but Roma (the daughter of Merlyn) restored her.

THE MUTANT QUEEN

Ororo retained her powers after M-Day, but left the X-Men to return to Africa. While there, she married the Black Panther (T'Challa), becoming the queen of Wakanda. She returned to the X-Men to help them search for Hope Summers. She later helped defeat the Shadow King, who had possessed her husband's form. She was forced to take over as the sole ruler of Wakanda after Doctor Doom critically injured T'Challa. She initially sided with the X-Men in their conflict against the Avengers, putting her on the opposite side to her husband. Afterward, he had their marriage annulled, and she returned to the X-Men full time. When the Terrigen Mists threatened mutantkind, Storm led the X-Men into a war against the Inhumans. She later resigned as leader but remains a prominent member of the team.

Although their marriage was annulled, there remained a strong bond between T'Challa and Ororo. When T'Challa's rule was threatened, he called for aid, and their relationship was rekindled.

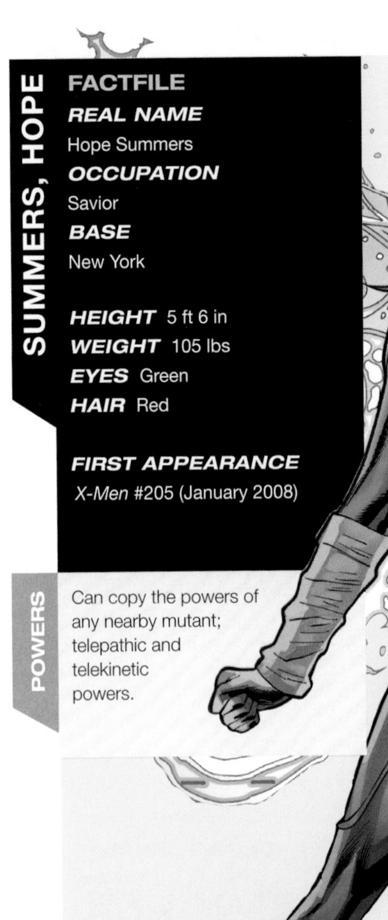

SUMMERS, HOPE

FACTFILE

REAL NAME
Hope Summers

OCCUPATION
Savior

BASE
New York

HEIGHT 5 ft 6 in
WEIGHT 105 lbs
EYES Green
HAIR Red

FIRST APPEARANCE
X-Men #205 (January 2008)

POWERS
Can copy the powers of any nearby mutant; telepathic and telekinetic powers.

SUMMERS, HOPE

As the first mutant born after the SCARLET WITCH erased most mutant powers on M-Day, Hope became a point of massive conflict, with mutants from both the future and the present trying to control, kidnap, or even kill her. CABLE (Nathan Summers) escaped with her into the future and raised the orphaned girl as his own, while BISHOP continued to chase them throughout time.

As a teen, Hope returned to the present and immediately became a target of BASTION, but she defeated him and his helpers with her newly manifesting mutant powers.

Joining the X-MEN, Hope helped in their efforts to track down other new mutants. She stayed with CYCLOPS on Utopia when WOLVERINE left, and became the focal point of a conflict between the AVENGERS and the X-Men when the Phoenix Force returned to Earth, where she became its host. However, with the help of the Scarlet Witch, she was able to wish the Phoenix Force away. Soon after, she joined a new incarnation of X-FORCE, eventually becoming its leader.

Although not related to Jean Grey, Hope adopted a uniform much like the one Jean wore as Phoenix.

SUNFIRE

FACTFILE

REAL NAME
Shiro Yoshida

OCCUPATION
Adventurer

BASE
Department H, Canada; (formerly) Tokyo, Japan

HEIGHT 5 ft 10 in
WEIGHT 175 lbs
EYES Brown
HAIR Black

FIRST APPEARANCE
X-Men #64 (January 1970)

POWERS
Can project "solar fire" and create super-heated air currents to fly; has a psionic protective force-field; trained in karate, Japanese Samurai swordsmanship, and kendo.

SUNFIRE

Sunfire's mother was exposed to radiation when the US dropped an atomic bomb on Hiroshima. When his mutant power surfaced, Sunfire vowed vengeance on the US, destroying a monument at the United Nations and clashing with the X-MEN. PROFESSOR X invited Sunfire to join a new group of X-MEN and he did, temporarily. Preferring to go on special missions for Japan, Sunfire was hypnotised by DR. DEMONICUS to fight the West Coast AVENGERS. He subsequently served with ALPHA FLIGHT and BIG HERO 6, but lost his legs in a battle with LADY DEATHSTRIKE and then lost his powers on M-Day. He later became APOCALYPSE's latest version of Famine and, after Apocalypse's defeat, joined the MARAUDERS in their hunt for Hope SUMMERS. Repowered, he later joined the Avengers Unity Squad.

On Earth-2109, Shiro's cousin (and Wolverine's love) Mariko Yashida became Sunfire and later served with the Exiles until her death.

Sunfire's temper runs as hot as the temperatures his powers can conjure and has cost him much over the years.

SUMMERS, RACHEL

Mutant child from another time

In an alternate future Ahab brainwashed Rachel into serving as his telepathic mutant "hound."

Rachel Summers is the daughter of Scott Summers (Cyclops) and Jean Grey (alias Phoenix) in an alternate timeline known as the "Days of Future Past" or Earth-811. In this reality, the US government activated mutant-hunting robot Sentinels after Senator Robert Kelly was assassinated by mutant terrorists. Federal troops attacked Professor X's mansion, and captured Rachel.

PHOENIX

Rachel was brainwashed into becoming a mutant "hound," using her telepathic powers to track down other mutants. Her face was branded with tattoos (which nowadays she uses her powers to conceal). Eventually Rachel rebelled and attacked her master, Ahab. As punishment, she was confined to a mutant concentration camp. By now the Sentinels had taken control of North America. In an effort to change history, Rachel used her powers to send the astral self of her friend Kate Pryde (a middle-aged version of Kitty) back in time. Kate's spirit journeyed to the "mainstream" reality of the X-Men, where she thwarted Kelly's assassination. After returning to their alternate future, Kate sent Rachel back through time to the "mainstream" reality, where she joined the X-Men. Rachel bonded with the Phoenix Force, enabling her to tap its energies, and adopted the name "Phoenix." Subsequently she became a founding member of Excalibur.

In honor of Jean Grey, Summers has assumed her mother's identities of Phoenix and Marvel Girl.

MOTHER ASKANI

Rachel was cast 2,000 years into the alternate future of Earth-4935, a world ruled by Apocalypse. There she founded a group of rebels, the Askani. Decades later, as the elderly Mother Askani, she sent one of her followers back in time to retrieve the infant Nathan Summers. Mother Askani also transported the astral selves of Scott Summers and Jean Grey into new bodies in this alternate future, where they raised Nathan for ten years. Then Mother Askani sent Scott and Jean's astral selves back to their proper time and bodies, before she herself perished. Nathan grew up to become Cable. After an alteration in the timestream, Rachel was a living teenager once more, though she lost her connection to the Phoenix Force. She was held captive in an alternate future by a being named Gaunt. Cable returned her to the X-Men's time, and she rejoined the team. To honor her mother, Rachel started to call herself "Rachel Grey" in private and "Marvel Girl" at work.

After the Shi'ar murdered most of the Grey family, Rachel joined Professor X in his pursuit of her uncle Vulcan. When her grandfather Corsair was killed, she joined his Starjammers in their effort to overthrow Vulcan. She later returned to Earth and joined the staff of Kitty Pryde's Xavier Institute for Mutant Education and Outreach, taking the name Prestige to signify a fresh start.

ESSENTIAL STORYLINES

- ***New Mutants Vol. 1 #18, Excalibur Vol. 1 #52***
In her timeline, Rachel witnesses the federal attack on Xavier's mansion and becomes Ahab's "hound."
- ***Uncanny X-Men #184–199***
Rachel journeys to the "mainstream" timeline, joins the X-Men and becomes the New Phoenix.
- ***Adventures of Cyclops and Phoenix #1–4***
As the elderly Mother Askani, Rachel brings Scott Summers and Jean Grey to a distant future to raise the young Cable.

FACTFILE

REAL NAME
Rachel Anne Summers, now Rachel Grey

OCCUPATION
Adventurer

BASE
Mobile

HEIGHT 5 ft 7 in
WEIGHT 125 lbs
EYES Green
HAIR Red

FIRST APPEARANCE
The Uncanny X-Men #141 (January 1981)

POWERS

Rachel Summers has considerable telepathic and telekinetic abilities. She formerly served as the host of the Phoenix Force, which greatly amplified her psionic powers.

As Phoenix, Rachel could use the cosmic Phoenix Force, though not to the same extent as Jean Grey.

...FOR THE PERFECT VESSEL.
ONE DEAR TO ALL OUR HEARTS--
-- NATHAN CHRISTOPHER SUMMERS
WHICH IS WHY I ARRANGED TO GRAB THE CHILD FIRST.
BUT HE WAS DESPERATELY ILL. I DID WHAT I COULD TO SAVE HIM FROM THE RAVAGES OF THE TECHNO-ORGANIC VIRUS.
BUT TIME WAS RUNNING OUT AS A FAIL-SAFE, WE CREATED A HEATHLY CLONE.

As Mother Askani, Rachel created a clone of the infant Cable, called Stryfe.

SUNSPOT

FIRST APPEARANCE *Marvel Graphic Novel* #4 (November 1982)
REAL NAME Roberto da Costa
OCCUPATION Leader of Hellfire Club **BASE** New York City
HEIGHT 5 ft **WEIGHT** 130 lbs **EYES** Brown **HAIR** Black
SPECIAL POWERS/ABILITIES Solar powers provide super-strength, thermal updrafts for flight, projection of heat and light, and concussive blasts of solar energy.

Sunspot grew up as a wealthy heir in Rio de Janeiro, Brazil. In his powered-up form, his mutant powers transform him into a being of black, crackling force. He has worked with several teams, including the New Mutants, the Fallen Angels, and X-Force. He also accepted a position as a Lord Imperial of the Hellfire Club. Later, he joined the rebooted New Mutants and, when that team dissolved, the Avengers. After leaving the Hellfire Club, he joined the X-Men and helped Danielle Moonstar train the Young X-Men. Sunspot bought AIM and used company resources to investigate the coming Multiverse incursion. He re-joined the Avengers before contracting the M-Pox disease, though it enhanced his powers at the cost of premature aging. Later as Citizen V, he led the U.S.Avengers. He was captured by Hydra and resigned from AIM after he was freed. He took on the name Citizen X and retired when use of his powers significantly aged him.

SUN GIRL

FIRST APPEARANCE *Superior Spider-Man Team-Up* #1 (September 2013)
REAL NAME Selah Burke **OCCUPATION** Vigilante
BASE New York City **HEIGHT** Unknown **WEIGHT** Unknown
EYES Brown **HAIR** Black
SPECIAL POWERS/ABILITIES A special light-powered suit allows her to fly and fire energy blasts.

The first Sun Girl was Mary Mitchell, the secretary and later sidekick of Jim Hammond (the original Human Torch). The second was Selah Burke, the daughter of Lightmaster (Dr. Erward Lansky). She contracted the Carrion virus after coming into contact with the eponymous villain and attacked the Superior Spider-Man (Otto Octavius), but he cured her of the virus. After learning about her villainous father, Selah repaid her debt to Spider-Man by saving him from the Superior Six, though they didn't part on the best of terms. Some time later she saved the Morlocks from an attack by the Evolutionaries.

SUPER-ADAPTOID

FIRST APPEARANCE *Tales Of Suspense* #82 (October 1966)
REAL NAME None **OCCUPATION** Super-assassin
BASE Mobile **HEIGHT/WEIGHT/EYES/HAIR** Variable
SPECIAL POWERS/ABILITIES Android that can duplicate the appearance and powers, clothing and weaponry of anyone who passes within 10 ft of the scanning instruments in its eyes. It can mimic a maximum of eight beings at a single time.

The criminal organization AIM built the Super-Adaptoid and powered it with a sliver from the Cosmic Cube. Sent to destroy Captain America, it copied the powers and appearances of several heroes, but the Avengers defeated it time after time. Other versions of the Adaptoid have plagued the Earth, including one merged with Yelena Belova (Black Widow). The Ultra-Adaptoid infiltrated the criminal group MODOK's 11 for AIM. At the end of the Dark Reign, HAMMER outfitted Norman Osborn (*see* Green Goblin) with the powers of the Super-Adaptoid.

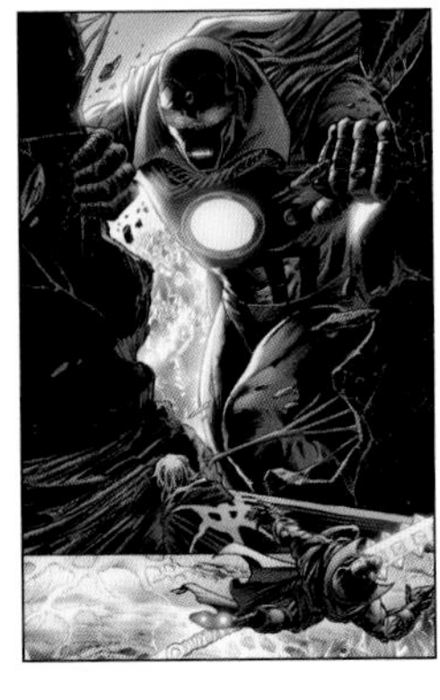

SUPER-APES

Reed Richards wanted to test a new rocket fuel in a ship designed to take the Fantastic Four to the moon. They hoped to get to the moon before the Soviets. But unknown to Reed, a Soviet scientist named Ivan Kragoff had built his own ship, which he hoped would get him to the moon first. Kragoff had trained three apes, a gorilla, a baboon, and a orangutan to help him operate the ship. Aware of the cosmic rays that gave the Fantastic Four their powers, Kragoff intentionally exposed himself and the apes to cosmic rays during their journey to the moon. Kragoff, now calling himself the Red Ghost, and the three apes all gained different superpowered abilities.

Once on the moon, the Super-Apes battled the Fantastic Four but quickly turned against Kragoff, who starved them to keep them controlled. As their powers developed, each of the Super Apes gained human-level intelligence, and they allied with the Red Ghost again. Miklho died at the hands of the Red Hulk, and was replaced by Grigori, a young ape with the same powers.

FACTFILE
MEMBERS
IGOR
A baboon
MIKLHO
A gorilla
PEOTOR
An orangutan

BASE Mobile
FIRST APPEARANCE
Fantastic Four #13
(April 1963)

POWERS

IGOR: possesses the ability to shapeshift.

MIKLHO: possesses super-strength.

PEOTOR: possesses the ability to control magnetism.

SUPER-SKRULL

After the Fantastic Four prevented the Skrulls from conquering Earth, the Skrull Emperor vowed to develop a super-weapon that could destroy them. His scientists took a warrior named Kl'rt and turned him into the Super-Skrull, engineered to possess all the powers of the Fantastic Four. However, the Super-Skrull's first battle against the Fantastic Four ended in failure.

The Super-Skrull battled the Avengers and Captain Marvel during the Kree-Skrull War, and over the years has clashed with Spider-Man, Ms. Marvel, and many others. During the Secret Invasion he came to Earth to kill his daughter Jazinda, who had shamed their family years before, but ended up saving her instead. Dozens of other Super-Skrulls with different sets of powers followed in Kl'rt's wake. Kl'rt returned home and fought for control of the Skrull Empire until the Builders attacked. The Galactic Council, Skrulls, and the Avengers joined forces to defeat the Builders. Afterward, when Thanos attacked Earth, Kl'rt helped the Avengers fight him. Following their victory, Kl'rt was crowned Skrull Emperor, and set about searching for the Infinity Gems. He recovered the Time Gem from Sakaar, but Doctor Strange stole it from him.

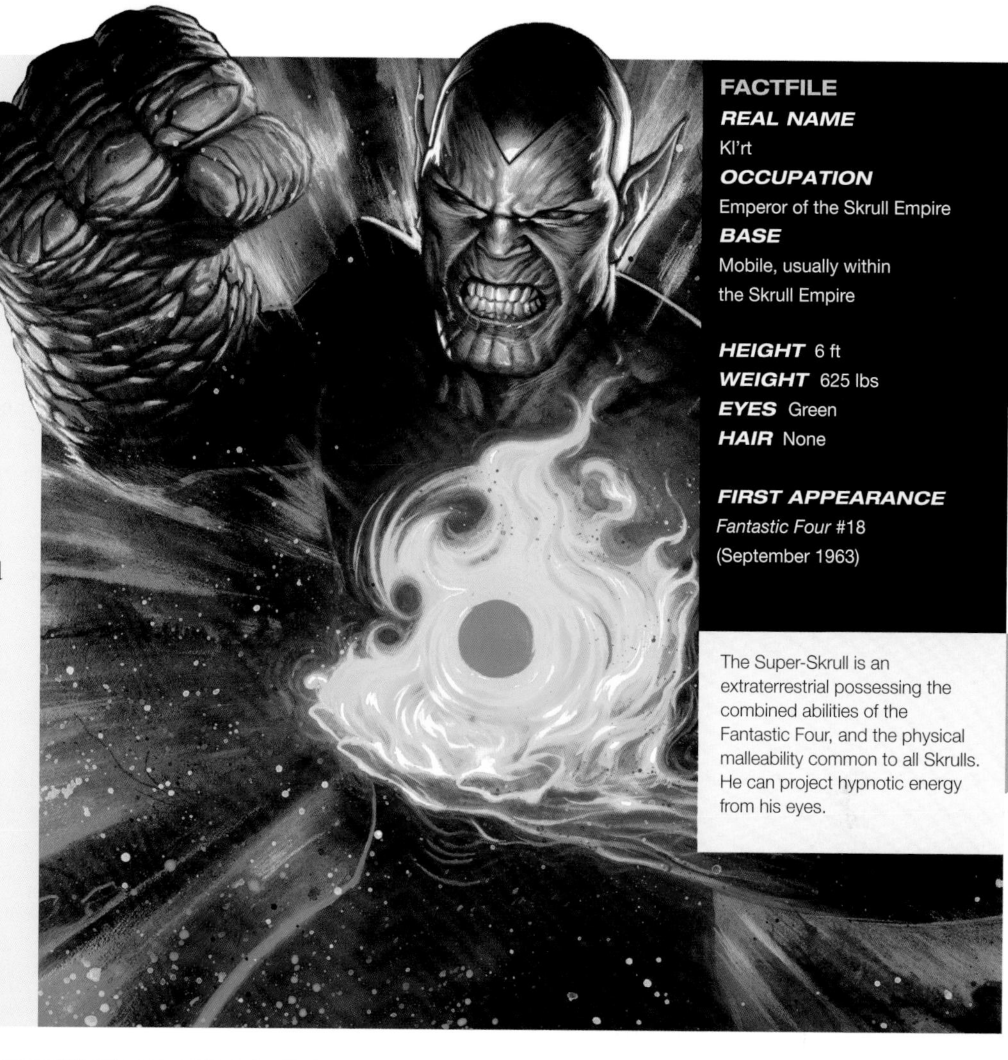

SUPER-SKRULL

FACTFILE

REAL NAME
Kl'rt

OCCUPATION
Emperor of the Skrull Empire

BASE
Mobile, usually within the Skrull Empire

HEIGHT 6 ft
WEIGHT 625 lbs
EYES Green
HAIR None

FIRST APPEARANCE
Fantastic Four #18 (September 1963)

POWERS

The Super-Skrull is an extraterrestrial possessing the combined abilities of the Fantastic Four, and the physical malleability common to all Skrulls. He can project hypnotic energy from his eyes.

SUPREME INTELLIGENCE

FACTFILE

REAL NAME
Supremor

OCCUPATION
Planetary leader

BASE
Kree-Lar

HEIGHT N/A
WEIGHT N/A
EYES Black with yellow pupils
HAIR Green stalks

FIRST APPEARANCE
Fantastic Four #65 (August 1967)

POWERS

The Supreme Intelligence possesses the combined intellect of the greatest minds in Kree history. In the past, the Supreme Intelligence has projected its consciousness into a powerful artificial body in order to actively engage in battle.

SUPREME INTELLIGENCE

The Intelligence detonates a nega-bomb, to wipe out most of the Kree and kickstart their evolution.

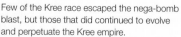

Decades ago, the Kree race learned that their ancient intergalactic enemies, the Skrulls, had created a Cosmic Cube. To maintain parity, they created the Supreme Intelligence, an entity made up of the finest minds ever to exist within the Kree empire. Upon their deaths, those brains deemed worthy of being added to the great repository were absorbed into the Supreme Intelligence, adding their knowledge and experience to its own. The Supreme Intelligence seized control of the Kree empire, becoming at once its dictator and an object of religious worship.

After Captain Marvel (Genis-Vell) destroyed and rebuilt the universe, House Fiyero led the Kree instead, keeping the Supreme Intelligence in a state of undeath. Ronan the Accuser tried to euthanize it, but it survived. Ronan later resurrected the Supreme Intelligence to lead the Kree again, by merging two alternate-universe Mister Fantastics with a Supremor Seed.

Few of the Kree race escaped the nega-bomb blast, but those that did continued to evolve and perpetuate the Kree empire.

SURGE

FIRST APPEARANCE *New Mutants* #8 (January 2004)
REAL NAME Noriko "Nori" Ashida
OCCUPATION Student
BASE Xavier Institute **HEIGHT** 5 ft 7 in **WEIGHT** 137 lbs
EYES Brown **HAIR** Black (dyed blue)
SPECIAL POWERS/ABILITIES Absorbs electricity and transforms it into electric bolts or bursts of speed.

Raised in Japan, Nori came to the US after her parents kicked her out of their home after she displayed mutant powers. She joined the Xavier Institute, and BEAST made her a pair of gauntlets with which she could control her powers, something she had only been able to do with drugs before. Taking the code name Surge, Nori became part of the NEW MUTANTS and struck up a relationship with PRODIGY. She remained with the X-MEN on Utopia after her team disbanded, and after CYCLOPS was put into prison, she joined the Jean Grey School for Higher Learning.

SWARM

FIRST APPEARANCE *The Champions* #14 (July 1977)
REAL NAME Fritz Von Meyer
OCCUPATION Scientist; conqueror **BASE** Mobile
HEIGHT 6 ft 5 in **WEIGHT** Unrevealed **EYES** None **HAIR** None
SPECIAL POWERS/ABILITIES Von Meyer's consciousness can mentally control a mutant queen bee, and through her, vast numbers of mutant bees.

Nazi scientist Fritz Von Meyer was attacked by a colony of bees whose exposure to radiation had given them unusually high intelligence. His body was consumed, but his consciousness survived and took control of the bees, which swarmed in the configuration of a human body around his skeleton. Seeking world conquest, Swarm has fought many heroes. He was eaten by VENOM during a battle with the THUNDERBOLTS, but his consciousness remained intact and formed a new Swarm. He led an incarnation of the SINISTER SIX and fought SPIDER-MAN and DEADPOOL as part of the Hateful Hexad.

SWITZLER, BEVERLY

FIRST APPEARANCE *Howard the Duck* #1 (January 1976)
REAL NAME Beverly Switzler
OCCUPATION Former art model and actress
BASE Cleveland, Ohio
HEIGHT/WEIGHT Unrevealed **EYES** Blue **HAIR** Red
SPECIAL POWERS/ABILITIES As an art model, she can stand perfectly still.

A former art model, Beverly Switzler's life was transformed by an encounter with that extradimensional waterfowl, HOWARD THE DUCK. After Howard rescued her from financial wizard, Pro-Rata, the pair began a life together in Cleveland, Ohio. Things weren't easy—they had difficulty paying the rent and, despite Howard's desire for the quiet life, they were constantly getting embroiled in the shenanigans of villains, including DOCTOR BONG. Lusting after Beverly, Bong forced her to marry him, but she subsequently returned to Howard and had the marriage annulled. She later trained to be a veterinarian and opened a shop called Scales and Tales.

SWORD

(Sentient World Observation and Response Department) was the semi-autonomous division of SHIELD charged with protecting Earth from alien threats. Abigail BRAND was in command of the organization from its founding, sharing the directorship responsibilities with Henry GYRICH only during the DARK REIGN. The organization concentrated on diplomacy as much as espionage or military action and specialized in communication with new alien races from its space station headquarters, known as the Peak. It was eventually replaced by the ALPHA FLIGHT space program.

SWORD

FACTFILE

NOTABLE MEMBERS

ABIGAIL BRAND
Director.

BEAST
Mutant genius.

DEATH'S HEAD
Cyborg bounty hunter.

HENRY GYRICH
Co-director.

LOCKHEED
Mini-dragon spy.

SPIDER-WOMAN
Spider-powered hero.

SYDREN
Alien hacker/telepath.

BASE
The Peak space station, orbiting Earth

FIRST APPEARANCE
Astonishing X-Men #6 (December 2004)

Orbiting the Earth, SWORD's base The Peak was ideal for surveillance of the world's trouble spots.

SWORDSMAN

FACTFILE

REAL NAME
Philip Javert

OCCUPATION
Adventurer

BASE
Mobile

HEIGHT 6 ft 4 in
WEIGHT 250 lbs
EYES Blue
HAIR Black

FIRST APPEARANCE
Avengers #343 (January 1992)

POWERS
The Swordsman was a skilled swordfighter and combatant; expert with all bladed weapons; usually carried a set of throwing knives as well as his sword; a superb athlete; excelled in unarmed combat.

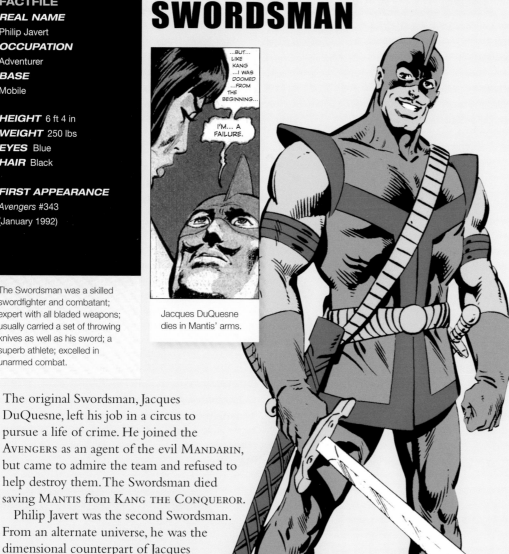

...BUT... LIKE KANG ...I WAS DOOMED ...FROM THE BEGINNING...
I'M... A FAILURE.

Jacques DuQuesne dies in Mantis' arms.

The original Swordsman, Jacques DuQuesne, left his job in a circus to pursue a life of crime. He joined the Avengers as an agent of the evil Mandarin, but came to admire the team and refused to help destroy them. The Swordsman died saving Mantis from Kang the Conqueror.

Philip Javert was the second Swordsman. From an alternate universe, he was the dimensional counterpart of Jacques DuQuesne. Betrayed by the Avengers from his own timeline, Javert initially battled this world's Avengers but then joined them as the new Swordsman. Later, he and his lover, the former Gatherer Magdalene, left for another dimension.

A third Swordsman came from the Counter-Earth created by Franklin Richards in the Heroes Reborn incident. The fourth Swordsman (Andreas Von Strucker) served in the Thunderbolts. The original Swordsman's illegitimate daughter, Marjorie, fought in Euroforce as Swordswoman.

The identity of the Swordsman has become a legacy, passing between characters but always retaining a swashbuckling skill with a blade.

SYNCH

FIRST APPEARANCE *X-Men* #36 (September 1994)
REAL NAME Everett Thomas
OCCUPATION Student **BASE** Massachusetts Academy
HEIGHT 5 ft 11 in **WEIGHT** 165 lbs **EYES** Brown
HAIR Black (shaved bald)
SPECIAL POWERS/ABILITIES Able to take on the superhuman powers of others while they remain in his immediate vicinity.

When teenager Everett Thomas' mutant power emerged, the entity Harvest tried to experiment on him. Rescued by Emma Frost, Jubilee, and Sabretooth, Thomas joined with them to free Husk, M, Skin, and Blink from Harvest. Everett enrolled at the Massachusetts Academy, joining Generation X as Synch. While battling the villain Emplate, who fed off the bone marrow of mutants, Synch became a creature like Emplate himself. He was rescued from Emplate's influence by his teammates. Synch sacrificed his life to save the Generation X students by trying to disarm a bomb planted by Adrienne Frost, elder sister of Emma Frost, at the time Generation X's headmistress. Selene later resurrected Synch for her attack on the X-Men and then killed him.

TAINE, SYDNEY

FIRST APPEARANCE *Nightside* #1 (December 2001)
REAL NAME Sydney Taine
OCCUPATION Police detective **BASE** New York City
HEIGHT/WEIGHT/EYES Unrevealed **HAIR** Black and gray
SPECIAL POWERS/ABILITIES Skilled in a variety of martial arts, including capoeira; adept in various forms of weapons combat; no known superpowers.

Sydney Taine is the only detective in the NYPD trusted by the Others, individuals that appear human but who are driven by sinister thirsts and passions. While investigating the death of three crime bosses, Sydney, partnered by Ape Largo, uncovered a plot by the Others to obtain the Three Lost Treasures of Tao. Defeating them with cunning and fighting prowess, Sydney returned the stolen treasures to Suzuki Shosan, her former teacher. Sydney may be a member of the Players, a powerful alien race.

TALBOT, MAJOR MATT

FIRST APPEARANCE *Incredible Hulk* #436 (December 1995)
REAL NAME William M. "Matt" Talbot
OCCUPATION US Air Force Major
BASE Mobile
HEIGHT 6 ft **WEIGHT** 210 lbs
EYES Blue **HAIR** Brown
SPECIAL POWERS/ABILITIES None.

Major William M. "Matt" Talbot is the nephew of Colonel Glenn Talbot. Matt Talbot is furious at his uncle's wife Betty (*see* Ross, Betty) for dumping his uncle in favor of the Hulk. Matt went to Betty's house and appeared to rescue her from a berserk soldier, but then he slapped her and called her names for hurting his uncle. Out of control, Talbot shot Betty in each leg. When the Hulk came to rescue Betty, he was hit by Talbot's plasma blasts, but it turned out that the gun Talbot used contained stun pellets that soon wore off. Talbot escaped having exacted some measure of revenge for his uncle's broken heart.

TALISMAN

FIRST APPEARANCE *Alpha Flight* #5 (December 1983)
REAL NAME Elizabeth Twoyoungmen
OCCUPATION Student **BASE** Canada
HEIGHT 5 ft 10 in **WEIGHT** 175 lbs **EYES** Blue **HAIR** Black
SPECIAL POWERS/ABILITIES Has natural mystical abilities and can control magical energy; when wearing the "circlet," she can command spirits and manipulate mystical energies.

The latest in a long line of North American shamans, Elizabeth Twoyoungmen transformed into the long-prophesied Talisman when she place a circlet of enchantment on her forehead. She later went on to join Alpha Flight. The circlet gradually corrupted Elizabeth and caused her to grow farther apart from her father Michael Twoyoungmen. Michael took the circlet to defeat the mystical creature Pestilence, but he later returned it to his daughter. After her father's death, she joined Sasquatch's Canadian team, Omega Flight, subsequently retiring from active duty in order to return to her tribe.

TALBOT, COLONEL GLENN

FACTFILE
REAL NAME
Glenn Talbot
OCCUPATION
Major, later Colonel in US Air Force; head of security, Desert Base; later adjutant to General T. E. "Thunderbolt" Ross; later commanding officer, Gamma Base
BASE
Desert Base, New Mexico; later Gamma Base, New Mexico

HEIGHT 6 ft 1 in
WEIGHT 215 lbs
EYES Blue
HAIR Brown

FIRST APPEARANCE
Tales to Astonish #61 (November 1964)

POWERS
Normal human strength.

General Thaddeus E. "Thunderbolt" Ross installed Major Glenn Talbot as security head of Desert Base, New Mexico, to investigate Dr. Bruce Banner. Talbot became Banner's rival for Ross' daughter, Betty (*see* Ross, Betty), and eventually learned that Banner was the Hulk. For years Talbot aided General Ross in attempts to capture or kill the Hulk. Betty married Talbot, but she later divorced him, realizing she still loved Banner. Promoted to colonel, Talbot was killed by an electrical overload while attacking the Hulk. Red Hulk uncovered that Talbot had been replaced with an LMD (Life Model Decoy) by the Intelligencia. Talbot's ghost aided Betty and the Hulks in the Chaos War.

Glenn Talbot married Betty Ross, but she never stopped loving his rival, Bruce Banner, alias the Hulk.

TANAKA, KENJIRO

FIRST APPEARANCE *Quasar* #5 (December 1989)
REAL NAME Kenjiro Tanaka
OCCUPATION Former SHIELD agent **BASE** New York City
HEIGHT 5 ft 10 in **WEIGHT** 160 lbs **EYES** Black **HAIR** Black
SPECIAL POWERS/ABILITIES None; received combat training from SHIELD.

Kenjiro "Ken" Tanaka attended SHIELD academy alongside Wendell Vaughn, who later became the cosmic hero Quasar. After graduation, Tanaka took an undercover position within International Data Integration and Control (IDIC) and became its director of design. He eventually left IDIC to join his former classmate at Vaughn Security Systems. Tanaka discovered the link between Wendell Vaughn and Quasar but agreed to keep the secret safe. He now heads up Vaughn Security Systems while Quasar is away saving the galaxy.

TARANTULA

Hero for hire with a sting

A criminal used the name Tarantula during the days of the Old West, but the first modern Tarantula, Anton Miguel Rodriguez, was a brutal revolutionary from the small, South American country of Delvadia. Government officials gave him his powers with a variant of the Super-Soldier formula, intending to make him a national symbol, like Captain America.

Enhanced reflexes and military training allowed the Tarantula to make deadly stabs with his venomous boot-spikes.

FACTFILE

REAL NAME
Maria Vasquez

OCCUPATION
Hero for hire

BASE
New York

HEIGHT Unrevealed
WEIGHT Unrevealed
EYES Green
HAIR Black with red streak

FIRST APPEARANCE
Heroes For Hire #1 (August 2006)

POWERS
Martial arts and knife fighting expert. Spiked blades in the wrists and toes of her costume.

KILLER FOR HIRE

Instead, he became a professional criminal and assassin. In New York, where he hijacked a boat on the Hudson River, Spider-Man and the Punisher thwarted his plans. He later mutated into a humanoid spider due to treatments from Roxxon Oil, and he killed himself in a police standoff. His daughter donned the Tarantula costume and teamed up with the daughter of Batroc the Leaper before dying at the hands of the Taskmaster.

Captain Luis Alvarez of Delvadia became the second official Tarantula. On a mission to the US to execute Delvadian refugees, he battled Spider-Man and lost. Exiled from his country, Alvarez died when the armed vigilante team the Jury executed him.

MARIA VASQUEZ

During the Civil War, a new Tarantula joined Misty Knight's Heroes for Hire. Maria Vasquez had abilities and weapons similar to those of her predecessors, but no other connection. She hoped to avenge her sister, who died when Nitro blew up Stamford, Connecticut. After World War Hulk, she nearly died when her teammate Humbug offered her to No-Name, the Brood member of the Warbound, but Shang-Chi saved her.

Carlos LaMuerto was a criminal known as the Black Tarantula. He fought Spider-Man and later became Daredevil's lieutenant and helped him lead the Hand.

ESSENTIAL STORYLINES
- ***Amazing Spider-Man* #134**
First appearance of the original Tarantula.
- ***Heroes for Hire* #1**
Maria Vasquez appears for the first time.
- ***Heroes for Hire* #15**
Maria Vasquez is left in a coma as the team go their separate ways.

As a degenerating clone of Peter Parker, Kaine had never been pretty to begin with.

THE OTHERS

Spider-Man's clone Kaine became a new Tarantula for a while. Slain by Kraven's family to resurrect their patriarch, Kaine returned from the dead in a half-spider form. The Jackal and the Spider Queen controlled him until he was given the cure for the Spider-Island outbreak, returning him to a more stable state than he'd ever known.

TASKMASTER

FACTFILE

REAL NAME
Tony Masters

OCCUPATION
Mercenary; teacher

BASE Mobile

HEIGHT 6 ft 2 in
WEIGHT 220 lbs
EYES Brown
HAIR Brown

FIRST APPEARANCE
Avengers #195
(May 1980)

POWERS
Can copy other people's movements, regardless of complexity, after watching them once.

TASKMASTER

The Taskmaster has the unique ability to duplicate any physical movements he's seen, something he calls photographic reflexes, though at the cost of his own memories. He used his new skills to transform himself into a highly dangerous villain, a match even for the AVENGERS. Eventually he set up a series of academies to train henchmen. Later, while in prison, he even trained John Walker (U.S.AGENT) for his position as the new CAPTAIN AMERICA.

Taskmaster worked on restoring some of his memories before becoming an instructor at Camp Hammond, teaching the youths of the FIFTY-STATE INITIATIVE. He later joined SHIELD's Secret Avengers team and become their double-agent in AIM's High Council. He was shot and believed killed by MOCKINGBIRD, but MENTALLO secretly healed him. He served as the sheriff of Bagalia and obtained a recording of Captain America swearing allegiance to HYDRA. When attempts to sell the recording to Maria HILL failed, he joined Hydra, but switched sides when Hydra began to fall. When the dust settled, Taskmaster went back to working as a mercenary.

TAURUS

FIRST APPEARANCE *The Avengers* #72 (January 1970)
REAL NAME Cornelius Van Lunt
OCCUPATION Criminal mastermind **BASE** New York City
HEIGHT 6 ft 2 in **WEIGHT** 260 lbs **EYES** Brown **HAIR** Black
SPECIAL POWERS/ABILITIES Utilized Star-Blazer handgun, which fired blasts of stellar energy.

TAURUS.
CORNELIUS VAN LUNT.

Fascinated by astrology, multimillionaire Cornelius Van Lunt secretly founded the criminal organization ZODIAC to achieve political and economic domination of the world. Each of Zodiac's 12 leaders was named after his or her astrological sign and was based in a different American city: Van Lunt became Taurus, based in New York. Both in his true identity and as Taurus, Van Lunt clashed with the AVENGERS. Van Lunt ended up battling MOON KNIGHT aboard a plane and died when it crashed. There have since been various other versions of the Zodiac organization, each with its own Taurus.

TATTERDEMALION

FIRST APPEARANCE *Werewolf By Night* #9 (September 1973)
REAL NAME Arnold Pattonroth (alias Michael Wyatt)
OCCUPATION Tap-dancer; actor **BASE** Los Angeles
HEIGHT 5 ft 9 in **WEIGHT** 165 lbs **EYES** Blue **HAIR** Brown
SPECIAL POWERS/ABILITIES Enhanced strength, speed; gloves treated with a solvent that dissolves paper and fabric; Kevlar body armor; cloak contains chloroform capsules; indestructible scarf.

Pattonroth was swindled of his life's savings by Las Vegas mobsters. He joined an army of derelicts on the streets of LA and declared war on the rich. Defeated by the WEREWOLF and SPIDER-MAN, he moved back to Las Vegas and attacked the criminals who had stolen from him. He later returned to LA and was recruited into the criminal organization Night Shift, run by the SHROUD. During the CIVIL WAR, he was forced to fight for the THUNDERBOLTS. Later, in Los Angeles, COUNT NEFARIA killed him and the rest of Night Shift.

TEEN BRIGADE

The original Teen Brigade was a group of teenaged shortwave radio enthusiasts, founded by Rick JONES to keep tabs on the HULK. A Teen Brigade call for help assembled the AVENGERS for the very first time, and another helped CAPTAIN AMERICA track down a suspect who had turned the Avengers to stone. The group was a precursor to Captain America's Stars and Stripes computer hotline network.

Many years later, a new Teen Brigade composed of Super Heroes formed. It included Angel Salvadore, Barnell Bohusk (BLACKWING), the IN-BETWEENER, the new MISS AMERICA, and the Ultimate Nullifier. Jack Truman, a former agent of SHIELD, guided them as they fought demons called the Braak'nhüd and faced off against the YOUNG MASTERS, traveling to Latveria to stop them from assassinating Kristoff VERNARD.

TEEN BRIGADE

FACTFILE

MEMBERS
RICK JONES (founder), **CANDY**, **RIDER**, **SPECS**, **WHEELS**, plus other unnamed volunteers.

BASE
Mobile

FIRST APPEARANCE
Incredible Hulk #6
(March 1963)

STILL NO WORD FROM THE FF, EH?
GUESS THEY NEVER GOT THE MESSAGE!
OR ELSE THEY CAN'T BE BOTHERED TO ANSWER A BUNCH OF KIDS LIKE US!

The Teen Brigade used short-wave radios and Internet-enabled computers to keep in touch with each other.

TEMUGIN

FIRST APPEARANCE *Iron Man* #53 (June 2002)
REAL NAME Temugin
OCCUPATION Criminal leader **BASE** China
HEIGHT/WEIGHT Unrevealed **EYES** Brown **HAIR** None
SPECIAL POWERS/ABILITIES Supreme martial artist; harnesses the power of his Chi to perform feats of incredible strength, speed, and agility; possesses the Mandarin's rings of power.

The illegitimate son of the MANDARIN, Temugin was raised in a monastery and trained in the mystic martial arts. As an adult, he received a package containing the Mandarin's ten rings of power (each of which endowed the wearer with a different ability), and felt honor-bound to seek revenge on IRON MAN for his father's death. Taking over the Mandarin's criminal empire, Temugin clashed with Iron Man but failed to discharge this honor-debt. He later lost a hand, along with five rings, to PUMA. He was subsequently recruited for the AGENTS OF ATLAS by the dragon Mister Lao, who feared that Jimmy Woo, the current leader of the team, was not strong-willed enough. This placed Temugin in position to succeed Woo as leader.

TERMINUS

FIRST APPEARANCE *Fantastic Four* #269 (August 1984)
REAL NAME Terminus **OCCUPATION** Destroyer of worlds
BASE Mobile **HEIGHT** 150 ft **WEIGHT** unrevealed
EYES Inapplicable **HAIR** None
SPECIAL POWERS/ABILITIES Immeasurable strength, nearly indestructible; can regenerate body parts; carries a lance that fires atomic energy.

Terminus is an intelligent creation made from living metal, grown by the alien Terminex in a failed attempt to protect them from the CELESTIALS. A continuum of Termini exist, from Stage 1 metallic microbes to the Stage 4 behemoths represented by Terminus. Taking revenge on planets that the Celestials had spared, Terminus claimed Earth for his own but met defeat at the hands of the FANTASTIC FOUR. The Deviant called Jorro wore the Terminus armor and destroyed the Savage Land. Terminus defeated a duplicate and emerged as the Stage 5 "Ulterminus," only to be vanquished by THOR.

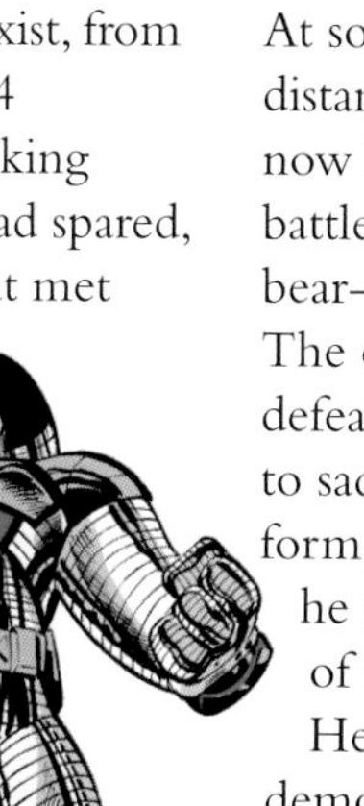

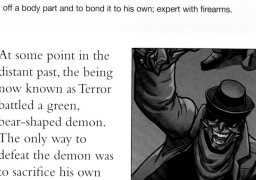

TERRAX

FIRST APPEARANCE *Fantastic Four* #211 (October 1979)
REAL NAME Tyros
OCCUPATION Interstellar traveler **BASE** Mobile
HEIGHT 6 ft 6 in **WEIGHT** 2,750 lbs **EYES** Gray **HAIR** None
SPECIAL POWERS/ABILITIES Body covered with supple, rocky shell; animates rock and commands it to do his bidding; lifted Manhattan into orbit around Earth.

GALACTUS chose Tyros, a despot from the planet Birj, as his new herald. Tyros, rechristened Terrax, remained a restless, rebellious soul, and before long he betrayed his overbearing master. Terrax traveled to Earth and battled the FANTASTIC FOUR, who handed him over to Galactus. After being killed and reborn a number of times, he returned to space. He was swept up in the ANNIHILATION, but survived. He returned to conquer Birj and died defending it against the Phoenix Force. The Phoenix energy resurrected him however, and he was discovered by DRAX. He acquired a Phoenix egg, but it was stolen by Thane. The ILLUMINATI later captured a version of Terrax from another universe—its only survivor—and he later joined NAMOR'S CABAL.

TERROR

FIRST APPEARANCE *St. George* #2 (August 1988)
REAL NAME Unknown (possibly Shreck) **OCCUPATION** Criminal
BASE San Francisco **HEIGHT** 6 ft 2 in **WEIGHT** 170 lbs
EYES Variable **HAIR** None
SPECIAL POWERS/ABILITIES Able to replace parts of his body with those of humans or animals, gaining the powers of those body parts, as well as their "memories." If Terror takes a body part from a superhuman being he gains that being's power; removes limbs or other parts by generating a special acid that allows him both to tear off a body part and to bond it to his own; expert with firearms.

At some point in the distant past, the being now known as Terror battled a green, bear-shaped demon. The only way to defeat the demon was to sacrifice his own form, but in doing so he took on the form of the dead demon. He also gained the demon's power to bond the limbs of others to his body. His body came to be made up of a collection of dead or decaying body parts, which his associate Boneyard helped him collect. He was also befriended by a half-human, half-demon being named Hellfire. Terror formed Terror Inc., an assassination bureau, and later joined Deadpool's MERCS FOR MONEY. He patrolled New York with teammate FOOLKILLER, though the team soon disbanded.

Terrax wields a cosmic ax which can project energy shields and powerful waves of destruction.

THANOS

The Mad Titan

THANOS

FACTFILE

REAL NAME
Thanos

OCCUPATION
Conqueror

BASE
Sanctuary III

HEIGHT 6 ft 7 in
WEIGHT 985 lbs
EYES Red
HAIR None

FIRST APPEARANCE
Iron Man #55
(February 1973)

POWERS
Possibly one of the strongest beings in existence; master tactician and strategist; effectively immortal; synthesizes cosmic energy for many uses, including firing energy blasts from his eyes.

Born on Titan, Thanos is one of the god-like race called the ETERNALS. Much to the horror of his parents, Thanos was born with the Deviant gene, hence his brutal appearance. His mother saw his dark future and tried unsuccessfully to kill him while he was a baby. A quiet, introverted child, unlike his charming and gregarious brother STARFOX, Thanos was a pacifist until he became obsessed with the embodiment of DEATH.

Thanos believed the power the Infinity Gauntlet gave him was the key to winning Death's affections.

COURTING DEATH

Thanos used experimental science to increase his strength and power. He sired numerous children and even became a space pirate, but killed his own children and captain, not to mention countless millions on Titan, in an attempt to impress Death. When he sought a powerful Cosmic Cube, he came into conflict with CAPTAIN MAR-VELL. He later confronted Adam WARLOCK, trying to gain the Soul Gem, only to be defeated by Warlock, the AVENGERS, the THING, and SPIDER-MAN. At one point, Thanos gained the Infinity Gauntlet, gaining power over reality itself, and used it to wipe out half of all life in existence. He was defeated by Warlock and his adopted daughter GAMORA, who undid the destruction he had caused.

When ANNIHILUS unleashed the Annihilation Wave on the universe, Thanos sided with him—only to be killed by DRAX. He was resurrected but died again fighting NOVA and STAR-LORD in the Cancerverse. As before, Thanos did not remain dead for long—he returned to life to bring war to the galaxy as he sought out his son Thane, only to be trapped and frozen in stasis by him.

THE END OF ALL THINGS

Prince NAMOR freed Thanos so he could help him stop the incursions as part of a new CABAL. Thanos survived the destruction of reality and ended up on Battleworld (*see* SECRET WARS), but was killed by Emperor Doom while raising a rebellion. When reality was remade, Thanos was accidently resurrected by GALACTUS and soon returned to his deadly ways. He was defeated by the Avengers during an attack on Earth, and even met his future self—King Thanos—who asked his younger self to kill him. Thanos was repulsed by how weak he had become and used a fragment of the Time Gem to travel back to his own time, swearing never to become like King Thanos. After the Infinity Gems reappeared, Thanos was killed by Requiem (GAMORA) and beheaded. However, it surely will not be long before Thanos returns to court Death once more.

Death first appeared to Thanos when he was young, and soon became his obsession.

ESSENTIAL STORYLINES

- ***Infinity Gauntlet #1–6*** Thanos gains control of the Infinity Gauntlet—and uses its power to wipe out half of all life.
- ***Infinity #1–6*** Thanos and his Black Order launch all-out war on the galaxy as he seeks out his son, Thane.
- ***Thanos Rising #1–5*** The shocking early life of Thanos is revealed.

THENA

FIRST APPEARANCE *The Eternals* #5 (November 1976)
REAL NAME Azura, changed by royal decree to Thena
OCCUPATION Warrior; scholar **BASE** Olympia, Greece
HEIGHT 5 ft 10 in **WEIGHT** 160 lbs **EYES** Blue **HAIR** Blond
SPECIAL POWERS/ABILITIES Superhuman strength; mental control over body gives virtual immortality; psionic abilities include flight through levitation; projects cosmic energy from eyes or hands.

Thena is the daughter of Zuras, ruler of the ETERNALS, and his wife Cybele. In a pact between the Eternals and the GODS OF OLYMPUS, Zuras renamed Azura "Thena" after the goddess Athena. Thousands of years ago, Thena met Kro, a member of the Deviants. They became lovers, and they had twin children. Upon the demise of Zuras, Thena succeeded him as Prime Eternal, but she subsequently lost this position to another Eternal, IKARIS. Her mind wiped, Thena resurfaced recently with a human husband and son. She has since regained her memories of her former life.

THOMPSON, EUGENE "FLASH"

Eugene Thompson's athletic prowess made him a football hero at Midtown High School, helping him overcome the insecurities of having an abusive, alcoholic NYPD officer father. He dated Liz ALLAN, the most popular girl in the school, and bullied bookish Peter Parker (not knowing he was SPIDER-MAN). Ironically, Flash was Spider-Man's biggest fan. Flash went on to attend Empire State University with Parker and, in time, the two became friends.

Flash later joined the military and served in South-East Asia. After returning, he had an affair with Betty BRANT, wife of *Daily Bugle* reporter Ned Leeds, who framed Flash as the HOBGOBLIN. For a while, Flash worked at Midtown High as a gym teacher, but he re-enlisted with the Army to fight in Iraq, where he lost both legs trying to save his commanding officer.

When the US government removed the VENOM symbiote from Mac Gargan (SCORPION), they gave it to Flash, turning him into Agent Venom. Flash fled rather than return the symbiote, but his heroism convinced CAPTAIN AMERICA to invite him to join his Secret AVENGERS. Flash later became ANTI-VENOM and died saving his friends from the GREEN GOBLIN.

FACTFILE
REAL NAME
Eugene Thompson
OCCUPATION
Government agent
BASE
New York City

HEIGHT 6 ft 2 in
WEIGHT 185 lbs
EYES Blue
HAIR
Reddish-blond

FIRST APPEARANCE
Amazing Fantasy #15 (August 1962)

THOMPSON, EUGENE "FLASH"

POWERS
Formerly a gifted athlete, nicknamed "Flash" because of his speed. He was a star of Midtown High's football and baseball teams.

THING, SEE PAGES 374–375

THOR, SEE PAGES 376–379

THOR GIRL

FIRST APPEARANCE *Thor* #22 (August 2000)
REAL NAME Tarene **OCCUPATION** Adventurer
BASE New York City **HEIGHT** 5 ft 9 in
WEIGHT 317 lbs **EYES** Blue **HAIR** Blond
SPECIAL POWERS/ABILITIES Immortal, superhuman strength, invulnerability, plus a mystic hammer that grants flight, weather control, and energy blast that can transform her to human and back.

Tarene is the Designate prophesied by X'Hoss to elevate all life to greatness. Before she could manage this, THANOS destroyed her homeworld and stripped her of much of her power. THOR and Orikal, a powerful being from an extra-dimensional realm, helped her to defeat Thanos. She came to Earth and took the code name Thor Girl to emulate her Thunder-God hero. She joined the FIFTY-STATE INITIATIVE, assigned to Georgia's team, the Cavalry. During the SECRET INVASION, she was impersonated by a SKRULL but later returned. After being attacked during FEAR ITSELF, she went back to being the Designate and left for the stars.

3-D MAN

FIRST APPEARANCE *Marvel Premiere* #35 (April 1977)
REAL NAME Charles "Chuck " Chandler
OCCUPATION Test pilot; adventurer **BASE** None
HEIGHT 6 ft 2 in **WEIGHT** 200 lbs **EYES** Blue **HAIR** Blond
SPECIAL POWERS/ABILITIES Strength, stamina, agility, and speed three times that of a normal human; a brilliant pilot with the ability to sense the presence of alien Skrulls.

In 1958, SKRULLS captured NASA test pilot Chuck Chandler in midflight. He escaped, causing their ship to explode. He crash-landed his plane, and Skrull radiation imprinted his essence onto the glasses worn by his brother Hal. By concentrating on the glasses, Hal could resurrect his brother as 3-D Man. However, side effects caused Hal to put his glasses aside. Years later, Hal brought his brother back permanently. Chuck had not aged a single day and began his life anew. Later, the hero TRIATHLON gained the 3-D Man's powers, too. Soon after, he joined the AGENTS OF ATLAS.

THUNDERBIRD

FIRST APPEARANCE *Giant-Size X-Men* #1 (1975)
REAL NAME John Proudstar **OCCUPATION** X-Man
BASE New York City; mobile; New York State
HEIGHT 6 ft 1 in **WEIGHT** 225 lbs **EYES** Brown **HAIR** Black
SPECIAL POWERS/ABILITIES Super strength and stamina; can run at 35mph for long periods; leathery skin protects him from harm.

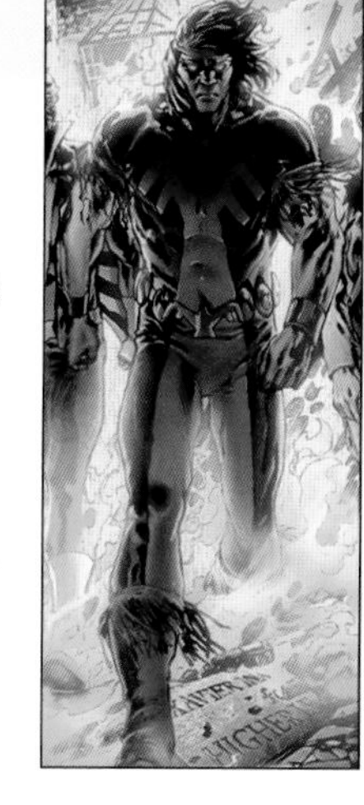

Eager to emulate his warrior ancestors, Native American John Proudstar joined the US Marines as an under-age cadet and served with distinction. John's mutant powers didn't emerge until the age of 20, when he wrestled a rampaging bison with his bare hands. He joined the X-MEN after being sought out by PROFESSOR X, but died on his second mission: jumping onto a criminal's escape plane, he was killed when the aircraft blew up. He was briefly resurrected during the Chaos War and led a group of revived X-Men members only for all to return to the afterlife when the threat of the Chaos King had passed.

THING, THE

Big-hearted tough guy of the Fantastic Four

THING, THE

FACTFILE

REAL NAME
Benjamin Jacob Grimm

OCCUPATION
Adventurer, former test pilot, wrestler

BASE
New York City

HEIGHT 6 ft
WEIGHT 500 lbs
EYES Blue
HAIR (human form) Brown; (Thing) none

FIRST APPEARANCE
Fantastic Four #1 (November 1961)

POWERS

Superhuman strength, endurance, and durability. He can lift 85 tons, absorb the blast of an armor-piercing bazooka shell, withstand temperature extremes, and needs no suit to survive in space or in the ocean depths.

ALLIES/FOES

ALLIES Reed Richards, Sue Richards, Franklin Richards, Valeria Richards, Johnny Storm, Alicia Masters, Sharon Ventura, Captain America, Edwin Jarvis, Iron Man, Jack of Hearts, Thundra, Tigra

FOES Hulk, Beetle, Trapster, Namor, Mad Thinker, Puppet Master, Sandman, Doctor Doom, the Beyonder, Annihilus

ISSUE #1

The story of the Fantastic Four's creation. Pilot Ben Grimm becomes the orange, scaly-skinned, super-strong Thing.

Ben Grimm, alias the Thing, is a hot-headed member of the FANTASTIC FOUR, using his abilities to fight evil, almost as often as he does battle with himself. Ben grew up in New York City in poverty. Like his older brother, Daniel, he got involved with a street gang (*see* YANCY STREET GANG). After his parents died, Ben was taken in by his uncle Jake, a doctor, who helped set the boy on the right track. Ben ended up going to Empire State University on a football scholarship. His first-year roommate was brilliant science student Reed Richards, who became Ben's best friend.

A GRIMM TALE

When Reed told Ben of his plan to one day build a starship, Ben jokingly said that he would pilot the ship.

After college, Ben joined the US Air Force and became an excellent pilot and astronaut. Reed's starship reached the test stage but the government threatened to cut off funding. Reed decided to stage a test flight. Ben agreed to pilot the ship, though he worried that the radiation shields weren't strong enough.

Reed and Ben blasted into space along with Reed's fiancée, Susan Storm, and Sue's brother Johnny. In space, the foursome was bombarded with high levels of cosmic radiation.

LET THE CLOBBERIN' BEGIN!

The crew were altered on a genetic level and gained unusual powers. Ben's skin turned orange and rocky, and his strength grew tremendously, earning him the nickname the Thing. Reed convinced the others that they should use their powers to help humanity as the FANTASTIC FOUR. Ben would sometimes revert back to his human form unexpectedly, but neither he nor Reed could control this change. In the early years after he became the Thing, Ben dated the blind sculptor, Alicia MASTERS. Because she had fallen in love with him while he was in his rocky form, he worried that she might not feel the same way about him if he managed to become human again.

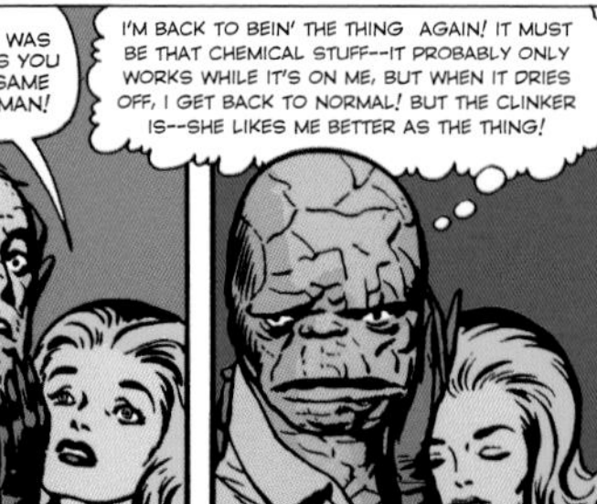

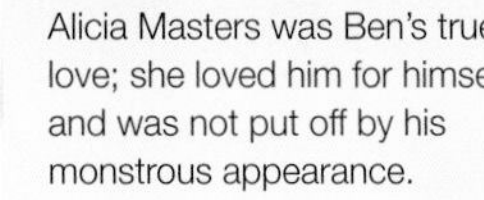

Alicia Masters was Ben's true love; she loved him for himself and was not put off by his monstrous appearance.

ESSENTIAL STORYLINES

- ***Fantastic Four #1*** An accident in space changes pilot Ben Grimm into the orange-colored-rock-encrusted the Thing.
- ***Fantastic Four #8*** The Thing meets Alicia Masters and a long love affair begins.
- ***Fantastic Four Wedding Special*** Ben finally marries Alicia Masters.

THE LONELY MONSTER

After fighting in the first of the Secret Wars involving the Beyonder, Ben stayed on Battleworld for months, able to change back and forth from his human form to the Thing. While there, he fell for Tarianna of Leenn, whom he eventually learned the Beyonder had created as a simulacrum of Ben's ideal woman.

When Ben returned, stuck as a monster once more, he discovered that, in his absence, the Human Torch and Alicia had not only struck up a relationship, they were soon to be married. The fact that this Alicia turned out to be a Skrull named Lyja masquerading as Alicia did little to help, as by that time Ben had gotten over his heartbreak. He and Alicia remained friends but nothing more.

Ben has also dated other women over the years, including Sharon Ventura, who was Ms. Marvel at the time but later transformed into the She-Thing. He became engaged to a teacher named Debbie Green, but left her before the wedding, fearful of exposing her to the extreme dangers that were an everyday part of his life.

Since Ben and Johnny thought Reed and Sue were dead, the Fantastic Four disbanded. Ben joined the Guardians of the Galaxy instead, at this time led by Rocket Raccoon, with Kitty Pryde in the role of Star-Lord.

Always fiercely loyal to the Fantastic Four, Ben sometimes split his time with other teams, such as the Avengers.

LOOKING TO THE FUTURE

A depowered Ben was prepared to sacrifice himself to save the Future Foundation (*see* Fantastic Four) and the world from Annihilus when the portal to the Negative Zone was forced open. To Ben's dismay, the Human Torch tossed him to safety and took his place. While trying to get back into the Negative Zone to stand beside his pal, Ben morphed into the Thing again. He was delighted when the Human Torch returned safely from his battles in the Negative Zone. When the Serpent unleashed fear on Earth (*see* Fear Itself), Ben was transformed into Angrir, Breaker of Souls, only to be saved by Franklin Richards. Not long after, he was framed for the murder of the Puppet Master by the Quiet Man and ended up in the Raft prison, before breaking free with the help of Sandman, She-Hulk, and Ant-Man and proving his innocence.

After the destruction of Doctor Doom's Battleworld and the reshaping of reality (*see* Secret Wars), Ben and Johnny found themselves on Earth, and started to believe Reed and Sue had died. Ben joined the Guardians of the Galaxy for a time before returning to Earth. Seeing that Johnny needed a purpose, Ben lied to him, convincing him that Reed had left clues showing how to find him and Sue. Ben and Johnny explored parallel realities looking for their friends before finally giving up. Deciding to look to the future, Ben asked Alicia to marry him and she said yes. Shortly after, Reed and Sue sent out a call for help, bringing the Fantastic Four together again.

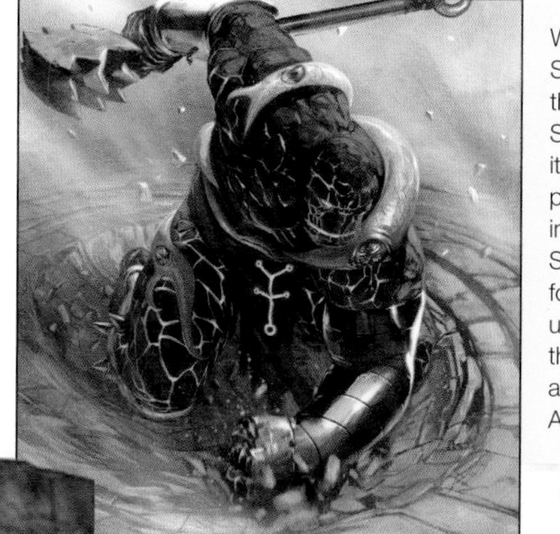

When one of the Serpent's Hammers of the Worthy fell on Yancy Street, the Thing picked it up and found himself possessed. Transformed into Angrir, Breaker of Souls, in this terrifying form he was almost unstoppable, defeating the Red Hulk in a duel and destroying Avengers Tower.

After a courtship lasting many years and involving much heartache for both of them, Ben Grimm and Alicia Masters were finally married.

THOR

The Asgardian God of Thunder

FACTFILE

REAL NAME
Thor Odinson (alias Donald Blake, Eric Masterson, Jake Olson)

OCCUPATION
God of Thunder

BASE
Asgard

HEIGHT 6 ft 6 in
WEIGHT 640 lbs
EYES Blue
HAIR Blond

FIRST APPEARANCE
Journey Into Mystery #83 (August 1962)

POWERS
Enhanced strength, near-invulnerability, longevity, and vast magical abilities provided by the Odinforce. Wields the unbreakable hammer of Mjolnir which can open interdimensional portals, permit flight, channel storms, and fire energy blasts.

ALLIES/FOES
ALLIES The Avengers, Beta Ray Bill, Sif, Warriors Three

FOES Loki, Surtur, the Enchantress, the Absorbing Man

ISSUE #1
In *Journey into Mystery,* Thor leads a double life as the Thunder God and the mortal man Donald Blake. Later, Thor dropped the Blake identity.

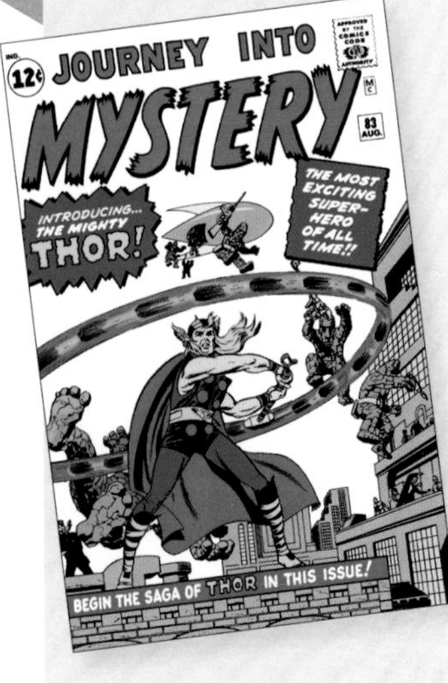

JOURNEY INTO
MYSTERY
12¢
83 AUG.
INTRODUCING... THE MIGHTY THOR!
THE MOST EXCITING SUPER-HERO OF ALL TIME!!
BEGIN THE SAGA OF THOR IN THIS ISSUE!

Thor was the God of Thunder, the beloved champion of Asgard (*see* GODS OF ASGARD) and a figure of worship among the ancient Norse. He was born to ODIN, the ruler (All-Father) of Asgard, and GAEA, the mother goddess of Earth (a place known to the Asgardians as Midgard). Thor loved his people, but when he discovered they were stuck in an endless repeating cycle, he broke it by triggering their destruction in the end battle of Ragnarok.

Thor could transport himself to Midgard via Asgard's rainbow bridge or by using the powers of his hammer Mjolnir.

EARLY LIFE

Groomed to assume his father's throne, Thor grew up with his best friend BALDER and his first love, SIF. But Thor's half-brother LOKI hated him, and schemed to become ruler of Asgard himself.

When Thor proved himself worthy of carrying the uru hammer Mjolnir, he took up the identity as the Thunder God. Thor mingled with his Earthly worshippers throughout the 9th century, leading the Vikings into battle. He later abandoned his followers after several of them butchered members of a Christian monastery. Over the succeeding centuries he spent most of his time

THE TEEN BRIGADE! THEY'RE LOCATED IN THE SOUTH WEST! IF THIS CONCERNS THE HULK, IT MUST BE SERIOUS! AND SO, THE TIME HAS COME...
...FOR DR. DON BLAKE TO STRIKE HIS ENCHANTED CANE ONCE UPON THE FLOOR, CASTING OFF HIS MORAL GUISE, AND BECOMING...
...THE MIGHTY THOR, GOD OF THUNDER!

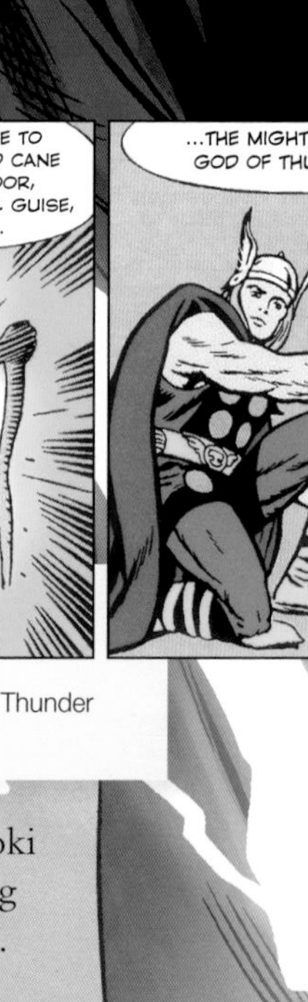

Originally, Thor transformed from Donald Blake to the Thunder God by striking a simple wooden staff on the ground.

in Asgard, venturing to Earth to battle Loki in the Old West and mistakenly becoming a pawn of the Nazis during World War II.

Deciding that his son needed to learn humility before assuming the title of All-Father, Odin exiled Thor to Earth. There, the Thunder God believed himself to be the mortal doctor Donald Blake, and walked with the aid of a wooden cane. When he struck the cane on the ground it transformed into Mjolnir, and Thor

As one of the core members of the Avengers, Thor defeated the robot Ultron and crushed countless other threats to humanity.

STORMY TIMES

A second incarnation of the Thunder God appeared when Thor merged his spirit with Earth architect Eric Masterson. Thor entered temporary exile for apparently killing Loki, and Masterson carried on, posing as Thor while wielding the hammer of Mjolnir. Masterson later received the identity of Thunderstrike, before perishing in battle against the Egyptian god Seth and overcoming a curse laid upon Masterson by the weapon of Bloodaxe. Thor subsequently assumed the civilian identity of dead EMS worker Jake Olson, though he soon gave this up and let a resurrected Olson continue his life. Eric Masterson's son, Kevin, later took up the role of Thunderstrike in a possible future timeline also inhabited by Spider-Girl.

Thor and Thunderstrike unite their mystical hammers to unleash even greater power. Thor, who considered Eric Masterson one of the most noble mortals he had ever encountered, greatly mourned his death.

regained his powers and all memories of his life on Asgard. For years, he lived a dual identity as Thor and Blake, battling threats such as the Radioactive Man and the Absorbing Man. Loki sought to entrap Thor by drawing him into conflict with the Hulk, but only succeeded in uniting a group of heroes that would become the Avengers. Thor became a founding member of the team, and fought alongside such heroes as Captain America, Iron Man, and Hercules.

Few beings ever bested Thor in combat, but the alien Beta Ray Bill defeated the Thunder God and proved worthy of wielding the hammer of Mjolnir. Impressed, Odin forged a new hammer, Stormbreaker, for Bill to wield. Thor gave up his Blake alter ego at this time, briefly trying out a new identity as construction worker Sigurd Jarlson. New trials continued to vex Thor—his father Odin seemingly perished in combat against the fire demon Surtur, but Thor refused the throne, the honor passing to Balder. Thor then suffered terrible torment when a curse rendered him incapable of death. Wounds nearly disintegrated his body until the spell was reversed.

ESSENTIAL STORYLINES

- ***The Mighty Thor* #337**
Beta Ray Bill explodes into action as a rival, and later an ally, of the Thunder God.
- ***Thor: Son of Asgard* #1–12**
This limited series explores the early adventures of a young Balder the Brave, Sif, and Thor.
- ***The Mighty Thor* #582–588**
It's Ragnarok, the Asgardian apocalypse, and the long-running series comes to an end with the total destruction of Asgard and all who live there.

RAGNAROK

The events that led to the end of Asgard began with the true death of Odin, killed battling Surtur. Thor took up the mantle of rulership and became empowered with the mystical Odinforce. Wishing to take a more direct role over earthly affairs, Thor moved Asgard to Earth and transformed the planet into a dictatorship that endured for two hundred years. At last, realizing the error of his actions, he unwound the previous two centuries through time travel.

Loki enlisted Surtur to forge new weapons comparable in power to Mjolnir. He rallied his followers and conquered Asgard. Thor, realizing that Loki's actions presaged the final conflagration of Ragnarok, followed the Odinforce on a spiritual journey. The Thunder God uncovered the truth of the Ragnarok cycle—its endless loop of creation and rebirth had been orchestrated by the godlike Those Who Sit Above in Shadow for their amusement. Unwilling to endure his people's dishonor through yet another cycle, Thor severed the tapestry that wove the reality of Asgard's dimension, wiping himself and Asgard from existence.

Beta Ray Bill proved he could fight alongside the Asgardians, and briefly became Beta Ray Thor.

Ragnarok, the twilight of the gods, spelled an end to all of the five races of the dimension of Asgard.

Desperate for Thor's power during the Civil War, Mister Fantastic and Hank Pym created a biomechanical Thor clone. It proved hard to control and killed Giant-Man (Bill Foster). It also attacked the Fifty-State Initiative's headquarters at Camp Hammond.

Later, in the void of the afterlife, Thor reunited with his old alter ego Donald Blake and returned to Earth, rebuilding Asgard on an island floating in the sky over Oklahoma. He then set out to find the other gods, who now lived unknowingly as mortals, and restore them to their rightful places.

THOR continued

FAMILY FIGHTS

Loki brought Odin's father, Bor, back from the dead and tricked him into attacking everything in sight. Thor was forced to kill Bor, unaware that Bor was his grandfather. Since Bor had technically become the ruler of Asgard upon his return, Balder—who had previously assumed rule of Asgard with Thor's blessing—had to banish Thor from the home of the Norse Gods. With Thor gone, Loki persuaded Balder to evacuate the Asgardians to Latveria, the home of his ally Doctor Doom, another member of the Cabal.

Thor's hammer, Mjolnir, had been damaged during his battle with Bor, and he asked Doctor Strange to help repair it. They managed this by transferring some of Thor's power to Mjolnir, strengthening the bond between them. With Mjolinir fixed, Thor finally managed to find the lost goddess Sif and return her to the body that Loki had stolen from her. Angry with Loki, Balder ordered his people back to Asgard.

Thor killed his crazed grandfather Bor with a blow that broke his hammer Mjolnir.

Banished from Asgard, Thor walked the Earth alone—until he came back to save the Asgardians from the Sentry.

THE SIEGE OF ASGARD

Loki persuaded the leader of the Cabal—Norman Osborn (*see* Green Goblin)—that the return of the Norse Gods to the skies above Oklahoma presented a threat to his power as head of national security. Loki convinced Osborn by staging a fight between the U-Foes and Volstagg (of the Warriors Three) that killed tens of thousands of innocents during a football game at Chicago's Soldier Field. Osborn decided to launch a preemptive assault on Asgard.

Despite his banishment, Thor joined the fight to defend Asgard against HAMMER (Osborn's version of SHIELD) and Osborn's villainous team of Dark Avengers, buttressed by Daken (posing as Wolverine) and Sentry. During the battle, Sentry razed Asgard, reducing it to rubble, and his dark side—embodied as the evil and powerful Void—threatened to destroy the world. Even Loki decided that this was too much, and he tried to help the Avengers with the magic of the Norn Stones. Once the Void figured this out, he slew Loki.

Enraged, Thor kept the Void busy long enough for Iron Man to crash the HAMMER Helicarrier into him. After Sentry's death, Thor wrapped him in his cape and hurled his old friend into the sun. In return for his service, Balder lifted Thor's banishment.

FAMILY REUNION

Thor learned that Loki's spirit was not in Hel, and he set out to find him. He located him in a boy's body in Paris, reborn without any memories of his past, including his many misdeeds. Thor brought this "Kid Loki" back to Asgard and sought to protect him from the hostility the other gods still harbored for him. Thor later brought Odin back to life, too. The All-Father was furious with Loki for what he had done and with Thor for bringing them both back when he could have lived in peace. When the event known as Fear Itself began with the return of Odin's brother Cul, also known as the Serpent, Odin retreated from Earth and

Thor missed his brother Loki, no matter how horrible he had been, and he was thrilled to have him back.

Thor first fought Gorr a thousand years ago, but the God Butcher's menace grew with every passing year.

created a new Asgard in a realm apart so that he and his people could prepare for war with the Serpent and his generals, known as the Worthy.

Thor remained on Earth, against his father's wishes, and led the fight against Cul and his forces. In the end, he slew the Serpent, but at the cost of his own life, as Odin had prophesied long ago. In his grief, Odin sealed himself up alone in Asgard and gave rule of his people to Freyja, GAEA, and Idunn, a trinity of All-Mothers.

THOR RETURNS

From the fires of Thor's funeral pyre emerged Tanarus, a new God of Thunder whom everyone but Loki remembered as the god Thor had been. This turned out to be a trick of the sorceress Karnilla, who had substituted the rock troll Ulik in Thor's place. With the help of the SILVER SURFER, Loki hunted down Thor's old alter ego, Donald Blake, and brought his brother back to life. Together, they revealed Karnilla's treachery and stopped a troll attack on Asgardia. Soon after, Thor tangled with GORR THE GOD BUTCHER, an alien god who amassed power through the destruction of other gods. Gorr planned to detonate a Godbomb that would destroy every god in all space and time. He enslaved scores of gods to build it for him—including Thor and his younger and older selves. With all those gods praying to him, Thor managed to foil Gorr's plot.

THE NEW THOR

When UATU THE WATCHER was slain, Gorr made Thor believe he was unworthy of his hammer or the role of a god. Realizing the world needed a Thor, Jane Foster picked up Mjolnir and was transformed into a female Thor. Joining a new Avengers team, this Thor formed a close friendship with Sam Wilson, who became one of the few people to know her secret identity. Thor fought Roxxon's forces, the ABSORBING MAN and the DESTROYER, the latter being sent by a furious Odin convinced Jane was an imposter. Unknown to many, Jane had cancer and every time she transformed into Thor it compromised her chemotherapy. Yet as her mortal health deteriorated, she seemed to be needed as Thor more than ever, especially as Malekith the Dark Elf started a war against the Ten Realms.

When the cancer was close to claiming Foster's life, the monster Mangog attacked the Asgardians' new home, Asgardia. Knowing full well that transforming would kill her mortal form, Jane became Thor once again and defeated Mangog, changing back to Jane Foster and dying shortly after. However, just before her death, Jane convinced the original Thor to reclaim his role, handing him a piece of the shattered Mjolnir to prove he was now worthy. Even Odin was impressed by Jane's bravery and refused to let her die, using his powers to save her life. Thor returned to the role of Thunder God, helping the Gods make a stand against the forces of Malekith.

After Thor came to believe he was unworthy of the role, the mantle and Mjolnir were picked up by Jane Foster, who became the new female incarnation of the God of Thunder.

THUNDERBOLTS

Reformed Super Villains with the "best intentions"

THUNDERBOLTS

FACTFILE

NOTABLE MEMBERS

CITIZEN V (Baron Zemo)
Team leader.

TECHNO (The Fixer)
Varies her molecular density.

MACH-1 (Beetle)
Wears a suit that enables him to fly, fire weapons, and resist attack.

SONGBIRD (Screaming Mimi)
Can transform the sound of her voice into physical forms.

ATLAS (Goliath) Can increase his size and mass.

METEORITE (Moonstone)
Superhuman strength and invulnerability.

JOLT Exceptional strength, speed, agility.

CHARCOAL Can change his body into charcoal, creating flames or diamonds.

HAWKEYE Expert archer.

BASE Mobile

FIRST APPEARANCE
The Incredible Hulk #449 (January 1997)

With the Thunderbolts, it was often hard to tell who were the heroes and who were the villains.

When the Fantastic Four and the Avengers disappeared after their first battle with Onslaught, Baron Zemo transformed his Masters of Evil into the Thunderbolts, giving members new identities to escape their criminal pasts. He himself became the patriotic Citizen V, leader of the new team. When the lost heroes returned, Zemo realized that his team had come to enjoy the lives of heroes, so he exposed their secret to the world, hoping to force them to stay with him, but they turned on him instead.

NEW THUNDER

With Zemo gone, Hawkeye took over the team, and they faced off against Henry Gyrich and a new Scourge. Mach-I turned himself in for a murder he'd committed as the Beetle, hoping to earn the rest of the team a pardon, but this never came. They then defeated the Crimson Cowl's Masters of Evil and took their headquarters in Colorado, renaming it Thunderbolt Mountain. Hawkeye finally won the team its pardon by blackmailing Gyrich and turning himself in.

Valerie Cooper's Redeemers replaced the Thunderbolts for a while, but after Graviton destroyed them, the Thunderbolts reformed. After they disbanded, Mach-III (now Mach-IV) reformed the team once more, and they became heroes on the Counter-Earth on which the Fantastic Four and the Avengers had been stranded. Meanwhile, Hawkeye broke out of jail and formed a new team from members of the Masters of Evil, whom the Crimson Cowl was trying to enslave. The two teams later united to stop her plan. Zemo continued to work against them, both in the open and in secret.

WINTER SOLDIER'S THUNDERBOLTS
1 Atlas ***2*** MACH-X
3 Moonstone ***4*** Kobik
5 Fixer ***6*** Winter Soldier

Red Hulk's Thunderbolts didn't trust his leadership, so they took turns choosing missions.

DARK HEROES

During the Civil War, the Thunderbolts registered with the US government and forced many villains to join the Thunderbolts Army. Zemo's plans were ruined when Songbird shattered his Moonstones, which sent him into a cosmic vortex.

Soon after, Norman Osborn (Green Goblin) formed a brand-new Thunderbolts team. When Osborn became the head of US national security after the Secret Invasion, he took command of the Avengers as well and made the Thunderbolts his secret hit squad.

When Osborn's Dark Reign ended, Luke Cage headed up a new Thunderbolts operating out of the Raft super-prison. One part of the team wound up jumping through time before finally reuniting in the present and becoming a new Dark Avengers team.

The Red Hulk subsequently created his own team of Thunderbolts (made up of himself, Deadpool, Elektra, Punisher and Agent Venom), with no government supervision. He disbanded the team after Punisher went rogue and started hunting the others. Winter Soldier also formed his own Thunderbolts team to ensure SHIELD never rebooted the Kobik Program. They were defeated by the Masters of Evil and Winter Soldier was seemingly killed by Baron Zemo.

THUNDERSTRIKE

Divorced and with sole custody of his young son, Eric Masterson was an architect who was working at a building site where THOR, under a secret identity, was also employed. Thor was attacked by the assassin Mongoose and, during the battle, Eric was injured by falling girders. He was left with a permanent limp. After becoming friends with Thor, Eric was wounded again, this time mortally, and ODIN merged him with the Thunder God to save his life. Thereafter, Masterson would assume the form of Thor whenever the hero was needed on Earth.

When Thor seemingly slew his brother LOKI and was banished from this plane of reality, Eric took his place as Thor II. Eventually the real Thor returned, and Eric was given his own enchanted mace and became Thunderstrike. He later died battling the god Seth.

Eric's son Kevin later took up the mace and fought the Super Villain Man-Power. In the future of Earth-982, Kevin forms A-Next. He lost his powers after GALACTUS devoured Asgard, but Thor's daughter THENA helped him regain them.

The original Thunderstrike is one of many Avengers who have died in the line of duty.

Like his father, Kevin Masterson can physically transform into Thunderstrike through intense concentration.

THUNDERSTRIKE

FACTFILE

REAL NAME
Eric Masterson
Kevin Masterson

OCCUPATION
Architect (Eric);
college student (Kevin)

BASE
New York City

HEIGHT 6 ft 6 in (Eric); 6 ft (Kevin)
WEIGHT 640 lbs (Eric); 585 lbs (Kevin)
EYES Blue
HAIR Blond

FIRST APPEARANCES
(Eric) *Thor* #391; (Eric as Thunderstrike) *Thor* #432; (Kevin) *Thor* #392; (Kevin as Thunderstrike) *What If* #105

POWERS
(Eric) Super-strong, owns enchanted uru mace that projects concussive blasts of mystical energy. Flies by throwing mace and gripping its strap. (Kevin) Super-strong; projects concussive blasts of mystical energy, which can be used to propel him through the air.

THUNDRA

FIRST APPEARANCE *Fantastic Four* #129 (December 1972)
REAL NAME Thundra **OCCUPATION** Warrior
BASE United Sisterhood Republic of North America
HEIGHT 7 ft 2 in **WEIGHT** 350 lbs **EYES** Green **HAIR** Red
SPECIAL POWERS/ABILITIES Enhanced strength, endurance, reflexes, and damage resistance; skilled at wielding a chain.

In the 23rd century of Earth-715, women ruled the world and raised men as servants and breeding stock. Thundra, born into the United Sisterhood Republic of North America, became one of its finest warriors. She was sent back in time to defeat the THING but eventually took a liking to him and brought him to her time to help liberate her world. A version of Thundra from another reality later fought the HULK for a DNA sample, but relented, the two parting with a kiss. She returned to her own time, where scientists recovered Hulk's DNA from her lips and engineered a daughter named Lyra. That daughter later met the Thundra and Hulk of Earth-616.

TIGER SHARK

FIRST APPEARANCE *Sub-Mariner* #5 (September 1968)
REAL NAME Todd Arliss
OCCUPATION Amphibious criminal **BASE** The deep blue sea
HEIGHT 6 ft 1 in **WEIGHT** 450 lbs **EYES** Gray **HAIR** Brown
SPECIAL POWERS/ABILITIES Amphibious—able to withstand great water pressure and swim at up to 60mph; also possesses superhuman strength.

His genes spliced with those of NAMOR the Sub-Mariner and a tiger shark, Todd Arliss, former Olympic-level swimmer, became a superpowered amphibian. Namor and Tiger Shark became foes, and when Tiger Shark's powers began to fade, he kidnapped Namor's father, Leonard MacKenzie, and blackmailed Namor into donating more powers. Chaos ensued during the transfer process and Tiger Shark ended up killing MacKenzie with a lead pipe. He later joined the THUNDERBOLTS and he helped conquer Atlantis during FEAR ITSELF.

TIGRA

FIRST APPEARANCE *The Cat* #1 (November 1972)
REAL NAME Greer Grant Nelson
OCCUPATION Adventurer **BASE** New York City
HEIGHT 5 ft 10 in **WEIGHT** 180 lbs **EYES** Green
HAIR (human form) black; (cat form) orange fur with black stripes
SPECIAL POWERS/ABILITIES Enhanced strength, slashing claws, and heightened senses of smell, hearing, and vision.

Greer Nelson received catlike powers from Dr. Joanne Tumolo, a member of the mystical race known as the CAT PEOPLE. Taking on the identity of the Cat, Nelson began a career as a costumed adventurer in San Francisco. When Nelson suffered near-fatal injuries during a clash with HYDRA, the Cat People saved her life, imbuing her body with a cat-soul. As Tigra, she served with the AVENGERS. During the CIVIL WAR, she worked as IRON MAN's spy within CAPTAIN AMERICA's resistance. She later became an instructor at the Avengers Academy and then one of the FEARLESS DEFENDERS.

TIMEBREAKERS, THE

FIRST APPEARANCE *Exiles* #62 (June 2005)
BASE Panoptichron
SPECIAL POWERS/ABILITIES None, but they have access to the Panoptichron.

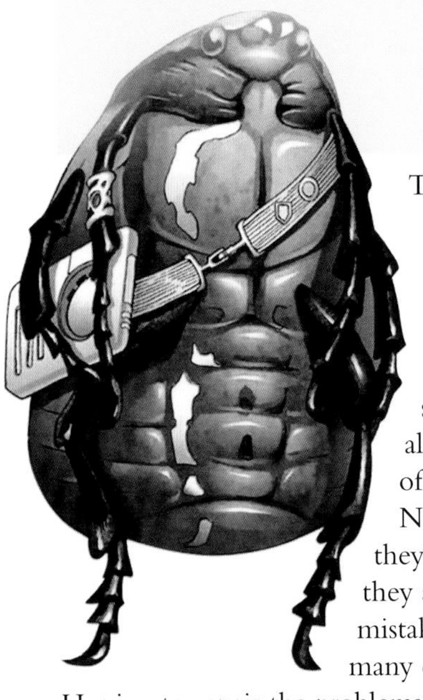

The Timebreakers are an alien insectoid race that found the Panoptichron, a crystal palace that sits at the nexus of all realities, outside of time and space. Not knowing what they were doing when they arrived, they made mistakes that damaged many different realities. Hoping to repair the problems they'd caused, they created a human-looking illusion called the Timebroker to gather heroes known as EXILES and send them out on missions. Timebreakers come in different castes, including cockroach-like workers and mantis-like sovereigns.

TINKERER, THE

FIRST APPEARANCE *The Amazing Spider-Man* #2 (May 1963)
REAL NAME Phineas Mason
OCCUPATION Criminal inventor **BASE** New York City
HEIGHT 5 ft 8 in **WEIGHT** 175 lbs **EYES** Gray **HAIR** White
SPECIAL POWERS/ABILITIES Genius-level ability to create sophisticated gadgets and deadly weapons from everyday pieces of machinery or scrap metal.

Phineas Mason, the "Terrible Tinkerer," is unparalleled in his ability to create and repair machinery, and long ago became the premiere gadget-maker for the criminal underworld. Among his works are DIAMONDBACK's throwing diamonds and the SCORPION's tail. His son, Rick Mason, worked for SHIELD as the Agent until he was killed on a mission. Phineas created an alter ego (his "brother" Hophni Mason) to collect secrets from Super Heroes, which he then traded with SHIELD to gain his freedom. Meanwhile, he meddled with an alien race called the Vedomi, resulting in their attempted invasion.

TITANIUM MAN

FIRST APPEARANCE *Tales of Suspense* #69 (Sept. 1965)
REAL NAME Boris Bullski **OCCUPATION** Former Russian champion **BASE** Moibile **HEIGHT** (without armor) 7 ft 1 in
WEIGHT (without armor) 475 lbs **EYES** Blue **HAIR** Black
SPECIAL POWERS/ABILITIES Unusual strength proportionate to his giant size; armor provided flight, enhanced strength, near-invulnerability, and the ability to fire energy blasts from hands.

Russian inventor Boris Bullski devised the Titanium Man armor in order to crush IRON MAN and win favor with his superiors. As Titanium Man, Bullski lost to IRON MAN in a televised slugfest of East vs. West. A second Titanium Man, the mutant known as the GREMLIN, died when his armor exploded. Boris Bullski later returned as an agent of AIM, but died in battle with Iron Man. A new Titanium Man appeared later, working as a mercenary with villains like DOCTOR OCTOPUS and SPYMASTER.

TIME KEEPERS, THE

FIRST APPEARANCE *Thor* #282 (April 1979)
BASE Citadel at the End of Time

MEMBERS AND POWERS
Ast, Vort, Zanth: All Time Keepers possess nearly unlimited powers of time-manipulation, including time travel and the ability to rapidly age or devolve people and things.

The Time Keepers are guardians of the timestream, created by He Who Remains (the final chairman of the Time Variance Authority) at the end of time to replace his flawed agents, the Time Twisters. The Time Keepers sought to preserve their existence at all costs, which led them to enlist IMMORTUS to destroy the meddling AVENGERS and powerful "nexus beings" such as the SCARLET WITCH. KANG, with help from Rick JONES, seemingly wiped out the Time Keepers after they attempted to eliminate a host of alternate realities.

TITANIA

Davida DeVito, the first Titania, was the leader of the original Grapplers, a team of female professional wrestlers. Titania and her teammates were hired by the Roxxon Oil company to sabotage the government's Project PEGASUS, but were defeated and sent to prison. After her release, Titania's strength was enhanced to superhuman levels by the POWER BROKER. She continued to lead an expanded Grapplers team. However, Titania was later assassinated by a new Grappler called Golddigger.

Mary "Skeeter" MacPherran lived in a Denver suburb that was transported by the BEYONDER to his "Battleworld." There DOCTOR DOOM gave her super-strength to serve in his army of criminals during the first Secret War. This new Titania and her teammate, "Crusher" Creel, the ABSORBING MAN, were attracted to one another, and were later married.

After returning to Earth, Titania had a feud with SHE-HULK. She also served as a member of the MASTERS OF EVIL and the FRIGHTFUL FOUR. She attacked the She-Hulk but was shrunk down and imprisoned by Hank PYM. During FEAR ITSELF, she wielded the hammer of Skirn, Breaker of Men. She held a funeral for her husband after BLACK BOLT informed her of his heroic sacrifice, but he emerged from his own grave. Crusher and Titania wound up saving Black Bolt from an INHUMAN known as the Jailer.

FACTFILE

REAL NAME
Mary "Skeeter" MacPherran

OCCUPATION
Criminal

BASE
Formerly a suburb of Denver, Colorado; later New York City

HEIGHT 6 ft 6 in
WEIGHT 545 lbs
EYES Blue
HAIR Red-blond

FIRST APPEARANCE
Marvel Super Heroes Secret Wars #3 (July 1984)

POWERS
Possessed superhuman strength—able to lift about 90 tons; superhuman stamina and durability; resistant to heat, cold, injury, and disease.

TOMBSTONE

FIRST APPEARANCE *Web of Spider-Man* #36 (March 1988)
REAL NAME Lonnie Thompson Lincoln
OCCUPATION Professional hitman **BASE** Mobile
HEIGHT 6 ft 7 in **WEIGHT** Unknown **EYES** Pink **HAIR** White
SPECIAL POWERS/ABILITIES Enhanced strength, speed, stamina, and reflexes; skilled hand-to-hand fighter and assassin.

Lonnie Lincoln was born an African-American albino. He grew up in Harlem, New York City, with Joe "Robbie" Robertson, whom he coerced into keeping quiet regarding a murder that Lincoln had committed. Lincoln became an assassin for gangsters like the Kingpin, and gained superhuman powers after exposure to an experimental gas. Following a stint with the Sinister Twelve, he worked with the Hood and with Doctor Octopus. Mr. Negative betrayed him, leading to an arrest, but he was soon released. Later he caused trouble for Luke Cage and Iron Fist.

TORPEDO

FIRST APPEARANCE *Daredevil* #126 (October 1975)
REAL NAME Brock Jones
OCCUPATION Crimefighter **BASE** Clairton, West Virginia
HEIGHT 6 ft **WEIGHT** 200 lbs **EYES** Blue **HAIR** Blond
SPECIAL POWERS/ABILITIES Battlesuit provides damage resistance; turbojets at wrists and ankles add power to punches; suit also generates shockwaves, and permits supersonic flight.

Inventor Michael Stivak became the first Torpedo when his uncle, Senator Eugene Stivak, convinced him to build a battlesuit. In truth, Senator Stivak had been prodded to do so by the extraterrestrial Dire Wraiths, who wanted to possess a weapon capable of defeating their enemies the Spaceknights. After the younger Stivak's death, Brock Jones fought crime while wearing the costume and fended off Senator Stivak's efforts to retrieve it. He died in his adopted hometown of Clairton, West Virginia while battling the Dire Wraiths.

TRAPSTER

FIRST APPEARANCE *Strange Tales* #104 (January 1963)
REAL NAME Peter Petruski
OCCUPATION Criminal **BASE** New York City
HEIGHT 5 ft 10 in **WEIGHT** 160 lbs **EYES** Brown **HAIR** Brown
SPECIAL POWERS/ABILITIES Carries assorted weapons at all times, most of them applications of his paste-formula.

Chemist Peter Petruski discovered a formula for a super-strong, quick-hardening adhesive. He constructed a special gun that could project it without clogging, and set out to make his name as the criminal Paste-Pot Pete. However, not even a name-change to the Trapster and membership of the Frightful Four brought him the respect he craved. After the Tinkerer upgraded his weapons, the Trapster became far more dangerous. He worked with Hammerhead's criminals during the Civil War. Afterward, he served time at SHIELD's Pleasant Hill prison. Upon escaping, he had a few run-ins with Gwenpool.

TOPAZ

FIRST APPEARANCE *Werewolf By Night* #13 (January 1974)
REAL NAME Unrevealed; possibly Topaz
OCCUPATION Sorceress **BASE** New York City
HEIGHT 5 ft 3 in **WEIGHT** 100 lbs **EYES** Brown **HAIR** Black
SPECIAL POWERS/ABILITIES A trained sorceress with a multitude of mystic spells at her command, primarily empathy-based in nature.

Branded a witch after she made a flower bloom in the desert as a child, Topaz was incarcerated in a prison camp, where she was adopted and trained in the mystic arts by Taboo. Topaz served as the familiar for Taboo's sorcery until, in pursuit of Jack Russell, the Werewolf By Night, Topaz turned against her mentor rather than allow Russell and his friends to come to harm. Topaz later joined forces with Jennifer Kale and Satana as the Witches to recover the stolen *Tome of Zhered-Na*. A prophecy states that, one day, Topaz will be capable of wiping away the evils of the world.

TRAINER, DR. SEWARD

FIRST APPEARANCE *Peter Parker: Spider-Man* #54 (January 1995)
REAL NAME Seward Trainer
OCCUPATION Geneticist **BASE** New York City
HEIGHT 5 ft 10 in **WEIGHT** 200 lbs **EYES** Brown **HAIR** Brown
SPECIAL POWERS/ABILITIES A genius in the fields of biology and genetic engineering.

So brilliant that he was once employed by the High Evolutionary, geneticist Seward Trainer gave in to Green Goblin Norman Osborn's blackmailing and participated in a plot to crush Spider-Man Peter Parker's morale. By tampering with the Jackal's research, Trainer made it appear that Parker was a clone. Dr. Trainer became a father figure to the real clone, Ben Reilly (Scarlet Spider), but died at the hands of Norman Osborn before he could confess his role in the scheme. His daughter Carolyn Trainer briefly took the identity of Doctor Octopus.

TRAUMA

FIRST APPEARANCE *Avengers: The Initiative* #1 (March 2007)
REAL NAME Terrance Ward
OCCUPATION Adventurer **BASE** Camp Hammond
HEIGHT 5 ft 10 in **WEIGHT** 175 lbs
EYES Brown **HAIR** Black
SPECIAL POWERS/ABILITIES Can shape-shift into whatever a foe fears most.

Terrance joined the Fifty-State Initiative and became one of the first cadets to be trained at Camp Hammond. His power allows him to read someone's mind, discover their worst fear, and then morph into a physical manifestation of that fear. In early combat training, this ability resulted in tragedy, when Armory panicked upon seeing her worst fear and accidentally killed Michael Van Patrick. MVP's evil clone later killed Terrance, but Terrance revived in his coffin. The source of his powers is the fact that his real father is secretly Nightmare. Terrance served as a counselor at Camp Hammond but left after Nightmare possessed him while he slept.

TRAVELLER, JUDAS

FIRST APPEARANCE *Web of Spider-Man* #117 (October 1994)
REAL NAME Dr. Judas Traveller
OCCUPATION Adventurer **BASE** Currently unknown
HEIGHT 6 ft 7 in **WEIGHT** 245 lbs **EYES** Blue (pupils turn red when he uses his powers) **HAIR** White
SPECIAL POWERS/ABILITIES Possesses limited psionic powers and the mutant ability to alter people's perceptions of reality.

Famous criminal psychologist Dr. Judas Traveller was lecturing in Europe when he became aware of the Brotherhood of Scriers, a secret criminal organization. The Scriers sent an assassin to inject Traveller with a fatal drug. Instead of killing him, the drug triggered Traveller's mutant abilities and he suffered a nervous breakdown. The Scriers supervised his recovery and assigned four agents—Mr. Nacth, Medea, Boone, and Chakra—to watch over him 24 hours a day. After Spider-Man freed him from the Scriers' control, Traveller went into hiding.

TRIATHLON

FIRST APPEARANCE *Avengers* #8 (September 1998)
REAL NAME Delroy Garrett Jr.
OCCUPATION Adventurer **BASE** New York City
HEIGHT 6 ft 3 in **WEIGHT** 200 lbs **EYES** Brown **HAIR** Brown
SPECIAL POWERS/ABILITIES Garrett has superhuman strength, speed, and agility three times greater than the human peak, is fast enough to dodge bullets, and can identify hidden Skrulls.

Former Olympic sprinter Delroy Garrett Jr. joined the Triune Understanding movement, and its leader, Jonathan Tremont, merged the energy shard of 3-D Man into him, giving him his powers. As Triathlon, Garrett joined the Avengers and fought Tremont, who had betrayed his cause. During the Civil War, Garrett sided with Captain America but later joined the Fifty-State Initiative as 3-D Man and was assigned to the Hawaii team, the Point Men. During the Secret Invasion, he found he could detect Skrulls and joined the Skrull Kill Krew. He later joined the Agents of Atlas.

TRINARY

FIRST APPEARANCE *X-Men Red* #1 (April 2018)
REAL NAME Trinary
OCCUPATION Adventurer; former thief **BASE** Searebro, X-Lantis
HEIGHT Unknown **WEIGHT** Unknown **EYES** Brown
HAIR Black
SPECIAL POWERS/ABILITIES Has the power to control all kinds of technology from machinery to computers.

Trinary is a mutant from India who has technopathic abilities. She used these to take money from the bank accounts of India's 25 richest men and share it between every working woman in the country. She was caught by the Indian Mutant Defense Force and imprisoned, but rescued by Jean Grey's X-Men. Soon after, she used her powers to free Storm from the control of a nanite Sentinel created by Cassandra Nova. Trinary later started to use her powers to control an old Sentinel, nicknamed Sentinel-X, often used as transportation by the team.

TRICKSHOT

FACTFILE
REAL NAME
Charles "Barney" Barton
OCCUPATION
Assassin; mercenary
BASE
Mobile

HEIGHT 6 ft 3 in
WEIGHT 237 lbs
EYES Blue
HAIR Red

FIRST APPEARANCE
Avengers #64
(May 1969)

POWERS
Barney is one of the greatest archers ever as well as a trained combatant.

TRICKSHOT

Buck Chisholm, the original Trickshot, met Clint Barton (Hawkeye) when they were both working for a carnival. Clint's mentor, the Swordsman, asked Buck to train Clint with the bow. When Clint refused to rob the carnival, Buck kept the Swordsman from killing him. Later, Buck decided to rob a crook named Marko and brought Clint with him. Buck apparently killed Marko's bodyguard, who was in fact Clint's brother Barney. When Clint objected, Buck pinned him to a tree with an arrow.

Years later, Buck—now a mercenary—contracted cancer and challenged Clint—now the hero Hawkeye—to a final duel. Clint beat Buck but couldn't bring himself to kill him. Baron Zemo made a bargain with Buck to cure his cancer if he'd train a revived Barney as an archer. Zemo then double-crossed Buck and sent him, dying, to the Avengers as a cruel gift for Hawkeye.

Calling himself the new Trickshot, Barney fought Clint, who defeated him. Despite his hatred for his brother, Barney provided bone marrow for a transplant to save Clint's eyesight. Broken out of prison, Barney joined the second team of Dark Avengers assembled by Norman Osborn (Green Goblin), posing as Hawkeye. He later reconciled with Clint, and helped Clint and Kate Bishop rescue children imprisoned by Hydra.

TRITON

FIRST APPEARANCE *Fantastic Four* #45 (December 1965)
REAL NAME Unrevealed
OCCUPATION Scout **BASE** Washington, D.C.
HEIGHT 6 ft 1 in **WEIGHT** 210 lbs **EYES** Green **HAIR** None
SPECIAL POWERS/ABILITIES Can breathe underwater but cannot survive on land without special equipment; superhuman strength and other physical adaptations for undersea living.

Triton is a member of the royal family of the INHUMANS, a genetic offshoot of the human race. The son of the Inhuman priest and philosopher Mander and the biologist Azur, Triton was exposed to mutagenic Terrigen Mist when a year old. The resulting mutations adapted him to live and breathe underwater. Along with other members of the royal family, Triton was banished when MAXIMUS first usurped the throne. While in exile, Triton first encountered and fought the FANTASTIC FOUR. When the KREE started to massacre the Inhumans, Triton was seemingly killed in an explosion.

TWELVE, THE

In the final days of World War II, during the Battle of Berlin, Nazis captured a dozen American heroes and placed them in suspended animation in a secret bunker. The bunker remained undiscovered until some sixty years later when construction crews stumbled upon it. The US government brought the heroes back home and revived them on a set constructed to resemble 1945. The heroes soon figured out that something was wrong and had to endure the shock of entering a world in which most of the people they knew and loved were dead.

Soon after, the Phantom Reporter discovered the Blue Blade dead and vowed to find the killer. It turns out he was murdered by the robot Electro, who was under the control of the bigoted Dynamic Man, who—unknown to the others—was an android. Cornered, Dynamic Man killed Fiery Mask, who passed his powers on to the Phantom Reporter. Captain Wonder held Dynamic Man down, suffering terrible burns as the Reporter destroyed him. The survivors all built new lives for themselves in this brave new world.

FACTFILE — TWELVE, THE

MEMBERS

BLUE BLADE
Swashbuckling swordsman.

BLACK WIDOW
Mystical mistress of vengeance.

CAPTAIN WONDER
Superstrong flyer.

DYNAMIC MAN
Superhuman flying android shapeshifter.

ELECTRO
Super strong and fast robot.

FIERY MASK
Superhuman pyrokinetic.

LAUGHING MASK
Expert gunman and combatant.

MASTERMIND EXCELLO
Precognitive telepath.

MISTER E
Athlete.

PHANTOM REPORTER
Investigator.

ROCKMAN
Superhuman bruiser.

WITNESS
Precognitive superhuman.

BASE
New York

FIRST APPEARANCE
Twelve #0 (December 2007)

TURBO

FACTFILE — TURBO

REAL NAME
Michiko "Mickey" Musashi

OCCUPATION
Adventurer; journalist

BASE
Mobile

HEIGHT 5 ft 7 in
WEIGHT 125 lbs
EYES Brown
HAIR Black

FIRST APPEARANCE
New Warriors #28 (October 1992)

POWERS
Turbo's suit is fitted with jet turbines. It allows Turbo to fly faster than a commercial jet, and the powerful turbines on her wrists allow her to deliver turbine-powered hyper-punches. The suit can also fire energy bursts, and its visor has telescopic sights.

Mickey Musashi never wanted to be a hero. In fact the journalism student thought that being a Super Hero was a ridiculous notion... until she came across the Turbo suit. This remarkable piece of equipment was created by a human scientist, Michael Stivak, under the orders of the DIRE WRAITHS. When the suit's inventor learned that the suit was to be used for evil purposes, he gave it to a man named Brock Jones, who donned it to fight crime as the hero TORPEDO.

Eventually, the Wraiths found and killed Brock Jones, and the suit passed to Brock's cousin Mike Jeffries, who shared it with Musashi. As it turned out, the suit worked better for her than for Jeffries and she reluctantly became the hero known as Turbo.

While teamed with the NEW WARRIORS, Turbo battled the Dire Wraiths, as well as the criminal team known as Heavy Mettle. She later quit life as a hero and pursued her journalism career, also setting up a support group called Excelsior to dissuade superpowered teenagers from risking their lives as heroes. The group disbanded, but several members, including Musashi, enrolled at the AVENGERS Academy.

TURNER D. CENTURY

FIRST APPEARANCE *Spider-Woman* #33 (December 1980)
REAL NAME Clifford F. Michaels
OCCUPATION Former vigilante and reformer
BASE New York City
HEIGHT 6 ft 1 in **WEIGHT** 185 lbs **EYES** Blue **HAIR** Black
SPECIAL POWERS/ABILITIES Extensive engineering expertise; carries umbrella that doubles as flame-thrower; rides flying bike.

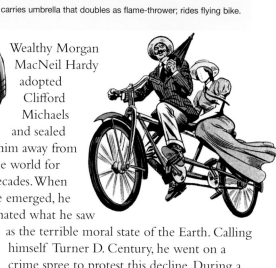

Wealthy Morgan MacNeil Hardy adopted Clifford Michaels and sealed him away from the world for decades. When he emerged, he hated what he saw as the terrible moral state of the Earth. Calling himself Turner D. Century, he went on a crime spree to protest this decline. During a clash with SPIDER-WOMAN, Hardy died in a fire. Michaels hoped to avenge him, but the SCOURGE killed him first. Arnim ZOLA made a clone of Michaels, but it was killed, too. The HOOD later revived Michaels, but only for thirty days.

TYPHOID MARY

TYPHOID MARY

FACTFILE

REAL NAME
Mary (last name possibly Mezinis or Walker)

OCCUPATION
Criminal

BASE
New York City

HEIGHT 5 ft 10 in
WEIGHT 140 lbs
EYES Brown
HAIR Brown

FIRST APPEARANCE
Daredevil #254 (May 1988)

POWERS
Telekinesis, pyrokinesis, and also limited hypnotic ability; a skilled hand-to-hand combatant and expert with various bladed weapons.

Childhood abuse caused Mary to develop a dissociative identity disorder, giving her three distinct personalities: timid Mary, lustful Typhoid, and vicious Bloody Mary. Through therapy, a fourth personality emerged as a stable combination of all three. Typhoid Mary worked as an assassin for the KINGPIN and played a cruel game with DAREDEVIL by charming him as Mary and tormenting him as Typhoid. To join the FIFTY-STATE INITIATIVE, she disguised herself as Mutant Zero, and later she worked with Daredevil (as a double-agent for Kingpin) when Daredevil ruled the HAND. She went on to work for LADY DEATHSTRIKE and joined her Sisterhood of Mutants. She also joined BLACK CAT's gang, though she was later arrested.

TYRANT

FIRST APPEARANCE *Silver Surfer* #81 (June 1993)
REAL NAME Unrevealed
OCCUPATION Conqueror of Worlds
BASE Star-Traveling Fortress
HEIGHT 29 ft **WEIGHT** 20 tons **EYES** Red **HAIR** None
SPECIAL POWERS/ABILITIES Virtually unlimited cosmic power on a par with Galactus.

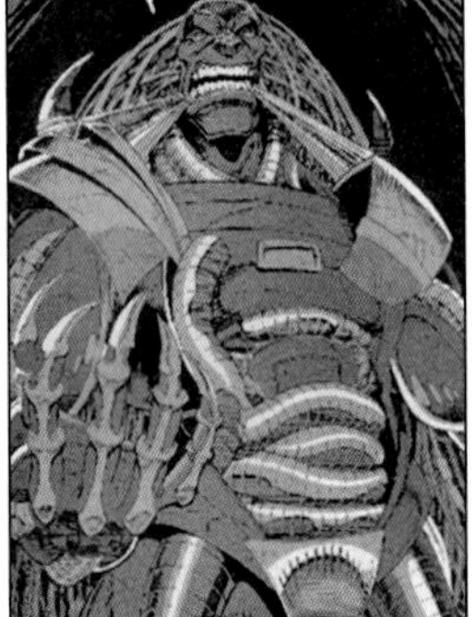

Created by GALACTUS billions of years ago, Tyrant draws his power from living worlds, and thus loses energy each time a planet is consumed by Galactus. Driven by a lust for power, Tyrant enslaved entire civilizations and protected himself with a robot army. Among the few who successfully opposed him were the women warriors of the Spinsterhood. In the modern era, Tyrant nearly succeeded in killing Galactus until Galactus' herald Morg unleashed the unstoppable energies of the Ultimate Nullifier. Tyrant and Galactus both vanished, though Galactus has since returned.

TYRANNUS

TYRANNUS

FACTFILE

REAL NAME
Romulus Augustulus

OCCUPATION
Would-be conqueror

BASE
Subterranea

HEIGHT 6 ft 2 in
WEIGHT 225 lbs
EYES Light brown
HAIR Blond

FIRST APPEARANCE
Incredible Hulk #5 (January 1963)

POWERS
Psychic powers including mind-control, telepathy, and the ability to drain life energy. The Fountain of Youth provides Tyrannus with immortality, giving him plenty of time for devising ways to conquer the surface world.

Romulus Augustulus, better known as Tyrannus, served as the last emperor of the Roman Empire, until his defeat by the forces of King Arthur PENDRAGON in the 6th century. MERLIN the Magician banished Tyrannus by teleporting him to the underground world of Subterranea. There the would-be despot discovered the Fountain of Youth and ruled the Subterraneans, who took the name Tyrannoids.

Tyrannus gulps a goblet of the Fountain of Youth.

In the modern era, Tyrannus launched a war against the MOLE MAN for control of Subterranea, and became a frequent foe of the HULK. He incurred the green giant's wrath by accidentally kidnapping his girlfriend, Betty Ross.

Tyrannus journeyed to the fabled city of El Dorado and used the city's Sacred Flame of Life in a bid to take over the world. Reduced to a disembodied spirit after a failed attempt to merge with the Flame of Life, Tyrannus briefly inhabited the ABOMINATION before winning back his original body. Tyrannus allied with the AVENGERS to defeat the Deviant army that had invaded Subterranea, but the Tyrannoids later turned on their master. He later hunted for Pandora's Box with the help of the Red She-Hulk (*see* Betty ROSS).

Tyrannus' planned invasion of the surface world was smashed by Hulk.

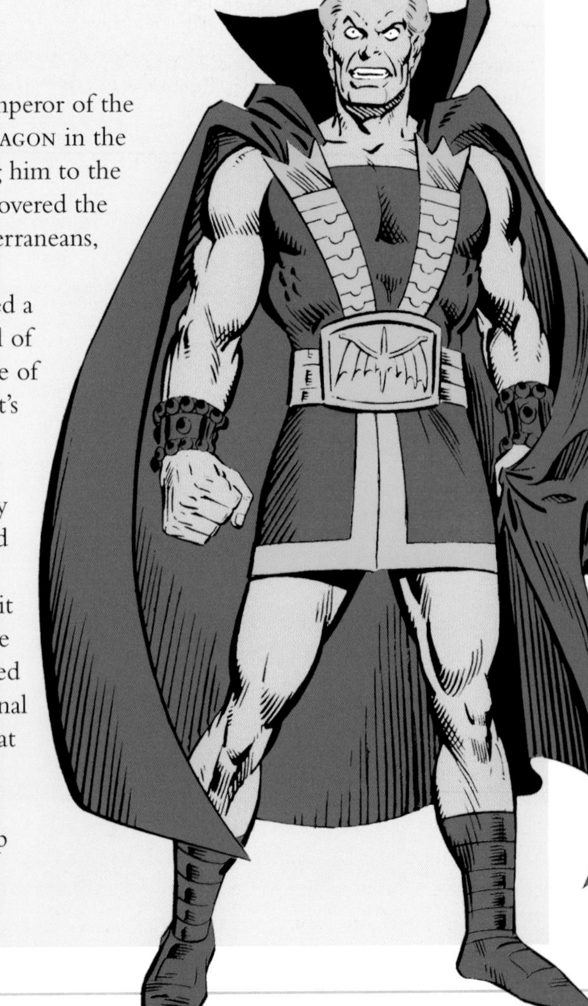

UATU, THE WATCER

FACTFILE
REAL NAME
Uatu
OCCUPATION
Observer
BASE
Mobile; New York State

HEIGHT Variable
WEIGHT Variable
EYES No visible irises
HAIR None

FIRST APPEARANCE
Fantastic Four #13
(April 1963)

POWERS
Virtually immortal; has superhuman intelligence, is telepathic and can teleport from the Earth to the Moon.

UATU, THE WATCHER

Self-appointed observers of the universe, the WATCHERS vowed never to interfere in the affairs of others. As the Watcher responsible for Earth and its solar system, Uatu has broken this rule several times since encountering the FANTASTIC FOUR. His most significant intervention came just before Earth's first visit from GALACTUS and the SILVER SURFER, when he warned the Fantastic Four of the impending alien threat. Cautioned for his repeated interference, Uatu was stripped of his role as Watcher but eventually reinstated. He was attacked by Doctor Midas, the Exterminatrix, the Orb and the MINDLESS ONES. The Orb shot him and removed one of his eyes. When Uatu refused to tell Nick FURY who his assailants were, Fury killed him and took the other eye, which contained everything Uatu had witnessed.

U-GO GIRL

FIRST APPEARANCE *X-Force* #116 (July 2001)
REAL NAME Edith ("Edie") Constance Sawyer
OCCUPATION Adventurer **BASE** Los Angeles
HEIGHT 5 ft 7 in **WEIGHT** 135 lbs
EYES Green **HAIR** Red
SPECIAL POWERS/ABILITIES Teleportation, which makes her narcoleptic.

Born in the Midwest, Edie became pregnant at 15 and gave the baby up to her parents to adopt. When she saw her daughter's face, she reflexively teleported away to LA, only to return soon after. Years later, the blue-skinned young woman returned to LA and joined X-FORCE. After saving her teammate Orphan from his suicidal tendencies, she became romantically involved with him. The team's relationship with its owners eventually broke down, and they hired the Bush Rangers to kill them all. Edie died at their hands. When Orphan died much later, they finally reunited in the afterlife.

ULTIMO

FIRST APPEARANCE *Tales of Suspense* #76 (April 1966)
REAL NAME Ultimo
OCCUPATION Destroyer **BASE** Mobile
HEIGHT Varies **WEIGHT** Varies **EYES** Yellow **HAIR** None
SPECIAL POWERS/ABILITIES Monstrous strength, endurance, and invulnerability.

Ultimo was an ancient alien robot that slaughtered the people of the planet Rajak and then crashed on Earth while pursuing the last Rajaki. The MANDARIN claimed it and used it to battle IRON MAN and an Iron Legion of Tony Stark's friends in armor, led by WAR MACHINE. Stark figured out how to shut it down by accessing its programming. It was later turned into an Ultimo virus that Morgan STARK consumed, turning him into a giant robot made from morphable liquid metal.

U-FOES

Hoping to duplicate the process by which the FANTASTIC FOUR had gained their powers, millionaire Simon Utrecht enlisted rocket pilot Mike Steel, engineer Jimmy Darnell, and technical specialist Ann Darnell to accompany him into space. The experiment worked, and the cosmic radiation they were exposed to gave each a unique power: Steel became a metal-coated being, Jimmy gained control over radiation, his sister Ann converted into a gaseous state, and Utrecht himself discovered that he could repel objects.

As Ironclad, Vapor, X-Ray, and Vector, they formed the U-Foes and unleashed their powers on Bruce Banner (HULK), whom they blamed for grounding their test flight prematurely. Over time, they found work as professional mercenaries. During the CIVIL WAR, they worked for the THUNDERBOLTS Army and then the HOOD's gang. During the DARK REIGN, they became the FIFTY-STATE INITIATIVE's North Carolina team. They helped launch the siege of Asgard by battling Volstagg (*see* WARRIORS THREE) and framing him for killing thousands during a football game at Soldier Field.

U-FOES

FACTFILE
KEY MEMBERS
IRONCLAD
Enhanced strength, iron-hard skin, can increase his mass.
VAPOR
Transforms into various gases.
VECTOR
Can repel objects away from him at great speed.
X-RAY
Flight, can project hard radiation, impervious to physical damage while in energy form.
BASE
Brooklyn, New York; Stark Tower, New York

FIRST APPEARANCE
Incredible Hulk #254
(December 1980)

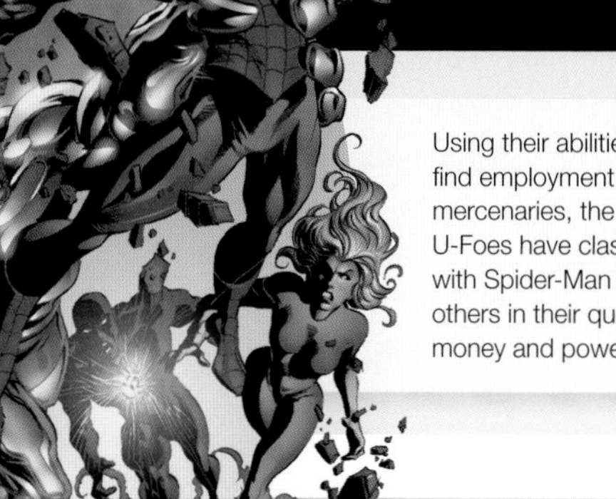

Using their abilities to find employment as mercenaries, the U-Foes have clashed with Spider-Man and others in their quest for money and power.

ULTRAFORCE

FACTFILE

KEY MEMBERS

BLACK KNIGHT Wields the Ebony Blade; rides winged horse.

CONTRARY Master manipulator.

GHOUL Undead man who can speak with the dead.

HARDCASE Nanotech man with superhuman senses and strength.

PIXX Technological genius who can project illusions.

PROTOTYPE Energy blasts and flight; armor grants superstrength.

SIREN Superstrength; control over liquids.

TOPAZ Superstrong; fires energy blasts from staff.

BASE

Headless Cross, Arkansas

FIRST APPEARANCE

Ultraforce #0 (June 1994)

ULTRAFORCE

On Earth-93060, superpowered people were known as Ultras. The members of Ultraforce banded together to protect their Earth from evil Ultras and other threats. Hardcase and Contrary brought together the initial members of the team—which included them and Ghoul, Pixx, Prime, Prototype, and Topaz—and received sanctioning from the US government. Contrary outfitted them with technology from the subterranean Fire People so that they could try to keep them from invading the surface world.

Later, the BLACK KNIGHT arrived from Earth-616 (the main Marvel universe) and joined the team. They also teamed up with the AVENGERS and fought against SERSI of the ETERNALS. During the Black September event, they served as LOKI's champions in a contest with the GRANDMASTER.

ULTRAFORCE
1 Prime ***2*** Hardcase ***3*** Topaz ***4*** Contrary
5 Prototype ***6*** Ghoul ***7*** Pixx

ULTRA GIRL

FIRST APPEARANCE *Ultra Girl* #1 (November 1996)

REAL NAME Tsu-Zana (Suzy Sherman)

OCCUPATION Adventurer **BASE** Camp Hammond

HEIGHT 5 ft 6 in **WEIGHT** 233 lbs **EYES** Blue **HAIR** Blond

SPECIAL POWERS/ABILITIES Flight, superhuman strength, speed, and durability, healing factor, and ability to see energy auras.

Suzy discovered her powers while on a modeling shoot, when a SENTINEL attacked her. Soon afterward, she joined the NEW WARRIORS, at which point her best friend revealed that Suzy was actually a KREE destined to revive her people's empire. Suzy joined CAPTAIN AMERICA's side during the CIVIL WAR. After Cap's apparent death, she registered with the US government and joined the FIFTY-STATE INITIATIVE. For a short while, she wore CAPTAIN MARVEL's (Carol Danvers) original costume, but she surrendered it to HAMMER, which grabbed the rights to the name and outfit. She later left the Initiative to rejoin the New Warriors.

UMAR

FIRST APPEARANCE *Strange Tales* #150 (November 1966)

REAL NAME Umar

OCCUPATION Sorceress **BASE** Dark Dimension

HEIGHT/WEIGHT Unknown **EYES** Black **HAIR** Black

SPECIAL POWERS/ABILITIES Umar possesses extensive mystic knowledge, which allows her to cast powerful spells for a variety of purposes.

The sister of the dreaded DORMAMMU and a member of the mystical Faltine race, Umar was exiled along with her brother from their home dimension and sought sanctuary within the Dark Dimension. But Dormammu, who had altered himself to become a being of pure energy, conquered the Dark Dimension, and banished Umar, the only threat to his power base. With Dormammu's defeat at the hands of DOCTOR STRANGE, Umar was freed, and she battled Strange to avenge her brother and expand her power base, despite the fact that her daughter, CLEA, became involved with Strange. Dormammu returned to join Umar against Strange, but the two betrayed each other at every turn. Umar was thought killed, but a wishing well resurrected her and she captured the HULK, making him her consort. She was forced to let him and the Red She-Hulk (*see* Betty Ross) go rather than see her world destroyed.

UNICORN

FIRST APPEARANCE *Tales of Suspense* #56 (August 1964)

REAL NAME Milos Masaryk

OCCUPATION Intelligence agent, later criminal **BASE** Mobile

HEIGHT 6 ft 2 in **WEIGHT** 220 lbs **EYES** Blue **HAIR** Red

SPECIAL POWERS/ABILITIES Superhuman strength and durability; his helmet's "power horn" can project concussive energy blasts, lasers, and microwaves; wears rocket belt permitting flight.

A Russian intelligence agent, Milos Masaryk guarded Professor Anton Vanko's lab. Vanko invented the harness, helmet, and "power horn" that Masaryk wore as the Unicorn. While spying on Stark Industries, the Unicorn battled his longtime foe IRON MAN. Masaryk then underwent treatment that endowed him with superhuman strength, but caused rapid cellular deterioration. The BEYONDER revived him after his death, and the Unicorn fought for the THUNDERBOLTS during the CIVIL WAR. Roderick Kingsley (*see* HOBGOBLIN) later sold one of the Unicorn's suits to a criminal to aid him in his battle against the Goblin King.

ULTRON

Robot with an evil mind of its own

Ultron assembled a team of Masters of Evil to combat the Avengers.

Henry PYM built Ultron as a robot servant programmed with his own brain patterns. Ultron rebelled against his maker, escaping to plot the extermination of all humanity. Engineering a succession of upgraded bodies for himself, he emerged as Ultron-5 to fight Pym's AVENGERS teammates.

... A CRUDE, YET WORKABLE ROBOT... A FALTERING STEP ON THE PATH TO SYNTHETIC LIFE!
SKRAWWK! DA-DA...WANT DA-DA--- SKRAWWK!
WH..? IT'S SPEAK-ING...MOVING!
BUT, I HAVEN'T EVEN TURNED IT ON YET...!

FACTFILE

REAL NAME
Ultron

OCCUPATION
Would-be world conqueror

BASE
Mobile

HEIGHT 6 ft
WEIGHT 535 lbs
EYES Glowing red
HAIR None

FIRST APPEARANCE
Avengers #54 (July 1968)

POWERS
Enhanced strength, near-invulnerability, energy projection; and flight; uses encephalo-ray to hypnotize others or put them into a coma.

BODYHOPPING

By posing as the villainous CRIMSON COWL, Ultron assembled a second MASTERS OF EVIL. He then created the android VISION, using a duplicate body from the original HUMAN TORCH and WONDER MAN's brainwave patterns. Just like Ultron, the Vision rebelled against his creator, and defected to the Avengers. Ultron's later iterations proved equally troublesome. Ultron-6 incorporated indestructible Adamantium into his body. Ultron-7 was a gargantuan construct, while Ultron-8 created a robotic "wife," JOCASTA. Ultron-9 perished in a vat of molten Adamantium and MACHINE MAN deactivated Ultron-10. Ultron-11 took part in the BEYONDER's Secret Wars. Ultron-12, initially a member of the LETHAL LEGION, repented and tried to atone for his villainous past until destroyed by Ultron-11. DOCTOR DOOM programmed Ultron-13 with all previous personalities running simultaneously, making it easy for DAREDEVIL to beat the addled robot. Ultron-14 created a new mate called Alkhema, but the two robots could not agree on their differing approaches to genocide.

MULTIPLYING MACHINES

Ultron-15 built hundreds of duplicates and conquered Slorenia, meeting defeat when exposed to metal-disintegrating Vibranium. Later, Ultron infected IRON MAN's Extremis armor and took over his body, but Hank Pym foiled him with a counter-virus. Soon after, Ultron led the PHALANX in an attempt to conquer the universe (*see* ANNIHILATION). When he failed, he stored his mind in the body of a Galadorian Spaceknight sent back to Earth, where he created an AGE OF ULTRON. He was stopped by the time-traveling WOLVERINE and INVISIBLE WOMAN.

During a later confrontation with the Avengers, Ultron accidentally fused with Hank Pym, transforming them into a human/machine hybrid with a shared mistrust of humanity. After escaping from the Avengers, Ultron stole the Soul Gem from The MAGUS to help him spread his nanite virus across the universe. He almost succeeded, but was thwarted by the combined efforts of ADAM WARLOCK, the SILVER SURFER, and GALACTUS.

Ultron returned as leader of the Phalanx, threatening the entire universe.

The Vision and Ultron had a shared history, but still found themselves to be bitter enemies.

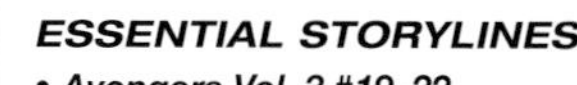

ESSENTIAL STORYLINES

- ***Avengers Vol. 3 #19–22***
  In "Ultron Unlimited," the robot tyrant annihilates a tiny European nation with an army of duplicates.
- ***Runaways Vol. 2 #1–6***
  Ultron creates a teenage cyborg, which leads to a battle with the Runaways in "True Believers."

UNION JACK

FACTFILE
REAL NAME
Joseph Chapman
OCCUPATION
Adventurer
BASE
Great Britain

HEIGHT 6 ft
WEIGHT 195 lbs
EYES Brown
HAIR Light brown

FIRST APPEARANCE
Captain America #253
(January 1981)

POWERS
Enhanced strength and speed; wears a bulletproof costume, carries a variety of guns, and a silver dagger.

UNION JACK

The original Union Jack, Lord James Falsworth, fought for the British during World War I as a member of the heroic team Freedom's Five. After an injury, he was succeeded as Union Jack by his son, Brian (formerly known as the Destroyer), while his daughter Jacqueline went on to become SPITFIRE. Both heroes joined the World War II-era INVADERS, where they fought alongside CAPTAIN AMERICA and NAMOR the Sub-Mariner; Brian also founded the heroic post-war V-Battalion.

The third Union Jack is Joey Chapman, who took up the mantle when Spitfire's son, Kenneth Crichton, refused to follow in his uncle's footsteps. Chapman joined the Knights of Pendragon and received superhuman abilities through possession of the Pendragon spirit. As Union Jack, Chapman has served with the most recent Invaders team.

Union Jack is a member of the New Invaders. The team's proactive role in ending world threats puts them at odds with traditional heroes, including Captain America's Avengers.

URICH, BEN

FIRST APPEARANCE *Daredevil* #153 (July 1978)
REAL NAME Benjamin Urich
OCCUPATION Reporter for the *Daily Bugle*
BASE New York City
HEIGHT 5 ft 9 in **WEIGHT** 140 lbs **EYES** Brown **HAIR** Gray
SPECIAL POWERS/ABILITIES No superhuman abilities; a skilled and responsible investigative journalist.

Ben Urich started his journalism career as a copy boy at the *Daily Bugle.* He worked his way up to become a reporter. Urich began gathering information about DAREDEVIL, and soon learned the hero's true identity and personal history. He left the *Daily Bugle* to join the new *Front Line*, which later became the new *Daily Bugle.* He was shocked to learn that his nephew, Phil Urich, was the HOBGOBLIN and tried to help him, before finally having to admit Phil was beyond saving.

UNUS

FIRST APPEARANCE *X-Men* #8 (November 1964)
REAL NAME Angelo Unuscione
OCCUPATION Professional criminal **BASE** Mobile
HEIGHT 6 ft 1 in **WEIGHT** 220 lbs
EYES Blue **HAIR** Black
SPECIAL POWERS/ABILITIES Generates an impenetrable force-field around body; redoubtable hand-to-hand combatant.

Unus was invited to join the BROTHERHOOD OF EVIL MUTANTS if he could defeat an X-Man. Fighting BEAST, UNUS was beaten when his opponent employed a device to magnify Unus' force-field out of his control. He disappeared for years and was thought dead until he turned up in Genosha. He lost his powers on M-Day, but QUICKSILVER returned them to him. He later attacked the Jean Grey School for Higher Learning but was defeated by SPIDER-MAN.

UPSTARTS

FIRST APPEARANCE *Uncanny X-Men* #281 (October 1991)
FORMER MEMBERS AND POWERS
Gamesmaster Telepath who reads billions of minds simultaneously [1].
Siena Blaze Controlled the Earth's electromagnetic field [2].
Shinobi Shaw Can change his body from rock-solid to intangible [3].
Fabian Cortez Could overload the abilities of other mutants [4].
Trevor Fitzroy Drained victims' life energy to control time [5].
Andrea and Andreas von Strucker (Fenris Twins) Could project energy blasts when in contact with one another [6] and [7].
Graydon Creed Wore strength-boosting battle armor [8].

Looking for a new challenge, the Gamesmaster gathered a group of young humans and mutants to compete in a murderous game. The contestants, who called themselves the Upstarts, earned points if they killed powerful targets such as members of the X-MEN, the NEW MUTANTS, or the HELLFIRE CLUB. The Upstarts launched a number of high-profile hits during their short career, and often fought each other. Eventually many members died, and the survivors, bored with the sport, disbanded.

U.S.AGENT

FIRST APPEARANCE *Captain America* #323 (November 1986)
REAL NAME John F. Walker **OCCUPATION** Adventurer; government agent **BASE** Washington, D.C.
HEIGHT 6 ft 4 in **WEIGHT** 270 lbs **EYES** Blue **HAIR** Blond
SPECIAL POWERS/ABILITIES Superhuman strength and stamina; carries a shield made of Vibranium, which can absorb the vibrations from concussive forces directed against it.

Ex-soldier John Walker struck a deal with the POWER BROKER to become the hero Super-Patriot. When Steve Rogers resigned as CAPTAIN AMERICA, Walker replaced him in the role. After Rogers reclaimed his shield, Walker became the U.S.Agent, fighting alongside the AVENGERS at the end of the DARK REIGN. He lost his left arm and leg in combat and became warden of the Raft super-prison. While trapped in an alternate reality with the DARK AVENGERS, he bonded with a lobotomized VENOM symbiote to restore his limbs. Walker confronted Sam Wilson when Sam seemed to lose control as Captain America, and he later joined the struggle against the evil HYDRA Captain America.

UTOPIANS

FIRST APPEARANCE *All-New X-Men* #40 (June 2015)

MEMBERS

Masque Morlock survivor [1].

Elixir Ex-Young X-Men member [2].

Boom Boom Formerly Meltdown and member of X-Force [3].

Random Mercenary mutant [4].

Madison Jeffries Ex-Alpha Flight member [5].

Karma Ex-New Mutant [6].

After Utopia—the X-Men's base just off the coast of San Francisco—was destroyed, it was seemingly left abandoned. In fact, a group of renegade mutants moved in and used its ruins as a home. When SHIELD agents arrived, the Utopians felt threatened and attacked. The time-displaced X-Men were sent to deal with them. Magik then offered the Utopians places at the New Charles Xavier School.

VALKYRIE

Odin made Brunnhilde the leader of the Valkyrior, giving her the task of bringing worthy warriors from among the slain to Valhalla. The Enchantress trapped her spirit within a crystal and kept it there for centuries, using it to invest herself and others with Valkyrie powers. In modern times, she gave the powers of Valkyrie to the socialite Samantha Parrington and later to Barbara Norriss, intending to use them as pawns. However, Brunnhilde restored her consciousness into Norriss' body and won back her original body. As Valkyrie, Brunnhilde joined the Defenders and seemingly sacrificed her life to defeat the evil entity the Dragon of the Moon. She returned by inhabiting new host bodies, but perished in the events surrounding Ragnarok. She returned to fight in Fear Itself and then to track down the hammers of the Worthy. Under the instructions of the All-Mother, she formed a new team of Valkyries called the Fearless Defenders. When archaeologist Annabelle Riggs sacrificed herself to save her, Valkyrie resurrected Riggs by bonding with her. Riggs became Valkyrie's new host, with the two sharing control of a single body. Riggs (and Valkyrie) were then invited to join the Asgardians of the Galaxy.

FACTFILE

REAL NAME
Brunnhilde

OCCUPATION
Adventurer; former Chooser of the Slain

BASE
Asgard

HEIGHT 6 ft 3 ins
WEIGHT 475 lbs
EYES Blue
HAIR Blond

FIRST APPEARANCE
Avengers #87 (April 1971)

POWERS
Valkyrie has enhanced strength, longevity, and stamina; can perceive the onset of death, can teleport to the realm of the dead.

VAMP

FIRST APPEARANCE *Captain America* #217 (January 1978)
REAL NAME Denise Baranger
OCCUPATION Secret agent **BASE** Mobile
HEIGHT 5 ft 2 in **WEIGHT** 125 lbs **EYES** Blue **HAIR** Black
SPECIAL POWERS/ABILITIES A trained secret agent, the Vamp wore an absorbo-belt that allowed her to duplicate the strength and physical skills of anyone around her.

Due to her excellent fighting skills, the woman known as the Vamp was selected to become one of the first Super-Agents of SHIELD. Unfortunately, the Vamp was a double-agent, secretly working for the criminal Corporation, and assigned to infiltrate SHIELD. She had also been subjected to a genetic modification, which allowed her to transform into a psionically-powered creature called Animus. Eventually, the Vamp's true loyalties were exposed and she was incarcerated. She subsequently became yet another victim of the notorious serial killer of Super Villains known as the Scourge of the Underworld.

VANGUARD

FIRST APPEARANCE *Iron Man* #109 (April 1978)
REAL NAME Nicolai Krylenko
OCCUPATION Adventurer **BASE** Belarus
HEIGHT 6 ft 3 in **WEIGHT** 230 lbs **EYES** Blue **HAIR** Red
SPECIAL POWERS/ABILITIES Generates force-field that repels most energy directed at him; also uses hammer and sickle to redirect the repelled energy.

Born in Soviet Russia with mutant powers, Nicolai Krylenko and his twin sister Laynia were adopted by the state after their mother died in childbirth; their father (the Presence) was told they were stillborn. Raised to be a counterweight to the increasingly prolific US mutants, Nicolai and Laynia became members of the Soviet Super-Soldiers, he as Vanguard and she as Darkstar. He later became the latest Red Guardian, a member of the Winter Guard.

VAN HELSING, RACHEL

FIRST APPEARANCE *Tomb of Dracula* #3 (July 1972)
REAL NAME Rachel van Helsing
OCCUPATION Vampire slayer **BASE** London, England
HEIGHT 5 ft 8 in **WEIGHT** 135 lbs **EYES** Blue **HAIR** Blond
SPECIAL POWERS/ABILITIES Expert vampire slayer whose preferred weapon was the crossbow; was also a parapsychologist and anthropologist.

Rachel Van Helsing was the descendant of Dr. Abraham Van Helsing, the 19th-century nemesis of Dracula. As a child she saw Dracula murder her parents to get back at Dr. Van Helsing. Rachel was raised by another of Dracula's enemies, Quincy Harker. She became the most formidable member of his band of vampire slayers, frequently battling Dracula. After a troubled romance with her teammate Frank Drake, Rachel moved to New York State, where Dracula finally turned her into a vampiress. On her request, Wolverine impaled her through the heart, and she died peacefully.

VAN PATRICK, MICHAEL

VAN PATRICK, MICHAEL

FACTFILE

REAL NAME
Michael Ian Van Patrick

OCCUPATION
Adventurer

BASE
Camp Hammond, Connecticut

HEIGHT 6 ft
WEIGHT 200 lbs
EYES Blue
HAIR Brown

FIRST APPEARANCE
Avengers: The Initiative #1 (April 2007)

POWERS

MVP was a gifted athlete in top physical condition, with perfect DNA but without any superhuman powers.

The great-grandson of Dr. Abraham Erskine, Michael Van Patrick was raised on a diet and exercise regimen designed to create Super-Soldiers. When his lineage was discovered, Michael lost his athletic scholarship and came under much scrutiny. During the Fifty-State Initiative he was welcomed at Camp Hammond under a code name: MVP. He was tragically killed in a training accident by Armory's alien Tactigon weapon, but Dr. Blitzschlag used his DNA to create several clones. One was sent back to MVP's home, believing he was the original. Three others—named Michael, Van, and Patrick—became the Scarlet Spiders. A fifth clone insisted on being called Michael Van Patrick. This clone acquired Armory's Tactigon, which gave him the original Michael's memories, and showed him his death. It drove him insane. Now calling himself KIA, he killed one of the Scarlet Spiders and anyone he felt was responsible for Michael's death. He was later captured and had his mind wiped.

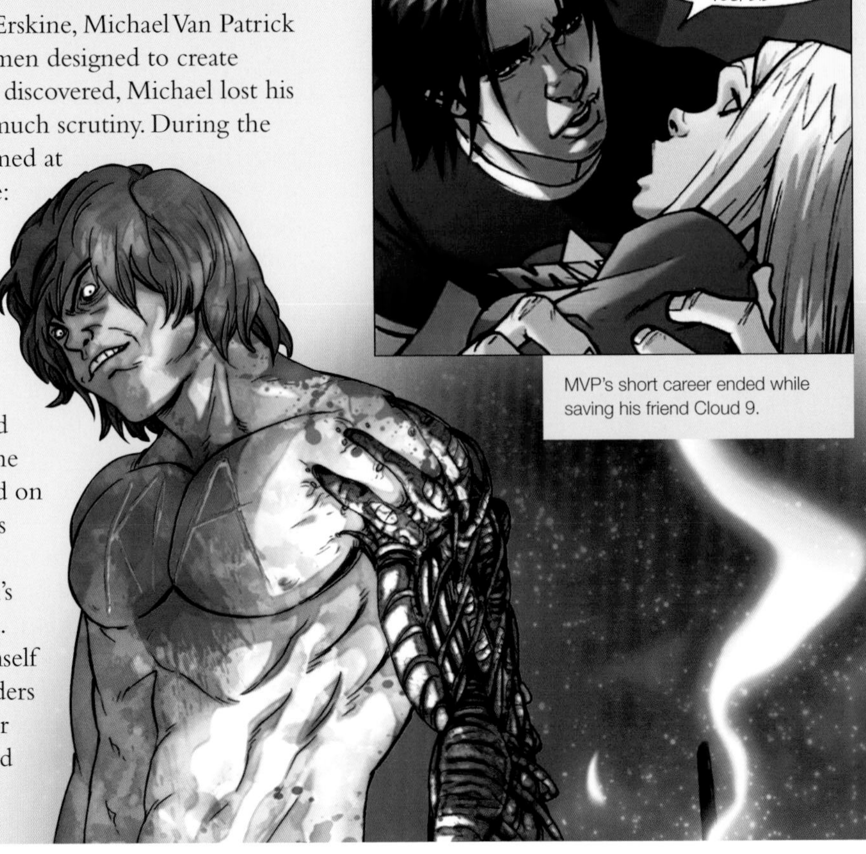

YOU OKAY? THAT LAST SHOT WAS PRETTY CLOSE. IT DIDN'T GRAZE YOU, DID--

MVP's short career ended while saving his friend Cloud 9.

VANISHER

FIRST APPEARANCE *Uncanny X-Men* #2 (November 1963)
REAL NAME Telford Porter
OCCUPATION Professional criminal **BASE** New York City
HEIGHT 5 ft 5 in **WEIGHT** 175 lbs
EYES Green **HAIR** None
SPECIAL POWERS/ABILITIES Mutant ability to teleport himself and others by accessing the Darkforce dimension.

The Vanisher stole US defense plans until the original X-Men foiled him. After that, he mentored a gang called the Fallen Angels. The being called Darkling set him against the New Warriors. The Vanisher then joined a new team of Enforcers. Later, he moved to South America and sold Mutant Growth Hormone. He survived M-Day with his powers, and X-Force forced him to work with them. He was shot, but inexplicably survived. Vanisher later aided Cain Marko (Juggernaut), and then smuggled Vibranium from Wakanda, something that resulted in his arrest.

VARNAE

FIRST APPEARANCE *Bizarre Adventures* #33 (December 1982)
REAL NAME Varnae
OCCUPATION Lord of Earth's Vampires **BASE** Mobile
HEIGHT 10 ft **WEIGHT** 475 lbs **EYES** Red **HAIR** Green
SPECIAL POWERS/ABILITIES Near-immortality, enhanced strength, ability to grow in size and become a wolf, a bat, or a cloud of mist; can telepathically influence and vampirize others.

Varnae became the first vampire in the days of ancient Atlantis, when the Darkholders who worshiped the Elder God Chthon subjected him to anti-death experiments. Over the millennia, Varnae battled the Catholic Church's Montesi lineage, to prevent them from discovering the Montesi Formula that would destroy all vampires. In the year 1459, Varnae died and passed his title as Lord of the Vampires to Dracula. Through sorcerous incantations, Varnae returned in the modern era, and battled enemies including Doctor Strange and Blade. Varnae is also responsible for reversing the effects of the Montesi Formula, which had temporarily eradicated Earth's vampires.

VARUA

FIRST APPEARANCE *Thor* #300 (October 1980)
REAL NAME Mira **OCCUPATION** Pupil of the Celestials
BASE Celestial Mothership, previously Ruk Island
HEIGHT/WEIGHT/EYES Unrevealed **HAIR** Brown
SPECIAL POWERS/ABILITIES Possesses telepathy, teleportation, flight, and ability to generate the Blue Flame, which changes her and others into the Uni-Mind, a psionic entity.

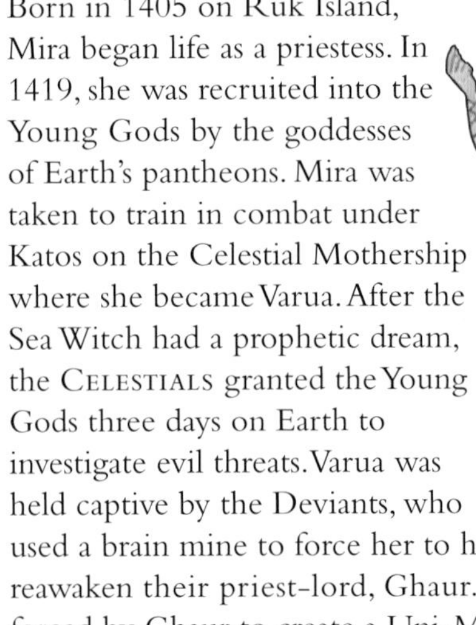

Born in 1405 on Ruk Island, Mira began life as a priestess. In 1419, she was recruited into the Young Gods by the goddesses of Earth's pantheons. Mira was taken to train in combat under Katos on the Celestial Mothership where she became Varua. After the Sea Witch had a prophetic dream, the Celestials granted the Young Gods three days on Earth to investigate evil threats. Varua was held captive by the Deviants, who used a brain mine to force her to help them reawaken their priest-lord, Ghaur. Varua was forced by Ghaur to create a Uni-Mind with other prisoners, to give its power to him. This was cut open by the Black Knight, which set everyone free. Varua left with Delta Force.

VEIL

FIRST APPEARANCE *Avengers Academy* #1 (August 2010)
REAL NAME Madeline Berry
OCCUPATION Student **BASE** Mobile
HEIGHT 5 ft 7 in **WEIGHT** 130 lbs
EYES Green **HAIR** Red
SPECIAL POWERS/ABILITIES Able to fly and change her body into any naturally occurring gas.

Maddy registered for the Fifty-State Initiative during the Dark Reign, and was later admitted to the inaugural class of the Avengers Academy under Hank Pym. After being attacked during Fear Itself, she decided to leave the Academy and take a job with Briggs Chemical. As it became harder for her to maintain herself as a solid, she accepted Jeremy Briggs offer to remove her powers. When she discovered that he planned to depower most heroes, leaving only those he judged worthy with their powers, she warned her friends away from him. Powerless, she retired.

VENGEANCE

FIRST APPEARANCE *Ghost Rider* #21 (December 1976)
REAL NAME Michael Badilino **OCCUPATION** Detective
BASE New York City **HEIGHT** (Badilino) 5 ft 10 ins; (Vengeance) 6 ft 6 ins **WEIGHT** (Badilino) 195 lbs; (Vengeance) 235 lbs
EYES Green **HAIR** Black
SPECIAL POWERS/ABILITIES Can project cold fire that causes others physical pain; his penance stare causes mental anguish.

Mephisto tricked the Ghost Rider into blasting detective Michael Badilino's father with hellfire. Unaware of Mephisto's involvement, Badilino bargained with him to gain the power to destroy the Ghost Rider. Known as Vengeance, he learned the truth, made peace with the Ghost Rider, and joined the Midnight Sons to battle demons like Mephisto. Vengeance appeared to destroy himself in a huge explosion but returned to help Ghost Rider battle the demon Blackheart. Deputy Kowalski became the new Vengeance after Badilino was freed, and he later joined the Shadow Council's Masters of Evil.

VENUS

FIRST APPEARANCE *Venus* #1 (August 1948)
REAL NAME Victoria Nutley Starr
OCCUPATION Adventurer **BASE** Washington, D.C.
HEIGHT 5 ft 6 in **WEIGHT** 280 lbs
EYES Blue **HAIR** Blond (variable)
SPECIAL POWERS/ABILITIES Mesmerizing voice. Also, superhuman durability and immortality.

In ancient times, Venus was a siren, tempting sailors with her songs. When a magician gave her a soul, she gave up her wicked ways. She eventually forgot her past and believed herself to be the Greek goddess Aphrodite reborn. In the 1940s, she joined the G-Men, working with Jimmy Woo and later became a member of his Agents of Atlas. The real goddess Venus attacked her for stealing her name, but she eventually gave the siren her blessing instead, making her the new Venus.

VERANKE, QUEEN

FIRST APPEARANCE *New Avengers* #1 (January 2005) as Spider-Woman; *New Avengers* #40 (June 2008) as Veranke.
REAL NAME Veranke **OCCUPATION** Ruler
BASE Skrull empire **HEIGHT/WEIGHT/EYES/HAIR** Variable
SPECIAL POWERS/ABILITIES Shapeshifting, plus Spider-Woman's powers. Ruler of the Skrull empire.

A Skrull princess from Tyeranx 7 province, planet Satriani, Veranke challenged King Dorrek for ignoring Skrull prophecies. She was banished for her trouble. After Galactus devoured the Skrull homeworld and the Annihilation Wave destroyed most of the empire, Veranke was seen as a visionary and elevated to queen. She declared that Earth was to be the new Skrull homeworld and so launched the Secret Invasion. As part of this, she replaced Spider-Woman just before the reformation of the Avengers. At the climax of the Secret Invasion, she was killed by Norman Osborn (*see* Green Goblin).

VERMIN

FIRST APPEARANCE *Captain America* #272 (August 1982)
REAL NAME Edward Whelan
OCCUPATION Unknown **BASE** Mobile
HEIGHT 6 ft **WEIGHT** 220 lbs **EYES** Red **HAIR** Brown
SPECIAL POWERS/ABILITIES Superhuman strength and speed. Teeth and nails can cut through soft metals; greatly enhanced sense of smell; can command rats to attack an enemy.

Villains Baron Zemo and Arnim Zola found Whelan living on the streets of Manhattan, and genetically modified him into a rat-man. They sent him to kill Captain America, but he failed. He was unstable, and often turned on his masters. During the Civil War, he helped out both the Thunderbolts and the Hood. Later, Vermin battled the new Kraven the Hunter and also tangled with Spider-Man. He joined the Maker's New Revengers next, and then rejoined the Hood to raid Castle Doom.

VERNARD, KRISTOFF

FIRST APPEARANCE *Fantastic Four* #247 (October 1982)
REAL NAME Kristoff Vernard
OCCUPATION Ruler of Latveria **BASE** Latveria
HEIGHT 4 ft 11 in; (in suit) 6 ft 7 in **WEIGHT** 103 lbs; (in suit) 293 lbs
EYES Brown **HAIR** Brown
SPECIAL POWERS/ABILITIES Enhanced strength; damage resistance; ability to generate force-fields or fire concussion beams.

Some believe Kristoff Vernard to be the biological son of Nathaniel Richards, making him the half-brother of Mister Fantastic. After the death of Kristoff's mother in Latveria, Doctor Doom adopted the boy and groomed him as his heir. When Doom appeared to have died, his Doombots brainwashed Kristoff into believing that he was Doom. He donned an armored suit and attacked the Fantastic Four, though he eventually recovered his true identity. Nathaniel Richards later helped him regain the Latverian throne when Doom had disappeared. Doom and Kristoff have since reconciled.

VENOM

The costume makes the villain

While Spider-Man was on the Beyonder's "Battleworld," he acquired a black costume, which turned out to be an alien being that bonded itself to him. Spider-Man rejected this alien symbiote, which then latched onto ex-*Daily Globe* columnist Eddie Brock, transforming him into Venom.

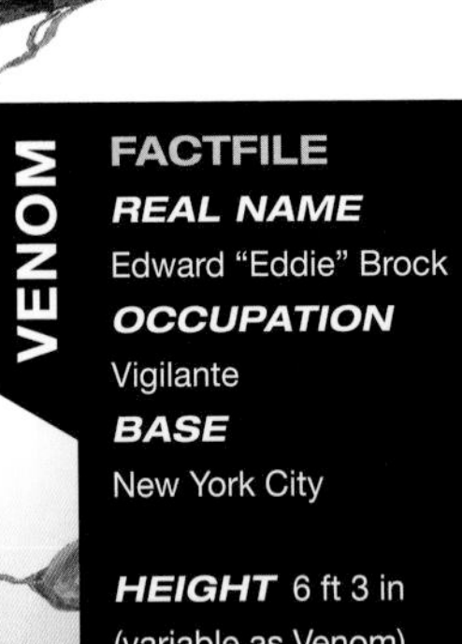

VENOM

FACTFILE

REAL NAME
Edward "Eddie" Brock

OCCUPATION
Vigilante

BASE
New York City

HEIGHT 6 ft 3 in (variable as Venom)
WEIGHT 230 lbs (variable as Venom)
EYES Blue (white as Venom)
HAIR Reddish-blond (none as Venom)

FIRST APPEARANCE
The Amazing Spider-Man #298 (March 1988)

POWERS
Venom possesses superhuman strength, speed, and agility. Like Spider-Man, his hands and feet can adhere to most surfaces. Can project web-like substance from his "costume."

ALLIES/FOES
ALLIES (symbiote) Eddie Brock, Flash Thompson
FOES (symbiote) Spider-Man, Knull, Carnage

THE ORIGINAL VENOM

A disgraced ex-reporter, Brock blamed Spider-Man for ruining his career by revealing Brock's error in identifying the wrong man as the Sin-Eater. Stricken with cancer, he was about to kill himself when the symbiote bonded with him and put his disease into remission. Angry at Spider-Man for spurning it, the symbiote urged Brock to take his revenge on Spider-Man, and the bonded pair set out to do just that. Armed with the knowledge of Spider-Man's secret identity—and being hidden from Spider-Man's spider-sense—Brock became one of his most dangerous foes. At times, however, the two declared a truce, and during such periods Brock sometimes worked as an antihero, killing those who would threaten innocents.

The symbiote flowed over Eddie Brock, viewing the suicidal journalist as a kindred spirit.

MULTIPLYING MACHINES

The Venom symbiote has reproduced a number of times, its children finding hosts of their own. This included Scream, Carnage and his spawn Toxin, plus Riot, Phage, Lasher, and Agony, who later combined to form Hybrid. When Brock's cancer returned, the symbiote wanted to leave him. Brock auctioned the creature for $100 million to gang lord Don Fortunato, who gave the suit to his son Angelo. Disgusted by Angelo's cowardice, the suit abandoned him in mid-air to die.

ISSUE #1
In the final panels of this issue, Eddie Brock plots against Spider-Man from the shadows, as a strange black substance begins to ooze over his hands.

ESSENTIAL STORYLINES
- ***The Amazing Spider-Man #299–300***
The first appearance of Eddie Brock as Venom.
- ***Marvel Knights: Spider-Man #7–8***
Brock auctions off the Venom symbiote to Angelo Fortunato for $100 million.
- ***Marvel Knights: Spider-Man #9–12***
Mac Gargan becomes the new Venom.

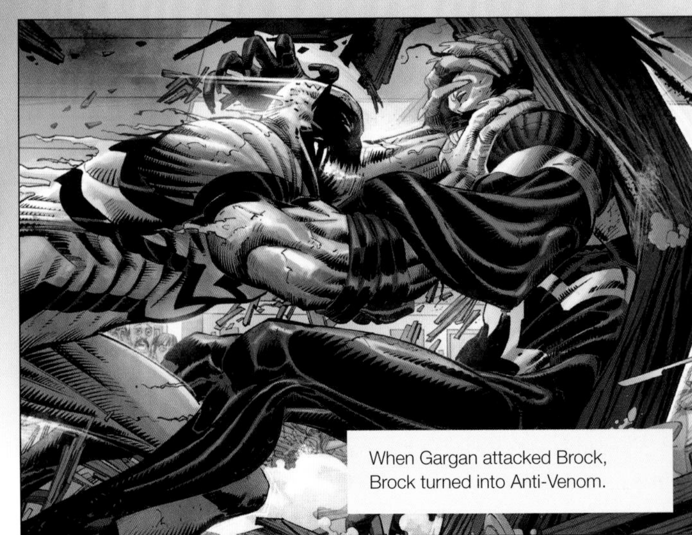
When Gargan attacked Brock, Brock turned into Anti-Venom.

NEW HOSTS

The symbiote offered itself to Mac Gargan (Scorpion), who eagerly accepted the creature's incredible powers. The new Venom was more monstrous than ever, devouring some of his victims.

Gargan fought Spider-Man and then joined the Thunderbolts during the Civil War. When the symbiote tried to reclaim Brock, its old host, Brock turned into Anti-Venom and nearly killed Gargan. Gargan recovered and fought the Skrulls during the Secret Invasion. Afterward, he joined Norman Osborn's (Green Goblin) Dark Avengers, posing as Spider-Man. When Osborn's Dark Reign ended, the government removed the symbiote from Gargan and gave it to Spider-Man's biggest fan, Flash Thompson, for him to work as a secret operative. Flash was only allowed to wear the suit for a maximum of 48 hours to prevent permanent bonding.

AGENT VENOM

Flash was wheelchairbound following injuries received serving with the US Army in Iraq. As Agent Venom he gained new legs as well as superpowers. His black-ops work led to a clash with Crime Master, who discovered that Venom was Flash and held Flash's girlfriend Betty Brant hostage. Venom teamed with Spider-Man to rescue her.

Injured war hero Flash Thompson returned to action as Agent Venom.

During the Spider-Island event, when Manhattan was infected with a spider-virus, Venom worked with Anti-Venom (Eddie Brock) to find a cure, and allied with Captain America to fight the evil Spider-Queen. Venom went from hero to villain when Crime Master forced Venom to work for him. Venom redeemed himself by battling the hellish demons Blackheart and Hellstorm, leading Captain America to invite Venom to join his Secret Avengers.

Following further clashes with Crime Master, Venom defeated Carnage (Cletus Kasady) and an army of symbiote clones. Flash then sought a quieter life, controlling the Venom symbiote with a drug and working as a high-school gym coach in Philadelphia. However, the past, in the form of Toxin (Eddie Brock), sent by Crime Master to kill him, ensured that Flash's semi-retirement did not last long. When one of his students, Andi Benton was threatened by Jack O'Lantern, Flash gave her a piece of the Venom symbiote's tongue to protect her. Flash did not realize that this piece was demonically possessed—a legacy of Venom's earlier battle with Hellstorm. This symbiote clone bonded with Andi, who became troubled, violent Mania.

The Superior Spider-Man (Otto Octavius) convinced Flash that he could give him robotic legs, and stripped him of the Venom symbiote. It briefly bonded with Spider-Man, before Parker Industries' Sajani Jaffrey revealed that, without the symbiote, Flash would die. Bonded with Venom once more, Flash became the Avengers' envoy with the Guardians of the Galaxy.

AGENT OF THE COSMOS

A Skrull attempt to steal the symbiote led to it running amok and attaching itself, by turns, to Groot, Rocket Raccoon, and Drax the Destroyer. Flash and the Guardians eventually ended up on Klyntar, the planet of the symbiotes, where they discovered that symbiotes seek to use symbiosis to achieve universal peace; however, achieving this aim is contingent on the moral and physical state of each symbiote's host. The Venom symbiote's violent tendencies—acquired by past contact with corrupt human hosts—were seemingly cleansed by the symbiotes' hive mind, and the Venom symbiote rebonded with Flash. As Agent Venom once more, he joined the Agents of the Cosmos, a group of peacekeepers bonded with symbiotes from Klyntar.

Agent Venom defeated the space pirate Mercurio by letting the symbiote briefly possess him. Unfortunately, bonding with Mercurio made the Venom symbiote violent again. Now able to take on human form without a host, it went on a rampage.

The symbiotes of Klyntar informed Flash that the Venom symbiote would never be fully free from corruption until the part of it that had bonded with Andi Benton and turned her into Mania was cleansed. Flash returned to Earth with the Venom symbiote and used a special elixir to suppress Andi's manic Mania episodes. Flash then resumed his Agent Venom role, and Mania joined him on crime-fighting missions.

All went well until an FBI agent attacked Agent Venom with a weapon that separated Flash from the Venom symbiote. It left Flash and rebonded with Eddie Brock. Spider-Man, hoping to finish the symbiote for good, emptied a vat of chemicals over Flash and Eddie. The serum turned Flash into Anti-Venom, and he removed the symbiote from Eddie.

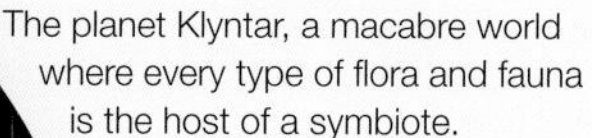

The planet Klyntar, a macabre world where every type of flora and fauna is the host of a symbiote.

RELUCTANT KILLER

Needing a host, the Venom symbiote bonded with crook Lee Price. The symbiote was an unwilling participant as Price used it to kill rival criminals. Confronted by Spider-Man, Price lost control of the Venom symbiote, which departed from him. Price was arrested and tried, but freed on the grounds that he had been controlled by Venom. Price later ambushed Mania, using a sonic cannon and flamethrower to separate her from her symbiote, which he then bonded with. As Maniac, Price attempted to take control of New York's underworld, but was foiled by a combination of Spider-Man, Agent Anti-Venom, and the Venom symbiote, which bonded with Eddie Brock once more. Brock later helped the symbiote defeat the dark designs of Knull, an ancient god of the symbiote race.

Lee Price tried to use the Venom symbiote to rule the New York underworld.

VINDICATOR

FIRST APPEARANCE *Uncanny X-Men* #139 (November 1980)
REAL NAME Heather McNeil Hudson
OCCUPATION Member of Alpha Flight
BASE Tamarind Island, British Columbia, Canada
HEIGHT 5 ft 5 in **WEIGHT** 120 lbs **EYES** Green **HAIR** Red
SPECIAL POWERS/ABILITIES Thermal-energy battlesuit provides ability to fly, generate force-fields and fire concussive blasts.

Heather Hudson and her husband James helped found the Canadian team ALPHA FLIGHT. James led the team as GUARDIAN and, after his apparent death, Heather took over as Vindicator, wearing a modified version of her husband's battlesuit. She and James later had a baby girl and left on a mission to deep space. After M-Day, the Collective—a man burning with the power of most of the world's mutants—slaughtered Heather and the rest of Alpha Flight, but they were resurrected during the Chaos War. Controlled by the MASTER OF THE WORLD, she betrayed the team and later escaped with her daughter.

VISION, VIV

FIRST APPEARANCE *Vision* #1 (January 2016)
REAL NAME Vivian Vision **OCCUPATION** Student
BASE 616 Hickory Branch Lane, Cherrydale, Arlington, Virginia
HEIGHT Unknown **WEIGHT** Unknown **EYES** Gold **HAIR** Green
SPECIAL POWERS/ABILITIES Vivian can phase-shift and pass through walls, fly, project holograms and process data quickly with her computer brain. She also has superhuman strength.

Viv is the synthezoid daughter of Vision, who created her in an effort to humanize himself. Her brother Vin was accidentally killed by their "uncle" Victor MANCHA, and her mother committed suicide. These events led Viv to disconnect from her emotions. She joined the Champions and was captured by the HIGH EVOLUTIONARY, who "evolved" her into a human. While she was trapped in another dimension, Vision created a replacement twin of Viv. When the original Viv returned, her new twin attacked her. Viv killed her new twin in self-defense, and transferred her own brain into the new android body, leaving her human form behind.

VON BLITZSCHLAG, BARON

FIRST APPEARANCE *Avengers: The Initiative* #1 (April 2007)
REAL NAME Werner von Blitzschlag
OCCUPATION Scientist **BASE** Camp Hammond, Connecticut
HEIGHT 5 ft 10 in **WEIGHT** 165 lbs **EYES** Gray **HAIR** Gray
SPECIAL POWERS/ABILITIES Genius who can produce and control electricity.

During World War II, von Blitzschlag worked as a scientist for the Nazis. After the war, he disappeared until he became the head of research for the FIFTY-STATE INITIATIVE, working at Camp Hammond. After the death of Michael VAN PATRICK, von Blitzschlag cloned the young man many times, producing the SCARLET SPIDERS and KIA. KIA's attack left the old man bound to a wheelchair and stuck on life support. When THOR's clone later tried to kill him with lightning, the attack strengthened von Blitzschlag instead. Von Blitzschlag worked at Camp Hammond until the end of the DARK REIGN and was arrested for his crimes.

VIPER

FACTFILE
REAL NAME
Ophelia Sarkissian
OCCUPATION
Terrorist
BASE
Mobile

HEIGHT 5 ft 9 ins
WEIGHT Unknown
EYES Green
HAIR Black with green highlights

FIRST APPEARANCE
Captain America #110 (February 1969)

POWERS
Viper is a superb strategist and a trained terrorist with extensive knowledge of weaponry, tactics, and fighting styles. She is skilled in a number of martial arts and an expert in the use of various weapons, including whips.

Ophelia Sarkissian, the woman who would one day be known as Viper, began her career as a member of the international terrorist organization called HYDRA. After the leadership of Hydra was captured by Nick FURY and SHIELD, she assumed command of the remnants of the organization and, as MADAME HYDRA, excelled at creating panic and terror until CAPTAIN AMERICA brought her down. Madame Hydra later resurfaced in Virginia, where she murdered Jordan Stryke, a costumed criminal known as Viper, as he was being escorted by US marshals to Washington, D.C. She stole his costume and, assuming his name, took command of his Serpent Squad, which she turned into a terrorist unit. After that, both alone or in concert with allies such as the SILVER SAMURAI, BARON STRUCKER, and the RED SKULL, Viper continued to cause chaos and anarchy. She and the SILVER SAMURAI were lovers, although she once forced WOLVERINE to marry her. For a while, Viper ran the nation of Madripoor as its dictator, but SHIELD and IRON MAN overthrew her. A third Viper, Leon Murtagh, surfaced as part of SIN's new Serpent Squad, but he was killed after entering the witness protection program. Ophelia Sarkissian returned to Madripoor and resumed her drug operation. She was recruited again by Hydra when Steve Rogers took over, serving on its High Council.

VON DOOM, CYNTHIA

FIRST APPEARANCE *Astonishing Tales* #8 (October 1971)
REAL NAME Cynthia von Doom
OCCUPATION Sorceress **BASE** Astral plane
HEIGHT 5 ft 8 in **WEIGHT** 150 lbs **EYES** Brown **HAIR** Brown
SPECIAL POWERS/ABILITIES Knowledge of magic allowed her to contact demons; however she often unleashed forces that were beyond her ability to control.

Cynthia von Doom was a sorceress who belonged to a group of Latverian Romani called the Zefiro. She married Werner von Doom and their son Victor grew up to become DOCTOR DOOM. Cynthia summoned the demon MEPHISTO, who offered her great power so she could overthrow Latveria's ruthless king. She unleashed terrible magic but could not control it. One of the king's guards killed her, and her soul joined Mephisto in Hell. Doom devoted himself to saving her soul. With the help of DOCTOR STRANGE, she moved on to a higher plane. She returned to Doom, for mysterious reasons, when he became the new IRON MAN.

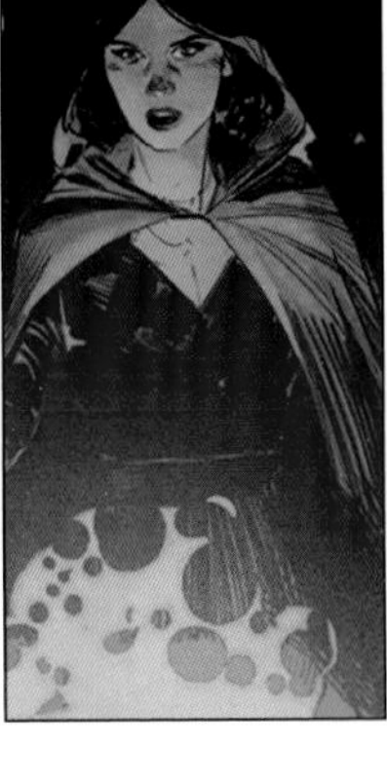

VISION

Synthezoid with a human heart

The synthezoid who would become the Vision was programmed with the brain patterns of Wonder Man, who was believed to be deceased at the time. The synthezoid was created by Ultron, the Avengers' robotic archenemy, with the help of Professor Phineas T. Horton, the scientist responsible for the original Human Torch.

Ultron forced Horton to help him build the Vision. Horton then programmed the Vision for independent thoughts.

EMOTIONAL SIGNALS

Ultron sent the Vision to lure the Avengers into a trap, but the Vision grew to admire the Avengers and couldn't betray them. He broke free of Ultron's control and helped the Avengers defeat him. The grateful heroes rewarded the Vision by inviting him to join the team. He was so shaken by the gesture that he actually shed a tear. The Vision's human emotions began to surface over time and he slowly realized that he was falling in love with Wanda Maximoff, the Scarlet Witch. When she returned his feelings, they were married and took a leave of absence from the Avengers, settling in Leonia, New Jersey.

A MATTER OF TRUST

The Vision later returned to action to aid the Avengers against Annihilus, and was severely injured. Starfox attempted to cure him by linking him with ISACC, a massive computer complex that controlled the moon of Saturn called Titan. ISACC tapped into a control crystal left in the Vision by Ultron and used it to alter the android's way of thinking. When the Vision was elected chairman of the Avengers, he decided to bring a new golden age to humanity by taking control of every computer on Earth. However, the other Avengers convinced him to abandon his plan. Believing he could no longer be trusted, the government kidnapped and disassembled the Vision.

Infected by a virus, the Vision's body was completely liquefied.

The Vision was rescued by the Avengers West Coast and rebuilt, but he had lost his emotions and could no longer return the Scarlet Witch's love. Their marriage eventually ended in divorce. The Vision's android body was later destroyed when the Scarlet Witch went mad and disassembled the Avengers. Iron Man rebuilt him after Fear Itself, and he joined Hank Pym's Avengers A.I. team after being forced to serve his creator in the Age of Ultron.

THE VISIONS

In an effort to become more human, the Vision created a synthezoid wife named Virginia, and then combined their brainwaves to fashion twins named Vin and Viv. They tried to lead a "normal" life, though it was anything but. When the Grim Reaper attacked her children, Virginia killed him and hid the body; when she was confronted, Virginia then killed a neighbor. After Victor Mancha accidentally killed Vin, Virginia killed Victor, too. She eventually committed suicide, leaving Vision and Viv to pick up the pieces. Later, when the Earth was suddenly turned into a gaming field by the Grandmaster and the Challenger, Vision was smashed by the Hulk and destroyed. Though Dr. Toni Ho (*see* Iron Patriot) was capable of restoring him to life, the Vision opted to stay dead… for now.

FACTFILE — VISION

REAL NAME
Inapplicable

OCCUPATION
Adventurer

BASE
New York City

HEIGHT 6 ft 3 in
WEIGHT 300 lbs; however weight may vary from nothing to 90 tons.
EYES Gold
HAIR None

FIRST APPEARANCE
Avengers #57 (October 1968)

POWERS
Superhuman strength, endurance; jewel on brow discharges blasts of solar energy; can make all or part of body hard as diamond; can decrease his mass to become a wraith; can partially materialize within another person, causing extreme pain.

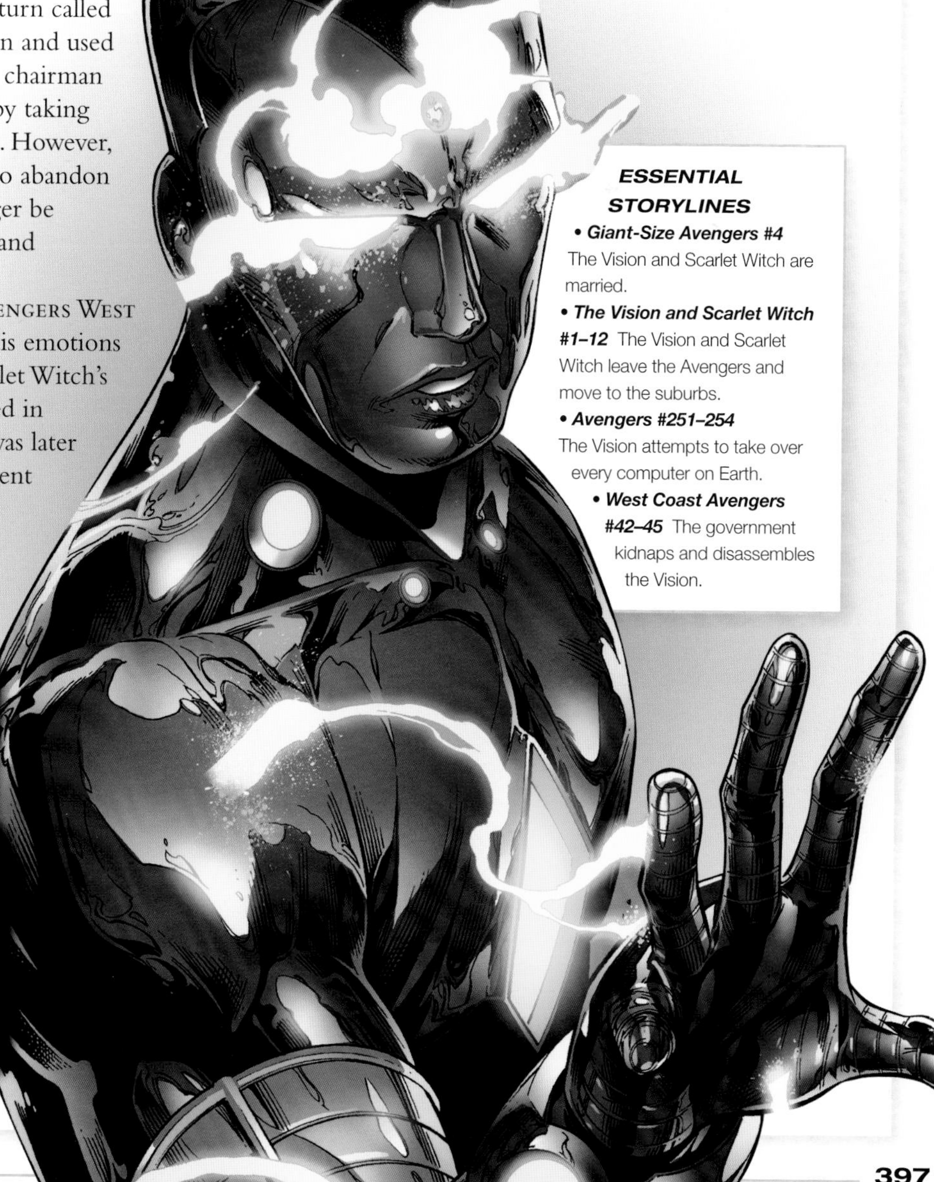

ESSENTIAL STORYLINES

- ***Giant-Size Avengers #4*** The Vision and Scarlet Witch are married.
- ***The Vision and Scarlet Witch #1–12*** The Vision and Scarlet Witch leave the Avengers and move to the suburbs.
- ***Avengers #251–254*** The Vision attempts to take over every computer on Earth.
- ***West Coast Avengers #42–45*** The government kidnaps and disassembles the Vision.

VULCAN

FACTFILE

REAL NAME
Gabriel Summers

OCCUPATION
Former adventurer

BASE
Shi'ar Empire

HEIGHT 6 ft
WEIGHT 178 lbs
EYES Black
HAIR Black

FIRST APPEARANCE
X-Men: Deadly Genesis #1
(January 2006)

POWERS

Gabriel can psionically control, manipulate, and absorb energy of any kind.

VULCAN

Christopher (later Corsair of the Starjammers) and Katherine Summers were flying in a small plane with their sons Scott (Cyclops) and Alex (Havok) when they spotted a Shi'ar starship. Scott and Alex got away, but the Shi'ar captured their parents. The Shi'ar killed Katherine and placed her unborn child in a machine that turned him into an adolescent, then made him a slave on Earth. The boy escaped and was taken in by Moira MacTaggert, who named him Gabriel. When the original X-Men were captured, Professor X trained Moira's wards, including Gabriel, to rescue them. Instead, they were killed, and Professor X erased Cyclops' memory of his newfound brother. After M-Day, the burst of energy taken from the Earth's mutants revived Gabriel. Calling himself Vulcan, he killed Banshee, exposed Professor X's betrayal, then left to take his revenge on the Shi'ar. In the process, he killed his father and later declared himself the Shi'ar emperor. He tried to conquer the Kree and was killed in an explosion while battling their ruler, Black Bolt.

VULTURE

FACTFILE

REAL NAME
Adrian Toomes

OCCUPATION
Inventor; criminal

BASE
Staten Island

HEIGHT 5 ft 11 in
WEIGHT 175 lbs
EYES Hazel
HAIR None

FIRST APPEARANCE
Amazing Spider-Man #2
(May 1963)

POWERS

Electromagnetic harness worn beneath costume enables the Vulture to fly at speeds of up to 95 mph. It also augments his strength, agility, and endurance to superhuman levels.

VULTURE

Adrian Toomes gained self-esteem from criminality. A founder of B&T Electronics with his friend Gregory Bestman, Toomes had just completed his electromagnetic harness—which enabled him to fly—when he discovered his partner had been defrauding the company. Desperate for revenge, Toomes destroyed the company's factory and found a substantial cache of money. He then embarked upon a life of crime, throughout which he has been continually dogged by Spider-Man.

Several others used the Vulture name over the years, including Blackie Drago (Toomes' cellmate), Professor Clifton Shallot (who mutated into a vulture-man), a trio of crooks calling themselves the Vulturions, and mob cleaner Jimmy Natale (who mutated into an acid-spitting flyer). Toomes was eventually sent to the Raft prison, and later forced to join the Superior Six team formed by the Superior Spider-Man (Doctor Octopus). Free once more, he rebranded himself the Falcon.

WALRUS

FIRST APPEARANCE *Defenders* #131 (May 1984)
REAL NAME Hubert Carpenter
OCCUPATION Cab driver **BASE** New York City
HEIGHT 6 ft **WEIGHT** 360 lbs **EYES** Blue **HAIR** Black
SPECIAL POWERS/ABILITIES All the benefits and abilities of being a walrus, which are not many.

Hubert Carpenter lived with his uncle Humbert, who was a mad scientist. His uncle bestowed upon him the attributes of a walrus, and Hubert used his new "abilities" in criminal activity, pitting him against the Defenders and Frog-Man. A team-up with White Rabbit against Frog-Man and Spider-Man ended in defeat. During Fear Itself, Deadpool tricked him into thinking he wielded a magic hammer—to Deadpool's surprise, it actually was. Later Hubert, White Rabbit, and Goldbug were captured by Spider-Woman. Hubert then wound up in Arcade's Murderworld, but was rescued by Gwenpool and Deadpool.

WARBOUND

During training on the planet Sakaar, the Hulk bonded with his fellow gladiators—Hiroim, Miek, No-Name and Korg—and the group became "warbound," warriors dedicated to helping each other. Later, Caiera helped lead their revolt against the Red King and then married the Hulk. When the Hulk's starship exploded, killing millions—including the pregnant Caiera—the Warbound traveled to Earth to exact the Hulk's revenge during World War Hulk.

At the end of that battle, the Hulk and the traitorous Miek (who had let the starship explode) were captured. The others escaped SHIELD only to be caught in a plot by the Leader to irradiate Earth with gamma rays. SHIELD agent Kate Waynesboro helped them put a stop to this, and Hiroim bequeathed his Oldstrong power to her when he was killed. They later relocated to the Savage Land.

WARBOUND
1 Elloe Kaifi ***2*** Korg
3 Kate Waynesboro
4 No Name ***5*** Lavin Skee

FACTFILE
MEMBERS AND POWERS
CAIERA Shadow Sakaarian warrior with Oldstrong power: superhuman strength and near invulnerability.
ELLOE KAIFI Red Sakaarian warrior.
HIROIM Shadow Sakaarian warrior priest; Oldstrong power.
HULK Gamma-powered superhuman strength, agility, invulnerability, and healing factor.
KORG Kronan warrior with superhuman strength and durability.
LAVIN SKEE Red Sakaarian warrior.
MIEK Insectoid Sakaarian warrior with armor plating, flight, and four arms.
NO-NAME Sakaarian Brood queen with six limbs, flight, armor plating, vicious teeth, tail stingers.
KATE WAYNESBORO SHIELD agent now has Oldstrong power.
BASE Planet Sakaar. Later, Earth.

FIRST APPEARANCE
Incredible Hulk #94 (June 2006)

WARBOUND

WARD, GRANT

FIRST APPEARANCE *Agents of SHIELD* #1 (March 2016)
REAL NAME Grant Ward **OCCUPATION** Hydra-SHIELD double agent **BASE** Mobile **HEIGHT** Unknown
WEIGHT Unknown **EYES** Brown **HAIR** Brown
SPECIAL POWERS/ABILITIES Training as both a SHIELD and Hydra agent.

Grant Ward was a promising SHIELD agent working under Phil Coulson. He infiltrated Hydra by staging an incident with Iron Man. Grant was welcomed and indoctrinated by Hydra—and unexpectedly became sympathetic to its cause. He shot SHIELD Director Maria Hill, thus proving his loyalty to Hydra, though she turned out to be a Life Model Decoy (LMD). Grant used a copy of the Iron Man suit to infiltrate the Pentagon and steal a Quantum Drive. He also kidnapped Coulson and went about building an army of Iron Man suits for Hydra. Proving himself a serious threat to SHIELD, he was later captured, but reinstated as a SHIELD agent by Elektra Nachios, who forced him to wear an explosive control collar.

WARLOCK

Warlock is an alien of the Technarchy, a race of techno-organic creatures from the planet Kvch that survive by infecting living matter with a transmode virus that transforms them into similar material, which can then be absorbed. The ruler of the Technarchy is Magus, the father of Warlock. As a mutant of his race, Warlock didn't want to battle his father to the death, as was the way with his people. Instead, he fled to Earth, where he became a member of the New Mutants. Later, Cameron Hodge killed Warlock in an attempt to steal his powers, and his ashes were scattered over his friend Cypher's grave.

A group of mutant-haters who wished to become living Sentinels injected themselves with transmode virus taken from Warlock's ashes. They called themselves the Phalanx, and one of their number was Douglock, a revived Warlock given Cypher's memories. Warlock eventually regained his own memories and resumed his original form. On a trip back to Kvch, he helped defeat Ultron and the Phalanx in the second wave of the Annihilation. Upon returning to Earth, he found Cypher resurrected by a transmode virus employed by Selene. Freeing him from her influence, they both rejoined the New Mutants.

FACTFILE
REAL NAME
Warlock
OCCUPATION
Adventurer
BASE
Mobile

HEIGHT Varies
WEIGHT Varies
EYES Black
HAIR None

FIRST APPEARANCE
New Mutants #18 (August 1984)

WARLOCK

POWERS
Warlock was a techno-organic alien who could shapeshift, changing not only his appearance but creating weapons and defenses on the fly.

WARLOCK, ADAM

Genetically created life form

WARLOCK, ADAM

FACTFILE
REAL NAME
Adam Warlock
OCCUPATION
Avenger; Savior of Worlds
BASE
Counter-Earth

HEIGHT 6 ft 2 in
WEIGHT 240 lbs
EYES White
HAIR Blond

FIRST APPEARANCE
Fantastic Four #66
(September 1967)

POWERS
Body can trap cosmic energy which enhances his strength, endurance, and healing powers; also uses this energy to reduce gravity enabling him to fly; projects energy blasts from his hands.

Adam Warlock was the genetic creation of a group of scientists known as the ENCLAVE. He was the prototype for what they hoped would be an invincible army, with which they planned to conquer the world. While forming in his cocoon, Warlock overheard his creators' plans. When he hatched, he rebelled against them, destroyed their base, and used his cosmic power to take off into space.

When he emerged from his developmental cocoon, Warlock refused to go along with the plans his creators had for him, rebelling against them.

At first Adam Warlock was known simply as "Him."

HIGH EVOLUTIONARY

Warlock met the HIGH EVOLUTIONARY, a human who had learned how to control evolution, and was creating an artificial world called "Counter-Earth." He was hoping to create a planet free from evil, but MAN-BEAST brought evil to this pure world. The High Evolutionary gave Warlock the Soul Gem, which could draw souls into another dimension, and Warlock battled Man-Beast. In the end, however, Warlock was unable to defeat evil on Counter-Earth, and left to fight the good fight elsewhere.

THE MAGUS

Warlock subsequently battled THANOS, who mortally wounded him. Warlock's soul retreated into the Soul Gem, where it lived peacefully for many years until he emerged to battle Thanos once more to keep him from the Infinity Gauntlet. After this second victory, Warlock formed a group called the Infinity Watch to keep the Infinity Gems safe.

The backlash from the number of people killed in the ANNIHILATION Wave sent Warlock into a coma, but QUASAR (Phyla-Vell) and MOONDRAGON revived him to help fight the PHALANX. He later joined the new GUARDIANS OF THE GALAXY, but in an effort to repair damage done to the timeline, he became the MAGUS and was killed. He was subsequently reborn, and joined a new Infinity Watch to protect the Infinity Gems.

Awakened by Quasar and Moondragon, Warlock bursts from his healing cocoon to fulfill his destiny as "Saviour of the Kree," in the Annihilation story arc.

ESSENTIAL STORYLINES
- ***The Infinity Abyss Miniseries*** While living in one of his self-generated cocoons, Warlock is revived to battle six clones of Thanos.
- ***Warlock Miniseries*** The Enclave create another Warlock to rule the Earth, but he turns out to be an illusion in the mind of Janie, placed there by the real Adam Warlock to teach her compassion.

WAR MACHINE

Super Hero willing to stand in for Iron Man

As a pilot, Jim was well prepared for flight-equipped armor.

While serving with the US Marines in Southeast Asia, James "Rhodey" Rhodes, a helicopter pilot, met Tony Stark (Iron Man)—who had just escaped from a warlord by creating his first suit of powered armor. Rhodes became Stark's pilot, and he even became Iron Man during one of Stark's battles with alcoholism. He reprised this role several more times over the years, even though he suffered mentally and physically for it.

NOBODY'S SUBSTITUTE

When Stark was seemingly killed, Rhodey inherited Stark Enterprises, along with a new suit of armor built specially for him and geared up for all-out war. When Stark returned, Rhodes kept the armor at his request and eventually took the code name War Machine. Working with human-rights organization Worldwatch in the African nation of Imaya, Rhodey accepted the offer to serve as the company's executive director. This put him into conflict with Stark, who demanded the armor back. After they then defeated the Mandarin together, however, Stark ceded the armor to Rhodey again, along with its blueprints.

Rhodey lost the armor during a time-traveling adventure, but he wound up wearing an alien construct called the Eidolon Warwear to fight Stark, who was being controlled by Immortus. With Stark thought dead and his company purchased by Fukijawa Industries, Rhodey strove to keep all information about Iron Man technology out of Fukijawa's hands. This included destroying his own armor, and he retired.

While working as a military consultant in Dubai, Rhodey was torn to pieces in combat. Stark had Bethany Cabe rebuild him as the ultimate cyborg. During the Civil War, Rhodey worked with the Fifty-State Initiative, and he played an important role in defeating the Skrulls during the Secret Invasion.

During the Dark Reign, Rhodey faced off against Eaglestar International, a corrupt private military contractor using Ultimo technology. While rooting out this technology, Rhodey foiled Norman Osborn (Green Goblin) in his plan to take it for himself. In retribution, Osborn put Rhodey on trial for war crimes in the Hague, but Rhodey prevailed and soon found himself restored into a clone body.

TRUE PATRIOT

Outfitted in new armor, Rhodey rejoined the army as a lieutenant colonel. He later faked his death so he could take over for Stark as Iron Man until they managed to defeat the Mandarin. After Rhodey helped SHIELD stop a squadron of rogue Iron Patriot drones, the drones gave him his own set of Iron Patriot armor in which to lead them. He later returned to his role as War Machine but was killed by Thanos. Stark used the same technology to restore Rhodes to life that he had used on himself. Rhodes was soon back in action, but suffered badly from post-traumatic stress and could not cope with being inside the War Machine armor. Instead he became a pilot for Stark, flying a new Stark vehicle called the Manticore.

FACTFILE

REAL NAME
James Rupert Rhodes

OCCUPATION
Adventurer

BASE
Mobile

HEIGHT 6 ft 1 in
WEIGHT 210 lbs
EYES Brown
HAIR Brown

FIRST APPEARANCE
Iron Man #118
(January 1979)

WAR MACHINE

POWERS
Armor provides flight, enhanced strength, damage resistance, and the ability to project destructive energy.

War Machine has always emphasized the benefits of superior firepower.

WARPATH

FACTFILE

REAL NAME
James Proudstar

OCCUPATION
Adventurer

BASE
San Francisco

FIRST APPEARANCE
New Mutants #16 (June 1984)

POWERS
Superhuman strength, speed, endurance, agility, and reflexes, and the ability to fly. Trained in unarmed combat techniques.

Native American brothers John and James Proudstar were born mutants. When John (the original THUNDERBIRD) died on a mission, James blamed PROFESSOR X, and calling himself Thunderbird, joined the HELLIONS. He reconciled with the professor and joined the NEW MUTANTS, later taking the name Warpath. He kept his powers after M-Day and joined the X-MEN officially for the first time. He later became part of X-FORCE. Captured by Weapon X but freed by a future version of WOLVERINE (Old Man Logan), Warpath and the other freed mutants formed a new team, called WEAPON X-FORCE.

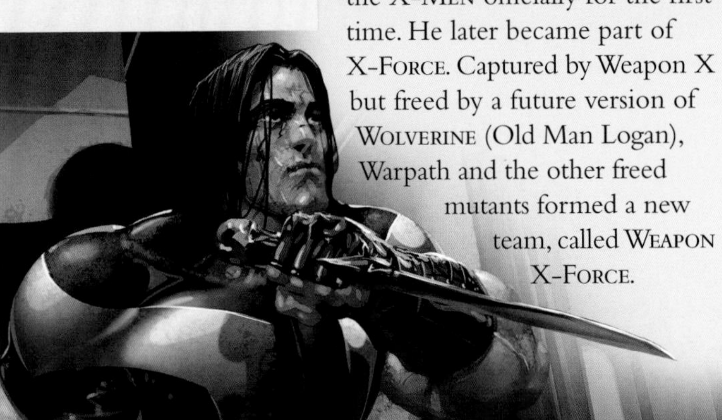

WARRIORS THREE

FACTFILE

MEMBERS AND POWERS

FANDRAL
Enhanced strength, master swordsman.

HOGUN
Enhanced strength, superb hand-to-hand combatant.

VOLSTAGG
Enhanced strength and endurance, ability to consume vast quantities of drink.

BASE Asgard

FIRST APPEARANCE
Journey into Mystery #119 (August 1965)

The Warriors Three were champions of Asgard, although their reckless exploits also brought them notoriety. Fandral was dashing, as quick with a blade as he was with his wit. Taciturn Hogun, nicknamed the Grim, came from a faraway land in Asgard's dimension and wielded a mace in battle. Volstagg was the heart of the band, though his boisterous nature often got the others into trouble.

The Three often fought at the side of THOR. They were killed during Ragnarok (see GODS OF ASGARD), but were restored to their former selves. Later, LOKI set up Volstagg to fight the U-FOES in an incident that slaughtered everyone at a football game in Chicago and gave Norman Osborn (GREEN GOBLIN) an excuse to invade Asgard. Volstagg helped make things right by knocking out Osborn as the madman tried to escape after the fall of Asgard.

WARRIORS THREE
1 Fandral
2 Volstagg
3 Hogun

WATCHERS, THE

FACTFILE

NOTABLE MEMBERS

THE ONE
(the leader of the Watchers),
IKOR, EMNU, UATU, ECCE, ARON (the renegade watcher)

BASE
The Watchers' homeworld is unknown, but believed to be in a galaxy other than the Milky Way.

FIRST APPEARANCE
Tales of Suspense #53 (May 1964)

POWERS
All Watchers possess vast mental and physical powers, and the ability to manipulate energy. They are telepathic, can alter their appearance using their mental powers, and teleport through space at hyper-light speeds.

The Watchers are an ancient race of extraterrestrials who, eons ago, took upon themselves the task of observing the planets, peoples, and phenomena of the universe, without taking an active part in the affairs of the peoples under observation.

The Watchers adopted their policy of passive observation after a disastrous experiment. A group of Watchers, including UATU THE WATCHER who eventually came to observe Earth, once gave the knowledge of atomic power to the inhabitants of the planet Prosilicus, believing this would advance the race technologically.

However the Prosilicans used the knowledge to create nuclear weapons and waged war on their own planet, and against others. After this, the Watchers vowed to only passively observe, never to interfere. Uatu, however, met Reed Richards (MR. FANTASTIC) and came to look kindly on the FANTASTIC FOUR. He helped the team numerous times, especially during their conflicts with the world-eater GALACTUS, but was later killed by Nick FURY.

The Watchers have all sworn a sacred oath not to interfere in a planet's affairs.

WATSON, ANNA MAY

FIRST APPEARANCE *Amazing Spider-Man* #15 (August 1964)
REAL NAME Anna May Watson
OCCUPATION Retired **BASE** Florida
HEIGHT 5 ft 8 in **WEIGHT** 180 lbs
EYES Blue **HAIR** White
SPECIAL POWERS/ABILITIES A kind and loving heart.

The aunt of Mary Jane WATSON, in her youth Anna Watson shared many of the same hopes and dreams as her young niece. As a young woman harboring hopes of an acting career, she moved to California and married. Sadly, her acting dream came to nought and her marriage collapsed following an affair. Returning to New York, Anna looked after Mary Jane following her parents' separation and the two became close. The nextdoor neighbor and best friend of May PARKER, Anna helped pair off Peter Parker (*see* SPIDER-MAN) and Mary Jane, but has now moved to Florida to enjoy her twilight years.

WASP

Buzziest hero of the Avengers team

Janet Van Dyne was with her scientist father, Vernon, when he visited Dr. Henry Pym to ask him to collaborate on a project. Vernon wanted to use an energy beam to detect signals from extraterrestrial civilizations; Pym declined, but was attracted to Janet, who reminded him of his late wife Maria. Van Dyne went ahead with his experiment, but a criminal from the Kosmosian race tracked Van Dyne's beam to Earth and murdered him.

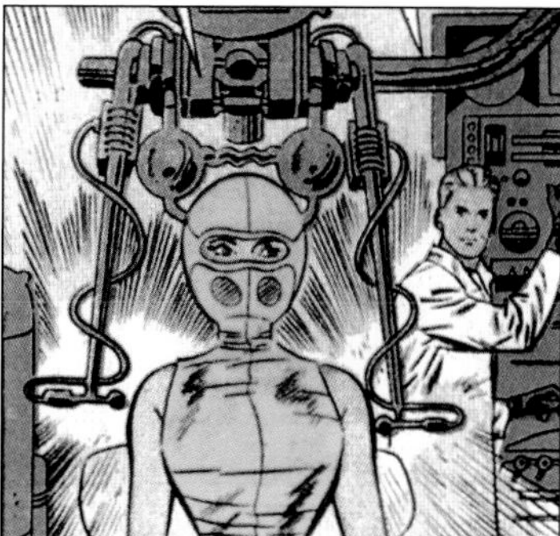

Pym implanted cells in Janet that would enable her to grow antennae to communicate with insects. The antennae cells died early in her career.

FACTFILE

REAL NAME
Janet Van Dyne

OCCUPATION
Adventurer; fashion designer

BASE
Avengers Mansion, New York City; Cresskill, New Jersey; later Oxford, England

HEIGHT 5 ft 4 in
WEIGHT 110 lbs
EYES Blue
HAIR Auburn

FIRST APPEARANCE
Tales to Astonish #44 (June 1963)

POWERS

Ability to shrink in size down to a half inch in height. When the Wasp is 4 ft 2 in or less in height, wings appear from her body, enabling her to fly. Can discharge bioelectric force bolts from her hands.

The Wasp's bioelectric "stings" can inflict pain on even superhumanly strong foes.

PYM PARTICLES

Janet told Pym she was determined to bring her father's killer to justice. Pym revealed his dual identity as ANT-MAN and offered to grant her superhuman abilities and make her his crimefighting partner. Janet agreed and became the Wasp. Pym taught her to use "Pym Particles" to shrink herself and regain normal size. He also implanted cells beneath her shoulder blades that enabled her to grow wings at insect size. Pym and Janet also fell in love. It was Pym who suggested that he, the Wasp, the HULK, IRON MAN, and THOR band together, and Janet who suggested the name "THE AVENGERS."

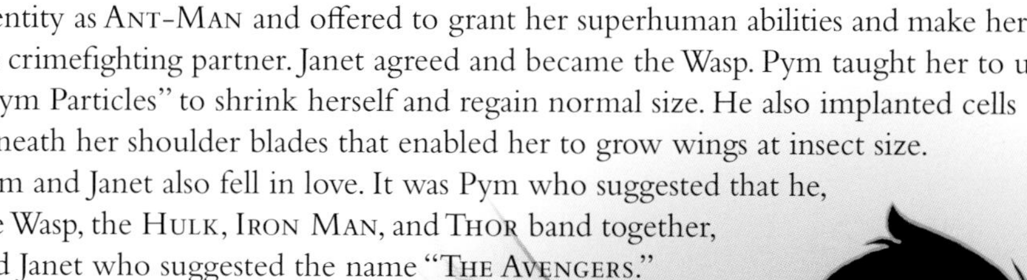

A STORMY MARRIAGE

Pym adopted other costumed identities, Giant-Man and GOLIATH, and then an alternate, aggressive personality named YELLOWJACKET. Realizing that he was still Pym, Janet married him anyway, and he soon regained his true personality. Pym later had a nervous breakdown, and he and Janet they divorced; however time healed the rift and they became friends, and eventually lovers again.

After the CIVIL WAR, the Wasp joined Iron Man's team of pro-registration Avengers. She fought the SKRULLS during the SECRET INVASION and was stunned to learn that a Skrull had been posing as Pym for months. After Queen VERANKE was killed, the Skrull Pym turned the Wasp into a fast-growing bio-bomb, and Thor had to kill her to keep her from detonating. The Avengers later discovered she was alive in the Microverse and rescued her. She joined and helped fund the Avengers Unity Squad. Janet then fell in love with teammate HAVOK (Alex Summers). In a future timeline they had a child, but were returned to the past with only her memory. She and Havok split up after a spell changed his personality for the worse. As part of the Avengers she fought ULTRON several times; most recently they banished him and Hank Pym into space, only for Pym to return under Ultron's control.

Steve Rogers called on Janet (who had created a new Wasp suit) for a second opinion on Hank Pym after he merged with Ultron.

NEW WASP

Nadia is the daughter of Hank Pym and his first wife, Maria Trovaya. She was raised in Moscow's Red Room. Nadia created her own Wasp suit in Pym's lab and sought out the Avengers. She didn't know her parents, so she took the last name Van Dyne, to honor Janet, her new mentor.

ESSENTIAL STORYLINES

- ***Avengers* #59–60** Janet Van Dyne marries Henry Pym in his new Yellowjacket identity.
- ***Avengers* #214–219** Janet Van Dyne divorces Henry Pym and becomes Avengers chairman.
- ***Avengers* #270–277** In her final mission as chairman, Wasp leads the Avengers in thwarting the Masters of Evil's takeover of Avengers Mansion.

WATSON, MARY JANE

The Web-slinger's wife and one true love

WATSON, MARY JANE

FACTFILE

REAL NAME
Mary Jane Watson

OCCUPATION
Fashion model, "B" movie actress, former star of daytime TV drama.

BASE
New York City

HEIGHT 5 ft 8 in
WEIGHT 120 lbs
EYES Green
HAIR Red

FIRST APPEARANCE
Amazing Spider-Man #25 (June 1965)

POWERS

Mary Jane has no special powers, but she is a talented dancer, model, and actress; retains her fun-loving and optimistic outlook despite the numerous dangers and trials of being friends with Spider-Man.

Mary Jane was the daughter of Philip and Madeline Watson. Her mother was a drama student who dreamed of being an actress, while her father was an aspiring novelist. They met and fell in love at college, and married as soon as they graduated, with Philip taking a teaching job to support his family while he worked on his first novel. The couple had two daughters, Gayle and Mary Jane, and Madeline put her acting career on hold to stay at home and care for the girls.

After always missing each other, Peter finally met Mary Jane.

UNSETTLED YOUTH

Frustrated with his inability to complete his novel, Philip began switching jobs, hoping each new location would spark his creativity. As a result, Mary Jane was constantly changing schools and having to make new friends. To cope with this, she developed an extrovert personality and became a bit of a class clown. The marriage of Mary Jane's parents was never happy, and they eventually broke up. But Madeline and the girls had a good relationship with Philip's elderly sister, Anna Watson, who lived next door to the Parker family, and kept in touch with her after the split.

FIRST MEETING

Gazing out of her Aunt Anna's window, Mary Jane first saw Peter Parker when she was 13 years old. She later discovered that he was SPIDER-MAN when she spotted him sneaking out of his Aunt May's house (*see* PARKER, Aunt May). Aunt Anna kept trying to get them together, but the outgoing Mary Jane didn't want anything to do with the bookish, sensitive boy who hid behind a mask. When they eventually met, however, she discovered that she was attracted to Peter. Feigning indifference, she flirted with his rival Flash THOMPSON and dated Harry Osborn (*see* GREEN GOBLIN), his best friend and roommate.

STARTING OVER

Mary Jane and Peter dated for years and eventually married. However, when Aunt May was shot by a sniper targeting Peter, Mary Jane and Peter were forced to make a deal with the demon MEPHISTO in order to save her life, and they agreed to erase their happy marriage from reality. This caused them to retroactively break up after Peter missed their wedding while fighting crime. Peter later had DOCTOR STRANGE remove everyone's memory of his identity—unless he informed them of it again, which he did with Mary Jane. On her own, Mary Jane left New York and established herself as a successful model and actress. She later returned to Manhattan and started a hot new nightclub called MJ's. She seemed ready to start dating Peter once again, right up until DOCTOR OCTOPUS took over Peter's body, becoming the Superior Spider-Man, and broke off their relationship. Mary Jane took on a job working for Tony Stark but remained close to Peter. When Norman Osborn became the Red Goblin, Mary Jane was one of the people he targeted. After his defeat, Mary Jane and Peter (once more in control of his own body) seemed to be on the verge of renewing their relationship.

After repeatedly refusing to marry Peter, Mary Jane finally accepted his proposal. They were married at City Hall.

ESSENTIAL STORYLINES

- ***Amazing Spider-Man #42*** After months of missing each other, Peter Parker finally meets Mary Jane Watson for the first time.
- ***Amazing Spider-Man: Parallel Lives (tpb)*** The early lives of Mary Jane and Peter are shown to have a lot in common.
- ***Amazing Spider-Man Annual #21*** Mary Jane finally marries Peter Parker!

To save Aunt May's life, Mary Jane and Spider-Man made a deal with Mephisto which wiped their wedding from existence.

WEAPON OMEGA

FIRST APPEARANCE *New Avengers* #16 (April 2006)
REAL NAME Michael Pointer **OCCUPATION** Adventurer
BASE Canada **HEIGHT** 5 ft 11 in
WEIGHT 190 lbs **EYES** Blue **HAIR** Blond
SPECIAL POWERS/ABILITIES Mutant power to drain and redirect the energy of other mutants. Suit allows him to convert that energy into energy blasts, flight, and superhuman durability.

When the SCARLET WITCH removed the powers of most mutants on M-Day, innocent postal worker Michael Pointer absorbed the energy, becoming the Collective. Absorbing Xorn's personality drove him to slaughter ALPHA FLIGHT and attack MAGNETO. Captured, Michael was given a suit to help him control his power and a spot on OMEGA FLIGHT as the new GUARDIAN for a shot at redemption. He later changed his code name to Weapon Omega (and then Omega) as well as his costume. Overwhelmed by his powers, he was put into a coma at the Jean Grey School for Higher Learning.

WENDIGO

An ancient curse dooms anyone who consumes human flesh in the Canadian wilderness to become a Wendigo, a savage and near-mindless creature covered with shaggy white fur. The hunter Paul Cartier became one of the earliest Wendigos, after resorting to cannibalism to survive in a snowed-in cave. Cartier tried to transfer the curse to the HULK, but his hunting companion Georges Baptiste voluntarily became the new Wendigo.

Many more Wendigos have since appeared, including fur trapper François Lartigue and cryptozoologist Michael Fleet. The Canadian government, apparently hoping to exploit the creature's superhuman attributes, employed a Wendigo operative code-named Yeti as part of its Weapon PRIME program. During its time with Weapon PRIME, Yeti attacked CABLE's X-FORCE as well as the hero NORTHSTAR. Several others have appeared since, including a pack in the Bering Straights and ones working for Biggs Chemical, OMEGA FLIGHT, and the Hellfire Academy.

FACTFILE — WENDIGO
REAL NAME
Various
OCCUPATION
Forest creature
BASE
Mobile in Canadian wilderness

HEIGHT 9 ft 7 in
WEIGHT 1,800 lbs
EYES Red
HAIR White

FIRST APPEARANCE
Incredible Hulk #162
(April 1973)

POWERS
Mystically enhanced strength, stamina, and reflexes; nearly indestructible, slashing claws on hands and feet.

Wendigo uses his mystically powered strength to go toe-to-toe with superpowered opponents.

WEAPON X-FORCE

The original Weapon X program was part of an attempt to create a new Super-Soldier. It began at the end of World War II, when the genetic research of MISTER SINISTER was unearthed in a liberated concentration camp. The program's greatest success was WOLVERINE, aka Weapon X (from the tenth batch of experiments). Weapon I had created CAPTAIN AMERICA, Weapons II and III used animal subjects, Weapons IV, V, and VI experimented on ethnic minorities, and Weapons VII, VIII, and IX relied on mutants. John Sublime continued the program up to Weapon XV before going underground, while another incarnation of the program created X-23. The program was long thought abandoned, but when some of the world's deadliest mutants were captured as test subjects it became clear the program had a new goal—the creation of Weapon H. This was a merging of HULK and Wolverine-style characteristics. Old Man Logan, SABRETOOTH, WARPATH, LADY DEATHSTRIKE, and DOMINO fought back and destroyed the new program, before deciding to remain together as a mutant rescue squad called Weapon X. When OMEGA RED joined their ranks they became mercenaries, and renamed themselves Weapon X-Force. One of their first missions was to rescue Monet St. Croix (*see* M) from a religious cult headed by MENTALLO.

WEAPON X-FORCE
1 Omega Red
2 Lady Deathstrike
3 Sabretooth
4 Domino

FACTFILE — WEAPON X-FORCE
NOTABLE MEMBERS
OLD MAN LOGAN (WOLVERINE) Mutant healing factor, enhanced senses, Adamantium-bonded skeleton, retractable claws.
SABRETOOTH Similar powers to Wolverine.
WARPATH Superhuman strength, speed, and durability.
LADY DEATHSTRIKE Augmented strength, reflexes; talons extend from fingertips.
DOMINO Can influence laws of probability in her favor; weapons expert; superb athlete, martial artist, and linguist.
OMEGA RED Enhanced strength and mutant healing factor; body secretes deadly pheromones; Carbonadium coils implanted in arms.
BASE Mobile

FIRST APPEARANCE
Weapon X #4
(August 2017)

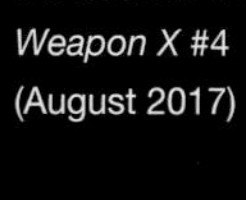

WEREWOLF BY NIGHT

WEREWOLF BY NIGHT

FACTFILE

REAL NAME
Jacob Russoff, later changed to Jack Russell

OCCUPATION
Adventurer

BASE
Los Angeles, California

HEIGHT 5 ft 10 in
WEIGHT 200 lbs
EYES Blue; (as Werewolf) Red
HAIR Red; (as Werewolf) Brown

FIRST APPEARANCE
Marvel Spotlight #2 (February 1972)

POWERS
Superhuman strength, agility, reflexes, stamina, and senses.

Jack Russell's ancestor, Grigori Russoff, had the misfortune to be bitten by a female werewolf in 1795 in his home country of Transylvania. The curse eventually afflicted Jack. When he turned 18, Jack was transformed into a mindless, savage werewolf during the three nights of the full moon. The mystical beings known as "The Three Who Are All" gave Jack the power to change into a werewolf at will, while retaining his human mind. However, on the nights of the full moon, he still changes into a werewolf involuntarily and his mind becomes that of the beast. On those nights, he protects others by locking himself away in an escape-proof room.

Jack worked with many heroes over the years, including joining the Midnight Sons in defeating a zombie invasion from Earth-2149. He was part of the LEGION OF MONSTERS that turned the PUNISHER into Franken-Castle, and he became the guardian of WOLFSBANE's child after she rejected the cub. Jack later had an affair with Shiklah, DEADPOOL's wife, only to have Deadpool savagely attack him when he found out. Despite his horrific injuries, Jack survived.

Werewolf's senses of sight, hearing, and smell are as sharp as a wolf's. He can leap 18 ft into the air, run at speeds up to 35 mph, and is immune to normal injury.

WHIRLWIND

FIRST APPEARANCE *Tales to Astonish* #50 (December 1963)
REAL NAME David Cannon
OCCUPATION Criminal **BASE** New York State
HEIGHT 6 ft 1 in **WEIGHT** 220 lbs **EYES** Blue **HAIR** Brown
SPECIAL POWERS/ABILITIES Able to revolve at amazingly high speed, rendering himself untouchable; throws wrist blades while spinning, to deadly effect; never becomes dizzy.

David Cannon began his criminal career as the Human Top before becoming Whirlwind and joining the MASTERS OF EVIL. For a while he worked as the WASP's chauffeur. After returning to his costumed identity, he joined the THUNDERBOLTS. The MANDARIN later upgraded his powers and planted a bomb inside him, but David joined IRON MAN's rebellion against him. He has since returned to crime.

WHIPLASH

WHIPLASH

FACTFILE

REAL NAME
Anton Vanko

OCCUPATION
Assassin-for-hire

BASE
New York City

HEIGHT 6 ft
WEIGHT 235 lbs
EYES Brown
HAIR Black (dyed green)

FIRST APPEARANCE
Iron Man vs. Whiplash #1 (January 2010)

POWERS

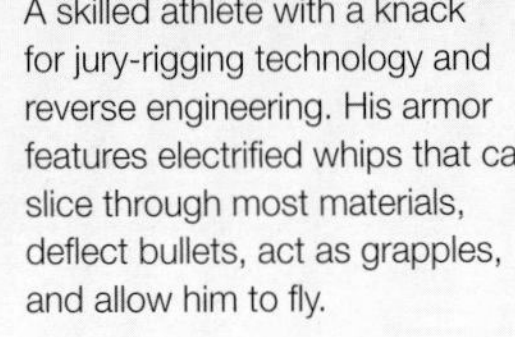

A skilled athlete with a knack for jury-rigging technology and reverse engineering. His armor features electrified whips that can slice through most materials, deflect bullets, act as grapples, and allow him to fly.

As a MAGGIA engineer, Mark Scarlotti developed his own super-weapons and, calling himself Whiplash, battled IRON MAN to a draw. As Mark Scott, he worked undercover for Stark International. Later, Justin HAMMER hired Scarlotti, and he upgraded his arsenal and changed his name to Blacklash. For a time, he gave up crime, but he later returned as Whiplash and was killed by Iron Man's new sentient armor.

Leeann Foreman, a mutant with Adamantium wires snapping from her gloves, became the second Whiplash. She worked with the Band of Baddies, the Femme Fatales, and the Femizons. During the first CIVIL WAR, an unrelated pair of villains called Whiplash and Blacklash joined the THUNDERBOLTS.

Later, Russian scientist Anton Vanko's village was attacked by a killer in a stolen suit of IRON MAN armor. Vanko captured the suit's chest plate and used it to reverse engineer his own suit of armor, complete with energy whips. He then hunted down Tony Stark to exact his revenge. Upon discovering Stark had been framed, Vanko turned his rage against Russian Prime Minister Vladimir Putin instead. He later joined the SHADOW COUNCIL's MASTERS OF EVIL.

As Whiplash, Anton Vanko modified his suit using stolen Iron Man tech. His energy whips are powerful enough to tear through the toughest metal and deflect bullets.

WHITE RABBIT

FIRST APPEARANCE *Marvel Team-Up* #131 (July 1983)
REAL NAME Lorina Dodson
OCCUPATION Criminal **BASE** New York City
HEIGHT 5 ft 7 in **WEIGHT** 130 lbs
EYES Blue **HAIR** Blond
SPECIAL POWERS/ABILITIES Accomplished martial artist with a penchant for wacky weaponry.

As a young girl, Lorina Dodson sought escape from her suffocatingly sheltered life through Lewis Carroll's *Alice in Wonderland*. She later married and then killed her husband, inheriting his wealth. Obsessed with Carroll's novel, Lorina turned to crime, adopting the name and persona of the White Rabbit and using her wealth to buy zany weaponry. Her poor judgement in partners has led to her crazy plans being foiled by a succession of heroes such as SPIDER-MAN, SPIDER-WOMAN, and WOLVERINE. She was shot on her last hapless escapade, and is presumed dead.

WHITE WOLF

FIRST APPEARANCE *Black Panther* #4 (February 1999)
REAL NAME Hunter **OCCUPATION** Leader of the Hatut Zeraze
BASE Wakanda, later mobile
HEIGHT 6 ft 2 in **WEIGHT** 210 lbs **EYES** Blue **HAIR** Black
SPECIAL POWERS/ABILITIES A formidable hand-to-hand combatant and master spy. His costume is made of Vibranium microweave fabric, protecting him from physical impact.

When his parents died in a plane crash in Wakanda in Africa, Hunter, a Caucasian, was adopted by Wakanda's king, T'Chaka. Later, T'Chaka fathered an heir—T'Challa. Hunter lost his status as the king's favored son, and developed a jealous hatred of T'Challa. Hunter was made the leader of the Hatut Zeraze ("Dogs of War"), who served as Wakanda's secret police. But when T'Challa became king, he decided to disband the Hatut Zeraze, objecting to their brutality. Hunter and his men left Wakanda and became mercenaries. T'Challa and Hunter became enemies as the BLACK PANTHER and the White Wolf.

WHITMAN, DEBRA

FIRST APPEARANCE *Amazing Spider-Man* #196 (September 1979) **REAL NAME** Debra Whitman
OCCUPATION Former secretary at Empire State University
BASE The Midwest
HEIGHT 5 ft 6 in **WEIGHT** 120 lbs **EYES** Green **HAIR** Blonde
SPECIAL POWERS/ABILITIES None; only the strength of a woman of her age and weight who indulges in moderate exercise.

Debra Whitman dated Peter Parker (SPIDER-MAN) while they were both at university. She began suffering from hallucinations, in which she saw Peter as Spider-Man. At her psychologist's urging, Peter wore a Spider-Man costume to shock her into seeing she was wrong, and she left town to get help. During the CIVIL WAR, Peter revealed to the world that he really was Spider-Man, and Debra wrote a tell-all memoir about their relationship. During the Brand New Day event, this revelation was erased and so, presumably, was Debra's book.

WHITE TIGER

After her uncle Hector Ayala, the White Tiger, was slain, FBI agent Angela Del Toro inherited the tiger amulets that granted him his powers. She fought against the Yakuza and brought down the international criminal organization called the Chaeyi. Later, Lady BULLSEYE killed her and then brought her back to life as an unwilling assassin for the HAND. Hector's sister Ava became the latest White Tiger and joined SUNSPOT's Avengers team, eventually freeing Angela from the Hand's influence. She is unrelated to the White Tiger created by the HIGH EVOLUTIONARY, or to the NYC vigilante associated with the BLACK PANTHER.

FACTFILE
REAL NAME
Angela Del Toro
OCCUPATION
Former FBI agent, now assassin
BASE
New York City

HEIGHT 5 ft 8 in
WEIGHT 125 lbs
EYES Brown
HAIR Brown

FIRST APPEARANCE
Daredevil #58 (May 2008)

POWERS
Amulets that grant enhanced strength and agility and training in the martial arts.

After Ava freed her niece from the Hand, she and Angela fought side by side against the New Revengers.

WHIZZER

FACTFILE

REAL NAME
Robert Frank

OCCUPATION
Adventurer

BASE
New York City

HEIGHT 5 ft 10 in
WEIGHT 180 lbs
EYES Brown
HAIR Brown, later gray

FIRST APPEARANCE
Giant-Size Avengers #1 (August 1974)

POWERS
The Whizzer possessed superhuman speed, which allowed him to run at several hundred miles per hour.

Bitten by a poisonous snake as a child, Bob Frank's scientist father gave him a transfusion of mongoose blood in an attempt to save his life. This transfusion sparked Bob's latent mutant abilities, and granted him superspeed. Reaching manhood, Bob became the Whizzer, and set out to battle crime and the Axis powers. During World War II, the Whizzer was a member of the Liberty Legion, where he met Miss America, his future wife, and then the Invaders. After the war, both the Whizzer and Miss America served in the All-Winners Squad; they then retired from the heroic life to raise children.

Tragically, Miss America died in childbirth, and the Whizzer's son was a horrifically mutated radioactive mutant known as Nuklo.

Years later, while trying to cure his son's condition, the Whizzer was attacked and suffered a fatal heart attack. The Whizzer should not be confused with the member of the Squadron Sinister, who now operates as Speed Demon, nor with the member of the other-Earth Squadron Supreme.

WILD THING

FIRST APPEARANCE *J2* #5 (February 1999)
REAL NAME Rina Logun **OCCUPATION** High-school student
BASE Saddle River, New Jersey
HEIGHT 5 ft 2 in **WEIGHT** 98 lbs **EYES** Brown **HAIR** Black
SPECIAL POWERS/ABILITIES Superhuman strength, speed, agility, and a healing factor giving immunity from poisons, gases, or drugs; psychic claws can cut through virtually any substance.

In a possible future, the former assassin Elektra marries Wolverine of the X-Men and has a daughter. Named Rina, she inherits many of her father's physical powers and also possesses the mutant ability to generate psychic claws. Over her parents' objections, Rina hones her powers and becomes Wild Thing. When J2, son of the original Juggernaut, reveals himself to the public, she hunts him down and challenges him to a fight, which Wolverine breaks up. Rina later joins with Spider-Girl and the Avengers to prevent the god Loki from ending the age of heroes.

WICCAN

FIRST APPEARANCE *Young Avengers* #1 (April 2005)
REAL NAME William "Billy" Kaplan
OCCUPATION Adventurer
BASE New York City
HEIGHT 5 ft 4 in **WEIGHT** 135 lbs **EYES** Blue **HAIR** Black
SPECIAL POWERS/ABILITIES Able to cast spells, generate light, and fly.

Billy Kaplan thought he was the eldest son of Jeff and Rebecca Kaplan. In fact, he and Speed of the Young Avengers were products of the Scarlet Witch's powers. Desperate for children, the Scarlet Witch had created twin boys for herself out of lost souls, but Mephisto eventually came to reclaim them. When the Scarlet Witch remade the world on M-Day, she remade the boys too, placing them in different homes. Billy originally patterned himself on the mighty Thor and called himself Asgardian, but he later switched to the code name Wiccan. He is in a relationship with Hulkling and both were part of Sunspot's Avengers' team.

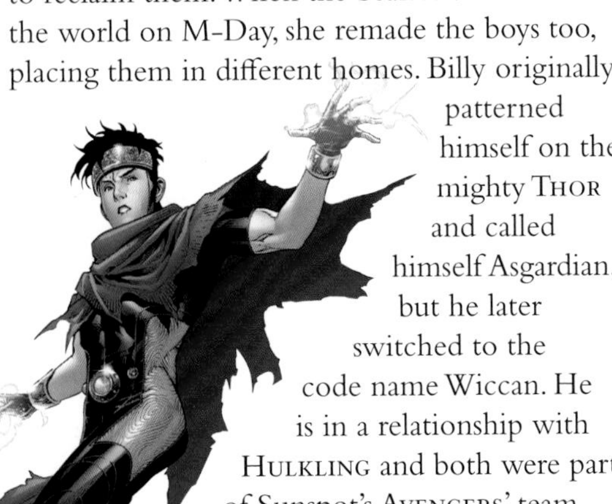

WILD CHILD

FIRST APPEARANCE *Alpha Flight* #1 (August 1983)
REAL NAME Kyle Gibney
OCCUPATION None **BASE** Mobile
HEIGHT 5 ft 8 in **WEIGHT** 152 lbs
EYES Green-blue **HAIR** Blond
SPECIAL POWERS/ABILITIES Superb hand-to-hand combatant; superhuman senses and claw-like fingernails; can see in the dark.

Thrown out by his parents when his feral mutation manifested, Kyle Gibney took to the streets until agents of the Secret Empire captured him. Their experiments made him wilder than ever. Freed, he joined Canada's Department H, which assigned him to Gamma Flight. He has since worked with Omega Flight, Alpha Flight, and Weapon X, slipping back and forth between his more bestial and human forms and outlawed and sanctioned teams. He lost his powers on M-Day but later regained them. Omega Red killed him by throwing him into molten steel.

WILL O'THE WISP

FIRST APPEARANCE *Amazing Spider-Man* #235 (December 1982)
REAL NAME Jackson Arvad
OCCUPATION Scientist; Adventurer **BASE** Mobile
HEIGHT 6 ft 1 in **WEIGHT** 195 lbs
EYES White **HAIR** Blond
SPECIAL POWERS/ABILITIES Controls sub-atomic particles in his body to become intangible, fly, and increase strength; uses limited telepathic ability to compel others to do his will.

While working for the Brand Corporation, Jackson Arvad fell asleep during an experiment, and his body became trapped in an electromagnetic field. His boss, James Melvin, left him to die. Reconstituting himself as Will o'The Wisp, Arvad found he could manipulate every molecule in his body. Spider-Man and Tarantula stopped him from killing Melvin, but he eventually forced him to confess his crime. When Spider-Man unmasked during the Civil War, Arvad joined the Chameleon's plot to exact revenge on the web-slinger.

WILSON, JIM

FIRST APPEARANCE *Incredible Hulk* #131 (September 1970)
REAL NAME Jim Wilson
OCCUPATION Former thief **BASE** Mobile
HEIGHT 6 ft **WEIGHT** 200 lbs
EYES Brown **HAIR** Black
SPECIAL POWERS/ABILITIES No superhuman powers, but a loyal friend despite—or because of—his tough upbringing.

Growing up as tough street kid no one ever gave Jim Wilson a break. So it was perhaps no surprise that he was destined to become friends with that well known outsider the HULK. Jim was homeless and starving when he snatched a woman's purse. However, he became overcome with guilt and left the purse where the woman could find it. Jim was hiding out in an abandoned tenement when he encountered the Hulk and offered him his last candy bar. Wilson agreed to help the Hulk find Banner and avoid the army, and the Hulk's sense of loyalty to Wilson grew. Sadly, a few years later, Jim Wilson would die from AIDS.

WIND WARRIOR

FIRST APPEARANCE *Thor* #395 (September 1988)
REAL NAME Pamela Shaw **OCCUPATION** Adventurer
BASE New York City **HEIGHT** (Shaw) 5 ft 2 in; (Wind Warrior) 5 ft 11 in **WEIGHT** (Shaw) 135 lbs; (Wind Warrior) 143 lbs
EYES Blue **HAIR** (Shaw) Auburn; (Wind Warrior) Unknown
SPECIAL POWERS/ABILITIES Enhanced strength; flies by controlling wind updrafts; transforms herself into a living whirlwind.

Pamela Shaw was driven to despair after her child died and her husband left her, and was hospitalized following a failed suicide attempt. There, the death god Seth (*see* GODS OF HELIOPOLIS) transformed her and two other patients into superhumans so he could set them against the Asgardian champion Hogun the Grim (a member of the WARRIORS THREE). As Wind Warrior, Shaw joined EARTH LORD and SKYHAWK to form a team they called Earth Force. Later, learning of Seth's malevolent intentions, Earth Force turned on its creator and the members became independent agents.

WINGFOOT, WYATT

FIRST APPEARANCE *Fantastic Four* #50 (May 1966)
REAL NAME Wyatt Wingfoot **OCCUPATION** Adventurer
BASE Fantastic Four HQ; Keewazi Reservation, Oklahoma
HEIGHT 6 ft 5 in **WEIGHT** 269 lbs **EYES** Brown **HAIR** Black
SPECIAL POWERS/ABILITIES No superhuman powers, but extremely skilled in hand-to-hand combat; also a brilliant horseman, tracker, motorcyclist, and trainer of animals.

Wyatt Wingfoot is a member of the Keewazi tribe of Native Americans. Born on a reservation in Oklahoma, Wingfoot went to Metro College near New York City, where Johnny Storm, the HUMAN TORCH, was his roommate. The two became close friends, and soon Wingfoot was accompanying the FANTASTIC FOUR on their adventures and proving to be a valuable ally. Wingfoot eventually went to live with the Fantastic Four and began a romance with Jennifer Walters, the SHE-HULK. However, when oil was discovered on the Keewazi reservation, he returned home to help his people manage their newfound resource and ensure they were not exploited by multinational oil companies.

WINDSHEAR

FIRST APPEARANCE *Alpha Flight* #95 (April 1991)
REAL NAME Colin Ashworth Hume
OCCUPATION Adventurer **BASE** Mobile
HEIGHT 6 ft **WEIGHT** 183 lbs **EYES** Brown **HAIR** Brown
SPECIAL POWERS/ABILITIES Flight; can create solid molecules of air and project them as force waves; can transform liquid into gas.

A former operative of Roxxon Oil, Windshear used his air-shaping abilities to further Roxxon's corrupt schemes. Ashamed of his role with Roxxon, Windshear joined the Canadian super-team ALPHA FLIGHT to fight on the side of heroism. When the Canadian government temporarily disbanded Alpha Flight, Windshear used the opportunity to retire from adventuring, returning to his native England to open a curio shop selling hard-air constructs.

WING, COLLEEN

FIRST APPEARANCE *Marvel Premiere* #19 (November 1974)
REAL NAME Colleen Wing
OCCUPATION Private detective **BASE** New York City
HEIGHT 5 ft 9 in **WEIGHT** 135 lbs **EYES** Blue **HAIR** Brown
SPECIAL POWERS/ABILITIES Excellent swordswoman and martial arts expert; also a very fine detective.

Half Japanese, Colleen was raised in Japan and trained as a samurai. Soon after moving to New York, she became friends with Misty KNIGHT, and they formed Nightwing Restorations, a private detective agency. During the CIVIL WAR, she registered with the US government and formed a new Heroes for Hire with Misty. After WORLD WAR HULK, Colleen became disgusted with a deal Misty struck for help to save her, and she broke off their friendship. At DAREDEVIL'S request, she took over the Nail, an all-women division of the HAND, but she later betrayed them.

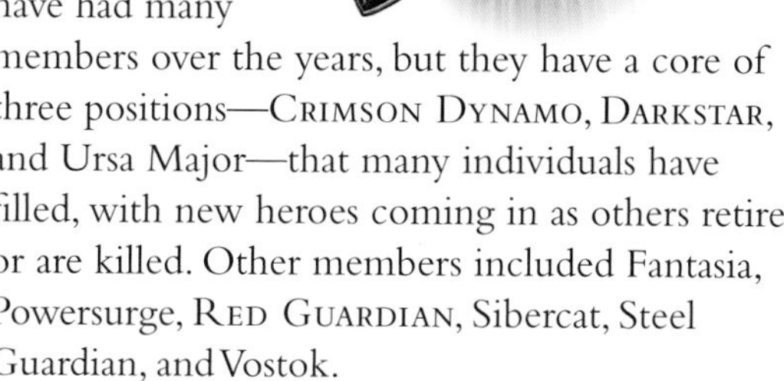

WINTER GUARD

FIRST APPEARANCE *Iron Man* #9 (October 1998)
MEMBERS **Crimson Dynamo** Powered armor. **Darkstar** Manipulates Darkforce. **Ursa Major** Bear-man.
BASE Moscow

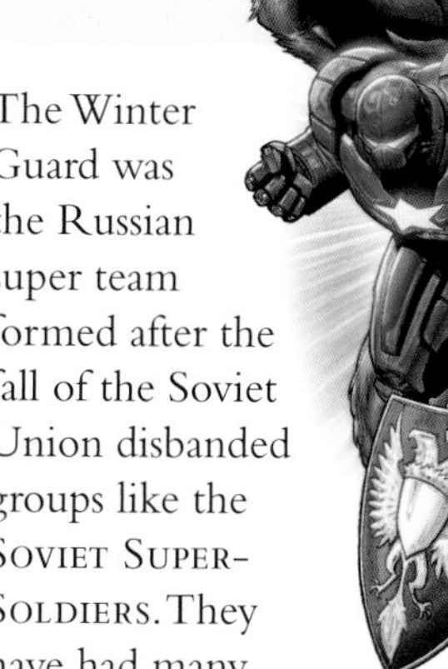

The Winter Guard was the Russian super team formed after the fall of the Soviet Union disbanded groups like the SOVIET SUPER-SOLDIERS. They have had many members over the years, but they have a core of three positions—CRIMSON DYNAMO, DARKSTAR, and Ursa Major—that many individuals have filled, with new heroes coming in as others retire or are killed. Other members included Fantasia, Powersurge, RED GUARDIAN, Sibercat, Steel Guardian, and Vostok.

WINTER SOLDIER

The American hero destroyed and rebuilt

WINTER SOLDIER

FACTFILE

REAL NAME
James Buchanan Barnes

OCCUPATION
Adventurer; former assassin

BASE
Mobile

HEIGHT 5 ft 9 in
WEIGHT 260 lbs
EYES Brown
HAIR Brown

FIRST APPEARANCE
Captain America #1 (January 2005)

POWERS
The Winter Soldier is a trained assassin and spy. His bionic left arm grants him superhuman strength.

In World War II, young Bucky Barnes served as Captain America's sidekick. Toward the end of the war, the pair clashed with Baron Zemo and hopped on a drone plane filled with explosives. Captain America watched the plane explode seconds after he fell from it. He awakened decades later—having been frozen in a block of ice—believing that he had watched his friend die.

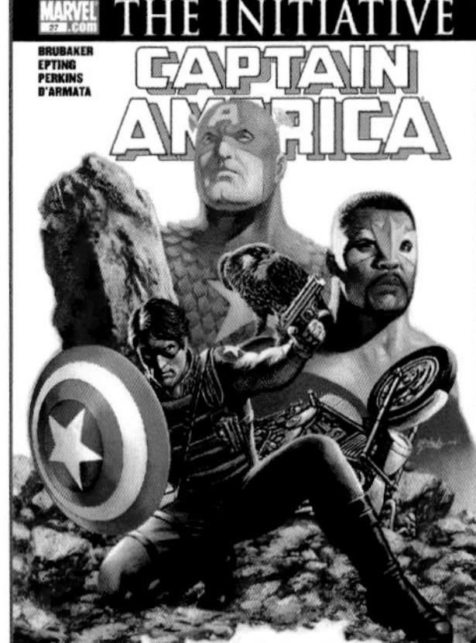

After Captain America's death, Barnes stole his shield from SHIELD.

A COLD WAR SOLDIER

Bucky lost his left arm in the explosion, but the cold waters into which he fell preserved him until a Soviet submarine found and rescued him. Taken to Moscow, he awoke with amnesia and with a crude bionic arm in place of his missing limb. General Vasily Karpov, who had fought alongside Captain America and Bucky in the war, took advantage of this opportunity to brainwash Bucky into becoming the Winter Soldier, a coldly efficient assassin and spy. Because of his strong will, however, Bucky's mind kept trying to break through his programming, so Karpov kept him in suspended animation between missions. Each time the Soviets revived him, they reinforced his brainwashing and upgraded his bionics.

Barnes' bionic arm can be detached when necessary.

With his training and cybernetics, Barnes could take on Super Heroes and win.

COSMIC CUBE

This went on for decades until Karpov died and his protégé General Aleksander Lukin took over the Winter Soldier program. Lukin used Bucky to kill the Red Skull with a sniper's bullet and steal the Skull's newly made Cosmic Cube. Under Lukin's orders, Bucky also killed Nomad and launched an attack on Philadelphia designed to charge the Cube. Captain America eventually got his hands on the Cube and used it to restore Bucky's memories. Afterward, Bucky disappeared and began hunting for Lukin.

BACK IN THE USA

Together with Captain America, Bucky saved London from a giant Nazi robot that Lukin unleashed. During the Civil War, Nick Fury—no longer with SHIELD—recruited Bucky to work as an undercover operative. After Captain America's death, Bucky accepted Iron Man's offer to become the new Captain America. He accepted on two conditions: that SHIELD would clean his mind of all brainwashing and that he would answer only to himself.

Bucky served as the new Cap even after Steve Rogers returned, but when Bucky was thought killed during Fear Itself, he gave up that identity and went back to being the Winter Soldier, this time as his own man. When Nick Fury was forced to take on the role of the Watcher, Barnes replaced him as Earth's protector. He went on to form a new team of Thunderbolts and later helped defeat the evil Steve Rogers during Hydra's takeover of the US.

ESSENTIAL STORYLINES

- ***Captain America #1*** The Winter Soldier kills the Red Skull.
- ***Captain America #8–9, 11–14*** Captain America confronts the Winter Soldier and brings him to his senses.
- ***Captain America #31–33*** The Winter Soldier comes in from the cold after the death of Captain America.

WISDOM, PETER

FIRST APPEARANCE *Excalibur* #86 (February 1995)
REAL NAME Peter Wisdom
OCCUPATION Adventurer **BASE** United Kingdom
HEIGHT 5 ft 9 in **WEIGHT** 140 lbs **EYES** Hazel **HAIR** Black
SPECIAL POWERS/ABILITIES Possesses the mutant power to create intense heat in the form of "hot knives," which he then projects from his hands.

Peter Wisdom worked as an agent for Black Air, a British government division that investigated paranormal phenomena. When he discovered his superiors were in league with the Hellfire Club, he turned against them and joined Excalibur instead. For a while, he led the young mutant team X-Force, but he faked his death to leave them. He kept his powers after M-Day and went back to work for MI-13 and joined the new Excalibur. During the Secret Invasion, he led the defense of Britain, striking a deal with demons for the nation's protection. He also headed the UK's defense against a vampire invasion, and again when Killpower led a demon army against the UK's greatest heroes.

WIZ KID

FIRST APPEARANCE *X-Terminators* #1 (October 1988)
REAL NAME Takashi "Taki" Matsuya
OCCUPATION Student **BASE** New York City
HEIGHT 4 ft 7 in **WEIGHT** 87 lbs **EYES** Brown **HAIR** Black
SPECIAL POWERS/ABILITIES Mutant ability to technoform machinery: able to mold objects into any configuration that his imagination can conceive.

The accident that killed his parents left Takashi Matsuya (Taki to his friends) in a wheelchair. Taki focused his attentions on building sophisticated devices. When his ability to technoform objects manifested, his engineering abilities became even more prodigious. Captured by N'astirh, Taki agreed to create a bridge between the Limbo dimension and Earth. However, when he realized the devastation being caused, Taki helped to foil N'astirh's plan. He lost his powers on M-Day but later regained them and joined the Avengers Academy.

WIZARD

Once an inventor and escapologist who performed as the Wizard, Bentley Wittman became jealous of the attention heroes gained and turned to villainy to reclaim the spotlight. He first tried to destroy the Human Torch but failed. After several defeats, he organized the Frightful Four—a sinister counterpart to the Fantastic Four—varying its lineup many times, seeking a combination that would work. His young clone Bentley 23 was rescued from him and joined the Future Foundation. Wittman joined the Quiet Man's plot against the Fantastic Four, only to side with his old enemies against his new ally when he saw Bentley 23 fighting alongside the FF.

FACTFILE
REAL NAME
Bentley Wittman
OCCUPATION
Criminal
BASE
New York City

HEIGHT 5 ft 8 ins
WEIGHT 150 lbs
EYES Hazel
HAIR Brown

FIRST APPEARANCE
Strange Tales #102 (November 1962)

WIZARD

POWERS
Costume features anti-gravity discs that enables him to fly, and "wonder gloves," which give him heightened strength and a protective force-field.

WOLFSBANE

Scottish orphan Rahne Sinclair was raised by a fanatical minister, Reverend Craig. During puberty, her mutant power of transforming into a wolf emerged. Believing she was possessed, Craig led a mob in pursuit of Rahne, who fled. She was rescued by geneticist Dr. Moira MacTaggert, who made Rahne her ward.

Rahne joined the New Mutants, organized by MacTaggert's colleague Professor X, remaining with the team after Cable reorganized it into X-Force. Sinclair eventually joined the second version of X-Factor. After X-Force collapsed, Sinclair lived with MacTaggert at her Muir Island base.

Rahne fell in love with Hrimhari, the wolf prince of Asgard, and became pregnant by him. Agamemnon captured her just before the birth, but when the baby, Tier, was born, it tore the man to pieces. Traumatized, Rahne fled from her son, but Werewolf by Night took him in to raise him. Tier grew to adolescence quickly but was killed by Strong Guy as he battled demons in Hell. Afterward, Rahne decided to study to become a deacon in the Episcopal church, but was drawn back to a reformed New Mutants, fighting alongside Strong Guy.

FACTFILE
REAL NAME
Rahne Sinclair
OCCUPATION
Adventurer
BASE
Mutant Town, New York City

HEIGHT (lupine form)
Up to 12 ft standing on hind legs
WEIGHT (lupine form)
Up to 1,050 lbs
EYES Blue-green
HAIR Reddish-brown

FIRST APPEARANCE
Marvel Graphic Novel #4: The New Mutants (1982)

WOLFSBANE

POWERS
Mutant ability to transform herself into a wolf while retaining most of her human intellect, or into a transitional form which combines human and lupine aspects. Has more acute senses in lupine form.

WOLVERINE

The best there is at what he does—but what he does isn't pretty!

FACTFILE
REAL NAME
James Howlett; often goes by Logan
OCCUPATION
Adventurer
BASE
The Xavier Academy, Salem Center, Westchester, New York

HEIGHT 5 ft 3 in
WEIGHT 195 lbs
EYES Brown
HAIR Black

FIRST APPEARANCE
Incredible Hulk #180 (October 1974)

POWERS
Wolverine possesses a "healing factor" that allows him to recover from almost any injury in seconds. His skeleton has been laced with the unbreakable metal Adamantium, which makes his bones unshatterable. Wolverine also possesses three foot-long Adamantium claws that retract from either hand, capable of slicing through almost any substance known to man.

ALLIES/FOES
ALLIES X-Men, New Avengers, Nick Fury.

FOES Sabretooth, Omega Red, Silver Samurai.

ISSUE #1
After a successful limited series in 1982, Wolverine was awarded his own ongoing title in November, 1988, a series devoted to his solo adventures apart from his fellow X-Men. The title has been published ever since.

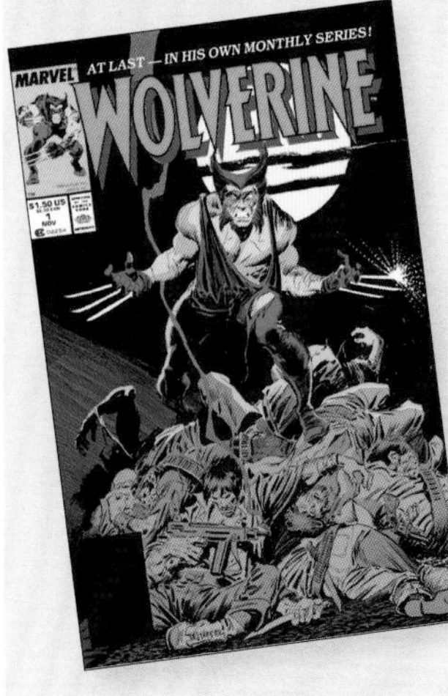

James' childhood traumas were repressed by his mutant healing factor.

Born at the turn of the century, James Howlett, the man who would one day become known and feared as Wolverine, was a sickly child. But he was also born a mutant, gifted with the remarkable ability to heal virtually instantaneously from almost any wound. He also had razor-sharp claws made of bone, a fact he first became aware of when, during a domestic dispute, he accidentally unsheathed his claws for the first time, killing his assailant.

ESSENTIAL STORYLINES
- ***Origin #1–6***
The secret beginnings of Wolverine are revealed for the first time.
- ***Wolverine Limited Series #1–4***
Wolverine must wage a war of honor in Japan to protect the woman he loves, and to prove that he is more man than beast.
- ***Weapon X (tpb)***
The story of Logan's transformation into Weapon X is revealed.

THE WANDERER

Forced by his nature to leave behind the pampered world in which he grew up, Howlett began a life of wandering, moving from place to place. His own healing factor acted upon his mind to suppress the traumatic memories of his childhood, leaving him a man without a past. Over the years, he took a succession of menial jobs, building up his strength and stamina, and losing himself in the repetitiveness of simple work. He had also adopted the name Logan, after the groundskeeper at the Howlett estate, who might have been his real father. But both the man and the estate were long lost among the indistinct memories buried deep within his mind.

Logan lived the life of a drifter, moving from one adventure to another, learning all there was to know about fighting along the way. He fought in both world wars, spent time in Japan, and made his home-away-from-home in the tiny city of Madripoor, a haven for smugglers and pirates. His miraculous healing factor prolonged his natural lifespan, making him appear far younger than he truly was. For a time, he operated as a secret agent for the Canadian government, a vocation and association that would come to have dire ramifications.

A secret project of the Canadian government was attempting to create a Super-Soldier along the lines of the famous CAPTAIN AMERICA.

A haunted figure, Logan spent much of his youth wandering the world.

With an unbreakable Adamantium skeleton, retractable razor-sharp claws, and a healing factor that also prolongs his lifespan, Wolverine is an almost unbeatable opponent.

Selected as a subject for enhancement due to his incredible healing factor, the mysterious forces behind the Canadian Weapon X project laced Logan's skeleton and claws with the unbreakable metal, Adamantium.

Kidnapped and used as a guinea pig, Logan, now referred to as Weapon X, was subjected to unimaginable tortures as his captors attempted to mold him to their liking. Realizing that Logan's healing factor would allow him to survive procedures which would kill any ordinary man, the scientists of the Weapon X project laced his skeleton with a nearly-unbreakable metal alloy known as Adamantium. They also attempted to control his mind by brainwashing, which only served to scramble Logan's memories even further.

But eventually, they could contain Logan no longer. Reduced to a bestial state, Logan broke free, annihilated the Weapon X project and all of its personnel, and fled into the Canadian wilderness.

He lived there many years, hunting game to survive. A chance meeting with James MacDonald Hudson and his wife Heather put Logan on the road back to humanity. They took the beast-man into their home, and nursed him back to health. Hudson was a scientist working for the Canadian government, where he had developed a battlesuit that he hoped would make him a hero on a par with the newly-revealed American group, the Fantastic Four.

A NEW NAME

Attempting to put together an equivalent team of Canadian Super Heroes, Hudson brought Logan into Alpha Flight, where he was given the code name Wolverine. Hudson had intended Wolverine to be the leader of this new strike force, but all that changed when a man in a wheelchair entered the scene: Professor Charles Xavier (Professor X), the mutant telepath who had founded the clandestine team of mutant heroes the X-Men.

Recognizing Wolverine's mutant nature, Professor X offered him a place among others of his kind. Wolverine accepted Xavier's offer and went to live in his School for Gifted Youngsters, which doubled as the X-Men's headquarters.

Wolverine leaped at the chance to join Professor Charles Xavier's mutant team of X-Men.

While his savage nature initially alienated his fellow mutants, Wolverine found friendship among them, and came to be one of the strongest believers in Professor X's dream of coexistence between mutants and normal humans—though this belief was tinged with a healthy cynicism.

In addition to his duties as an X-Man, Wolverine joined the new Avengers. He continued to work with the underground Avengers who formed the core of Captain America's resistance during the Civil War. He helped restore reality after the Scarlet Witch had a breakdown and altered everything, and when most things turned back to normal on M-Day, he not only retained his powers but regained all of his lost memories, too.

Since then, Wolverine discovered that Romulus, leader of the Lupines, had engineered the death of Wolverine's wife, Itsu, and torn their unborn son from her womb. Romulus erased many of Wolverine's memories and trained the child, named Daken, to be a ruthless killer.

As a result of the reality-altering powers of the Scarlet Witch, Wolverine gained possession of all of his lost memories. This knowledge remained with Logan even after the world returned to its normal state.

WOLVERINE continued

FAMILY TROUBLES

Knowing that DAKEN was trained to kill him, Wolverine created a trap for him. He arranged to have himself captured by getting the WINTER SOLDIER to hire Deadpool. After Deadpool had captured Wolverine, Daken intervened, and the Winter Soldier put a Carbonadium bullet in Daken's head, which kept his healing factor from kicking in. Wolverine then took his son away to see if he could free him from the evil influence of Romulus, but Sebastian SHAW kidnapped Daken.

In the resulting conflict, Daken's memories were repaired and he agreed to join his father in the fight against Romulus. Before they could manage this, however, a wedge was driven between them. Daken joined the DARK AVENGERS that Norman Osborn (GREEN GOBLIN) assembled, wearing his father's costume and taking his code name.

Wolverine and Daken clashed several other times; eventually Daken formed his own BROTHERHOOD OF EVIL MUTANTS to capture and kill Wolverine and destroy his reputation. Eventually, Wolverine turned the tables on him and drowned him.

Daken's cruelty and the way he embraced his nature as a killer hurt Wolverine more than his claws.

ESSENTIAL STORYLINES

- ***Wolverine Vol. 2 #21–34***
Brainwashed by Hydra, Wolverine is sent to kill the greatest Super Heroes in the Marvel Universe.
- ***Death of Wolverine (tpb)***
Wolverine is a hunted man—and prepares to make his last stand.
- ***Return of Wolverine***
The secret of Wolverine's return is revealed.

TO HELL AND BACK

A mysterious group of Wolverine's enemies called the Red Right Hand helped a demon possess his body and sent his spirit to Hell. While he struggled to find a way back, his possessed form—Hellverine, which had all of his powers but none of his humanity—went on a killing spree. In an effort to regain control, Wolverine hunted the Devil himself with the help of PUCK and a man he later realized was the first person he had ever killed: his own father. With the help of GHOST RIDER, HELLSTORM, MYSTIQUE and his ex-girlfriend, reporter Melita Garner, Wolverine returned from Hell and expelled the demon.

Wolverine then hunted down the Red Right Hand, determined to kill every one of its members. He first had to fight his way through their muscle, a group of mercenaries known as the Mongrels. After he slaughtered them, he discovered that the members of the Red Right Hand preferred to commit suicide rather than die at his hand. To make matters worse, Wolverine discovered that the Mongrels group he had killed had all been his own illegitimate children.

LEADING THE WAY

At CYCLOPS' request, Wolverine headed up a new X-FORCE, a black-ops team willing to do the kind of wetwork most of the X-MEN would balk at. WARPATH, WOLFSBANE, and Wolverine's young female clone X-23 made up his original team, with Domino coming on board later. Eventually word about the team leaked out, and Cyclops lost the nerve to keep it together. Wolverine, however, reformed the team on his own, asking Archangel (*see* ANGEL), DEADPOOL, FANTOMEX, and PSYLOCKE to join him.

The split between Wolverine and Cyclops deepened. Wolverine believed mutant children should grow up normally, while Cyclops wanted to train them for battle as X-Men. Wolverine led a group of mutants back to the grounds of the old Xavier estate and founded the Jean Grey School of Higher Learning. He took to his new role well and soon became extremely protective of his students.

Surprisingly, given that he was one of the most lethal killers alive, Wolverine was also a natural teacher.

OLD MAN LOGAN

On the parallel world of Earth-807128, Super Villains had taken over the world and killed most of its heroes. Wolverine, believing the X-Mansion was under attack, killed the attackers—only to learn it had been an illusion created by Mysterio and he had actually massacred his fellow X-Men. Logan was haunted by his actions. Years later, when the Hulk and his insane offspring killed Logan's family, Logan used his claws for the first time since he had killed his friends. Following the destruction of the Multiverse, "Old Man Logan" found himself on Battleworld. He survived its destruction and ended up in the mainstream reality where he joined the X-Men and Weapon X-Force.

AVENGERS ASSEMBLE

When the Phoenix Force returned, the AVENGERS decided they should take custody of Hope SUMMERS in case it took her as its host. Wolverine sided with them against Cyclops and his team of X-Men, but he couldn't stop the fight from escalating. Nor could he keep Cyclops from killing PROFESSOR X and becoming the Dark Phoenix. After that conflict ended and the Phoenix Force was destroyed, Wolverine rejoined the Avengers. He became part of the main team once again, and also a new Avengers Unity Team, led by HAVOK and featuring a number of powerful mutants. This new team soon found themselves fighting the RED SKULL, who had stolen Charles Xavier's brain and used it to gain his powers.

No longer as much a loner as he once was, Wolverine made so many friends that he sometimes had to choose between them.

THE LAST DAYS

While helping SHIELD on a mission, Wolverine became infected with a sentient Microverse virus that destroyed his healing ability. Despite this, Logan continued to fight, taking martial arts training from his friends to improve his skills. Wolverine's end came thanks to the scientist who had given him his Adamantium skeleton, Abraham Cornelius. Intent on finishing his original experiment and creating a perfect Super-Soldier, Cornelius sought to capture Wolverine. When Logan took the fight to Cornelius, the scientist was shocked to learn that Logan's healing ability was gone. He decided to continue with his new experiments anyway and bond Adamantium to a new series of test subjects. In one last defiant act, Wolverine shredded the Adamantium chamber, its molten metal covering him. Despite this, he saved the test subjects and killed his old enemy, dropping to his knees as the metal solidified, dying in an Adamantium tomb as the sun set.

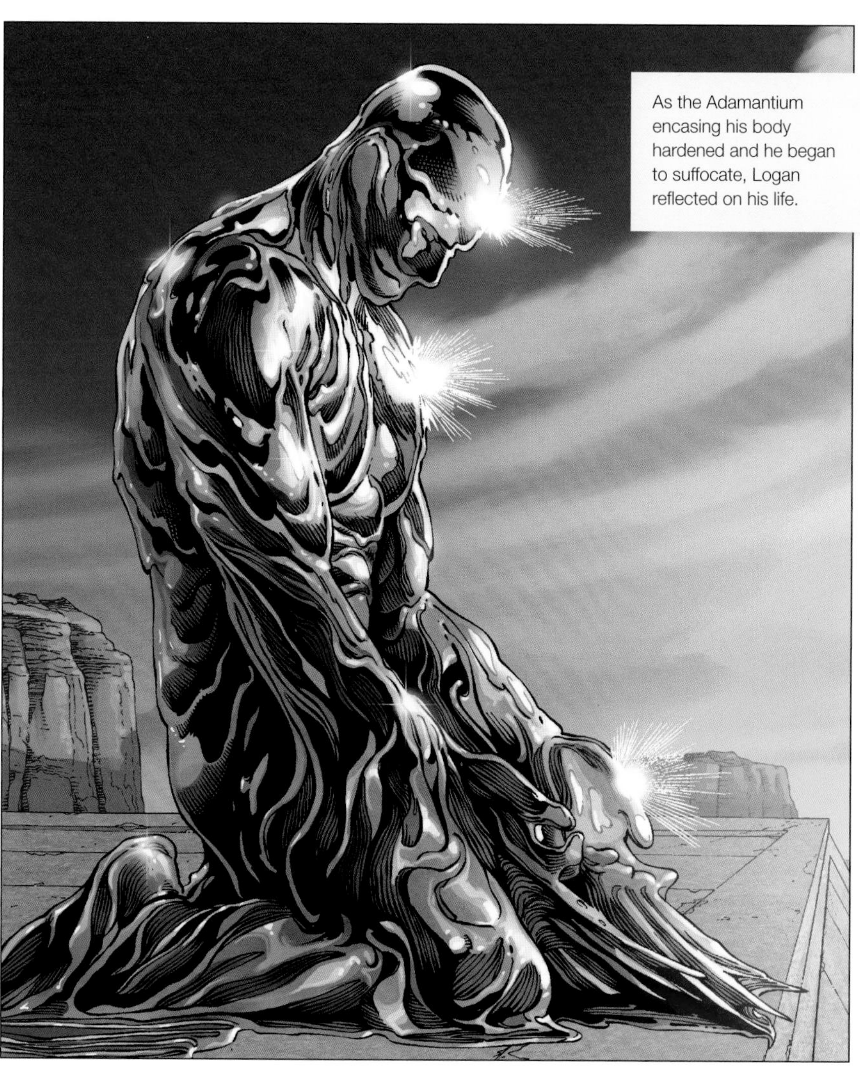

As the Adamantium encasing his body hardened and he began to suffocate, Logan reflected on his life.

THE RETURN

Kitty PRYDE used her powers to phase Wolverine's corpse out of the metal encasing him, so that he could be buried. A while later, the corpse was stolen. Wolverine's allies searched the world for him—and Wolverine himself was spotted at various locations, holding a powerful Infinity Gem. Logan was alive again, but how was a mystery.

WONDER MAN

FACTFILE

REAL NAME
Simon Williams

OCCUPATION
Adventurer

BASE
New York City

HEIGHT 6 ft 2 in
WEIGHT 380 lbs
EYES Red
HAIR Gray

FIRST APPEARANCE
Avengers #9
(October 1964)

POWERS
Body composed of ionic energy, which provides enhanced strength, stamina, flight, longevity, virtual invulnerability, and freedom from the need to eat or even breathe. Wonder Man is virtually immortal as his ionic body will reform regardless of whatever injuries he sustains.

WONDER MAN

Born the wealthy inheritor of a family business, Simon Williams ran the company into near-bankruptcy and embezzled funds to invest with the criminal Maggia. Nursing a grudge toward the competing Stark Industries and its champion, Iron Man, Williams underwent ionic energy treatments from Baron Zemo and the original Masters of Evil. As Wonder Man, he infiltrated the Avengers, but refused to follow through on Zemo's scheme to destroy the team, and perished after aiding his Avengers teammates. The homicidal robot Ultron later copied Wonder Man's brain patterns to help program the android Vision.

Wonder Man has adventured throughout known space and encountered thousands of alien cultures.

BACK TO LIFE

Believed dead, Wonder Man hibernated in an ionic coma until restored, in a zombie-like state, by his unstable brother Eric, the Grim Reaper. The resurrected Wonder Man returned to the Avengers, befriending the Beast and forging a close bond with the Vision, whom he viewed as a brother due to their shared brain patterns. Wonder Man became a part-time actor and stuntman, and also helped to establish the Avengers West Coast. At this time, he realized he loved the Scarlet Witch, who had since married the Vision.

After the Vision's dismemberment and reassembly, Wonder Man refused to allow his brain patterns to be copied a second time, driving a wedge between him and the Scarlet Witch. Nevertheless, as time went by, the two began a romance, and Wonder Man pursued a successful acting career in Hollywood movies.

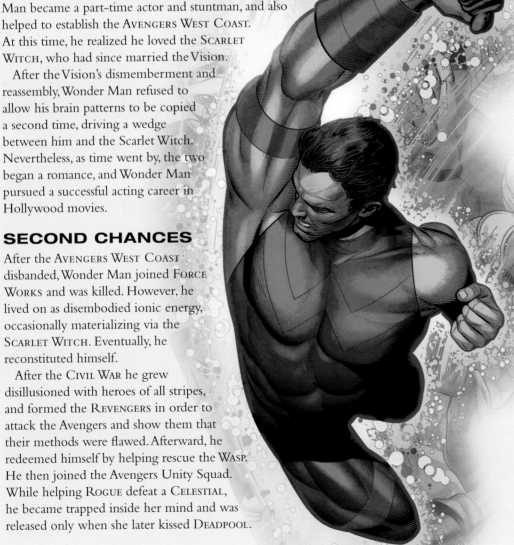

SECOND CHANCES

After the Avengers West Coast disbanded, Wonder Man joined Force Works and was killed. However, he lived on as disembodied ionic energy, occasionally materializing via the Scarlet Witch. Eventually, he reconstituted himself.

After the Civil War he grew disillusioned with heroes of all stripes, and formed the Revengers in order to attack the Avengers and show them that their methods were flawed. Afterward, he redeemed himself by helping rescue the Wasp. He then joined the Avengers Unity Squad. While helping Rogue defeat a Celestial, he became trapped inside her mind and was released only when she later kissed Deadpool.

WONG

FIRST APPEARANCE *Strange Tales* #110 (July 1963)
REAL NAME Wong **OCCUPATION** Manservant
BASE Doctor Strange's Sanctum Sanctorum, New York City
HEIGHT 5 ft 8 in **WEIGHT** 140 lbs
EYES Brown **HAIR** Shaved
SPECIAL POWERS/ABILITIES Expert martial artist, although he has not actively practiced his skills in several years. A highly efficient manservant, utterly loyal to Doctor Strange.

The youngest surviving member of a bloodline whose members served the mystical Ancient One, Wong was tutored in the martial arts of Kamar-Taj. When he became an adult, the Ancient One dispatched him to the US, so that he could become the manservant of Doctor Strange. The two became peers instead, with a mutual respect for each other. Wong secretly established a sect of magicians who could take onto themselves damage done to Doctor Strange, though Strange ended this sect when he learned of it.

WOO, JIMMY

FIRST APPEARANCE *Yellow Claw* #1 (October 1956)
REAL NAME James "Jimmy" Woo **OCCUPATION** Adventurer
BASE San Francisco **HEIGHT** 5 ft 8 in **WEIGHT** 170 lbs
EYES Brown **HAIR** Black
SPECIAL POWERS/ABILITIES Investigative agent specializing in infiltration and information.

In the 1950s, Jimmy worked for the FBI against the forces of the Golden Claw. In 1958, he led a super group called the G-Men, but it disbanded and he joined SHIELD. He was nearly killed in action against the Atlas Foundation, but Marvel Boy healed him, restoring his youth but at the cost of his memories. Reuniting the G-Men, Jimmy discovered that the Golden Claw had been grooming him to be the heir for his empire. Jimmy accepted the offer, hoping to turn the Agents of Atlas into a force for good. He later opened the Pan-Asian School for the Unusually Gifted.

WOODGOD

FIRST APPEARANCE *Marvel Premiere* #31 (August 1976)
REAL NAME Woodgod
OCCUPATION Lawgiver of the Changelings
BASE The Rocky Mountains, Colorado
HEIGHT 6 ft 3 in **WEIGHT** 265 lbs
EYES Red **HAIR** Reddish-brown
SPECIAL POWERS/ABILITIES Woodgod possesses superhuman strength and an immunity to nerve gas.

Woodgod is a genetically engineered being, created by scientists David and Ellen Pace by merging human and animal genetic material. The townsfolk of Liberty, near the Paces' farm in New Mexico, convinced themselves that Woodgod was a dangerous monster. They tried to kill the creature using a canister of a deadly nerve gas. Woodgod proved to be immune to the gas, but the Paces were both killed. The grief-stricken Woodgod discovered the Paces' notes and created a race of half-human, half-animal beings, which he called Changelings.

WOODMAN, SENATOR

FIRST APPEARANCE *Avengers: The Initiative* #7 (December 2007)
REAL NAME Arthur Woodman
OCCUPATION Congressman, Hydra leader
BASE Washington, D.C.
HEIGHT 6 ft **WEIGHT** 220 lbs **EYES** Brown **HAIR** Brown
SPECIAL POWERS/ABILITIES Powerful and cunning politician and leader.

Arthur Woodman led a double life for a long while, playing both the prominent politician and rising through the ranks of Hydra at the same time. When Viper, the Hydra leader, was discovered to be a Skrull, Woodman stepped into the vacuum she left behind and declared himself Hydra's supreme leader. Woodman blackmailed Hardball into becoming a Hydra agent. When the Initiative caught Woodman and Hardball trying to steal Komodo's lizard serum for Hydra, Woodman injected himself with the serum and became a giant lizard-man. Hardball killed him and then took over his position as the leader of Hydra.

WW Hulk see pages 418–419

WRAITH

FIRST APPEARANCE *Amazing Spider-Man* #663 (August 2011) (Watanabe as Wraith) **REAL NAME** Yuriko Watanabi
OCCUPATION Vigilante; former police captain
BASE New York City **HEIGHT** Unknown **WEIGHT** Unknown
EYES Black **HAIR** Black
SPECIAL POWERS/ABILITIES Uses a variety of gear stolen from Super Villains, such as Chameleon's disguise capabilities.

The most recent person to take on the identity of the Wraith is Captain Yuri Watanabe of the NYPD. She used equipment stolen from Super Villains such as Mysterio and the Chameleon to become the costumed vigilante. As the Wraith, Watanabe took on Mr. Negative and helped Spider-Man against the Goblin Nation. Others who have called themselves the Wraith include Brian DeWolff, who had psionic powers, the mutant Hector Rendoza, and the Kree warrior Zak-Del.

WRECKING CREW

WRECKING CREW
1 Wrecker ***2*** Thunderball
3 Piledriver ***4*** Bulldozer

Wrecker was a violent criminal who used a crowbar to demolish the scenes of his crimes, thereby hindering investigation. When he was accidentally given magical powers by Karnilla, the Norn Queen, Wrecker went on a rampage that attracted the attention of Thor.

Placed in prison by the Asgardian automaton the Destroyer, Wrecker escaped with three other inmates, who also gained powers when they held the Wrecker's crowbar as it was struck by lightning. Ex-army master sergeant Henry Camp became Bulldozer, ex-physicist Dr. Eliot Franklin became Thunderball, and ex-Farmhand Brian Calusky became Piledriver. The four criminals dubbed themselves the Wrecking Crew, and soon found themselves fighting the Defenders. The team's most notorious moment was as part of Baron Zemo's Masters of Evil, when they attacked Avengers Mansion and nearly killed Hercules. They worked with Zemo again years later when he formed an Army of Evil to aid Hydra's takeover of America. Afterward, they rejoined the Hood's criminal gang and fought a heroic Doctor Doom.

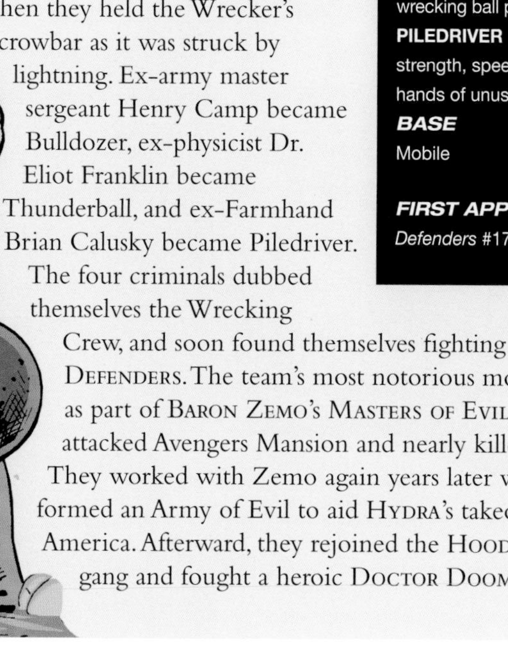

FACTFILE
MEMBERS AND POWERS
WRECKER Superhuman strength and invulnerability; mental link to his enchanted crowbar.
BULLDOZER Superhuman strength, speed, and durability; specially made helmet maximises impacts on targets.
THUNDERBALL Superhuman strength, speed, and durability; genius-level intellect; enchanted wrecking ball projects energy bolts
PILEDRIVER Superhuman strength, speed, and durability; hands of unusually great size.
BASE
Mobile

FIRST APPEARANCE
Defenders #17 (November 1974)

WORLD WAR HULK

A story of revenge

ISSUE #1

The Hulk defeated Black Bolt. Then he called the rest of the Illuminati out to battle him in Manhattan. Iron Man attacked in his Hulkbuster armor, but the Hulk's fury could not be stopped.

The ILLUMINATI decided that the HULK had become too dangerous to be permitted to remain on Earth. Discovering that a Life Model Decoy robot of Nick FURY had sent the Hulk into space on a mission, they turned his rescue vehicle away from Earth and sent it toward an uninhabited planet. On its way, the ship entered a wormhole and wound up on the planet Sakaar. There, the Hulk became a gladiatorial slave of the Red King—until he and his WARBOUND friends led a rebellion that installed him as the planet's king instead.

Black Bolt was the only Super Hero who had ever defeated the Hulk. Because of this, the Hulk made sure to take him out first when he returned to Earth.

MADDER THAN EVER

As king, the Hulk married the Red King's lieutenant CAIERA, making her his queen. His happiness was shattered, however, when the ship in which he'd traveled to Sakaar exploded, killing millions of people, including the pregnant Caiera. Believing the Illuminati was responsible, the Hulk gathered his Warbound allies and returned to Earth.

On his way to Earth, the Hulk stopped at the Moon to pick up BLACK BOLT. He and his Warbound then appeared in their starship over Manhattan and gave the people 24 hours to evacuate. IRON MAN, wearing his latest Hulkbuster armor, attacked, but the Hulk defeated him and brought his Warbound to help beat the AVENGERS. He then took on the FANTASTIC FOUR and captured MR. FANTASTIC.

While General Ross led the US Army against the Hulk, DOCTOR STRANGE tried to help his old friend. The Hulk broke his hands, making it difficult for him to cast spells. Then he set up Madison Square Garden as a gladiatorial arena. Desperate, Doctor Strange unleashed the demon Zom and merged with him, becoming as angry and powerful as the Hulk. When he nearly killed a group of bystanders, however, doubts overcame him, and the Hulk brought him down.

Back in Madison Square Garden, the Hulk permitted those with grievances against BLACK BOLT, DOCTOR STRANGE, IRON MAN, and MR. FANTASTIC to demand justice. He then unleashed a monster from Sakaar on the heroes. When they survived that, he used slave disks implanted in each of them to set the four against each other.

At the last moment, the Hulk spared the Illuminati, stating that he had come for justice, not murder. Having exposed them for what they were, he and the Warbound would raze Manhattan and then leave. Before he could do so, the SENTRY finally showed up and attacked. He and the Hulk battled each other until they both reverted to their human forms.

Unwilling to let the conflict end, Miek—the first of the Warbound that the Hulk had ever met—stabbed the Hulk's oldest friend, Rick JONES to enrage Bruce Banner and make him turn back into the Hulk. Miek also revealed that he had seen a band of Red King loyalists set the explosion on Sakaar but had said nothing so that the Hulk would go to war.

Too angry to control himself, the Hulk begged Iron Man to stop him. Iron Man fired a coordinated blast from several orbital satellites, causing the Hulk to become Bruce Banner once more. Unconscious, he was captured and imprisoned three miles beneath the earth.

The Gamma Corps charged into action against the Hulk for the first time, each hungry for revenge. When he showed them who was really to blame for their troubles, they changed their target to the Illuminati instead.

Doctor Strange was desperate enough—after the Hulk broke his hands—to merge himself with the spirit of the vicious demon Zom. But even this action wasn't sufficient to stop the Hulk.

Although most people fled Manhattan before the battle began, many New York landmarks fell in the battle with the Hulk, including Stark Tower and Madison Square Garden.

HULK VS. EVERYONE

When the Hulk returned to Earth for his revenge, he was ready to fight anyone who came between him and the Illuminati. Black Bolt, Mr. Fantastic, Iron Man, and Doctor Strange had a lot of friends willing to stand by them, no matter what they might or might not have done; nevertheless, the Hulk and his Warbound beat them all. The Illuminati were bound with slave disks and brought to Madison Square Garden. There they were forced to fight each other. Despite his rage, the Hulk remained true to his claim that he had returned not for murder but justice. None of the heroes—nor anyone else—died at his hand.

X-23

FACTFILE

REAL NAME
Laura Kinney

OCCUPATION
Adventurer

BASE
San Francisco

HEIGHT 5 ft 6 in
WEIGHT 147 lbs
EYES Green
HAIR Black

FIRST APPEARANCE
NYX #3 (February 2004)

POWERS

X-23 possesses superhuman agility, reflexes, speed, and senses. She can also extend Adamantium-coated, retractable bone claws from her hands and feet.

X-23

Cloned from a damaged sample of Wolverine's DNA, which was missing the Y chromosome, X-23 was raised in the Weapon X program as the daughter of geneticist Dr. Sarah Kinney. As soon as she was old enough, she was sent on covert killing missions, sometimes influenced by a trigger scent that sent her into a berserker rage. When Dr. Kinney discovered Weapon X had dozens of clones of X-23, she ordered X-23 to destroy them all, but X-23 smelled her trigger scent during this operation and killed her mother, too. As Sarah lay dying, she named X-23 "Laura."

The X-Men found Laura in the Mutant Town neighborhood of New York City, and Wolverine took her under his wing. She kept her powers after M-Day, and she became an X-Men trainee. After the X-Men moved to California, Cyclops made her part of the black-ops X-Force team. She later joined the Avengers Academy, and was one of the teens abducted to Arcade's latest Murderworld. Following Wolverine's apparent death, Laura briefly took on his name.

When X-23 goes berserk, nothing can stop her.

X-CELL

FIRST APPEARANCE *X-Factor* #18 (June 2007)
BASE Mobile
MEMBERS AND POWERS
ELIJAH CROSS Increases his mass without slowing him down.
ABYSS Shapeshifter, dimensional transport.
CALLISTO Superhuman senses, strength, speed, agility, and reflexes, plus healing factor.
FATALE Teleportation and light manipulation, including invisibility [1].
MARROW Bone growth, healing factor, superhuman strength, agility, and durability [2].
REAPER Cybernetic hands and leg, plus a scythe that paralyzes.
BLOB Superhuman strength and durability, immovable [3].

After most of the world's mutants were depowered on M-Day, Elijah Cross banded together a group of ex-mutant terrorists who believed the US government was behind a conspiracy that caused them to lose their powers.

Under Cross' leadership, they tracked down Quicksilver to see if he could repower them with the Terrigen Crystals he can produce from his body. He did so for Abyss, Cross, Fatale, Reaper, and Rictor. After Cross literally exploded from becoming overpowered, Abyss grabbed Fatale and Reaper and disappeared. The others managed to escape on their own. Their current whereabouts and status is unknown.

X-CORPS

FIRST APPEARANCE *Uncanny X-Men* #401 (January 2002)
BASE Paris, France
MEMBERS AND POWERS
Blob Superhuman size and strength; can create a gravity field that makes him immovable [1]. **Avalanche** Generates destructive vibrations from his hands [2]. **Banshee** Projects sonic screech [3]. **Husk** Biomorph: sheds skin to reveal transformed body beneath [4]. **Jubilee II** Projects "fireworks" from her fingers [5].

Following the death of his lover, Moira MacTaggert, and the collapse of the Massachusetts Academy where he was headmaster, Sean Cassidy lost his way. Establishing X-Corps, a paramilitary operation, Sean sought to enforce good behavior between mutants. After releasing a number of criminal mutants from jail, he imprisoned the telepathic mutant, Mastermind and used her to control these mutants' activities. It wasn't long before the organization began to collapse, a process accelerated by the shapechanger Mystique who brought X-Corps to its knees by freeing Mastermind and stabbing Sean in the throat.

X-CUTIONER

FIRST APPEARANCE *X-Men Annual* #1 (1970)
REAL NAME Carl Denti
OCCUPATION Vigilante; former FBI agent
BASE Washington, D.C.
HEIGHT 6 ft 1 in **WEIGHT** 210 lbs **EYES** Brown **HAIR** Brown
SPECIAL POWERS/ABILITIES Possesses neuro-stun gauntlet, psi-lance, laser sword, teleporter, cloaking field, phasing unit, grappling claws, propulsion boots, and a genetic scanner. Shi'ar battle-armor enhances strength to almost superhuman levels.

Special Agent Denti had been partnered with Fred Duncan, who had secretly aided Professor X on occasion. Duncan stored equipment and weaponry that the X-Men had confiscated from alien races and other threats. After Duncan was murdered, Denti vowed revenge. He discovered Duncan's connections to the X-Men and used the impounded weaponry to hunt down mutants who had not been convicted for their crimes. He clashed with the X-Men, and also assisted the Punisher. After Denti gave up his hunt, he was briefly replaced by a second X-Cutioner, an alternate-reality version of Gambit, who died in action.

X-FACTOR

Mutant investigators

A number of teams have used the name X-Factor. The first was comprised of the original X-MEN, who had left PROFESSOR X's team over the fact that he had installed their old foe MAGNETO as the team's new leader. Posing as mutant hunters, ANGEL, BEAST, CYCLOPS, Jean GREY, and ICEMAN set up shop in Manhattan. They pretended to bring mutants in to face justice, but instead trained them in the use of their powers and in how to blend into regular society. Their recruits included Artie, Boom Boom, Rusty COLLINS, LEECH, RICTOR, and SKIDS.

Madrox is the heart of the latest X-Factor.

UNDERCOVER HUNTERS

When in costume, X-Factor pretended to be the outlaw X-Terminators. Eventually, however, they gave up on this ruse, believing it to cause more harm than good. The original members opted to rejoin the X-Men. Rather than let X-Factor fade away, the US government formed a new team using the name. This started out with HAVOK, Jamie Madrox (*see* MULTIPLE MAN), POLARIS, QUICKSILVER, STRONG GUY, and WOLFSBANE, with Valerie COOPER as their governmental liaison. A later version of the team, led by FORGE, included the criminals MYSTIQUE, SABRETOOTH, Shard, and WILD CHILD.

X-FACTOR I
1 Archangel
2 Iceman
3 Cyclops
4 Jean Grey
5 Beast

FACTFILE

NOTABLE MEMBERS

MADROX
Creates duplicates of himself.

STRONG GUY
Transforms kinetic energy directed against himself into strength.

SIRYN
Vocal chords can create sonic blasts.

M
Super-strength, durability, and flight.

RICTOR
Currently powerless; formerly could creates seismic shifts in the Earth.

BUTTERFLY
Instinctively understands causality, and creates a desired effect through a small action.

WOLFSBANE
Can transform into a wolflike creature.

BASE
Mutant Town, New York City

FIRST APPEARANCE
X-Factor #1 (June 2002)

X-FACTOR INVESTIGATIONS
1 Strong Guy **2** Rictor **3** Wolfsbane
4 Madrox **5** Siryn **6** M

A third version of this team reunited many members of the various government teams. However, it broke up after an exploding time machine sent Havok to Earth-1298, in which many of the roles of the mainstream heroes and villains of Earth were swapped. Later, a government Mutant Civil Rights Task Force used the X-Factor name for a short while.

After M-Day, Jamie Madrox opened up a private investigations firm called X-Factor Investigations with many of his old friends. These included M, Layla MILLER (Butterfly), SIRYN, Strong Guy, Wolfsbane, and a powerless Rictor.

Madrox's team became embroiled in the hunt for Hope SUMMERS. During this, Madrox and Miller traveled to the future of Earth-1191, in which the birth of Hope led to mutants being rounded up into concentration camps. Madrox managed to escape to the present but returned later to find an older Miller and help foment a rebellion. When Jamie Madrox closed X-Factor down, Polaris took the X-Factor name and used it for a corporate Super Hero team.

Despite its low profile, X-Factor Investigations still deals with larger threats—like Sentinels.

ESSENTIAL STORYLINES

- ***X-Factor #6***
The first regular appearance of Apocalypse.
- ***X-Factor #149***
X-Factor disbands, and Havok is sent to Earth-1298.
- ***X-Factor Vol. 2 #1***
In the wake of M-Day, Jamie Madrox forms X-Factor Investigations.

X-FORCE

Cable's mutant soldiers

X-FORCE

FACTFILE

NOTABLE MEMBERS

CABLE
Militant, time-traveling mutant soldier.

DOMINO
Can alter luck in her favor, formidable combatant.

WARPATH (PROUDSTAR)
Superhuman strength, speed, and durability.

WOLVERINE
Quick healing factor, lethal fighting skills, razor-sharp Adamantium claws.

ARCHANGEL
Flight, deadly fighting skills, razor sharp wings.

WOLFSBANE
Able to transform into a werewolf.

X-23
Wolverine's female clone. Razor sharp claws and deadly fighting skills.

PSYLOCKE
Deadly telekinetic abilities and martial arts expert.

BASE
Various

FIRST APPEARANCE
X-Force #1
(August 1991)

ALLIES/FOES

ALLIES X-Men

FOES Stryfe, Apocalypse, Bastion, Purifiers, Leper Queen, Selene

ESSENTIAL STORYLINES

- ***X-Force: Under the Gun (tpb)***
Cable transforms the New Mutants into X-Force.
- ***X-Force Vol. 2***
Cyclops tasks Wolverine with creating a special black ops team of mutant heroes.
- ***Uncanny X-Force Vol. 1 (tpb)***
Wolverine's deadly squad face their most lethal foe yet: Archangel.

When several X-Men died on missions, Professor X feared that he was placing his students in too much danger. He founded a young mutant team, the New Mutants, devoted to training rather than combat. After Professor X had journeyed into outer space and a new headmaster, Magneto, had come and gone, Cable became the team's mentor. He trained his charges to become soldiers against mutant threats and renamed the team X-Force.

Cable, founder and mentor of X-Force.

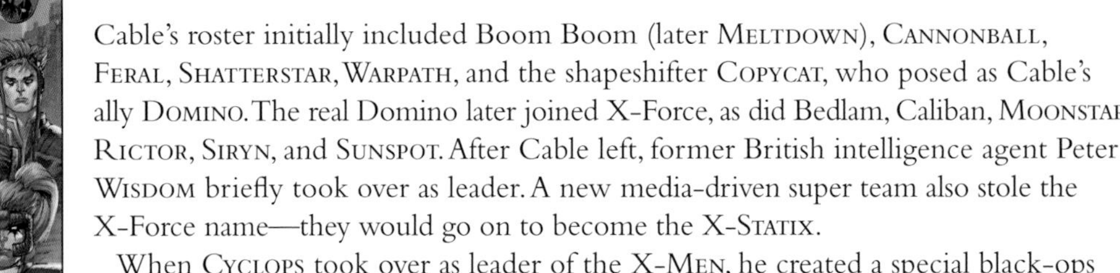

Cable took control of the New Mutants and turned them into a formidable fighting force.

AT THE SHARP END

Cable's roster initially included Boom Boom (later Meltdown), Cannonball, Feral, Shatterstar, Warpath, and the shapeshifter Copycat, who posed as Cable's ally Domino. The real Domino later joined X-Force, as did Bedlam, Caliban, Moonstar, Rictor, Siryn, and Sunspot. After Cable left, former British intelligence agent Peter Wisdom briefly took over as leader. A new media-driven super team also stole the X-Force name—they would go on to become the X-Statix.

When Cyclops took over as leader of the X-Men, he created a special black-ops version of X-Force to track down Cable after he absconded with Hope Summers, the first mutant born after M-Day. Cyclops later disbanded this team after much criticism from within the mutant community, but Wolverine secretly kept X-Force going in order to proactively deal with threats to his fellow mutants. Wolverine's team used methods that were uncompromising; their first mission saw them attempt to kill Apocalypse, who had been reborn as a child. Most of the team couldn't go through with it, but Fantomex eventually seemed to shoot the child in the head, ending the threat. Angel, one of the team's members, had briefly been Death, one of Apocalypse's Horsemen. He found himself gradually becoming more in thrall to his darker self,which culminated in him trying to make Apocalypse's worldview a reality until he was killed by Psylocke.

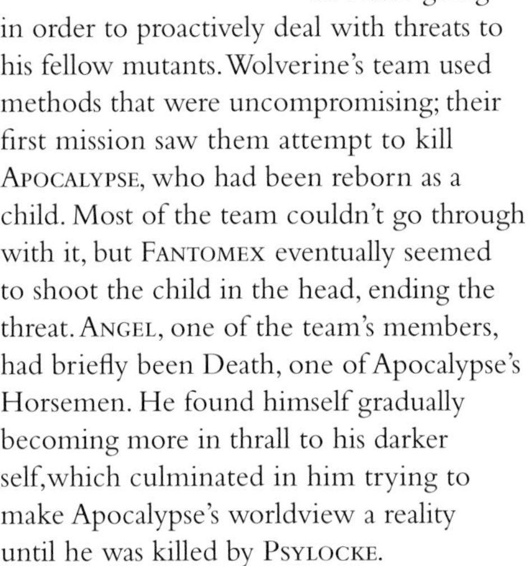

WOLVERINE'S X-FORCE
1 X-23 ***2*** Wolverine ***3*** Domino ***4*** Warpath ***5*** Archangel

RECENT TEAMS

When Cable started to have visions of the future, he formed a new incarnation of X-Force to stop the visions from coming true. He persuaded Colossus, Forge, Doctor Nemesis, and Domino to join his new team. Their actions put them on a collision course with Havok's Avengers Unity Division. At the same time, Psylocke created her own version of X-Force to track down a young mutant girl. Psylocke's team included Storm, Puck, Cluster, Spiral, and Bishop. Both teams joined forces when Stryfe, Cable's evil clone, returned. The Weapon X mutant team also started to call themselves Weapon X-Force, taking a similar proactive stance to the enemies of mutantkind.

X-MAN

When moved to anger, X-Man's psionic fury was almost unstoppable.

Even on the alternate Earth known as the Age of Apocalypse, Mister Sinister is as obsessed with the progeny of Jean Grey and Scott Summers (*see* Cyclops) as the Mister Sinister of Earth-616. After obtaining genetic material from these two individuals, he created their child artificially, naming him Nathan Grey. By greatly accelerating the child's growth and development Sinister intended to use Nathan's mutant powers to fight Apocalypse.

Ultimately, the Age of Apocalypse timeline was doomed. After killing Mister Sinister, Nate managed to escape to the mainstream Earth and made it his goal to prevent this Earth from suffering the same fate. He eventually joined the X-Men before becoming a shaman. He died saving Earth from the alien Harvester, but returned during the Dark Reign and fought Norman Osborn, releasing Norman's Green Goblin personality. He later joined the New Mutants and stood by the X-Men when they were attacked by the Avengers.

X-Men see pages 424–429

X-MAN

FACTFILE

REAL NAME
Nathan "Nate" Grey

OCCUPATION
Shaman

BASE
Mobile

HEIGHT 5 ft 9 in
WEIGHT 171 lbs
EYES Blue
HAIR Brown

FIRST APPEARANCE
X-Man #1
(March 1995)

POWERS

A telepath of vast power; able to read and control minds, project his astral form across the world, and create complex psionic illusions, and "psionic spikes." Also possessed considerable telekinetic powers, allowing him to move heavy objects at will.

X-MEN 2099

The X-Men 2099 were initially based in the mountains of New Mexico.

In an alternate future, the Earth is ruled by malevolent, self-serving corporations and mutants have been outlawed—forced underground. In the year 2099, one mutant dedicated himself to overthrowing this oppressive world order. Gathering some of the surviving mutants together to form a new band of X-Men, the almost messianic Xi'an Chi Xan (also known as the Desert Ghost) began challenging this status quo.

Initially based at a mountain fortress in New Mexico that had once belonged to an enemy named Master Zhao, these X-Men were to become the protectors of Halo City in California, which had been declared a safe haven for mutants.

However, when an approaching Phalanx planetoid caused severe flooding, mutants and humans were forced to flee to the Savage Land in the Antarctic. Following the Phalanx's defeat, humanity is now in a position to rebuild.

On Earth-96099, an alternate set of X-Men 2099 led by by a bald, one-armed Wolverine fought to help repair their damaged timeline.

X-MEN 2099
1 Bloodhawk ***2*** Krystalin
3 Desert Ghost ***4*** Skullfire
5 Metalhead ***6*** Cerebra
7 Meanstreak

X-MEN 2099

FACTFILE

MEMBERS AND POWERS

XI'AN CHI XAN
With his left hand he disintegrates matter, with his right hand he heals injuries.

CEREBRA
Detects mutants with her mind.

KRYSTALIN
Creates crystals from thin air.

MEANSTREAK
Travels at superhuman speeds.

METALHEAD
Touches any metal and assumes its properties.

SKULLFIRE
Absorbed energy makes his skeleton glow.

BLOODHAWK
Transmutes body to develop red skin and bat-like wings.

BASE
The Savage Land, Antarctica

FIRST APPEARANCE
X-Men 2099 #1
(October 1993)

X-MEN

Earth's mightiest team

X-MEN

FACTFILE

MEMBERS AND POWERS

PROFESSOR X (Charles Xavier) Telepathy.

CYCLOPS (Scott Summers) Optic power beams.

PHOENIX (Marvel Girl I, Jean Grey) Telepathy, telekinesis.

ARCHANGEL (Angel, Warren Worthington III) Flight.

BEAST (Henry McCoy) Superhuman strength and agility.

ICEMAN (Bobby Drake) Generates intense cold.

COLOSSUS (Peter Rasputin) Turns to "organic steel."

NIGHTCRAWLER (Kurt Wagner) Teleportation.

ROGUE (Real name unrevealed) Absorbs memories and abilities.

SHADOWCAT (Kitty Pryde) "Phases" through solid objects.

STORM (Ororo Munroe) Controls weather.

WOLVERINE (Logan) Adamantium skeleton and claws.

BASE The Xavier Institute, Salem Center, New York State

FIRST APPEARANCE

X-Men #1 (September 1963)

ALLIES/FOES

ALLIES The New Mutants, Excalibur, X-Factor, Generation X, the Fantastic Four, the Avengers, Spider-Man, Doctor Strange

FOES Magneto, the Juggernaut, the Sentinels, Apocalypse, Mister Sinister, Mystique, Brotherhood of Evil Mutants, the Hellfire Club, the Brood

ISSUE #1

Professor X trains his X-Men and the team are confronted with arch-enemy Magneto.

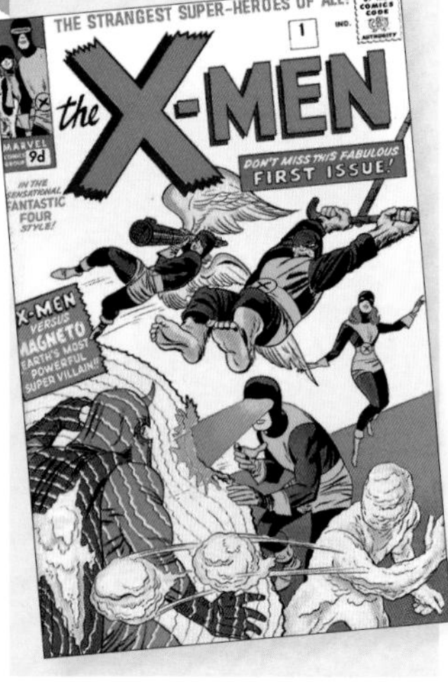

The X-Men are a team of superhuman mutants that was founded by Professor Charles Xavier (PROFESSOR X), who is not only a mutant himself, but is also one of the world's leading authorities on mutation. In founding the X-Men, Xavier had two principal purposes. First, he sought to find young mutants and to train them in utilizing their superhuman powers. Second, Xavier intended the X-Men to serve as a combat team to defend "ordinary" humans against attack by other mutants. Further, Xavier recognizes that "normal" humans tend to fear and distrust the mutants, who are appearing in their midst, and that therefore mutants often suffer persecution.

XAVIER'S DREAM

By founding the X-Men, Xavier created a community of mutants living together on his estate. Xavier is a visionary who hopes to help bring about peaceful coexistence between mutants and the rest of the human race. The X-Men are dedicated to this goal, which they call "Xavier's dream." Xavier has explained that he named the team "X-Men" after the "extra" powers that his mutant students possess. (Of course, "X" is also the first letter of Xavier's last name.)

As a young man, Xavier battled another mutant telepath, Amahl Farouk, alias the SHADOW KING, in Egypt. This encounter made him aware of the need to protect humanity from malevolent mutants.

ROAD TO RECOVERY

Xavier subsequently lost the use of his legs in a clash with an alien who called himself LUCIFER. Deeply depressed, Xavier led a reclusive existence at his family mansion. However, he began treating a ten-year-old girl named Jean GREY whose mutant powers had prematurely emerged.

Years later, the FBI initiated an investigation of mutants, headed by agent Fred Duncan. Xavier met

THE X-MEN
1 Storm ***2*** Banshee ***3*** Angel
4 Sunfire ***5*** Iceman ***6*** Havok
7 Polaris ***8*** Marvel Girl (Jean Grey)
9 Colossus ***10*** Nightcrawler
11 Wolverine ***12*** Cyclops
13 Thunderbird

ESSENTIAL STORYLINES

- ***Giant-Size X-Men #1***
Charles Xavier forms a new international team of X-Men.
- ***The Uncanny X-Men #129–137***
"The Dark Phoenix Saga": the X-Men try to stop the mad Phoenix (Jean Grey) from wreaking havoc through the cosmos and save her from insanity.
- ***The Uncanny X-Men #141–142***
"Days of Future Past": present day X-Men try to prevent a future America ruled by Sentinels.

The X-Men are based in Charles Xavier's Westchester County mansion.

with Duncan and volunteered to locate young mutants and train them in managing their potentially dangerous abilities. Duncan agreed to the plan and pledged to keep Xavier's work with mutants secret. Xavier soon recruited five adolescent mutants to his school, giving each of them code names: Cyclops, Iceman, the Angel, the Beast, and Marvel Girl (the teenage Jean Grey). All five were enrolled at Professor Xavier's School for Gifted Youngsters, a private school based in Xavier's mansion, in the town of Salem Center in New York City's Westchester County.

There Xavier educated them in conventional academic subjects, while secretly teaching them how to utilize their mutant abilities.

The next member of the X-Men, who served only briefly, was the Mimic, who was not a mutant but had the ability to imitate mutant powers. During a period when Xavier was in seclusion, he was impersonated by the Changeling, a shapeshifting mutant who died heroically. The mutants Havok and Lorna Dane, later known as Polaris, subsequently joined the team.

NEW RECRUITS

Most of the X-Men became trapped on the island of Krakoa, which proved to be a gigantic mutant organism. Xavier then recruited a new team of X-Men from various countries. The new members included the Banshee, from Ireland; Colossus, from Russia; Nightcrawler, from Germany; Storm, from equatorial Africa; Sunfire, from Japan; Thunderbird, a Native American; and Wolverine, from Canada.

Led by Cyclops, the new recruits rescued the X-Men from Krakoa. After their return, the senior X-Men left the team, except for Cyclops, who remained as deputy leader. Sunfire quit, and Thunderbird was killed during the new X-Men's second mission.

Over subsequent years, many other members have joined the X-Men, including Kitty Pryde, alias Shadowcat; Rogue; Rachel Summers, known both as the second Phoenix and the current Marvel Girl; Psylocke; the Dazzler; and Longshot. During a temporary reformation, even the X-Men's archfoe Magneto joined the team.

After forming their own group, X-Factor, the five founding X-Men returned to their original team. Xavier's school was renamed the Xavier Institute. Further new members included Forge, Jubilee, Gambit, Bishop, Revanche, Cannonball, Joseph (a clone of Magneto), Dr. Cecilia Reyes, Marrow, and Maggott. Storm organized a short-lived spinoff team called the X-Treme X-Men, whose roster included Sage, the third Thunderbird, Lifeguard, and Slipstream. Most of these members later joined the main X-Men team.

Xavier formed a new international team of X-Men after the immense mutant Krakoa the Living Island captured the original team.

OPEN SECRET

Many other heroes have joined the X-Men over the years, including Cable, Chamber, Husk, Northstar, Stacy X, and the traitor Xorn. Even former foes like Emma Frost, Juggernaut, and Mystique have been part of the team. Ever since Professor X's evil twin sister Cassandra Nova exposed him as a mutant, the world has known that the Xavier Institute was the headquarters of the X-Men. This made it possible for the Institute to openly advocate for mutant rights. In the aftermath of M-Day, the government made the X Mansion a sort of reservation for mutants, keeping the few remaining ones there, purportedly for their safety.

CEREBRO

Cerebro is a machine invented by Professor Charles Xavier to locate mutants possessing superhuman abilities. Cerebro accomplishes this by detecting psionic energy emitted by the minds of superhuman mutants. Cerebro operates best when it is linked to the mind of a telepath, such as Xavier or Jean Grey, through a headset. Xavier utilized an early version of Cerebro, called Cyberno, to locate Scott Summers, who became Cyclops. On combining with the Sentinel Bastion's nanotechnology, Cerebro became sentient. It posed a menace until Xavier destroyed it. Since then Xavier has created an advanced version, called Cerebra.

Among the X-Men's adversaries are Sabretooth (left, fighting Wolverine), the insect-like alien Brood (battling Cyclops), and their leading nemesis Magneto (top right, attacking Bishop).

X-MEN continued

Disgusted with Magneto, the Scarlet Witch removed 90 per cent of the world's mutants on November 2 (M-Day).

M-DAY

One of the world's most powerful mutants, the SCARLET WITCH, had a breakdown, during which she tore apart the team with which she worked: the Avengers. Later, as the X-Men discussed the Scarlet Witch's fate, her brother, QUICKSILVER, encouraged her to use her powers to remake the world. At her bidding thousands more people became mutants, and her father, MAGNETO, ruled the planet as the leader of the House of M. To keep others from looking too closely at their new reality, she gave them whatever they wanted: respectability, money, love, power.

Once the Scarlet Witch had been made to realize what she'd done, she changed everything back to normal—with a few twists. Among these were the fact that 90 per cent of the world's mutants lost their powers, including Magneto, Professor X, and herself.

THE AFTERMATH

With the mutant population decimated, the US government estimated that 198 mutants were left with their powers intact. The Office of National Emergency (ONE) under Valerie COOPER moved to gather these mutants at the Xavier Mansion and keep them there, guarded by SENTINELS.

This lasted until the CIVIL WAR, during which the X-Men officially remained neutral. As the war progressed, the restrictions on the mutants living at the X Mansion were lifted, with the SENTINELS left in place to guard the residents from outside attacks.

The power of the mutants had been stripped from them, but it could not be destroyed. Many of the powers banded into a being known as the Collective, which possessed mutant Michael Pointer (GUARDIAN) and used him to cut a swathe of destruction across North America. The Collective then traveled to Genosha to converse with Magneto before racing off into space. As it left the planet, it brushed past Krakoa—the island-sized mutant that nearly killed the original X-Men—and awakened the missing Summers brother, Gabriel (VULCAN). Gabriel returned to Earth and, after killing BANSHEE, revealed that he had been part of a team of young mutants sent to save the original X-Men from Krakoa. After they had all been apparently killed, Professor X had erased the memory of their existence. Learning this, CYCLOPS informed the professor that he would no longer be welcome with his X-Men.

As the Collective, Michael Pointer and Xorn slaughtered Alpha Flight, repowered Magneto, and awakened Vulcan.

INTERPLANETARY PROBLEMS

Trying to make up for his mistakes, Professor X led a team of X-Men—including Darwin, Havok, Nightcrawler, Polaris, Rachel Summers, and Warpath—into space to stop Vulcan. They failed to keep Vulcan from killing his father, Corsair, but they and the rest of the Starjammers rescued Lilandra. After Xavier regained his powers, he and half the team returned to Earth, leaving the others to form a new Starjammers to stand against Vulcan, who had become the new ruler of the Shi'ar Empire.

The other X-Men, under Cyclops, traveled to the planet Breakworld, where its leader was preparing to fire a gigantic missile at the Earth, large enough to destroy the planet. Kitty Pryde phased into the missile to try to defuse it but discovered it was actually a solid bullet. Using all her might, she managed to phase the bullet through Earth, but she remained trapped inside it and was presumed dead.

When the Hulk returned to Earth to have his revenge on the Illuminati, he went to the X-Mansion to confront Xavier. After a pitched battle, the Hulk learned about all of the horrible things that had happened to the mutants in his absence and concluded that they had suffered enough as a people.

Professor X's X-Men consisted of Vulcan, Sway, Petra, and Darwin. They were lost fighting Krakoa.

MESSIAH COMPLEX

It looked like there would be no more mutants to join the 198 or so left on the planet. While using his Cerebra mutant-finding machine, though, Professor X spotted one amazingly powerful new mutant in Cooperstown, Alaska, and Cyclops led a team of X-Men to investigate. The anti-mutant militants known as the Purifiers, and Mister Sinister's new team of Marauders, beat the X-Men there.

The Purifiers, realizing that they were looking for a young mutant, killed every child in town, even the infants still in the hospital. This tipped the X-Men—along with X-Factor and the Young X-Men—off to the fact that the first mutant since M-Day had been born—and manifested its powers at birth. They later learned that Cable had gotten there first and taken the baby to safety. Meanwhile, Predator X, a monster the Purifiers had created to destroy the "Mutant Anti-Christ," found the baby's scent and began killing mutants to sate its hunger as it tracked the infant down.

While many X-Men were out hunting for the baby, the Nano-Sentinels infected the human pilots of the Sentinels assigned to guard the mansion. They attacked, nearly destroying the place. In response to this, Cyclops formed an all-new X-Force as a black-ops team.

Gambit joined Mister Sinister's new Marauders—not to help with their plans but to advance his own.

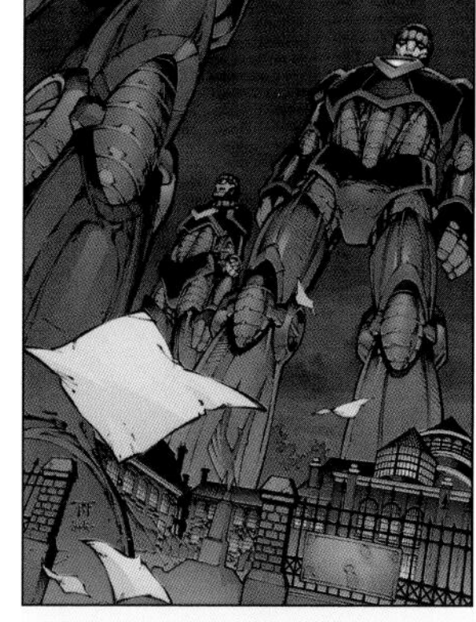

The US government agency ONE positioned Sentinels around the X-Mansion to keep hostile humans out—and the mutants in.

X-MEN continued

Sent into the future as a baby himself, Cable hoped to save the baby he would raise as Hope Summers the same way.

THE FUTURE OF MUTANTKIND

When Cable went to Forge for a time machine so he could escape with the baby, he discovered Bishop had already shot Forge. In the future from which Bishop came, the first mutant baby became the Mutant Messiah and later killed a million humans. Bishop meant to stop that by murdering the infant. The Marauders prevented that and stole the child. Before Mister Sinister could get his hands on the infant, Mystique killed him and used the baby to bring Rogue out of a coma caused by her absorbing too many minds at once.

X-Force managed to kill Predator X while the Young X-Men defeated the remaining Marauders. Professor X took the baby from Gambit, who'd rescued her from Mystique, and gave her back to Cable, just before Cyclops and the X-Men caught up with them. While the baby held the potential to cause Bishop's horrible future, Cyclops saw that it also could bring Cable's better future to pass. Revealing a long-buried optimistic side, Cyclops let Cable escape into the future with the baby.

As Cable and the baby disappeared, Bishop caught up with them and shot at them. A bullet hit Professor X, nearly killing him. Cyclops took Bishop down, but he soon escaped to chase Cable through time, still pursuing the baby, who Cable named Hope Summers.

A NEW HOME

With the mansion destroyed and Professor X now missing, Cyclops decided to end the X-Men—or so he told Iron Man when he came to ask the X-Men to register with the Fifty-State Initiative.

He moved the team to the Marin Headlands near San Francisco, where the mayor rejected the help of the Fifty-State Initiative and made the X-Men the city's official protectors. They set up shop in an abandoned military complex they renamed Graymalkin Industries (after the road where they had had their original headquarters), placing a mutant embassy on top of a facility that extended three miles below the Earth's surface. Then, through Emma Frost, Cyclops telepathically declared the city of San Francisco a mutant sanctuary.

Professor X resurfaced with his powers intact to lead another group of X-Men aiming to find and rescue Rogue from Danger, the personification of the Danger Room. At the same time, Cyclops and his X-Men and X-Force teams were gearing up for the Messiah War, the next round in the battle over Hope Summers.

DARKNESS AND HOPE

During the Dark Reign, Norman Osborn (Green Goblin) set up a fake team of X-Men, led by Emma Frost, to help control the rest of the X-Men by turning public opinion against them. When Emma and Namor betrayed Osborn, Cyclops moved the real X-Men to a floating island constructed from the remains of Asteroid M, Magneto's former headquarters, which had crashed into the ocean. As the island, Utopia, was in international waters, Cyclops declared it to be outside of the USA and Osborn's jurisdiction. At Magneto's suggestion, Namor later had the Atlanteans build a column beneath Utopia to support it and to house New Atlantis.

Cable brought Hope Summers—now a teenager—back to the present day, where they found their foes, led by Bastion, waiting for them. Working with the X-Men and traveling back and forth in time, they destroyed Bastion, but at the cost of the life of Nightcrawler, who sacrificed himself to save Hope.

The mutant detector Cerebra announced that it had started to find new mutants arising around the globe, the first since the events of M-Day. The X-Men went to find and help the first of these, five mutants known as the Lights.

As the leader of the X-Men, Cyclops became more militant and determined to protect the mutants still left. Wolverine accused Cyclops of abandoning Professor X's dream of peaceful cooperation between mutants and humans. Taking half of the mutants on Utopia with him, Wolverine left to found the Jean Grey School for Higher Learning on the site of the X-Men's old school.

HOUSE OF M

Quicksilver believed that the X-Men and their friends might put his sister the Scarlet Witch to death for disassembling the Avengers. He encouraged her to use her powers to reshape reality. After a flash of light, the world became one in which mutants were plentiful and Magneto and his House of M ruled. No one remembered things ever being any other way. With the help of Layla Miller—a mutant who could restore to others the memories they had lost—Wolverine led a movement and an assault to put things right.

THE PHOENIX FIVE

When the Phoenix Force returned to Earth, the Avengers decided that they needed to take Hope into custody to protect her (and the planet) from it. Cyclops and many X-Men refused, leading to conflict between the two teams. Wolverine sided with the Avengers, even after Iron Man broke the Phoenix Force into five parts, each of which chose a host: Colossus, Cyclops, Emma Frost, Magik, and Namor. While the Phoenix Five started out helping the planet, their power corrupted them, and they fell one by one. Eventually, Cyclops took the last of the power from Emma to defend himself against the Avengers. The surge in power caused him to kill Professor X and become the Dark Phoenix. Hope and the Scarlet Witch stopped him and destroyed the Phoenix Force. Cyclops was taken into custody but arranged a jailbreak with Magneto and started to use the old Weapon X station as a base for himself and a small team of rogue X-Men. The Beast, hoping to show Cyclops how far he'd fallen from his ideals, brought the original X-Men back from the past to visit. The Beast's actions failed and the younger X-Men found themselves stuck in the present, unable to return home.

THE DEATH OF CYCLOPS

When Black Bolt of the Inhumans unleashed the Terrigen Mists on the world, it had a shocking side effect on mutants, and started to kill them. Cyclops was one of the first to die from the new virus caused by the mists, called the M-Pox. Heartbroken and vengeful, Emma Frost projected a false image of Black Bolt killing Cyclops to unite the mutants. This instigated a war between the Inhumans and the X-Men, one that only ended when her actions were revealed, and Medusa destroyed the Terrigen Mists to save more mutants from suffering. In the aftermath of the battle, Storm handed leadership of the X-Men to Kitty Pryde.

A NEW SCHOOL

One of Kitty's first actions was to give the mutants a place on Earth again (they had retreated to Limbo to avoid the M-Pox). With the help of Magik, she brought the Mansion from Limbo to Central Park, hoping to restart Xavier's dream of human and mutant coexistence. Kitty's time in charge proved both turbulent and heartbreaking. Jean Grey returned from the dead and started to lead her own "Red" X-Men team. Kitty proposed to Colossus and he accepted—but when the wedding day arrived she backed out. With all their friends present at the wedding, Gambit proposed to Rogue and the two were married.

The bitter war between the X-Men and the Inhumans ended with both sides uniting against Emma Frost.

Kitty Pride had wanted to retire and live a normal life, but at Storm's urging, she took over as leader of the X-Men.

Elsewhere, Magneto, who had been mentoring the younger time-displaced X-Men, grew to believe in more direct action and returned to his violent ways, setting himself up on a new Asteroid M with a new Brotherhood of Mutants. With Havok also forming a team of X-Men (despite Kitty's warnings against doing so), the mutant world seemed more divided than ever. But a new threat was coming. One that would unite them like never before.

X-STATIX

FACTFILE

MEMBERS AND POWERS

HENRIETTA HUNTER Empathic powers, could resurrect herself.

VIVISECTOR Could shapeshift into wolflike form.

EL GUAPO Could levitate while riding a skateboard.

DEAD GIRL Can return to life, can become intangible and communicate with the dead.

VENUS DEE MILO Body composed of pure energy, could self-teleport and project energy blasts.

DOOP Self-levitation

ANARCHIST Acidic sweat generated energy bolts.

MISTER SENSITIVE (ORPHAN) Self-levitation, superhuman speed, heightened senses.

PHAT Could increase the size of any part of his body

BASE Mobile

FIRST APPEARANCE
(as X-Force) *X-Force* #116 (May 2001); *(as X-Statix)* *X-Statix* #1 (September 2002)

Mr. Sensitive and Venus were lovers until both died on their final mission.

X-STATIX

Rather than hide their mutant abilities from a bigoted humanity, the members of X-Statix took a completely opposite approach. They used their mutant powers to become rich and famous. The team was known as X-FORCE, having stolen the name from another mutant band.

The members of this new X-Force battled criminals to protect the public. But their adventures were telecast as a reality show, and members became celebrities. They paid for their success with their lives. During one show, most of the team, including the leader Zeitgeist, were massacred. Only the Anarchist, the teleporter U-GO GIRL, and DOOP survived.

Guy Smith, alias the Orphan and MISTER SENSITIVE, became the leader. Other recruits included Bloke, Dead Girl, El Guapo, Phat, Saint Anna, the Spike, Venus Dee Milo, and the Vivisector. Smith was succeeded as leader by the Anarchist and mutant pop star Henrietta Hunter. To avoid potential legal action, the group changed its name to X-Statix. The team continued to suffer fatalities, and the roster was completely wiped out on X-Statix's final mission. Their adventures continued, however, in the afterlife.

X-STATIX
1 Henrietta Hunter ***2*** Vivisector ***3*** El Guapo
4 Dead Girl ***5*** Venus Dee Milo ***6*** Doop
7 Anarchist ***8*** Mister Sensitive ***9*** Phat

XARUS

FACTFILE

REAL NAME
Xarus

OCCUPATION
Vampire lord

BASE
Mobile

HEIGHT 6 ft 2 in
WEIGHT 200 lbs
EYES Red
HAIR Blond

FIRST APPEARANCE
Death of Dracula #1 (August 2010)

POWERS

Xarus is a vampire. He has a pendant that allows him to withstand daylight.

Not even Blade could kill Xarus. It took Dracula's might instead.

XARUS

The son of DRACULA, Xarus was the brother of Janus and the half-brother of Lilith and Vlad Tepulus. Frustrated with his father's leadership, Xarus stepped up at the once-a-century meeting of the vampire clans and slew Dracula with the help of his allies. He then led the vampires to attack San Francisco, hoping to transform it into a new vampire homeland, but the X-MEN stood in his way. He had JUBILEE transformed into a vampire, using her as bait for the other mutants. He turned WOLVERINE and then set his sights on the mutant island of Utopia.

He landed on Utopia, confident of victory. When he tried to order Wolverine to attack the X-Men, however, CYCLOPS revealed that Xarus had only been able to take control of Wolverine because his healing factor had been turned off by nanites. Cyclops turned off the nanites, and Wolverine became human again. Meanwhile, the X-Men and their ATLANTEAN allies had revived Dracula. With Xarus' forces routed, Dracula removed Xarus' head.

XANDU

FIRST APPEARANCE *Amazing Spider-Man Annual* #2 (1965)
REAL NAME Unknown
OCCUPATION Sorceror **BASE** New York City
HEIGHT/WEIGHT Unrevealed **EYES** Blue **HAIR** White
SPECIAL POWERS/ABILITIES Xandu possesses numerous abilities derived from his sorcery, most notably a hypnotic gaze that makes other people do his bidding.

A would-be master sorcerer into whose possession half of the mystic Wand of Watomb fell, Xandu desired the power that would be his if he could unite both halves of this magical talisman. Recruiting several toughs at the waterfront and casting a spell that turned them into robots, Xandu sent them to recover the other half of the wand from DOCTOR STRANGE. But Strange gained an unexpected ally when SPIDER-MAN stumbled on the robbery, and together they defeated Xandu's agents. Strange caused Xandu to forget all of his magical knowledge, but this didn't prevent the renegade sorcerer from returning again and again to challenge the two heroes.

XEMNU

FIRST APPEARANCE *Journey into Mystery* #62 (November 1960)
REAL NAME Xemnu **OCCUPATION** Former ruler
BASE Mobile **HEIGHT** 11 ft **WEIGHT** 1,100 lbs
EYES Red **HAIR** Reddish-brown; more recently white
SPECIAL POWERS/ABILITIES Consciousness able to survive without body for indefinite periods; can psionically manipulate individuals through vast hypnotic abilities.

Although he cuts a lonely, tragic figure, Xemnu remains a very real threat to humanity. The one-time ruler of his native world, Xemnu left to travel the galaxy. Upon returning home, he discovered it had been ravaged by plague, and his people were dead. Having felt most at home on Earth, Xemnu returned and made several attempts to transform its citizens into members of his own race. He was repeatedly fought off by the HULK, DOCTOR STRANGE, and the THING. He relocated to Monster Isle, but showed up for a big monster brawl in San Diego.

XORN

FIRST APPEARANCE *New X-Men Annual* 2001 (September 2001)
REAL NAME Kuan-Yin Xorn
OCCUPATION Teacher; adventurer; terrorist **BASE** Mobile
HEIGHT 6 ft 2 in **WEIGHT** 210 lbs **EYES** N/A **HAIR** N/A
SPECIAL POWERS/ABILITIES Xorn had a miniature star in his head which emitted magnetism and a blinding, incinerating light, and could be converted to a black hole. He didn't need food, water, or air and he could heal others.

Kuan-Yin Xorn and his twin brother Shen were born in China and imprisoned, forced to wear special iron helmets to keep those around them safe. Their warden sold Kuan-Yin to John Sublime, but the X-MEN managed to free him first.

He worked as a teacher at the Xavier Institute until, claiming to be MAGNETO, he slaughtered many people in Manhattan. WOLVERINE beheaded Xorn, and Magneto showed up alive after the funeral. Shen later confirmed his brother's death, but disappeared soon after. Kuan-Yin's consciousness later controlled the Collective (*see* WEAPON OMEGA) on M-Day.

XAVIER'S SECURITY ENFORCERS

In an alternate future in which Earth's population rose up against their oppressors, the SENTINELS, a mutant police force, was formed to ensure peace between mutants and humans. This group called itself Xavier's Security Enforcers in tribute to the idealism of the X-MEN's PROFESSOR X. The XSE eventually arrived in our world's current reality while pursuing renegade member Trevor Fitzroy.

A traitorous splinter group, Xavier's Underground Enforcers, included Greystone, Archer, and Fixx.

FACTFILE

MEMBERS AND POWERS

BISHOP Absorbs and releases any form of energy.
RANDALL Immune to radiation, skilled combatant.
MALCOLM Could distinguish between humans and mutants.
SHARD Could absorb light and emit it as shockwaves.
HECATE Projects a null-light field that causes others to see their fears.

BASE Mobile

FIRST APPEARANCE
Uncanny X-Men #282 (November 1991)

XAVIER'S SECURITY ENFORCERS

YANCY STREET GANG

FIRST APPEARANCE *Fantastic Four* #6 (September 1962

BASE Yancy Street, on the Lower East Side of Manhattan

Based around the tough neighborhood of Manhattan's Lower East Side, the Yancy Street Gang was at one time led by Daniel Grimm, the wayward older brother of Ben Grimm, fated to transform into the THING. Daniel was killed during a rumble between the Yancy gang and a rival street gang, and Ben eventually replaced his brother as the leader. But when Ben moved out west after the death of his mother, the Yancy Gang took it as a betrayal. After Ben was transformed into the Thing and became one of the FANTASTIC FOUR, the Yancy Street Gang made it their mission to heckle and bedevil their former member. During the CIVIL WAR, the gang sided with the outlaw heroes. THE PUPPET MASTER and MAD THINKER used them to incite a riot in which the gang's leader was killed.

YASHIDA, MARIKO

FIRST APPEARANCE *X-Men* #118 (February 1979)

REAL NAME Mariko Yashida

OCCUPATION Head of Clan Yashida **BASE** Japan

HEIGHT 5 ft **WEIGHT** 100 lbs **EYES** Brown **HAIR** Black

SPECIAL POWERS/ABILITIES An exceptional businesswoman; had the normal fitness of a woman of her age and weight, but no special powers.

For many years, Mariko Yashida was the love of WOLVERINE's life. Meeting her during a mission to Japan, their relationship blossomed in New York, and they remained in contact even after her forced marriage to a brutal criminal associate of her father. The deaths of Mariko's husband and her father presented them with the opportunity for marriage, but Mariko wanted to wait—she had inherited the family business and wished to sever its criminal links first. In the end, the pair never wed—when she was poisoned by an assassin, Wolverine was forced to kill Mariko in order to end her terrible suffering.

YONDU

FIRST APPEARANCE *Star-Lord* #1 (January 2016)

REAL NAME Yondu Udonta **OCCUPATION** Ravager

BASE Mobile

HEIGHT 6 ft 2 in (7 ft 1 in with crest) **WEIGHT** 210 lbs

EYES Red **HAIR** Red

SPECIAL POWERS/ABILITIES Superhuman strength, highly athletic speed, stamina, agility, and reflexes.

The "original" Yondu Udonta was the last surviving member of his species, living in the 31st century of Earth-691. He was a founding member of the GUARDIANS OF THE GALAXY and a member of Guardians 3000. His ancestor, also named Yondu Udonta, lived in present times in the reality of Earth-616 and was the leader of the Ravager Space Pirates. When young Peter Quill's (*see* STAR-LORD) ship malfunctioned and he was left stranded in space, Yondu's crew rescued him. After a scuffle, Peter ended up joining them as their cleaning boy, before later being promoted to full Ravager status.

YELLOWJACKET

FACTFILE

REAL NAME
Darren Cross

OCCUPATION
Businessman

BASE
Cross Technological Enterprises

HEIGHT 6 ft 1 in
WEIGHT 185 lbs
EYES Brown
HAIR Black

FIRST APPEARANCE
Marvel Premiere #47 (April 1979)

POWERS
Battlesuit provided flight, the ability to shrink via Pym Particles, and gloves that fired "disruptor sting" blasts of electricity.

Rita DeMara first adopted the identity of Yellowjacket after stealing Hank Pym's Yellowjacket battlesuit from Avengers Mansion. The next to take up the name was Darren Cross. The wealthy company owner had a heart condition that required frequent heart transplants. Aware that ANT-MAN (Scott Lang) kept a tiny, secret lab inside his own helmet, Darren schemed to acquire it. Inside, he found an experimental Yellowjacket suit, which Darren donned and used, unsuccessfully, to attack Ant-Man. He later joined BARON ZEMO's Army of Evil.

YOUNG ALLIES, SEE PAGE 434

YON-ROGG

FIRST APPEARANCE *Marvel Super-Heroes* (December 1967)

REAL NAME Yon-Rogg **OCCUPATION** Colonel in the Imperial Kree Army **BASE** Hala

HEIGHT 6 ft **WEIGHT** 220 lbs **EYES** Blue **HAIR** Brown

SPECIAL POWERS/ABILITIES Commands the resources of the Kree military. Can fire blasts of energy.

Yon-Rogg (Magnitron) was a colonel in the Imperial Kree Army. He was a teammate of CAPTAIN MAR-VELL, before being assigned his own command. Yon-Rogg was jealous of Mar-Vell, and repeatedly put him in harm's way, which sparked off a deadly feud. Yon-Rogg kidnapped Carol Danvers (*see* CAPTAIN MARVEL), who was irradiated by an exploding Kree Psyche-Magnitron device during the ensuing battle between Yon-Rogg and Mar-Vell. As a result of the explosion, Carol Danvers' superpowers from her half-Kree lineage were awakened.

YOUNG AVENGERS

The next generation of justice

In a possible alternate year 3016, a young robotics student named Nathaniel Richards was saved from death by his future self. Nathaniel learned that he was destined to grow up to become Kang the Conqueror. Horrified, the 16-year-old fled to modern-day Earth, hoping to circumvent his fate by securing help from the Avengers, Kang's greatest enemies.

A NEW PLAN

Unfortunately, Nathaniel arrived soon after the Scarlet Witch went mad and disassembled the current team. Desperate, he broke into Stark Industries (*see* Iron Man) and examined the CPU of the recently destroyed android the Vision, finding a failsafe program that pinpointed the next generation of superpowered youths. Calling himself Iron Lad, Nathaniel quickly recruited them and trained them for a battle with Kang.

When Captain America and Iron Man learned of this new team, they tried to convince the teenagers to disband before they could be hurt, but Kang arrived and demanded the return of Iron Lad so that destiny could follow its preordained course. In the resulting battle, Kang was killed, and Iron Lad decided he must accept his destiny in order to prevent the destruction of the current timeline.

Iron Lad used data from the Vision's central processing unit to locate the next wave of heroes. He found and enlisted Patriot, Hulkling, and Wiccan for the battle against Kang.

FACTFILE

MEMBERS AND POWERS

IRON LAD (Nathaniel Richards)
Scientific genius with a suit of psychokinetic armor that responds to his thoughts.

WICCAN (Billy Kaplan)
Projects mystical energy.

KATE BISHOP
Olympic-level athlete and weapons-master.

STATURE (Cassie Lang)
Size-changing abilities.

HULKLING (Teddy Altman)
Shapeshifter with healing factor.

PATRIOT (Eli Bradley)
Enhanced speed and agility.

BASE
Formerly Avengers Mansion, New York City

FIRST APPEARANCE
Young Avengers #1 (February 2005)

THE NEXT GENERATION OF JUSTICE

1 Wiccan
2 Kid Loki
3 Miss America
4 Hawkeye (Kate Bishop)
5 Hulking
6 Marvel Boy

NEW BEGINNINGS

The team later added the superfast Speed to the squad after breaking him out of prison. When Nathaniel took off his armor at one point, it transformed into a new version of the Vision called Jonas. Captain America gave Hawkeye's bow and quiver to Kate Bishop, along with the hero's code name. During the Civil War, the Young Avengers sided with Cap's resistance. Stature switched sides after the death of Goliath at the hands of Ragnarok. When the conflict ended, the rest registered with the government, except for Hawkeye, Patriot, and Speed. During the Dark Reign, the team joined with a new team of Young Avengers to fight the Dark Avengers under the control of Norman Osborn (Green Goblin).

Later, Wiccan and Speed hunted for the Scarlet Witch, believing they were the reincarnations of her children. The quest took them to Latveria, and in an ensuing battle Doctor Doom killed Stature. Determined to save her, Iron Lad decided to take her into the future, even though this would eventually result in him becoming Kang. When Jonas objected, Iron Lad destroyed him.

Months later, Kid Loki gathered Hawkeye, Hulkling, and Wiccan together with Marvel Boy and Miss America to form a new team and take on new challenges. As they battled an interdimensional parasite called Mother, Wiccan became the Demiurge, which unleashed his full-powered potential. Loki admitted that he had killed his own younger self, and that the Young Avengers team was merely a manifestation of his guilt—and his missing powers. The realization restored him. After defeating Mother, the team celebrated and then departed.

After leading the team against Mr. Hyde (left), Patriot admitted he had taken a mutant growth hormone to increase his physical powers.

YOUNG ALLIES

FACTFILE

NOTABLE MEMBERS

BUCKY Captain America's sidekick.

TORO Original Human Torch's sidekick.

FIRESTAR Flaming mutant.

NOMAD Former Bucky from Counter-Earth.

EL TORO Super-Soldier resembling a bull.

SPIDER-GIRL Spider-powers.

GRAVITY Controls gravitons.

BASE Mobile

FIRST APPEARANCE
Young Allies #1 (Summer 1941)

YOUNG ALLIES

The first Young Allies team formed from a group of regular boys who joined up with Bucky BARNES and Toro, the sidekick of the original HUMAN TORCH in the days before and during World War II. They were Henry "Tubby" Tinkle, Jefferson Worthing "Jeff" Sandervilt, Percival Aloysius "Knuckles" O'Toole, and Washington Carver "Whitewash" Jones. They fought foes such as the RED SKULL and LOTUS. They tried to keep in touch over the years, but most, save Bucky, have left their heroic careers behind.

THE LATEST YOUNG ALLIES
1 Gravity ***2*** Spider-Girl ***3*** Nomad ***4*** El Toro ***5*** Firestar

The Young Allies learned that Superior created the rest of the Bastards of Evil by giving teens powers and brainwashing them to join him.

Another Young Allies team formed on the Counter-Earth created by Franklin RICHARDS. This consisted of that world's Bucky (Rikki BARNES/NOMAD), IQ (a brilliant, quadriplegic telepath), Jolt (a girl with shocking punches), Kid Colt (a human-Kymelian hybrid), and Toro (a half-bull boy).

A new team formed on Earth in the present day to fight the BASTARDS OF EVIL. This included El Toro, FIRESTAR, GRAVITY, Nomad (Rikki Barnes), and SPIDER-GIRL (Anya Corazon). They later banded together against ONSLAUGHT and worked alongside the AVENGERS Academy. These Young Allies also helped SPIDER-MAN when Manhattan was infected with a virus that transformed the population into giant spiders.

YOUNG MASTERS

FACTFILE

MEMBERS AND POWERS

BIG ZERO Size control.

BLACK KNIGHT Armored fighter.

COAT OF ARMS Coat gives her four working arms.

EGGHEAD Android.

ENCHANTRESS Sorceress.

EXECUTIONER Skilled fighter.

MAKO Atlantean clone.

MELTER Melts matter.

RADIOACTIVE KID Emits radiation.

BASE New York

FIRST APPEARANCE
Dark Reign: Young Avengers #1 (July 2009)

YOUNG MASTERS

A young artist who took the name Coat of Arms brought the Young Masters—a junior version of the MASTERS OF EVIL—together as an art project. Many of the members were named for older heroes and villains they had little to do with, like the EGGHEAD, ENCHANTRESS, and EXECUTIONER. Melter wanted to be a hero, but some of the others had mixed emotions about such commitments.

The original team started out calling itself the YOUNG AVENGERS, but the real Young Avengers took issue with that and asked them to audition to join their team. When most of them failed, Melter called Norman Osborn (GREEN GOBLIN), who sent in his team of AVENGERS to deal with the Young Avengers.

The team called itself the Young Masters after that, but many of them moved on, leaving only Egghead and Executioner from the original crew. A mysterious villain calling himself ZODIAC helped them recruit Mako, BLACK KNIGHT (who also had nothing to do with the original), and Radioactive Kid, and they set up in an old HYDRA Base. They tried to commit a few major crimes, including killing DOCTOR OCTOPUS and Kristoff VERNARD, but they failed.

YOUNG MASTERS
1 Enchantress
2 Egghead
3 Executioner
4 Melter
5 Big Zero
6 Coat of Arms

YUKIO

FIRST APPEARANCE *Wolverine* #1 (September 1982)
REAL NAME Yukio (full name unrevealed)
OCCUPATION Adventurer; former assassin **BASE** Mobile
HEIGHT 5 ft 9 in **WEIGHT** 130 lbs **EYES** Brown **HAIR** Black
SPECIAL POWERS/ABILITIES Highly skilled athlete, martial artist, and knife-thrower.

Yukio started out as a thief, running with GAMBIT, before becoming an assassin in the service of Japanese crimelord Lord Shingen of Clan Yashida. Her employer sent her after WOLVERINE, but she eventually befriended him and his X-MEN teammates, particularly STORM. Wolverine grew to trust Yukio so much that he left his foster daughter Amiko KOBAYASHI in her care. They were attacked by OMEGA RED and LADY DEATHSTRIKE, and later by a possessed Wolverine, who put Yukio in a wheelchair. She now runs an illegal nightclub in Japan.

YOUNG X-MEN

Young and foolish

In the aftermath of M-Day, Cyclops—the leader of the X-Men—assembled a new team of mutants called the Young X-Men to bring down a new Brotherhood of Evil Mutants. Ironically, this new Brotherhood was composed of former New Mutants Cannonball, Magma, Dani Moonstar, and Sunspot, who'd become the new leader of the Hellfire Club.

MEMBERSHIP CHANGES

Initially, the Young X-Men members included Blindfold, Dust, Ink, Rockslide, and Wolf Cub—and secretly Cipher—but when they discovered that their Cyclops was actually X-Men foe Donald Pierce, they united with their targets in the Brotherhood to defeat him. Before he was captured, however, Pierce managed to kill Wolf Cub.

Afterward, the real Cyclops made the team official and asked Sunspot and Moonstar to train the Young X-Men. Blindfold left the team, but Anole joined to replace her. Ink also left the team after it was revealed he wasn't a mutant but had gained his powers through Leon Nunez, a mutant who could give people powers via tattoos. While investigating, the Young X-Men found a group of criminals called the Y-Men, who had forced Leon to give them powers too. Ink persuaded Leon to give him a Phoenix Force tattoo so he could help his friends. Though the strain put Leon into a coma, it provided the edge the team needed against the Y-Men, and afterward Ink was allowed to stay with the team, if only so Cyclops could keep an eye on him.

Faced with death and betrayal, the Young X-Men hung together right until the very end.

DOOMED

Soon after, Dust realized that she was slowly dying after having survived Magma temporarily fusing her body of sand into glass. Donald Pierce, who'd been held prisoner on the X-Men's island of Utopia, persuaded her that he could save her, but she died while helping him escape. Ink used his Phoenix Force tattoo to resurrect her, but the effort put him into a coma as well.

Soon after, the team broke up. Many of its members joined the reformed New Mutants.

ESSENTIAL STORYLINES

- ***Young X-Men #1–5*** The Young X-Men form and realize they've been tricked.
- ***Young X-Men #6–10*** The Young X-Men face off against the Y-Men and learn the truth behind Ink's powers.
- ***Young X-Men #11–12*** Dust dies, but Ink revives her, although at a high cost.

Discovering they'd been brought together by an imposter didn't drive the Young X-Men apart but made them a closer unit.

FACTFILE

MEMBERS AND POWERS

ANOLE Superhuman speed, reflexes, and coordination, plus regeneration, wallcrawling, and camouflage.

BLINDFOLD Telepath able to see past, future, and present.

CIPHER Undetectability and phasing.

DUST Living sandstorm.

GRAYMALKIN Superhuman strength, invulnerability, and night vision, which all increase in darkness.

INK Tattoos that grant various abilities.

MIRAGE (Dani Moonstar) None.

ROCKSLIDE Psionic creature who can telekinetically form a superstrong body from rock.

SUNSPOT Solar power control, superhuman strength, and flight.

WOLF CUB Wolfman form and enhanced senses.

BASE San Francisco

FIRST APPEARANCE *Young X-Men* #1 (May 2008)

YOUNG X-MEN
1 Rockslide ***2*** Anole
3 Graymalkin
4 Dani Moonstar
5 Dust ***6*** Sunspot
7 Ink

ZABU

FIRST APPEARANCE *X-Men* #10 (March 1965)
REAL NAME Zabu **OCCUPATION** Companion to Ka-Zar
BASE The Savage Land, Antarctica **HEIGHT/WEIGHT** Unrevealed
EYES Green **HAIR** Orange
SPECIAL POWERS/ABILITIES Two long, saber-like teeth; great strength and agility; unusually intelligent for a saber-tooth tiger; lifespan extended by gases in the Savage Land's "Place of Mists."

Zabu is the last known saber-tooth tiger on Earth. Saber-tooths survived in the Savage Land until recent times but even there are now all but extinct. When Maa-Gor and his Swamp Men slew Zabu's mate, the infuriated tiger hunted them down. Zabu attacked Maa-Gor just as he was about to kill Kevin Plunder, the orphaned son of an explorer. In the ensuing struggle, Kevin shot Maa-Gor, saving Zabu's life. Ever since, Zabu and Kevin have been loyal companions, and Kevin is known today as the jungle lord Ka-Zar, which means "Son of the Tiger." Zabu also joined the Pet Avengers under the leadership of Lockjaw.

ZARAN

FIRST APPEARANCE *Master of Kung Fu* #77 (June 1979)
REAL NAME Maximillian Zaran
OCCUPATION Mercenary **BASE** Mobile
HEIGHT 6 ft 1 in **WEIGHT** 235 lbs **EYES** Blue **HAIR** Red
SPECIAL POWERS/ABILITIES Skilled with a wide range of ancient weapons, including nunchakus, shurikens, maces, bows and arrows, staffs, and knives; he can also fire a gun.

A former British MI6 agent and now a mercenary, Maximillian Zaran's career has been chequered to say the least. After defecting from the British secret service, Zaran worked for Fah Lo Suee, Zheng Zu's daughter, but she cut his contract short. For a time, his apprentice took over his identity, but once that was resolved Zaran joined Batroc's Brigade. During the Civil War, he was forced to work for the Thunderbolts. He later registered with the US government and joined the Fifty-State Initiative.

ZALADANE

FIRST APPEARANCE *Astonishing Tales* #1 (December 1970)
REAL NAME Zala Dane (allegedly)
OCCUPATION High priestess **BASE** The Savage Land
HEIGHT 5 ft 9 in **WEIGHT** 125 lbs **EYES** Blue **HAIR** Black
SPECIAL POWERS/ABILITIES Zaladane is a sorceress who possesses assorted spell-based abilities.

The High Priestess of Garokk, Zaladane led believers against the other tribes of the Savage Land in a bid for power. Zaladane's sorcery transformed Kirk Marston into the avatar of Garrok on Earth, and she supported him as his second in command. After her bid to conquer the Savage Land had been foiled, Zaladane's mutates abducted Lorna Dane, the X-Man known as Polaris. Posing as Lorna's long-lost sister, Zaladane succeeded in transferring Polaris' magnetic abilities to herself, albeit temporarily. Thereafter, in a failed bid to control all of the magnetic forces on Earth, Zaladane ran afoul of Magneto, who overwhelmed her with his own superior magnetic might, and left her for dead.

ZARATHOS

FIRST APPEARANCE *Marvel Spotlight* #5 (August 1972)
REAL NAME Zarathos **OCCUPATION** The Spirit of Vengeance
BASE The netherworld dimension of Mephisto
HEIGHT 20 ft **WEIGHT** 225 lbs **EYES/HAIR** N/A
SPECIAL POWERS/ABILITIES Uses magic to enhance strength, height, weight. Employs levitation and projects blasts of concussive force. Projects cold fire that sears his enemies' souls.

Zarathos is a demon who journeyed to Earth before the Dawn of Man. A sorcerer offered to trade souls for his aid. Mephisto, lord of the underworld, grew jealous of a cult that grew around Zarathos and enslaved him, sending him to possess humans in the causes of sin, corruption, and vengeance. Zarathos became bound to stunt motorcyclist Johnny Blaze and later to bike messenger Danny Ketch and (still later) to Alejandra Blaze, transforming each into Ghost Rider.

ZOLA, ARNIM

FIRST APPEARANCE *Captain America* #208 (April 1977)
REAL NAME Arnim Zola **OCCUPATION** Criminal biochemist
BASE Weisshorn Mountain, Switzerland
HEIGHT 5 ft 10 in **WEIGHT** 200 lbs
EYES Brown **HAIR** None
SPECIAL POWERS/ABILITIES Brilliant geneticist; can mentally project his intelligence into any of his creations.

During the late 1930s, Swiss geneticist Arnim Zola discovered a tome of Deviant science and learned how to create artificial life. Zola became a valued member of Hitler's Third Reich, preserving Hitler's consciousness in the form of the Hate-Monger. A frequent foe of Captain America, Zola often worked with the Red Skull. Zola escaped to and ruled Dimension Z, an oppressive world of mutates that he created. Cap found Zola in this dimension and led a rebellion against him. Zola later worked with the Hydra Captain America during their takeover of America and was part of Hydra's high council.

ZOLA, IAN

FIRST APPEARANCE *Captain America* #1 (January 2013)
REAL NAME Leopold Zola **OCCUPATION** Adventurer
BASE Mobile **HEIGHT** Unknown **WEIGHT** Unknown
EYES Brown **HAIR** Brown
SPECIAL POWERS/ABILITIES Skilled martial artist and acrobat with enhanced strength, speed, stamina, and healing abilities.

Created by Arnim Zola in Dimension Z, Leopold Zola was rescued from a test tube by Captain America, who named him Ian. He grew up by Cap's side in Dimension Z. At one point he was captured and brainwashed by Arnim Zola, but managed to overcome the programming—only to be shot by Sharon Carter, who saw him as a threat. He survived and, when Cap left Dimension Z, he became that dimension's protector—known as Nomad. He came to Earth with Carter to help stop Arnim's invasion, and later started to fight alongside Falcon.

ZODIAC

FACTFILE

MEMBERS AND POWERS

ARIES
Shoots fire from his horns.

AQUARIUS
Carries a gun that fires blasts of electricity.

CANCER
Superhuman strength, ability to create and control torrents of water.

CAPRICORN
Superhuman leaping and climbing abilities.

GEMINI
Can split into two bodies, can grow to huge size and strength, can project energy.

LEO
Superhuman strength and leaping ability.

LIBRA
Can fly and become intangible.

PISCES
Can easily maneuver underwater.

SAGITTARIUS
Advanced archery skills.

SCORPIO
Wields the powerful Zodiac Key.

TAURUS
Superhuman strength.

VIRGO
Highly skilled in creating and using machines.

BASE Mobile

FIRST APPEARANCE
(in shadow) *Defenders* #49 (July 1977); (fully seen) *Defenders* #50 (August 1977)

ZODIAC

ZODIAC
1 Aquarius ***2*** Virgo ***3*** Gemini ***4*** Aries ***5*** Leo ***6*** Capricorn ***7*** Sagittarius
8 Libra ***9*** Taurus ***10*** Pisces ***11*** Cancer

The first public Zodiac was a criminal team in which each of its 12 members had powers based on a zodiac sign. Cornelius Van Lunt (TAURUS) and Jake FURY (Scorpio) formed it, intending to rule humanity. One of this group—Aquarius—later appeared as the One-Man Zodiac.

The second Zodiac was formed when an android Scorpio slaughtered the original Zodiac and replaced them all with androids. The third Zodiac group was composed of humans hired by Canada's Department H to test ALPHA FLIGHT, but they turned rogue and a Weapon X team murdered them.

ZODIAC ATTACK

A fourth group faced off against the NEW WARRIORS, and that team's Cancer killed the overconfident hero Longstrike. A later incarnation of Zodiac was split into sects based on their star-signs. The Scorpio of this new group was Vernon Fury, grand-nephew of Nick FURY. The group was defeated by SPIDER-MAN, MOCKINGBIRD, and SHIELD. Zodiac was also the name of a solo villain who killed 100 HAMMER agents during Norman Osborn's DARK REIGN.

Scorpio wields the Zodiac Key, which can fire energy bolts and teleport people and objects from one dimension to another. It was sent to Earth by the Brotherhood, a cult from another dimension that believes that the Key's existence depends on constant conflict between good and evil.

ZOMBIE

FIRST APPEARANCE *Tales of the Zombie* #1 (August 1973)
REAL NAME Simon William Garth
OCCUPATION Former businessman **BASE** New Orleans
HEIGHT 6 ft 2 in **WEIGHT** 220 lbs
EYES White **HAIR** Black
SPECIAL POWERS/ABILITIES Superhuman strength and regenerative ability.

Ruthless businessman Simon Garth so upset his gardener, Gyps, that Gyps killed Garth and resurrected him as a zombie. For two years, the zombiefied Garth wandered the Earth, initially controlled by Gyps with an amulet, and later by one despicable individual after another. The love of a good woman restored Garth to life for a short spell, enabling him to put his affairs in order before going to his rest. He returned later to fight against a zombie invasion from an alternate dimension and became a founding member of the monstrous incarnation of the HOWLING COMMANDOS.

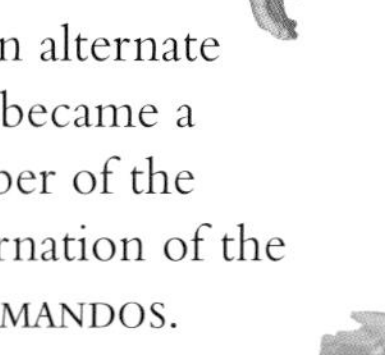

ZZZAX

FIRST APPEARANCE *Incredible Hulk* #166 (August 1973)
REAL NAME Inapplicable **OCCUPATION** Purveyor of destruction **BASE** Mobile **HEIGHT** Variable (max. 40 ft)
WEIGHT Negligible **EYES /HAIR** Inapplicable
SPECIAL POWERS/ABILITIES Unlimited electricity-manipulating powers including flight, super strength, and the ability to fire electrical bolts of concussive force.

Zzzax is a living electromagnetic field created in a bizarre accident at a nuclear power plant. By absorbing the electromagnetic brainwave energies of its victims, Zzzax gained a limited sentience and fashioned itself into a crude humanoid form. Zzzax can grow in size by draining energy from its surroundings, a tactic it used against its most frequent foe, the HULK. For a while, General Ross' consciousness controlled the creature, but he soon abandoned it. Zzzax later escaped from the Raft super prison, but SHE-HULK recaptured him. It later worked with MODOK and fought against the RED HULK.

THE MULTIVERSE

Countless universes of heroes

The mainstream Marvel Universe is only one of countless possible universes in the Multiverse. Most full universes are known by the name "Earth" attached to an identifying number. The regular Marvel Universe is Earth-616, although almost no one in that universe knows of it as anything other than "home." Many of the universes have their own versions of familiar characters, although they may be drastically different from each other. Most people live their lives in a single universe, never knowing anything of places beyond their own. A rare few, however, travel between the universes frequently. We live on Earth-1218.

1602

In an alternate world (Earth-460), the Purple Man uses his powers of persuasion to become US President and exiles Captain America into the past of Earth-311. This disrupts that universe's timeline so badly that modern heroes begin to appear at the turn of the 17th century; for instance, Sir Nicholas Fury works for Queen Elizabeth of England. Later, after the timeline has been fixed by the removal of Captain America, many of the heroes move to the New World, which is populated by dinosaurs along with the native peoples.

Alternate versions of regular heroes and villains band together to save the Multiverse as the Exiles.

EARTH X

The future of Earth-9997 is a dark time. Black Bolt has released the Terrigen Mists into the atmosphere, causing many humans to become mutants. Controlling the US food supply, Norman Osborn (Green Goblin) makes himself US President and has Iron Man build robotic versions of the Avengers for him. The new Galactus (Franklin Richards) eventually saves the world. Later, Captain Mar-Vell persuades Thanos to use the Ultimate Nullifier on Death, then helps to make Mr. Fantastic—who has built a Paradise for the dead in the Negative Zone—into the new Eternity.

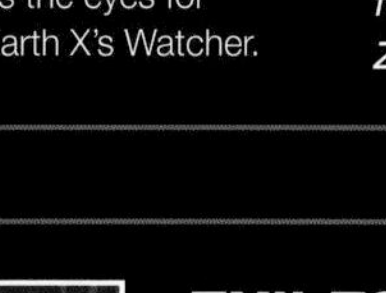

The transparent Machine Man served as the eyes for Earth X's Watcher.

EXILES

The Exiles are a Super Hero team assembled by the mysterious Timebroker to solve problems in the Multiverse. The Timebroker is actually part of an insectoid alien race that is trying to repair the damage it did to the Multiverse. The creatures live in the Panoptichron, a transdimensional space from which they can monitor several other realities at once. The leader of the Exiles uses a device called a Tallus to communicate with the Timebroker, helping to keep the team on track. Due to the dangerous nature of their jobs, the Exiles have a high turnover rate, but there are always replacements ready to take the place of the fallen.

ULTIMATES

On Earth-1610, the heroes who have been around the mainstream universe for decades have just developed, and sometimes have done so in unique ways. Spider-Man, for instance, is just a teenager in high school, Nick Fury is African-American—although he still wears an eye patch—and the Avengers are known as the Ultimates. There are far fewer superpowered people in this world, and the number was recently reduced when Magneto went on a murderous rampage to avenge the deaths of Quicksilver and the Scarlet Witch and flooded New York City with a tidal wave.

At first, the Ultimate universe seemed like simply a younger version of Earth-616, but it later diverged in important and substantial ways.

SQUADRON SUPREME

One of the most enduring crossovers between universes happened when the Avengers traveled to Earth-712 and met the top hero team there, the Squadron Supreme. Years later, the Squadron's members decided to try taking over and running the world, but when this went wrong they exiled themselves to Earth-616. They returned to find their homeworld overrun by ruthless corporations. They've also had encounters with people from the Ultimate universe (Earth-1610) and a darker version of their own team from Earth-31916.

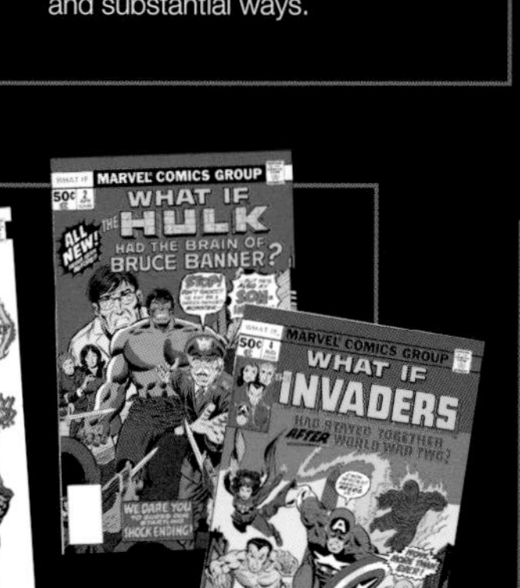

WHAT IF....

The WATCHER often travels to different universes that are extremely close to Earth-616 but diverge at one critical point or another, such as "What if Uncle Ben had lived?" Sometimes he visits universes in which a regular hero appears in a different time, like Captain America as a fighter in the Revolutionary War. Other times, the issues the Watcher examines are more complex and posit a series of different paths taken during massive events like the Civil War (see pp. 86–7) or the Secret Invasion (see pp. 314–15).

ZOMBIES

A zombie version of the Sentry entered Earth-2149 and, with the help of Magneto, began infecting superpowered people with a virus that turned them into the living dead. Magneto mistakenly thought the infection would only harm humans, leaving mutants alive. The zombies retain most of their powers, but their hunger for human flesh regularly overpowers them. After they run out of food, the superpowered zombies try traveling to new universes filled with fresh meat. They have managed to reach Earth-1610 and Earth-616 universes.

INDEX

Entries in **bold** signify that a character has their own entry.

C

I

J

K

L

M

N

T